Lecture Notes in Artificial Intelligence 9387

Subseries of Lecture Notes in Computer Science

More information about this series at http://www.springer.com/series/1244

Qingliang Chen · Paolo Torroni
Serena Villata · Jane Hsu
Andrea Omicini (Eds.)

PRIMA 2015: Principles and Practice of Multi-Agent Systems

18th International Conference
Bertinoro, Italy, October 26–30, 2015
Proceedings

Springer

Editors
Qingliang Chen
Jinan University
Guangzhou
China

Jane Hsu
National Taiwan University
Taipei
Taiwan

Paolo Torroni
DISI
Università di Bologna
Bologna
Italy

Andrea Omicini
DISI
Università di Bologna
Bologna
Italy

Serena Villata
Inria - Sophia Antipolis-Méditerranée
Sophia Antipolis
France

ISSN 0302-9743   ISSN 1611-3349   (electronic)
Lecture Notes in Artificial Intelligence
ISBN 978-3-319-25523-1   ISBN 978-3-319-25524-8   (eBook)
DOI 10.1007/978-3-319-25524-8

Library of Congress Control Number: 2015951757

LNCS Sublibrary: SL7 – Artificial Intelligence

Springer Cham Heidelberg New York Dordrecht London

Printed on acid-free paper

Springer International Publishing AG Switzerland is part of Springer Science+Business Media
(www.springer.com)

Preface

Welcome to the proceedings of the 18th International Conference on Principles and Practice of Multi-Agent Systems (PRIMA 2015) held in Bertinoro, Italy, during October 26–30, 2015.

Originally started as a regional (Asia-Pacific) workshop in 1998, PRIMA has become one of the leading and influential scientific conferences for research on multi-agent systems. Each year, PRIMA brings together active researchers, developers and practitioners from both academia and industry to showcase, share and promote research in several domains, ranging from foundations of agent theory and engineering aspects of agent systems, to emerging interdisciplinary areas of agent-based research.

The 2015 edition was a very special one, because this was the very first time that PRIMA was brought to Europe since it emerged as a full-fledged international conference in 2009. Previous successful editions were held in Nagoya, Japan (2009), Kolkata, India (2010), Wollongong, Australia (2011), Kuching, Malaysia (2012), Dunedin, New Zealand (2013), and Gold Coast, Australia (2014).

We received 94 submissions from 30 countries. Each submission was carefully reviewed by at least three members of the Program Committee (PC) composed of 184 prominent world-level researchers and 27 additional reviewers. The review period was followed by PC discussions moderated by Senior Program Committee (SPC) members. The PRIMA SPC has been part of the PRIMA reviewing scheme since 2010, and this year it included 22 members. At the end of the reviewing process, in addition to the technical reviews, each paper received a summary meta-review by an SPC member. The PC and SPC included researchers from 139 institutions located in 33 countries world–wide.

Of the 94 submissions, PRIMA 2015 accepted 29 papers, with an acceptance rate of 31 %. In addition, 24 contributions were accepted as promising, but not fully mature early innovation papers. All papers were presented at the conference. Each paper was also invited to display a poster so as to enable further discussion. In addition to paper presentations and poster sessions, the conference itself also included three workshops, two tutorials, three keynote talks, and a demo session.

We nominated three papers for the PRIMA 2015 Best Paper Award:

- "Verification of Asynchronous Mobile-Robots in Partially–Known Environments", by Sasha Rubin, Florian Zuleger, Aniello Murano, and Benjamin Aminof
- "Potential of Heterogeneity in Collective Behaviors: a Case Study on Heterogeneous Swarms", by Daniela Kengyel, Heiko Hamann, Payam Zahadat, Gerald Radspieler, Franz Wotawa and Thomas Schmickl
- "Designing a Source-Level Debugger for Cognitive Agent Programs", by Vincent Koeman and Koen Hindriks

Authors of selected papers were invited to submit extended versions of their work to several scientific journals, to further the impact of PRIMA 2015 via special issues and fast tracks. A special issue of *Fundamenta Informaticae* will be devoted to more theoritical work, whereas one by the *Knowledge Engineering Review* will focus on emerging perspectives in the PRIMA scope. Finally, the *Journal of Autonomous Agents and Multi-Agent Systems* will fast-track the processing of extended PRIMA best papers.

We would like to thank all individuals, institutions, and sponsors that supported PRIMA 2015. Mainly we thank the conference delegates and the authors, who answered our call for papers by submitting state-of-the-art research papers from all over the world, confirming the role that PRIMA has gained as a leading international conference in multi-agent system research. Without them, none of this would have been possible. We also thank EasyChair for the use of their conference management system, which allowed us to handle the reviewing process of a conference of this size, from the early stages until the production of the present volume.

We are indebted to our PC and SPC members and additional reviewers for spending their valuable time by providing careful reviews and recommendations on the submissions, and for taking part in follow-up discussions. We are proud that all PRIMA submissions received informative and constructive feedback. We nominated three PC members for the PRIMA 2015 Best PC Member Award: Michael Winikoff, Stéphane Airiau, and Fabio Paglieri; and three SPC members for the PRIMA 2015 Best SPC Member Award: Rafael Bordini, Yves Demazeau, and Tony Bastin Roy Savarimuthu. A special mention was made of additional reviewers Chiara Bassetti, Dave De Jonge, and Fuyuki Ishikawa for providing very thorough and insightful reviews.

Special thanks to some individuals who have consistently supported this conference, in particular the senior advisors of PRIMA 2015, Aditya Ghose, Guido Governatori, and Makoto Yokoo, and the staff members and students of the Università di Bologna's Department of Computer Science and Engineering (DISI), especially Marco Prandini, Enrico Denti, and Stefano Mariani for their efforts in the local and financial organization and management of the website: http://prima2015.apice.unibo.it. We also thank the workshop and tutorial chairs, Matteo Baldoni, Mohammad Namazi, and Cristina Baroglio, the conference secretariat in Bertinoro, in particular Roberta Partisani and Michela Schiavi, Editorial Director Alfred Hofmann, and Editors-in-Chief Damian Niwinski, Peter McBurney, Simon Parsons, Peter Stone, and Carles Sierra. Last but not least, special thanks for to the wonderful invited talks given by Marc Cavazza, Michael Mäs, and Franco Zambonelli.

Finally, we are very grateful to the sponsors who supported PRIMA financially, making the conference accessible to a larger number of delegates, and supporting the participation of keynote speakers:

- The Bertinoro Centre for Informatics, http://bici.eu
- The Università di Bologna's Department of Computer Science and Engineering, http://disi.unibo.it

– The European Coordinating Committee for Artificial Intelligence, http://eccai.org
– Springer's *Lecture Notes in Computer Science*, http://springer.com/computer/lncs

We hope you enjoy the proceedings!

August 2015

Qingliang Chen
Paolo Torroni
Serena Villata
Jane Hsu
Andrea Omicini

Organization

General Co-chairs

Jane Hsu   National Taiwan University, Taiwan
Andrea Omicini   Università di Bologna, Italy

Program Co-chairs

Qingliang Chen   Jinan University, China
Paolo Torroni   Università di Bologna, Italy
Serena Villata   Inria Sophia Antipolis, France

Workshop Chairs

Matteo Baldoni   Università di Torino, Italy
Mohammad Namazi   University of Wollongong, Australia

Tutorial Chair

Cristina Baroglio   Università di Torino, Italy

Finance and Organization Chairs

Enrico Denti   Università di Bologna, Italy
Marco Prandini   Università di Bologna, Italy

Web Chair

Stefano Mariani   Università di Bologna, Italy

Senior Advisors

Aditya Ghose   University of Wollongong, Australia
Guido Governatori   NICTA, Australia
Makoto Yokoo   Kyushu University, Japan

Senior Program Committee

Bo An   Nanyang Technological University, Singapore
Tina Balke   Dassault Systèmes/Quintiq, The Netherlands

Rafael Bordini	Pontifícia Universidade Católica do Rio Grande do Sul, Brazil
Hoa Khanh Dam	University of Wollongong, Australia
Mehdi Dastani	University of Utrecht, The Netherlands
Paul Davidsson	Malmö University, Sweden
Yves Demazeau	CNRS, France
Frank Dignum	University of Utrecht, The Netherlands
Rino Falcone	Institute of Cognitive Sciences and Technologies, CNR, Italy
Guido Governatori	NICTA, Australia
Katsutoshi Hirayama	Kobe University, Japan
Takayuki Ito	Nagoya Institute of Technology, Japan
Zhi Jin	Peking University, China
Nicolas Maudet	Université Paris 6, France
Julian Padget	University of Bath, UK
David Pynadath	University of Southern California, USA
Bastin Tony Roy Savarimuthu	University of Otago, New Zealand
Karl Tuyls	University of Liverpool, UK
Harko Verhagen	Stockholm University/KTH, Sweden
Bo Yang	Jilin University, China
Makoto Yokoo	Kyushu University, Japan
Jie Zhang	Nanyang Technological University, Singapore

Program Committee

Thomas Ågotnes	University of Bergen, Norway
Stéphane Airiau	Université Paris 6, France
Huib Aldewereld	Delft University of Technology, The Netherlands
Natasha Alechina	University of Nottingham, UK
Leila Amgoud	Institut de Recherche en Informatique de Toulouse, France
Giulia Andrighetto	Institute of Cognitive Sciences and Technologies, CNR, Italy
Grigoris Antoniou	University of Huddersfield, UK
Alexander Artikis	NCSR Demokritos, Greece
Guillaume Aucher	University of Rennes 1/Inria, France
Fatma Başak Aydemir	University of Trento, Italy
Nicola Basilico	University of Milan, Italy
Ana L.C. Bazzan	Universidade Federal do Rio Grande do Sul, Brazil
Francesco Belardinelli	Université d'Evry, France
Salem Benferhat	Université d'Artois, France
Jamal Bentahar	Concordia University, Canada
Floris Bex	Utrecht University, The Netherlands
Pierre Bisquert	National Institute for Agricultural Research, France
Olivier Boissier	ENS Mines Saint-Etienne, France

Elise Bonzon   Paris Descartes University, France
Vicent Botti   Universitat Politècnica de València, Spain
Felix Brandt   Technische Universität München, Germany
Daniela Briola   University of Genova, Italy
Nils Bulling   Delft University of Technology, The Netherlands
Ddac Busquets   Imperial College London, UK
Elena Cabrio   Inria Sophia Antipolis, France
Patrice Caire   University of Luxembourg, Luxembourg
Cristiano Castelfranchi   Institute of Cognitive Sciences and Technologies,
                              CNR, Italy
Marc Cavazza   University of Teesside, UK
Marcello Ceci   University of Bologna, Italy
Federico Cerutti   University of Aberdeen, UK
Yin Chen   South China Normal University, China
Shih-Fen Cheng   Singapore Management University, Singapore
Amit Chopra   Lancaster University, UK
Paolo Ciccarese   Harvard Medical School and Massachusetts General
                              Hospital, USA
Marco Comerio   University of Milano-Bicocca, Italy
Massimo Cossentino   High Performance Computing and Network Institute,
                              CNR, Italy
Stefania Costantini   University of L'Aquila, Italy
Mathieu D'Aquin   The Open University, UK
Célia Da Costa Pereira   Université Nice Sophia Anipolis, France
Nirmit Desai   IBM T.J. Watson Research Center, USA
Marina De Vos   University of Bath, UK
Mathijs De Weerdt   Delft University of Technology, The Netherlands
Isabella Distinto   ISTC-CNR Laboratory for Applied Ontology, Trento,
                              Italy
Juergen Dix   Technical University of Clausthal, Germany
Sylvie Doutre   Institut de Recherche en Informatique de Toulouse,
                              France
Jérôme Euzenat   Inria and University of Grenoble, France
Xiuyi Fan   Imperial College London, UK
Catherine Faron Zucker   Université Nice Sophia Anipolis, France
Michael Fisher   University of Liverpool, UK
Nicoletta Fornara   Università della Svizzera Italiana, Switzerland
Katsuhide Fujita   Tokyo University of Agriculture and Technology,
                              Japan
Naoki Fukuta   Shizuoka University, Japan
Simone Gabbriellini   GEMASS, CNRS and Paris-Sorbonne, France
Yang Gao   Nanjing University, China
Guglielmo Gemignani   University of Rome La Sapienza, Italy
Vladimir Gorodetsky   St. Petersburg Institute for Informatics and Automation
                              of the Russian Academy of Sciences, Russia
Davide Grossi   University of Liverpool, UK

Nicola Guarino   ISTC-CNR Laboratory for Applied Ontology, Trento,
                               Italy
Akin Gunay   Nanyang Technological University, Singapore
James Harland   RMIT University, Australia
Koen Hindriks   Delft University of Technology, The Netherlands
Reiko Hishiyama   Waseda University, Japan
Xiaowei Huang   University of Oxford, UK
Anthony Hunter   University College London, UK
Wojciech Jamroga   Polish Academy of Sciences, Poland
Yichuan Jiang   Southeast University, China
Ozgur Kafali   North Carolina State University, USA
Tony Kakas   University of Cyprus, Cyprus
Shohei Kato   Nagoya Institute of Technology, Japan
Sabrina Kirrane   Insight Centre for Data Analytics, Ireland
Yasuhiko Kitamura   Kwansei Gakuin University, Japan
Sébastien Konieczny   CNRS and Centre de Recherche en Informatique de
                               Lens, France
Andrew Koster   Samsung Research Institute, Brazil
Bob Kowalski   Imperial College London, UK
Kazuhiro Kuwabara   Ritsumeikan University, Japan
Jérôme Lang   Université Paris-Dauphine, France
Kate Larson   University of Waterloo, Canada
Joao Leite   New University of Lisbon, Portugal
Ho-Fung Leung   The Chinese University of Hong Kong, China
Beishui Liao   Zhejiang University, China
Churn-Jung Liau   Academia Sinica, Taiwan
Marco Lippi   University of Bologna, Italy
Chanjuan Liu   Peking University, China
Fenrong Liu   Tsinghua University, China
Rey-Long Liu   Tzu Chi University, Taiwan
Brian Logan   University of Nottingham, UK
Alessio Lomuscio   Imperial College London, UK
Maite Lopez-Sanchez   University of Barcelona, Spain
Emiliano Lorini   Institut de Recherche en Informatique de Toulouse,
                               France
Marco Luetzenberger   Distributed Artificial Intelligence Laboratory Berlin,
                               Germany
Xudong Luo   Sun Yat-Sen University, China
Patrick MacAlpine   University of Texas at Austin, USA
Samhar Mahmoud   King's College London, UK
Xinjun Mao   National University of Defense Technology, China
Elisa Marengo   Free University of Bozen-Bolzano, Italy
Viviana Mascardi   University of Genova, Italy
Shigeo Matsubara   Kyoto University, Japan
Toshihiro Matsui   Nagoya Institute of Technology, Japan

Sandip Sen	University of Tulsa, USA
Luciano Serafini	Fondazione Bruno Kessler, Italy
Yuping Shen	Sun Yat-Sen University, China
Zhongzhi Shi	Chinese Academy of Sciences, China
Carles Sierra	Artificial Intelligence Research Institute, CSIC, Spain
Marija Slavkovik	University of Bergen, Norway
Leon Sterling	Swinburne University of Technology, Australia
Alina Strachocka	University of Warsaw, Poland
Kaile Su	Griffith University, Australia
Valentina Tamma	University of Liverpool, UK
Yuqing Tang	Carnegie Mellon University, USA
Andrea Tettamanzi	Université Nice Sophia Antipolis, France
Michael Thielscher	The University of New South Wales, Australia
Matthias Thimm	University of Koblenz, Germany
Michaël Thomazo	Technical University of Dresden, Germany
Xiangrong Tong	Yantai University, China
Francesca Toni	Imperial College London, UK
Fujio Toriumi	The University of Tokyo, Japan
Nicolas Troquard	Université Paris-Est Créteil, France
Kagan Tumer	Oregon State University, USA
Luca Tummolini	Institute of Cognitive Sciences and Technologies, CNR, Italy
Paolo Turrini	Imperial College London, UK
Andreea Urzica	University Politehnica of Bucharest, Romania
Leon van der Torre	University of Luxembourg, Luxembourg
Wiebe van der Hoek	University of Liverpool, UK
Wamberto Vasconcelos	University of Aberdeen, UK
Matteo Venanzi	University of Southampton, UK
Maria Esther Vidal	Universidad Simon Bolivar, Venezuela
Mirko Viroli	University of Bologna, Italy
Toby Walsh	NICTA and University of New South Wales, Australia
Can Wang	Commonwealth Scientific and Industrial Research Organisation, Australia
Chongjun Wang	Nanjing University, China
Kewen Wang	Griffith University, Australia
Wanyuan Wang	Southeast University, China
Zhe Wang	Griffith University, Australia
Michael Winikoff	University of Otago, New Zealand
Brendon J. Woodford	University of Otago, New Zealand
Feng Wu	University of Sicence and Technology of China, China
Lijun Wu	University of Electronic Science and Technology, China
Adam Wyner	University of Aberdeen, UK
Pinar Yolum	Bogazici University, Turkey

Neil Yorke-Smith   American University of Beirut, Lebanon
Yifeng Zeng   Teesside University, UK
Zhiqiang Zhuang   Griffith University, Australia

Additional Reviewers

Balbo, Flavien   Nide, Naoyuki
Banfi, Jacopo   Pianini, Danilo
Bassetti, Chiara   Ramos, Gabriel de Oliveira
Beck, Zoltan   Rebhuhn, Carrie
Cardoso, Henrique   Sabatucci, Luca
Charrier, Tristan   Santos, Fernando
Chen, Yingke   Sapienza, Alessandro
De Jonge, Dave   Shams, Zohreh
Havur, Giray   Szreter, Maciej
Ishikawa, Fuyuki   Tirea, Monica
Kokkinogenis, Zafeiris   Yliniemi, Logan
Li, Naiqi   Razo-Zapata, Iván
Lopes, Fernando   Zhan, Jieyu
Gustavo Nardin, Luis

Contents

Regular Papers

Solving F³MDPs: Collaborative Multiagent Markov Decision Processes with Factored Transitions, Rewards and Stochastic Policies

Julia Radoszycki, Nathalie Peyrard, and Régis Sabbadin[✉]

INRA-MIAT (UR 875), 31326 Castanet-Tolosan, France
{julia.radoszycki,nathalie.peyrard,regis.sabbadin}@toulouse.inra.fr

Abstract. Multiagent Markov Decision Processes provide a rich framework to model problems of multiagent sequential decision under uncertainty, as in robotics. However, when the state space is also factored and of high dimension, even dedicated solution algorithms (exact or approximate) do not apply when the dimension of the state space and the number of agents both exceed 30, except under strong assumptions about state transitions or value function. In this paper we introduce the F³MDP framework and associated approximate solution algorithms which can tackle much larger problems. An F³MDP is a collaborative multiagent MDP whose state space is factored, reward function is additively factored and solution policies are constrained to be factored and can be stochastic. The proposed algorithms belong to the family of Policy Iteration (PI) algorithms. On small problems, where the optimal policy is available, they provide policies close to optimal. On larger problems belonging to the subclass of GMDPs they compete well with state-of-the-art resolution algorithms in terms of quality. Finally, we show that our algorithms can tackle very large F³MDPs, with 100 agents and a state space of size 2^{100}.

Keywords: Multiagent markov decision processes · Policy gradient · Inference in graphical models

1 Introduction

Markov Decision Processes (MDPs) form a suitable tool for modelling and solving problems of multiagent sequential decision under uncertainty [19]. However, direct application to domains like robotics, environmental management, etc., is not straightforward when the state representation is also factored. Several algorithms have been proposed for MDPs with factored state and action spaces (FA-FMDPs, [8,11]). However, they usually do not apply when the numbers of agents and of state variables both exceed 20-30, except when drastic assumptions about state transitions or value functions hold (see Section 2).

This work was funded by ANR-13-AGRO-0001-04.

Q. Chen et al. (Eds.): PRIMA 2015, LNAI 9387, pp. 3–19, 2015.
DOI: 10.1007/978-3-319-25524-8_1

In this article, we propose a new framework, F^{3}MDP, which can be applied to the approximate resolution of general multiagent MDPs with additive rewards. F^3 stands for triply factored, since we consider factored stochastic policies in addition to factored transitions and rewards. To solve F^{3}MDPs, we propose a generic gradient-based Policy Iteration (PI) algorithm. We show that the evaluation of stochastic policies amounts to computing marginal probabilities in a Bayesian network, which can be done exactly or approximately, using state-of-the art tools. The policy update phase amounts to computing small changes in the parameters of the stochastic policies, either along a single coordinate, or along the gradient of the policy value. The latter can be computed either by finite differences, or by computing the marginals of a modified Bayesian network.

In Section 2, we provide some background on FA-FMDPs and on the resolution of multiagent factored MDPs or Dec-POMDPs, related to our approach. In Section 3, we present our main contribution. We introduce the F^{3}MDP framework and the generic gradient-based PI algorithm. In Section 4, we present extensive experiments on FA-FMDPs, both random and inspired by a disease management problem.

2   Background

2.1   FA-FMDP

The method we propose in this paper is dedicated to the resolution of stationary, finite or infinite-horizon multiagent factored MDPs (FA-FMDPs), where the transition function is represented by a Dynamic Bayesian Network (DBN, [16]). We consider the case of FA-FMDPs whose reward function is a sum of small scope reward functions. Such an FA-FMDP is an MDP $\mathcal{P} =< \mathcal{S}, \mathcal{A}, P, R, T >$ with:

- Factored state space: $\mathcal{S} = \prod_{i=1}^{n} \mathcal{S}_i$, where each $\mathcal{S}_i$ is a finite set. The state of the system at time $t \in \{0, \dots, T\}$ is noted: $s^t = (s_1^t, ..., s_n^t) \in \mathcal{S}$.
- Factored action space: $\mathcal{A} = \prod_{j=1}^{m} \mathcal{A}_j$, where each $\mathcal{A}_j$, the action space of agent j, is a finite set. The action at time $t \in \{0, \dots, T-1\}$ is noted: $a^t = (a_1^t, ..., a_m^t) \in \mathcal{A}$.
- Factored transition function: $\forall t \in \{0, \dots, T-1\}, P(s^{t+1}|s^t, a^t) = \prod_{i=1}^{n} P_i(s_i^{t+1}|pa_P(s_i^{t+1}))$ where $pa_P(s_i^{t+1}) = pa_P^S(s_i^{t+1}) \bigcup pa_P^A(s_i^{t+1})$, $pa_P^S(s_i^{t+1}) \subset \{s_j^t, j = 1...n, s_{j'}^{t+1}, j' = 1...n, j' \neq i\}$ and $pa_P^A(s_i^{t+1}) \subset \{a_k^t, k = 1...m\}$. Synchronous arcs are allowed, but the underlying directed graph must be acyclic.
- Additive reward function: $R(s^t, a^t) = \sum_{\alpha=1}^{r} R_\alpha (pa_R(R_\alpha^t))$, where $pa_R(R_\alpha^t) \subset \{s_j^t, j = 1...n\} \cup \{a_k^t, k = 1...m\}$. $R(s^t, a^t)$ is assumed positive and bounded.
- $0 < T \leq +\infty$ the horizon of the problem.

A stationary policy for an MDP is defined as a mapping $\delta : \mathcal{S} \mapsto \mathcal{A}$, which decides the global action a^t according to the global state s^t. Its value for a given initial state $s^0 \in \mathcal{S}$ is $V_\delta^{R,T}(s^0) = \mathbb{E}\left[\sum_{t=0}^{T} \gamma^t R^t \mid s_0, \delta\right]$, where $0 < \gamma \leq 1$ is a given *discount factor*[1]. Solving an MDP amounts to finding a policy δ^* which has maximal value for all initial states : $\forall s^0 \in \mathcal{S}, \forall \delta : \mathcal{S} \mapsto \mathcal{A}, V_{\delta^*}(s^0) \geq V_{\delta}(s^0)$ (there always exists such a deterministic policy [19]).

Since optimal solutions of FA-FMDPs are out of reach, we will not try to find a policy which is optimal for all states. We will consider a given initial distribution on states $P^0(s^0)$, and search for a policy maximizing the expected value with respect to P^0 : $V_{\delta}^{R,T}(P^0) = \sum_{s^0} P^0(s^0) V_{\delta}^{R,T}(s^0)$. In order to be stored in memory, the initial distribution must be represented as a Bayesian network. Furthermore, we will limit our search to stationary policies, even in the finite horizon case where the optimal policy may not be stationary, since they can be more concisely described and are easier to interpret and compute.

2.2   Related Work in Collaborative Multiagent MDPs

In FA-FMDPs, deterministic optimal policies are lists of *global* mappings δ_j^*: $\mathcal{S} \rightarrow \mathcal{A}_j$. Computing and even representing such global policies may quickly become too difficult when n increases. Therefore, most approaches for solving large FA-FMDPs have tried to remediate this effect by computing approximate policies. These policies are either (i) factored policies, $\left(\prod_{i \in I_j} \mathcal{S}_i \right) \rightarrow \mathcal{A}_j$, where all $I_j \subset \{1, \ldots, n\}$ have small cardinality or (ii) factored parameterized policies, where each local policy is moreover parameterized.

In the first family of approaches, several algorithms have been proposed for collaborative multiagent MDPs that approximate the value function (see for example [8], [26], [25]). *Decentralized POMDPs* (Dec-POMDPs, [1]) consider a factored action space (decentralized multiagent setting) and local observations, generating factored policies. However, the state space is most often *not factored* and of small size, compared to the action space [4]. There are some exceptions, however, where the state space is also factored. [5] consider independent observations and transitions. [12] assume $V_{\delta}^{R,T}(s^0)$ factorizes as a sum of functions of reduced scopes of the initial state, a property which holds only in some specific subclasses of Dec-POMDPs, mostly when there are independent transitions. They propose an EM algorithm for solving Dec-POMDPs which has great scalability, and solves problems where $|\mathcal{S}| \approx 2^{58}$, $|\mathcal{A}| \approx 2^{40}$, $|\Omega| \approx 2^{47}$.

Still in the first family, [17] propose an approach based on *collaborative graphical Bayesian games*. The limiting factor for this approach is the horizon T (the largest horizon considered is $T = 6$, with 100 agents). Graph-based MDPs (GMDPs [3, 21]) form a sub-class of FA-FMDPs which also belong to the first family. In the GMDP framework, a single agent and a single reward function are associated to each state variable and rewards, transition and policies are assumed to have identical factorization structure. The algorithms proposed for the GMDP framework either make an approximation of the value function as a sum of functions of small scopes of the initial state ([6,18]), or a multiplicative approximation ([3]).

---

[1] The problem can be undiscounted, in the finite-horizon case, in which case $\gamma = 1$.

In the second family of approaches, [10] propose a stochastic gradient descent algorithm to optimize policies in form of finite-state machine controllers for factored MDPs (the action space is not factored and of small size). Still in the second family, [2,22] propose reinforcement learning algorithms which optimize parameterized policies for FA-FMDPs. The approach of [22] was applied to problems with at most 40 agents (and fewer state variables). The simulation-based value function gradient computation proposed in [2] can be applied to larger problems. However, it is not feasible for problems involving thousands of parameters, which will be the case when considering *stochastic factored policies* as we do.

The approach we propose is similar in spirit to the two approaches, in that we deal with general FA-FMDPs and use approximations of marginal probabilities of the corresponding DBN to evaluate policies. Then, while the EM approach of [12] is a *planning as inference* approach, directly modelling a policy optimization problem as an inference problem, we only use inference to evaluate policies and maintain interleaved parameters' update phases. As far as we know, no planning as inference approach has yet been proposed that would succeed in solving general FA-FMDPs with as many variables as we do.

In the next section, we propose a new approach, belonging to the first family, where *stochastic factored policies* with an a priori defined structure are considered. Our approach has the originality to mix inference methods for graphical models for policy evaluation (as in *planning as inference* methods) and continuous optimization algorithms for policy updates (as in policy gradient methods). Its generality allows to easily incorporate any new inference method for graphical models, or any new continuous optimization algorithm, in order to improve the quality or the speed of the resolution.

3   F³MDP

3.1   Stochastic Factored Policies and F³MDP

An F³MDP is an FA-FMDP with additive reward and stochastic factored policies (SFP). SFPs extend deterministic factored policies. They are defined as: $\delta(a^t|s^t) = \prod_{j=1}^{m} \delta_j(a_j^t|pa_\delta(a_j^t))$ where the $\delta_j(\cdot|pa_\delta(a_j^t))$ are conditional probability distributions and $pa_\delta(a_j^t) \subset \{s_i^t, i = 1...n\} \cup \{a_k^t, k = 1...m, k \neq j\}$. We only consider factored policies for which the graph of dependencies corresponding to both the transition and the SFP is acyclic (see Figure 1). The problem we tackle is that of optimizing SFPs for a given structure. An F³MDP is thus a tuple $\mathcal{P} =< \mathcal{S}, \mathcal{A}, T, P, pa_\delta, R, P^0 >$. This framework is a particular case of factored Dec-POMDP [17] where the agent's observations are subsets of the state variables and the observation function is deterministic. It is useful in frameworks like agriculture management where the agents, the farmers, can only observe the fields they own (which are potentially disconnected) in the landscape. In the case of full observability, choosing the best policy structure, *i.e.* defining $\{pa_\delta(a_j^t), j = 1...m\}$ is an important and complex question that we leave for further research. Figure 1 shows an example of transition, reward and policy structures for an F³MDP with two agents and two state variables.

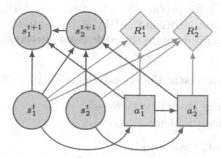

Fig. 1. Example of transition (in blue), reward (in green) and policy (in red) structures of an F³MDP with two agents and two state variables. $pa_P(s_1^{t+1}) = \{s_1^t, a_1^t, s_2^{t+1}\}$, $pa_P(s_2^{t+1}) = \{s_1^t, s_2^t, a_2^t\}$, $pa_R(R_1^t) = \{s_1^t, a_1^t\}$, $pa_R(R_2^t) = \{s_1^t, s_2^t, a_2^t\}$, $pa_\delta(a_1^t) = \{s_1^t\}$ and $pa_\delta(a_2^t) = \{a_1^t, s_2^t\}$. Here agent 2 observes the decision of agent 1 before acting.

A given SFP δ, together with transition functions and a given factored distribution on initial states P^0 define a DBN in which the probability of a trajectory $(s, a)^{0:T} = < s^0, a^0, ...a^{T-1}, s^T >$ is:

$$P_\delta^T((s, a)^{0:T}) = P^0(s^0) \times \prod_{t=0}^{T-1} \left(\prod_{i=1}^{n} P_i(s_i^{t+1} | pa_P(s_i^{t+1})) \prod_{j=1}^{m} \delta_j(a_j^t | pa_\delta(a_j^t)) \right).$$

The value of a given SFP δ for a given initial distribution P^0, in the finite horizon case[2] with horizon T, is defined as:

$$V_\delta^{R,T}(P^0) = \sum_{(s,a)^{0:T}} P_\delta^T((s, a)^{0:T}) \left(\sum_{t=0}^{T} \gamma^t R(s^t, a^t) \right). \tag{1}$$

Computing this expectation requires the evaluation of only some local marginals of $P_\delta^T((s, a)^{0:T})$:

$$V_\delta^{R,T}(P^0) = \sum_{t=0}^{T} \gamma^t \sum_{\alpha=1}^{r} \sum_{pa_R(R_\alpha^t)} b_\alpha^t(pa_R(R_\alpha^t)) R_\alpha(pa_R(R_\alpha^t)),$$

where $b_\alpha^t(\cdot)$ is the marginal distribution over variables influencing reward α at time t. It is computed by marginalizing $P_\delta^T((s, a)^{0:T})$ over all other state and action variables from time 0 to time T. Note that the value is a sum of functions with reduced scopes $\{pa_R(R_\alpha^t)\}_{\alpha \in \{1...r\}, t \in \{0,...,T\}}$. This decomposition is exact and follows directly from the hypotheses of the framework.

There exist many implemented algorithms allowing to compute exact values or approximations of the marginals $b_\alpha^t(\cdot)$, such as the exact Junction Tree

---

[2] In the infinite horizon case with discount, the infinite sum can be approximated by a (large enough) finite horizon time T.

algorithm (JT, e.g. [24]), for problems with small treewidth, or the approximate Loopy Belief Propagation algorithm (LBP, [7]). Monte-Carlo (MC) algorithms can also be applied to approximate the SFP value directly.

3.2   Optimizing Stochastic Factored Policies in F^3MDP

When we look for optimal stochastic factored policies, we are facing a continuous constrained optimization problem:

F^3MDP Optimization Problem

$$\underset{\bar{\delta} \in (\mathbb{R}^+)^N}{\text{maximize}} \quad V_{\bar{\delta}}^{R,T}(P^0)$$

$$\text{subject to} \quad \sum_{a_j \in \mathcal{A}_j} \delta_j(a_j | pa_\delta(a_j)) = 1, \ \forall j, \forall pa_\delta(a_j)$$

where $\bar{\delta}$ is the vector of coordinates $\{\delta_j(a_j | pa_\delta(a_j)), \ \forall j, \forall pa_\delta(a_j)\}$. The number of coordinates of $\bar{\delta}$ is:

$$N = \sum_{j=1}^{m} |\mathcal{A}_j| \prod_{k/A_k \in pa_\delta^A(a_j)} |\mathcal{A}_k| \prod_{k/S_k \in pa_\delta^S(a_j)} |\mathcal{S}_k| \tag{2}$$

When $\forall j = 1...m, |\mathcal{A}_j| = |\mathcal{A}_1|, |pa_\delta^A(a_j)| = |pa_\delta^A(a_1)| = z$ and $\forall i = 1...n, |\mathcal{S}_i| = |\mathcal{S}_1|,$ $|pa_\delta^S(a_j)| = |pa_\delta^S(a_1)| = y$, we have $N = m|\mathcal{A}_1|^{z+1}|\mathcal{S}_1|^y$ which is much smaller than the number of parameters of a deterministic global policy ($m|\mathcal{S}| = m|\mathcal{S}_1|^n$) when $z << m$ and $y << n$.

Theorem. *The decision version of the F^3MDP problem is NP^{PP}-complete.* See appendix for the proof.

3.3   Approximate Policy Iteration Algorithms

The F^3MDP optimization problem will not be solved exactly in practice since (i) we will often only have access to an approximation of $V_{\bar{\delta}}^{R,T}(P^0)$ and (ii) the problem may have many local maxima since it was not shown to be convex (most of continuous optimization algorithms are local optimization algorithms which are guaranteed to converge to the global optimum only when the function is convex). Thus we propose a family of *Policy Iteration*-like algorithms, alternating *approximate evaluations* and *local improvements* of policies:

- Evaluation step: Given current SFP δ^q, $V_{\delta^q}^{R,T}(P^0)$ is evaluated, using for instance, JT, LBP or MC.
- Update step: δ^q is improved to δ^{q+1}, using either a *Gradient Ascent* (GA) or a *Coordinate Ascent* (CA) approach (see [14]).

Gradient Ascent Algorithms. PI-like *gradient-ascent* algorithms provide a local maximum in $\bar{\delta}$ of the (potentially approximate) value $V_{\bar{\delta}}^{R,T}(P^0)$[3]. A simple re-parameterization allows us to get rid of the constraints. We write:

$$\forall j, \forall a_j, \forall pa_\delta(a_j) \; \delta_j(a_j|pa_\delta(a_j)) = \frac{e^{\theta_j(a_j|pa_\delta(a_j))}}{\sum_{a'_j \in A_j} e^{\theta_j(a'_j|pa_\delta(a_j))}},$$

where the coordinates $\theta_j(a_j|pa_\delta(a_j))$ take real values. θ has the same structure as δ, and we define the vector of real-valued coordinates $\bar{\theta}$ analogously to $\bar{\delta}$ (both have the same number of coordinates). Once reparameterized, the optimization problem becomes:

$$\max_{\bar{\theta} \in \mathbb{R}^N} V_{\bar{\theta}}^{R,T}(P^0), \tag{3}$$

where N is defined in Equation (2).

Using gradient-ascent approaches to solve the maximization problem of Equation 3 requires to be able to compute the gradient $\nabla_{\bar{\theta}} V_{\bar{\theta}}^{R,T}(P^0)$, either analytically, or numerically. It can be shown that the components $\frac{\partial V_{\bar{\theta}}^{R,T}(P^0)}{\partial \bar{\theta}_k}$ can be expressed as the marginals of a DBN, derived from the one defining $V_{\bar{\theta}}^{R,T}(P^0)$. Thus, in theory, the gradient can be computed in the same way as $V_{\bar{\theta}}^{R,T}(P^0)$ itself, using e.g. the JT algorithm. However, this is often too costly in practice. Therefore, we present a finite-difference approximation of the gradient, which we used in the experiments: $\forall k = 1...N$,

$$\frac{\partial V_{\bar{\theta}}^{R,T}(P^0)}{\partial \bar{\theta}_k} \approx \frac{V_{\bar{\theta}^+}^{R,T}(P^0) - V_{\bar{\theta}}^{R,T}(P^0)}{\epsilon}, \tag{4}$$

where $\bar{\theta}_k^+ = \bar{\theta}_k + \epsilon$ and $\forall l \neq k$ $\bar{\theta}_l^+ = \bar{\theta}_l$. $V_{\bar{\theta}}^{R,T}(P^0)$ and $V_{\bar{\theta}^+}^{R,T}(P^0)$ are computed or approximated, using JT, LBP or MC. ϵ is a small, positive, step value. Note that a change in a single component $\bar{\theta}_k$ induces a change in several coordinates of $\bar{\delta}$. Indeed, the policy $\bar{\delta}^+$ associated to $\bar{\theta}^+$ is given by :

$$\bar{\delta}_k^+ = \frac{\bar{\delta}_k e^\epsilon}{1 + (e^\epsilon - 1)\bar{\delta}_k}$$

$$\bar{\delta}_g^+ = \frac{\bar{\delta}_g}{1 + (e^\epsilon - 1)\bar{\delta}_k}, \forall g \in G(k) \tag{5}$$

$$\bar{\delta}_g^+ = \bar{\delta}_g, \forall g \notin G(k),$$

where $G(k)$ is defined as follows: If $\bar{\delta}_k = \delta_j(a_j|pa_\delta(a_j))$, then $g \in G(k)$ *iff* there exists $a'_j \neq a_j$, $\bar{\delta}_g = \delta_j(a'_j|pa_\delta(a_j))$. Once computed the approximation of the gradient by finite differences (using the formulas for $\bar{\theta}^+$ or $\bar{\delta}^+$ and the chosen evaluation method), the update of parameter vector $\bar{\theta}$ is given by :

$$\bar{\theta}^{q+1} = \bar{\theta}^q + \eta_q \nabla_{\bar{\theta}^q} V_{\bar{\theta}^q}^{R,T}(P^0) \tag{6}$$

---

[3] They provide in fact a critical point, *i. e.* a point for which the gradient is the null vector, which is a necessary but not sufficient condition to have a maximal point.

There exist several ways to choose the step η_q used in Equation (6) for updating $\bar{\theta}^q$ in the gradient direction at iteration q [14]. It can be *fixed* once and for all. Alternately, it can be chosen *optimal*, i.e. leading to the maximal increase in $V_{\bar{\theta}}^{R,T}(P^0)$. The *Wolfe conditions* step choice method can be seen as an intermediate method which performs well in practice. In our experiments, we compared these three choice methods.

Coordinate Ascent Algorithms. In the case of binary agent spaces, using the fact that $\forall j, \forall pa_\delta(a_j)$, $\delta_j(a_j = 2|pa_\delta(a_j)) = 1 - \delta_j(a_j = 1|pa_\delta(a_j))$, we can build directly an unconstrained optimization problem, whose parameter vector is

$$\tilde{\delta} = \{\delta_j(a_j = 1|pa_\delta(a_j)), \forall j, \forall pa_\delta(a_j)\}.$$

This also reduces the number of coordinates to optimize to $N' = \frac{N}{2}$ and the optimization problem becomes:

$$\underset{\tilde{\delta} \in [0,1]^{\frac{N}{2}}}{\text{maximize}} V_{\tilde{\delta}}^{R,T}(P^0) \tag{7}$$

Coordinate ascent is a derivative-free algorithm. It consists in cycling among the $\frac{N}{2}$ coordinates $\delta_j(a_j = 1|pa_\delta(a_j))$ and trying to locally improve the value by modifying the current coordinate $\tilde{\delta}_k$. Modifications can consist in considering a *fixed step* modification of the current coordinate, or optimizing the value by changing the local coordinate (using the *golden section search* algorithm, see [14]). If all coordinates have been left unchanged after a full cycle, a local maximum has been found.

Since action variables are binary, the constraints are box-constraints and the coordinate ascent algorithm is guaranteed to converge to a local maximum of $V_{\tilde{\delta}}^{R,T}(P^0)$. Note that gradient ascent can compute the coordinates of the gradient in parallel, while coordinate ascent is inherently sequential.

4   Experiments

We have performed extensive experiments on F³MDP problems with infinite horizon, which is the most difficult case for our algorithm. In all experiments we took a discount factor of $\gamma = 0.9$.

The different solution algorithms we have empirically tested are named in the form *Optim-Eval*, where *Optim* is the optimization method (CA or GA) and *Eval* is the evaluation method used, exact (JT) or approximate (LBP or MC).

Our code is in Matlab and uses calls to functions of the libDAI library [15] for JT and LBP evaluation. We have used a Scilab implementation of the *Mean-Field Approximate Policy Iteration* (MF-API) algorithm to solve GMDP problems [21]. In GMDPs, the transition, the reward and the policy are supposed to have the same structure, and the objective is to find the best deterministic factored policy. MF-API is based on a *mean field* evaluation of deterministic factored policies, *ie* a 'more approximate' method than *loopy belief propagation*. Moreover, there is no guarantee with this algorithm to improve the value of the policy at each iteration. Experiments have been conducted on a 16 core server, and the gradient ascent algorithm has been parallelized, using the Matlab Parallelization toolbox.

In Section 4.1, a comparison of the different evaluation algorithms is provided. In Section 4.2, we provide a comparison of the different PI-like algorithms on small problems ($n = 6$ binary state variables, $m = 6$ agents with binary action spaces and $r = 6$ reward functions), for which an optimal *global* policy can be computed. We have used the Matlab MDP toolbox: http://www.inra.fr/mia/T/MDPtoolbox to compute optimal global policies. In Section 4.3, we provide an evaluation on large problems of random structure (15 state variables, and 15 agents with binary or ternary action spaces). Finally, in Section 4.4, we illustrate the use of our PI-like algorithms on a large disease management problem on a grid (25 binary state variables and 25 agents for the first grid, 100 binary state variables and 100 agents for the second grid). We have found no other implementation of an algorithm dedicated to F³MDP solution which can tackle so large problems. In Section 4.2, we used a *natural policy structure*, in which $pa_\delta(a_j)$ is the union of the state variables which (i) either appear in a common reward factor R_α with a_j or (ii) influence a state variable jointly with a_j (i.e. appear jointly in one set $pa_P(s_i^{t+1})$).

4.1 Policy Evaluation Methods

In order to choose an approximate evaluation method, the marginal evaluation method is important, but the horizon approximation, $\hat{T}$, also. Both may have an impact on the evaluation error and the computation time. We have tested the impact of the horizon approximation on small F³MDP problems, for which we can go as far as $\hat{T} = 100$ (Table 1).

Table 1. Mean relative error and mean evaluation time for stochastic policies on 100 small random F³MDP ($n = 6$ binary state variables, $m = 6$ agents with binary action spaces, $r = 6$ reward functions). For Monte-Carlo evaluation, the average value is taken over 4000 trajectories.

Evaluation method	MRE	mean time (sec)
MC $\hat{T} = 40$	0.01	23.45
JT $\hat{T} = 20$	0.11	0.085
LBP $\hat{T} = 20$	0.11	0.049
MC $\hat{T} = 100$	6.8×10^{-4}	66.05
JT $\hat{T} = 100$	2.4×10^{-5}	1.1
LBP $\hat{T} = 100$	0.009	0.23

The error obtained when $\hat{T} = 20$ is significant (10%), but not worse with LBP than with JT. MC provides good results for $\hat{T} = 40$ (1% error), and all methods are quite precise for $\hat{T} = 100$, but are too slow to be incorporated in an optimization algorithm.

Therefore, we have chosen to use the LBP algorithm with $\hat{T} = 20$ in the evaluation step of our PI-like algorithms, as it offers a good compromise between computation time and approximation error. The MC approach with $\hat{T} = 40$ (and 4000 trajectories) is used for comparing the values of the policies returned by these algorithms, when exact evaluation is impossible.

4.2   Small F^3MDP Problems

We have performed a series of experiments on small F^3MDP problems for which the exact optimal (global and not factored) policy can be computed, in order to evaluate the policies returned by several *Optim-Eval* instanciations of our PI-like algorithm (Table 2). The uniform policy is used for initializing the algorithms. Note that the value of η_q is 0.1 in CA algorithms, where policy parameters belong to $[0, 1]$, while it is 10 or 20 in GA algorithms where parameters can take any real value.

The Mean Relative Error (MRE) between the optimal and approximate policies is given, as well as the mean computation time. Since the optimal policy is global, it may not possess the natural structure assumed in our algorithms. Thus, the computed MRE is an upper bound of the MRE with respect to the optimal factored policy.

Using the CA-JT or GA-JT algorithm, we get policies whose MRE is 2% of the optimal global policy. Using GA-LBP or CA-LBP with various line search methods gives similar results with MRE 12%. We also tried GA-JT for an assumed random policy structure (with the same size as the natural policy structure), and obtained an MRE of 0.048 (0.02 with the natural structure) and a mean execution time of 3.66 minutes (3.25 minutes with the natural structure). We may reasonably think thus that, when no constrained policy structure is given in the problem, the natural structure we proposed is a good choice. Here GA is not parallelized, except when agents have ternary action spaces (in this case there starts to be a computation time difference).

More generally, the slower is a given Optim-Eval algorithm, the greater it is in terms of quality. The exact resolution is faster but it does not allow to find the best factored policy with the constrained structure, while CA-JT or GA-JT provide a locally optimal factored policy with this structure.

4.3   Large Random Problems

On random F^3MDPs and GMDPs, with 15 agents, 15 state variables and 15 reward functions, the optimal global policy can no more be computed. We have compared (i) CA-LBP, GA-LBP and MF-API on GMDPs with binary action spaces and (ii) CA-LBP, GA-LBP and a uniform stochastic policy, on F^3MDPs (Table 3). For F^3MDPs, we assumed a policy structure chosen at random, with at most 9 parent variables per action variable. Algorithms were initialized with the greedy policy in the case of GDMPs, and with the uniform policy otherwise. The greedy policy is the deterministic factored policy which chooses actions that maximize immediate rewards. For these problems, the parallelizability of

Table 2. Mean relative error to the optimal global policy of small random F^{3}MDPs, having $n = 6$ binary state variables, $m = 6$ agents with binary action spaces and $r = 6$ reward functions, averaged over 100 problems. The last two lines correspond to 100 problems with $n = m = r = 5$ and ternary action spaces.

Computed policy - step	MRE	mean time
Binary action spaces		
GA-JT - $\eta_q = 20$	0.0200	3.25 min
GA-LBP - $\eta_q = 20$	0.1228	1.88 min
GA-LBP - $\eta_q = 10$	0.1214	2.47 min
GA-LBP - Wolfe step	0.1216	2.48 min
GA-LBP - optimal step	0.1217	2.63 min
CA-JT - $\eta_q = 0.1$	0.0222	5.14 min
CA-LBP - $\eta_q = 0.1$	0.1228	1.53 min
Exact (global policy)	-	1.95 min
Ternary action spaces		
GA-LBP - $\eta_q = 20$	0.1288	39.74s
Exact (global policy)	-	43.44s

Table 3. Monte-Carlo evaluation of solution policies of large random F^{3}MDPs and GMDPs (15 agents and 15 state variables). Values are averaged over 5 problems. GA is parallelized (8 cores).

Computed policy - initial policy - step	Value (MC)	mean time
GMDPs		
CA-LBP - greedy - $\eta_q = 0.1$	99.492	6.31 min
GA-LBP - greedy - Wolfe step	99.538	39.91 sec
CA-LBP - uniform - $\eta_q = 0.1$	97.508	22.58 min
GA-LBP - uniform - Wolfe step	99.472	1.25 min
MF-API - greedy	99.684	1.16 sec
F^{3}MDPs, binary action spaces		
GA-LBP - uniform - Wolfe step	85.65	9.18 min
CA-LBP - uniform - $\eta_q = 0.1$	86.738	74.24 min
F^{3}MDPs, ternary action spaces		
GA-LBP - uniform - Wolfe step	76.47	14.97 min
CA-LBP	not applicable	–
Uniform policy	65,542	–

the GA-LBP algorithm makes it far faster than the CA-LBP algorithm, to the price of a slight loss in quality.

On GMDPs, our PI-like algorithms provide good quality SFPs, compared to MF-API, but they are slower. These good results in terms of quality, as the ones obtained on small problems, encourage to apply PI-like algorithms on large non-GMDP problems.

4.4 Large Disease Management Problems

We have considered very large F^3MDP problems, inspired by the disease management problem modelled in the GMDP framework in [3,21]. Crop fields are distributed on 5×5 or 10×10 grids. One binary state variable (uninfected or infected crop) and one binary action variable ("normal" cropping system or "treated" and left fallow) are attached to each crop field. Each binary action variable is chosen independently by agents. Disease can spread to neighbouring fields only. In the 10×10 grid case, the total number of parameters of an SFP is $N = 5184$.

To make the initial GMDP model more realistic, we considered that treatment occurs before disease spread and reduces the probability of contamination of neighbouring fields. In this case, the problem is not a GMDP anymore. The probability of infection becomes: $P(\epsilon, p_1, n_1, p_2, n_2) = \epsilon + (1-\epsilon)(1-(1-p_1)^{n_1}(1-p_2)^{n_2})$. p_1 (resp. p_2) is the probability of short distance contamination without (resp. with) treatment, n_1 (resp. n_2) is the number of non treated (resp. treated) infected neighbouring fields and ε is the probability of long-distance contamination. The form of the reward function is the same as in [21], with maximal reward $\rho = 100$. Table 4 displays the results for $\epsilon = 0.01$, $p_1 = 0.6$, $p_2 = 0.4$ and $\hat{T} = 20$ for LBP evaluation (using $\hat{T} = 40$ led to similar results). We compared the CA-LBP and GA-LBP policies with the uniform stochastic policy and the greedy policy. CA-LBP improves the value of the greedy policy by 30% in the case of the 5×5 grid and 23% in the case of the 10×10 grid, while GA-LBP converges to the greedy policy.

Table 4. Monte-Carlo evaluation of policies in the disease management problem.

Computed policy - step	Value (MC)	mean time
5×5 grid, uniform start		
Uniform	10367	-
Greedy	13191	-
CA-LBP - $\eta_q = 0.1$	17264	1h16
GA-LBP - Wolfe step	13195	21min20
10×10 grid, uniform start		
Uniform	40495	-
Greedy	52575	-
CA-LBP - $\eta_q = 0.1$	65068	43h42
GA-LBP - Wolfe step	52574	10h20

Finally, we considered a surveillance network situation inspired by the disease management problem, in which factored expert policies are likely to perform well. Namely, we have considered the 5×5 disease management problem, but each agent chooses the management action in each crop, given the same information: 4 sites (site of coordinates (2,2) and the three symmetric ones) are monitored

Table 5. Monte-Carlo evaluation of policies in the disease management problem with surveillance network.

Computed policy - step - $\hat{T}$	Value (MC)	mean time
5 × 5 grid, $p = 0.2$, uniform start		
Uniform	11393	-
Greedy	13953	-
Policy 1	18911	-
Policy 2	18349	-
CA-LBP - $\eta_q = 0.1$ - $\hat{T} = 20$	15055	47.25min
GA-LBP - Wolfe step - $\hat{T} = 20$	14427	43.18sec
GA-LBP - Wolfe step - $\hat{T} = 40$	14480	3.8min

and everyone knows their state at the current time step. MF-API does not apply to this non-GMDP problem. The CA-LBP and GA-LBP policies are compared to the uniform policy, to the greedy policy and to expert policies, consisting in treating a crop (i) if one of the closest observed crops is infected (Policy 1) or (ii) if at least 3 observed crops are infected (Policy 2).

The results showed that CA-LBP and GA-LBP improve over uniform or greedy, GA-LBP being faster but slightly worse than CA-LBP (Table 5). However, expert policies do better. In this example, expert policies are local maxima of $V_\theta^{R,T,LBP}(P^0)$. They are fixed points of CA-LBP and GA-LBP. In the general case, when factored expert policies are available, initializing CA-LBP or GA-LBP with them is a good way to evaluate them and to determine whether they can be improved or are local maxima.

5   Concluding Remarks

We have proposed a generic framework, F³MDP, and a family of solution algorithms for solving large size FA-FMDPs, by computing stochastic factored policies. Using this framework, we are able to deal with collaborative multiagent MDPs with up to 100 agents and 2^{100} states.

Experiments have shown that the algorithms compute policies of better or equivalent value than existing algorithms, when these are available. When problems are too large to solve with current approaches, the policies computed by our algorithms improve over simple arbitrary policies. When expert knowledge about solution policies is available, our approach can use it as an initialization, and either improve these expert policies, or show that they cannot be locally improved. Expert policies may also suggest a policy structure.

A reasonable use of CA-LBP and GA-LBP is thus to apply them on F³MDPs in an iterative loop Expert Policy - Optimization - Expert interpretation. Note also that the flexibility of our approach allows us to use in alternation the different algorithms : (i) use a few steps of GA-LBP to get fast close to a local optimum then (ii) use of CA-LBP (if actions are binary) to eventually improve the current value and (iii) in the end, use CA-MC or GA-MC, to optimize an asymptotically unbiased estimation of the policy value.

The framework we propose here admits some other natural extensions. For instance, partial observability is already handled, given that stochastic factored policies only have access to partial observation (it is obvious in the last experiment). It can be straightforwardly extended to the case of Dec-POMDPs with factored state space, by considering observations and factored observation functions, in addition to factored transitions and SFPs. The principle of the approach presented here would be unchanged, provided that the dependency graph determined by transitions, SFPs *and* observation functions is acyclic.

References

1. Bernstein, D., Givan, R., Immerman, N., Zilberstein, S.: The complexity of Decentralized Control of Markov Decision Processes. Mathematics of Operations Research **27**(4), 819–840 (2002)
2. Buffet, O., Aberdeen, D.: The Factored Policy-Gradient Planner. Artificial Intelligence **173**, 722–747 (2009)
3. Cheng, Q., Liu, Q., Chen, F., Ihler, A.: Variational Planning for Graph-Based MDPs. Advances in Neural Information Processing Systems **26**, 2976–2984 (2013)
4. Dibangoye, J.S., Amato, C., Buffet, O., Charpillet, F.: Exploiting separability in multiagent planning with continous-state MDPs. In: Proceedings of the 13th International Conference on Autonomous Agents and Multiagent Systems (2014)
5. Dibangoye, J. S., Amato, C., Doniec, A.: Scaling up decentralized MDPs through heuristic search. In: Proceedings of the 28th Conference on Uncertainty in Artificial Intelligence, pp. 217–226 (2012)
6. Forsell, N., Sabbadin, R.: Approximate linear-programming algorithms for graph-based Markov decision processes. In: Proceedings of the 17h European Conference on Artificial Intelligence, pp. 590–594 (2006)
7. Frey, B., Mackay, D.: A revolution: belief propagation in graphs with cycles. In: Advances in Neural Information Processing Systems, pp. 479–485 (1998)
8. Guestrin, C., Koller, D., Parr, R.: Multiagent Planning with factored MDPs. In: Advances in Neural Information Processing Systems, pp. 1523–1530 (2001)
9. Hoey, J., St-Aubin, R., Hu, A., Boutilier, C.: SPUDD: stochastic planning using algebraic decision diagrams. In: Proceedings of the 15th Conference on Uncertainty in Artificial Intelligence, pp. 279–288 (1999)
10. Kim, K-E., Dean, T., Meuleau, N.: Approximate solutions to factored Markov decision processes via greedy search in the space of finite state controllers. In: Proceedings of the 5th International Conference on Artificial Intelligence Planning Systems, pp. 323–330 (2000)
11. Kim, K.-E., Dean, T.R.: Solving factored MDPs with large action space using algebraic decision diagrams. In: Ishizuka, M., Sattar, A. (eds.) PRICAI 2002. LNCS (LNAI), vol. 2417, pp. 80–89. Springer, Heidelberg (2002)
12. Kumar, A., Zilberstein, S., Toussaint, M.: Scalable multiagent planning using probabilistic inference. In: Proceedings of the 22th International Joint Conference on Artificial Intelligence (2011)
13. Littman, M., Goldsmith, J., Mundhenk, M.: The Computational Complexity of Probabilistic Planning. Journal of Artificial Intelligence Research **9**, 1–36 (1998)

14. Luenberger, D.G., Ye, Y.: Linear and Nonlinear Programming, 3rd edition. Springer (2008)
15. Mooij, J.M.: libDAI: A Free and open Source C++ Library for Discrete Approximate Inference in Graphical Models. Journal of Machine Learning Research **11**, 2169–2173 (2010)
16. Murphy, K.: Dynamic Bayesian networks: representation, inference and learning. PhD Thesis, School of Computer Science, University of California, Berkeley (2002)
17. Oliehoek, F.A., Whiteson, S., Spaan, M.T.J.: Approximate solutions for factored dec-PODMPs with many agents. In: Proceedings of the 12th International Conference on Autonomous Agents and Multiagent Systems (2013)
18. Peyrard, N., Sabbadin, R.: Mean field approximation of the policy iteration algorithm for graph-based Markov decision processes. In: Proceedings of the European Conference on Artificial Intelligence, pp. 595–599 (2006)
19. Puterman, M.: Markov Decision Processes. John Wiley and Sons (1994)
20. Raghavan, A., Joshi, S., Fern, A., Tadepalli, P., Khardon, R.: Planning in factored action spaces with symbolic dynamic programming. In: Proceedings of the 26th AAAI Conference on Artificial Intelligence (2012)
21. Sabbadin, R., Peyrard, N., Forsell, N.: A Framework and a Mean-Field Algorithm For The Local Conrtol of Spatial Processes. International Journal of Approximate Reasoning **53**(1), 66–86 (2012)
22. Sallans, B., Hinton, G.E.: Reinforcement Learning with Factored States and Actions. Journal of Machine Learning Research **5**, 1063–1088 (2004)
23. St-Aubin, R., Hoey, J., Boutilier, C.: APRICODD: approximate policy construction using decision diagrams. In: Advances in Neural Information Processing Systems, pp. 1089–1095 (2000)
24. Yedidia, J.S., Freeman, W.T., Weiss, Y.: Constructing Free-Energy Approximations and Generalized Belief Propagation Algorithms. IEEE Transactions on Information Theory **51**(7), 2282–2312 (2005)
25. Kok, J.R., Vlassis, N.: Collaborative Multiagent Reinforcement Learning by Payoff Propagation. Journal of Machine Learning Rsearch **7**, 1789–1828 (2006)
26. Guestrin, C., Lagoudakis, M., Parr, R.: Coordinated reinforcement learning. In: Proceedings of the 19th International Conference on Machine Learning (2002)

Appendix: Demonstration of the Complexity Result

We prove here the Theorem of Section 3.2. In order to show that the F³MDP problem is NP^{PP}-hard, we will use a polynomial time reduction from the $EMAJSAT$ problem, which is known to be NP^{PP}-complete [13].

Definition 1. *$EMAJSAT$ problem.*

Let ϕ be a boolean formula over variables $X_1, \ldots, X_n$, with m clauses ($\phi = (C_1 \wedge \ldots \wedge C_m)$), and let $k \in \{1, \ldots, n\}$ be a fixed integer. The $EMAJSAT$ decision problem consists in asking whether there exists an instantiation $(x_1, \ldots, x_k)$ of the variables $(X_1, \ldots, X_k)$ such that, for the majority of the possible instantiations $(x_{k+1}, \ldots, x_n)$ of $(X_{k+1}, \ldots, X_n)$ ϕ is satisfied.

We are going to show a polynomial transformation of any instance (ϕ, k) of $EMAJSAT^4$ into a F^3MDP instance $(\mathcal{P}, \frac{1}{2})$: an instance $\mathcal{P}$ is positive iff there exists an SFP δ^*, with structure defined by the $\{pa_\delta(a_j)\}_{j=1..m}$, of value $V_{\delta^*}^{R,T}(P^0) > \frac{1}{2}$. So, we are going to exhibit a transformation from $EMAJSAT$ instances into F^3MDP instances such that the answer to the $EMAJSAT$ problem is yes iff there exists a (deterministic) factored policy δ^* of value greater than $\frac{1}{2}$.

We build a F^3MDP with binary decision variables $(X_1^t, \ldots, X_k^t)$, and with state variables $(X_{k+1}^t, \ldots, X_n^t, C_1^t, \ldots, C_m^t, Y_1^t, \ldots, Y_k^t)$. All variables take values in $\{0, 1\}$, except variables Y_l^t, which take values in $\{-1, 0, 1\}$. The initial probability distribution, the transition probabilities and the reward functions are defined as:

- $P^0(X_i^0 = 0) = P^0(X_i^0 = 1) = \frac{1}{2}, \forall i = k+1, \ldots, n$.
- $P^0(C_j^0 = 0) = 1, \forall j = 1, \ldots, m$.
- $P^0(Y_l^0 = -1) = 1, \forall l = 1, \ldots, k$.
- $P_i(X_i^{t+1} = x_i | X_i^t = x_i) = 1, \forall i = k+1, \ldots, n, \forall x_i \in \{0, 1\}$. The values of the variables X_i^0 are drawn uniformly at random at the beginning, and then remain unchanged through time.
- $P_{n+1}(C_1^{t+1} = 1 | C_1^t = 1 \vee (C_1^t = 0 \wedge X^t \models C_1)) = 1$ et $\forall j = 2...m$, $P_{n+j}(C_j^{t+1} | C_j^t = 1 \vee (C_j^t = 0 \wedge C_{j-1}^t = 1 \wedge X^t \models C_j)) = 1$. The local transition probabilities linked to variables C_j are such that, for any instantiation $X^0 = (x_1, \ldots, x_n)$, at $t = 1$ C_1^1 takes value 1 iff $(x_1, \ldots, x_n) \models C_1$, and then, at any time t, C_j^t takes value 1 iff if $(x_1, \ldots, x_n) \models C_1 \wedge \ldots \wedge C_j$.
- $P_l(Y_l^{t+1} = x_l | X_l^t = x_l) = 1, \forall l = 1, \ldots, k, \forall x_l \in \{0, 1\}, \forall t = 0, \ldots, T - 1$. Variables Y_l are gadgets, which will be used jointly with gadget reward functions, to ensure that non-deterministic policies cannot be optimal.
- Reward functions $\{R_l, l = 1 \ldots k\}$ are defined on pairs of variables (X_l, Y_l). $R_l(x_l, y_l) = 0$ if $x_l = y_l$ and $R_l(x_l, y_l) = -K$ if $x_l \neq y_l$, where $K > \frac{1}{\gamma^{2m}}$.
- Reward function R_{k+1} is defined on variable C_m : $R_{k+1}(c_m) = \frac{1}{\gamma^m}$ if $c_m = 1$ and $R_{k+1}(c_m) = 0$ if $c_m = 0$.

With this definition and the definition of the transition functions, it is guaranteed that any possible trajectory $x^0, \ldots, x^T$ incurs a positive or null sum of rewards iff $x^0 = x^1 = \ldots = x^T$ and a negative reward else. We consider, in addition, that the horizon of the F^3MDP is $T = m$. Furthermore, we consider that $pa_\delta(X_l^t) = \emptyset, \forall l = 1 \ldots k$.

Note that the reduction is polynomial in time. All transition tables and reward functions have bounded size. In particular, since we consider 3-clauses, in $P_{n+j}(C_j^{t+1} | pa_P(C_j^{t+1}))$, $pa_P(C_j^{t+1})$ involves five variables at most. In order to complete the proof, we have to show that : (i) the optimal policy δ^* of this

---

[4] We exhibit a polynomial time reduction from $EMAJSAT$ with 3-clauses to F^3MDP, benefiting from the known fact that an $EMAJSAT$ instance can be rewritten as an equivalent $EMAJSAT$ instance, containing only 3-clauses (which may contain polynomially more clauses and variables).

F^3MDP is deterministic, and (ii) δ^* has value greater than $\frac{1}{2}$ iff if the answer to the EMAJSAT problem is yes.

Fact (i) is proved by first showing that the value of an arbitrary stochastic policy δ for the F^3MDP model of an EMAJSAT instance (see equation (1)), is upper bounded by a sum over all trajectories with variables $(X_1^t = x_1, \ldots, X_n^t = x_n)$ constant in time of a function $g(x_1, \ldots, x_n)$:

$$\forall \delta, V_\delta^{R,T}(P^0) \leq \sum_{x_1, \ldots, x_n} (\delta(x_1, \ldots, x_k))^m \, P^0(x_{k+1}, \ldots, x_n) g(x_1, \ldots, x_n),$$

where $g(x_1, \ldots, x_n) = 1$ if $(x_1, \ldots, x_n) \models \phi$ and 0 else. Then, the deterministic policy of optimal value, $\delta^*(\emptyset) = (x_1^*, \ldots, x_k^*)$, is defined by:

$$(x_1^*, \ldots, x_k^*) = \arg \max_{x_1, \ldots, x_k} \sum_{x_{k+1}, \ldots, x_n} P^0(x_{k+1}, \ldots, x_n) g(x_1, \ldots, x_n),$$

For any SFP δ, we have $\delta(x_1, \ldots, x_k) \leq 1, \forall x_1, \ldots, x_k$ and thus $V_\delta^{R,T}(P^0) \leq V_{\delta^*}^{R,T}(P^0)$. So, the deterministic factored policy δ^* is optimal for the F^3MDP.

To prove fact (ii), let us consider a deterministic factored policy δ, corresponding to a vector $(x_1, \ldots, x_k)$. P^0 determines a set of values $(x_{k+1}, \ldots, x_n)$ at random (all vectors have identical probability $\frac{1}{2^{n-k}}$). Once all variables values are fixed at time $t = 0$, it is easy to check that transitions are deterministic, and that $C_m^m = 1$ iff $(x_1, \ldots, x_n) \models C_1 \wedge \ldots \wedge C_m$. If this is verified, the corresponding trajectory incurs a discounted sum of rewards $\gamma^m R_{k+1}(1) = 1$. Thus, the value of any determistic factored policy $\delta = (x_1, \ldots, x_k)$ is:

$$V_\delta^{R,T}(P^0) = \sum_{x_{k+1}, \ldots, x_n \, s.t. \{x_1, \ldots, x_n\} \models \phi} \frac{1}{2^{n-k}}$$

This value is greater than $\frac{1}{2}$ iff a majority of the 2^{n-k} instantiations $\{x_{k+1}, \ldots, x_n\}$ satisfy ϕ. So, EMAJSAT reduces to the F^3MDP problem, and the F^3MDP problem is NP^{PP}-hard. It is easier to show that the F^3MDP problem belongs to the NP^{PP} class (omitted here due to limited space), and thus that the F^3MDP problem is NP^{PP}-complete.

Managing Autonomous Mobility on Demand Systems for Better Passenger Experience

Wen Shen[✉] and Cristina Lopes

Department of Informatics, University of California, Irvine, CA 92697, USA
{wen.shen,lopes}@uci.edu

Abstract. Autonomous mobility on demand systems, though still in their infancy, have very promising prospects in providing urban population with sustainable and safe personal mobility in the near future. While much research has been conducted on both autonomous vehicles and mobility on demand systems, to the best of our knowledge, this is the first work that shows how to manage autonomous mobility on demand systems for better passenger experience. We introduce the Expand and Target algorithm which can be easily integrated with three different scheduling strategies for dispatching autonomous vehicles. We implement an agent-based simulation platform and empirically evaluate the proposed approaches with the New York City taxi data. Experimental results demonstrate that the algorithm significantly improve passengers' experience by reducing the average passenger waiting time by up to 29.82% and increasing the trip success rate by up to 7.65%.

Keywords: Autonomous vehicles · Mobility on demand · AMOD Systems · Agent-based simulation

1 Introduction

As urbanization accelerates and city population continues to grow, more traffic is generated due to the increasing demand for personal mobility as well as the upswing of private car ownership [11]. This results in many severe problems such as traffic congestion, air pollution and limited public space available for the construction of parking areas and roads [4]. To solve these problems, it is in urgent need of building a transportation system that not only satisfies people's mobility demand but is also more sustainable, efficient and reliable. Although autonomous mobility on demand (AMOD) systems, which, due to some technical, economical and governmental obstacles left to be overcome, are still in their infancy, they hold very promising prospectus in meeting the need. This is because AMOD systems have great potential to provide a safer, near instantly available solution for personal mobility. Once such services have become highly available and affordable, the collective transport solutions will eventually transcend the traditional private ownership, which will significantly reduce the traffic congestion, pollution and land use for parking purpose through system-wide optimization and coordination. Besides, autonomous vehicles can also avoid

© Springer International Publishing Switzerland 2015
Q. Chen et al. (Eds.): PRIMA 2015, LNAI 9387, pp. 20–35, 2015.
DOI: 10.1007/978-3-319-25524-8_2

accidents caused by human errors, making them safer than conventional cars driven by human drivers [18].

In recent years, much research has been conducted on autonomous vehicles. However, most of the research focuses on the control of a single autonomous vehicle to perform various tasks including picking up passengers and parking. While interesting and important, it leaves much other territory uninvestigated, especially methodologies on managing systems of autonomous vehicles for personal mobility. To bridge the gap and address the transportation problems brought by city expansion and population growth, we study how to dispatch AMOD systems to improve passengers' experience. In doing so, we introduce the *Expand and Target* (EAT) algorithm. We then conduct agent-based simulation using the AMOD simulation platform based on the *MobilityTestbed* [7][6] and the New York City taxi data [10].

The rest of the paper is organized as follows: Section 2 briefly discusses the background and related work on autonomous vehicles, mobility on demand(MOD) systems, and AMOD systems; Section 3 introduces three scheduling strategies and the *Expand and Target* algorithm for managing AMOD systems; Section 4 talks about the experiments for evaluating the proposed dispatching approaches for AMOD systems. Section 5 concludes this paper and presents potential directions for further investigation.

2 Related Work

2.1 Autonomous Vehicles

An autonomous or automated vehicle is a vehicle capable of fulfilling transport tasks such as motion and braking without the control of a human driver [18]. The development of autonomous vehicles relies on advances in computer vision, sensing technology, wireless communication, navigation, robotic control as well as technologies in automobile manufacturing [3]. Significant progresses have been achieved in these fields over the past several decades. For example, LIDAR and vision-based detection techniques (e.g., stereo vision) are extensively studied in pedestrian, lane and vehicle detection [27][15][24]. Vehicular communication systems make it possible for individual vehicles to share information (e.g., traffic congestion, road information) from other vehicles in the vicinity, which can potentially improve the operational safety of autonomous vehicles [26].

The shift from conventional cars to autonomous vehicles can substantially reduce traffic accidents caused by human errors, given the fact that the operation of autonomous vehicles does not involve human intervention [3]. It also increases mobility for people who are unable or unwilling to drive themselves [3].

As technology advances, many prototypes of autonomous cars have been designed and developed. Some examples of these include Google driver-less car [21], Vislab's BRAiVE [5], and BMW's M235i [17], just to name a few. These cars are also successfully tested in various real-world traffic environments, making it possible and desirable to be integrated with MOD systems.

2.2 Mobility on Demand Systems

To reduce private car ownership while also meeting the need for personal urban mobility, Mitchell et al. introduces MOD systems [23][8]. The original purpose of MOD systems is to complement mass transportation systems such as subways and buses, providing commuters with the mobility for the first mile and the last mile. A notable prototype is the CityCar [22].

The vehicles in current MOD systems are mainly light electric vehicles across the main stations around the city , guided by human drivers or guideways, which limits the scope of mobility and the development of the MOD systems. If autonomous vehicles were integrated into the MOD systems, the AMOD systems would transform mobility and revolutionize the transportation industry by offering more flexible and more convenient solutions for urban personal mobility.

2.3 Autonomous Mobility on Demand Systems

Due to lack of infrastructure, little research has been done on autonomous MOD systems. Among the very few studies, Spieser et.al. [29] provides analytical guidelines for autonomous MOD systems using Singapore taxi data. The results show that AMOD systems could meet the mobility need of the same population with only 1/3 of the taxis that are current in operation. Zhang et al. [30] presents a similar analysis using a queueing-theoretical model with trip demand data in Manhattan, New York City. While interesting and innovative, the research leaves a number of issues unexplored. For instance, how to efficiently manage autonomous vehicles to enhance passengers' experience?

Although numerous research addresses taxi dispatching problems using various methodologies including techniques in multi-agent systems [2][28][13][1][12], no or at least little research addresses methodologies on dispatching AMOD systems for better user experience. Unlike conventional taxi dispatching systems where it is often difficult to coordinate because of human factors (e.g., the drivers may not follow the dispatcher's instructions carefully), the AMOD systems make it possible to implement a much higher level of autonomy through delicate, system-wide coordination. Moreover, it is challenging to achieve near instantly availability using conventional approaches. We try to bridge this gap by introducing a new algorithm-the *Expand and Target* algorithm to effectively manage AMOD systems.

3 Managing Autonomous Mobility on Demand Systems

In this section, we first discuss three scheduling strategies that are either commonly used in the taxi dispatching field or frequently studied in literature: the No-Scheduling Strategy (NSS), the Static-Scheduling Strategy (SSS), and the Online-Scheduling Strategy(OSS) [19].

For effective management of AMOD systems, we introduce the *Expand and Target* (EAT) algorithm. This algorithm enables managing authorities of

AMOD systems to automatically and effectively dispatch autonomous vehicles and meanwhile update adjacency schedule as well for better passenger experience: first, it increases the possibility of finding global optimal solutions; second, it reduces computation time by avoiding looping all the possible vehicles; third, it connects isolated areas with other dispatching areas and updates the adjacency schedule automatically, which increases the dispatch success rate.

We then discuss methodologies on integrating the scheduling strategies with the EAT algorithm to improve passengers' experience, especially to reduce the average passenger waiting time and increase the trip success rate.

3.1   Scheduling Strategies

No-Scheduling Strategy. In this strategy, the dispatcher assigns the nearest idle taxi to an incoming call. If such a taxi can not be found, then the call will be rejected. The dispatcher does not update the dispatching schedule. That is why we call it the No-Scheduling Strategy or NSS. The NSS is the most commonly used strategy in taxi dispatching applications [28].

Static-Scheduling Strategy. In SSS, the dispatcher keeps a schedule of the dispatching process and updates it by appending an incoming call to the list of processed requests. When a new call comes, the dispatcher searches for the nearest taxi from all the vehicles (both idle and busy). It then estimates the time from current position to the pickup location based on current traffic condition. For a idle taxi, the dispatcher simply computes a trip plan directly from the taxi's current location to the pickup location. While for a taxi that is busy, the dispatcher then calculates the remaining time needed for the taxi to complete the current trip and then calculate a trip plan from the end point of the trip to the pickup location. Then the dispatcher estimates the total time needed for this taxi to arrive at the pickup location. In this way, the dispatcher selects a taxi that can reach the passenger to be picked up in the quickest time. The dispatcher does update the schedule of the dispatching process, but it never reschedules or reassigns the requests. This strategy broadens the choice of taxis, but it scales poorly due to one-time scheduling.

Online-Scheduling Strategy. The OSS is similar to the static approach except that in the online strategy the schedules are always re-computed in response to traffic variations such as delays or speedups. It is more cost efficient than SSS but requires more computational power.

3.2   The Expand and Target Algorithm

We formally introduce the *Expand and Target* algorithm (see Algorithm 1). The basic idea of the algorithm is described as follows:

- When the dispatcher receives a call c, it first identifies the neighborhood a_c that c originates from.

- If area a_c has no adjacent areas, it then searches for the nearest available vehicle in area a_c: if found, it assigns the vehicle to the call, and returns the assignment; if not, it searches for the nearest available vehicle in all dispatching areas: if found, it adds the vehicle's area a_i as a neighbor of area a_c (by doing so, it removes the isolated dispatching area and updates the adjacency schedule), assigns the vehicle to the call, and returns the assignment; if not found, it rejects the call. Meanwhile, it updates the schedule.
- If area a_c has other adjacent areas $\tilde{B}_{a_c}$ where the service is available, then we define the dispatching area for call c as B_{a_c}. Instead of searching for the nearest available vehicle in a_c, it first expands the dispatching area for c: $B_{a_c} \leftarrow \tilde{B}_{a_c} \cup a_c$. We call this process as *expand*. The expansion is necessary because it diminishes the possibility of finding local minimum: For example, when a call is from the border of several areas, it is not sufficient to decide whether a nearest available vehicle is in the current dispatching area or from other areas without considering all the neighborhoods.
- After expansion, then *target*: it searches for the nearest available vehicle in B_{a_c}: if found, it assigns the vehicle to the call, returns the assignment and terminates; if not found, then continues to expand the dispatching area B_{a_c} using the previous strategy.

The *Expand and Target* algorithm dynamically expands the search space and targets the autonomous vehicles, in which the expansion and targeting can be viewed as a multi-agent, self-adaptive process. The algorithm assumes that the dispatching system processes passengers' requests in a First-Come, First-Served (FCFS) manner. It is also suitable for dispatching systems using other policies such as batch processing. However, modification of the algorithm is necessary for such applications (though we do not explore it in this work).

3.3   Integration

To improve the performance of the dispatching system, we combine the three scheduling strategies discussed in section 3.1 and the EAT algorithm, resulting in three integrated approaches: NSS-EAT, SSS-EAT, and OSS-EAT. The incorporation is straightforward: when applying the EAT algorithm for dispatching autonomous vehicles, the dispatcher computes the nearest available vehicles using the three different scheduling strategies respectively. There is a commonly used searching method for taxi dispatching: when a call comes, the dispatcher first searches for a nearest available taxi in the current dispatching area; if such a taxi not found, then searches for an available taxi in an adjacent area. If the taxi does not have adjacent areas, the dispatcher then rejects the call. We also integrate this method with the three scheduling strategies as three control groups: NSS, SSS, and OSS.

3.4   The Autonomous Mobility on Demand Simulation Platform

We implement the simulation platform for AMOD systems on top of the *MobilityTestbed* [7][6]. The *MobilityTestbed* is an agent-based, open-source simulation

---

Algorithm 1. *Expand and Target*

Precondition: c -an incoming call, V - autonomous vehicles in operation, and A-dispatching adjacency schedule

1: **procedure** EXPAND AND TARGET(c, V, A)
2:    identify $c's$ dispatching area $a_c \in A$
3:    **if** area a_c has adjacent areas (immediate neighbors) $\tilde{B}_{a_c} \subseteq A$ **then**
4:       //begin to *expand:*
5:       $B_{a_c} \leftarrow a_c \cup \tilde{B}_{a_c}$
6:       //begin to *target:*
7:       **if** there are available vehicles in area B_{a_c} **then**
8:          in area B_{a_c}, search for the nearest available vehicle $v \in V$
9:          **return** assignment pair (v, c)
10:      **else**
11:         **while** a in B_{a_c} **do**
12:            continue to *expand* within A
13:         **end while**
14:         **return** reject the call c
15:      **end if**
16:   **else**
17:      **if** there are available vehicles in area c **then**
18:         in area c, search for the nearest vehicle $v \in V$
19:         **return** assignment pair (v, c)
20:      **else**
21:         **if** there are available vehicles in area A **then**
22:            in area A, search for the nearest vehicle $v \in V$
23:            //begin to *update:*
24:            set the dispatching area v as a neighbor of area a_c
25:            **return** assignment pair (v, c)
26:         **else**
27:            reject the call c
28:         **end if**
29:      **end if**
30:   **end if**
31: **end procedure**

---

framework (written in Java) tailored for modeling and simulating on-demand transport systems. It consists of three layers: the *AgentPolis* simulator [16], the Testbed Core and the mechanism implementation [7][6]. The first two layers provide the Testbed API while the third layer enables users to implement their own mechanisms or strategies for various on-demand transport systems. The mechanism implementation includes three agent logic blocks: the driver agent logic, the dispatcher agent logic and the passenger agent logic. In AMOD systems, no drivers are needed, so we replace the driver logic with the autonomous vehicle agent logic. The *MobilityTestbed* does not work properly with large datasets (e.g., a trip demand file larger than 1GB) due to poor memory management schemes. Thus, We modify the Testbed Core to make the platform be able to support large datasets.

This testbed also contains other components such as experiment management, benchmark importer, and visualization and reporting. However, the original experiment management component can only produce overall statistics, whereas in real-world scenarios it is important and necessary to log the operational data periodically for future use. The benchmark importer component provides benchmark data for studying on-demand transport systems, but it is customized for traditional on-demand transport service and only deal with small datasets. The visualization and reporting component, using Google Earth to visualize daily mobility pattern of passengers and vehicles, does not work properly with large-scale datasets. For these reasons, we discard all the three components. To meet the needs of the experiment, we implement the data logger component which enables the platform to efficiently log the operational data periodically.

An overview of the AMOD platform based on the *MobilityTestbed* is shown in Fig. 1. The simulation platform is composed of two layers- the mechanism implementation layer and the simulation platform core layer, and an extension- the data logger. The mechanism implementation includes three logic blocks: the vehicle agent logic, the dispatcher agent logic, and the passenger agent logic. The simulation platform core is built on the basis of the *MobilityTestbed* which consists of the testbed core and the *AgentPolis* platform.

4   Experimental Analysis

To empirically evaluate the performance of the *Expand and Target* algorithm on managing AMOD systems, we implement six different dispatching approaches using the AMOD simulation platform on the basis of the *MobilityTestbed* and OpenStreetMap [14]. We then perform experiments using the 2013 New York City taxi data [10] and analyze the experimental results.

4.1   Evaluation Metrics

To evaluate the performance of the dispatching system from the passengers' perspective, we select the following two metrics: the Average Passenger Waiting

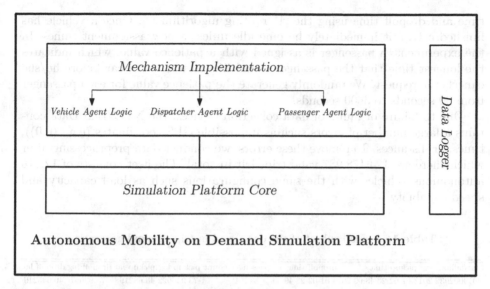

Fig. 1. An overview of the Autonomous Mobility on Demand Simulation Platform based on *MobilityTestbed*.

Time (T_{APW}) and the Trip Success Rate (R_{TS}). This is because they are considered as the two most important indicators of passenger satisfaction (quality of service) [19].

The average passenger waiting time is formulated as the following equation:

$$T_{APW} = \frac{\sum_{i \in N}(T_i^p - T_i^r)}{|N|}, \tag{1}$$

where T_i^p and T_i^r are the pickup time and the request time of call i, respectively. N is the set of calls and $|N|$ is the number of calls in set N.

The trip success rate is defined as below:

$$R_{TS} = \frac{n_s}{n}, \tag{2}$$

where n_s is the number of successful trips and n is the number of calls.

4.2   The Datasets

We choose the 2013 New York City Taxi Data [10] to generate the trip demand. This raw data takes up for about 21.23GB in CSV format, in which each row represents a single taxi trip (including demand information). Table 1 shows a small sample of data which we use in the experiments. In order to compute the average passenger waiting time, the request time of the calls is needed. However, there is no such information available in this dataset. To solve this problem, we use the actual pickup time as the request time. We compute the pickup time and dropoff time using the A^* routing algorithm [9]. Once a vehicle has finished a trip, it immediately become idle unless a new assignment comes. In the experiment, a passenger is assigned with a patience value, which indicates the longest time that the passenger would like to wait for a car before he/she cancels the request. We randomly generate the patience value for each passenger from 60 seconds to 3600 seconds.

Due to failure or faults of data collection devices, the NYC Taxi Data contains a large number of errors such as impossible GPS coordinates (e.g., (0,0)), times, or distances. To remove these errors, we conduct data preprocessing after which there are 124,178,987 valid trips left in total. The fleet consists of 12,216 autonomous vehicles with the same configurations such as load capacity and speed capability.

Table 1. A small subset of the data used in trip demand generation

medallion	pickup time	dropoff time	passenger count	pickup log	pickup lat	dropoff log	dropoff lat
2013002932	2013-01-02 23:43:00	2013-01-02 23:49:00	4	-73.946922	40.682198	-73.92067	40.685219
2013009193	2013-01-02 23:43:00	2013-01-02 23:54:00	2	-74.004379	40.747887	-73.983376	40.766918
2013007140	2013-01-02 23:46:00	2013-01-02 23:55:00	1	-73.869743	40.772369	-73.907898	40.767262
2013008400	2013-01-02 23:50:12	2013-01-02 23:56:41	3	-73.984756	40.768322	-73.983276	40.757259

The initial dispatching adjacency (see Fig. 2) is generated from the Pediacities New York City Neighborhoods GeoJSON data [25], in which there are 310 neighborhood boundaries in total. Fig. 3 shows the final adjacency schedule (71 neighborhood boundaries) using the *Expand and Target* algorithm with New York taxi data.

As for the navigation map, we use the OpenStreetMap data for New York City obtained from MAPZEN metro extracts [20] on April 9th, 2015. The size of the OSM XML data file is about 2.19GB.

4.3   Experimental Settings

In the experiment, we implement the three integrated approaches described in section 3: the NSS-EAT, the SSS-EAT, and the OSS-EAT. For comparison, we also implement the three scheduling using the common approach described in Section 3.3 as control groups: NSS, SSS, and OSS. The six AMOD systems share the same experimental setup except the dispatching approaches.

In the simulation, the vehicle speed limit is 25 Miles/hour (40.2336 Km/hour). The maximum load capacity of an autonomous vehicle is 4 and the maximum speed capacity is 100 Miles/hour. The A^* algorithm is selected as the routing algorithm. All other parameter settings are default as used in the *MobilityTestbed*. The simulation is conducted on a quad-core 2.3 GHz machine with 16 GB of RAM.

Fig. 2. Initial adjacency schedule from Pediacities New York City Neighborhoods Geo-Json data shown on OpenStreetMap

Fig. 3. Final adjacency schedule using the *Expand and Target* algorithm shown on OpenStreetMap

4.4   Experimental Results

We compare both the average passenger waiting time (see Table 2) and the trip success rate (see Table 3) of the AMOD systems using the six different dispatching approaches with the 2013 New York City Taxi Data (from 01-01-2013 to 12-31-2013).

Table 2 and Table 4 show that the EAT algorithm significantly reduces the average waiting time, both monthly and yearly, with all the three scheduling strategies. When the AMOD system follows the no-scheduling strategy, the EAT algorithm shortens the monthly average passenger waiting time by up to 49.74% (2.82 *mins*). The average passenger waiting time of the whole year is reduced by 29.82%, from 8.14 *mins* to 6.27 *mins*. Considering the total number of the trips in the year 2013, it saves 3,870,245.09 hours' time for the passengers as well as substantial reduction on operational cost and green gas emission (though we do not calculate it due to limited availability of the parameters). In the static-scheduling strategy scenarios, the EAT algorithm improves the system's performance by 26.42%, bringing the overall average waiting time down from 7.80 *mins* to 6.17 *mins*. As for the systems with online-scheduling strategy, the yearly average waiting time is also diminished greatly by 26.51%. Though the EAT algorithm considerably improves systems' performance irrespective of the scheduling strategies, it works best when associated with the NSS scenario. This is because it is more prone to local minimum in the NSS scenario than the others, while the EAT algorithm counteracts the effect by systematically expanding the search space and updating the dispatching adjacency schedule.

From Table 3 and Table 4, we can see that the EAT algorithms increases the trip success rate for systems with all the three scheduling strategies. The improvement for both NSS and SSS systems is slight, and below 5% in most months of the year. However, the improvement for the OSS system is significant, and can be up to 11.12% monthly and 7.65% for the whole year. The reason behind is that the combination of OSS and EAT provides the dispatcher sufficient search space of vehicles and updated information of the traffic information to target an optimal assignment.

Fig. 4 and 5 shows the daily average passenger waiting time and the trip success rate of the AMOD systems using the six dispatching paradigms in April 2013. They demonstrate that the OSS-EAT system performs the best among all the six systems, in measurement of both daily average passenger waiting time and trip success rate. The NSS system has the highest daily average waiting time in most case, however, it performs better than OSS according to the comparison of daily trip success rate. The reason is not clearly known to us yet, though it may be owing to the OSS system's constantly updating of the traffic information.

In summary, the EAT algorithm significantly improves the performance of AMOD systems with all the three scheduling strategies according to both the metrics. Specifically, it significantly reduces the average passenger waiting time by up to 29.82%. It increases the trip success rate by up to 7.65%.

Table 2. A comparison of the average passenger waiting time (in minutes) of the AMOD systems using the six different dispatching approaches with the 2013 New York City Taxi Data.

	NSS		SSS		OSS	
	w/ EAT	w/o EAT	w/ EAT	w/o EAT	w/ EAT	w/o EAT
Jan	6.71	8.87	6.68	8.01	6.03	7.45
Feb	6.99	9.11	6.82	8.17	6.12	7.62
Mar	7.43	9.21	7.39	9.15	6.98	8.51
Apr	5.67	8.49	5.66	7.23	5.01	6.74
May	5.11	7.30	5.04	6.78	4.78	6.08
June	6.85	8.43	6.76	8.10	6.14	7.97
July	6.68	8.56	6.37	7.81	6.19	7.55
Aug	4.88	6.67	4.85	6.50	4.64	6.16
Sept	8.60	10.28	8.52	10.21	7.33	8.68
Oct	6.98	8.83	6.83	8.75	6.17	7.78
Nov	5.89	7.64	5.73	7.65	5.22	7.06
Dec	4.16	5.65	4.05	6.18	3.91	5.30
year	6.27	8.14	6.17	7.80	5.62	7.11

Table 3. A comparison of the trip success rate(in percentage %) of the AMOD systems using the six different dispatching approaches with the 2013 New York City Taxi Data.

	NSS		SSS		OSS	
	w/ EAT	w/o EAT	w/ EAT	w/o EAT	w/ EAT	w/o EAT
Jan	87.32	79.96	89.44	87.46	90.79	86.87
Feb	83.67	89.04	92.69	89.61	93.63	89.64
Mar	92.16	89.04	92.69	89.61	93.63	89.64
Apr	80.20	77.70	81.93	79.26	82.31	76.82
May	89.96	88.10	94.05	89.69	96.77	90.96
June	83.11	80.66	85.34	83.07	89.27	81.81
July	86.05	84.76	89.14	85.17	91.79	85.61
Aug	89.27	84.79	91.09	87.86	94.01	85.71
Sept	79.87	76.04	82.31	80.00	85.91	80.48
Oct	82.79	80.55	85.32	81.62	89.79	81.35
Nov	74.99	72.61	78.35	71.65	81.27	76.51
Dec	79.52	76.23	83.65	81.40	87.66	78.89
year	83.91	80.97	86.79	83.12	89.59	83.22

Table 4. Performance improvement (in percentage %) of the AMOD systems on average passenger waiting time (T_{APW} (min)) and trip success rate (R_{TS} %) brought by the *Expand and Target* algorithm.

	NSS		SSS		OSS	
	$T_{APW}(min)$	$R_{TS}(\%)$	$T_{APW}(min)$	$R_{TS}(\%)$	$T_{APW}(min)$	$R_{TS}(\%)$
Jan	32.19	**9.20**	19.91	2.26	23.55	4.51
Feb	30.33	1.63	19.79	5.17	24.51	6.29
Mar	23.96	3.50	23.82	3.44	21.92	4.45
Apr	**49.74**	3.22	27.74	3.37	34.53	7.15
May	42.86	2.11	34.52	4.86	27.20	6.39
June	23.07	3.04	19.82	2.73	29.80	9.12
July	28.14	1.52	22.61	4.66	21.97	7.22
Aug	36.68	5.28	34.02	3.68	32.76	9.68
Sept	19.53	5.04	19.84	2.89	18.42	6.75
Oct	26.50	2.78	28.11	4.53	26.09	10.37
Nov	29.71	3.28	31.94	**9.35**	35.25	6.22
Dec	35.82	4.32	**52.59**	2.76	**35.55**	**11.12**
year	29.82	3.63	26.42	4.42	26.51	7.65

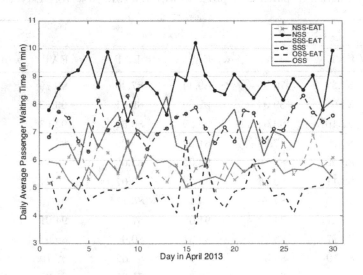

Fig. 4. Daily average passenger waiting time of AMOD systems using six different dispatching approaches (New York Taxi Data, April 2013)

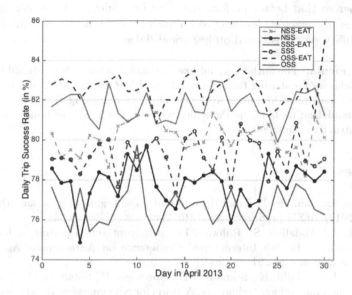

Fig. 5. Daily trip success rate (in percentage %) of AMOD systems using six different dispatching approaches (New York Taxi Data, April 2013)

5   Conclusion and Future Work

Autonomous mobility on demand systems, which, though still in their infancy, have very promising prospects in providing urban population with sustainable and safe personal mobility service in the near future. While a lot of research has been done on autonomous vehicles and mobility on demand systems, to the best of our knowledge, this is the first work that shows how to manage autonomous mobility on demand systems for better passenger experience.

To reduce the average passenger waiting time and increase the trip success rate, we introduce the *Expand and Target* algorithm which can be easily integrated with three different scheduling strategies for dispatching autonomous vehicles. We implement the autonomous mobility on demand simulation platform and conduct an empirical study with the 2013 New York City Taxi Data. Experimental results demonstrate that the algorithm significantly improves the performance of the autonomous mobility on demand systems: it reduces the overall average passenger waiting time by up to 29.82% and increases the trip success rate by up to 7.65%; it saves millions of hours of passengers' time annually.

While the results are impressive, there is still a long way to go towards a society with near instantly available personal mobility. To facilitate research in this emerging field, we are developing a robust, open-source, agent-based simulation platform for autonomous mobility on demand systems from scratch. Another interesting direction is to investigate and design novel mechanisms to encourage passengers truthfully report their travel demand well in advance to the dispatcher so that better performance can be achieved. Moreover, it would be useful to study machine learning techniques that can accurately predict passengers' mobility patterns based on historical data.

Acknowledgments. The authors would like to thank Michal Jakob, Michal Certicky and Martin Schaefer for sharing the source code of the *MobilityTestbed* and the *Agent-Polis* platform, and providing other technical support regarding the development of the AMOD simulation tool. The authors also wish to thank the anonymous reviewers for their constructive comments.

References

1. Agussurja, L., Lau, H.C.: Toward large-scale agent guidance in an urban taxi service (2012). arXiv preprint arXiv:1210.4849
2. Alshamsi, A., Abdallah, S., Rahwan, I.: Multiagent self-organization for a taxi dispatch system. In: 8th International Conference on Autonomous Agents and Multiagent Systems, pp. 21–28 (2009)
3. Anderson, J.M., Nidhi, K., Stanley, K.D., Sorensen, P., Samaras, C., Oluwatola, O.A.: Autonomous vehicle technology: A guide for policymakers. Rand Corporation (2014)
4. Beirão, G., Cabral, J.S.: Understanding attitudes towards public transport and private car: A qualitative study. Transport policy **14**(6), 478–489 (2007)
5. Broggi, A., Buzzoni, M., Debattisti, S., Grisleri, P., Laghi, M.C., Medici, P., Versari, P.: Extensive tests of autonomous driving technologies. IEEE Transactions on Intelligent Transportation Systems **14**(3), 1403–1415 (2013)
6. Čertickỳ, M., Jakob, M., Píbil, R.: Analyzing on-demand mobility services by agent-based simulation. Journal of Ubiquitous Systems & Pervasive Networks **6**(1), 17–26 (2015)
7. Čertickỳ, M., Jakob, M., Píbil, R., Moler, Z.: Agent-based simulation testbed for on-demand transport services. In: Proceedings of the 2014 International Conference on Autonomous Agents and Multi-agent Systems, pp. 1671–1672 (2014)
8. Chong, Z., Qin, B., Bandyopadhyay, T., Wongpiromsarn, T., Rebsamen, B., Dai, P., Rankin, E., Ang Jr, M.H.: Autonomy for mobility on demand. In: Intelligent Autonomous Systems 12, pp. 671–682. Springer (2013)
9. Delling, D., Sanders, P., Schultes, D., Wagner, D.: Engineering route planning algorithms. In: Lerner, J., Wagner, D., Zweig, K.A. (eds.) Algorithmics of Large and Complex Networks. LNCS, vol. 5515, pp. 117–139. Springer, Heidelberg (2009)
10. Donovan, B., Work, D.: New york city taxi data 2010–2013 (2014). http://publish.illinois.edu/dbwork/open-data/
11. Downs, A.: Still Stuck in Traffic: Coping with Peak-hour Traffic Congestion. Brookings Institution Press (2005)
12. Gan, J., An, B., Miao, C.: Optimizing efficiency of taxi systems: scaling-up and handling arbitrary constraints. In: Proceedings of the 2015 International Conference on Autonomous Agents and Multiagent Systems, pp. 523–531 (2015)
13. Glaschenko, A., Ivaschenko, A., Rzevski, G., Skobelev, P.: Multi-agent real time scheduling system for taxi companies. In: 8th International Conference on Autonomous Agents and Multiagent Systems (AAMAS 2009), pp. 29–36. Budapest, Hungary (2009)

14. Haklay, M., Weber, P.: Openstreetmap: User-generated street maps. IEEE Pervasive Computing **7**(4), 12–18 (2008)
15. Huang, A.S., Moore, D., Antone, M., Olson, E., Teller, S.: Finding multiple lanes in urban road networks with vision and lidar. Autonomous Robots **26**(2–3), 103–122 (2009)
16. Jakob, M., Moler, Z., Komenda, A., Yin, Z., Jiang, A.X., Johnson, M.P., Pěchouček, M., Tambe, M.: Agentpolis: towards a platform for fully agent-based modeling of multi-modal transportation. In: Proceedings of the 11th International Conference on Autonomous Agents and Multiagent Systems, vol. 3, pp. 1501–1502 (2012)
17. Lavrinc, D.: BMW builds a self-driving car - that drifts. Wired Magazine (2014)
18. Lozano-Perez, T., Cox, I.J., Wilfong, G.T.: Autonomous robot vehicles. Springer Science & Business Media (2012)
19. Maciejewski, M., Nagel, K.: Simulation and dynamic optimization of taxi services in MATSim. VSP Working Paper (2013)
20. MAPZEN: Mapzen metro extracts: New york City (2015). https://mapzen.com/data/metro-extracts
21. Markoff, J.: Google cars drive themselves, in traffic. New York Times (2010)
22. Mitchell, W.J.: Intelligent cities. UOC Papers **5**, 1541–1885 (2007)
23. Mitchell, W.J.: Reinventing the automobile: Personal urban mobility for the 21st century. MIT Press (2010)
24. Moghadam, P., Wijesoma, W.S., Feng, D.J.: Improving path planning and mapping based on stereo vision and lidar. In: Proceedings of the 10th International Conference on Control, Automation, Robotics and Vision, pp. 384–389. IEEE (2008)
25. Ontodia: Pediacities neighborhoods of New York city (2015). http://catalog.opendata.city/dataset/pediacities-nyc-neighborhoods
26. Papadimitratos, P., La Fortelle, A., Evenssen, K., Brignolo, R., Cosenza, S.: Vehicular communication systems: Enabling technologies, applications, and future outlook on intelligent transportation. IEEE Communications Magazine **47**(11), 84–95 (2009)
27. Premebida, C., Ludwig, O., Nunes, U.: Lidar and vision-based pedestrian detection system. Journal of Field Robotics **26**(9), 696–711 (2009)
28. Seow, K.T., Dang, N.H., Lee, D.H.: A collaborative multiagent taxi-dispatch system. IEEE Transactions on Automation Science and Engineering **7**(3), 607–616 (2010)
29. Spieser, K., Treleaven, K., Zhang, R., Frazzoli, E., Morton, D., Pavone, M.: Toward a systematic approach to the design and evaluation of automated mobility-on-demand systems: a case study in singapore. In: Road Vehicle Automation, pp. 229–245. Springer (2014)
30. Zhang, R., Pavone, M.: Control of robotic mobility-on-demand systems: a queueing-theoretical perspective (2014). arXiv preprint arXiv:1404.4391

Norm Establishment in a Single Dimension Axelrod Model

Vinay Katiyar and David Clarance[(⊠)]

Tata Research Development & Design Centre,
Plot 54-B, Hadapsar Industrial Estate, Pune 411013, India
{vinay.katiyar,david.clarance}@tcs.com

Abstract. In Axelrod norm models (Axelrod, 1986), the existence of a norm is described in terms of two variables, namely Boldness and Vengefulness. This tradition operates on the assumption that these two variables are independent. In this paper we seek to investigate behavior when this assumption is violated. In particular, we postulate a linear negative relationship between the two. We find that in such a world, norm establishment is possible without a Metanorm. Further we prove that this state is an Evolutionary Stable State (ESS). Finally, we explore the role of initial states in bringing about varied behavior in the presence of multiple ESSs.

1   Introduction

Norms are behavioral prescriptions that play an important role in guiding behavior in human systems. These prescriptions can exist as formal centralized directives or as unwritten codes of acceptable behavior. The emergence, spread and establishment of norms has been studied across disciplines and in various forms. Anthropologists [1], sociologists [2, 3] and economists [4, 5] amongst others have approached the phenomenon of norms from different perspectives. On the computational side of the spectrum, the multi-agent study of norms has progressed in various directions. Neumann [6] broadly categorized the agent based simulation literature into two traditions: Systems of interactions with game-theoretic foundations and systems with cognitively richer agents with its roots in artificial intelligence. Further, Savarimuthu et al. [7] have divided these models into nine categories, some of which are off-line design, learning, cognition, culture and evolution and sanction, with some models falling in more than one category. On the basis of these classifications, this paper borrows from the evolutionary game theoretic tradition where norm enforcement is based on individual sanctions with Axelrod's classic paper [8] being the point of reference.

In Axelrodian norm models, a game theoretic approach is taken where a set of agents with bounded rationality take binary decisions.   The existence of a norm is described in terms of two factors, namely *boldness* and *vengefulness*. *Boldness* refers to the propensity of an agent to defy a norm i.e. higher the boldness, higher the likelihood of norm violation. *Vengefulness* describes an agent's tendency to punish non-conformers of that norm. High *vengefulness* translates to a high probability of punishing a defector. A state of high *boldness* and low *vengefulness* describes norm

© Springer International Publishing Switzerland 2015
Q. Chen et al. (Eds.): PRIMA 2015, LNAI 9387, pp. 36–48, 2015.
DOI: 10.1007/978-3-319-25524-8_3

collapse. The opposite – low *boldness* and high *vengefulness* – characterizes norm establishment.

Axelrod's model serves as a benchmark in this tradition and several models have been built on the basis of these two variables [10, 12, 13, 14, 15]. However in these models, *boldness* and *vengefulness* have been taken to be independent. In this paper, we seek to examine a case where this assumption is violated. We forward the claim that the independence of these variables is a substantial assumption both in terms of realism as well as in bringing about the model's results. A violation of this independence can take many forms. There could be a linear or non-linear relationship between *boldness* and *vengefulness*. This relationship could be positive or negative. To see how much such an assumption contributes to the results of Axelrod's model we start with one possible violation and create a model where we postulate a linear negative relationship between *boldness* and *vengefulness* and analyze its effects on norm establishment and spread.

We start with a brief review of Axelrod's original paper, followed by a description of some concepts from Galan and Izquierdo [9] that we will use later in the paper. Following that we describe the model's framework and its parameters. In section 4 we discuss the experiments conducted and their results. We conclude with a discussion of our contribution to the literature on norms and our future work in this direction.

2   Axelrod's Norm Model

Axelrod describes the existence of a norm to the extent that individuals take a certain decision and are punished if they do not [8]. He uses an evolutionary approach where agents are not perfectly rational. In this approach a strategy that results in a higher payoff for the agent under consideration is more likely to be reused, while one that does not fare well is more likely to be discarded. Payoffs are arrived at on the basis of the "norms game" which is described below.

At the beginning of the norms game, an agent has an option to defect or to cooperate, that is, whether to reject a norm or to adhere to it. A. An agent's decision to defect depends on his level of *boldness*. If the agent chooses to defect, he receives a payoff of T while all the other agents are hurt by an amount H. The defector is caught defecting with a probability S. If an agent i observers a player j defecting, agent i can choose to punish j depending upon S and his *vengefulness*. If i does punish j, then j gets a negative payoff (P). i's payoff also decreases as there is a cost, E, of enforcing the punishment. In a given population, each agent makes one choice in a generation. After the scores are calculated, each agent with a score that is below the average population score does not reproduce. Those with a score greater than one standard deviation above the mean reproduce once in the next generation. An agent with a score lying between the mean and one standard deviation above the mean has two offspring. The population is kept constant in every generation.

Axelrod showed that this game results in a collapse of norms, that is a state where Boldness is high and Vengefulness is low. He then proposed a secondary process of a *metanorm* that would further enforce the norm. Axelrod's *metanorm* is a mechanism in which an agent who observes and does not punish another agent's defection is punished. He showed that in the presence of this *metanorm*, the primary norm is established.

3   Characterisation of Evolutionary Stable States (ESSs)

Galan and Izquierdo [9] re-implemented and analysed Axelrod's models. In a series of experiments which included running the model for a greater number of generations, using different mutation rates, changing the payoff matrix and using different selection mechanisms they found that Axelrod's *metanorm* game results were not as reliable as earlier thought to be. He had shown that if initial conditions were favourable enough the Metanorm could prevent defection in every case. While Axelrod had reported the results from 5 runs consisting of 100 generations each, Galan and Izquierdo ran the model for 1000 runs consisting of 1 million generations each. They found that in approximately 70% of the runs, norm collapse was observed by the end. Using this as an example they called for several measures to be taken in agent based modelling including replication, sensitivity analysis and of complementing simulation with analytical work.

To do so we use a concept of point stability which they call Evolutionary Stable State [ESS] to check if a certain pair of values of *boldness* and *vengefulness* is truly a point of global stability as suggested by experiments. Galan and Izquierdo define a state to be an ESS if the following conditions are satisfied:

A is the set of all agents, b_i and v_i are the level of Boldness and Vengefulness of agent i. I is the set of all incumbent agents and m is the mutant agent.

1.   Every agent in the population **A** receives the same payoff.

$$\text{Exp}(\text{Payoff}_i) = \text{Exp}(\text{Payoff}_j) \; \forall \, i, j \, \in A \qquad (1)$$

2.   A single mutant agent m who changes his strategy (let s_m be the new strategy) gets a strictly lower expected payoff than any of the other agents in the incumbent population, $I \in A - \{m\}$.

$$\text{Exp}(\text{Payoff}_m) < Exp(\text{Payoff}_i) \, , \forall \, m \, \in A; \; \forall \, i \, \in I \, ; \; \forall \, (b_m, v_m) \qquad (2)$$

3.   The mutant agent does not distort the composition of the population,

$$\text{Exp}(\text{Payoff}_i) = \text{Exp}(\text{Payoff}_j) \, \forall \, i, j \, \in I(m \notin I), \forall \, m \, \in A; \; \forall \, b_m, v_m \qquad (3)$$

Given this description of an ESS, the necessary conditions for a state being an ESS, assuming continuity of agent's properties, for *boldness* is

For all mutant agents m,

$$\frac{\partial(\text{Payoff}_m)}{\partial b_m} = \frac{\partial(\text{Payoff}_i)}{\partial b_m} \ \forall \, i \in I$$

OR

$$b_m = 1 \text{ AND } \frac{\partial(\text{Payoff}_m)}{\partial b_m} \geq \frac{\partial(\text{Payoff}_i)}{\partial b_m} \ \forall \, i \in I \qquad (4)$$

OR

$$b_m = 0 \text{ AND } \frac{\partial(\text{Payoff}_m)}{\partial b_m} \leq \frac{\partial(\text{Payoff}_i)}{\partial b_m} \ \forall \, i \in I$$

Similarly, the conditions for *vengefulness* can be define by replacing b_m with v_m in equation (4). Let this corresponding equation for vengefulness be Equation (5)

Equations (4) and (5) are used to show that the only ESS in the "norm game" is the state of norm collapse with $v_i = 0$ and $b_i = 1$. In the "Metanorm game" Galan and Izquierdo find two ESSs, one with norm collapse as observed before and one where the norm is established with $v_i = 1$ and $b_i = 4/169$.

In this paper, we provide analytical examples and mathematical proofs based on the concepts defined above to substantiate results derived from simulations.

4   Model Description

We retain the base Axelrod model of the "norm game" but reduce the strategy space to one dimension. *Boldness* and *vengefulness* are inversely related at the level of the agent. As *boldness* increases/decreases, *vengefulness* decreases/increases. If *boldness* is given by b_i for agent i, then *vengefulness* is $1 - b_i$ for agent i. The two collapse into one variable that we call *Prosocialness* (*ps*). High *prosocialness* refers to low *boldness* and therefore high *vengefulness* while low *prosocialness* refers to the opposite. *Prosocialness* lies between 0 and 1. A detailed description of the model follows.

1.   There are 100 agents and each agent has complete visibility.

2.   As before, an agent makes a binary decision to cooperate or defect. The decision to defect depends on the level of Prosocialness, e.g. if Prosocialness is 0.7, then the agent defect with a probability of 0.3 and punishes defectors with a probability of 0.7. If he defects he earns a higher payoff (D) as compared to the payoff from cooperation (C). Defection imposes a hurt cost (H) to the other agents. Upon defection an agent is liable to be punished with a cost P if he is seen by other agents and if the agents choose to punish him. There is an enforcement cost to punishment (E). At the end of each run, the scores are calculated for each agent. Table 1 summarizes payoffs for the norm game between two agents A and B.

Table 1. Payoff Matrix

	Reward to A	Hurt to B	Punishment by B if B sees A violate	Enforcement cost for B if punishing A
Agent A violates norm	D	H	P	E
Agent A complies with norm	C	-	-	-

3. The expected score for the ith individual agents at the end of a single run is given by the following equation:

$$G_i = \alpha_i + (H \times \sum_{\substack{j=1 \\ j \neq i}}^{N} \beta_j) + (P \times \gamma_i \times \sum_{\substack{j=1 \\ j \neq i}}^{N} \delta_{ji}) + (E \times \sum_{\substack{j=1 \\ j \neq i}}^{N} \theta_{ij}) \quad (6)$$

Where,

$$\alpha_i = \begin{cases} D \text{ if agent i has violated the norm} \\ C \text{ if agent i has not violated the norm} \end{cases}$$

$$\beta_j = \begin{cases} 1 \text{ if agent j has violated the norm} \\ 0 \text{ if agent j has not violated the norm} \end{cases}$$

$$\gamma_i = \begin{cases} 1, \text{ if agent i has violated the norm} \\ 0, \text{ if agent i has not violated the norm} \end{cases}$$

$$\delta_{ji} = \begin{cases} 1, \text{If j sees i violating norm and punishes} \\ 0, \qquad\qquad \text{Otherwise} \end{cases}$$

$$\theta_{ij} = \begin{cases} 1, \text{If i sees j violating norm and punishes} \\ 0, \qquad\qquad \text{Otherwise} \end{cases}$$

4. Each agent with a score below the mean randomly chooses an agent with a score above the mean and tends towards the latter's level of *prosocialness* by 0.1 units. Suppose at time t, agent i possess a score $Score_{it}$ and a Prosocialness level ps_{it} and agent j possess a score of $Score_{jt}$ and a *Prosocialness* level of ps_{jt}. Let the mean score at the end of time t be m. Assume that $Score_i < m < Score_j$. *prosocialness* values in the next period (t + 1) will be,

$$If \ ps_{it} > ps_{jt} , ps_{it+1} = \begin{cases} ps_{it} + 0.1 \ if \ (ps_{it} - ps_{jt}) > 0.1 \\ ps_{it} , \qquad if \ (ps_{it} - ps_{jt}) \leq 0.1 \end{cases} \quad (7)$$

$$If\ ps_{it} < ps_{jt},\ ps_{it+1} = \begin{cases} ps_{it} - 0.1 \ if\ (ps_{it} - ps_{jt}) > 0.1 \\ ps_{it}, \quad if\ (ps_{it} - ps_{jt}) \leq\ 0.1 \end{cases} \tag{8}$$

5. In every generation a mutation occurs in the population. With probability m, an agent randomly changes his level of *prosocialness* to any level between 0 and 1. Mutation is an efficient system to ensure that the model reaches a global equilibrium by not getting caught in a local equilibrium.

5   Experiments and Results

We run the following experiments on the model described above.

1. The base norm game using Axelrod's parameters
2. Varying initial states.
3. Speed of convergence across different initial distributions of *prosocialness*.

Some common parameters used across the experiments are Mutation rate (μ) = 0.001 and probability of being seen (S) = 0.50. We performed 30 runs for each experiment and each run consisted of 1000 generations. NetLogo 4.1.3 [11] was used as the modelling environment. This agent based programmable environment allows for autonomous agents, parameterization and in general met all our requirements.

5.1   Single Dimension Norm Game

We begin by running the model with Axelrod's payoff matrix. The values are given below.

Table 2. Axelrod's payoff matrix

	Reward to A	Hurt to B	Punishment by B if B sees A violate	Enforcement cost for B if punishing A
Agent A violates norm	3	-1	-9	-2
Agent A complies with norm	0	-	-	-

Each agent receives a *prosocialness* level based on a random draw from a uniform distribution lying between 0 and 1. The game is played for 1000 generations. We record the average *prosocialness* and the number of cooperators and defectors at the end of each generation. Figure 1 show the number of cooperators and defectors for 1000 generations. We see that by the end all the agents cooperate. This shows that the norm has been established. Further note that this takes place relatively quickly (within 150 generations).

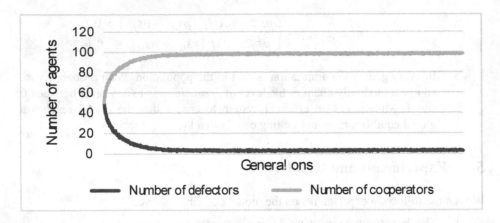

Fig. 1. Norm establishment in the modified Norm Game

Figure 2 demonstrates how this happens. Agents with high *prosocialness* increase while those who low *prosocialness* get crowded out. Each curve in the figure represents the number of agents lying between a certain *prosocialness* range. A *prosocialness* range peaks to the right of the *prosocialness* range which lies just below it. This shows that agents with higher levels of *prosocialness* receive higher payoffs and hence are reproduced in subsequent generations. The system seems to settle at a *prosocialness* level of 1.

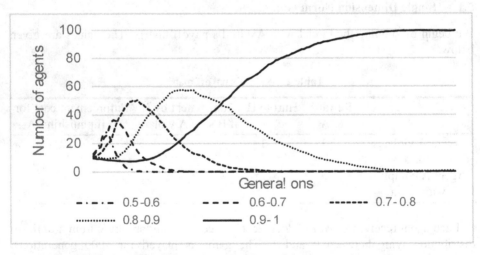

Fig. 2. Agents at different ranges of Prosocialness across generations

To check if this is indeed the case, taking into account Galan and Izquierdo's concern we conduct a mathematical analysis of an approximation of the model to search for Evolutionary Stable States.

5.2   ESSs in the One Dimension Norm Game

We begin by stating Galan and Izquierdo's [9] necessary conditions in terms of our model. From equation (4 and 5) and assuming continuity of the agent's properties the necessary conditions for a set of agents being an ESS are as follows:

For all mutant agents m,

$$\frac{\partial \text{Exp}(\text{Payoff}_m)}{\partial \text{ps}_m} = \frac{\partial \text{Exp}(\text{Payoff}_i)}{\partial \text{ps}_m} \ \forall\, i \in I \tag{9}$$

OR

$$\text{ps}_m = 1 \ \text{AND} \ \frac{\partial \text{Exp}(\text{Payoff}_m)}{\partial \text{ps}_m} \geq \frac{\partial \text{Exp}(\text{Payoff}_i)}{\partial \text{ps}_m} \ \forall\, i \in I \tag{10}$$

OR

$$\text{ps}_m = 0 \ \text{AND} \ \frac{\partial \text{Exp}(\text{Payoff}_m)}{\partial \text{ps}_m} \leq \frac{\partial \text{Exp}(\text{Payoff}_i)}{\partial \text{ps}_m} \ \forall\, i \in I \tag{11}$$

Each statement described above in equation (9), (10) and (11) will be examined. However before that we prove a supporting result that in an ESS, each agent must play the same strategy. This result is then used in further proofs.

Statement 1: A necessary condition that a state is an ESS is that each agent must play the same strategy.

Proof: Since for ESS each agent must receive the same payoff, from Equation (1) we have:

$$\text{Exp}(\text{Payoff}_i) = \text{Exp}(\text{Payoff}_k) \ \forall\, i, k \in A \tag{12}$$

Let

$$F = \text{Exp}(\text{Payoff}_i) - \text{Exp}(\text{Payoff}_k) = 0 \tag{13}$$

Therefore we have,

$$\frac{\partial F}{\partial \text{ps}_m} = \frac{P}{2}(\text{ps}_k - \text{ps}_i) + \frac{E}{2}(\text{ps}_k - \text{ps}_i) = 0 \ \rightarrow \ \text{ps}_k = \text{ps}_i \tag{14}$$

Since i and k are arbitrary, each agent must play the same strategy in an ESS.

Statement 2: $ps = 1$ and $ps = 0$ are ESSs.

Proof: The expected payoff to player i is given by,

$$\text{Exp}\,[Payoff_i] = [\text{ps}_i.\,C + (1 - \text{ps}_i)D] + \left[H.\textstyle\sum_{j=1,j\neq i}^{n}(1 - \text{ps}_j)\right] + \tag{15}$$
$$\left[P.\,(1 - \text{ps}_i).\left(\tfrac{1}{2}\right).\ \textstyle\sum_{j=1,j\neq i}^{n}(\text{ps}_j)\right] + \left[E.\,\text{ps}_i.\left(\tfrac{1}{2}\right)\textstyle\sum_{j=1,j\neq i}^{n}(1 - \text{ps}_j)\right]$$

Further,

$$\frac{\partial \text{Exp(Payoff}_i)}{\partial ps_m} = -H + P(1 - ps_i).\left(\frac{1}{2}\right) - E.ps_i.\left(\frac{1}{2}\right) \tag{16}$$

$$\frac{\partial \text{Exp(Payoff}_m)}{\partial ps_m} = -D - P.\left(\frac{1}{2}\right).\Sigma_{j=1,j\neq m}^{n}(ps_j) + E.\left(\frac{1}{2}\right).\Sigma_{j=1,j\neq m}^{n}(1 - ps_j) \tag{17}$$

Now since all the players follow the same strategy in an ESS (as proved in statement 1)
Let,

$$ps_i = PS, \quad \forall i \in I \tag{18}$$

Therefore, from equation 16, 17 and 18 we have,

$$\frac{\partial \text{Exp(Payoff}_i)}{\partial ps_m} = -H + \frac{P}{2} - \frac{(P+E)}{2}.PS \tag{19}$$

and,

$$\frac{\partial \text{Exp(}Payoff_m)}{\partial ps_m} = -D - \frac{P}{2}.(n-1).PS + \frac{E}{2}.(n-1).(1-PS) \tag{20}$$

Using Axelrod's parameters (Table 2) and from Equation 19 and 20,

$$\text{For PS = 1,} \quad \frac{\partial \text{Exp(Payoff}_m)}{\partial ps_m} > \frac{\partial \text{Exp(Payoff}_i)}{\partial ps_m} \text{ for n} \geq 3 \tag{21}$$

And,

$$\text{For PS = 0,} \quad \frac{\partial \text{Exp(Payoff}_m)}{\partial ps_m} < \frac{\partial \text{Exp(Payoff}_i)}{\partial ps_m} \text{ for n} \geq 2 \tag{22}$$

Hence for reasonable $n \geq 3$, PS = 0 and PS = 1 are ESSs.

Statement 3: There exists no *prosocialness* level that lies between 0 and 1 and is an ESS.

Proof: From equation 9, 18, 19 and 20 we have,

$$PS = \frac{2n-3}{11(n-2)} \tag{23}$$

From Equation 23, we find that PS decreases from 0.27 to 0.18 as n increases from 3 to ∞. In our model the number of agents are 100, therefore, $PS \approx 0.18$. The expected payoff of an agent with $PS = 0.18$ is -160.72. However this is not an ESS because an agent with prosocialness 0.1 or 0 has a expected score of -160.40 and -160 respectively and can easily invade a state where all agents are at PS = 0.18.

5.3   Norm Emergence under Different Initial States

The analysis presented above suggests that two ESSs exist. We observed only one ESS (norm establishment with ps = 1) in the first set of results that we presented. A question that arises is as follows: Under what conditions do we observe the model settling at the second ESS (norm collapse with ps = 0)? In this section we seek to address this question by varying the initial conditions of the model.

Table 3. Results of Experiments

Experiment no.	Mean	Defectors	Co-operators	Status
1	0.00	99.97	0.03	Collapse
2	0.10	99.20	0.80	Collapse
3	0.20	18.27	81.73	Established
4	0.30	6.13	93.87	Established
5	0.40	8.00	92.00	Established
6	0.50	5.63	94.37	Established
7	0.60	7.67	92.33	Established
8	0.70	5.97	94.03	Established
9	0.80	0.50	99.50	Established
10	0.90	0.30	99.70	Established
11	1.00	0.07	99.93	Established

We run the norm model with Axelrod's parameters by setting the initial distribution of *prosocialness* as a normal distribution with means 0, 0.1, 0.2 and so on up to 1 respectively. The standard deviation in each case is set to 0.1. Each level was repeated 30 times for 1000 generations. The results are presented in Table 2. We can clearly see that the norm is established across most distributions. However when *prosocialness* is normally distributed with means 0 and 0.1 we observe that the norm collapses. This substantiates our finding in Section 5.2.

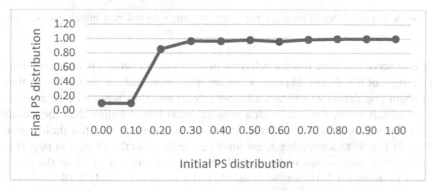

Fig. 3. Average PS at the end of the simulations across distributions

Figure 3 shows the average final prosocialness at each initial prosocialness distribution. We find that the point where the system changes its behavior lies between 0.1 and 0.2. In the simulations of the above experiment we find that to the right of this point, the model tends to reach a state of norm establishment and below this point we observe norm collapse. To explore this further we calculate approximate expected payoffs.

Figure 4 shows the expected payoff for different levels of *prosocialness* for the incumbent population and two mutants. Each point has three bars associated with it. The center bar shows the average payoff of the incumbent population. The bar to the right shows the expected payoff of a mutant whose *prosocialness* is higher (by 0.1 units) than the incumbent population. Similarly the bar to the left indicates the payoff of a mutant with lower *prosocialness*. Therefore this figure shows whether a mutant has potential to invade the incumbent population.

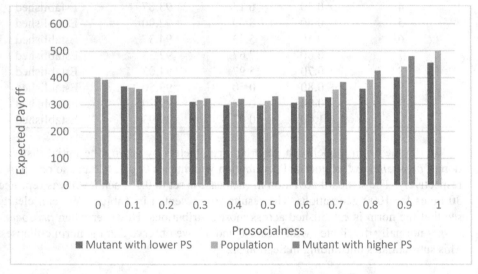

Fig. 4. Expected Payoff for incumbents and mutants with different initial distributions.

We observe that here too the behavior of the system changes between 0.1 and 0.2. To the right of this threshold point, a mutant with *prosocialness* that is higher than the incumbent population will obtain a higher payoff and thus reproduce on average. To the left of this point, a mutant with a *prosocialness* that is higher than the incumbent population will receive a payoff that is lower. Therefore at this threshold point, the change in payoff to a mutating agent must be the same as the change in payoff to the incumbent population when the mutant changes his strategy. This is the condition defined in statement 3. Hence the threshold point is approximately 0.18.

5.4   Convergence in the Modified Norm Game

Finally we analyze the number of generations required for a modified norm game to reach a steady state based on the initial distribution. We define convergence as the point where 90% of the population is at the same level of Prosocialness and hence uses the same strategy. We do not use a 100% criterion as mutation can cause one single agent to change his *prosocialness* and hence bias the results. The results are presented in Figure 5.

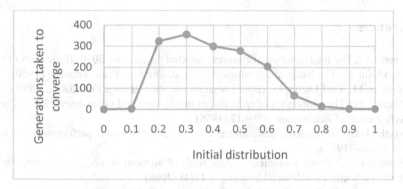

Fig. 5. Number of generations required for convergence.

We see that in general, the closer the initial distribution is to its ESS, the faster there is convergence. The points to the left of 0.2 converge almost immediately to a *prosocialness* of 0, while the time taken for the points to the right of 0.2 depend on the distance from the point of *prosocialness* 1.

6   Conclusion

Norm models have traditionally assumed the independence of two variables – *boldness* and *vengefulness* – that describe Axelrod's world. We have attempted to investigate the effects of a violation of such an assumption. In particular we postulate a linear negative relationship between the two. We find that in such a system, norms are established without the enforcement of a Metanorm. We show through simulation (Figure 1, 2), mathematically (Section 5.2) and through an analytical approximation (Figure 4) that norm establishment is an Evolutionary Stable State. However, we also find that there is an alternate stable state of Norm Collapse and that where the system ultimately ends up depends on the initial distribution. Finally we show that the time required for a system to converge depends on the initial distribution as well.

Through this paper we have attempted to throw light on the importance of relationships between psychological variables at the level of an agent in an agent based system. Different assumptions lead to different consequences and hence building a relevant model must start with establishing correct micro-foundations. While this paper has looked at a population where the two variables are negatively related in a linear fashion, there are other relations possible. These could be linear or non-linear, positive or negative. In the future we would like to explore different possible combinations individually and together (mixed populations) to see how they affect norm establishment and spread in Axelrodian norm systems.

Acknowledgement. We would like to acknowledge the inputs received from our colleagues Vivek Balaraman, Meghendra Singh and Mayuri Duggirala that greatly improved this research work.

References

1. Geertz, C.: The interpretation of cultures: Selected essays, vol. 5019. Basic books (1973)
2. Durkheim, E.: The Rules of Sociological Method. The Free Press, Glencoe (1950)
3. Hechter, M., Karl-Dieter, O., (eds): Social norms. Russell Sage Foundation (2001)
4. Akerlof, G.: The economics of caste and of the rat race and other woeful tales. The Quarterly Journal of Economics, 599–617 (1976)
5. North, D.C.: Institutions, institutional change, and economic performance. Cambridge Univ Press (1990)
6. Neumann, M.: Homo socionicus: a case study of simulation models of norms. Journal of Artificial Societies and Social Simulation **11**(4) (2008)
7. Savarimuthu, B., Tony, R., Stephen, C.: Norm creation, spreading and emergence: A survey of simulation models of norms in multi-agent systems. Multiagent and Grid Systems **7**(1), 21–54 (2011)
8. Axelrod, R.: The Evolution of Norms. The American Political Science Review **80**(4), 1095–1111 (1986)
9. Galan, J.M., Izquierdo, L.R.: Appearances can be deceiving: Lessons learned re-implementing Axelrod's' evolutionary approach to norms. Journal of Artificial Societies and Social Simulation **8**(3) (2005)
10. Axelrod, R.: The evolution of cooperation. Basic Books, New York (1984)
11. Wilensky, U.: NetLogo: Center for Connected Learning and Computer-Based Modeling. Northwestern University, Evanston (1999). http://ccl.northwestern.edu/netlogo/
12. Balaraman, V., Meghendra, S.: Exploring norm establishment in organizations using an extended axelrod model and with two new metanorms. In: Proceedings of the 2014 Summer Simulation Multiconference. Society for Computer Simulation International (2014)
13. Matsumoto, M.: Relationship between Norm-internalization and Cooperation in N-person Prisoners' Dilemma Games. Transactions of the Japanese Society for Artificial Intelligence **21**, 167–175 (2006)
14. Mahmoud, S., et al.: Efficient norm emergence through experiential dynamic punishment. In: ECAI, vol. 12 (2012)
15. Mahmoud, S., et al.: Optimised reputation-based adaptive punishment for limited observability. In: 2012 IEEE Sixth International Conference on Self-Adaptive and Self-Organizing Systems (SASO). IEEE (2012)

Multi-agent Systems Meet Aggregate Programming: Towards a Notion of Aggregate Plan

Mirko Viroli[✉], Danilo Pianini, Alessandro Ricci, Pietro Brunetti, and Angelo Croatti

University of Bologna, Bologna, Italy
{mirko.viroli,danilo.pianini,a.ricci,p.brunetti,a.croatti}@unibo.it

Abstract. Recent works foster the idea of engineering distributed situated systems by taking an aggregate stance: design and development are better conducted by abstracting away from individuals' details, directly programming overall system behaviour instead. Concerns like interaction protocols, self-organisation, adaptation, and large-scaleness, are automatically hidden under the hood of the platform supporting aggregate programming. This paper aims at bridging the apparently significant gap between this idea and agent autonomy, paving the way towards an aggregate computing approach for multi-agent systems. Specifically, we introduce and analyse the idea of "aggregate plan": a collective plan to be played by a dynamic team of cooperating agents.

1 Introduction

Self-organisation mechanisms support adaptivity and resilience in complex natural systems at all levels, from molecules and cells to animals, species, and entire ecosystems. A long-standing aim in computer science is to find effective engineering methods for exploiting such mechanisms to bring similar adaptivity and resilience to a wide variety of complex, large-scale applications—in smart mobility, crowd engineering, swarm robotics, etc. Practical adoption, however, poses serious challenges, since self-organisation mechanisms often trade efficiency for resilience and are often difficult to predictably compose to meet more complex specifications.

On the one hand, in the context of multi-agent systems, self-organisation is achieved relying on a weak notion of agency: following a biology inspiration, agents execute simple and pre-defined behaviour, out of which self-organisation is achieved by emergence [13]—ant foraging being a classical example. This approach however hardly applies to open and dynamic contexts in which what is the actual behaviour to be followed by a group of agents is to be decided (or even synthesised) at run-time.

On the other hand, a promising set of results towards addressing solid engineering of open self-organising systems are being achieved under the umbrella of *aggregate programming* [5]. Its main idea is to shift the focus of system programming from the individual's viewpoint to the aggregate viewpoint: one no

Q. Chen et al. (Eds.): PRIMA 2015, LNAI 9387, pp. 49–64, 2015.
DOI: 10.1007/978-3-319-25524-8_4

longer programs the single entity's computational and interactive behaviour, but rather programs the aggregate (i.e., the collective). This is achieved by abstracting away from the discrete nature of computational networks, by assuming that the overall executing "machine" is a sort of computational continuum able to manipulate distributed data structures: self-organisation mechanisms sit under the hood, and are the key for automatically turning aggregate specifications into individual behaviour. Aggregate programming is grounded in the computational field calculus [10], its incarnation in the Protelis programming language [29], on studies focussing on formal assessment of resiliency properties [35], and building blocks and libraries built on top to support applications in the context of large scale situated systems [3].

This paper aims at bridging the apparently significant gap between aggregate programming and agent autonomy, paving the way towards a fruitful cooperation by which stronger notions of agents (including deliberation and planning capabilities) can closely relate to self-organisation mechanisms. This is achieved by considering an aggregate program as a plan, what we call an "aggregate plan", operationally guiding the cooperative behaviour of a team of agents. Agents can create aggregate plans or receive them from peers, and can deliberate to execute them or not in different moments of time. The set of agents executing an aggregate plan forms a cooperating "dynamic team", coherently bringing about the social goal that the plan is meant to achieve, typically expressed in terms of a final distributed data structure used as input for other processes or to feed actuators (i.e., to make agents/devices move). The inner mechanisms of aggregate computing smoothly support entering/quitting the team, making overall behaviour spontaneously adapt to such dynamism as well as being resilient to changes in environment conditions.

The remainder of this paper is organised as follows: Section 2 overviews aggregate computing, Section 3 compares it with multi-agent systems and illustrates the aggregate plan idea, Section 4 described an example scenario of a distributed rescue activity by autonomous entities, Section 5 compares with alternative MAS approaches, and finally Section 5 concludes and discusses future works.

2   Aggregate Computing

Most paradigms of distributed systems development, there including the multi-agent system approach, are based on the idea of programming each single individual of the system, in terms of its computational behaviour (goals, plans, algorithm, interaction protocol), typically considering a finite number of "roles", i.e., individual classes. This approach is argued to be problematic: it makes it complicated to reason in terms of the effect of composing behaviours, and it forces the programmer to mix different concerns of resiliency and coordination—using middlewares that externalise coordination abstractions and interaction mechanisms only partially alleviate the problem [38,7].

These limits are widely recognised, and motivated work toward aggregate programming across a variety of different domains, as surveyed in [2]. Historically such works addressed different facets of the problem: making device interaction implicit (e.g., TOTA [23]), providing means to compose geometric and topological constructions (e.g., Origami Shape Language [25]), providing means for summarising from space-time regions of the environment and streaming these summaries to other regions (e.g., TinyDB [21]), automatically splitting computational behaviour for cloud-style execution (e.g., MapReduce [11]), and providing generalisable constructs for space-time computing (e.g., Proto [24]).

Aggregate computing, based on the field calculus computational model [10] and its embodiment in Protelis programming language [29], lies in the above approaches and attempts a generalisation starting from the works on space-time computing [5], which are explicitly designed for distributed operation in a physical environment filled with embedded devices.

2.1   Computing at the Aggregate Level

The whole approach starts from the observation that the complexity of large-scale situated systems must be properly hidden "under-the-hood" of the programming model, so that composability of collective behaviour can be more easily supported and allow to better address the construction of complex systems. Aggregate programming is then based on the idea that the "machine" being programmed is a region of the computational environment whose specific details are abstracted away (perhaps even to a pure and uniform spatial continuum): the program is specified as a manipulation of data constructs with spatial and temporal extent across that region. Practically, since such "machine" is ultimately a collection of communicating devices, the semantics of aggregate programming is given as a mapping to a self-organising algorithm involving local interactions between such devices.

As an example, consider the problem of designing crowd steering services based on fully distributed, peer-to-peer interactions between crowd members' smart-phones. In this example, smart-phones could interact to collectively estimate the density and distribution of crowding, seen as a distributed data structure mapping each point of space to a real-value indicating the crowd estimation, namely, a *computational field* (or simply *field*) of reals [23,10]. This can be in turn used as input for actual steering services: warning systems for people nearby dense regions (producing a field of booleans holding true where warning has to be set), dispersal systems to avoid present or future congestion (producing a field of directions suggested to people via their smartphones), steering services to reach points-of-interest (POI) avoiding crowded areas (producing a field of pairs of direction and POI name). Building such services in a fully-distributed, resilient, and composable/reusable way is very difficult, as it comes to achieve self-* behaviour by careful design of each device's interaction with neighbours. With aggregate programming, on the other hand, one instead naturally reasons in terms of an incremental construction of continuous-like computational fields, with the programming platform taking care of turning aggregate programs into programs for the single device.

2.2   Constructs

The *field calculus* [10] captures the key ingredients of aggregate computation into a tiny language suitable for grounding programming and reasoning about correctness – recent works addressed type soundness [10] and self-stabilisation [35] – and is then incarnated into a Java-oriented language called Protelis [29], which we here use for explanation purposes. The unifying abstraction is that of computational field, and every computation (atomic or composite) is about functionally creating fields out of fields. Hence, a program is made of an expression e to be evaluated in space-time (ideally, in a continuum space-time, practically, in asynchronous rounds in each device of the network) and returning a field evolution. Four mechanisms are defined to hierarchically compose expressions out of values and variables, each providing a possible syntactic structure for e.

Application: $\lambda(e_1, \ldots, e_n)$ applies "functional value" λ to arguments $e_1, \ldots, e_n$, using call-by-value semantics and in a point-wise manner (output in a space-time point depend on inputs at the same point). λ can either be a "built-in" primitive (any non-aggregate operation to be executed locally, like mathematical, logical, or algorithmic functions, or calls to sensors and actuators), a user-defined function (that encapsulates reusable behaviour), or an anonymous function value $(x_1, \ldots, x_n)$->e (treated as a value, and hence possibly passed also as argument, and ultimately, spread to neighbours to achieve open models of code deployment [10])—in the latter case Protelis ad-hoc syntax is λ.apply$(e_1, \ldots, e_n)$.

Dynamics: rep(x<-v){e} defines a local state variable x initialised with value v and updated at each node's computation round with the result of evaluating the update expression e (which mentions x to mean the old value).

Interaction: nbr(e) gathers by observation a map at each neighbour to its latest resulting value of evaluating e. A special set of built-in "hood" functions can then be used to summarise such maps back to ordinary expressions, e.g., minHood(m) finds the minimum value in the range of map m.

Restriction: if(e){e$_1$} else {e$_2$} implements branching by partitioning the network into two regions: where e evaluates to true e$_1$ is evaluated, elsewhere e$_2$ is evaluated. Notably, because if is implemented by partition, the expressions in the two branches are encapsulated and no action taken by them can have effects outside of the partition.

The above informal description roughly amounts to a denotational semantics of Protelis, given as a transformation of data structures dislocated in space-time [5]. An operational semantics, describing an equivalent system of local operations and message passing between devices [10], can be sketched as follows. Given a network of interconnected devices D that runs a main expression e_0, computation proceeds by asynchronous rounds in which a device $\delta \in D$ evaluates e_0. The output of each round at a device is an ordered tree of values, called *value-tree*, tracking the result of computing each sub-expression encountered during evaluation of e_0. Such an evaluation is performed against the most recently received value-trees of neighbours, and the produced value-tree is conversely made available to all neighbours (e.g., via broadcast in compressed form) for their next round. Most specifically: nbr(e) uses the most recent value of e at the same position in its neighbours' value-trees, rep(x<-v){e} uses the value of x from the previous round, and if(e){e$_1$} else {e$_2$} completely erases the non-taken branch in the value-tree (allowing interactions through construct nbr with only neighbours that took the same branch, called "aligned neighbours").

2.3 Building Blocks and APIs

An example of aggregate program is the definition of a general building block G as reported in Figure 1(top) and thoroughly discussed in [4]. It is a highly reusable "spreading" operator executing two tasks: it computes a field of shortest-path distances from a source region (indicated as a boolean field holding true on sources) according to the supplied function metric (yielding a map from neighbours to a distance value), then propagates values along the gradient of the distance field away from source, beginning with value initial and accumulating along the gradient with function accumulate. A complementary operator is C, which accumulates information back to the source down the gradient of a supplied potential field; beginning with an idempotent null, at each device, the local value is combined with "uphill" values using a commutative and associative function accumulate, to produce a cumulative value at each device in the source. Another operator S can be used to elect a set of leaders with approximate distance grain from each other.

On top of such building blocks one can incrementally define general-purpose APIs. Some examples are shown in Figure 1(center), which culminate in functions **share** and **meanPathObstacles**. The former is used to gather information from an input field with a suitable accumulation function, broadcast it back so that all devices agree on the result, and do so by sub-regions of a given size partitioning the whole network. The latter computes in a fully-distributed and network-independent way the complex task of gathering in a source node the average amount of "obstacle" nodes (e.g. nodes sensing high traffic, or high-pollution) that one would encounter if travelling towards a destination according to a shortest-path: such information could be used to estimate the appropriateness of moving towards that destination.

Finally, to support openness and dynamism of code injection and management, our model support higher-order functions, allowing code (i.e., functions) to be passed around and be treated as data to diffuse. This allows to store a minimal code in each device, as show in Figure 1(bottom): function **deploy** is used to let function g be spread from sources and be executed remotely, while **virtual-machine** uses it to extract from environmental sensors the function to be injected, the injection point, and the range of diffusion. This means that a complex behaviour like that of functions **share** and **meanPathObstacles** needs not be statically present in each device, but could have been injected dynamically, received, and then executed by the set of involved devices.

```
// Spreads 'initial' out of 'source', using a given 'metric' and 'accumulate' update function
def G(source, initial, metric, accumulate) {
  rep(dv <- [Infinity, initial]) { // generates a field of pairs: distance + value
    mux(source) { // mux is a built-in ternary conditional operator
      [0, initial] // value of the field at a source
    } else { // lexicographic minimum of pairs obtained from neighbours
      minHood([nbr(dv.get(0)) + metric.apply(), accumulate.apply(nbr(dv.get(1)))])
    } // adding distance and accumulating.. then selcting min
  }.get(1) // of the pair only second component is returned
}
// Spreads 'initial' out of 'source', using a given 'metric' and 'accumulate' update function
def C(potential, accumulate, local, null) { ... }
// Elects leaders distant approximately 'grain' using a given 'metric'
def S(grain, metric) { ... }
```

```
// Computes minimum distance to 'source'
def distanceTo(source) {
  G(source, 0, () -> {nbrRange}, (v) -> {v + nbrRange})
}
// Broadcasts 'value' out of 'source'
def broadcast(source, value) {
  G(source, value, () -> { nbrRange }, (v) -> {v})
}
// Share values obtained 'accumulation' over 'field' done into regions of 'regionSize'
def share(field,accumulation,null,regionSize){
  let leaders = S(regionSize,() -> { nbrRange });
  broadcast(leaders,C(distanceTo(leaders),accumulate,field,null))
}
// Activates nodes on a path region with 'width' size connecting 'src' and 'dst'
def channel(src, dest, width) {
  distanceTo(src) + distanceTo(dest) <= broadcast(src,distanceTo(dest)) + width
}
// Gathers in sink the sum of 'value' across 'region'
def summarize(sink, region, value) {
  C(if (region) {distanceTo(sink)} else {Infinity}, +, value, 0)
}
// Gathers average level of obstacles 'obs' in the 'size'-path from 'src' to 'dest'
def meanPathObstacles(src, dest, size, obs) {
  summarize(src, channel(src, dest, size), obs)/summarize(src, channel(src, dest, size), 1)
}
```

```
// Evaluate a function field, running 'g' within 'range' meters from 'source', 'no-op' elsewhere
def deploy (range, source, g, no-op) {
  if (distance-to(source) < range) { broadcast(source,g).apply() } else {no-op.apply() }
}
// The entry-point function executed to run the virtual machine on each device
def virtual-machine () {
  deploy(sns-range, sns-injection-point, sns-injected-fun, ()->0)
}
```

Fig. 1. Building blocks G, C, and S (top), elements of upper-level APIs (center), VM bootstrapping code (bottom)

As one may note, an aggregate program never explicitly mentions a device's individual behaviour: it completely abstracts away from inner details of network shape and communication technology, and only assumes the network is dense enough for devices to cooperate by proximity-based interaction. Additionally, it is showed that operators G, C and S, along with construct if and function application mechanisms, form a self-stabilising set [4], hence any complex behaviour built on top is self-stabilising to any change in the environment, guaranteeing resilience to faults and unpredicted transitory changes.

3   Aggregate Computing and Multi-agent Systems

In this section we draw a bridge between the agent-based approach and aggregate computing: after discussing commonalities and differences, we introduce and discuss the notion of aggregate plan.

3.1   Multi-agent Systems vs Aggregate Computing

Multi-agent systems and aggregate computing have some common assumptions that worth being recapped, and which form the basic prerequisite for identifying a common operating framework. First, they both aim at distributed solutions of complex problems, namely, by cooperation of individuals that, though being selfish, they are also social and hence be willing to bring about "social" goals and objectives. Second, they both assume agents are situated in a physical or logical environment, and work by perceiving a local context and acting on it, there including exchanging messages and sensing/acting on the environment. Finally, both approaches have been used to achieve self-organisation, typically by engineering nature-inspired solutions (mostly from biology for agents, and from physics for aggregate computing [39]).

On the other hand, multi-agent systems and aggregate computing have key differences, both conceptually and methodologically. First, with aggregate computing one programs the collective behaviour of individuals, whereas most agent approaches provide languages to program an agent behaviour, either as a reactive component exchanging messages adhering to given protocols, or as a proactive component with declarative goals, a deliberation cycle, and carrying on plans. Traditionally, weak forms of aggregation are considered in the MAS community as well, including the use of coordination mechanisms and tools (e.g. via artifacts [27] or protocols [18]), social/organisational norms [1], commitments [22], and so on. However, they either provide mere declarative constraints to agent interaction (i.e., they do not operationally describe the aggregate behaviour to carry on), or manage interactions between a typically small number of agents.

Second, agents feature autonomy as key asset. At least in the "stronger" notion of agency, agents do not follow pre-determined algorithms, but provide mechanisms to dynamically adapt their behaviour to the specific contingency: they have some even minimal ability to negatively reply to an external request, and to deviate from a previously agreed cooperative behaviour. On the other hand, in aggregate computing, individuals execute the same program in quite a rigid fashion: it is thanks to higher-order functions as developed in [10] that individuals can be given very simple initial programs which are unique system-wise, and later can execute different programs as a result of what function they receive and start executing. This mechanism is actually key for the adoption of aggregate computing mechanisms in multi-agent systems.

3.2 Aggregate Programs as Collective Plans

Though many ways of integrating aggregate computing and MAS exist (see a discussion in last section), in this paper we develop on the notion of "aggregate plan": a plan that an agent can either create or receive from peers, and can deliberate to execute or not in different moments of time, and which specifies an aggregate behaviour for a team of agents.

Life-cycle of Aggregate Plans. In our model, aggregate plans are expressed by anonymous functions of the kind ()->e, where e is a field expression possibly calling API functions available as part of each agent's library—functions like those shown in Figure 1 (center). One such plan can be created in two different ways, by suitable functions (whose detail we abstract away): first, it can be a sensor (like sns-injected-function in Figure 1 (bottom)) to model the plan being generated by the external world (i.e. a system programmer) and dynamically deployed; second, it can model a local planner (e.g., a function plan-creation) that synthesises a suitable plan for the situation at hand. When the plan is created, it should then be shared with other agents, typically by a broadcasting pattern, like the one implemented by function deploy—though, the full power of field calculus can be used to rely on more sophisticated techniques for constraining the target area of broadcasting.

Agents are to be programmed with a virtual-machine-like code that makes it participate to this broadcast pattern, so as to receive all plans produced remotely in the form of a field of pairs of a description of the plan and its implementation by the anonymous function. Among the plans currently available, by the restriction operator if the agent can autonomously decide which one to actually execute, using as condition the result of a built-in deliberation function that has access to the plan's description.

Note that if/when an aggregate plan is in execution, it will make the agent cooperatively work with all the other agents that are equally executing the same aggregate plan. This "dynamic team" will then coherently bring about the social goal that this plan is meant to achieve, typically expressed in terms of a final distributed data structure, used as input for other processes or to feed actuators (i.e., to make agents/devices move). The inner mechanisms of aggregate computing smoothly support entering/quitting the team, making overall behaviour spontaneously self-organise to such dynamism.

Mapping Constructs, and Libraries. As a plan is in execution, the operations of aggregate programming that it includes can be naturally understood as "instructions" for the single agent, as follows:

- Function application amounts to any pure computation an agent has to execute, there including algorithmic, deliberation, scheduling and planning activities, as well as local action and perception.
- Repetition construct is instead used to make some local result of execution of the aggregate plan persist over time, e.g. modelling belief update.

- Restriction can be used inside a plan to temporarily structure the plan in sub-plans, allowing each agent to decide which of them should be executed, i.e., which sub-team has to be dynamically joined.
- Neighbour field construction is the mechanism by which information about neighbour agents executing the same (sub-)plan can be observed, supporting the cooperation needed to make the plan be considered as an aggregate one.

As explained in previous section, one of the assets of aggregate programming is its ability of defining libraries of reusable components of collective behaviour, with formally provable resilience properties. Seen in the context of agent programming, such libraries can be used as libraries of reusable aggregate plans, built on top of building blocks:

- Building block G is at the basis of libraries of "distributed action", namely, cooperative behaviour aimed at acting over the environment or sets of agents in a distributed way. Examples include, other than broadcasting information (broadcast) and reifying distances (distanceTo), also the possibility of forecasting events, creating network partitions, clusters or topological regions in general.
- Building block C conversely supports libraries of "distributed perception", namely, cooperative behaviour aimed at perceiving the environment or information about a set of agents in a distributed way. They allow gathering "aggregate" values over space-time regions, like sums, average, maximum, semantic combination [32], as well as computing consensus values [12].
- Building block S supports libraries requiring forms of explicit or implicit leader elections, often needed to aggregate and then spread-back consensus values.

The combination of building blocks G, C, S, and others [4], allow to define more complex elements of collective adaptive behaviour, generally used to intercept distributed events and situations, compute/plan response actions, and actuate them collectively.

4   Case Study

As an exemplification of the above mentioned concepts, we propose a cooperative teamwork case study. We imagine that a situation of emergency occurs in a urban scenario. A group of rescuers is responsible of visiting the areas where an unknown number of injured victims are likely to be located, and decide in which order to assist them (e.g., to complete a *triage*). We suppose rescuers carry a smart device, and are able to communicate with each other the position of victims in their field of view. Such devices are equipped with a small VM code (a minimal aggregate plan), which is responsible of computing and selecting a collaborative strategy for exploring the area, and of displaying a coordinate to go to. Rescuers do not initially know the exact position of victims: they are required to get to the area by visiting a set of coordinates assigned by the mission control, explore the surroundings, and assist any people they encounter that require treatment.

4.1 An Aggregate Computing Approach

Our devices start with a simple plan, suggesting directions to reach given coordinates assigned by the mission control.

As a rescuer sees a victim, it creates and injects a second, more advanced plan, working as follows: if the rescuer sees a victim and nobody else is assisting her, then it simply takes charge of assisting. If somebody else is already assisting her, instead, the rescuer moves towards the closest known victim if any, relying on the aggregate knowledge of all the other rescuers, namely taking into account all the victims that had been seen by any other rescuer—namely, performing a distributed observation. As a consequence, rescuers will tend to come close to the areas where victims have already been found but not assisted yet. The idea behind the plan is that it is likely that many victims are grouped, and as such calling for more rescuers may raise the probability of finding them all. If no victims have been discovered or all have been assisted, then the dynamic aggregate plan is quit, and the initial plan of reaching the target destination (former exploration strategy) is executed.

The collaborative strategy requires agents to collectively compute fields like `remaining`, mapping each agent to the list of positions of nearby victims to be assisted. Building, maintaining and manipulating distributed and situated data structures like this one, and do so in a resilient way [35], is a fundamental brick of any aggregate plan, and specifically, of the dynamic plan that in this scenario an agent may decide to play. Aggregate computing can be used to smoothly solve the problem by the following sub-plan:

- by function **share** a field of known `victims` can be created by the union of single agent's knowledge about victims, as reflected by their visual perception;
- similarly, again by function **share**, a field of victims currently `assisted` can be created based on information coming from the agents actually assisting;
- by set subtraction, the field `remaining` is built that provides information about victims not assisted yet;
- if field `victims` is empty, the plan is quit;
- otherwise, if there are no known `remaining`, the agent moves to the closest `assisted` – where it is likely to find new victims;
- otherwise, the agent moves to the closest `remaining`, assisting the victim as she is reached.

Once this plan and the original one are alive, each agent can autonomously decide which one to follow.

4.2 Simulation

We have chosen to simulate our case study in an urban environment. There, two groups of victims are displaced, and a group of rescuers starts its mission from in-between those two groups. Initially, coordinates are generated by the mission control, and are given to rescuers. Once the first victim is encountered,

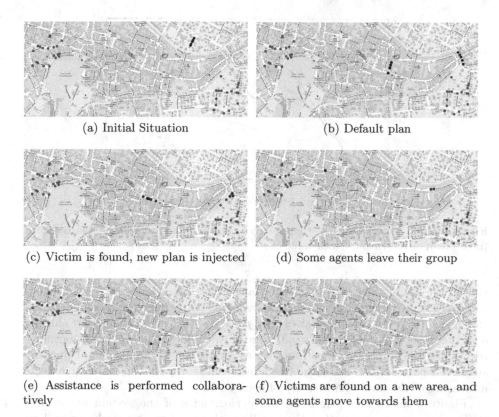

(a) Initial Situation

(b) Default plan

(c) Victim is found, new plan is injected

(d) Some agents leave their group

(e) Assistance is performed collaboratively

(f) Victims are found on a new area, and some agents move towards them

Fig. 2. Simulation of the case study. Rescuers that follow their initial plan are pictured in black, rescuers that are acting collaboratively are in blue, and rescuers that are assisting are marked in purple. Victims are in red, until they receive assistance and switch to green. The rescuers initially split in two groups, but when the first victim is found, some of those going towards the other victim group decide to change their plan and act collaboratively.

the aggregate plan becomes available. To simulate autonomous behaviour, we assign a certain probability p that an agent accepts to follow the aggregate plan: if it does not, it keeps moving towards the given coordinates. Each ten minutes each agent reconsiders its decision to follow the aggregate plan, again according to probability p.

We used Alchemist [28] as simulation platform. Alchemist supports simulating on real-world maps, exploiting OpenStreetMaps data and imagery, and leveraging Graphhopper for navigating agents along streets. The actual city used as scenario is the Italian city of Cesena.

Section 4.2 shows some snapshots from a run executed with $p = 0.75$. Rescuers (black dots) visit the coordinates starting from a random one; as such, they initially split in two sub-groups. At some point, one of them finds a victim. The second plan becomes available, and some of the agents, both in the close

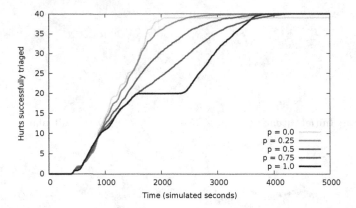

Fig. 3. Impact of our measure of autonomy p on the numer of victims assisted with time. Mean of 100 runs for each value of p.

sub-group and in the group far away change their behaviour and start walking towards such a victim. The number of rescuers that change their original direction and follows the new plan raises with p. With $p = 1$, all of them start chasing a victim as soon as found, with $p = 0$ none of them does, and every one continues to visit its waypoints. $1 - p$ can be seen as a measure of the likelihood that the suggested plan is rejected by the freedom of autonomy: in this sense, it reflects a measure of the level of autonomy of each agent.

Figure 3 shows how p impacts the performance of the system in our scenario. Our expectation is that the results with very low p strongly depend on how fortunate is the initial waypoints choice. In case the selection is rough or approximate, the rescuers may end up not finding all the victims. The chart confirms this expectation: the line for $p = 0$ rises very quickly (agents divide their load pretty evenly), but the final result is that in 99 out of 100 runs some of the victims are not discovered. It is worth observing the behaviour for $p = 1$: initially, all the rescuers walk towards the first group that is found. Only when this group is completely assisted, they start looking for more victims on different places, hence the flat part of the black line. Once the second group is found, all the rescuers are attracted towards that area, and the assisting procedure is quickly completed: as shown, in fact, the number of successfully assisted victims steeply rises. Intermediate values of p show a progressive change in behaviour between the two extremes. A very solid and globally quick result is obtained with $p = 0.25$, suggesting that the system takes advantage from both autonomy in choice and collective decisions.

5   Related MAS Approaches

Alternative ways to implement the case study and similar systems with MASs range from purely subjective approaches (agents realise coordination) to objective approaches (the coordination burden is externalised to coordination media and/or organisation mechanisms) [26].

The simplest example for the subjective case is given by a well-known platform like JADE [6], which does not provide any specific support to coordination but only relies on speech-act/FIPA based communication protocols. In this case, the design of such protocols should take into the account all the issues that we implicitly manage at the aggregate level and achieve self-organisation. So, our approach sits at a rather higher abstraction level and hence defines a much more convenient engineering framework—JADE could of course be possibly used as a low-level platform to support our agent-to-agent interactions.

More complex subjective approaches exploit Distributed AI techniques for MAS coordination and teamwork—such as distributed scheduling and planning [16,20,33]. A main example for the first case is given by Generalized Partial Global Planning (GPGP) and the TAEMS Framework for Distributed Multi-agent systems [19]. A main example for the second case is given by approaches based on Distributed (Partially Observable) Markov Decision Problems (Distributed (PO)MDPs) and Distributed Constraint Optimization Problems (DCOPs) [34]. While these approaches have been proven to be effective in realistic domains, taking into the account the uncertainty of agent's actions and observations, they typically fail to scale up to large numbers of agents [34], which aggregate computing smoothly addresses by construction.

On the objective side, a viable approach would be to rely on specific coordination artifacts [27] (like tuple spaces and their variants). Using models/infrastructures like TuCSoN [14,36], or the chemical-inspired SAPERE approach [37], one could couple each device with a networked shared space in which tuple-like data chunks can be injected, observed, and get diffused, aggregated, and evaporated by local coordination rules. Although proper coordination rules could in principle be instrumented to achieve a similar management of computational fields, the functional nature of aggregate computing – that is crucial to support reusability and composability – is difficult to mimic, if not by an automatic compilation process.

A different objective approach is rooted on organisation/normative models and structures, e.g., using Moise and a supporting platform like JaCaMo [7]—which integrates the organisation dimension (based on Moise) with the agent dimension (based on the Jason agent programming language) and the environment one (based on the CArtAgO framework). In this case, the solution would account to explicitly define the coordination among agents in terms of the structural/functional/normative view of the organisation of the MAS. The coordination aspect would be handled in particular by defining missions and social schemas. The level of self-organisation supported in this case is limited to the way in which individual agents are capable to achieve the individual goals that are assigned and distributed by the organisational infrastructure, executing the "organisation program". The functional description of the coordination to be enacted at the organisation level – specified by missions – is essentially a shared plan explicitly defining which goals must be done and in which order.

This approach is not feasible in the application domains for which aggregate computing has been devised, where it is not possible (or feasible) in general to define a priori such a shared static global plan. That is, it is possible to specify what is the desired goal (e.g. what kind of spatial distribution of the human/agents we want to obtain), but not its functional decomposition in subtasks/subgoals to be assigned to the individual agents/roles.

6   Conclusion and Future Works

In this work we started analysing a bridge between multi-agent systems to aggregate programming. Aggregate programming can be useful in MAS as an approach that allows to specify the behaviour and goal of the MAS at the global level, as a kind of *shared plan* abstracting from the individual autonomous behaviour. This makes our work strongly related to existing literature in MAS dealing with cooperative planning in partially observable stochastic domains [17], and decision making in collaborative contexts adopting formalized frameworks based on a notion of shared plans [15]. In that perspective, there are many interesting directions that can be explored in future work. A first one is to explore aggregates composed by intelligent agents based on specific model/architecture such as the BDI one, promoting a notion of *aggregate stance* that may integrate with classical *intentional stance* [8]. A second direction is to explore the link with approaches that investigate the use *stigmergy* and coordination based on implicit communication in the context of aggregates of intelligent agents [9,30]; Finally, it would be interesting to integrate aggregate programming with agent-oriented programming [31] and current agent programming languages, making it possible to conceive agent programs that e.g. exploit both local plans – like in the case of a BDI agent language like Jason – and global plans as conceived by the aggregate level.

References

1. Artikis, A., Sergot, M.J., Pitt, J.V.: Specifying norm-governed computational societies. ACM Trans. Comput. Log. 10(1) (2009)
2. Beal, J., Dulman, S., Usbeck, K., Viroli, M., Correll, N.: Organizing the aggregate: languages for spatial computing. In: Formal and Practical Aspects of Domain-Specific Languages: Recent Developments, chap. 16, pp. 436–501. IGI Global (2013). http://arxiv.org/abs/1202.5509
3. Beal, J., Pianini, D., Viroli, M.: Aggregate programming for the internet of things. IEEE Computer (2015)
4. Beal, J., Viroli, M.: Building blocks for aggregate programming of self-organising applications. In: IEEE Workshop on Foundations of Complex Adaptive Systems (FOCAS) (2014)
5. Beal, J., Viroli, M.: Space–time programming. Philosophical Transactions of the Royal Society of London A: Mathematical, Physical and Engineering Sciences 373(2046) (2015)

6. Bellifemine, F.L., Poggi, A., Rimassa, G.: Developing multi-agent systems with JADE. In: Castelfranchi, C., Lespérance, Y. (eds.) ATAL 2000. LNCS (LNAI), vol. 1986, p. 89. Springer, Heidelberg (2001)
7. Boissier, O., Bordini, R.H., Hübner, J.F., Ricci, A., Santi, A.: Multi-agent oriented programming with jacamo. Science of Computer Programming 78(6), 747–761 (2013)
8. Bratman, M.E.: Intention, Plans, and Practical Reason. Harvard University Press, Nov. 1987
9. Castelfranchi, C., Pezzulo, G., Tummolini, L.: Behavioral implicit communication (BIC): Communicating with smart environments via our practical behavior and its traces. International Journal of Ambient Computing and Intelligence 2(1), 1–12 (2010)
10. Damiani, F., Viroli, M., Pianini, D., Beal, J.: Code mobility meets self-organisation: a higher-order calculus of computational fields. In: Graf, S., Viswanathan, M. (eds.) Formal Techniques for Distributed Objects, Components, and Systems. LNCS, vol. 9039, pp. 113–128. Springer, Heidelberg (2015)
11. Dean, J., Ghemawat, S.: MapReduce: simplified data processing on large clusters. Communications of the ACM 51(1), 107–113 (2008)
12. Elhage, N., Beal, J.: Laplacian-based consensus on spatial computers. In: 9th International Conference on Autonomous Agents and Multiagent Systems (AAMAS 2010), pp. 907–914. IFAAMAS (2010)
13. Fernandez-Marquez, J.L., Serugendo, G.D.M., Montagna, S., Viroli, M., Arcos, J.L.: Description and composition of bio-inspired design patterns: a complete overview. Natural Computing 12(1), 43–67 (2013)
14. Gardelli, L., Viroli, M., Casadei, M., Omicini, A.: Designing self-organising environments with agents and artefacts: A simulation-driven approach. International Journal of Agent-Oriented Software Engineering 2(2), 171–195 (2008)
15. Grosz, B.J., Hunsberger, L., Kraus, S.: Planning and acting together. AI Magazine 20(4), 23–34 (1999)
16. Grosz, B.J., Kraus, S.: Collaborative plans for complex group action. Artificial Intelligence 86(2), 269–357 (1996)
17. Kaelbling, L.P., Littman, M.L., Cassandra, A.R.: Planning and acting in partially observable stochastic domains. Artif. Intell. 101(1–2), 99–134 (1998)
18. Kalia, A.K., Singh, M.P.: Muon: designing multiagent communication protocols from interaction scenarios. Autonomous Agents and Multi-Agent Systems 29(4), 621–657 (2015)
19. Lesser, V., Decker, K., Wagner, T., Carver, N., Garvey, A., Horling, B., Neiman, D., Podorozhny, R., Prasad, M., Raja, A., Vincent, R., Xuan, P., Zhang, X.: Evolution of the GPGP/TAEMS domain-independent coordination framework. Autonomous Agents and Multi-Agent Systems 9(1–2), 87–143 (2004)
20. Levesque, H.J., Cohen, P.R., Nunes, J.H.T.: On acting together. In: Proceedings of the Eighth National Conference on Artificial Intelligence, AAAI 1990, vol. 1, pp. 94–99. AAAI Press (1990)
21. Madden, S.R., Szewczyk, R., Franklin, M.J., Culler, D.: Supporting aggregate queries over ad-hoc wireless sensor networks. In: Workshop on Mobile Computing and Systems Applications (2002)
22. Mallyak, A.U., Singh, M.P.: An algebra for commitment protocols. Autonomous Agents and Multi-Agent Systems 14(2), 143–163 (2007)
23. Mamei, M., Zambonelli, F.: Programming pervasive and mobile computing applications: The TOTA approach. ACM Trans. on Software Engineering Methodologies 18(4), 1–56 (2009)

24. MIT Proto. http://proto.bbn.com/ (retrieved on January 1, 2012)
25. Nagpal, R.: Programmable Self-Assembly: Constructing Global Shape using Biologically-inspired Local Interactions and Origami Mathematics. Ph.D. thesis, MIT (2001)
26. Omicini, A., Ossowski, S.: Objective versus subjective coordination in the engineering of agent systems. In: Klusch, M., Bergamaschi, S., Edwards, P., Petta, P. (eds.) Intelligent Information Agents. LNCS (LNAI), vol. 2586, pp. 179–202. Springer, Heidelberg (2003)
27. Omicini, A., Ricci, A., Viroli, M.: Artifacts in the A&A meta-model for multi-agent systems. Autonomous Agents and Multi-Agent Systems 17(3), June 2008
28. Pianini, D., Montagna, S., Viroli, M.: Chemical-oriented simulation of computational systems with Alchemist. Journal of Simulation (2013)
29. Pianini, D., Viroli, M., Beal, J.: Protelis: Practical aggregate programming. In: Proceedings of ACM SAC 2015, pp. 1846–1853. ACM, Salamanca, Spain, (2015)
30. Ricci, A., Omicini, A., Viroli, M., Gardelli, L., Oliva, E.: Cognitive stigmergy: towards a framework based on agents and artifacts. In: Weyns, D., Van Dyke Parunak, H., Michel, F. (eds.) E4MAS 2006. LNCS (LNAI), vol. 4389, pp. 124–140. Springer, Heidelberg (2007)
31. Shoham, Y.: Agent-oriented programming. Artif. Intell. 60(1), 51–92 (1993)
32. Stevenson, G., Ye, J., Dobson, S., Pianini, D., Montagna, S., Viroli, M.: Combining self-organisation, context-awareness and semantic reasoning: the case of resource discovery in opportunistic networks. In: ACM SAC, pp. 1369–1376. ACM (2013)
33. Tambe, M.: Towards flexible teamwork. J. Artif. Int. Res. 7(1), 83–124 (1997)
34. Taylor, M.E., Jain, M., Kiekintveld, C., Kwak, J., Yang, R., Yin, Z., Tambe, M.: Two decades of multiagent teamwork research: past, present, and future. In: Guttmann, C., Dignum, F., Georgeff, M. (eds.) CARE 2009 / 2010. LNCS, vol. 6066, pp. 137–151. Springer, Heidelberg (2011)
35. Viroli, M., Beal, J., Damiani, F., Pianini, D.: Efficient engineering of complex self-organising systems by self-stabilising fields. In: IEEE Conference on Self-Adaptive and Self-Organising Systems (SASO 2015) (2015)
36. Viroli, M., Casadei, M., Omicini, A.: A framework for modelling and implementing self-organising coordination. In: Proceedings of ACM SAC 2009, volume III, pp. 1353–1360. ACM, March 8–2, 2009
37. Viroli, M., Pianini, D., Montagna, S., Stevenson, G., Zambonelli, F.: A coordination model of pervasive service ecosystems. Science of Computer Programming, June 18, 2015
38. Weyns, D., Omicini, A., Odell, J.: Environment as a first class abstraction in multiagent systems. Autonomous Agents and Multi-Agent Systems 14(1), 5–30 (2007)
39. Zambonelli, F., Viroli, M.: A survey on nature-inspired metaphors for pervasive service ecosystems. International Journal of Pervasive Computing and Communications 7(3), 186–204 (2011)

CAMP-BDI: A Pre-emptive Approach for Plan Execution Robustness in Multiagent Systems

Alan White[✉], Austin Tate, and Michael Rovatsos

School of Informatics, Centre for Intelligent Systems and their Applications,
Artificial Intelligence Applications Institute, University of Edinburgh, Edinburgh, UK
a.g.white@sms.ed.ac.uk, a.tate@ed.ac.uk, mrovatso@inf.ed.ac.uk

Abstract. Belief-Desire-Intention agents in realistic environments may face unpredictable exogenous changes threatening intended plans and debilitative failure effects that threaten reactive recovery. In this paper we present the CAMP-BDI (Capability Aware, Maintaining Plans) approach, where BDI agents utilize introspective reasoning to modify intended plans in avoidance of anticipated failure. We also describe an extension of this approach to the distributed case, using a decentralized process driven by structured messaging. Our results show significant improvements in goal achievement over a reactive failure recovery mechanism in a stochastic environment with debilitative failure effects, and suggest CAMP-BDI offers a valuable complementary approach towards agent robustness.

Keywords: Multiagent teamwork · Belief-desire-intention · Planning · Capability · Robustness

1 Introduction

The Belief-Desire-Intention (BDI) approach is widely applied towards intelligent agent behaviour, including within realistic domains such as emergency response. Realistic environments are stochastic and dynamic; exogenous change during execution can threaten the success of planned activities, risking both intention failure and debilitative consequences. Current BDI architectural implementations typically employ reactive approaches for failure mitigation, replanning or repairing plans after failure; *Jason* agents (Bordini and Hbner [2006]), for example, define recovery plans explicitly triggered by goal failure(s). This may risk additional costs associated with recovering from debilitated post-failure states – or even risk recovery being *impossible*. Continuous short-term planning helps handle uncertainty, but risks inadvertently stymieing long-term goals – such as if resource requirements are not identified and subsequently lost to contention.

We suggest agents embodied with capability knowledge can use introspective reasoning to proactively avoid plan failure. The CAMP-BDI (Capability Aware, Maintaining Plans) approach presented in this paper allows agents to modify intended plans when they are threatened by exogenous change – supporting use of long term planning whilst allowing response to unanticipated world states. We contribute the following components as part of our approach;

© Springer International Publishing Switzerland 2015
Q. Chen et al. (Eds.): PRIMA 2015, LNAI 9387, pp. 65–84, 2015.
DOI: 10.1007/978-3-319-25524-8_5

- An algorithm for anticipatory plan repair behaviour, henceforth referred to as *maintenance*
- Extension to the distributed hierarchical team case, using structured communication to drive individual adoption of responsibility for, and performance of, maintenance
- A supporting architecture, providing the capability, dependency, and obligation knowledge required to support introspective reasoning during maintenance
- A policy mechanism allowing runtime tailoring of maintenance behaviour

An experimental implementation of CAMP-BDI was evaluated against a reactive replanning system, using a logistics environment where unpredictable exogenous events could occur during intention execution. Our results were gathered over multiple experimental runs, for several probabilities of negative failure consequences. Our proactive approach was observed to hold a significant advantage in goal achievement over a reactive approach, and to offer greater efficiency (in terms of planning calls) at higher probabilities of negative failure consequences (i.e. where it was more likely failure led to a world state that increased difficulty of recovery planning).

2   Motivating Example

Our motivating example is a logistics domain, where goals require delivery of cargo to a set location in a stochastic, dynamic, continuous and non-deterministic environment. Uncertainty arises from agent health state, weather conditions (rainstorms may flood roads or cause landslips), or emergence of 'danger zones' (hostile insurgent activity at a given location). Failure risks negative consequences including vehicle damage (and, if already damaged, being rendered unusable), stranding off-road, or cargo destruction with possible toxic contamination rendering roads unusable. Figure 1 depicts a *Truck* agent travelling a planned route from location A to M, when road $F{\rightarrow}M$ is rendered unusable by flooding – threatening *Truck*'s intended activity, $move(F, M)$.

We target environments where exogenous change causes divergence from the beliefs held at intention formation, failure risks debilitation, and resource contention prevents continual planning. This requires a *pre-emptive* approach; anticipating failure risks and proactively altering plans to compensate. Behaviour

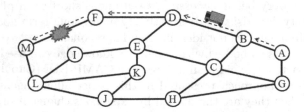

Fig. 1. Example of *Truck* executing a plan to travel from A to M.

must extend to both local and multiagent contexts; i.e. if *Truck* cannot maintain sufficient confidence in meeting an obligation, the dependent agent should be able to compensate by modifying it's local (dependent) intended plan.

3 Architecture Components

In order to support a *pre-emptive* approach and allow introspective examination of intended plans, CAMP-BDI agents require the following meta-knowledge components. We suggest these can be regarded as subsets of agent *Beliefs*, although storage and retrieval semantics will be implementation-specific; the key element is that CAMP-BDI agents must specifically distinguish and consequently use this information in maintenance reasoning. Due to our approach of plan modification to avoid threatened failure, we adopt Simari and Parsons [2006]'s definition of an intention i as combining a goal and plan; i.e. $i = \{i_{goal}, i_{plan}\}$.

3.1 Capabilities

Capabilities define meta-knowledge regarding activities performable, and goals achievable, by agents. Our capability model provides the information required for introspective maintenance reasoning – it is also used to provide a representation of such information when conveyed within a dependency contract, allowing our algorithms to employ the same reasoning approach for both locally performed *and* delegated activities.

We define an activity a as similar to a *task* in a Hierarchical Task Network; where successful execution of a achieves some given state transition. A planned activity may represent either an atomic action or a (sub)goal, where performance of the latter entails execution of some subplan (i.e. an ordered sequence of activities). A capability $c(a)$, denoting the holding agents ability to perform a, has the following fields;

$$c(a) = <s, g(a), pre(a), eff(a), conf(a, B_a)>$$

- s: signature with name n and t parameters ($s=n(t_1,..., n_t)$); a specific capability instance c within the MAS can be uniquely identified by combining s and (identifier of) the agent holding $c(a)$.
- $g(a)$: defines an associated goal – a set of atoms ground to a. This can be used to distinguish between a defined purpose of a and its side-effects; i.e. *fly* and *drive* would achieve the same goal state (to arrive at some location), but with different total effects ($eff(a)$, below).
- $pre(a)$: preconditions (belief atoms) defining where a can be achieved - specifically, where use of $c(a)$ is not *guaranteed to fail*
- $eff(a)$: the complete set of post-effects of using $c(a)$ – i.e. $eff(a) = g(a) \cup$ side-effects($c(a)$).
- $conf$: $a \times B_a \rightarrow [0:1]$; the *confidence* function; estimates the quality (in this context indicating likelihood of success) of using $c(a)$ to perform a, where belief set B_a gives the execution context. This supports identification of where

exogenous change decreases optimality of a planned a – i.e. $conf(driveAlong(F, M), B)$ is lower where $B \ni slippery(F,M)$ than $B \ni dry(F,M)$.

In summary, holding $c(a)$ indicates that agent can achieve $g(a)$, with total post-effects $eff(a)$, provided $pre(a)$ holds in the execution context B_a, with the level of quality indicated by $conf$.

3.1.1   Capability Typology

We define the *type* of a capability using two, overlapping categories;

Complexity: Primitive and Composite capabilities can be viewed as equivalent to basic and high level activities (Dhirendra *et al.* [2010]). *Primitive* capabilities represent atomic activities; *Composites* represent knowledge of one *or more* plans to perform some activity, or the ability to *form* a plan under specified preconditions. Each plan in an agent's plan library is represented by *exactly* one composite capability, meaning plans:capabilities have an $n:1$ relationship.

The activities found *within* plans will themselves correspond to capabilities. Composites can be seen as representing refinement options for (sub)goal activities within plans (i.e. requiring execution of some subplan), and also support continual planning by allowing reasoning whether plans exist for (as-yet unrefined) subgoals.

Locality: *Internal* capabilities represent activities an agent can perform itself; *External* capabilities represent those advertised by others, where a can be performed by delegation; as any decomposition is identified and performed by the resultant obligant(s) (i.e. the advertising agent), external capabilities are always primitive (e.g. are atomic from the *dependant*'s perspective).

3.1.2   The Confidence Function

Certain state combinations may impact the likelihood of activity success, without being significant enough to include within preconditions (the *qualification problem* defined by McCarthy [1958]). The confidence function ($conf(a, B_a)$) is used to allow reasoning whether exogenous change has increased *risk* of failure, even where preconditions are not violated. A numerical value allows semantic-independent comparison between different internal and/or external capabilities for the same s, and supports varying levels of granularity (e.g.$yes=1$, $maybe=0.5$, $no=0$).

Estimation depends on both the capability type and a itself. If a is unground, confidence indicates the *general* ability of that agent to achieve g in B_a – an *abstract* estimation. If a is ground, additional semantic information can be used for *specific* estimation. *Primitive* capabilities will use a predefined calculation for both abstract and specific estimation – such as considering both past execution results (similar to Dhirendra *et al.* [2010]) and states in B_a. Implementation is domain and agent specific, requiring appropriate analysis of both.

External capabilities use a fixed, abstract confidence value as received in the relevant capability advertisement. Agents are unlikely to be able to share semantic knowledge required for *specific* estimation, as recipients may lack the modelling or sensory ability required to interpret. However, *specific* estimates are provided for delegated activities through the external capability field of contracts (see 3.2). We treat the actual advertisement process as implementation specific.

Composite capability confidence derives from the set of plans represented by that capability ($P_{capability}$). *Plan* confidence is the minimum held in a constituent activity (below, with *conf* expanded to consider a plan p as the first argument, where B_p is the execution context of the first activity in p); B_a requires updating with a_n's effects to estimate the execution context of a_{n+1}.

$$conf(p, B_p) = min_{a \in p} conf(a, B_a)$$

We assume the highest confidence plan is always selected for a goal. Composite capability confidence is taken as the highest of a selectable plan (where preconditions hold – if none are selectable, 0 is returned), where a_{goal} is the activity being performed using the composite capability and $B_{a_{goal}}$ it's execution context.

$$conf(a_{goal}, B_{a_{goal}}) = max_{\substack{p \in P_{capability} \\ pre(p) \subset B_{a_{goal}}}} conf(p, B_{a_{goal}})$$

This equates to formation and traversal of an AND-OR tree, similar to goal-plan trees described in Thangarajah *et al.* [2003], representing all potential plan and subplan execution 'paths' required to decompose and achieve a_{goal}. The return value derives from visiting every leaf activity ($O(n)$ worst case complexity, for n leaf nodes), originating from either a primitive or external capability confidence value. We assume cyclical loops cannot occur due to the decompositional nature of plans; this property is also required to prevent infinite loops in agent activity itself. Use of advertised confidence for external capabilities – rather than requesting potential dependants calculate a value locally – restricts semantic knowledge requirements to the advertising agent.

There is considerable scope for domain specific optimization of confidence calculation for both primitive and composite types. Average-case complexity can also be improved in contexts where a minimum threshold is being tested by using α-β pruning based on that threshold value. Finally, composite capabilities representing runtime planning abilities will require custom implementation of confidence estimation, similar to that used by primitive capabilities.

3.2 Obligation and Dependency Contracts

Our approach assumes dependency *contracts* are formed as early as possible, in advance of execution, to reserve agent capabilities and protect against possible agent resource contention. CAMP-BDI agents are aware of their obligation (to perform some activity upon request) *and* dependency (activities to be performed by some obligant) contracts. Contracts define mutual beliefs between dependants and obligants regarding a delegated activity – our algorithms require the following fields be represented and established during contract formation;

- The **activity** to be performed by the obligant(s) for the dependant.
- **Causal link** states; states that will be established by planned dependant, as effects of activities in the plan, prior to execution of the delegated activity.
- An **external capability**, used by obligant(s) to convey the (anticipated) post-effects and confidence for the activity – the latter estimating the execution context using the causal link states. If there is more than one obligant, the individual obligant capabilities will be merged;
  - *Confidence* is set as the *minimum* individual obligant confidence
  - *Preconditions* are formed as the conjunction of all obligant preconditions
  - *Effects* are set as the union of all obligant post-effects
- A **maintenance policy**, used to guide maintenance behaviour (see 3.3).

3.3 Maintenance Policies

A maintenance policy defines specific fields, applied to a defined set of agents and/or capabilities, where both field values and the applicable agent-capability set are modifiable during runtime;

- **Threshold**: the minimum confidence (quality) value for an activity; runtime modification of this value also allows compensation for over-sensitive confidence estimation
- **Priority**: guides relative prioritisation within maintenance behaviour, when multiple activities in an i_{plan} are identified as under threat

Maintenance policies are used to tailor maintenance behaviour; agent-capabilities associated with activities that have greater (probability or severity) failure consequences can be given lower thresholds and higher priorities. This assists balancing the additional computational costs of maintenance (lower threshold values act to increase the likelihood of an agent attempting to identify a confidence-raising modification of the i_{plan}) against the benefits of avoiding failure.

Contract maintenance policies merge dependant and obligant policies – these are matched respectively to the capability mapped to the dependent's i_{goal} (where i_{plan} contains the delegated activity) and to that associated with the obligant and delegated activity (obligant's i_{goal}). To restrict changes to a minimal subset of the overall distributed plan, the merged maintenance policy uses the most constrained field values (lowest threshold and highest priority values) to ensure obligants must have attempted maintenance before informing dependants of confidence changes.

4   The CAMP-BDI Algorithm

The reasoning cycle (algorithm 1) of a CAMP-BDI agent extends Rao and Georgeff [1995]'s generic BDI algorithm with contract formation and maintenance steps (the former to support information requirements of the latter). Intentions are selected before the *maintain* function attempts to diagnose and correct threats to i_{plan}, the performance of which may result in subsequent modification. The maintain function is also called following receipt of *obligationMaintained* messages, which convey changes in how obligants will perform a delegated activity and also signifies they have performed any required (possible) local maintenance. The *formAndUpdateContracts* function forms new, and updates existing, dependency and obligation contracts; this executes after *maintain*, to account for plan modifications and/or inherited dependency contract changes.

The *maintain* function (Algorithm 2) first forms a priority-ordered list (agenda) of maintenance tasks – each representing a threatened activity. The agent iterates through this agenda, terminating when a maintenance task is successfully handled *or* the agenda emptied. The function *handleMaintenanceTask* attempts to modify i_{plan} to address the issue represented by a given maintenance task, returning true if successful (false if i_{plan} is unchanged).

Separating agenda formation and handling allows the former to prioritize amongst the complete set of threatened activities. Decoupling of agenda formation (i.e. threat diagnosis) and handling processes also facilitates investigation into alternate approaches for either.

In our motivating example (Fig. 1), *handleAgenda* would identify – using the associated capability's *pre* field – that flooding of $F \rightarrow M$ violates the preconditions of $move(F, M)$, and insert a corresponding maintenance task into the agenda. A subsequent *handlingMaintenanceTask* call for that maintenance task would (attempt to) modify i_{plan} such that i_{goal} can be achieved, either by avoiding use of $move(F,M)$ or (if capable) removing the flooded state of $F \rightarrow M$.

If there are multiple possible intentions ($I \neq \emptyset$), the agent only attempts to maintain the specific $i \in I$ that has been selected for execution. We view intention selection as goal driven behaviour, such that maintenance changes to improve an i_{plan} will not invalidate the original choice to *select* that i. This avoids the cost of maintaining *every* potential intention prior to selection – especially as maintenance of unselected intentions risks being rendered futile by subsequent agent activity. We terminate after the first successfully handled maintenance task, as modifications may invalidate other maintenance tasks in the agenda; this also provides a guaranteed termination point. An alternative is to iteratively diagnose and handle until either an empty agenda is formed or handling fails, but this is likely to result in significantly higher computational cost.

4.1 Maintenance Tasks

Maintenance tasks are data structures which define a threatened activity, details of the threat and handling requirements. A maintenance task mt defines an activity a, task *type* (*preconditions* or *effects*), estimated execution context B_a for a, estimated confidence $conf_a$ of a given B_a, and the maintenance policy mp_a associated with a and used to set confidence thresholds;

$$mt = < a, type, B_a, conf_a, mp_a >$$

Algorithm 1. The CAMP-BDI reasoning cycle with changes from Rao and Georgeff [1995]'s generic algorithm highlighted as **bold** text, denoting maintenance activities and contract formation/updates.

---

initializeState();
while *agent is alive* do
    $D \leftarrow$ optionGenerator(*eventQueue, I, B*);
    $i \leftarrow$ deliberate(*D, I, B*);
    if $i \neq null$ *& i not waiting on a dependency to complete* then
       $i \leftarrow$ updateIntentions(*D, I, B*);
       $B_i \leftarrow$ **estimated execution context of** i;
       maintain(i**,** B_i**);**
       formAndUpdateContracts(i**);**
       execute();

    for *each obligationMaintained message* $\in$ *eventQueue* **do**
       $i_{dependency} \leftarrow$ **the associated dependant intention;**
       $B_{dependency} \leftarrow$ **estimated execution context of** $i_{dependency}$**;**
       maintain($i_{dependency}$**,** $B_{dependency}$**);**
       formAndUpdateContracts($i_{dependency}$**);**

    for *each obligation contract* $\in$ *agent's Obligations* **do**
       if $i = \emptyset$ **then**
          $i_{ob_{goal}} \leftarrow$ **activity defined in** *obligation*;
          $i_{ob_{plan}} \leftarrow$ **cached plan for** *obligation* **(to achieve** $i_{ob_{goal}}$**);**
          $i_{ob} \leftarrow i_{ob_{goal}}, i_{ob_{plan}}$**;**
          $B_{ob} \leftarrow$ **execution context estimated using (causal links in** *obligation* $\cup$ *B***);**
          maintain(i_{ob}**,** B_{ob}**);**
       formAndUpdateContracts(i_{ob}**);**

    getNewExternalEvents();
    $I \leftarrow$ dropSuccessfulAttitudes();
    $I \leftarrow$ dropImpossibleAttitudes();
    $I \leftarrow$ postIntentionStatus();

Capability knowledge facilitates introspective reasoning for maintenance task generation. Activities are mapped to – in precedence order – internal capabilities, contract-contained external capabilities, and finally advertised external capabilities; this assumes activities are only delegated where necessary and that agents adopt the least complex (fewest activities) approach for performing any activity. If an activity can be met by several external capabilities, that with highest general confidence is selected; mirroring the most likely criteria for obligant selection. Maintenance tasks are ordered in an agenda first by (mp_a defined) priority, then by precedence within the plan.

Preconditions maintenance task are generated where a's preconditions do not hold in B_a, but it is valuable to preserve a within the plan – either due to it fulfilling a goal state, or to avoid (the costs of) cancelling a pre-existing

---

Algorithm 2. The *maintain* function

Data: i – An intention; a plan i_{plan} to meet some goal i_{goal}
$\quad$ B_i – The estimated execution context of the first activity in i_{plan}
$handled \leftarrow$ false;
$agenda \leftarrow$ new empty Agenda;
$agenda \leftarrow$ the agenda returned by formAgenda($i_{goal}, i_{plan}, B_i, agenda$);
while $\neg$ *handled* & $\neg$ *agenda.isEmpty()* **do**
$\quad \lfloor$ *handled* $\leftarrow$ handleMaintenanceTask(*agenda*.removeTop());

update Dependency contracts;
if i *is an Obligation* **then**
$\quad \lfloor$ update contract and send to the dependant in an *obligationMaintained*
$\quad$ message;

---

dependency contract for a. This type indicates maintenance should first attempt to restore precondition states before considering modifications to replace a.

Effects maintenance tasks arise where either preconditions do not hold and a does not require preservation, or $conf_a$ is under $mp_a.threshold$ (a is of unacceptable quality and at risk of failure). This indicates a should be replaced by an activity sequence that will achieve the same post-execution effects as a.

4.2 Agenda Formation

Agenda formation (algorithm 3) employs recursion to support hierarchical plan structures (i.e. where composite activities are achieved through sub-plans). Each leaf activity (primitive activity *or* a composite which does not yet have an associated subplan, as may occur when employing continual planning) is iterated through in scheduled execution order. The *getCapability* function associates each activity with it's representative capability; this knowledge is used to identify threats and insert representative maintenance tasks into the agenda, with B_a finally being updated with activity effects (estimating the execution context for the subsequent activity). The *consolidate* function merges multiple maintenance tasks for the same subplan into a single maintenance task within the agenda, where appropriate. This consolidated maintenance task represents a need to maintain the entire subplan containing those activities – avoiding recurrent costs of re-diagnosing and handling each threatened activity individually, over multiple reasoning cycles.

4.3 Handling Maintenance Tasks

Handling a maintenance task (mt) requires modification of the i_{plan} containing $mt.a$, by identification and subsequent insertion of a new *maintenance plan* into i_{plan}. This behaviour is performed through the *handleMaintenanceTask* function (as called within the reasoning cycle given by Algorithm 1), which uses submethods *handlePreconditionsTask* (Algorithm 4) and *handleEffectsTask*

Algorithm 3. The *formAgenda* function

Data: g – a goal met, or composite activity performed, by p
  p – plan of n activities $\{a_0, a_1, ..., a_n\}$ to perform g
  agenda – priority ordered list of maintenance tasks; empty in initial
  (top-level) call
  B_a – estimated execution context of a_0 in p
Result: *agenda* updated with maintenance tasks for p
  B_a updated with post-effects of p (used by recursion)
$B_{start} \leftarrow$ copy of B_a (for execution context estimation);
for *each activity* $a \in p$ **do**
  if a *is abstract* **then**
    return *agenda*, B_a;
  $c_a \leftarrow$ getCapability(a);
  if $c_a = null$ **then**
    Add *effects* type maintenance task for a in B_a to *agenda*;
    Update B_a with effects of goal a;
  else if c_a *primitive* $\|$ *(c_a composite & (a is not decomposed into a subplan))*
  then
    if *maintenance task mt found for leaf activity* a **then**
      add *mt* to *agenda*;
      Update B_a with c_a.eff(a);
  else if c_a *composite & (a is decomposed into a subplan)* **then**
    $p_a \leftarrow$ subplan decomposing a;
    agenda, $B_a \leftarrow$ formAgenda(a, p_a, B_a, *agenda*);
  agenda $\leftarrow$ consolidate(g, *agenda*, B_{start});
return *agenda*, B_a;

Algorithm 4. The *handlePreconditionsTask* function

Data: *task* – a maintenance task
Result: **true** if a plan was found and inserted
$i_{mt} \leftarrow$ plan containing *task.a*;
$c_a \leftarrow$ getCapability(*task.a*);
Define planning problem *prob$_a$*, with initial state = *task.B_{mt}* and goal =
c_a.pre(*task.a*);
if *acceptable plan plan$_a$ solving prob$_a$ found* **then**
  Insert *plan$_a$* into i_{mt} as predecessor of *task.a*, and **return** true;
return false;

(Algorithm 5) for the *preconditions* and *effects* types respectively. Capability knowledge is used to define an operator specification (reflecting currently accessible capabilities) and form the maintenance planning problem.

If a *preconditions* maintenance task cannot be handled, the algorithm generates and attempts to handle an equivalent *effects* maintenance task – relaxing

---

Algorithm 5. The *handleEffectsTask* function

Data: *task* – a maintenance task
Result: true if a plan was found and inserted
$i_{mt} \leftarrow$ intended plan containing *task.a*;
if i_{mt} *is a hierarchical plan* **then**
    $p_{mt} \leftarrow$ subplan of i_{mt} containing *a*;
else
    $p_{mt} \leftarrow i_{mt}$;
$B_{mt} \leftarrow task.B_a$;
if *a not last in* i_{mt} ∥ *a has subsequent dependencies* **then**
    $c_a \leftarrow$ getCapability(*a*);
    Define planning problem $prob_a$, with initial state $= B_{mt}$ and goal $=$
    c_a.effects(*a*);
    if *acceptable plan* $plan_a$ *found for* $prob_a$ **then**
        Replace *a* in p_{mt} with $plan_a$;
        return true;

if *a not first in* i_{mt} ∥ *a has preceding dependencies* **then**
    $a \leftarrow$ goal achieved by p_{mt};
    $c_a \leftarrow$ getCapability(*a*);
    Define $prob_a$, with initial state $= B_{mt}$ and goal $= c_a$.effects(*a*);
    if *acceptable plan* $plan_a$ *found for* $prob_a$ **then**
        Replace p_{mt} from *a* inclusive with $plan_a$;
        return true;

while $a \neq$ *root goal of* i_{mt} **do**
    $a \leftarrow$ goal activity for p_{mt};
    $B_{mt} \leftarrow$ estimated execution context of *a*;
    $c_a \leftarrow$ getCapability(*a*);
    Define $prob_a$, with initial state $= B_{mt}$ and goal $= c_a$.effects(*a*);
    if *acceptable plan* $plan_a$ *found for* $prob_a$ **then**
        Replace p_{mt} with $plan_a$;
        return true;

  return false;

---

the (preconditions maintenance) problem to allow replacement of *mt.a* rather than fail from violated preconditions. For example, if *Truck* cannot restore preconditions for *move(F,M)* by unblocking road $F{\rightarrow}M$, it will attempt to find an alternate method to achieve the required goal state *at(M)*.

4.3.1 Performing Preconditions Maintenance

Preconditions maintenance (Algorithm 4) attempts to generate a plan reestablishing preconditions of *mt.a*, to be inserted prior to *mt.a* (similar to *prefix* plan repair as defined by Komenda *et al.* [2014]). Generated maintenance plans are only inserted where their confidence is above $mt.mp_a.threshold$. This condition attempts to prevent subsequent maintenance of the i_{plan} arising from insertion of a suboptimal confidence plan, but is *not* applied if $mt.a$ is immediately due to execute – we deem any non-zero confidence plan preferable over guaranteed failure. In our motivating example (Fig. 1), successful preconditions maintenance would insert a (sub)plan which, when completed, removes the *flooded* state of road $F \to M$ before $move(F, M)$ executes.

4.3.2   Performing Effects Maintenance

Effects maintenance attempts to substitute a subset of the plan containing $mt.a$, with a new (sub)plan achieving identical effects. In our previous motivating example (Fig. 1), successful effects maintenance would substitute a new subplan for $move(F, M)$ which achieves the associated i_{goal} – e.g. reforming the i_{plan} such that *Truck* (given a current location at D) will now travel through a (higher confidence offering) route $D \to E \to I \to L$.

Our algorithm (algorithm 5) adopts a similar approach to HTN plan repair – we use upwards recursion to re-refine composite activities (subgoals or the root i_{goal}), terminating when either an acceptable confidence (greater than $mt.mp_a.threshold$) maintenance plan is found and inserted, or the algorithm has reached the level of i_{goal} (i.e. attempted and failed to reform the entire i_{plan}). We trade-off the potential cost of multiple planning calls at goal/subgoal levels against the stability costs of complete replanning (Fox *et al.* [2006]).

The algorithm also considers potential costs from dependency cancellation, either from performing communication or the loss of external capability. Changes in circumstance after initial contract formation may render potential obligants subsequently unable to accept dependencies, even where now-cancelled dependency contracts previously existed – potentially stymieing maintenance planning if that external capability was necessary. To account for dependencies, we attempt two more restricted scope planning operations at the lowest level of iteration (the subplan containing $mt.a$). Firstly, if dependency contracts have been formed for $mt.a$ or it's successors in that subplan, the algorithm first attempts to generate a maintenance plan that directly and solely replaces $mt.a$; retaining successive activities and their associated dependency contracts. If any dependencies precede $mt.a$, the algorithm may also attempt *suffix* plan repair (Komenda *et al.* [2014]); where the generated maintenance plan replaces $mt.a$ and it's successors in that subplan, but preserves preceding activities. These two more constrained cases attempt to reduce disruption to a *distributed* plan performing team, at the cost of (potentially) requiring multiple planner calls.

The algorithm will, in the worst case, iterate and attempt to plan all levels of a hierarchical i_{mt}, including at the initial p_{mt} level twice (once for a failed preconditions maintenance task, and once for the replacement of $mt.a$ only), equivalent to $O((n+2)p)$ complexity (where n is the number of plan levels, and p the cost of planning). This, however, may still entail significant *actual* computational cost due to multiple planner invocations.

We are also investigating potential optimizations, including using policies to define conditions where planning is intractable (i.e. if *Truck* had been damaged to the extent *any* plan would have too low confidence) – allowing handling to terminate early and effectively delegate to any dependent. Another alternative is use of heterogeneous planners, allowing computationally restricted agents to employ less flexible, but faster, approaches such as HTN planning or libraries. Finally, it is trivial to modify the effects maintenance algorithm to only perform top-level modification, if minimizing computational cost takes precedence over maximizing plan stability.

5   Distributed Behaviour

MASs use co-operative teams of agents to achieve goals unattainable by individuals; activity failure impacts other team members and threatens the success of distributed plans. In our approach, we assume hierarchical agent teams arise from delegation to, and decomposition into plans by, obligants. We define a decentralized approach as the distribution of knowledge and capability across agents often renders centralized approaches infeasible for realistic domains. We apply the previously defined individual maintenance algorithms to the distributed context, using structured communication to drive successive adoption of maintenance responsibility by individual agents at increasingly abstract levels of the decompositional team hierarchy (Fig. 2).

The supporting architecture is critical in supporting this behaviour; dependency and obligation contracts allow *specific* capability information to be provided for a delegated activity. Placing external capabilities within contracts makes this information available to dependants, whilst offsetting semantic *knowledge* requirements to the actual obligant(s). As both internal and external capabilities share the same representative model, this allows an agent's maintenance reasoning to regard delegated activities in the same manner as those (to be) performed locally.

If an agent maintains an i_{plan} where the i_{goal} meets an obligation, the (waiting) dependent agent is messaged after maintenance completes. Dependants are viewed as quiescent during execution of a delegated activity; this allows maintenance of a dependency to be triggered in response to obligants completing their local maintenance. Obligants will maintain intentions both when performing (as

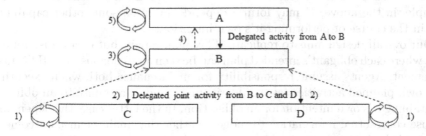

Fig. 2. The adoption of responsibility process in a hierarchical team, where B is an obligant of A, and C and D are obligants for a joint activity in B's plan.

an intention) an obligation, or when not presently pursuing any intention (Algorithm 1) – in the latter case, such that idle agents will act to maintain mutual beliefs with their dependent regarding the *future* achievement (or otherwise) of that delegated activity.

Dependants adopt maintenance responsibility if and when their obligants are unable to maintain confidence in their subpart of a greater distributed plan; restricting changes in a distributed plan to the 'lowest' (most specific) agent level. We informally refer to this as 'percolation' of maintenance responsibility – in that responsibility gradually moves upwards in the team hierarchy, until an agent has maintained an intention and produced an outcome acceptable to both itself and any direct dependant. In our motivating example, if *Truck* is unable to reach M (despite local maintenance), the dependant may alter it's own i_{plan} to instead use a Helicopter (not hindered by flooding) as an obligant to achieve the delivery i_{goal}.

We can summarize the resultant behaviour in general terms (Fig. 2) as follows;

1. Agents C and D call *maintain* within local reasoning cycle(s).
2. C and D individually perform post-maintenance messaging; each sends a *obligationMaintained* message to B that includes contracts updated to account for any maintenance changes.
3. B calls it's *maintain* method upon receipt of *obligationMaintained* messages from all obligants. Information in the messaged, updated contracts is used to update the contract held by B for that dependency, which will itself be sent on to A after *maintain* completes.
4. B sends A post-maintenance messaging, again using *obligationMaintained* messages.
5. A calls *maintain* upon receipt of B's post-maintenance message); as A is not an obligation, no further messaging is required.

Contracts are employed to help synchronize this behaviour through defining a common maintenance policy for that activity, applied by both obligant(s) and dependant. As both share confidence threshold triggers, for a dependent to diagnose and attempt to handle an effects maintenance task the obligant must have first attempted the same. Although the above example indicates a linear approach to dependency formation, indirect 'self dependencies' can emerge – for example, in the above, D may form a dependency upon some other capability of A in the course of performing it's own intention.

Our overall design aims to replicate HTN plan repair, but over a distributed plan; where each obligant's intended plan can be seen as analogous to an HTN task refinement. Agents assume responsibility for maintenance both when executing their own planned activities (as in Algorithm 1), and in response to an obligant maintaining it's own intention for an obligation. In the latter case, the dependant can use contractual information to judge whether that maintenance outcome is acceptable by it's *own* standards and modify the dependant i_{plan} if not.

6 Evaluation

CAMP-BDI was implemented by extending the *Jason* agent framework (Bordini and Hbner [2006]). We compared a MAS of CAMP-BDI agents against a system using reactive replanning, in our previously described motivating logistics domain. Three types of post-failure debilitation could occur, with defined probabilities for cargo damage, cargo spillage (requiring roads to be decontaminated), and for agent damage (with graded degrees and associated confidence loss). We evaluated performance under four probabilities: 0.2, 0.4, 0.6 and 0.8; representing 20, 40, 60 and 80% chance of an activity failure resulting in debilitation. These probabilities were applied individually for each debilitation type, albeit with cargo damage/spillage debilitation only possible if the failed activity was to load, unload or move whilst carrying cargo. Results for ten experimental runs, performed under fixed simulation seeds, were averaged and are presented in Fig. 3. A system with *no* failure mitigation was used as a worst-case indicator.

Our results show CAMP-BDI enjoyed significant advantage in goal success rate over replanning, increasing with the likelihood of debilitative failure consequences (Fig. 3a); CAMP-BDI maintained around 95% goal achievement for all consequence probability ranges, whilst replanning dropped from achieving 61.9% of goals at probability 0.2, to 26.6% at 0.8. In all three graphs CAMP-BDI shows fairly consistent performance; *avoidance* of failure (Fig. 3b) meant changes in *consequence* probability were unlikely to impact performance. In contrast, acceptance of failure as a 'trigger point' for reactive recovery meant replanning faced increasing difficulty in recovering (and achieving goals) from post-failure states as debilitation became more likely.

Worst case behaviour remained more variable (although always worst), as these agents would fail goals *immediately* upon activity failure regardless of

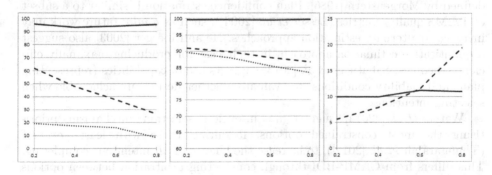

(a) y-axis; Average goals achieved (%) (b) y-axis; Average activity success (%) (c) y-axis; Average planner calls per goal achieved

Fig. 3. Experimental results; x-axis denotes post-failure damage probability. CAMP-BDI results are shown as solid lines, Replanning dashed, and Worst-Case dotted.

debilitation (or otherwise) – unlike replanning, where agents would pursue the intended goal until all options were exhausted, potentially failing in multiple activities (with resultant accumulated debilitation) before recovery attempts finally became futile. Goal and activity success rates of the *worst case* system were similarly variable; as no recovery mechanism was employed, each goal failure could be attributed to a single activity failure. This contrasts with reactive replanning, where agents would pursue an intended goal until all reactive replanning options were exhausted; each goal failure was potentially associated with multiple activity failures and consequent debilitations.

One obvious concern with a proactive approach is *cost*, particularly with CAMP-BDI's use of planning. Toyama and Hager [1997] note reactive approaches hold an advantage in only expending their costs following definitive, rather than potential, failure. Indeed, our results show CAMP-BDI performed significantly more planning calls at lower consequence probabilities (Fig. 3c); 9.91 calls per goal, compared to 5.62 for replanning at the lowest consequence probability. As the probability of post-failure debilitation increased, reactive replanning became significantly *less* efficient; an average 19.51 planning calls were required for each goal achieved at the highest consequence probability, compared to 11.03 for CAMP-BDI. This reflects an increasingly likelihood of debilitation stymieing *reactive* recovery – suggesting maintenance costs can be balanced against those incurred by failure. It may also still be preferable to employ a higher cost proactive approach, in domains where failure risks sufficiently severe consequences – such as if delivery goals are concerned with transport of nuclear waste or essential medical supplies.

7   Related Work

CAMP-BDI draws from a variety of existing work; our capability model captures the concepts of *know-how-to-perform*, *can-perform* and *know-how-to-achieve* defined by Morgenstern [1986]. Plan confidence estimation is similar to a subset of TÆMS quality metrics (Lesser *et al.* [2004]), such as q_min; future work may investigate alternate estimation approaches. He and Ioerger [2003] also suggest a quantitative estimation approach, in their case for producing maximally efficient schedules. Sabatucci *et al.* [2013] suggests use of capabilities (representing plans and viability conditions) to evaluate whether desires are achievable when selecting intentions.

Waters *et al.* [2014] suggest an intention selection mechanism prioritising the most constrained options, favouring those with least *coverage* (Thangarajah *et al.* [2012]), to increase the chance of *all* intentions completing. This differs from CAMP-BDI through considering arbitration between options in order to maximize intention throughput, rather than to ensure a specific intention succeeds. Whilst not explored in this paper, CAMP-BDI capability knowledge could facilitate similar reasoning during desire and intention selection. Plan execution monitoring approaches, such as SIPE (Wilkins [1983]), and plan repair approaches, such as O-Plan (Drabble *et al.* [1997]), share conceptual similarities with CAMP-BDI as both respond to divergence from expected states. CAMP-BDI differs through explicit focus on a multi-agent context, and use of confidence estimation to identify suboptimal activities.

Braubach *et al.* [2005] define two types of goals driving agent proactivity; those to *achieve* some state, and those to *maintain* it (over some defined period or under set conditions). Duff *et al.* [2006] further distinguishes reactive and proactive maintenance goals; the former requiring re-establishment of the state once violated, the latter constraining goal and plan adoption to prevent violation. In the reactive case, these drive adoption of achievement goals to re-establish violated (maintained) states; CAMP-BDI could consequently be used to maintain resultant intentions.

Precondition maintenance in CAMP-BDI can be viewed as similar in outcome to inferring proactive maintenance goals, corresponding to precondition states, and active until the relevant activity executes. Effects maintenance can be viewed as somewhat similar, in the sense that the loss of high-confidence associated states trigger plan modification; although our approach does not necessarily entail re-establishment of specific states if maintenance planning can identify an acceptable, alternate combination of activities. We also assume that plan formation mechanisms, used both in intention formation and maintenance planning, will be implemented to recognise and respect any maintenance goals.

Work by Hindriks and Van Riemsdijk [2007] uses (limited) lookahead similar to CAMP-BDI, with regard to respecting proactive maintenance goals. They identify potential violations from adopted goals and plans using a goal-plan tree to anticipate future effects of adopted intentions. However, plans in this approach are treated as pre-defined and immutable; anticipated violation is suggested as best addressed by goal relaxation to allow alternative plan options. This may not be a viable approach in certain domains, if goals cannot be safely relaxed.

Duff *et al.* [2006] suggest a similar predictive approach, again using a goal-plan tree to filter goal adoption based upon effects of potentially usable plans. CAMP-BDI varies by more explicitly considering exogenous change, rather than potential goal/plan adoption, as a source of violation. Our approach also differs by focusing upon ensuring *existing* intentions avoid failure after exogenous change – proactive maintenance goals are typically employed more as constraints upon the *formation* and adoption of desires or intentions (although this encompasses adoption of subgoals and subplans in continual approaches).

Continual planning handles uncertainty by deferring planning decisions (desJardins *et al.* [2000]) – including decomposing certain abstract activities only upon execution. CAMP-BDI supports this approach, using composite capabilities to reason whether abstract activities can be met by (sub)plans. If planning incorporates sensing – representing knowledge requirements through preconditions and effects – these can be represented similarly within capabilities.

Markov Decision Processes (MDPs) are an alternate approach for acting within stochastic domains, using state transition probabilities and rewards to generate a *policy* defining the optimal activity in every possible state. Partially Observable MDPs (POMDPs) remove total knowledge assumptions through a probability map of state observations, used to infer actual states and define a solveable MDP. Whilst MDP approaches offer optimal behaviour, complexity issues render them intractable as state space increases. Schut *et al.* [2002] show BDI agents can handle relatively simple domains that are intractable for MDPs and approximate MDP performance (depending on time costs of runtime planning). Attempts to improve tractability typically involve abstraction – simplifying state spaces at the cost of optimality (Boutilier and Dearden [1994]).

Although BDI is viewed as a (time-efficient) alternative to MDP approaches, work has been performed to reconcile both; Simari and Parsons [2006] identify similarities and suggests possible mapping between policies and plans. Pereira *et al.* [2008] extend that work by defining an algorithm to form deterministic plans (for libraries) from POMDP policies – although this assumes the latter are formable offline. There is a risk that transition probability information is unavailable, or impractical to *learn* under domain time constraints. An MDP specification of a complex domain can also be non-intuitive, restricting practical usability; Meneguzzi *et al.* [2011] suggest a method to map more intelligible HTN domains onto MDPs – defining probabilities based upon state presence within operator preconditions, rather than probabilities in the *environment.* We defined CAMP-BDI under the assumption in realistic domains it is necessary to use deterministic plans, due to the above intractability and domain knowledge issues. A relationship can be envisaged between confidence estimation and MDP transition probabilities – although the former only requires a scalar *quality* estimate, rather than requiring exact probability estimation.

8 Conclusion

In this paper, we contribute CAMP-BDI – an approach towards distributed plan execution robustness using pre-emptive plan modification or *maintenance.* We have described the provision of capability knowledge, dependency contracts and dynamically modifiable policies to support pre-emptive maintenance through introspection, and depicted a structured messaging approach for extending that individual agent behaviour to perform decentralized, distributed maintenance. Whilst we do not argue *all* failures can be prevented – that CAMP-BDI can replace reactive methods – we suggest it offers a valuable complementary approach. Finally, our supporting architecture may be useful for other robustness approaches or improving desire and intention selection; this helps justify the analytical costs involved in defining capability specifications.

CAMP-BDI does require gathering domain and agent information to model capability knowledge; consideration whether to employ our approach must balance the analytical and computational costs against the likelihood and severity of failure costs. We believe this domain analysis is a reasonable requirement, as such knowledge is used to form planning operators (or plan libraries) for agents. Even if fully granular and/or probabilistic confidence estimation is not possible, we view it as plausible for 'risky' world states to be identified and incorporated. Time-weighted success records can potentially be used for confidence estimation; similar to Dhirendra *et al.* [2010]'s use in learning plan execution contexts.

Our future work intends to focus upon maximizing gains from failure avoidance whilst minimizing planning costs; such as using policies to regulate maintenance behaviour, investigating potential specification of proactive maintenance goals within policies, and methods to focus 'computational expenditure' where avoiding failure is of greatest importance. Optimization of confidence estimation and agenda formation remains another aspect of interest, although we anticipate many of the most effective approaches will be domain specific.

Acknowledgments. This work was funded with support from EADS Innovation Works. Alan White would like to extend additional thanks to Dr. Stephen Potter for his invaluable help and advice. The authors and project partners are authorized to reproduce and distribute reprints and online copies for their purposes, notwithstanding any copyright annotation hereon.

References

Bordini, R.H., Hübner, J.F.: BDI agent programming in agentspeak using jason (tutorial paper). In: Toni, F., Torroni, P. (eds.) CLIMA 2005. LNCS (LNAI), vol. 3900, pp. 143–164. Springer, Heidelberg (2006)

Boutilier, C., Dearden, R.: Using abstractions for decision theoretic planning with time constraints. In: Proceedings of the 12th National Conference on Artificial Intelligence, pp. 1016–1022. Morgan Kaufmann, San Francisco, CA (1994)

Braubach, L., Pokahr, A., Moldt, D., Lamersdorf, W.: Goal representation for BDI agent systems. In: Bordini, R.H., Dastani, M., Dix, J., El Fallah Seghrouchni, A. (eds.) PROMAS 2004. LNCS (LNAI), vol. 3346, pp. 44–65. Springer, Heidelberg (2005)

desJardins, M.E., Durfee, E.H., Ortiz, C.L. Jr., Wolverton, M.J.: A Survey of Research in Distributed, Continual Planning (2000)

Singh, D., Sardinia, S., Padgham, L., Airiau, S.: Learning context conditions for BDI plan selection. In: Proceedings of the 9th International Conference on Autonomous Agents and Multiagent Systems: Volume 1 - Volume 1, AAMAS 2010, pp. 325–332. International Foundation for Autonomous Agents and Multiagent Systems, Richland (2010)

Drabble, B., Dalton, J., Tate, A.: Repairing plans on-the-fly. In: Proceedings of the NASA Workshop on Planning and Scheduling for Space (1997)

Duff, S., Harland, J., Thangarajah, J.: On proactivity and maintenance goals. In: AAMAS 2006, pp. 1033–1040 (2006)

Fox, M., Gerevini, A., Long, D., Serina, I.: Plan stability: replanning versus plan repair. In: Proc. ICAPS, pp. 212–221. AAAI Press (2006)

He, L., Ioerger, T.R.: A quantitative model of capabilities in multi-agent systems. In: Proceedings of the International Conference on Artificial Intelligence, IC-AI 2003, vol. 2, pp. 730–736, June 23–26, 2003, Las Vegas, Nevada, USA (2003)

Hindriks, K.V., van Riemsdijk, M.B.: Satisfying maintenance goals. In: Baldoni, M., Son, T.C., van Riemsdijk, M.B., Winikoff, M. (eds.) DALT 2007. LNCS (LNAI), vol. 4897, pp. 86–103. Springer, Heidelberg (2008)

Komenda, A., Novák, P., Pechoucek, M.: Domain-independent multi-agent plan repair. J. Network and Computer Applications **37**, 76–88 (2014)

Lesser, V., Decker, K., Wagner, T., Carver, N., Garvey, A., Horling, B., Neiman, D., Podorozhny, R., Prasad, M.N., Raja, A., Vincent, R., Xuan, P., Zhang, X.Q.: Evolution of the GPGP/TÆMS Domain-Independent Coordination Framework. Autonomous Agents and Multi-Agent Systems 9(1–2), 87–143 (2004)

McCarthy, J.: Programs with common sense. In: Proceedings of the Teddington Conference on the Mechanisation of Thought Processes, pp. 77–84 (1958)

Meneguzzi, F., Tang, Y., Sycara, K., Parsons, S.: An approach to generate MDPs using HTN representations. In: Decision Making in Partially Observable, Uncertain Worlds: Exploring Insights from Multiple Communities, Barcelona, Spain (2011)

Morgenstern, L.: A first order theory of planning, knowledge, and action. In: Proceedings of the 1986 Conference on Theoretical Aspects of Reasoning About Knowledge, TARK 1986, pp. 99–114, San Francisco, CA, USA. Morgan Kaufmann Publishers Inc. (1986)

Pereira, D.R., Gonçalves, L.V., Dimuro, G.P., Costa, A.C.R.: Constructing BDI plans from optimal POMDP policies, with an application to agentspeak programming. In: Proc. of Conf. Latinoamerica de Informática, CLEI, vol. 8, pp. 240–249 (2008)

Rao, A.S., Georgeff, M.P.: BDI agents: from theory to practice. In: Proceedings of the First International Conference on Multi-Agent Systems (ICMAS 1995), pp. 312–319 (1995)

Sabatucci, L., Cossentino, M., Lodato, C., Lopes, S., Seidita, V.: A possible approach for implementing self-awareness in JASON. In: EUMAS 2013, pp. 68–81 (2013)

Schut, M.C., Wooldridge, M.J., Parsons, S.: On partially observable MDPs and BDI models. In: d'Inverno, M., Luck, M., Fisher, M., Preist, C. (eds.) UKMAS Workshops 1996-2000. LNCS (LNAI), vol. 2403, p. 243. Springer, Heidelberg (2002)

Simari, G.I., Parsons, S.: On the relationship between MDPs and the BDI architecture. In: Proceedings of the Fifth International Joint Conference on Autonomous Agents and Multiagent Systems, AAMAS 2006, pp. 1041–1048, New York, NY, USA. ACM (2006)

Thangarajah, J., Padgham, L., Winikoff, M.: Detecting and avoiding interference between goals in intelligent agents. In: IJCAI 2003, pp. 721–726 (2003)

Thangarajah, J., Sardina, S., Padgham, L.: Measuring plan coverage and overlap for agent reasoning. In: Proceedings of the 11th International Conference on Autonomous Agents and Multiagent Systems, AAMAS 2012, vol. 2, pp. 1049–1056, Richland, SC. International Foundation for Autonomous Agents and Multiagent Systems (2012)

Toyama, K., Hager, G.: If at first you don't succeed. In: Proc. AAAI, pp. 3–9, Providence, RI (1997)

Waters, M., Padgham, L., Sardina, S.: Evaluating coverage based intention selection. In: Proceedings of Autonomous Agents and Multi-Agent Systems (AAMAS), pp. 957–964, Paris, France, May 2014. IFAAMAS. Nominated for Jodi Best Student Paper award (2014)

Wilkins, D.E.: Representation in a domain-independent planner. In: Proceedings of the 8th International Joint Conference on Artificial Intelligence, pp. 733–740, Karlsruhe, FRG, August 1983 (1983)

Optimizing Long-Running Action Histories in the Situation Calculus Through Search

Christopher Ewin[1](✉), Adrian R. Pearce[1], and Stavros Vassos[2]

[1] National ICT Australia and Computing & Information Systems,
The University of Melbourne, Melbourne, Australia
cjewin@student.unimelb.edu.au, adrianrp@unimelb.edu.au
[2] Department of Computer, Control, and Management Engineering,
Sapienza University of Rome, Rome, Italy
vassos@dis.uniroma1.it

Abstract. Agents are frequently required to perform numerous, complicated interactions with the environment around them, necessitating complex internal representations that are difficult to reason with. We investigate a new direction for optimizing reasoning about long action sequences. The motivation is that a reasoning system can keep a window of executed actions and simplify them before handling them in the normal way, e.g., by updating the internal knowledge base. Our contributions are: (i) we extend previous work to include sensing and non-deterministic actions; (ii) we introduce a framework for performing heuristic search over the space of action sequence manipulations, which allows a form of disjunctive information; finally, (iii) we provide an offline precomputation strategy. Our approach facilitates determining equivalent sequences that are easier to reason with via a new form of search. We demonstrate the potential of this approach over two common domains.

As agents evolve, sense, and interact with the environment, the difficulty of maintaining and reasoning about a representation of the world around them increases. This is particularly significant in cases where an agent possesses incomplete information, either in terms of its initial knowledge base or the effects of its actions, due to the complexity of reasoning over this uncertainty. Yet actions frequently occur that are capable of simplifying the underlying representation of an agent's knowledge base. An agent may, for example, be able to eliminate uncertainty regarding particular facts by sensing, communicating with other agents, or performing an action that brings the environment to a known state of affairs.

We investigate a new direction for optimizing reasoning over long action sequences by means of analyzing and manipulating the sequence before reasoning with it. Consider a long-lived agent that operates for days or months and is constantly performing actions while also reasoning about them, e.g., by means of an agent program that interleaves search and execution. Keeping the whole action history (possibly thousands or millions of actions) and relying on a regression mechanism for answering queries about the current (and future states) is impractical, therefore a progression mechanism is highly motivated.

© Springer International Publishing Switzerland 2015
Q. Chen et al. (Eds.): PRIMA 2015, LNAI 9387, pp. 85–100, 2015.
DOI: 10.1007/978-3-319-25524-8_6

However, always progressing up to the final state may occasionally blow up the size of the KB due to incomplete information and the way it is encoded in the final state, which is an unnecessary effort if a subsequent action makes fluent values known. We consider an approach that allows to combine both reasoning mechanisms. The agent may progress only up to a point but leave a final sequence of actions for which queries about the current state will be answered by means of regression. Before progressing over an action sequence, reordering and eliminating actions can significantly reduce the effort needed to reach the final state.

One simple example is the case of a "resetting" action that makes all previous actions in the sequence obsolete; therefore when reasoning over the whole sequence of actions we can in fact simplify our deliberation method to only consider the last "resetting" action and the actions that come after this. This is just a special case, while in general there are many other ways to optimize reasoning by manipulating an action sequence.

The work of [4] investigated this idea in the context of the situation calculus [10, 11] which provides a general and well-studied logical formalism for representing a dynamic domain as a first-order logical theory. Given a basic action theory and a sequence of actions, the authors articulated the logical conditions that allow the manipulation of an action sequence in two basic ways while preserving the answer to all queries at the final state and future states of the domain. These two basic operations are (i) *swapping* the order of two consecutive actions and (ii) *eliminating* on action from the action sequence as being obsolete.

Such operations form the basis for investigating how transforming action sequences can achieve computational gains in the context of a desired reasoning task, e.g., performing *projection* queries that query the truth of conditions in a future state of affairs or *updating* or *progressing* the domain representation to reflect the current state of affairs after a sequence of actions has been performed. In this paper we introduce a new search framework for finding equivalent action sequences that are optimal with respect to the effort required to perform reasoning on the resulting final state. In order to achieve this it is necessary to investigate a number of aspects, building on [4].

In particular, (i) we extend previous work on the conditions of reordering and eliminating action to account for sensing and nondeterministic actions; (ii) we introduce a rewriting framework for transforming sequences and propose a local search setting for finding equivalent sequences with a minimal size based on the notion of *dominatable pairs*; (iii) we adopt a view similar to databases, while also allowing a form of disjunctive information, and investigate a more refined local search setting where the intermediate effort for updating the representation is taken into account based on the notions of *progression speedup* and *progression slowdown*; (iv) we facilitate an *offline* precomputation strategy allowing efficient online detection of swappability and elimination potential. Finally, to illustrate the applicability of our results and framework, we show example runs over two well-known domains.

1   Situation Calculus Basic Action Theories

The situation calculus as presented in [11] is a three-sorted first-order (FO) language $\mathcal{L}$ with equality. The sorts are used to distinguish between actions, situations, and objects (everything else). A *situation* represents a world history as a sequence of actions. The constant S_0 is used to denote the initial situation where no actions have occurred. Sequences of *actions* are built using the function symbol do, such that $do(a, s)$ denotes the successor situation resulting from performing action a in situation s. We will typically use a to denote a variable of sort action and α to denote a term of sort action, and similarly s and σ for situations.

A *relational fluent* is a predicate whose last argument is a situation, and thus whose truth value can change from situation to situation. For example, $RobotAt(l, \sigma)$ may be used to represent that the robot lies at location l in situation σ. Actions need not be executable in all situations, and the predicate atom $Poss(\alpha, \sigma)$ states that action α is executable in situation σ. Actions may also have a sensing result: the special function $sr(\alpha, \sigma)$ denotes the sensing outcome of action α when executed in situation σ [14].

We will restrict our attention to a language $\mathcal{L}$ with a finite number of relational fluent symbols, an infinite number of constant symbols, and a finite number of action symbols. Often we will focus on sentences in $\mathcal{L}$ that refer to a particular situation. For this purpose, for any situation term σ, we define the set of *uniform formulas in* σ to be all those first-order (FO) or second-order (SO) formulas in $\mathcal{L}$ that do not mention any other situation terms except for σ, do not mention $Poss$, and where σ is not used by any quantifier [7]. Finally, we use δ to denote a sequence of actions of the form $\langle \alpha_1, \ldots, \alpha_n \rangle$, and $do(\delta, S_0)$ as a shorthand for the situation term $do(\alpha_n, \cdots do(\alpha_1, S_0))$.

Within $\mathcal{L}$, one can formulate action theories that describe how the world changes as the result of the available actions. We focus on a variant of the *basic action theories (BATs)* [11] of the following form,[1]

$$\mathcal{D} = \mathcal{D}_{ap} \cup \mathcal{D}_{ss} \cup \mathcal{D}_{sr} \cup \mathcal{D}_{una} \cup \mathcal{D}_0 \cup \mathcal{D}_{fnd}, \text{ where:}$$

1. $\mathcal{D}_{ap}$ is the set of action precondition axioms (PAs), one per action symbol A, of the form $Poss(A(\boldsymbol{y}), s) \equiv \Pi_A(\boldsymbol{y}, s)$, where $\Pi_A(\boldsymbol{y}, s)$ is FO and uniform in s. PAs characterize when actions are physically possible.
2. $\mathcal{D}_{ss}$ is the set of successor state axioms (SSAs), one per fluent symbol F, of the form $F(\boldsymbol{x}, do(a, s)) \equiv \Phi_F(\boldsymbol{x}, a, s)$, where $\Phi_F(\boldsymbol{x}, a, s)$ is FO and uniform in s. SSAs describe how fluents change between situations as the result of actions.
3. $\mathcal{D}_{sr}$ is the set of sensing-result axioms (SRAs), one for each action symbol A, of the form $sr(A(\boldsymbol{y}), s) = r \equiv \Theta_A(\boldsymbol{y}, r, s)$, where $\Theta_A(\boldsymbol{y}, r, s)$ is FO and uniform in s. SRAs relate sensing outcomes with fluents.
4. $\mathcal{D}_{una}$ is the set of unique-names axioms for actions.
5. $\mathcal{D}_0$, the *initial knowledge base (KB)*, is a set of FO sentences uniform in S_0 describing the initial situation S_0.

---

[1] For legibility, we typically omit leading universal quantifiers.

6. $\mathcal{D}_{fnd}$ is the set of domain independent axioms of the situation calculus, formally defining the legal situations. A SO induction axiom is included in $\mathcal{D}_{fnd}$.

2 Transforming Extended Action Sequences

We build upon [4] to consider reordering and dominating actions in the presence of sensing actions and incomplete information. First, we review the notions of *always swappable* and *always dominated* actions.

Definition 1 ([4]). *Actions α and α' are* always swappable *wrt $\mathcal{D}$ iff for all $F(\boldsymbol{x}, s)$ in $\mathcal{L}$, $\mathcal{D} - \mathcal{D}_0 \models \forall \boldsymbol{x}.F(\boldsymbol{x}, do(\langle \alpha, \alpha' \rangle, S_0)) \equiv F(\boldsymbol{x}, do(\langle \alpha', \alpha \rangle, S_0))$. Action α is* always dominated *by α' wrt $\mathcal{D}$ iff for all $F(\boldsymbol{x}, s)$, $\mathcal{D} - \mathcal{D}_0 \models \forall \boldsymbol{x}. F(\boldsymbol{x}, do(\langle \alpha, \alpha' \rangle, S_0)) \equiv F(\boldsymbol{x}, do(\alpha', S_0))$.*

Intuitively, when the specified condition holds then we can perform these transformations in any action sequence δ in which α' comes exactly after α and preserve the final state we arrive after all actions in the sequence are executed.

Example 1. Consider a mobile robot whereby its position can be controlled only by the action $moveTo(l)$, which unconditionally moves the robot to location l. Allow the robot's position in situation σ to be represented by the fluent $RobotAt(v, \sigma)$. The SSAs for $RobotAt(v, \sigma)$ can then be expressed as follows:

$$\gamma_F^+(\boldsymbol{v}, a, \sigma) \equiv a = moveTo(l) \wedge v = l, \; \gamma_F^-(\boldsymbol{v}, a, \sigma) \equiv a = moveTo(l) \wedge \neg v = l.$$

Allow similarly the robot's direction to be represented by a fluent $RobotDir(v, \sigma)$ and controlled by an action $turnTo(l)$. The SSAs for $RobotDir(v, \sigma)$ are then:

$$\gamma_F^+(\boldsymbol{v}, a, \sigma) \equiv a = turnTo(l) \wedge v = l, \; \gamma_F^-(\boldsymbol{v}, a, \sigma) \equiv a = turnTo(l) \wedge \neg v = l.$$

From Definition 1 we can observe that actions $moveTo$ and $turnTo$ are always swappable, but neither action dominates the other.

We now reintroduce the definitions of the so-called *single-value fluents*. These are treated in a way such that for a fluent $F(\boldsymbol{x}, v, s)$, the arguments $\boldsymbol{x}$ are considered as the *input* and the argument v as the (single) *output* of the fluent.

Definition 2 ([4]). Single-value *fluents are fluents for which the following holds: $\mathcal{D} \models \forall \boldsymbol{x}, v\{F(\boldsymbol{x}, v, s) \supset \neg \exists v'(F(\boldsymbol{x}, v', s) \wedge v' \neq v)\}$.*

For example, $RobotAt(v, \sigma)$ may be naturally be considered a single value fluent with an empty $\boldsymbol{x}$ term, requiring that the robot can be at only one location in a given situation.

In this context it is natural to consider the so-called *resetting actions* that preserve the property of single-value fluents. We will typically assume that successor state axioms (SSAs) have the following form: $F(\boldsymbol{x}, v, do(a, s)) \equiv \gamma_F^+(\boldsymbol{x}, v, a, s) \vee F(\boldsymbol{x}, v, s) \wedge \neg \gamma_F^-(\boldsymbol{x}, v, a, s)$, where γ_F^+ and γ_F^- are FO formulas uniform in s encoding the positive and negative effects, respectively, of action a on fluent F at situation s.

Definition 3 ([4]). *The SSA for $F(\boldsymbol{x}, v, s)$ has resetting-actions iff $\gamma_F^+(\boldsymbol{x}, v, a, s)$ is a disjunction of formulas of the form: $\exists \boldsymbol{z}(a = A(\boldsymbol{y}) \wedge v = y_i \wedge \phi(\boldsymbol{y}, s))$, and $\gamma_F^-(\boldsymbol{x}, v, a, s)$ is a disjunction of formulas of the form: $\exists \boldsymbol{z}(a = A(\boldsymbol{y}) \wedge \neg v = y_i \wedge \phi(\boldsymbol{y}, s))$, where A is an action symbol, $\boldsymbol{y}$ contains $\boldsymbol{x}$, $\boldsymbol{z}$ corresponds to the remaining variables of $\boldsymbol{y}$, y_i is a variable in $\boldsymbol{y}$, and $\phi(\boldsymbol{y}, s)$ (called a* context formula*) is a FO formula uniform in s. We also require that γ_F^+, γ_F^- come in pairs in the sense that for each disjunct in γ_F^+ there is one in γ_F^- that is identical except for the atom $v = y_i$.*

A ground resetting action "sets" a fluent atom to be true for a particular ground input and ground output (both given as arguments of the action), and at the same time "unsets" it to be false for all other outputs for the given input. The SSAs modelled in Example 1 both have resetting actions. For ground resetting actions we can rewrite the instantiated γ formulas in a normal form that exposes the objects that are affected by the action, as in [4, Lemma 1], and extract the *effect-set* from an SSA, which explicitly characterises the possible effects of actions.

Definition 4 ([4]). *Let α be a ground resetting action. The effect set Φ of α is the set: $\{\phi \supset F(\boldsymbol{c}, d) \mid \boldsymbol{x} = \boldsymbol{c} \wedge v = d \wedge \phi$ appears in (the simplified) $\gamma_F^+(\boldsymbol{x}, v, \alpha, s)\}$.*

We now extend this setting to account for sensing actions.

Definition 5. *A is a* resetting sensing action *iff it has a sensing-result axiom (SRA) of the form $sr(A(\boldsymbol{y}), s) = r \equiv \bigwedge_i [\phi_i(\boldsymbol{y}, r, s) \supset \bigvee_j F_{ij}(\boldsymbol{x}_{ij}, z_{ij}, s)]$, where $\{\boldsymbol{x}_{ij}, z_{ij}\} \subseteq \{\boldsymbol{y}, r\}$.*

Recall that sensing actions differ from physical actions in that they can only "filter" models of the BAT by means of adding an atom of the form $sr(\alpha, \sigma)$ to the theory, hence requiring that the right-hand side of the corresponding SRA holds. We model a sensing action as a set of implications (the conjuncts i), each of which provides under the context condition ϕ_i, disjunctive information about fluent atoms that are built using the arguments of the action and the sensing result. We define the effect set for such actions similarly to physical actions.

Definition 6. *Let α be a ground sensing resetting action along with a sensing result. The effect set Φ of α is the set of all those formulas $\phi_i \supset \bigvee_{ij} F_{ij}(\boldsymbol{c}_{ij}, d_{ij})$ that appear in the instantiated (and simplified similarly as Definition 4) SRA. The* expanded effect set Φ^* *is the set where each element of Φ is broken down to j elements of the form $\phi_i \supset F_{ij}(\boldsymbol{c}_{ij}, d_{ij})$.*

The resetting sensing actions require special treatment within the existing framework, and except for the normal effect set we will use also expanded version that characterizes all fluent terms that *may* be affected by a sensing action.

Sensing actions can be reordered in a manner similar to physical actions. The key difference is that sensing actions may be reordered even if they affect the contexts of other actions, as a fluent unaffected by action α, that was sensed after performing action α must have held the same value prior to performing α. The following theorems identify sound methods for determining whether two actions can be swapped.

Theorem 1. *Any two consecutive resetting sensing actions are always swappable.*

Theorem 2. *Let action α_1 be a resetting sensing action with expanded effect set Φ_1^*, and α_2 be a (physical) resetting action with effect set Φ_2, that occurs immediately before or after α_1. Then α_1 and α_2 are always swappable if for all elements of Φ_2 of the form $\phi_1 \supset F_1(c_1, d_1)$, there does not exist an element of Φ_1^* of the form $\phi_2 \supset F_2(c_2, d_2)$ such that $F_1 = F_2, c_1 = c_2$ or s.t. ϕ_1 mentions $F_2(c_2, e)$ for some e.*

Theorem 3. *Theorem 10 of [4] that specifies the condition according to which α_2 always dominates α_1, holds also with resetting sensing actions when the expanded effect set is used instead, for action α_1.*

We now turn our attention to actions with nondeterministic effects. A nondeterministic action can be modelled as corresponding to a set of actions with deterministic effects, and assuming that the agent does not know which of them was performed [1]. This is typically handled in an epistemic version of situation calculus, but one can also model the notion of the agent *knowing some sentence to hold* in this setting, by means of entailment as follows.

Definition 7. *We assume that the domain includes for each single-value fluent $F(x, v, s)$ a particular resetting action $A_F(x, v)$ with only effect to set the output of F to be v for the input x. A widening ground action α^* is defined as a finite set of resetting actions $\{A_F(c, d_1), \ldots, A_F(c, d_n)\}$ for some fluent F. For a ground sequence δ^* with widening actions and a FO sentence $\phi(do(\delta^*, S_0))$, we define the unfolding of ϕ as the resulting sentence after recursively replacing all subformulas of the form $\phi(do(\alpha^*, \sigma)$ by $\forall a.(a = \alpha_1 \vee \cdots \vee a = \alpha_n) \supset \phi(do(a, \sigma))$, where $\alpha^* = \{\alpha_1, \ldots, \alpha_n\}$ is a widening action.*

The notion of the effect set then generalizes naturally to widening actions, and our previous results about always swappable and always dominatable also apply.

Definition 8. *The effect set Φ of a widening action $\alpha^* = \{\alpha_1, \ldots, \alpha_n\}$ is the union of the effect sets of actions α_i.*

Theorem 4. *Widening actions follow the same conditions as physical actions for always swappable and always domination, using the corresponding definition for effect sets.*

Our framework then allows for a practical alternative for reasoning with widening actions in the context of regular BATs, as by reordering and eventually eliminating such actions we can in some cases arrive back to having regular action sequences and reason using the standard methods.

3   A Rewriting System and Search Framework

Section 2 and results in [4] show how to reorder and eliminate actions in the context of single-valued fluents. We now look into finding preferred transformations. First, we introduce some notation and a search framework.

Definition 9. *Let δ be an action sequence of the form $\langle \alpha_1, \ldots, \alpha_n \rangle$, and $1 \leq i \leq n-1$. We use r_i to denote the swapping the position of actions α_i and α_{i+1}, and $r_i(\delta)$ to denote the resulting sequence. Similarly, we use e_i to denote the elimination of action α_i in δ, and $e_i(\delta)$ for the result.*

Definition 10. *$\mathcal{A}^{\mathcal{D}} = (A, \rightarrow)$ is an abstract rewrite system, where A is the set of all finite sequences of ground actions in a BAT $\mathcal{D}$, and $\rightarrow$ is a binary relation between sequences s.t. $\delta \rightarrow \delta'$ iff there exists an i, $1 \leq i \leq n-1$, where n is the size of δ, s.t. $\delta' = r_i(\delta)$ and actions α_i, α_{i+1} are always swappable in δ wrt $\mathcal{D}$ or $\delta' = e_i(\delta)$ and action α_{i+1} dominates α_i δ wrt $\mathcal{D}$. Also, $\overset{*}{\rightarrow}$ is the reflexive transitive closure of $\rightarrow$.*

Essentially $\delta \rightarrow \delta'$ is true when we can perform exactly one step of reordering or eliminating, while $\delta \overset{*}{\rightarrow} \delta'$ is true when δ' can be derived by a finite number of steps. This characterizes a class of sequences that are equivalent as follows.

Definition 11. *For a sequence δ we define the set $FSE(\delta)$ of* final-state equivalent *sequences as the set $\{ \delta' \mid \delta \overset{*}{\rightarrow} \delta' \}$.*

Observe that the set $\{ \delta' \mid \delta \overset{*}{\rightarrow} \delta' \}$ is finite, as the permutations of a finite sequence δ are finite and sequences can only shrink to a smaller size, not grow. Depending on which type of reasoning task we intend to apply over the action sequence, the conditions that identify a preferred sequence may vary greatly. Without yet committing to a particular reasoning task, one natural way is to consider minimal length so that shorter sequences are to be preferred over longer ones.

Finding a sequence in $FSE(\delta)$ with a global minimal size can be posed as an *optimization problem* where the objective function is the size of the sequence. For example, a hill-climbing local search algorithm would work as follows: start from the original sequence; at every iteration look into the current sequence δ and all successors δ' such that $\delta \rightarrow \delta'$; keep a successor with minimal size smaller than δ and continue; if one does not exist then return δ. Other methods could be employed in a similar manner, e.g., simulated annealing.

The size of sequences is not a good choice though for evaluating the successors toward a global minimal. This is because often it will be necessary to perform several reordering steps before an elimination step can take place, which leads to large plateaus. A better approach is to use a heuristic cost function that evaluates our progress towards making the current sequence shorter. A simple way to quantify this is to look over all pairs of actions in δ such that one can dominate the other and measure how far they are to each other.

Definition 12. *We define the set of* dominatable pairs *$Dom(\delta)$ as $\{ (\alpha, \alpha') \mid \alpha$ always dominates α' in δ wrt $\mathcal{D} \}$. The* dominatable pairs distance heuristic *h^{ei} is* the function $h^{e_i}(\delta) = \sum_{(\alpha,\alpha') \in Dom(\delta)} dist(\alpha, \alpha')$, where $dist(\alpha, \alpha')$ is the distance of the actions in terms of their index in δ.

Note that hill-climbing with h^{e_i} is nonetheless not optimal. As with any greedy local search algorithm that does not occasionally backtrack to sequences with a lower heuristic cost value, hill-climbing with h^{e_i} may decide to eliminate an action too early. This is illustrated with the following example.

Example 2. Consider $\delta = \langle \alpha_1, \alpha_2, \alpha_3, \alpha_4 \rangle$ and $\Phi_1, \Phi_2, \Phi_3, \Phi_4$ the effect sets of actions as follows: $\Phi_1 = \{G(\boldsymbol{x}, v) \supset F(\boldsymbol{x}, v)\}$, $\Phi_2 = \{\top \supset G(\boldsymbol{x}, v)\}$ $\Phi_3 = \{\top \supset F(\boldsymbol{x}, v)\}$ $\Phi_4 = \{\top \supset F(\boldsymbol{x}, v), G(\boldsymbol{x}, v) \supset H(\boldsymbol{x}, v)\}$. Then applying hill-climbing with heuristic h^{e_i} will perform only one transition $\delta \to_{e_3} \delta'$, resulting in a sequence of length 3. The optimal approach follows the transitions: $\delta \to_{r_2} \langle \alpha_1, \alpha_3, \alpha_2, \alpha_4 \rangle$ $\to_{e_1} \langle \alpha_3, \alpha_2, \alpha_4 \rangle \to_{r_1} \langle \alpha_2, \alpha_3, \alpha_4 \rangle \to_{e_2} \langle \alpha_2, \alpha_4 \rangle$, resulting in a length 2. Note that this cannot be obtained by any transformation from δ'.

More sophisticated heuristics can be specified based on the dominatable pairs, also taking into account the interactions between the pairs through their effect sets. In this way, for instance, an appropriate causal ordering can be defined that requires certain eliminating steps to occur before others, avoiding the problem illustrated in Example 2. We now look into optimizing the effort required to reason wrt particular actions.

4   A Case of DBs with Disjunctive Information

Depending on the reasoning task we want to perform, the particular actions in the sequence and their order may affect greatly the effort needed. We investigate this in a setting inspired by databases. We focus on a particular type of KB with disjunctive information, and look into the impact of manipulating action sequences in the effort required to progress, i.e., update, the KB to the final state after all actions are executed.

The KB is a *database of possible closures* that explicitly specifies a set of possible worlds for single-valued fluents.

Definition 13. *Let τ be a fluent atom of the form $F(\boldsymbol{c}, w, S_0)$ with ground input $\boldsymbol{c}$ and output w. The* atomic closure χ *of τ on d is the sentence: $\forall w.F(\boldsymbol{c}, w, S_0) \equiv (w = d)$. The* closure of vector $\boldsymbol{\tau} = \langle \tau_1, \ldots, \tau_n \rangle$ *of distinct fluent atoms on a ground input vector $\boldsymbol{d} = \langle d_1, \ldots, d_n \rangle$ of constants is the conjunction $(\chi_1 \wedge \ldots \wedge \chi_n)$, where each χ_i is the atomic closure of τ_i on d_i.*

A closure of $\boldsymbol{\tau}$ expresses complete information about the output of all input-grounded fluents in $\boldsymbol{\tau}$. For example, consider $RobotAt(x, s)$ and $RobotDir(x, s)$ that represent information about the location and the direction of the robot. Let χ_1 be the the atomic closure of $RobotAt(w, S_0)$ on loc_1 and χ_2 the atomic closure of $RobotDir(w, S_0)$ on *north*; , that is:

$$\forall w.\, RobotAt(w, S_0) \equiv (w = loc_1), \tag{χ_1}$$
$$\forall w.\, RobotDir(w, S_0) \equiv (w = north). \tag{χ_2}$$

χ_1 and χ_2 express complete information about the location and the direction of the robot. We can combine closure statements to express incomplete information.

Definition 14. *A* possible closures axiom (PCA) *for a vector of input-grounded fluents τ is a disjunction of the form $(\chi_1 \vee \cdots \vee \chi_n)$, where each χ_i is a closure of τ on a vector of constants d_n of the same size.*

A PCA for τ expresses *disjunctive information* about the output of all fluents in τ, by stating how such outputs can be combined together (in n possible ways).

Example 3. Let χ_1 and χ_2 represent as before the atomic closures of $RobotAt(w, S_0)$ on loc_1 and $RobotDir(w, S_0)$ on *north* respectively. Let χ_3 be the closure of $RobotAt(w, S_0)$ on loc_2 and χ_4 the closure of $RobotDir(w, S_0)$ on *east*, which both express complete information. Then $((\chi_1 \wedge \chi_2) \vee (\chi_3 \wedge \chi_4))$ is a PCA for $\langle RobotAt(w, S_0), RobotDir(w, S_0) \rangle$ which states two possible combinations for the location and direction.

Using a set of PCAs we now define the form of the KB we want to consider.

Definition 15. *A* database of possible closures (DBPC) *is a set $\mathcal{D}_0 = \{\Xi^{\tau_1}, \ldots, \Xi^{\tau_\ell}\}$, where each Ξ^{τ_i} is a PCA for τ_i s.t. $\tau_i \cap \tau_j = \emptyset$, for all distinct $i, j \in \{1, \ldots, \ell\}$. For every i, each disjunct of Ξ^{τ_i} is called a* possible closure *wrt $\mathcal{D}_0$.*

So, for every fluent atom τ with a ground input either the output of τ is completely unknown in S_0 (i.e., τ is not mentioned in $\mathcal{D}_0$) or there is just one PCA Ξ_{τ_i} (with $\tau \in \tau_i$) that specifies its output value in several possible "partial worlds" (one per disjunct in the PCA). A PCA can be viewed also as a database table which lists as rows, the possible partial worlds for a set of input-ground fluent atoms. We will refer to the number of ground-input atoms in a PCA as the *width*, and the number of disjuncts in PCA as the *depth* of the PCA. Note that as the DBPC evolves under the effects of actions, more input-ground fluents may need to be put together in a PCA in order to express the resulting state, affecting the size of a PCA through the combinations of values that need to be explicitly represented by means of a cross product. This increase or decrease of the width and depth of the DBPC provides then a means for evaluating action sequences wrt to the effort needed to update to the final state.

Definition 16. *Let be the Φ the effect set of α, consisting of elements of the form $\phi \supset \bigvee_n F(c, d)$. We define the* progression speedup factor $h_+(\alpha)$ *of α as the total number of elements in Φ such that (i) $n = 1$ (ii) $F(c, d)$ appears in a PCA in $\mathcal{D}_0$ with depth greater than 1 and (iii) condition (ii) is not true for any fluent atom mentioned in ϕ. We define the* progression slowdown factor $h_-(\alpha)$ *of α as the total number of fluent atoms mentioned in ϕ in the elements of Φ such that the atom appears in a PCA in $\mathcal{D}_0$ with depth greater than 1 plus the number of members of the effect set with $n > 1$.*

Note that sensing actions with an equivalent speedup factor are inherently more desirable than physical actions as they allow all partial worlds inconsistent with the sensed fluent to be removed, reducing the depth of the PCA. This is demonstrated in the following example:

Example 4. Consider the robot described above with the initial situation $\mathcal{D}_0 = \{((\chi_1 \wedge \chi_2) \vee (\chi_3 \wedge \chi_4))\}$. The PCAs for the initial situation can be represented by the following table:

RobotAt	RobotDir
loc_1	north
loc_2	east

After performing the action *moveTo*(loc_3) in the initial situation, the PCAs can be represented by the following table:

RobotAt	RobotDir
loc_3	north
loc_3	east

Now allow an action *senseLocation*, which returns the current location of the robot. If the robot is initially at loc_1, then the PCAs after performing this action in the initial situation can be represented by the following table:

RobotAt	RobotDir
loc_1	north

Observe also that the notions of speedup and slowdown can help distinguish between action sequences of the same size. In particular we can specify heuristic cost functions for identifying the best permutation of a sequence that cannot be simplified further by elimination steps. As this relates to reordering actions, we use the r_i notation to denote the heuristic functions.

Definition 17. *The following are heuristic cost functions based on the effort imposed by intermediate updates when progressing to the final state:*

- speedup heuristic $h_+^{r_i}(\delta) = \sum_{\alpha \in \delta} -h_+(\alpha)$;
- slowdown heuristic $h_-^{r_i}(\delta) = \sum_{\alpha \in \delta} h_-(\alpha)$;
- balanced heuristic $h_b^{r_i}(\delta) = \sum_{\alpha \in \delta} h_-(\alpha) - h_+(\alpha)$.

Hill-climbing using these heuristics is not optimal, however. A key observation is that they take into account only of disjunctive information in the initial state, rather than considering the evolution of disjunctive information as actions occur in the sequence. A more sophisticated approach would keep track of the fluents mentioned in the PCAs and compare these to the fluents mentioned in the effect set.

Example 5. Consider a simplified version of the Wumpus World domain [12, Chapter7] with a *senseBreeze*(y_1, y_2) action, which senses whether one of two surrounding locations contains a pit, and a *sensePit*(y) action, which senses whether a particular location contains a pit. Allow fluent *IsPit*(x, s) to capture whether (from the point of view of the agent) that x contains a pit, and let the initial situation be represented by the PCAs $(\chi_1), (\chi_2), (\chi_3), (\chi_4)$, with each χ_i being the closure of *IsPit* on loc_i. Now consider the sequence $\langle senseBreeze(loc_1, loc_2), sensePit(loc_1) \rangle$ and assume that both sensing actions return *true*. Progressing wrt the first action leads to the following DBPC, which contains a single PCA shown as a table.

$IsPit(loc_1)$	$IsPit(loc_2)$
true	true
false	false
true	true

According to Definition 17, $senseBreeze(loc_1, loc_2)$ has a speedup heuristic value of 0 and a slowdown heuristic value of 1, while $sensePit(loc_1)$ has a speedup of -1 and a slowdown 0. This motivates us to consider reordering the $sensePit(loc_1)$ actions towards the start of the action sequence using Theorem 1. This leads to the sequence $\langle sensePit(loc_1), senseBreeze(loc_1, loc_2)\rangle$, which is final-state equivalent wrt Definition 1. The DBPC after the first action in this sequence can be represented as follows (which happens to be equivalent to the DBPC in the final situation):

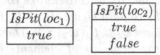

$IsPit(loc_1)$
true

$IsPit(loc_2)$
true
false

As expected, the DBPC for the final situation is the same for both sequences. Note though that for the reordered sequence, table sizes are maintained between 1×1 and 1×2, as compared with the 2×3 table produced for the original sequence, with a corresponding reduction in the cost progression.

5   An Offline Precomputing Step

We now examine the approach of precomputing actions off-line, in order to determine whether any pair of actions can be reordered or eliminated. This approach leads to a considerable increase in the efficiency of the online reasoning task, at the cost of producing and maintaining a version of the effect sets for each pair of action symbols in the domain. As an added benefit, the expensive offline reasoning need only be executed once for every pair of action symbols in the domain, rather than for every pair of ground actions in an action sequence. We take each pair of unground action symbols in the domain, and reformulate the γ^+, γ^- formulas of SSAs according to the following lemma:

Lemma 1. *Let α be the unground resetting action $A(\boldsymbol{y})$. Then, for each action symbol A in the domain, $\gamma_F^+(\boldsymbol{x}, v, \alpha, s)$ is logically equivalent to a formula of the form $(\boldsymbol{x} = \boldsymbol{w}_1 \wedge v = z_1 \wedge \phi_1(s)) \vee \cdots \vee (\boldsymbol{x} = \boldsymbol{w}_m \wedge v = z_m \wedge \phi_m(s))$, where each of the $\boldsymbol{w}_1, \ldots, \boldsymbol{w}_m$ is a vector of variables contained in $\boldsymbol{y}$, each z_i is a variable in $\boldsymbol{y}$ and $\phi_1(s), \ldots, \phi_m(s)$ are first-order and uniform in s. Each combination of $\boldsymbol{w}_i, z_i$ must be distinct. Similarly, $\gamma_F^-(\boldsymbol{x}, \alpha, s)$ is logically equivalent to a formula of the form $(\boldsymbol{x} = \boldsymbol{w}_1 \wedge \neg v = z_1 \wedge \phi_1(s)) \vee \cdots \vee (\boldsymbol{x} = \boldsymbol{w}_m \wedge \neg v = z_m \wedge \phi_m(s))$.*

We now define a variation of the effect sets that encapsulates the same property for unground actions:

Definition 18. *Let α be an unground resetting action of the form $A(\boldsymbol{y})$. The effect set Φ of α is the set: $\{\phi \supset F(\boldsymbol{x}, v) \mid \boldsymbol{x} = \boldsymbol{w} \wedge \phi \wedge v = z$ appears in $\gamma_F^+(\boldsymbol{x}, v, \alpha, s)\}$.*

We are now able to split the process of determining whether two actions can be reordered into two parts: First, a more complex off-line precomputing step that produces a set of equality relations between variables mentioned in the action terms, which we call the *online determination set (ODS)*. Second, a comparatively simple online procedure that verifies whether the equality relations hold. We consider the case of *conjunctive resetting actions*, which have contexts that are comprised of quantifier-free conjunctions of fluent atoms. We note that these results are similar for resetting sensing actions.

Definition 19. *Let F be a fluent symbol, x be a vector of variables and ϕ a situation-suppressed conjunctive context formula. Then $arg(F, x, \phi)$ is the smallest set such that for all y, v if $F(y, v)$ appears in ϕ then $y \neq x$ is in $arg(F, x, \phi)$.*

Theorem 5. *Let actions α_1 and α_2 be consecutive conjunctive resetting actions with effect sets Φ_1, Φ_2. Let Φ_1 contain elements of the form $\phi_1 \supset F_1(w_1, z_1)$ and Φ_2 contain elements of the form $\phi_2 \supset F_2(w_2, z_2)$. Then the offline precomputing step is as follows: For all combinations of elements in Φ_1 and Φ_2, add $w_1 = w_2 \supset z_1 \neq z_2$, $arg(F_1, w_1, \phi_2)$ and $arg(F_2, w_2, \phi_1)$ to the ODS. Then α_1 and α_2 are always swappable if all formulas in the ODS evaluate to true.*

Now, to eliminate α_1 it is necessary to establish that the eliminating action α_2 *will* set the value of all fluents that *could* have been set by a_1. That is, the context of α_1 implies the context of α_2 for all fluents. To facilitate offline precomputing for this task, we define a procedure $eval(\phi)$, which establishes conditions between variables so that ϕ is a valid formula.

Definition 20. *Let ϕ be a quantifier-free formula. $eval(\phi)$ is disjunction of all unifications expressed as equality atoms between variables mentioned in ϕ, for which ϕ is a valid formula*

Theorem 6. *Let action α_1 and α_2 be consecutive conjunctive resetting action with effect sets Φ_1, Φ_2. Let $\phi_1[F(w)]$ refer to the disjunction of all ϕ_1 for which $\phi_1 \supset F(w, z)$ is in Φ_1 for any z, and $\phi_2[F(w)]$ refer to the disjunction of all ϕ_2 for which $\phi_2 \supset F(w, z)$ is in Φ_2 for any z. Then the offline precomputing step is as follows:*

- *For all w, add $eval(\phi_1[F(w)] \supset \phi_2[F(w)])$ to the ODS.*
- *For all elements of Φ_1 of the form $\phi_1 \supset F(w_1, z_1)$, for each element of Φ_2 of the form $\phi_2 \supset F(w_2, z_2)$ add $arg(F, w_1, \phi_2)$ to the ODS.*

Then α_1 and α_2 are always swappable if all formulas in the ODS evaluate to true.

Theorem 7. *Determining whether two actions can be reordered or eliminated can be done in time linear in the size of the ODS after off-line precomputing has been completed.*

6   Basic Optimization Scenarios

We now give some insights about the effectiveness of these technique using two well-known domains, namely Sokoban [18] and the Wumpus World [12, Chapter7]. Progression and action sequence optimization are performed using a C program that runs a greedy search over the space of possible action sequence manipulations, using a combination of the dominatable pairs and progression speedup heuristics defined earlier, with a horizon of 10 actions. The offline precomputing step is also employed to simplify the effort required to determine action sequence modifications. Logical reasoning is performed using an Indigolog program [3].

We follow the modeling of Sokoban as a planning domain [5] and generate long action sequences of length 5000 actions, by employing a simple agent whose goal is to avoid repeated states. For the Wumpus World we consider action sequences generated by the agent described in [13] in maps of size 8×8 and 10×10. Note that while Sokoban is well suited for using progression for query answering, the Wumpus World, due to the type of incomplete information that needs to be represented, is well suited for using regression. As we want to evaluate our framework over both approaches, we solve projection queries via progression in Sokoban and via regression in the Wumpus World.

We formalise the domains using resetting actions and perform reasoning for answering a projection query that attempts to 'map' the domain by identifying the locations of all known blocks/pits. For each action, the Indigolog program implements a *Poss* axiom, providing the conditions under which the action can be executed, as well as one or more effect axioms. For example, the *moveFwd* action is specified as follows:

```
poss(moveFwd(L), neg(offTheEdge(L))).
causes(moveFwd(X), locRobot, Y, Y=X).
```

The top level control program is implemented as a series of prioritised interrupts which specify the agent behaviour. Each interrupt consists of a guard or condition under which it can be executed, and a small program to run. *locRobot*, *aliveWumpus* and *noGold* are all fluents in the domain.

```
proc(mainControl,
  prioritized_interrupts(
    [interrupt([dir], and(aliveWumpus=true,
      in_line(locRobot,dir,locWumpus)), [shoot(dir)] ),
    interrupt(isGold(locRobot)=true, [pickGold(locRobot)]),
    interrupt(inDungeon=true,
    if(noGold>0,[goto(loc(1,1)),climb],
    [smell(locRobot),
      senseBreeze(locRobot),
      senseGold(locRobot),
      explore_grid
    ]))
    ])
).
```

Table 1. Experimental results for Sokoban

Sequence	opt.	query	total	length
Original Progressed	-	1.45	1.45	5000
Optimized Progressed	0.15	0.00	**0.15**	**3**

Table 2. Experimental results for Wumpus World

Sequence	opt.	query	total	length
Original Regressed (8×8)	-	17.2	17.2	104
Optimized Regressed (8×8)	0.3	15.1	**15.4**	**77**
Original Regressed (10×10)	-	41.0	41.0	167
Optimized Regressed (10×10)	0.6	37.2	**37.8**	**125**

We report the runtime following two approaches: *(i)* applying the reasoning method (regression or progression) over the original action sequence in order to answer the projection query, and *(ii)* optimizing first the sequence before applying the reasoning method. The results are reported in Table 1 and 2. Columns *opt* and *query* represent the average time in milliseconds taken over 10 sequences.

We observe that the structure of Sokoban permits many elimination operations, with a substantial resultant speedup, that is in fact faster than progression. This is a very interesting result as progression works extremely well for planning domains like Sokoban. For Wumpus World, none of the actions affecting the agent's knowledge of pit locations could be eliminated, hence the performance improvement was far less significant. In a richer setting with overlapping sensing information and physical action, this could prove much more beneficial, drastically and efficiently simplifying the action sequence to a minimal length.

7 Related and Future Work

Our work is inspired by the idea of database query optimization and is based on the framework of [4]. Here, we facilitate optimization search for finding minimal *final state equivalent* sequences, using offline/online techniques for more efficient query answering. Parallels to classical planning exists [2] where pairs of actions are classified and removed. Reordering actions is not considered by these approaches, to-date. Note in the approach by Chrpa *et al.* preconditions of *each action* must be considered, in contrast to our approach.

Löwe *et al.* [9] consider similar properties in the context of Dynamic Epistemic Logic planning. They define event models as being *self-absorbing* or *commutative*, and demonstrate tractability results for models of this type. Löwe's self-absorbing actions corresponds to a special case of our dominatable actions whereby both the dominatable and the dominating action are the same, while commutative actions are similar to our reorderable actions. Yu *et al.* [19] use these same notions to demonstrate the decidability of of explanatory diagnosis for multi-agent systems under certain conditions.

The state representation that was used as the basis for evaluating the reasoning effort related to particular actions and action sequences, namely a DBPC, is similar in expressiveness to other KB forms in the literature for incomplete information, such as the so-called $proper^+$ KBs [8]. With DBPCs we aimed for a setting that is as close to the database case as possible, which allows to reuse database functionality in the implementation of reasoning systems. In our future work we intend to look into this type of implementation and a thorough investigation of the joint use of h^{e_i} and h^{r_i} heuristics in order to construct combined heuristics.

Notice that ideas presented here could also be applied in other action formalisms such as the fluent calculus [16] and the event calculus [6,15]. Indeed, our work shares some similarity to those that utilise constraints solvers, such as the Flux system for implementing fluent calculus theories [17] which uses (among other things) constraints to represent the effects implied to fluents with arithmetic arguments. In Flux these constraints specify how the old value of fluents relates to the new one, and are appended to the constraint store as the action history grows. Periodically, Flux's constraint store invokes heuristic techniques for simplifying the history by eliminating redundant constraints. Our work could be used to advantage in this setting to optimise action histories in more informed ways inspired by temporal action properties, e.g., the effect of sensing, instead of more low-level constraints.

8   Conclusions

We have shown how transforming action sequences facilitates a rewriting and local search setting where the effort for updating can be based on notions of *progression speedup* and *progression slowdown*, and the minimal size of the sequence can be estimated using the notion of *dominatable pairs*. The expanded framework incorporates sensing and widening actions, the effects of which strongly motivate reordering and elimination of actions. This work sets the ground for developing novel optimization strategies and hybrid approaches in reasoning about action, for utilisation in synchronous, concurrent and even asynchronous reasoning tasks.

We have further demonstrated a process for partially determining action sequences transformations offline, enabling an agent to more efficiently compute desirable transformations. For long running executions, such as agents operating over protracted time periods, our approach provides a mechanism for answering queries efficiently over the large action sequences generated.

Acknowledgments. NICTA is funded by the Australian Government through the Department of Communications and the Australian Research Council through the ICT Centre of Excellence Program.

References

1. Bacchus, F., Halpern, J.Y., Levesque, H.J.: Reasoning about noisy sensors (and effectors) in the situation calculus. In: Dorst, L., Voorbraak, F., van Lambalgen, M. (eds.) RUR 1995. LNCS, vol. 1093. Springer, Heidelberg (1996)
2. Chrpa, L., McCluskey, T.L., Osborne, H.: Determining redundant actions in sequential plans. In: ICTAI, pp. 484–491 (2012)
3. De Giacomo, G., Levesque, H.: An incremental interpreter for high-level programs with sensing. In: Levesque, H., Pirri, F. (eds.) Logical Foundations for Cognitive Agents. Artificial Intelligence, pp. 86–102. Springer, Heidelberg (1999)
4. Ewin, C., Pearce, A.R., Vassos, S.: Transforming situation calculus action theories for optimised reasoning. In: Proceedings of the Fourteenth International Conference on Knowledge Representation and Reasoning, pp. 448–457 (2014)
5. Helmert, M.: Domains - ipc-2008, deterministic part (2010). http://ipc.informatik.uni-freiburg.de/Domains (accessed February 13, 2015)
6. Kowalski, R., Sergot, M.: A logic-based calculus of events. New Gen. Comput. **4**(1), 67–95 (1986)
7. Lin, F., Reiter, R.: How to progress a database. Artificial Intelligence **92**(1–2), 131–167 (1997)
8. Liu, Y., Levesque, H.J.: Tractable reasoning with incomplete first-order knowledge in dynamic systems with context-dependent actions. In: Proceedings of the 19th International Joint Conference on Artificial intelligence, IJCAI 2005, pp. 522–527 (2005)
9. Löwe, B., Pacuit, E., Witzel, A.: DEL planning and some tractable cases. In: van Ditmarsch, H., Lang, J., Ju, S. (eds.) LORI 2011. LNCS, vol. 6953, pp. 179–192. Springer, Heidelberg (2011)
10. McCarthy, J., Hayes, P.J.: Some philosophical problems from the standpoint of artificial intelligence. Machine Intelligence **4**, 463–502 (1969)
11. Reiter, R.: Knowledge in Action: Logical Foundations for Specifying and Implementing Dynamical Systems. MIT Press (2001)
12. Russell, S., Norving, P.: Artificial Intelligence: A Modern Approach, second edn. Prentice Hall (2003)
13. Sardina, S., Vassos, S.: The wumpus world in indigolog: a preliminary report. In: Proceedings the Nonmonotonic Reasoning, Action and Change Workshop at IJCAI (NRAC 2005), pp. 90–95 (2005)
14. Scherl, R., Levesque, H.J.: Knowledge, action, and the frame problem. Artificial Intelligence **144**(1–2), 1–39 (2003)
15. Shanahan, M.: The event calculus explained. In: Veloso, M.M., Wooldridge, M.J. (eds.) Artificial Intelligence Today. LNCS (LNAI), vol. 1600, pp. 409–430. Springer, Heidelberg (1999)
16. Thielscher, M.: From situation calculus to fluent calculus: State update axioms as a solution to the inferential frame problem. Artificial Intelligence **111**(1–2), 277–299 (1999)
17. Thielscher, M.: FLUX: A logic programming method for reasoning agents. Theory and Practice of Logic Programing **5**(4–5), 533–565 (2004)
18. Wikipedia: Sokoban - Wikipedia, the free encyclopedia (2015). http://en.wikipedia.org/wiki/Sokoban (accessed February 13, 2015)
19. Yu, Q., Wen, X., Liu, Y.: Multi-agent epistemic explanatory diagnosis via reasoning about actions. In: Proceedings of the Twenty-Third International Joint Conference on Artificial Intelligence, IJCAI 2013, pp. 1183–1190. AAAI Press (2013)

Semantics for Modelling Reason-Based Preferences

Erica Calardo[1], Guido Governatori[2](✉), and Antonino Rotolo[1]

[1] CIRSFID, University of Bologna, Bologna, Italy
[2] Software Systems Research Group, NICTA, Brisbane, QLD, Australia
guido.governatori@nicta.com.au

Abstract. In [13] the authors developed a logical system based on the definition of a new non-classical connective ⊗ originally capturing the notion of reparative obligation. The operator ⊗ and the system were proved to be appropriate for rather handling well-known contrary-to-duty paradoxes. Later on, a suitable model-theoretic possible-world semantics has been developed [4,5]. In this paper we show how a version of this semantics can be used to develop a sound and complete logic of preference and offer a suitable possible-world semantics. The semantics is a sequence-based non-normal one extending and generalising semantics for classical modal logics.

1 Introduction

Theoretical and computational research in social choice theory is now recognised as relevant and is well-established in the MAS community. Indeed, it deals with the problem of how to aggregate in MAS individual preferences into a social or collective preference in order to achieve a rational collective decision [11].

Preliminarily to any useful contribution in this area we need to develop suitable formalisms and reasoning methods to represent and handle agents' preferences. In the current literature, we find several approaches, among which the most remarkable in computational social choice theory are perhaps the following [2]:

- conditional preference networks, or CP-nets [1];
- prioritised goals [7,17].

The second approach uses logical formalisms to describe the goals of the agents whose preferences are modelled as propositional formulae. This allows for a manageable and purely qualitative representation of preferences. Very recently, a new proposal in this perspective has been advanced [16], which presents a modal logic where a binary operator is meant to syntactically express preference orderings between formulae: each formula of this logic determines a preference ordering over alternatives based on the priorities over properties that the formula express. The authors recall that such types of formalisms are in fact capable of representing not just orderings over alternatives but the reasons that lead to the preferences [18]. The formalism is then interestingly used in [16] to originally treat the problem of collective choice in MAS as aggregation of logical formulae. The logic in

© Springer International Publishing Switzerland 2015
Q. Chen et al. (Eds.): PRIMA 2015, LNAI 9387, pp. 101–117, 2015.
DOI: 10.1007/978-3-319-25524-8_7

[16] is clearly inspired by the work in [3], which in turn has a number of similarities with a system that was independently developed in [13] and where a Gentzen system was proposed in a different but related area—deontic logic—to reason about orderings on obligations. The idea that reasoning about preferences is crucial in deontic logic was introduced in semantic settings long time ago [15] (for recent discussions, [14,21]). [13] is however based on the syntactic introduction of the new non-classical operator $\otimes$: the reading of an expression like $a \otimes b \otimes c$ is that a is primarily obligatory, but if this obligation is violated, the secondary obligation is b, and, if the secondary (CTD) obligation b is violated as well, then c is obligatory. These constructions can be used as well to reason about preferences. Thus, following the approach in [13], let $\Vdash$ be a non-classical consequence relation used to characterise conditional preferences. An expression like

$$Resident \Vdash \neg Pay\_Taxes \otimes \neg Pay\_Interest \otimes Pay\_Minimum$$

can be intuitively viewed as a conditional preference statement meaning the following:

1. if I'm resident in Italy, i.e. if *Resident* is the case, then not paying taxes is my actual preference, but,
2. if it happens that I pay taxes, then my actual preference is rather not to pay any interest, but
3. if I pay any interest, then my actual preference is pay a minimum.

Very recently, we have also devised a new semantics for $\otimes$ logics, which extends neighbourhood models with sequences of truth sets [4,5]. In this paper we take advantage of our previous work and offer some technical results for a new preference logic. Our intent is to take the token from [16] and go deeper into semantically investigating such modal logics.

The layout the paper is as follows. Section 2 presents the basic logical system for $\otimes$ to represent and reason about preferences. The logic recalls some intuitions from [4,5,13]. Section 3 defines a sequence neighbourhood semantics suitable for the system which adjusts the one proposed in [4,5]. Sections 5 and 6 provide, respectively, soundness and completeness results. Some conclusions end the paper.

2   A Logic for Reason-Based Preferences

Let us present in this section a new variant of the logic presented in [4,5,13], a logic which was originally devised for modelling deontic reasoning and which is here revised to reason about preferences. The language consists of a countable set of atomic formulae. Well-formed-formulae are then defined using the usual Boolean connectives and the n-ary connective $\otimes$, which is intended to syntactically formalise preference ordering among reasons. The language also includes the modal operator Pr denoting the actual preferred reason or state of affairs: in other words, $\mathsf{Pr}p$ means that p is preferred. The interpretation of an expression

$a \otimes b$ is that b is a the most preferred reason or state of affairs, but, if a is not the case then b is preferred.

Let $\mathscr{L}$ be a language consisting of a countable set of propositional letters $Prop = \{p_1, p_2, \dots\}$, the propositional constant $\perp$, round brackets, the boolean connective $\rightarrow$, the unary operator Pr, and a set of n-ary operators $\otimes^n$ for $n \in \mathbb{N}$, $n > 0$.

Definition 1 (Well Formed Formulae). *Well formed formulae (wffs) are defined as follows:*

- *Any propositional letter $p \in Prop$ and $\perp$ are wffs;*
- *If a and b are wffs, then $a \rightarrow b$ is a wff;*
- *If a is a wff and no operator $\otimes^n$ and Pr occurs in a, then $\mathsf{Pr}a$ is a wff;*
- *If $a_1, \dots, a_n$ are wffs and no operator $\otimes^n$ and Pr occurs in any of them, then $a_1 \otimes^n \cdots \otimes^n a_n$ is a wff, where $1 \le n;$*[1]
- *Nothing else is a wff.*

We use WFF to denote the set of well formed formulas.

Other Boolean operators are defined in the standard way, in particular $\neg a =_{def} a \rightarrow \perp$ and $\top =_{def} \perp \rightarrow \perp$.

We say that any formula $a_1 \otimes^n \cdots \otimes^n a_n$ is an $\otimes$-*chain*. The formation rules allow us to have $\otimes$-chain of any (finite) length, and the arity of the operator is equal to number of elements in the chain; accordingly we drop the index m from $\otimes^m$. Moreover, we will often use the prefix notation $\bigotimes_{i=j}^{n} a_i$ for $a_j \otimes \cdots \otimes a_n$. In addition we use the following notation: $\bigotimes_{i=j}^{n} a_i \otimes b \otimes \bigotimes_{k=l}^{m} c_k$, where $i, j \in \{0, 1\}$. The "a" part and "c" part are optional, i.e., they are empty when $i = 0$ or $j = 0$, respectively. Otherwise the expression stands for the following chain of $n+1+m$ elements: $a_1 \otimes \cdots \otimes a_n \otimes b \otimes c_1 \otimes \cdots \otimes c_m$

Let us define a Gentzen-style sequent calculus for $\otimes$.

Definition 2 (Sequents). *Let $\vdash$ and $\Vdash$ be two binary consequence relations defined over $\mathscr{P}(WFF) \times WFF$. Thus expressions $\Gamma \vdash a$ and $\Gamma \Vdash a$ are sequents where Γ is a finite (and possibly empty) set of wffs, and a is a wff.*

We use $\vdash$ for the consequence relation of classical propositional logic (see [10] for an appropriate set of rules), and $\Vdash$ for the consequence relation for the preference logic of $\otimes$. The following axiom and rules define the sequent calculus $\mathsf{E}^{\otimes}$ for $\Vdash$:

$$\Gamma, a \Vdash a \tag{ID}$$

This axiom allows us to use assumptions in $\Vdash$.

$$\frac{\vdash a}{\Gamma \Vdash a} \tag{PC}$$

---

[1] We will use the prefix form $\otimes^1 a$ for the case of $n = 1$.

The rule above allows us to import classical consequences in $\Vdash$.

$$\frac{\Gamma \Vdash a \qquad \Delta \Vdash a \to b}{\Gamma, \Delta \Vdash b} \tag{MP}$$

The combination of (ID), (PC) and (MP) enables us to use the full power of classical propositional logic in the right-hand side of the preference consequence relation.

$$\frac{\Gamma, a \Vdash b \qquad \Delta \Vdash a}{\Gamma, \Delta \Vdash b} \tag{Cut}$$

$$\frac{\Vdash a_j \equiv a_k}{\Gamma \Vdash (\bigotimes_{i=1}^{n} a_i) \equiv (\bigotimes_{i=1}^{k-1} a_i) \otimes (\bigotimes_{i=k+1}^{n} a_i)} \qquad \text{(where } j < k\text{)} \quad \text{(}\otimes\text{-shortening)}$$

$$\frac{\Gamma \Vdash \bigotimes_{k=0}^{p} a_k \otimes (\bigotimes_{i=1}^{n} b) \otimes \bigotimes_{l=0}^{q} c_l \qquad \Delta, \{\neg b_1, \ldots, \neg b_n\} \Vdash \bigotimes_{j=1}^{m} d_j}{\Gamma, \Delta, \Vdash \bigotimes_{k=0}^{p} a_k \otimes (\bigotimes_{i=1}^{n} b) \otimes \bigotimes_{j=1}^{m} d_j} \tag{$\otimes$-I}$$

$$\frac{\Gamma \Vdash (\bigotimes_{i=0}^{n} b_i) \otimes c \otimes \bigotimes_{j=0}^{m} d_j \qquad \Delta \Vdash \bigwedge_{i=0}^{n} \neg b_i}{\Gamma, \Delta \Vdash \mathsf{Pr}c} \tag{Pr-detachment}$$

$$\frac{\Gamma \Vdash \mathsf{Pr}a}{\Gamma \Vdash \neg\mathsf{Pr}\neg a} \tag{$\otimes$-D}$$

$$\frac{\Gamma \Vdash \bigotimes_{i=1}^{n} a_i}{\Gamma \Vdash \bigotimes_{i=1}^{n-1} a_i} \qquad \text{(where } n > 1\text{)} \tag{$\otimes$-$\bot$}$$

$$\frac{\Vdash b \equiv c}{\Gamma \Vdash (\bigotimes_{i=0}^{n} a_i \otimes b \otimes \bigotimes_{j=0}^{m} d_j) \equiv (\bigotimes_{i=0}^{n} a_i \otimes c \otimes \bigotimes_{j=0}^{m} d_j)} \tag{$\otimes$-RE}$$

A few comments are in order.

The rule ($\otimes$-shortening) corresponds to duplication and contraction[2]: for example, $a \otimes b \otimes a$ is equivalent to $a \otimes b$. Intuitively, if I prefer not to get any damage, but if this happens I prefer to be compensated, and, if the damage is not compensated, then I prefer not to get any damage, this just means that my primary preference is not to get any damage and my secondary preference is to be compensated.

(Pr-detachment) is nothing but a rule allowing for detaching actual preferences from $\otimes$-chains, i.e, those preferences that hold in a given context. They

---

[2] Contraction in a logical sense, which is different from the one usually adopted in preference theory and which is captured by the subsequent derived rule ($\otimes$-contraction) (see Section 4). For this reason, we prefer to use in this first case the term "shortening".

reflect the intuitive reading of the $\otimes$ operator. Indeed, if $a \otimes b$, the primary preference should hold, and, if a is factually false ($\neg a$), then b must be preferred, i.e., $\mathsf{Pr}b$.

($\otimes$-I) is a peculiar introduction rule for $\otimes$. Let us illustrate ($\otimes$-I) by considering a simple instance of it as applied to a concrete example:

$$\frac{\Vdash \neg Pay\_Taxes \otimes \neg Pay\_Interest \qquad Pay\_Taxes \wedge Pay\_Interest \Vdash \otimes Pay\_Minimum}{\Vdash \neg Pay\_Taxes \otimes \neg Pay\_Interest \otimes Pay\_Minimum}$$

The sequent of the left-hand side states that my primary preference is not to pay taxes, but if this happens then my preference is not pay any interest (for example, by paying them in due time without delay). The sequent of the right-hand side rather states that, if I pay taxes and pay with interest (e.g., because I was late), then my preference is to pay the minimum amount. Hence, ($\otimes$-I) states that there is a chain of preferences dealing iteratively with the fact that my primary preference (not to pay any taxes) is not satisfied.

Schemata ($\otimes$-**D**) and ($\otimes$-$\perp$) ensure respectively internal and external consistency of preferences, similarly as in standard modal logic [6]. ($\otimes$-**D**) is nothing but a simple generalisation of modal **D** [6], stating that it is not possible to have both $\mathsf{Pr}a$ and $\mathsf{Pr}\neg a$, indeed we have the following derivation:

$$\frac{\dfrac{\Gamma \Vdash \mathsf{Pr}a}{\Gamma \Vdash \neg \mathsf{Pr}\neg a} \qquad \Delta \Vdash \mathsf{Pr}\neg a}{\Gamma, \Delta \Vdash \perp}$$

The logic of $\otimes$ inherits the standard consistency rule (i.e., derive $\Gamma, \Delta \Vdash \perp$ from $\Gamma \Vdash a$ and $\Delta \Vdash \neg a$) from the underlying classical propositional consequence relation $\vdash$. This clearly holds for any $\otimes$-chain. Given the preference chain $n =\Vdash a \otimes b \otimes c$—meaning that a is preferred, and the second best preference is b, and the third best preferred one is c—asserting that n does not hold, i.e., $\Vdash \neg(a \otimes b \otimes c)$ amounts to a contradiction. But what about if we just assert that b is not the second best preference with respect to a, or that a is not actually preferred without having $\neg a$? These two cases are subsumed by n, thus they should result in a contradiction as well. ($\otimes$-$\perp$) ensure this effect by allowing us to derive all the initial (starting from the leftmost element) sub-chains of an existing $\otimes$-chain. In other words, if

$$\Vdash \neg Pay\_Taxes \otimes \neg Pay\_Interest \otimes Pay\_Minimum$$

then we can conclude that the following hold, too:

$$\Vdash \neg Pay\_Taxes \otimes \neg Pay\_Interest$$
$$\Vdash \neg Pay\_Taxes.$$

Finally, it should be intuitively clear that ($\otimes$-**RE**) generalises for $\otimes$-formulae the weakest inference rule for modal logics, i.e., the closure of $\square$ (here Pr) under logical equivalence [6].

3 Sequence Semantics

Let us introduce the semantic structures that we use to interpret $\otimes$-formulas. In fact, they are just an extension of neighbourhood frames for classical modal logics.

Definition 3. *A sequence frame is a tuple* $\mathscr{F} = \langle W, \mathscr{C} \rangle$ *where:*

- *W is a non empty set of worlds;*
- *$\mathscr{C}$ is a neighbourhood function with the following signature*[3]

$$\mathscr{C}: W \mapsto 2^{((2^W)^n)} \qquad \text{for } n \in \mathbb{N}.$$

In general, a sequence frame is nothing but a structure where the standard neighbourhood function is replaced by a function that establishes an order between elements (i.e., sets of worlds) of each neighbourhood associated to every world. Figure 1 offers a pictorial representation of the intuition.

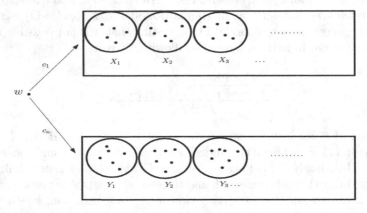

Fig. 1. Sequence basic structure: $X_1, X_2, X_3, \cdots \subseteq W$ and $Y_1, Y_2, Y_3, \cdots \subseteq W$

The following definitions introduce the notion of redundancy and the operations of *zipping* and *s-zipping*, i.e., operations that, respectively, remove repetitions or redundancies occurring in $\otimes$-chains and in sequences of sets of worlds. Intuitively, these operations are necessary because, despite the fact the language allows for building expressions like $a \otimes b \otimes a$, these must be semantically evaluated using the sequences of sets of worlds $\langle \|a\|_V, \|b\|_V \rangle$ (see rule ($\otimes$-shortening)).

Definition 4. *A formula A is* redundant *iff* $A = \bigotimes_{i=1}^{n} a_i$, $n > 1$ *and* $\exists a_j, a_k$, $1 \leq j, k \leq n$, $j \neq k$, *such that* $a_j \equiv a_k$.

Definition 5. *Let $A = \bigotimes_{i=1}^{n} a_i$ be any redundant formula. We say that the non-redundant B is* zipped *from A iff B is obtained from A by applying recursively the operations below:*

---

[3] As done sometimes with the standard neighbourhood function, we use the notation $\mathscr{C}_w$ to denote $\mathscr{C}(w)$.

1. If $n = 2$, i.e., $A = a_1 \otimes a_2$, and $a_1 \equiv a_2$, then B, the zipped from, is Pra_1;
2. Otherwise, if $n > 2$, then for $1 \leq k \leq n$, if $a_j \equiv a_k$, for $j < k$, delete $\otimes a_k$ from the sequence.

Let $X = \langle X_1, \ldots, X_n \rangle$ be such that $X_i \in 2^W$ $(1 \leq i \leq n)$. We analogously say that Y is s-zipped from X iff Y is obtained from X by applying the operations below:

1. If $n = 2$ and $X_1 = X_2$, then its s-zipped from Y is $\langle X_1 \rangle$;
2. Otherwise, if $n > 2$, then for $1 \leq k \leq n$, if $X_j = X_k$, for $j < k$, delete X_k from the sequence.

Definition 6 (Models with Sequences and Truth of Formulae). *A model $\mathscr{M}$ is a pair $\langle \mathscr{F}, V \rangle$ where $\mathscr{F}$ is a frame and V is a valuation such that:*

- *for any non-redundant $\bigotimes_{i=1}^n a_i$, $\models_w^V \bigotimes_{i=1}^n a_i$ iff there is a $c_j \in \mathscr{C}_w$ such that $c_j = \langle \|a_1\|_V, \ldots, \|a_n\|_V \rangle$;*
- *for any redundant $\bigotimes_{i=1}^n a_i$, $\models_w^V \bigotimes_{i=1}^n a_i$ iff*
  - $\bigotimes_{f=1}^k a_f$ *is zipped from $\bigotimes_{i=1}^n a_i$, and*
  - $\models_w^V \bigotimes_{f=1}^k a_f$.
- $\models_w^V \mathsf{Pra}$ *iff there is a $c_l \in \mathscr{C}_w$ such that:*
  - $c_l = \langle \|a_1\|_V, \ldots, \|a_n\|_V \rangle$;
  - *for some $k \leq n$, $\|a_k\|_V = \|a\|_V$;*
  - *for $1 \leq j < k$, $w \notin \|a_j\|_V$.*

Figure 2 pictorially illustrates the types of models used for evaluating $\otimes$-formulae. In fact, we use only finite sequences, of sets of worlds, closed under s-zipping. A formula $\bigotimes_{i=1}^n a_i$ is true iff the corresponding appropriate finite sequence of sets of worlds (without redundancies) is in $\mathscr{C}_w$. Notice that the evaluation clause for Pra works using sequences of length 1 or with longer sequences whenever a is the k's element of the $\otimes$-chain and the previous a_j are such that $w \notin \|a_j\|_V$, i.e., the previous preferences have not been satisfied in w.

Definition 7 (Truth of Sequents). *Let $\Gamma \Vdash a$ be any sequent. Then,*

$$\models_w^V \Gamma \Vdash a \text{ iff, if } \forall w' \in W \text{ such that } \models_{w'}^V \Gamma, \text{ then } \models_{w'}^V a.$$

4 Choice Consistency: Contraction and Expansion

It is almost standard in social choice theory to assume two rationality conditions of choice (which are related with the fact that a choice function is rationalis-able) [11]: *contraction consistency* and *expansion consistency*. The former one is "is concerned with keeping a chosen alternative choosable as the set is expanded by adding alternatives dominated [...] in other choices", while the latter one "is concerned with keeping a chosen alternative choosable as the set is contracted by dropping other alternatives" [20, page 65]. More precisely, contraction states that if an agent chooses some alternative from a set S of alternatives and this

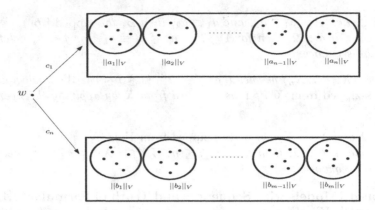

Fig. 2. Sequence models where finite sequences are used to evaluate the formulae $\bigotimes_{i=1}^{n} a_i, \ldots, \bigotimes_{i=1}^{m} b_i$

alternative remains available in a subset S' of S, then the agent chooses it from S'. Expansion somehow works in the opposite direction and requires that, given two sets S and S' of alternatives such that $S \subseteq S'$, for all pairs of alternatives in S, if one agent chooses them from S, then the agent still chooses from S' both of them or does not choose none of them. [11]. Although it has been argued that one possibility, among others, to avoid Arrow's impossibility result is precisely is to relax one of those principles [2,11], these last are usually taken as basic standards of rationality in choice theory.

Notice that such conditions hold as well in the framework proposed in [16], where a simple semantic formulation is proposed, but no syntactic formalisation is given. Our logic, too, satisfies both conditions and a simple formalisation is possible.

Let us begin by considering contraction. Within our formalism, choices are ordered via the $\otimes$ operator, while a simple way to select arbitrary sets of alternatives is done by arbitrarily considering propositional formulae in the antecedents of $\Vdash$-sequents. Hence, contraction can be easily represented as follows:

$$\frac{a \Vdash \bigotimes_{i=1}^{n} b_i \qquad c \vdash a}{c \Vdash \bigotimes_{i=1}^{n} b_i} \qquad (\otimes\text{-contraction})$$

$(\otimes$-contraction$)$ is clearly a derived rule, as it corresponds in our setting to logical monotonicity with respect to $\Vdash$. In fact, suppose that any state where c holds is also a state where a holds:

$$\frac{\dfrac{c \vdash a}{c \Vdash a} \qquad a \Vdash \bigotimes_{i=1}^{n} b_i}{c \Vdash \bigotimes_{i=1}^{n} b_i}$$

From the semantic point of view, it is plain to see that $(\otimes$-contraction$)$ rule does not require any specific frame condition because, by construction, if, for all worlds $w \in \|a\|_V$ and $\models^V_w \bigotimes^n_{i=1} b_i$, since $\|c\|_V \subseteq \|a\|_V$ then for all $v \in \|c\|_V$ we trivially have that $\models^V_v \bigotimes^n_{i=1} b_i$.

The formulation of expansion is intuitive as well:

$$\frac{a \Vdash \bigotimes^n_{i=1} b_i \qquad c \Vdash \bigotimes^n_{i=1} b_i}{\Vdash ((a \vee d) \to \bigotimes^n_{i=1} b_i) \equiv ((c \vee d) \to \bigotimes^n_{i=1} b_i)} \qquad (\otimes\text{-expansion})$$

Here, pairs of alternatives (more generally, pairs of sets of alternatives) are selected by assuming the truth of a and c and we state that a certain choice from $\bigotimes^n_{i=1} b_i$ is considered in both alternatives. Now, if pick up larger sets (which are determined by disjunctively adding any arbitrary propositional formula d), then either the same choice is preserved or it is abandoned in both alternatives.

Indeed, ($\otimes$-expansion) holds, since inference rule (PC) allows us to import in $\Vdash$-logic all consequences of classical logic[4]. The same idea can be easily checked in our sequence semantics. Indeed, it is plain to see that ($\otimes$-expansion) rule does not require, too, any specific frame condition: if, for any worlds $w \in \|a\|_V$ and $v \in \|c\|_V$ we have that $\models^V_w \bigotimes^n_{i=1} b_i$ and $\models^V_v \bigotimes^n_{i=1} b_i$, since $\|a\|_V \subseteq \|a \vee d\|_V$ and $\|c\|_V \subseteq \|c \vee d\|_V$, then, by simple set-theoretic considerations, for all worlds $w' \in \|a \vee d\|_V$ and $v' \in \|c \vee d\|_V$ we have either (i) $\models^V_{w'} \bigotimes^n_{i=1} b_i$ and $\models^V_{v'} \bigotimes^n_{i=1} b_i$, or (ii) $\not\models^V_{w'} \bigotimes^n_{i=1} b_i$ and $\not\models^V_{v'} \bigotimes^n_{i=1} b_i$.

5   Soundness Results

5.1   System $E^\otimes$

Let us prove in this section soundness results for the rules of system $E^\otimes$, which consists of the following rules: ($\otimes$-shortening), (Pr-detachment), ($\otimes$-**RE**), ($\otimes$-**I**), ($\otimes$-**D**), ($\otimes$-$\perp$).

Lemma 1. ($\otimes$-**RE**) *is valid in the class of all sequence frames.*

Proof. The result for ($\otimes$-**RE**) trivially follows from the fact that the valuation clause for any $\otimes$-formula $\bigotimes^n_{i=1} a_i$, at any world w and with any valuation V, requires the existence of a sequence $c \in \mathscr{C}_w$ of truth sets $\langle \|a_1\|_V, \ldots, \|a_n\|_V \rangle$. Then since for any i, $\|a_i\|_V = \|b_i\|_V$ ($a_i \equiv b_i$ for any frame and any valuation by assumption) there is also a sequence $\langle \|b_1\|_V, \ldots, \|b_n\|_V \rangle \in \mathscr{C}_w$.

Also ($\otimes$-shortening) holds in general:

Lemma 2. ($\otimes$-shortening) *is valid in the class of all sequence frames.*

Proof. The proof follows directly from the valuation clause of redundant formulae, and from the definition of *redundancy*, *zipping*, and *s-zipping*.

---

[4] The proof is a rather long, cumbersome, but in fact a routine exercise in sequent calculi for classical propositional logic and is omitted. Just notice that $((a \to b) \wedge (c \to b)) \to (((a \vee d) \to b) \equiv ((c \vee d) \to b))$ is a tautology.

Lemma 3. (Pr-detachment) *is valid in the class of all sequence frames.*

Proof. The proof trivially follows from the valuation clause for the operator Pr.

As we have shown, ($\otimes$-contraction rule) is a derived rule and does not need any specific investigation. In fact, it is plain to semantically see by construction that, if, for all $w \in Y$ and $\models_w^V \bigotimes_{i=1}^n a_i$ and $w \in Y$, if $X \subseteq Y$ then for all $v \in X$ we have $\models_v^V \bigotimes_{i=1}^n a_i$.

Let us now study additional rules that are not validated the class of all sequence frames. Let us first consider the introduction rule for $\otimes$, which requires extra semantic conditions.

Definition 8. *Let $\mathscr{F} = \langle W, \mathscr{C} \rangle$ be a frame. We say that $\mathscr{F}$ is $\otimes$-extended iff for any $w \in W$ and $c_i = \langle X_1, \ldots, X_n \rangle \in \mathscr{C}_w$, if $\exists i, j$, such that $i \leq j \leq n$ and $\forall k, i \leq k \leq j, w \in W - X_k$, then $\langle Y_1, \ldots, Y_m \rangle \in \mathscr{C}_w$, then there exists $c' \in \mathscr{C}_w$ such that c' is s-zipped from $\langle X_1, \ldots, X_j, Y_1, \ldots, Y_m \rangle$.*

Lemma 4. ($\otimes$-I) *is valid in the class of $\otimes$-extended sequence frames.*

Proof. Let us assume for simplicity that all the formulae are zipped. Suppose, for reductio, that $\otimes$-I does not hold in an $\otimes$-extended frame. Thus there is a world w such that

$$\models_w^V \bigwedge \Gamma \wedge \bigwedge \Delta \qquad \not\models_w^V \overset{p}{\underset{k=0}{\bigotimes}} a_k \otimes (\overset{n}{\underset{i=1}{\bigotimes}} b_i) \otimes \overset{m}{\underset{j=1}{\bigotimes}} d_j. \tag{1}$$

This means that

$$\langle \|a_0\|_V, \ldots, \|a_p\|_V, \|b_1\|_V, \ldots, \|b_n\|_V, \|d_1\|_V, \ldots, \|d_m\|_V \rangle \notin \mathscr{C}_w. \tag{2}$$

From the assumption the premises of $\otimes$-I are true in w, and $\models_w^V \bigwedge \Gamma$, thus $\models_w^V \bigotimes_{k=0}^p a_k \otimes (\bigotimes_{i=1}^n b_i) \otimes c$. Hence

$$\langle \|a_0\|_V, \ldots, \|a_p\|_V, \|b_1\|_V, \ldots, \|b_n\|_V, \|c\|_V \rangle \in \mathscr{C}_w. \tag{3}$$

Suppose that $w \in \|\neg b_i\|$ (for $1 \leq i \leq n$); therefore $\models_w^V \bigwedge_{i=1}^n \neg b_i$. In addition, again from the assumption, $\models_w^V \bigwedge \Delta \wedge \bigwedge_{i=1}^n \neg b_i$. From this and the truth of the second premise of $\otimes$-I in w we obtain that $\models_w^V \bigotimes_{j=1}^m d_j$, which means that

$$\langle \|d_1\|_V, \ldots, \|d_m\|_V \rangle \in \mathscr{C}_w \tag{4}$$

on the hypothesis that $w \in \|\neg b_i\|$ for $1 \leq i \leq n$. Since the frame is $\otimes$-extended

$$\langle \|a_0\|_V, \ldots, \|a_p\|_V, \|b_1\|_V, \ldots, \|b_n\|_V, \|d_1\|_V, \ldots, \|d_m\|_V \rangle \in \mathscr{C}_w \tag{5}$$

which contradicts (2).

Let us consider rules for ensuring consistency, i.e., ($\otimes$-**D**) and ($\otimes$-$\perp$).

Definition 9 (Seriality). *Let $\mathscr{F} = \langle W, \mathscr{C} \rangle$ be a frame. We say that $\mathscr{F}$ is serial iff $\forall w \in W$ and $\forall c_i = \langle X_1, \ldots, X_n \rangle \in \mathscr{C}_w$, there is no $c_j = \langle Y_1, \ldots, Y_m \rangle \in \mathscr{C}_w$ such that $Y_j = W - X_k$ if for all X_g, Y_h, $g < k \leq n$, $h < j \leq m$, $w \notin X_g$, $w \notin Y_h$.*

Lemma 5. $(\otimes\text{-}\mathbf{D})$ *is valid in the class of serial sequence frames.*

Proof. The proof is straightforward. Consider any arbitrary sequent $\Gamma \Vdash \mathsf{Pr}a$ and suppose there is a serial frame $\mathscr{F}$, a valuation V, and a world w such that

$$\models_w^V \Gamma \Vdash \mathsf{Pr}a \tag{6}$$

and

$$\not\models_w^V \Gamma \Vdash \neg\mathsf{Pr}\neg a. \tag{7}$$

Hence, there is a world v such that $\models_v^V \mathsf{Pr}a$ and $\not\models_v^V \neg\mathsf{Pr}\neg a$. By the valuation clause for Pr, this implies that

1. there exists an $\otimes$-chain $\bigotimes_{j=1}^m d_j$ true at v where (a) $d_1 = a$, or (b) $d_h = a$, $1 < h \leq m$, and $\models_v^V \Vdash \bigwedge_{l=1}^{h-1} \neg d_l$,
2. there exists an $\otimes$-chain $\bigotimes_{i=1}^n b_i$ true at v where (i) $b_1 = \neg a$, or (ii) $b_k = \neg a$, $1 < k \leq n$, and $\models_v^V \Vdash \bigwedge_{j=1}^{h-1} \neg b_j$.

From 1 we have that $\langle \|a\|_V, \|d_2\|_V, \ldots, \|d_m\|_V \rangle \in \mathscr{C}_v$ or $\langle \|d_1\|_V, \ldots, \|d_{h-1}\|_V, \|a\|_V,$ $\|d_{h+1}\|_V, \ldots, \|d_m\|_V \rangle \in \mathscr{C}_v$ and $v \notin \|d_1\|_V, \ldots, \|d_{k-1}\|_V$.

From 2 we have that $\langle W - \|a\|_V, \|b_2\|_V, \ldots, \|b_n\|_V \rangle \in \mathscr{C}_v$ or $\langle \|b_1\|_V, \ldots, \|b_{k-1}\|_V,$ $W - \|a\|_V, \|b_{k+1}\|_V, \ldots, \|b_n\|_V \rangle \in \mathscr{C}_v$ and $v \notin \|b_1\|_V, \ldots, \|b_{k-1}\|_V$.

Hence, $\mathscr{F}$ is not serial, thus leading to a contradiction.

Definition 10 ($\otimes$-seriality). *Let $\mathscr{F} = \langle W, \mathscr{C} \rangle$ be a frame. We say that $\mathscr{F}$ is $\otimes$-serial iff for any $w \in W$ and for any finite sequence $c_i = \langle X_1, \ldots, X_n \rangle \in \mathscr{C}_w$, $n > 1$, the sequence $\langle X_1, \ldots, X_{n-1} \rangle \in \mathscr{C}_w$.*

Lemma 6. $(\otimes\text{-}\bot)$ *is valid in the class of $\otimes$-serial sequence frames.*

Proof. The proof is straightforward. Consider any arbitrary sequent $\Gamma \Vdash \bigotimes_{i=1}^n a_i$ and suppose there is an $\otimes$-serial frame $\mathscr{F}$, a valuation V, and a world w such that

$$\models_w^V \Gamma \Vdash \bigotimes_{i=1}^n a_i \tag{8}$$

and

$$\not\models_w^V \Gamma \Vdash \bigotimes_{i=1}^{n-1} a_i. \tag{9}$$

Hence, there is a world v such that $\models_v^V \bigotimes_{i=1}^n a_i$ and $\not\models_v^V \bigotimes_{i=1}^{n-1} a_i$. By the valuation clause for $\otimes$-chains, this implies that

1. there exists a sequence $\langle \|a_1\|_V, \ldots, \|a_n\|_V \rangle \in \mathscr{C}_v$, and
2. there is no sequence $\langle \|a_1\|_V, \ldots, \|a_{n-1}\|_V \rangle \in \mathscr{C}_v$.

Thus, $\mathscr{F}$ is not $\otimes$-serial, contrary to the assumption.

6 Semantic Completeness

6.1 Completeness of $\mathsf{E}^\otimes$

In this section we shall provide a semantic completeness theorem via canonical models for $\mathsf{E}^\otimes$, as defined in Section 2.

Definition 11. *Two sequents $\Gamma \Vdash a$ and $\Delta \Vdash b$ are inconsistent if and only if $\Gamma \cup \Delta$ is a consistent set (i.e., $\Gamma, \Delta \nVdash \bot$) and $\Vdash a \wedge b \to \bot$.*

Let us start by constructing the worlds of a canonical model:

1. Let W^C be the set of all possible maximal consistent sets of formulae in the language of $\mathsf{E}^\otimes$, constructed with a standard Lindenbaum procedure.
2. Take any $w \in W^C$. Let:
   (a) $w_0^+ := w$;
   (b) Let $\Gamma_1, \Gamma_2, \ldots$ be an enumeration of all the possible sequents in the language (where $Cl(v)$ is the closure of v under all the rules of the logic). Set $w_{n+1}^+ := Cl(w_n^+ \cup \{\Gamma_n\})$ if $\bigcap W^C \cup \{\Gamma_n\}$ is consistent; $w_{n+1}^+ := w_n^+$ otherwise.
   (c) $w^+ := \bigcup_{n \in \mathbb{N}} w_n^+$.
3. Set $W^+ := \{w^+ \mid w \in W^C\}$

Notice that clause (2b) of this construction guarantees that the set of sequents is the same for any v^+.

Definition 12 ($\mathsf{E}^\otimes$-Canonical Models). *A sequence model with sequences $\mathscr{M} := \langle W^+, \mathscr{C}, V \rangle$ is a canonical model for $\mathsf{E}^\otimes$ if and only if:*

1. *For any propositional letter $p \in Prop$, $\|p\|_V := |p|_{\mathsf{E}^\otimes}$, where $|p|_{\mathsf{E}^\otimes} := \{w \in W^+ \mid p \in w\}$*
2. *Let $\mathscr{C} := \bigcup_{w \in W} \mathscr{C}_w$, where for each $w \in W$, $\mathscr{C}_w := \{\langle \|a_1\|_V, \ldots, \|a_n\|_V \rangle \mid a_1 \otimes \cdots \otimes a_n \in w\} \cup \{\langle \|a\|\rangle_V \mid \mathrm{Pra} \in w\}$, where each a_i is a meta-variable for a Boolean formula and $a_1 \otimes \cdots \otimes a_n$ is zipped.*

Lemma 7 (Truth Lemma). *For any $w \in W^+$ and for any formula or sequent A, $A \in w$ if and only if $\models_w^V A$.*

Proof. Given the construction of the canonical model, this proof is easy and can be given by induction on the length of an expression A. We consider only a few relevant cases.

Assume A has the form $a_1 \otimes \cdots \otimes a_n$ and is redundant (clearly the case for non redundant formulae is easier and does not need to be considered here).

Suppose $a_i \otimes \cdots \otimes a_n \in w$. Then, by $\otimes$-shortening, we have that the formula $b_1 \otimes \cdots \otimes b_j$, the *zipped* form of A, is also in w. By definition of canonical model we have that there is a sequence $\langle \|b_1\|_V, \ldots, \|b_j\|_V \rangle \in \mathscr{C}_w$. Following from the semantic clauses given to evaluate $\otimes$-formulae, it holds that $\models_w^V a_1 \otimes \cdots \otimes a_n$.

Now suppose that $\models_w^V a_1 \otimes \cdots \otimes a_n$. By definition, there is a zipped formula $b_1 \otimes \cdots \otimes b_j$ such that $\models_w^V b_1 \otimes \cdots \otimes b_j$. Thus, C_w contains an ordered j-tuple $\langle \|b_1\|_V, \ldots, \|b_j\|_V \rangle$. By definition of $\mathscr{C}_w$ it follows that $b_1 \otimes \cdots \otimes b_j \in w$ and by $\otimes$-shortening, all the *unzipped* forms of $b_1 \otimes \cdots \otimes b_j$ are also in w, including $a_1 \otimes \cdots \otimes a_n$.

If, on the other hand, A has the form $\mathsf{Pr}b$ and $\mathsf{Pr}b \in w$, then $\langle \|b\|_V \rangle \in \mathscr{C}_w$ and, by definition $\models_w^V \mathsf{Pr}b$. Conversely, if $\models_w^V \mathsf{Pr}b$, then there is an s-zipped sequence $\langle \|c_0\|_V, \ldots, \|c_n\|_V, \|b\|_V, \|d_1\|_V, \ldots, \|d_m\|_V \rangle \in \mathscr{C}_w$ and for $0 \le i \le n$, $w \notin \|c\|_i$. Thus, since any c_i is Boolean and w is maximal, $\neg c_0, \ldots, \neg c_n \in w$. Moreover $\bigotimes_{i=0}^n c_i \otimes b \otimes \bigotimes_{j=1}^m d_j \in w$. Hence by the Pr-detachment rule, $\mathsf{Pr}b \in w$.

If A is a sequent $\Gamma \Vdash a$ belonging to w, take any $v^+ \in W^+$ s.t. $\models_{v^+}^V \bigwedge \Gamma$. By induction hypothesis, $\Gamma \subseteq v^+$. By construction of v^+, $\Gamma \Vdash a \in v^+$, hence $a \in v^+$ and by induction hypothesis $\models_{v^+}^V a$. Thus, $\models_{v^+}^V \Gamma \Vdash a$. Conversely, assume $\Gamma \Vdash a \notin w^+$. By construction of w^+ it means that Γ is consistent with $\bigcap W^C$, i.e., $\Gamma \subseteq \bigcap W^C$ and $\Gamma \subseteq w^+$. By induction hypothesis, $\models_{w^+}^V \bigwedge \Gamma$. Also, $a \wedge b \to \bot$ for some $b \in \bigcap W^C$, hence $a \notin w^+$ and by induction hypothesis $\not\models_{w^+}^V a$.

For any sequent or formula A that is not derivable in $\mathsf{E}^\otimes$ it holds that $A \notin \bigcap W^+$ and hence for any $w^+ \in W^+$, $\not\models_{w^+}^V A$ by Lemma 7.

Lemma 8. *The canonical frame for* $\mathsf{E}^\otimes$ *is:*

1. $\otimes$-*Extended (as in Definition 8)*;
2. *Serial (as in Definition 9)*;
3. $\otimes$-*Serial (as in Definition 10)*.

Proof. The proof is straightforward.

1. Consider a world w^+ such that (i) $\bigotimes_{i=0}^p a_i \otimes \bigotimes_{j=1}^n b_j \otimes \bigotimes_{l=0}^q c_l \in w^+$ and (ii) $\neg b_1, \ldots, \neg b_n \Vdash \bigotimes_{k=1}^m d_k \in w^+$. From (i) by Lemma 7

$$\models_{w^+}^V \bigotimes_{i=0}^p a_i \otimes \bigotimes_{j=1}^n b_j \otimes \bigotimes_{l=0}^q c_l \tag{10}$$

and thus

$$\langle \|a_0\|_V, \ldots, \|a_p\|_V, \|b_1\|_V, \ldots, \|b_n\|_V, \|c_0\|_V, \ldots, \|c_q\|_V \rangle \in \mathscr{C}_{w^+}. \tag{11}$$

Suppose $w^+ \in W - \|b_i\|$ for $1 \le i \le n$. Again by Lemma 7, $\neg b_i \in w^+$ (for $1 \le i \le n$), then from (ii) and the construction of w^+, $\bigotimes_{k=1}^m d_k \in w^+$, and

$\bigotimes_{i=0}^{p} a_i \otimes \bigotimes_{j=1}^{n} b_j \otimes \bigotimes_{k=1}^{m} d_k \in w^+$. Thus, by Lemma 7,

$$\models_{w^+}^{V} \bigotimes_{k=1}^{m} d_k \tag{12}$$

$$\models_{w^+}^{V} \bigotimes_{i=0}^{p} a_i \otimes \bigotimes_{j=1}^{n} b_j \otimes \bigotimes_{k=1}^{m} d_k \tag{13}$$

which means

$$\langle \|d_1\|_V, \ldots, \|d_m\|_V \rangle \in \mathscr{C}_{w^+} \tag{14}$$

$$\langle \|a_0\|_V, \ldots, \|a_p\|_V, \|b_1\|_V, \ldots, \|b_n\|_V, \|d_1\|_V, \ldots, \|d_m\|_V \rangle \in \mathscr{C}_{w^+}. \tag{15}$$

which show that the canonical model is $\otimes$-extended.

2. If, for reductio, there are a world w^+ and two sequences belonging to $\mathscr{C}_{w^+}$

$$\langle \|a_1\|_V, \ldots, \|a_m\|_V, \|b\|_V, \|c_1\|_V, \ldots, \|c_m\|_V \rangle$$
$$\langle \|d_1\|_V, \ldots, \|d_j\|_V, -\|b\|_V, \|e_1\|_V, \ldots, \|e_k\|_V \rangle,$$

$w^+ \notin \|a_i\|_V$ for each i and $w^+ \notin \|d_i\|_V$ for each i, it would follow that both Pra, and Pr$\neg a$ belong to w^+, although by $\otimes$-D $\neg$Pr$\neg a \in w^+$.

3. The proof for $\otimes$-seriality is trivial and follows directly from the construction of the canonical model and the presence of $\otimes$-$\bot$.

Corollary 1. *The logic* $\mathsf{E}^{\otimes}$ *is sound and complete with respect to the class of sequence frames that are extended, serial, and* $\otimes$-*serial.*

7   Conclusion and Related Work

This paper offered a semantic study of the $\otimes$ operator originally introduced in [13] to model deontic reasoning and contrary-to-duty obligations. We showed that a suitable Gentzen-style sequent calculus incorporating $\otimes$-expressions can be characterised in a class of structures extending neighbourhood frames with sequences of sets of worlds. We argued that the formalism and the semantics can be employed, with some adjustments, to grasp various forms of reasoning about reason-based preferences. In this perspective, our contribution may offer useful insights for establishing connections between the proof-theoretic and model theoretic approaches to preference reasoning. Also, we showed that the logic validates both Contraction and Expansion Consistency [11,16], thus satisfying two basic rationality conditions in social choice theory.

The current logic falls within the research on prioritised goals [7,17], i.e., on formalisms for describing the goals of the agents whose preferences are modelled as propositional formulae. This allows for a purely qualitative representation of preferences. Before the recent developments in MAS [2], the most extensive (and, still the most advanced) work on preferences was done in the context of deontic logic. A first line of inquiry was mainly semantic-based: deontic sentences are interpreted in settings with ideality orderings on possible worlds or states [15]. This approach is quite flexible: depending on the properties of the preference or ideality relation, different deontic logics can be obtained. This semantic approach has been fruitfully renewed in the '90 for example by [19,22], and most recently by works such as [14,21], which have confirmed the vitality of this line of inquiry. The second line was proof-theoretic: in this second area, the Gentzen system proposed in [13] was definitely seminal for us in developing the current proposal. [13] is based on the introduction of the non-classical binary operator $\otimes$: the reading of an expression like $a \otimes b$ is that a is primarily obligatory, but is this obligation is violated, the secondary obligation is b. Inference rules introduced by [13]—in particular, ($\otimes$-shortening) and ($\otimes$-I)—are proposed here, too.

In the context of preference logics several proposals can be mentioned [7,17,18]. However, two works have specifically inspired our effort: [16] and [3]. [16] is very recent and presents a modal logic where a binary operator is meant to syntactically express preference orderings between formulae: each formula of this logic determines a preference ordering over alternatives based on the priorities over properties that the formula express. While the formalism is interesting in that it can represent not just orderings over alternatives but the reasons that lead to the preferences [18], the modal logic for expressing individual preferences is in fact equivalent to **S5**, which amounts to being a very strong and simple option (indeed, the main concern in this work is preference aggregation): as we argued, weaker but very expressive logics can be adopted. The qualitative choice logic (QCL) of [3] is a propositional logic for representing alternative, ranked options for problem solutions, using a substructural ordered disjunction. It offers a much richer alternative with respect to [16], showing a number of similarities with [13] (the two formalisms have been developed independently) and the one discussed here. A major differences is, for instance, that the $\otimes$-detachment produces conclusions that are modalised and not just factual. The semantics and proof theory of [3], though based on similar intuitions, are however technically different from ours: semantics is based on the degree of satisfaction of a formula in a particular (classical) model. Consequences of QCL theories can be computed through a compilation to stratified knowledge bases which in turn can be compiled to classical propositional theories. The consequence relation of [3] satisfies properties usually considered intended in nonmonotonic reasoning, such as cautious monotonicity and cumulative transitivity.

The preference operator $\otimes$ has been combined with Defeasible Logic to provide a computationally oriented approach to modelling alternative goals of rational agents to then select plans [8,9]. More recently [12] investigates different forms of $\otimes$ detachment to identify different types of goal like mental attitudes for agents.

A number of open research issues are left for future work. Among others, we plan to explore decidability questions using, for example, the filtration methods. The fact that neighbourhoods contain sequences of sets of worlds instead of sets is not expected to make the task significantly harder than the one in standard neighbourhood semantics for modal logics.

Second, we expect to enrich the language and allow for nesting of $\otimes$-expressions, thus having formulae like $a \otimes \neg(b \otimes c) \otimes d$. We argued in [13] that the meaning of those formulae is not clear in deontic reasoning. However, a semantic analysis of them in the sequence semantics can clarify the issue. Indeed, in the current language we can evaluate in any world w formulae like $\neg(a \otimes b)$, which semantically means that there is no sequence $\langle \|a\|_V, \|b\|_V \rangle \in \mathscr{C}_w$. Conceptually, expressions like that may express meta-preferences, i.e., preferences about preference orderings. However, this reading poses interesting conceptual and technical problems.

Finally, we plan to apply the our framework to social choice theory by checking how our analysis impacts on the collective choice rules proposed in [16].

Acknowledgments. NICTA is funded by the Australian Government and the Australian Research Council through the ICT Centre of Excellence program. Antonino Rotolo was supported by the Unibo FARB 2012 project *Mortality Salience, Legal and Social Compliance, and Economic Behaviour: Theoretical Models and Experimental Methods.*

References

1. Boutilier, C., Brafman, R.I., Domshlak, C., Hoos, H.H., Poole, D.: Cp-nets: A tool for representing and reasoning with conditional ceteris paribus preference statements. J. Artif. Intell. Res. (JAIR) **21**, 135–191 (2004)
2. Brandt, F., Conitzer, V., Endriss, U.: Computational social choice. In: Multiagent Systems, MIT Press (2012)
3. Brewka, G., Benferhat, S., Le Berre, D.: Qualitative choice logic. Artif. Intell. **157**(1–2), 203–237 (2004)
4. Calardo, E., Governatori, G., Rotolo, A.: A preference-based semantics for CTD reasoning. In: Cariani, F., Grossi, D., Meheus, J., Parent, X. (eds.) DEON 2014. LNCS, vol. 8554, pp. 49–64. Springer, Heidelberg (2014)
5. Calardo, E., Governatori, G., Rotolo, A.: A sequence semantics for deontic logic. Under submission (2015)
6. Chellas, B.F.: Modal Logic: An Introduction. Cambridge University Press (1980)
7. Coste-Marquis, S., Lang, J., Liberatore, P., Marquis, P.: Expressive power and succinctness of propositional languages for preference representation. In: Principles of Knowledge Representation and Reasoning: Proceedings of the Ninth International Conference (KR2004), pp. 203–212, Whistler, Canada, June 2–5, 2004 (2004)
8. Dastani, M., Governatori, G., Rotolo, A., van der Torre, L.W.N.: Preferences of agents in defeasible logic. In: Zhang, S., Jarvis, R.A. (eds.) AI 2005. LNCS (LNAI), vol. 3809, pp. 695–704. Springer, Heidelberg (2005)
9. Dastani, M., Governatori, G., Rotolo, A., van der Torre, L.W.N.: Programming cognitive agents in defeasible logic. In: Sutcliffe, G., Voronkov, A. (eds.) LPAR 2005. LNCS (LNAI), vol. 3835, pp. 621–636. Springer, Heidelberg (2005)
10. Fitting, M.: Proof Methods for Modal and Intuitionistic Logics. Springer (1983)
11. Gaertner, W.: A Primer in Social Choice Theory: Revised Edition. Oup Oxford (2009)

12. Governatori, G., Olivieri, F., Scannapieco, S., Rotolo, A., Cristani, M.: The rational behind the concept of goal. Theory and Practice of Logic Programming, forthcoming

13. Governatori, G., Rotolo, A.: Logic of violations: A Gentzen system for reasoning with contrary-to-duty obligations. Australasian Journal of Logic **4**, 193–215 (2006)

14. Hansen, J.: Conflicting imperatives and dyadic deontic logic. J. Applied Logic **3**(3–4), 484–511 (2005)

15. Hansson, B.: An analysis of some deontic logics. Nous **3**, 373–398 (1969)

16. Jiang, G., Zhang, D., Perrussel, L., Zhang, H.: A logic for collective choice. In: Proceedings of the 2015 International Conference on Autonomous Agents and Multiagent Systems, AAMAS 2015, pp. 979–987, Istanbul, Turkey, May 4–8, 2015 (2015)

17. Lang, J.: Logical preference representation and combinatorial vote. Ann. Math. Artif. Intell. **42**(1–3), 37–71 (2004)

18. Osherson, D., Weinstein, S.: Preference based on reasons. The Review of Symbolic Logic **5**, 122–147 (2012)

19. Prakken, H., Sergot, M.J.: Contrary-to-duty obligations. Studia Logica **57**(1), 91–115 (1996)

20. Sen, A.: Social choice theory: A re-examination. Econometrica **45**(1), 53–89 (1977)

21. van Benthem, J., Grossi, D., Liu, F.: Priority structures in deontic logic. Theoria (2013)

22. van der Torre, L.: Reasoning about obligations: defeasibility in preference-based deontic logic. PhD thesis, Erasmus University Rotterdam (1997)

Strategy-Proof Cake Cutting Mechanisms for All-or-Nothing Utility

Takamasa Ihara[✉], Shunsuke Tsuruta, Taiki Todo, Yuko Sakurai,
and Makoto Yokoo

Kyushu University, Fukuoka, Japan
{ihara,tsuruta}@agent.inf.kyushu-u.ac.jp,
{todo,ysakurai,yokoo}@inf.kyushu-u.ac.jp

Abstract. The cake cutting problem must fairly allocate a divisible good among agents who have varying preferences over it. Recently, designing strategy-proof cake cutting mechanisms has caught considerable attention from AI and MAS researchers. Previous works assumed that an agent's utility function is additive so that theoretical analysis becomes tractable. However, in practice, agents have non-additive utility functions over a resource. In this paper, we consider the all-or-nothing utility function as a representative example of non-additive utility because it can widely cover agents' preferences for real-world resources, such as the usage of meeting rooms, time slots for computational resources, bandwidth usage, and so on. We first show the incompatibility between envy-freeness and Pareto efficiency when each agent has all-or-nothing utility. We next propose two strategy-proof mechanisms that satisfy Pareto efficiency, which are based on a serial dictatorship mechanism, at the sacrifice of envy-freeness. To address computational feasibility, we propose an approximation algorithm to find a near-optimal allocation in time polynomial in the number of agents, since the problem of finding a Pareto efficient allocation is NP-hard. As another approach that abandon Pareto efficiency, we develop an envy-free mechanism and show that one of our serial dictatorship based mechanisms satisfies proportionality in expectation, which is a weaker definition of proportionality. Finally, we evaluate the efficiency obtained by our proposed mechanisms by computational experiments.

1 Introduction

Mechanism design, which is a subfield of microeconomics and game theory develops collective decision making rules for multiple agents. Such a rule is expected to satisfy several desirable properties, such as social efficiency, while each agent addresses her own utility, i.e., is self-interested. Due to the growing needs for agent technology and the Internet's popularity, vigorous research on mechanism design has been conducted in the AI and MAS research communities.

Cake cutting, which is a fundamental model of *fair division* [8], addresses fair sharing of a whole cake that is usually done as an interval [0, 1]. This abstract model can be applied in practice for sharing a divisible good, such as a meeting

© Springer International Publishing Switzerland 2015
Q. Chen et al. (Eds.): PRIMA 2015, LNAI 9387, pp. 118–133, 2015.
DOI: 10.1007/978-3-319-25524-8_8

room's usage, time slots for computational resources, bandwidth usage, and so on. Several cake cutting algorithms have been developed, such as cut-and-choose and moving-knife [2]. In cake cutting, envy-freeness (EF) is one of the most studied fairness properties. Cake allocation is said to be envy-free if, under it, no agent envies any other agent. For instance, when there are only two agents, any allocation produced from the cut-and-choose protocol satisfies EF.

Recently, AI and MAS researchers have studied such cake cutting problems as mechanism design and proposed strategy-proof (SP) cake cutting mechanisms [3,7,11]. A cake cutting mechanism asks each agent to declare her utility function of the cake instead of indicating the point at which she would prefer to cut the cake. In an SP cake cutting mechanism, it is guaranteed that reporting a true utility function is a dominant strategy.

Although several SP mechanisms have been proposed in cake cutting, previous works assume that an agent's utility function is additive and thus discount non-additive utility functions. An all-or-nothing utility function is binary and simple, but it is also a representative example of non-additive utility. As a typical real-world example, we select the following two examples. If we are allocated a shorter time slot than required for a meeting room, we cannot hold our meeting. Furthermore, when narrower bandwidth than is required is allocated for watching a movie, the movie will be interrupted while we are watching it. In these examples, even if each agent is allocated a piece which is less than her requirement, her utility remains at 0.

We first show that there exist no cake cutting mechanisms that satisfy Pareto efficiency (PE) and EF when an agent's utility function is all-or-nothing; we need to abandon either PE or EF. We develop two SP mechanisms based on a serial dictatorship mechanism (SD): a randomized serial dictatorship mechanism (RSD) and a sorted serial dictatorship mechanism (SSD) by abandoning EF. In an SD, for a given ordering of agents, the agent who is ordered first is assigned her top choice in a set of all possible outcomes. The agent ordered second is assigned her top choice among a set of the remaining possible outcomes, which is reduced based on the first agent's choice, and so on. In an RSD, we randomly sort the agents with equal probabilities and in an SSD, we sort the agents by an increase of a required length. These mechanisms satisfy SP and PE.

However, we also show that the problem of finding a PE allocation is NP-hard. Thus, we propose an approximate algorithm to find an allocation close to a PE allocation in the polynomial time of the number of agents. We apply this approximate allocation algorithm to an RSD and an SSD, which are called as an RSD by fixing the order of the allocation pieces (RSDF) and SSD by fixing the order of the allocation pieces (SSDF).

We also propose a modified SSDF that satisfies EF at the sacrifice of PE. To guarantee EF, we cannot use the random order of the agents. If we randomly sort the agents, some losers envy the winners, since who wins depends on the order of the agents. Therefore, we modify an SSDF by dividing the agents into groups by the required length and sorting the groups of agents by an increase of

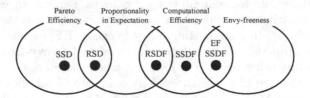

Fig. 1. Our results

the required length. If all allocation results (the winner candidates) are identical for all the permutations of the agents in a dictator group, we allocate the pieces to the winner candidates and go to the next turn. Otherwise, stop the procedure and do not go to the next turn.

We finally show that there exist no mechanisms to simultaneously guarantee both EF and proportionality in expectation (PPE). However, as a positive result, we show that an RSD satisfies PPE. To sum up, our research results obtained in this paper are shown in Fig. 1. Since we showed the incompatibility between PE and EF, they are disjoint. For a similar reason, EF and PPE are also disjoint. RSDF, SSDF, and EF-SSDF are computationally efficient, because each mechanism can determine an allocation in the polynomial time of the number of agents. We compare the efficiency obtained by each proposed mechanism using computational experiments and show that SSD outperforms the rest of computational efficient mechanisms.

2   Related Works

Traditional Envy-Free Cake Cutting: Gamow and Stern [8] proposed a cake cutting protocol that returns an envy-free allocation when only three agents exist. Brams and Taylor [5] extended the results and proposed an algorithm that returns an envy-free allocation by discrete procedures for any number of agents. In another way, Austinproposed an algorithm that returns an envy-free allocation for two agents, based on the well-known moving-knife protocol.

Mechanism Design for Cake Cutting: Brams et al. [4] investigated the effects of strategic manipulations in cake cutting. Chen et al. [7] proposed a polynomial-time cake cutting mechanism that satisfies strategy-proofness, proportionality, envy-freeness, and Pareto efficiency under piecewise uniform utility (valuation) functions. Mossel and Tamuz [11] proposed a randomized cake cutting mechanism that satisfies strategy-proofness, proportionality, and Pareto efficiency under additive utility functions. Aziz and Ye [3] proposed a randomized cake cutting mechanism that satisfies strategy-proofness and proportionality under piecewise uniform and piecewise constant utility functions and is a special case of additive utility functions.

Scheduling: Liu and Layland [10] discussed the problem of multiprogram scheduling on a single processor. Garey and Johnson [9] showed that the problem of examining whether all tasks are scheduled when both start-time and deadline of a task are given is NP-complete. Carroll and Grosu [6] augmented the divisible load theory with incentives and considered a case when processors might misreport their true processing power.

3 Preliminaries

3.1 Model

Let $N = \{1, 2, \ldots, n\}$ be a set of agents and $n = |N|$ be the number of agents. The cake is represented as an interval $[0, 1]$. Let $\text{len}(I) = y - x$ be the length of a closed interval $I = [x, y] \subseteq [0, 1]$ with $x \leq y$. Also, let $\text{len}(X) = \sum_{I \in X} \text{len}(I)$ be the length of piece X of a cake, where $I \in X$ indicates each disjoint interval that consists of piece X.

We assume that the utility function of each agent $i \in N$ is all-or-nothing; binary utility, either 1 or 0.

Definition 1 (All-or-Nothing Utility Function). *Agent $i \in N$ is interested in interval $r_i = [s_i, e_i] \subseteq [0, 1]$ and requires a piece whose length is not shorter than $d_i \in (0, e_i - s_i]$ in interval r_i. r_i is called a reference interval to agent i.*

When piece X_i is allocated for agent i, her utility is defined as

$$U_i(X_i) = \begin{cases} 1 \ \exists I \ \text{s.t.} \ I \subseteq X_i \ \text{and} \ \text{len}(I \cap r_i) \geq d_i, \\ 0 \ \text{otherwise.} \end{cases}$$

For example, this utility function represents an agent's preference such that she wants to use a meeting room for two hours in the afternoon. If an agent wants to use the room for two hours from 13:00 through 15:00, the length of her reference interval equals her required length.

By definition, any utility function U_i is automatically non-atomic. We also assume that it is normalized.

Non-atomic: $U_i([x, x]) = 0$ for any $x \in [0, 1]$,
Normalized: $U_i([0, 1]) = 1$.

Note that we can treat open/half-open intervals as closed intervals with respect to agents' utilities by the non-atomicity property.

Let $\mathcal{U}$ be the set of all possible all-or-nothing utility functions, which is common among all agents. Let $U = (U_i)_{i \in N}$ denote a profile of the utility functions of agents N, $U_{-i} = (U_j)_{j \in N \setminus \{i\}}$ denote a profile of the utility functions of agents N except for agent i, and (U_i, U_{-i}) denote a profile of utility functions when agent i reports U_i and the other agents report U_{-i}.

Feasible *allocation* A of the cake to a set of agents N is represented as a tuple $(A_i)_{i \in N}$, where A_i indicates an allocation to a specific agent $i \in N$, $A_i \cap A_j = \emptyset$ for any pair $i, j (\neq i) \in N$, and $\bigcup_{i \in N} A_i \subseteq [0, 1]$. Let $\mathcal{A}_N$ denote the set of all feasible allocations to N.

Mechanism f is a union of functions $f^N : \mathcal{U}^n \to \mathcal{A}_N$. That is, f^N maps a profile of utility functions reported by N to A_N. For simplicity, we usually abbreviate f^N to f. For given profile U of utility functions, let $f(U)$ denote the pieces of cake returned by mechanism f, and let $f_i(U)$ denote the pieces of cake allocated to agent i according to $f(U)$.

3.2   Properties

We introduce desirable properties for cake cutting mechanisms. Fairness and efficiency are considered necessary properties for the mechanisms and we also require mechanisms to guarantee strategy-proofness. We first introduce envy-freeness (EF) which is one representative fairness property.

Definition 2 (Envy-Freeness (EF)). *Cake cutting mechanism f is said to satisfy* envy-freeness *if for any $U \in \mathcal{U}^n$, any $U_i \in \mathcal{U}$, and any $i, j \ (\neq i) \in N$, $U_i(A_i) \geq U_i(A_j)$.*

We next introduce an efficiency property called Pareto efficiency (PE), which guarantees the quality of the allocations obtained by the mechanisms. PE is a well-studied efficiency property in mechanism design literature. For a given allocation obtained by a PE mechanism, there exists no other allocation that weakly raises the utilities of all agents and strictly raises the utility of at least one.

Definition 3 (Pareto Efficiency (PE)). *For a given N and $U \in \mathcal{U}^n$, allocation $A' \in \mathcal{A}_N$ is said to* Pareto dominate *another allocation $A \in \mathcal{A}_N$ if $U_i(A_i') \geq U_i(A_i)$ holds for any $i \in N$, with inequality strict for a $j \in N$. Cake cutting mechanism f is said to satisfy* Pareto efficiency *if for any $U \in \mathcal{U}^n$, there exists no allocation $A' \in \mathcal{A}_N$ where Pareto dominates A.*

Finally, we define an incentive property called strategy-proofness (SP), which guarantees that reporting a true utility function to a mechanism is the best strategy; truth-telling is a dominant strategy, for every agent.

Definition 4 (Strategy-Proofness (SP)). *Cake cutting mechanism f is said to guarantee* strategy-proofness *if for any $i \in N$, any $U_{-i} \in \mathcal{U}^{n-1}$, any $U_i \in \mathcal{U}$, and any $U_i' \in \mathcal{U}$,*

$$U_i(f_i((U_i, U_{-i}))) \geq U_i(f_i((U_i', U_{-i}))).$$

Truthfully declaring agent i's reference interval $[s_i, e_i]$ and required length d_i is the optimal strategy for maximizing utility regardless of other participants' declarations. The *revelation principle* states that we can restrict our attention to direct revelation protocols that are strategy-proof without loss of generality.

4   Incompatibility

We show that even if we do not require cake cutting mechanisms to satisfy SP, there exists no cake cutting mechanisms that satisfy PE and EF, when each agent has all-or-nothing utility.

Theorem 1. *There exists no cake cutting mechanism that satisfies Pareto efficiency and envy-freeness, when each agent's utility function is all-or-nothing.*

Proof. For the sake of contradiction, we assume there exists a cake cutting mechanism f that satisfies Pareto efficiency and envy-freeness. We first consider the following case: there are only two agents $N = \{1, 2\}$, who have the same utility function, i.e., for $i \in \{1, 2\}$, $r_i = [0, 1]$ and $d_i = 1$. We consider the following two cases.

Case 1: We assume a whole cake $[0, 1]$ goes to agent 1, but agent 2 does not obtain any pieces of its. Obviously, agent 2's utility is 0. However, by trading agent 1's allocated whole cake to agent 2, agent 2's utility increases from 0 to 1. Thus, agent 2 envies agent 1. WLOG, we prove that agent 1 envies agent 2 if we assume agent 2 obtains a whole cake. Thus, envy-freeness is not satisfied.

Case 2: Next consider other allocation results rather than Case 1. For such an allocation, both the utilities of agents 1 and 2 are 0. If a designer allocates a whole cake to either agent, the utility of the agent who allocates the cake increases from 0 to 1, while the other agent's utility remains 0. Pareto efficiency is not satisfied.   □

5   SP and PE Cake Cutting Mechanisms

Based on the incompatibility between PE and EF, we first investigate a strategy-proof cake cutting mechanism that satisfies PE by abandoning EF. Our proposed mechanism is based on a serial dictatorship that satisfies strategy-proof and Pareto efficiency [1]. In a serial dictatorship mechanism (SD), for a given ordering of agents, the agent who is ordered first is assigned her top choice from a set of all possible outcomes. The agent ordered second is assigned her top choice among a set of the remaining possible outcomes, which is reduced by the first agent's choice, and so on. By doing such a processing, Pareto efficent allocation can be done because if an agent can't get allocation, then other agent always gets the interval she wants.

5.1   Randomized Serial Dictatorship Mechanism

In this subsection, we propose a randomized serial dictatorship mechanism (RSD).

Mechanism 1 (Randomized Serial Dictatorship Mechanism)

1. *Randomly order agents with equal probability.*
2. *For the k-th agent $(k = 1, \ldots, n)$, ask about her reference interval $[s_k, e_k]$ and required length d_k as a dictator.*
3. *From the first agent to the n-th agent, select the k-th agent as a dictator and determine her allocation to maximize her utility without changing the utilities for the $k - 1$ agents who have been already asked.*

Theorem 2. *RSD satisfies strategy-proofness and Pareto efficiency.*

Proof. We first show that RSD satisfies SP. A mechanism designer determines agent i's allocation to maximize her utility, while guaranteeing that the utility of each agent whose assignment was already determined is unchanged even if a winner's assigned piece is moved. If there exists a piece of cake such that agent i's utility is 1, she receives it with a utility of 1. Agent i does not change the pieces of cake that can be assigned to her by manipulating her declaration. Thus, the best strategy for agent i is to truthfully declare her reference interval $[s_i, e_i]$ and required length d_i.

We next show that RSD satisfies PE. We assume that agent i is a loser, because she cannot receive any pieces of a cake and her utility is 0. This indicates that her required length does not remain within her reference interval. If agent i's utility increases from 0 to 1, some winners, who are assigned to the pieces within agent i's reference interval, lose their assigned pieces and their utilities decrease from 1 to 0. As a result, there exists no other allocation that weakly raises the utilities of all agents and strictly raises the utility of at least one. □

We show an example to explain how a RSD mechanism works.

Example 1. We assume 6 agents and each agent declaration is as follows:

agent 1: $[s_1, e_1] = [0.25, 0.7]$, $d_1 = 0.4$,   **agent 2**: $[s_2, e_2] = [0.2, 0.4]$, $d_2 = 0.15$,

agent 3: $[s_3, e_3] = [0, 1]$, $d_3 = 0.2$,   **agent 4**: $[s_4, e_4] = [0.4, 0.85]$, $d_4 = 0.3$,

agent 5: $[s_5, e_5] = [0.25, 0.45]$, $d_5 = 0.15$, **agent 6**: $[s_6, e_6] = [0.5, 1]$, $d_6 = 0.25$.

To simplify our explanation, we assume that a mechanism designer determines the order of agents as 1, 2, 3, 4, 5, and 6.

agent 1: $[0.25, 0.65]$ is assigned to agent 1.

agent 2: No piece is assigned to agent 2, since a mechanism designer cannot find a piece of length 0.15 within agent 2's reference interval $[0.2, 0.4]$, while guaranteeing that agent 1's utility is 1 by moving agent 1's assignment of length 0.4 within her reference interval $[0.25, 0.7]$.

agent 3: $[0.25, 0.65]$ goes to agent 1 and $[0.65, 0.85]$ goes to agent 3.

agent 4: No piece is assigned to agent 4.

agent 5: No piece is assigned to agent 5.

agent 6: $[0.25, 0.65]$ goes to agent 1, $[0, 0.2]$ goes to agent 3, and $[0.65, 0.9]$ goes to agent 6.

As a result, the winners are agents 1, 3, and 6. The length of the union of the allocated pieces is $0.4 + 0.2 + 0.25 = 0.85$.

5.2   Sorted Serial Dictatorship Mechanism

Next, we develop a sorted serial dictatorship mechanism (SSD) as another type of an SD mechanism. In an SSD, agents are sorted in increasing order by the required length d_i.

Mechanism 2 (Sorted Serial Dictatorship Mechanism)

1. *Ask each agent about her reference interval $[s_i, e_i]$ and required length d_i.*
2. *Sort the agents in increasing order of d_k. When there exist multiple agents with a certain length, their order is randomly determined with equal probability.*
3. *From the first agent to the n-th agent, select the k-th agent as a dictator and determine her allocation to maximize her utility without changing the utilities for the $k-1$ agents who have already been asked.*

Theorem 3. *SSD satisfies strategy-proofness and Pareto efficiency.*

Proof. We show that no agent improves her utility by manipulating her required length, since the SSD is the same as the RSD without determining the order of the agents using each agent's required length.

Based on the definition of all-or-nothing utility, declaring d'_i such that $d'_i < d_i$ is useless, since the agent's utility is 0 even if she receives d'_i in her reference interval. Furthermore, when she declares d'_i such that $d'_i > d_i$, her turn is later than her original turn that was determined by truthfully declaring d_i. This implies that the pieces allocatable for her when she declares d'_i are reduced compared with the case of truth-telling; her utility is not improved by declaring a longer length than d_i.

As a result, to determine the order of agents, agent i has no incentive to declare a longer or shorter length than the original d_i.   □

We show an example to explain how an SSD mechanism works.

Example 2. We consider the same problem setting used in Example 1. A mechanism designer first sorts the agents by the increase of d_i. In this example, the order of agents is determined as 2, 5, 3, 6, 4, and 1.

agent 2: $[0.2, 0.35]$ is assigned.
agent 5: No piece is assigned to agent 5.
agent 3: $[0.2, 0.35]$ goes to agent 2, and $[0.35, 0.55]$ goes to agent 3.
agent 6: $[0.2, 0.35]$ goes to agent 2, $[0.35, 0.55]$ goes to agent 3, and $[0.55, 0.8]$ goes to agent 6.
agent 4: agent 4 obtains $[0.4, 0.7]$, and it still holds that agents 2, 3, 6 have a utility of 1: $[0.2, 0.35]$ goes to agent 2, $[0, 0.2]$ goes to agent 3, and $[0.7, 0.95]$ goes to agent 6.
agent 1: No piece is assigned to agent 1.

As a result, the winners are agents 2, 3, 4, and 6. The length of the union of the allocated pieces is $0.15 + 0.2 + 0.25 + 0.3 = 0.9$.

6   Integer Programming for Determining Pareto Efficient Allocation

We propose an integer programming (IP) formula for finding a Pareto efficient allocation in RSD and SSD. In an SD, according to the given order of the agents, each agent chooses the best outcome from a set of all the outcomes she can choose. For the k-th agent, her assignment is determined to maximize her utility without changing the utilities of the $k-1$ agents who were previously determined before agent k. For the k-th agent, we formalize the following formulation to maximize an allocation decision variable by listing the allocation decision valuables assigned to the $k-1$ agents who were already asked.

We define some notations. For agent $i \in N$, let y_i be a 0/1 decision variable that denotes that agent i's utility is 1. Let a_i be the starting point of the piece allocated to agent i. $x_{i,j}$ is a 0/1 decision variable where $a_i < a_j$ is satisfied. In words, $x_{i,j} = 1$ holds if the starting point of the piece allocated to agent i is placed ahead of agent j's start point. Otherwise, $x_{i,j} = 0$ holds. We denote a large positive real number as M. Let W be a set of winners who were determined until k-th agent's turn comes.

Definition 5 (IP formulation to find the best allocation for the k-th agent). *The problem of finding the k-th agent's best allocation in a serial dictatorship mechanism is modeled as follows.*

$$\max y_k$$
$$\text{s.t. } \forall j \in W, e_j \geq a_j + d_j, -(\text{i})$$
$$e_k \geq a_k + d_k - M(1 - y_k), -(\text{ii})$$
$$\forall i, j \in W \cup \{k\}, \ a_j \geq a_i + d_i - M(1 - x_{i,j}), -(\text{iii})$$
$$\forall i, j \in W \cup \{k\}, \ x_{i,j} + x_{j,i} = 1, -(\text{iv})$$
$$y_k \in \{0, 1\},$$
$$\forall i, j \in W \cup \{k\}, \ x_{i,j} \in \{0, 1\}.$$

If we have $y_k = 1$, agent k is added to a list of winners W.

The objective function maximizes agent k's decision variable. Constraint (i) ensures that the end point of the reference interval for agent $j \in W$ is not smaller than the starting point of her allocated piece plus her required length, since agent j was determined to be a winner. Constraint (ii) ensures that if agent k is a winner, the end point of her reference interval is not smaller than the starting point of a piece allocated to her plus her required length. Constraint (iii) ensures that if agents i and j win, the piece allocated to agent i does not conflict with the piece allocated to agent j. Constraint (iv) ensures that if agents i and j win, the order of the pieces allocated to them is consistent.

Next compare the efficiency obtained in our proposed mechanisms with the optimal allocation in the terms of the number of winners. A PE allocation in a SD is not always the optimal allocation, since an SD narrows the outcome space

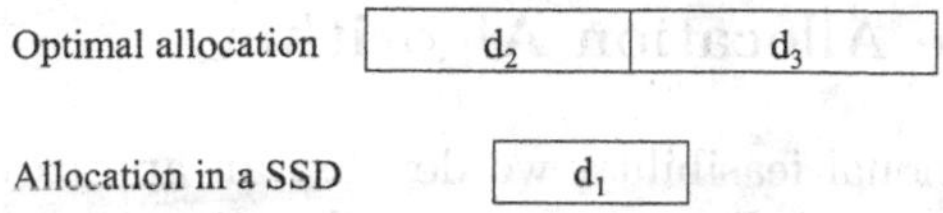

Optimal allocation $\boxed{\begin{array}{c|c} d_2 & d_3 \end{array}}$

Allocation in a SSD $\boxed{\ d_1\ }$

Fig. 2. Comparison between an optimal allocation and an allocation in an SSD

by giving the order of agents. We find the optimal number of winners by solving an IP formula. In an IP formula that maximizes the number of winners, we put constraints (i) – (iv) in an IP formula defined in Def. 5 for all $i \in N$ instead of $W \cup \{k\}$.

Theorem 4. *In an RSD, for all possible permutation of the agents, $1/(n-1)$ is the worst-case ratio of the number of winners that can be obtained by an RSD over the optimal number of winners.*

Proof. In the worst-case analysis, we consider the situation where there are two options to determine an allocation; either 1 winner or $n-1$ winners. We assume that 1 agent requires a whole cake $[0, 1]$, and $n-1$ agents require disjoint pieces with length of $1/(n-1)$. Their reference intervals are also disjoint: agent 2's reference interval $[0, 1/(n-1)]$, agent 3's reference interval $[1/(n-1), 2/(n-1)]$, and so on. When agent 1 is the first-ordered, the number of winners in a RSD is 1, which is the worst-case. On the other hand, the optimal number of winner is obviously $n-1$. Thus, the worst-case ratio is $1/(n-1)$.   □

Theorem 5. *The worst-case ratio of the number of winners can be obtained by an SSD against the optimal number of winners is $1/2$.*

Proof. We prove this theorem using Fig. 2 by assuming the following: agent 1 requires d_1 within $[d_2/2, d_2/2 + d_1]$, agent 2 requires d_2 within $[0, d_2]$, and agent 3 requires d_3 within $[d_2, d_2 + d_3]$. We also assume that $d_1 < d_2 < d_3$ holds.

In an optimal allocation, agents 2 and 3 receive a piece of cake. On the other hand, when we apply a SSD, the order of the agents is determined as 1, 2, and 3, based on a required length. Agent 1's is the first-ordered and obtains a piece of cake. Agents 2 and 3 do not get any cake.

As shown as this situation, when we sort the agents by the increase of required length d_i, a piece assigned to one agent conflicts with at most two agents' assignments. Thus, the worst-case ratio is $1/2$.   □

Theorem 6. *The problem of finding an efficient allocation in a serial dictatorship mechanism (SD) is NP-hard.*

Proof. The allocation problem for the k-th agent is determining whether there exists an allocation such that all agents including the k-th agent and the winners who were determined before the k-th agent get a piece of cake. The problem defined in Def. 5 corresponds to a sequencing problem with release times and deadlines, which is known to be NP-complete [9]. Thus, a Pareto efficient allocation problem for an SD is NP-hard.   □

7 Approximate Allocation Algorithm

To address computational feasibility, we develop an approximate algorithm to find an allocation close to a Pareto efficient allocation in a reasonable amount of time. Intuitively, we consider that an agent who get left side of a cake will get left side of a cake even if the number of agent increases. Specifically, our proposed allocation algorithm allocates the pieces such that an agent can obtain a utility of 1 from the left side of cake without changing the order of the allocated pieces before the current dictator's turn. We examine whether there remains a piece with k-th agent's required length in her reference interval by moving the winners' allocated pieces by keeping the relations among the allocated pieces.

Algorithm 1. Approximate allocation algorithm

Approximate allocation algorithm(OL)

```
w = 0
for i ← 1 to n do
    for j ← 0 to w do
        L = WL
        k = w
        while k ≥ j do
            L[k + 1] = L[k]
            k = k - 1
        end while
        L[j] = OL[i]
        t = true
        x = 0
        for l ← 0 to w do
            if x ≤ e_{L[l]} - d_{L[l]} then
                a_{L[l]} = max(x, s_{L[l]})
                x = a_{L[l]} + d_{L[l]}
            else
                t = false
                break
            end if
        end for
        if t = true then
            WL = L
            w = w + 1
            break
        end if
        j = j + 1
    end for
end for
```

Algorithm 1 represents the pseudocode of the approximate allocation algorithm. OL denotes the order of agents, WL denotes a list of the current winners, and L denotes a list of the tentative current winners. We apply this algorithm to find an allocation for each agent in an RSD and an SSD instead of calculating the formulation given in Def. 5 to find the best allocation for each dictator. We call an RSD and an SSD using this approximate algorithm an RSD by fixing the order of the allocated pieces (RSDF) and an SSD by fixing the order of the allocated pieces (SSDF). We show that the computational time of our approximate algorithm is polynomial for the number of agents.

Fig. 3. The points where an approximate algorithm examins whether a piece of agent 3 can be allocated

Theorem 7. *Our proposed approximate algorithm produces a solution in $O(n^3)$.*

Proof. Assume at most n agents. For each one, we examine at most n possibilities to allocate the pieces for all n agents. The computational time of examining one possibility is $O(n)$. As a result, the computational time for our approximate algorithm is $O(n^3)$.   □

We finally analyze the worst-case ratio to compare between our mechanism and Pareto efficient allocation in terms of the number of winners.

Theorem 8. *The worst-case ratio between the number of winners obtained by our algorithm and Pareto efficient allocation is $2/n$.*

Proof. The allocation result of our algorithm for the first and second agents is the same as a PE allocation, since both algorithm examine whether a piece with the second agent's required length can be allocated either to the left or to the right of the first agent's allocated piece. For the third agent, our approximate algorithm examines only 3 possibilities to put a piece with her required length (Fig. 3). On the other hand, we examines 3! possibilities to find a PE allocation by changing the order of the allocated pieces. Even if our approximate algorithm cannot allocate any pieces to the the third agents or later-ordered agents, a PE allocation can achieve n winners. As a result, the worst-case ratio is $2/n$.   □

Example 3. We show how an RSDF works by considering the same problem setting used in Example 1. To simplify our explanation, we assume that a mechanism designer determines the order of agents as 1, 2, 3, 4, 5, and 6.

agent 1: [0.25, 0.65] is assigned to agent 1.
agent 2: No piece is assigned to agent 2.
agent 3: [0.25, 0.65] goes to agent 1 and [0.65, 0.85] goes to agent 3.
agent 4: No piece is assigned to agent 4.
agent 5: No piece is assigned to agent 5.
agent 6: No piece goes to agent 6, since there does not exist no pieces such that agent 6 obtains the utility of 1 by fixing the order of the allocated pieces among the winners, i.e., 1 and 3, from the left most point of cake, that is, 0.

The winners are agents 1 and 3. The length of the union of the allocated pieces is $0.4 + 0.2 = 0.6$.

8   Envy-Free Cake Cutting Mechanism

We propose an EF cake cutting mechanism when an agent's utility function is all-or-nothing by modifying SSDF. In an SSDF, the agents are sorted by the increase of required length d_i, but they are randomly sorted with equal probability when there exist multiple with a certain required length as an exceptional procedure. Thus, our obtained allocation result depends on the order of the agents, and some losers might envy the winners. To avoid such a dissatisfaction, we divide the agents into groups by the required length d_i. Those who require a certain length belong to a single group.

Mechanism 3 (Envy-Free SSDF, EF-SSDF)

1. *Ask each agent about her reference interval $[s_i, e_i]$ and her required length d_i.*
2. *Allocate a piece with d_i when agent i's reference interval does not overlap any other agent's reference.*
3. *Divide the agents into groups by d_i among the agents except those who were allocated a piece in the previous procedure.*
4. *Sort the groups by an increase of d_i. We denote the k-th group as g_k.*
5. *From the first group, i.e., $k = 1$, allocate the pieces to all the agents in g_k, if all the allocation results are identical for all the permutations of agents in group g_k, go to the next group g_{k+1}. Otherwise, the agents in g_k cannot obtain any pieces of cake, and stop the mechanism. To determine the allocation for each order, we apply our approximate algorithm.*

Theorem 9. *An EF-SSDF satisfies strategy-proofness and envy-freeness.*

Proof. We show that EF-SSDF satisfies EF, since we show that it satisfies SP in the same manner as SSD. In EF-SSDF, when a set of winner candidates is identical independently of the order of the agents in a group, each winner candidate obtains a piece of the required length in her reference interval. Thus, the agents in a group do not envy each other. Furthermore, no losers envy the winners, since the piece obtained by each winner is shorter than each loser's required length or does not conflict with her reference interval.   □

Example 4. This example shows how a EF-SSDF works by considering the same problem setting used in Example 1.

In an EF-SSDF, agents 2 and 5 belong to the first-ordered group g_1, since they require $d_2 = d_5 = 0.15$, which is the shortest length among the 6 agents. We consider two types of orders of agents: $2 \rightarrow 5$ and $5 \rightarrow 2$. When agent 2 is the first-ordered, she is a winner candidate. On the other hand, agent 5 is a winner candidate when agent 5 is the first-ordered. The mechanism is stopped since the winner candidates are different in both cases. As a result, no pieces are allocated to the agents.

9   Proportionality in Expectation

Next we consider proportionality which is another well-known fairness property like EF. Based on the definition of all-or-nothing utility, since obviously no mechanism satisfies proportionality, we introduce a weaker notation of it.

Definition 6 (Proportionality in Expectation (PPE)). *Randomized cake cutting mechanism f is said to guarantee* proportionality in expectation, *if for any $i \in N$, any $U \in \mathcal{U}^n$, and any $U_i \in \mathcal{U}$, $U_i(f_i(U)) \geq \frac{1}{n}$.*

If a randomized cake cutting mechanism satisfies PPE, for any $i \in N$, agent i's expected utility is at least $1/n$. We show the impossibility theorem in which no mechanisms simultaneously satisfy EF and PPE; fortunately, our proposed mechanisms satisfy PPE.

Theorem 10. *Under the all-or-nothing utility function, envy-freeness is incompatible with proportionality in expectation.*

Proof. We assume that there exist a randomized cake cutting mechanism that satisfies both of EF and PPE. Let's consider how to allocate a cake for a set of agents N such that $[s_i, e_i] = [0, 1]$ and $d_i = 1$ holds for any $i \in N$. If the whole cake goes to agent $j \in N$, she is envied by the other agents. Thus, we cannot allocate a whole cake to a single agent because of PPE. Furthermore, the other allocation rules (except allocating a whole cake to an agent) do not work since no agent can obtain a utility of 1. Thus, no mechanisms satisfy both EF and PPE. □

Theorem 11. *Our proposed randomized cake cutting mechanisms, such as RSD and RSDF, satisfy proportionality in expectation.*

Proof. In a randomized SD, each agent can be the first-ordered with probability $1/n$. Thus, each agent's expected utility is at least $1/n$. □

10   Experimental Simulations

We experimentally evaluate the number of winners obtained by our proposed mechanism to show that our approximate algorithm is reasonably efficient. The simulations were run on Intel(R) Core(TM) i7-3960X CPU processors with 32.0GB RAM. The test machine ran Windows 7 Professional. We used CPLEX Studio12.5, a general-purpose mixed integer programming package.

We denote the number of varieties of required length d_i as div. For example, when $div = 1$ set, the length required by all agents is identical. d_i is randomly chosen from $[0.10 - 0.01(div - 1), 0.10 + 0.01(div - 1)]$. s_i and e_i are also randomly selected from $[0, 1 - d_i]$ and from $[s_i + d_i, 1]$. We set the number of agents to $n = 15$ and $n = 30$. We vary div from 3 to 9 when $n = 15$ and from 5 to 15 when $n = 30$. Figures 4(a) and 4(b) shows the average number of winners for solving 100 problem instances.

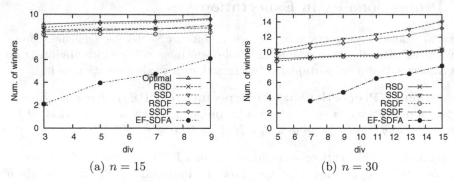

(a) $n = 15$ (b) $n = 30$

Fig. 4. Average number of winners

Table 1. Run time of each program when $n = 30$

div	RSD	SSD	RSDF	SSDF	EF-SSDF
5	2.2×10^5 ms	3.0×10^5 ms	1.5×10^2 ms	1.6×10^2 ms	over 5.0×10^6 ms
15	2.3×10^5 ms	5.1×10^5 ms	1.7×10^2 ms	1.7×10^2 ms	1.4×10^3 ms

Figure 4 shows the average number of winners obtained by each mechanism. When $n = 15$, we could calculate the optimal allocation and SSD obtained almost the same number of winners as the optimal result on average. While the RSD, SSD, RSDF and SSDF mechanisms are stable against the increase in div and the increase in the number of winners is small, EF-SSDF has a large increase since the increase in div reduces the possibilities of quickly stopping the mechanism. The sorted SDs outperforms the randomized SDs. Furthermore, RSDF and SSDF effectively find an allocation close to RSD and SSD (Tab. 1).

Figure 5 show the average utility obtained by each mechanism by varing required length when $n = 15$ and $div = 15$. Although we theoretically show that

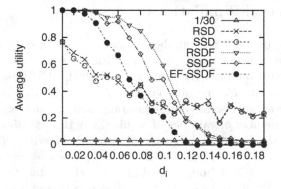

Fig. 5. Average utility

the expected utility obtained by the randomized SDs is at least $1/n$, RSD and RSDF get better average utility than $1/30$. Furthermore, the sorted SDs cannot guarantee PPE theoretically, but when the required length is relatively small, i.e., lower than 0.12, the sorted SDs including EF-SSDF obtain an average utility that exceeds $1/30$.

11 Conclusion

We investigated strategy-proof cake cutting mechanisms for the all-or-nothing utility and proposed SP mechanisms based on a serial dictatorship mechanisms. We also developed an approximate algorithm that effectively finds an allocation close to Parato efficient allocation. Furthermore, we showed that our randomized SD mechanisms satisfy proportionality in expectation. Future work will consider cake cutting with more complex situations, or analyzing the effect of a different type of manipulation from SP, such as false-name-manipulations.

Acknowledgments. This research was partially supported by JSPS KAKENHI Grant Number 24220003, 15H02751, and 15K12101.

References

1. Abdulkadiroğlu, A., Sönmez, T.: Random serial dictatorship and the core from random endowments in house allocation problems. Econometrica **66**(3), 689–701 (1998)
2. Aziz, H., Ye, C.: New cake cutting algorithms: a random assignment approach to cake cutting. The Computing Research Repository abs/1307.2908 (2013)
3. Brams, S.J., Jones, M.A., Klamler, C.: Better ways to cut a cake. Notices of the American Mathematical Society **53**(11), 1314–1321 (2006)
4. Brams, S.J., Taylor, A.D.: An envy-free cake division protocol. American Mathematical Monthly, 9–18 (1995)
5. Carroll, T.E., Grosu, D.: Strategyproof mechanisms for scheduling divisible loads in bus-networked distributed systems. IEEE Transactions on Parallel and Distributed Systems **19**(8), 1124–1135 (2008)
6. Chen, Y., Lai, J.K., Parkes, D.C., Procaccia, A.D.: Truth, justice, and cake cutting. Games and Economic Behavior **77**(1), 284–297 (2013)
7. Gamow, G., Stern, M.: Puzzle-math. Macmillan (1958)
8. Garey, M.R., Johnson, D.S.: Two-processor scheduling with start-times and deadlines. SIAM Journal on Computing **6**(3), 416–426 (1977)
9. Liu, C.L., Layland, J.W.: Scheduling algorithms for multiprogramming in a hard-real-time environment. Journal of the ACM (JACM) **20**(1), 46–61 (1973)
10. Maya, A., Nisan, N.: Incentive compatible two player cake cutting. In: Goldberg, P.W. (ed.) WINE 2012. LNCS, vol. 7695, pp. 170–183. Springer, Heidelberg (2012)
11. Mossel, E., Tamuz, O.: Truthful fair division. In: Kontogiannis, S., Koutsoupias, E., Spirakis, P.G. (eds.) SAGT 2010. LNCS, vol. 6386, pp. 288–299. Springer, Heidelberg (2010)

Leximin Asymmetric Multiple Objective DCOP on Factor Graph

Toshihiro Matsui[1]([⊠]), Marius Silaghi[2], Tenda Okimoto[3],
Katsutoshi Hirayama[3], Makoto Yokoo[4], and Hiroshi Matsuo[1]

[1] Nagoya Institute of Technology, Gokiso-cho Showa-ku, Nagoya 466-8555, Japan
{matsui.t,matsuo}@nitech.ac.jp
[2] Florida Institute of Technology, Melbourne, FL 32901, USA
msilaghi@fit.edu
[3] Kobe University, 5-1-1 Fukaeminami-machi Higashinada-ku, Kobe 658-0022, Japan
{tenda,hirayama}@maritime.kobe-u.ac.jp
[4] Kyushu University, 744 Motooka Nishi-ku, Fukuoka 819-0395, Japan
yokoo@is.kyushu-u.ac.jp

Abstract. Leximin AMODCOP has been proposed as a class of Multiple Objective Distributed Constraint Optimization Problems, where multiple objectives for individual agents are optimized based on the leximin operator. This problem also relates to Asymmetric DCOPs with the criteria of fairness among agents, which is an important requirement in practical resource allocation tasks. Previous studies explore only Leximin AMODCOPs on constraint graphs limited to functions with unary or binary scopes. We address the Leximin AMODCOPs on factor graphs that directly represent n-ary functions. A dynamic programming method on factor graphs is investigated as an exact solution method. In addition, for relatively dense problems, we also investigate several inexact algorithms.

Keywords: Distributed constraint optimization · Asymmetric · Multiple objectives · Leximin · Egalitarian

1 Introduction

Multiple Objective Distributed Constraint Optimization Problems (MODCOPs) [1,7] have been studied as an extension to DCOPs [2,8,12,16]. With MODCOPs, agents cooperatively solve multiple objective problems. As a class of MODCOPs, Leximin AMODCOP, where multiple objectives for individual agents are optimized based on the leximin operator, has been proposed [15]. This problem also relates to Asymmetric DCOPs with a criteria of fairness among agents [3,10,11]. The fairness among agents is an important requirement in practical resource allocation tasks [5,9–11]. For example, in a smart grid, autonomous consumers should share power resource without unfairness on their preferences considering relationship among them. Leximin is a well-known egalitarian social welfare that represents the fairness/unfairness among agents. Since maximization based on leximin ordering improves equality among agents, the Leximin AMODCOP is considered as a fundamental class of DCOPs.

© Springer International Publishing Switzerland 2015
Q. Chen et al. (Eds.): PRIMA 2015, LNAI 9387, pp. 134–151, 2015.
DOI: 10.1007/978-3-319-25524-8_9

The previous study [15] has proposed the Leximin AMODCOP on constraint graphs for binary and unary functions. Constraint graphs of Asymmetric DCOPs are represented as directed arc graphs, where nodes and directed arcs/edges stand for variables and functions, respectively [3,9]. Therefore, the direction of edges should be handled in solution methods. On the other hand, this class of problems is well represented with factor graphs. In factor graphs, nodes stand for variables or functions while non-directed edges stand for scopes of functions. Since a function is separately treated as a node in factor graphs, the function node is owned by an agent, where the function represents the preferences of the agent. Therefore, there are no directions of edges that represent ownership of the functions. Namely, asymmetric functions are naturally represented as factor graphs without any modifications. In addition, factor graphs directly represent n-ary functions.

In this paper, we evaluate several solution methods to Leximin AMODCOPs on factor graphs. A dynamic programming method on factor graphs is investigated as an exact/approximation solution method in conjunction with other inexact algorithms also applied to the factor graphs.

2   Preliminary

In the following, we present preliminaries of our study. Several definitions and notations are inherited from the previous literatures [6,15].

2.1   DCOP

A distributed constraint optimization problem (DCOP) is defined as follows.

Definition 1 (DCOP). *A DCOP is defined by (A, X, D, F), where A is a set of agents, X is a set of variables, D is a set of domains of variables, and F is a set of objective functions. The variables and functions are distributed to the agents in A. A variable $x_n \in X$ takes values from its domain defined by the discrete finite set $D_n \in D$. A function $f_m \in F$ is an objective function defining valuations of a constraint among several variables. Here f_m represents utility values that are maximized. We also call the utility values of f_m, objective values. $X_m \subset X$ defines the set of variables that are included in the scope of f_m. $F_n \subset F$ similarly defines a set of functions that include x_n in its scope. f_m is defined as $f_m(x_{m0}, \cdots, x_{mk}) : D_{m0} \times \cdots \times D_{mk} \rightarrow \mathbb{N}_0$, where $\{x_{m0}, \cdots, x_{mk}\} = X_m$. $f_m(x_{m0}, \cdots, x_{mk})$ is also simply denoted by $f_m(X_m)$. The aggregation $F(X)$ of all the objective functions is defined as follows: $F(X) = \sum_{m \ s.t. \ f_m \in F, X_m \subseteq X} f_m(X_m)$. The goal is to find a globally optimal assignment that maximizes the value of $F(X)$.*

Each agent locally knows its own variables and related functions. A distributed optimization algorithm is performed to compute the globally optimal solution.

2.2   Factor Graph, Max-Sum Algorithm and Bounded Max-Sum Algorithm

The factor graph [2] is a representation of DCOPs, and is a bipartite graph consisting of variable nodes, function nodes and edges. An edge represents a relationship between a variable and a function. Figure 1(a) shows a factor graph consisting of three variable nodes and three function nodes. As shown in the case of a ternary function f_2, the factor graph directly represents n-ary functions.

The Max-Sum algorithm [2] is a method for solving a DCOP by exploiting its factor graph. Each node of the factor graph corresponds to an 'agent' referred to as variable node or function node. Each such node communicates with neighborhood nodes using messages to compute globally optimal solutions. A message represents an evaluation function for a variable. A node computes/sends a message for each variable that corresponds to a neighborhood node. Here the nodes of functions in F_n are called the *neighborhood function nodes* of variable node x_n. Similarly, the nodes of variables in X_m are called the *neighborhood variable nodes* of function node f_m. A message payload $q_{x_n \to f_m}(x_n)$ that is sent from variable node x_n to function node f_m is represented as follows.

$$q_{x_n \to f_m}(x_n) = \begin{cases} 0 & \text{if } F_n = \{f_m\} \\ \sum_{f_{m'} \in F_n \setminus \{f_m\}} r_{f_{m'} \to x_n}(x_n) & \text{otherwise} \end{cases} \quad (1)$$

A message payload $r_{f_m \to x_n}(x_n)$ that is sent from function node f_m to variable node x_n is represented as follows.

$$r_{f_m \to x_n}(x_n) = \max_{\varepsilon \in D_{X_m \setminus \{x_n\}}} \left(f_m(\varepsilon, x_n) + \sum_{x_{n'} \in X_m \setminus \{x_n\}} q_{x_{n'} \to f_m}(\varepsilon \| x_{n'}) \right) \quad (2)$$

Here $\max_{\varepsilon \in D_{X_m \setminus \{x_n\}}}$ denotes the maximization for all assignments of variables in $X_m \setminus \{x_n\}$. A variable node x_n computes a marginal function that is represented as $z_n(x_n) = \sum_m \text{ s.t. } f_m \in F_n r_{f_m \to x_n}(x_n)$. Since $z_n(x_n)$ corresponds to global objective values for variable x_n, the variable node of x_n chooses the value of x_n that maximizes $z_n(x_n)$ as its solution. See [2] for the details of the algorithm.

In the cases where a factor graph contains cycles, the Max-Sum algorithm is an inexact method that may not converge, since the computation on different paths cannot be separated. In Bounded Max-Sum algorithm [13], a cyclic factor graph is approximated to a maximum spanning tree (MST) using a preprocessing that eliminates the cycles. For the computation of MST, the impact of edge e_{ij} between function f_i and variable x_j is evaluated as weight value $w_{ij} = \max_{X_i \setminus \{x_j\}} \left(\max_{x_j} f_i(X_i) - \min_{x_j} f_i(X_i) \right)$. When a set of variables $X_i^c \in X_i$ is eliminated from the scope of function f_i, the function is approximated to $\tilde{f}_i = \min_{X_i^c} f_i(X_i)$. Then, the Max-Sum algorithm is applied to the spanning tree as an exact solution method. In this computation, a couple of bottom-up and top-down processing steps based on a rooted tree are performed similarly to DPOP [12].

2.3   Multiple Objective DCOP for Preferences of Agents

Multiple Objective DCOPs. Multiple objective DCOP [1] (MODCOP) is a generalization of the DCOP framework. With MODCOPs, multiple objective functions are defined over the variables. The objective functions are simultaneously optimized based on appropriate criteria. The tuple with the values of all the objective functions for a given assignment is called the *objective vector*.

Definition 2 (Objective Vector). *An objective vector* $\mathbf{v}$ *is defined as* $[v_0, \cdots, v_K]$, *where* v_j *is an objective value. The vector* $\mathbf{F}(X)$ *of objective functions is defined as* $[F^0(X^0), \cdots, F^K(X^K)]$, *where* X^j *is the subset of* X *on which* F^j *is defined.* $F^j(X^j)$ *is an objective function for objective* j. *For assignment* $\mathcal{A}$, *the vector* $\mathbf{F}(\mathcal{A})$ *of the functions returns an objective vector* $[v_0, \cdots, v_K]$. *Here* $v_j = F^j(\mathcal{A}^j)$.

Since there is a trade-off among objectives, objective vectors are compared based on Pareto dominance [4,14]. Multiple objective problems generally have a set of Pareto optimal solutions that form a Pareto front.

Social Welfare. With a social welfare that defines an order on objective vectors, traditional solution methods for single objective problems can be applied to choose a Pareto optimal solution. There are several criteria of social welfare [14] and scalarization methods [4]. A traditional social welfare is defined as the summation $\sum_{j=0}^{K} F^j(\mathcal{A}^j)$ of objectives. The maximization of this summation ensures Pareto optimality. However, it does not capture the equality on these objectives. *Maximin* maximizes the minimum objective value. While maximin improves the worst case, it is not Pareto optimal. Maximin is also improved with summation that breaks ties of maximin ordering. See literatures [4,14] for the details of above criteria. The study in [9] addresses a multiple objective Asymmetric DCOP whose social welfare is based on Theil index. This social welfare also represents inequality/fairness among agents. However, a local search algorithm is employed to solve the problem, since the social welfare is non-monotonic.

Another social welfare, called *leximin*, is defined with a lexicographic order on objective vectors whose values are sorted in ascending order.

Definition 3 (Sorted Vector). *A sorted vector based on vector* $\mathbf{v}$ *is the vector, where all the values of* $\mathbf{v}$ *are sorted in ascending order.*

Definition 4 (Leximin). *Let* $\mathbf{v}$ *and* $\mathbf{v}'$ *denote vectors of the same length* $K+1$. *Let* $[v_0, \cdots, v_K]$ *and* $[v'_0, \cdots, v'_K]$ *denote sorted vectors of* $\mathbf{v}$ *and* $\mathbf{v}'$, *respectively. Also, let* $\prec_{leximin}$ *denote the relation of the leximin ordering.* $\mathbf{v} \prec_{leximin} \mathbf{v}'$ *if and only if* $\exists t, \forall t' < t, v_{t'} = v'_{t'} \wedge v_t < v'_t$.

The maximization on the leximin ordering ensures Pareto optimality. The leximin is an 'egalitarian' criterion, since it reduces the inequality on objectives.

Leximin Asymmetric MODCOP on Preferences of Agents. Leximin Asymmetric MODCOP (Leximin AMODCOP) [15] is a class of MODCOP, where each objective stands for a preference of an agent. This problem also relates to extended Asymmetric DCOPs with fairness or envy among agents [3,5,9–11]. Here each agent individually has its set of objective functions whose aggregated value represents the preference of the agent. On the other hand, several agents relate each other, since the subsets of their variables are contained in the scope of the same function. A Leximin AMODCOP is defined as follows [15].

Definition 5 (Leximin AMODCOP). *A Leximin AMODCOP is defined by* (A, X, D, F), *where* A, X *and* D *are similarly defined as for the DCOP in Definition 1. Agent* $i \in A$ *has its local problem defined on* $X_i \subseteq X$. $\exists (i, j)$ *s.t.* $i \neq j, X_i \cap X_j \neq \emptyset$. F *is a set of objective functions* $f_i(X_i)$ *for all* $i \in A$. *The function* $f_i(X_i) : D_{i_0} \times \cdots \times D_{i_k} \to \mathbb{R}$ *represents the objective value for agent* i *based on the variables in* $X_i = \{x_{i_0}, \cdots, x_{i_k}\}$. *For an assignment* $\mathcal{A}$ *of variables, the global objective function* $\mathbf{F}(\mathcal{A})$ *is defined as* $[f_0(\mathcal{A}_0), \cdots, f_{|A|-1}(\mathcal{A}_{|A|-1})]$. *Here* $\mathcal{A}_i$ *denotes the projection of the assignment* $\mathcal{A}$ *on* X_i. *The goal is to find the assignment* $\mathcal{A}^*$ *that maximizes the global objective function based on the leximin ordering.*

In general cases, Leximin AMODCOPs are NP-hard, similar to DCOPs.

The operations in the solution methods for DCOPs are extended for the leximin. The evaluation values are replaced by the sorted objective vectors, and the comparison on objective values is extended with the leximin. Also, the addition of objective values is extended as a concatenation operation of objective values. The 'addition' of sorted vectors is defined as follows [15].

Definition 6 (Addition on Vectors). *Let* $\mathbf{v}$ *and* $\mathbf{v}'$ *denote vectors* $[v_0, \cdots, v_K]$ *and* $[v'_0, \cdots, v'_{K'}]$. *The addition* $\mathbf{v} \oplus \mathbf{v}'$ *of the two vectors gives a vector* $\mathbf{v}'' = [v''_0, \cdots v''_{K+K'+1}]$ *where each value in* $\mathbf{v}''$ *is a distinct value in* $\mathbf{v}$ *or* $\mathbf{v}'$. *Namely,* $\mathbf{v}''$ *consists of all values in* $\mathbf{v}$ *and* $\mathbf{v}'$. *As a normalization, the values in* $\mathbf{v}''$ *are sorted in ascending order.*

In Bounded Max-Sum algorithm and our proposed method, partial solutions and related evaluation values are aggregated in a bottom up manner on a tree structure. This aggregation can be naturally extended for the leximin based on the similar operation whose correctness has been proven in [15].

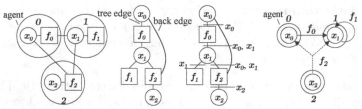

(a) factor graph/AMODCOP (b) pseudo tree   (c) separators   (d) constraint graph/AMODCOP

Fig. 1. AMODCOP on factor graph

Figure 1(a) shows a factor graph of the (Leximin) AMODCOP, where each agent i has a variable x_i and a function f_i. Since factor graphs directly represent n-ary functions, any asymmetric problems are well figured using this graph structure. Note that scope X_i of f_i should contain x_i. On the other hand, Figure 1(d) shows the constraint graph of the same problem. It requires directed arcs to represent the ownership of the functions. Solution methods for such constraint graphs have to handle the direction of edges. Moreover, a hyper-edge is necessary to represent an n-ray (ternary) function f_2.

For cyclic factor graphs, the traditional Max-Sum algorithm is inexact. Namely, an objective value is redundantly aggregated via different paths [2, 17]. A possible approach to avoid the redundant aggregation is the computation based on a spanning tree of the factor graph, similar to the Bounded Max-Sum algorithm [13]. However, this approximation is not very promising, since it eliminates several relationships between functions and variables. That may decrease the actual minimum objective value and the solution quality on leximin ordering.We therefore employ different types of algorithms.

3   Solution Methods for Leximin AMODCOPs on Factor Graphs

As an exact solution method for Leximin AMODCOPs, we introduce a dynamic programming algorithm based on pseudo trees of factor graphs. Then, we also introduce an approximation method and a local search algorithm. Here we assume that there are communication channels between any pairs of agents.

3.1   Dynamic Programming Based on Pseudo Tree

Several solution methods employ pseudo trees [8,12] to decompose problems on constraint graphs. On the other hand, there are a few similar studies for factor graphs [6]. We employ a solution method based on pseudo trees on factor graphs[1].

Pseudo Trees on Factor Graphs. A pseudo tree on a factor graph is constructed in a preprocessing of the main optimization method. Here we employ a DFS tree for a factor graph. The DFS graph traversal is initiated from a variable node and performed for all nodes ignoring their types. Edges of the original factor graph are categorized into tree edges and back edges based on the DFS tree. Figure 1(b) shows a pseudo tree for the factor graph of Fig. 1(a). Based on the factor graph and DFS tree, several related nodes are defined for each variable/function node i as follows.

- Nbr_i: the set of i's neighborhood nodes.

---

[1] While the previous study employs cross-edge pseudo trees and a search algorithm [6], we employ DFS trees and dynamic programming methods for the sake of simplicity. The pseudo trees based on DFS trees have no cross-edges and do not need a dedicated technique in [6].

- $Nbrh_i/Nbrl_i$: the set of i's neighborhood nodes in higher/lower depth.
- $prnt_i$: the parent node of i.
- $Chld_i$: the set of i's child nodes.
- Sep_i the set of separators: i.e., the variables related both to the subtree rooted at i and to i's ancestor nodes.
- $\overline{Sep_i}$: the set of non-separator variables that i has to consider in addition to the separators.
- $Seph_j^i$: the set of function nodes that are higher neighborhood nodes of variable node j. Here j is contained in Sep_i.

The separators and non-separators are defined for variable node i as follows.

$$Sep_i = \begin{cases} \{\,\} & \text{if } i \text{ is the root node} \\ \{i\} \cup \bigcup_{j \in Chld_i} Sep_j & \text{otherwise} \end{cases} \tag{3}$$

$$\overline{Sep_i} = \begin{cases} \{i\} & \text{if } i \text{ is the root node} \\ \{\,\} & \text{otherwise} \end{cases} \tag{4}$$

$$Seph_i^i = \begin{cases} \{\,\} & \text{if } i \text{ is the root node} \\ Nbrh_i & \text{otherwise} \end{cases} \tag{5}$$

$$Seph_k^i = \bigcup_{j \in Chld_i} Seph_k^j, \text{ where } k \in Sep_i \wedge k \neq i \wedge (i \text{ is non-root node}). \tag{6}$$

The set of separators Sep_i is empty in the root node, while other nodes aggregate their own variable and separators of child nodes (Eq. (3)). Only root node i has non-separator i (Eq. (4)). Non-root nodes set their own $Seph_i^i$ as $Nbrh_i$ (Eq. (5)). For other nodes k in separators Sep_i, node i sets $Seph_k^i$ aggregating $Seph_k^j$ of child nodes j (Eq. (6)).

For function node i, the separators and non-separators are defined as follows.

$$Sep_i = \left(Nbrh_i \cup \bigcup_{j \in Chld_i} Sep_j \right) \setminus \overline{Sep_i} \tag{7}$$

$$\overline{Sep_i} = \{ l \mid l \in Nbrl_i, \; Seph_l^{\prime i} = \{\,\} \} \tag{8}$$

$$Seph_k^{\prime i} = \begin{cases} \left(\bigcup_{j \in Chld_i, k \in Sep_j} Seph_k^j \right) \setminus \{i\} & \text{if } k \in Nbrl_i \\ \bigcup_{j \in Chld_i, k \in Sep_j} Seph_k^j & \text{otherwise} \end{cases} \tag{9}$$

$$Seph_k^i = Seph_k^{\prime i}, \text{ where } k \in Sep_i. \tag{10}$$

Each node sets separators Sep_i aggregating $Nbrh_i$ and separators of child nodes. Then, non-separators $\overline{Sep_i}$ are eliminated from Sep_i (Eq. (7)). Here non-separators in $\overline{Sep_i}$ are the variable nodes whose topmost neighborhood function node is i (Eq. (8) and (9)). For child nodes j and nodes k in separators Sep_j, node i aggregates $Seph_k^j$. Then, i is eliminated if k is i's neighborhood variable (Eq. (9)). After Sep_i is set, $Seph'^i_k$ is also used to set $Seph^i_k$ for k in Sep_i (Eq. (10)). In above equations, if function node i is the highest neighborhood node of variable node k, then k is not included in Sep_i. This computation is performed in a bottom-up manner from leaf nodes to the root node. It is possible to integrate the computation into the backtracking of the DFS traversal for the pseudo tree. Figure 1(c) illustrates separators of the pseudo tree shown in Fig. 1(b). For $i = f_1$, $\overline{Sep}_{f_1} = \{\ \}$, $Sep_{f_1} = \{x_1\}$ and $Seph^{f_1}_{x_1} = \{\ \}$. For $i = x_2$, $Sep_{x_2} = \{x_2\}$, $\overline{Sep}_{x_2} = \{\ \}$ and $Seph^{x_2}_{x_2} = \{f_2\}$. For $i = f_2$, $Seph'^{f_2}_{x_2} = \{\ \}$, $\overline{Sep}_{f_2} = \{x_2\}$, $Sep_{f_2} = \{x_0, x_1\}$, $Seph^{f_2}_{x_0} = \{\ \}$ and $Seph^{f_2}_{x_1} = \{\ \}$. For $i = x_1$, $Sep_{x_1} = \{x_0, x_1\}$, $\overline{Sep}_{x_1} = \{\ \}$, $Seph^{x_1}_{x_1} = \{f_0\}$ and $Seph^{x_1}_{x_0} = \{\ \}$. Similar computations are performed for the other nodes.

Dynamic Programming. Exploiting the pseudo tree on a factor graph, a dynamic programming method consisting of two phases is performed. The computation of the first phase is represented as follows.

$$g_i^*(Sep_i) = \max_{\substack{leximin \\ \overline{Sep}_i}} g_i(Sep_i \cup \overline{Sep}_i) \tag{11}$$

$$g_i(Sep_i \cup \overline{Sep}_i) = \begin{cases} \bigoplus_{j \in Chld_i} g_j^*(Sep_j) & \text{if } i \text{ is a variable node} \\ f_i(X_i) \oplus \bigoplus_{j \in Chld_i} g_j^*(Sep_j) & \text{otherwise} \end{cases} \tag{12}$$

Note that the above expressions include the cases such that $Sep_i = \{\ \}$ (the root variable node) or $\overline{Sep}_i = \{\ \}$ (non-root variable nodes and leaf function nodes). In expression (12), for each assignment $\mathcal{A}$ of $Sep_i \cup \overline{Sep}_i$, compatible assignments $\mathcal{A}_i$ of X_i and $\mathcal{A}_{Sep_j}$ of Sep_j are aggregated. This computation is performed in a bottom-up manner. As a result, each node i has its optimal objective vectors $g_i^*(Sep_i)$ for the assignments of its separators and the subtree rooted at i.

The computation of the second phase is performed in a top-down manner. The optimal assignment d_i^* of the root variable node i, that is also represented as $\mathcal{A}^*_{\overline{Sep}_i} = \{d_i^*\}$, is determined so that $g^*(\mathcal{A}^*_{Sep_i}) = g(\mathcal{A}^*_{Sep_i} \cup \mathcal{A}^*_{\overline{Sep}_i})$. Namely, $g^*(\{\}) = g(\mathcal{A}^*_{\overline{Sep}_i})$. The optimal assignments of other variable nodes are determined by their parent or ancestor node. For each child node j of i, its optimal separator Sep_j is determined by i so that $\mathcal{A}^*_{Sep_j} \subseteq \mathcal{A}^*_{Sep_i} \cup \mathcal{A}^*_{\overline{Sep}_i}$, where $g^*(\mathcal{A}^*_{Sep_i}) = g(\mathcal{A}^*_{Sep_i} \cup \mathcal{A}^*_{\overline{Sep}_i})$. Note that the above expressions also include the cases such that $Sep_i = \{\ \}$ or $\overline{Sep}_i = \{\ \}$. In the actual computation of the first phase, each agent i propagates $g_i^*(Sep_i)$ to $prnt_i$. Then, in the second phase, each agent i propagates $\mathcal{A}^*_{Sep_j}$ for each j in $Chld_i$.

This solution method inherits most parts of the correctness and the time/space complexity from conventional methods based on dynamic programming such as DPOP [12] and Bounded Max-Sum [13]. The overhead of operations on sorted vectors for leximin can be estimated as almost $O(n)$ for a sequential comparison of values of vectors, where n is the size of sorted vector. The sorting of values can be implemented as red-black tree whose time complexity is $O(\log n)$ [15].

3.2   Approximation Method

In the above exact dynamic programming method, each node i computes a table of objective vectors $g_i^*(Sep_i)$ for corresponding separators Sep_i. Therefore, the solution method is not applicable for the large number of separators. In such cases, several approximation methods can be applied to eliminate several back edges and corresponding separators. However, if the relationship between a variable and a function is completely eliminated, the value of the variable is determined ignoring the actual values of other variables in the scope of the function. As a result, the actual minimum objective value cannot be well controlled. That may decrease the quality of solutions, since leximin ordering is very sensitive to the minimum objective value. Here we employ another approach that fixes several values of variables. To eliminate separators, we define a threshold value $maxnsep$ for the maximum number of separators. Based on the threshold value $maxnsep$, the approximation is iteratively performed as multiple rounds. Each round consists of the following steps.

- (Step 1) selection of the node with the maximum number of separators (Fig. 2(a)).
- (Step 2) selection/fixation of the variable of the largest impact in the separators (Fig. 2(b)).
- (Step 3) notification of the fixed variable (Fig. 2(c)).

In Step 1, each node i reports the number of separators in Sep_i and its identifier. In actual computation, the computation is initiated by the root node in a top-down manner (Fig. 2(1)). The information of the number of separators is then aggregated in a bottom-up manner (Fig. 2(2)). Based on the aggregated information, an agent j who has the maximum number is selected to eliminate one of its separators. If $|Sep_j|$ is less than or equal to the threshold value $maxnsep$, the iteration of rounds is terminated. Otherwise, the root node notifies j so that j eliminates a separator (Fig. 2(3)).

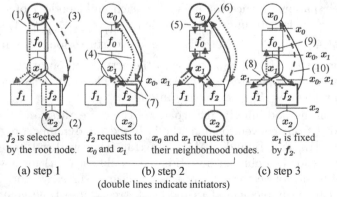

f_2 is selected f_2 requests to x_0 and x_1 request to x_1 is fixed
by the root node. x_0 and x_1 their neighborhood nodes.   by f_2.

(a) step 1   (b) step 2   (c) step 3
(double lines indicate initiators)

Fig. 2. Flow of approximation

In Step 2, node j eliminates a separator by fixing its value. First, for each separator x_k in Sep_j, node j requests the variable node of x_k to evaluate the impact of variable x_k (Fig. 2(4)). Then, for each neighborhood (function) node of f_l in Nbr_k, each variable node k of separator x_k requests function node of f_l to evaluate its impact (Fig. 2(5)). Each function node of f_l then returns the information of $f_l^{\perp}(x_k) = \min_{X_i \setminus \{x_k\}} f_i(X_i)$ to variable node of separator x_k (Fig. 2(6)). $f_l^{\perp}(x_k)$ represents the lower bound of f_l for x_k. Then, for each f_l, the boundaries are aggregated into sorted vectors so that $h_k^{\perp}(x_k) = \bigoplus_{f_l \in Nbr_k} f_l^{\perp}(x_k)$. Then, lower bound $h_k^{\perp\perp} = \min_{leximin x_k} h_k^{\perp}(x_k)$ and upper bound $h_k^{\perp\top} = \max_{leximin x_k} h_k^{\perp}(x_k)$ of $h_k^{\perp}(x_k)$ are computed. Variable node of x_k returns $h_k^{\perp\perp}$ and $h_k^{\perp\top}$ to node j (Fig. 2(7)). Now, node j determine the separator $x_{\hat{k}}$ to be fixed so that $\hat{k} = \operatorname{argmin}_{leximin k} h_k^{\perp\perp}$.

Note that the length of sorted objective vectors $h_k^{\perp\perp}$ can be different. In such cases, ∞ is employed as a padding value. As a result, a longer vector that affects more functions is selected in the case of a tie. We infer from the above expression that $x_{\hat{k}}$ is a 'risky' variable, since it's choice may be restricted to yield lower objective values in future computations of the approximation. Therefore, we prefer to fix this variable in advance. The value of $x_{\hat{k}}$ is fixed to $d_{\hat{k}}$ so that $h_{\hat{k}}^{\perp\top} = h_{\hat{k}}^{\perp}(d_{\hat{k}})$. Here we prefer the value corresponding to the maximum lower bound.

In Step 3, node j propagates the information of $D_{\hat{k}} = \{d_{\hat{k}}\}$ to its parent node and child nodes (Fig. 2(8)). The propagation is terminated when Sep_i or Sep_j s.t. $j \in Ch_i$ in a node i do not contain $x_{\hat{k}}$. Then, the information of termination is returned to node j (Fig. 2(9)). Then, node j notifies the root node of the termination of a round (Fig. 2(10)).

Note that the above algorithm is a base line to clarify the flow of information. We believe that there are several opportunities to optimize the message paths. This approximation method is a heuristic algorithm focusing on the worst case. Such a pessimistic approach is relatively reasonable for leximin ordering, since the minimum objective value has a major influence on the quality of the solutions. The upper bound objective value of each function, whose related variables are fixed, is calculated by maximizing its objective values for the fixed variables. However, the upper bound objective vector of an approximated solution cannot be directly calculated, since the objective values are evaluated on leximin ordering. Instead of that, the upper bound objective vector can be solved as the optimal solution of an approximated problem with the upper bound values of the functions. It also means that the technique of Bounded Max-Sum to calculate upper bound objective values is unavailable for leximin ordering.

3.3 Local Search

Another inexact approach is based on local search methods. Here we employ a local search method from a previous study [9]. While the original method is designed for constraint networks, we adapt the method to (Leximin) AMOD-COPs with factor graphs. This local search is cooperatively performed by each

1 Preprocessing:

2 let $Nbr_{x_i}^-$ denote $(Nbr_i$ of $x_i) \setminus \{f_i\}$. let $Nbr_{f_i}^-$ denote $(Nbr_i$ of $f_i) \setminus \{x_i\}$.

3 $ANbr_{x_i} \leftarrow \bigcup_j$(the owner agent of f_j in $Nbr_{x_i}^-$).

4 $ANbr_{f_i} \leftarrow \bigcup_j$(the owner agent of x_j in $Nbr_{f_i}^-$). $ANbr_i \leftarrow ANbr_{x_i} \cup ANbr_{f_i}$.

5 send $ANbr_i$ to j in $ANbr_i$. receive $ANbr_j$ from all j in $ANbr_i$.

6 $BANbr_i \leftarrow ANbr_i \cup \bigcup_{j \in ANbr_i} ANbr_j$.

8 Main procedure:

9 choose the initial assignment d_i^{cur} of x_i. // locally maximize f_i.

10 **until**(cutoff){

11   send d_i^{cur} to all agents j in $ANbr_{x_i}$. receive d_j^{cur} from all agents j in $ANbr_{f_i}$.

12    $\mathcal{A}_i^{cur} \leftarrow \{(x_i, d_i^{cur})\} \cup \bigcup_{x_j \text{ in } Nbr_{f_i}^-}(x_j, d_j^{cur})$.

13    $v_i^{cur} \leftarrow f_i(\mathcal{A}_i^{cur})$. send v_i^{cur} to agents j in $ANbr_i$. receive v_j^{cur} from agents j
        in $ANbr_i$.

14    $\mathbf{v}_i^{cur} \leftarrow \{v_i^{cur}\} \oplus \bigoplus_{j \text{ in } ANbr_i} \{v_j^{cur}\}$.

15   choose the new assignment d_i^{new} under $\mathcal{A}_i^{cur} \setminus \{(x_i, d_i^{cur})\}$.

16    $\mathcal{A}_i^{new} \leftarrow \{(x_i, d_i^{new})\} \cup \bigcup_{x_j \text{ in } Nbr_{f_i}^-}(x_j, d_j^{cur})$. $v_i^{new} \leftarrow f_i(\mathcal{A}_i^{new})$.

17   send d_i^{new} to all agents j in $ANbr_{x_i}$. receive d_j^{new} from all agents j in $ANbr_{f_i}$

18   **foreach**(x_k in $Nbr_{f_i}^-$){

19      $\mathcal{A}_{i,k}^{new} \leftarrow \{(x_i, d_i^{cur})\} \cup (x_k, d_k^{new}) \cup \bigcup_{x_j \text{ in } Nbr_{f_i}^- \setminus \{x_k\}}(x_j, d_j^{cur})$.
          $v_{i,k}^{new} \leftarrow f_i(\mathcal{A}_{i,k}^{new})$.

20   send $v_{i,k}^{new}$ to the owner agent of x_k.

21   }

22   receive v_j^{new} from all agents j in $ANbr_{x_i}$.

23    $\mathbf{v}_i^{new} \leftarrow \{v_i^{new}\} \oplus \bigoplus_{j \text{ in } ANbr_{x_i}} \{v_j^{new}\} \oplus \bigoplus_{k \text{ in } ANbr_i \setminus ANbr_{x_i}} \{v_k^{cur}\}$.

24   **if**($\mathbf{v}_i^{cur} \prec_{leximin} \mathbf{v}_i^{new}$){ $v_i^{dif} \leftarrow \max(0, v_i^{new} - v_i^{cur})$. }**else**{ $v_i^{dif} \leftarrow 0$. }

25   send v_i^{dif} to all agents j in $BANbr_i$. receive v_j^{dif} from all agents j in $BANbr_i$

26   **if**($v_i^{dif} = \max_{j \text{ in } BANbr_i \cup \{i\}} v_j^{dif}$){ $d_i^{cur} \leftarrow d_i^{new}$. } // tie is broken by agent
        IDs.

27 }

Fig. 3. local search (procedures of node i)

agent with its neighborhood agents. Since each agent i has its own variable node x_i and function node f_i, the neighborhood agents $ANbr_i$ of agent i are defined as a set of agents who have a neighborhood node of x_i or f_i. Note that we denote the neighborhood nodes of x_i and f_i as Nbr_i and Nbr_i, respectively. In addition, each agent i has to know its second order neighborhood agents $BANbr_i$. $BANbr_i$ is referred in decision making among agents. Since the variable of i's neighborhood agent j affects the functions of j's neighborhood agents including i, agent i should agree with agents within two hops. The above computations are performed in a preprocessing (Fig. 3, lines 1-6).

After the initialization (Fig. 3, line 9), the local search is iteratively performed as multiple rounds (lines 10-27). Each round consists of the following steps.

- (Step 1) notification of current assignments (lines 11 and 12).
- (Step 2) evaluation of current assignments (lines 13 and 14).
- (Step 3) proposal of new assignments (lines 15-17).
- (Step 4) evaluation of new assignments (lines 18-23).
- (Step 5) update of assignments (lines 24-26).

In Step 1, each agent i notifies the agents, whose functions relate to x_i, of the current assignment d_i^{cur} of its own variable x_i. Then, agents update the related current assignments. In Step 2, each agent i evaluates the value of its own function f_i for the current assignment. The valuation of f_i is announced to neighborhood agents. Then, agents update the current valuations. In addition, using the valuations, a sorted vector is generated. These valuations are stored for future evaluation. In Step 3, each agent i chooses its new assignment d_i^{new} that improves the valuation of f_i under the current assignment of other variables. Agent i then announces the new assignment d_i^{new} to the agents whose functions relate to x_i. In Step 4, each agent i evaluates the value of its own function f_i assuming that an assignment d_k^{cur} in the current assignment is updated to d_k^{new} by an agent who has x_k. Agent i then returns the valuation to the agent of x_k. This process is performed for all variables in the scope of f_i. Each agent of x_k receives and stores the valuation for d_k^{new}. Then, using the valuations, x_k generates a sorted vector for the case of d_k^{new}. In Step 5, each agent i compares the sorted vectors for the cases of d_i^{cur} and d_i^{new}. If the sorted vector for d_i^{new} is preferred, the improvement d_i^{dif} of the valuation of its own function f_i is evaluated. Otherwise, d_i^{dif} is set to 0. Then, agent i notifies agents, within two hops, of the improvement d_i^{dif}. When its own improvement d_i^{dif} is the greatest value in the agents $BANbr_i$, d_i^{cur} is updated by d_i^{new}.

4   Evaluation

4.1   Settings

Example Problems and Evaluation Values. We experimentally evaluated the proposed method. A class of Leximin AMODCOPs is used to generate test problems. The problems consist of n agents who have a ternary variable x_i ($|D_i| = 3$) and a function f_i of arity a. Objective values of the functions were randomly set as follows. g9_2: a rounded integer value based on a gamma distribution with $(\alpha = 9, \beta = 2)$, similar to [13]. u1-10: an integer value in $[1, 10]$ based on uniform distribution. Results were averaged over 25 instances of the problems. We evaluated the following criteria for a sorted objective vector $\mathbf{v}$. scl: a scalarized value of $\mathbf{v}$ shown below. sum: the total value of values in $\mathbf{v}$. min: the minimum value in $\mathbf{v}$. wtheil/theil: WTheil social welfare and Theil index shown below. As a normalization, each criterion (except 'theil') is divided by the corresponding criterion of the upper limit vector. The upper limit vector is defined as the vector consisting of $\max_{X_i} f_i(X_i)$ for all agent i.

Scalarization of Sorted Vectors (scl). To visualize sorted vectors, we introduce a scalar measurement. The scalar value represents the location on a dictionary that is compatible with a lexicographic order on the leximin. Here the minimum objective value $v^\perp$ and the maximum objective value $v^\top$ are given. With these limit values, for a sorted vector $\mathbf{v}$, a scalar value $s(\mathbf{v}) = s(\mathbf{v})_{(|A|-1)}$ that represents $\mathbf{v}$'s location on the dictionary is recursively calculated as $s(\mathbf{v})_{(k)} = s(\mathbf{v})_{(k-1)} \cdot (|v^\top - v^\perp| + 1) + (v_k - v^\perp)$ and $s(\mathbf{v})_{(-1)} = 0$. Here v_k is the kth objective value in sorted vector $\mathbf{v}$. Since we consider the values in $[v^\perp, v^\top]$ as the characters in $\{c_0, \cdots, c_{v^\top - v^\perp}\}$ that construct a word in the dictionary, $|v^\top - v^\perp| + 1$ is considered as the number of characters in the 'alphabet'. In the case where $|v^\top - v^\perp|$ and the number of variables are large, we can use multiple precision variables in the actual implementation. Below, we simply use 'scl' that denotes s($\mathbf{v}$).

Social Welfare Based on Theil Index (Wtheil/Theil). In a previous study [9], a social welfare based on Theil Index has been employed. Originally, Theil index is a criterion of unfairness defined as $T = \frac{1}{N}\sum_N^i \left(\frac{x_i}{\bar{x}} \ln \frac{x_i}{\bar{x}}\right)$. Here $\bar{x}$ denotes the average value for all x_i. T takes zero if all x_i are equal. The social welfare is defined as $WTheil = \bar{x}e^{-T}$ so that the average (summation) is integrated to the fairness. We compared the results with Theil Index and WTheil.

Bounded Max-Sum Algorithm. As addressed in Subsection 2.3, the Bounded Max-Sum algorithm can be adapted to leximin optimization problems. We evaluated such a Bounded Max-Sum (Bounded Max-Leximin) algorithm. While there are opportunities to modify the impact values of edges for minimum spanning trees, we found that other types of impact values were not very effective. Therefore, we simply employed the spanning trees of the original algorithm.

4.2   Results

First, we compared different criteria of optimization. In this experiment, we employed exact algorithms based on dynamic programming, except the case of WTheil as shown below. The aggregation and maximization operators of the solution method were replaced by other operators similar to the previous study [5]. Those operators are correctly applied to the dynamic programming based on pseudo trees. Table 1 shows the results of the comparison. Here 'ptmaxleximin' denotes the proposed method based on pseudo trees. Compared methods maximize the summation ('ptmaxsum') and the minimum value ('ptmaximin'), respectively. Additionally, 'ptmaximinsum' is an improved version of 'ptmaximin' that maximizes the summation when two minimum values are the same. Moreover, we also evaluated an exact solution method that maximizes WTheil ('maxwtheil'). Since WTheil cannot be decomposed into dynamic programming, we employed a centralized solver based on tree search. Due to the time/space complexity of the solution methods, we evaluated the case of $n = 15$ and $a = 3$.

Table 1. Comparison with different optimization criteria ($n = 15$, $a = 3$)

prb.	opt. criteria	scl	sum	min	wtheil	theil
g9_2	maxwtheil	0.563	0.815	0.637	**0.799**	0.031
	ptmaximin	0.698	0.735	**0.752**	0.730	0.017
	ptmaximinsum	**0.699**	0.769	**0.752**	0.763	0.019
	ptmaxsum	0.513	**0.818**	0.596	0.797	0.037
	ptmaxleximin	**0.699**	0.759	**0.752**	0.755	**0.016**
u1-10	maxwtheil	0.636	**0.888**	0.668	**0.879**	0.010
	ptmaximin	0.688	0.840	**0.722**	0.832	0.010
	ptmaximinsum	0.691	0.882	**0.722**	0.874	0.009
	ptmaxsum	0.599	**0.888**	0.632	0.878	0.013
	ptmaxleximin	**0.692**	0.875	**0.722**	0.869	**0.008**

* Problems were solved by exact algorithms.
* scl, sum, min and wtheil are ratio values to
the upper limit vector.
* To be maximized: scl, sum, min, wtheil. To be
minimized: theil.

Table 2. Size of pseudo tree (a=3)

n	depth	#leafs	avg. #branches	max. $|Sep_i|$	max. $\prod_{k \in Sep_i} |D_k|$
10	16	3	1.15	6	1558
20	30	7	1.18	11	447460
30	42	11	1.20	15	462162351
40	55	14	1.20	19	1.165E+11
50	65	18	1.21	25	1.156E+13

* Each factor graph consists of n variable
nodes and n function nodes.

The results in Table 1 shows that 'ptmaxleximin' always maximizes sorted vectors on leximin ordering ('scl'). Similarly, 'ptmaxsum' and 'maxwtheil' always maximize summation ('sum') and wtheil, respectively. 'ptleximin', 'ptmaximin' and 'ptmaximinsum' maximize the minimum value ('min'). While 'ptmaximinsum' relatively increases 'scl' in average, Theil index ('theil') of 'ptleximin' is less than 'that of ptmaximinsum'. Therefore, it is considered that 'ptleximin' improves fairness among agents. Table 2 shows the size of pseudo trees in the case of $a = 3$. Due to the size of $|Sep_i|$, even in the case of $n = 20$, the exact solution method is not applicable. Therefore, we did not compared exact methods and approximate methods.

Next, we evaluated approximate methods and local search methods. Figures 4-7 show the results in the case of g9_2 and $a = 3$. Here we evaluated the following methods. bms: the original Bounded Max-Sum algorithm. bmleximin: a Bounded Max-Sum algorithm whose values and operators are replaced for leximin. lsleximin100/1000: the local search method shown in Subsection 3.3, where the cutoff round is 100 or 1000. ptmaxleximin1/4/8: the approximation method shown in Subsection 3.2, where the maximum size of $|Sep_i|$ is 1, 4 or 8. ptmaxleximin8_ub: the upper bound of 'ptmaxleximin8' that is addressed in Subsection 3.2. While we also evaluated a local search which employs WTheil, the results resemble that of 'lsleximin'. It is considered that the both criteria resemble and only work as a threshold in the local search. Therefore, we show the results of 'lsleximin'. Figure 4 shows the result of 'scl'. The values of 'bms' and 'bmleximin' are relatively low, since those algorithms eliminate edges of factor graphs. As a result, actual values of several variables are ignored by other nodes. That decreases the minimum objective value and 'scl'. However, the results of 'bmleximin' are slightly better than that of 'bms'. When the maximum size of $|Sep_i|$ is sufficient, 'ptmaxleximin' is better than other methods. On the other hand, with the number of fixed variables, the quality of solutions decreases. The local search method outperforms 'ptmaxleximin' around thirty agents. Also, the local search method is better than Bounded Max-Sum/Leximin methods. Figures 5 and 6 show the results of 'sum' and 'min'. The results show that 'min' mainly affects the quality of 'scl'. Figure 7 shows the results of Theil index.

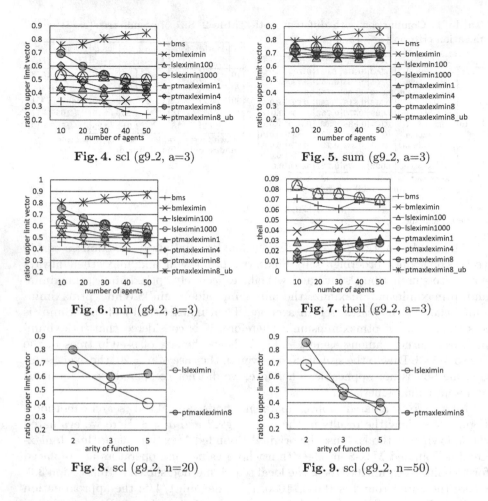

Fig. 4. scl (g9_2, a=3)

Fig. 5. sum (g9_2, a=3)

Fig. 6. min (g9_2, a=3)

Fig. 7. theil (g9_2, a=3)

Fig. 8. scl (g9_2, n=20)

Fig. 9. scl (g9_2, n=50)

Even if 'ptmaxleximin' loses the best quality on leximin ordering, it still holds relatively low unfairness.

Figures 8 and 9 show the results for different arities. Basically, the quality of solutions decreases with arities. On the other hand, the influence on 'ptmaxleximin' is not monotonic in the case of $n = 20$. It is considered that the heuristic of approximation is affected both of arity and the number of nodes. Figures 10 and 11 show the cases of u1-10 and $a = 3$. While the results resemble the cases of g9_2 and $a = 3$, 'ptmaxleximin' is slightly better. It is considered that relatively uniform objective values mitigate the influence of the approximation.

While we presented base line approximation algorithms for the sake of simplicity, we evaluated the total number of synchronized message cycles and the total number of messages. Note that the current evaluation is not in the main scope of this study. Tables 3 and 4 show the results of 'lsleximin' and 'ptmaxleximin', respectively. While the approximation method requires relatively large

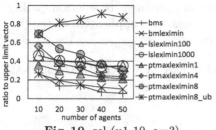

Fig. 10. scl (u1-10, a=3)

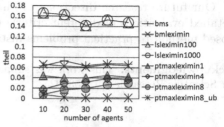

Fig. 11. theil (u1-10, a=3)

Table 3. Total number of cycles/messages (g9_2, n=50, a=3, lsleximin)

cutoff round	#converg.	#cyc.	#cyc. in converg.			#msg.	#msg. in converg.		
			min.	ave.	max.		min.	ave	max.
100	4	457	121	254	436	119903	31590	66249	113990
1000	6	3886	121	372	676	1017571	31590	98736	181640

Table 4. Total number of cycles/messages (g9_2, n=50, a=3, ptmaxleximin)

lmt. $|Sep_i|$	#cyc.					#msg.				
	step1	step2	step3	DP	total	step1	step2	step3	DP	total
1	4303	129	1386	128	5946	6639	3184	2075	198	12097
8	2480	73	936	128	3617	3829	2729	1422	198	8178

number of cycles, the total number of messages is less than that of local search, where agents basically multicast messages to their neighborhood agents.

5 Related Works and Discussions

While pseudo trees on factor graph have been proposed in [6], we employ the factor graphs to eliminate the directions of edges in the cases of Asymmetric DCOPs on constraint graphs [3]. As a result, the obtained solution methods do not handle the direction of edges that was necessary in the previous studies [3, 10]. In addition, the factor graph directly represents n-ary functions.

Theil based social welfare WTheil has been proposed in [9]. However, that social welfare cannot be decomposed into dynamic programming. We evaluated exact algorithms that optimize leximin and WTheil, relatively. In our experiment, the result shows that leximin is better than WTheil on the criteria of leximin, maximin and Theil Index.

6 Conclusions

We propose solution methods for the leximin multiple objective optimization problems with preferences of agents and employing factor graphs. A dynamic programming method on factor graphs is employed as an exact/approximation solution method in conjunction with other inexact algorithms also applied to factor graphs. The experimental results show the influences brought by the approximation method on the leximin social welfare and factor graphs.

Our future research directions will include improvement of solution quality, detailed evaluations of different criteria of fairness, and application of the proposed method to practical problems instances.

Acknowledgments. This work was supported in part by KAKENHI Grant-in-Aid for Scientific Research (C), 25330257.

References

1. Fave, D., Maria, F., Stranders, R., Rogers, A., Jennings, N.R.: Bounded decentralised coordination over multiple objectives. In: 10th International Conference on Autonomous Agents and Multiagent Systems, vol. 1, pp. 371–378 (2011)
2. Farinelli, A., Rogers, A., Petcu, A., Jennings, N.R.: Decentralised coordination of low-power embedded devices using the max-sum algorithm. In: 7th International Joint Conference on Autonomous Agents and Multiagent Systems, pp. 639–646 (2008)
3. Grinshpoun, T., Grubshtein, A., Zivan, R., Netzer, A., Meisels, A.: Asymmetric distributed constraint optimization problems. J. Artif. Intell. Res. **47**, 613–647 (2013)
4. Marler, R.T., Arora, J.S.: Survey of multi-objective optimization methods for engineering. Structural and Multidisciplinary Optimization **26**, 369–395 (2004)
5. Matsui, T., Matsuo, H.: Considering equality on distributed constraint optimization problem for resource supply network. In: 2012 IEEE/WIC/ACM International Joint Conferences on Web Intelligence and Intelligent Agent Technology, vol. 2, pp. 25–32 (2012)
6. Matsui, T., Matsuo, H.: Complete distributed search algorithm for cyclic factor graphs. In: 6th International Conference on Agents and Artificial Intelligence, pp. 184–192 (2014)
7. Matsui, T., Silaghi, M., Hirayama, K., Yokoo, M., Matsuo, H.: Distributed search method with bounded cost vectors on multiple objective dcops. In: Principles and Practice of Multi-Agent Systems - 15th International Conference, pp. 137–152 (2012)
8. Modi, P.J., Shen, W., Tambe, M., Yokoo, M.: Adopt: Asynchronous distributed constraint optimization with quality guarantees. Artif. Intell. **161**(1–2), 149–180 (2005)
9. Netzer, A., Meisels, A.: SOCIAL DCOP - social choice in distributed constraints optimization. In: 5th International Symposium on Intelligent Distributed Computing, pp. 35–47 (2011)
10. Netzer, A., Meisels, A.: Distributed envy minimization for resource allocation. In: 5th International Conference on Agents and Artificial Intelligence, vol. 1, pp. 15–24 (2013)
11. Netzer, A., Meisels, A.: Distributed local search for minimizing envy. In: 2013 IEEE/WIC/ACM International Conference on Intelligent Agent Technology, pp. 53–58 (2013)
12. Petcu, A., Faltings, B.: A scalable method for multiagent constraint optimization. In: 19th International Joint Conference on Artificial Intelligence, pp. 266–271 (2005)

13. Rogers, A., Farinelli, A., Stranders, R., Jennings, N.R.: Bounded approximate decentralised coordination via the Max-Sum algorithm. Artif. Intell. **175**(2), 730–759 (2011)
14. Sen, A.K.: Choice, Welfare and Measurement. Harvard University Press, Cambridge (1997)
15. Matsui, T., Silaghi, M., Katsutoshi, H., Makoto, Y., Matsuo, H.: Leximin multiple objective optimization for preferences of agents. In: 17th International Conference on Principles and Practice of Multi-Agent Systems
16. Zivan, R.: Anytime local search for distributed constraint optimization. In: Twenty-Third AAAI Conference on Artificial Intelligence, pp. 393–398 (2008)
17. Zivan, R., Peled, H.: Max/min-sum distributed constraint optimization through value propagation on an alternating dag. In: 11th International Conference on Autonomous Agents and Multiagent Systems, pp. 265–272 (2012)

Dynamic Coalition Formation in Energy Micro-Grids

Muhammad Yasir$^{(\boxtimes)}$, Martin Purvis, Maryam Purvis,
and Bastin Tony Roy Savarimuthu

Department of Information Science, University of Otago, Dunedin, New Zealand
{muhammad.yasir,martin.purvis,maryam.purvis,
tony.savarimuthu}@otago.ac.nz

Abstract. In recent years the notion of electrical energy micro-grids, in which communities share their locally-generated power, has gained increasing interest. Typically the energy generated comes from renewable resources, which means that its availability is variable-sometimes there may be energy surpluses and at other times energy deficits. This energy variability can be ameliorted by trading energy with a connected main electricity utility grid. But since main electricity grids are subject to faults or other outages, it can be advantageous for energy micro-grids to form coalitions and share their energy among themselves. In this work we present our model for the dynamic formation of such micro-grid coalitions. Our agent-based model, which is scalable and affords autonomy among the micro-grids participating in the coalition (agents can join and depart from coalitions at any time), features methods to reduce overall discomfort, so that even when all participating micro-grids in a coalition experience deficits; they can share energy so that overall discomfort is minimized. We demonstrate the efficacy of our model by showing empirical studies conducted with real energy production and consumption data.

Keywords: Renewable energy · Multi-agent systems · Coalition formation · Micro-grids

1   Introduction

A micro-grid (MG) is a local energy system that provides for the generation, storage, and consumption of electrical power within a community [8]. The function of a micro-grid is to utilize the distributed local renewable energy resources (such as wind and sun) and to satisfy power needs locally, thus minimizing the reliance on nearby utility grids. As a result, the power losses during transmission are reduced. Typically, a MG is connected to the nearby utility grid, so it can sell during surplus generation (generation is more than demand) or buy during deficient generation (generation is less than demand) power from an energy utility company. However, renewable energy sources are intermittent in nature and vary from hour to hour, and even from minute to minute, depending upon local conditions [8].

© Springer International Publishing Switzerland 2015
Q. Chen et al. (Eds.): PRIMA 2015, LNAI 9387, pp. 152–168, 2015.
DOI: 10.1007/978-3-319-25524-8_10

This means that at any time, a MG may have an excess or shortage of power generation. Different energy management strategies are used to mitigate the impact of supply variations, such as storage devices (batteries, fly wheels, capacitors, etc.), forecasting techniques, demand load management, and backup generators. One of the approaches to address this issue is the interconnection of nearby micro-grids which, by trading among the communities, can reduce the impact of irregularity with respect to renewable energy sources [8]. An agent-based architecture for local energy distribution among micro-grids has been presented in Yasir *et al.* [22], where each micro-grid represents a community which has its own power generation based on renewable energy sources and also has its own electric energy demand which varies hourly. Every community has a coordinator agent which, when it has a power surplus or deficit, is responsible for power trading with other interconnected communities or to the utility grid. We use that architecture as a basis on top of which we build our energy trading model.

Due to the centralized nature of existing electric generation and distribution systems, any technical fault or natural disaster can cause a wide-area blackout. Such power outages from the utility grid will also affect communities having MGs (hereafter interchangeably referred to simply as "communities"). Ordinarily MGs are not able to fulfill all their power needs by themselves all the time. So when a MG does not meet its demand, then the community will suffer hardship from having to cope with an insufficient energy supply. For brevity, we will refer to this hardship as "discomfort", and we note that the discomfort level (as discussed further below) is a nonlinear function of the energy deficit. So if the energy deficit is doubled, then the discomfort level is more than doubled. In order to address this problem, we believe that a useful approach is the formation of coalitions among the communities. A coalition here is considered to be a group of MGs that can distribute their electric power among each other. By operating in coalitions, communities can reduce their overall discomfort level, even when there is no additional external supply of energy.

In multi-agent systems, a coalition can be defined as a group of agents who decide to cooperate in order to achieve joint goals [14]. According to [19], coalition formation includes three activities: coalition structure generation, solving the optimization problem of each coalition, and dividing the obtained value among the agents. In this paper, our work is focused on the first activity of the coalition formation. We introduce a cooperation mechanism for dynamic coalition formation to reduce the overall discomfort level of the communities present in the system over time. The goal of our mechanism is not to find the optimal solution, but to find a satisfactory coalition match for the community in a non-deterministic environment (where community demand and generation vary hourly without advance knowledge) by relying on recent power and generation data.

The major contributions of this paper are twofold: 1) We have developed an algorithm for dynamic coalition formation to reduce discomfort at two levels: individual community level and at the system level (i.e. aggregation of communities). 2) We have investigated different power sharing mechanisms within the coalition and their impact on the discomfort level of the community and the system.

The rest of the paper is organized as follows. Related work on coalition formation in smart grids is discussed in Section 2. In Section 3 we present the problem scheme addressed in this work. Section 4 presents our approach to addressing that problem. Experiments and discussion are covered in Section 5. Section 6 presents conclusions and future work.

2 Related Work

Coalition formation in smart grids has been widely studied in the multi-agent system community (see for example [18] [16] [11] [6]), and much of this work has centered around two objectives: 1) reducing power losses and loads over the utility grids by forming local coalitions among MGs and customers. 2) optimizing monetary outcomes by trading power locally among MG participants.

Work in the first of these two areas has been conducted by studying coalitions among MGs, between MGs and consumers, or between MGs and the utility grid [17][3][6][13]. For example Chakraborty et al. [3] seek to reduce transmission losses by encouraging power-trading among MGs based on locality. Wei et al. [6] employ a game-theoretic coalition formation strategy to minimize power losses. However, although these approaches seek to reduce transmission losses, they do not address the coalition-formation process itself, as there are no mechanisms for how distantly located MGs can form efficient coalitions. Also these studies assume that the main utility grid is always available, so they have not considered circumstances when the coalitions may be cut off from such grids.

Other MG coalition studies have focused on optimizing monetary outcomes (the 2nd objective presented above) [4][5][13]. Some work has examined coalitions of plug-in hydroelectric vehicles (PHEV), which can form coalitions in order to have sufficient aggregate power to qualify for power trading markets [4][5]. In such approaches there is a broker that represents the coalition, and the individual PHEVs have little autonomy. Mondal et al. [13] describe a model for MGs competing with each other to attract consumer customers. In their work there is no cooperation between the MGs, and hence no coalitions are formed.

In contrast, the goal of our coalition formation mechanism is to form coalitions among the MGs in such a way that the members of a coalition complement their weather and demand patterns. As a result, the coalition becomes more resilient even during calamitous conditions and tries to reduce the aggregate discomfort of the members. In our model, each community also has the autonomy to join or leave the coalition by considering its demands, generation, and discomfort.

3 Problem Model

The scenario presented in our work concerns situations where communities having MGs must rely on their production to meet their demand. In cases of their own energy surpluses or deficits, they cannot get energy supplements from or sell excesses back to the grid, which is now cut off from them. When a community encounters an energy deficit, it will suffer "discomfort" because of the power shortage. We know from previous studies [1] [2] [20] that people or communities are willing to pay more than 100% of the original electric tariff if the power outage lasted for more than 24 hours. So we have assumed that there is a continuous polynomial function that can represent the discomfort of the community. So when a deficit increases, the discomfort level increases non-linearly. Supposing that dmd_i is the demand of the community at a given time i, where i is any hour of the day. gen_i is the generation of the community at given time i, def_i is the deficit of the community at time i, then we can calculate it as:

$$def_i = Max[\frac{dmd_i - gen_i}{dmd_i}, 0] * maxRange \qquad (1)$$

For simplicity we normalize the value of def_i between 0 and 10, where 0 means no deficit (i.e. generation is more than or equal to the demand) and 10 means extreme deficit (i.e. no generation is produced locally). In Equation 1, maxRange represents the maximum range of normalization i.e. 10.

The function for calculating the discomfort level is presented in Equation 2. The value of discomfort is assumed to lie between 0 and 10 (where 0 means no discomfort and 10 means extreme discomfort). This function takes def_i as an input and gives the discomfort level for time i. Mathematically this function can be expressed as:

$$f(def_i) = a * def_i + b * (def_i)^2 + c * (def_i)^3 \qquad (2)$$

where a = 0.1, b = -0.01 and c = 0.01. A plot of this function is given in Figure 1.

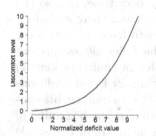

Fig. 1. Discomfort because of deficit

For example, at a particular hour of the day, say at 10 am, a community generates the electric power of 200 kWh, and its demand for that hour is 350 kWh. So, by using Equation 1, we calculate the normalized deficit value to be 4.28. By inserting this value into Equation 2, the value of discomfort for this hour becomes 1.02. The specific values used in this function are not important and have been chosen for illustration. We do believe, however, that the non-linear shape of this function is generally representative of how discomfort is related to power consumption deficits.

Communities are assumed to be dispersed across a varied geography such that some communities may sometimes have surplus power generation(have more available power than their consumer demand levels require) due to good wind or sun, while at the same time others may face deficits and thereby suffer discomfort. The idea of coalition formation among the communities is to help communities that suffer from extreme discomfort by receiving support from those who have a much smaller level of discomfort. A community in a coalition that offers assistance at one time would expect to receive reciprocal assistance when it encounters energy deficit at a later point in time. To illustrate why this would be beneficial, let us consider a simplified example of just two communities, C1 and C2. Suppose that during a certain hour of the day C1 has enough energy generation that exactly matches its demand (and hence has a discomfort level of 0), while C2 has no energy generation at all (and so has a discomfort level of 10). During another hour of the same day, both communities C1 and C2 each have a power deficit level of 5 and so have discomfort levels of 1.5. This means that during the first hour period the aggregate discomfort of C1 and C2 is 10, and during the second hour period the aggregate discomfort level of the two is 3 (computed using Equation 2, also shown in Figure 1). So over the two hour period, the aggregate discomfort level is 13.0.

If C1 and C2 were to form a coalition for mutual assistance, then during the first hour C1 might offer 10% of its power to C2. This would result in a discomfort level of 0.1 for C1 and a discomfort level of 7.48 for C2. During the other mentioned hour of the day, C2 would reciprocate by giving 10% of its power back to C1, meaning that C2's power deficit will be 6 and C1's deficit will be 4. Their corresponding discomfort values for this period would then be 2.4 for C2 and 0.88 for C1, making their aggregate discomfort level is 7.48 + 0.1 + 2.4 + 0.88 = 10.86. So even though C2 would give up some power when it is in a deficit, it benefits from being in the coalition. Note that the new comfort level is smaller than the discomfort level of 13 when no coalition is formed.

So operating within a coalition is likely to have beneficial results for all parties. The most effective coalitions will be those for which the excesses and deficits of community members complement each other. The worst periods for some coalition members match up with better periods for others, who may even have energy excesses during those periods.

Of course, energy generation conditions may change over time, and so the most effective coalition combinations over a geographic area may thereby change, too. It would be best if we would allow MG communities to have the autonomy of moving to a new coalition if it so desires. So in the following we present our examination of communities that operate in four different configurations: 1) Standalone - there are no coalitions and no energy sharing. 2) Fixed coalitions - there is a single, unchanging coalition arrangement. 3) Dynamic coalitions - communities have the option of joining a different coalition at the beginning of every day. 4) Centralized system - all communities are members of one single coalition.

For all coalition configurations (thus not the standalone configuration), a community may share its power with others when it has relatively low discomfort. Similarly, a community can receive power from the coalition if it has a relatively high discomfort level. The details of energy sharing within coalitions are described in the next section. The dynamic coalition arrangement allows communities to change coalitions, and this coalition formation mechanism is described in the next section. The centralized system considers a single large coalition that is managed centrally. This system affords optimal energy swapping, but offers less autonomy and has the vulnerability of a single point of failure and high transmission losses.   Since MGs are located at dispersed geographical locations, there will always be transmission losses associated with energy transfer. These transmission losses are determined by the following formula:

$$P_i^{Loss} = (Q_i^2 * R/U^2) + \theta * Q_i \tag{3}$$

where: P_i^{Loss} is the transmission power loss during one hour (i) in watts (W) from one community to another, Q_i is the total amount of power transmitted during hour i in kWh, R is the resistance of the distribution line between two MGs, U is the optimal voltage of the line, and θ is the fraction of power lost in the transformer during step up and step down process. The power lost during transmission is taken into account by the receiving MG.

4 System Model

In this section, we present the dynamic coalition formation mechanism. As with any coalition formation, the goal is to reduce the overall discomfort level of communities present in the coalition. The value of a coalition $(v(c_j))$ is represented by:

$$v(c_j) = \sum_{i=1}^{s} discomfort\_of\_community_i \tag{4}$$

where j is the coalition number, s is the number of communities present in the coalition j. The goal of coalition formation is to minimize the value of $v(c_j)$.

At the start of every day, two processes run in a coalition. In the first process, communities in the coalition calculate the amount they can give and take to/from the coalition for the next 24 hours by using their predicted demand and forecasted generation categorized into the best and worst hours. We assume that the forecasted wind pattern for the next 24 hours is up to 93% accurate [9]. Typically a community has twelve best and worst hours in a day. However, sometimes the best and worst hours may not be equal in number. Best hours are the hours in which a community has no discomfort or less discomfort. During those hours, the community can help other members of the coalition by sharing some proportion of its generation. Worst hours are the hours in which a community has less generation or no generation and it suffers from extreme discomfort. In other words, the community suffers more discomfort and seeks some power from the other members of the coalition to get some relief from its discomfort. Hence as a result, its overall discomfort of the day will be reduced.

In the second process, a community is selected to be the coordinator agent for the coalition. In this work, the coordinator agent is selected by lexicographic order. The responsibility of the coordinator agent is to broadcast an invitation message to other communities outside its coalition, identify the potential members of the coalition for joining the coalition, and manage the power-sharing distribution within the coalition.

There are two main phases of our coalition mechanism. The operational phase deals with the power distribution within the coalition, and the recruitment phase deals with recruiting other communities to join the coalition. First we discuss the operational phase. At the beginning of every hour, the coordinator agent calculates the total amount of electric power from coalition members who commit to give to the coalition and distributes the amount proportionally among the members of the coalition who are expecting the power from the coalition for the particular hour. We assume that communities do not cheat and reveal correct information about their give and take commitment.

A community can make a commitment about the amount of power to be given or taken from the coalition by using two approaches: dynamic offer and fixed offer. In a dynamic offer a community curtails a calculated at-the-time percentage of its generation from its 12 best hours and gives to its coalition. In return, the community expects the same amount back from the coalition during its 12 worst hours. However, in fixed offer, a community has a certain fixed value (in percentage) to curtail its generation from its best hours and then expect the same amount to return back during its worst hours.

Algorithm 1 gives the pseudo-code of the fixed and dynamic offer of a community to a coalition. At the beginning of each day, all communities in the system calculate their best and worst hours of the next 24 hours by using predicted demand and forecasted wind and sun information (line 1 of Algorithm 1). After identifying the best and the worst hours of the next 24 hours, a community aggregates the discomfort of the best and worst hours (line 4). For a fixed offer, the community selects the fixed arbitrary value of percentage for curtailing its generation from best hours (line 6 of Algorithm 1). If the selected value helps in reducing the aggregate discomfort of the day, then the community makes the offer otherwise the community does not participate in the coalition(lines 7-12 of Algorithm 1). However, for a dynamic offer (lines 13 to 30 of Algorithm 1), the community looks at all the possibilities of curtailing its generation (from 1% to 100%) from the best hours and observes its potential impact on the worst hours (lines 14 to 23 of Algorithm 1). After assessing all the possibilities, the community picks the best possible proportion (in percentage) for curtailing its generation among all the possibilities (line 26) and then calculates the amount of electricity to be given and taken to/from the coalition for the next 24 hours (line 27 of Algorithm 1).

We now discuss, the recruitment phase. From a recruitment perspective, we assume that the coalition is always looking for new communities to join the coalition in order to reduce a coalition's discomfort level. The coordinator agent collects the best and worst hours information from all the members of the coalition and categorizes the hours of the day into best hours and worst hours of the coalition. For recruiting the new community in the coalition, the coalition follows the following steps: at the start of every day, the coordinator agent of each coalition calculates the average discomfort of each hour of the next day by collecting best and worst hours information from the members of the coalition. The twelve hours with the lowest discomfort are ranked as the "best hours", while the remaining twelve hours are marked as the "worst hours". The "best hours" imply hours of the day during which the coalition can commit to sharing some of its power with newcomer communities. The "worst hours" signify hours when the coalition seeks to gain power assistance from a potential newcomer community. After calculating best and worst hour information, the coordinator agent

---

Algorithm 1. Algorithms for fixed and dynamic offer of a community

---

    input : Generation & demand of next 24 hours

    output: Give & take amount for exisitng coalition

1 Calculate best and worst hours slot

2 Total_discomfort_in_best_hours $= \sum discomfort\_in\_best\_hour\_discomfort$

3 Total_discomfort_in_worst_hours $= \sum discomfort\_in\_worst\_hour\_discomfort$

4 Total_actual_discomfort = Total_discomfort_in best_hours +
                                  Total_discomfort_in_worst_hours

5 **Algorithm for fixed offer**

6 | set certain value of α // **value in percentage of generation**
    | **curtailment**

7 | Total_new_discomfort = Compatibility Check(Best & worst hours, α)

8 | **if** $Total\_new\_discomfort < Total\_actual\_discomfort$ **then**

9 | Make Offer(α) // **amount to be given and taken from the**
      | **coalition**

10 | **else**

11 | No offer

12 | **end**

13 **Algorithm for dynamic offer**

14 | set i = 1% // **cutail of generation in percentage**

15 | **while** $i \leq 100$ **do**

16 | Total_new_discomfort = Compatibility Check(Best & worst hours,i)

17 | **if** $Total\_new\_discomfort < Total\_actual\_discomfort$ **then**

18 | Store order-pair (i, Total_new_discomfort) into discomfort-track-list

19 | **else**

20 | break

21 | **end**

22 | increment in i by 1

23 | **end**

24 | **if** *discomfort-track-list* **then**

25 | Sort discomfort-track-list in ascending order w.r.t Total_new_discomfort

26 | Pick the first order pair from discomfort-track-list & set the value of α

27 | Make Offer(α) // **amount to be given and taken from the**
     | **coalition**

28 | **else**

29 | No offer

30 | **end**

---

broadcasts the invitation message to join its coalition along with the information of its average discomfort for the worst and best hours. A new community must remain with the coalition it joins for at least one day. In addition to what each coalition coordinator agent does, all communities also calculate their own discomfort level at the end of each day (see Algorithm 2). If the existing discomfort level of the community is less than its rolling average discomfort, then the community is not interested in leaving its present coalition and will reject all invitation messages (line 10 of Algorithm 2). Otherwise, the community analyzes which coalition's invitation suits it best. The community identifies the matched and non-matched hours. Matched hours are those hours in which the invitation-receiving community's best and worst hours match the inviting coalition's worst and best hours. While the remaining hours of the invitation-receiving community are declared as non-matched hours (line 2 of Algorithm 2). An invitation-receiving community can only make offers to the inviting coalition if the matched hours are present (line 3 of Algorithm 2).

The offer mentions how much electric power it can expect from coalition during the community's worst hours and how much power a community can give to the coalition during the coalition's worst hours. The offer could be either a dynamic offer or a fixed offer. The community then makes offer for matched (by using Algorithm 1) and non-matched hours (by using Algorithm 3). For non-matched hours offer, a community calculates its average discomfort level over the next 24 hours (line 1 of Algorithm 3). If the community employs a dynamic offer mechanism, then the community offers a certain percentage of its generation (line 5 of Algorithm 3) to the coalition if the non-matched hour's discomfort is lower than the average discomfort of the next 24 hours. For example, if average discomfort of the day is 5 and the discomfort of the non-matched hour 4 is 3, then the value of ψ is 20% ((5-3)/10). However, if the non-matched hour's discomfort is higher than the average discomfort of the next day, then community expects certain percentage of its deficit from the coalition (line 7 of Algorithm 3). In contrast to dynamic offers, for a fixed offer of non-matched hours, a community always uses fixed proportions for making offers for give and take to/from the coalition. The offer made in non-matched hours either by using the dynamic or fixed offer mechanism is always less than the offer made in matched hours. Once a coalition receives an offer from a community, it calculates how much the coalition's average discomfort level would be decreased by inducting this community. This calculation is done by adding and subtracting the power (the amount offered by the prospective newcomer community) from the next day's data of the coalition and recalculating what the discomfort level would be. As part of this calculation, the coalition also takes into consideration the location of the prospective new member by calculating the expected transmission losses associated with this community during power trading. These losses result in deficits that affect the coalition's discomfort level. The coalition then ranks the offers in descending order in terms of how much they would reduce its discomfort level, and then it selects the top community from the list and sends its willingness to recruit the community. After receiving the willingness signal from the coalition, the prospective community also performs the same calculations done by the coalition and selects the best coalition that helps in reducing its own discomfort level. The community then sends a joining message to that coalition, while sending a refusal message to any other coalition.

Once the community joins the coalition, the community and coalition must fulfill their commitments. We assume that there is no cheating in fulfilling these commitments. However, sometimes the community or the coalition is unable to comply with their commitments because they were not able to generate the

---

Algorithm 2. A community's analysis of invitation

---

1 **if** *current's day discomfort value* $\geq$ *rolling average discomfort* $+ \beta$ *value* **then**
   | // **where** β **is the threshold value;**
2 | find matched and non-matched hours between community and invited
   | coalition;
3 | **if** *matched hours are found* **then**
4 | | **if** *community's best hours* $=$ *coalition's worst hour & Vice versa* **then**
   | | | // **matched hours;**
5 | | | Make offer ;
6 | | | Send offer to coalition;
7 | | **else**
8 | | | Make offer for non-matched hours // **Algorithm 3**
9 | **else**
10 | | Reject coalition's invitation
11 **else**
12 | Reject coalition's invitation

---

required power due to the intermittent nature of renewable sources such as wind
and sun.

5   Simulation Results

In our experiments, we investigated two questions: 1) What would be the impact
on discomfort level of a community present in a coalition as compared to a
community in no coalition? 2) What is the impact of different power-sharing
mechanisms on the discomfort level (of a community and the system) in dynamic
coalition formation.

5.1   Experimental Setup

Our experiments involved forty communities (C1 to C40). Each community has
an average hourly consumption of 1150 kWh and a wind turbine or array of
solar photovoltaic (PV) of 2000 kW generation capacity. However, the power
generation values for an individual community will vary, due to the dispersed
geography involving different wind speeds and solar radiations.

It could be possible that a community having renewable energy generation
(either wind or solar PV) always or most of the time has surplus. Similarly, it
is possible that a community has no surplus or most of the time it faces deficit
of generation. For our model, we have chosen a general configuration such that
most of the communities are in deficit most of the time. However, our mechanism
is also applicable to situations where communities have a surplus most of the
time. In our system, 13 communities have arrays of solar PV and the rest of

---

Algorithm 3. Algorithm for making offers during non-matched hours by a community

---

1 Calculate the average discomfort of the day;
2 **if** *offer mechanism is dynamic* **then**
3   **foreach** *non-matched hours* **do**
4   **if** *average discomfort of the day* $\geq$ *discomfort of non-matched hour* **then**
5   ψ = (average discomfort of the day) - (discomfort of non-matched hour);
            // ψ is the proportion of generation a community is willing to give to coalition for the hour
6   **else**
7   η = (discomfort of the non-matched hour) - (average discomfort of the day);
            // η is the proportion of its deficit a community is expecting to take from coalition

8 **else**
    // offer mechanism is fixed;
9   α is the certain fixed value (in percentage);
10   **if** *average discomfort of the day* $\geq$ *discomfort of non-matched hour* **then**
11   community can give α of its generation to coalition
12   **else**
13   community expects α of its deficit from the coalition

---

them have wind turbines. The power generated by a wind turbine is calculated by using the formula [12]:

$$P = 1/2\rho AV^3 C_p \tag{5}$$

where P is the power in watts (W), ρ is the air density in kilograms per cubic meter (kg/m^3), A is the swept rotor area in square meters (m^2), V is the wind speed in meters per second (m/s), and C_p is the power co-efficient.

We obtained the wind speed (V) data of forty different New Zealand areas from the National Institute of Water and Atmospheric (NIWA) database [21]. We also obtained hourly power consumption data of forty different places from the Property Services office of the University of Otago [15]. The assumptions made while running our experiments are as follows. All communities are situated at sea level, so the air density value of is 1.23 kg/m^3. The blade length of the wind turbines is 45 meters (m). The cut-in and cut-out wind speeds of the turbines are 3 and 25 meters per second (m/s), respectively. Theoretically the maximum value of Cp is 59%, which is known as the Betz limit [12]. However, in practice the value of Cp is in between 25%-45% [12], depending upon the height and size of the turbine. The value of the power co-efficient (Cp) is 0.4 (i.e. 40%). Similarly, the power generated by a solar PV is calculated by using the formula [7]:

$$E = A * r * H * PR \tag{6}$$

where E is the power in kilowatt-hour (KWh), A is the total solar panel area

(m^2), r is the yield of solar panel (%). The value of r for PV module of 4kWp is 15%, H is the solar radiation in kilo-Watt per meter square (kW/m^2), PR is performance ratio, which ranges between 0.5 and 0.9, with a default value of 0.75. We obtained the solar radiation (H) data of 13 different New Zealand areas from the National Renewable Energy Laboratory [10].

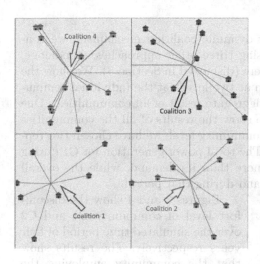

Fig. 2. Proximity based coalition

The simulation runs for 4 years (i.e. 48 months). At the start of the simulation, there are four coalitions present in the environment. Communities are initially assigned to each coalition on the basis of proximity, i.e. communities located in the same region of the grid belong to one coalition (see Figure 2). In Figure 2, house symbols represent a community. The arrow points to the centroid of the coalition. The communities within a coalition can transfer power among each other by using nearest point in the transmission line. The transmission lines are the black horizontal and vertical lines intersecting at the center of the figure. Transmission loss is calculated by using Equation 3. The initial value of R (resistance in Equation 3) in our experimental setup is 0.2 ohms per km. The value of θ is 0.02. The value of U is 33 kV. We setup the distribution network within a square region of 500 km x 500 km.

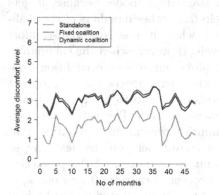

Fig. 3. C1: Standalone vs. Coalition

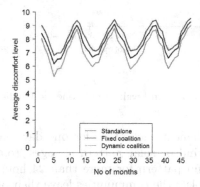

Fig. 4. C2: Standalone vs. Coalition

5.2   Results

All communities in the environment used our dynamic coalition formation mechanism. As stated above, we examined two areas: a) the effect of coalition sharing and b) the effect of dynamic versus fixed offer.

Coalition vs no Coalition

In order to measure the effects of our dynamic coalition mechanism, we conducted comparative experiments by using three other approaches: standalone, fixed coalition, and the centralized system (discussed in Section 3). We show the effectiveness of our coalition mechanism at two levels: at the individual community level and at the system level (the aggregate result of all communities). Due to space constraints, we are not able to show the results of all the communities present in the environment. So at the community level, we have chosen two representative communities (C1 and C2). The total power generation for C1 during the simulated four years period was more than its demand, while the overall generation of C2 was less than its demand during that period.

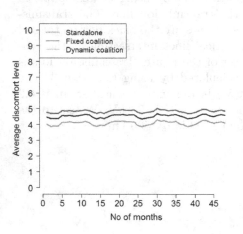

Fig. 5. System level: Standalone vs. Coalition

Figures 3 and 4 show the discomfort level of community C1 and C2 over the simulated time period of four years respectively. The results show that the community employing the standalone (no coalition) approach suffers much more discomfort, as no other community is able to help the standalone community. The community staying in a fixed coalition does better compared to the community in standalone mode, because, it gets help from other members of the coalition when it has severe discomfort levels. However, when the community employs our dynamic coalition approach, it experiences lower discomfort levels compared to using the alternative approaches. This is because, communities present in a coalition that complement each other for one day may not complement on the next day, as the wind or solar pattern changes from minute to minute and the prediction of wind pattern for more than 24 hours is not very accurate [9]. So our approach lets the communities leave their original coalition (created on the basis of proximity) and join the coalition that has a contrasting wind pattern or solar radiation. Similarly, Figure 4 illustrates the discomfort level of community C2 for the simulated time period of four years. Again, when the community operates under the dynamic coalition formation suffers less discomfort compared to

the community configurations using the fixed coalition and the standalone approach. Figure 5 shows the average discomfort of all 40 communities (i.e. the
system level result) in three configurations. It highlights that the dynamic coalition is the best in reducing the discomfort of all the communities. The results
(Figure 3-5) clearly show that the dynamic coalition formation mechanism not
only helps in reducing the discomfort in the individual community, but it is also
helpful in reducing discomfort at the societal level. By employing our dynamic
coalition formation approach, communities find the coalitions that complement
the best and worst hours of each other. As a result, there is an overall reduction
in the discomfort at the system level.

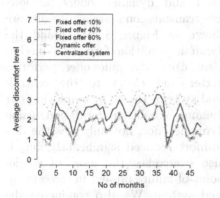

Fig. 6. Comparison of C1's discomfort   **Fig. 7.** Comparison of C2's discomfort
in different approaches   in different approaches

Dynamic Coalition: Fixed vs Dynamic Offers

In Section 4, we described two methods (fixed and dynamic) of making offering
in the dynamic coalition formation mechanism. We compared these two methods with the centralized system at the community and at the system level. In
the fixed offer mechanism, we ran the experiments by varying the value of α
(Algorithm 1) i.e. 10%, 40% , and 80%.

Figure 6 depicts the result when C1 employed the two approaches for dynamic
coalition formation. The result shows that the fixed offer approach does not give
the optimal reduction in discomfort unless the community knows the best value
of α. However, in dynamic offers, C1 does not need to know the value of α
which gives the least possible discomfort. In our experiments, after trial and
error we found that the optimal value of α in fixed offers is 40%. Any increase
or decrease in the optimal value of α (i.e. 10% or 80%) results in the increase
of discomfort level. 40% is the optimal value of α for the configuration we had
in our experiments. However, this is likely to change based on the underlying
data (e.g. sun and wind), whereas dynamic offers always finds the best possible
value to offer, which results in reducing its discomfort without any trial and error

method on any data set. We also found that the dynamic coalition formation by using dynamic offers is also significantly closer to the centralized system which is considered to be the optimally arranged power sharing mechanism. However, because of the centralized system's single-point-of-failure nature, it is not resilient. Similarly, Figure 7 shows the result of C2, where a similar trend of result was observed. The dynamic offer mechanism gives the highest reduction in discomfort and is closer to the centralized system approach.

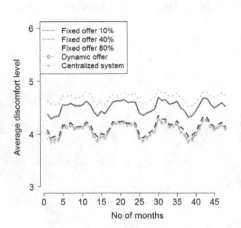

Fig. 8. System's discomfort level in low losses configuration

At the system level, it was also evident that the dynamic coalition with dynamic offers performs better than others. We ran our dynamic coalition formation mechanism using fixed and dynamic offers on low-loss transmission systems. Results are shown in Figure 8. We found the dynamic coalition formation mechanism using dynamic offer performs better and closer to the centralized system. Hence by employing our dynamic coalition formation using dynamic offer, not only was the discomfort reduced significantly, but it also overcomes the issue of single-point-of-failure present in the centralized system. We also conducted the same set of experiments on high transmission loss systems and found the same trends also exist.

6   Conclusion and Future Work

In this paper, we have presented our dynamic coalition-formation mechanism for micro-grids when they operate in a situation where there is no available support from a main utility grid. The goal of the coalition formation is to reduce the discomfort of communities because of deficit power generation.

Experiments show that our mechanism of dynamic coalition formation using dynamic offers is effective in reducing discomfort level (i.e. discomfort) of a communities. We have also shown that, compared to the standalone, fixed coalition, and dynamic coalition formation using fixed offer approaches, the dynamic coalition with dynamic offers outperforms and reduces the discomfort level at community and at the system level by considerable amounts. We believe the mechanism presented in this paper can be used by remote (rural) communities to reduce their discomfort by improving the availability of power required through local power sharing, while avoiding the reliance of the main utility grid.

For future work, we intend to introduce a split and merge algorithm for the coalition, so that coalitions could merge with other coalitions in order to more optimally reduce transmission losses.

References

1. Carlsson, F., Martinsson, P.: Does it matter when a power outage occurs? A choice experiment study on the willingness to pay to avoid power outages. Energy Economics **30**(3), 1232–1245 (2008)
2. Carlsson, F., Martinsson, P., Akay, A.: The effect of power outages and cheap talk on willingness to pay to reduce outages. Energy Economics **33**(5), 790–798 (2011)
3. Chakraborty, S., Nakamura, S., Okabe, T.: Scalable and optimal coalition formation of microgrids in a distribution system. In: IEEE PES Innovative Smart Grid Technologies, pp. 1–6, Europe, October 2014
4. de O Ramos, G., Burguillo, J.C., Bazzan, A.L.: Dynamic constrained coalition formation among electric vehicles. Journal of the Brazilian Computer Society **20**(1), 8 (2014)
5. Decker, K.S., Kamboj, S., Kempton, W.: Deploying power grid-integrated electric vehicles as a multi-agent system. In: 10th International Conference on Autonomous Agents and Multi-agent Systems, AAMAS, pp. 13–20, Taipei (2011)
6. Fadlullah, Z.M., Nozaki, Y., Takeuch, A., Kato, N.: A survey of game theoretic approaches in smart grid. In: International Conference on Wireless Communications and Signal Processing, WCSP, Nanjing (2011)
7. Ganguli, S., Singh, J., Engineering, I., Engineering, E., Sangrur, T.: Estimating the Solar Photovoltaic generation potential and possible plant capacity in Patiala. International journal of Applied Engineering Research **1**(2), 253–260 (2010). Dindigul
8. Jacobson, M.Z., Delucchi, M.A.: Providing all Global Energy with Wind, Water, and Solar Power, Part I: Technologies, Energy Resources, Quantities and Areas of Infrastructure, and Materials. Energy Policy **39**(3), 1154–1169 (2011)
9. Labortay, N.R.E.: Solar and Wind Forecasting. http://www.nrel.gov/electricity/transmission/resource_forecasting.html. [Accessed on 10 April 2015]
10. Labortay, N.R.E.: Solar Radiation Research. http://www.nrel.gov/solar_radiation/facilities.html/. [Accessed on 13 May 2015]
11. McArthur, S., Davidson, E., Catterson, V., Dimeas, A.: Multi-Agent Systems for Power Engineering ApplicationsPart I: Concepts, Approaches, and Technical Challenges. Power Systems **22**(4), 1743–1752 (2007)
12. Miller, A., Muljadi, E., Zinger, D.S.: A Variable Speed Wind Turbine Power Control. Energy Convers. **12**(2), 181–186 (1997)
13. Mondal, A., Misra, S.: Dynamic coalition formation in a smart grid: a game theoretic approach. In: 2013 IEEE International Conference on Communications Workshops (ICC), pp. 1067–1071. IEEE, Budapest (2013)
14. Oliveira, P., Pinto, T., Morais, H., Vale, Z.A., Praça, I.: MASCEM an electricity market simulator providing coalition support for virtual power players. In: 15th International Conference on Intelligent System Applications to Power Systems, 2009, ISAP 2009, pp. 1–6. IEEE, Curitiba (2009)
15. Pietsch, H.: Property service Division. http://www.propserv.otago.ac.nz/. [Accessed on 25 September 2014]
16. Ramchurn, S.D., Vytelingum, P., Rogers, A., Jennings, N.R.: Putting the 'Smarts' Into the Smart Grid: A Grand Challenge for Artificial Intelligence. Communications of the ACM, 86–97 (2012)
17. Saad, W., Han, Z., Poor, H.: Coalitional game theory for cooperative micro-grid distribution networks. In: 2011 IEEE International Conference on Communications Workshops (ICC), pp. 1–5. IEEE, Kyoto (2011)

18. Saad, W., Han, Z., Poor, H.V., Bas, T.: Game Theoretic Methods for the Smart Grid. Sig. Process. Mag. IEEE **29**(5), 86–105 (2012)
19. Sandholm, T., Larson, K., Andersson, M., Shehory, O., Tohmé, F.: Coalition structure generation with worst case. Artif. Intell. **111**(1–2), 209–238 (1999)
20. Shaalan, A.M.: Outages Cost Estimation for Residential Sector. Journal of King Abdulaziz University **12**(2), 69–79 (2000)
21. The National Climate Database. NIWA, The National Institute of Water and Atmospheric Research (2014)
22. Yasir, M., Purvis, M.K., Purvis, M., Savarimuthu, B.T.R.: Agent-based community coordination of local energy distribution. Ai & Society, December 2013

On the Hierarchical Nature
of Partial Preferences

Luigi Sauro[✉]

Department of Electrical Engineering and Information Technologies,
Università di Napoli "Federico II", Naples, Italy
luigi.sauro74@gmail.com

Abstract. In this work we generalize classical Decision Theory by considering that a preference relation might not be total. Incomplete preferences may be helpful to represent those situations where, due to lack of information, the decision maker would like to maintain different options *alive* and defer the final decision. In particular, we show that, when totality is pulled out, different formalizations of classical Decision Theory become not equivalent. We provide a hierarchical characterization of such formalizations and show that some derived properties of classical Decision Theory, such as justification, no longer hold. Consequently, whenever profitable, justification has to be reintroduced into the theory as an independent axiom.

1 Introduction

In recent years, "Economic Paradigms in Multiagent Systems" has become a fruitful area of research.[1] Decision Theory and its axiomatic formalization of preferences play a foundational role of such paradigms, thus, when we *import* an economic paradigm into our field (e.g. Game Theory or Social Mechanism Design), we are tacitly importing such a model of agent's preferences.

In his pioneering work on Decision Theory [11], when delineating the very basic properties of a preference relation $\prec$, Savage makes the following point: given two potential outcomes f and g, it cannot be the case that $f \prec g$ and $g \prec f$ at the same time. Clearly, this is logically equivalent to saying that either $f \not\prec g$ or $g \not\prec f$, which leads to three possible cases: *(i)* $f \not\prec g$ and $g \prec f$, *(ii)* $f \prec g$ and $g \not\prec f$, or *(iii)* $f \not\prec g$ and $g \not\prec f$. Then, he postulates that these three cases are the only possible judgments concerning f and g. In particular, the last case ($f \not\prec g$ and $g \not\prec f$) allegedly implies that f and g are equivalent in the sense that in any situation wherein these are the only two possible options, the decision maker does not mind delegating to coin flipping. Consequently, in classical Decision Theory a very fundamental property of a preference relation is its totality.

From the theory's very start, the hidden assumptions underlying this model of an *economic man* has raised some criticisms, among which Simon's was one of the most influential:

---

[1] A somewhat tautological piece of evidence is its being one of the topics of this conference.

© Springer International Publishing Switzerland 2015
Q. Chen et al. (Eds.): PRIMA 2015, LNAI 9387, pp. 169–184, 2015.
DOI: 10.1007/978-3-319-25524-8_11

"This man is assumed to have knowledge of the relevant aspects of his environment which, if not absolutely complete, is at least impressively clear and voluminous. He is assumed also to have a well-organized and stable system of preferences, and a skill in computation that enables him to calculate, for the alternative courses of action that are available to him, which of these will permit him to reach the highest attainable point on his preference scale" [12].

Based on his criticism, Simon moved towards a problem-solving perspective which was extremely influential in the field of Artificial Intelligence.[2] However, it would be wrong to look at Decision Theory and Problem Solving as Eteocles and Polynices. To some extent, Simon's criticism was already considered by the founders of Decision Theory:

"It is conceivable and may even in a way be more realistic to allow for cases where the individual is neither able to state which of two alternatives he prefers nor that they are equally desirable. How real this possibility is, both for individuals and for organizations, seems to be an extremely interesting question, but it is a question of fact. It certainly deserves further study." [10].

Several relevant application domains would advocate the foregoing considerations. Preferences often result from complex trade-offs between different attributes (functionalities, cost, Quality of Service, information disclosure risks, etc.) a generic user may only have a vague idea of. Moreover, in some cases the decision maker is actually a collectivity where internal debate does not easily end up with a total preference.

Finally, from a MAS perspective, we generally develop software agents acting *on behalf of* real users. Clearly, a related issue is how users' preferences are actually transferred to the delegated agents. If an agent admits total preferences only, a user would be forced to pre-emptively disabimguate all (possibly unexpected) options and typically one is reluctant to identify indecisions due to lack of knowledge or still trembling desires with indifference. Furthermore, albeit the user conforms with a classical economic man, her preference relation could be so voluminous and lacking of regularities that it could not be entirely and efficiently injected into the software agent – even if ceteris paribus techniques are adopted [7]. The foregoing arguments end up with the following consideration, if Savage judged sufficient to consider three possible options (choose f, choose g, and flip a coin), we propose a fourth one for the delegated agent: defer the decision and ask the user again. This involves distinguishing between indifference and incomparability.

Besides foundational issues and motivations, you may think that, from a technical point of view, dealing with incomplete preferences is quite a straightforward task: it simply suffices to replace totality with reflexivity. In this work, we show that this is not the case. Indeed, Classical Decision Theory can be modelled by several formalizations which turn out to be variants of the same theory.

---

[2] Together with Newell, he won the Turing Award in 1975.

However, we show that their equivalence is inherently guaranteed by the totality axiom; as a consequence, by weakening totality in favour of reflexivity, the resulting axiomatic systems characterize different notions of partial preference. Clearly, any debate concerning which of these should be adopted would profit from formal properties. Thus, we first start to delineate the hierarchical structure underlying such axiomatizations. Then, we point out some basic properties that can be derived in any of the considered theory. Finally, we also identify a justification property which may be useful to model how preferences are injected from a user into the software agent. It turns out that the justification property cannot be derived from any of the axiomatizations taken into account, therefore, you have to buy it as an independent axiom. We also show that the justification property allows to prove that gambling over incomparable alternatives never comes up with a better outcome.

In Section 2, we show two motivating scenarios where considering preferences as incomplete seems to be appropriate. In Section 3, we introduce four equivalent variants of classical Decision Theory and enlighten mutual dependencies of their axioms. Section 4 shows the hierarchical nature of different notions of partial preferences obtained from the previous classical systems by replacing totality with reflexivity. Section 5 shows some shared properties of partial preferences whereas Section 6 focuses on the independent justification property. Section 7 examines previous investigations on partial preferences. Conclusions end the paper.

2   Motivating Scenarios

In this section we introduce two scenarios where partial preferences seem to provide a more natural way to describe a decision maker, or a software agent behaving on its behalf, compared with total preferences.

In the first scenario, Bob wants to learn to play the piano and posts a request on a consumer-to-consumer social network. Soon after, he receives offers from two musicians, Carl and Mary. Carl provides two options: a 5 people class for 15 dollars per person or a one-to-one class for 35 dollars. Mary offers two similar options: a 3 people class for 20 dollars per person or a one-to-one class for 40 dollars. Furthermore, they both offer a trial lesson. Regarding Carl's options, Bob thinks that 5 people are too many for a class, thus he prefers the one-to-one option. On the contrary, he judges the price difference between Mary's options somewhat excessive, hence he prefers the 3 people class. If someone asked Bob *"Do you prefer Mary's 3 people class or Carl's one-to-one class?"*, Bob would probably answer *"I do not know, I first have to attend the trial lessons"*. Notice that this is different from saying that the two options are equivalent, because in that case Bob would simply flip a coin and choose one of them. On the contrary, it is more natural to think that these options are initially *incomparable* and Bob will use the trial lessons to disambiguate them.

More generally, in the absence of complete information it might be difficult for an individual to figure out a consistent total order over the bids and choose one of them in a single step. On the contrary, making a decision can be viewed as a multiple step process where offers are initially filtered according to a partial preference relation. Then, depending on the resulting offers, an individual can acquire further information and possibly refine her ranking.

In the second scenario, Alice's father has finally agreed to buy her a smartphone, and now she is browsing Ebay for possible offers. Unfortunately, the list is huge and patience is not Alice's forte. So, she would like to be assisted by a software agent to filter out undesired options. The software agent accepts constraints such as maximum cost and size, color restrictions, etc., and also a preference relation as a total order over bids. Then, according to the specified preference relation, the agent returns the best offer. Clearly, Alice's desires are influenced by several attributes such as operating system, color, weight, brand, and so on. For instance, she has a preference over operating systems in the following decreasing order: OS1, OS2, and OS3; over colors: blue, red, black, white; and over brands: Brand1, Brand2, Brand3. Furthermore, out of benevolence for her father, given a specific model, the cheaper the better. However, such preferences over single attributes do not constitute a total order. Moreover, Alice cannot establish a priority over attributes, for instance she prefers a Brand3 phone with operating system OS1 to a Brand2 with operating system OS2, but she prefers a Brand1 OS2 phone to a Brand2 OS1. Alice soon realizes that providing a total order to the software agent is frustrating and requires about the same effort as comparing all the offers by herself. This scenario reveals the following issue: in designing a software agent that behaves on behalf of real users, we have to take into account how users can *instruct* the agent about their own preferences. In electronic markets where the number of offers can be huge, it could be unfeasible to transfer an exact representation of users' desires into a software agent. In this case, the agent should make do with an approximate representation of users' desires as a partial order and return a restricted list of choices from which the user can select the preferred one. As a further advantage, the user retains the ability to apply unforeseen, situation-specific knowledge and preferences that have not been formalized in advance.

3   Classical Preferences

In this section we introduce classical preference relations through four distinct formalizations. Then, by proving their mutual equivalence, we show the various interdependencies between their axioms. Such a result will be used in the next section when we weaken such theories by allowing preferences to be partial.

First, some preliminary notions are needed. Let $\mathcal{A}$ be a finite set of alternatives and $\Delta(\mathcal{A})$ the class of all probability distributions over $\mathcal{A}$. In the decision making jargon, elements of $\Delta(\mathcal{A})$ are also called *lotteries* or *outcomes*. Given two lotteries $f, g \in \Delta(\mathcal{A})$ and a real number $\alpha \in [0, 1]$, we denote with $\alpha f + (1 - \alpha)g$, in short $\langle \alpha, f, g \rangle$, the convex combination of f and g such that $\langle \alpha, f, g \rangle(a) = \alpha f(a) + (1 - \alpha)g(a)$, for all $a \in \mathcal{A}$. Furthermore, for an alternative $a \in \mathcal{A}$, $[a]$ denotes the degenerate distribution that assigns probability 1 to a and probability 0 to all the other alternatives.

A (classical) preference relation $\preceq$ is a binary relation over lotteries in $\Delta(\mathcal{A})$ which satisfies the following axioms:

1. $f \preceq g$ or $g \preceq f$;
2. if $f \preceq g$ and $g \preceq h$, then $f \preceq h$;
3. for each $0 \leq \alpha \leq 1$ and h, $f \preceq g$ iff $\langle \alpha, f, h \rangle \preceq \langle \alpha, f, h \rangle$;
4. if $h \prec \langle \alpha, f, g \rangle$ (resp. $\langle \alpha, f, g \rangle \prec h$), for all $0 < \alpha < 1$, then $f \not\prec h$ (resp. $h \not\prec g$).

where, as usual, $f \sim g$ means that $f \preceq g$ and $g \preceq f$, whereas $f \prec g$ means that $f \preceq g$ and $g \not\preceq f$.

The first two axioms force $\preceq$ to be a total (hence reflexive) transitive relation, that is a total preorder. Axiom 3 states that the preference between f and g is preserved by *diluition* with h and, conversely, if we have a certain preference between diluited lotteries, the same preference holds between the undiluited lotteries f and g. Finally, axiom 4 is a very weak form of continuity, it just prevents the case where the strict preference between a singleton h and the closed line of all convex combinations involving f and g goes in one direction for one end-point and in precisely the opposite direction for the entire remainder of the segment.

It is worth noting that axioms 1–4 are not the only way to define classical preference relations. Different equivalent axiomatizations have been proposed in literature. For instance in [9] Myerson replaces 3 with axioms

6. if $f \prec g$ and $0 \leq \alpha < \beta \leq 1$, then $\langle \beta, f, g \rangle \prec \langle \alpha, f, g \rangle$;
7. if $f_1 \preceq g_1$, $f_2 \preceq g_2$, and $0 \leq \alpha \leq 1$, then $\langle \alpha, f_1, f_2 \rangle \preceq \langle \alpha, g_1, g_2 \rangle$;
8. if $f_1 \prec g_1$, $f_2 \preceq g_2$, and $0 \leq \alpha \leq 1$, then $\langle \alpha, f_1, f_2 \rangle \prec \langle \alpha, g_1, g_2 \rangle$;

and axiom 4 with the axiom

9. if $h \preceq f$ and $f \preceq g$, then there exists some $0 \leq \alpha \leq 1$ such that $f \sim \langle \alpha, g, h \rangle$.

Informally, axiom 6 establishes that $\preceq$ is monotonic under convex combinations. Axiom 7 asserts a substitution principle: given a lottery between f_1 and f_2, if we substitute each of them with a better outcome (i.e. g_1 and g_2, respectively), then we obtain a better lottery. Axiom 8 is a strict version of 7. Finally, axiom 9 is a different notion of continuity assuring that the convex combinations of two outcomes f and g encompass all possible gradations of the preference relation between f and g.

Clearly, we can also consider mixed cases where only axiom 3 is replaced with axioms 6–8 (respectively, axiom 4 with 9). Doing so, we obtain four different axiomatizations of the Classical Decision Theory, namely CDT_0, CDT_1, CDT_2, and CDT_3 (see Table 1). Generally speaking, we say that a set of axioms T_2 *entails* another set of axioms T_1, $T_1 \leq T_2$, if and only if all the preference relations satisfying T_2 satisfy T_1 as well. We show that CDT_0–CDT_3 are equivalent in the sense that they characterize the same set of preference relations. First, we need some preliminary results that point out the interdependencies among the

Table 1. The four axiomatizations of classical preference relations CDT_0, CDT_1, CDT_2, and CDT_3.

	Axioms 1,2	Axiom 3	Axioms 6, 7, 8	Axiom 4	Axiom 9
CDT_0	✓		✓	✓	
CDT_1	✓	✓		✓	
CDT_2	✓		✓		✓
CDT_3	✓	✓			✓

axioms introduced above.[3] Lemma 1 shows that to obtain axioms 6, 7 and 8 from axiom 3, totality is not needed. In particular, any preorder (i.e. transitive and reflexive relation) which satisfies axiom 3 also satisfies axioms 6, 7 and 8.

Lemma 1. *Let $\preceq$ be reflexive. Axioms 2 and 3 imply axioms 6, 7 and 8.*

Proof. Assume that $f \prec g$ and $0 \leq \alpha < \beta \leq 1$. Let $\gamma' = \beta - \alpha$, $\gamma = \frac{\alpha}{1-\gamma'}$ and $h = \langle \gamma, f, g \rangle$. Since $0 \leq \alpha < \beta \leq 1$, both γ' and γ are in the interval $[0,1]$. Since $f \prec g$, axiom 3 implies $\langle \gamma', f, h \rangle \prec \langle \gamma', g, h \rangle$. Moreover, it is easy to see that $\langle \gamma', f, h \rangle = \langle \beta, f, h \rangle$ and $\langle \gamma', g, h \rangle = \langle \alpha, f, g \rangle$. Consequently, axiom 6 holds.

Assume that $f_1 \preceq g_1$, $f_2 \preceq g_2$, and $0 \leq \alpha \leq 1$. Due to axiom 3 and $f_1 \preceq g_1$, $\langle \alpha, f_1, f_2 \rangle \preceq \langle \alpha, g_1, f_2 \rangle$. Analogously, axiom 3 and $f_2 \preceq g_2$ imply that $\langle \alpha, g_1, f_2 \rangle \preceq \langle \alpha, g_1, g_2 \rangle$. Finally, by transitivity $\langle \alpha, f_1, f_2 \rangle \preceq \langle \alpha, g_1, g_2 \rangle$, hence axiom 7 holds.

Finally, assume that $f_1 \prec g_1$, $f_2 \preceq g_2$, and $0 \leq \alpha \leq 1$. As in the previous case, by axiom 3, $\langle \alpha, f_1, f_2 \rangle \prec \langle \alpha, g_1, f_2 \rangle$ and $\langle \alpha, g_1, f_2 \rangle \preceq \langle \alpha, g_1, g_2 \rangle$ which means that $\langle \alpha, f_1, f_2 \rangle \prec \langle \alpha, g_1, g_2 \rangle$. Therefore, also axiom 8 holds.

The following lemma goes in the opposite direction, however to obtain axiom 3 from 2, 7, and 8 we require $\preceq$ to be a total preorder.

Lemma 2. *Axioms 1, 2, 7, and 8 imply axiom 3.*

Proof. Let h be a lottery and $0 \leq \alpha \leq 1$. Let $f_1 = f$, $g_1 = g$ and $f_2 = g_2 = h$, if $f \preceq g$, then by axiom 7 we have that $\langle \alpha, f, h \rangle \preceq \langle \alpha, g, h \rangle$.

Conversely, assume that for some gamble h and $0 \leq \alpha \leq 1$, $\langle \alpha, f, h \rangle \preceq \langle \alpha, f, h \rangle$. We apply the contrapositive of axiom 8, from $\langle \alpha, g, h \rangle \not\prec \langle \beta, f, h \rangle$ we obtain $g \not\prec f$. Then, since $\preceq$ is a total relation, it holds that $f \preceq g$.

The following two lemmas concern axioms 4 and 9. As expected, axiom 9 defines a stronger notion of continuity which alone suffices to derive axiom 4. Conversely, we can get axiom 9 back from 4 with the help of totality and the strict substitution principle.

Lemma 3. *Axioms 1, 8 and 4 imply axiom 9.*

---

[3] Notice that, at the best of our knowledge, such an analysis of axioms' interdependencies has not been shown elsewhere. In particular, it will also used in Section 4 to show the hierarchical nature of partial preferences.

Proof. Assume $h \preceq f \preceq g$, notice that if $h \sim f$ (resp. $f \sim g$) axiom 9 trivially holds with $\alpha = 0$ (resp. $\alpha = 1$). It remains the case $h \prec f \prec g$. Let $A = \{\alpha \in [0,1] \mid f \prec \langle \alpha, g, h \rangle\}$ and $B = \{\alpha \in [0,1] \mid \langle \alpha, g, h \rangle \prec f\}$. Clearly, $A \cap B = \emptyset$, $1 \in A$ and $0 \in B$.

Assume that β_1 and β_2 are in A and $\beta_1 < \beta_2$, this means that $f \prec h_1$ and $f \prec h_2$ where $h_1 = \langle \beta_1, g, h \rangle$ and $h_2 = \langle \beta_2, g, h \rangle$. It is easy to verify that for each $\beta_1 \leq \beta \leq \beta_2$, there exists an $0 \leq \alpha' \leq 1$ such that $\langle \beta, g, h \rangle = \langle \alpha', h_1, h_2 \rangle$. Then, by applying axiom 8 with $f_1 = f_2 = f$, $g_1 = h_1$, and $g_2 = h_2$, it holds that $f \prec \langle \alpha', h_1, h_2 \rangle$. Consequently, A is an interval of $[0,1]$. Similarly, it can be shown that B is an interval as well.

Let δ be the greatest lower bound of A and γ the least upper bound of B – clearly, the least upper bound of A is 1 and the greatest lower bound of B is 0. In case $\gamma < \delta$, by the totality axiom we would have that for all $\lambda \in (\gamma, \delta)$ $f \sim \langle \lambda, g, h \rangle$ and hence the thesis. Assume then that $\gamma = \delta$. Let $k = \langle \gamma, g, h \rangle$, notice that for each $0 < \alpha' < 1$, $\langle \alpha', k, h \rangle \prec f$ and $f \prec \langle \alpha', g, k \rangle$, then by axiom 4 $f \nprec k$ and $k \nprec f$. By totality, $f \nprec k$ implies $k \preceq f$ and $k \nprec f$ implies $f \preceq k$, consequently $f \sim k$ and hence the thesis.

Lemma 4. *Axiom 9 implies axiom 4.*

Proof. By contradiction, assume that $f \prec h$ and for all $0 < \alpha' < 1$, $h \prec \langle \alpha', f, g \rangle$. Let $k = \langle \alpha, f, g \rangle$, for some $0 < \alpha < 1$. since $f \prec h$ and $h \prec k$, by axiom 9 there exists a $\beta \in [0,1]$ such that $h \sim \langle \beta, f, k \rangle$. Therefore, we have that $h \sim \langle \gamma, f, g \rangle$, where $\gamma = \beta + (1 - \beta)\alpha$ belongs to the interval $[\alpha, 1]$. This is a contradiction because for all $\alpha' \in [\alpha, 1)$ $h \prec \langle \alpha', f, g \rangle$ and for $\alpha' = 1$, $f \prec h$.

Analogously, it can be proved that if for all $0 < \alpha' < 1$, $\langle \alpha', f, g \rangle \prec h$, then $h \nprec g$. Consequently, axiom 4 holds.

As final result, we use the previous lemmas to show that CDT_0, CDT_1, CDT_2, and CDT_3 are variants of the same theory.

Theorem 1. *Theories CDT_0, CDT_1, CDT_2, and CDT_3 are equivalent.*

Proof. Let $\preceq$ be a relation satisfying CDT_0. By the definition of CDT_0 and Lemma 2, $\preceq$ satisfies axiom 3 and hence CDT_1. Assume now that $\preceq$ satisfies CDT_1, by Lemma 1 $\preceq$ satisfies axioms 1, 8, and 4. Therefore, due to Lemma 3, $\preceq$ also satisfies axiom 9 and hence CDT_3. In turn, if $\preceq$ satisfies CDT_3, by applying Lemma 1, it satisfies CDT_2 as well. Finally, Lemma 4 assures that each $\preceq$ satisfying CDT_2 satisfies CDT_0 as well. In summary, it holds that

$$CDT_0 \geq CDT_1 \geq CDT_3 \geq CDT_2 \geq CDT_0.$$

Consequently, these formalizations are all equivalent.

4   Partial Preferences

In this section we assume that outcomes may be incomparable and subsequently preference relations are modelled as (possibly partial) preorders. For this reason, we weaken the totality in favour of reflexivity:

1'. $f \preceq f$;

In particular, we focus on the theories PDT_0, PDT_1, PDT_2 and PDT_3 obtained by replacing axiom 1 with 1' in CDT_0, CDT_1, CDT_2 and CDT_3, respectively.

It is worth noting that the proof of CDT_0–CDT_3 equivalence makes use of axiom 1 in Lemmas 2 and 3. We show that by weakening totality with reflexivity PDT_0–PDT_3 are no longer equivalent. Lemma 5 simply applies Lemma 1 and 4 to reveal the entailment relations among PDT_0–PDT_3.

Lemma 5. *The following conditions hold: (i) $PDT_0 \leq PDT_1$, (ii) $PDT_0 \leq PDT_2$, (iii) $PDT_1 \leq PDT_3$, and (iv) $PDT_2 \leq PDT_3$.*

Proof. Conditions (i) and (iv) are a direct consequence of Lemma 1, whereas conditions (ii) and (iii) derives from Lemma 4.

The following Lemmas 6–9 show that the entailment relations in Lemma 5 are actually strict.

Lemma 6. *There exists a preference relation that satisfies PDT_1 and does not satisfy axiom 9. Consequently, PDT_1 does not entail PDT_2 and PDT_3.*

Proof. Let $\mathcal{A} = \{a, b, c\}$ and $\preceq$ be the preference relation $\preceq$ satisfying the following two conditions:

1. $f \sim g$ iff $f = g$;
2. $f \prec g$ iff $f(a) < g(a)$.

First, we show that that $\preceq$ satisfies PDT_1. Reflexivity and transitivity are immediate. With respect to axiom 3, we distinguish two cases. The first case concerns condition 1. For all $\alpha \in [0, 1]$ and $\forall h \in \Delta(\mathcal{A})$, the following chain of implications holds:

$$f \sim g \Leftrightarrow f = g$$
$$f = g \Leftrightarrow \langle \alpha, f, h \rangle = \langle \alpha, g, h \rangle$$
$$\langle \alpha, f, h \rangle = \langle \alpha, g, h \rangle \Leftrightarrow \langle \alpha, f, h \rangle \sim \langle \alpha, g, h \rangle.$$

The second case takes into account condition 2, in particular for all $\alpha \in [0, 1]$ and $h \in \Delta(\mathcal{A})$

$$f \prec g \Leftrightarrow f(a) < g(a)$$
$$f(a) < g(a) \Leftrightarrow \alpha f(a) + (1 - \alpha)h(a) < \alpha g(a) + (1 - \alpha)h(a) \Leftrightarrow \langle \alpha, f, h \rangle \prec \langle \alpha, g, h \rangle.$$

With respect to axiom 4, *per absurdum* assume that for each $\alpha \in (0, 1)$, $h \prec \langle \alpha, f, g \rangle$ and $f \prec h$. On the one hand, $f \prec h$ implies $f(a) < h(a)$, that is $h(a) = f(a) + \delta$, with $\delta > 0$. On the other hand, for each $0 < \alpha < 1$, $h(a) < \alpha f(a) + (1 - \alpha)g(a)$. Now, let $\gamma = \frac{g(a) - f(a) - \delta}{g(a) - f(a)}$. Since $\delta > 0$, we have $\gamma < 1$. Moreover, it is easy to verify that $\alpha f(a) + (1 - \alpha)g(a) < h(a)$, for all $\gamma < \alpha < 1$, a contradiction. Analogously, it can be proved that if for each $\alpha \in (0, 1)$, $\langle \alpha, f, g \rangle \prec h$, then $h \not\prec g$.

It remains to prove that $\preceq$ does not satisfy axiom 9. Let f, g and h be defined as follows:

$$g = \frac{1}{2}[a] + \frac{1}{2}[b] + 0[c]$$
$$f = 0[a] + 0[b] + 1[c]$$
$$h = \frac{1}{8}[a] + \frac{1}{4}[b] + \frac{5}{8}[c]$$

By condition 2, $f \prec h \prec g$ and by condition 1 $\langle \alpha, f, g \rangle \sim h$ iff $h = \langle \alpha, f, g \rangle$. However, a and b have the same probability in any convex combination of f and g, whereas they have different probabilities in h. This means that there does not exist an α such that $h = \langle \alpha, f, g \rangle$.

Lemma 7. *PDT_0 does not entail PDT_2.*

Proof. Consider the set of alternatives $\mathcal{A} = \{a, b, c\}$ and the preference relation $\preceq$ defined in Lemma 6. We already know that $\preceq$ satisfies PDT_1 and yet it does not satisfy axiom 9 and hence PDT_2. However, due to Lemma 5, $\preceq$ also satisfies PDT_0.

Lemma 8. *There exists a preference relation that satisfies PDT_2 and does not satisfy axiom 3. Consequently, PDT_2 does not entail PDT_1 and PDT_3.*

Proof. Let $\mathcal{A} = \{a, b\}$ and $\preceq$ be the preference relation defined as follows, for all $f, g \in \Delta(\mathcal{A})$,

$$f \preceq g \text{ iff } \frac{1}{g(b)} \leq \frac{1}{f(b)} \text{ or } f = g = [a].$$

Notice that, since $\frac{1}{0}$ is undefined, $[a]$ is comparable only with itself. Moreover, in case $f \neq [a]$ and $g \neq [a]$, we have that $g(b) - f(b) \geq 0$ (resp. $g(b) - f(b) > 0$) iff $f \preceq g$ (resp. $f \prec g$).

First, we show that all the axioms of PDT_2 are satisfied. Reflexivity and transitivity hold by construction. Assume that $f \prec g$ and $0 \leq \alpha < \beta \geq 1$. First, notice that neither f nor g are $[a]$, which is incomparable with all the other lotteries. Let $h = \langle \beta, f, g \rangle$ and $k = \langle \alpha, f, g \rangle$. It's straightforward to see that $h(b) - k(b) = (\beta - \alpha)(g(b) - f(b))$. Since $\beta > \alpha$ and $g(b) > f(b)$, $h(b) - k(b) > 0$, subsequently $\langle \alpha, f, g \rangle \prec \langle \beta, f, g \rangle$ and hence axiom 6 is satisfied.

Assume that $f_1 \preceq g_1$ and $f_2 \preceq g_2$. For some $0 \leq \alpha \leq 1$, let $h = \langle \alpha, f_1, f_2 \rangle$ and $k = \langle \alpha, g_1, g_2 \rangle$. Then, $h(b) - k(b) = \alpha(g_1(b) - f_1(b)) + (1 - \alpha)(g_2(b) - f_2(b))$. Now, consider the following four cases: Case 1) $f_1 = [a]$ and $f_2 = [a]$. In this case also $g_1 = g_2 = [a]$, therefore trivially $h \preceq k$. Case 2) $f_1 = [a]$ and $f_2 \neq [a]$. Then, $g_1 = [a]$ and $g_2 \neq [a]$ which means that both h and k are not $[a]$. Moreover, since $h(b) - k(b) = (1 - \alpha)(g_2(b) - f_2(b))$ and $g_2(b) - f_2(b)$ is a positive number by hypothesis, it holds that $h \preceq k$. Case 3) $f_1 \neq [a]$ and $f_2 = [a]$. Analogously to the previous case, it follows that $h(b) - k(b) = \alpha(g_1(b) - f_1(b)) \geq 0$, $h \preceq k$. Case 4) $f_1 \neq [a]$ and $f_2 \neq [a]$. This means that also $g_1 \neq [a]$ and $g_2 \neq [a]$ and hence both $g_1(b) - f_1(b)$ and $g_2(b) - f_2(b)$ are positive by construction. Then,

$h(b) - k(b) = \alpha(g_1(b) - f_1(b)) + (1 - \alpha)(g_2(b) - f_2(b)) \geq 0$, which means that $h \preceq k$. Since in all four cases $h \preceq k$, axiom 7 holds. Analogously, in can be shown that axiom 8 is satisfied as well.

Finally, let the antecedent of axiom 9 hold, $h \preceq f \preceq g$. If $h = [a]$, then f and g are equal to $[a]$ too, this means that any $\alpha \in [0, 1]$ verifies $f \sim \langle \alpha, g, h \rangle$. Therefore, assume that $h \neq [a]$ and consequently $0 < h(b) \leq f(b) \leq g(b) \leq 1$. We distinguish two cases. In the first case $h \sim g$, this means that $h(b) = g(b)$ and hence, as before, any $\alpha \in [0, 1]$ verifies $f \sim \langle \alpha, g, h \rangle$. In the second case, $h \prec g$ (equivalently $h(b) < g(b)$). Then, by setting $\alpha = \frac{f(b)-h(b)}{g(b)-h(b)}$, it is easy to verify that α belongs to the interval $[0, 1]$ and $\alpha h(b) + (1-\alpha)g(b) = f(b)$. Consequently, $f \sim \langle \alpha, g, h \rangle$.

It remains to prove that axiom 3 is not satisfied. Let $f = [a]$, $g = [b]$, $h = \frac{1}{2}[a] + \frac{1}{2}[b]$ and $\alpha = \frac{1}{2}$. We have that $\langle \alpha, f, h \rangle = \frac{3}{4}[a] + \frac{1}{4}[b]$ and $\langle \alpha, g, h \rangle = \frac{1}{4}[a] + \frac{3}{4}[b]$, consequently $\langle \alpha, f, h \rangle \preceq \langle \alpha, g, h \rangle$. However, since f and g are incomparable, $f \npreceq g$.

Lemma 9. PDT_0 *does not entail* PDT_1.

Proof. Consider $\mathcal{A}$ and $\preceq$ as defined in Lemma 8. We already know that $\preceq$ satisfies PDT_2 and yet it does not satisfy axiom 3 and hence PDT_1. However, due to Lemma 5, $\preceq$ also satisfies PDT_0.

Finally, Theorem 2 summarizes the previous lemmas.

Theorem 2. *The following relations hold:* $PDT_0 < PDT_1$, $PDT_0 < PDT_2$, $PDT_1 < PDT_3$, *and* $PDT_2 < PDT_3$. *Moreover, neither* $PDT_1 \leq PDT_2$ *nor* $PDT_2 \leq PDT_1$.

Theorem 2 shows that the four axiomatizations PDT_0–PDT_3 actually characterize different sets of preference relations. Clearly, this gives room to debate which of them is the most appropriate in general (if any) or with respect to a specific application domain. It is out of the scope of the present work to go further on foundational considerations, conversely we help fuel the debate by showing some formal properties. A first of such properties is provided by Theorem 2 itself, PDT_0–PDT_3 are not unrelated but lie in a hierarchy of strict entailments.

5   Common Properties of Partial Preferences

In this section, we show some properties that are valid in all PDT_0–PDT_3; as such, they cannot be used to advocate any of them. Clearly, due to Theorem 2, it will suffice to show that such properties hold in PDT_0.

Given two distributions $f, g \in \Delta(\mathcal{A})$, we write $f \to g$ in case there exist $\epsilon > 0$ and two alternatives a_1 and a_2 such that *(i)* $[a_1] \prec [a_2]$, *(ii)* $g(a_1) = f(a_1) - \epsilon$, $g(a_2) = f(a_2) + \epsilon$, and *(iii)* for all $a \neq a_1, a_2$, $g(a) = f(a)$. Informally, when $f \to g$, g can be obtained from f by shifting a positive amount of probability from an alternative a_1 to a strictly preferred alternative a_2. Then, denote by $f \Rightarrow g$ the transitive closure of $\to$.

Theorem 3. *Let $\preceq$ be a preference relation satisfying PDT_0 and $f, g \in \Delta(\mathcal{A})$. If $f \Rightarrow g$, then $f \prec g$.*

Proof. It suffices to show that $f \rightarrow g$ implies $f \prec g$. Assume that for some a_1 and a_2, where $[a_1] \prec [a_2]$, there exists $\epsilon > 0$ such that $f(a_1) = g(a_1) + \epsilon$ and $f(a_2) = g(a_2) - \epsilon$. Let $\gamma = g(a_1) + g(a_2) = f(a_1) + f(a_2)$, $\alpha = \frac{f(a_2)}{\gamma}$ and $\beta = \frac{g(a_2)}{\gamma}$. Then, g can be written as $\langle \gamma, g', h \rangle$ and f as $\langle \gamma, f', h \rangle$, where h is a probability distribution such that $h(a_1) = h(a_2) = 0$, $g' = \langle \beta, [a_2], [a_1] \rangle$ and $f' = \langle \alpha, [a_2], [a_1] \rangle$. Since $[a_1] \prec [a_2]$ and $\alpha < \beta$, Axiom 6 implies that $f' \prec g'$. Then, due to Axiom 8, $f \prec g$. $\blacksquare$

Another property that can be proved in PDT_0 is dominance: if each alternative coming from a distribution f is worse than all the alternatives from g, then $f \preceq g$. Preliminarily, given a distribution $f \in \Delta(\mathcal{A})$, the *support* of f, $supp(f) = \{a \in \mathcal{A} \mid f(a) > 0\}$, is the set of alternatives to which f assigns positive probability.

Theorem 4. *Let $\preceq$ be a preference relation satisfying PDT_0 and $f, g \in \Delta(\mathcal{A})$. If $[a] \preceq [a']$, for all $a \in supp(f)$ and $a' \in supp(g)$, then $f \preceq g$.*

Proof. We first show that for all $a \in supp(f)$, $[a] \preceq g$. The proof is by induction on the cardinality n of $supp(g)$ where the case $n = 1$ is trivial. Assume $n > 1$, then g can be written as $\langle \alpha, [a'], g' \rangle$, where a' is a generic alternative from $supp(g)$ and $g'(a') = 0$. Clearly, the distribution $[a]$ can also be written as $\langle \alpha, [a], [a] \rangle$. By assumption $a \preceq a'$ and, since the cardinality of g' is $n - 1$, by induction $[a] \preceq g'$. Then, by applying Axiom 7 we have $[a] \preceq g$.

Now, the proof is by induction on the cardinality m of $supp(f)$ where the base case $m = 1$ has been proved above. Assume $m > 1$ and let $a \in supp(f)$, then f can be written as $\langle \alpha, [a], f_{-a} \rangle$, where $f_{-a}(a) = 0$ and $f_{-a}(a') = \frac{f(a')}{1 - f(a)}$ for all $a' \in supp(f) \setminus \{a\}$. We already proved that $[a] \preceq g$ and by induction hypothesis it holds also that $f_{-a} \preceq g$. Then, by writing g as $\langle \alpha, g, g \rangle$ and applying Axiom 7 we have that $f \preceq g$. $\blacksquare$

From Theorem 4, it is immediate to show that distributions over equivalent alternatives are equivalent themselves.

Corollary 1. *Let $\mathcal{A}' \subseteq \mathcal{A}$ be a subset of alternatives such that $[a_1] \sim [a_2]$, for all $a_1, a_2 \in \mathcal{A}'$. Then, for all lotteries f and g, if $supp(f) \subseteq \mathcal{A}'$ and $supp(g) \subseteq \mathcal{A}'$, then $f \sim g$.*

6 The Justification Axiom

Clearly, by assuming possibly incomplete preferences, besides totality, some other properties are lost too. Thus, an important issue is whether it is worth regaining some of them. For instance, assume that f and g are incomparable lotteries and let $0 \leq \alpha < \beta \leq 1$. Then, is it admissible that $\langle \alpha, f, g \rangle \prec \langle \beta, f, g \rangle$? In [5] it has been advocated that this may look inappropriate and, to some extent, the incomparability between distributions should persist also when they are combined. For this reason a further axiom is considered:

10. if $0 \leq \alpha \leq 1$, and $\langle \alpha, f_1, f_2 \rangle \prec \langle \alpha, g_1, g_2 \rangle$, then there exist $j, k \in \{1, 2\}$ such that $f_j \prec g_k$.

Informally, the lottery $\langle \alpha, f_1, f_2 \rangle$ can be seen as a random choice which picks f_1 with probability α and f_2 with probability $1 - \alpha$. Comparing $\langle \alpha, f_1, f_2 \rangle$ with another lottery $\langle \alpha, g_1, g_2 \rangle$ involves comparing four possible draws: (f_1, g_1), (f_1, g_2), (f_2, g_1), and (f_2, g_2).[4] If there is no draw in which the second component is strictly better than the first one, axiom 10 requires that $\langle \alpha, g_1, g_2 \rangle$ is not strictly preferred to $\langle \alpha, f_1, f_2 \rangle$.

In the perspective of the user-agent interaction, axiom 10 can be also seen as follows: assume that the user tells the agent that $\frac{1}{2}[a] + \frac{1}{2}[b]$ is strictly preferred to $\frac{1}{2}[c] + \frac{1}{2}[d]$. According to axiom 10, then, the agent will ask the user to justify this claim in terms of degenerate lotteries. Consequently, such an axiom establishes a bottom-up direction where the agent expects to be instructed on the simple alternatives first and then on more complex lotteries.

The following theorem tells us that axiom 10 is independent from PDT_0–PDT_3. Clearly, it suffices to show that axiom 10 is not entailed by PDT_3.

Theorem 5. *There exists a preference relation that satisfies PDT_3 and does not satisfy axiom 10.*

Proof. We have to show that there exists a preference relation that satisfies PDT_3 and does not satisfy axiom 10. Let $\mathcal{A} = \{a, b, c\}$ and $\preceq$ be the preference relation defined as follows:

1. $f \sim g$ iff $f = g$;
2. $f \prec g$ iff $f(c) = g(c)$ and $f(b) < g(b)$.

First, we show that $\preceq$ satisfies PDT_3. Axioms 1 and 2 are trivial. Regarding axiom 3, given a real number $\alpha \in [0, 1]$ and a lottery $h \in \Delta(\mathcal{A})$, let $k_1 = \langle \alpha, f, h \rangle$ and $k_2 = \langle \alpha, g, h \rangle$. By condition 1, it holds that:

$$f \sim g \Leftrightarrow f = g \Leftrightarrow k_1 = k_2 \Leftrightarrow k_1 \sim k_2.$$

Moreover, by condition 2, we also have that $f \prec g$ iff $f(c) = g(c)$ and $f(b) < g(b)$ iff $k_1(c) = k_2(c)$ and $k_1(b) < k_2(b)$ iff $k_1 \prec k_2$. Therefore, axiom 3 is satisfied.

With respect to axiom 9, if $f \sim g$ (resp. $h \sim f$), then f is trivially equivalent to a convex $\langle \alpha, h, g \rangle$ with $\alpha = 0$ (resp. $\alpha = 1$). Therefore, assume that $h \prec f \prec g$. In this case, by construction, $h(c)$, $f(c)$, and $g(c)$ are the same value v. This means that the projection of h, f and g on the alternatives a and b lie on the same straight line given by the equation $x + y = 1 - v$. Consequently, it is straightforward to see that

$$\alpha = \frac{g(b) - f(b)}{g(b) - h(b)}$$

makes $f = \langle \alpha, h, g \rangle$. Moreover, since $h(b) < f(b) < g(b)$, α is in the interval $(0, 1)$. Consequently, axiom 9 is satisfied by $\preceq$. It remains to show that $\preceq$ does

---

[4] With probabilities α^2, $\alpha(1 - \alpha)$, $\alpha(1 - \alpha)$ and $(1 - \alpha)^2$, respectively.

not satisfy Axiom 10. Let f_1, f_2, g_1, and g_2 be the following lotteries:

$$f_1 = \frac{7}{40}[a] + \frac{1}{8}[b] + \frac{7}{10}[c]$$

$$f_2 = \frac{23}{40}[a] + \frac{1}{8}[b] + \frac{3}{10}[c]$$

$$g_1 = \frac{1}{8}[a] + \frac{1}{4}[b] + \frac{5}{8}[c]$$

$$g_2 = \frac{3}{8}[a] + \frac{1}{4}[b] + \frac{3}{8}[c]$$

Let f be $\langle\frac{1}{2}, f_1, f_2\rangle$ and g be $\langle\frac{1}{2}, g_1, g_2\rangle$. Notice that for each $i, j \in \{1, 2\}$, $f_i(c) \neq g_j(c)$ which means that f_i and g_j are incomparable. However, it is straightforward to see that

$$f = \frac{3}{8}[a] + \frac{1}{8}[b] + \frac{1}{2}[c]$$

$$g = \frac{1}{4}[a] + \frac{1}{4}[b] + \frac{1}{2}[c]$$

and hence, by construction, $f \prec g$.

Axiom 10 assures that if the supports of two lotteries f and g are pairwise incomparable, then no strict preference between f and g can be derived. In what follows $f \nleq g$ means that f and g are incomparable according to a partial preference $\preceq$.

Lemma 10. *Let $f, g \in \Delta(\mathcal{A})$ be such that, for all $a \in supp(f)$ and $a' \in supp(g)$, $[a] \nleq [a']$. Then, either $f \nleq g$ or $f \sim g$.*

Proof. Let $n_f = |supp(f)|$ and $n_g = |supp(g)|$, we proceed by induction on $n_f + n_g$. If $n_f + n_g = 2$, the thesis is obviously true. Otherwise, assume w.l.o.g. that $n_f > 1$ and let $a \in supp(f)$. We can write f as $\langle f(a), [a], f_{-a}\rangle$, where $f_{-a}(a) = 0$ and $f_{-a}(a') = \frac{f(a')}{1-f(a)}$ for all $a' \in supp(f) \setminus \{a\}$. Since the support of f_{-a} is smaller than the one of f, we can apply the inductive hypothesis to the pair f_{-a}, g, obtaining that either $f_{-a} \nleq g$ or $f_{-a} \sim g$. We can also apply the inductive hypothesis to the pair $[a], g$, obtaining that $[a] \nleq g$ or $[a] \sim g$. Assume by contradiction that $f \bowtie g$ for some $\bowtie \in \{\prec, \succ\}$. By axiom 10, it holds $[a] \bowtie g$ or $f_{-a} \bowtie g$, which is a contradiction.

Finally, the following generalization of Lemma 10 shows that alternatives that are either incomparable or equivalent lead to distributions that are themselves either incomparable or equivalent.

Theorem 6. *Let $f, g \in \Delta(\mathcal{A})$ be such that, for all $a \in supp(f)$ and $a' \in supp(g)$, either $[a] \sim [a']$ or $[a] \nleq [a']$. Then, $f \nleq g$ or $f \sim g$.*

Proof. The proof is very similar to the one of Lemma 10, where only the base case is affected by the weakened assumption.

Finally, axiom 10 has been motivated above by analysing which preferences between $f = \langle \alpha, f_1, f_2 \rangle$ and $g = \langle \alpha, g_1, g_2 \rangle$ are admissible on the basis of the preferences on the possible draws (f_1, g_1), (f_1, g_2), (f_2, g_1), and (f_2, g_2). In Table 2 we perform such an analysis extensively. In particular, for each entry, the left-hand side $\bowtie_1 \bowtie_2 \bowtie_3 \bowtie_4$, with $\bowtie \in \{\sim, \prec, \succ, \lesssim\}$, is a consistent combination $f_1 \bowtie_1 g_1$, $f_1 \bowtie_2 g_2$, $f_2 \bowtie_3 g_1$, and $f_2 \bowtie_4 g_2$, whereas the right-hand side shows which preference relations between f and g are consistent with PDT_0 plus axiom 10.[5] For example, the first entry is the case $f_1 \sim g_1$, $f_1 \sim g_2$, $f_2 \sim g_1$, and $f_2 \sim g_2$, then according to axiom 7, $f \sim g$ is the only possibility. Conversely, in some

Table 2. Extensive analysis of axiom 10 in PDT_0.

---

[5] Table 2 has been generate automatically via a Prolog program.

other cases (e.g. $\prec\npreceq\succ\npreceq$) no axiom can be applied, consequently f can be in any relationship with g.

Table 2 provides a close look on how the considered axioms propagate a preference under convex combinations. In some cases f and g are comparable even if some of the underlying draws are not so (e.g. $\prec\npreceq\npreceq\sim$ results in $f \prec g$). Somewhat conversely, f and g can be incomparable even if all the underlying draws are comparable (e.g. $\prec\succ\prec\succ$ admits $f \npreceq g$).

7 Related Works

In Decision Theory, a theoretical investigation on partial preferences can be found in [2,3,8]. Differently from our aim to compare different formulations, each of these works considers a specific axiomatic system and investigates whether utility functions can be used to represent partial preferences and how they have to be generalized to gain a (sort of) Expected Utility Theorem back. In particular, the axiomatic system in [3] is essentially PDT_1, whereas it can been seen that the one used in [8] entails PDT_3. Therefore, it is a natural question whether some notion of generalized utility can be developed also for PDT_0.

Recently, partial preferences have been employed in procurement auctions modelling multi-cloud provisioning scenarios [1,4,6]. Somewhat surprisingly, it has been shown that extending second price auctions to partial preferences does not yield truthful mechanisms, since overbidding may be profitable in some contexts. This means that partial preferences may significantly change the theoretical properties of a mechanism. However, in these works partial preferences have been defined as *ad hoc* conditions over bids.[6] Therefore, we are confident that the axiomatizations presented in this work enable to employ partial preferences uniformly in the field of Mechanism Design and to estimate their impact.

Finally, the present paper starts from the seminal extended abstract [5] where, at the best of our knowledge, the justification axiom has been taken into consideration for the first time. Here, we generalize and extend [5] in several aspects. First, in [5] a single axiomatic system is considered whereas here we focus on comparing different axiomatic systems and show they are not equivalent. Secondly, we complete [5], where no continuity axiom is present, by considering two different notions of continuity. Finally, we prove that the justification property cannot be derived from the previously considered axioms and hence has to be taken as an independent axiom.

8 Conclusions

In this work we challenged the customary decision-theoretic assumption of totality of the preference relations, on the basis of two real-world scenarios. This is not a straightforward task, since different formalizations of the classical theory,

---

[6] Actually, what is referred to as *preference* in [1] is rather a notion of dominance among strategies.

once totality is weakened in favour of reflexivity, are no longer equivalent. We delineated a complete hierarchy for four different axiomatizations PDT_0–PDT_3 on the basis of standard entailment. We have also shown that some basic notions, such as dominance, are still valid also in the weaker axiomatizations of partial preferences. Somewhat conversely, we identified a classical property that cannot be derived PDT_0–PDT_3 (and hence it has to be bought as an independent axiom). On the one hand, we show that such a property grasps possibly desirable conditions on how incomparability propagates over lotteries; on the other hand, it delineates an agent-user interface where, even if the latter is not required to provide a complete preference, the former may ask to justify some instructions when they seems to be groundless.

References

1. Anisetti, M., Ardagna, C.A., Bonatti, P.A., Damiani, E., Faella, M., Galdi, C., Sauro, L.: E-Auctions for multi-cloud service provisioning. In: Proc. of the IEEE International Conf. on Services Computing, SCC 2014, Anchorage, AK, USA, 27 June–2 July 2014
2. Aumann, R.J.: Subjective programming. Econometric Res. Prog. Re-search memorandum vol. 22, Princeton University (1961). Also in Shelly, M.W., Bryan, G.L., (eds.) Human judgments and optimality. Wiley, New York (1964)
3. Aumann, R.J.: Utility Theory without the Completeness Axiom. Econometrica **30**(3), 445–462 (1962)
4. Bonatti, P.A., Faella, M., Galdi, C., Sauro, L.: Towards a mechanism for incentivating privacy. In: Atluri, V., Diaz, C. (eds.) ESORICS 2011. LNCS, vol. 6879, pp. 472–488. Springer, Heidelberg (2011)
5. Bonatti, P.A., Faella, M., Sauro, L.: Partial preferences for mediated bargaining. In: Proc. of the 2nd International Workshop on Strategic Reasoning, SR14, Grenoble, France, 5–6 April 2014
6. Bonatti, P.A., Faella, M., Galdi, C., Sauro, L.: Auctions for partial heterogeneous preferences. In: Proc. of Mathematical Foundations of Computer Science 2013–38th International Symposium, MFCS 2013, Klosterneuburg, Austria, 26–30 August 2013
7. Boutilier, C., Brafman, R.I., Domshlak, C., Hoos, H.H.: CP-nets: A Tool for Representing and Reasoning with Conditional Ceteris Paribus Preference Statements. Journal of Articial Intelligence Research **21**, 135–191 (2004)
8. Dubra, J., Maccheroni, F., Ok, E.A.: Expected utility theory without the completeness axiom. Journal of Economic Theory **115**(1), 118–133 (2004)
9. Myerson, R.B.: Game Theory: Analysis of Conict. Harvard University Press (1997)
10. van Neumann, J., Morgenstern, O.: Theory of Games and Economic Behavior. Princeton University Press (1994)
11. Savage, L.J.: The Foundations of Statistics. Wiley, NewYork (1954)
12. Simon, H.: A Behavioral Model of Rational Choice. Q. J. Econ. **69**(1), 99–118 (1955). doi:10.2307/1884852

Verification of Asynchronous Mobile-Robots in Partially-Known Environments

Sasha Rubin[2], Florian Zuleger[1]($\boxtimes$), Aniello Murano[2], and Benjamin Aminof[1]

[1] Technische Universität Wien, Vienna, Austria
zuleger@forsyte.at
[2] Università Degli Studi di Napoli "Federico II", Naples, Italy

Abstract. This paper establishes a framework based on logic and automata theory in which to model and automatically verify that multiple mobile robots, with sensing abilities, moving asynchronously, correctly perform their tasks. The motivation is from practical scenarios in which the environment is not completely know to the robots, e.g., physical robots exploring a maze, or software agents exploring a hostile network. The framework shows how to express tasks in a logical language, and exhibits an algorithm solving the *parameterised* verification problem, where the graphs are treated as the parameter. The main assumption that yields decidability is that the robots take a bounded number of turns. We prove that dropping this assumption results in undecidability, even for robots with very limited ("local") sensing abilities.

1 Introduction

Autonomous mobile robots are designed to achieve some task in an environment without a central control. Foundational tasks include, for example, rendezvous (gather all robots in a single position) and reconfiguration (move to a new configuration in a collision-free way) [14,15,25]. This paper studies robots in *partially known* environments, i.e., robots do not have global information about the environment, but may know some (often topological) information (e.g., whether the environment is connected, or that it is a ring of some unknown size) [14]. The motivation for studying partially known environments is that in many practical scenarios the robots are unaware of the exact environment in which they are operating, e.g., mobile software exploring a hostile computer network, or physical robots that rendezvous in an environment not reachable by humans.

To illustrate, here is an *example reconfiguration problem.* Suppose that k robots find themselves on different internal nodes of a binary tree, and each robot has to reach a different leaf in a collision free way. Each robot can sense

---

Benjamin Aminof and Florian Zuleger were supported by the Austrian National Research Network S11403-N23 (RiSE) of the Austrian Science Fund (FWF) and by the Vienna Science and Technology Fund (WWTF) through grant ICT12-059. Aniello Murano was supported by FP7 EU project 600958-SHERPA. Sasha Rubin is a Marie Curie fellow of the Istituto Nazionale di Alta Matematica.

© Springer International Publishing Switzerland 2015
Q. Chen et al. (Eds.): PRIMA 2015, LNAI 9387, pp. 185–200, 2015.
DOI: 10.1007/978-3-319-25524-8_12

if its left (or right) child is occupied by a robot. One protocol for solving this problem (assuming a large enough tree) is for each robot to execute 'go to the left child, then repeatedly go the right child' until a leaf is reached. Each move is guarded by a test that the child it wants to move to is not currently occupied.

As the example illustrates, we make the following modeling choices: environments are discrete (rather than continuous), robots have finite memory (rather than being oblivious, or being Turing powerful), robots are nondeterministic (rather than probabilistic), robots move asynchronously (rather than synchronously), and robots can sense the positions and the internal states of each robot no matter where they are, i.e., they can perform "remote" tests (but cannot leave information at visited positions).[1] The assumption that robots move asynchronously is motivated as follows: processes in distributed systems have no common notion of time since they may be running with different internal clocks, and thus a standard abstraction is to assume that processes' actions are interleaved, see [26]. There are two main ways to interleave the robots: an adversary tries to make sure that the robots do not succeed [16], and a co-operator tries to help the robots succeed (reminiscent of schedulers in strategic reasoning [7]).

In this paper we provide a framework for modeling and verifying that multiple mobile robots achieve a task (under adversarial and co-operative interleavings) in a partially-known environment. We now explain how we model the fact that environments are partially-known. Fix a class $\mathcal{G}$ of environments (e.g., $\mathcal{G}$ is the set of all lines, or all grids, or all rings). The *parameterised verification problem* states: Given robots $\overline{R}$, decide if they solve the task T on all graphs $G \in \mathcal{G}$. Requiring the robots to solve the task T on all graphs from a class $\mathcal{G}$ is how we model that the robots operate in partially-known environments — the robots know they are in a graph from $\mathcal{G}$, but they do not know which one. In contrast, the classic (non-parameterised) verification problem states: Given robots $\overline{R}$ and a graph $G \in \mathcal{G}$, decide if robots $\overline{R}$ solve the task T on G. In that setting, the robots can be designed to exploit the exact structure (size, etc.) of the graph.

Aims and Contributions. The aim of this work it to provide a formal framework in which one can reason (both mathematically and computationally) about multiple mobile-robots, with sensing abilities, moving asynchronously in a discrete, static, partially-known environment. We prove that parameterised verification is undecidable already for line-environments, and even for robots with limited tasks (e.g., halting) which can only detect collisions. I.e., a robot can only sense which other robots share its current position. This undecidability result also holds for robots that move synchronously. On the other hand, we prove that parameterised verification is decidable for scenarios in which the number of times that the robots take turns is bounded.[2] This decidability result is very robust:

---

[1] The ability to sense positions is a form of vision, while the ability to sense internal states is a form of communication

[2] In the example reconfiguration problem, there is some ordering of the robots that switches turns at most k times in which the stated robot-protocol succeeds. Also, for every ordering of the robots that switches turns a sufficiently large number of times, the protocol succeeds ("ordering" and "switching" are formalised in Section 3).

it holds on a very general class of graphs called *context-free sets of graphs* which include e.g., rings, trees, series-parallel graphs, but not grids; it also holds with very powerful abilities called *position-tests* which allow each robot to remotely test the positions of all the robots using formulas which include, e.g., the ability to test connectivity, as well as *state-tests* that allow each robot to remotely test the internal state of the other robots; it holds for tasks that are expressible using a new logic MRTL (Multiple-Robot Task Logic), which can express many natural tasks, e.g., reconfiguration, gathering, and "safe" variations (i.e., complete the task without touching dangerous positions).

Related Work. The work closest to ours is [30] which also considered the parameterised verification problem for multi-robot systems. However, in that paper, the decidability result (and the corresponding logic RTL) was only for one-robot systems (i.e., $k = 1$), and the undecidability result for $k = 2$ was for multiple robots that move *synchronously* and have *remote* tests.

The distributed-computing community has proposed and studied a number of models of robot systems, e.g., recently [8,10,13,17,18,24]. This literature is mostly mathematical, and *theorems from this literature are parameterised*, i.e., they may involve graph-parameters (e.g., the maximum degree, the number of vertices, the diameter), memory parameters (e.g., the number of internal states of the robot protocol), and the number of robots may be a parameter. Only recently has there been emphasis on formal analysis of correctness of robots in a parameterised setting [4,22,23,27,29,30]. In these formal analyses, typically it is the *number of agents* that is treated as the parameter [4,22,23,27]. In contrast, in this paper (as in [30]) we apply formal methods to the parameterised verification problem in which it is the *environment that is parameterised*.

Also, the formal-verification community has placed emphasis on distributed models in which processes are stationary and interact by sending messages (e.g., in a broadcast or rendezvous manner) or by using guarded commands. The parameterised verification problem for such distributed processes is, in general, undecidable [31]. By simplifying the systems (e.g., restricting the mode of communication, the abilities of the processes, the specification languages, etc.) one can get decidable parameterised verification, recently e.g., [1–3,12].

We refer the reader to [30, Section 7] for an up-to-date and detailed discussion of the connections between multi-robot systems, classic automata theory (i.e., graph-walking automata) and distributed systems (in particular, token-passing systems). Finally, we mention that there is a smattering of work on parameterised *synthesis* (called *generalised planning* in the AI literature) [11,19–21].

2 Background: Automata Theory

Write B^* and B^ω for the sets of finite and infinite sequences over alphabet B, respectively. The empty sequence is denoted ϵ. Write $[n]$ for the set $\{1, 2, \cdots, n\}$.

Graphs and Trees. A Σ-*graph*, or *graph*, G, is a tuple (V, E, Σ, λ) where V is a finite set of *vertices*, $E \subseteq V \times V$ is the *edge relation*, Σ is a finite set of *edge* *labels*, and $\lambda : E \to \Sigma$ is the *edge labeling function*. A Δ-*ary tree* (for $\Delta \in \mathbb{N}$) is a Σ-graph (V, E, Σ, λ) where (V, E) is a tree, $\Sigma = [\Delta] \cup \{up\}$, and λ labels the edge leading to the node in direction i (if it exists) by i, and the edge leading to the parent of a node (other than the root) is labelled by up. We may rename the labels for convenience, e.g., for binary trees ($\Delta = 2$) we let $\Sigma = \{lc, rc, up\}$ where lc replaces 1 and rc replaces 2.

Monadic Second-Order Logic. Formulas are interpreted in Σ-graphs G. Define the set of monadic second-order formulas $\mathsf{MSOL}(\Sigma)$ as follows. Formulas of $\mathsf{MSOL}(\Sigma)$ are built using *first-order variables* $x, y, \cdots$ that vary over vertices, and *set variables* $X, Y, \cdots$ that vary over sets of vertices. The *atomic formulas* (when interpreted over Σ-graphs) are: $x = y$ (denoting that vertex x is the same as vertex y), $x \in X$ (denoting that vertex x is in the set of vertices X), $edg_\sigma(x, y)$ (denoting that there is an edge from x to y labeled $\sigma \in \Sigma$) and true (the formula that is always true). The formulas of $\mathsf{MSOL}(\Sigma)$ are built from the atomic formulas using the Boolean connectives (i.e., $\neg, \vee, \wedge, \to$) and variable quantification (i.e., $\forall, \exists$ over both types of variables). A variable that is not quantified is called *free*. The fragment of $\mathsf{MSOL}(\Sigma)$ which does not mention set variables is called *first-order logic*, denoted $\mathsf{FOL}(\Sigma)$. Write $\mathsf{MSOL}_k(\Sigma)$ for formulas with at most k many free first-order variables and no free set-variables. We abbreviate $z_1, \cdots, z_k$ by $\overline{z}$. We write $\phi(x_1, \cdots, x_k)$ to mean that the free variables from the formula ϕ are amongst the set $\{x_1, \cdots, x_k\}$ – note that the formula $\phi(x_1, \cdots, x_k)$ does not need to use all of the variables $x_1, \cdots, x_k$. For a graph G, and $v_1, \cdots, v_k \in V$, we write $G \models \phi(v_1, \cdots, v_k)$ to mean that ϕ holds in G with variable x_i simultaneously substituted by vertex v_i (for all $i \in [k]$ for which x_i occurs free in ϕ). Here are some examples of formulas and their meanings: The formula $\forall x(x \in X \to x \in Y)$ means that $X \subseteq Y$. Similarly, there are formulas for the set operations $\cup, \cap, =$, and relative complement $X \setminus Y$. The formula $edg(x, y) := \bigvee_{\sigma \in \Sigma} edg_\sigma(x, y)$ means that there is an edge from x to y (here Σ is assumed to be finite). The formula $E^*(x, y) := \forall Z[(closed_E(Z) \wedge x \in Z) \to y \in Z]$ where $closed_E(Z)$ is $\forall a \forall b[(a \in Z \wedge E(a, b)) \to b \in Z]$ defines the transitive closure of E. Generally, MSOL can express the 1-ary transitive closure operator (e.g., [30]).

The Validity Problem and Courcelle's Theorem. A *sentence* is a formula with no free variables. Let Φ be a set of sentences, and let $\mathcal{G}$ be a set of graphs. The Φ-*validity problem of* $\mathcal{G}$ is to decide, given $\phi \in \Phi$, whether for all graphs $G \in \mathcal{G}$, it holds that $G \models \phi$. Unfortunately, the $\mathsf{MSOL}(\Sigma)$-validity problem for the set $\mathcal{G}$ of all Σ-graphs is undecidable. However, Courcelle's Theorem states that MSOL-validity of context-free sets of graphs is uniformly decidable, i.e., there is an algorithm that given a description of a context-free set of graphs $\mathcal{G}$ and an MSOL-sentence ϕ decides if every graph in $\mathcal{G}$ satisfies ϕ [9]. Context-free sets of graphs are the analogue of context-free sets of strings, and can be described by graph grammars, equations using certain graph operations, or MSOL-transductions of the set of trees. Formally, $\mathcal{G}$ is *context-free* if it is MSOL-definable and of bounded clique-width [9]. Examples include, for a fixed alphabet, the set of labeled lines, rings, trees, series-parallel graphs, cliques, but not the set of grids.

Automata and Regular Expressions. Ordinary *regular-expressions* over a finite alphabet B are built from the sets $\emptyset$, $\{\epsilon\}$, and $\{b\}$ ($b \in B$), and the operations union $+$, concatenation $\cdot$, and Kleene-star $*$. Kleene's Theorem states that the languages definable by regular expressions over alphabet B are exactly those recognised by finite automata over alphabet B. An ω-*regular expression* over alphabet B is inductively defined to be of the form: exp^ω, $exp \cdot r$, or $r + r'$, where exp is an ordinary regular-expression over B, and r, r' are ω-regular expressions over B. An ω-regular language is one defined by an ω-regular expression. A variation of Kleene's Theorem says that the languages definable by ω-regular expressions over alphabet B are exactly the languages recognised by Büchi automata over alphabet B (which are like finite automata except they take infinite words as input, and accept if some accepting state occurs infinitely often).

3   The Model of Robot Systems

In this section we provide a framework for modeling multi-robot systems parameterised by their environment. Environments are modeled as Σ-graphs G and robots are modeled as regular languages of instructions. An instruction either tells the robot to move along an edge, or to test robot positions (e.g., a robot can learn which other robots are at the same vertex as it is, or if there is a robot north of it). Tests are formalised as logical formulas.

Instructions for Robots. Fix a number k of robots and a set of edge labels Σ. A *command* is a symbol from $\{\uparrow_\sigma : \sigma \in \Sigma\} \cup \{\circlearrowleft\}$. The command $\uparrow_\sigma$ tells the robot to move from its current vertex along the edge labeled σ, and the command $\circlearrowleft$ tells the robot to stay at its current vertex. A *position-test* is a formula from $\mathsf{MSOL}_k(\Sigma)$. A *state-test* is an expression of the form "robot i is in state q", where $i \in [k]$ and q is a symbol denoting a state of a robot (formally we may assume that all robots have states from $\mathbb{N}$, and that $q \in \mathbb{N}$)[3]. A position test $\tau(x_1, \cdots, x_k)$ allows the robot to test that $\tau(x_1, \cdots, x_k)$ holds in G, where x_i is the current vertex of robot R_i in G. Simple tests include "$x_i = x_j$" which tests if robots i and j are in the same vertex (i.e., collision detection), and "$edg(x_i, x_j) \vee edg(x_j, x_i)$" which tests if robots i and j are adjacent. A *test* is a state-test or a position-test. The *instruction set* $\mathrm{INS}_{\Sigma,k}$ consists of all expressions of the form $\tau \to \kappa$ where τ is a test and κ is a command.

Robots, Configurations, Runs. A k-*robot ensemble* is a vector of robots $\langle R_1, \cdots, R_k \rangle$ where each *robot* $R_i = \langle Q_i, \delta_i \rangle$, each Q_i is a finite set of *states*, and each $\delta_i \subset Q_i \times \mathrm{INS}_{\Sigma,k} \times Q_i$ is a finite *transition* relation. For technical convenience, we assume that robot i does not test its own state, i.e., no *ins* in a transition $(p, ins, q) \in \delta_i$ contains any occurrences of state-tests of the form "robot i is in state j". We designate a subset $I_i \subseteq Q_i$ of the states of robot i

---

[3] Note that, for ease of exposition, we do not explicitly allow Boolean combinations of state-tests. However, these can be indirectly performed by chaining state-tests (remembering the previous test results in the local state) to perform conjunctions, and using nondeterminism for disjunctions.

as *initial* states, and a subset $A_i \subseteq Q_i$ of its states as *accepting* states. A state $p \in Q_i$ is called *halting* if the only transition the robot has from p is (p, true, p). Thus we model a halting robot as one that forever stays in the same state and does not move. The halting states are denoted $H_i \subseteq Q_i$.

Fix a Σ-graph G. A *configuration* c of $\langle R_1, \cdots, R_k \rangle$ on graph G is a pair $\langle \overline{v}, \overline{q} \rangle \in V^k \times \prod_{i \in [k]} Q_i$. A configuration is *initial* if $\overline{q} \in \prod I_i$. For a test τ and a configuration $c = \langle \overline{u}, \overline{p} \rangle$, define $c \Vdash \tau$ to mean that configuration c makes τ true in G. Formally, if τ is a position test then define $c \Vdash \tau$ iff $G \models \tau(\overline{u})$, and if τ is a state-test, say "robot i is in state j", then define $c \Vdash \tau$ iff $p_i = j$. The following definition of $\vdash_i$ expresses that one configuration results from another after robot i successfully executes an instruction, while the rest are idle: for $i \in [k]$ and configurations $c = \langle \overline{w}, \overline{q} \rangle, d = \langle \overline{v}, \overline{p} \rangle$, write $c \vdash_i d$ if $p_j = q_j$ and $w_j = v_j$ for all $j \neq i$, and there exists a transition $(p_i, \tau \to \kappa, q_i) \in \delta_i$ (i.e., of robot R_i) such that $c \Vdash \tau$ (i.e., the current configuration satisfies the test τ) and, if $\kappa = \uparrow_\sigma$ then $\lambda(w_i, v_i) = \sigma$, and if $\kappa = \circlearrowleft$ then $w_i = v_i$.

Schedules and Runs. A *schedule* is a finite or infinite sequence $\mathcal{S} = s_1 s_2 s_3 \cdots$ where $s_i \in [k]$. A *run* ρ of $\langle R_1, \cdots, R_k \rangle$ on G *starting with an initial config-uration* c *according to schedule* $\mathcal{S}$ is a finite or infinite sequence $c_1 c_2 c_3 \cdots$ of configurations such that $c_1 = c$ and for all i, $c_i \vdash_{s_i} c_{i+1}$. The *set (resp. sequence) of positions of a run* $\alpha = \langle \overline{v}_1, \overline{p}_1 \rangle \langle \overline{v}_2, \overline{p}_2 \rangle \cdots$ is the set of positions $\{\overline{v}_1, \overline{v}_2, \cdots \}$ (resp. sequence $\overline{v}_1 \overline{v}_2 \cdots$ of positions) of its configurations. In a similar way define the *set (resp. sequence) of positions of robot i on a run*.

Orderings. A *(finite) k-ordering* is a string $\alpha \in [k]^+$, say of length $N + 1$, such that $\alpha_i \neq \alpha_{i+1}$ for $1 \leq i \leq N$. Write $||\alpha|| = N$ to mean that $|\alpha| = N + 1$, and say that α *is N-switching*. E.g., 171 is 2-switching. Say that a schedule $\mathcal{S}$ *follows* α if $\mathcal{S}$ is in $\alpha_1^* \alpha_2^* \cdots \alpha_N^* \alpha_{N+1}^*$ or $\alpha_1^* \alpha_2^* \cdots \alpha_N^* \alpha_{N+1}^\omega$, i.e., robot α_1 is scheduled for some (possibly no) time, then robot α_2 is scheduled, and so on, until α_{N+1} which can be scheduled forever. Similarly, an *infinite k-ordering* of k robots is a string $\alpha \in [k]^\omega$ such that $\alpha_i \neq \alpha_{i+1}$ for all $i \in \mathbb{N}$. In this case write $||\alpha|| = \infty$. A schedule *follows* α if the schedule is in the set $\alpha_1^* \alpha_2^* \cdots$.

Robot Tasks. Robots should achieve some task in their environment. We give some examples of foundational robot tasks [25]: A robot ensemble *deploys* or *reconfigures* if they move, in a collision-free way, to a certain target configuration. A robot ensemble *gathers* if, no matter where each robot starts, there is a vertex z, such that eventually every robot is in z. A robot ensemble *collaboratively explores* a graph if, no matter where they start, every node is eventually visited by at least one robot. All of these tasks have *safe* variations: the robots complete their task without entering certain pre-designated "bad" nodes.

Multi-Robot Task Logic — MRTL. We now define MRTL, a logic for formally expressing robot tasks. We first define the syntax and semantics, and then we give some example formulas. Later (in Lemma 1) we prove that, when restricted to bounded-switching orderings, MRTL formulas (and therefore many interesting natural tasks) can be converted into MSOL formulas over graphs.

MRTL Syntax. Fix $k \in \mathbb{N}$ and Σ. Formulas of MRTL_k are built, as in the definition of $\mathsf{MSOL}(\Sigma)$ from Section 2, from the following atomic formulas: $x = y$, edg_σ (for $\sigma \in \Sigma$), $x \in X$, true, and the following <u>additional atomic formulas</u> (with free variables $\overline{X}, \overline{x}, \overline{y}$ each of size k) $Reach_Q, Halt_Q^K, Infty_Q$ and $Rept_Q^K$ where $Q \in \{\exists, \forall\}$ and $\emptyset \neq K \subseteq [k]$. Denote by MRTL the set of formulas $\cup_k \mathsf{MRTL}_k$.

MRTL Semantics. Formulas of MRTL_k are interpreted over graphs G, and with respect to k-robot ensembles $\overline{R}$ and a set of orderings Ω. Define the satisfaction relation $\models_{\overline{R},\Omega}$:

- $G \models_{\overline{R},\Omega} Reach_\exists(\overline{X}, \overline{x}, \overline{y})$ iff $\boxed{\text{there is}}$ an ordering $\alpha \in \Omega$ and there is a finite run of $\overline{R}$ on G that uses a schedule that follows α, such that the run starts with some initial configuration of the form $\langle \overline{x}, \overline{p} \rangle$ (i.e., $\overline{p} \in \prod I_i$), ends with a configuration of the form $\langle \overline{y}, \overline{q} \rangle$ (i.e., $\overline{q} \in \prod Q_i$), and for each $i \in [k]$, the set of positions of robot i on this run is contained in X_i.
- $G \models_{\overline{R},\Omega} Halt_\exists^K(\overline{X}, \overline{x}, \overline{y})$ means the same as $Reach_\exists$ except that the last tuple of states $\overline{q}$ has the property that $i \in K$ implies that $q_i \in H_i$ (i.e., every robot in K is in a halting state).
- $G \models_{\overline{R},\Omega} Infty_\exists(\overline{X}, \overline{x}, \overline{y})$ means the same as $Reach_\exists$ except that the run is infinite and, instead of ending in $\overline{y}$, it visits $\overline{y}$ infinitely often.
- $G \models_{\overline{R},\Omega} Rept_\exists^K(\overline{X}, \overline{x}, \overline{y})$ means the same as $Reach_\exists$ except that the run is infinite, and infinitely often it reaches a configuration of the form $\langle \overline{y}, \overline{q} \rangle$ such that $i \in K$ implies that q_i is an accepting state (i.e., $q_i \in A_i$).
- $G \models_{\overline{R},\Omega} Reach_\forall(\overline{X}, \overline{x}, \overline{y})$ is the same as $Reach_\exists$ except replace "there is an ordering $\alpha \in \Omega$ and there is a finite run..." by "$\boxed{\text{for every}}$ ordering $\alpha \in \Omega$ there is a finite run ...". In a similar way, define $Halt_\forall^K, Infty_\forall$ and $Rept_\forall^K$.

Extend the satisfaction relation to all formulas of MRTL_k in the natural way.

Example 1. The statement $G \models_{\overline{R},\Omega} (\forall \overline{x})(\exists \overline{y})(\exists \overline{X}) Reach_\exists(\overline{X}, \overline{x}, \overline{y}) \wedge (\wedge_{i,j} y_i = y_j)$ means that, no matter where the robots start in G, there is an ordering $\alpha \in \Omega$, and a run according to a schedule that follows α, such that the robots $\overline{R}$ gather at some vertex of the graph G. Replacing $Reach_\exists$ by $Reach_\forall$ means, no matter where the robots start in G, for every ordering $\alpha \in \Omega$, the robots have a run according to a schedule that follows α such that the robots gather at a vertex of the graph. Note that by conjuncting with $\wedge_i X_i \cap B = \emptyset$ where B is an MSOL-definable set of "bad" vertices, one can express "safe gathering".

Example 2. Consider the statement $G \models_{\overline{R},\Omega} (\forall \overline{x})(\exists \overline{y})[\mathrm{NONLEAF}(\overline{x}) \wedge \mathrm{DIFF}(\overline{x}) \rightarrow (\mathrm{LEAF}(\overline{y}) \wedge \mathrm{DIFF}(\overline{y}) \wedge Reach_\forall(V^k, \overline{x}, \overline{y})]$ where G is a tree, $\mathrm{NONLEAF}(\overline{x})$ is an MSOL-formula expressing that every x_i is not a leaf, $\mathrm{LEAF}(\overline{y})$ is an MSOL-formula expressing that every y_i is a leaf, and $\mathrm{DIFF}(\overline{z})$ is an MSOL-formula expressing that $z_i \neq z_j$ for $i \neq j$. The statement says that, as long as the robots start on different internal nodes of the tree G, for every ordering $\alpha \in \Omega$ there is a run of the robots $\overline{R}$ according to a schedule that follows α in which the robots reconfigure and arrive at different leaves.

4   Reasoning about Robot Systems

We formalise the parameterised verification problem for robot protocols and then study its decidability. The parameterised verification problem depends on a (typically infinite) set of graphs $\mathcal{G}$, a set of k-robot ensembles $\mathcal{R}$, a k-robot task written as an MRTL_k formula T, and a set of k-orderings Ω.

Definition 1. *The **parameterised verification problem** $\mathsf{PVP}_{\mathrm{T},\Omega}(\mathcal{G},\mathcal{R})$ is: given a robot ensemble $\overline{R}$ from $\mathcal{R}$, decide whether for every graph $G \in \mathcal{G}$, $G \models_{\overline{R},\Omega}$ T (i.e., the robots $\overline{R}$ achieves the task T on G with orderings restricted to Ω).*

Example 3. Let $\mathcal{G}$ be the set of all binary trees, $\mathcal{R}$ be the set of all k-robot ensembles, let $\Omega_b := \{\alpha \in [k]^* : ||\alpha|| = b\}$ be the set of b-*switch orderings*, and let T be the task expressing that if the robots start on different internal nodes of a tree then they eventually reconfigure themselves to be on different leaves of the tree, no matter which ordering from Ω_b is chosen (cf. Example 2). We will see later that one can decide $\mathsf{PVP}_{\mathrm{T},\Omega_b}(\mathcal{G},\mathcal{R})$ given $b \in \mathbb{N}$. So, one can decide, given b, whether the protocol from the reconfiguration example (in the Introduction) succeeds for every ordering with b switches.

In Section 4.1 we show that the PVP is undecidable even on lines, for simple tasks, and allowing the robots very restricted testing abilities, i.e., a robot can sense which of the other robots shares the same position with it, called "local collision tests". In Section 4.2 we show that we can guarantee decidability merely by restricting the scheduling regime while allowing the robots full testing abilities, including testing positions and states of other robots "remotely".

4.1   Undecidability of Multi-Robot Systems on a Line

Our undecidability proof proceeds by reducing the halting problem of two counter machines to the parameterised verification problem. An *input-free 2-counter machine* (2CM) [28] is a deterministic program manipulating two non-negative integer counters using commands that can increment a counter by 1, decrement a counter by 1, and check whether a counter is equal to zero. We refer to the "line numbers" of the program code as the "states" of the machine. One of these states is called the *halting state*, and once it is entered the machine *halts*. Observe that a 2CM has a single computation, and that if it halts then the values of both counters are bounded by some integer n. The *non-halting problem for 2CMs* is to decide, given a 2CM $\mathfrak{M}$, whether it does not halt. This problem is known to be undecidable [28], and is usually a convenient choice for proving undecidability of problems concerning parameterised systems due to the simplicity of the operations of counter machines.

Let $\mathcal{G}$ be the set of all graphs that are finite lines. Formally, for every $n \in \mathbb{N}$ there is a graph $L_n = (V_n, E_n, \Sigma, \lambda_n) \in \mathcal{G}$, where $\Sigma = \{l, r\}$, $V_n = [n]$, $E_n = \cup_{i<n}\{(i, i+1), (i+1, i)\}$, and the label λ_n of an edge of the form $(i, i+1)$ is r, and of the form $(i+1, i)$ is l. We now describe how, given a 2CM $\mathfrak{M}$, one

can construct a robot ensemble $\overline{R}$ which can, on long enough lines, simulate the computation of $\mathfrak{M}$. Our robots have very limited sensing abilities: a robot can only sense if it at one of the two ends of the line or not, and it can sense which of the other robots are in the same node as it is ("collision detection"). Note that a robot does not know that another robot has collided with it (and then moved on) if it is not scheduled while they both occupy the same node.

The basic encoding uses two counter robots C_1 and C_2. The current position of C_i on the line corresponds to the current value of counter i, and it moves to the right to increment counter i and to the left to decrement it. Each of these robots also stores in its finite memory the current state of the 2CM. One difficulty with this basic encoding is how to ensure that the two counter robots always stay synchronised in the sense that they both agree on the next command to simulate, i.e., we need to prevent one of them from "running ahead". A second difficulty is how to update the state of the 2CM stored by a counter robot when it simulates a command that is a test for zero of the other counter. Note that both of these difficulties are very easy to overcome if one robot can remotely sense the state/position of the other robot. Since we disallow such powerful sensing these difficulties become substantially harder to overcome. The basic idea used to overcome the first difficulty is to add synchronisation robots and have a counter robot move only if it has collided with the appropriate synchronization robot. Thus, by arranging that the synchronization robots collide with the counter robots in a round-robin way the latter alternate their simulation turns and are kept coordinated. In order to enforce this round-robin behavior we have to change the encoding such that only every other position on the line is used to encode the counter values. Thus, an increment or a decrement is simulated by a counter robot moving two steps (instead of one) in the correct direction. The basic ingredient in addressing the second difficulty is to add a *zero-test* robot that, whenever one counter is zero, moves to the position of the other counter's robot, thus signaling to it that the first counter is zero.

Theorem 1. *For every 2CM $\mathfrak{M}$, there is a robot ensemble $\overline{R}$ which, for every $n \geq 5$, simulates on the line L_n any prefix of the computation of $\mathfrak{M}$ in which the counters never exceed the value $(n-3)/2$.*

Proof. The ensemble $\overline{R}$ consists of 9 robots: the *counter* robots C_0, C_1, four *synchronisation* robots R_0, R_1, R_2, R_3, a *zero-test* robot T, a *zero* robot Z that marks the zero position of the counters, and a *mover* robot M whose role is to ensure that the robots can simulate more than one command of $\mathfrak{M}$ only if their starting positions on the line are as in the *initialised configuration* escribed below (($\ddagger$)). The value of a counter is encoded as half the distance between the corresponding counter robot and the Z robot (e.g., if Z is in node 3 and C_1 is in node 7 then the value of counter 1 is 2).

($\ddagger$) (*initialised configuration*): robots R_2, R_3 are in node 1, robots R_0, R_1 are in node 2, and the rest are in node 3.

The definition of the transitions of the robots has the important property that there is only one possible run starting from the initialised configuration, i.e., at each point in time exactly one robot has exactly one transition with a test that evaluates to true. We assume that each robot remembers if it is at an odd or even node. This can be done even without looking at the node by storing the parity of the number of steps taken since the initialised configuration (‡).

Each command of the 2CM $\mathfrak{M}$ is simulated by the ensemble using 4 phases. For every $i \in \{0, 1, 2, 3\}$, phase i has the following internal stages: (1) the synchronization robots arrange themselves to signal to robot R_i that it can start moving to the right (this mechanism is described below ($\star$)). (2) robot R_i moves to the right until it collides with robot C_j (where $j = i \bmod 2$). It is an invariant of the run that this collision is at an even node if i is odd, and vice-versa. (3) robot C_j moves one step to the left or to the right, in order to simulate the relevant half of the current command of $\mathfrak{M}$, as described below (†). (4) robot R_i moves to the right until it reaches the end of the line. Observe that if during this stage R_i collides with C_j then (unlike in stage 2) it is on a node with the same parity as i (by the invariant, and since C_j moved one step in stage 3). This parity information is used by C_j to know that it should not move, and by R_i to know that it can continue moving to the right. (5) robot R_i moves to the left until it reaches the beginning of the line (see ($\star$)), which ends the phase (here, as in the previous stage, the parity information is used to ignore collisions with C_j). In case the other counter (i.e., counter $1 - j$) is zero, stage (2) of phases $0, 1$ are modified as follows: when robot R_i enters node 3 from the left it collides with Z, C_{1-j} and T; then, T and R_1 move to the right together, where T always goes first, and then R_i follows in lock-step; at the end of stage 2 both T and R_i collide with C_j, thus signalling to the latter that counter $1 - j$ is zero. A similar modification to stages (4) and (5) makes T and R_i move in lock-step fashion all the way to the right and then back to the left depositing T back in node 3.

(†): The operation performed by C_j in stage (3) of each phase is as follows. In phase 0 robot C_0 simulates the first half of the command, in phase 1 robot C_1 simulates the first half of the same command, in phase 2 robot C_0 simulates the second half of the command and in phase 3 C_1 does so. For example, if the command is "increment counter 0" then in phase 0 robot C_0 moves right one step (and updates its simulated state of $\mathfrak{M}$ to be the next command of $\mathfrak{M}$), in phase 1 robot C_1 moves right one step (and updates its simulated state of $\mathfrak{M}$), in phase 2 robot C_0 moves again one step to the right (thus encoding an incremented counter), and in phase 3 robot C_0 moves left one step (thus, returning to its previously encoded value). Simulating the other three increment and decrement commands is done similarly. The only other command we need to simulate is of the form "if counter i is zero goto state p else goto state q". Since this command does not change the value of any counter it is simulated by each counter robot going right in the first half of the simulation and left in the second half. The internal state of $\mathfrak{M}$ is updated to p or q depending on the value of the counter. When simulating the first half of the command, robot C_j knows that counter j (resp. $1 - j$) is zero iff it sees Z (resp. T) with it.

($\star$): We now show that every arrangement of the synchronization robots uniquely determines which one of them its turn it is to move. Let

NEXT$(i) := i+1 \bmod 4$, PREV$(i) := i-1 \bmod 4$. An *initial arrangement for phase* i is of the following form: $R_{\text{PREV(PREV}(i))}, R_{\text{PREV}(i)}$ are in node 1, and $R_i, R_{\text{next}(i)}$ are in node 2. Note that the initialised configuration ($\ddagger$) contains the initial arrangement for phase 0. We let the initial arrangement for phase i signal that the next robot to move is $R_{\text{PREV(PREV}(i))}$, which moves to the right, thus completing stage (1) of phase i. Hence, at the beginning of stage 2 the arrangement is such that only $R_{\text{PREV}(i)}$ is left in node 1, which signals that R_i is the next robot to move, as needed for stage (2). Just before the end of stage (5), robot R_i returns to node 2 from the left, and the above arrangement repeats itself. Hence, again it is R_i that moves, however, this time to the left (as indicated by its now different internal memory). The resulting arrangement at the end of phase i is thus: $R_{\text{prev}(i)}, R_i$ are in node 1 and $R_{\text{NEXT}(i)}, R_{\text{PREV(PREV}(i))}$ are in node 2. Observe that this is exactly the initial arrangement for phase NEXT(i), as required. Note that since robots have collision tests a robot can tell by sensing which other robots are with it (and which are not) exactly which arrangement of the ones described above it is in, and thus if it is allowed to move or not.

Finally, we describe how to amend the construction above by incorporating the robot M to ensure that robots can only simulate the 2CM if they happen to begin in the initialised configuration ($\ddagger$), and otherwise the system deadlocks after a few steps without any robot entering a halting state.[4] Add to every transition of robot R_i, for $i \in \{0,1,2,3\}$, the additional guard that M is on the same node with it. Thus, M enables the synchronisation robots to move, and if M ever stops, then so does the simulation. Robot M behaves as follows. It first verifies that the rest of the robots are in the initialised configuration by executing the following sequence (and stopping forever if any of the conditions in the sequence fail to hold): check that it is alone on the right-hand side of the line, move left until it collides with C_0, C_1, Z, T, move one step left and check that it collides with R_0, R_1, move one step left and check it is on the left-hand side of the line and collides with R_2, R_3. Once it verified that the robots are on the nodes specified by ($\ddagger$), it starts "chasing after" the currently active synchronisation robot, i.e., it remembers which robot is active and the direction it moves in, and moves in that direction (if it does not currently collide with that robot).   □

From the previous theorem we can easily deduce that $\mathfrak{M}$ halts iff there is a run of the ensemble $\overline{R}$ (on a long enough line, and that fully simulates the run of $\mathfrak{M}$) and in which the robots C_0, C_1 halt. We thus get:

Corollary 1. *Let $k = 9$, $\mathcal{G}$ be the set of lines, $\mathcal{R}$ the set of k-robot ensembles consisting of robots whose only tests are local collision tests and the ability to test the left (resp. right) end of the line, Ω the set of all k-orderings, and T the MRTL formula $(\forall \overline{x})(\forall \overline{y})(\forall \overline{X}) \neg Halt_{\exists}^{\{1\}}(\overline{X}, \overline{x}, \overline{y})$.[5] Then $\mathsf{PVP}_{\mathrm{T},\Omega}(\mathcal{G}, \mathcal{R})$ is undecidable.*

---

[4] One can modify the construction to remove the need for the M robot, however we find the exposition with M clearer.

[5] The formula expresses "for every initial configuration, and every scheduling of the robots, robot 1 never enters a halting state".

Suitable changes to the construction in Theorem 1 yield that other tasks, such as "certain robots gather" or "certain robots reconfigure", are also undecidable.

Remark 1. Note that in the construction, starting from the initialised configuration, at most one robot can move at any time. Thus, allowing all robots that can act to act, as in the synchronous model, does not change anything. So, with minor modifications to deal with the initialisation phase, the theorem also holds for the synchronous model. This strengthens the previously known fact that the PVP is undecidable for synchronous robots on a line with remote testing abilities (i.e., robot l can test if "robots i and j are in the same node") [30].

4.2   Decidability of Multi-Robot Systems with Bounded Switching

The previous section shows that decidability cannot be achieved in very limited situations. However, we now suggest a limitation on the *orderings* which guarantees decidability without requiring any other restrictions. Thus it works on many classes of graphs, robots, and tasks. We first describe, at a high level, the approach we use to solve (restricted cases of) the parameterised verification problem $\mathsf{PVP}_{T,\Omega}(\mathcal{G},\mathcal{R})$, cf. [30]. Suppose we can build, for every k-ensemble $\overline{R}$ of robots, a formula $\phi_{\overline{R},T,\Omega}$ such that for all graphs $G \in \mathcal{G}$ the following are equivalent: i) $G \models \phi_{\overline{R},T,\Omega}$ and ii) $\overline{R}$ achieves task T on G with orderings restricted to Ω. Then, for every $\mathcal{R}$ and $\mathcal{G}$, we would have reduced the parameterised verification problem $\mathsf{PVP}_{T,\Omega}(\mathcal{G},\mathcal{R})$ to the $\Phi_{\mathcal{R},T,\Omega}$-validity problem for $\mathcal{G}$ where $\Phi_{\mathcal{R},T,\Omega}$ is the set of formulas $\{\phi_{\overline{R},T,\Omega} : \overline{R} \in \mathcal{R}\}$. We now show how to build an MSOL-formula $\phi_{\overline{R},T,\Omega}$ in case T is a formula of MRTL and Ω is a finite set of finite orderings.

We begin with a lemma that will be used as a building block. In the simplest setting, the lemma says that for every $i \in [k]$ there is an MSOL formula with free variables $\overline{x}, \overline{y}$ that holds on a graph G if and only if robot i can move in G from x_i to y_i while all the other robots are frozen, i.e., $x_j = y_j$ for $j \neq i$.

Lemma 1 (From Robots to MSOL). *Fix k, and let $\overline{R}$ be a k-robot ensemble over instruction set $\mathrm{INS}_{\Sigma,k}$. For every $\overline{p}, \overline{q} \in \prod Q_i$ (k-tuples of states) and ordering $\alpha \in [k]^{+}$, one can effectively construct an $\mathsf{MSOL}(\Sigma)$ formula $\psi_{\alpha,\overline{p},\overline{q}}(\overline{X}, \overline{x}, \overline{y})$ with free variables X_i, x_i, y_i ($i \in [k]$) such that for every graph G: $G \models \psi_{\alpha,\overline{p},\overline{q}}(\overline{X}, \overline{x}, \overline{y})$ if and only if there exists a run c of $\overline{R}$ on G according to a schedule that follows α, starting from configuration $c_1 = \langle \overline{x}, \overline{p} \rangle$ and reaching, for some $T \in \mathbb{N}$, the configuration $c_T = \langle \overline{y}, \overline{q} \rangle$, such that for all $i \in [k]$, the set of positions of robot i on $c_1 c_2 \cdots c_T$ is contained in X_i.*

Similarly one can construct $\psi_{\alpha,\overline{p},\overline{q}}^{\infty}(\overline{X}, \overline{x}, \overline{y})$ so that for every graph G: $G \models \psi_{\alpha,\overline{p},\overline{q}}^{\infty}(\overline{X}, \overline{x}, \overline{y})$ if and only if there exists a run c of $\overline{R}$ on G according to a schedule that follows α, starting from configuration $c_1 = \langle \overline{x}, \overline{p} \rangle$ and reaching the configuration $\langle \overline{y}, \overline{q} \rangle$ infinitely often, and such that the set of positions of robot i on the run is contained in X_i ($i \in [k]$).

Proof. Fix k and $\overline{R}$. We start with an auxiliary step. For $i \in [k]$, states $p_i, q_i \in Q_i$, and $\overline{s} = (s_1, \cdots, s_{i-1}, s_{i+1}, \cdots, s_k)$ with $s_j \in Q_j$, we define an MSO-formula

$\phi_{i,p_i,q_i,\bar{s}}$ with free variables $X, x, y, \bar{z}$ where $\bar{z} = (z_1, \cdots, z_{i-1}, z_{i+1}, \cdots, z_k)$ such that $G \models \phi_{i,p_i,q_i,\bar{s}}$ if and only if the k-ensemble robot $\bar{R}$ has a run according to a schedule in i^* in which robot i starts in position x and state p_i, and reaches position y and state q_i while only visiting vertices in X, and for $j \neq i$, robot j is in vertex z_j and state s_j and does not move or change state. This is done as follows. Each robot $R_i = \langle Q_i, \delta_i \rangle$ is a finite automaton (without initial or final states) over the finite alphabet $\text{INS}_{\Sigma,k}$. By Kleene's theorem, we can build a regular expression exp_i (that depends on $p_i, q_i, \bar{s}$) over $\text{INS}_{\Sigma,k}$ for the language of the automaton R_i with initial state p_i and final state q_i. By induction on the regular expressions we build MSOL formulas (with free variables $X, x, y, \bar{z}$):

- $\varphi_\emptyset :=$ false and $\varphi_\epsilon := x = y \wedge x \in X$,
- if $\tau \in \text{MSOL}_k(\Sigma)$ is a position-test then
  - $\varphi_{\tau \to \uparrow_\sigma} := \tau(z_1, \cdots, z_{i-1}, x, z_{i+1}, \cdots, z_k) \wedge edg_\sigma(x, y) \wedge x, y \in X$,
  - $\varphi_{\tau \to \circlearrowleft} := \tau(z_1, \cdots, z_{i-1}, x, z_{i+1}, \cdots, z_k) \wedge x = y \wedge x \in X$,
- if τ is a state-test, say "robot j is in state l" (for $j \neq i$ and $l \in Q_j$) then, if $s_j = l$ then
  - $\varphi_{\tau \to \uparrow_\sigma} := edg_\sigma(x, y) \wedge x, y \in X$,
  - $\varphi_{\tau \to \circlearrowleft} := x = y \wedge x \in X$,
  and otherwise if $s_j \neq l$, then $\varphi_{\tau \to \uparrow_\sigma}$ and $\varphi_{\tau \to \circlearrowleft}$ are defined to be false,
- $\varphi_{r+s} := \varphi_r \vee \varphi_s$,
- $\varphi_{r \cdot s} := \exists w [\varphi_r(X, x, w, \bar{z}) \wedge \varphi_s(X, w, y, \bar{z})]$,
- $\varphi_{r^*} := \forall Z[(cl_{\varphi_r}(X, Z, \bar{z}) \wedge x \in Z) \to y \in Z]$ where $cl_{\varphi_r}(X, Z, \bar{z})$ is defined as $\forall a, b [(a \in Z \wedge \varphi_r(X, a, b, \bar{z})) \to b \in Z]$.

Then, define $\phi_{i,p_i,q_i,\bar{s}}$ to be $\varphi_{exp_i}(X, x, y, \bar{z})$. To prove the lemma proceed by induction on the length l of α. Base case: For $\alpha = i \in [k]$, define $\psi_{i,\bar{p},\bar{q}}(\bar{X}, \bar{x}, \bar{y})$ by $\bigwedge_{j \neq i} x_j = y_j \wedge X_j = \{x_j\} \wedge \phi_{i,p_i,q_i,\bar{s}}(X_i, x_i, y_i, x_1, \cdots, x_{i-1}, x_{i+1}, \cdots, x_k)$, where $\bar{s} = (p_1, \cdots, p_{i-1}, p_{i+1}, \cdots, p_k)$, if $q_j = p_j$ for all $j \neq i$, and otherwise the formula is defined as false. Inductive case: For $\alpha \in [k]^+, i \in [k]$, define $\psi_{\alpha \cdot i, \bar{p}, \bar{q}}(\bar{X}, \bar{x}, \bar{y})$ by $\exists \bar{z} \bigvee_{\bar{r}} [\psi_{\alpha, \bar{p}, \bar{r}}(\bar{X}, \bar{x}, \bar{z}) \wedge \psi_{i, \bar{r}, \bar{q}}(\bar{X}, \bar{z}, \bar{y})]$ and $\bar{r}$ varies over $\prod Q_i$. This completes the construction of ψ_α. The construction of ψ_α^∞ is similar. □

In Lemma 1, a variable X_i designates a set containing – but not necessarily equal to – the positions of robot i along the run. If one wishes X_i to designate the exact set of positions visited by robot i (in order to express, e.g., "exploration"), then one needs to modify the construction of $\phi_{i,p_i,q_i,\bar{s}}$ in the proof of the lemma.[6] The required modifications are straightforward except for those to the definition of φ_{r^*}, which are more complicated.[7]

---

[6] In [30] it is wrongly stated that one can transform an MSOL formula that says that there is a run (satisfying some property) that stays within a set X, to one that says that it also visits all of X, by simply requiring that X be a minimal set for which a run satisfying the property exits.

[7] Recall that φ_{r^*} has free variables $X, x, y, \bar{z}$, and its semantic in this case is that robot i can reach y from x (with the other robots' positions being $\bar{z}$), visiting exactly X, using a concatenation of sub-paths each satisfying φ_r. Intuitively, φ_{r^*} existentially quantifies over the stitching points of these sub-paths and uses appropriate sub-formulas that are all satisfied iff one can find sub-paths that can be stitched to lead from x to y and that cover all the positions in X.

Observe that this lemma can be used to express both collaborative and adversarial scheduling. For instance, if Ω is a finite set of orderings, the formula $\bigvee_{\alpha \in \Omega} \psi_{\alpha,\overline{p},\overline{q}}(\overline{X}, \overline{x}, \overline{y})$ says that there is an ordering $\alpha \in \Omega$ that the robots can follow to go from $\overline{x}$ to $\overline{y}$ while staying in $\overline{X}$, i.e., the ordering is chosen collaboratively, while $\bigwedge_{\alpha \in \Omega} \psi_{\alpha,\overline{p},\overline{q}}(\overline{X}, \overline{x}, \overline{y})$ expresses that the ordering is chosen adversarially.

Putting everything together, we solve the PVP for finite sets of orderings (and thus for adversarial or co-operative b-switch orderings $\Omega_b := \{\alpha : ||\alpha|| = b\}$).

Theorem 2. *There is an algorithm that given an edge-label set Σ, a number of robots $k \in \mathbb{N}$, a formula T of $MRTL_k$, a finite set Ω of finite k-orderings, and a description of a context-free set of Σ-graphs $\mathcal{G}$, decides $PVP_{T,\Omega}(\mathcal{G}, \mathcal{R})$, where $\mathcal{R}$ is the set of all k-ensembles of robots over $INS_{\Sigma,k}$.*

Proof. Given $\overline{R} \in \mathcal{R}$ build the formula $\phi_{\overline{R},T,\Omega}$ by replacing every atomic formula in T by its definition with respect to $\overline{R}$. E.g., $Reach_\exists(\overline{X}, \overline{x}, \overline{y})$ is replaced by $\bigvee_{\alpha \in \Omega} \bigvee_{\overline{p}} \bigvee_{\overline{q}} \psi_{\alpha,\overline{p},\overline{q}}(\overline{X}, \overline{x}, \overline{y})$, where $\overline{p}$ varies over $\prod_{i \in [k]} I_i$ and $\overline{q}$ varies over $\prod_{i \in [k]} Q_i$. Now, a routine induction on the structure of the formula T shows that $G \models_{\overline{R},\Omega} T$ if and only if $G \models \phi_{\overline{R},T,\Omega}$. By Lemma 1 the formula $\phi_{\overline{R},T,\Omega}$ is in $MSOL(\Sigma)$. Finally, apply the fact that the MSOL-validity problem for context-free sets of graphs $\mathcal{G}$ is uniformly decidable [9]. □

5 Discussion

In [6,30] (see also the discussion before Theorem 1) it was shown that the PVP is undecidable for two synchronous robots on a line, reachability tasks, and allowing the robots "remote" position-tests. In Section 4.1 we substantially strengthen this result and prove that the problem is still undecidable even if we only allow robots "local" position-tests or even just local "collision tests", both for robots that move synchronously and asynchronously. The fact that the proof works for both the synchronous and asynchronous models (Remark 1), strongly suggests that limiting the robots' sensing capabilities may not be a very fruitful direction for decidability. In Section 4.2 we showed that for asynchronous robots, if one imposes a bound on the number of times the robots can switch, then PVP is decidable for very general tasks (i.e., those expressible in a new logic called MRTL), large classes of graphs (i.e., the context-free sets of graphs), and allowing robots very powerful testing abilities (i.e., MSOL position-tests *and* state-tests). This is the first parameterised decidability result of the PVP for *multiple* robots where the environment is the parameter. Thus, our work indicates that if practitioners want formal guarantees on the correctness of the robot protocols they design, then they could design them in the framework given in this paper (i.e., finite-state, bounded-switching, powerful testing abilities).

A main limitation of our decidability result is the fact that the set of grids is not context-free — grids are the canonical workspaces since they abstract 2D and 3D real-world scenarios. However, this limitation is inherent and not confined to our formalisation since the parameterised verification problem even for one robot ($k = 1$) on a grid with only "local" tests is undecidable [6,30]. A second limitation is that robots do not have a rich memory (e.g., they cannot remember a map of where they have visited). Extending the abilities to allow for richer memory and communication will result in undecidability, unless it is done in a careful way. Also, the complexity of the decision procedure we gave is very high. Again this is inherent in the problem since, e.g., already for one robot on trees the PVP with the "explore and halt" task is ExpTime-complete [30]. We leave for future research the problem of finding decidability results with reasonable complexity for multi-robot systems that are rich enough to capture protocols found in the distributed computing literature, e.g., [5,14,15,24].

References

1. Aminof, B., Jacobs, S., Khalimov, A., Rubin, S.: Parameterized model checking of token-passing systems. In: McMillan, K.L., Rival, X. (eds.) VMCAI 2014. LNCS, vol. 8318, pp. 262–281. Springer, Heidelberg (2014)
2. Aminof, B., Kotek, T., Rubin, S., Spegni, F., Veith, H.: Parameterized model checking of rendezvous systems. In: Baldan, P., Gorla, D. (eds.) CONCUR 2014. LNCS, vol. 8704, pp. 109–124. Springer, Heidelberg (2014)
3. Aminof, B., Rubin, S., Zuleger, F., Spegni, F.: Liveness of parameterized timed networks. In: Halldórsson, M.M., Iwama, K., Kobayashi, N., Speckmann, B. (eds.) ICALP 2015. LNCS, vol. 9135, pp. 375–387. Springer, Heidelberg (2015)
4. Auger, C., Bouzid, Z., Courtieu, P., Tixeuil, S., Urbain, X.: Certified impossibility results for byzantine-tolerant mobile robots. In: Higashino, T., Katayama, Y., Masuzawa, T., Potop-Butucaru, M., Yamashita, M. (eds.) SSS 2013. LNCS, vol. 8255, pp. 178–190. Springer, Heidelberg (2013)
5. Bender, M.A., Slonim, D.K.: The power of team exploration: Two robots can learn unlabeled directed graphs. Technical report, MIT (1995)
6. Blum, M., Hewitt, C.: Automata on a 2-dimensional tape. In: SWAT (FOCS), pp. 155–160 (1967)
7. Čermák, P., Lomuscio, A., Mogavero, F., Murano, A.: MCMAS-SLK: a model checker for the verification of strategy logic specifications. In: Biere, A., Bloem, R. (eds.) CAV 2014. LNCS, vol. 8559, pp. 525–532. Springer, Heidelberg (2014)
8. Cohen, R., Fraigniaud, P., Ilcinkas, D., Korman, A., Peleg, D.: Label-guided graph exploration by a finite automaton. T. Algorithms (TALG) 4(4), 42 (2008)
9. Courcelle, B., Engelfriet, J.: Book: Graph structure and monadic second-order logic. a language-theoretic approach. Bull. EATCS 108, 179 (2012)
10. Das, S.: Mobile agents in distributed computing: Network exploration. Bull. EATCS 109, 54–69 (2013)
11. De Giacomo, G., Felli, P., Patrizi, F., Sardiña, S.: Two-player game structures for generalized planning and agent composition. In: Fox, M., Poole, D., (eds.) AAAI, pp. 297–302 (2010)
12. Delzanno, G.: Parameterized verification and model checking for distributed broadcast protocols. In: Giese, H., König, B. (eds.) ICGT 2014. LNCS, vol. 8571, pp. 1–16. Springer, Heidelberg (2014)
13. Diks, K., Fraigniaud, P., Kranakis, E., Pelc, A.: Tree exploration with little memory. Journal of Algorithms 51(1), 38–63 (2004)

14. Flocchini, P., Prencipe, G., Santoro, N.: Computing by mobile robotic sensors. In: Nikoletseas, S., Rolim, J.D., (eds.) Theoretical Aspects of Distributed Computing in Sensor Networks, EATCS, pp. 655–693. Springer (2011)
15. Flocchini, P., Prencipe, G., Santoro, N.: Distributed Computing by Oblivious Mobile Robots. Synthesis Lectures on Distributed Computing Theory. Morgan & Claypool (2012)
16. Flocchini, P., Prencipe, G., Santoro, N., Widmayer, P.: Hard tasks for weak robots: the role of common knowledge in pattern formation by autonomous mobile robots. In: Aggarwal, A.K., Pandu Rangan, C. (eds.) ISAAC 1999. LNCS, vol. 1741, p. 93. Springer, Heidelberg (1999)
17. Fraigniaud, P., Ilcinkas, D., Peer, G., Pelc, A., Peleg, D.: Graph exploration by a finite automaton. Theoretical Computer Science 345, 331–344 (2005)
18. Gasieniec, L., Radzik, T.: Memory efficient anonymous graph exploration. In: Broersma, H., Erlebach, T., Friedetzky, T., Paulusma, D. (eds.) WG 2008. LNCS, vol. 5344, pp. 14–29. Springer, Heidelberg (2008)
19. Hu, Y., De Giacomo, G.: Generalized planning: synthesizing plans that work for multiple environments. In: Walsh, T., (ed.) IJCAI, pp. 918–923. AAAI (2011)
20. Khalimov, A., Jacobs, S., Bloem, R.: PARTY parameterized synthesis of token rings. In: Sharygina, N., Veith, H. (eds.) CAV 2013. LNCS, vol. 8044, pp. 928–933. Springer, Heidelberg (2013)
21. Khalimov, A., Jacobs, S., Bloem, R.: Towards efficient parameterized synthesis. In: Giacobazzi, R., Berdine, J., Mastroeni, I. (eds.) VMCAI 2013. LNCS, vol. 7737, pp. 108–127. Springer, Heidelberg (2013)
22. Kouvaros, P., Lomuscio, A.: Automatic verification of parameterised multi-agent systems. In: Gini, M.L., Shehory, O., Ito, T., Jonker, C.M., (eds.) AAMAS, pp. 861–868 (2013)
23. Kouvaros, P., Lomuscio, A.: A counter abstraction technique for the verification of robot swarms. In: Bonet, B., Koenig, S., (eds.) AAAI, pp. 2081–2088 (2015)
24. An, H.-C., Krizanc, D., Rajsbaum, S.: Mobile agent rendezvous: a survey. In: Flocchini, P., Gkasieniec, L. (eds.) SIROCCO 2006. LNCS, vol. 4056, pp. 1–9. Springer, Heidelberg (2006)
25. Kranakis, E., Krizanc, D., Rajsbaum, S.: Computing with mobile agents in distributed networks. In: Rajasekaran, S., Reif, J., (eds.) Handbook of Parallel Computing: Models, Algorithms, and Applications, CRC Computer and Information Science Series, pp. 8–1 – 8–20. Chapman Hall (2007)
26. Lynch, N.A.: Distributed Algorithms. Morgan Kaufmann (1996)
27. Millet, L., Potop-Butucaru, M., Sznajder, N., Tixeuil, S.: On the synthesis of mobile robots algorithms: the case of ring gathering. In: Felber, P., Garg, V. (eds.) SSS 2014. LNCS, vol. 8756, pp. 237–251. Springer, Heidelberg (2014)
28. Minsky, M.L.: Computation: finite and infinite machines. Prentice-Hall Inc (1967)
29. Murano, A., Sorrentino, L.: A game-based model for human-robots interaction. In: Workshop "From Objects to Agents" (WOA), CEUR Workshop Proceedings, vol. 1382, pp. 146–150. CEUR-WS.org (2015)
30. Rubin, S.: Parameterised verification of autonomous mobile-agents in static but unknown environments. In: Weiss, G., Yolum, P., Bordini, R.H., Elkind, E., (eds.) AAMAS, pp. 199–208 (2015)
31. Suzuki, I.: Proving properties of a ring of finite-state machines. Inf. Process. Lett. 28(4), 213–214 (1988)

Potential of Heterogeneity in Collective Behaviors: A Case Study on Heterogeneous Swarms

Daniela Kengyel[1]([✉]), Heiko Hamann[2], Payam Zahadat[1], Gerald Radspieler[1], Franz Wotawa[3], and Thomas Schmickl[1]

[1] Artificial Life Laboratory at the Department of Zoology,
Karl-Franzens University Graz, Graz, Austria
`daniela.kengyel@uni-graz.at`
[2] Department of Computer Science, University of Paderborn, Paderborn, Germany
`heiko.hamann@uni-paderborn.de`
[3] Institute for Software Technology, Graz University of Technology, Graz, Austria

Abstract. Research in swarm robotics and collective behaviors is often focused on homogeneous swarms. However, heterogeneity in behaviors can be advantageous as we know, for example, from studies on social insects. Our objective is to study the hypothesis that there are potential advantages of heterogeneous swarms over homogeneous swarms in an aggregation scenario inspired by behaviors of juvenile honeybees. Even without task switching – that is, with predefined, static roles for certain swarm fractions – we find in our case study that heterogeneous swarms can outperform homogeneous swarms for a predetermined set of basic behaviors. We use methods of evolutionary computation to define behaviors imitating those found in honeybees (random walkers, wall followers, goal finders, immobile agents) and also to find well-adapted swarm fractions of different predetermined behaviors. Our results show that nontrivial distributions of behaviors give better aggregation performance.

1 Introduction

In the field of swarm robotics the swarm was, at least early on, defined as (quasi-)homogeneous [3]. This homogeneity referred primarily to the hardware of the swarm robots because that would allow for mass production and consequently for inexpensive swarms. The idea of mass production is followed to date as seen in the kilobot robot [27] and experiments with 1000 robots [28]. Still, a new trend pushes towards heterogeneous swarm research, such as the Swarmanoid project [9]. Heterogeneity in the morphology of swarm members is also seen in natural systems, such as polymorphism in ants [17]. Another concept is to have heterogeneity in the behavior[1]. A swarm with heterogeneous behaviors can still be homogeneous concerning its hardware, hence, still allowing for

---

[1] The term 'behavior' is used in its biological sense here, that is, it describes a set of an organism's actions. Within the computer science community it would be similar to an agent's strategy or policy and should not be mixed up with low-level behaviors on the level of atomic actions (e.g., turning, gripping).

© Springer International Publishing Switzerland 2015
Q. Chen et al. (Eds.): PRIMA 2015, LNAI 9387, pp. 201–217, 2015.
DOI: 10.1007/978-3-319-25524-8_13

mass production. The idea of heterogeneous behaviors in a swarm is that swarm members have predetermined behavioral roles. For example, the polyethism of honeybees [32], that is, taking over different tasks at different times in a bee's life, could be interpreted as a concept of heterogeneous behaviors because the bees rarely switch their general tasks. This is in contrast to frequent task switching in common task allocation and division of labor problems which could be interpreted as temporary heterogeneous behavior [6,7,29,37]. However, each swarm member is typically capable of executing any of the tasks and tasks are switched on demand. There is also the concept of behavioral castes "to describe groups of individuals that perform the same set of tasks in a given period." [10] If tasks are performed for longer periods, agents might specialize, possibly even permanently and hence form heterogeneous behaviors [26]. In natural systems there are examples of swarms that are heterogeneous in their morphology and that have morphology-dependent task switching behaviors [17,35]. In artificial swarms there are also examples of heterogeneous swarms such the aboved mentioned Swarmanoid swarm robot project [9] or software approaches such as multi-type ant colony optimization (MACO) [25]. Swarms that allow for frequent task switching show generally high adaptivity to different work loads and environmental conditions [4,23], but there are also task switching costs (e.g., switching times) that decrease the efficiency [14,22]. Still, dynamic task switching is advantageous in many situations and, for example, highly developed in many species of social insects. Task partitioning and task switching behaviors are also subject to research in evolutionary swarm robotics [11]. The evolution of heterogeneous behaviors in a multiagent system is reported by [36].

In the following investigations we focus on an extreme case by not allowing any task switching. Agents start with a predetermined behavior and keep it for the whole experiment. The motivation is to simplify the swarm system and to investigate the potential capabilities of such a static non-task-switching system. We hypothesize that swarms with predetermined and fixed behavioral heterogeneity can outperform homogeneous swarms for certain sets of predetermined behaviors. This idea is inspired by the behavior of juvenile honeybees that were found to show several behavioral roles in an aggregation behavior while not switching between them during the whole experiment [20,34]. Such a complex swarm system with heterogeneous behaviors is an interesting research object in itself but also as an inspiration for how to design swarm robotic systems. We focus on an aggregation task in which the swarm has to find a single target area or to choose between two target areas. In the latter case, the behavior can also be interpreted as a collective-decision making process [12,15,34]. This setting is subject to many studies on an algorithm for homogeneous swarms called BEECLUST [1,2,5,13,16,18,19,21,30,31]. The BEECLUST algorithm (see Fig. 1) is actually inspired by the above mentioned behavior of young honeybees. Agents controlled by the BEECLUST algorithm move around randomly (step 1 and step 2 create trajectories of straight lines interrupted by rotations due to collision avoidance), whenever they meet another swarm member (step 3)

```
1.) Each agent moves straight until it
    perceives an obstacle O within
    sensor range.
2.) If O is a wall the agent turns
    away and continues with step 1.
3.) If O is another agent, the agent
    measures the local potential field value.
    The higher the scalar field value the
    longer the agent stays still.
    After this waiting period, the
    agent turns away from the other
    agent and continues with step 1.
```

Fig. 1. The BEECLUST algorithm [30].

they stop, measure the local potential field value (e.g., temperature, light, gas concentration), wait for a time proportional to that value, and continue to move randomly afterwards. As a result, the robots form clusters, which is followed by a competition of growing and 'dissolving' robot clusters until one big cluster remains with robots leaving and returning occasionally. The BEECLUST algorithm simplifies the situation found in bees by reducing the different behavior types to only one: random walk. BEECLUST implements a homogeneous approach. The following work can be viewed as an extension of the BEECLUST algorithm to the domain of heterogeneous behavior. In contrast to the study reported in [20], here we investigate behavior compositions with arbitrary numbers that are optimized by evolutionary algorithms, we rely on a mathematical model to represent the individual behavior types, and we investigate different environments.

In this paper, we investigate the above mentioned hypothesis whether a swarm that is heterogeneous in its behavior can outperform a homogeneous swarm under the condition that there are only predetermined basic behaviors and agents are not allowed to switch between them. The motivation is our finding in the behavior of juvenile honeybees that take behavioral roles and never switch them during the run of the experiment [20,34]. Aggregation at appropriate spots within the bee hive is essential for survival of honeybees and hence we follow that the observed heterogeneous swarm behavior is a well adapted product of natural evolution. In this study, we investigate whether we can reproduce that behavior in simulated agents and test the hypothesis whether heterogeneity outperforms homogeneity in the investigated setting. The results of this study might help to make the right design decisions for systems of swarm robots, such as considering a heterogeneous approach in the first place and then choosing appropriate compositions of predetermined behaviors.

In the following, we limit our case study to a selection of four predetermined behavior types inspired by the biological system of juvenile honeybees. Our study might be considered as an example of biomimicry research due to this choice. However, we also motivate this choice by the opinion that these naturally evolved behaviors might be well adapted to the investigated task of aggregation. The definition of the four behavior types found in juvenile honeybees and a novel model to describe them are our next steps.

2   Four Behavior Types in Juvenile Honeybees

Honeybees (*Apis mellifera*) of age younger than 24 hours show four types of behaviors when allowed to move in a bounded temperature field [34]. The experiments were done in a circular arena surrounded by walls that cannot be climbed by the bees. Heat lamps create a distinct temperature field and it is known that juvenile honeybees have a preference for areas of $36°C$ [21,31]. Each of the four behavior types consists of up to two actions: moving and stopping. Except for one type (immobile) all behavior types are combinations of both actions. Switching between the two actions is not considered task switching. The types differ in their movement pattern; there are: *random walker* (no bias found, neither due to walls nor due to temperature), *wall follower* (bias towards walls), *goal finder* (bias towards warmer areas), and *immobile agent* (no or slow movement only). See Fig. 2 for typical trajectories assigned to their respective behavior type based on tracking data of young honeybees. Note, that the young honeybees never switch between the different behavior types during an experiment.

3   Mathematical Model of the Behavior Types

The behaviors of our agents are directly inspired by the behaviors observed in young honeybees. These behaviors are logically separated in two components: individual behavior aspects differ according to the four identified types and the collective behavior aspects that are identical across all types except for the immobile agents that do not show a reaction to social interactions because they only stay stopped always.

3.1   Individual Behavior

We give a general, unified model here that is parametrized to describe all four behavior types. These behavior types are instantiated through different sets of parameters (see Section 3.3). An agent has a position $\mathbf{x} = (x_0, x_1)^\mathsf{T}$ (arena limits are $\sqrt{x_0^2 + x_1^2} < 1$), a heading $\phi \in [0, 2\pi)$, and a nominal velocity $v \in [0, 5]$ which is downscaled by discretization to $v/100$ per time step. An agent can measure an environmental feature, which is temperature in the case of young honeybees but it could also be light, ground color, gas concentration, etc. The environmental feature is modeled by a potential field $P(\mathbf{r})$, $\mathbf{r} \in \mathbb{R}^2$. An agent's turning behavior depends on the environmental feature and/or random effects. The parameter $\alpha \in [0, 1]$ is a weighting factor that determines how intensively an agent follows the gradient of the potential field. A 100% greedy agent following the gradient is defined by $\alpha = 1$. An agent that moves randomly is defined by $\alpha = 0$. Any intermediate value of α defines a corresponding agent that follows the gradient to some extent but is also subject to noise. We define the change of an agent's heading (for simplicity without units) by

$$\frac{d\phi(t)}{dt} = \alpha \, \min\left(\text{atan}\left(\frac{\partial P(\mathbf{x}(t))}{\partial x_0}, \frac{\partial P(\mathbf{x}(t))}{\partial x_1}\right), \phi_{\max}\right)$$
$$+ (1 - \alpha)\xi(\sigma, t), \tag{1}$$

for a stochastic process ξ based on Gaussian noise with zero mean, standard deviation σ, and maximal turning angle $\phi_{\max} = 7/18\pi$ ($\phi_{\max} = 70°$). An agent's velocity (for simplicity without units) is defined by

$$\frac{d\mathbf{x}}{dt} = \begin{pmatrix} \cos \phi(t) \\ \sin \phi(t) \end{pmatrix} v(t)m(t), \tag{2}$$

for its current nominal speed $v(t)$ and $m(t) \in \{0, 1\}$ giving the agent's current state: $m = 0$ for *stopped*, $m = 1$ for *moving*. Note that the nominal speed v is irrelevant in state stopped ($m = 0$). The transitions between *stopped* and

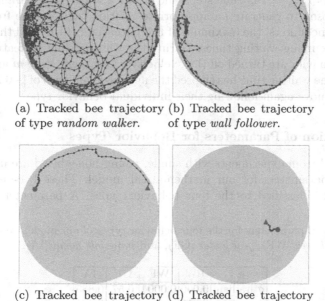

(a) Tracked bee trajectory of type *random walker*.

(b) Tracked bee trajectory of type *wall follower*.

(c) Tracked bee trajectory of type *goal finder*.

(d) Tracked bee trajectory of type *immobile agent*.

Fig. 2. Typical tracked trajectories of young honeybees (same length of experiment), assigned to the four behavior types, start of trajectory at triangle, end at circle, 36°C target area at the left hand side of the arena.

moving are modeled as probabilistic state machine with probability to move again P_{move} and probability to stop P_{stop}. Finally, the change of an agent's nominal speed v over time is modeled by a simple Markov chain. The interval of possible velocities $[0, 5]$ is discretized as a set of 51 velocities. For each of these discrete velocities v we have a probability of increasing the velocity $P_{\text{incr}}(v)$ by one step (i.e., $v' = v + 1/50$) and a symmetrical probability of decreasing the speed $1 - P_{\text{incr}}(v)$ (i.e., we force a change). These probabilities P_{incr} define the velocity distribution that results from our model.

3.2   Social Behavior

The agents' social behavior, that is the interactions between agents, are homogeneous across all behavior types. They follow the definition of the behavioral model of young honeybees [34] and the definition of the BEECLUST algorithm [30]. Once two agents perceive each other, they stop their motion, measure the local value of the potential field P, and wait for a certain period. This waiting time w is modulated proportionally to the measured potential field value P. It is defined by the function

$$w(P) = \frac{t_{\max}P^2}{\theta + P^2}, \tag{3}$$

for parameters $t_{\max} = 132$ time steps and $\theta = 1.4 \times 10^4$. The parameters $t_{\max}$ and θ are chosen to generate an appropriate relation between the frequency of robot-robot encounters, the maximum of the potential field P, and the resulting interval of occurring waiting times. During the waiting time all features of the individual behavior are turned off (i.e., velocity v and agent state m are not relevant). Once the waiting time has elapsed the agents do a u-turn of $[-0.25\pi, 0.25\pi]$ and start to move again following their individual behavior type.

3.3   Evolution of Parameters for Behavior Types

Data acquired from experiments with single, young honeybees[2] are used to find appropriate parameters for our mathematical model. These bee-derived data were manually classified to the four behavior types. A parameter set (σ, α,

Table 1. Typical parameters for the four behavior types of our model: *random walker* (RW), *wall follower* (WF), *goal finder* (GF), and *immobile agent* (IA).

	RW	WF	GF	IA
σ [radian]	0.090	0.0004	0.57	0.885
α	0.016	0	0.99	0.481
P_{stop}	0	0	0.007	0.163
P_{move}	0	0	0.024	0.002

---

[2] unpublished, publication in preparation.

P_{stop}, P_{move}, P_{incr}) for each behavior type is evolved using a simple genetic algorithm. The population size is 100, we evolve for 100 generations, the mutation rate is 0.25, we select based on proportionate selection, and 30 repetitions per evaluation are done. In each evaluation the agent operates in an arena with only one goal area to avoid side-effects of the symmetrical setting investigated in the swarm experiments. The agent is initially positioned far from that goal area with random orientation and random speed. The agent's behavior is defined by the considered parameter set and it is simulated for 1.5×10^4 time steps. During the simulation all turns and changes of velocity are stored in a histogram of turning angles and a histogram of velocities. The fitness function is a weighted sum of two features: First, it rewards similarities in the histograms of the simulated agent to the histograms acquired from the bee data. Second, type-specific qualities, that are not directly represented by the histograms of turning angles and velocities, are rewarded. In the case of the *goal finder*, turns towards the goal (i.e., maximum in the potential field P) are rewarded. The gradient of the potential field $(\frac{\partial P(\mathbf{x})}{\partial x_1}, \frac{\partial P(\mathbf{x})}{\partial x_2})^{\mathsf{T}}$ defines the optimal direction for each position $\mathbf{x}$. For each time step, the difference between the agent's direction and the optimal direction is calculated. The sum of these differences is part of the fitness function and hence imposes a minimization problem. In the case of the *wall follower*, time spent close to the wall is rewarded. This is done by defining three areas: a ring-shaped area R_{wall} directly at the wall $\mathbf{x} \in A_{\text{wall}} : \sqrt{x_0^2 + x_1^2} > 0.47$, a circular area far from the wall $\mathbf{x} \in A_{\text{center}} : \sqrt{x_0^2 + x_1^2} < 0.4$, and a second ring in between $\mathbf{x} \in A_{\text{neutral}} : 0.47 < \sqrt{x_0^2 + x_1^2} < 0.4$. In each time step, the agent is rewarded by a score of $+1$ when positioned on A_{wall}, it receives a penalty of -1 when positioned on A_{center}, and it is treated neutral (± 0) when positioned on A_{neutral}. This score needs to be maximized to evolve a wall following agent. In the case of the *immobile agent*, staying stopped is rewarded which is

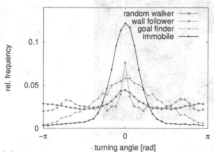

(a) Histogram of turning angles for all 4 behavior types.

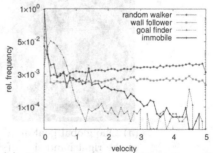

(b) Histogram of velocities for all 4 behavior types (note logarithmic scale on vertical axis).

Fig. 3. Histograms of turning angles and velocities for all four behavior types based on the mathematical model and parameters as given in table 1 (averaged over 200 repetitions of simulations, 1.5×10^4 time steps each).

implemented by minimizing the agent's average speed. In the case of the *random walker*, no type-specific quality is defined.

The results of these evolutionary runs are shown in table 1 (except for the 50 values of P_{incr}). The resulting histograms of turning angles and velocities (due to $P_{incr}(v)$) for these four behavior types as defined by our model and the parameters given in table 1 are shown in Fig. 3. These results do not allow for a simple interpretation but a few features can be discussed here. The lowest peak for turning angle 0 is found for the *random walker* which indicates that the turning angle distribution is close to a uniform distribution. The *random walker* is also one of the fastest. The next peak for angle 0 is that of the *goal finder* but it also has low values for extreme turning angles. Hence, the *goal finder* approaches the goal area in a rather straight trajectory. In addition, the *goal finder* moves slowly. The *wall follower* has a distribution of turning angles that is close to a uniform distribution similarly to the *random walker*. However, the maximal turning angle σ is small, which leads to the behavior of a *wall follower*. Additionally there are two more peaks for big turning angles which are the required corrections when following the curved wall around the circular arena. The *wall follower* moves rather fast. In the case of the *immobile agent* the turning angle is of limited relevance, instead its low average velocity is of more importance.

4   Setup of Experiments

In the following experiments, the agents move in a circular arena with either one goal area or two goal areas (see Fig. 4). Following our inspiration from the honeybee experiments we define the potential field P as a temperature field here.

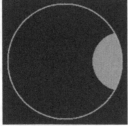 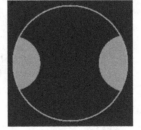

(a) One global goal area at the right hand side of the arena.

(b) A local goal area at the left-hand side and a global goal area at the right-hand side.

Fig. 4. Experimental setup of the arena; the global goal area is located at the right-hand side of the arena and contains temperatures between $36°C$ and $30°C$. The local goal area at the left-hand side of the arena contains temperatures between $32°C$ and $30°C$. Each of the goal areas covers 11% of the arena.

The potential field P is chosen in a way that there is a global optimum at the right-hand side and an optional local optimum at the left-hand side of the arena.

In our experimental settings, these optima are located at the wall, see Fig. 4. In the first experiment 4(a), there is a semi-circle area around the global optimum on the right side. This area is called *global goal area* and has temperatures of 30°C to 36°C ranging from the boundary between the border of the semi-circle and black area to the wall. In the second experimental setup we create a choice-experiment. Additionally to the *global goal area* on the right side, there is a semi-circle area around the local optimum on the left side. This area is called *local goal area* and has a maximal temperature of 32°C at the outer side and 30°C at the boundary between the border of the semi-circle and black area. Each of the goal areas covers 11% of the total arena.

5   Evolution of Behavior Type Compositions

A variation of evolutionary algorithms, called wolf-pack-inspired evolutionary algorithm [38], is used to evolve the composition of behavior types in the swarm. The algorithm maintains overlapping generations and considers a fixed maximum population size. Proportional selection (fitness-based) is used to select individuals (i.e., compositions of behavior types) for mutation that fill empty places in the population. In every generation, one of the individuals, that have not been evaluated yet, is evaluated (alternatively the least evaluated individual if all the individuals have been evaluated already). The algorithm maintains the hierarchy in the population and keeps its diversity by removing older individuals with an equal or lower fitness than a newly evaluated individual (with a probability factor). The fitness function is defined by

$$F = G - L \qquad (4)$$

where G is the number of agents within the global goal area and L is the number of agents within the local goal area (if there is one).

6   Results

For both experimental settings (one global goal and choice-experiment), we investigate the potential of heterogeneous swarms. As described in the above section, we use evolutionary algorithms to adapt the swarm's behavior-type composition to the environment. The experiments are based on a fixed swarm size $N = 15$. The results are based on $n = 18$ independent runs of the evolutionary algorithm and the population of compositions was initialized to a random uniformly distributed setting of behavior types. The evolved approach is compared to the fitness of several homogeneous swarm settings (Fig. 5) that were evaluated in $n = 100$ independent simulation runs (no evolution because composition is predetermined). In the first three homogeneous swarm settings we use a swarm size of $N = 15$. For the last two settings we used a swarm size of $N = 12$ to test for a potential density dependency.

First we focus on the experiment with only one goal area (Fig. 5(a)). The median fitness for 15 *random walkers* is 7, for 15 *goal finders* it is 5, for 15 *wall followers* it is 9, for 12 *random walkers* it is 6, and for 12 *wall followers* it is 8. For the heterogeneous swarm optimized by evolution the median fitness is 10 ($n = 18$). The evolved behavior-type composition is found to be significantly better than the homogeneous swarms (based on Wilcoxon rank sum test, $p < 0.05$).

Figure 5(b) shows the results of the choice experiment (*global goal area* and *local goal area*). Here we compare the evolved heterogeneous behavior-type composition (first box plot, labeled 'Evo') to homogeneous behavior-type compositions.

The median fitness for 15 *random walkers* is 2, for 15 *goal finders* it is 0, for 15 *wall followers* it is 3, for 12 *random walkers* it is 2, and for 12 *wall followers* it is 2. For the heterogeneous swarm optimized by evolution the median fitness is 5.5 ($n = 18$). The evolved behavior-type composition is found to be significantly better than the homogeneous swarms (based on Wilcoxon rank sum test, $p < 0.05$). Hence, our heterogeneous approach is the most effective variant of all tested configurations. The results for 12 *random walkers* and 12 *wall followers* indicate no dependency on density. The motivation of this test is based on results we report below and the consideration that *immobile agents* might potentially be used to virtually decrease the agent density.

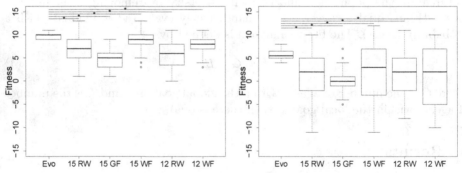

(a) Setting with one goal area at the wall. (b) Setting with a *global goal area* and a *local goal area* (choice experiment).

Fig. 5. Comparison of the best fitness between one evolved heterogeneous setting and several homogeneous swarm settings for one goal area at the wall (left) and the choice experiment on the right (*global goal area* and *local goal area*); heterogeneous swarm (labeled 'Evo'), homogeneous swarms with only *random walkers* (RW), *goal finders* (GF), or *wall followers* (WF). In both settings, the heterogeneous swarm is significantly better than all homogeneous swarms (based on Wilcoxon rank sum test, $p < 0.05$). Other significances are not shown.

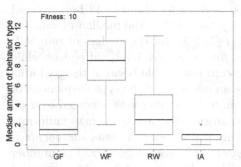

(a) Results of the evolution with one goal area. The plot shows the median amount of behavioral types that are used to compose a heterogeneous swarm with the highest fitness.

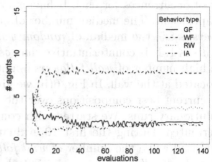

(b) Type frequencies of the best composition over evaluations

Fig. 6. Results of evolved swarm compositions with one goal area and all four behavioral types: *random walker* (RW), *goal finder* (GF), *wall follower* (WF), and *immobile agent* (IA).

Next, we evolve behavior-type compositions for different environments (one or two goal areas) and different initializations of the composition populations. We start with the setting that has only one goal area (see Fig. 4(a)). The evolutionary approach is as described above, that is, the initial population of compositions is sampled from a random uniform distribution. For our analysis, we take the best composition of the last population from each evolutionary run. The box plots shown in Fig. 6(a) give a summary of these best compositions. The num-

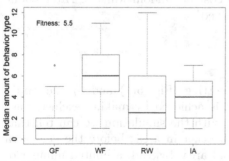

(a) Median number of behavior types as they occur in the best swarm composition.

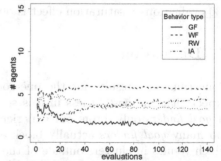

(b) Development of the best composition that is evaluated at each time step.

Fig. 7. Results of the evolution for the choice experiment (*local goal area* and *global goal area*) and all four behavioral types: *random walker* (RW), *goal finder* (GF), *wall follower* (WF), *immobile agent*) (IA).

ber of occurrences for each behavior type is given for the $n = 18$ best evolved compositions. The median number of *goal finders* is 1.5, the median of *wall followers* is 8.5, the median of *random walkers* is 2.5, and the median of *immobile agents* is 1. It is counterintuitive that *goal finders* are relatively infrequent while the high number of *wall followers* might seem reasonable because the goal area is located at the wall. In Fig. 6(b) we give an overview of the type frequencies of the current best compositions over the number of evaluations averaged over all evolutionary runs. We started with compositions that are in average uniformly distributed. During the first 10 evaluations the number of *immobile agents* is decreased while the number of *wall followers* is increased quickly. The number of *random walkers* increases initially but then decreases again. The number of *goal finders* is decreased over a long period during the first 40 evaluations. After about 100 evaluations a saturation effect is observed.

Next we investigate the choice experiment (*local goal area* on the left side and a *global goal area* on the right side of the arena). The box plots of Fig. 7(a) give the number of agents for each behavior type as they occurred in the best compositions of $n = 20$ independent evolutionary runs. The median number of *goal finders* is 1, the median of *wall followers* is 6, the median of *random walkers* is 2.5, and the median of *immobile agents* is 4. As expected the number of *goal finders* is smaller in comparison to the setting with only one goal (cf. Fig. 6(a)) because *goal finders* merely follow the gradient and the swarm separates between the two goal areas. The number of *wall followers* is decreased, the number of *random walkers* is increased in its variance, and the number of *immobile agents* is increased in comparison to the one-goal setting. Especially the increase of *immobile agents* is counterintuitive because they are of no direct use to maximize the fitness function. In Fig. 7(b) we give an overview of the type frequencies of the current best compositions over the number of evaluations averaged over all evolutionary runs. Starting from approximately uniformly distributed compositions the number of *immobile agents* first decreases and is then increased slowly over about 120 evaluations at the cost of random walkers. After about 130 evaluations a saturation effect is observed.

7   Discussion

Concerning the results for the one-goal setting (Fig. 5(a) and 6) one would expect that the best fitness in this setup is achieved by making exclusive use of *goal finders* only. From our experience with the simulation we can tell that too many *goal finders* actually block each other in areas before the goal area which results in clusters outside of the goal area. Instead, a limited number of *goal finders* turns out to be useful because such deadlock situations are then avoided. They serve as seeds within the goal area and help agents of other types to form clusters inside the goal area more easily, which is an example of how the different behavior types create opportunities of cooperation between agents. Most of the agents of the evolved heterogeneous swarms are *wall followers*. With only one goal area present, the *wall followers* always end up in the goal area and form a cluster. In comparison, the number of *random walkers* is low. Their approach to the goal area is slower because they might form clusters within the center of the arena. Eventually, they join the cluster in the goal area and join the *wall followers*. Therefore, in this setup a high amount of *wall followers* is the better choice. In an extended study, that is in preparation, we have also done experiments with goals not positioned at the walls. The number of *wall followers* decreases for that setting as expected but the qualitative result of our study is not influenced by the positions of the goal areas.

Concerning the results for the choice experiment (Fig. 5(b) and 7) the small number of *goal finders* is explained by the fact that they are not able to distinguish between a global and a local goal area because they merely follow the local gradient. Hence, they are not able to increase fitness ($F = G - L$). This is also indicated by the zero median for homogeneous *goal finder* swarms (Fig. 5(b)). Still, *goal finders* might be useful in a heterogeneous swarm to mark the goal areas and to serve as social seeds that attract others. Compared to the results of the experiment with only one goal area, the median amount of *immobile agents* is higher. Intuitively it seems inappropriate to use any *immobile agent* because they never enter the goal area when placed outside of it initially. However, they are part of many evolved swarm compositions although the optimization algorithm is effective [38] and we also do not enforce that all four behavior types have to be included in the solution. Thus, additional experiments are required to investigate the role of *immobile agents* and to find a sound explanation of why *immobile agents* are useful for the swarm in both our model and also in the natural swarms of honeybees. We can only speculate that *immobile agents* might have the functionality of a barrier and might slow down or even block agents that switch between goals. That way *immobile agents* might prevent other agents from visiting the *local goal area* and hence might stabilize the whole decision-making process. However, this requires more investigations and will be done in future work.

8   Conclusion

In this paper we have investigated swarms of agents that are heterogeneous in their behaviors. The idea is to simplify the swarm system by predefining static roles for certain swarm fractions. Even for the investigated extreme case without task switching, the heterogeneous swarm outperforms homogeneous swarms in the investigated aggregation scenario for the selected, predetermined behavior types. For now, all our results are based on one set of predetermined behaviors and one kind of collective task. However, the selection of behaviors was not arbitrary but inspired by results from biological experiments with juvenile bees. Still, the generalization of this work is left for future work.

The evolved compositions of behavior types indicate a rather complex underlying system that creates nontrivial distributions of behaviors which might even be perceived as counterintuitive. While the behavior types themselves were simple and predefined here, it is of course an option to determine the behavior types also by evolutionary computation or other methods of machine learning. However, for applications of swarm robotics, such as nanorobotics [24], it is attractive to make use of simple predetermined behaviors.

The effectivity of the evolved behavior compositions is certainly interesting, raises questions, and allows for different interpretations. While the four behavior types all score low in homogeneous swarms, they allow for a much more efficient aggregation behavior once combined. Obviously cooperation among different types is crucial and teamwork of a diverse team is essential. A tempting interpretation is that the results might be compared to findings in natural swarms that rely on certain degrees of leadership [8]. Only leadership is difficult to define here. The goal-oriented and greedy behavior of the *goal finder* is not helpful for the swarm per se. It requires a *random walker* and a *wall follower* to make use of the social seed within the goal area created by a *goal finder*. Hence, we observe a sophisticated interplay of agents with different approaches and capabilities that outperform their homogeneous counterparts as a heterogeneous swarm.

Also note that the use of simulations is potentially the only means to investigate the concept of predetermined behavioral roles in the natural complex system of young honeybees. Following the common standards of experiment design in biology it is not an option to use the same subjects (bees) in several replications of the experiment. In our case here an initial experiment would be necessary to label the bee with its behavioral role and in a second experiment we could create the desired swarm composition of behavior types. However, the bee might be influenced by the initial experiment and show a different behavior. Hence, simulations are a useful tool to investigate this complex system of interacting honeybees.

The results of this study support a core idea of swarm robotics that the interplay of several simple behaviors generates complex behaviors due to multiple interactions. This case study's main result is that heterogeneous swarms based on predetermined behaviors without task switching can perform well. Our approach is not limited to the study of the BEECLUST algorithm. Also other collective behaviors can be explored, such as heterogeneity in the stimulus-response functions of bees in their waggle-dance behavior [33]. In future work, we plan to do a complete sensitivity analysis of the many paramters in our model. In addition, we plan to work our way towards a generalization of our approach, for example, allowing different sets of predetermined or even learned behaviors. Although this study was guided by the biological inspiration of young honeybees' behavior, our future research will focus more on engineering applications of heterogeneous swarms in (evolutionary) swarm robotics.

Acknowledgments. This work is supported by: Austrian Science Fund (FWF): P19478-B16 and P23943-N13 (REBODIMENT); EU FP7 FET-Proactive 'ASSISI$_{bf}$', no. 601074; EU H2020 FET '*flora robotica*', no. 640959.

References

1. Arvin, F., Turgut, A.E., Bazyari, F., Arikan, K.B., Bellotto, N., Yue, S.: Cue-based aggregation with a mobile robot swarm: a novel fuzzy-based method. Adaptive Behavior **22**(3), 189–206 (2014)
2. Arvin, F., Turgut, A.E., Yue, S.: Fuzzy-based aggregation with a mobile robot swarm. In: Dorigo, M., Birattari, M., Blum, C., Christensen, A.L., Engelbrecht, A.P., Groß, R., Stützle, T. (eds.) ANTS 2012. LNCS, vol. 7461, pp. 346–347. Springer, Heidelberg (2012)
3. Beni, G.: From swarm intelligence to swarm robotics. In: Şahin, E., Spears, W.M. (eds.) Swarm Robotics 2004. LNCS, vol. 3342, pp. 1–9. Springer, Heidelberg (2005)
4. Berman, S., et al.: Optimized stochastic policies for task allocation in swarms of robots. Robotics, IEEE Transactions on **25**(4), 927–937 (2009)
5. Bodi, M., Thenius, R., Szopek, M., Schmickl, T., Crailsheim, K.: Interaction of robot swarms using the honeybee-inspired control algorithm beeclust. Mathematical and Computer Modelling of Dynamical Systems **18**(1), 87–100 (2012)
6. Bonabeau, E., Dorigo, M., Theraulaz, G.: Swarm Intelligence: From Natural to Artificial Systems. Oxford Univ Press (1999)
7. Campbell, A., Wu, A.S.: Multi-agent role allocation: issues, approaches, and multiple perspectives. Autonomous Agents & Multi-Agent Systems **22**, 317–355 (2011)
8. Couzin, I.D., Krause, J., Franks, N.R., Levin, S.A.: Effective leadership and decision-making in animal groups on the move. Nature **433**, 513–516 (2005)
9. Dorigo, M., et al.: Swarmanoid: a novel concept for the study of heterogeneous robotic swarms. IEEE Robotics & Automation Magazine **20**(4), 60–71 (2013)
10. Dorigo, M., Bonabeau, E., Theraulaz, G.: Ant algorithms and stigmergy. Future Generation Computer Systems **16**(9), 851–871 (2000)
11. Ferrante, E., Dúeñez Guzmán, E., Turgut, A.E., Wenseleers, T.: Evolution of task partitioning in swarm robotics. In: et al., V.T. (ed.) Proceedings of the Workshop on Collective Behaviors and Social Dynamics of the European Conference on Artificial Life (ECAL 2013) (2013)
12. Garnier, S., Gautrais, J., Asadpour, M., Jost, C., Theraulaz, G.: Self-organized aggregation triggers collective decision making in a group of cockroach-like robots. Adaptive Behavior **17**(2), 109–133 (2009)
13. Hamann, H.: Towards swarm calculus: Urn models of collective decisions and universal properties of swarm performance. Swarm Intelligence **7**(2–3), 145–172 (2013)
14. Hamann, H., Karsai, I., Schmickl, T.: Time delay implies cost on task switching: A model to investigate the efficiency of task partitioning. Bulletin of Mathematical Biology **75**(7), 1181–1206 (2013)
15. Hamann, H., Meyer, B., Schmickl, T., Crailsheim, K.: A model of symmetry breaking in collective decision-making. In: Doncieux, S., Girard, B., Guillot, A., Hallam, J., Meyer, J.-A., Mouret, J.-B. (eds.) SAB 2010. LNCS, vol. 6226, pp. 639–648. Springer, Heidelberg (2010)
16. Hereford, J.M.: Analysis of BEECLUST swarm algorithm. In: Proc. of the IEEE Symposium on Swarm Intelligence (SIS 2011), pp. 192–198. IEEE (2011)
17. Hölldobler, B., Wilson, E.: The ants. Belknap Press of Harvard University (1990)
18. Kengyel, D., Schmickl, T., Hamann, H., Thenius, R., Crailsheim, K.: Embodiment of honeybee's thermotaxis in a mobile robot swarm. In: Kampis, G., Karsai, I., Szathmáry, E. (eds.) ECAL 2009, Part II. LNCS, vol. 5778, pp. 69–76. Springer, Heidelberg (2011)

19. Kengyel, D., Thenius, R., Crailsheim, K., Schmickl, T.: Influence of a social gradient on a swarm of agents controlled by the beeclust algorithm. Advances in Artificial Life. In: Proceedings of the 12th European Conference on the Synthesis and Simulation of Living Systems, ECAL 2013 12, pp. 1041–1048 (2013)

20. Kengyel, D., Wotawa, F., Schmickl, T.: Towards swarm level programming: The role of different movement patterns in swarm systems. Swarm Intelligence (2014), submitted

21. Kernbach, S., Thenius, R., Kornienko, O., Schmickl, T.: Re-embodiment of honeybee aggregation behavior in an artificial micro-robotic swarm. Adaptive Behavior 17, 237–259 (2009)

22. Khaluf, Y., Birattari, M., Hamann, H.: A swarm robotics approach to task allocation under soft deadlines and negligible switching costs. In: del Pobil, A.P., Chinellato, E., Martinez-Martin, E., Hallam, J., Cervera, E., Morales, A. (eds.) SAB 2014. LNCS, vol. 8575, pp. 270–279. Springer, Heidelberg (2014)

23. Labella, T.H., Dorigo, M., Deneubourg, J.L.: Division of labor in a group of robots inspired by ants' foraging behavior. ACM Transactions on Autonomous and Adaptive Systems (TAAS) 1(1), 4–25 (2006)

24. Lenaghan, S., Wang, Y., Xi, N., Fukuda, T., Tarn, T., Hamel, W., Zhang, M.: Grand challenges in bioengineered nanorobotics for cancer therapy. IEEE Transactions on Biomedical Engineering 60(3), 667–673 (2013)

25. Liu, X., Li, X., Shi, X., Huang, K., Liu, Y.: A multi-type ant colony optimization (maco) method for optimal land use allocation in large areas. International Journal of Geographical Information Science 26(7), 1325–1343 (2012)

26. Lorenz, K.: Vergleichende Verhaltensforschung: Grundlagen der Ethologie. Springer (1978)

27. Rubenstein, M., Ahler, C., Hoff, N., Cabrera, A., Nagpal, R.: Kilobot: A low cost robot with scalable operations designed for collective behaviors. Robotics and Autonomous Systems 62(7), 966–975 (2014)

28. Rubenstein, M., Cornejo, A., Nagpal, R.: Programmable self-assembly in a thousand-robot swarm. Science 345(6198), 795–799 (2014)

29. Schmickl, T., Crailsheim, K.: TaskSelSim: a model of the self-organization of the division of labour in honeybees. Mathematical and Computer Modelling of Dynamical Systems 14, 101–125 (2008)

30. Schmickl, T., Hamann, H.: BEECLUST: a swarm algorithm derived from honeybees. In: Xiao, Y. (ed.) Bio-inspired Computing and Communication Networks. CRC Press, March 2011

31. Schmickl, T., Thenius, R., Möslinger, C., Radspieler, G., Kernbach, S., Crailsheim, K.: Get in touch: Cooperative decision making based on robot-to-robot collisions. Autonomous Agents and Multi-Agent Systems 18(1), 133–155 (2008)

32. Seeley, T.D.: Adaptive significance of the age polyethism schedule in honeybee colonies. Behavioral Ecology and Sociobiology 11, 287–293 (1982)

33. Seeley, T.D.: Honey bee foragers as sensory units of their colonies. Behavioral Ecology and Sociobiology 34, 51–62 (1994)

34. Szopek, M., Schmickl, T., Thenius, R., Radspieler, G., Crailsheim, K.: Dynamics of collective decision making of honeybees in complex temperature fields. PLoS ONE 8(10), e76250 (2013)

35. Wilson, E.: The relation between caste ratios and division of labour in the ant genus Pheidole (Hymenoptera: Formicidae). Behav. Ecol. Sociobiol. 16, 89–98 (1984)

36. Yong, C.H., et al.: Coevolution of role-based cooperation in multiagent systems. IEEE Transactions on Autonomous Mental Development 1(3), 170–186 (2009)

37. Zahadat, P., Crailsheim, K., Schmickl, T.: Social inhibition manages division of labour in artificial swarm systems. In: Lio, P., Miglino, O., Nicosia, G., Nolfi, S., Pavone, M. (eds.) 12th European Conference on Artificial Life (ECAL 2013), pp. 609–616. MIT Press (2013)
38. Zahadat, P., Schmickl, T.: Wolfpack-inspired evolutionary algorithm and a reaction-diffusion-based controller are used for pattern formation. In: Proceedings of the 2014 Conference on Genetic and Evolutionary Computation, pp. 241–248. GECCO 2014, ACM, New York, USA (2014)

Multi-agent Path Planning
in Known Dynamic Environments

Aniello Murano[1], Giuseppe Perelli[2]([✉]), and Sasha Rubin[1]

[1] Università di Napoli "Federico II", Naples, Italy
[2] University of Oxford, Oxford, England
perelli.gi@gmail.com

Abstract. We consider the problem of planning paths of multiple agents in a dynamic but predictable environment. Typical scenarios are evacuation, reconfiguration, and containment. We present a novel representation of abstract path-planning problems in which the stationary environment is explicitly coded as a graph (called the arena) while the dynamic environment is treated as just another agent. The complexity of planning using this representation is PSPACE-complete. The arena complexity (i.e., the complexity of the planning problem in which the graph is the only input, in particular, the number of agents is fixed) is NP-hard. Thus, we provide structural restrictions that put the arena complexity of the planning problem into PTIME(for any fixed number of agents). The importance of our work is that these structural conditions (and hence the complexity results) do not depend on graph-theoretic properties of the arena (such as clique- or tree-width), but rather on the abilities of the agents.

1 Introduction

The path-planning problem is to find collision-free paths for mobile agents in an environment that may contain obstacles [10,20,27,32]. Obstacles, which may not always be stationary, are *known* if their size, locations, motions, etc. are fixed ahead of planning.

For example, consider a building consisting of rooms, corridors between certain pairs of rooms, and a set of exits. Initially, a fixed number of people are positioned in various rooms, and a flood begins in one of the rooms. At each time step every agent can either stay where it is or move through a corridor to an adjacent room. Suppose the flood spreads radially (i.e., at each time step it reaches all adjacent rooms that are accessible via a corridor). The path planning problem is to exhibit a sequence of actions for the agents that ensures they can reach an exit before the flood traps them.

Other applications are to space exploration, warehouse management, intelligent transportation, assembly or disassembly, and computer games (see [16] and the references therein).

This work has been partially supported by the FP7 EU project 600958-SHERPA and the ERC Advanced Grant "RACE" (291528) at Oxford. Sasha Rubin is a Marie Curie fellow of the Istituto Nazionale di Alta Matematica.

© Springer International Publishing Switzerland 2015
Q. Chen et al. (Eds.): PRIMA 2015, LNAI 9387, pp. 218–231, 2015.
DOI: 10.1007/978-3-319-25524-8_14

The AI literature on planning has established that planning is intractable, e.g., propositional STRIPS planning is PSPACE-COMPLETE [2]. To gain deeper insight into what makes planning hard, one must study structural properties of the problem, e.g., [19]:

> For many discrete planning problems that we would like a computer to solve, the state space is enormous (e.g., 10^{100} states). Therefore, substantial effort has been invested in constructing implicit encodings of problems in hopes that the entire state space does not have to be explored by the algorithm to solve the problem.

In this paper we propose an implicit representation ("encoding" in the language above) of path-planning problems of mobile agents in which obstacles are known, and agents should collaborate, rather than compete, to achieve some goal. Know but dynamic environments, such as the flood in the example above, are treated as agents.

Since our representation is exponentially compact, the associated decision problem is PSPACE-complete (Theorems 1 and 2). This is true even for a fixed number of agents, i.e., this high space complexity is not the result of the availability of more and more agents. The *restricted path-planning problem* assumes that all the data is fixed in advance, except for the arena which is the input. We prove that the complexity of the restricted path-planning problem, called the *arena complexity* in the abstract, may be NP-hard (Proposition 1); it is not known if it can be PSPACE-hard. Thus, we describe cases that are solvable in PTIME in which the agent behaviour is restricted (Theorem 3): every agent is either monotone or of bounded-extent. Informally, an agent is monotone if its set of positions can only expand over time (or, only shrink over time). A typical example is the flood: once a room is flooded it stays flooded. An agent is of bounded-extent if it can only occupy a set of positions of bounded size (where the bound does not depend on the size of the arena). A typical example are people: each person in the building can occupy only one room at a time, no matter how large the room is.

1.1 Related Work

Much work in robotics focuses on geometric reasoning, e.g., [18,30,32]. Although our environment is discrete (i.e., a finite graph), it may represent a discretisation of the geometric structure of the environment, e.g., a vertex may represent an area not occupied by any of the obstacles. For a discussion of the subtle issues involved in such a translation, see for instance [16].

Standard ways to deal with the fact that planning has, in general, high computational complexity, is to use abstractions and heuristics, see for instance a recent survey on path planning [27]. In contrast, in this paper we isolate computationally tractable but interesting path-planning scenarios.

Standard ways to encode planning problems are logic-based: e.g., the situation calculus is a first-order logic in which the main objects are finite sequences of actions; and in the set-theoretical representation (such as STRIPS or the multi-agent extension MA-STRIPS [1]) every state is an evaluation of a fixed number of Boolean variables [10]. In contrast, our representation is graph-theoretic and represents the positions of the agents on a graph. Although our planning problems can be expressed in these logical formalisms, this would hide the graphical nature of the problem, see Section 5.

Our representation is related to multi-robot path-planning problems and puzzles [8,15,23,26,28]. In [15,26,28] the goal is to rearrange a group of robots in a given graph, without colliding with each other or with obstacles. The non-optimal version of that problem is in PTIME [15]. We can encode the variation in which more than one agent may move at a time [28], see Example 2. The motion-planning problems and puzzles of [8,12] are PSPACE-complete. We use one such puzzle to prove a PSPACE-hard lower bound on our path-planning problems, see Theorem 2.

Monotonicity has been used to get PTIME algorithms in the setting of propositional temporal planning [4]. That work studies a propositional representation of planning problems in which the fluents (i.e., literals) are required to be monotone, e.g., once removed a fluent can never be added in any plan of the planning problem. In contrast, the natural translation of our representation into the propositional planning encoding does not preserve monotonicity, see Section 4.

Most of the planning literature, including this paper, focuses on attainment goals of the form "a target configuration can be reached from some initial configuration" [19]. In particular then, we can also model goals of the form "every agent eventually reaches its target vertex in a collision-free way".

Our formalisation and results are inspired by formal methods. Other work in planning with the similar inspirations are an automata-theoretic approach to planning [5], and planning as model checking [11,13,21,24,25,31]. These papers also supply centralised planning algorithms, however their representation is based on transition-systems, and hence is not compact, as ours is.

2   Representation of the Path-Planning Problem

We describe how we represent the path-planning problem. Informally, all moving entities (people, floods, fires) are considered to be agents. Agents operate in a finite graph (V, E). At any given time, an agent can occupy a subset V, called its position (e.g., a person occupies a single vertex, and a flood may occupy more than one vertex). One may specify the legal positions $\mathcal{L}$ of the agents, e.g., that agents cannot occupy overlapping vertices. An agent's movements are governed by its mobility relation Δ that relates its current position to its next possible position (the fact that Δ is a relation, rather than a function, models that moves may be nondeterministic). In Section 3 we will discuss how to specify $\mathcal{L}$ and Δ (in particular these objects can be defined algorithmically, or by formulas, e.g., of first-order logic).

Formally, let $k \in \mathbb{N}$ (representing the number the agents). An *arena* is a finite directed graph $\mathcal{A} = (V, E)$. Subsets of V are called *positions*. A *(k-)configuration* *(over $\mathcal{A}$)* is an expansion of $\mathcal{A}$ by k many positions, i.e., $\langle V, E, P_1, \cdots, P_k \rangle$ where each $P_i \subseteq V$ is called the *position of agent i (in the configuration)*. Note that an agent can be in more than one vertex, e.g., a flood. A *mobility relation (over $\mathcal{A}$)* is a subset Δ of $2^V \times 2^V$ such that $(X, Y) \in \Delta$ implies $Y \subseteq X \cup E(X)$, where $E(X) := \{v \in V \mid \exists u \in X. (u, v) \in E\}$. The idea is that $(X, Y) \in \Delta$ means that a player can move from position X to position Y but only along edges.

A *(path-)planning domain* is a tuple $\mathcal{D} = \langle \mathcal{A}, \mathcal{L}, \Delta_1, \cdots, \Delta_k \rangle$ where $\mathcal{A} = (V, E)$ is an arena, $\mathcal{L}$ is a set of k-configurations of $\mathcal{A}$, called the *legal configurations*, and each Δ_i is a mobility relation over $\mathcal{A}$. For k-configurations c, d over $\mathcal{A}$ write $c \vdash d$ to mean that d results from c via simultaneous application of Δ_is, formally: for $c = \langle V, E, P_1, \cdots, P_k \rangle$ and $d = \langle V, E, Q_1, \cdots, Q_k \rangle$ define $c \vdash d$ iff $(P_i, Q_i) \in \Delta_i$ for all $i \leq k$. An *execution starting in configuration c* is a finite or infinite sequence π of configurations of $\mathcal{A}$ such that $\pi_1 = c$ and for all i, a) $\pi_i \in \mathcal{L}$, and b) $\pi_i \vdash \pi_{i+1}$.

A *(path) planning instance* is a tuple $\mathcal{P} = \langle \mathcal{D}, \mathcal{I}, \mathcal{G} \rangle$ where $\mathcal{I}$ and $\mathcal{G}$ are sets of k-configurations over $\mathcal{A}$ called the *initial configurations* and *goal configurations*. An execution π of $\mathcal{P}$ is called a *solution* if $\pi_1 \in \mathcal{I}$ and there exists j such that $\pi_j \in \mathcal{G}$.

Example 1 (Evacuation). To model the flood example from the introduction with one person take $k = 2$, i.e., one agent is a person, and the other agent is the flood. Consider an initial configuration of the form $\langle V, E, \{p\}, \{f\} \rangle$, i.e., the person starts in some vertex s, and the source of the flood is in some vertex f. The goal configurations are of the form $\cup_{X \subseteq V} \langle V, E, \{t\}, X \rangle$ for some vertex t. The mobility of the person relates $\{v\}$ to all those $\{w\}$ such that $(v, w) \in E$ or $v = w$, i.e., the person can move to an adjacent position, or stay where it is. The mobility of the flood relates X to the single set $X \cup E(X)$, i.e., the flood expands radially. Thus a typical configuration in an execution is of the form $\langle V, E, \{v\}, F \rangle$ for some $v \in V$ and $F \subseteq V$. Finally, to specify that the person cannot move into a flooded area, define the set of legal configurations $\mathcal{L}$ to be those of the form $\langle V, E, \{v\}, F \rangle$ such that $v \notin F$.

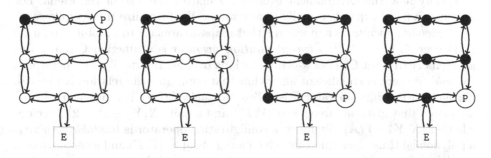

Fig. 1. An evolution of a flood scenario. Player P cannot reach the exit E

In Figure 1 we represent a possible evolution of an instance of the Evacuation scenario. The graph represents three floors of a building, connected by two lifts located at the sides. Each floor has three connected rooms. Moreover, there is an exit point E at the basement, that is reachable from the central room of the first floor. In the initial configuration, the flood is located in the leftmost top room of the building, while Player P is in the rightmost top. At each step in time, the flood spreads from flooded rooms to the connected unflooded rooms, while P moves to some available room. Unfortunately for P, he gets stuck after three units of time without reaching the exit point. It is not hard to see that, in case the initial position of P is on a side of the second floor (or anywhere in the first floor), he can safely reach the exit point.

Example 2 (Reconfiguration). The abstract path-planning problem requires a set of k mobile robots to re-arrange themselves into a target configuration without colliding with each other or fixed obstacles [28]. This can be modeled as follows. There is one initial configuration, say $\langle V, E, \{v_1\}, \cdots, \{v_k\}\rangle$, and one goal configuration, say $\langle V, E, \{t_1\}, \cdots, \{t_k\}\rangle$. The mobility relation for each agent is the same as the mobility relation for the person in the previous example. Define the set of legal configurations $\mathcal{L}$ to be those of the form $\langle V, E, \{v_1\}, \cdots, \{v_k\}\rangle$ such that $v_i \neq v_j$ for $i \neq j$. This captures the fact that players should not collide.

Example 3 (Containment). Consider a variation of the flooding example in which the goal of the people is to erect barriers in some of the rooms in order to stop the flood from reaching a certain vertex (or cover a set of vertices). This can be modeled by having extra agents that represent barriers. Each barrier is associate with exactly one agent. When a barrier is placed on an unflooded vertex then the flood cannot enter that vertex (this can be coded in the legal-configurations). Agents can carry barriers with them or drop them when they move rooms (this is also expressed in the legal-configurations).

3   Complexity of the Path-Planning Problem

In order to talk about the decision problem for path-planning, we need a way to specify how the environment evolves no matter the size of the arena. For instance, a flood expands radially in any arena. We formalize this as follows.

A *mobility operator* is a function F that maps an arena $\mathcal{A}$ to a mobility relation $F(\mathcal{A})$ over $\mathcal{A}$. For $k \in \mathbb{N}$, a k-*configuration operator* is a function C that maps an arena $\mathcal{A}$ to a set $C(\mathcal{A})$ of k-configurations over $\mathcal{A}$. Informally, an operator is *tractable* if there is an efficient algorithm that computes the relation it induces. Formally, a mobility operator F is called *tractable* if there is a polynomial time algorithm that given an arena $\mathcal{A} = \langle V, E\rangle$, and a pair $(X, Y) \in 2^V \times 2^V$, decides whether $(X, Y) \in F(\mathcal{A})$. Similarly, a configuration operator is *tractable* if there is a polynomial time algorithm that, given an arena $\mathcal{A} = \langle V, E\rangle$ and a configuration $c = \langle V, E, P_1, \cdots, P_k\rangle$ over $\mathcal{A}$ decides whether $c \in C(\mathcal{A})$. Note that the operators in Examples 1 and 2 are tractable.

We assume, for the rest of this paper, that all operators are tractable.

Remark 1. This tractability assumption implies $\vdash$ is tractable, i.e., there is a PTIME algorithm that given $\mathcal{A}$ and k-configurations c, d over $\mathcal{A}$, decides whether $c \vdash d$.

Observe that fixing the following *planning data*

- $k \in \mathbb{N}$,
- mobility operators F_i (for each $i \leq k$),
- configuration operators $\mathsf{L}, \mathsf{I}, \mathsf{G}$, and
- an arena $\mathcal{A} = \langle V, E \rangle$,

uniquely determines a path-planning domain and a path-planning instance, i.e., the planning domain $\mathcal{D} = \langle \mathcal{A}, \mathsf{L}(\mathcal{A}), \mathsf{F}_1(\mathcal{A}), \cdots, \mathsf{F}_k(\mathcal{A}) \rangle$ and the planning instance $\mathcal{P} = \langle \mathcal{D}, \mathsf{I}(\mathcal{A}), \mathsf{G}(\mathcal{A}) \rangle$. Call this $\mathcal{P}$ the *planning instance induced by the given planning data*, or simply the *induced planning instance*.

Definition 1. *The path-planning problem asks, given as input the planning data* $k, \mathsf{F}_1, \cdots, \mathsf{F}_k, \mathsf{L}, \mathsf{I}, \mathsf{G}, \mathcal{A}$, *whether the induced path-planning instance has a solution. The restricted path-planning problem fixes* $k, \mathsf{F}_1, \cdots, \mathsf{F}_k, \mathsf{L}, \mathsf{I}, \mathsf{G}$ *and asks, given an arena* $\mathcal{A}$ *as input, whether or not the induced path-planning instance has a solution.*

Remark 2. In order to talk about the complexity of this decision problem (and also of the notion of a tractable operator), we should specify how these objects are coded. We use any natural encoding. E.g., sets V are identified with sets of the form $\{1, 2, \cdots, N\}$; the number of robots k is written in unary; relations (such as $E \subseteq V \times V$ and $P \subseteq V$) are coded by listing their elements; and a tractable operator is coded as the state diagram of a PTIME Turing machine (in Remark 4 we will see how to express operators as formulas rather than machines). The *size* of the planning data is the number of bits of its encoding. Note that the size of an arena $\mathcal{A} = \langle V, E \rangle$ is $O(|V|^2)$, and the size of a k-configuration over $\mathcal{A}$ is $O(|V|^2 + |V|k)$.

Theorem 1. *The path-planning problem can be solved in* PSPACE, *or time exponential in* $|V|$ *and* k.

Proof. The number of configurations is $O(2^{|V|k})$, and thus the brute force algorithm takes EXPTIME in $|V|$ and k. However, since each configuration can be written in polynomial space (in the size of V and k), one can search the reachable configuration space using a nondeterministic polynomial-space algorithm. That is, the algorithm stores the current configuration c on its tape, nondeterministically guesses (in PTIME) a legal configuration d (and writes it on its tape), and then verifies that $c \vdash d$ (by Remark 1 the $\vdash$ relation is computable in PTIME). The algorithm begins by guessing (in PTIME) a configuration in $\mathsf{I}(\mathcal{A})$ and proceeds until the current configuration is in $\mathsf{G}(\mathcal{A})$. This algorithm halts if and only if the induced planning problem has a solution. Now use the fact that NPSPACE = PSPACE. $\square$

Corollary 1. *For every* $k, \mathsf{F}_1, \cdots, \mathsf{F}_k, \mathsf{L}, \mathsf{I}, \mathsf{G}$ *the restricted path-planning problem can be solved in* PSPACE, *or time exponential in* $|V|$.

Since there are motion-planning problems that are PSPACE-hard (e.g., [8,12]), the path-planning problem is also PSPACE-hard. For instance, *generalised rush-hour* is a generalisation of a children's puzzle in which the objective is to slide cars in a grid-environment in order for a target car to reach a certain exit co-ordinate. Solving generalised rush-hour is PSPACE-complete [8].

Theorem 2. *The path-planning problem is* PSPACE-*hard.*

Proof. We describe a reduction from generalised rush-hour (GRH) to path-planning problems. Note that although [8] prove PSPACE-hardness when the GRH instances consist of cars (1×2 vehicles) and trucks (1×3 vehicles), it is known that using only cars suffice [29]. An instance of GRH consists of the width w and height h of the grid, a number n of cars, and for each car an orientation (horizontal or vertical) and co-ordinates of the head of each car (x_i, y_i). We assume that the first car is the designated car, and that it has horizontal orientation. Each car can only move, forwards or backwards, in the direction of its orientation. The goal is to move the cars, one at a time, until the head of the designated car reaches the right-hand-side of the grid.[1]

The main problem we have to solve is that in GRH one car moves at a time, while in our path-planning problems agents move concurrently. We solve this problem by treating the set of all cars as a single agent, i.e., let $k = 1$. This introduces the problem that we need to be able to distinguish between different cars. This is solved by placing each car on a disjoint copy of the grid. That is, a GRH configuration is encoded by the arena $w \times h \times n$ grid so that if the head of the ith car is (currently) at co-ordinate (a, b) then: if the car is horizontal then this car is coded by the vertices $a \times b \times i$ and $(a + 1) \times b \times i$, and if the car is vertical then this car is coded by the vertices $a \times b \times i$ and $a \times (b + 1) \times i$.

More precisely, given an instance of GRH define planning-data as follows. Let $k = 1$, let the arena be the $w \times h \times n$ grid, formally it has $V = [w] \times [h] \times [n]$ and $E = \{((x, y, z), (x', y', z')) : |x - x'| = 1 \text{ xor } |y - y'| = 1 \text{ xor } |z - z'| = 1\}$. We only describe how the operators map grid arenas of the form $a \times b \times c$ for $a, b, c \in \mathbb{N}$ (on other arenas the maps may be arbitrary). The legal configuration operator $\mathcal{L}$ maps the grid arena $a \times b \times c$ to the set of configurations in which there is exactly one car on each of the c-levels; the $\mathcal{G}$ operator maps the grid arena $a \times b \times c$ to the set of legal configurations in which the head of the first car has y-coordinate equal to b; the $\mathcal{I}$ operator maps the grid arena $w \times h \times n$ to the configuration encoding the initial layout of the GRH; the mobility operator maps the grid arena $a \times b \times c$ to the relation over $V = [a] \times [b] \times [c]$ that relates X to Y if the only difference between X and Y is that for some co-ordinate $i \leq c$, every element in $X \cap [a] \times [b] \times [i]$ moves one coordinate forwards in the

---

[1] The original definition of GRH unnecessarily allows any of the cars to be the target, the exit to be anywhere on the perimeter, and the target car to be horizontal or vertical [8].

direction of the orientation or every element moves one co-ordinate backwards in the direction of orientation. This completes the description of the reduction. It is not hard to see that the GRH has a solution if and only if the planning instance induced by the constructed data has a solution.   □

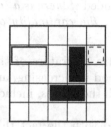
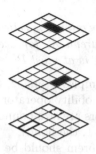

Fig. 2. A representation of the encoding for Generalised Rush Hour (GRH) to path-planning problem. On the left, an instance of GRH. The white rectangle represents the position of the designated car, the black rectangles represent the position of the other cars, the dashed square represents the exit point. On the right, the path-planning representation.

It is not clear if there exists a restricted path-planning problem that is PSPACE-hard. We remark that the proof just given does not work since a reduction would have to map an instance of generalised rush-hour (which includes the initial layout) to an arena $\mathcal{A}$ (which does not include the initial configuration). We do know the following:

Proposition 1. *There exists $k, \mathsf{F}_1, \cdots, \mathsf{F}_k, \mathsf{L}, \mathsf{I}, \mathsf{G}$ such that the restricted path-planning problem is NP-hard.*

Proof. We reduce from the NP-complete problem that asks if a given vertex colouring of a graph by 3 colours is a proper colouring, i.e., that no two adjacent vertices have the same colour. The idea is to use $k = 3$ agents, the initial configurations are arbitrary colourings (i.e., I maps $\mathcal{A}$ to $\langle \mathcal{A}, P_1, P_2, P_3 \rangle$ such that $P_i \cap P_j = \emptyset$ for $i \neq j$), the mobility relations map A to the identity relation on 2^V (i.e., agents do not move), every configuration is a legal configuration (i.e., L maps A to the set of all 3-configurations), and the goal configurations are proper colourings (i.e., G maps $\mathcal{A}$ to $\langle \mathcal{A}, P_1, P_2, P_3 \rangle$ such that $(x, y) \in E$ and $x \in P_i, y \in P_j$ implies $i \neq j$). It is immediate that the reduction that maps $\mathcal{A}$ to the data $k = 3, \mathsf{F}_1, \mathsf{F}_2, \mathsf{F}_3, \mathsf{L}, \mathsf{I}, \mathsf{G}$ is computable in PTIME, and that $\mathcal{A}$ is 3-colourable if and only if the constructed restricted path-planning problem has a solution.   □

We now identify a general subclass of path-planning problems that are solvable in PTIME. We use the following definitions.

Definition 2. *A mobility relation Δ is called:*

- increasing *if* $(X, Y) \in \Delta \Rightarrow X \subseteq Y$,
- decreasing *if* $(X, Y) \in \Delta \Rightarrow Y \subseteq X$,
- monotone *if it is increasing or decreasing,*
- size-decreasing *if* $(X, Y) \in \Delta \Rightarrow |X| \geq |Y|$.

A mobility operator F *is called* increasing *(resp. decreasing, monotone, size-preserving) if every mobility relation* $F(\mathcal{A})$ *is increasing (resp. decreasing, monotone, size-preserving).*

A configuration operator C *is called* size-bounded *if there is a constant* $B \in \mathbb{N}$ *such that for every arena* $\mathcal{A}$, *for every* $i \leq k$, *the cardinality of* P_i *in every configuration in* $C(\mathcal{A})$ *is at most* B.

Note that in Examples 1 and 2, the mobility operators of the players are size-preserving, the mobility operator of the flood is increasing, and the initial-configuration operators are size-bounded (for all the agents, including, although we don't need this fact, the flood).

The following theorem should be contrasted with the fact that Theorem 1 implies that the time-complexity of restricted path-planning problems is exponential in $|V|$.

Theorem 3. *Fix* $B \in \mathbb{N}$, *and consider the planning problem in which one restricts the input* $\langle k, \mathsf{L}, \mathsf{I}, \mathsf{G}, \mathsf{F}_1, \cdots, \mathsf{F}_k \rangle$ *so that* I *is size-bounded (by* B), *and each mobility operator* F_i *is monotone or size-decreasing. The time complexity of the restricted planning problem is polynomial in* $|V|$.

Proof. The number N of reachable configurations is bounded above by a polynomial in $|V|$. Indeed: $N \leq \prod_{i \leq k} m_i |V|^{n_i}$ where $m_i = 1, n_i = 1$ if the mobility operator for agent i is monotone, and $m_i = 2, n_i = B$ if the mobility operator for agent i is size-preserving (since the number of subsets of V of size at most B is bounded above by $2|V|^B$). In particular, the product is $|V|^{O(k)}$, i.e., polynomial in $|V|$ and exponential in k. Now, since the successor configuration relation $\vdash$ is computable in PTIME (see Remark 1) we can build the reachable configuration space in PTIME. Since the initial-configuration and goal-configuration operators are tractable, we can compute the set of initial configurations and the set of goal configurations in PTIME. Now we test if there is a path from some initial configuration to some goal configuration, which can be done in time quadratic in N. □

Remark 3. Thus, the planning instances from Examples 1 and 2 are solvable in PTIME. The algorithm in the proof of Theorem 3 shows that Example 1 is solvable in time $O(|V|^2)$. With k people and one flood the algorithm runs in time $O(|V|^{k+1})$.

Remark 4. The reader who prefers logical specification languages (i.e., FOL) to computational ones (i.e., Turing Machines) may express their operators as formulas. Indeed, since the program-complexity of FOL (i.e., the complexity of model-checking FOL on finite structures in which the formula is fixed and the structure varies) is in PTIME, deduce that every FOL-definable operator is tractable.

Informally, the descriptions of the operators in Examples 1 and 2 can be expressed as formulas of FOL in appropriate signatures.

More precisely, fix unary predicate symbols $P_1, \cdots, P_k, A, B$ and a binary predicate symbol E (we use standard notation, e.g., [7]). We assume we have symbols for equality and set containment with their usual interpretations. A mobility operator F is FOL-*definable* if there is a first-order formula ϕ in the signature $S = (E, A, B)$, such that for every S-structure $\mathcal{M} = (V^{\mathcal{M}}, E^{\mathcal{M}}, A^{\mathcal{M}}, B^{\mathcal{M}})$ we have that $\mathcal{M} \models \phi$ if and only if $(A^{\mathcal{M}}, B^{\mathcal{M}}) \in F((V^{\mathcal{M}}, E^{\mathcal{M}}))$. For instance, the mobility operator for the flood in Example 1 is definable using a FOL-formula that states that A and B are singletons, say $A = \{a\}, B = \{b\}$, and that $(a, b) \in E$, e.g.,

$$\exists x \in A. \exists y \in B. \forall z. (z \in A \to x = z) \land (z \in B \to y = z) \land (x, y) \in E.$$

Similarly, a configuration operator C is FOL-*definable* if there is a first-order formula ϕ in the signature $(E, P_1, \cdots, P_k)$ such that for every S-structure $\mathcal{M} = (V^{\mathcal{M}}, E^{\mathcal{M}}, P_1^{\mathcal{M}}, \cdots, P_k^{\mathcal{M}})$ we have that $\mathcal{M} \models \phi$ if and only if $\mathcal{M} \in C((V^{\mathcal{M}}, E^{\mathcal{M}}))$. For instance, a simple variation of the legal configurations in Example 2 is definable by the FOL-formula $\bigwedge_{i \neq j} \neg \exists x. x \in P_i \land x \in P_j$.

4 Comparison with Other Representations

The goal of this section is to analyse the translations of the abstract path-planning problems considered in this paper into standard representations of planning problems, i.e., the set-theoretical representation and the classical representation [10]. We illustrate by encoding the flood problem of Example 1.

A planning problem in the set-theoretical representation is a tuple $\mathcal{S} = \langle P, A, I, G \rangle$ where:

- P is a finite set of *atoms*,
- $\iota \subset P$ is the *initial state*,
- $G \subset P$ is the set of *goal propositions*,
- A is a set of *actions*, each action a is a tuple $\langle pre^+(a), pre^-(a), add(a), del(a) \rangle$ of subsets of P.

A *state* is a subset of P. A *plan* is any sequence (possibly empty sequence $\langle \rangle$) of actions $\pi = \langle a_1, a_2, \cdots, a_N \rangle$. The state $a(s)$ produced by applying action a to state s is defined as follows: if $pre^+(a) \subseteq s$ and $pre^-(a) \cap s = \emptyset$, then $s' := (s \cup add(a)) \setminus del(a)$, and otherwise $s' := s$. The state produced by applying a plan π to a state s is defined inductively: $\langle \rangle (s) := s$ and $\langle \pi, a \rangle (s) := a(\pi.s)$. A plan π is a *solution* if $G \subseteq \pi(\iota)$.

For simplicity of exposition we now encode the flood scenario of Example 1 into the set-theoretical representation. Let $\langle V, E \rangle$ be the underlying graph, $q, r \in V$ be the starting positions of the person and the flood, respectively, and $t \in V$ the exit. Every vertex v of the graph is associated with two atoms p_v, f_v. The meaning of p_v is that the person currently occupies vertex v, and the meaning of

f_v is that vertex v is flooded. The initial state is $\iota = \{p_q, f_r\}$. The goal G is the set $\{t_v\}$. For every triple $\langle v, w, F \rangle \in E \times 2^V$ with $v, w \notin F$, there is an action a defined as follows:

- $pre^+(a) = \{p_v\} \cup \{f_z : z \in F\}$ (if the person is at v and F is flooded...),
- $pre^-(a) = \{f_z : z \notin F\}$ (and nowhere else is flooded...),
- $rem(a) = \{p_v\}$ (then remove the person from v...),
- $add(a) = \{p_w\} \cup \{f_z : \exists x \in F.(x, z) \in E\}$ (and place the person at w and expand the flood).

Then the person can escape the flood if and only if the planning problem $\mathcal{S}$ has a solution.

The translation into the classical representation (i.e., states are ground literals in a first-order relational signature) is similar. In brief, there is a constant v for each vertex, constants p and f for the agents, a relation $at(x, y)$ that says that agent x occupies vertex y, and for each triple $(v, w, F) \in E \times 2^V$ there is an action with precondition $\{at(p, v)\} \cup \{at(f, z) : z \in F\} \cup \{at(f, z) : z \notin F\}$ and effects $\{at(p, w), \neg at(p, v)\} \cup \{at(f, z) : z \in E(F)\}$.

We now present a simple analysis. First, the size of both of the representations is exponential in $|V|$. In contrast, the size of the representation in Example 1 is polynomial in $|V|$. Second, since the actions of the agents are concurrent, none of the actions are monotone, e.g., it is note the case that once a tuple is removed from at (or a variable in the set-theoretic representation is removed) it is not added later. In contrast, our representation neatly separates the abilities of the multiple agents (i.e., some are monotone, others are not) even though the agents behave concurrently. Third, consider the *interaction graph* for the set-theoretic representation [3]: its vertices are the atoms, and there is an edge from atom x to atom y if there is some action a such that $x \in pre^+(a) \cup pre^-(a) \cup rem(a) \cup add(a)$ and $y \in rem(a) \cup add(a)$. The main result in [3] implies that if there is no bound on the size of the strong connected components of the interaction graph then the planning problem (i.e., the existence problem) is not in PTIME unless an established complexity-theoretic assumption fails. Note that the arena $\mathcal{A} = \langle V, E \rangle$ embeds in the interaction graph. Thus there is no bound on the size of the strongly connected components of the interaction graphs, even in the flood example. In contrast, since our framework is tailored for path-planning problems (and not general planning problems), we were able to exhibit PTIME algorithms for such path-planning problems on arbitrary arenas (Theorem 3).

5   Summary and Future Work

We exhibited a natural representation of path-planning problems in which the arena and the positions of the agents in the arena are coded in a natural graph-theoretic way, rather than as an evaluation of Boolean propositions (as in, e.g., the set-theoretical representation). Our formalism can represent static environments (e.g., fixed obstacles are coded by the lack of an edge in the graph) and dynamic but predictable environments (e.g., flooding). We gave a PSPACE algorithm for solving the planning problem in these settings, which is also solvable in time exponential in the number of robots k and the size of the arena $|V|$.

By restricting the abilities of the agents (to be monotone or size-preserving), we showed that the planning problem can be solved in time polynomial in the size of the arena, i.e., for a fixed number of agents k but a varying arena, these restricted planning problems are PTIME in the size of the arena $|V|$. The same ideas can also be used to get PTIME algorithms for b-bounded piecewise monotone mobility relations, e.g., for $b = 1$ the flood starts spreading, but at some point in time stops spreading and begins to recede. The reason is that the size of the configuration space blows up, for each b-bounded piecewise monotone agent, by a multiplicative factor of $|V|^b$.

The main open question in this work is the exact complexity of restricted planning-problems, i.e., is there a restricted planning-problem that is PSPACE-hard? We know that there is a restricted planning-problem with three agents that is NP-hard (Proposition 1).

This paper opens up many avenues for extending the model and studying the complexity: optimal planning, e.g., there are costs associated with moving that need to be minimised [19] — our paper only deals with feasible planning, i.e., "does there exist a plan"; adversarial agents that are non-deterministic or probabilistic [6,9,14,17,22] — our paper only covers, implicitly, deterministic adversaries, such as the flood; and more expressive goals, such as those expressible in temporal logics, [5,24] or quantitative goals — our paper only deals with attainment/reachability goals; imperfect information, e.g., one does not know the exact starting position of the flood, or one does not know the speed of the flood.

References

1. Brafman, R.I., Domshlak, C.: From one to many: planning for loosely coupled multi-agent systems. In: Rintanen, J., Nebel, B., Beck, J.C., Hansen, E.A., (eds.) ICAPS, pp. 28–35. AAAI (2008)
2. Bylander, T.: The computational complexity of propositional strips planning. Artificial Intelligence **69**(1), 165–204 (1994)
3. Chen, H., Giménez, O.: Causal graphs and structurally restricted planning. J. Comput. Syst. Sci. **76**(7), 579–592 (2010)
4. Cooper, M.C., Maris, F., Régnier, P.: Monotone temporal planning: Tractability, extensions and applications. J. Artif. Intell. Res. (JAIR) **50**, 447–485 (2014)
5. De Giacomo, G., Vardi, M.Y.: Automata-theoretic approach to planning for temporally extended goals. In: Biundo, S., Fox, M. (eds.) ECP 1999. LNCS, vol. 1809. Springer, Heidelberg (2000)
6. Dean, T.L., Givan, R., Kim, K.: Solving stochastic planning problems with large state and action spaces. In: Simmons, R.G., Veloso, M.M., Smith, S.F., (eds.) AIPS, pp. 102–110. AAAI (1998)
7. Enderton, H.: A mathematical introduction to logic. Academic Press (1972)
8. Flake, G.W., Baum, E.B.: Rush hour is pspace-complete, or "why you should generously tip parking lot attendants". Theoretical Computer Science **270**(1–2), 895–911 (2002)

9. Geffner, H., Bonet, B.: A Concise Introduction to Models and Methods for Automated Planning. Synthesis Lectures on Artificial Intelligence and Machine Learning. Morgan & Claypool (2013)
10. Ghallab, M., Nau, D.S., Traverso, P.: Automated planning - theory and practice. Elsevier (2004)
11. Giunchiglia, F., Traverso, P.: Planning as model checking. In: Biundo, S., Fox, M. (eds.) ECP 1999. LNCS, vol. 1809. Springer, Heidelberg (2000)
12. Hopcroft, J., Schwartz, J., Sharir, M.: On the complexity of motion planning for multiple independent objects; PSPACE-hardness of the "warehouseman's problem. Technical report, Courant Institute of Mathematical Sciences, New York (1984)
13. Jamroga, W.: Strategic planning through model checking of ATL formulae. In: Rutkowski, L., Siekmann, J.H., Tadeusiewicz, R., Zadeh, L.A. (eds.) ICAISC 2004. LNCS (LNAI), vol. 3070, pp. 879–884. Springer, Heidelberg (2004)
14. Kaelbling, L.P., Littman, M.L., Cassandra, A.R.: Planning and acting in partially observable stochastic domains. Artificial intelligence 101(1), 99–134 (1998)
15. Kornhauser, D., Miller, G., Spirakis, P.: Coordinating pebble motion on graphs, the diameter of permutation groups, and applications. In: FOCS, pp. 241–250. IEEE (1984)
16. Krontiris, A., Sajid, Q., Bekris, K.: Towards using discrete multiagent pathfinding to address continuous problems. In: Proc, AAAI Workshop on Multiagent Pathfinding (2012)
17. Lamiri, M., Xie, X., Dolgui, A., Grimaud, F.: A stochastic model for operating room planning with elective and emergency demand for surgery. European Journal of Operational Research 185(3), 1026–1037 (2008)
18. J.-C. Latombe. Robot motion planning, volume 124 of International Series in Engineering and Computer Science. Springer, 2012
19. LaValle, S.M.: Planning Algorithms. Cambridge University Press (2006)
20. Lumelsky, V.J., Stepanov, A., et al.: Dynamic path planning for a mobile automaton with limited information on the environment. Automatic Control, IEEE Transactions on 31(11), 1058–1063 (1986)
21. Mogavero, F., Murano, A., Vardi, M.Y.: Relentful strategic reasoning in alternating-time temporal logic. Journal of Logic and Computation (2014) (to appear)
22. Murano, A., Sorrentino, L.: A game-based model for human-robots interaction. In: Workshop "From Objects to Agents" (WOA) CEUR Workshop Proceedings, vol. 1382, pp. 146–150. CEUR-WS.org (2015)
23. Papadimitriou, C.H., Raghavan, P., Sudan, M., Tamaki, H.: Motion planning on a graph (extended abstract). In: FOCS, pp. 511–520. IEEE (1994)
24. Pistore, M., Traverso, P.: Planning as model checking for extended goals in nondeterministic domains. In: Walsh, T., (ed.) IJCAI, pp. 479–486. IJCAI/AAAI (2001)
25. Pistore, M., Vardi, M.Y.: The planning spectrum - one, two, three, infinity. J. Artif. Intell. Res. (JAIR) 30, 101–132 (2007)
26. Röger, G., Helmert, M.: Non-optimal multi-agent pathfinding is solved (since 1984). In: Borrajo, D., Felner, A., Korf, R.E., Likhachev, M., López, C.L., Ruml, W., Sturtevant, N.R., (eds.) SOCS. AAAI (2012)
27. Souissi, O., Benatitallah, R., Duvivier, D., Artiba, A., Belanger, N., Feyzeau, P.: Path planning: a 2013 survey. In: Industrial Engineering and Systems Management (IESM), pp. 1–8, October 2013
28. Surynek, P.: An application of pebble motion on graphs to abstract multi-robot path planning. In: ICTAI, pp. 151–158. IEEE (2009)

29. Tromp, J., Cilibrasi, R.: Limits of Rush Hour Logic Complexity. In: CoRR, abs/cs/0502068 (2005)
30. van den Berg, J., Snoeyink, J., Lin, M.C., Manocha, D.: Centralized path planning for multiple robots: optimal decoupling into sequential plans. In: Robotics Science and Systems V (2009)
31. van der Hoek, W., Wooldridge, M.:Tractable multiagent planning for epistemic goals. In: AAMAS, pp. 1167–1174. ACM (2002)
32. Wilfong, G.T.: Motion planning in the presence of movable obstacles. Ann. Math. Artif. Intell. **3**(1), 131–150 (1991)

Module Checking for Uncertain Agents

Wojciech Jamroga[1] and Aniello Murano[2]([⊠])

[1] Institute of Computer Science, Polish Academy of Sciences, Warsaw, Poland
w.jamroga@ipipan.waw.pl
[2] Dipartimento di Ingegneria Elettrica e Tecnologie dell'Informazione, Università
degli Studi di Napoli Federico II, Naples, Italy
aniello.murano@unina.it

Abstract. *Module* checking is a decision problem proposed in late 1990s
to formalize verification of open systems, i.e., systems that must adapt their
behavior to the input they receive from the environment. It was recently
shown that module checking offers a distinctly different perspective from
the better-known problem of *model* checking. Module checking has been
studied in several variants. Syntactically, specifications in temporal logic
CTL and strategic logic ATL have been used. Semantically, the environment was assumed to have either perfect or imperfect information about
the global state of the interaction. In this work, we rectify our approach
to imperfect information module checking from the previous paper. Moreover, we study the variant of module checking where also the system acts
under uncertainty. More precisely, we assume that the system consists of
one or more agents whose decision making is constrained by their observational capabilities. We propose an automata-based verification procedure
for the new problem, and establish its computational complexity.

Keywords: Module checking · Strategic logic · Imperfect information

1 Introduction

Module checking [20,22] is a formal method to automatically check for correctness of *open systems*. The system is modeled as a *module* that interacts with
its environment, and correctness means that a desired property must hold with
respect to all possible interactions. The module can be seen as a transition
system with states partitioned into ones controlled by the system and by the
environment. The environment represents an external source of nondeterminism, because at each state controlled by the environment the computation can
continue with any subset of its possible successor states. In consequence, we have
an infinite number of computation trees to handle, one for each possible behavior of the environment. Properties for module checking are usually specified in
temporal logics CTL or CTL* [9,11].

It was believed for a long time that module checking of CTL/CTL* is a special (and rather simplistic) case of *model* checking strategic logics ATL/ATL* [2].
Because of that, active research on module checking subsided shortly after its
conception. The belief has been recently refuted in [17]. There, it was proved

© Springer International Publishing Switzerland 2015
Q. Chen et al. (Eds.): PRIMA 2015, LNAI 9387, pp. 232–247, 2015.
DOI: 10.1007/978-3-319-25524-8_15

that module checking includes two features inherently absent in the semantics of ATL, namely irrevocability and nondeterminism of strategies. This made module checking an interesting formalism for verification of open systems again.

In [18], we extended module checking to handle specifications in the more expressive logic ATL. However, [18] focused on modules of perfect information, i.e., ones where all the participants have, at any moment, complete and accurate knowledge of the current global state of the system. The assumption is clearly unrealistic, as almost all agents must act under uncertainty. In this paper, we focus on that aspect, and investigate verification of open systems that include uncertain agents. In fact, our study in [18] mentioned systems where the environment might have imperfect information. However, our treatment of such scenarios did not really capture the feasible patterns of behavior that can be produced by uncertain environments. Here, we give a new interpretation to the problem. Moreover, we generalize ATL module checking to modules that include uncertainty also on the part of the system. Finally, we investigate formal properties of the new problem in terms of expressive power, automata-based algorithms, and computational complexity.

Related Work. Module checking was introduced in [20,22], and later extended in several directions. In [21], the basic CTL/CTL* module checking problem was extended to the setting where the environment has imperfect information about the state of the system. In [7], it was extended to infinite-state open systems by considering pushdown modules. The pushdown module checking problem was first investigated for perfect information, and later, in [4,6], for imperfect information. [3,13] extended module checking to μ-calculus specifications, and in [26] the module checking problem was investigated for bounded pushdown modules (or *hierarchical modules*). Recently, module checking was also extended to specifications in alternating-time temporal logics ATL/ATL* [18]. From a more practical point of view, [24,25] built a semi-automated tool for module checking in the existential fragment of CTL, both in the perfect and imperfect information setting. Moreover, an approach to CTL module checking based on tableau was exploited in [5]. Finally, an extension of module checking was used to reason about three-valued abstractions in [10,14–16].

It must be noted that literature on module checking became rather sparse after 2002. This should be partially attributed to the popular belief that CTL module checking is nothing but a special case of ATL model checking. The belief has been refuted only recently [17], which will hopefully spark renewed interest in verification of open systems by module checking.

2   Verification of Open Multi-Agent Systems

We first recall the main concepts behind module checking of multi-agent systems.

2.1   Models and Modules

Modules in *module checking* [20] were proposed to represent open systems – that is, systems that interact with an environment whose behavior cannot be determined in advance. Examples of modules include: an ATM interacting with customers, a steel factory depending on fluctuations in iron supplies, a Mars explorer adapting to the weather conditions, and so on. In their simplest form, modules are represented by unlabeled transition systems with the set of states partitioned into those "owned" by the system, and the ones where the next transition is controlled by the environment.

Definition 1 (Module). *A module is a tuple* $M = \langle AP, St_s, St_e, q_0, \rightarrow, PV \rangle$, *where AP is a finite set of (atomic) propositions, $St = St_s \cup St_e$ is a nonempty finite set of states partitioned into a set St_s of* system *states and a set St_e of* environment *states, $\rightarrow \subseteq St \times St$ is a (global) transition relation, $q_0 \in St$ is an initial state, and $PV : St \rightarrow 2^{AP}$ is a valuation of atomic propositions that maps each state q to the set of atomic propositions that are true in q.*

Modules can be seen as a subclass of more general models of interaction, called *concurrent game structures* [2].

Definition 2 (CGS). *A* concurrent game structure (CGS) *is a tuple* $M = \langle AP, \mathrm{Agt}, St, Act, d, o, PV \rangle$ *including nonempty finite set of propositions AP, agents $\mathrm{Agt} = \{1, \ldots, k\}$, states St, (atomic) actions Act, and a propositional valuation $PV : St \rightarrow 2^{AP}$. The function $d : \mathrm{Agt} \times St \rightarrow 2^{Act}$ defines nonempty sets of actions available to agents at each state, and the (deterministic) transition function o assigns the outcome state $q' = o(q, \alpha_1, \ldots, \alpha_k)$ to each state q and tuple of actions $\alpha_i \in d(i, q)$ that can be executed by Agt in q.*

We will write $d_i(q)$ instead of $d(i, q)$, and denote the set of collective choice of group A at state q by $d_A(q) = \prod_{i \in A} d_i(q)$. We will also use $AP^M, \mathrm{Agt}^M, St^M$ etc. to refer to the components of M whenever confusion can arise.

A pointed CGS *is a pair (M, q_0) of a CGS and an initial state in it.*

2.2 Multi-Agent Modules

Multi-agent modules have been proposed in [18] to allow for reasoning about open systems that are themselves implemented as a composition of several autonomous processes.

Definition 3 (Multi-agent Module). *A multi-agent module is a pointed concurrent game structure that contains a special agent called "the environment" ($e \in \mathrm{Agt}$). We call a module k-agent if it consists of k agents plus the environment (i.e., the underlying CGS contains $k + 1$ agents).*

The module is alternating *iff its states are partitioned into those owned by the environment (i.e., $|d(a, q)| = 1$ for all $a \neq e$) and those where the environment is passive (i.e., $|d(e, q)| = 1$). That is, it alternates between the agents' and the environment's moves. Moreover, the module is* turn-based *iff the underlying CGS is turn-based.*[1]

---

[1] A CGS is turn-based iff every state in it is controlled by (at most) one agent. That is, for every $q \in St$, there is an agent $a \in \mathrm{Agt}$ such that $|d(a', q)| = 1$ for all $a' \neq a$.

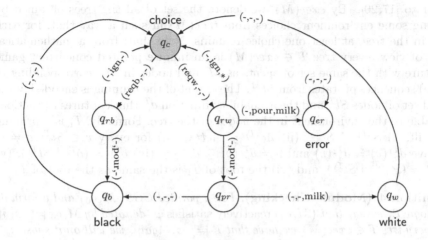

Fig. 1. Multi-agent coffee machine M_{caf}

We note in passing that the original modules from [20] were turn-based (and hence also alternating). On the other hand, the version of module checking for imperfect information in [21] assumed that the system and the environment can act simultaneously.

Example 1. A multi-agent coffee machine is presented in Figure 1. The module includes two agents: the brewer (br) and the milk provider ($milky$). The brewer's function is to pour coffee into the cup (action $pour$), and the milk provider can add milk on top (action $milk$). Moreover, each of them can be faulty and ignore the request from the environment (ign). Note that if br and $milky$ try to pour coffee and milk at the same time, the machine gets to an error state. Finally, the environment has actions $reqb, reqw$ available in state q_c, meaning that it requests black (resp. white) coffee. Since the module is alternating, we adhere to the popular convention of marking system states as white, and environment states as grey.

2.3   Module Checking

The generic module checking problem can be defined as follows. Assume a modal logic $\mathcal{L}$ whose formulae are interpreted in pointed concurrent game structures according to the semantic relation $\models_{\mathcal{L}}$.[2] For example, $\mathcal{L}$ can be the computation tree logic CTL [9,11] or alternating-time temporal logic ATL [2]. Given a CGS M, the set of all infinite computations of M starting from the initial state q_0 is described by an St-labeled tree that we call *the computation tree of M* and

---

[2] We will omit the subscript whenever it is clear from the context.

denote by $tree(M)$. The tree is obtained by unwinding M from q_0 in the usual way. We omit the formal construction for lack of space, and refer the interested reader to [17,20]. By $exec(M)$, we denote the set of all the trees obtained by pruning some environment choices from $tree(M)$ in such a way that, for each node in the tree, at least one choice remains. Note that, from a mathematical point of view, every tree $T \in exec(M)$ is an infinite pointed concurrent game structure with the same set of agents as M, and nodes in St^T corresponding to (some) sequences of states from St^M. The extent of the pruning is encoded in the actual set of nodes St^T and the availability function d_e^T that captures the actions available to the environment in the nodes of the tree. Formally, T_1 is a pruning of T_2 iff: (i) $St^{T_1} \subseteq St^{T_2}$, (ii) $Act^{T_1} \subseteq Act^{T_2}$, (iii) for every $v \in St^{T_1}, a \neq e$, we have $d_a^{T_1}(v) = d_a^{T_2}(v)$ and $\emptyset \neq d_e^{T_1}(v) \subseteq d_e^{T_2}(v)$, (iv) $o^{T_1} = (o^{T_2} \mid St^{T_1})$, (v) $PV^{T_1} = (PV^{T_2} \mid St^{T_1})$, and (vi) the root of T_1 is the same as the root of T_2.

Definition 4 (Module Checking). *For a pointed CGS (M, q_0) and a formula φ of logic $\mathcal{L}$, we say that (M, q_0) reactively satisfies φ, denoted by $M, q_0 \models_{\mathcal{L}}^r \varphi$, iff for every tree $T \in exec(M)$ we have that $T \models_{\mathcal{L}}^r \varphi$. Again, we will omit subscripts if they are clear from context. The problem of deciding whether M reactively satisfies φ is called* module checking *[22].*

Note that, for most modal logics, $M \models_{\mathcal{L}}^r \varphi$ implies $M \models_{\mathcal{L}} \varphi$ but the converse does not hold. Also, $M \not\models_{\mathcal{L}}^r \varphi$ is in general not equivalent to $M \models_{\mathcal{L}}^r \neg\varphi$.

Example 2. Consider the coffee machine from Example 1 with the CTL specification EFwhite saying that there exists at least one possible path where eventually white coffee will be served. Clearly, $M_{caf} \models_{CTL} $ EFwhite. On the other hand, $M_{caf} \not\models_{CTL}^r $ EFwhite. Think of a line of customers who never order white coffee. It corresponds to an execution tree of M_{caf} that prunes off all nodes labeled with q_{rw}, and such a tree cannot satisfy EFwhite.

2.4   Reasoning about Strategic Behavior: Alternating Time Logic

Alternating-time temporal logic ATL/ATL* [2] generalizes the branching-time logic CTL/CTL* [9,11] by means of *strategic modalities* $\langle\langle A \rangle\rangle$. Informally, $\langle\langle A \rangle\rangle\gamma$ expresses that the group of agents A has a collective strategy to enforce temporal property γ. The language ATL* is given by the grammar below:

$$\varphi ::= \mathsf{p} \mid \neg\varphi \mid \varphi \wedge \varphi \mid \langle\langle A \rangle\rangle\gamma,$$
$$\gamma ::= \varphi \mid \neg\gamma \mid \gamma \wedge \gamma \mid \mathsf{X}\gamma \mid \gamma \,\mathsf{U}\, \gamma.$$

where $A \subseteq \mathrm{Agt}$ is any subset of agents, and p is a proposition. Temporal operators X, U stand for "next" and "until", respectively. The "sometime" and "always" operators can be defined as $\mathsf{F}\gamma \equiv \top \,\mathsf{U}\, \gamma$ and $\mathsf{G}\gamma \equiv \neg\mathsf{F}\neg\gamma$. Also, we can use $[A]\gamma \equiv \neg\langle\langle A \rangle\rangle\neg\gamma$ to express that no strategy of A can prevent property γ. Similarly to CTL, ATL is the syntactic variant in which every occurrence of a strategic modality is immediately followed by a temporal operator.

Given a CGS, we define the strategies and their outcomes as follows. A *strategy* for agent a is a function $s_a : St \to Act$ such that $s_a(q) \in d_a(q)$.[3] A *collective strategy* for a group of agents $A = \{a_1, \ldots, a_i\}$ is simply a tuple of individual strategies $s_A = \langle s_{a_1}, \ldots, s_{a_i} \rangle$. The "outcome" function $out(q, s_A)$ returns the set of all paths that can occur when agents A execute strategy s_A from state q on. Finally, for a path $\lambda \in St^\omega$, we use $\lambda[i]$ to denote the ith state on λ, and $\lambda[i..\infty]$ to denote the ith suffix of λ. The semantics $\models_{ATL}$ of alternating-time logic is defined below:

$M, q \models \mathsf{p}$ iff $q \in PV(\mathsf{p})$, for $\mathsf{p} \in AP$;
$M, q \models \neg\varphi$ iff $M, q \not\models \varphi$;
$M, q \models \varphi_1 \wedge \varphi_2$ iff $M, q \models \varphi_1$ and $M, q \models \varphi_2$;

$M, q \models \langle\!\langle A \rangle\!\rangle \gamma$ iff there is a collective strategy s_A for A such that, for every $\lambda \in out(q, s_A)$, we have $M, \lambda \models \gamma$.

$M, \lambda \models \varphi$ iff $M, \lambda[0] \models \varphi$;
$M, \lambda \models \neg\gamma$ iff $M, \lambda \not\models \gamma$;
$M, \lambda \models \gamma_1 \wedge \gamma_2$ iff $M, \lambda \models \gamma_1$ and $M, \lambda \models \gamma_2$;
$M, \lambda \models \mathsf{X}\gamma$ iff $M, \lambda[1, \infty] \models \gamma$; and
$M, \lambda \models \gamma_1 \mathsf{U} \gamma_2$ iff there is an $i \in \mathbb{N}_0$ such that $M, \lambda[i, \infty] \models \gamma_2$ and $M, \lambda[j, \infty] \models \gamma_1$ for all $0 \le j < i$.

Example 3. Consider the CGS from Figure 1. Clearly, $M_{caf} \not\models \langle\!\langle br \rangle\!\rangle \mathsf{F}\mathsf{white}$: the brewer cannot provide the customer with white coffee on its own. In fact, even both coffee agents together cannot guarantee that, since the customer may never order white coffee: $M_{caf} \not\models \langle\!\langle br, milky \rangle\!\rangle \mathsf{F}\mathsf{white}$. On the other hand, they can produce black coffee regardless of what the customer asks for: $M_{caf} \models \langle\!\langle br, milky \rangle\!\rangle \mathsf{F}\mathsf{black}$. Finally, they can deprive the customer of coffee if they consistently ignore her requests: $M_{caf} \models \langle\!\langle br, milky \rangle\!\rangle \mathsf{G}(\neg\mathsf{black} \wedge \neg\mathsf{white})$.

Embedding CTL* in ATL*. The path quantifiers of CTL* can be expressed in the standard semantics of ATL* as follows [2]: $\mathsf{A}\gamma \equiv \langle\!\langle \emptyset \rangle\!\rangle \gamma$ and $\mathsf{E}\gamma \equiv \langle\!\langle \mathrm{Agt} \rangle\!\rangle \gamma$. We point out that the above translation of E does *not* work for several extensions of ATL*, e.g., with imperfect information, nondeterministic strategies, and irrevocable strategies. On the other hand, the translation of A into $\langle\!\langle \emptyset \rangle\!\rangle$ does work for all the semantic variants of ATL* considered in this paper. Thanks to that, we can define a translation $atl(\varphi)$ from CTL* to ATL* as follows. First, we convert φ so that it only includes universal path quantifiers, and then replace every occurrence of A with $\langle\!\langle \emptyset \rangle\!\rangle$. For example, $atl(\mathsf{EG}(\mathsf{p}_1 \wedge \mathsf{AF}\mathsf{p}_2)) = \neg\langle\!\langle \emptyset \rangle\!\rangle \mathsf{F}(\neg\mathsf{p}_1 \vee \neg\langle\!\langle \emptyset \rangle\!\rangle \mathsf{F}\mathsf{p}_2)$. Note that if φ is a CTL formula then $atl(\varphi)$ is a formula of ATL. By a slight abuse of notation, we will use path quantifiers A, E in ATL formulae whenever it is convenient.

---

[3] Unlike in the original semantics of ATL* [2], we use *memoryless* rather than *perfect recall* strategies. It is well known, however, that the semantics based on the two notions of strategy coincide for all formulae of ATL, cf. [2,27].

2.5   Module Checking of ATL* Specifications

ATL* module checking has been proposed and studied in [18]. The problem can be defined by the straightforward combination of our generic treatment of module checking from Section 2.3 and the semantics of ATL* presented in Section 2.4.

Example 4. Consider the multi-agent coffee machine M_{caf} from Example 1. Clearly, $M_{caf} \not\models^r \langle\langle br, milky \rangle\rangle$Fwhite because the environment can keep requesting black coffee. On the other hand, $M_{caf} \models^r \langle\langle br, milky \rangle\rangle$Fblack: the agents can provide the user with black coffee whatever she requests. They can also deprive the user of coffee completely – in fact, the brewer alone can do it by consistently ignoring her requests: $M_{caf} \models^r \langle\langle br \rangle\rangle$G($\neg$black $\wedge$ $\neg$white).

The above formulae can be also used for *model* checking, and they would actually generate the same answers. So, what's the benefit of *module* checking? In module checking, we can *condition the property to be achieved on the behavior of the environment*. For instance, users who never order white coffee can be served by the brewer alone: $M_{caf} \models^r$ AG$\neg$reqw $\rightarrow$ $\langle\langle br \rangle\rangle$Fblack. Note that the same formula in model checking trivially holds since $M_{caf} \not\models$ AG$\neg$reqw. Likewise, we have $M_{caf} \models$ AG$\neg$reqb $\rightarrow$ $\langle\langle br \rangle\rangle$Fwhite, whereas module checking gives a different and more intuitive answer: $M_{caf} \not\models^r$ AG$\neg$reqb $\rightarrow$ $\langle\langle br \rangle\rangle$Fwhite. That is, the brewer cannot handle requests for white coffee on its own, even if the user never orders anything else.

3   Imperfect Information

In Section 2, we summarized the main developments in module checking for multi-agent systems with perfect information. That is, we implicitly assumed that both the system and the environment always know the precise global state of the computation. The framework was extended to handle uncertain environments in [21] (for temporal logic specifications) and [18] (for specifications of strategic ability). In this paper, we revise and extend our previous work from [18]. The novel contribution is threefold. First, we give a new interpretation of ATL module checking for uncertain environments (Section 3.1). The one proposed in [18], while mathematically sound, arguably does not capture the feasible patterns of behavior that can be produced by uncertain environments. Secondly, we generalize the problem to modules that include uncertainty also on the part of the system (Section 3.2). Thirdly, we investigate formal properties of the new problem, in terms of expressive power (Section 4) as well as algorithms and computational complexity (Section 5).

3.1   Handling Environments with Imperfect Information

So far, we have only considered multi-agent modules in which the environment has complete information about the state of the system. In many practical scenarios this is not the case. Usually, the agents have some private knowledge that the environment cannot access. As an example, think of the coffee machine from Example 1. A realistic model of the machine should include some internal variables that the environment (i.e., the customer) is not supposed to know during the interaction, such as the amount of milk in the container or the amount of coins available for giving change. States that differ only in such hidden information are indistinguishable to the environment. While interaction with an "omniscient" environment corresponds to an arbitrary pruning of transitions in the module, in case of imperfect information the pruning must coincide whenever two computations look the same to the environment.

To handle such scenarios, the definition of multi-agent modules was extended as follows [18].

Definition 5 (Multi-agent Module with Uncertain Environment). *A multi-agent module with uncertain environment is a multi-agent module further equipped with an indistinguishability relation $\sim_e \subseteq St \times St$ that encodes uncertainty of the environment. We assume $\sim_e$ to be an equivalence.*

We will additionally require that the available choices of the environment are consistent with its indistinguishability relation.

Definition 6 (Uniformity of Modules). *A multi-agent module with uncertain environment is* uniform *wrt relation $\sim_e$ iff $q \sim_e q'$ implies $d_e(q) = d_e(q')$.*

In [18], we assumed that an uncertain environment can only prune whole subtrees of the execution tree, and when it does, it must do it uniformly. This was arguably a very rough treatment of how the environment can choose to behave. We propose a more subtle treatment below.

Let M be a uniform multi-agent module with uncertain environment. First, we extend the indistinguishability relation to the nodes in the computation tree of M. Formally, two nodes v and v' in $tree(M)$ are indistinguishable ($v \cong v'$) iff (1) the length of v, v' in $tree(M)$ is the same, and (2) for each i, we have $v[i] \sim_e v'[i]$. Secondly, we will only consider prunings of $tree(M)$ that are imperfect information-consistent. Formally, $T \in tree(M)$ is imperfect information-consistent iff it is uniform wrt $\cong$. We denote the set of such prunings by $exec^i(M)$. Clearly, $exec^i(M) \subseteq exec(M)$.

The module checking problem for uncertain environments is defined analogously to the perfect information case:

Definition 7 (Module Checking for Uncertain Environments). *Given a multi-agent module with uncertain environment M and a formula φ of logic $\mathcal{L}$, the corresponding module checking problem is defined by the following clause:*
$$M \models_{\mathcal{L}}^{r,i} \varphi \quad \text{iff} \quad T \models_{\mathcal{L}} \varphi \text{ for every } T \in exec^i(M).$$

Example 5. Consider an extension of the multi-agent coffee machine from Example 1, where the environment can choose to reset the machine while it is preparing coffee. If the machine is reset after the coffee is poured but before it is served, the system proceeds to the error state. Moreover, pressing reset in the error state

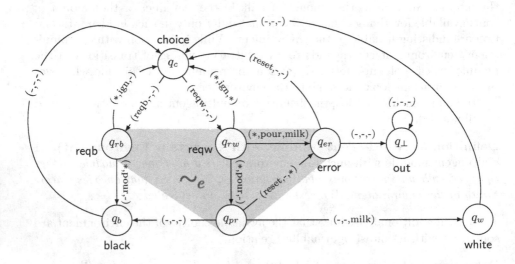

Fig. 2. Multi-agent coffee machine with reset M_{caf2}

initiates a recovery procedure that brings the system back to the initial state q_c. On the other hand, if the system is not reset while in the error state then it proceeds to the "out of order" state q_{out}, and requires intervention of an external repair crew. Furthermore, we assume that the environment has no access to the local states of the system agents $br, milky$. Since states $q_{rb}, q_{rw}, q_{pr}, q_{er}$ should intuitively differ only in local states of those agents, they are indistinguishable to the environment (see Figure 2). Note that we do not label states grey and white anymore, as the module is not alternating.

Let us define the "recovery formula" as $\varphi_{recv} \equiv \text{AG}(\text{error} \rightarrow \text{AXchoice})$, saying that the system always recovers after an error. Now we have for example that $M_{caf2} \models^{r,i} \varphi_{recv} \rightarrow \text{AG}\neg\text{white}$. This is because the user cannot distinguish between situations when an error has occurred, and ones where the coffee has been poured and waits for milk to be added. If she chooses to reset the machine in the first kind of nodes, she has to do reset also in the latter, and then white coffee can never be completed. Thus, for such behaviors of the user, the agents cannot provide her with white coffee anymore: $M_{caf2} \models^{r,i} \varphi_{recv} \rightarrow \neg\langle\langle br, milky\rangle\rangle\text{Fwhite}$.

On the other hand, the agents retain the ability to serve black coffee whenever it is requested – in fact, the brewer can make it on its own: $M_{caf2} \models^{r,i} \varphi_{recv} \rightarrow \text{AG}(\text{reqb} \rightarrow \langle\langle br\rangle\rangle\text{Fblack})$. Moreover, for such inputs, the agents cannot crash the system: $M_{caf2} \models^{r,i} \varphi_{recv} \rightarrow \neg\langle\langle br, milky\rangle\rangle\text{Fout}$, which is rather a good thing. Finally, even if the user never tries recovery, the agents can keep the system from crashing, and serve white coffee whenever it is requested (they simply avoid pouring coffee and milk at the same time). Formally, let $\varphi_{norecv} \equiv \text{AG}(\text{error} \rightarrow$

AX¬choice); then, $M_{caf2} \models^{r,i} \varphi_{norecv} \rightarrow \langle\langle br, milky\rangle\rangle G\neg out$ and $M_{caf2} \models^{r,i}$ $\varphi_{norecv} \rightarrow AG(reqw \rightarrow \langle\langle br, milky\rangle\rangle F white)$.

3.2   Imperfect Information Module Checking

The treatment of module checking, presented in the previous section, allows for uncertainty on the part of the environment, but assumes perfect information on the part of the system. That is, the agents that comprise the system can always fully observe the global state of the system, including each other's variables as well as the local state of the environment. Is this assumption realistic? Clearly not. One can perhaps use perfect information models when the hidden information is irrelevant for the agent's decision making, i.e., the agents need only their local views to choose their course of action (cf. the coffee machine example) but even that is seldom justified.

Definition 8 (Multi-agent Module with Imperfect Information). *A multi-agent module with imperfect information is a multi-agent module further equipped with indistinguishability relations $\sim_a \subseteq St \times St$, one per agent $a \in \mathrm{Agt}$.*

Each multi-agent module with imperfect information M is required to be uniform wrt every relation $\sim_a$ in M.

Now we proceed analogously to Section 3.1. Let M be a multi-agent module with imperfect information, and $\mathcal{L}$ be a suitable logic. Two nodes v and v' in $tree(M)$ are indistinguishable to the environment ($v \cong_e v'$) iff (1) the length of v, v' in $tree(M)$ is the same, and (2) for each i, we have $v[i] \sim_e v'[i]$. Then, $exec^i(M)$ consists of all the prunings in $exec(M)$ that are uniform wrt $\cong_e$. The corresponding module checking problem is again defined by the clause:

$$M \models^{r,i}_{\mathcal{L}} \varphi \quad \text{iff} \quad T \models_{\mathcal{L}} \varphi \text{ for every } T \in exec^i(M).$$

One thing remains to be settled. What logic is suitable for specification of agents with imperfect information? In this paper, we use a semantic variant of ATL* proposed in [27]. First, a (memoryless) strategy s_a is *uniform* iff $q \sim_a q'$ implies $s_a(q) = s_a(q')$. A collective strategy s_A is uniform iff it consists of uniform individual strategies. Then, the semantics $\models_{ATL_i}$ of "ATL* with imperfect information" is obtained by replacing the clause for $\langle\langle A \rangle\rangle\gamma$ as follows:

$M, q \models \langle\langle A \rangle\rangle\gamma$ iff there is a uniform collective strategy s_A such that, for every $a \in A$, every q' with $q \sim_a q'$, and every $\lambda \in out(q', s_A)$, we have $M, \lambda \models \gamma$.

Example 6. Let us go back to the multi-agent coffee machine with reset from Example 5. We will now additionally assume that *milky* cannot detect the *pour* action of the brewer, formally: $q_{rw} \sim_{milky} q_{pr}$. Let us denote the resulting multi-agent model by M_{caf3}. Then, the agents are still able to keep the machine from crashing, even for users that do no recovery, but they are not able anymore to guarantee that white coffee requests are served. Formally, $M_{caf3} \models^{r,i} \varphi_{norecv} \rightarrow \langle\langle br, milky\rangle\rangle G\neg out$ (the right strategy assumes that *milky* never pours milk), and $M_{caf3} \not\models^{r,i} \varphi_{norecv} \rightarrow AG(reqw \rightarrow \langle\langle br, milky\rangle\rangle F white)$ (in a uniform strategy, if *milky* decides to do no action at q_{rw}, it has to do the same at q_{pr}).

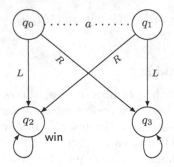 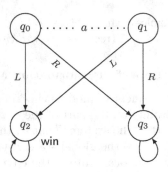

Fig. 3. Variants of the "poor duck problem" from [8]

4   Expressive Power of Imperfect Information Module Checking

In this section, we show that ATL module checking offers a distinctly different perspective when imperfect information is added. Before we proceed, we briefly recall the notions of distinguishing power and expressive power (cf. e.g. [29]).

Definition 9 (Distinguishing and Expressive Power). Let $L_1 = (\mathcal{L}_1, \models_1)$ and $L_2 = (\mathcal{L}_2, \models_2)$ be two logical systems over the same class of models $\mathcal{M}$. By $[\![\phi]\!]_{\models} = \{(M, q) \mid M, q \models \phi\}$, we denote the class of pointed models that satisfy ϕ in the semantics given by $\models$. Likewise, $[\![\phi, M]\!]_{\models} = \{q \mid M, q \models \phi\}$ is the set of states (or, equivalently, pointed models) that satisfy ϕ in a given structure M.

L_2 is at least as expressive as L_1 (written: $L_1 \preceq_e L_2$ iff for every formula $\phi_1 \in \mathcal{L}_1$ there exists $\phi_2 \in \mathcal{L}_2$ such that $[\![\phi_1]\!]_{\models_1} = [\![\phi_2]\!]_{\models_2}$.

L_2 is at least as distinguishing as L_1 (written: $L_1 \preceq_d L_2$ iff for every model M and formula $\phi_1 \in \mathcal{L}_1$ there exists $\phi_2 \in \mathcal{L}_2$ such that $[\![\phi_1, M]\!]_{\models_1} = [\![\phi_2, M]\!]_{\models_2}$.[4]

Note that $L_1 \preceq_e L_2$ implies $L_1 \preceq_d L_2$ but the converse is not true. For example, it is known that CTL has the same distinguishing power as CTL*, but strictly less expressive power. We also observe that module checking ATL* can be seen as a logical system where the syntax is given by the syntax of ATL*, and the semantics is given by $\models^r$. For module checking "ATL* with imperfect information", the semantics is given by $\models^{r,i}$. Thus, we can use Definition 9 to compare the expressivity of both decision problems.

Theorem 1. *The logical system* (ATL*, $\models^{r,i}$) *has incomparable distinguishing power (and thus also incomparable expressive power) to* $(ATL*, \models^r)$.

Proof. First we prove that there are multi-agent modules M, M' that satisfy the same formulae of ATL* wrt the semantic relation $\models^r$, but are distinguished by

---

[4]   Equivalently: for every pair of pointed models that can be distinguished by some $\phi_1 \in \mathcal{L}_1$ there exists $\phi_2 \in \mathcal{L}_2$ that distinguishes these models.

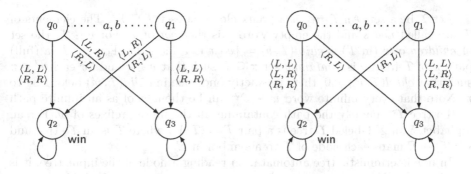

Fig. 4. "Coordinated poor duck problem" with 2 agents a and b

an ATL* formula wrt the semantic relation $\models^{r,i}$. As M, take the "poor duck" model from Figure 3 (left) with q_0 be the initial state, and add the environment agent e in such a way that it never influences the evolution of the system (i.e., $|d_e(q)| = 1$ for all $q \in St$). Moreover, let M' be a modified variant of M where the outgoing transitions from q_1 are swapped, see Figure 3 (right). Clearly, $exec(M) = exec^i(M) = \{T(M)\}$, and analogously for M' (there is only one way how the environment can act). Thus, the semantic relation $\models^r$ (resp. $\models^{r,i}$) coincides on M and M' with $\models_{ATL}$ (resp. $\models_{ATL_i}$). Furthermore, M, M' are in strategic bisimulation [1], and hence they satisfy the same formulae of ATL* wrt $\models_{ATL}$. On the other hand, $M \not\models_{ATL_i} \langle\!\langle a \rangle\!\rangle F$win and $M' \models_{ATL_i} \langle\!\langle a \rangle\!\rangle F$win.

Secondly, we prove that there are multi-agent modules M, M' that satisfy the same formulae of ATL* wrt the semantic relation $\models^{r,i}$, but are distinguished by an ATL* formula with the semantic relation $\models^r$. As M and M', take now the left hand side and right hand side models from Figure 4, respectively. Again, the initial is q_0 and the environment is idle in all states. We leave it for the reader to check that in both models all the coalitions can only enforce trivial path properties (i.e., ones that hold on all paths starting from q_0, q_1) by using uniform strategies. Thus, M and M' satisfy the same formulae of ATL_i^*. On the other hand, $M \not\models_{ATL} \langle\!\langle a \rangle\!\rangle F$win and $M' \models_{ATL} \langle\!\langle a \rangle\!\rangle F$win.

5   Algorithms and Complexity

Our algorithmic solution to the problem of ATL* module checking with imperfect information exploits the automata-theoretic approach. It combines and extends that ones used to solve the *CTL* module checking with imperfect information* and the *ATL* model checking with perfect information* problems. Precisely, we make use of *alternating parity tree automata* on infinite tress and reduce the addressed decision problem to the checking for automata emptiness. In this section we first introduce some preliminary definition regarding these automata and then we show how to use them to our purpose. For the sake of clarity we also give a proper definition of infinite labeled trees.

Let Υ be a set. An Υ-*tree* is a prefix closed subset $T \subseteq \Upsilon^*$. The elements of T are called *nodes* and the empty word ε is the *root* of T. For $v \in T$, the set of *children* of v (in T) is $child(T, v) = \{v \cdot x \in T \mid x \in \Upsilon\}$. For $v \in T$, a (full) path π of T from v is a *minimal* set $\pi \subseteq T$ such that $v \in \pi$ and for each $v' \in \pi$ such that $child(T, v') \neq \emptyset$, there is exactly one node in $child(T, v')$ belonging to π. Note that every infinite word $w \in \Upsilon^\omega$ can be thought of as an infinite path in the tree Υ^*, namely the path containing all the finite prefixes of w. For an alphabet Σ, a Σ-labeled Υ-tree is a pair $T = \langle T, V \rangle$ where T is an Υ-tree and $V : T \rightarrow \Sigma$ maps each node of T to a symbol in Σ.

In nondeterministic tree automata, on reading a node of the input tree, it is possible to send at most one copy of the automaton in every single child, in accordance with the nondeterministic transition relation. Alternating tree automata, instead, are able to send several copies of the automaton along the same child, by means of a transition relation that uses positive Boolean combinations of directions and states. The formal definition of alternating tree automata follows. For more details we refer to [12,28].

Definition 10. *An alternating tree automaton (ATA, for short) is a tuple $\mathcal{A} = < \Sigma, D, Q, q_0, \delta, F >$, where Σ is the alphabet, D is a finite set of directions, Q is the set of states, $q_0 \in Q$ is the initial state, $\delta : Q \times \Sigma \rightarrow \mathcal{B}^+(D \times Q)$ is the transition function associating to each state and alphabet symbol a positive Boolean combination of pairs (d, q), where d is a direction and q is a state, and F is the accepting condition defined later.*

To give an intuition on how an *ATA* $\mathcal{A}$ works, assume that it is in a state q, reading a node tree labeled by σ and $\delta(q, \sigma) = ((0, q_1) \vee (1, q_2)) \wedge (1, q_1)$. Then the automaton can just send two copies in direction 1 with state q_1 and q_2, respectively. The connectives $\vee$ and $\wedge$ in δ represent, respectively, choice and concurrency. Nondeterministic tree automata are alternating tree automata in which the concurrency feature is not allowed. A run of an alternating tree automaton $\mathcal{A}$ on a Σ-labeled tree $< T, V >$, with $T = D^*$, is a $(D^* \times Q)$-labeled $\mathbb{N}$-tree $< T_r, r >$ such that the root is labeled with (ε, q_0) and the labels of each node and its successors satisfy the transition relation. A run $\langle T_r, r \rangle$ is accepting iff all its infinite paths satisfy the acceptance condition. In this paper we are interested in the parity acceptance condition and, as its special case, the Büchi acceptance condition. A parity condition F maps all states of the automaton to a finite set of colors $C = \{C_{\min}, \ldots, C_{\max}\} \subset \mathbb{N}$. Thus, $F : Q \rightarrow C$. For a path π, let $m(\pi)$ be the maximal color that appears infinitely often along π. Then, π satisfies the parity condition F iff $m(\pi)$ is even. The Büchi acceptance condition is a parity condition with only two colors, i.e., $C = \{1, 2\}$. By $L(\mathcal{A})$ we denote the set of trees accepted by $\mathcal{A}$. We say that the automaton is not empty if $L(\mathcal{A}) \neq \emptyset$. We name ATA along with the parity and Büchi conditions PATA and BATA for short, respectively. In both cases of PATA and BATA emptiness can be checked in EXPTIME [12].

In ATL* module checking with (im)perfect information given a module M and an ATL* formula φ we check whether $M \models^{r,(i)} \varphi$ by checking whether

$T \models \varphi$ for every $T \in exec^{(i)}(M)$. Consequently, $M \not\models^{r,(i)} \varphi$ iff there exists a tree $\overline{T} \in exec^i(M)$ such that $\overline{T} \models \neg\varphi$. In the perfect information case, to solve this problem one can build a PATA $\mathcal{A}$, accepting all such $\overline{T}$ trees and reduce the model checking question "does $M \models^r \varphi$?" by checking for the automaton emptiness. In particular, the automaton uses one direction for each possible decision and, input trees and run trees have exactly the same shape. In the case of imperfect information, we are forced to restrict our reasoning to uniform strategies and this deeply complicates the construction of the automaton. Indeed, not all the trees in $exec^i(M)$ can be taken into consideration but only those coming from uniform strategies. This has to be taken into account both on the side of the environment agent, while performing the pruning, and the other players playing in accordance with the modalities indicated by the ATL* formula. Uniformity forces to use the same action in indistinguishable states. To accomplish this, the automaton takes as input not trees T from $exec^i(M)$, but rather corresponding "thin" trees T' such that each node v' in T' is meant to represent all nodes H in T that are indistinguishable to v'. Then, the automaton will send to v just $|H|$ different states all with the same direction, to force all of them to respect the same strategy. Thus, the input tree can be seen as a profile of uniform strategies, e.g., once a uniform strategy has been fixed, it collects all the possible outcomes obtained by combining this strategy with all possible uniform strategies coming from the other players. It is worth noting that the run tree has the shape of the desired $\overline{T} \in exec^i(M)$. In a way this is the witness of our automata approach.

To give few more details, let $[St]_{\sim i}$ be the equivalence class build upon the states that are indistinguishable to agent i. We use as directions of the automaton $\Pi_i[St]_{\sim i}$. Agents can then choose actions upon their visibility. The automaton has to accept trees corresponding to uniform strategy profiles whose composition with the module satisfy $\neg\varphi$. Thus, a run of the automaton proceeds by simulating an unwinding of the module, pruned at each step according to the strategy profile and the satisfiability of the formula is checked on the fly. Starting from an ATL* formula the automaton we obtain is an exponential PATA. In case of ATL, the automaton is a polynomial BATA. Since the module-checking problem with imperfect information is 2EXPTIME-complete for CTL* and EXPTIME-complete for CTL even in case the formula is of bounded size, we get the following result.

Theorem 2. *The module-checking problem with imperfect information is* 2EXPTIME-*complete for ATL* and* EXPTIME-*complete for ATL. For formulae of bounded size the problem is* EXPTIME-*complete in both cases.*

6   Conclusions

We have presented an extension of the module checking problem that handles specifications of strategic ability for modules involving imperfect information. As usual for computational problems, the key features are expressivity and complexity. We show that this new variant of module checking fares well in both respects.

On one hand, the computational complexity is the same as that of module checking CTL/CTL* with imperfect information. On the other hand, ATL/ATL* module checking under imperfect information has incomparable expressive power to ATL/ATL* module checking for perfect information, which means that the two variants of the problem offer distinctly different perspectives at verification of open systems.

In the future, we plan to characterize the correspondence of imperfect information module checking to an appropriate variant of model checking (in the spirit of [17]). We are also going to look at the relation of module checking to model checking of temporal logics with propositional quantification [19,23]. Last but not least, we would like to apply the framework to verification of agent-oriented programs.

Acknowledgements. Aniello Murano acknowledges the support of the FP7 EU project 600958-SHERPA. Wojciech Jamroga acknowledges the support of the FP7 EU project ReVINK (PIEF-GA-2012-626398).

References

1. Ågotnes, T. , Goranko, V., Jamroga, W.: Alternating-time temporal logics with irrevocable strategies. In: Proceedings of TARK XI, pp. 15–24 (2007)
2. Alur, R., Henzinger, T.A., Kupferman, O.: Alternating-time Temporal Logic. J. ACM **49**, 672–713 (2002)
3. Aminof, B., Legay, A., Murano, A., Serre, O., Vardi, M.Y.: Pushdown module checking with imperfect information. Inf. Comput. **223**(1), 1–17 (2013)
4. Aminof, B., Murano, A., Vardi, M.Y.: Pushdown module checking with imperfect information. In: Caires, L., Vasconcelos, V.T. (eds.) CONCUR 2007. LNCS, vol. 4703, pp. 460–475. Springer, Heidelberg (2007)
5. Basu, S., Roop, P.S., Sinha, R.: Local module checking for CTL specifications. Electronic Notes in Theoretical Computer Science **176**(2), 125–141 (2007)
6. Bozzelli, L.: New results on pushdown module checking with imperfect information. In: Proceedings of GandALF, EPTCS, vol. 54, pp. 162–177 (2011)
7. Bozzelli, L., Murano, A., Peron, A.: Pushdown module checking. Formal Methods in System Design **36**(1), 65–95 (2010)
8. Bulling, N., Jamroga, W.: Comparing variants of strategic ability: How uncertainty and memory influence general properties of games. Journal of Autonomous Agents and Multi-Agent Systems **28**(3), 474–518 (2014)
9. Clarke, E., Emerson, E.: Design and synthesis of synchronization skeletons using branching time temporal logic. In: Kozen, D. (ed.) Logics of Programs. LNCS, vol. 131, pp. 52–71. Springer, Heidelberg (1981)
10. de Alfaro, L., Godefroid, P., Jagadeesan, R.: Three-valued abstractions of games: uncertainty, but with precision. In: Proceedings of LICS, pp. 170–179. IEEE Computer Society (2004)
11. Emerson, E.: Temporal and modal logic. In: van Leeuwen, J. (ed.) Handbook of Theoretical Computer Science, vol. B, pp. 995–1072. Elsevier Science Publishers (1990)

12. Emerson, E., Jutla, C.: Tree automata, mu-calculus and determinacy. In: Proceedings of the 32nd Annual Symposium on Foundations of Computer Science, pp. 368–377. IEEE (1991)
13. Ferrante, A., Murano, A., Parente, M.: Enriched μ-calculi module checking. Logical Methods in Computer Science 4(3–1), 1–21 (2008)
14. Gesell, M., Schneider, K.: Modular verification of synchronous programs. In: Proceedings of ACSD, pp. 70–79. IEEE (2013)
15. Godefroid, P.: Reasoning about abstract open systems with generalized module checking. In: Alur, R., Lee, I. (eds.) EMSOFT 2003. LNCS, vol. 2855, pp. 223–240. Springer, Heidelberg (2003)
16. Godefroid, P., Huth, M.: Model checking vs. generalized model checking: semantic minimizations for temporal logics. In: Proceedings of LICS, pp. 158–167. IEEE Computer Society (2005)
17. Jamroga, W., Murano, A.: On module checking and strategies. In: Proceedings of the 13th International Conference on Autonomous Agents and Multiagent Systems AAMAS 2014, pp. 701–708 (2014)
18. Jamroga, W., Murano, A.: Module checking of strategic ability. In: Proceedings of the 14th International Conference on Autonomous Agents and Multiagent Systems AAMAS 2015, pp. 227–235 (2015)
19. Kupferman, O.: Augmenting branching temporal logics with existential quantification over atomic propositions. Journal of Logic and Computation 9(2), 135–147 (1999)
20. Kupferman, O., Vardi, M.: Module checking. In: Alur, R., Henzinger, T.A. (eds.) CAV 1996. LNCS, vol. 1102. Springer, Heidelberg (1996)
21. Kupferman, O., Vardi, M.: Module checking revisited. In: Grumberg, O. (ed.) CAV 1997. LNCS, vol. 1254, pp. 36–47. Springer, Heidelberg (1997)
22. Kupferman, O., Vardi, M., Wolper, P.: Module checking. Inf. Comput. 164(2), 322–344 (2001)
23. Da Costa, A., Laroussinie, F., Markey, N.: Quantified CTL: expressiveness and model checking. In: Koutny, M., Ulidowski, I. (eds.) CONCUR 2012. LNCS, vol. 7454, pp. 177–192. Springer, Heidelberg (2012)
24. Martinelli, F.: Module checking through partial model checking. Technical report, CNR Roma - TR-06 (2002)
25. Martinelli, F., Matteucci, I.: An approach for the specification, verification and synthesis of secure systems. Electronic Notes in Theoretical Computer Science 168, 29–43 (2007)
26. Murano, A., Napoli, M., Parente, M.: Program complexity in hierarchical module checking. In: Cervesato, I., Veith, H., Voronkov, A. (eds.) LPAR 2008. LNCS (LNAI), vol. 5330, pp. 318–332. Springer, Heidelberg (2008)
27. Schobbens, P.Y.: Alternating-time logic with imperfect recall. Electronic Notes in Theoretical Computer Science 85(2), 82–93 (2004)
28. Thomas, W.: Automata on infinite objects. Handbook of Theoretical Computer Science 2 (1990)
29. Wang, Y., Dechesne, F.: On expressive power and class invariance. CoRR, abs/0905.4332 (2009)

Towards Systematic Evaluation of Multi-agent Systems in Large Scale and Dynamic Logistics

Rinde R.S. van Lon$^{(\boxtimes)}$ and Tom Holvoet

iMinds-DistriNet, KU Leuven, 3001 Leuven, Belgium
{Rinde.vanLon,Tom.Holvoet}@cs.kuleuven.be

Abstract. A common hypothesis in multi-agent systems (MAS) literature is that decentralized MAS are better at coping with dynamic and
large scale problems compared to centralized algorithms. Existing work
investigates this hypothesis in a limited way, often with no support for
further evaluation, slowing down the advance of more general conclusions. Investigating this hypothesis more systematically is time consum-
ing as it requires four main components: (1) formal metrics for the variables of interest, (2) a problem instance generator using these metrics,
(3) (de)centralized algorithms and (4) a simulation platform that facilitates the execution of these algorithms. Present paper describes the construction of an instance generator based on previously established formal
metrics and simulation platform with support for (de)centralized algorithms. Using our instance generator, a benchmark logistics dataset with
varying levels of dynamism and scale is created and we demonstrate how
it can be used for systematically evaluating MAS and centralized algorithms in our simulator. This benchmark dataset is essential for enabling
the adoption of a more thorough and systematic evaluation methodology, allowing increased insight in the strengths and weaknesses of both
the MAS paradigm and operational research methods.

1 Introduction

In pickup and delivery problems (PDPs) a fleet of vehicles is tasked with transporting customers or goods from origin to destination [23,27]. In dynamic PDPs
the orders describing the vehicles' tasks arrive during the operating hours [1],
necessitating online assignment of vehicles to orders. The dynamic nature and
potential large scale of this problem makes exact algorithms often infeasible.

Decentralized multi-agent systems (MASs) are often presented as a good
alternative to centralized algorithms [3,6,29], MASs are especially promising for
large scale and dynamic problems due to their ability to make quick local decisions. Previous work has shown that MASs can sometimes outperform centralized
algorithms in specific cases [3,18,19,20]. However, to the best of our knowledge
there has never been a systematic effort to compare centralized algorithms to
decentralized MASs with varying levels of dynamism and scale.

Although the previously mentioned papers each do a thorough evaluation of
a MAS applied to a logistics problem, it is often hard to do further comparisons
using these papers because of the lack of available problem data, source code or

© Springer International Publishing Switzerland 2015
Q. Chen et al. (Eds.): PRIMA 2015, LNAI 9387, pp. 248–264, 2015.
DOI: 10.1007/978-3-319-25524-8_16

both. It has been argued before that this is a problem in science in general [8], and in multi-agent systems literature in particular [16].

In this paper we introduce a dataset generator and a benchmark dataset of the dynamic pickup and delivery problem with time windows (PDPTW) with support for varying three variables. The degree of dynamism and urgency of a dynamic PDPTW are two variables that were introduced before [14]. The proposed dataset contains an additional variable, scale, that we define in the context of PDPTW as a multiplier applied to the number of vehicles and orders in a problem. Using this dataset it will be possible to systematically investigate the following hypotheses in the context of PDPTW:

- Multi-agent systems perform better when compared to centralized algorithms on very dynamic problem instances
- Multi-agent systems perform better when compared to centralized algorithms on more urgent problem instances
- Multi-agent systems perform better when compared to centralized algorithms on large scale problem instances

Investigating these hypotheses should lead to insight in the performance of both decentralized MASs and centralized algorithms for PDPTWs. These insights can then be used to make more informed decisions when designing a system that needs to cope with dynamic, urgent and large scale problems. Additionally, the dataset generator, the benchmark dataset instance and the simulator [15] that we use are open sourced. This improves the reproducibility of the current paper while presenting an opportunity for other researchers to investigate the above hypotheses using their own algorithms.

The paper is organized as follows. First, the relevant literature is discussed (Section 2) and we define dynamic PDPTWs including the measures for dynamism, urgency and scale and the measure for algorithm performance (Section 3). This is followed by a description of the dataset generator and dataset benchmark instance (Section 4). It is demonstrated how the hypotheses of dynamism, urgency and scale can be investigated using the proposed benchmark instance (Section 5), leading to the conclusion that the benchmark dataset facilitates a systematic and long term research effort into these hypotheses (Section 6).

2   Related Work

Several literature surveys discuss the dynamic vehicle routing problem (VRP) and its special case, dynamic PDPTW [1,5,24,26]. The dynamic PDPTW is often treated as a stochastic problem where some a priori information is known about the orders. This section only discusses papers that do not use a priori information but view the problem from a completely dynamic perspective.

2.1   Centralized Algorithms

Madsen et al. [17] developed an insertion heuristic for the dynamic dial-a-ride-problem (DARP) with time windows for moving elderly and disabled people.

Potvin et al. [25] presented a learning system based on linear programming that can learn an optimal policy taking into account decisions of an expert in past scenarios. Mitrović-Minić et al. [22] presented an approach based on two time horizons: a short time horizon aimed at achieving the short-term goal of minimization of distance traveled, and a longer time horizon aimed at achieving the long-term goal of facilitating the insertion of future requests. Gendreau et al. [4] introduced a dynamic version of tabu search with a neighboring structure based on ejection chains. When new requests arrive, the algorithm reacts by insertion and ejection moves and with local search.

2.2 Multi-Agent Systems

An alternative approach to the dynamic PDPTW is using a decentralized MAS instead of a centralized planner. Fischer et al. [3] used a MAS with the extended contract net protocol for cooperative transportation scheduling and they showed that its performance was comparable to existing operational research (OR) techniques. Mes et al. [20] compared traditional heuristics with a distributed MAS that uses a Vickrey auction to bid for new pickup and delivery requests when they appear, showing that the MAS approach performs often better than traditional heuristics. In subsequent work Mes and Van der Heijden [21] further improved the performance of the MAS by introducing a look-ahead mechanism in which bidding uses value functions to estimate the expected future revenue of inserting a new order in an agent plan. Máhr et al. [19] thoroughly evaluated a MAS with auctions and a mixed-integer program on real world data of a PDPTW. Their results show that both approaches have comparable performance. Glaschenko et al. [6] discussed the deployment of a MAS for a taxi company in London, adopting the MAS led to an increase of taxi fleet utilization by 5 - 7 %.

3 Dynamic Pickup-and-Delivery Problems

We base our definition of dynamic PDPs on [14] which is an adaptation of the definition of [4]. In PDPs there is a fleet of vehicles responsible for the pickup-and-delivery of items. The dynamic PDP is an online problem, the customer transportation requests are revealed over time during the fleet's operating hours. It is further assumed that the fleet of vehicles has no prior knowledge about the total number of requests nor about their locations or time windows.

3.1 Formal Definition

For describing the dynamic PDP we adopt the formal definition of [14]. A *scenario*, which describes the unfolding of a dynamic PDP, is defined as a tuple:

$$\langle \mathcal{T}, \mathcal{E}, \mathcal{V} \rangle := \text{scenario},$$

where

$$[0, \mathcal{T}) := \text{time frame of the scenario,} \qquad \mathcal{T} > 0$$
$$\mathcal{E} := \text{list of events,} \qquad |\mathcal{E}| \geq 2$$
$$\mathcal{V} := \text{set of vehicles,} \qquad |\mathcal{V}| \geq 1$$

$[0, \mathcal{T})$ is the period in which the fleet of vehicles $\mathcal{V}$ has to handle all customer requests. The events represent customer transportation requests. Since we consider the purely dynamic PDPTW, all events are revealed between time 0 and time $\mathcal{T}$. Each event $e_i \in \mathcal{E}$ is defined by the following variables:

$$a_i := \text{announce time}$$
$$p_i := [p_i^L, p_i^R] = \text{pickup time window,} \; p_i^L < p_i^R$$
$$d_i := [d_i^L, d_i^R) = \text{delivery time window,} \; d_i^L < d_i^R$$
$$pst_i := \text{pickup service time span}$$
$$dst_i := \text{delivery service time span}$$
$$ploc_i := \text{pickup location}$$
$$dloc_i := \text{delivery location}$$
$$tt_i := \text{travel time from pickup location to delivery location}$$

Reaction time is defined as:

$$r_i := p_i^R - a_i = \text{reaction time} \qquad (1)$$

The time window related variables of a transportation request are visualized in Figure 1.

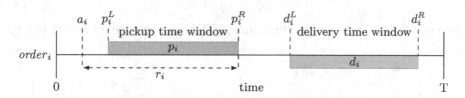

Fig. 1. Visualization of the time related variables of a single order event $e_i \in \mathcal{E}$.

Furthermore we assume that:

- vehicles start at a depot and have to return after all orders are handled;
- the fleet of vehicles $\mathcal{V}$ is homogeneous;
- the cargo capacity of vehicles is infinite (e.g. courier service);
- the vehicle is either stationary or driving at a constant speed;
- vehicle diversion is allowed, this means that a vehicle is allowed to divert from its destination at any time;

- vehicle fuel is infinite and driver fatigue is not an issue;
- the scenario is completed when all pickup and deliveries have been made and all vehicles have returned to the depot; and,
- each location can be reached from any other location.

Vehicle schedules are subject to both hard and soft constraints. The opening of time windows is a hard constraint, hence vehicles need to adhere to these:

$$sp_{ij} \geq p_i^L \tag{2}$$

$$sd_{ij} \geq d_i^L \tag{3}$$

Here, sp_{ij} is the start of the pickup operation of order event e_i by vehicle v_j; similarly, sd_{ij} is the start of the delivery operation of order event e_i by vehicle v_j. The time window closing (p_i^R and d_i^R) is a soft constraint incorporated into the objective function, it is defined similarly to [4] and needs to be minimized:

$$min := \sum_{j \in \mathcal{V}} \left(vtt_j + td\left\{bd_j, \mathcal{T}\right\} \right) + \sum_{i \in \mathcal{E}} \left(td\left\{sp_{ij}, p_i^R\right\} + td\left\{sd_{ij}, d_i^R\right\} \right) \tag{4}$$

where

$$td\left\{\alpha, \beta\right\} := max\left\{0, \alpha - \beta\right\} = \text{tardiness} \tag{5}$$

Here, vtt_j is the total travel time of vehicle v_j; bd_j is the time at which vehicle v_j is back at the depot. In summary, the objective function computes the total vehicle travel time, the tardiness of vehicles returning to the depot and the total pickup and delivery tardiness.

We further impose the following hard constraints on the construction of scenarios to ensure consistency and feasibility of individual orders:

$$r_i \geq 0 \tag{6}$$

$$d_i^R \geq p_i^R + pst_i + tt_i \tag{7}$$

$$d_i^L \geq p_i^L + pst_i + tt_i \tag{8}$$

These constraints are visualized in Figure 2. The reaction time constraint (eq. 6)

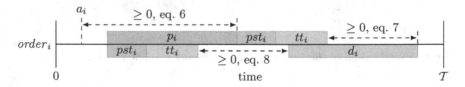

Fig. 2. Visualization of the time window constraints of an order event $e_i \in \mathcal{E}$.

ensures that an order is always announced before its due date. The time window constraints (eq. 7 and eq. 8) ensure that pickup and delivery time windows are compatible with each other. Hence, a pickup operation started at any time within p_i guarantees feasibility of a delivery within d_i given that a vehicle is available and respecting vehicle capacity, service time and travel time constraints.

3.2   Dynamism

In this section we describe the measure for the degree of dynamism first defined in [14]. Informally, a scenario that changes continuously is said to be dynamic while a scenario that changes occasionally is said to be less dynamic. In the context of PDPTWs a change is an event that introduces additional information to the problem, such as the events in $\mathcal{E}$. More formally, the degree of dynamism, or the continuity of change, is defined as:

$$dynamism := 1 - \frac{\sum_{i=0}^{|\Delta|} \sigma_i}{\sum_{i=0}^{|\Delta|} \bar{\sigma}_i} \tag{9}$$

where

$$\Delta := \{\delta_0, \delta_1, \ldots, \delta_{|\mathcal{E}|-2}\} = \{a_j - a_i | j = i+1 \wedge \forall a_i, a_j \in \mathcal{E}\} \tag{10}$$

$$\theta := \text{perfect interarrival time} = \frac{T}{|\mathcal{E}|} \tag{11}$$

$$\sigma_i := \begin{cases} \theta - \delta_i & \text{if } i = 0 \text{ and } \delta_i < \theta \\ \theta - \delta_i + \dfrac{\theta - \delta_i}{\theta} \times \sigma_{i-1} & \text{if } i > 0 \text{ and } \delta_i < \theta \\ 0 & \text{otherwise} \end{cases} \tag{12}$$

$$\bar{\sigma}_i := \theta + \begin{cases} \dfrac{\theta - \delta_i}{\theta} \times \sigma_{i-1} & \text{if } i > 0 \text{ and } \delta_i < \theta \\ 0 & \text{otherwise} \end{cases} \tag{13}$$

This measure can compute the degree of dynamism of any scenario.

3.3   Urgency

In [14] urgency is defined as the maximum reaction time available to the fleet of vehicles in order to respond to an incoming order. Or more formally:

$$urgency\,(e_i) := p_i^R - a_i = r_i \tag{14}$$

To obtain the urgency of an entire scenario the mean and standard deviation of the urgency of all orders can be computed.

3.4   Scale

Assigning a scale level to a PDP instance allows to conduct a scalability experiment to investigate the existence of a correlation between the scale of a PDP and the computation time and solution quality of an algorithm.

In the context of computer systems scaling up is defined as maintaining a fixed execution time per task while scaling the workload up in proportion to the number of processors applied to it [7]. Analogously, scaling in the context of PDPs can be defined as maintaining a fixed computation time per order while scaling the workload (number of orders) up in proportion to the number of vehicles in the fleet.

However, there are three factors that limit the usefulness of this definition. First, it is known that PDPTWs are NP-hard [27], therefore an exact algorithm for a PDPTW requires time that is superpolynomial in the input size. Therefore, maintaining a fixed computation time per order when using an exact algorithm is infeasible. When using an anytime algorithm (an algorithm that can be stopped at any moment during its execution to return a valid solution) such as a heuristic, maintaining a fixed computation time per order is trivial, but will likely have an influence on the solution quality.

Second, the previously mentioned notion of urgency influences the amount of available computation time. Within an order's urgency period three activities need to be performed, first a vehicle needs to be selected, then the selected vehicle needs to drive towards the pickup location and it needs to perform the actual pickup operation. The longer the computation of the vehicle selection takes, the less time remains for the driving and picking up.

Third, depending on the degree of dynamism there may be many orders with a small interarrival time. Each order that arrives while a computation takes place forces a premature halt and subsequent restart of the algorithm. Therefore, maintaining a fixed computation time per order is nonsensical for PDPTWs.

For these reasons, we define scaling in PDPTWs as *maintaining a fixed objective value per order while scaling the number of orders up in proportion to the number of vehicles in the fleet*. Using this definition, scaling up a scenario $\langle \mathcal{T}, \mathcal{E}, \mathcal{V} \rangle$ with a factor α will create a new scenario $\langle \mathcal{T}, \mathcal{E}', \mathcal{V}' \rangle$ where $|\mathcal{V}'| = |\mathcal{V}| \cdot \alpha$ and $|\mathcal{E}'| = |\mathcal{E}| \cdot \alpha$. To compute the objective value per order, the global objective value needs to be divided by the number of orders.

4   Dataset

This section describes the construction of the scenario generator that creates scenarios with specific levels of dynamism, urgency and scale. Using the scenario generator a benchmark dataset is constructed.

4.1   Scenario Generator

To create a scenario generator capable of generating scenarios with specific levels of scale, dynamism and urgency we adapted the generator developed in [14].

Controlling Dynamism of Time Series. Based on [14] we assigned a time series generator method to a specific range of dynamism levels such that the entire range $[0, 1]$ is covered (Table 1).

Table 1. Overview of dynamism ranges and the corresponding time series generator used for generating scenarios in that range.

Dynamism range	Time series generator
[0, .475)	non-homogeneous Poisson process
[.475, .575)	homogeneous Poisson process
[.575, .675)	Normal distribution
[.675, 1]	Uniform distribution

The non-homogeneous Poisson process that is used for $[0, .475)$ has an intensity function based on a sine wave with the following parameters:

$$\lambda(t) = a \cdot \sin(t \cdot f \cdot 2\pi - \pi \cdot p) + h \tag{15}$$
$$a = 1 \qquad\qquad\qquad\qquad \text{amplitude} \qquad (16)$$
$$f = 1 \qquad\qquad\qquad\qquad \text{frequency} \qquad (17)$$
$$p \sim \mathcal{U}(0, 1) \qquad\qquad\qquad \text{phase shift} \qquad (18)$$
$$h \sim \mathcal{U}(-.99, 1.5) \qquad\qquad\qquad \text{height} \qquad (19)$$

In order to keep the total number of events constant with different levels of dynamism, the amplitude and height parameters are rescaled such that the total area under the intensity function equals $|\mathcal{E}|$.

For the $[.475, .575)$ range we used the homogeneous Poisson process, with the (constant) intensity function defined as:

$$\lambda(t) = \frac{|\mathcal{E}|}{T} = 30 \tag{20}$$

The normal distribution for the $[.575, .676)$ range is the truncated normal distribution $\mathcal{N}\left(\frac{T}{|\mathcal{E}|}, 0.04\right)$ with a lower bound of 0 and a standard deviation of 0.04. If a value x was drawn such that $x < 0$, a new number was drawn from the distribution. Truncating a normal distribution actually shifts the mean, hence the mean was rescaled to make sure the effective mean was equal to $\frac{T}{|\mathcal{E}|}$.

In the $[.675, 1]$ range a uniform distribution with mean $\frac{T}{|\mathcal{E}|}$ and a maximum deviation from the mean, σ, is used. The σ value is (for each scenario again) drawn from the truncated normal distribution $\mathcal{N}(1, 1)$ with bounds $[0, 15]$. If a value σ is obtained from the distribution such that $\sigma > 15$ or $\sigma < 0$ a new value is drawn. Since the mean is not scaled, the effective mean of σ is higher than 1.

Generating Comparable Scenarios with Different Dynamism, Urgency and Scale Levels. The generator should be able to generate a set of scenarios where all settings are the same except for dynamism, urgency and scale levels. Also, any interactions between variables should be minimized, e.g. dynamism should not correlate with time window intervals. This ensures that any effect measured is solely caused by the difference in dynamism, urgency and or scale.

Because the dataset generator is stochastic, the number of events $|\mathcal{E}|$ and the degree of dynamism of a scenario can not be directly controlled. To construct a consistent dataset, scenarios that do not have exactly $|\mathcal{E}|$ events are rejected. For each desired dynamism level a bin with an acceptable deviation is defined, only generated scenarios with a dynamism value that lies within a bin are accepted.

We further define the concept of *office hours* as the period $[0, \mathcal{O})$ in which new orders are accepted. To ensure feasibility of individual orders we need to take into account the travel time, service time durations and urgency:

$$\mathcal{O} = \mathcal{T} - pst_{max} - dst_{max} - \begin{cases} 2 \cdot tt_{max} & \text{if } u < \frac{1}{2} \cdot tt_{max} \\ 1\frac{1}{2} \cdot tt_{max} - u & \text{otherwise} \end{cases} \qquad (21)$$

Here, pst_{max} and dst_{max} are the maximum pickup and delivery service times respectively, tt_{max} is the maximum travel time between a pickup and delivery location, and u is urgency.

The pickup and delivery time windows have to be randomly chosen while respecting the constraints as set out by the urgency level and the announce time. The p_i^R is defined as the sum of a_i and u, hence it follows that p_i^L needs to be between a_i and the sum of a_i and u:

$$p_i^L = \begin{cases} \sim \mathcal{U}(a_i, p_i^R - 10) & \text{if } u > 10 \\ a_i & \text{otherwise} \end{cases} \qquad (22)$$

Here, 10 is the minimum pickup time window length unless urgency is less than 10, in that case the urgency level equals the pickup time window length. The upper bound of d_i^R can be defined as:

$$ubd_i^R = \mathcal{T} - tt(dloc_i, depot_{loc}) - dst_i \qquad (23)$$

This translates as the latest possible time to start the delivery operation such that the delivery time window constraints are met and the vehicle can still be back at the depot on time. The lower bound of d_i^L was already defined in eq. 8:

$$lbd_i^L = p_i^L + pst_i + tt_i \qquad (24)$$

We define a minimum delivery time window length of 10, which then results in an upper bound of d_i^L:

$$ubd_i^L = ubd_i^R - 10 \qquad (25)$$

Based on these bounds we draw the opening of the delivery time window from the following uniform distribution:

$$d_i^L \sim \mathcal{U}(lbd_i^L, \max(lbd_i^L, ubd_i^L)) \qquad (26)$$

To find d_i^R we need to redefine the lower bound (from eq. 7) by using the actual value of d_i^L:

$$lbd_i^R = \min(\max(p_i^R + pst_i + tt_i, d_i^L + 10), ubd_i^R) \qquad (27)$$

Finally, the closing of the delivery time window is defined as:

$$d_i^R \sim \mathcal{U}\left(lbd_i^R, ubd_i^R\right) \tag{28}$$

For the pickup and delivery service times we choose $pst_i = dst_i = 5$ minutes.

All locations in a scenario are points on the Euclidean plane. It has a size of 10 by 10 kilometer with a depot at the center of this square. Vehicles start at the depot and have a constant travel speed of 50 km/h. All pickup and delivery locations are drawn from a two dimensional uniform distribution $\mathcal{U}_2(0, 10)$.

4.2 Benchmark Dataset

The benchmark dataset that we created for this paper has three levels for each of the dimensions of interest resulting in a total of $3 \cdot 3 \cdot 3 = 27$ scenario categories. The dimensions of interest are dynamism, urgency and scale, the used values are listed in Table 2a, the other parameters are listed in Table 2b. Since the

Table 2. Overview of the parameters used to generate the benchmark dataset.

(a) Dimensions

Dimension	Values		
Dynamism	.2	.5	.8
Urgency	5	20	35
Scale	1	5	10

(b) Settings

Parameter	Value
T	8 hours
$|\mathcal{E}|$	scale · 240
$|\mathcal{V}|$	scale · 10

generation of the order arrival times is a stochastic process the exact degree of dynamism can not be controlled. Therefore, we define a dynamism bin using a radius of 1% around each dynamism value. For this dataset, we consider a scenario with dynamism d where $b - .01 < d < b + .01$ to have dynamism b, where b is one of the dynamism bins listed in Table 2a.

For each scenario category 50 instances are generated, resulting in a total of $50 \cdot 27 = 1350$ scenarios. Each scenario is written to a separate file with the following name format: **dynamism-urgency-scale-id.scen**, for example **0.20-5-1.00-0.scen** depicts a scenario with 20% dynamism, an urgency level of 5 minutes, a scale of 1 and id 0. This format allows easy selection of a subset of the dataset. The scenario file contains the entire scenario in JavaScript Object Notation (JSON). Time in a scenario is expressed in milliseconds, distance in kilometer and speed in kilometer per hour. A scenario is considered to be finished when all vehicles are back at the depot and the current time is $\geq T$.

The open source discrete time simulator RinSim [15] version 4.0.0 [13] has native support for the scenario format. With RinSim it is easy to run the scenario with centralized algorithms and multi-agent systems, allowing researchers to only have to focus on their algorithms. For reproducibility, the code of the dataset generator is released [11] as well as the dataset scenarios [10] and all other code and results [9].

5   Demonstration

As a demonstration a centralized algorithm is compared with a decentralized multi-agent system on 10 instances of each category in the benchmark dataset, resulting in a total of 270 experiments per approach. For reproducibility, the code and results of this experiment are published on an accompanying web page [9]

5.1   Heuristics

Just as in [14] two well known heuristics are used, the cheapest insertion heuristic (Algorithm 1) and the 2-opt optimization procedure (Algorithm 2). Since the 2-opt procedure requires a complete schedule as input, it uses the cheapest insertion heuristic to construct a complete schedule first. Both these algorithms have been used in earlier work for vehicle routing problems [2,28].

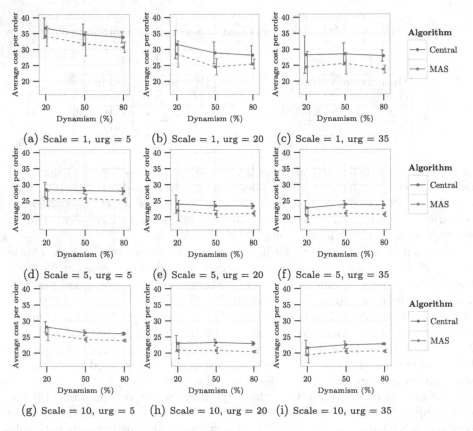

Fig. 3. Comparison with mean relative cost versus dynamism for all levels of scale and urgency. The error bars indicate one standard deviation around the mean.

```
Input: ⟨𝒯, ℰ, 𝒱⟩;                                    /* A scenario as input */
Data: 𝒮;                                             /* the current schedule or ∅ */
𝒮_best = ∅
foreach e ∈ ℰ, e ∉ 𝒮 do
    /* generate all PDP insertion points in the current schedule:          */
    insertions = generate_insertion_points(𝒮)
    for i ∈ insertions do
        /* construct a new schedule by inserting e at insertion i          */
        𝒮_new = construct(𝒮,e,i)
        if cost(𝒮_new) < cost(𝒮_best) then
        |   𝒮_best = 𝒮_new
        end
    end
end
```

Algorithm 1. Cheapest insertion heuristic, source code available in [12].

```
Input: 𝒮
𝒮_best = 𝒮
swaps = generate_swaps(𝒮)
foreach e ∈ swaps do
    𝒮_new = swap(𝒮,e)
    if cost(𝒮_new) < cost(𝒮_best) then
    |   𝒮_best = 𝒮_new
    end
end
/* If a better schedule has been found, we start another iteration         */
if 𝒮_best ≠ 𝒮 then
|   2-opt(𝒮_best)
end
```

Algorithm 2. 2-opt procedure, source code available in [12].

5.2 Centralized Algorithm

Each time a new order is announced the cheapest insertion heuristic is executed to produce a new schedule for the fleet of vehicles. It is assumed that execution of the algorithm is instantaneous with respect to the dynamics of the simulations.

5.3 Contract Net Protocol Multi-Agent System

The multi-agent system implementation is based on the contract net protocol (CNP) as described by Fischer et al. [3]. For each incoming order an auction is organized, when the auction is finished the order will be assigned to exactly one vehicle. All vehicles always bid on each order, the bid contains an estimate of the additional cost that including the new order in the vehicles assignment would incur. This estimate is computed using the cheapest insertion heuristic as described in Algorithm 1. The vehicle with the lowest bid will win the auction and receive the order. Each vehicle computes a route to visit all its pickup and delivery sites using the 2-opt procedure described in Algorithm 2.

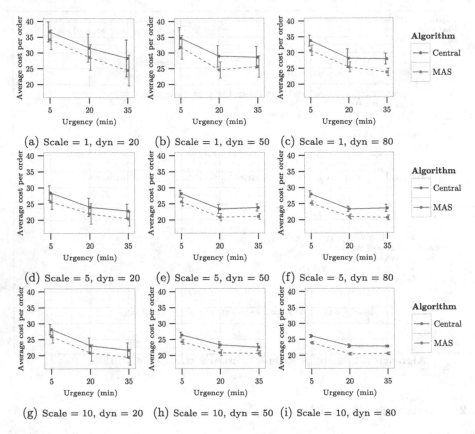

(a) Scale = 1, dyn = 20   (b) Scale = 1, dyn = 50   (c) Scale = 1, dyn = 80

(d) Scale = 5, dyn = 20   (e) Scale = 5, dyn = 50   (f) Scale = 5, dyn = 80

(g) Scale = 10, dyn = 20   (h) Scale = 10, dyn = 50   (i) Scale = 10, dyn = 80

Fig. 4. Comparison with mean relative cost versus urgency for all levels of scale and dynamism. The error bars indicate one standard deviation around the mean.

5.4   Results and Analysis

The results[1] of the experiments are plotted along the dynamism, urgency and scale dimension in Figures 3, 4 and 5 respectively. Although all results indicate that the MAS performs better than the centralized algorithm, the current experiment is too limited to verify the hypotheses posed in this paper. Instead, we discuss the behavior of both algorithms with respect to the dimensions of interest.

Dynamism. Figure 3 shows that the level of dynamism has very little influence on the performance of both the MAS and the centralized algorithm. This lack of effect is very consistent among all urgency and scale settings.

---

[1] In [9] the raw results are published.

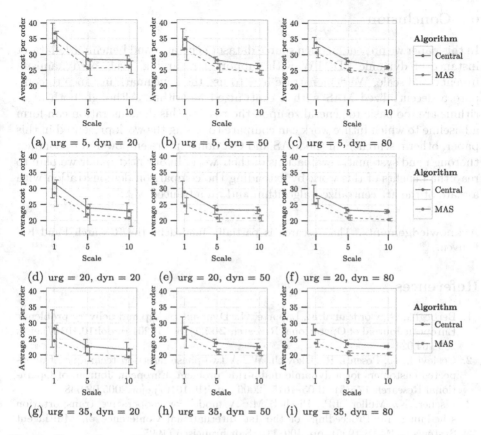

Fig. 5. Comparison with mean relative cost versus scale for all levels of urgency and dynamism. The error bars indicate one standard deviation around the mean.

Urgency. In Figure 4 a clear trend can be observed for both algorithms, the less urgent orders are, the lower the average cost per order is. This effect can be explained by the fact that when orders are less urgent, vehicles have more time to handle other nearby orders first while still respecting the time windows.

Scale. Contrary to what one would expect, Figure 5 shows that the larger scale the problem is the lower the average cost of an order. This surprising result can be explained by the fact that computation time is ignored in our current setup, this means that the algorithms have enough time to deal with greater complexity of larger scale problems. The lower average cost per order can be explained by the fact that with more vehicles the average distance of a new order to the closest vehicle is smaller, resulting in reduced average travel times and tardiness.

6 Conclusion

In this paper we present an open source dataset generator and benchmark dataset instance of dynamic PDPTW with support for varying levels of dynamism, urgency and scale. We demonstrate how to use the benchmark instance to compare a decentralized MAS with a centralized algorithm. Although both algorithms are too basic to generalize upon the results, this demonstration can form a baseline to which future work can compare to. Using the work presented in this paper, other researchers in the MAS and OR domains are empowered to conduct thorough and systematic evaluations of their work. In our next paper we plan to reap the benefits of this work by extending the comparison demonstration with a state of the art centralized algorithm and an advanced MAS.

Acknowledgements. This research is partially funded by the Research Fund KU Leuven.

References

1. Berbeglia, G., Cordeau, J.F., Laporte, G.: Dynamic pickup and delivery problems. European Journal of Operational Research **202**(1), 8–15 (2010). doi:10.1016/j.ejor. 2009.04.024
2. Coslovich, L., Pesenti, R., Ukovich, W.: A two-phase insertion technique of unexpected customers for a dynamic dial-a-ride problem. European Journal of Operational Research **175**(3), 1605–1615 (2006). doi:10.1016/j.ejor.2005.02.038
3. Fischer, K., Müller, J.P., Pischel, M.: A model for cooperative transportation scheduling. In: Proceedings of the 1st International Conference on Multiagent Systems (ICMAS 1995), pp. 109–116, San Francisco (1995)
4. Gendreau, M., Guertin, F., Potvin, J.Y., Séguin, R.: Neighborhood search heuristics for a dynamic vehicle dispatching problem with pick-ups and deliveries. Transportation Research Part C: Emerging Technologies **14**(3), 157–174 (2006). doi:10.1016/j.trc.2006.03.002
5. Gendreau, M., Potvin, J.Y.: Dynamic vehicle routing and dispatching. In: Crainic, T., Laporte, G. (eds.) Fleet Management and Logistics. Centre for Research on Transportation, pp. 115–126. Springer, NewYork (1998). doi:10.1007/978-1-4615-5755-5_5
6. Glaschenko, A., Ivaschenko, A., Rzevski, G., Skobelev, P.: Multi-agent real time scheduling system for taxi companies. In: Proceedings of 8th International Conference on Autonomous Agents and Multiagent Systems (AAMAS), pp. 29–36 (2009)
7. Gunther, N.J.: Guerrilla Capacity Planning: A Tactical Approach to Planning for Highly Scalable Applications and Services. Springer-Verlag New York Inc., Secaucus (2006). doi:10.1007/978-3-540-31010-5
8. Ince, D.C., Hatton, L., Graham-Cumming, J.: The case for open computer programs. Nature **482**(7386), 485–488 (2012). doi:10.1038/nature10836
9. van Lon, R.R.S.: Code and results, PRIMA 2015, August 2015. doi:10.5281/zenodo. 27365
10. van Lon, R.R.S.: Dynamism, urgency and scale dataset, August 2015. doi:10.5281/zenodo.27364

11. van Lon, R.R.S.: PDPTW dataset generator: v1.0.0, August 2015. doi:10.5281/zenodo.27362
12. van Lon, R.R.S.: RinLog: v2.0.0, August 2015. doi:10.5281/zenodo.27361
13. van Lon, R.R.S.: RinSim: v4.0.0, August 2015. doi:10.5281/zenodo.27360
14. van Lon, R.R.S., Ferrante, E., Turgut, A.E., Wenseleers, T., Vanden Berghe, G., Holvoet, T.: Measures for dynamism and urgency in logistics. In: CW Reports, vol. CW686. Department of Computer Science, KU Leuven, August 2015
15. van Lon, R.R.S., Holvoet, T.: RinSim: a simulator for collective adaptive systems in transportation and logistics. In: Proceedings of the 6th IEEE International Conference on Self-Adaptive and Self-Organizing Systems (SASO 2012), pp. 231–232. Lyon (2012). doi:10.1109/SASO.2012.41
16. van Lon, R.R.S., Holvoet, T.: Evolved multi-agent systems and thorough evaluation are necessary for scalable logistics. In: 2013 IEEE Workshop on Computational Intelligence In Production And Logistics Systems (CIPLS), pp. 48–53 (2013). doi:10.1109/CIPLS.2013.6595199
17. Madsen, O.B.G., Ravn, H.F., Rygaard, J.M.: A heuristic algorithm for a dial-a-ride problem with time windows, multiple capacities, and multiple objectives. Annals of Operations Research 60(1), 193–208 (1995). doi:10.1007/BF02031946
18. Máhr, T., Srour, J.F., de Weerdt, M., Zuidwijk, R.: Agent performance in vehicle routing when the only thing certain is uncertainty. In: Proceedings of 7th International Conference on Autonomous Agents and Multiagent Systems (AAMAS). Estorial (2008)
19. Máhr, T., Srour, J.F., de Weerdt, M., Zuidwijk, R.: Can agents measure up? a comparative study of an agent-based and on-line optimization approach for a drayage problem with uncertainty. Transportation Research: Part C 18(1), 99–119 (2010). doi:10.1016/j.trc.2009.04.018
20. Mes, M., van der Heijden, M., van Harten, A.: Comparison of agent-based scheduling to look-ahead heuristics for real-time transportation problems. European Journal of Operational Research 181(1), 59–75 (2007). doi:10.1016/j.ejor.2006.02.051
21. Mes, M., van der Heijden, M., Schuur, P.: Look-ahead strategies for dynamic pickup and delivery problems. OR Spectrum 32(2), 395–421 (2010). doi:10.1007/s00291-008-0146-3
22. Mitrović-Minić, S., Krishnamurti, R., Laporte, G.: Double-horizon based heuristics for the dynamic pickup and delivery problem with time windows. Transportation Research Part B - Methodological 38(8), 669–685 (2004). doi:10.1016/j.trb.2003.09.001
23. Parragh, S.N., Doerner, K.F., Hartl, R.F.: A survey on pickup and delivery problems. Part II: Transportation between pickup and delivery locations. 58(2), 81–117 (2008)
24. Pillac, V., Gendreau, M., Gueret, C., Medaglia, A.L.: A review of dynamic vehicle routing problems. European Journal of Operational Research 225(1), 1–11 (2013). doi:10.1016/j.ejor.2012.08.015
25. Potvin, J., Dufour, G., Rousseau, J.: Learning vehicle dispatching with linear-programming models. Computers & Operations Research 20(4), 371–380 (1993). doi:10.1016/0305-0548(93)90081-S
26. Psaraftis, H.: Dynamic vehicle routing: Status and prospects. Annals of Operations Research 61, 143–164 (1995). doi:10.1007/BF02098286
27. Savelsbergh, M.W.P., Sol, M.: The general pickup and delivery problem. Transportation Science 29(1), 17–29 (1995). doi:10.1287/trsc.29.1.17

28. Solomon, M.M.: Algorithms for the vehicle routing and scheduling problems with time window constraints. Operations Research **35**(2), 254–265 (1987). doi:10.1287/opre.35.2.254
29. Weyns, D., Boucké, N., Holvoet, T.: Gradient field-based task assignment in an agv transportation system. In: Proceedings of 5th International Conference on Autonomous Agents and Multiagent Systems (AAMAS), pp. 842–849 (2006). doi:10.1145/1160633.1160785

Paraconsistent Multi-party Persuasion in TalkLOG

Barbara Dunin-Kęplicz and Alina Strachocka[(✉)]

Institute of Informatics, University of Warsaw, Banacha 2, 02-097 Warsaw, Poland
{keplicz,astrachocka}@mimuw.edu.pl

Abstract. Some conflicts appearing in multi-agent settings may be resolved via communication. In this paper, besides *conflicts of opinions*, paradigmatically resolved by *persuasion*, we study resolution of *conflicting justifications of opinions*. To cope with agents' *ignorance* and *inconsistencies*, often arising from perception and interactions, our formal framework TalkLOG employs a 4-valued logic with two additional logical values: *unknown* and *inconsistent*. Within TalkLOG we study such properties of persuasion as: termination, soundness and completeness. Another critical issue is complexity of agents' communication, typically interleaved with reasoning. In TalkLOG tractability of both aspects is obtained thanks to the implementation tool: rule-based 4-valued language 4QL.

1 Requirements for Resolving Conflicts via Persuasion

The overall goal of this research is a communication protocol for resolving conflicts by a group of agents situated in dynamic and unpredictable environments where up-to-date, unambiguous and complete information is hardly obtainable. Within our dialogue system, TalkLOG, we introduce a new approach to logical modeling of conversing agents, obeying the following principles of communication:

1. Agents' informational stance is **paraconsistent** (i.e., tolerating inconsistencies) and **paracomplete** (i.e., tolerating lack of information). Particularly, inconsistent and incomplete conclusions do not terminate reasoning, but can be further dealt with.
2. Agents are able to complete and disambiguate missing and ambiguous information.
3. **Flexible, multi-party** conversations are considered.
4. **Tractable** protocols are built to allow for practical applicability.
5. **Dynamics** of communication model involves beliefs change during dialogue.

Contemporary approaches to flexible communication draw upon Walton and Krabbe's semi-formal theory of dialogue, adapting the normative models of human communication to multi-agent settings. The dialogue that aims at resolving conflicts in their typology is **persuasion**, characterized as follows: "The

---

Supported by the Polish National Science Centre grants 2011/01/B/ST6/02769 and CORE 6505/B/T02/2011/40.

Q. Chen et al. (Eds.): PRIMA 2015, LNAI 9387, pp. 265–283, 2015.
DOI: 10.1007/978-3-319-25524-8_17

initial situation of a *persuasion dialogue* (or *critical discussion*), is a clash or conflict of points of view. The *main goal* is a resolution of the initial conflict by verbal means. This means that if the dialectical process is to be successful at least one of the parties involved in the conflict will have to *change its point of view* at some stage in the dialogue. The *internal aim of each party* is to persuade the others to take over its point of view" [1].

In the whole spectrum of approaches to persuasion starting from the seminal volume [1], through more formal works [2,3], the two-party, two-valued models prevail. Only recently multi-party aspects have been studied [4,5], while non-classical approaches [6,7] did not treat inconsistencies as first-class citizens. In contrast to them, the contribution of this paper is a formal, dynamic model of a tractable, paraconsistent and paracomplete multi-party persuasion, featuring *Classical* and *Deep Persuasion*, to solve *conflicts of opinions* and *conflicts of justifications of opinions*, respectively. Opposed to [6,7], our solution is built upon the four-valued logic of [8] with an intuitive semantics behind the two new truth values: *unknown* (u) and *inconsistent* (i). Such choice permits to rationally cope with agents' ignorance and inconsistencies usually resulting from agents' interactions and the complexity of the environment.

Another critical issue is complexity of agents' communication, typically inter-leaved with reasoning. Instead of reasoning in logical systems of high complexity, in TalkLOG we query paraconsistent knowledge bases. To this end we use 4QL - a DATALOG¬¬-like four-valued rule-based query language. In the light of the new perspective we prove such properties of paraconsistent persuasion as: termination, convergence to the merged outcome, soundness and completeness; similarly to our results obtained for inquiry [9].

The paper is structured as follows. First, in Section 2 related work is reviewed. Next, Section 3, briefly recalls the underpinnings of our solution. The main matter convey Sections 4 and 5, concerning formalization of persuasion and analysis of its properties, respectively. Finally, Section 6 concludes the paper.

2   Related Work

Walton and Krabbe introduced two types of semi-formal persuasion dialogues: permissive (PPD - everyday conversations) and rigorous (RPD - model of rea-soned argument). Their "persuasion dialogue generally takes the form of a sequence of *questions and replies, or attacks and defenses* where each side takes a turn to make a move. A *move is a sequence of locutions* advanced by a par-ticipant at a particular point in the sequence of dialogue" [1]. As in PPD and RPD replies cannot be postponed, since each player's move has to pertain to the adversary's preceding move, these dialogue types do not offer a more nuanced handling of the burden of proof, which is important for increased flexibility of interlocutors. Moreover no formal properties are given.

PWA protocol [3], although suffered from similar modeling limitations (see also [10] for discussion) was a formal approach allowing to analyze formal proper-ties, among others, termination and outcomes of dialogues. Prakken's system [2] was the first to allow alternative replies and postponing replies, thus permitting much flexibility in persuasion. Conflict resolution in [3] hinged on the preference relation between arguments, while in [2] on the priorities of reasoning rules. Still all above mentioned approaches were two-party and required that support of an argument was consistent.

Multi-party aspects were introduced to persuasion by Bonzon et al. [4], where agents shared the set of arguments, but had different attack relations among them. Although agents were privately assigned to two adverse groups, they independently proposed moves to the central authority who selected the move to play. The outcomes were juxtaposed with the merged argumentation system [11].

Several argumentation systems dealt with ignorance or inconsistency, although not necessarily applied to persuasion. Sawamura et al. [7] proposed a framework for multiple-valued argumentation (LMA) where agents can argue using multi-valued knowledge base. In [6] ASPIC+, a framework for structured argumentation with possible inconsistent knowledge bases and defeasible rules was given. However, none of these formalisms handles inconsistency or lack of information the way 4QL does. Usually the inconsistent premises yield conclusions (e.g., 'undecided') which terminate the reasoning process, thus cannot be further dealt with, unlike in our approach.

3   4QL as an Implementation Tool

TalkLOG uses the logical language introduced in [12–14]. This allows to encode agents' informational stance in the rule-based query language 4QL[1] defined in [12], further developed in [13], and based on the 4-valued logic of [8]. 4QL features:

- Possibly many, perhaps distributed information sources.
- Four logical values (t, f, i, u).
- Unrestricted negation (in premises and conclusions of rules).
- Simple tools: rules, modules and multi-source formulas to formulate and enrich (lightweight versions of) (Local) Closed World Assumption, autoepistemic reasoning, default reasoning, defeasible reasoning, etc.
- Modular architecture to deal with unknown or inconsistent conclusions without enforcing termination of the reasoning process.
- PTime complexity of computing queries while capturing all tractable queries.

For convenience, both the underlying 4-valued logic and 4QL are recalled from [8,12–14] in Appendix[2]. In what follows all sets are finite except for sets of formulas; domain and language are fixed and the programs and rules are ground. We deal with the classical first-order language over a given vocabulary without function symbols. Γ denotes the set of all facts; Π denotes the set of all rules.

The semantics of 4QL is defined by *well-supported models*, i.e., models consisting of (positive or negative) ground literals, where each literal is a conclusion of a derivation starting from facts. For any set of rules, such a model is uniquely determined and computable in deterministic polynomial time $O(N^k)$ where N

---

[1] Open-source implementation of 4QL is available at 4ql.org.

[2] Availalble at http://4ql.org/downloads/appendix.pdf .

is the size of domain and $k = max(s, t)$ where s is the maximal arity of relations and t is the maximum number of free variables. As we deal here with ground programs, $t = 0$. When s is a bound constant, what takes place in qualitative not quantitative reasoning, being all practical applications of 4QL, tractability is achieved.

4   Persuasion in TalkLOG

Although traditionally persuasion arises from a conflict of **opinions** [1], the following example illustrates other possibilities.

Example 1 (John & Mark). Two friends John and Mark are saving up money together (expressed by $save(money)$) and every week they are paying an agreed amount into their common bank account. However, John wants to buy a motor-cycle with that money (expressed by the rule $save(money) :\!- buy(moto)$) and Mark plans to open a small bar ($save(money) :\!- buy(bar)$). As there is no out-spoken initial conflict of opinions regarding saving money ($save(money)$ is **t** for both of them), classically, no persuasion can commence. However, the concealed disagreement concerns their motivations.   ◁

In TalkLOG, if the friends want to resolve the issue immediately (instead of fight-ing over saved money later), they can enter into a discussion about their *differing motivations*. Ultimately, as an outcome from such dialogue, they would:

- abandon one of the goals and focus on the other, or
- continue to save money for both goals, or
- give up on saving at all since they could not come to an agreement.

We formalize motivation (warrant or justification) as the *proper proof* of a for-mula (see Def. 2). To this end, the notion of the *dependence set of a literal ℓ from a program P* is needed. Intuitively, it consists of literals reachable via backward chaining on P from ℓ.

Definition 1 (Dependence Set). Let ℓ be a literal and P a 4QL program. The *dependence set* of ℓ from P, denoted $\mathcal{D}_{P,\ell}$ is the set of literals such that:

- $\neg\ell, \ell \in \mathcal{D}_{P,\ell}$,
- if there is a rule $\ell' :\!- b_{11}, \ldots, b_{1i_1} \mid \ldots \mid b_{m1}, \ldots, b_{mi_m}$ in P, such that $\ell' \in \mathcal{D}_{P,\ell}$ then $\forall_{j \in 1..m} \forall_{k \in 1..i_j} b_{jk}, \neg b_{jk} \in \mathcal{D}_{P,\ell}$.   ◁

The *proof* of a literal ℓ from a program P is a subprogram S of P generated from the dependence set $\mathcal{D}_{P,\ell}$ by taking all rules and facts of P whose conclusions are in $\mathcal{D}_{P,\ell}$. Notice that proof may contain rules whose premises evaluate to **f** or **u**, thus do not influence the value of ℓ. The definition of *proper proof* disregards such rules.

Definition 2 (Proof, Proper Proof). Let ℓ be a literal, P a 4QL program and $\delta \in \Gamma \cup \Pi$ a fact or a rule. The *proof* of l from P is a 4QL program $S \subseteq P$ such that $\delta \in S$ iff $head(\delta) \in \mathcal{D}_{P,\ell}$. The *proper proof* (p-proof) or *warrant* of l from P denoted $\Phi_{l,P}$, is a subset of $S_{l,P}$ such that $\delta \in \Phi_{l,P}$ iff $body(\delta)(\mathcal{M}_{S_{l,P}}) \in \{\mathbf{t}, \mathbf{i}\}$.   ◁

By equal/different motivations we mean equal/unequal p-proofs. By *equal opinions* we mean equal valuations of the formulas representing opinions. Obviously, equality of warrants entails equality of opinions, but not the other way around. We differentiate between cases where *initial situation* concerns *conflict of opinions* or *conflict of warrants* and we are interested in *how* the initial conflict is resolved, i.e., whether a *common opinion* or a *common warrant* has been reached. Although [1] distinguish three types of points of view (opinions) towards a topic of persuasion: positive, negative and one of doubt, in TalkLOG, the 'doubtful' point of view is expanded, distinguishing the cases when the doubt results from ignorance or from inconsistency.

Definition 3 (Initial Conflict on Topic). Let:

- $\varphi \in \mathbb{C}$ be a ground literal, representing the topic of dialogue,
- P_1 and P_2 be two 4QL programs of agents A_1 and A_2,
- $\mathcal{M}_{P_1}$ and $\mathcal{M}_{P_2}$ be the well-supported models of P_1 and P_2 respectively,
- Φ_{φ,P_1} and Φ_{φ,P_2} be the p-proofs of φ from P_1 and P_2 respectively.

Then:
- an *initial conflict on topic* φ between A_1 and A_2 occurs when:
  - $\varphi(\mathcal{M}_{P_1}) \neq \varphi(\mathcal{M}_{P_2})$, or   [conflict of opinion]
  - $\Phi_{\varphi,P_1} \neq \Phi_{\varphi,P_2}$ [conflict of warrant]
- A_1 and A_2 share a *common opinion on* φ if $\varphi(\mathcal{M}_{P_1}) = \varphi(\mathcal{M}_{P_1})$,
- A_1 and A_2 share a *common warrant on* φ if $\Phi_{\varphi,P_1} = \Phi_{\varphi,P_2}$.

The goal of **Classical Persuasion** is a common opinion, while of **Deep Persuasion** - common warrant. Unless stated otherwise, the formalism concerns both dialogues.

4.1 Locutions and Moves

In TalkLOG, the *content* of a locution is either an opinion (belief) of an agent, represented by a literal φ together with its value v; or a piece of evidence, represented by a fact or a rule δ together with its membership function $\mu(\delta)$ (see Definition 4 below).

Definition 4. Let P be a 4QL program and $\delta \in \Gamma \cup \Pi$ be a fact or a rule. Then:

$$\mu_P(\delta) \stackrel{\text{def}}{=} \begin{cases} \mathbf{t} \text{ when } \delta \in P \wedge \neg\delta \notin P; \\ \mathbf{f} \text{ when } \delta \notin P \wedge \neg\delta \in P; \\ \mathbf{i} \text{ when } \delta, \neg\delta \in P; \\ \mathbf{u} \text{ } otherwise. \end{cases}$$

Definition 5. A *locution* is a tuple of the form $\langle Agent, Dialogue, SpeechAct, Content \rangle$ for simplicity denoted further as $SpeechAct_{Agent}^{Dialogue}\langle Content \rangle$, where:

- *Agent* is the identifier of the sender of the utterance: $Agent \in \mathcal{X}_{Ag}$,
- *SpeechAct* is the type of locution: $SpeechAct \in \{assert, assertBel, concede, why, retract, adopt, retractBel\}$,
- *Dialogue* is the identifier of the dialogue: $Dialogue \in \mathcal{X}_{Dial}$,

- *Content* is the propositional content of locution, dependent on speech act type.   ◁

The format and intended meaning of locutions permitted in TalkLOG persuasion[3], i.e.:

- assertions of evidence or beliefs,
- questioning evidence or beliefs,
- concessions, retraction or adoption of evidence,
- retraction of beliefs,

are given in Tab. 1, where $x \in \mathcal{X}_{Ag}$, $d \in \mathcal{X}_{Dial}$ and:

- $\varphi \in \mathbb{C}$ is a ground literal, $\delta \in \Gamma \cup \Pi$ is a fact or a rule,
- $v, \mu(\delta), v' \in \mathbb{T}$ is a truth value, such that $v' \neq \mathbf{u}$,
- B is a body of a rule.[4]

Table 1. Formats and intended meaning of permissible locutions in TalkLOG persuasion.

Locution Type	Format	Intended Meaning
assert	$assert_x^d \langle \delta, \mu(\delta) \rangle$	asserting attitude towards evidence δ
concede	$concede_x^d \langle \delta, \mu(\delta) \rangle$	conceding/agreeing with evidence δ
assertBel	$assertBel_x^d \langle \varphi, v \rangle$	asserting attitude towards an opinion φ
assertBel	$assertBel_x^d \langle B, v \rangle$	asserting attitude towards an opinion B
why	$why_x^d \langle \varphi, v' \rangle$	questioning opinion φ
retract	$retract_x^d \langle \delta \rangle$	retracting evidence δ
adopt	$adopt_x^d \langle \delta \rangle$	adopting evidence δ
retractBel	$retractBel_x^d \langle \varphi, v \rangle$	retracting opinion φ

The set of all locutions that match the format presented in Tab. 1 is denoted $\mathcal{U}$. A **move** is a sequence of locutions uttered by the same agent in the same timepoint. *Moves* denotes the set of all permissible persuasion moves (where neither agent's knowledge base nor its beliefs can change during a move), so in a single move an agent cannot:

- assert different points of view towards the same belief,
- assert and retract the same belief,
- both (concede or assert) and (retract or adopt) a piece of evidence.

4.2   Dialogue Stores

TalkLOG persuasion merges two approaches:

- resolving conflicts of opinions via argumentation (and embedded 4QL mechanisms),

---

[3] We skip 'operational' locutions like $requestAll, join, leave$ for simplicity.

[4] $assertBel \langle B, v \rangle$ is a notation for a sequence of *assertBel* concerning literals in B.

- employing dedicated conflict resolution methods to adjudicate between conflicting pieces of evidence. To this end we have chosen social choice theory methods [15] (particularly, voting) for resolving conflicts unsolvable via argumentation.

In the mentalistic approach [16–18] the semantics of locutions was defined by means of their pre- and post-conditions; for a related paraconsistent semantics consult [19]. However, recently pre-conditions are realized via *relevance function* (see Section 4.3), while post-conditions – as updates of so-called *dialogue stores*. TalkLOG persuasion requires: Query (QS), Dispute (DS), Resolved Dispute (RDS) and Commitment Stores (CS). This permits to validate correctness of moves using public information [20] (i.e., these stores' content) rather than internal states of agents.

QS QS contains beliefs and questions uttered by agents. Agents may inspect QS to find questions that need answering or opinions of others that can be questioned.

DS DS contains pieces of evidence put forward by agents to support a belief or respond to a question. Agents may query DS to support or undermine a piece of evidence submitted by another agent.

RDS contains both traces of resolved conflicts as well as unanimously accepted pieces of evidence. To comply with those decisions, participants are required to adopt a piece of evidence accepted by the group (using *adopt*) or abandon one (using *retract* locution) via voting, but consult e.g., [21].

CS CS contains the agreed-upon pieces of evidence, which once accepted are never deleted. The fact that CS grows monotonically is important for both complexity considerations and analysis of the properties of TalkLOG persuasion.

QS contains tuples of the form $\langle Q, F, V, X \rangle$ where $Q \in \{bel, why\}$ denotes tuple type, $F \in \mathbb{C}$ ground literal, $V \in \mathbb{T}$ a point of view towards the formula, and $X \in \mathcal{X}_{Ag}$ the sender. QS Update Function defines how QS changes after a move:

- $assertBel_A(\varphi, v)$ results in creating a new tuple $\langle bel, \varphi, v, A \rangle$,
- $why_A(\varphi, v)$ results in creating a new tuple $\langle why, \varphi, v, \perp \rangle$,
- $retractBel_A(\varphi, v)$ results in removing $\langle bel, \varphi, v, A \rangle$ from QS, and, if that was the last opinion v about φ in QS, removing also tuple $\langle why, \varphi, v, \perp \rangle$ (if one exists).

Definition 6. Let $F_d^t : \{bel, why\} \times \mathbb{C} \times \mathbb{T} \times \mathcal{X}_{Ag}$ and $m^t = u_1; \ldots; u_k$ be the move received at time t. Then, QS *Update Function* $update_{QS} : F_d^t \times Moves \to F_d^t$ is:

$$update_{QS}(S, u_1; \ldots; u_k) \overset{\text{def}}{=} \begin{cases} update_{QS}(step_{QS}(S, u_1), u_2; \ldots; u_k) & \text{if } k > 1 \\ step_{QS}(S, u_1) & \text{if } k = 1, \end{cases}$$

where $step_{QS} : F_d^t \times \mathcal{U} \to F_d^t$ is a one-step update function defined as follows:

$$step_{QS}(S,u) \stackrel{\text{def}}{=} \begin{cases} S \cup \{\langle why, \varphi, v, \bot\rangle\} & \text{if } u = why_A^d\langle\varphi,v\rangle; \\ S \cup \{\langle bel, \varphi, v, A\rangle\} & \text{if } u = assertBel_A^d\langle\varphi,v\rangle; \\ S \setminus \{\langle bel, \varphi, v, A\rangle\} & \text{if } u = retractBel_A^d\langle\varphi,v\rangle \wedge \\ & \exists_{\langle bel,\varphi,v,A'\rangle \in S} \text{ s.t. } A' \neq A; \\ S \setminus \{\langle bel, \varphi, v, A\rangle, \langle why, \varphi, v, \bot\rangle\} & \text{if } u = retractBel_A^d\langle\varphi,v\rangle \wedge \\ & \neg\exists_{\langle bel,\varphi,v,A'\rangle \in S} \text{ s.t. } A' \neq A; \\ S & \text{otherwise.} \end{cases}$$

Definition 7 (Query Store). Let m^t be the move received at time t, and $update_{QS}$ be the QS Update Function. Then, *Query Store* of persuasion d at time t, initiated by A_{init}, is a finite set of tuples, denoted $QS_d^t : \{bel, why\} \times \mathbb{C} \times \mathbb{T} \times \mathcal{X}_{Ag}$, s.t.:

$$QS_d^t \stackrel{\text{def}}{=} \begin{cases} \{\langle bel, s, v_i, A_{init}\rangle\} & \text{if } t = 0 \\ update_{QS}(QS_d^{t-1}, m^t) & \text{otherwise} \end{cases}$$

Dispute Store contains tuples of form $\langle \delta, n_t, n_f, n_i, n_u\rangle : (\Gamma \cup \Pi) \times \mathbb{N}^4$. We will write:
$$DS[\delta, k] \stackrel{\text{def}}{=} n_k, \quad DS[\neg\delta, k] \stackrel{\text{def}}{=} DS[\delta, \neg k], \text{ where } k \in \mathbb{T}.$$

We use $DS[\delta]$ to test if an entry for δ is in DS, and $DS[\delta, k]{+}{+}$ to increment n_k counter for δ:

$$DS[\delta] \stackrel{\text{def}}{=} \begin{cases} \mathsf{t} & \text{iff } \langle \delta, n_t, n_f, n_i, n_u\rangle \in DS; \\ \mathsf{f} & \text{iff } \langle \delta, n_t, n_f, n_i, n_u\rangle \notin DS; \end{cases}$$

$$DS[\delta, k]{+}{+} \stackrel{\text{def}}{=} \{\langle x, n_t, n_f, n_i, n_u\rangle \in DS | x \neq \delta\} \cup$$
$$\{\langle \delta, x_t, x_f, x_i, x_u\rangle \in DS : x_k = DS[\delta, k] + 1\}$$

DS Update Function defines the way DS is updated after each move:

- *assert* results in creating a new tuple for the propositional content of assertion (unless already exist) and increasing the support counter for the asserted value,
- *concede* increases the support counter for the uttered value if the relevant tuple exist in DS.

Definition 8. Let $m^t = u_1; \ldots; u_k$ be the move received at time t, $\delta \in \Gamma \cup \Pi$; $v \in \mathbb{T}$ and $V_d^t : (\Gamma \cup \Pi) \times \mathbb{N}^4$. Then, *DS Update Function* $update_{DS} : V_d^t \times Moves \to V_d^t$ is:

$$update_{DS}(S, u_1; \ldots; u_k) \stackrel{\text{def}}{=} \begin{cases} update_{DS}(step_{DS}(DS, u_1), u_2; \ldots; u_k) & \text{if } k > 1 \\ step_{DS}(DS, u_1) & \text{if } k = 1 \end{cases}$$

where $step_{DS} : V_d^t \times \mathcal{U} \to V_d^t$ is a one-step update function defined as follows:

$$step_{DS}(DS, u) \stackrel{\text{def}}{=} \begin{cases} X[\delta, v]{+}{+} & \text{where } X = DS \cup \{\langle \delta, 0, 0, 0, 0\rangle\} \text{ and} \\ & u = assert_A^d\langle\delta, v\rangle \text{ and } DS[\delta] = \mathsf{f}; \\ DS[\delta, v]{+}{+} & \text{if } (u = assert_A^d\langle\delta, v\rangle \vee u = concede_A^d\langle\delta, v\rangle) \\ & \text{and } DS[\delta] = \mathsf{t}; \\ DS & \text{otherwise.} \end{cases}$$

Definition 9 (Dispute Store). Let m^t be the move received at time t and $update_{DS}$ be the DS Update Function. Then, *Dispute Store* of persuasion d at time t is a finite set of tuples, denoted as $DS_d^t : (\Gamma \cup \Pi) \times \mathbb{N}^4$ such that:

$$DS_d^t \overset{\text{def}}{=} \begin{cases} \emptyset & \text{if } t = 0 \\ update_{DS}(DS_d^{t-1}, m^t) & \text{otherwise} \end{cases}$$

The entries in RDS are of the form $\langle(\neg)\delta, i\rangle$ or $\langle(\neg)\delta, o\rangle$, meaning the piece of evidence is either admitted (*"in"*) or rejected (*"out"*). After each increase of support counter in DS for δ, the voting function is called, which, if there are enough casting votes, adjudicates about δ (unlike the argumentation approach where each move may change the status of an argument). Recall, that each agent A_i votes with its $\mu_{P_{A_i}}(\delta)$.

Definition 10. Let $Status = \{i, o\}$, $\delta \in \Gamma \cup \Pi$, and $n \in \mathbb{N}$ be the number of dialogue participants. Then, a *voting function* VF is any function $VF : (\Gamma \cup \Pi) \times \mathbb{N}^5 \to Status^2$, such that $VF(\delta, n_t, n_f, n_i, n_u, n) = \emptyset$ iff $n_t + n_f + n_i + n_u \neq n$, and if $\delta \in \Pi$ (a rule) then $VF(\delta, n_t, n_f, n_i, n_u, n) \neq \langle i, i\rangle$.

From several possible outcomes of voting over δ, we forbid accepting antithetic rules (expressed by $\langle i, i\rangle$). If $\langle a, b\rangle$ is the outcome for δ, then a is the status of δ and b of $\neg\delta$.

Definition 11 (Resolved Dispute Store). Let m^t be the move received at time t, and:
- DS_d^t be the Dispute Store of dialogue d at time t,
- VF be a voting function,
- $\delta \in \Gamma \cup \Pi$; $v \in \mathbb{T}$; $s_1, s_2 \in Status$,
- $n \in \mathbb{N}$ be the number of dialogue participants.

Then, *Resolved Dispute Store* of persuasion d at time t is a finite set of tuples denoted as $RDS_d^t : (\Gamma \cup \Pi) \times Status$ such that:
- $RDS_d^0 = \emptyset$
- $RDS_d^t = RDS_d^{t-1} \cup X$, where: $X = \{\langle\delta, s_1\rangle \cup \langle\neg\delta, s_2\rangle \mid$
  (a) $concede_S^d\langle\delta, v\rangle \in m^t \vee assert_S^d\langle\delta, v\rangle \in m^t$,
  (b) $\langle s_1, s_2\rangle = VF(\delta, DS_d^t[\delta, t], DS_d^t[\delta, f], DS_d^t[\delta, i], DS_d^t[\delta, u], n)\}$.
- $RDS_d^t = RDS_d^{t-1}$ otherwise.   ◁

Commitment Store is updated always after RDS is updated with an entry with status "in". The final value of the Deep Persuasion topic is evaluated within the context of this store. In fact, CS is just an evolving 4QL program [22].

Definition 12 (Commitment Store). Let:
- RDS_d^t be the Resolved Dispute Store of dialogue d at time t,
- m^t be the message received at time t,
- $\delta \in \Gamma \cup \Pi$; $v \in \mathbb{T}$.

Then, *Commitment Store* of a persuasion dialogue d at time t is a 4QL program denoted CS_d^t such that:

- $CS_d^0 = \emptyset$
- $CS_d^t = CS_d^{t-1} \cup X$, where $X = \{\delta \mid$
  (a) $concede_A^d \langle \delta, v \rangle \in m^t \vee assert_A^d \langle \delta, v \rangle \in m^t$,
  (b) $\langle \delta, i \rangle \in RDS_d^t\}$,
- $CS_d^t = CS_d^{t-1}$ otherwise.   ◁

The conclusion of persuasion on topic s with initial value v_i is the final value v_f of s, together with the justification (p-proof) Φ_{s,CS_d^t} for that value, obtained in the dialogue. For the purpose of this paper we distinguish two termination conditions:

- **Impasse**: when no agent has a relevant move to make,
- **Common Opinion**: when all agents agree on the value of the topic.

Definition 13. Let CS_d^t be the Commitment Store of Deep Persuasion d terminating at t, with the topic s of initial value v_i. Then, the *conclusion* of d is $c = \langle v_f, S \rangle$ where:

- $v_f = s(\mathcal{M}_{CS_d^t})$, where $\mathcal{M}_{CS_d^t}$ is the well-supported model of CS_d^t,
- $S = \Phi_{s,CS_d^t}$, i.e., S is the p-proof of s from CS_d^t.

Definition 14. Let QS_d^t be the Query Store and CS_d^t be the Commitment Store of Classical Persuasion d terminating at t with n participants $A_1, \ldots, A_n$, with the topic s of initial value v_i. Then, the *conclusion* of d is $c = \langle v_f, S \rangle$ where:

- $n = |\langle bel, s, v_f, X \rangle \in QS_d^t : X \in \{A_1, \ldots A_n\}|$,
- $S = \Phi_{s,CS_d^t}$, i.e., S is the p-proof of s from CS_d^t.

Obtaining conclusion of terminated Deep Persuasion amounts to computing the well-supported model of CS_d^t just once, at the end of dialogue. Thus, this problem is in $O(N^k)$ (see Section 3) where N is the size of domain and k is the maximal arity of relations. Obtaining conclusion of terminated Classical Persuasion is in $O(N) = |QS_d^t|$ (QS_d^t may possibly contain all beliefs of agents at termination time).

4.3   Move and Locution Relevance

To ensure coherence and focus of persuasion, the notion of **move relevance** is employed after [23]. As move is a sequence of locutions, relevance of each locution is verified on the basis of dialogue stores' content at the given timepoint t and the locution content (arbitrarily, irrelevant locutions are ignored). For ease of presentation, dialogue stores are updated after each relevant locution, so that locution relevance can be defined without reference to preceding locutions in the move. Relevant locutions are:

1. Assertions of a belief $assertBel_S^d \langle \psi, v \rangle$ if it concerns:
   (a) the topic of the dialogue,
   (b) a belief asserted by another agent,
   (c) premisses or head of a rule present in DS, or a fact present in DS.
2. Questions about a belief $why_S^d \langle \varphi, v \rangle$ if the opinion $v \in \{t, f, i\}$ about φ is in QS.

3. Assertions of a fact or rule $assert^d_S\langle\delta,v\rangle$ if
    (a) a question about a belief concerning $head(\delta)$ is in QS,
    (b) it is present in DS (an assertion works as concession then).
4. Concessions of a fact or a rule $concede^d_S\langle\delta,v\rangle$ present in DS.
5. Retractions of a belief $retractBel^d_S\langle\varphi,v\rangle$ if relevant belief of agent S is in QS.
6. Adoptions of a fact or a rule $adopt^d_S\langle\delta,v\rangle$ if $\langle\delta,i\rangle \in RDS$.
7. Rejections of a fact or a rule $reject^d_S\langle\delta,v\rangle$ if $\langle\delta,o\rangle \in RDS$.

An irrelevant move is a move without relevant locutions. Notice that an irrelevant locution $u_i \in m^t$ may be relevant at $t' \neq t$, but a non-permissible move m^t will not be permissible at any other time t'. Lemma 1 illustrates that in a single move an agent can always utter its entire p-proof of a formula.

Lemma 1. *If $\Phi_{s,P} \neq \emptyset$ and $s(\mathcal{M}_P) = v$, then while $\langle why, s, v, \bot\rangle \in QS$ there exists a relevant move $m = u_1;\dots;u_n$ s.t.[5]:*

$$\Phi_{s,P} = \bigcup \{\delta[\mu_P(\delta) \in \{\mathsf{t},\mathsf{i}\}], \neg\delta[\mu_P(\delta) \in \{\mathsf{f},\mathsf{i}\}] \in P :$$
$$\exists_{i\in 1..n}\, u_i = assert\langle\delta, \mu_P(\delta)\rangle \vee u_i = concede\langle\delta, \mu_P(\delta)\rangle\}.$$

Proof follows from move/locution relevance definition.

4.4 Working Example

The standard example [2] is adapted to the 3-agent case introducing agent Tom and additional steps 4' and 8'. The agents share an ontology, where module *top* contains top-level beliefs while module *news* beliefs about a specific information source (here a newspaper). At $t = 0$, Paul's program P^0 consists of modules top^0_P and $news^0_P$: $P^0 = \{top^0_P, news^0_P\}$. Olga's and Tom's programs are denoted likewise. Table 2 concisely presents evolving programs of three agents. We refer to their elements by numbers (e.g., rule $\neg\mathtt{safe(car)} \mathbin{:-} \mathtt{high(maxspeed, car)}$ from

Table 2. Evolving Programs of Paul, Olga and Tom.

	Module *top* :	P^0	O^0	T^0	$O^{4'}$	P^9
1.	$safe(car) \mathbin{:-} has(airbag, car).$	×				×
2.	$\neg safe(car) \mathbin{:-} news.reports(airbagExplosions, car),$			×		
	$news.reliable(airbagExplosions) \in \{\mathsf{t}, \mathsf{u}, \mathsf{i}\}.$					
3.	$\neg safe(car) \mathbin{:-} high(maxspeed, car).$		×	×	×	×
4.	$has(airbag, car).$	×		×	×	×
5.	$high(maxspeed, car).$		×	×	×	×
	Module *news* :	P^0	O^0	T^0	$O^{4'}$	P^9
6.	$\neg reliable(airbagExplosions) \mathbin{:-}$	×				×
	$concerns(airbagExplosions, technology).$					
7.	$reports(airbagExplosions, car).$	×	×	×	×	×
8.	$concerns(airbagExplosions, technology).$	×	×	×	×	×

---

[5] $[\cdot]$ is the Iverson bracket.

Table 3. Evolving Beliefs of Paul, Olga and Tom.

	Literals from module top :	P^0	O^0	T^0	$O^{4'}$	P^9
A.	$safe(car)$	t	f	f	f	i
B.	$has(airbag, car)$	t	u	t	t	t
C.	$high(maxspeed, car)$	u	t	t	t	t

	Literals from module $news$:	P^0	O^0	T^0	$O^{4'}$	P^9
D.	$reliable(airbagExplosions)$	f	u	u	u	f
E.	$reports(airbagExplosions, car)$	t	t	t	t	t
F.	$concerns(airbagExplosions, technology)$	t	t	t	t	t

Table 4. Conduct of Paul, Olga & Tom persuasion on subject $safe(car)$.

t	S	m^t	ΔQS^t	DS^t	RDS^t	CS^t
1	P	$assertBel\langle A, \mathbf{t}\rangle$	$+\langle bel, A, \mathbf{t}, P\rangle$	$\emptyset$	$\emptyset$	$\emptyset$
2	O	$why\langle A, \mathbf{t}\rangle$	$+\langle why, A, \mathbf{t}, \bot\rangle$	$\emptyset$	$\emptyset$	$\emptyset$
3	P	$assert\langle 1, \mathbf{t}\rangle$; $assertBel\langle B, \mathbf{t}\rangle$; $assert\langle 4, \mathbf{t}\rangle$	$+\langle bel, B, \mathbf{t}, P\rangle$	$\langle 1,1,0,0,0\rangle$, $\langle 4,1,0,0,0\rangle$	$\emptyset$	$\emptyset$
4	T	$concede\langle 4, \mathbf{t}\rangle$; $assertBel\langle A, \mathbf{f}\rangle$	$+\langle bel, A, \mathbf{f}, T\rangle$	$\langle 1,1,0,0,0\rangle$, $\langle 4,2,0,0,0\rangle$	$\emptyset$	$\emptyset$
4'	O	$concede\langle 4, \mathbf{u}\rangle$; $assertBel\langle A, \mathbf{f}\rangle$	$+\langle bel, A, \mathbf{f}, O\rangle$	$\langle 1,1,0,0,0\rangle$, $\langle 4,2,0,0,1\rangle$	$\langle 4, i\rangle$, $\langle \neg 4, o\rangle$	4
5	P	$why\langle A, \mathbf{f}\rangle$	$+\langle why, A, \mathbf{f}, \bot\rangle$,	$\langle 1,1,0,0,0\rangle$, $\langle 4,2,0,0,1\rangle$	$\langle 4, i\rangle$, $\langle \neg 4, o\rangle$	4
6	T	$assert\langle 2, \mathbf{t}\rangle$; $assertBel\langle E, \mathbf{t}\rangle$; $assertBel\langle D, \mathbf{u}\rangle$;	$+\langle bel, E, \mathbf{t}, T\rangle$, $+\langle bel, D, \mathbf{u}, T\rangle$	$\langle 1,1,0,0,0\rangle$, $\langle 4,2,0,0,1\rangle$, $\langle 2,1,0,0,0\rangle$	$\langle 4, i\rangle$, $\langle \neg 4, o\rangle$	4
7	P	$concede\langle 2, \mathbf{u}\rangle$; $assertBel\langle D, \mathbf{f}\rangle$; $assert\langle 6, \mathbf{t}\rangle$; $assertBel\langle F, \mathbf{t}\rangle$	$+\langle bel, D, \mathbf{f}, P\rangle$, $+\langle bel, F, \mathbf{t}, P\rangle$	$\langle 1,1,0,0,0\rangle$, $\langle 4,2,0,0,1\rangle$, $\langle 2,1,0,0,1\rangle$, $\langle 6,1,0,0,0\rangle$	$\langle 4, i\rangle$, $\langle \neg 4, o\rangle$,	4
8	O	$adopt\langle 4, \mathbf{t}\rangle$; $assert\langle 3, \mathbf{t}\rangle$; $assertBel\langle C, \mathbf{t}\rangle$; $assert\langle 5, \mathbf{t}\rangle$	$+\langle bel, C, \mathbf{t}, O\rangle$,	$\langle 1,1,0,0,0\rangle$, $\langle 4,2,0,0,1\rangle$, $\langle 2,1,0,0,1\rangle$, $\langle 6,1,0,0,0\rangle$, $\langle 3,1,0,0,0\rangle$, $\langle 5,1,0,0,0\rangle$	$\langle 4, i\rangle$, $\langle \neg 4, o\rangle$,	4
8'	T	$concede\langle 3, \mathbf{t}\rangle$; $concede\langle 5, \mathbf{t}\rangle$		$\langle 1,1,0,0,0\rangle$, $\langle 4,2,0,0,1\rangle$, $\langle 2,1,0,0,1\rangle$, $\langle 6,1,0,0,0\rangle$, $\langle 3,2,0,0,0\rangle$, $\langle 5,2,0,0,0\rangle$	$\langle 4, i\rangle$, $\langle \neg 4, o\rangle$,	4
9	P	$concede\langle 3, \mathbf{u}\rangle$; $concede\langle 5, \mathbf{u}\rangle$		$\langle 1,1,0,0,0\rangle$, $\langle 4,2,0,0,1\rangle$, $\langle 2,1,0,0,1\rangle$, $\langle 6,1,0,0,0\rangle$, $\langle 3,2,0,0,1\rangle$, $\langle 5,2,0,0,1\rangle$	$\langle 4, i\rangle$, $\langle \neg 4, o\rangle$, $\langle 3, i\rangle$, $\langle \neg 3, o\rangle$, $\langle 5, i\rangle$, $\langle \neg 5, o\rangle$	4, 3, 5
9b	P	$adopt\langle 3, \mathbf{t}\rangle$; $adopt\langle 5, \mathbf{t}\rangle$; $retractBel\langle A, \mathbf{t}\rangle$	$-\langle bel, A, \mathbf{t}, P\rangle$, $-\langle why, A, \mathbf{t}, \bot\rangle$,	$\langle 1,1,0,0,0\rangle$, $\langle 4,2,0,0,1\rangle$, $\langle 2,1,0,0,1\rangle$, $\langle 6,1,0,0,0\rangle$, $\langle 3,2,0,0,1\rangle$, $\langle 5,2,0,0,1\rangle$	$\langle 4, i\rangle$, $\langle \neg 4, o\rangle$, $\langle 3, i\rangle$, $\langle \neg 3, o\rangle$, $\langle 5, i\rangle$, $\langle \neg 5, o\rangle$	4, 3, 5

module *top* has number 3 and at $t = 0$ is present in Olga's and Tom's programs, as indicated by $\times$ in columns O^0 and T^0). Program P^0 uniquely determines the well-supported model for modules top_P^0 and $news_P^0$ ($\mathcal{M}_{top_P^0}$ and $\mathcal{M}_{news_P^0}$ resp.), as given in Table 3. We refer to beliefs by capital letters (e.g., A for $safe(car)$, thus $\mathcal{M}_{top_P^0} = \{A, \neg A, B, C\}$, but $\mathcal{M}_{top_O^0} = \{\neg A, C\}$).

The complete dialogue conduct is given in Table 4, where column 4 shows the **change** in Query Store between consecutive moves. We elaborate only on the first few steps:

1	Paul:	"My car is safe."	$assertBel\langle A, \mathsf{t}\rangle$
2	Olga:	"Why is your car safe?"	$why\langle A, \mathsf{t}\rangle$
3	Paul:	"Since it has an airbag."	$assert\langle 1, \mathsf{t}\rangle$; $assertBel\langle B, \mathsf{t}\rangle$; $assert\langle 4, \mathsf{t}\rangle$
4	Tom:	"That is true, but this does not make your car safe."	$concede\langle 4, \mathsf{u}\rangle$; $assertBel\langle A, \mathsf{f}\rangle$
4'	Olga:	"Yes, exactly."	$concede\langle 4, \mathsf{u}\rangle$; $assertBel\langle A, \mathsf{f}\rangle$
5	Paul:	*"Why does that not make my care safe?*	
6	Tom:	*"Since the newspapers recently reported on airbags expanding without cause.*	
7	Paul:	*"Yes, that is what the newspapers say but that does not prove anything, since newspaper reports are very unreliable sources of technological information."*	
8	Olga:	*"Still your car is still not safe, since its maximum speed is very high."*	
8'	Tom:	*"That's right."*	
9	Paul:	*OK, I was wrong that my car is safe."*	

Notice that after Olga's concession (Tab. 4, step 4') her program should change, adopting the fact has(airbag, car). Thus, her belief structure may change such that new reasoning lines become available and/or the already uttered beliefs are no longer up-to-date. The technical contribution of our solution allows to model such dialogues.

In step 9b Paul retracts his original belief. However, he still disagrees with others on that matter as $safe(car)$ is f for Olga and Tom but it is i for Paul at time $t = 9$ (see Table 3). Note that Impasse criterion is not met yet, since there are still relevant moves to make, e.g., a concession of rule 1 by Olga and Tom.

5 Selected Properties

The following assumptions about participating agents allow us to verify quality and completeness of the obtained results.

[**Cooperativeness**]. We deal with a finite set of n cooperative agents who do not withhold information. This implicitly constraints the number of queries to dialogue stores per one locution. Agents' belief bases are encoded as finite, ground 4QL programs $P_1, \ldots, P_n$, that share a common ontology.

[**Activeness**]. In between *join* and *leave*, an agent must make at least one relevant move.

[**Compliance**]. Agents' programs change during dialogue according to the current state of RDS.

[**Sincerity**]. Agents do not lie about their beliefs nor contents of their programs.

[**Pragmatism**]. Particular agents cannot repeat *assert* and *concede* locutions.

Agents communicate one-to-all without coordination. Their final beliefs are expressed by the well-supported models $\mathcal{M}_{P_1}, \ldots, \mathcal{M}_{P_n}$ of the programs. Note that agents **can** repeat *assertBel* locutions, provided they are separated by *retractBel*: simply in the light of new evidence agents' beliefs may change.

Theorem 1. *Persuasion dialogues terminate.*

Proof. Regardless the termination criterion, termination of persuasion follows trivially from the fact that we deal with finite 4QL programs, and from the assumptions of activeness (disallowing joining and leaving dialogue endlessly), pragmatism (disallowing repeating specific locutions), sincerity (disallowing inventing beliefs or evidence), compliance (disallowing infinitely expanding programs, since in the course of dialogue agents' programs change only to reflect resolved conflicts, so the size of CS can be bounded by the union of all participants' programs).   ◁

Theorem 2. *Persuasion terminating on Impasse is a Deep Persuasion.*

Proof Assume d is a persuasion dialogue on topic s terminating at t on Impasse criterion, with participants $A_1, \ldots, A_n$, s.t. A_i's program at t is P_i^t. Then, A_i's p-proof of s at t is Φ_{s, P_i^t}, A_i's value of s at t is $s(\mathcal{M}_{P_i^t}) = v_i^t$ and dialogue conclusion is $c = \langle v_f, \Phi_{s, CS_d^t} \rangle$, where CS_d^t is the Commitment Store of d at t and $v_f = s(\mathcal{M}_{CS_d^t})$. Assume d is not a Deep Persuasion, i.e., $\exists_i \Phi_{s, P_i^t} \neq \Phi_{s, CS_d^t}$. We will consider the two cases separately: either v_f is not commonly shared by all agents, or it is.

Case 1: $\exists_i v_i^t \neq v_f$. First assume $v_i^t \neq \mathsf{u}$, so $\Phi_{s, P_i^t} \neq \emptyset$. Then, agent A_i has either:

1a. not revealed its current belief, thus could not (properly) prove it, or

1b. uttered its current belief but failed to provide a p-proof of it,

1c. uttered its current belief and provided a proof but other agents did not vote for it,

1d. uttered its current belief and provided a proof but other agents refuted it.

(1a) $\overset{\text{def}}{\equiv} \langle bel, s, v_i^t, A_i \rangle \notin QS_d^t$. Since *assertBel* concerning dialogue topic can be uttered at any time (unless already present in QS), this contradicts our assumptions ($\notmid$) that d terminated on Impasse.

(1b) $\overset{\text{def}}{\equiv} \exists_{\delta \in \Phi_{s, P_i^t}} DS_d^t[\delta] = \mathsf{f}$. Consider $\neg$ (1a) $\wedge$ (1b) holds. But, $\langle why, s, v_i^t, \bot \rangle \in QS_d^t$ since *why* can be uttered at any time by anyone, if the relevant belief is present in QS and the relevant tuple for *why* wasn't uttered yet. Thus, on Lemma 1, agent A_i has a relevant move consisting of all the facts and rules from Φ_{s, P_i^t}, thus $\notmid$.

(1c) $\overset{\text{def}}{\equiv} \exists_{\delta \in \Phi_{s, P_i^t}} : \langle \delta, \sigma \rangle, \langle \neg \delta, \sigma \rangle \notin RDS_d^t$ where $\sigma \in Status$. If $\neg$(1a) $\wedge \neg$(1b) $\wedge$ (1c), then there is an agent who did not vote for entry δ. But asserting an attitude towards a piece of evidence is possible at any time (provided it is not a repetition), thus $\frac{l}{r}$.

(1d) $\overset{\text{def}}{\equiv} \exists_{\delta \in \Phi_{s,P_i^t}} \delta \notin CS_d^t$. If $\neg$ (1a) $\wedge \neg$(1b) $\wedge \neg$ (1c) $\wedge$ (1d) holds, at least one rule or fact δ from A_i's p-proof of s was not accepted by others. Since A_i still regards δ as an element of p-proof at time t, it didn't comply with group decision, thus $\frac{l}{r}$.

So finally we have $\neg$ (1a) $\wedge \neg$ (1b) $\wedge \neg$ (1c) $\wedge \neg$ (1d), so $\forall_{\delta \in \Phi_{s,P_i^t}} \delta \in CS_d^t$ so $\Phi_{s,P_i^t} \subseteq CS_d^t$. Also $\forall_i CS_d^t \subseteq P_j^t$ (compliance). But $\exists_i : v_i^t \neq v_f = s(\mathcal{M}_{CS_d^t})$, so $P_i^t \setminus CS_d^t \cap \Phi_{s,P_i^t} \neq \emptyset$ but then $\frac{l}{r}$.

Back to *Case 1* when $v_i^t = \mathfrak{u}$. Then, A_i cannot provide a proof ($\Phi_{s,P_i^t} = \emptyset$), but $v_f \neq \mathfrak{u}$, so $\Phi_{s,CS_d^t} \neq \emptyset$. Assuming A_i is compliant, $CS_d^t \subseteq P_i^t$ but since $\Phi_{s,CS_d^t} \neq \emptyset$ and $\Phi_{s,P_i^t} = \emptyset$ there is a nonempty relevant piece of $P_i^t \setminus CS_d^t \neq \emptyset$ which influences the p-proof Φ_{s,P_i^t} and which was not shared by A_i, thus $\frac{l}{r}$.
Case 2.($\forall_i v_i^t = v_f$). If $v_f = \mathfrak{u}$ then $\forall_i \Phi_{s,P_i^t} = \Phi_{s,CS_d^t} = \emptyset$ trivially. Case when $v_f \neq \mathfrak{u}$ and $\exists_i \Phi_{s,P_i^t} \neq \Phi_{s,CS_d^t}$ is analogous to (1c) and (1d) above.   ◁

Since the common warrant may be obtained earlier than termination time t imposed by Impasse, formally Deep Persuasion covers a wider set of dialogues than persuasion ending on Impasse. Since we cannot determine at runtime whether a common warrant has been reached, in practice we use Impasse criterion and in the sequel we restrict the notion of Deep Persuasion to Deep Persuasion ending on Impasse.

Theorem 3. *Persuasion terminating on Common Opinion is a Classical Persuasion.*

Proof. Trivially from sincerity.   ◁

5.1   Soundness, Completeness and Convergence to Merged Outcome

The merging operator $\sum(s)$ used in analysis of persuasion properties reflects the nature of dialogue and is a consensual merge (see [11]) exploiting a voting mechanism (see Definition 10) for conflict resolution. Merging is an iterative procedure, achieved by joining p-proofs of the merge parameter s and resolving conflicts on the way. The result of merging is a 4QL program defined as follows:

$$\left(\sum_{i=1}^n P_i\right)(s) \overset{\text{def}}{=} \bigcup_{IT=0}^{ITMAX} \left(\bigcup_{\delta \in \bigcup \Phi^{IT}} IN(\delta)\right),$$

where for $IT \geq 0$, $k \in \mathbb{T}$:

- $\bigcup \Phi^{IT} \overset{\text{def}}{=} \bigcup_{i=1..n} \Phi_{s,P_i^{IT}}$,
- $ITMAX \overset{\text{def}}{=} IT : \forall_{i=1..n} : P_i^{IT+1} = P_i^{IT}$,
- $P_i^{IT+1} = P_i^{IT} \cup \bigcup_{\delta \in \bigcup \Phi^{IT}} IN(\delta) \setminus \bigcup_{\delta \in \bigcup \Phi^{IT}} OUT(\delta)$,
- $IN(\delta) = \{\delta[a = i], \neg\delta[b = i] : \langle a, b \rangle \in VF(\delta, n_{\mathfrak{t}}^\delta, n_{\mathfrak{f}}^\delta, n_{\mathfrak{i}}^\delta, n_{\mathfrak{u}}^\delta, n)\}$,
- $OUT(\delta) = \{\delta[a = o], \neg\delta[b = o] : \langle a, b \rangle \in VF(\delta, n_{\mathfrak{t}}^\delta, n_{\mathfrak{f}}^\delta, n_{\mathfrak{i}}^\delta, n_{\mathfrak{u}}^\delta, n)\}$
- $n_k^\delta = |\{i \in 1..n : \mu_{P_i^{IT}}(\delta) = k\}|$.

In each iteration, the conflicts in the union of all agents' p-proofs are resolved by voting[6], whose outcomes (sets IN and OUT) are then used to update the programs. The procedure stops naturally when agents' programs stop changing. The proof of s from such a merge is $\Phi_{s,(\sum_{i=1..n} P_i)(s)}$ while the value of the topic s is $s(\mathcal{M}_{(\sum_{i=1}^n P_i)(s)})$.

Informally, **soundness** of persuasion means that any conclusion obtained in the dialogue equals the conclusion obtained by a single agent reasoning from a merged knowledge bases of dialogue participants. On the other hand, **completeness** of persuasion means that any conclusion obtained by reasoning from **merged knowledge bases** of participants is obtainable by persuasion carried out by these agents.

Definition 15. Persuasion dialogue d on subject s is *sound* iff whenever it terminates at t with conclusion $c = \langle v_f, S \rangle$, then if $s(\mathcal{M}_{CS_d^t}) = v_f$ then $s(\mathcal{M}_{(\sum_{i=1}^n P_i)(s)}) = v_f$.

Definition 16. Persuasion dialogue d on subject s is *complete* iff whenever it terminates at t with conclusion $c = \langle v_f, S \rangle$, then if $s(\mathcal{M}_{(\sum_{i=1}^n P_i)(s)}) = v_f$ then $s(\mathcal{M}_{CS_d^t}) = v_f$.

Theorem 4. *Classical Persuasion is not sound and not complete.*

Proof. As a counterexample consider group of agents $G = \{A, B\}$ with programs $P_A = \{a :- b; b\}$ and $P_B = \{a :- \neg b; \neg b\}$ participating in dialogue d on subject a. Assume A starts with $assertBel_A^d \langle a, \mathbf{t} \rangle$. From 2 possible moves, B chooses to reply with $assertBel_B^d \langle a, \mathbf{t} \rangle$. Since $|\langle bel, a, \mathbf{t}, X \rangle \in QS_d^2 : X \in G| = |G|$, dialogue ends at $t = 2$ with a conclusion $c = \langle \mathbf{t}, \emptyset \rangle$ (CS_d^2 is empty). However, conclusion c' obtained using any merging operator VF (see Def. 10) on A and B's programs is $c' = \langle \mathbf{u}, \emptyset \rangle$. ◁

A subset of Deep Persuasion dialogues called **Iterated Deep Persuasion** can be distinguished when additional restrictions are put on agents regarding querying dialogue stores, namely, when the below steps are repeated one after another in a loop:

A. while (exists other relevant move) do not query DS nor RDS;
B. while (exists other relevant move) do not query RDS;
C. while (exists relevant move) play move; *(i.e., query RDS)*

Theorem 5. *Iterated Deep Persuasion is sound and complete.*

Proof. In Iterated Deep Persuasion, in each iteration IT (starting with $IT = 0$):
Loop A. Agents cannot see new evidence of other agents. Thus each agent i individually (e.g. in one relevant move) reveals only its whole current p-proof $\Phi_{s,P_i^{IT}}$ to others (interleaved with any $assertBel$ or *why* locutions). So $\bigcup \Phi^{IT} \stackrel{def}{=} \bigcup_{i=1..n} \Phi_{s,P_i^{IT}}$ is publicly available in DS after this phase.

---

[6] Note P not Φ in the subscript $\mu_{P_i^{IT}}(\delta)$, since one may vote for δ even if absent from the p-proof.

Loop B. Agents receive access to evidence of others (can query DS). Each agent i reveals its attitude towards any $\delta \in \bigcup \Phi^{IT}$ (even if not in its p-proof of s), so after this phase $\forall_{\delta \in \bigcup \Phi^{IT}}$ we have all $n_k^{\delta} = |\{i \in 1..n : \mu_{P_i^{IT}}(\delta) = k\}|$, where $k \in \mathbb{T}$. Thus, voting begins and $\forall_{\delta \in \bigcup \Phi^{IT}}$ we obtain the sets $IN(\delta)$ and $OUT(\delta)$ s.t.:

$IN(\delta) = \{\delta[a = i], \neg\delta[b = i] : \langle a, b \rangle \in VF(\delta, n_t^{\delta}, n_f^{\delta}, n_i^{\delta}, n_u^{\delta}, n)\}$, and

$OUT(\delta) = \{\delta[a = o], \neg\delta[b = o] : \langle a, b \rangle \in VF(\delta, n_t^{\delta}, n_f^{\delta}, n_i^{\delta}, n_u^{\delta}, n)\}$.

After this step, $RDS^{IT+1} = RDS^{IT} \cup$

$$\bigcup_{\delta \in \bigcup \Phi^{IT}} \{\langle \delta, i \rangle : \delta \in IN(\delta)\} \cup \bigcup_{\delta \in \bigcup \Phi^{IT}} \{\langle \delta, o \rangle : \delta \in OUT(\delta)\}.$$

Loop C. Agents receive access to RDS thus eventually each agent's program is updated as follows:

$$P_i^{IT+1} = P_i^{IT} \cup \bigcup_{\delta \in \bigcup \Phi^{IT}} IN(\delta) \setminus \bigcup_{\delta \in \bigcup \Phi^{IT}} OUT(\delta)$$

Since this is a Deep Persuasion, agents play until Impasse, i.e., when $\forall_i : P_i^{IT+1} = P_i^{IT}$ (when agents' programs stop changing, in loop C all final relevant moves are played if exist). Then, at termination time tt:

$$CS_d^{tt} = \bigcup \{\delta : \langle \delta, i \rangle \in RDS_d^{tt}\} = \bigcup_{IT=0}^{ITMAX} \bigcup_{\delta \in \bigcup \Phi^{IT}} IN(\delta) = \left(\sum_{i=1}^{n} P_i\right)(s),$$

so $\Phi_{s, (\sum_{i=1}^{n} P_i)(s)} = \Phi_{s, CS_d^{tt}}$.   ◁

Theorem 6. *Deep and Classical Persuasion possibly converges to the merged outcome.*

Proof. Immediately from Thm. 5 and the fact that Classical Persuasion subsumes Deep.

6   Conclusions

We presented a formalization of multi-party, paraconsistent and paracomplete persuasion in TalkLOG, where agents can argue about beliefs with use of pieces of evidence. Classical Persuasion [1] was investigated and extended to account for more types of initial conflicts of opinion due to the 4-valued approach. Moreover we distinguished Deep Persuasion, which solves conflicts of justifications of opinions, more common in tightly-coupled groups. We succeeded to obtain a unified treatment of both dialogue types, which, in TalkLOG, are differentiated only by termination criterion.

Our model is somewhat complex as it deals with 4 dialogue stores, retaining the effects of agents' moves and resolved conflicts. Such architecture permits to achieve a protocol with public semantics. Specifically, we show that obtaining conclusion of a terminated dialogue is tractable. Our contribution advances the research on computational models of persuasion as we explicitly consider dynamics of belief revision in the course of dialogue. Moreover, we depart from the traditional notion of conflict based on inconsistency, allowing instead for a custom voting mechanism for conflict resolution.

The outcomes of TalkLOG dialogues are juxtaposed with the merged outcomes of the individual informational stances of participants. A non-trivial merge operator (inspired by [11]) exploited the same voting mechanism as in dialogue. Finally, Classical Persuasion turned out to be neither sound nor complete, as the same opinion may be justified by different, in extreme cases even antithetic justifications, which may not be discovered. Thus, we naturally reached deeper than just opinions, namely at their justifications, what led us to distinguishing a new type of dialogue: Deep Persuasion. In a special class of Deep Persuasion, i.e., Iterated Deep Persuasion, soundness and completeness was obtained (assuming again the same voting mechanism in dialogue and merge) at the price of limiting flexibility of agents' communication.

The results were obtained in a paraconsistent, nonmonotonic, multi-party and dynamic setting. Extending this research, we will provide the proof of soundness and completeness of all Deep Persuasion dialogues and investigate more specific complexity results, following our previous work on inquiry [9].

Acknowledgments. The study is co-financed by the European Union under the European Social Fund. Project PO KL „Information technologies: Research and their interdisciplinary applications”, Agreement UDA-POKL.04.01.01-00-051/10-00 and by Warsaw Center of Mathematics and Computer Science.

References

1. Walton, D., Krabbe, E.: Commitment in Dialogue: Basic Concepts of Interpersonal Reasoning. State University of New York Press, Albany (1995)
2. Prakken, H.: Formal systems for persuasion dialogue. The Knowledge Engineering Review **21**(2), 163–188 (2006)
3. Parsons, S., Wooldridge, M., Amgoud, L.: Properties and complexity of some formal inter-agent dialogues. J. Log. Comput. **13**(3), 347–376 (2003)
4. Bonzon, E., Maudet, N.: On the outcomes of multiparty persuasion. In: McBurney, P., Parsons, S., Rahwan, I. (eds.) ArgMAS 2011. LNCS, vol. 7543, pp. 86–101. Springer, Heidelberg (2012)
5. Kontarinis, D., Bonzon, E., Maudet, N., Moraitis, P.: Regulating multiparty persuasion with bipolar arguments: discussion and examples. In: Modles Formels de l'interaction (MFI 2011) (2011)
6. Prakken, H.: An abstract framework for argumentation with structured arguments. Argument and Computation **1**(2), 93–124 (2010)
7. Takahashi, T., Sawamura, H.: A logic of multiple-valued argumentation. In: AAMAS, pp. 800–807. IEEE Computer Society (2004)
8. Vitória, A., Małuszyński, J., Szałas, A.: Modeling and reasoning with paraconsistent rough sets. Fundamenta Informaticae **97**(4), 405–438 (2009)
9. Dunin-Kęplicz, B., Strachocka, A.: Tractable inquiry in information-rich environments. In: Proceedings of the IJCAI 2015. AAAI Press (2015, to appear)

10. Prakken, H.: Models of persuasion dialogue. In: Simari, G., Rahwan, I. (eds.) Argumentation in Artificial Intelligence, pp. 281–300. Springer, NewYork (2009)
11. Coste-Marquis, S., Devred, C., Konieczny, S., Lagasquie-Schiex, M., Marquis, P.: On the merging of Dung's argumentation systems. Artif. Intell. **171**(10–15), 730–753 (2007)
12. Małuszyński, J., Szałas, A.: Partiality and inconsistency in agents' belief bases. In: KES-AMSTA of Frontiers in Artificial Intelligence and Applications, vol. 252, pp. 3–17. IOS Press (2013)
13. Szałas, A.: How an agent might think. Logic J. IGPL **21**(3), 515–535 (2013)
14. Małuszyński, J., Szałas, A.: Living with inconsistency and taming nonmonotonicity. In: de Moor, O., Gottlob, G., Furche, T., Sellers, A. (eds.) Datalog 2010. LNCS, vol. 6702, pp. 384–398. Springer, Heidelberg (2011)
15. Brandt, F., Conitzer, V., Endriss, U.: Computational social choice. Multiagent systems, pp. 213–283 (2012)
16. FIPA: (2002). http://www.fipa.org/
17. Cohen, P.R., Levesque, H.J.: Performatives in a rationally based speech act theory. In: Meeting of the Association for Computational Linguistics, pp. 79–88 (1990)
18. Fisher, M.: Representing and executing agent-based systems. In: Proceedings of the ECAI-1994 Workshop on Agent Theories, Architectures, and Languages, pp. 307–324 (1994)
19. Dunin-Kęplicz, B., Strachocka, A., Szałas, A., Verbrugge, R.: Paraconsistent semantics of speech acts. Neurocomputing **151**, 943–952 (2015)
20. Chopra, A.K., Artikis, A., Bentahar, J., Colombetti, M., Dignum, F., Fornara, N., Jones, A.J.I., Singh, M.P., Yolum, P.: Research directions in agent communication. ACM TIST **4**(2), 20 (2013)
21. Dunin-Kęplicz, B., Szałas, A., Verbrugge, R.: Tractable reasoning about group beliefs. In: Dalpiaz, F., Dix, J., van Riemsdijk, M.B. (eds.) EMAS 2014. LNAI. Springer, Heidelberg (2014)
22. Alferes, J.J., Brogi, A., Leite, J., Moniz Pereira, L.: Evolving logic programs. In: Flesca, S., Greco, S., Leone, N., Ianni, G. (eds.) JELIA 2002. LNCS (LNAI), vol. 2424, p. 50. Springer, Heidelberg (2002)
23. Prakken, H.: Coherence and flexibility in dialogue games for argumentation. Journal of Logic and Computation **15**, 1009–1040 (2005)

A Micro Study on the Evolution of Arguments in Amazon.com's Reviews

Simone Gabbriellini[1] and Francesco Santini[2($\boxtimes$)]

[1] GEMASS, CNRS & Paris-Sorbonne, Paris, France
`simone.gabbriellini@cnrs.fr`
[2] Department of Mathematics and Computer Science,
University of Perugia, Perugia, Italy
`francesco.santini@dmi.unipg.it`

Abstract. In this work we present an exploratory study on arguments in Amazon.com reviews. We manually extract positive (in favour of purchase) and negative (against it) arguments from each review concerning a selected product. Moreover, we link arguments to the rating score and length of reviews. For instance, we show that negative arguments are quite sparse during the first steps of such social review-process, while positive arguments are more equally distributed. In addition, we connect arguments through attacks and we compute Dung's extensions to check whether they capture such evolution through time. We also use Preference-based Argumentation to exploit the number of appearances of each argument in reviews.

1 Introduction

Recent surveys have reported that 50% of on-line shoppers spend at least ten minutes reading reviews before making a decision about a purchase, and 26% of on-line shoppers read reviews on Amazon prior to making a purchase.[1]

This paper reports an exploratory study of how customers use arguments in writing such reviews. We start from a well acknowledged result in the literature on on-line reviews: the more reviews a product gets, the more the rating tends to decrease [26]. Such rating is, in many case, a simple scale from 1 to 5, where 1 is a low rating and 5 is the maximum possible rating.

This fact can be explained easily considering that first customers are more likely to be enthusiast of the product, then as the product gets momentum, more people have a chance to review it and inevitably the average rating tends to stabilise on some values lower than 5. Such process, with a few enthusiast

---

S. Gabbriellini—The author is supported by ANR (Agence Nationale de la Recherche) within the project DIFFCERAM (n. ANR-12-CULT-0001-01).

F. Santini—The author is supported by GNCS-INDAM "Efficient Methods for Argumentation-based Decision Support".

[1] http://www.forbes.com/sites/jeffbercovici/2013/01/25/
how-amazon-should-fix-its-reviews-problem/.

© Springer International Publishing Switzerland 2015
Q. Chen et al. (Eds.): PRIMA 2015, LNAI 9387, pp. 284–300, 2015.
DOI: 10.1007/978-3-319-25524-8_18

innovators followed by a majority that gets convinced by the formers (on a lower level of enthusiasm), is a typical pattern in diffusion studies [26].

However, the level of disagreement in product reviews remains a challenge: does it influence what other customers will do? In particular, what does it happen, on a lower level, that justifies such diminishing trend in ratings? Since reviewing a product is a communication process, and since we use arguments to communicate our opinions to others (and possibly convince them) [23], it is evident that late reviews should contain enough negative arguments to explain such a negative trend in ratings.

Our present study can be considered as "micro" because we focus on a single product only, even if with a quite large number of reviews (i.e., 253). Unfortunately, due to the lack of well-established tools for the automated extraction of arguments and attacks, we cannot extend our study "in the large" and draw more general considerations. We extracted by hand, for each review about the selected product, both positive and negative arguments expressed, the associated rating (from one to five stars), and the time when the review has been posted. Afterwords, we analyse our data in terms of:

– how positive/negative arguments are posted through time.
– how many positive/negative arguments a review has (through time).

In particular, we argue that the reason why average ratings tend to decrease as a function of time depends not only on the fact that the number of negative reviews increases, but also on the fact that negative arguments tend to permeate positive reviews, decreasing de facto the average rating of these reviews.

One interesting way to reason with arguments is to adopt a computational argumentation approach. An *Abstract Argumentation Framework* (*AAF*), or System, as introduced in a seminal paper by Dung [14], is simply a pair $\langle A, R \rangle$ consisting of a set A whose elements are called arguments and of a binary relation R on A, called "attack" relation. An abstract argument is not assumed to have any specific structure but, roughly speaking, an argument is anything that may attack or be attacked by another argument. The sets of arguments (or *extensions*) to be considered are then defined under different semantics, which are related to varying degrees of scepticism or credulousness.

The rest of the paper is structured as follows. Section 2 sets the scene where we settle our work: we introduce related proposals that aggregate Amazon.com reviews in order to produce an easy-to-understand summary of them. In Sec. 3 we report the basic notions behind AAFs, as pioneered by Dung in 1995 [14]; we also introduce Preference-based Argumentation [1], which we use with the purpose to take advantage of the number of times each argument appears in review: we consider it as a strength-score for arguments. Afterwards, in Sec. 4 we describe the Amazon.com dataset from where we select our case-study. Section 5 plots how both positive and negative arguments dynamically change through time, zooming inside reviews with a more granular approach. In Sec. 6 we match Dung's semantics to the results advanced in Sec. 5; in particular, we show that the increase of negative arguments during the final part of the review process is also captured by the stable semantics, using its preference-based variant [1]. Finally, Sec. 7 wraps up the paper and hints direction for future work.

2   Literature Review

Electronic Word-of-Mouth (e-WoM) is the passing of information from person to person, mediated through any electronic means. Over the years it has gained growing attention from scholars, as more and more customers started sharing their experience online [2,28,32,19,10]. Since e-WoM somewhat influences consumers' decision-making processes, many review systems have been implemented on a number of popular Web 2.0-based e-commerce websites (e.g., Amazon.com[2] and eBay.com[3]), product comparison websites (e.g., BizRate.com[4] and Epinions.com[5]), and news websites (e.g., MSNBC.com[6] and SlashDot.org[7]).

Unlike recommendation systems, which seek to personalise each user's Web experience by exploiting item-to-item and user-to-user correlations, review systems give access to others' opinions as well as an average rating for an item based on the reviews received so far. Two key facts have been assessed so far:

- *reporting bias*: customers with more extreme opinions have a higher than normal likelihood of reporting their opinion [2];
- *purchasing bias*: customers who like a product have a greater chance to buy it and leave a review on the positive side of the spectrum [11].

These conditions produce a J-shaped curve of ratings, with extreme ratings and positive ratings being more present. Thus a customer who wants to buy a product is not exposed to a fair and unbiased set of opinions. Scholars have started investigating the relation between reviews, ratings, and disagreement among customers [24,13]. In particular, one challenging question is: *does the disagreement about the quality of a product in previous reviews influence what new reviewers will post?*

A common approach to measure disagreement in reviews is to compute the standard deviation of ratings per product, but more refined indexes are possible [25]. The next step is to detect correlations among disagreement as a function of time [13,25]. We aim, however, at modelling a lower level, micro-founded mechanism that could account for how customers' reviewing behaviour evolves over time. We want to analyse reviews not only in terms of rating and length, but also in terms of what really constitutes the review itself, i.e., the arguments used by customers. We aim at explaining disagreement as a consequence of customers' behaviour, not only at describing it as a correlation among variables (an

---

[2] http://www.amazon.com.

[3] http://www.ebay.com.

[4] http://www.bizrate.com.

[5] http://www.epinions.com.

[6] http://www.msnbc.com.

[7] http://slashdot.org.

analytical and micro-founded modelling of social phenomena is well detailed in [22,20,27] - for an application in on-line contexts, see [16]).

However, before automatically reasoning on arguments, we have first to extract them from a text corpora of on-line reviews. On this side, research is still dawning, even if already promising [29,31]. In addition, we would like to mention other approaches that can be used to summarise the bulk of unstructured information (in natural language) provided by customer reviews. The authors of [21] summarise reviews by $i)$ mining product features that have been commented on by customers, $ii)$ identifying opinion sentences in each review and deciding whether each opinion sentence is positive or negative, and, finally, $iii)$ summarising the results. Several different techniques have been advanced to this, e.g., sentiment classification, frequent and infrequent features identification, or predicting the orientation of opinions (positive or negative). Even if never citing the word "argument", we think [21] is strictly related to argument mining.

3   Abstract Argumentation Frameworks and Tools

In this section we briefly summarise the background information related to classical Abstract Argumentation Frameworks (AAFs) [14] and Preference-based Argumentation (PAF) [1].

Definition 1 (AAF). *An Abstract Argumentation Framework (AAF) is a pair $F = \langle A, R \rangle$ of a set A of arguments and a binary relation $R \subseteq A \times A$, called the attack relation. $\forall a, b \in A$, aRb (or, $a \rightarrowtail b$) means that a attacks b. An AAF may be represented by a directed graph whose nodes are arguments and edges represent the attack relation. A set of arguments $S \subseteq A$ attacks an argument a, i.e., $S \rightarrowtail a$, if a is attacked by an argument of S, i.e., $\exists b \in S.b \rightarrowtail a$.*

Definition 2 (Defence). *Given $F = \langle A, R \rangle$, an argument $a \in A$ is defended (in F) by a set $S \subseteq A$ if for each $b \in A$, such that $b \rightarrowtail a$, also $S \rightarrowtail b$ holds.*

The "acceptability" of an argument can be defined under different semantics σ, depending on the frequency of its membership to some sets, called *extensions*: such semantics characterise a collective "acceptability" for arguments. In Def. 3 we only report the original semantics given by Dung [14]: $\sigma = \{adm, com, prf, stb, gde\}$, which respectively stand for admissible, complete, preferred, stable, and grounded semantics.

Definition 3 (Semantics [14]). *Let $F = \langle A, R \rangle$ be an AAF. A set $S \subseteq A$ is conflict-free (in F), denoted $S \in cf(F)$, iff there are no $a, b \in S$, such that $a \rightarrowtail b$ or $b \rightarrowtail a \in R$. For $S \in cf(F)$, it holds that i) $S \in adm(F)$, if each $a \in S$ is defended by S; ii) $S \in com(F)$, if $S \in adm(F)$ and for each $a \in A$ defended by S, $a \in S$ holds; iii) $S \in prf(F)$, if $S \in adm(F)$ and there is no $T \in adm(F)$ with $S \subset T$; iv) $S \in stb(F)$, if for each $a \in A \backslash S$, $S \rightarrowtail a$; v) $S = gde(F)$ if $S \in com(F)$ and there is no $T \in com(F)$ with $T \subset S$.*

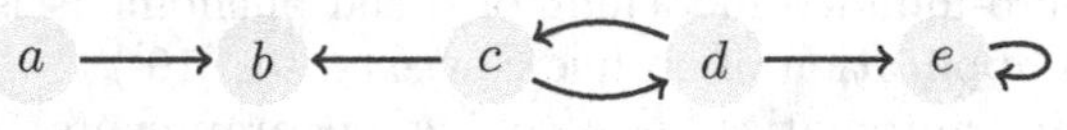

Fig. 1. An example of AAF.

We also recall that the different requirements in Def. 3 define an inclusion hierarchy on the extensions: from the most to the least stringent we have $stb(F) \subseteq prf(F) \subseteq com(F) \subseteq adm(F)$.

Moreover, we can also define a strength level for each argument, given any of the semantics in Def. 3. A sceptically accepted argument proves to be stronger than a credulously accepted one.

Definition 4 (Arguments acceptance-state). *Given one of the semantics σ in Def. 3 and a framework F, an argument a is* i) *sceptically accepted iff $\forall S \in \sigma(F), a \in S$,* ii) *$a$ is credulously accepted if $\exists S \in \sigma(F), a \in S$ and a is not sceptically accepted.*

Example 1. Consider $F = \langle A, R \rangle$ in Fig. 1, with $A = \{a, b, c, d, e\}$ and $R = \{a \rightarrowtail b, c \rightarrowtail b, c \rightarrowtail d, d \rightarrowtail c, d \rightarrowtail e, e \rightarrowtail e\}$. In F we have $adm(F) = \{\emptyset, \{a\}, \{c\}, \{d\}, \{a, c\}, \{a, d\}\}$, $com(F) = \{\{a\}, \{a, c\}, \{a, d\}\}$, $prf(F) = \{\{a, d\}, \{a, c\}\}$, $stb(F) = \{\{a, d\}\}$, and $gde(F) = \{a\}$. Hence, argument a is sceptically accepted in $com(F)$, $prf(F)$ and $stb(F)$, while it is only credulously accepted in $adm(F)$.

Definition 5 (Preference-based Argumentation [1]). *A preference-based argumentation framework is a triplet $\langle A, R, Pref \rangle$ where $Pref$ is a partial preordering (reflexive and transitive binary relation) on $A \times A$. The notion of defence (see Def. 2) changes accordingly: let a and b be two arguments, we define $b \rightarrowtail a$ iff $R(b, a)$ and not $a > b$.*

In the following of the paper we exploit two different reasoning-tools based on Argumentation. *ConArg*[8] [7,8,5] (ARGumentation with CONstraints) is an Abstract Argumentation reasoner based on the *Gecode* library[9], which is an open, free, and efficient C++ environment where to develop constraint-based applications. To encode preference-based problems we instead use the *ASPARTIX*[10] system [15]. *ASPARTIX* relies on a fixed disjunctive *Datalog* program that takes an instance of an argumentation framework as input, and uses an Answer-Set solver for satisfying the semantics specified users. To specify the pre-ordering on arguments, a fact *pref/2* can be used. For example: $pref(a, b)$ specifies that argument a has a higher priority than argument b.

---

[8] http://www.dmi.unipg.it/conarg/.

[9] http://www.gecode.org.

[10] http://www.dbai.tuwien.ac.at/proj/argumentation/systempage/.

4   Dataset

Amazon.com allows users to submit their reviews to the web page of each product, and the reviews can be accessed by all users. Each review consists of the reviewer's name (either the real name or a nickname), several lines of comments, a rating score (ranging from one to five stars), and the time-stamp of the review. All reviews are archived in the system, and the aggregated result, derived by averaging all the received ratings, is reported on the Web-page of each product. It has been shown that such reviews provide basic ideas about the popularity and dependability of corresponding items; hence, they have a substantial impact on cyber-shoppers' behaviour [11]. It is well known that the current Amazon.com reviewing system has some noticeable limits [30]. For instance, *i)* the review results have the tendency to be skewed toward high scores, *ii)* the ageing issue of reviews is not considered, and *iii)* it has no means to assess reviews' helpfulness if the reviews are not evaluated by a sufficiently large number of users.

For our purposes, we retrieved the "Clothing, Shoes and Jeweller" products section of Amazon[11]. The dataset contains approximately 110k products and spans from 1999 to July 2014, for a total of more than one million reviews. The whole dataset contains 143.7 millions reviews.

We summarise here a quick description of such dataset:[12]

- the distribution of reviews per product is highly heterogeneous;
- the disagreement in ratings tends to rise with the number of reviews until a point after which it starts to decay. Interestingly, for some highly reviewed products, the disagreement remains high: this means that only for specific products opinions polarise while, on average, reviewers tend to agree;[13]
- more recent reviews tend to get shorter, irrespectively of the number of reviews received, which is pretty much expectable: new reviewers might realise that some of what they wanted to say has already been stated in previous reviews;
- more recent ratings tend to be lower, irrespectively of the number of reviews received.

To sum up, it seems that the disagreement in previous reviews does not affect much latest ratings - except for some cases which might correspond to products with polarised opinions. This result has already been found in the literature [24]. However, it has also already been challenged by Nagle and Riedl [25], who found that a higher disagreement among prior reviews does lead to lower ratings. They ascribe their new finding to their more accurate way of measuring the disagreement in such J-shaped distributions of ratings.

---

[11] Courtesy of Julian McAuley and SNAP project (source: http://snap.stanford.edu/data/web-Amazon.html and https://snap.stanford.edu).

[12] Space constraints prevented us to show more detailed results here, but additional plots are available in the form of research notes at http://tinyurl.com/pv5owct.

[13] Polarisation only on specific issues has already been observed in many off-line contexts, see [3].

Table 1. Positive and negative arguments, with their number of appearances in reviews between 2009 and July 2014.

ID	Positive arguments	#App.	ID	Negative arguments	#App.
A	the kid loved it	78	a	it has a bad quality	18
B	it fits well	65	b	it is not sewed properly	17
C	it has a good quality/price ratio	52	c	it does not fit	12
D	it has a good quality	44	d	it is not full	11
E	it is durable	31	e	it is not as advertised	8
F	it is shipped fast	25	f	it is not durable	7
G	the kid looks adorable	23	g	it has a bad customer service	4
H	it has a good price	21	h	it is shipped slow	3
I	it has great colors	21	i	it smells chemically	3
J	it is full	18	j	you can see through it	3
K	it did its job	11	k	it cannot be used in real dance class	2
L	it is good for playing	11	l	it has a bad quality/price ratio	2
M	it is as advertised	9	m	it has a bad envelope	1
N	it can be used in real dance classes	7	n	it has a bad waistband	1
O	it is aesthetically appealing	7	o	it has bad colours	1
P	it has a good envelope	2	p	it has high shipping rates	1
Q	it is a great first tutu	2	q	it has no cleaning instructions	1
R	it is easier than build your own	2	r	it is not lined	1
S	it is sewed properly	2	s	it never arrived	1
T	it has a good customer service	1	t	it was damaged	1
U	it is secure	1			
V	it is simple but elegant	1			
W	you can customize it	1			
X	you cannot see through it	1			

One of the main aims of this work is to understand how it is that new reviews tend to get lower ratings. Our hypothesis is that this phenomenon can be explained if we look at the level of arguments, i.e., if we consider the dynamics of the arguments used by customers, more than aggregate ratings.

Since techniques to mine arguments from a text corpora are yet in an early development stage, we focus on a single product and extract arguments by hand. We randomly select a product, which happens to be a ballet tutu for kids, and we examine all the 253 reviews that this product received between 2009 and July 2014. From the reviews, we collect a total of 24 positive arguments and 20 negative arguments, whose absolute frequencies are reported in Tab. 1.

There are of course many issues that arise when such a process is done by hand. First of all, an argument might seem positive to a reader and negative to another. For the purpose of this small example, we coded arguments together and, for each argument, tried to achieve the highest possible agreement on its polarity. A better routine, for larger studies, would be to have many coders operate autonomously and then check the consistency of their results. However, we didn't find case where an argument could be considered both positive and negative, maybe because the product itself didn't allow for complex reasoning. When we encountered a review with both positive and negative arguments, like "the kid loved it, but it is not sewed properly", we split the review counting one positive argument and one negative argument. The most interesting thing emerging from this study is the fact that, as reviews accumulate, they tend to contain more negative bits, even if the ratings remain high.

5   Analysis

In Fig. 2, the first plot on the left shows the monthly absolute frequencies of positive arguments in the specified time range. As it is easy to see, the number of positive arguments increases as time goes by, which can be a consequence of a success in sales: more happy consumers are reviewing the product. At the same time, the first plot on the right shows a similar trend for negative arguments, which is a signal that, as more customers purchase the product, some of them are not satisfied with it. According to what we expect from the literature (see Sec. 2), the higher volume of positive arguments is a consequence of the J-shaped curve in ratings, i.e., a consequence of reporting and selection biases. What is

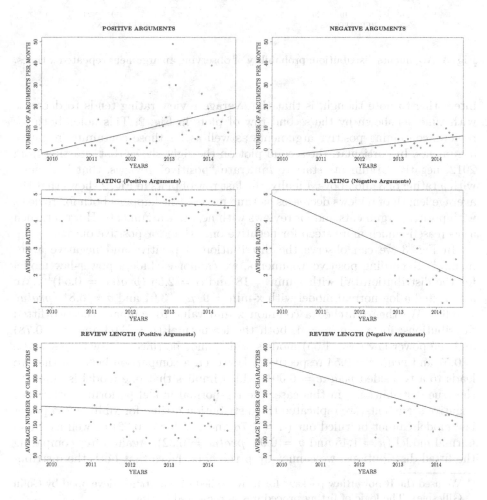

Fig. 2. Argument trends: (row1) absolute frequency of arguments per month, (row2) average rating of reviews per month, (row3) average review-length per month.

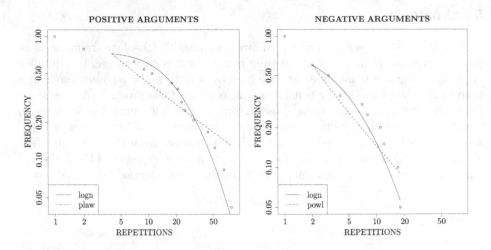

Fig. 3. Arguments distribution: probability of observing an argument repeated x times.

interesting to note though, is that the average review rating tends to decrease with time, as shown by the second row of plots in Fig. 2. This holds both for reviews containing positive arguments as well as for those containing negative arguments. In particular, the second plot on the right shows that, starting from 2012, negative arguments start to infiltrate "positive" reviews, that is reviews with a rating of 3 and above. Finally, the last row of plots in Fig. 2 shows that the average length of reviews decreases as time passes; this happens both for reviews with positive arguments and for reviews with negative arguments. However, such a decrease is much more steep for negative ones than for positive ones.

In Fig. 3 we can observe the distribution of positive and negative arguments.[14] Regarding positive arguments, we cannot exclude a power-law model for the distribution tail with x-min = 18 and α = 2.56 ($pvalue$ = 0.54)[15]. We also tested a log-normal model with x-min = 9, μ = 3.01 and σ = 0.81 ($pvalue$ = 0.68). We then searched a common x-min value to compare the two fitted distributions: for $x - min$ = 4, both the log-normal (μ = 3.03 and σ = 0.78) and the power-law (α = 1.55) models still cannot be ruled out, with $p - value$ = 0.57 and $pvalue$ = 0.54 respectively. However, a comparison between the two leads to a two-sided $pvalue$ = 0.001, which implies that one model is closer to the true distribution - in this case, the log-normal model performs better. For negative arguments, we replicated the distribution fitting: for xmin = 2, a power law model cannot be ruled out (α = 1.78 and p-value = 0.22) as well as a log-normal model (μ = 1.48 and σ = 0.96, $pvalue$ = 0.32). Again, after comparing the fitted distributions, we cannot drop the hypotheses that both the distribu-

---

[14] We used the R poweRlaw package for heavy tailed distributions (developed by Colin Gillespie). The logic of fitting procedures is presented in [18].

[15] We used the relatively conservative choice that the power law is ruled out if $pvalue$ = 0.1, as in [12].

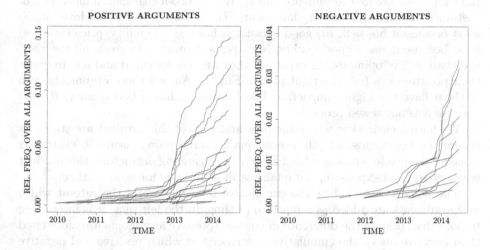

Fig. 4. Relative cumulated frequencies for each positive and negative argument.

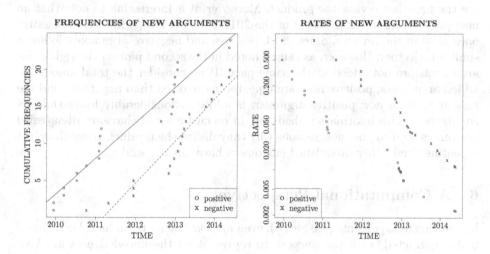

Fig. 5. Left plot: cumulative frequencies of new positive and negative arguments per month. Right plot: rate of new positive and negative arguments over total arguments per month.

tions are equally far from the true distribution (two-sided *pvalue* = 0.49). In this case, too few data are present to make a wise choice.

The plots in Fig. 4 show the cumulative frequencies of each single arguments as a function of time. The frequencies are calculated over all the arguments (repeated or new) across all reviews, so to give an idea of how much a single argument represents customers' opinion. Among the positive arguments (plot on the left), there are four arguments that represent, taken together, almost 44% of customers' opinions. These arguments are: *i)* good because the kid loved it, *ii)* good because it fits well, *iii)* good because it has a good quality/price ratio, *iv)* good because it has a good quality. Negative arguments represent, all together, less than 20% of opinions. As expected, they are less repeated and less frequent than positive ones (see the right plot in Fig. 4). Among these arguments, two of them have the higher impact: *i)* bad because it has a bad quality, *ii)* bad because it is not sewed properly.

We have a clear view where the pros and cons of this product are stated as arguments: not surprisingly, the overall quality is the main reason why customers consider the product as a good or bad deal. Even among detractors, this product is not considered expensive, but quality still is an issue for most of them.

The plots in Fig. 5 show the cumulative frequencies and the rate at which new arguments are added as a function of time. In the left plot, it is interesting to note that, despite the difference in volume (positive arguments are more cited than negative ones), the cumulative frequencies at which positive and negative arguments are added are almost identical. Positive arguments start being posted earlier than negative ones, consistently with the fact that enthusiast customers are the first that review the product. Moreover, it is interesting to note that no new positive argument is added in the 2011-2013 interval, while some negative ones arise in the reviews. Since 2013, positive and negative arguments follow a similar trajectory. However, as can be noted in the second plot on the right, new arguments are not added at the same pace. If we consider the total amount of added arguments, positive ones are repeated more often than negatives, and the rate at which a new positive argument is added is considerably lower than its counterpart. This information sheds a light on customers' behaviour: dissatisfied customers tend to post new reasons why they dislike the product, more than just repeating what other dissatisfied customers have already said.

6   A Computational Perspective

In addition to arguments (see Sec. 5), even attacks among them have been "manually" extracted, with the purpose to represent all the knowledge as an AAF (see Sec. 3). For some couples of arguments, this has been very easy: some positive arguments are the exact negation of what stated in the relative negative argument (and vice versa). For instance, looking at Tab. 1, *the tutu has a good quality* (D) and *the tutu has a bad quality* (a), or *the tutu fits well* (B) and *the tutu does not fit* (c). For the sake of completeness, such easy-to-detect (bidirectional) attacks are $\{B \leftrightarrow c, C \leftrightarrow l, D \leftrightarrow a, E \leftrightarrow f, F \leftrightarrow h, I \leftrightarrow o, J \leftrightarrow d, M \leftrightarrow e, N \leftrightarrow k, P \leftrightarrow m, S \leftrightarrow b, T \leftrightarrow g, X \leftrightarrow j\}$. Furthermore, we have identified some other unidirectional and bidirectional attacks; the complete list of arguments is visually reported with the graphical representation of the whole AAF, in Fig. 6. Note that we also have two unidirectional attacks between two positive arguments ($Q \rightarrow N$ and $V \rightarrow J$), and one bidirectional attack between two negative arguments ($s \leftrightarrow h$). Some of the reported attacks need the full sentences (or

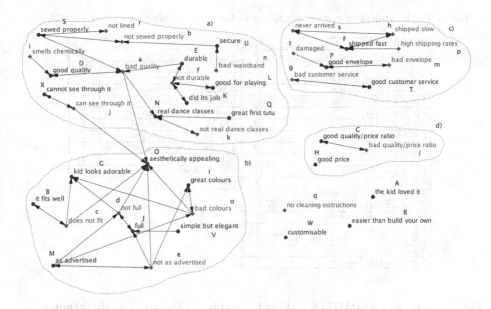

Fig. 6. The final and complete AAF extracted from 253 reviews.

even the whole reviews) related to the extracted arguments, in order to be comprehended at full. Even if sometimes connections are hidden at first sight, we tried to be as more linear as possible, thus avoiding too much subtle criticisms.

The complete AAF is represented in Fig. 6: circles represent positive arguments, while diamonds represent negative ones. We have clustered most of the arguments into four main subsets: *a)* product quality, *b)* product appearance, *c)* shipping-related information, and *d)* price-related information. Four arguments do not belong to any of these subsets (see Fig. 6).

By executing ConArg over the AAF in Fig. 6 we obtain $\{A, H, Q, R, V, W, i, k, m, n, p, q, t\}$ as the grounded extension. Such subset also corresponds to the set of sceptically accepted arguments while considering the stable semantics (see Sec. 3). The complete set of stable (and semi-stable) extensions counts 256 different instances, which exactly correspond also to the set of preferred extensions. We also retrieve 6.651 complete extensions.

However, we consider all such information hard to be somehow analysed and interpreted. For this reason we switch to considering preferences, i.e., PAF (see Sec. 3). The main reason is that we can exploit further information concerning a preference score associated with arguments: we consider the total number of times each argument appears in the 253 reviews about the tutu. In practice, we define a preference ordering based on the third and sixth columns in Tab. 1. For instance, argument M (*the tutu is as advertised*) is preferred w.r.t argument e (*the tutu is NOT as advertised*), since $9 > 8$, that is it appears (slightly) more frequently. Therefore, we completely define the partial order as requested by

Table 2. The subset of arguments taken in the single stable extension with PAF.

ID	Positive	#App.	ID	Negative	#App.
A	the kid loved it	78	b	it is not sewed properly	17
B	it fits well	65	d	it is not full	12
C	it has a good quality/price ratio	52	e	it is not as advertised	8
D	it has a good quality	44	g	it has a bad customer service	4
E	it is durable	31	i	it smells chemically	3
F	it is shipped fast	25	j	you can see through it	3
G	the kid looks adorable	23	n	it has a bad waistband	1
H	it has a good price	21	p	it has high shipping rates	1
J	it is full	18	q	it has no cleaning instructions	1
K	it did its job	11	r	it is not lined	1
L	it is good for playing	11	s	it never arrived	1
M	it is as advertised	9	t	it was damaged	1
N	it can be used in real dance classes	7			
O	it is aesthetically appealing	7			
P	it has a good envelope	2			
R	it is a great first tutu	2			
V	it is easier than build your own	2			
W	it is simple but elegant	1			
X	you can customize it	1			

Def. 5 and we run ASPARTIX looking for stable extensions. The single outcome-extension is represented in Tab. 2.

In order to show how the evolution of an AAF through time is computationally captured in Dung's semantics, we draw an AAF considering all the reviews up to the end of 2013. On the other hand, we reckon it is not meaningful to consider a screenshot of years 2010 (2 positive args), 2011 (7 positive args and 1 negative), and 2012 (12 positive and 5 negative args.). The 2013 AAF is in Fig. 7: it contains 19 positive and 8 negative arguments, and it has been obtained by projecting the AAF in Fig. 6 on arguments $\{A, B, C, D, E, F, G, H, I, J, K, L, O, P, R, S, V, W, X, a, b, c, d, e, i, k, l\}$. The number of appearances is reported in parentheses, for the sake of a compact representation. On such AAF we obtain 4 stable (and preferred) extensions, and 9 complete ones. The grounded extension is $\{A, E, F, H, K, L, P, R, V, W, X, b, d, e, i, k\}$: the only arguments that survive to the following two years of reviews are $\{A, H, R, V, W, i, k\}$. Even in this case, we use PAF (see Sec. 3) to consider the number of appearances. The resulting stable extension is 2013 $= \{A, B, C, D, E, F, G, H, I, J, K, L, O, P, R, V, W, X, b, d, e, i, k\}$. We notice that only S (*sewed properly*) is excluded, defeated by *not sewed properly*, which is repeated just one time more ($2 > 1$). Therefore, 18 out of 19 positive arguments are taken, while 3 out of 8 negative arguments are discarded.

The stable extension in Fig. 6 (i.e., with the final AAF) is $Jul2014 = \{A, B, C, D, E, F, G, H, J, K, L, M, N, O, P, Q, R, V, W, b, d, e, g, i, j, n, p, q, r, s, t\}$. Hence, according to the fact that after 2013 many new negative arguments appear (see Sec. 5), we notice that the number of negative arguments increases in the stable extension: $\{g, j, n, p, q, q, r, s, t\}$ are the new negative arguments in Jul2014, while only argument k disappears w.r.t 2013. Moreover, the most frequent negative arguments ($\{b, d, e\}$) are taken both in 2013 and Jul2014: they survive even in the final rush of reviews. Positive arguments remain substantially the same from 2013 to Jul2014: only $\{M, N, Q\}$ pop up, while $\{I, X\}$ disappear in Jul2014.

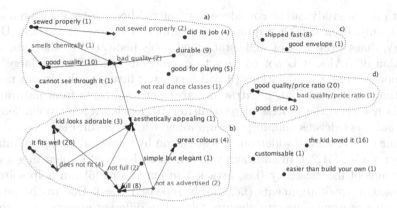

Fig. 7. The AAF extracted at the end of 2013.

Finally, we can notice that the new (Jul2014) negative arguments related to the product ($\{j,n,q,r\}$) are associated to reviews with a high rating ($j = 4/4/5$, $n = 4$, $q = 4$, $r = 3$), while those ones associated with the service ($\{g,p,s,t\}$) are associated with reviews with a low rating ($g = 1/3/1/1$, $p = 4$, $s = 1$, $t = 2$).

7 Discussion and Conclusions

In this paper we have proposed a first exploratory study on how to use Abstract Argumentation to understand if using arguments can improve our knowledge about social trends in product reviews. More in particular, we "enter" into an *Amazon.com* review and we achieve a more granular view of it by considering the different arguments expressed in each of the 253 reviews about the selected product (a ballerina tutu). What we observe is that the frequency of negative arguments (*against* purchasing the tutu) increases after some time, while the distribution of positive arguments (*in favour of* purchasing the tutu) is more balanced between the considered period. Moreover, while positive arguments are always associated with high ratings (i.e., 4 or 5), negative arguments are associated with low (as expected) but also high ratings. In addition, negative arguments are more frequently associated with shorter reviews, while enthusiasts tend to be less concise. To summarise, the aim is to "explode" reviews into arguments and then try to understand how the behaviour of reviewers changes through time, from the point of view of arguments.

In the second part of the paper, we link computational Abstract Argumentation to the arguments extracted during the first sections. We use Preference-based Argumentation [1] in order to take into account strength-scores, i.e, the number of appearances of each argument in all the reviews. The goal here is dual: first we show how the single outcome-extension (obtained by considering the stable semantics) changes before and after negative arguments start increasing. Moreover, we show how such extension can represent a simple and significant screen-shot of what reviewers believe about the considered product.

Our present study can be considered as "micro" because we focus on a single product only, even if with a quite large number of reviews (i.e., 253). Unfortunately, due to the lack of well-established tools dedicated to the automated extraction of AAFs, it is not so easy to extend our study "in the large" and draw more general considerations (it will be part of future work). In our manual extraction we noticed that, if extracting abstract arguments from natural language is not easy, the process of recognising attacks is even more challenging, due to subtle criticisms and, in general, ambiguities of natural languages.

In the future, we will widen our investigation by taking advantage of mining-techniques, e.g., [31,29]. In addition, we plan to understand if tolerating a given low amount of inconsistency (i.e., attacks) in extensions [6] can help softening the impact of weak arguments (i.e., rarely repeated ones). Due to the possible partitioning of arguments into clusters related to different aspects of a product (e.g., either its *quality* or *appearance*), we also intend to apply coalition-oriented semantics, as proposed in [9]. Moreover, we can exploit *Value-based AAFs* [4] to associate each argument with a value representing a different product aspect (e.g., shipping).

Following [17], we also plan to implement an Agent-Based Model with Argumentative Agents to explore the possible mechanisms, from a user's perspective, that give raise to such trends and correlations among positive and negative arguments.

References

1. Amgoud, L., Cayrol, C.: On the acceptability of arguments in preference-based argumentation. In: UAI 1998: Proceedings of the Fourteenth Conference on Uncertainty in Artificial Intelligence, pp. 1–7. Morgan Kaufmann (1998)
2. Anderson, E.W.: Customer satisfaction and word of mouth. Journal of Service Research **1**(1), 5–17 (1998)
3. Baldassarri, D., Bearman, P.: Dynamics of political polarization. American Sociological Review **72**, 784–811 (2007)
4. Bench-Capon, T.J.M.: Persuasion in practical argument using value-based argumentation frameworks. J. Log. Comput. **13**(3), 429–448 (2003)
5. Bistarelli, S., Rossi, F., Santini, F.: Benchmarking hard problems in random abstract AFs: the stable semantics. In: Computational Models of Argument - Proceedings of COMMA. Frontiers in Artificial Intelligence and Applications, vol. 266, pp. 153–160. IOS Press (2014)
6. Bistarelli, S., Santini, F.: A common computational framework for semiring-based argumentation systems. In: ECAI 2010–19th European Conference on Artificial Intelligence. FAIA, vol. 215, pp. 131–136. IOS Press (2010)
7. Bistarelli, S., Rossi, F., Santini, F.: Enumerating extensions on random abstract-AFs with Argtools, Aspartix, ConArg2 and Dung-O-Matic. In: Bulling, N., van der Torre, L., Villata, S., Jamroga, W., Vasconcelos, W. (eds.) CLIMA 2014. LNCS, vol. 8624, pp. 70–86. Springer, Heidelberg (2014)

8. Bistarelli, S., Rossi, F., Santini, F.: A first comparison of abstract argumentation reasoning-tools. In: ECAI 2014–21st European Conference on Artificial Intelligence. FAIA, vol. 263, pp. 969–970. IOS Press (2014)
9. Bistarelli, S., Santini, F.: Coalitions of arguments: An approach with constraint programming. Fundam. Inform. **124**(4), 383–401 (2013)
10. Chatterjee, P.: Online reviews do consumers use them? In: Gilly, M.C., Myers-Levy, J. (eds.) Proceedings of the ACR 2001, pp. 129–134. Association for Consumer Research (2001)
11. Chevalier, J., Mayzlin, D.: The effect of word of mouth on sales: Online book reviews. Journal of Marketing **43**(3), 345–354 (2006)
12. Clauset, A., Shalizi, C., Newman, M.: Power-law distributions in empirical data. SIAM Review **51**(4), 661–703 (2009)
13. Dellarocas, C.: The digitization of word of mouth: promise and challenges of online feedback mechanisms. Management Science **49**(10), 1407–1424 (2003)
14. Dung, P.M.: On the acceptability of arguments and its fundamental role in nonmonotonic reasoning, logic programming and n-person games. Artif. Intell. **77**(2), 321–357 (1995)
15. Egly, U., Gaggl, S.A., Woltran, S.: Answer-set programming encodings for argumentation frameworks. Argument and Computation **1**(2), 147–177 (2010)
16. Gabbriellini, S.: The evolution of online forums as communication networks: An agent-based model. Revue Francaise de Sociologie **4**(55), 805–826 (2014)
17. Gabbriellini, S., Torroni, P.: A new framework for ABMs based on argumentative reasoning. In: Kamiński, B., Koloch, G. (eds.) Advances in Social Simulation. AISC, vol. 229, pp. 25–36. Springer, Heidelberg (2014)
18. Gillespie, C.: Fitting heavy tailed distributions: the powerlaw package. Journal of Statistical Software **64**(2) (2015)
19. Goldenberg, J., Libai, B., Muller, E.: Talk of the network: a complex systems look at the underlying process of word-of-mouth. Marketing Letters **12**(3), 211–223 (2001)
20. Hedstrom, P.: Dissectin the Social: on the Principles of Analytical Sociology, 1st edn. Cambridge University Press (2005)
21. Hu, M., Liu, B.: Mining and summarizing customer reviews. In: Proceedings of the Tenth ACM SIGKDD International Conference on Knowledge Discovery and Data Mining, KDD 2004, pp. 168–177. ACM (2004)
22. Manzo, G.: Educational choices and social interactions: A formal model and a computational test. Comparative Social Research **30**, 47–100 (2013)
23. Mercier, H., Sperger, D.: Why do humans reason? Arguments for an argumentative theory. Behavioral and Brain Sciences **34**(2), 57–74 (2011)
24. Moe, W.W., Schweidel, D.A.: Online product opinions: Incidence, evaluation, and evolution. Marketing Science **31**(3), 372–386 (2012)
25. Nagle, F., Riedl, C.: Online word of mouth and product quality disagreement. In: ACAD MANAGE. Proc. Meeting Abstract Supplement. Academy of Management (2014)
26. Rogers, E.: Diffusion of Innovations, 5th edn. Simone & Schuster (2003)
27. Squazzoni, F.: Agent-Based Computational Sociology, 1st edn. Wiley (2012)
28. Stokes, D., Lomax, W.: Taking control of word of mouth marketing: the case of an entrepreneurial hotelier. Journal of Small Business and Enterprise Development **9**(4), 349–357 (2002)

29. Villalba, M.P.G., Saint-Dizier, P.: A framework to extract arguments in opinion texts. IJCINI **6**(3), 62–87 (2012)
30. Wang, B.C., Zhu, W.Y., Chen, L.J.: Improving the amazon review system by exploiting the credibility and time-decay of public reviews. In: Proceedings of the 2008 IEEE/WIC/ACM International Conference on Web Intelligence and Intelligent Agent Technology, WI-IAT 2008, vol. 3, pp. 123–126. IEEE Computer Society (2008)
31. Wyner, A., Schneider, J., Atkinson, K., Bench-Capon, T.J.M.: Semi-automated argumentative analysis of online product reviews. In: Computational Models of Argument - Proceedings of COMMA 2012. FAIA, vol. 245, pp. 43–50. IOS Press (2012)
32. Zhu, F., Zhang, X.: The influence of online consumer reviews on the demand for experience goods: the case of video games. In: Proceedings of the International Conference on Information Systems, ICIS, p. 25. Association for Information Systems (2006)

The Long-Term Benefits of Following Fairness Norms: A Game-Theoretic Analysis

Emiliano Lorini[1]([⊠]) and Roland Mühlenbernd[2]

[1] IRIT-CNRS, Toulouse University, Toulouse, France
lorini@irit.fr
[2] University of Tübingen, Tübingen, Germany

Abstract. In this study we present a game-theoretic model of guilt in relation to sensitivity to norms of fairness. We focus on a specific kind of fairness norm à la Rawls according to which a fair society should be organized so as to admit economic inequalities to the extent that they are beneficial to the less advantaged agents. We analyze the impact of the sensitivity to this fairness norm on the behavior of agents who play a repeated Prisoner's Dilemma and learn via fictitious play. Our results reveal that a great sensitivity to the fairness norm is beneficial in the long term when agents have the time to converge to mutual cooperation.

1 Introduction

Prototypical human and artificial societies (*e.g.*, a community, an organization) are populated by agents who have repeated encounters and can decide either to collaborate with the others thereby acting cooperatively, or to exploit the work of the others thereby acting selfishly. In a game-theoretic setting this kind of situations can be represented as an iterated Prisoner's Dilemma (PD) in which agents in the population have repeated one-to-one interactions with others (*i.e.*, at each round two agents in the population meet and play one-shot PD).

The aim of this work is to study how fairness norms tend to emerge in this kind of societies in which agents are assumed (i) to be rational in the sense of being expected utility maximizers, and (ii) to learn from their past experiences. In the paper, we focus on a special kind of fairness norm à la Rawls [20] according to which a fair society should be organized so as to admit economic inequalities to the extent that they are beneficial to the less advantaged agents.

Our analysis is based on the general assumption that agents in the society are heterogenous in the sense of being more or less sensitive to the fairness norm, where an agent's degree of norm sensitivity captures the extent to which the fairness norm has been internalized by the agent. Norm internalization is a concept

---

Nobody argues that the art of navigation is not founded on astronomy because sailors cannot wait to calculate the Nautical Almanac. Being rational creatures they go to sea with it already calculated; and all rational creatures go out upon the sea of life with their minds made up on the common questions of right and wrong, as well as on many of the far more difficult questions of wise and foolish.
J.S. Mill, Utilitarianism [16, Chap.2]

© Springer International Publishing Switzerland 2015
Q. Chen et al. (Eds.): PRIMA 2015, LNAI 9387, pp. 301–318, 2015.
DOI: 10.1007/978-3-319-25524-8_19

that has been widely discussed in the literature in social sciences and multi-agent systems [2,1,3,10,11]. The idea is that if a given norm is internalized by an agent then there is no need for an external sanction, a reward or punishment to ensure norm compliance. The agent is willing to comply with the norm because, if she does not do this, she will feel (morally) bad. We study the conditions under which an agent's disposition to follow the fairness norm à la Rawls (*i.e.*, the agent's sensitivity to the fairness norm) increases the agent's individual benefit in the long term. In other words, we aim at providing an utilitarian explanation of the internalization of the fairness norm à la Rawls, that is to say, we aim at explaining why rational agents with learning capabilities should become motivated to follow the fairness norm à la Rawls even without external enforcement (*e.g.*, external sanctions, punishment).

The rest of the paper is organized as follows. In Section 2 we present a game-theoretic model of guilt aversion which provides the static foundation of our analysis. The main idea of the model is that agents in a game are motivated both by their personal utilities and by the goal of avoiding guilt feeling. It is assumed that guilt feeling is triggered in case of the violation of an internalized norm. Specifically, the intensity of guilt feeling is proportional to the agent's sensitivity to the norm. In Section 3, we provide a dynamic extension of our model in order to formally specify repeated interactions and learning in a game-theoretic setting. The learning approach we use is the well-known fictitious play [7].[1] Section 4 provides some mathematical results about convergence for fictitious play in the case of iterated PD in which agents are assumed to be more or less sensitive to the fairness norm à la Rawls. Our mathematical analysis of convergence for fictitious play is partial, as it only covers a subset of the set of possible values of norm sensitivity for the agents in the population. Thus, in Section 5, we present some computational results about convergence for fictitious play which complements the analysis of Section 4. Finally, in Section 6, we present some experimental results in the case of iterated PD which highlight the relationship between an agent's degree of sensitivity to the fairness norm à la Rawls and her individual benefit in the long term. Our results reveal that a great sensitivity to this fairness norm is beneficial in the long term when agents have the time to converge to mutual cooperation. As a side note, we would like to remark that a preliminary version of this work by one of the authors has appeared in [9]. One limitation of this previous work is that it was only applied to a specific instance of the Prisoner's Dilemma and not to the entire class. A second limitation is that, differently from the present work, it was not supported by in-depth mathematical analysis of convergence for the fictitious play process. Finally, it did not contain any analysis of the way an agent's sensitivity to the fairness norm influences her benefit in the long term.

---

[1] We preferred fictitious play over alternative 'learning from the past' models, since it is i) deterministic, thus manageable to be analyzed formally, and ii) well-established in the field.

2   Game-Theoretic Model of Guilt Aversion

In this section, we present our game-theoretic model of guilt and of its influence on strategic decision making. We assume that guilt feeling originates from the agent's violation of a certain norm. Specifically, the intensity of an agent's guilt feeling depends on two parameters: (i) how much the agent is responsible for the violation of the norm, and (ii) how much the agent is sensitive to the norm. As emphasized in the introduction, in our model the agent's sensitivity to the norm captures the extent to which the norm is internalized by the agent.

Our model assumes that an agent has two different motivational systems: an endogenous motivational system determined by the agent's desires and an exogenous motivational system determined by the agent's internalized norms. Internalized norms make the agent capable of discerning what from his point of view is *good* (or *right*) from what is *bad* (or *wrong*). If an agent has internalized a certain norm, then she thinks that its realization ought to be promoted because it is *good* in itself. A similar distinction has also been made by philosophers and by social scientists. For instance, Searle [21] has recently proposed a theory of how an agent may want something without desiring it and on the problem of reasons for acting based on moral values and independent from desires. In his theory of morality [13], Harsanyi distinguishes a person's *ethical preferences* from her *personal preferences* and argues that a moral choice is a choice that is based on ethical preferences.

2.1   Normative Game and Guilt-dependent Utility

Let us first introduce the standard notion of normal-form game.

Definition 1 (Normal-form game). *A normal-form game is a tuple $G = (N, (S_i)_{i \in N}, U)$ where:*

- *$N = \{1, \ldots, n\}$ is a finite set of agents or players;*
- *for every $i \in N$, S_i is agent i's finite set of strategies;*
- *$U : N \longrightarrow (\prod_{i \in N} S_i \longrightarrow \mathbb{R})$ is an utility function, with $U(i)$ being agent i's personal utility function mapping every strategy profile to a real number (i.e., the personal utility of the strategy profile for agent i).*

For every $i \in N$, elements of S_i are denoted by $s_i, s_i', \ldots$ Let $2^{Agt*} = 2^N \setminus \{\emptyset\}$ be the set of all non-empty sets of agents (*alias* coalitions). For notational convenience we write $-i$ instead of $N \setminus \{i\}$. For every $J \in 2^{Agt*}$, we define the set of strategies for the coalition J to be $S_J = \prod_{i \in J} S_i$. Elements of S_J are denoted by $s_J, s_J', \ldots$ We write S instead of S_N and we denote elements of S by $s, s', \ldots$ Every strategy s_J of coalition J can be seen as a tuple $(s_i)_{i \in J}$ where agent i chooses the individual strategy $s_i \in S_i$. For notational convenience we write $U_i(s)$ instead of $U(i)(s)$. As usual a mixed strategy for agent i is a probability distribution over S_i. Agent i's set of mixed strategies is denoted by Σ_i and elements of Σ_i are denoted by $\sigma_i, \sigma_i', \ldots$ The set of mixed strategy profiles is defined to be $\Sigma = \Sigma_1 \times \ldots \times \Sigma_n$

	C	D
C	R, R	S, T
D	T, S	P, P

Fig. 1. Prisoner's dilemma (with player 1 being the row player and player 2 being the column player).

and its elements are denoted by $\sigma, \sigma', \ldots$ The utility function U_i reflects agent i's endogenous motivational system, *i.e.*, agent i's desires.

A well-known example of normal-form game is the Prisoner's Dilemma (PD) in which two agents face a social dilemma. The PD is represented in Figure 2.1.

Each agent in the game can decide either to cooperate (action C) or to defect (action D) and has an incentive to defect. Indeed, it is assumed that, if an agent defects, she gets a reward that is higher than the reward obtained in the case of cooperation, no matter what the other agent decides to do. In other words, cooperation is strongly dominated by defection. The social dilemma lies in the fact that mutual defection, the only Nash equilibrium of the game, ensures a payoff for each agent that is lower than the payoff obtained in the case of mutual cooperation. The Prisoner's Dilemma can be compactly represented as follows.

Definition 2 (Prisoner's Dilemma). *A Prisoner's Dilemma (PD) is a normal-form game* $G = (N, (S_i)_{i \in N}, U)$ *such that:*

- $N = \{1, 2\}$;
- *for all* $i \in N$, $S_i = \{C, D\}$;
- $U_1(C, C) = R$, $U_1(D, D) = P$, $U_1(C, D) = S$ *and* $U_1(D, C) = T$;
- $U_2(C, C) = R$, $U_2(D, D) = P$, $U_2(C, D) = T$ *and* $U_2(D, C) = S$;

and which satisfies the following two conditions:

(C1) $T > R > P > S$,
(C2) $S = 0$.

Condition **(C1)** is the typical one in the definition of the Prisoner's Dilemma. Condition **(C2)** is an extra *normality* constraint which is not necessarily assumed in the definition of PD. It is assumed here to simplify the analysis of the evolution of fairness norms.

The following definition extends the definition of normal-form game with a *normative* component. Specifically, we assume that every outcome in a game is also evaluated with respect to its ideality degree, *i.e.*, how much an outcome in the game conforms to a certain norm. Moreover, as pointed above, we assume that an agent in the game can be more or less sensitive to the norm, depending on how much the norm is internalized by her.

Definition 3 (Normative game). *A normative game is a tuple* $NG = (N, (S_i)_{i \in N}, U, I, \kappa)$ *where:*

- $(N, (S_i)_{i \in N}, U)$ *is a normal-form game;*

- $I : \prod_{i \in N} S_i \longrightarrow \mathbb{R}$ is a function mapping every strategy profile in S to a real number measuring the degree of ideality of the strategy profile;
- $\kappa : N \longrightarrow \mathbb{R}_{\geq 0}$ is a function mapping every agent in N to a non-negative real number measuring the agent's sensitivity to the norm.

For notational convenience we write κ_i instead of $\kappa(i)$ to denote agent i's sensitivity to the norm.

Following current psychological theories of guilt [12], we conceive guilt as the emotion which arises from an agent's self-attribution of responsibility for the violation of an internalized norm (*i.e.*, a norm to which the agent is sensitive). Specifically, intensity of guilt feeling is defined as *the difference between the ideality of the best alternative state that could have been achieved had the agent chosen a different action and the ideality of the current state, — capturing the agent's degree of responsibility for the violation of the norm —, weighted by the agent's sensitivity to the norm.* The general idea of our model is that the intensity of guilt feeling is a monotonically increasing function of the agent's degree of responsibility for norm violation and the agent's sensitivity to the norm.

Definition 4 (Guilt). *Let $NG = (N, (S_i)_{i \in N}, U, I, \kappa)$ be a normative game. Then, the guilt agent i will experience after the strategy profile s is played, denoted by $Guilt(i,s)$, is defined as follows:*

$$Guilt(i,s) = \kappa_i \times (\max_{s_i' \in S_i} I(s_i', s_{-i}) - I(s))$$

The following definition describes how an agent's utility function is transformed depending on the agent's feeling of guilt. In particular, the higher the intensity of guilt agent i will experience after the strategy profile s is played, the lower the (transformed) utility of the strategy profile s for agent i. Note indeed that the value $Guilt(i,s)$ is either positive or equal to 0. Guilt-dependent utility reflects both agent i's desires and agent i's moral considerations determined by her sensitivity to the norm.

Definition 5 (Guilt-dependent utility). *Let $NG = (N, (S_i)_{i \in N}, U, I, \kappa)$ be a normative game. Then, the guilt-dependent utility of the strategy profile s for agent i is defined as follows:*

$$U_i^*(s) = U_i(s) - Guilt(i,s)$$

It is worth noting that the previous definition of guilt-dependent utility is similar to the definition of regret-dependent utility proposed in regret theory [14]. Specifically, similarly to Loomes & Sugden's regret theory, we assume that the utility of a certain outcome for an agent should be trasformed by incorporating the emotion that the agent will experience if the outcome occurs.

2.2   Fairness Norms

In the preceding definition of normative game an agent i's utility function U_i and ideality function I are taken as independent. There are different ways of linking the two notions.

For instance, Harsanyi's theory of morality provides support for an utilitarian interpretation of fairness norms which allows us to reduce an agent i's ideality function I to the utility functions of all agents [13]. Specifically, according to the Harsanyi's view, a fairness norm coincides with the goal of maximizing the collective utility represented by the weighted sum of the individual utilities.

Definition 6 (Normative game with fairness norm à la Harsanyi). *A normative game with fairness norm à la Harsanyi is a normative game $NG = (N, (S_i)_{i \in N}, U, I, \kappa)$ such that for all $s \in S$:*

$$I(s) = \sum_{i \in N} U_i(s)$$

An alternative to Harsanyi's utilitarian view of fairness norms is Rawls' view [20]. In response to Harsanyi, Rawls proposed the *maximin* criterion of making the least happy agent as happy as possible: for all alternatives s and s', if the level of well-being in the worst-off position is strictly higher in s than in s', then s is better than s'. According to this well-known criterion of distributive justice, a fair society should be organized so as to admit economic inequalities to the extent that they are beneficial to the less advantaged agents.Following Rawls' interpretation, a fairness norm should coincide with the goal of maximizing the collective utility represented by the individual utility of the less advantaged agent.

Definition 7 (Normative game with fairness norm à la Rawls). *A normative game with fairness norm à la Rawls is a normative game $NG = (N, (S_i)_{i \in N}, U, I, \kappa)$ such that for all $s \in S$:*

$$I(s) = \min_{i \in N} U_i(s)$$

In this paper we focus on fairness norm à la Rawls. In particular, we are interested in studying the relationship between the agents' sensitivities to this kind of norm and their behaviors in a repeated game such as the Prisoner's Dilemma in which the agents learn from their past experiences. To this aim, in the next section, we provide a dynamic extension of our model of guilt aversion.

3   Dynamic Extension

In the dynamic version of our model, we assume that every agent in a given normative game has probabilistic expectations about the choices of the other agents. These expectations evolve over time. The following concept of history captures this idea.

Definition 8 (History). *Let $NG = (N, (S_i)_{i \in N}, U, I, \kappa)$ be a normative game. A history (for NG) is a tuple $H = ((\omega_{i,j})_{i,j \in N}, (c_i)_{i \in N})$ such that, for all $i, j \in N$:*

- $\omega_{i,j} : \mathbb{N} \longrightarrow \Delta(S_j)$ *is a function assigning to every time* $t \in \mathbb{N}$ *a probability distribution on* S_j,
- $c_i : \mathbb{N} \longrightarrow S_i$ *is a choice function specifying the choice of agent* i *at each time point* $t \in \mathbb{N}$.

For every $t \in \mathbb{N}$ and $s_j \in S_j$, $\omega_{i,j}(t)(s_j)$ denotes agent i's subjective probability at time t about the fact that agent j will choose action $s_j \in S_j$. For notational convenience, we write $\omega_{i,j}^t(s_j)$ instead of $\omega_{i,j}(t)(s_j)$. For all $i, j \in N$, $t \in \mathbb{N}$ and $s_{-i} \in S_{-i}$ we moreover define:

$$\omega_i^t(s_{-i}) = \prod_{j \in N \setminus \{i\}} \omega_{i,j}^t(s_j)$$

$\omega_i^t(s_{-i})$ denotes agent i's subjective probability at time t about the fact that the other agents will choose the joint action s_{-i}.

The following definition introduces the concept of agent i's expected utility at time t. Notice that the concept of utility used in the definition is the one of guilt-dependent utility of Definition 5. Indeed, we assume a rational agent is an agent who maximizes her expected guilt-dependent utility reflecting both the agent's desires and the agent's moral considerations determined by her sensitivity to the norm.

Definition 9 (Expected utility at time t). *Let* $NG = (N, (S_i)_{i \in N}, U, I, \kappa)$ *be a normative game, let* $H = ((\omega_{i,j})_{i,j \in N}, (c_i)_{i \in N})$ *be a history for* NG *and let* $t \in \mathbb{N}$. *Then, the expected utility of action* $s_i \in S_i$ *for the agent* i *at time* t, *denoted by* $EU_i^t(s_i)$, *is defined as follows:*

$$EU_i^t(s_i) = \sum_{s'_{-i} \in S_{-i}} \omega_i^t(s'_{-i}) \times U_i^*(s_i, s'_{-i})$$

As the following definition highlights, an agent is rational at a given time point t, if and only if her choice at time t maximizes expected utility.

Definition 10 (Rationality at time t). *Let* $NG = (N, (S_i)_{i \in N}, U, I, \kappa)$ *be a normative game, let* $H = ((\omega_{i,j})_{i,j \in N}, (c_i)_{i \in N})$ *be a history for* NG *and let* $t \in \mathbb{N}$. *Then, agent* i *is rational at time* t *if and only if* $EU_i^t(c_i(t)) \geq EU_i^t(s_i)$ *for all* $s_i \in S_i$.

We assume that agents learn via fictitious play [7], a learning algorithm introduced in the area of game theory and widely used in the area of multi-agent systems (see, *e.g.*, [22]). The idea of fictitious play is that each agent best responds to the empirical frequency of play of her opponents. The assumption underlying fictitious play is that each agent believes that her opponents are playing stationary strategies that do not depend from external factors such as the other agents' last moves.

Definition 11 (Learning via fictitious play). *Let* $NG = (N, (S_i)_{i \in N}, U, I, \kappa)$ *be a normative game and let* $H = ((\omega_{i,j})_{i,j \in N}, (c_i)_{i \in N})$ *be a history for* NG. *Then,* *agent i learns according to fictitious play (FP) along H, if and only if for all $j \in N \setminus \{i\}$, for all $s_j \in S_j$ and for all $t > 0$ we have:*

$$\omega_{i,j}^t(s_j) = \frac{obs_{i,j}^t(s_j)}{\sum_{s_j' \in S_j} obs_{i,j}^t(s_j')}$$

where $obs_{i,j}^0(s_j) = 0$ and for all $t > 0$:

$$obs_{i,j}^t(s_j) = \begin{cases} obs_{i,j}^{t-1}(s_j) + 1 & \text{if } c_j(t-1) = s_j \\ obs_{i,j}^{t-1}(s_j) & \text{if } c_j(t-1) \neq s_j \end{cases}$$

Note that $obs_{i,j}^t(s_j)$ in the previous definition denotes the number of agent i's past observations at time t of agent j's strategy s_j.

Two notions of convergence for fictitious play are given in the literature, one for pure strategies and one for mixed strategies. Let $H = ((\omega_{i,j})_{i,j \in N}, (c_i)_{i \in N})$ be a history. Then, H converges in the pure strategy sense if and only if there exists a pure strategy $s \in S$ and $\bar{t} \in \mathbb{N}$ such that for all $i \in N$:

$$c_i(t) = s_i \text{ for all } t \geq \bar{t}$$

On the contrary, H converges in the mixed strategy sense if and only if there exists a mixed strategy $\sigma \in \Sigma$ such that for all $i \in N$ and for all $s_i \in S_i$:

$$\lim_{\bar{t} \to \infty} \frac{|\{t \leq \bar{t} : c_i(t) = s_i\}|}{\bar{t} + 1} = \sigma_i(s_i)$$

Clearly, convergence in the pure strategy sense is a special case of convergence in the mixed strategy sense.

It has been proved [18] that for every *non-degenerate* 2×2 game (*i.e.*, two-player game where each player has two strategies available) and for every history H for this game, if all agents are rational and learn according to fictitious play along H, then H converges in the mixed strategy sense. The fact that the game is *non-degenerate* just means that, for every strategy of the second player there are no different strategies of the first player which guarantee the same payoff to the first player, and for every strategy of the first player there are no different strategies of the second player which guarantee the same payoff to the second player.[2] A generalization of this result to $2 \times n$ games has been given by [5].

4 Mathematical Analysis in the PD with Fairness Norm à la Rawls

In this section, we provide convergence results for fictitious play in the case of iterated Prisoner's Dilemma in which players are more or less sensitive to the fairness norm à la Rawls.

---

[2] Miyazawa [17] assumed a particular tie-breaking rule to prove convergence of fictitious play in 2×2 games.

	C	D
C	R, R	$-\kappa_1 P, T - \kappa_2 R$
D	$T - \kappa_1 R, -\kappa_2 P$	P, P

Fig. 2. Prisoner's Dilemma with transformed utilities according to fairness norm à la Rawls.

The first thing we can observe is that for any possible combination of norm sensitivity values for the two players, the behaviors of both players will converge to mixed strategies. In particular:

Theorem 1. *Let $NG = (N, (S_i)_{i \in N}, U, I, \kappa)$ be a normative game with fairness norm à la Rawls such that $(N, (S_i)_{i \in N}, U)$ is the Prisoner's Dilemma and let $H = ((\omega_{i,j})_{i,j \in N}, (c_i)_{i \in N})$ be a history for NG. Moreover, assume that every agent in N learns according to fictitious play along H and is rational for all $t \geq 0$. Then, H converges in the mixed strategy sense.*

Proof. For all possible values of κ_1 and κ_2, the transformed PD in which the utility function U_i is replaced by U_i^* for all $i \in \{1, 2\}$ is non-degenerate. The transformed PD is represented in Figure 2. Hence, the theorem follows from the fact that, as observed in the previous section, fictitious play is guaranteed to converge in the class of non-degenerate 2×2 games. $\square$

Our second result is the following theorem about convergence in the pure strategy sense. The theorem highlights that if at the beginning of the learning process every player has a uniform probability distribution over the strategies of the other player and the value of norm sensitivity is lower than the following threshold for cooperativeness

$$\theta_{tc} = \frac{P + T - R}{R - P}$$

for both players, then the two players will always play mutual defection. On the contrary, if at the beginning of the learning process every player has a uniform probability distribution over the strategies of the other player and the value of norm sensitivity is higher than the threshold θ_{tc} for both players, then the two players will always play mutual cooperation.

Theorem 2. *Let $NG = (N, (S_i)_{i \in N}, U, I, \kappa)$ be a normative game with fairness norm à la Rawls such that $(N, (S_i)_{i \in N}, U)$ is the Prisoner's Dilemma and let $H = ((\omega_{i,j})_{i,j \in N}, (c_i)_{i \in N})$ be a history for NG. Moreover, assume that every agent in N learns according to fictitious play along H and is rational for all $t \geq 0$, and that $\omega_{i,j}^0(s_j) = 0.5$ for all $i, j \in \{1, 2\}$ and for all $s_j \in \{C, D\}$. Then:*

- *if $\kappa_1 < \theta_{tc}$ and $\kappa_2 < \theta_{tc}$ then $c_1(t) = c_2(t) = D$ for all $t \geq 0$,*
- *if $\kappa_1 > \theta_{tc}$ and $\kappa_2 > \theta_{tc}$ then $c_1(t) = c_2(t) = C$ for all $t \geq 0$.*

Proof. Assume that every agent in N learns according to fictitious play along H and is rational for all $t \geq 0$, and that $\omega_{i,j}^0(s_j) = 0.5$ for all $i,j \in \{1,2\}$ and for all $s_j \in \{C,D\}$. We are going to prove that, for all $i,j \in \{1,2\}$, if $\kappa_i > \frac{P+T-R}{R-P}$ then $EU_i^0(C) > EU_i^0(D)$ and that if $\kappa_i < \frac{P+T-R}{R-P}$ then $EU_i^0(D) > EU_i^0(C)$.

First of all, let us compute the values of $EU_i^0(D)$ and $EU_i^0(C)$:

$$EU_i^0(D) = 0.5 \times P + 0.5 \times (T - \kappa_i \times (R - S))$$
$$= 0.5 \times P + 0.5 \times (T - \kappa_i \times R)$$
$$= 0.5 \times (P + T - \kappa_i \times R)$$

$$EU_i^0(C) = 0.5 \times R + 0.5 \times (S - \kappa_i \times (P - S))$$
$$= 0.5 \times R + 0.5 \times (-\kappa_i \times P)$$
$$= 0.5 \times (R - \kappa_i \times P)$$

It follows that $EU_i^0(D) > EU_i^0(C)$ if and only if $P + T - \kappa_i \times R > R - \kappa_i \times P$. The latter is equivalent to $\kappa_i < \frac{P+T-R}{R-P}$. Therefore, we have $EU_i^0(D) > EU_i^0(C)$ if and only if $\kappa_i < \frac{P+T-R}{R-P}$. By analogous argument, we can prove that $EU_i^0(C) > EU_i^0(D)$ if and only if $\kappa_i > \frac{P+T-R}{R-P}$.

It is routine task to verify that, for all possible values of κ_1 and κ_2 in the original normative game NG, the strategy profile (D, D) is a *strict Nash equilibrium* in the transformed PD depicted in Figure 2 in which the utility function U_i is replaced by U_i^* for all $i \in \{1,2\}$. Hence, by Proposition 2.1 in [8] and the fact that every agent is rational for all $t \geq 0$, it follows that if $\kappa_1 < \frac{P+T-R}{R-P}$ and $\kappa_2 < \frac{P+T-R}{R-P}$ then $c_1(t) = c_2(t) = D$ for all $t \geq 0$.

It is also a routine to verify that, if $\kappa_i > \frac{T-R}{R-S}$ for all $i \in \{1,2\}$, then the strategy profile (C, C) is a *strict Nash equilibrium* in the transformed PD depicted in Figure 2. Hence, by Proposition 2.1 in [8], the fact that every agent is rational for all $t \geq 0$ and the fact that $\frac{P+T-R}{R-P} > \frac{T-R}{R-S}$, it follows that if $\kappa_1 > \frac{P+T-R}{R-P}$ and $\kappa_2 > \frac{P+T-R}{R-P}$ then $c_1(t) = c_2(t) = C$ for all $t \geq 0$. □

5 Computational Results in the PD with Fairness Norm à la Rawls

Theorem 2 shows that if both κ-values are smaller than the threshold for cooperativeness θ_{tc}, both players converge to mutual defection, whereas if both κ-values are greater than this threshold, both players converge to mutual cooperation. Note that this does not cover the whole space of tuples of κ-values, c.f. how do agents operate, if one value is smaller and the other value is greater that θ_{tc}? In these terms we are faced with the more general question: for which combination of κ-values do agents converge to mutual cooperation or to mutual defection under fictitious play?

To examine the convergence behavior of players under fictitious play for different κ-values, we conducted multiple computations of repeated interactions, for different game parameters and a large subset of the κ^2-space. We recorded the results and we managed to deduce the conditions determining the convergence behavior that pertain perfectly with the data. These conditions are as follows.

For all normative games with fairness norm à la Rawls $NG = (N, (S_i)_{i \in N}, U, I, \kappa)$ and history $H = ((\omega_{i,j})_{i,j \in N}, (c_i)_{i \in N})$ for NG that we computed such that $(N, (S_i)_{i \in N}, U)$ is the Prisoner's Dilemma, every agent in N learns according to fictitious play along H, is rational for all $t \geq 0$, and $\omega_{i,j}^0(s_j) = 0.5$ for all $i, j \in \{1, 2\}$ and for all $s_j \in \{C, D\}$, the following three conditions were satisfied:

1. if $(\kappa_1 - lim_{mx}) \times (\kappa_2 - lim_{mx}) < curv_{mx}$ then $\exists t' \in \mathbb{N} : c_1(t) = c_2(t) = D$ for all $t \geq t'$,
2. if $(\kappa_1 - lim_{mx}) \times (\kappa_2 - lim_{mx}) > curv_{mx}$ then $\exists t' \in \mathbb{N} : c_1(t) = c_2(t) = C$ for all $t \geq t'$,
3. if $(\kappa_1 - lim_{mx}) \times (\kappa_2 - lim_{mx}) = curv_{mx}$ then both players converge to a mixed strategy,

whereby:

$$curv_{mx} = \left(\frac{PT}{(R+P)(R-P)} \right)^2$$

$$lim_{mx} = \frac{P^2 + R(T-R)}{(R+P)(R-P)}$$

Note that the equation $(\kappa_1 - lim_{mx}) \times (\kappa_2 - lim_{mx}) = curv_{mx}$ defines a separating curve between the convergence to mutual cooperation and mutual defection: for at least one of both κ-values being less than given, the first condition holds and fictitious play converges to mutual defection, whereas for at least one of both κ-values being greater than given, the second condition holds and fictitious play converges to mutual cooperation. For each pair of κ-values that fulfills the equation, the third condition holds and fictitious play converges to a mixed strategy for each player. This curve can be defined as a function for the convergence to a mixed strategy f_{mx} over κ_1-values[3]:

$$f_{mx}(\kappa_1) = \frac{curv_{mx}}{\kappa_1 - lim_{mx}} + lim_{mx}$$

The function f_{mx} is depicted in Figure 3. A necessary condition of function f_{mx} to be correct is that it has an intersection point for $\kappa_1 = \kappa_2 = \theta_{tc}$, as proved in Theorem 3. An implication of function f_{mx} to be correct is the fact that the value lim_{mx} is the asymptote of the function f_{mx}, as proved in Theorem 4, and therefore determines a lower bound for κ-values that enable the convergence to mutual cooperation. Finally, note that the value $curv_{mx}$ determines the curvature of the function. Since lim_{mx} and $curv_{mx}$ both depend on the parameters of

---

[3] Note that the function forms an *anallagmatic* curve, c.f. it inverts into itself.

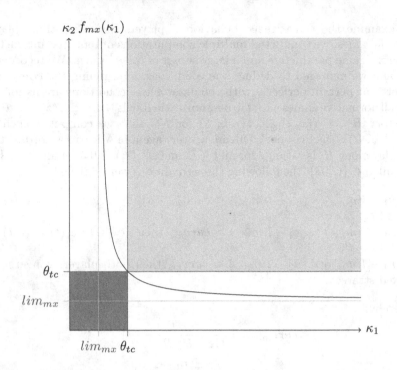

Fig. 3. The dark gray/light gray area shows in accordance with Theorem 2 that if both κ-values are smaller than the threshold for cooperativeness $\theta_{tc} = \frac{P+T-R}{R-P}$, both players behave according to mutual defection (dark gray area), whereas if both κ-values are greater than this threshold, both players behave according to mutual cooperation (light gray area). The curve represents the function for non-convergence f_{mx} and defines for which combination of κ-values players converge to mutual cooperation (right of/above the curve), converge to mutual defection (left of/below the curve) or converge to a combination of mixed strategies (points of the curve). Note that i) lim_{mx} is the asymptote of the function f_{mx}, thus it defines a lower bound for mutual cooperation, and ii) $\kappa_1 = \kappa_2 = \theta_{tc}$ is an intersection point of the curve.

the PD game, the asymptote and curvature of a function f_{mx} can strongly differ among different games. Figure 4 shows the different curves of function f_{mx} for different game parameters.

Theorem 3. $\kappa_1 = \kappa_2 = \theta_{tc}$ *is an intersection point of function* f_{mx}.

Proof. We are going to show that $f_{mx}(\theta_{tc}) = \theta_{tc}$:

$$f_{mx}(\theta_{tc}) = \frac{curv_{mx}}{\theta_{tc} - lim_{mx}} + lim_{mx}$$

$$= \frac{\left(\frac{PT}{(R+P)(R-P)}\right)^2}{\frac{P+T-R}{R-P} - \frac{P^2+R(T-R)}{(R+P)(R-P)}} + lim_{mx}$$

$$= \frac{\left(\frac{PT}{(R+P)(R-P)}\right)^2}{\frac{(R+P)(P+T-R)}{(R+P)(R-P)} - \frac{P^2+R(T-R)}{(R+P)(R-P)}} + lim_{mx}$$

$$= \frac{\left(\frac{PT}{(R+P)(R-P)}\right)^2}{\frac{(R+P)(P+T-R)-(P^2+R(T-R))}{(R+P)(R-P)}} + lim_{mx}$$

$$= \left(\frac{PT}{(R+P)(R-P)}\right)^2 \times \frac{(R+P)(R-P)}{(R+P)(P+T-R)-(P^2+R(T-R))} + lim_{mx}$$

$$= \left(\frac{PT}{(R+P)(R-P)}\right)^2 \times \frac{(R+P)(R-P)}{PT} + lim_{mx}$$

$$= \frac{PT}{(R+P)(R-P)} + lim_{mx}$$

$$= \frac{PT}{(R+P)(R-P)} + \frac{P^2+R(T-R)}{(R+P)(R-P)}$$

$$= \frac{PT+P^2+R(T-R)}{(R+P)(R-P)}$$

$$= \frac{PT+P^2+RT-R^2}{(R+P)(R-P)}$$

$$= \frac{(P+T-R)(R+P)}{(R+P)(R-P)}$$

$$= \frac{P+T-R}{R-P} = \theta_{tc}$$

$\square$

Theorem 4. lim_{mx} *is the asymptote of function* f_{mx}.

Proof. We are going to show that $\lim\limits_{\kappa \to +\infty} f_{mx}(\kappa) = lim_{mx}$:

$$\lim_{\kappa \to +\infty} f_{mx}(\kappa) = \lim_{\kappa \to +\infty} \left(\frac{curv_{mx}}{\kappa - lim_{mx}} + lim_{mx}\right)$$

$$= \lim_{\kappa \to +\infty} \left(\frac{curv_{mx}}{\kappa - lim_{mx}}\right) + lim_{mx}$$

$$= lim_{mx}$$

$\square$

6   Tournaments and Experimental Results

Let's assume we have a mixed population in terms of sensitivity to fairness norm κ. There might be individuals with high κ-values, with low κ-values or with no sensitivity to that norm at all. In such a setup it is reasonable to ask how beneficial fairness norm sensitivity might be. Is a low, middle or high sensitivity rather detrimental or profitable - especially in comparison with the outcome of the other individuals of the population?

To get a general idea of how beneficial a particular degree of sensitivity to the fairness norm might be, we tested the performance of agents with different κ-values in a tournament. Such a tournament was inspired by Axelrod's tournament of the repeated Prisoner's Dilemma [4]. In Axelrod's tournament a number of agents play the repeated Prisoner's Dilemma - pairwise each agent against every other agent - for a particular number of repetitions. Each agent

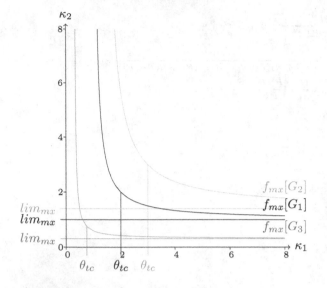

Fig. 4. Exemplary Prisoner's Dilemma games G_1 ($T = 3, R = 2, P = 1$), G_2 ($T = 4, R = 3, P = 2$) and G_3 ($T = 7, R = 6, P = 2$) and their corresponding values θ_{tc}, lim_{mx} and $curv_{mx}$ (right table). The graph shows the corresponding curves of the function f_{mx} for each game. Note that the value $curv_{mx}$ behaves anti-proportional to the curvature of the function.

updates her behavior according to a rule defined by its creator. The score of each encounter is recorded, and the agent with the highest average utility over all encounters wins the tournament.

In our tournament we also define a number of n agents $0, 1, 2, ..., n - 1$, where each agent plays against each other agent for a number of repetitions t_{max}. In distinction from Axelrod's tournament, all agents i) play the Prisoner's Dilemma as a normative game with fairness norm à la Rawls, and ii) have the same update rule: fictitious play. Although the agents have the same update rule, they differ in another crucial aspect: their sensitivity to the fairness norm. To keep things simple, we predefine that their sensitivity is i) bounded above by a value $\kappa_{max} \in \mathbb{R}_{>0}$, and ii) equally distributes among the n agents, just by ascribing sensitivity to the fairness norm $\kappa_i = \frac{i \times \kappa_{max}}{n-1}$ to agent i.[4] A tournament works as follows: for each pair of agents i, j we conducted a normative game with fairness norm à la Rawls based on the Prisoner's Dilemma for a number of t_{max} repetitions, whereby agents i and j learn according to fictitious play along their common history. For each agent i her average utility TU_i - called *tournament*

---

[4] Note that to ascribe a value of fairness norm sensitivity $\kappa = \frac{i \times \kappa_{max}}{n-1}$ to agent i ensures that agent 0 has a sensitivity to the fairness norm of 0, agent $n - 1$ has one of κ_{max}, and all other agents' sensitivity to the fairness norm are equally distributed between these boundaries.

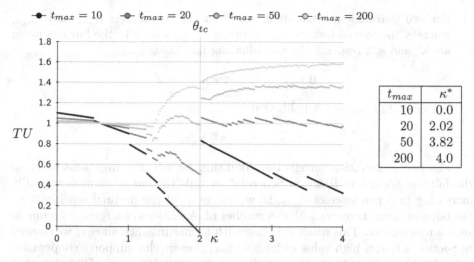

Fig. 5. The resulting tournament utilities of four different tournaments with 200 agents each, pairwise playing a normative game with fairness norm à la Rawls based on a Prisoners Dilemma game with $T = 3$, $R = 2$, $P = 1$ and $S = 0$. The right table shows for each t_{max} parameter the appropriate optimal sensitivity to the fairness norm κ^* of the tournament's winner.

utility - is computed, which is the average utility value an agent scored over all interactions.

For a given set of agents A that participate in such a tournament, the winner is the agent $i \in A$ who obtains the maximal tournament utility TU_i. We refer to the winner's κ_i value as the optimal fairness norm sensitivity κ^*, with respect to her tournament utility:

$$\kappa^* = \kappa_i \text{ with } i = \arg\max_{j \in A} TU_j$$

We computed 4 tournaments, each with 200 agents playing a normative game NG with fairness norm à la Rawls based on a Prisoner's Dilemma with $T = 3$, $R = 2$, $P = 1$ and $S = 0$. For such a game θ_{tc} is 2, and to ensure an equal portion of cooperative and non-cooperative agents, we set $\kappa_{max} = 2 \times \theta_{tc} = 4$. The tournaments differed in the parameter for t_{max}, here we chose the values 10, 20, 50 and 200. Figure 5 shows the performance of each agent in the appropriate tournament and the appended table shows the κ^* value of each tournament's winner.

The results of the tournaments indicate that the optimal sensitivity to the fairness norm is by any means dependent of t_{max} and θ_{tc}. To verify this indication we computed a great number of further tournaments with different t_{max} and κ_{max} values. The results support de facto - without any exception - the following two observations:

1. For two tournaments that differ solely in the parameters t_{max} and t'_{max}, whereby the tournaments' optimal values of sensitivity to the fairness norm are κ^* and κ'^*, respectively, the following fact holds:

$$\text{if } t_{max} > t'_{max} \text{ then } \kappa^* \geq \kappa'^*$$

2. For every tournament it holds that:

$$\kappa^* = 0 \text{ or } \kappa^* > \theta_{tc}$$

The first observation unveils one condition for which a high sensitivity to the fairness norm à la Rawls is beneficial. It tells us that κ^* is monotonically increasing in dependence of t_{max}, i.o.w. the value of the optimal sensitivity to the fairness norm increases with the number of repetitions of a repeated game in such a tournament. This result is in line with former insights, since i) we showed in Section 4 that a high value of fairness norm sensitivity supports cooperative behavior, and ii) we know from studies of repeated Prisoner's Dilemma that cooperative behavior is especially beneficial in combination with reputation [19], a virtue that needs repetition to be established.

The second observation says that it is optimal either to have no sensitivity to the fairness norm at all, or to have a sensitivity to the fairness norm that ensures *preliminary cooperativeness*[5]. Which of both cases holds depends inter alia on the number of repetitions t_{max}. By all means, it is never the case that $0 < \kappa^* \leq \theta_{tc}$. This stresses the fact that a great fairness norm sensitivity is only beneficial if it not only enables a line of mutual cooperation, but it also implies preliminary willingness to start it.

7   Conclusion and Perspectives

Our study presents a game-theoretic model of guilt in relation to sensitivity to the norm of fairness à la Rawls. We i) employed this model on the Prisoner's Dilemma, and ii) worked out the convergence behavior under fictitious play for any combination of the fairness norm sensitivity of both players. We found out that a particular threshold for cooperation θ_{tc} plays a crucial role: it defines for which combinations both agents cooperate of defect from the beginning, and for which combinations they might learn to cooperate or to defect. In a final experimental setup, we analyzed the performance of multiple agents with different values of sensitivity to the fairness norm involved in a tournament of repeated games. We revealed that i) a great sensitivity to the fairness norm is the more beneficial, the higher the number of repetitions of the repeated game is, and ii) the threshold for cooperation θ_{tc} defines a lower bound for a great sensitivity to the fairness norm to be beneficial at all.

---

[5] As we have shown in Theorem 2, if agents have a sensitivity to fairness $\kappa > \theta_{tc}$, their first move is to cooperate. This behavioral characteristic can be seen as preliminary cooperativeness.

A further observation - that was not elaborated here - was the fact that a great sensitivity to a fairness norm is the more beneficial in a population, the more other agents have a great sensitivity to that norm. This fact let us presume that fairness norm sensitivity i) is a reasonable value for explaining multiple cooperation in multi-player games like the public goods game, and ii) is a good candidate to be analyzed under stability aspects of population dynamics, e.g. as an *evolutionary stable strategy* [15], a standard concept in evolutionary game theory. Such analyses are currently in progress and will be part of subsequent studies. This line of future work will allow us to relate our analysis with existing naturalistic theories of fairness according to which sensitivity to fairness norm might be the product of evolution (see, *e.g.*, [6]).

References

1. Andrighetto, G., Villatoro, D., Conte, R.: Norm internalization in artificial societies. AI Communications **23**, 325–339 (2010)
2. Andrighetto, G., Villatoro, D., Conte, R.: The role of norm internalizers in mixed populations. In: Conte, R., Andrighetto, G., Campenni, M. (eds.) Minding Norms: Mechanisms and Dynamics of Social Order in Agent Societies, pp. 153–174. Oxford University Press, Oxford (2013)
3. Aronfreed, J.M.: Conduct and Conscience: The Socialization of Internalized Control Over Behavior. Academic Press, New York (1968)
4. Axelrod, R.: The Evolution of Cooperation. Basic books (1984)
5. Berger, U.: Fictitious play in 2xn games. Journal of Economic Theory **120**, 139–154 (2005)
6. Binmore, K.: Natural justice. Oxford University Press, New York (2005)
7. Brown, G.W.: Iterative solution of games by fictitious play. In: Koopmans, T.C. (ed.) Activity Analysis of Production and Allocation, pp. 374–376. John Wiley, New York (1951)
8. Fudenberg, D., Levine, D.K.: The Theory of Learning in Games. MIT Press, Cambridge (1998)
9. Gaudou, B., Lorini, E., Mayor, E.: Moral guilt: an agent-based model analysis. In: Kamiński, B., Koloch, G. (eds.) Advances in Social Simulation. AISC, vol. 229, pp. 95–106. Springer, Heidelberg (2014)
10. Gintis, H.: The hitchhiker's guide to altruism: Gene-culture co- evolution, and the internalization of norms. Journal of Theoretical Biology **220**(4), 407–418 (2003)
11. Gintis, H.: The genetic side of gene-culture coevolution: internalization of norms and prosocial emotions. Journal of Economic Behavior and Organization **53**, 57–67 (2004)
12. Haidt, J.: The moral emotions. In: Davidson, R.J., Scherer, K.R., Goldsmith, H. H. (eds.) Handbook of Affective Sciences, pp. 852–870. Oxford University Press (2003)
13. Harsanyi, J.: Cardinal welfare, individualistic ethics, and interpersonal comparisons of utility. Journal of Political Economy **63**, 309–321 (1955)
14. Loomes, G., Sugden, R.: Regret theory: An alternative theory of rational choice under uncertainty. Economic Journal **92**(4), 805–824 (1982)
15. Smith, J.M., Price, G.R.: The logic of animal conflict. Nature **246**, 15–18 (1973)
16. Mill, J.S.: Utilitarianism. Parker, Son & Bourn, West Strand (1863)

17. Miyazawa, K.: On the convergence of the learning process in a 2x2 non-zero-sum two-person game, vol. 3. Princeton University Econometric Research Program (1961)
18. Monderer, D., Shapley, L.S.: Fictitious play property for games with identical interests. Journal of Economic Theory **68**, 258–265 (1996)
19. Nowak, M., Sigmund, K.: Evolution of indirect reciprocity. Nature **437**, 1291–1298 (2005)
20. Rawls, J.: A Theory of Justice. Harvard University Press, Cambridge (1971)
21. Searle, J.: Rationality in Action. MIT Press, Cambridge (2001)
22. Vidal, J.M.: Learning in multiagent systems: an introduction from a game-theoretic perspective. In: Alonso, E., Kudenko, D., Kazakov, D. (eds.) Adaptive Agents and Multi-agent Systems, pp. 202–215. Springer-Verlag, Berlin (2003)

Using Preferences in Negotiations over Ontological Correspondences

Terry R. Payne$^{(\boxtimes)}$ and Valentina Tamma

Department of Computer Science, University of Liverpool, Liverpool L69 3BX, UK
{T.R.Payne,V.Tamma}@liverpool.ac.uk

Abstract. The alignment of disparate ontology is of fundamental importance to support opportunistic communication within open agent systems, and as such has become an established and active research area. Traditional alignment mechanisms typically exploit the lexical and structural resemblance between the entities (concepts, properties and individuals) found within the ontologies, and as such often require agents to make their ontology available to an oracle (either one of the agents themselves or a third party). However, these approaches are used irrespectively of whether they are suitable given the intended models underlying the ontologies and hence their overlap, and usually require the disclosure of the full ontological model. This prevents the agents from strategically disclosing only part of their ontological model on the grounds of privacy or confidentiality issues. In this paper we present a dialogue based mechanism that allows two agents with limited or no prior knowledge of the other's ontological model to determine whether it is possible to achieve some form of alignment between the two ontologies. We show how two agents, each possessing incomplete sets of private, heterogeneous (and typically ambiguous) correspondences, can derive an unambiguous alignment from a set of ambiguous, but mutually acceptable correspondences generated using an inquiry dialogue. The termination properties of the dialogue are formally proved, and the presentation and instantiation of an abstract preference-based argumentation is given. We demonstrate how ambiguity can be eliminated through the use of *undercuts* and *rebuttals*, given preference relations over the arguments.

1 Introduction

For an agent system to behave appropriately in uncertain or unknown environments it should have an internal representation, or world model, of what it perceives in the environment surrounding it. This representation is often internal to the agent, and defined within some logical theory (*ontology*) that is not always fully shared with other agents, even within complex collaborative models, although it models common assumptions regarding how pertinent information and knowledge is modelled, expressed and interpreted. When interoperation between heterogenous systems is required, often joint operations are preceded by an integration phase where the different knowledge models are reconciled and possible implicit assumptions are clarified. However, this lack of explicit shared

© Springer International Publishing Switzerland 2015
Q. Chen et al. (Eds.): PRIMA 2015, LNAI 9387, pp. 319–334, 2015.
DOI: 10.1007/978-3-319-25524-8_20

semantics can compromise more dynamic and opportunistic applications (e.g. e-commerce, open-data or mobile systems).

Knowledge integration has traditionally depended on the creation of *alignments* between pairs of ontologies, where an alignment consists of a set of *correspondences* between related entities. Many systems have been proposed that *align* pairs of ontologies to find these sets of correspondences, known as *alignments* [2]; however, most rely on the ontologies to be fully shared, and no single approach can provide a panacea for all ontology pairs. This raises the question *"what alignments or alignment mechanisms should be used by two agents to align their ontologies?"* The question is further exacerbated in those cases when neither agent may be prepared to disclose all of its ontology. The notion of privacy preserving information sharing has been advocated by a number of previous efforts [1,5,6,13], which include use-cases that require some form of privacy preservation in either the schema or data (or both); including monitoring healthcare crises, facilitating e-commerce, outsourcing, and end-to-end integration. More recently, the notion of preserving privacy when matching schemas and ontologies was proposed to facilitate interoperation between different parties when the possibility of sharing ontological knowledge is reduced [6,13].

The existence of alternate, pre-computed alignments has been exploited by several recent alignment negotiation approaches, which aggregate the constituent correspondences [7,11,12,16]. However, certain correspondences may be found frequently by different alignment approaches, whereas others could be spurious or erroneous, and only appear rarely, resulting in different levels of confidence or *weight*. Alignment systems may also map entities from one ontology to different entities in the other ontology, leading to *ambiguity*. Combining these would result in undesirable behaviour, such as incoherence and inconsistency within the ontologies, and thus render the alignment unusable. Furthermore, if we assume that agents can acquire such alignments through past experience, it follows that different agents will typically be aware only of a subset of the possible correspondences between two ontologies, and thus the knowledge of one agent can be very different to that of another. Hence, agents need to agree on what correspondences are the most relevant to resolve ambiguous combinations, whilst behaving rationally; i.e. only disclosing and proposing *viable* correspondences whilst minimising the total number of beliefs disclosed.

In [15], we formally defined a novel inquiry dialogue that allows agents to assert, counter, accept and reject correspondences shared by their peers. It assumed that the agents had acquired correspondences from past encounters, or from publicly available alignment systems, that were kept private, and that each agent associated some *weight* to each known correspondence. As this knowledge was *asymmetric* and *incomplete* (i.e. neither agent involved in the dialogue is aware of all of the correspondences, and their private weight for each correspondence could vary greatly), the agents engaged in an inquiry dialogue to: 1) ascertain the joint acceptability of each correspondence; and to 2) select an unambiguous set of correspondences which reduced the possibility of the resulting alignment being incoherent. In this paper we significantly extend this work with an argumentation framework that permits the agents to independently and deterministically resolve ambiguous cases (i.e. where several solutions could result from the combination of different correspondences) resulting from the dialogue. This framework instantiates the abstract argumentation system presented in [3,4,14] and determines consensus over the final alignment through the use of *undercuts* and *rebuttals*, given preference relations over the arguments. This paper characterises the properties of the dialogue in terms of the agents' mental attitudes and their effect on the dialogue termination.

This contribution complements the empirical analysis of the *Correspondence Inclusion Dialogue* in [15] which demonstrated that the approach finds viable solutions (typically 95% of the optimal solution found centrally with complete information), and that the precision of the final alignment increases by up to 40% (when compared to the average performance of using individual alignments in that dataset), whilst only slightly affecting recall.

The remainder of this paper is organised as follows: the *Correspondence Inclusion Dialogue* is first summarised in Section 2, followed by termination and complexity proofs for this dialogue in Section 3. A complete walkthrough based on that originally published in [15] is then provided to illustrate the dialogue (Section 4), and highlight the need for a mechanism for resolving ambiguity. The preference-based argumentation framework is then introduced, and its application to the selection of correspondences is presented and illustrated by means of examples in Section 5. The contribution of the paper is discussed in Section 6, and the paper then concludes in Section 7.

2 The Correspondence Inclusion Dialogue

In [15], the *Correspondence Inclusion Dialogue*(*CID*) was presented which enabled two agents to exchange knowledge about ontological correspondences resulting in an alignment that satisfies the following: 1) each agent is aware of a set of correspondences, each with an associated *weight*; 2) there should be no *ambiguity* with respect to either the source entities in the resulting alignment, or the target entities; 3) if there are alternative choices of correspondences, the selection is based on the combined, or *joint weight* of both agents; 4) that no correspondences should be selected where their joint weight is less than some defined *evidence-threshold*; and 5) the number of correspondences disclosed (i.e. whose weight is shared in the dialogue) should be *minimised*. The rationale behind this dialogue exploits the fact that whilst the agents involved seek to minimise the disclosure of their ontological knowledge, some exchange of ontological knowledge (at least the exchange of a subset of candidate correspondences) is necessary to determine a consensual set of correspondences that will form the final alignment. Thus, whilst the agents are assumed to be inherently self interested, there is also the assumption that the agents will collaborate to determine an alignment that can facilitate communication [10], as it is in the interest of all rational agents involved to be able to communicate successfully.

2.1   Ontologies, Correspondences and Beliefs

The agents negotiate over the viability of different correspondences that could be used to align the two agents' ontologies. The dialogue therefore assumes that each agent commits to an *ontology* $\mathcal{O}$, which is an explicit and formally defined vocabulary representing the agent's knowledge about the environment, and its background knowledge (domain knowledge, beliefs, tasks, etc.). $\mathcal{O}$ is modelled as a set of axioms describing classes and the relations existing between them[1] and Σ is the *ontology signature*; i.e. the set of class and property names used in $\mathcal{O}$. To avoid confusion, the sender's ontology is denoted $\mathcal{O}^x$, whereas the recipient's ontology is $\mathcal{O}^{\hat{x}}$. For agents to interoperate in an encounter, they need to determine an *alignment* $\mathcal{AL}$ between the two vocabulary fragments $\mathcal{O}^x$ and $\mathcal{O}^{\hat{x}}$ for that encounter. An alignment [9] consists of a set of *correspondences* that establish a logical relationship between the entities (classes, properties or roles, and instances) belonging to each of the two ontologies, and a set of logical relations[2]. The universe of all possible correspondences is denoted $\mathcal{C}$. The aim of the dialogue is to select an *unambiguous* set of viable correspondences, $\mathcal{AL} \subseteq \mathcal{C}$, which maps between the entities in $\mathcal{O}^x$ and $\mathcal{O}^{\hat{x}}$, and whose joint weight is at least as great as the admissibility threshold ϵ. The function $\mathsf{ent}(c)$ returns the set of entities e, e' for a correspondence c.

Definition 1. *A* **correspondence** *is a triple denoted* $c = \langle e, e', r \rangle$ *such that* $e \in \Sigma^x$, $e' \in \Sigma^{\hat{x}}$, $r \in \{=\}$.

Agents associate a private, static *weight*[3] κ_c to a correspondence c (where $0 \leq \kappa_c \leq 1$) that represents the confidence the agent has in the correctness of c. The tuple $\langle c, \kappa_c \rangle$ is a **belief** an agent holds on c. We refer to beliefs sent by x as ϕ, the beliefs sent by $\hat{x}$ (to x) as ψ, and the set of all beliefs is denoted $\mathcal{B}$. The function $\mathsf{corr} : \mathcal{B} \mapsto \mathcal{C}$ returns the correspondence c for some belief.

Each agent manages a private knowledge base, known as the *Alignment Store* (Δ), which manages the beliefs an agent has over its correspondences, and a public knowledge base, or *Joint Belief Store* (JB), which contains correspondences that have been shared. We distinguish between the sender's stores, Δ^x and JB^x, and the recipient's stores, $\Delta^{\hat{x}}$ and $JB^{\hat{x}}$, respectively. The sender's joint belief store JB^x ($JB^{\hat{x}}$ for the receiver) contains beliefs that are exchanged as part of the dialogue and hence contains beliefs sent and received by x (conversely $\hat{x}$). Throughout the dialogue, both agents will be aware of all of the beliefs shared[4]; i.e. $JB^x = JB^{\hat{x}}$.

Within the dialogue, the agents try to ascertain the *unambiguous* correspondences (i.e. where no entity appears more than once in the alignment) to include

---

[1] Here we restrict the ontology definition to classes and roles.

[2] We only consider *logical equivalence* (as opposed to *subsumption* ($\sqsubseteq$)), as it has the property that correspondences are symmetric; i.e. $\langle e, e', = \rangle$ is logically equivalent to $\langle e', e, = \rangle$, and thus can be easily used by either agent.

[3] Although no assumptions are made regarding how this value is determined, it could for example reflect the probability in the validity of the correspondence.

[4] For this reason, we will not distinguish between the two stores JB^x and $JB^{\hat{x}}$ in the remainder of this paper.

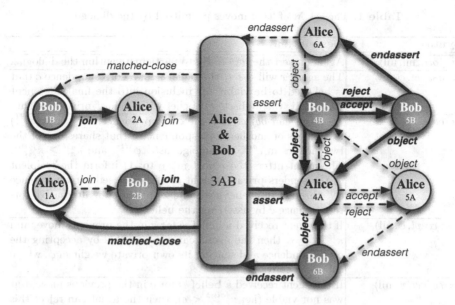

Fig. 1. The dialogue as a state diagram. Nodes indicate the agent whose turn it to utter a move. Moves uttered by Alice are labelled with a light font / dashed edge, whereas those uttered by Bob are labelled with a heavy font / solid edge.

in the final alignment $\mathcal{AL}$, such that the joint weight of the correspondences in $\mathcal{AL}$ are maximised, and greater than or equal to the *admissibility threshold*, ϵ. This is used to filter out correspondences with a low κ_c, whilst minimising the number of beliefs disclosed. The function joint : $\mathcal{C} \mapsto [0,1]$ returns the *joint weight* for some correspondence $c \in \mathcal{C}$. This results in either: 1) κ_c^{joint} for the average of both weights for both agents (if both weights have been disclosed); or 2) κ_c^{est} for a conservative, upper estimate if only one of the two weights is known, such that $\kappa_c^{est} \geq \kappa_c^{joint}$ [15].

Each agent takes it in turn to propose a belief regarding some correspondence, and the other participant confirms that the actual joint weight is not below threshold; i.e. $\kappa_c^{joint} \geq \epsilon$. If a correspondence c is ambiguous (i.e. an alternative, viable correspondence exists, which could be considered), then the agents can propose an alternative correspondence using the *object* move. As agents exchange beliefs, they determine the joint weight κ_c^{joint} for each correspondence c.

2.2 The Inquiry Dialogue Moves

The dialogue consists of a sequence of communicative acts, or *moves*, whereby agents take turns to assert the candidacy of some correspondence c (and its associated weight) for inclusion in a mutually acceptable alignment, $\mathcal{AL}$, and respond to such assertions by: 1) confirming the acceptability of c; 2) rejecting the acceptability of c; or 3) proposing alternate correspondences in the case of

Table 1. The set $\mathcal{M}$ of legal moves permitted by the dialogue.

Syntax	Description
$\langle x, join, \text{nil}, \text{nil} \rangle$	Agents assert the *join* move to participate within the dialogue.
$\langle x, assert, \phi, \text{nil} \rangle$	The agent x will *assert* the belief ϕ for a correspondence c that is believed to be viable for inclusion into the final alignment $\mathcal{AL}$, and is the undisclosed belief with highest private weight.
$\langle x, object, \phi, \phi^{att} \rangle$	An agent can *object* to some correspondence $c^{att} = \mathsf{corr}(\phi^{att})$ if it knows of another correspondence c that shares one of the two entities in c^{att}, i.e. $\mathsf{ambiguous}(\phi, \phi^{att})$, and $\kappa_c^{est} \geq \kappa_{c^{att}}^{joint}$. The agent utters the *object* move to: 1) inform the recipient of the senders private weight of the disclosed correspondence c^{att} through the belief ϕ^{att}; and 2) propose an alternative correspondence c by asserting the belief ϕ.
$\langle x, accept, \phi, \text{nil} \rangle$	If the agent received a belief ψ for c in the previous move, and $\kappa_c^{joint} \geq \epsilon$, then the agent can confirm this by accepting the correspondence and sharing its own private weight in ϕ, where $\mathsf{corr}(\phi) = \mathsf{corr}(\psi)$.
$\langle x, reject, \psi, \text{nil} \rangle$	If the agent received a belief ψ for c in the previous move, but was not viable (i.e. $\kappa_c^{joint} < \epsilon$), then the agent can reject this simply by returning the original belief ψ.
$\langle x, endassert, \text{nil}, \text{nil} \rangle$	If an agent has no more objections to make about the correspondences negotiated since the previous assert, it can then indicate this by uttering an *endassert* move. Once both agents have uttered this move sequentially, a new *assert* move can be uttered, or the dialogue can close.
$\langle x, close, \text{nil}, \text{nil} \rangle$	If an agent has no more correspondences that could be viable, but that have not been disclosed, then it utters a *close* move. However, the dialogue does not terminate until both agents utter a sequence of *close* moves (known as a *matched-close*).

ambiguity. Each agent discloses its private *belief* regarding c, and the agents goals are to rationally identify an unambiguous set of correspondences deemed viable by both agents, given an *admissibility threshold* ϵ. It assumes that only two agents (referred to as *Alice* and *Bob*) participate in the dialogue, and that each agent plays a role in each dialogue move, i.e. the agent is either a *sender* x or *recipient* $\hat{x}$.

The set of possible *moves* $\mathcal{M}$ permitted by the dialogue are summarised in Table 1. The syntax of each move at time s is of the form $m_s = \langle x, \tau, \phi, \phi^{att} \rangle$, where x represents the identity of the agent making the move; τ represents the move type; ϕ is a tuple that represents the belief that agent x has for a correspondence and the weight it associates to that correspondence; whereas ϕ^{att} represents a belief for some correspondence that the agent is countering. For some moves, it may not be necessary to specify one or either beliefs; in which case they will be empty or unspecified (represented as *nil*).

Agents take turns to utter *assert* moves (i.e. to transition from state 3AB in Figure 1). A sender x can also make multiple moves in certain circumstances, such as an *accept* or *reject* move (see states labelled 4A for *Alice* and 4B for *Bob* in Figure 1). This enables an agent to accept or reject a disclosed correspondence before making some other move (such as raising a *object* move), or signalling its intention to end a negotiation round (through an *endassert* move).

2.3 Alignment Ambiguities

Ambiguities occur when more than one correspondence maps several entities in the source ontology to a single entity in the target ontology (or vice versa). This can result in logical incoherence (i.e. generate unsatisfiable concepts). Objections can be made to an ambiguous belief, once it has been asserted. An ambiguity can be determined if there is some entity that exists in the correspondences of two beliefs.

Definition 2. *An* **ambiguity** *occurs given beliefs* ϕ, ϕ', $\phi \neq \phi'$ *(denoted* ambiguous(ϕ, ϕ')*) iff* ent(corr(ϕ)) $\cap$ ent(corr(ϕ')) $\neq \varnothing$.

In the remainder of this paper, we present proofs for the properties of the dialogue summarised above, and describe how the instantiation of a preference-based argumentation system is used to identify unambiguous alignments.

3 Dialogue Properties

The ontology inquiry dialogue allows agents to identify viable correspondences for inclusion in the final alignment, by determining arguments whose acceptability is negotiated on the grounds of joint weight.

In the dialogue, the strategy underlying the assertion and the acceptance of correspondences determine the agents' mental attitudes. We follow [14] in their classification and characterise the agents according to the stance taken when facing assertion and acceptance. Let j and k be two agents engaged in an ontology inquiry dialogue[5]. We redefine the *careful, cautious* and *credulous* attitudes within the context of this dialogue:

Definition 3.

- *An agent* j *is said to have a* careful assertion attitude *if it can assert any correspondence* $c \in \Delta^j$ *with weight* κ_c *if no stronger correspondence* c' *exists in the alignment store* Δ^j, *i.e* $\forall c' \in \Delta^j : \kappa_c \geq \kappa_{c'}$.
- *An agent* j *is said to have a* cautious acceptance attitude *if it can accept any correspondence* c *previously asserted by* k *with weight* κ_c *if no stronger correspondence* c' *exists in the alignment store* Δ^j.
- *An agent* j *is said to have a* credulous acceptance attitude *if it can accept any* admissible correspondence *previously asserted by* k, *i.e. a correspondence* c *with weight* κ_c *if* $\kappa_c \geq \epsilon$, *where* ϵ *is the admissibility threshold.*

---

[5] In this case j and k refer to the actual name of the agents rather than the role they play in the dialogue.

Given the formal definition of the moves for the ontology inquiry dialogue [15] summarised in Table 1 it can be derived that an agent always displays a *careful* assertion attitude, but it displays a *credulous* acceptance attitude when presented with the assertion of an admissible unambiguous correspondence. If the correspondence is ambiguous then it shows a *cautious* attitude.

These attitudes determine the whether the dialogue terminates and the number of moves necessary for termination.

Proposition 1. *The ontology inquiry dialogue with the set of moves* $\mathcal{M}$ *in Table 1 will always terminate.*

Proof. Both j and k have finite alignment stores Δ^j and Δ^k, as the set of possible correspondences $\mathcal{C}$ is finite. In the dialogue the agents can propose the inclusion of a correspondence in $\mathcal{AL}$ only once; when a correspondence is disclosed, it is added to the joint belief store JB and its inclusion in the final alignment is determined by the argumentation system.

The dialogue consists of a sequence of *interactions*, i.e. moves delimited by $assert - endassert$ that determines the candidacy of a correspondence c. When c is asserted, it is either accepted, or countered with an *object* move which, in turn, can be rejected. However, once a correspondence has been disclosed it can no longer be retracted. If the dialogue does not end before every possible correspondence is considered for inclusion, then it will end once the (finite) set of *assert* moves regarding the possible correspondences (i.e. $\subseteq (\Delta^j \cup \Delta^k)$ as we will only assert correspondences that are viable and grounded) have all been made once.

Whilst is proposition guarantees that the dialogue terminates, it does not offer much information regarding the length of the dialogue. The results of [14] show how the dialogue formalism and mental attitudes of the agents determine the precise bound.

Proposition 2. *An ontology inquiry dialogue between the agents j and k will terminate in $O(|\Delta^j \cup \Delta^k|)$ steps.*

Proof. Agents in the dialogue will assert *carefully* and will accept either *credulously* or *cautiously*, depending on whether the asserted correspondence is ambiguous. Hence, they will only assert a viable correspondence c that has the highest weight, and can only accept a proposition c that is viable and unambiguous. Likewise, ambiguous correspondences will be accepted only if they have the highest joint weight amongst the possible candidates. The ontology inquiry dialogue can thus be seen as a series of interactions between j and k, delimited by the $assert - endassert$ moves, each aiming to establish the candidacy of the correspondences. Hence the dialogue starts with one agent asserting c, to which the second agent will either respond with an *accept* move, with a *reject* or an *object* move. If c is either accepted or rejected, it will be followed by an *endassert* that terminates the current interaction, and a new interaction can be initiated. If the second agent believes more strongly in a correspondence c' that shares one

```
<terminated> Environment [Java Application] /System/Library/Java/JavaVirtualMachines/1.6.0.jdk/Contents/Home/bin/java (Oct 5, 2013, 8:39:16 PM)
 3  Alice -> Bob:ASSERT     <0.9, {http://l#b = http://h#z}>
 4  Bob -> Alice:OBJECT     <0.8, {http://l#b = http://h#x}> to <0.0, {http://l#b = http://h#z}>
 5  Alice -> Bob:OBJECT     <0.8, {http://l#a = http://h#x}> to <0.5, {http://l#b = http://h#x}>
 6  Bob -> Alice:ACCEPT     <0.6, {http://l#a = http://h#x}>
 7  Bob -> Alice:OBJECT     <0.4, {http://l#b = http://h#w}> to <0.0, {http://l#b = http://h#z}>
 8  Alice -> Bob:ACCEPT     <0.6, {http://l#b = http://h#w}>
 9  Bob -> Alice:OBJECT     <0.8, {http://l#b = http://h#x}> to <0.4, {http://l#b = http://h#w}>
10  Alice -> Bob:ACCEPT     <0.5, {http://l#b = http://h#x}>
11  Alice -> Bob:ENDASSERT
12  Bob -> Alice:ENDASSERT
13  Alice -> Bob:CLOSE
14  Bob -> Alice:CLOSE
```

Fig. 2. Messages exchanged between *Alice* and *Bob*.

of the entities mapped in c, then it answers to the assertion with an *object* move that proposes c', a correspondence not yet disclosed that has the highest weight. Now, the first agent can either accept this correspondence c', or reject it, or try to find a plausible alternative to object to it. This process will continue until the first agent receives a correspondence $\bar{c}$ that it can accept (either because it has an acceptable joint weight or because it cannot find any other correspondence to object to it). Analogously the second agent will only have the choice of accepting or rejecting $\bar{c}$ (as it has no other possible alternative).

The agents will take turns in iterating over these interactions until they have no more correspondences to propose for inclusion in $\mathcal{AL}$. This happens because both agents can only construct a finite number of moves as the number of correspondences to consider are finite and agents cannot propose a correspondence twice or retract it, and therefore the dialogue terminates. Each of the interactions can have a worst case length that is $O(|\Delta^j|)$ or $O(|\Delta^k|)$ depending on which agent made the *assert* move, and each proposition in Δ^j and Δ^k can only be asserted once, independently on how many interactions the agents go through during the dialogue hence there can be at most $O(|\Delta^j \cup \Delta^k|)$.

4 Inquiry Dialogue Example

We illustrate the dialogue by means of an example. Two agents, *Alice* and *Bob*, each possess a private ontological fragment, that provides the conceptualisation for the entities that they use to communicate. Each agent has acquired a subset of correspondences, and has associated a weight κ_c to each correspondence (Table 2), in the range $[0, 1]$. Not every correspondence is known to every agent; for example, *Alice* only knows about the correspondences $\langle b, z, = \rangle$, whereas she knows nothing about $\langle c, y, = \rangle$. The weight κ_c associated with each known correspondence c is also initially private. In Table 2 we summarise κ_c and joint(c) for each c for the two agents, and illustrate the correspondences between the entities in the two ontologies. We assume that both agents utilise a quality, or *evidence threshold* $\epsilon = 0.45$ to filter out correspondences with a low joint(c).

The example dialogue between *Alice* and *Bob* is presented in Figure 2. The turn order is non-deterministic; in this example, *Alice* makes the first *assert*.

Table 2. The private and joint *weights* for sample correspondences [15], and how they map between ontological entities. Propositions representing the candidacy of correspondence c is given by p.

p	c	κ_c^{Alice}	κ_c^{Bob}	κ_c^{joint}
i	$\langle a, x, = \rangle$	0.8	0.6	**0.7**
j	$\langle b, x, = \rangle$	0.5	0.8	**0.65**
k	$\langle b, w, = \rangle$	0.6	0.4	**0.5**
l	$\langle b, z, = \rangle$	0.9	—	**0.45**
m	$\langle c, y, = \rangle$	—	0.2	**0.1**

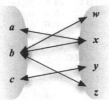

The two agents initiate the dialogue by both uttering the *join* move (omitted from Figure 2). Each exchange is shown, with its move identifier. As each belief disclosed states the agent's individual weight, values will differ depending on the sender. For example, *Bob* discloses $\kappa_{\langle b,x,=\rangle}^{Bob} = 0.8$ in move 4, whereas in *Alice's* response in move 5, she discloses $\kappa_{\langle b,x,=\rangle}^{Alice} = 0.5$. Each agent maintains an estimate of the other agents *upper bound*, which reflects the maximum weight an agent has in its undisclosed correspondences[6].

Move 3: *Alice* selects one of her undisclosed correspondences with the highest κ_c; in this case, $\langle b, z, = \rangle$. Initially, *Alice* assumes *Bob's* upper bound is 1, and estimates the upper bound estimate for correspondence c (denoted $joint_{est}(c)$) to be $\frac{1}{2}(0.9 + 1.0) = 0.95$. As this is above her ϵ, she asserts the tuple $\langle 0.9, \langle b, z, = \rangle \rangle$.

Move 4: As *Bob* was previously unaware of this correspondence, he calculates the actual $joint(\langle b, z, = \rangle)$ as $\frac{1}{2}(0.9 + 0.0) = 0.45$. Furthermore, *Bob* knows of an alternative correspondence $\langle b, x, = \rangle$ that shares the entity b with *Alice's* asserted correspondence. He knows, from *Alice's* previous assertion, that she will possess no correspondences with κ_c greater than 0.9 (as she would have asserted a belief with the highest κ_c), and therefore estimates an upper bound on $joint_{est}(\langle b, x, = \rangle)$ to be $\frac{1}{2}(0.9 + 0.8) = 0.85$. As this is greater than the actual value for $joint(\langle b, z, = \rangle) = 0.45$, he utters an *object* move, disclosing the alternative correspondence to *Alice's* correspondence, with his κ_c values for both.

Moves 5-6: *Alice* has a lower $\kappa_{\langle b,x,=\rangle} = 0.5$, and thus calculates $joint(\langle b, x, = \rangle) = \frac{1}{2}(0.5 + 0.8) = 0.65$. As $\langle a, x, = \rangle$ shares the entity x but has a higher $joint_{est}(\langle a, x, = \rangle) = \frac{1}{2}(0.8 + 1.0) = 0.9$, *Alice* utters her own objection. *Bob* computes the actual value $(joint(\langle a, x, = \rangle) = \frac{1}{2}(0.8 + 0.6) = 0.7)$; as he has no other correspondences that could object to *Alice's* objection, he accepts it.

To ensure that each agent takes turns in the negotiation, they *follow* an *accept* or *reject* move with another utterance.

Moves 7-8: *Bob* could now follow the acceptance by closing the negotiation or raising an alternative objection to one of the earlier proposed correspondences (including those he disclosed). One such alternative is the correspondence $\langle b, w, = \rangle$, which again has the entity b in common with *Alice's* original assertion. *Alice* accepts the candidacy of this correspondence.

---

[6] Note that the *upper bound* is not detailed here, but more information on how it is used within the dialogue can be found in [15].

Moves 9-10: At this point, *Bob* has no further correspondences that he wants to disclose. However, whilst checking for possible objections, he discovers that joint($\langle b, x, = \rangle$) $\geq$ joint($\langle b, w, = \rangle$), yet neither he or *Alice* had raised this objection. Despite the fact that both agents know the actual joint weights for both correspondences, he utters the objection to *Alice's* move. As this includes correspondences that have already been disclosed, *Alice* simply responds by accepting this objection (move 10).

Moves 11-14: *Alice* utters an *endassert*, signalling that she has no further objections to the correspondences exchanged so far. *Bob* also has no further objections, so also utters an *endassert*. At this point, as neither agent has any other correspondences to assert, they both issue a *close* utterance, and the dialogue ends.

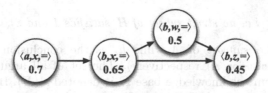

Fig. 3. The Final Attack Graph $\langle Ag, \triangleright \rangle$.

Each agent can now review the objections that were raised during the negotiation rounds, and from these, resolve their attack graphs (Figure 3). As attacks are resolved by finding the node with the highest value, attacks from $\langle a, x, = \rangle$ are resolved first. It attacks $\langle b, x, = \rangle$, which can no longer attack either $\langle b, w, = \rangle$ or $\langle b, z, = \rangle$. The next highest node is then considered (in this case $\langle b, w, = \rangle$), which attacks $\langle b, z, = \rangle$. Thus the only nodes remaining in the graph are $\langle a, x, = \rangle$ and $\langle b, w, = \rangle$, which are added to the final alignment.

5 Arguing about Correspondence Inclusion

The abstract argumentation system presented in [3,14] forms the basis of our approach to determine an alignment that resolves ambiguous correspondences, and is generated whilst minimising the number of correspondences disclosed. In [15], a heuristic approach for resolving ambiguous correspondences using an *attack graph* $\langle Ag, \triangleright \rangle$ was given, based on Dung's Abstract Argumentation Framework [8]; where $Ag \subseteq JB$ represented the set of viable but possibly ambiguous beliefs, and $\langle \phi, \phi' \rangle \in \triangleright$ represented the attack relations between beliefs (such that ϕ would attack ϕ', and vice versa). Attacks were resolved by comparing the joint weights of the beliefs in each attack relation. In this section, we replace this heuristic approach with a preference-based argumentation system that instantiates the general framework presented in [14] to support the selection of mutually acceptable alignments. In this instantiation, agents generate and resolve propositions that assert the viability of correspondences for inclusion in $\mathcal{AL}$.

In the argumentation system, the inclusion of a correspondence is modelled as a member of a possibly inconsistent knowledge base Σ with no deductive closure, which contains formulas of a propositional language $\mathcal{L}$. Each proposition p_c denotes the fact that the correspondence c is included in the final alignment $\mathcal{AL}$, whereas if $\neg p_c$ holds then c is not to be included in $\mathcal{AL}$. Under these conditions, an argument in favour of including a correspondence c in $\mathcal{AL}$ is defined as:

Definition 4. *An argument is a pair* $A = (H, h_c)$ *where* h_c *is a proposition of* $\mathcal{L}$ *representing the inclusion of some correspondence* c *in the alignment* $\mathcal{AL}$*, and* H *is a subset of* Σ *such that:*

1. *H is consistent;*
2. *$H \vdash h_c$; and*
3. *H is minimal (i.e. no strict subset of H satisfies 1 and 2).*

H is called the *support* of A while h_c is the conclusion of A (denoted support(A) and conclusion(A) respectively). The set of all arguments that can be constructed from the knowledge base Σ is denoted $\mathcal{A}(\Sigma)$. However, as Σ is inconsistent, arguments in $\mathcal{A}(\Sigma)$ will conflict, such that one argument can *rebut* or *undercut* another as follows:

Definition 5. *Let A_1 and A_2 be two arguments of $\mathcal{A}(\Sigma)$.*

- *A_1 rebuts A_2 iff $h_1 \equiv \neg h_2$ where $h_1 = $ conclusion(A_1) and $h_2 = $ conclusion(A_2).*
- *A_1 undercuts A_2 iff $h_1 = $ conclusion(A_1), and $\exists h_2 \in$ support(A_2) such that $h' \equiv \neg h$.*

An argument can *rebut* a second argument iff the conclusion of one is the negated conclusion of the other, whereas an argument is *undercut* iff there exists some conclusion from another argument that directly contradicts (i.e. negates) a proposition in the support of the first argument.

Example 1. Given the knowledge base $\Sigma = \{i, \neg i, j, i \leftrightarrow \neg j\}$ and three arguments: $a_1 = (\{j\}, j)$, $a_2 = (\{i, i \leftrightarrow \neg j\}, \neg j)$, and $a_3 = (\{\neg i\}, \neg i)$ then a_1 *rebuts* a_2, as the conclusion of $a_1 = j$ contradicts the conclusion of $a_2 = \neg j$; whereas a_3 *undercuts* a_2, as the conclusion of $a_3 = \neg i$ contradicts i in the support of a_2.

The knowledge base Σ is constructed by each agent throughout the dialogue, based on the beliefs added to JB. Each correspondence that is considered viable (resulting from an *accept* or *object* move) is represented in Σ by a proposition. Ambiguous pairs of correspondences (based on *object* moves) are modelled by propositional formulae that admit one, but not both correspondences. Thus, if we have two viable, ambiguous correspondences represented by the propositions p and q, we can say $p \leftrightarrow \neg q$ in support of one correspondence, and $q \leftrightarrow \neg p$ in support of the other. This results in inconsistency within Σ, which can be resolved through the use of a *rebut* or an *undercut*.

Example 2. If the correspondence $\langle c, y, = \rangle$ is accepted (Table 2), and its candidacy is represented by the proposition m, then $\{m\} \subseteq \Sigma$. If two new viable but ambiguous correspondences, $\langle b, w, = \rangle$ and $\langle b, z, = \rangle$ (represented by the propositions k and l respectively) appear in an *object* move, then $\{k, l, k \leftrightarrow \neg l, l \leftrightarrow \neg k\} \subseteq \Sigma$.

To capture the fact that some correspondences have a stronger joint weight than others, we assume that any set of propositions representing the candidacy of those correspondences has a preference order over it:

Definition 6. *CorrPref* $\subseteq \mathcal{C} \times \mathcal{C}$ *is a preference relation such that given two correspondences c and c', c is preferred to c' (CorrPref(c, c')) iff c is more strongly believed than c', i.e.* $\kappa_c^{joint} > \kappa_{c'}^{joint}$.

This results in a total preordering on the propositions in Σ. The preference relation needs to be *strict* to ensure that one argument can always defeat another (i.e. to resolve *symmetric* attacks). We also consider the inherent order in which a correspondence c is added to the Joint Belief Store JB. We say before(c, c') holds iff c is added to the JB before c', and preference over the set of propositions is defined as:

Definition 7. *Let $p_c, p_{c'}$ be propositions in Σ, where p_c $(p_{c'})$ states the inclusion of the correspondence c (c') in the final alignment $\mathcal{AL}$. The ordering p_c is preferred to $p_{c'}$ $(p_c \succcurlyeq p_{c'})$ is determined by:*

$$p_c \succcurlyeq p_{c'} = \begin{cases} CorrPref(c, c') & \text{if } \kappa_c^{joint} > \kappa_{c'}^{joint} \\ \text{before}(c, c') & \text{if } \kappa_c^{joint} = \kappa_{c'}^{joint} \end{cases}$$

The relation $p_c \succcurlyeq p_{c'}$ captures the fact that the two agents mutually prefer some correspondences over others, and this is reflected both in the joint weight and sequence in which beliefs are disclosed. This ordering induces a stratification of the knowledge base Σ into disjoint sets $\Sigma_1, \Sigma_2, \cdots, \Sigma_n$, such that the propositions stated in Σ_i are all equally preferred and are more preferred than those in Σ_j, where $j > i$. The preference level of a non-empty subset H of Σ, level(H), denotes the number of the highest numbered stratum that has a member in H.

Definition 8. *Let A_1 and A_2 be two arguments in $\mathcal{A}(\Sigma)$. A_1 is preferred to A_2 according to Pref iff* level(support(A_1)) $\geq$ level(support(A_2)).

Following [14], we denote by $\gg^{Pref}$ the strict preordering associated with *Pref*, and if *Pref*(A_1, A_2) we say that A_1 *is stronger than* A_2. These definitions permit us to define the instantiation of the argumentation system that we use to generate $\mathcal{AL}$. We first define: *Rebut* $\subseteq \mathcal{A}(\Sigma) \times \mathcal{A}(\Sigma)$ as the binary relation representing the defeat relation between arguments's conclusions; and *Undercut* $\subseteq \mathcal{A}(\Sigma) \times \mathcal{A}(\Sigma)$ as the binary relation representing the defeat relation between arguments. We can say:

Definition 9. *An argumentation system AS is a triple $\langle \mathcal{A}(\Sigma), \mathcal{R}, Pref \rangle$ such that:*

- $\mathcal{A}(\Sigma)$ *is the set of the arguments built from Σ;*
- $\mathcal{R}$ *represents all of the defeat relationships between arguments; i.e. $\mathcal{R} =$ Rebut $\cup$ Undercut; and*

- *Pref is the strict total preordering on $\mathcal{A}(\Sigma) \times \mathcal{A}(\Sigma)$.*

The preference order allows us to characterise the different types of relationships that can hold between arguments:

Definition 10. *Let A_1, A_2 be two arguments of $\mathcal{A}(\Sigma)$.*

- *If A_2 defeats A_1 then A_1 defends itself against A_2 iff $A_1 \gg^{Pref} A_2$. Otherwise, A_1 does not defend itself.*
- *A set of arguments S defends A iff: $\forall B$ defeats A and A does not defend itself against B, $\exists C \in S$ such that C defeats B and B does not defend itself against C.*

Based on [8], we can say $S \subseteq \mathcal{A}(\Sigma)$ is *conflict free* iff $\forall X, Y \in S, (X, Y) \notin \mathcal{R}$. The status of the arguments can then be evaluated as follows:

Definition 11. *Given AS, for any $X \in \mathcal{A}(\Sigma)$, X is acceptable with respect to some $S \subseteq \mathcal{A}(\Sigma)$ iff $\forall Y$ s.t. $(Y, X) \in \mathcal{R}$ implies $\exists Z \in S$ s.t. $(Z, Y) \in \mathcal{R}$. Let $S \subseteq A$ be conflict free. Then S is an admissible extension iff $X \in S$ implies X is acceptable w.r.t. S.*

- *S is an* admissible *extension iff $X \in S$ implies X is acceptable w.r.t. S;*
- *S is a* complete *extension iff $X \in S$ whenever X is acceptable w.r.t. S;*
- *S is a* preferred *extension iff it is a set inclusion maximal complete extension;*
- *S is the* grounded *extension iff it is the set inclusion minimal complete extension;*
- *S is a* stable *extension iff it is preferred and $\forall Y \notin S, \exists X \in S$ s.t. $(X, Y) \in \mathcal{R}$.*

The definitions for the *complete, preferred, grounded* and *stable* semantics are discussed further in [8]. However, we can say that X is *sceptically* (or *credulously*) justified under the *complete, preferred, grounded* or *stable* semantics if X belongs to all (respectively at least one) of these extensions.

Example 3. The agents, *Alice* and *Bob,* have acquired a subset of correspondences between their respective ontologies based on the dialogue described in Section 4, with the propositions p used to refer to the correspondences presented in Table 2. When the dialogue concludes, each agent generates its own stratified version of the knowledge base Σ, containing the following propositions:

$$\Sigma_{0.7} = \{i, i \leftrightarrow \neg j\}$$
$$\Sigma_{0.65} = \{j, j \leftrightarrow \neg i, j \leftrightarrow \neg k, j \leftrightarrow \neg l\}$$
$$\Sigma_{0.5} = \{k, k \leftrightarrow \neg j, k \leftrightarrow \neg l\}$$
$$\Sigma_{0.45} = \{l, l \leftrightarrow \neg j, l \leftrightarrow \neg k\}$$

The eight arguments in favour of (or arguing against) the viability of each correspondence can now be generated, which form the argumentation system AS, whereby the preference ordering is based on the levels of each stratum.

$$a_1 = (\{i, i \leftrightarrow \neg j\}, \neg j) \quad a_5 = (\{j, j \leftrightarrow \neg l\}, \neg l)$$
$$a_2 = (\{j, j \leftrightarrow \neg i\}, \neg i) \quad a_6 = (\{l, l \leftrightarrow \neg j\}, \neg j)$$
$$a_3 = (\{j, j \leftrightarrow \neg k\}, \neg k) \quad a_7 = (\{k, k \leftrightarrow \neg l\}, \neg l)$$
$$a_4 = (\{k, k \leftrightarrow \neg j\}, \neg j) \quad a_8 = (\{l, l \leftrightarrow \neg k\}, \neg k)$$

Given these arguments, we find that a_1 *undercuts* a_2, as $\neg j$ contradicts j, and a_1 is *preferred* to a_2 as $\mathsf{level}(\mathsf{support}(a_1)) \geq \mathsf{level}(\mathsf{support}(a_2)) = 0.7 \geq 0.65$. As there are no other attacks on a_1 (i.e. it defended itself), its conclusion $\neg j$ will *undercut* arguments a_3 and a_5, as its support is also preferred to that of a_3 and a_5. The arguments a_7 and a_8 are no longer attacked by a_3 and a_5. However, a_7 *undercuts* a_8 as $\neg l$ contraddicts $l \leftrightarrow \neg k$, and $0.5 \geq 0.45$. Finally, a_7 *undercuts* a_6, as the conclusion $\neg l$ contradicts l in the support of a_6, and $\mathsf{support}(a_7) \gg^{Pref} \mathsf{support}(a_6)$. The conclusions of the remaining arguments, a_1, a_4 and $a_7 = \neg j \wedge \neg l$, resulting in the alignment $\mathcal{AL} = \{\langle a, x, = \rangle, \langle b, w, = \rangle\}$.

6   Discussion

One difference between the approach presented here and the work presented by [14] is on the outcome of a dialogue. Proposition 5.6 in their paper proves that an inquiry dialogue can terminate unsuccessfully; however this is not the case here. In our dialogue, and given the agents mental attitudes, the agents will take turns to propose the inclusion of correspondences that have a high weight (for unknown correspondences the agents estimate the weights based on past exchanges). Hence the dialogue will generate the set of all the correspondences for which the agents agree that are viable candidates for inclusion in the final alignment $\mathcal{AL}$ that are then stored in each of the agent's joint belief stores.

The final alignment is determined by the argumentation process where each agent independently resolves the argumentation graph. The strict ordering over the propositions asserting correspondences and the undercut relation guarantee that the two argumentation graphs are deterministic and always reach the same conclusion, therefore ensuring that both agents converge to the same set of mutually believed correspondences, the final alignment. If such set of correspondences does not exist, the alignment generated will be the empty alignment. In our case, therefore, an alignment will always be computed as result, as long as the alignment stores of the agents are not empty. Then the question is whether the alignment constructed is optimal. In [15] we empirically show that in the majority of cases our mechanisms finds the optimal solution and when suboptimal solutions are found, they do not degrade the performance of the alignment.

7   Conclusions

This paper extends the work of [15] by providing further proofs over the properties of the *Correspondence Inclusion Dialogue*, and by instantiating and exploiting an existing abstract preference-based argumentation system. We defined the preference order based on the joint weight of each correspondence discussed using the inquiry dialogue, and demonstrated how the inclusion of a correspondence in the mutually acceptable final alignment could be modelled propositionally.

References

1. Agrawal, R., Evfimievski, A., Srikant, R.: Information sharing across private databases. In: Proceedings of the ACM SIGMOD 2003 International Conference on Management of Data, pp. 86–97. ACM (2003)
2. Aguirre, J.L., Eckert, K., Euzenat, J., Ferrara, A., van Hage, W.R., Hollink, L., Meilicke, C., Nikolov, A., Ritze, D., Scharffe, F., Shvaiko, P., Sváb-Zamazal, O., dos Santos, C.T., Jiménez-Ruiz, E., Grau, B.C., Zapilko, B.: Results of the ontology alignment evaluation initiative 2012. In: Shvaiko, P., Euzenat, J., Kementsietsidis, A., Mao, M., Noy, N.F., Stuckenschmidt, H. (eds.) CEUR Workshop Proceedings on OM, vol. 946. CEUR-WS.org (2012)
3. Amgoud, L., Cayrol, C.: On the acceptability of arguments in preference-based argumentation. In: Cooper, G.F., Moral, S. (eds.) UAI, pp. 1–7. Morgan Kaufmann (1998)
4. Amgoud, L., Vesic, S.: Rich preference-based argumentation frameworks. International Journal of Approximate Reasoning 55(2), 585–606 (2014)
5. Clifton, C., lu, M.K., Doan, A., Schadow, G., Vaidya, J., Elmagarmid, A., Suciu, D.: Privacy-preserving data integration and sharing. In: Proceedings of the 9th ACM SIGMOD Workshop on Research Issues in Data Mining and Knowledge Discovery, pp. 19–26. ACM (2004)
6. Cruz, I.F., Tamassia, R., Yao, D.: Privacy-preserving schema matching using mutual information. In: Data & Applications Security XXI, pp. 93–944602. Springer (2007)
7. Doran, P., Tamma, V., Payne, T.R., Palmisano, I.: Dynamic selection of ontological alignments: a space reduction mechanism. In: Proc. IJCAI, pp. 2028–2033 (2009)
8. Dung, P.: On the Acceptability of Arguments and its Fundamental Role in Nonmonotonic Reasoning, Logic Programming and n-person Games. Artificial Intelligence 77(2), 321–358 (1995)
9. Euzenat, J., Shvaiko, P.: Ontology Matching. Springer-Verlag (2007)
10. Grice, H.P.: Logic and conversation. In: Cole, P., Morgan, J.L. (eds.) Syntax and Semantics: Speech Acts, vol. 3, pp. 41–58. Academic Press, San Diego (1975)
11. Laera, L., Blacoe, I., Tamma, V., Payne, T., Euzenat, J., Bench-Capon, T.: Argumentation over ontology correspondences in MAS. In: Proceedings of AAMAS 2007, pp. 1285–1292 (2007)
12. Meilicke, C.: Alignment Incoherence in Ontology Matching. Ph.D. thesis, Dissertation, Universität Mannheim, Mannheim (2011)
13. Mitra, P., Liu, P., Pan, C.C.: Privacy-preserving ontology matching. In: AAAI Workshop on Context and Ontologies (2005)
14. Parsons, S., Wooldridge, M., Amgoud, L.: Properties and complexity of some formal inter-agent dialogues. J. Logic and Computation 13(3), 347–376 (2003)
15. Payne, T.R., Tamma, V.: Negotiating over ontological correspondences with asymmetric and incomplete knowledge. In: Proc. AAMAS 2014, pp. 517–524 (2014)
16. dos Santos, C.T., Quaresma, P., Vieira, R.: Conjunctive queries for ontology based agent communication in MAS. In: Proc. AAMAS 2008, pp. 829–836 (2008)

Designing a Source-Level Debugger
for Cognitive Agent Programs

Vincent J. Koeman[✉] and Koen V. Hindriks

Delft University of Technology, Delft, The Netherlands
v.j.koeman@tudelft.nl

Abstract. When an agent program exhibits unexpected behaviour, a developer needs to locate the fault by debugging the agent's source code. The process of fault localisation requires an understanding of how code relates to the observed agent behaviour. The main aim of this paper is to design a source-level debugger that supports single-step execution of a cognitive agent program. Cognitive agents execute a decision cycle in which they process events and derive a choice of action from their beliefs and goals. Current state-of-the-art debuggers for agent programs provide insight in how agent behaviour originates from this cycle but less so in how it relates to the program code. As relating source code to generated behaviour is an important part of the debugging task, arguably, a developer also needs to be able to suspend an agent program on code locations. We propose a design approach for single-step execution of agent programs that supports both code-based as well as cycle-based suspension of an agent program. This approach results in a concrete stepping diagram ready for implementation and is illustrated by an implementation of a source-level debugger for the GOAL agent programming language in the Eclipse development environment.

1 Introduction

Debugging is the process of detecting, locating, and correcting faults in a computer program [10]. A large part of the effort of a programmer consists of debugging a program. This makes efficient debugging an important factor for both productivity and program quality [26]. Typically, a defect is detected when a program exhibits unexpected behaviour. In order to locate the cause of such behaviour, it is essential to explain how and why it is generated [8].

A source-level debugger is a very useful and important tool for fault localization that supports the suspension and single-step execution of a program [19]. Single-step execution is based on breakpoints, i.e., points at which execution can be suspended [10]. Stepping through program code allows for a detailed inspection of the program state at a specific point in program execution and the evaluation of the effects of specific code sections.

Debuggers typically are source-level debuggers. However, most debuggers available for agent programs do not provide support for suspending at a particular location in the source code. Instead, these debuggers provide support

© Springer International Publishing Switzerland 2015
Q. Chen et al. (Eds.): PRIMA 2015, LNAI 9387, pp. 335–350, 2015.
DOI: 10.1007/978-3-319-25524-8_21

for suspension at specific points in the reasoning or decision cycle of an agent. The problem is that these points are hard to relate to the agent program code. In addition, these debuggers only show the current state, but do not show the current point in the code where execution will continue. It thus is hard for a programmer to understand how code relates to effects on agent behaviour. Although the role of an agent's decision cycle in the generation of an agent's behaviour is very important, we believe that source-level debugging is also very useful for agent-oriented programming.

In this paper, we propose a design of a source-level debugger for agent programming. Arguably, such a tool provides an agent programmer with a better understanding of the relation between an agent's program code and its behaviour. Part of the contribution of this paper is to propose a design approach that is applicable to programming languages for cognitive agents.

The paper is organised as follows. In Section 2, we discuss related work on (agent program) debugging. We also discuss the features of a few agent programming languages in some detail, as these are important for the design of a debugger for such languages. In addition, we discuss their current debugging tools. Section 3 presents the design of a source-level debugger for agent programs. We identify design principles and requirements that we use in our design, and features that a source-level debugger for agent programs should have. A concrete design is provided for the GOAL agent programming language [7] and some initial results about the use of this debugger are discussed. Section 4 concludes the paper with recommendations for future work.

2   Issues in Debugging Cognitive Agent Programs

In this section, we briefly discuss what is involved in debugging a software system, and analyse the challenges that a developer of cognitive agent programs faces.

2.1   Debugging and Program Comprehension

[11] provides a model of debugging derived from a general, somewhat oversimplified model of troubleshooting that consists of four debugging subtasks: (i) program comprehension, (ii) testing, (iii) locating the error, and (iv) repairing the error. Program comprehension, the first subtask in the model, is an important subtask in the debugging process as a programmer needs to figure out why a defect occurs before it can be fixed [13,14]. [6] argues that the main aim of program comprehension during debugging is to understand which changes will fix the defect. Based on interviews with developers, [16] concludes that the debugging process is a process of iterative *hypothesis refinement* (cf. [24]). Gathering information to comprehend source code is an important part in the process of hypothesis generation. [15] also emphasizes the information gathering aspect in program comprehension and the importance of *navigating source code*, which they report is by far the most used information source during debugging (cf. [19]). Similarly, [5] suggests to provide a variety of navigation tools at different

levels of granularity. In addition, *reproducing the defect* and *inspecting the system state* are essential for fault diagnosis and for identifying the root cause and a potential fix. It is common in debugging to try to replicate the failure [15,16]. In this process, the expected output of a program needs to be compared with its actual output, for which knowledge of the program's execution and design is required. *Testing* is not only important for reproducing the defect and for identifying relevant parts of code that are involved, but also for verifying that a fix actually corrects the defect [24].

[5] identifies that it is difficult to locate a fault because a fault and the symptoms of a defect are often far removed from each other (*cause/effect chasm*). As debugging is difficult, tools are important because they provide insight into the behaviour of a system, enabling a developer to form a mental model of a program [16,24] and facilitating navigation of a program's source code (at runtime) [15]. A source-level debugger is a tool that is typically used for controlling execution, setting breakpoints, and manipulating a runtime state. The ability to set breakpoints, i.e., points at which program execution can be suspended [10], by means of a source-level debugger is one of the most useful dynamic debugging tools available and is in particular useful for locating faults [19,24].

2.2 Challenges in Designing a Source-Level Debugger

Even though much of the mainstream work on debugging can be reused, the agent-oriented programming paradigm is based on a set of abstractions and concepts that are different from other paradigms [9,21]. The agent-oriented paradigm is based on a notion of a *cognitive agent* that maintains a *mental state* and derives its choice of action from its *beliefs* and *goals* which are part of this state. In a sense, agent-oriented programming is programming with mental states.

Compared to other programming paradigms, agent-oriented programming introduces several challenges that complicate the design of a source-level debugger (cf. [14]). For example, many languages for programming cognitive agents are **rule-based** [1,20]. In rule-based systems, fault localization is complicated by the fact that errors can appear in seemingly unrelated parts of a rule base [25]. Moreover, a rule base does not define an order of execution. Due to this absence of an execution order, agent debugging has to be based on the specific evaluation strategy that is employed. Moreover, cognitive agent programs repeatedly execute a **decision cycle** which not only *controls the choice of action* of an agent (e.g., which plans are selected or which rules are applied) but also specifies how and when particular *updates of an agent's state* are performed (e.g., how and when percepts and messages are processed, or how and when goals are updated). This style of execution is quite different from other programming paradigms, as a decision cycle imposes a control flow upon an agent program, and may introduce updates of an agent's state that are executed independently of the program code at fixed places in the cycle or when a state changes due to executing instructions in the agent program. This raises the question of *how to integrate these updates into a single-step debugger*.

An agent's decision cycle provides a set of points that the execution can be suspended at, i.e. *breakpoints*. These points do not necessarily have a corresponding code location. For example, receiving a message from another agent is an important state change that is not present in an agent's source, i.e., there is no code in the agent program that makes it check for new messages. Thus, two types of breakpoints can be defined: *code-based* breakpoints and (decision) *cycle-based* breakpoints. Code-based breakpoints have a clear location in an agent program. Cycle-based breakpoints, in contrast, do not always need to have a corresponding code location. Together, these are referred to as the set of *pre-defined* breakpoints that a single-step debugger offers. When single-stepping through a program, these points are traversed. A user should also be able to mark specific locations in an agent's source at which execution will always be suspended, even when not explicitly stepping. To facilitate this, a debugger has to identify such a marker (e.g., a line number) with a code-based breakpoint. These markers are referred to as *user-defined* breakpoints. A user should also be able to suspend execution upon specific decision cycle events, especially when those do not have a corresponding location in the source. This can for example be indicated by a toggle in the debugger's settings. Such an indication is referred to as a *user-selectable* breakpoint.

2.3   Languages and Debugging Tools for Cognitive Agents

In this section, we will briefly discuss specific debugging tools as illustrations of state-of-the-art debugging of cognitive agent programs. Moreover, we discuss the main language features and the decision cycle of such an agent program, which is most important in defining the semantics of a language. By understanding the building blocks of a specific agent programming language, we can identify the specific challenges that we will face in designing a source-level debugger for such a language. Due to space constraints, we focus on two different languages that are representative for both rule-based and Java-based agent programming languages respectively: Jason [2] and Jadex [17]. In addition, being the target of our implementation, we also discuss the GOAL language [7], which is also rule-based. We have looked at the debugging tools that are currently available for several other AOP languages like 2APL, Agent Factory, Jack, Jadex, and JIAC [1,20] as well, from which we could confirm that source-level debugging is not employed by any of them. Debugging is performed in a separate runtime application that is able to step through a decision cycle in parts or as a whole. When debugging or running an agent program, its source is not shown, and no indication of the currently executed line of code is given.

For the selected platforms, we describe the *basic language elements and abstractions* available for programming cognitive agents, whether any *embedded languages* are used, e.g., for knowledge representation, and the *decision cycle* that specifies how an agent program is executed. We also summarize the *functionality of the debugging tools* that are available. The latest Eclipse plug-in has been used as a starting point for the description of each programming language, as the published papers about these languages often differ from the current implementations because the languages are continuously developed.

Jason is a multi-agent programming language based on an extended version of AgentSpeak [2]. A dedicated *rule-based language* is used for the formalization of agent concepts. This language does not make use of any explicit *embedded language*, but a variant of Prolog is used that supports annotations to for example record the source of a belief. An agent is defined by a set of beliefs and a set of plans. A Jason agent is a reactive planning system: events trigger plans. A plan has a head that consists of a trigger event and a conjunction of belief literals representing a context. A plan also has a body, which is a sequence of basic actions or (sub)goals the agent has to achieve (or test) when the plan is triggered. A stack of (partially initiated) plans is called an intention. An intention indicates a course of action to handle a certain event. If a certain action in a plan fails or there is no applicable plan for a (sub)goal in the plan being executed, the whole failed plan is removed from the intention, and an internal event associated with that same intention is generated, allowing a programmer to specify how a particular failure is handled. If no such plan is available, the whole intention is discarded.

Decision Cycle. At the start of the decision cycle of a Jason agent, the list of current events is updated, and a single event is selected for processing. For this event, a set of applicable plans is determined, from which a single applicable plan has to be chosen: the intended means for handling the event. Plans for internal events are pushed to the current intention, whilst plans for external events create a new intention. Finally, a single intention has to be selected to be executed in the cycle. When all formulae in the body of a plan have been executed (removed), the whole plan is removed from the intention, and so is the achievement goal that generated it (if applicable). To handle the situation in which there is no applicable plan for a relevant event, a configuration option is provided to either discard such events or insert them back at the end of the event queue.

Debugging Tools. Jason provides a separate runtime that includes a debugger. This debugger can show the current and previous mental states of an agent, though a user cannot edit a mental state. It is possible to execute one or more (complete) decision cycles in a stepwise fashion, in which the agents can use different execution modes. In the default asynchronous mode, an agent goes to its next decision cycle as soon as it has finished its current cycle. In the synchronous mode, all agents execute one decision cycle at every "global execution step". There is no easy access to program code while stepping or for relating state changes to code executed, although there is a general console that displays log messages, accompanied by several customizable logging mechanisms that can be used by an agent. A plan can be annotated with a 'breakpoint' property which indicates that execution should be suspended when any of the agents start executing an intention with an instance of that plan. There are no other points like the evaluation of a plan's head or any cycle-based events at which this can be done.

Jadex is a language for programming intelligent software agents [17]. In its latest version (BDI V3), Jadex uses annotated Java code to designate agent concepts; there are no *rule-based* elements or *embedded languages*. Beliefs are represented in an object-oriented fashion, and operations against a beliefbase can be issued in a descriptive set-oriented query language. Goals are represented as explicit objects contained in a goalbase that is accessible to the reasoning component as well as to plans. An agent can have goals that are not currently associated with a plan. Four types of goals are supported: perform (an action), achieve (a world state), query (information about the world), and maintain. A plan is a function with an annotation that specifies the circumstances under which a plan may be selected. The function's body provides a predefined course of action. In addition, a context condition can be stated that must be true for the plan to continue executing. Capabilities represent a grouping mechanism for the elements of an agent, allowing closely related elements to be put together into a reusable (scoped) module which encapsulates certain functionality.

Decision Cycle. A Jadex agent has no explicit decision cycle, but, similar to Jack [23], when an agent receives an event, the reasoning engine builds up a list of applicable plans for an event or goal from which candidate(s) are selected and instantiated for execution. Jadex provides settings to influence the event processing individually for event types and instances, though as a default, messages are posted to a single plan, whilst for goals many plans can be executed sequentially until the goal is reached or finally fails (when no more plans are applicable). Selected plans are placed in the ready list, from which a scheduler will execute plans in a step-by-step fashion until a 'waitFor' method is called (i.e., waiting for the completion of an action or a specific event) or the plan significantly affects the internal state of the agent (i.e., by creating or dropping a goal). After a plan waits or is interrupted, the state of the agent can be properly updated, facilitating another plan to be scheduled after a certain goal has been created for example.

Debugging Tools. A BDI V3 agent can be debugged by stepping an agent through each plan step (as described above) whilst inspecting its mental state in a separate runtime. A user cannot modify the mental state at runtime, and no code location is indicated whilst debugging. No user-defined or user-selected breakpoint mechanism is available either. The Jadex developers suggest the standard Java debugger can be used as well. However, the Java debugger does not operate at the level of abstraction of a cognitive agent, which makes it more difficult for a user to relate program code to agent behaviour. For example, the annotations on functions create an execution flow that is not based on function calls (like regular Java), and will thus create jumps in the execution flow that can be unclear for a user when not visualized properly.

GOAL is an agent programming language that uses a dedicated *rule-based language* for the formalization of agent concepts [7]. GOAL is designed to allow for any *embedded knowledge-representation (KR) language* to be used, although currently only SWI-Prolog is supported. A mental state consists of a belief base, a goal base, a percept base, and a mailbox. Declarative goals specify the state of the environment that an agent wants to establish and are used to derive an agent's choice of action. Agents commit blindly to their goals, i.e., they drop (achieve) goals only when they have been completely achieved. Agents may focus their attention on a subset of their goals by using modules. A module can be viewed as an abstract action that groups a set of decision making rules.

Decision Cycle. The decision cycle of a GOAL agent starts with the processing of percept rules, allowing an agent to update its mental state according to the current perception of the environment. Next, using this updated mental state, an action is selected for execution by processing the rules that are present in the currently executed module. If the precondition of a selected action holds, its postcondition will be used to update the agent's mental state, after which a new cycle starts. Multiple actions can be executed at once by using an 'action-combo', i.e., a combination of actions. A mental state update can lead to the accomplishment of a goal, i.e., when a belief is inserted that matches a goal, that goal is automatically deleted. In addition, the currently executed module can change when it is exited, either by an exit-condition or an explicit command, or when a new module is called. An exit-condition allows the termination of a module when there are no more active goals or when no applicable action can be determined (anymore). A call to a module will push that module on the agent's module stack so that when it is exited again, execution of the module that made the call to the exited module will resume at that point.

Debugging Tools. The previous debugger for GOAL offers similar features to the debugger of 2APL [4], i.e., facilitating the inspection of the mental state of a single agent in a separate runtime and allowing specific steps of a decision cycle to be executed in a stepwise fashion. Examples of such steps are the entry of a module, rule condition evaluation, and action execution. This process of suspending on specific cycle-based breakpoints can be controlled by a user through a list of toggles. In addition, there is a user-defined breakpoint mechanism that suspends execution when a specific line of code is executed. Although no code location is indicated whilst debugging, this mechanism does operate at the source-level. Various tabs of logging output can be used to discern an agent's execution trace. Finally, actions to alter the mental state of an agent can be executed, and the mental state can be queried as well.

3   Design Approach for a Debugger for Cognitive Agents

In this section, we propose a design approach for a source-level agent debugging tool that is aimed at providing a better insight into the relationship between program code and the resulting behaviour. A number of principles and requirements will be introduced to guide the design of a stepping diagram.

3.1 Principles and Requirements

We will list some important principles and requirements for a source-level debugger that will be taken into account when designing such a debugger in the next section. As our main objective is to allow an agent developer to detect faults through understanding the behaviour of an agent, an important principle is **usability**. More specifically, [19] indicates that a programmer should be able to focus on the declarative semantics of a program, e.g. its rules, checking whether a rule is applicable, how it interacts with other rules, and what role the different parts of a rule play [25]. This is related to [5], which indicates that a debugger should employ a traversal method for resolving large cause/effect chasms, but without the need to go through indirect steps, intermediate subgoals, or unrelated lines of reasoning. Side-effects pose an additional challenge, as they might be part of a cause/effect chain, but cannot always be easily related to locations in the code. Therefore, **transparency** is an important principle that can be supported by providing a one-to-one mapping between what the user sees and what the interpreter is doing whilst explicitly showing any side effects that occur [18]. A debugger should also strive for temporal, spatial, and semantic **immediacy** [22]. Temporal immediacy means that there should be as little delay as possible between an effect and the observation of related events. Spatial immediacy means that the physical distance (on the screen) between causally related events should be minimal. Semantic immediacy means that the conceptual distance between semantically related pieces of information should be kept to a minimum. As source-level debuggers aim to correlate code with observed effects, immediacy is an important motivation for the use of such a debugger.

Breakpoints are an essential ingredient of single-step execution. Their main purpose is to facilitate navigating the code and run (generated states) of a program. As discussed in Section 2, a debugger for cognitive agent programming languages can define two types of breakpoints: code-based and cycle-based. We propose that for a source-level debugger, **code-based breakpoints should be preferred** over cycle-based breakpoints when they serve similar navigational purposes. In other words, when breakpoints show the same state, the code-based breakpoint should be used as a starting point, as it is important to highlight the code to increase a user's understanding of the effects of the program. A good example illustrating this point is the reception of percepts in the decision cycle of a GOAL agent. As percepts are processed in the event module, the entry of this module is a code-based breakpoint that can be identified with the processing of percepts, i.e., the received percepts can be displayed when entering the event module. This reduces the amount of steps that are required and improves the understanding of the purpose of the event module as well.

In addition, [3] indicates that a user should be able to **control the granularity** of the debugging process. In other words, a user should be able to navigate the code in such a way that a specific fault can be investigated conveniently.

For example, a user should be able to skip parts of an agent program that are (seemingly) unrelated to the fault, and examine (seemingly) related parts in more detail. The common way to support this is to define three different step actions: step into, step over, and step out. The stepping flow to follow after each of these actions will have to be defined in order to provide a user with the different levels of granularity that are required.

[8] and [19] indicate that at any breakpoint, a detailed **inspection of an agent's mental state** should be facilitated. The information about an agent's state should be visualized and customizable in multiple ways to support the different kinds of searching techniques that users employ. In addition, the work of [5] indicates that support for **evaluable mental state expressions** should be provided. This will aid a user by supporting, for example, posing queries about specific rule parts to identify which part fails. [19] indicates that modifying the program's state and continuing with a new state should be supported as well. Thus, we propose that support for the **modification of a mental state** should be provided. A user could for example be allowed to execute actions in a similar fashion to posing queries in order to perform operations on an agent's state.

3.2   Designing a Stepping Diagram

We propose a design approach for a source-level debugger for cognitive agent programs as a set of steps. First, possible code-based breakpoints will be defined by using the programming language's syntax (Step 1). The relevance of these code-based breakpoints to a user's stepping process needs to be evaluated, leading to a set of points at which events that are important to an agent's behaviour take place (Step 2a). In addition, the agent's decision cycle needs to be evaluated for important events that are not represented in the agent's source in order to determine cycle-based breakpoints (Step 2b). These points will then be used to define a stepping flow, i.e., identifying the result of a stepping action on each of those points in a stepping diagram (Step 3). Finally, other required features such as user-defined breakpoints (Step 4), visualization of the execution flow (Step 5) and state inspection (Step 6) need to be handled. As an example, we will provide a detailed design for the GOAL agent programming language, and briefly discuss the potential design of a source-level debugger for some other agent programming languages that were discussed in Section 2 as well.

Step 1: Syntax Tree. Inspired by [24], we propose that an agent's syntax tree can be used as the starting point for defining the single-step execution of an agent program. Figure 1 (top part) illustrates an already slightly modified syntax tree for a GOAL agent (see Section 2). Note that each node represents a specific type, but not an instance. For example, one module usually consists of multiple rules, as indicated by the labels on the edges. To slightly simplify this tree, we have abstracted away the program level of a module and identify a module with a set of rules. KR-specifics and syntactic sugar like nested rules have been left out as well. An edge indicates a syntactic link, whilst a broken edge indicates a semantic link.

Relevant semantic links need to be added in order to represent program execution flow that is not based on the syntax structure alone.

Step 2a: Code-Based Breakpoints. The idea is that each node in a syntax tree can be a possible code-based breakpoint ('step event'). However, as the actual source of some nodes is fully represented by their children, these non-terminal nodes can be left out of the stepping process. Moreover, some nodes might not be relevant to a user in order to understand an agent's behaviour. Here, we define a node that is relevant to agent behaviour as a point at which (i) an agent's mental state is inspected or modified, or (ii) a module is called and entered.

State inspections allow a user to identify mismatches between the expected and the actual result of such an inspection. In other words, if a user expects a condition to fail, he should be able to confirm this (and the other way around). Changes to a (mental) state are important to the exhibited behaviour of an agent and it should always be possible to inspect it, as should module calls or entries as they are important to the execution flow of an agent. In Figure 1, the breakpoints thus identified have been indicated at the corresponding syntax node.

Step 2b: Cycle-Based Breakpoints. There are points at which important behaviour occurs that a user would want to suspend the execution upon that are not present in an agent's syntax tree. For example, achieving a goal involves an important mental state inspection (looking for a corresponding belief) and modification (removing the goal) that are not represented in an agent program's source. Points like these that have no fixed correspondence in the code we call cycle-based breakpoints. To include such a breakpoint, a toggle (setting) can be added that provides a similar mechanism to user-defined breakpoints by always suspending the execution upon such an event. The need for these cycle-based breakpoints and additional explanations highlight an important challenge specific to agent-oriented programming. This results in the fact that we cannot 'simply' construct a source-level debugger by using an agent's source code only. Thus, a combination of both the syntax and the semantics of an agent is required to account for all possible changes of an agent's behaviour.

Step 3: Stepping Flow. Next, for each identified breakpoint, we need to determine the result of a stepping action, i.e., the flow of stepping. Based on the syntax tree, the stepping actions can be defined as follows:

- **Into:** traverse downward from the current node in the syntax diagram until we hit the next breakpoint. In other words, follow the edges going down in the tree's levels until an indicated node is reached. If the current node is a leaf (i.e., we cannot go down any further), perform an over-step.
- **Over:** traverse to the next node (i.e., to the right) on the current level until we hit the next breakpoint. If there are none, perform an out-step.

– **Out:** traverse upward from the current node until we hit the next breakpoint, whilst remaining in the current context. In other words, the edges going back up in the tree's levels should be traced until any applicable node, and then from there back down again until any indicated node is reached (like an into-step). Here, applicable refers to a 'one-to-many' edge of which not all cases have been processed yet.

On the bottom part of Figure 1, the flow for the step into and step over actions on each breakpoint has been illustrated. For readability, the step out action has been left out. Note that the broken edge indicates a link to the event module. This special module is executed after each action that has been performed in order to process any new percepts or messages that have been received by the agent. After the event module has been processed, depending on the rule evaluation order, either the first rule in the module or the rule after the performed action will be evaluated. In addition, a module's exit conditions might have been fulfilled at this point as well, which means that the flow may return to the action combo in which the call to the exited module was made.

The extensive definition of an out-step is needed because, for example, when stepping out of a user-defined action, purely following the edges until the previous (upper) breakpoint would result in reaching the module node, whilst we actually want to step to the next rule. Following this reasoning, the same result would be obtained even when doing a step-into from the post-condition node. Therefore, when traversing upward, we consider all nodes. In the mentioned example, both the action combo and the rule nodes have been processed completely already, so we will reach the module node. If the module contains any more rules, this node will be still be applicable, and thus we traverse downward until the first indicated node, which in this case is the next rule evaluation. If there are no more rules to be executed, we continue upwards, exiting the current module entirely, thus arriving back at the point where the call to the module was made (or finishing the execution when we were in a top-level module).

The stepping flow after a user-selectable breakpoint can be dictated by the existing (surrounding) node. For example, achieving a goal is only possible after either executing a mental state action or applying a post-condition, so the stepping actions from the relevant node should be used when stepping away from a goal-achieved breakpoint.

Step 4: User-Defined Breakpoints. User-defined breakpoints are usually line-based. In other words, a user can indicate a specific line to break on, instead of a code part. This breaking will always be done, even when not explicitly stepping. Line-based user-defined breakpoints are a widely used mechanism of convenience. However, some breakpoints can be at the same line as other break-points. In this case, we pick the breakpoints that are on a higher level in the tree in order to allow a user to still step into a lower level. In the case of GOAL, actions and post-conditions cannot be used as a user-defined breakpoint, whilst module entries, rule evaluations, and pre-conditions can.

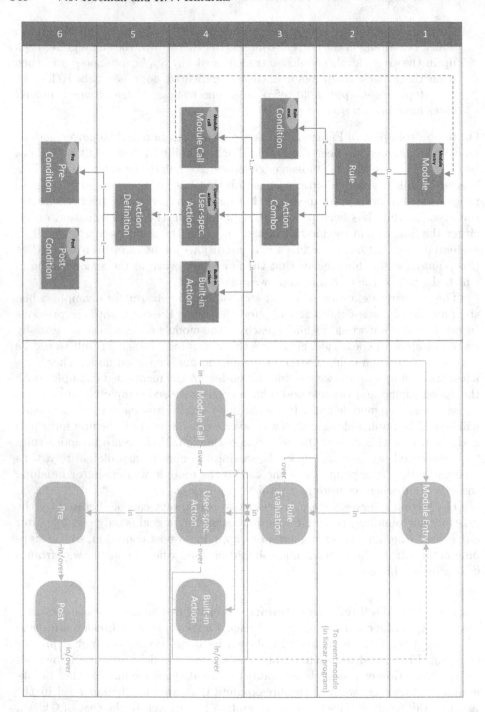

Fig. 1. A GOAL syntax tree with the relevant breakpoints indicated on the nodes that are present at the different levels on one side, and the stepping flow between those breakpoints illustrated on the other.

Step 5: Visualization. Each time the execution is suspended, the code that is about to be executed is highlighted, and any relevant evaluations of (e.g., the values of variables referenced in a rule) of this highlighted code should be displayed. These evaluations will improve a user's understanding of the execution flow. For example, if a rule's condition has no solutions, a user will not expect the rule's action to be the next point at which the execution is suspended. Note that such info is (usually) absent in cycle-based debuggers.

Problems can arise when the code evaluation does not help in making the execution flow clear to a user. For example, stepping into an action's precondition is a step that can lead to a completely different module, i.e., location in the code base, which might be unexpected. Another example is the completion of an action combo in a linear program, which can result in leaving the current module depending on its exit conditions. To help a user understand these jumps through code, the code evaluations that are shown can be augmented with additional information indicating the source of the step. For example, when at a precondition, besides the evaluation of the condition a user could also see "selected external action: ...", which gives a hint about the reason why we arrived at the action's precondition. Similar explanations can be provided after other steps that might not be clear to a user.

Step 6: State Inspection. Finally, the inspection and modification of a mental state will not be discussed in detail here, as this is a more standard feature. However, care should be taken to conveniently support all of those operations, as they are important to the debugging process. In particular, we have added features that allow the mental state of a GOAL agent to be *sorted* and *filtered* (by search queries). This helps a user make sense of a mental state, especially if it is very large. In addition, a single interactive console is provided in which both mental state queries and actions can be performed in order to respectively *inspect* or *modify* a mental state.

Application to Other Agent Programming Languages. Although we do not have space to discuss this in detail here, the same design steps discussed above can be applied to other programming languages in a similar fashion. The syntax and accompanying decision cycle of a Jason agent, for example, can be used in the same manner as described above. Although a Jason agent does not have modules, it does consist of a number of (plan) rules. Obvious code-based breakpoints would be the attempt to unify an event with a plan's triggering event, the following unification of a relevant plan's context, and finally the execution of an applicable plan's body. Special care would have to be taken to inform a user about cycle-based breakpoints that do not have a corresponding in the agent program, like the selection of events and intentions. For Jadex, the set of available annotations that indicate the cognitive agent constructs can be used as the base for the syntax tree. In contrast to the default Java debugging flow, the 'evaluation' of such an annotation is an important points of interest.

Care would have to be taken to make sure the execution flow between the annotated functions or classes is clear to a user.

3.3 Evaluation

GOAL uses the Eclipse platform to provide a full-fledged development environment for agent programmers, integrating all agent and agent-environment development tools in a single well-established setting [12]. It includes a state-of-the-art editor that features syntax highlighting, auto-completion, a code outline, code templates, bracket matching, and code folding. Exchangeable support for embedded KR languages is provided as well, and a testing framework for the validation of agents based on temporal operators has been created. To evaluate the source-level agent debugger design for GOAL, an implementation has been created in this plug-in.[1] For this implementation, some preliminary qualitative studies have been performed on different groups of users at different times. These evaluations were mainly performed through various online and offline surveys. Even though it is difficult to precisely pinpoint the effects of just the source-level debugging itself, we have obtained some useful qualitative feedback.

Before, we often got feedback about the difficulty of debugging an agent. Now, we receive feedback about fundamental difficulties such as debugging multiple agents at once, indicating interesting directions for future work. Qualitative evaluations show that users prefer the developed source-level debugger over a cycle-based debugger, showing a promising positive trend that warrants further evaluation of the usability of our work.

4   Conclusions and Future Work

We have proposed a source-level debugger design for agents that takes code stepping more serious than existing solutions, aimed at providing a better insight into the relationship between program code and the resulting behaviour. We identified two different types of breakpoints for agent programming: code-based and cycle-based. The former are based on the structure of an agent program, whereas the latter are based on an agent's decision cycle. We proposed concrete design steps for designing a debugger for cognitive agent programs. By using the syntax and decision cycle of an agent programming language, a set of pre-defined breakpoints and a flow between them can be determined in a structured manner, and represented in a stepping diagram. Based on such a diagram, features such as user-defined breakpoints, visualization of the execution flow, and state inspection can be handled as well. We have provided a concrete design for the GOAL agent programming language, and briefly argued that our design approach can be applied to other agent programming languages as well. A qualitative evaluation by users has shown that they prefer the source-level (i.e., code-based) over a purely cycle-based debugger.

---

[1] See http://goalhub.github.io/eclipse for a demonstration of the debugger implementation and instructions on how to install GOAL in Eclipse.

In this work, we have focused on debugging challenges related to rule-based reasoning and agent decision cycles. However, there are more challenges in debugging cognitive agents that need to be addressed. One of these is the fact that agents are (usually) connected to an **environment**. Two problems need to be dealt with: (i) it can no longer be assumed that an environment is *deterministic* which makes it difficult to reproduce a defect, and (ii) such environments typically cannot be *suspended instantly* which makes it difficult to understand the context of a defect. Another problem is the fact that debugging **multiple agents** at once is significantly more complicated than debugging a single agent. This problem was mentioned the most in the qualitative feedback we obtained. In addition, many programming languages for cognitive agents embed **knowledge representation (KR) languages** like Prolog or a Web Ontology Language (OWL). Some agent programming languages also embed (instead of extend) an object-oriented programming language such as Java. This introduces the additional problem of how to employ the debugging frameworks that are available for the embedded languages. Finally, to further analyse the effectiveness of a source-level debugger in agent programming in general, a detailed design of a source-level debugger for other agent programming languages can be of interest. It would be specifically interesting to investigate the effect of a more complicated decision cycle on the usability of a source-level debugger.

References

1. Bordini, R.H., Dastani, M., Dix, J., Seghrouchni, A.E.F. (eds.): Multi-Agent Programming: Languages, Platforms and Applications. Springer, US (2005)
2. Bordini, R.H., Hübner, J.F., Wooldridge, M.: Programming Multi-Agent Systems in AgentSpeak using Jason. John Wiley & Sons, Ltd, October 2007
3. Collier, R.: Debugging agents in agent factory. In: Bordini, R.H., Dastani, M., Dix, J., El Fallah Seghrouchni, A. (eds.) PROMAS 2006. LNCS (LNAI), vol. 4411, pp. 229–248. Springer, Heidelberg (2007)
4. Dastani, M.: 2apl: a practical agent programming language. Autonomous Agents and Multi-Agent Systems **16**(3), 214–248 (2008)
5. Eisenstadt, M.: My hairiest bug war stories. Communications of the ACM **40**(4), 30–37 (1997)
6. Gilmore, D.J.: Models of debugging. Acta Psychologica **78**(1–3), 151–172 (1991)
7. Hindriks, K.V.: Programming rational agents in goal. In: Seghrouchni, E.F.A., Dix, J., Dastani, M., Bordini, R.H. (eds.) Multi-Agent Programming: Languages, Tools and Applications, pp. 119–157. Springer, US (2009)
8. Hindriks, K.V.: Debugging is explaining. In: Rahwan, I., Wobcke, W., Sen, S., Sugawara, T. (eds.) PRIMA 2012. LNCS, vol. 7455, pp. 31–45. Springer, Heidelberg (2012)
9. Hindriks, K.V.: The shaping of the agent-oriented mindset. In: Dalpiaz, F., Dix, J., van Riemsdijk, M.B. (eds.) EMAS 2014. LNCS, vol. 8758, pp. 1–14. Springer, Heidelberg (2014)
10. ISO: ISO/IEC/IEEE 24765:2010 systems and software engineering - vocabulary. Technical report, Institute of Electrical and Electronics Engineers, Inc. (2010)
11. Katz, I.R., Anderson, J.R.: Debugging: An analysis of bug-location strategies. Human-Computer Interaction **3**(4), 351–399 (1987)

12. Koeman, V.J., Hindriks, K.V.: A fully integrated development environment for agent-oriented programming. In: Demazeau, Y., Decker, K.S., Bajo Pérez, J., De la Prieta, F. (eds.) PAAMS 2015. LNCS, vol. 9086, pp. 288–291. Springer, Heidelberg (2015)
13. Lam, D.N., Barber, K.S.: Comprehending agent software. In: Proceedings of the Fourth International Joint Conference on Autonomous Agents and Multiagent Systems. AAMAS 2005, pp. 586–593. ACM, New York (2005)
14. Lam, D.N., Barber, K.S.: Debugging agent behavior in an implemented agent system. In: Bordini, R.H., Dastani, M., Dix, J., El Fallah Seghrouchni, A. (eds.) PROMAS 2004. LNCS (LNAI), vol. 3346, pp. 104–125. Springer, Heidelberg (2005)
15. Lawrance, J., Bogart, C., Burnett, M., Bellamy, R., Rector, K., Fleming, S.: How programmers debug, revisited: An information foraging theory perspective. IEEE Transactions on Software Engineering $39(2)$, 197–215 (2013)
16. Layman, L., Diep, M., Nagappan, M., Singer, J., Deline, R., Venolia, G.: Debugging revisited: Toward understanding the debugging needs of contemporary software developers. In: ACM / IEEE International Symposium on Empirical Software Engineering and Measurement, pp. 383–392, October 2013
17. Pokahr, A., Braubach, L., Lamersdorf, W.: Jadex: a bdi reasoning engine. In: Bordini, R.H., Dastani, M., Dix, J., El Fallah Seghrouchni, A. (eds.) Multi-Agent Programming, Multiagent Systems, Artificial Societies, and Simulated Organizations, vol. 15, pp. 149–174. Springer, US (2005)
18. Rajan, T.: Principles for the design of dynamic tracing environments for novice programmers. Instructional Science $19(4–5)$, 377–406 (1990)
19. Romero, P., du Boulay, B., Cox, R., Lutz, R., Bryant, S.: Debugging strategies and tactics in a multi-representation software environment. International Journal of Human-Computer Studies $65(12)$, 992–1009 (2007)
20. Seghrouchni, A.E.F., Dix, J., Dastani, M., Bordini, R.H. (eds.): Multi-Agent Programming: Languages. Tools and Applications. Springer, US (2009)
21. Sudeikat, J., Braubach, L., Pokahr, A., Lamersdorf, W., Renz, W.: Validation of BDI agents. In: Bordini, R.H., Dastani, M., Dix, J., El Fallah Seghrouchni, A. (eds.) PROMAS 2006. LNCS (LNAI), vol. 4411, pp. 185–200. Springer, Heidelberg (2007)
22. Ungar, D., Lieberman, H., Fry, C.: Debugging and the experience of immediacy. Communications of the ACM $40(4)$, 38–43 (1997)
23. Winikoff, M.: Jack intelligent agents: an industrial strength platform. In: Bordini, R.H., Dastani, M., Dix, J., El Fallah Seghrouchni, A. (eds.) Multi-Agent Programming, Multiagent Systems, Artificial Societies, and Simulated Organizations, vol. 15, pp. 175–193. Springer, US (2005)
24. Yoon, B.d., Garcia, O.: Cognitive activities and support in debugging. In: Proceedings of Fourth Annual Symposium on Human Interaction with Complex Systems, pp. 160–169, March 1998
25. Zacharias, V.: Tackling the debugging challenge of rule based systems. In: Filipe, J., Cordeiro, J. (eds.) Enterprise Information Systems. LNBIP, vol. 19, pp. 144–154. Springer, Heidelberg (2009)
26. Zeller, A.: Why Programs Fail, Second Edition: A Guide to Systematic Debugging, 2nd edn. Morgan Kaufmann Publishers Inc., San Francisco (2009)

Reflecting on Agent Programming
with AgentSpeak(L)

Rem W. Collier[✉], Seán Russell, and David Lillis

School of Computer Science, University College Dublin, Dublin, Ireland
{rem.collier,sean.russell,david.lillis}@ucd.ie

Abstract. Agent-Oriented Programming (AOP) researchers have successfully developed a range of agent programming languages that bridge the gap between theory and practice. Unfortunately, despite the in-community success of these languages, they have proven less compelling to the wider software engineering community. One of the main problems facing AOP language developers is the need to bridge the cognitive gap that exists between the concepts underpinning mainstream languages and those underpinning AOP. In this paper, we attempt to build such a bridge through a conceptual mapping that we subsequently use to drive the design of a new programming language entitled ASTRA, which has been evaluated by a group of experienced software engineers attending an Agent-Oriented Software Engineering Masters course.

Keywords: Agent-Oriented programming · AgentSpeak(L) · ASTRA

1 Introduction

The Agent-Oriented Programming (AOP) paradigm is nearly 25 years old. Since its inception, a number of established AOP languages have emerged, with the most prominent being: 2/3APL [1,2], GOAL [3] and Jason [4]. However, while these languages have received much critical success within the AOP community, they have been less well received by the wider software engineering community.

A useful barometer for the view of this wider community has been the students enrolled on an Agent-Oriented Software Engineering (AOSE) module that is part of a Masters in Advanced Software Engineering offered at University College Dublin since 2005. Students on this course typically have 5 or more years of industrial software engineering experience and are senior software engineers in their respective companies. During the course, the students are exposed to an AgentSpeak(L)-based language, which has been one of AF-AgentSpeak [5], Jason [4], and our most recent agent-programming language, ASTRA [6].

Each year, the students have been asked to provide informal feedback on the AOP language(s) used and to comment on whether they would consider using such a language in a live industry application. The common response has been "no", with typical criticisms being the lack of tool support and the perceived learning curve required to master an AOP language.

© Springer International Publishing Switzerland 2015
Q. Chen et al. (Eds.): PRIMA 2015, LNAI 9387, pp. 351–366, 2015.
DOI: 10.1007/978-3-319-25524-8_22

The lack of tool support seems strange given the existence of mind inspectors [7], advanced debugging techniques [8,9], and a range of analytical tools [10,11]. However, after delving deeper, it became apparent to us that the criticisms were directed more closely towards the quality of the Integrated Development Environments (IDEs) provided and their limitations in terms of practical features such as code completion, code navigation and formatting support. Over the years, it has become apparent that developers become uneasy when stripped of their traditional supports and that this engenders a feeling that the languages are not production quality.

Conversely, the perceived learning curve is less unexpected. AOP, with its origins in Distributed Artificial Intelligence, is underpinned by a quite different set of concepts to mainstream software engineering, where there is a clear evolution from procedural programming languages to Object-Oriented Programming (OOP) languages. Individuals attempting to learn about AOP are confronted with a range of concepts - beliefs, desires and intentions; speech acts; plans - that bear little relation to mainstream programming concepts. For many, this can act as a significant barrier to learning how to program in an AOP language.

Perhaps the most common explanation of the relationship between AOP and OOP is the comparison table presented in [12]. This table presents a very high-level view of AOP and OOP that treats AOP as a specialisation of OOP. Unfortunately, it provides little practical detail. For example, how does the state of an object relate to the state of an agent? is there any correlation between how behaviours are specified in OOP and how they are specified in agents? when and how will a behaviour be executed?

Answering these questions requires a more detailed comparison of AOP and OOP. However, when attempting to create a deeper comparison, it quickly becomes evident that it is not possible. The main reason for this is that AOP, unlike OOP, does not promote or enforce a consistent conceptual model (i.e. a standard view of state, methods, messages, etc.). Instead, different languages can, and are, based around quite different approaches. For example, AgentSpeak(L) style languages are essentially event-driven languages. They define context-sensitive event handlers that map events to partial plans. Conversely, GOAL is, at its heart, an action selection language where rules identify the context in which each action should be executed. The consequence of this diversity is that it is more appropriate to compare specific styles of AOP language with OOP rather than trying to over-generalise.

In this paper, we focus on understanding the relationship between AgentSpeak(L) and OOP with the goal of trying to reduce the perceived cognitive gap. Our approach is to start by identifying a mapping between AgentSpeak(L) and OOP concepts in Section 2, which we then reflect on in Section 3. The purpose of the reflection is to try to understand how to improve the design of AgentSpeak(L) to better support developers wishing to learn the language. Following on from this, we introduce a new member of the AgentSpeak(L) family called ASTRA that has been designed in response to the findings of the previous section. Full details of ASTRA are not provided in this paper. Instead, we focus on only the most pertinent features. Finally, in Section 4 we present the relevant results of a wider survey carried out on the most recent class of the M.Sc. in Advanced Software Engineering.

2   Relating AgentSpeak(L) to OOP

AgentSpeak(L) can be prosaically described as an event-driven language where event handlers are fired based on both the triggering event and some context. Events, which are either external (environment-based) or internal (goal-based), are generated and added to an event queue. Events are then removed from this queue and matched to a rule which is then executed. The matching process checks both that the rule applies to the event and that the rule can be executed based on a rule context that defines valid program states in which the rule may be applied.

More commonly, the event handlers are known as **plan rules**; the program state is modeled as a set of **beliefs**, that are realized as atomic predicate logic formulae; the **events** are also modeled as atomic predicate formulae (with some additional modifiers); and the execution of plan rules is achieved through creation and manipulation of **intentions**. Finally, external events are generated through changes to the agent's state (i.e. the adoption or retraction of a belief), and internal events are generated through the declaration of **goals**.

It follows then, that an AgentSpeak(L) agent consists of an event queue, a set of beliefs (state), a set of plan rules (event handlers), and a set of intentions that are used to represent the execution of plan rules. Given that AOP is commonly viewed as a specialization of OOP, and that agents are a special type of object, the following outlines how AgentSpeak(L) concepts relate to OOP concepts from the perspective of an OOP developer:

Beliefs are equivalent to fields. As indicated above, beliefs form the state of an agent. In OOP, state is defined in terms of a set of **fields** that hold values (or object references). If we consider a field, such as `int value;` this could be modeled as a belief `value(0)`. Here, the value 0 is chosen as it is the default value for integer fields in many OOP languages. To be fully precise, beliefs and fields are not the same. Whereas fields can be modeled using beliefs, beliefs actually encompass more than this, including environment information, global variables, etc.

Plan Rules are equivalent to methods. A plan rule associates a plan with a triggering event and a context. Plans define behaviours and are basically blocks of procedural code that are executed whenever a matching event is processed and the rules context is satisfied. In OOP languages, procedural code is defined within methods and is executed whenever the method signature is matched to a message that has been received by the object. Accordingly, the AgentSpeak(L) equivalent of a method signature is the triggering event (specifically the identifier and the number of arguments). The context has no real equivalent in OOP, however, it can be viewed as providing a form of method overloading based on state (i.e. when there are multiple rules matching a given event, the context is used to identify which of the rules should be executed).

Goals are equivalent to method calls. Goals generate events. The are then matched to rules, which are subsequently executed. Method calls generate messages that are matched to methods that are executed. Typically, goals are declared from within a plan. The result is that the plan component of the selected rule is pushed onto the program (intention) stack and executed.

Events are equivalent to messages. Within AgentSpeak(L), events play a similar role to messages in OOP. Events are used to trigger plan rules in the same way that, for OOP languages, messages are used to invoke methods. This can be somewhat confusing because "message" is also the term used for communication between agents, however this is not the focus here. In OOP, the set of messages that can be handled by an object is known as the **interface** of the object. This set of messages corresponds to the signatures of the methods that are defined in the objects implementing class(es). Given our view of events being equivalent to OOP messages, then in AgentSpeak(L) the interface of an agent is the set of events that it can handle.

Intentions are equivalent to threads Intentions represent the plans that the agent has selected based upon the matching of events to plan rules. The AgentSpeak(L) interpreter processes the intentions by executing the instructions contained within the plan. In cases where the instruction is a sub-goal, this results in an additional plan being added to the intention which must be executed before the next instruction in the initial plan can be executed. In most programming languages, this activity is modelled by the program (call) stack. Intentions are simply the AgentSpeak(L) equivalent of this. Given that an agent can have multiple concurrent intentions whose execution is interleaved, it is natural to view an intention as being the equivalent of a thread.

The above mappings are intended to relate the concepts of AgentSpeak(L) to those present in OOP. The objective behind this is to try to reduce the cognitive gap faced by individuals who know OOP and wish to learn an AOP language. The benefit of doing this is that someone who is proficient in OOP can use these mappings as a starting point for their study of the language.

3   Exploring the Implications

The mapping developed in Section 2 is not only potentially useful to developers aiming to learn AgentSpeak(L), but it is also useful from a language developer's perspective as it raises questions about the set of features that may be appropriate for AgentSpeak(L)-style languages. In this section, we explore some of the consequences of adopting the above mapping.

3.1   Beliefs are Like Fields

Understanding the role of beliefs in AOP languages can be one of the most challenging concepts to grasp. Certainly, at a high-level it is clear that beliefs are the state, but many find it difficult to understand how beliefs relate to the state of an object. As was discussed above, one simple way of associating beliefs with object state is to demonstrate that beliefs are like fields. Fields are OOP's mechanism for defining the state of an object. Fields typically associate a label with a container for values, for example `String name = "Rem";` associates the field name, of type String with the value "Rem", which is itself a String literal. In AgentSpeak(L), it is possible to do something similar, namely to declare a fact, whose predicate corresponds to the field name, and which takes a single argument, the value associated with the field, for example `name("Rem");`.

In OOP, there are a couple of operations that can be performed on a field: (1) assigning a new value, for example, `name = "George";`; and (2) comparing a value, for example `name.equals("Rem")`. In AgentSpeak(L), performing these operations can be achieved as follows: (1) to assign a new value, you must first drop the existing belief and then adopt a new belief with the new value, for example, `-name("Rem");+name("George")`; and (2) to compare the value, you can either perform a query of the agents beliefs, for example, `?name("Rem")` or as part of a plan rule context, for example `<te> : name("Rem") <- ....` It should be noted here that the assignment operation, which is an atomic operation in OOP is not an atomic operation in AgentSpeak(L).

An interesting observation of the above is that, in transitioning from OOP (nominally Java) to AgentSpeak(L) the type of the field has been lost. Types can be a powerful feature of a programming language that can be used to statically verify the correctness of code. Specifically, in OOP, they can be used to identify situations where the wrong type of data is assigned to a field, or where the wrong type of data is passed to a method. Typically, AOP languages have used dynamically typed variables - this reflects the logical origins of AOP, where dynamically typed variables are common. For some developers, who come from a background where the languages they have used are strongly typed, this can be another significant hurdle to overcome.

One option for AOP language developers is to introduce a **type system** to their language [13]. Within AOP, type systems can be applied at the (multi-) agent level, and at the language level. (Multi-)agent types refer to the association of types with agent instances, which can be used for engendering reuse [14] of agent code or to support run-time substitution of agent instances [15].

The second use of type systems is to apply types to the terms of logical formulae, as is typically done in ontology languages, such as RDF [16]. The potential benefits of this are:

- **improved readability:** the meaning of the belief is clearer when the types are known.
- **static type checking:** compile-time checks can be used to reduce the number of run-time errors.

To take full advantage of static typing, a number of additional supports are required: correct forms for beliefs and (potentially) goals must be specified using an ontological representation; signatures representing the potential actions must be be specified in a similar way.

```
 1  Algorithm SelectionSort(A, n):
 2    for j=1 to n-1 do
 3      minIndex = j
 4      for k=j+1 to n-1 do
 5        if (A[minIndex] < A[k]) then
 6          minIndex =k
 7      if (minIndex <> j) then
 8        temp = A[j]
 9        A[j] = A[j+1]
10        A[j+1] = temp
11    return A
```

```
 1  !do_sort([7, 5, 12, 15, 3]);
 2
 3  +!do_sort(L) <-
 4    _size(L, S);
 5    !outerLoop(L, S, 0);
 6    ?sorted(L2);
 7    _print(L2).
 8
 9  +!outerLoop(L, S, X) <-
10    +min_index(X);
11    !innerLoop(L, S, X);
12    ?min_index(Z);
13    -min_index(Z);
14    !update(L, S, X, Z).
15
16  +!update(L, S, X, Z) : X < Z <-
17    _swap(L, X, Z, L2);
18    !outerLoop(L2, S, X+1).
19
20  +!update(L, S, X, Z) <-
21    !outerLoop(L, S, X+1).
22
23  +!outerLoop(L, S, X) <-
24    +sorted(L).
25
26  +!innerLoop(L, S, X) : X < S <-
27    _elementAt(L, X, T);
28    !compare(L, X, T);
29    !innerLoop(L, S, X+1).
30
31  +!innerLoop(L, S, X) <-
32    _skip().
33
34  +!compare(L,X,T):min_index(Y)<-
35    _elementAt(L, Y, S);
36    !compare(L, X, Y, S, T).
37
38  +!compare(L, X, Y, S, T)
39    : S < T <-
40    -min_index(Y);
41    +min_index(X).
42
43  +!compare(L, X, Y, S, T) <-
44    _skip().
```

| Pseudo code | AgentSpeak(L) code |

Fig. 1. Two implementations of Selection Sort algorithm

3.2   Plans Rules as Methods

The equivalence of plan rules and methods posits a simple question: if algorithms are a typical way for defining behaviour in OOP and methods are the common mechanism for implementing algorithms, would it not be natural for somebody learning AgentSpeak(L) to attempt to implement some established algorithms using the agent language?

To investigate this in more detail, we decided to implement a common algorithm using AgentSpeak(L). The choice of algorithm itself is not important, as the question really being asked here is: can somebody learning an AOP language apply their existing algorithmic problem solving skills easily in that language?

The result is illustrated in Figure 1. The left hand piece of code is standard pseudo code for the selection sort algorithm. The right-hand piece of code is the AgentSpeak(L) implementation of that algorithm. As can be seen, the AgentS-peak(L) solution is far more complicated than the pseudo code - it is over 3 times longer; one method has been mapped to 9 rules (the first rule in the AgentS-peak(L) program actually calls the sorting algorithm); and it is not even all of the code because 5 primitive actions are used (_size(....), _elementAt(...), _swap(...), _print(...), and _skip()). In fact, there are a number of clear issues with the AgentSpeak(L) solution:

1. **Rule explosion** occurs because in AgentSpeak(L) loops and selections are implemented using rules. In fact, 2 rules are typically required for both if statements and loops. In both cases, one rule is required where the guard is true and one where the guard is false. Both rules must be provided in all cases, even if they do nothing (failure to match an internal event to a rule is equated to failure to achieve a sub-goal as there are no valid event handlers for the given event).

2. **Returning results** is an issue in AgentSpeak(L) because the basic version of the language does not allow values to be returned from a sub-goal call. Instead, the value must be stored in a belief (in the global state) and upon completion of the sub-goal, the value must be retrieved by querying the global state. Such a convoluted approach clearly is not scalable given AgentSpeak(L) supports multiple concurrent intentions.

3. **Hidden code** arises because AgentSpeak(L) has such limited semantics that it is not able to directly perform simple operations such as swapping two values. Instead a number of custom primitive actions are also needed (these are not included in the code count) to implement this basic functionality. In the code any statement that is prefixed by a _ is a primitive action.

4. **Loss of readability** due to the number of rules and the convoluted control flow that results from it understanding the agent code is far more difficult than understanding the pseudo code.

Admittedly, many would question the value in implementing a sorting algorithm using an agent language, but again, the issue here is not the actual algorithm, but that algorithms cannot be easily implemented in AgentSpeak(L). Given the amount of time and effort that is put into teaching programmers to think algorithmically, it seems inefficient to be promoting languages that do not try to leverage those skills.

3.3   Intentions as Threads

In the mapping, we equate intentions with threads. Agents are commonly presented as being active objects, with their own thread of control. However, the reality is that AgentSpeak(L) agents are more like multi-threaded processes, with each intention being an individual thread. If this view is adopted as the correct analogy for intentions, then our languages must be designed with this in mind.

AgentSpeak(L) is not designed with such a view in mind. As was mentioned above, sub-goals cannot return values. Instead, the value must be stored in the global state of the agent and retrieved once the sub-goal has completed. It is easy to see that such a scenario does not work well if intentions are like threads. This is especially the case since intentions are normally interleaved, with the agent executing one action for one intention per iteration of its execution cycle.

Consider, for example, an agent with two intentions, A and B, that both need to sort a (different) list of numbers using the selection sort code of figure 1. On iteration i, intention A stores the sorted list in its global state. On the next iteration (i+1), intention B stores its sorted list in the global state. Two iterations later (after A and B have completed their sub-goals), A then attempts to retrieve the sorted list from the memory. The agent has two beliefs - one for each sorted list - based on the given program, it is ambiguous as to which of the sorted lists will be returned. The result is that either A or B will have the incorrect sorted list. Naturally, this problem can be overcome, but only by further increasing the complexity of the program!

One solution would be to introduce support for mutual exclusion into AgentSpeak(L). This would overcome the issue, but would require the mutual exclusion to be applied prior to the first invocation of the `!outerLoop(L, S, X)` sub-goal. The natural alternative is to allow sub-goals to return values.

3.4   Events are Like Messages

Perhaps the most contentious part of the mapping is the association of AOP events and OOP messages. This can seem contentious because messages are a well-defined concept in multi-agent systems that drive speech act based interaction between agents. Further, it conflicts with Shoham's analysis, which argues that message passing in AOP is equivalent to message passing in OOP. In reality, there is no conflict. The reason for the seeming inconsistency is that Shoham compares agents and objects from an external (and high-level) perspective, whereas our comparison of AgentSpeak(L) and OOP is more low-level. Further, the design of AgentSpeak(L) did not consider inter-agent communication.

There are two basic approaches to handling the receipt of messages in AgentSpeak(L). The first approach is the approach adopted in Jason. Here, a subset of KQML is identified and the chosen speech acts are closely integrated with the language. For example, receipt of a **tell** message results in the adoption a belief based on the content of the message together with an annotation identifying the sender of the message. Invoking a behaviour based on the receipt of a tell message thus requires the creation of a plan rule whose triggering event matches the belief adoption event created by the receipt of the message. The sending of messages is then supported through the provision of an internal action `.send(...)`. This approach fits the mapping presented in this paper because the semantics of the receipt of messages are hidden from the programmer.

An alternative approach is to introduce a new **message event** type to model the receipt of a message. This approach is more loosely coupled in that the receipt of a message does not have a direct impact on the agent. Instead, the programmer must implement a rule to handle the receipt of the message. The advantage of this approach is that it is left to the programmer to determine how the agent responds to the receipt of a message. For example, if an agent is informed of some new fact, then the programmer can provide a rule to define whether or not the agent should adopt the content as a belief. As before, sending of messages can be achieved through a custom action (or alternatively, a custom plan operator).

Irrespective of the model chosen, it is clear that AOP messages are not the same as OOP messages as ultimately, the behaviour resulting from the receipt of the message is realised through the processing of an event. What is interesting to note from the second model is the idea of increasing the number of event types supported by the language. The benefit of adding new event types is that the events can be specified in a way that all of the relevant data is encoded in the event. This can result in a solution that is clearer and easier to follow that trying to reduce every event to an annotated belief. The cost comes from the fact that the implemented language must handle more event types.

4   ASTRA: AgentSpeak(L) with Bells and Whistles

The mapping presented in this paper is aimed at reducing the cognitive gap for developers who are familiar with OOP and who wish to learn an AOP language. In order to evaluate whether such a mapping can help, we have developed a new implementation of AgentSpeak(L) called ASTRA. ASTRA is based upon Jason, but includes a number of features that are inspired by the mapping presented in this paper. In line with the rest of this paper, the syntax of ASTRA is based upon Java syntax, which has been chosen so that the language will seem more familiar to the user. In this section, we present only the most pertinent details of ASTRA that reflect the points made in the paper. For more information on the language, the reader is directed to [6].

4.1   The ASTRA Type System

ASTRA as a statically typed language that provides a typical set of primitive types for use. Because ASTRA is built on Java, and in an effort to improve the cohesion between the agent layer and the supporting functionality in the Java layer, the set of primitive types is based upon Java's type system. While not exhaustive, all the necessary types are provided for, including 4 and 8 byte integers (mapped to Java's `int` and `long` types), 4 and 8 byte floating point numbers (mapped to `float` and `double` types) as well as representations for character and boolean values (mapped to `char` and `boolean` types).

In addition, ASTRA also supports the non-primitive types of character strings which maps to the Java `String` class and a list type which maps to a custom implementation of the `java.util.List` interface. Finally, ASTRA allows the use of generic objects through the object type. Instances of objects cannot be directly represented within the language but can be stored and passed to internal and environment operations.

ASTRA uses modules to represent internal libraries. The design of these libraries is inspired by the use of annotations in CArtAgo [17]. Libraries allow four kinds of annotation: terms, formulae, sensors and actions. Terms represent basic calculations that can return a value. Formula methods are constructors that return any logical formula instance in ASTRA (these can be simple boolean values or more complex formulae). Sensors generate beliefs that are added to the agent's state. Actions represent internal actions that can be performed, returning a boolean value indicating if the action was successfully performed. Figure 2 shows the declaration of a module containing a single term and action.

All of the components of the modules are typed. This enables the static verification of types for any usage of the library as well as for any value returned. Terms, actions and formulae can be used in a manner intuitive to OOP programmers: Figure 3 shows an example of the use of a term to determine the largest of two numbers before using an action to print it.

Modules must first be declared by linking the class to a name within the agent, this declaration is shown in line 5 of the example. A consequence of this method of declaration is that a single agent can create several copies of the same module, each with a different name and state.

```
1  package ex;
2
3  import astra.core.Module;
4
5  public class MyModule extends
       Module {
6
7  @TERM
8  public int max(int a, int b){
9    return Math.max(a, b);
10  }
11
12  @ACTION
13  public boolean printN(int n){
14    System.out.println(n);
15    return true;
16  }
17  }
```

```
1  package ex;
2
3
4  agent Bigger {
5    module MyModule m;
6
7
8    initial num(45, 67);
9    initial !init();
10
11
12    rule +!init() {
13      query(num(int X,int Y));
14      int n = m.max(X,Y);
15      m.printN(n);
16    }
17
18  }
```

Fig. 2. Java code declaring a module with a term and action

Fig. 3. ASTRA code declaring and using a module

It should be noted that ASTRA is not alone in considering strong typing to be important in agent programming. The simpAL agent programming language [13] also supports typing, and includes the ability to extend strong typing to environment artifacts and to the agents themselves.

4.2   Extended Plan Syntax

ASTRA includes a number of extensions to the traditional AgentSpeak(L) plan syntax. These extensions are added to combat the issues noted in Section 3.2.

The usefulness of constructs such as these is emphasised by Jason's inclusion of some of these procedural-style constructs (e.g. if statements, loops) in its extended version of AgentSpeak(L). ASTRA attempts to provide a more complete mapping between procedural-style pseudocode, as well as AOP features.

If statement the most basic form of flow control
While loop traditional method of repetition in programming
Foreach loop repeats the same actions for every matching binding of a formula
Try-recover block allows for the recovery from failed actions
Local variable declaration declares a variable for use within a plan rule
Assignment allows the value of a local variable to be changed
Query bind the values of beliefs to variables
Wait pauses execution until condition if true
When performs block of code when condition is true
Send sends message to another agent
Synchronized provides for mutual exclusion in critical sections

Figure 4 shows an implementation of selection sort as a single rule in ASTRA. While this demonstrates only some elements of the extended plan syntax, when compared to the Agentspeak(L) implementation given in Figure 1 it is much easier to understand.

```
1   rule +!sort(list L, list R) {
2     R = L;
3     int j = 0;
4     while (j < P.size(R)) {
5       int minIndex = j;
6       int k = j+1;
7       while (k < P.size(R)) {
8         if (P.valueAsInt(R, minIndex) > P.valueAsInt(R, k))
9           minIndex = k;
10        k++;
11      }
12      if (minIndex ~= j) {
13        R = P.swap(R, minIndex, j);
14      }
15      j++;
16    }
17  }
```

Fig. 4. ASTRA rule for Selection Sort

4.3   Mutual Exclusion Support

In Section 3.3, the link between intentions and threads was established. This introduces potential difficulties in the form of race conditions since multiple intentions are, interleaved by their very nature. As such, it is necessary to provide functionality to offset these difficulties. To facilitate removal of these high-level race conditions, ASTRA includes support for synchronized blocks - sections of the agent program that are labeled as critical sections.

Code contained within a synchonized block can only be executed by a single intention at a time. Synchronized blocks are declared using the synchronized keyword but also require an identifier for the block. This allows multiple blocks to be declared representing a common critical section. Once an intention enters a synchronized block, all synchronized blocks with the same identifier are locked and cannot be entered until the current intention is completed.

Figure 5 shows an example of ASTRA code with race conditions. This program invokes the !init() goal twice, creating 2 intentions. In this situation, there is no way to know the output of the program. If both intentions query the belief at the same time the agent will only output the value of X at 0 and 1 (initial and incremented once). Figure 6 shows the same program with mutual exclusion added through the use of a synchronized block. In this situation, the output is guaranteed show the values of X at 0, 1 and 2.

```
1  agent Racy {
2    module Console C;
3
4    initial ct(0);
5    initial !init(), !init();
6
7
8    rule +!init() {
9      query(ct(int X));
10     +ct(X+1);
11     -ct(X);
12   }
13
14
15   rule +ct(int X) {
16     C.println("X = " + X);
17   }
18 }
```

Fig. 5. ASTRA code with race conditions

```
1  agent Racy {
2    module Console C;
3
4    initial ct(0);
5    initial !init(), !init();
6
7    rule +!init() {
8      synchronized (ct_tok) {
9        query(ct(int X));
10       +ct(X+1);
11       -ct(X);
12     }
13   }
14
15   rule +ct(int X) {
16     C.println("X = " + X);
17   }
18 }
```

Fig. 6. ASTRA code with mutual exclusion

5   Evaluation

In order to evaluate the concepts discussed in this paper, a survey was conducted using 20 students from the M.Sc. in Advanced Software Engineering programme in University College Dublin. The participants completed an Agent-Oriented Software Engineering module as a component of their degree. The students are full-time software engineers with an average experience of 7.65 years in industry. The degree is completed part-time over a number of years where each module is taught intensely for a single week of lectures and practical instruction.

Participants were asked to indicate their level of agreement with statements relating to general agent-oriented programming as well as more specific areas of interest to this work. The results were captured on a 5-point Likert scale. The questions presented form only a subset of the overall survey that was performed, full details of the survey and responses can be view in [18, pp.181–187].

The first group of questions relate to agent-oriented programming languages in general and their benefit to the participant.

Q1 Agents are a useful level of abstraction.
Q2 I would consider using an AOP language in my (future) work.
Q3 AOP languages make distributed programming easier.
Q4 AOP languages make concurrent programming easier.
Q5 Studying AOP languages enhanced my understanding of distributed computing

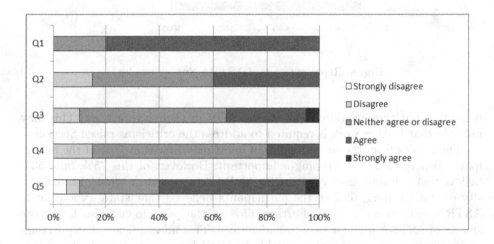

Fig. 7. Representation of Agents Survey results

The second group of questions relate to the participants' perception of some features of ASTRA and the impact this had on their ability to learn the language.

Q6 Static typing, and the verification this enables, are important.
Q7 Static typing is a necessary feature of AOP languages.
Q8 Static typing makes ASTRA code easy to read.
Q9 ASTRA was easy to learn.
Q10 I found it easy to apply my existing programming knowledge to ASTRA.
Q11 The syntax of ASTRA made it easy to understand.
Q12 There is a steep learning curve for ASTRA.
Q13 The lack of a debugger made ASTRA more difficult to learn.
Q14 ASTRA offers a good level of abstraction for programming distributed systems.

The results from the first group of questions show that the participants generally consider agents to be a useful level of abstraction. However, only 40%

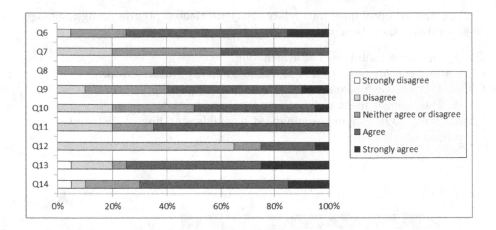

Fig. 8. Representation of ASTRA Survey results

indicated that they would consider using AOP in their future work. This may indicate that further work is required to address the criticisms raised Section 1.

The results from the second group of questions show that 75% of the participants believe that static typing is important. However, of this 75%, only 53% believe that it is a necessary feature for AOP languages. Regardless of the necessity of static typing, 65% of the participants believed that static typing made ASTRA code easier to read. Further, 65% of the participants also found the syntax of ASTRA made it easy to understand. This may indicate that provision of constructs more commonly available in OOP languages eases the transition from procedural languages to ASTRA.

In terms of learning ASTRA, the majority of participants disagreed that there is a steep learning curve. However, 75% of participants did believe that the lack of a debugger made the learning process more difficult. While this agrees with the informal feedback received previously, it is unclear whether this is a result of the level of experience of the participants. The amount of industry experience may make it more likely that the participants would utilise this level of support more than less experienced students of AOP languages.

6   Conclusions

In this paper, we have presented a practical conceptual mapping between AgentSpeak(L) and Object-Oriented Programming (OOP). The purpose of this mapping has been to attempt to find a way of reducing the cognitive gap for developers, experienced in OOP, who wish to learn Agent-Oriented Programming (AOP). In developing the mapping, we are not attempting to reduce one paradigm to the other, but instead aim to provide a stepping stone that will help developers wishing to learn AOP make their first steps.

In addition to the benefit such a mapping provides for those wishing to learn AgentSpeak(L), a second benefit is that it provides language designers with valuable insights into how their languages might be used in practice. To this end, Section 3 reflects on the mappings and identifies a number of possible issues and potential opportunities:

1. the potential of using a type system to improve the link between the agent and object layers and to reduce run-time defects through static type checks.
2. the provision of an extended suite of plan operators including a subset that mirror the typical constructs offered in procedural languages to support the use of existing algorithmic problem solving skills when developing agent behaviours and the curtailing of rule explosion that was evident in Figure 1.
3. the provision of mutual exclusion support for intentions to facilitate management of critical sections.
4. the use of an extended suite of event types rather than attempting to force all events to conform to AgentSpeak(L)'s original model of belief and goal events.

While we believe that we have come to these conclusions through a novel route, we do not claim to be the first to reach them. Certainly, Jason includes support for atomic behaviours and has an extended suite of plan operators. In terms of the latter, we do believe that our perspective offers some benefit: while Jason does include support for if statements and for and while loops, we do not believe that it offers support for local variable declaration or assignment, both of which are considered a core concept in pseudo code.

The principal outcome of our work has been to drive the development of ASTRA, an implementation of AgentSpeak(L) that is targeted towards reducing the cognitive gap. In 2014, ASTRA was made available to students on the M.Sc. in Advanced Software Engineering mentioned in the introduction. Students learned ASTRA over a 5-day period, during which they wrote a range of programs. On the last day, they were assigned a complex problem to solve [18, pp.167–180] and were asked to complete a questionnaire relating to both the problem and more generally agents. Details of the results of the relevant parts of this questionnaire are presented in Section 5. We believe that the feedback positively reflects our decision to include both the language level type system and the suite of plan operators into ASTRA.

References

1. Dastani, M.: 2APL: a practical agent programming language. Autonomous Agents and Multi-Agent Systems **16**(3), 214–248 (2008)
2. Dastani, M., van Birna Riemsdijk, M., Meyer, J.J.C.: Programming multi-agent systems in 3APL. In: Multi-agent programming, pp. 39–67. Springer (2005)
3. Hindriks, K.V.: Programming rational agents in GOAL. In: El Fallah Seghrouchni, A., Dix, J., Dastani, M., Bordini, R.H., (eds.) Multi-Agent Programming, pp. 119–157. Springer, US (2009)

4. Bordini, R.H., Hübner, J.F., Wooldridge, M.: Programming Multi-agent Systems in AgentSpeak using Jason. John Wiley & Sons (2007)
5. Russell, S., Jordan, H., O'Hare, G.M.P., Collier, R.W.: Agent factory: a framework for prototyping logic-based AOP languages. In: Klügl, F., Ossowski, S. (eds.) MATES 2011. LNCS, vol. 6973, pp. 125–136. Springer, Heidelberg (2011)
6. Astra language website. http://www.astralanguage.com/ (accessed June 21, 2015)
7. Collier, R.: Debugging agents in agent factory. In: Bordini, R.H., Dastani, M., Dix, J., El Fallah Seghrouchni, A. (eds.) PROMAS 2006. LNCS (LNAI), vol. 4411, pp. 229–248. springer, Heidelberg (2007)
8. Hindriks, K.V.: Debugging is explaining. In: Rahwan, I., Wobcke, W., Sen, S., Sugawara, T. (eds.) PRIMA 2012. LNCS, vol. 7455, pp. 31–45. Springer, Heidelberg (2012)
9. Lam, D.N., Barber, K.S.: Debugging agent behavior in an implemented agent system. In: Bordini, R.H., Dastani, M., Dix, J., El Fallah Seghrouchni, A. (eds.) PROMAS 2004. LNCS (LNAI), vol. 3346, pp. 104–125. Springer, Heidelberg (2005)
10. Botia, J.: Debugging huge multi-agent systems: group and social perspectives (2005)
11. Doan Van Bien, D., Lillis, D., Collier, R.W.: Space-time diagram generation for profiling multi agent systems. In: Braubach, L., Briot, J.-P., Thangarajah, J. (eds.) ProMAS 2009. LNCS, vol. 5919, pp. 170–184. Springer, Heidelberg (2010)
12. Shoham, Y.: Agent-oriented programming. Artificial intelligence 60(1), 51–92 (1993)
13. Ricci, A., Santi, A.: Typing multi-agent programs in simpal. In: Dastani, M., Hübner, J.F., Logan, B. (eds.) ProMAS 2012. LNCS, vol. 7837, pp. 138–157. Springer, Heidelberg (2013)
14. Dhaon, A., Collier, R.W.: Multiple Inheritance in AgentSpeak (L)-Style Programming Languages. In: Proceedings of the 4th International Workshop on Programming based on Actors Agents & Decentralized Control, pp. 109–120. ACM (2014)
15. Baldoni, M., Baroglio, C., Capuzzimati, F.: Typing multi-agent systems via commitments. In: Dalpiaz, F., Dix, J., van Riemsdijk, M.B. (eds.) EMAS 2014. LNCS, vol. 8758, pp. 388–405. Springer, Heidelberg (2014)
16. Emmons, I., Collier, S., Garlapati, M., Dean, M.: Rdf literal data types in practice. In: The 7th International Workshop on Scalable Semantic Web Knowledge Base Systems (SSWS 2011)
17. Ricci, A., Viroli, M., Omicini, A.: CArtAgO: a framework for prototyping artifact-based environments in MAS. In: Weyns, D., Van Dyke Parunak, H., Michel, F. (eds.) E4MAS 2006. LNCS (LNAI), vol. 4389, pp. 67–86. Springer, Heidelberg (2007)
18. Russell, S.: Real-time monitoring and validation of waste transportation using intelligent agents and pattern recognition. Ph.D. thesis, University College Dublin (2015)

Checking the Reliability of Information Sources in Recommendation Based Trust Decision Making

Kamilia Ahmadi[✉] and Vicki H. Allan

Computer Science Department, Utah State University, Logan, UT, USA
k.ahmadi@aggiemail.usu.edu

Abstract. Trust is one of the measures commonly used to evaluate the effectiveness of agents in cooperative societies. For building trust of a specific target, agents utilize their direct experiences and recommendations from agents who had mutual experience with the target. Some agents may provide false data due to misjudgment. Some others may have biased or extreme behavior toward evaluating others. Having the possibility of false data necessitate the existence of reliability checking mechanisms in building trust. This research focuses on showing the effect of reliability checking mechanisms on recommendation-based trust decision making.

Keywords: Recommendation-based trust · Decision making · Anti-bias filtering · Outlier detection

1 Introduction

Multi-agent systems solve problems that are beyond the capability of a single agent. Agents are autonomous, self-interested, and goal-driven, and interact with each other to pursue the goals of the system [15]. The notion of cooperation plays an essential role in the success of a multi agent system. In such a society, agents might not be certain about the competencies and capabilities of others. Even worse, agents need to consider the possibility of intentionally deceptive or erroneous information spread from peers. This possibility increases the uncertainty associated with interactions. In addition, it introduces a significant degree of complexity to decision-making approaches, such as task delegation and information sharing in the society of agents [9,16].

Trust is a social control mechanism that reduces the uncertainty of interactions, and helps in forming expectations about others. Agents who repeatedly fail to complete promised tasks are socially excluded from activities. This social control mechanism creates a form of supervision of the whole system in which all agents are involved [8].

Some of the agents may intentionally provide false information while others may do so because of misjudgment. Incorrect information has a direct effect

© Springer International Publishing Switzerland 2015
Q. Chen et al. (Eds.): PRIMA 2015, LNAI 9387, pp. 367–382, 2015.
DOI: 10.1007/978-3-319-25524-8_23

on the accuracy of trust-based decision making. There are various sources of false data such as correlated evidence (unintentional bias) and extreme opinions (intentional bias). Correlated bias happens when multiple agents have a single experience and use that in giving opinions about a trustee. The receiver considers them different experiences while they are referencing the same experience. Extreme agents are another main source of false data, as rely more on negative experiences than positive ones [3,10,16]. To avoid these sources of error, we need a mechanism for checking the reliability of provided information. Approaches for handling these situations include building reliability factor of recommenders, detecting and removing the unfair ratings along with gathering more and recent opinions [7,11,13].

In this research, agents use recommendation-based trust for evaluating the choice of peers on which to rely. Agents use their so-called neighbors for recommendations and they are categorized as Normal, Biased, or Extreme in terms of expressing their opinions. Normal agents reflect their actual experiences with the target while other modify it in different ways. Our society is robust, adaptive, and decentralized giving agents the opportunity of changing their neighbors to select strong peers. This reorganization is done without any external control or a single source of management. In our model agents are heterogenous in terms of their risk behaviors which is modeled as a continuous measure. Continuous measure of agent's risk results in having agents with a range of risk behavior rather than just three distinct types (Risk Seeking, Risk Neutral and Risk Averse). This risk measure affects the agents' interpretation of rewards. Risk-seeking agents have an optimistic attitude toward the reward, while risk-averse agents are pessimistic and undervalue the actual reward of tasks. However, risk neutral agents are objective and see the actual reward of an action. Reliability checking mechanisms is used to check the accuracy of provided information in building trust. Utilizing reliability mechanisms, agents have a more accurate evaluation of their peers, aiding them in the selection of cooperation partners.

2   Previous Work

Zhang et al (2008) proposed a *personalized* approach to deal with the problem of unfair ratings [16]. Unfair rating occurs when a buying agent needs to rely on some other agents for evaluating the trustworthiness of the seller agent. This approach uses the private experience of buyer and adviser, along with public knowledge of the adviser. They use a time window to exclude the old and repeated ratings in order to avoid the situation where some advisers may flood the system. Also, their approach provides a mechanism for buyers to rate the public knowledge. In this model, a central unit of public knowledge is needed to help buyers to evaluate the advisers. Since our model is decentralized, we do not have a central unit of knowledge. Therefore, this personalized approach is not applicable.

Josang et al (2009) use a statistical filtering technique for excluding unfair ratings [9]. In their model, unfair ratings are shown in cases where agents have unfairly positive or negative opinions about other agents. They have two approaches of dealing with this issue, termed *endogenous* and *exogenous* discounting. The assumption of endogenous discounting is that unfair ratings are recognized by statistical properties of provided opinions. The exogenous discounting method relies on external factors, such as the reputation of rater. This reputation is used to determine the weight of the rating and comes from external sources. The drawback of this model is the lack of effectiveness in the case of a high percentage of unfair behavior (more than 30 percent of all of the opinions). It seems that the model loses its effectiveness in the case of high numbers of inconsistent behaviors. Our desired model checks the reliability of the provided information regardless of the amount of unfair behaviors.

Burnett (2010) uses recommendation-based trust in ad-hoc societies [3]. Direct experiences are used to build trust. When an agent has no direct experience with a target, it uses the experiences of other nearby agents to build trust in the target. In highly dynamic societies, agents leave the community or newcomers join frequently. Therefore, building trust based on experiences is not always feasible. Burnett proposes a stereotyping method to build trust. Stereotyping tries to build trust based on predefined features for those agents without relevant experiences. In decision making, agents consider the context of the decision using concepts such as risk, reward and cost of the action to satisfy the controls of the system. Sources of unreliable recommendations in Burnett's model are biased agents. Agents may have different types of bias named perceptual bias, behavioral bias, prejudice, and affinity. There are anti-bias filtering mechanisms like monitoring the agents, building reliability factors of recommenders and two stage learning phase mechanism. Although this model satisfies some of our desired properties, there is a mismatch with our proposed model. Our model is a self-adaptive one, which adapts itself based on history and has some sort of dynamicity while the focus of Burnett's model is on ad-hoc organizations. Therefore, some approaches of Burnett's model are not employable in this research.

3 Our Proposed Model

Reliability checking mechanisms are necessary to check the accuracy of provided information in recommendation-based trust. There are various sources of false data like correlated evidence and biased/extreme agents. Normally when there is a high chance of false data, there is a big variance between provided opinions. Approaches for handling these situations include building reliability factor of recommenders, detecting the unfair recommendations and gathering more and recent opinions. More opinions help reduce the variance of data. Recent data is more accurate than old data, especially in dynamic societies. Agents should not depend on the recommendations which reflect old experiences [5,8,11]. In building trust, agents use the reliability checking mechanisms to evaluate the provided information from recommenders. Our self-adaptive society allows agents to evaluate their cooperation peers and change their organizational link with them in a decentralized way. Utilizing reliability checking mechanisms, we provide agents with a better evaluation mechanism of selecting their cooperation peers, along with avoiding tendentious recommendations.

3.1   Task Domain

In our model, a task is represented as an incoming stream of multiple requested services. These services are nodes (subtasks) of the tree. Each service instance (*SI*) has a known skill and computation time. There is sequential dependency between subtasks, which means that the parent *SI* must be executed before its child *SI*. When all of the nodes in the tree are executed, the task is complete [1]. Figure 1 shows the tree structure of a task.

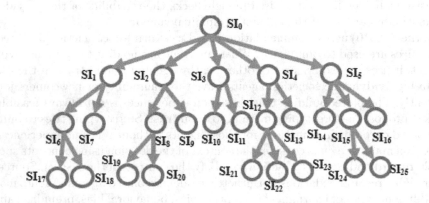

Fig. 1. Nodes represent a service instance (SI). Arrows represent sequential dependency between nodes of the tree. Each SI needs a special skill (S) and a computational amount (C).

Each subtask has a deadline associated with it along with the specified amount of utility associated with a complete task. The utility of a task is the amount of reward (utility) the agent gets for investing resources on this subtask and finishing it before its deadline. Multiple agents need to cooperate with each other in order to finish a task. Agents get reward if all of the task's nodes are completed before deadline. Therefore, the reward each agent gets not only depends on its effort on finishing its own part before deadline but also it relies on the performance of other agents who cooperated in finishing the task. In our model, nodes with more dependents have bigger reward associated with them since they are more critical in success of finishing the task tree. Thus agents have incentive to give better priority to these nodes in their working queue (details of the prioritization mechanism are explained in section 3.5). Expected time is the average estimated time for finishing the task. If the agent cannot finish the task by the expected time, the only punishment is decreasing its expected reward. This mechanism aims to reward a sooner finishing time, which is better for the system. Equation 1 and Equation 2 show the relationship between utility and time. Here t stands for time.

$$AssignedUtility_{task} = \sum_{i=0}^{|SI_i|} (Utility(SI_i)) \qquad (1)$$

$$Utility_{task} = AssignedUtility_{task} - (t_{task}^{taken} - t_{task}^{expected}) \qquad (2)$$

3.2   Agents' Characteristics

Based on the agent model in [6], each agent has a set of skills Sx and known computational capacity Cx needed for executing tasks and management. Formally, an agent is defined in the form of Equation 3.

$$Agent_x = \langle S_x, C_x \rangle \qquad (3)$$

The amount of computational capacity is defined per time step and agents cannot exceed it. Agents' skills can be overlapping and their capabilities and resources are limited in order to model real systems. Agents cooperate in finishing a task and each agent executes a particular task and allocates the dependent tasks to the capable neighbors. For executing a task, the agent must have the skill required by the task and the cumulative load of the task has to be less than the agent's computational capacity. In order to explore various approaches, there are three main types of agents defined in our model. Agents are categorized based on the approaches they use to recommend others and they are termed *biased*, *extreme*, and *normal* agents.

Biased agents form prejudiced opinions about other agents due to the existence of some attributes in the trustee. Features include difference of risk behavior, personality, place of the target agent in the hierarchy and skill set. Biased agents are positive toward agents that have similar features as they have (fewer differences). Examples of this bias are numerous in human societies; members of a same culture or nationality behave preferentially toward persons of the same culture or nationality. Another important factor for biased agents is the place of the trustee in hierarchy of their peer organization. Biased agents believe that if the agent is proficient one, it should have better ranking in the hierarchy. Therefore, agents behave negatively irrespective of other evidences [3].

Extreme agents focus on negative experiences in making opinion. For example if they had 10 experiences with trustee and just one was negative, they rely mostly on the bad experience. These agents are pessimistic and cautious in evaluating others, regardless of the other good experience they might have had with trustee [14].

Normal agents are neither biased nor extreme. These agents evaluate the trustee based solely on their mutual experiences. They simply average the functionality of the trustee based on their experiences and try to be accurate using the history.

3.3   Self-Adaptive Agent Organization

An agent organization is defined as a set of agents and organizational links that regulate the interaction between agents. Formally, organization is defined with a tuple containing a set of agents and a set of organizational links based on

Equation 4. Every link is in the form of Equation 5 which $type_i$ denotes the relationship between $agent_x$ and $agent_y$.

$$Organization = \langle Agents, Links \rangle \qquad (4)$$

$$Link = \langle Agent_x, Agent_y, Type_i \rangle \qquad (5)$$

In our case, the links control sources of recommendation as well as delegation of tasks. There are four levels of relationship between agents (listed in order of importance): (a) superior (obligation to satisfy), (b) subordinate (preferred delegation), (c) peer (low frequency of interaction) and (d) acquaintance (knowing existence but having no interaction). The type of relationship between agents specifies the amount of information they have about each other and shows the preferences of agents in the task-passing mechanism. Figure 2 shows an example of the organizational structure of agents.

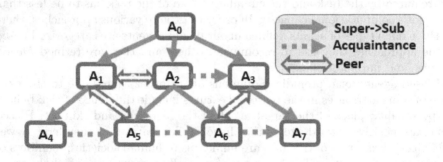

Fig. 2. Example of organizational structure.() shows services of self. shows services of subordinates. [] shows services of peers.

In our self-adaptive, agent organization, agents have the opportunity of evaluating their neighbors and can promote or demote their organizational links with them in every iteration. The evaluation process is called Meta-Reasoning and uses Satisfaction Measures based on Equation 6 and reliability factor of agents. In the beginning, all of the agents have the reliability factor equal to 1. Then, agents decrease the amount of reliability factor for those neighbors who have been recognized as source of unfair recommendation in different situations. Each agent aims to have more reliable and high satisfactory neighbor around it for cooperation. In Equation 6, i stands for iteration, t indicates current iteration, and $numProvidedRequests$ is the number of times the agent cooperated out of all of the times it has been requested for cooperation. Variable h is in the range of $[1, t-1]$ and shows the amount of history that will be considered.

$$satisfaction = \frac{\sum_{i=t-h}^{t-1} numProvidedRequests}{\sum_{i=t-h}^{t-1} numRequsts} \qquad (6)$$

Reorganization includes removing existing relations and creating new ones. There is an associated load with it while gives the system the opportunity of earning utility via new relations in future. Based on the specific type of relation between two agents, there are different possibilities of modifying the organizational links. Evaluation functions estimate the amount of utility and load associated with changing a current relation between $agent_x$ and $agent_y$ to a new type of relation. Loads consist of management load, communication load and load of changing the relation, and are estimated based on history. Utility is estimated based on past experiences with the type of new relation and the effectiveness of $agent_y$ in terms of earned utility. More details on self-adaptive agent organization can be found in our earlier publication in [2].

3.4 Recommendation-Based Trust

$Agent_x$ builds trust about a specific target based on experiences that can be direct or from third parties. Although direct experiences ($|D|$ in Equation 7) have a stronger effect on the process of building trust, $agent_x$ also considers the experiences provided by third parties in order to have better judgement. The number of recommendations $agent_x$ needs to build trust about a target depends on the risk behavior of $agent_x$. Risk-averse agents need more recommendations and more positive recommendations than risk-seeking ones. As we explained in section 3.3, each agent keeps the most reliable and high satisfactory neighbor around itself. Recommenders are picked from the neighbors which recently interacted with the target ($|R|$), superiors of target ($|S|$), and agents with the most iterations with the target ($|M|$). Then, $agent_x$ combines the experiences with different weights (ξ_i) to determine the amount of trust for the target based on Equation 7. Weights are based on the reliability of recommendation providers along with a heuristic that establishes a preference order among the recommenders.

$$Trust_{x \to z} = \sum_{i \in \{|D|,|R|,|S|,|M|\}} \xi_i * Trust_{x \to z}^i \tag{7}$$

Since the primary goal of each agent is earning more utility, agents need to have a motivation for providing a recommendation. Agents make opinion just based on their direct experience with the target while trust is build based on both direct experience and opinions from third-parties. One might think that agents provide information now for others as a part of cooperation, and they can expect that others will compensate for them in future. However, in most cases (as in human societies), the expectation of future compensation is not a sufficient reason to cooperate. Agents need to have a mechanism of mutual benefit between trustor and recommender. In our model, giving an opinion is considered as one kind of cooperation, and recommenders get a slight amount of the subtask's reward. This mechanism increases the incentive of recommenders to cooperate and works as social control on the false information providers.

3.5 Agents' Queue Reprioritization Using Agent' Strategy

Each agent has a limited amount of time and resources. While each agent is able respond to one request per time-step, it might receive more than one request per time step. Therefore, agents needs to prioritize requests in a waiting queue. For prioritization purpose, agents benefit from Equation 8 which considers different factors associated with the requested task. Factors are tasks deadline (D), tasks utility (U), and strength of relationship with requestor (SR).

$$Priority = \alpha_1 \times D + \alpha_2 \times U + \alpha_3 \times SR \qquad (8)$$

Each agent has a different weighting scheme ($a1, a2, a3$). This triplet is called the strategy of the agent and indicates the order of importance of each factor. Agents might be deadline-driven or greedily prefer gaining utility. Others may prefer to satisfy their superiors to keep their relationship strong. Upon receiving new request agents reprioritize their whole queue [1].

3.6 Evaluating Neighbors for Task Delegation Purposes

Finishing a task requires cooperation between multiple agents. Each agent utilizes task-passing mechanism and allocates subtasks to different level of neighbors. Figure 3 demonstrates this task-passing mechanism.

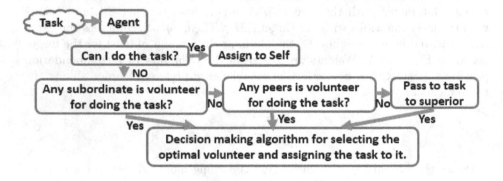

Fig. 3. Process of assigning a task to an agent. Priority of task passing starts from agent's subordinates, then peers and finally superiors.

Based on the task passing process, $agent_x$ starts from first level of neighbors (which are subordinates) and runs the decision making algorithm (our earlier publication [1]) to identify the best one from all of the volunteers. If there is no capable subordinate, $agent_x$ goes through the same steps in the next level of neighbors to find the optimal agent.

In the decision making algorithm, first $Agent_x$ sends a request to the target agents containing the characteristics of the requested task. After receiving the request, agents who are capable of doing the task (in term of having the skills needed for with task and enough computational capacity) send their responses to $agent_x$. Responses includes their best, average and worst case estimation time of doing the task (which was specified in the request) along with the associated probabilities of finishing the task by their estimated time. For estimations, each agent utilizes the reprioritization algorithm explained in section 3.5 to find the anticipated place of the task in its queue and following equations. Best case scenario denotes the case where neither the preceding tasks in queue, nor the requested task are delayed. Average case estimation allows half of the tasks to be delayed, while the other half is not delayed. Finally, Worst case represents the case where all tasks, including the requested task, are delayed. In all of the equations the number of tasks in the queue is considered as n.

$$T(BestCase) = \frac{\sum_{i=1}^{n} compNeeded_i}{AvgAgentCompPerIteration} \tag{9}$$

$$P(BestCase) = (1 - p(lateness))^n \tag{10}$$

$$T(AverageCase) = \frac{\sum_{i=1}^{n} compNeeded_i}{AvgAgentCompPerIteration} + \frac{n}{2} \times T(lateness) \tag{11}$$

$$P(AverageCase) = C_{\frac{n}{2}}^{n} \times (p(lateness)^{\frac{n}{2}}(1 - p(lateness))^{\frac{n}{2}}) \tag{12}$$

$$T(WorstCase) = \frac{\sum_{i=1}^{n} compNeeded_i}{AvgAgentCompPerIteration} + n \times T(lateness) \tag{13}$$

$$P(WorstCase) = 1 - P(BestCase) - P(AverageCase) \tag{14}$$

After all of the estimations, $Agent_x$ removes responses which are dominated by other responses. Then it updates trust value for the remaining agents and uses trust value to evaluate received responses. The next step includes mapping the estimated times of the responses to utility using Equation 2. After finding the reward of the task, $Agent_x$ calculates its interpretation of utility (IU)of the responses based on Equation 15 and its own risk measure. Risk-seeking agents have an optimistic attitude toward the reward, while risk-averse agents are pessimistic and undervalue the actual reward of tasks. However, risk neutral agents are objective and see the actual reward of an action.

$$IU = Reward^{RiskMeasure} \tag{15}$$

$Agent_x$ selects the optimal agent based on Expected Utility Theory [3,12]. Based on Equation 16, $agent_x$ evaluates different choices and selects the agent with the highest expected utility.

$$E(c) = IU_{Best} \times P_{Best} + IU_{Average} \times P_{Average} + IU_{Worst} \times P_{Worst} \tag{16}$$

3.7   Sources of False Data and Reliability Checking Mechanisms

One of the primary sources of false data is called Correlated Evidence. This problem happens when multiple agents observe a single interaction and use it in making opinion about the trustee. Agents make opinion just based on their direct experience with the target while trust is build based on both direct experience and opinions from third-parties. Since the experience is not identified in opinions, the third party receives several communications which seems to be different experiences while they all refer to a single interaction [8]. The tree structure task domain which we used, prevents the occurrence of correlated evidence. In our task domain, each task divides to multiples subtasks, and each subtask is assigned to one agent. If the agent finishes the subtask successfully, the completed subtask is used as a positive mutual experience between the agent who passed the subtask and the agent who executed it. This experience reflects the amount of utility the executer earned by accomplishing the subtask. In a case of task failure, this failure negatively influences the mutual experience between parties. Since each subtask is being done by just one agent, there are not any common experiences between multiple agents; therefore, this model does not struggle with the problem of correlated evidence.

The first step toward building trust is gathering recommendations. Then $agent_x$ checks the age of gathered opinions. Recent data seems to be more accurate than old data especially in our dynamic model. In our society, relations between agents, reliability values, and personality of agents are evolving over time. Therefore, agents should not confide in recommendations which primarily reflect old experiences. For satisfying the acceptability of data, $agent_x$ excludes old experiences in making opinion.

The other possible source of false data is opinions coming from biased and extreme agents. As described in section 3.2, these agents do not provide opinions based fairly on experiences. Therefore, their provided information is not persuasive. Normally when there is a high chance of false data, there is a big variance between provided opinions. In statistics, an *outlier* is an observation point that is distant from other observations and the opinions that are divergent from the majority have the high chance of being inaccurate or deceptive [8].

In our model, agents provide their opinions in the numerical range of $[0, 100]$. Suppose $agent_x$ gathered 10 opinions about $agent_y$, 9 out of the 10 report a value between $[80, 100]$ and just one recommender reports 10. Relying on the majority of the agents' opinions, there is a high chance of false data in this scenario as there is a large variance between gathered recommendations. There might be a biased or extreme agent on behind of that different opinions which needs to be detected.

In order to detect outlier points, we used the modified Z-score based on the [4]. In Equations 17 and 18, $\tilde{x}$ and $\tilde{Y}$ denotes the median of the data. Then any point of the data that has the modified Z-score with an absolute value of greater than 3.5 is labeled as an outlier [4]. When $agent_x$ detects the outliers, it removes them and gathers more opinions from possible recommenders.

$$M_i = 0.6745 * (x_i - \tilde{x})/MAD \tag{17}$$

$$MAD = median(|Y_i - \tilde{Y}|) \tag{18}$$

Building Reliability Factor is another ways of dealing with unfair recommendation providers. After detecting the outliers, $agent_x$ updates the reliability value of provider agents identified as outliers. Building reliability values about recommenders is similar to monitoring the agents over time. Instead of pursuing all of the behaviors of the agents, agents keep a numerical value and update it after each mutual experience of getting recommendation. Since getting recommendations adds cost to the system, it is not possible to gather the opinions of all potential recommenders. Costs include the message passing (communication cost) for gathering recommendations and different levels of anti-biasing mechanism. Therefore, agents mainly get recommendations based on the reliability value of agents. Agents who do not have good reliability values are excluded from participating in providing recommendations. Besides, since in our model agents get utility for providing recommendation (which is an incentive for participating in providing recommendations), this is a punishment for agents with a low reliability value. Also as mentioned in section 3.3, the reliability value is one of the factors used in evaluating neighbors for adaptation. Thus, adaptation helps agents to have strong and more reliable agents in their neighborhood for cooperation.

4   Experiments and Results

4.1   What is the Effect of Anti-bias Filtering in System's Profit?

We evaluate the effectiveness of the reliability checking mechanism based on the performance of the organization measured as the system profit. Since agents cooperatively execute a task, the accuracy of selecting peers leads in having better completion rate of tasks and higher utility of the system. Reliability checking mechanism helps the agents to evaluate their partners and pass the tasks to the most suitable one. The system profit during each iteration is computed as the summation of the profits of all individual agents. We use Equation 19 to calculate the profit of agents per iteration using the amount of earned utility and the total cost of that iteration. Costs include communication cost, reorganization cost and cost of anti-bias filtering mechanisms. Cost is calculated using Equation 21.

$$Profit_{org} = Utility_{org} - Cost_{org} \qquad (19)$$

$$Utility_{org} = \sum_{i \in \{tasks\}} Utility(task_i) \qquad (20)$$

$$Cost_{org} = Cost * \sum_{x \in \{Agents\}} numMesseges_x + \sum_{y \in \{AntiBiasMechanisms\}} Cost_y +$$
$$R * \frac{\sum_{x \in \{Agents\}} numReorg_x}{2} \qquad (21)$$

This experiment compares the profit of the system in two situations. In both of these situations, agents use a decision-making algorithm described in section 3.6 while one utilizes reliability checking mechanism in building trust. Both of the methods respect the hierarchy of the agent organization for delegating tasks; they delegate the tasks in the following order: subordinates, peers, superiors, and finally acquaintances. Using reliability checking mechanism, agents have a better evaluation of others along with identifying unfair information providers. Figure 4 shows the effectiveness of reliability checking mechanism in the profit of the system. Anti-bias filtering helps agents to avoid the effect of malicious opinions that lead them toward making more efficient decision in task passing. In this experiment, 60 percent of agents are normal and the rest are biased (20 percent) and extreme agents (20 percent). To avoid random effect on our results, the graph shows the average profit of 100 runs of the simulation with 100 agents.

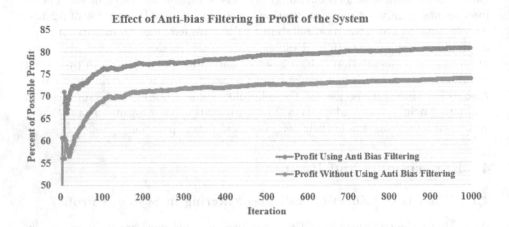

Fig. 4. Effect of Reliability Checking Mechanism on the profit of the system.

4.2   Does Anti-bias Filtering Always Help?

Anti-bias filtering mechanism imposes some costs to the system. Costs include gathering recommendations, detecting and removal of unfair ratings, asking for new recommendations to replace unfair recommendations, and building reliability factors. Since the primary goal of agents is to increase the profit of the system, they are interested in using reliability-checking mechanism if it benefits the system. This experiment is designed to show the effect of anti-bias filtering mechanism on the system's profit in different configuration of the simulation. In each situation, we change the ratio of normal agents versus biased/extreme agents. Figure 5 shows the result of this experiment.

As it can be seen from the results, when majority of agents are biased/extreme, reliability checking mechanism is not effective since it imposes a cost to the system while not resulting in more benefit for the system. When most of agents are biased or extreme, the marking of unfair recommendation gets less efficient and may even results in removing fair recommendations due to their difference with the average of other recommendations. Furthermore, it is interesting to see that when all the agents are normal ($N = 1$), use of the anti-bias filtering results in less profit for the system. This is also due to zero (or even negative) benefit versus the imposed cost of reliability checking to the system.

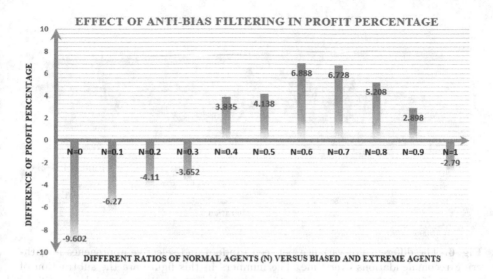

Fig. 5. Effect of Reliability Checking Mechanism on different configuration of the system. N stands for the ratio of normal agents. For example when N=0.1 means that 10 percent of agents are normal and the other 90 percent are biased/extreme agents. The numbers on the bars demonstrate the subtraction of the profit of the system using anti-bias filtering from the profit of the system in the absence of anti-bias filtering in decision making.

4.3   How Does Being Selective in Gathering Recommendation Help?

As we mentioned in the section 3.7, higher variance of the data indicates a higher chance of unfair rating among gathered recommendations. In our framework, agents adapt in every iteration in order to keep reliable and strong agents around themselves. Agents use their neighbors in cooperatively executing tasks along with using their opinions in building trust about a target agent. Therefore, our structural organization along with being selective in gathering recommendations from neighbors results in reducing the chance of false data. This experiment is designed to show the effectiveness of our proposed framework in reducing the variance of recommendations in two situations. The first situation denotes the case where agents are selective in gathering recommendations while they get random recommendations in second situation. In this experiment, recommendations are in the range of [0, 100] and the results are the average of 100 runs for 100 agents in the simulation over time in order to avoid the randomness effect.

The result (in Figure 6) shows the difference of variance between random and selective approaches. The numbers in this figure are the subtraction of variance of recommendations in the selective approach from the random approach. This figure demonstrates that the variance of gathered recommendations is lower when agents are selective in getting recommendation comparing to when they get recommendations from random agents. Another interesting observation is the

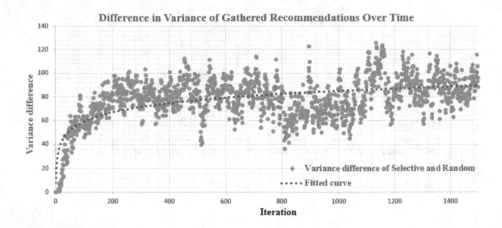

Fig. 6. The difference of variance between random and selective approaches in gathering recommendations over time. The numbers in this figure are the subtraction of variance of recommendations in selective approach from random approach.

variation of variances' differences over time. In early iterations, there are not that many mutual experiences between agents, therefore the opinions are almost the same without significant difference of being selective or random. While by passing time, agents have enough experiences and information about each other which specifically leads to having more accurate reliability values about each other. Therefore, when using anti-bias filtering mechanism, agents identify unreliable sources over time and avoid getting recommendation from them. As the result, the variance differences reach a plateau after some time.

5   Conclusion and Future Work

In this research, agents have the opportunity of evaluating their cooperation peers utilizing recommendation-based trust in a self-adaptive society. A self-adaptive society lets the agents evaluate the effectiveness of their neighbors based on the history and promote or demote the relationship with them in order to keep the most useful and reliable cooperative neighbors around them. Each agent builds trust about another agent using its own mutual experience with target along with the recommendation of agents who had experience it in order to have a variation of opinions.

Agents use the recommendation of other agents in building trust. Therefore, having reliability mechanisms to check the accuracy of provided information is necessary. Reliability checking mechanism used in this paper includes checking the age of data, detecting the outlier opinions, gathering more opinion, and building reliability values for agents. In addition, recommenders receive reward in order to give incentive to the agents for their participation.

In this model, we have three different types of agents. Biased agents making opinion about a target not only based on the quality of their mutual experiences, but also due to the existence of special features. Extreme agents are strict about negative experiences and they can be considered as cautious agents who are trying to notify all agents about any possibility of failure or lost. Normal agents are the ones who neither biased, nor extreme. These agents try to reflect their opinion exactly based on the history of experiences. Results show that reliability checking mechanism helps the agents in better profit rate and less task failure. Besides, it shows that by passing the times agents are less likely to use the recommendation of biased and extreme agents.

Possible Future work is to extend biased and extreme agents to be more complex. In this work, our biased opinions are only based on the existence of some features. We can have different types of bias, like perceptual bias or behavioral bias. It also would be interesting model other unfair behaviors pf agents such as randomly recommending other rather than modelling biased and extreme behaviors, there are other possibilities for . We can have more sophisticated anti-bias filtering using Bayesian probability and statistical methods.

References

1. Ahmadi, K.: Decision Making Using Trust and Risk in Self-Adaptive Agent Organizati by Kamilia Ahmadi. Master's thesis, Utah State University, April 2014. http://digitalcommons.usu.edu/etd/2159/
2. Ahmadi, K., Allan, V.H.: Efficient self adapting agent organizations. In: Proceedings of the 5th International Conference on Agents and Artificial Intelligence, pp. 294–303. SciTePress - Science and Technology Publications (2013). http://dx.doi.org/10.5220/0004261902940303
3. Burnett, C.: Trust Assessment and Decision-Making in Dynamic Multi-Agent Systems (2011). http://citeseerx.ist.psu.edu/viewdoc/summary?doi=10.1.1.303.3137
4. Crosby, T.: How to Detect and Handle Outliers. Technometrics **36**(3), 315–316 (1994). http://dx.doi.org/10.1080/00401706.1994.10485810
5. Falconem, R., Sapienza, A., Castelfranchi, C.: Trusting information sources through their categories. In: Demazeau, Y., Decker, K.S., Bajo Pérez, J., De la Prieta, F. (eds.) PAAMS 2015. LNCS, vol. 9086, pp. 80–92. Springer, Heidelberg (2015)
6. Gershenson, C.: Artificial Societies of Intelligent Agents. Social Science Research Network Working Paper Series, May 2003. http://ssrn.com/abstract=371641
7. Ghaffarizadeh, A., Allan, V.H.: History Based Coalition Formation in Hedonic Context Using Trust. International Journal of Artificial Intelligence & Applications **4**(4), 1–8 (2013). http://dx.doi.org/10.5121/ijaia.2013.4401
8. Grandison, T., Sloman, M.: A Survey of Trust in Internet Applications. Commun. Surveys Tuts. **3**(4), 2–16 (2000). http://dx.doi.org/10.1109/comst.2000.5340804
9. Jøsang, A., Golbeck, J.: Challenges for robust trust and reputation systems. In: 5th International Workshop on Security and Trust Management (STM 2009), Saint (2009). http://citeseerx.ist.psu.edu/viewdoc/summary?doi=10.1.1.460.8885
10. Jøsang, A., Guo, G., Pini, M.S., Santini, F., Xu, Y.: Combining recommender and reputation systems to produce better online advice. In: Torra, V., Narukawa, Y., Navarro-Arribas, G., Megías, D. (eds.) MDAI 2013. LNCS, vol. 8234, pp. 126–138. Springer, Heidelberg (2013)

11. Koster, A., Schorlemmer, M., Sabater-Mir, J.: Opening the black box of trust: reasoning about trust models in a BDI agent. Journal of Logic and Computation **23**(1), exs003–58 (2012). http://dx.doi.org/10.1093/logcom/exs003
12. Traub, M., Kaminka, G.A., Agmon, N.: Who goes there?: selecting a robot to reach a goal using social regret. In: The 10th International Conference on Autonomous Agents and Multiagent Systems, AAMAS 2011, vol. 1, pp. 91–98. International Foundation for Autonomous Agents and Multiagent Systems, Richland, SC (2011). http://portal.acm.org/citation.cfm?id=2030484
13. Venanzi, M., Rogers, A., Jennings, N.R.: Trust-based fusion of untrustworthy information in crowdsourcing Applications. In: Proceedings of the 2013 International Conference on Autonomous Agents and Multi-agent Systems, AAMAS 2013, pp. 829–836. International Foundation for Autonomous Agents and Multiagent Systems, Richland, SC (2013). http://portal.acm.org/citation.cfm?id=2485052
14. Whitby, A., JÃsang, A., Indulska, J.: Filtering Out Unfair Ratings in Bayesian Reputation Systems (2004). http://citeseerx.ist.psu.edu/viewdoc/summary?doi=10.1.1.60.1789
15. Wooldridge, M.: An Introduction to MultiAgent Systems. Wiley Publishing, 2nd edn. (2009). http://portal.acm.org/citation.cfm?id=1695886
16. Zhang, J., Şensoy, M., Cohen, R.: A detailed comparison of probabilistic approaches for coping with unfair ratings in trust and reputation systems. In: Sixth Annual Conference on Privacy, Security and Trust, pp. 189–200. IEEE, October 2008. http://dx.doi.org/10.1109/pst.2008.16

Supporting Human-Robot Teams in Space Missions Using ePartners and Formal Abstraction Hierarchies

Tibor Bosse[1,2(✉)], Jurriaan van Diggelen[2], Mark A. Neerincx[2], and Nanja J.J.M. Smets[2]

[1] Department of Computer Science, VU University Amsterdam,
De Boelelaan 1081, 1081 HV Amsterdam, The Netherlands
t.bosse@vu.nl
[2] Department of Perceptual and Cognitive Systems, TNO,
Kampweg 5, 3769 DE Soesterberg, The Netherlands
{jurriaan.vandiggelen,mark.neerincx,nanja.smets}@tno.nl

Abstract. Human space flight is a prototypical example of a complex, dynamic, and safety-critical domain in which missions are performed by collaborative teams of humans and technical systems. In such domains, intelligent electronic partners (*ePartners*) can play a useful role in supporting human-robot teams in their problem solving process whenever a non-nominal situation is encountered. To enhance the supportive capabilities of such ePartners, this paper presents an approach to formally represent the functionality of human-robot teams in terms of different levels of abstraction. By establishing formal relations between domain knowledge at different abstraction levels and introducing reasoning rules to navigate through these relations, ePartners are endowed with a number of supportive functions, such as the ability to reason about the mission status, make suggestions in non-nominal situations, and provide explanations. The approach is applied to a use case in the context of a manned space mission to Mars. It has been implemented within a mobile application to assist robot-astronaut teams during space missions, and has been tested in a pilot experiment at the European Space Research and Technology Centre.

Keywords: ePartners · Human-robot teams · Abstraction hierarchy · Reasoning · Space missions

1 Introduction

A team of astronauts has landed on Mars. As part of their mission, three 'actors' are involved in an Extra-Vehicular Activity (EVA): an engineer named Hannah, an astronaut named Albert, and a real-sized prototype of a Mars-rover, called *Eurobot*. Albert is dedicated to the task of setting up a cache for exploratory traverses at a remote location. While he uses the rover for transportation over the Mars surface towards his destination, Hannah monitors him from the habitat using wireless network communication. Suddenly, when Albert is halfway to the desired location, the rover experiences an error: one of the wheels fails to turn back to the original position. Since the malfunctioning wheel is expected to cause a higher load on the rover's battery,

© Springer International Publishing Switzerland 2015
Q. Chen et al. (Eds.): PRIMA 2015, LNAI 9387, pp. 383–399, 2015.
DOI: 10.1007/978-3-319-25524-8_24

following the original plan runs the risk of having to abandon the rover, walk back to the habitat and lose valuable mission time. So what should Albert do? He discusses the possibilities with Hannah, and several options come to their minds. Albert could abort the mission and directly return to the habitat, but this would waste mission time. He could set up the cache closer to the habitat, but this would reduce the benefit of the cache. Or should he perhaps replace the current battery by one of the reserve batteries (foreseen for the cache), to ensure his mission will not strand? All of these options seem to make some sense, but how to decide which one is the best?

This simple scenario illustrates a fundamental challenge of human space flight beyond Low Earth Orbit (LEO): dealing with unforeseen conditions and events (which will be inevitably present in these space missions) that require dynamic adjustments of the astronaut-automation team operation. These conditions and events can be failures of machines, environmental barriers or dysfunction of humans due to high workload or unforeseen health issues. Most often, an adequate solution cannot be established by one person alone, but results from collaboration and/or negotiation of a team of astronauts and computers (e.g., wicked problem solving [5]). This is because the solution may require knowledge, expertise, and capabilities that are distributed over different team members and computer systems. Furthermore, there may not be one optimal solution to a problem, but different solutions may exist with different pros and cons. Such compromises can only be made by involving all interested parties in the problem solving process (cf. [6]). Additionally, during these deep-space missions, support to the astronauts by ground control is often not a viable solution due to expected communication constraints.

Given that such wicked problems of the type described above often occur under time pressure, such incidents remain highly problematic. In this paper, we propose a solution that involves using intelligent electronic partners (*ePartners*) that are able to assist in the problem solving process [13]. The solution is illustrated for the domain of human space flight, but in principle it applies to any safety-critical domain involving collaborative missions of humans and technical systems in complex and dynamic environments. More specifically, an approach is proposed to formally represent the functionality of human-robot teams during safety-critical missions in terms of different levels of abstraction. By establishing formal relations between knowledge at different abstraction levels and introducing reasoning rules to navigate through these relations, ePartners are endowed with the ability to relate low-level problems (e.g., a wheel is turned in a different angle) to higher level conclusions about the mission as a whole (e.g., 'safety is endangered'). As a result, they are able to support humans during safety-critical missions, e.g., by reasoning about the mission status, making suggestions in non-nominal situations, and providing explanations. The approach is inspired by research in the area of Cognitive Work Analysis (CWA) [17]. The informal task models from CWA are made machine readable using techniques in Business Process Management [1].

The remainder of this paper is structured as follows. First, in Section 2, our perspective on the use of ePartners within safety-critical missions is explained. Next, in Section 3, a mission scenario and corresponding requirements for the envisioned ePartner are discussed, which were developed in the context of the MECA-HEART project. In Section 4, a framework is proposed that enables ePartners to reason through abstraction levels. An implementation of the framework is presented in Section 5, and a pilot experiment to obtain initial feedback on its usability is described in Section 6. Section 7 concludes the paper with a discussion.

2   ePartners

In [13], the use of intelligent agents as digital assistants is proposed as a means to support humans and automation actors during safety-critical missions under dynamic and high-demanding conditions. In general, such ePartners could assist in the problem solving process in the following three main ways:

- They are aware of the current context in which the problem has occurred. They inform their users of the constraints which are imposed by these contextual factors (e.g. resources being temporarily unavailable), but also suggest opportunities which are provided by the current context.
- They complement existing procedural rules (which are effective for solving the simpler problems) by supporting knowledge-based solutions. These solutions stem from a joint intelligent activity in which expertise and knowledge of a problem, possessed by humans and computer systems, is brought together and used to solve the problem.
- They streamline communication among (human or machine) team members. They provide a consistent, pervasive and explanatory interface to different machine components (explanatory agent), and are capable of translating between languages/ abstraction levels.

To further illustrate the ePartners' problem-solving support, consider the scenario sketched in the introduction. Here, it is assumed that each of the three 'actors' (i.e., astronaut Albert on EVA, remote engineer Hannah, and the Eurobot) has an ePartner to support the team operations. An example situation where these ePartners could play an important role is after an anomaly of the rover (e.g., the 'wheel problem' mentioned above). At this point, the actors enter a team decision making process that is commonly characterised as Sense, Assess, Decide, Plan and Act [17]; see Figure 1. The role of the ePartners in this process is to relieve humans as much as possible from skill- and rule-based tasks (such as Sense and Assess). Another role is to ensure that all relevant (human and machine) stakeholders are kept in the loop at the knowledge-based tasks such as Decide. The envisioned core functions of an ePartner are:

- Procedural rules such as responding fast to an anomaly can be performed fully automatically (e.g., using standard fault detection, isolation and recovery (FDIR) procedures).
- The procedural responses, which implement local rover intelligence, are complemented by the ePartner response that can apply its global intelligence (about the environment, mission goals, etc.) to establish a knowledge-based solution. The dashed line indicates the process that leads to a better solution (i.e. re-planning the mission). This process is enabled by the ePartner and would not

have occurred without it. Without the ePartner the local solution (i.e. rover shuts down) would have been the end solution.

- The cognitive task load of the human is minimised, but humans are taken into the loop if needed. For example, this is the case when the decision is made to change the mission objective.
- The Eurobot's ePartner knows the rover and serves as a communication intermediary that can interpret the rover's sensor logs and raise the level of abstraction to a level which is shared among all team members.

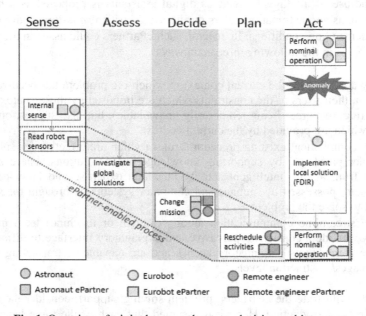

Fig. 1. Overview of a joint human-robot team decision making process.

3   Scenario and Requirements

The project MECA-HEART (Mission Execution Crew Assistant - Human E-partner Agent Robot Teaming) is a follow-up on the MECA project [2,12]. Within MECA (and related projects), consortium members have been working on the type of problems mentioned above for a number of years. Using the situated Cognitive Engineering (sCE) design methodology [11], a uniform Requirements Baseline (RB) has been established, which integrates a vast amount of state-of-the art ePartner knowledge, concepts, and techniques developed by international academic and industry parties and by the MECA consortium members themselves. The resulting RB (see [14]) was used to develop first MECA prototypes and use these in a series of tests in analogue long duration space missions.

The particular MECA-HEART prototype aims to demonstrate MECA within its envisioned technological environment, and to test its requirements baseline with the design rationale. To this end, an ePartner will be developed that functions with humans in a space context, while being integrated with "real" space technologies such as robots or alarm handling systems. It is envisioned that MECA will serve as a uniform, user-friendly and trusted access point to all systems that the astronaut has to interact with. This relieves the astronaut from uncoordinated streams of heterogeneous inputs from various systems.

To focus the scope of these activities, a detailed mission scenario in the domain of manned a manned space flight beyond Low Earth Orbit has been developed. A description of the context of the mission is as follows:

> Six astronauts and four rovers of varying types and sizes have landed on Mars. Basic infrastructure, like a habitat, electricity and wireless network communication is available. The rovers are ready for deployment and are currently in the habitat. Part of the crew, consisting of two persons and one rover, is dedicated to the task of setting up a cache for exploratory traverses at a remote location. The shelter for the cache is currently stored in the habitat and can be carried by the rover to the planned location. At the location, the shelter can be set up as a self-construction kit by unfolding it and by fixing it on the ground by drilling holes in the surface and by placing the poles of the shelter in these holes. The robot is equipped with a drill to do the drilling. The shelter is planned to be placed on a relatively flat location around 12 km from the habitat. The exact location of the shelter has not been decided yet as it depends on the presence of medium-sized stones that may make the area unsuitable as an exploratory cache location, but are too small to be detected on imagery made available to the crew. Communication with ground control on Earth is possible from the habitat, but is delayed 8 minutes (one way) for the distance between Mars and Earth at the time shortly after landing, and sometimes unavailable due to interference with the Sun.

> The plan is carried out by an engineer who remains in the habitat, called Hannah, and an astronaut on EVA, called Albert. Albert uses the Eurobot rover for transportation over the Mars surface, and to help him with heavy work such as moving rocks and drilling holes. Hannah monitors the robot and Albert from the habitat, and has access to various types of sensor data on the EVA team, which is sent to the habitat periodically in predefined packages. The transmission cycle time for these packages has to be specified manually. Furthermore, for most sensors (e.g. rover's battery, spacesuit air pressure, etc.) threshold values have been built in that automatically communicate alarms to the habitat.

The initial plan of setting up the cache distinguishes four phases (to which we will refer as use cases):

1. *preliminary preparation*: Albert and the robot are still in the habitat. Together with Hannah, they pick a site on the map, and make a plan of the mission.
2. *clearing the surface*: Albert and the Eurobot travel to the planned location, and clear the surface for the remote cache, while being monitored by Hannah from the habitat.
3. *construction*: Albert and the Eurobot construct the cache on the location, while being monitored by Hannah from the habitat.
4. *return to habitat*: Albert and the Eurobot return back to habitat, while being monitored by Hannah from the habitat.

Two variants of the scenario have been established: a problem scenario (a sequence of events without ePartner support), and a design scenario (a sequence of events with ePartner support). The scenario is summarised in Figure 2 and 3. Green lines show the nominal situation, blue lines show an off-nominal situation and red lines show a failed mission. Figure 2 shows the problem scenario in which only one branch results in a successful mission. As shown, several off-nominal situations may occur, such as a robot wheel failure (as mentioned in the introduction), a battery failure and a communication failure. The design scenario (shown in Figure 3) shows the actors having ePartner support (indicated by its logo) which should result in a successful mission in each branch.

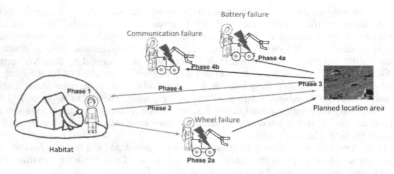

Fig. 2. Problem scenario with nominal and off nominal branches.

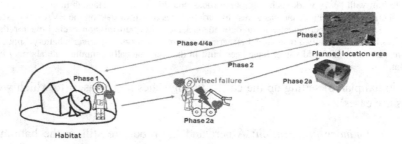

Fig. 3. Design scenario with nominal and off nominal branches.

Following the sCE method, these scenarios have been related to a set of (additional) requirements for the ePartner, thus refining the RB developed earlier. Some examples of these requirements are the following[1]:

- The ePartner shall monitor the current status of all actors and resources
- The ePartner shall raise an alarm when the status of some resource matches a certain condition

---

[1] As this paper focuses on the development phase rather than the requirements engineering phase, the details of the use cases and requirements are not included in this paper. However, they are available in the following document: [14].

- The ePartner shall support crew in decision making process based on given goals and constraints
- The ePartner shall propose resource reallocations that could solve process-related problems
- The ePartner shall explain any proposed solutions to the user

To satisfy the requirements, one of the main capabilities that the ePartner should have is the ability to reason about the various aspects of the mission at *different levels of abstraction*. For instance, in case a problem occurs at the level of an individual resource (e.g., a wheel is turned in a different angle, a communication system fails, or an astronaut experiences stress), the system should be able to relate this to higher level conclusions about the status of the mission as a whole (e.g., 'safety is endangered' or 'mission efficiency is compromised'), possibly via steps at intermediate levels. Moreover, the system should be able to explain its reasoning process to the user(s) in such a way that it is understandable and contains an appropriate level of detail. Our detailed approach to realise this functionality is presented in the next section.

4 Reasoning through Abstraction Levels

In this section, a framework is presented that enables ePartners to reason about safety-critical missions at different levels of abstraction. First, as a conceptual framework to refer to various aspects of a mission, the notion of abstraction hierarchy is introduced. Next, we illustrate how the relevant information within such a hierarchy can be represented formally. Finally, a set of reasoning rules is introduced that allow ePartners to reason about the dynamics of a mission.

4.1 Abstraction Hierarchy

The concept of abstraction hierarchy [16,17] refers to the hierarchical description of the functionality of a socio-technical system. It is the result of an analytical process called *Work Domain Analysis*. More specifically, an abstraction hierarchy has the form of a graph with a number of layers, where the nodes at the upper layer denote the purpose(s) of the system (e.g., 'setting up a cache for exploratory traverses at a remote location') and the nodes at the lowest layer denote the physical objects (or resources) involved in the system (e.g., astronauts, robots, batteries, ...). Typically, the following five layers are used: *purpose – values – functions – processes – objects*. Nodes at one level can be connected to nodes at the next lower level, thereby expressing means-end relationships (for instance, a process 'construct cache' might require several physical resources, such as an astronaut on EVA, a rover, and a drill).

Based on the cache construction mission scenario described above, an abstraction hierarchy was developed, of which a fragment is shown in Figure 4. Note that this hierarchy deviates at some points from the traditional 5-layered model introduced above. First, the two highest layers (purpose and values) are not used. Second, the notion of *task* is introduced, where a process is defined as a sequence of tasks in a particular configuration. Hence, tasks can be considered more elementary sub-steps of processes, such as *drive to location*, *clear area* and *drill holes*. Figure 4 depicts a separate layer for the tasks, where the view has 'zoomed in' onto one of the tasks (namely *cache construction*). Third, two additional layers have been added for so-called *capabilities* and *functionalities*. These two new concepts have been introduced to be able to establish relationships between, respectively, functions vs. processes, and tasks vs. resources, in a flexible manner. After all, it is not always desirable to make direct connections between these layers; for instance, instead of directly stating that task *fix cache* requires resource *Albert*, it is more expressive to state that task *fix cache* requires some functionality (e.g., 'being able to fix a cache'), and that resource *Albert* provides this functionality. In a similar manner, capabilities can be used as flexible connections between functions and processes.

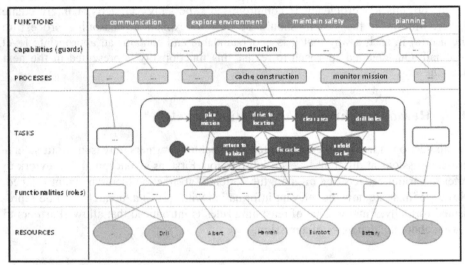

Fig. 4. Partial abstraction hierarchy for the cache construction mission.

4.2 Knowledge Representation

In the literature, abstraction hierarchies are mostly used in an informal manner, for instance as guidelines for human engineers during interface design. Instead, in the current paper we propose a mechanism to formalise abstraction hierarchies. As a result, the information at the different layers, as well as the relations between them, will be machine-readable. This will enable intelligent systems such as the proposed ePartner to process the information, and use it to generate dedicated support.

To formally model the semantics of abstraction hierarchies, the Object-Role Modeling (ORM) framework is used. ORM models use graphical symbols that are based on first order predicate logic and set theory, to enable modellers to create an unambiguous definition of an arbitrary universe of discourse [7]. As ORM is one of the standards used by the European Space Agency, and many ORM models are already available in the space domain, using it for our purpose was a logical decision.

For the current project, an ORM ontology has been created to express all relevant information for the cache construction mission scenario (i.e. all concepts and connections such as the ones shown in Figure 4). This ontology has been developed in the form of a number of ORM models. An example ORM model (for a *Process*) is visualised in Figure 5, where the rounded rectangles denote objects and the smaller boxes denote **ó**les, or relationships between objects. As can be seen in this figure, it contains, among others, some of the concepts shown at the left hand side of Figure 4; for instance, a *Process* may have a *Task*, a *Task* may be followed by another *Task*, a *Task* requires a *Functionality*, and a *Functionality* may be provided by a *Resource*[2]. By filling in these relations with scenario-specific information as shown in the right hand side of Figure 4, propositions such as these may be formulated:

> *Process 'cache construction' has Task 'plan mission'*
> *Task 'plan mission' is followed by Task 'drive to location'*
> *Task 'drive to location' requires Functionality 'transportation'*
> *Resource 'Eurobot' provides Functionality 'transportation'*

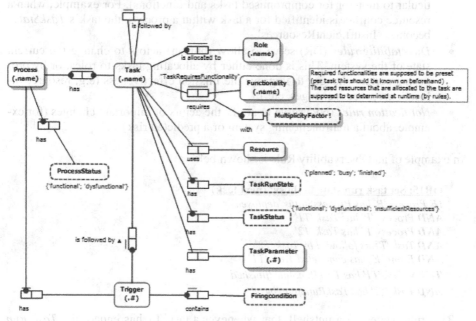

Fig. 5. Example ORM model for a *Process*.

4.3   Reasoning Rules

So far, the ORM models can be used to express static information about the mission, such as the fact that a task requires a particular functionality. However, an additional mechanism is required to let the system *reason* about the *dynamics* of the mission. Such reasoning is relevant, for instance, to conclude that the status of a task changes

---

[2] This last relationship is not shown in Figure 5, as it is part of a separate ORM model.

once that task has been completed, but also to relate a malfunction in a resource to the conclusion that a task, a process, or even the entire mission may be compromised. One step further, it may be used by the system to come up with (several alternative) solutions in case of problems, and with explanations about why a particular solution would be a good one (i.e., by predicting the consequences of a suggested option). Hence, for all of these derivations, some dynamic reasoning rules are required that enable the system to make inferences and navigate between layers of the abstraction hierarchy in a flexible manner.

To this end, a number of reasoning rules have been specified at a semi-formal level. In total, four sets of rules (inspired by [9]) are distinguished:

- *Observability rules* (OR) serve to update the status of functions, processes, tasks, resources, parameters, etc. This is done either based on user input or based on rules that propagate the status of entities between different levels of the abstraction hierarchy.
- *Predictability rules* (PR) aim to predict the status of various entities (in particular to monitor for compromised tasks and functions). For example, when a resource conflict is identified for a task within a process, the task's *TaskStatus* becomes 'InsufficientResources'.
- *Directability rules* (DR) serve to allow (human) actors to change the current state of the system. This is done either by allocating tasks to roles, or by proposing certain changes to improve the mission effectiveness (e.g. resource allocations, process changes, etc.).
- *Notification rules* (NR) serve to notify the actors of important changes (for example, about a malfunctioning system or a predicted risk).

An example of an Observability Rule is shown below:

OR15: Set task run state to 'busy' (next task)
IF Process 'P' has ProcessStatus 'deployed'
AND Process 'P' has Task 'T1'
AND Process 'P' has Task 'T2'
AND Task 'T1' is followed by Task 'T2'
AND Event 'E' has completed Task 'T1'
THEN Task 'T1' has TaskRunState 'finished'
AND Task 'T2' has TaskRunState 'busy'

This rules states, in a nutshell, that whenever a task T1 has ended, the *Task Run State* (see Figure 5) of that task is changed to *finished*, and that of the next task within that process is changed to *busy*. In total, about 40 of such reasoning rules have been established for this case study. The majority of these rules are domain independent, but a few of them are specific for the cache construction mission. An example of such a specific rule is a Predictability Rule that concludes that a transportation task has insufficient resources in case the wheels of the robot are turned in such a position that they will use more battery power for the planned route than what is currently available. The complete list of rules is provided in [15].

5   Implementation

To be able to demonstrate the usability of the ePartner in practice, it has been implemented as a distributed software architecture. The architecture consists of two main components: the MECA-HEART server (which comprises an SQL knowledge base, a Django server, and a rule engine written in Python), and the MECA-HEART app. As the technical details of the server are beyond the scope of this paper, they are not further described here. Instead, in the remainder of this section we will focus on a description of the app (from a user perspective), as this is the primary means of interaction between the user and the system.

The MECA-HEART app takes the form of an Android app running on a high-resolution, large-screen tablet. It makes use of a graphical user interface, to which user can provide input via touch, keyboard (where applicable), and voice (text dictation). An example screenshot of the interface is shown in Figure 6. The application screen is divided into different fragments, some of which are visible all the time, and others are shown or hidden depending on the context of operation:

- *Menu bar*: The Menu bar is always displayed at the top of the screen, and provides general context and control for the whole application. It contains the MECA logo, a main menu (consisting of several tabs representing the main objects managed by the system), and a settings button. The tabs displayed in the main menu refer, among others, to some of the layers in the abstraction hierarchy, namely *functions*, *processes*, *tasks* and *resources* (see Figure 4).

- *Embodied Conversational Agent (ECA)*: The ECA is a fragment occupying the left side of the screen, visible all the time, providing a constant and clear interface representing the ePartner providing continuous support to the user to monitor the mission context, the status of all mission elements and offering to the user interactive ways to communicate. It contains several components, including the user's name, an avatar representing the ePartner, a question box, and a list of active notifications. Below the notifications, a small map shows the surface area where the mission scenario develops and the approximate location of the main resources. Finally, below this map, a real time image is displayed which is sent from a webcam mounted on the Eurobot.

- *Overview fragment*: This fragment is shown in the central part of the screen (spanning to the right when the Details fragment is not visible). When one of the tabs of the Main menu is selected, the Overview fragment shows the list of the selected type, queried from the KB. Each item of the list includes an icon representing the type of object (function, process, task, or resource), its name and a sort description, its current status and health, and the time when it was updated. When an item is selected, it is highlighted and its details are displayed in the Details fragment that is shown at the right side of the Overview fragment. The item's background color can change to yellow, indicating that its health is off-nominal.

- *Details fragment*: When an item is selected at the list of the Overview fragment, more details about it are displayed in the Details fragment that opens at the right side. The fragment hides automatically when another item is selected from the Main menu and the list of objects is loaded into the Overview fragment. The contents of the Details fragment depend on the specific object that is selected at the Overview fragment list. The example screenshot shown in Figure 6 provides details of resource *Albert*. Depending on the type of resource selected, the details change, including some attributes that are specific of each type of resource.

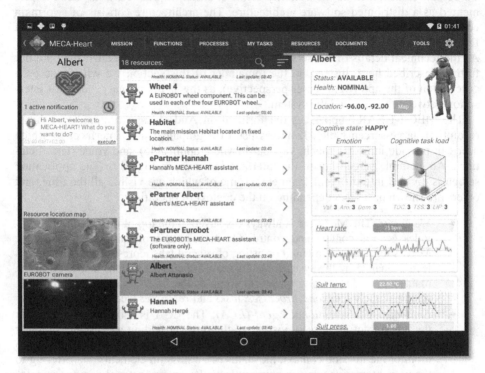

Fig. 6. Screenshot of the application's user interface, showing details of resource *Albert*.

The prototype has been set up in such a way that it can easily be integrated with external systems (e.g., robots or alarm handling systems) or tablet applications (e.g., personal agendas or chat functions). Note that, whenever the status of a resource changes (e.g., the location of a robot, the heart rate of an astronaut, or the position of a wheel), and this information is written to the knowledge base, the corresponding information in the Details fragment is updated automatically (depending on the value of the update delay setting). Additionally, the reasoning rules described in Section 4.3 automatically process the updated information, enabling the system to draw higher-level conclusions about the mission. For example, when the position of a wheel changes, the system will derive (using one of the Predictability rules) that the corresponding task is compromised, which will propagate (using some of the Observability rules) to the conclusion that the entire mission is endangered. As a result, the user will receive a warning notification (derived based on one of the Notification rules), and the system will make a proposal to solve the problem (using one of the Directability rules). In principle, the results of all of these steps can be visualised in one of the three fragments of the user interface. However, to prevent the user from being overloaded with a multitude of detailed warnings at the resource level (also referred to as "alarm flood"), the system provides feedback in terms of higher-level conclusions (such as 'the mission is endangered'). Only if the user explicitly asks for more detailed explanation, (s)he is able to view more details about the underlying reasoning process. This approach allows the user to devote his or her cognitive resources to higher cognitive processes (cf. Ecological Interface Design [18]).

6   Pilot Experiment

As a preliminary test of the usability of the ePartner within a (semi-)realistic environment, a pilot experiment has been conducted at the European Space Research and Technology Centre (ESTEC) in Noordwijk, the Netherlands. The design of the experiment is explained in Section 6.1. The initial results are discussed in Section 6.2.

6.1   Design

The main aim of the experiment was to assess the appropriateness and accuracy of the scenario, procedures, material, measurements, software and hardware, and to obtain feedback from domain experts. Based on the results, the prototype, test-setting and methods would be improved, thereby creating the necessary conditions for a quantitative experiment at a later stage of the project.

The participant in the experiment was an adult male operator at ESTEC with experience in the space domain. He was asked to play a role as part of a team in a scenario based evaluation: he conducted the evaluation as Albert, who had to go on EVA with the rover to set-up a shelter for the cache. The other team member was played by a MECA-HEART member and conducted the evaluation as Hannah, who stayed in the habitat to monitor the mission. The scenario was played two times: first with ePartner, and later without ePartner. In the condition with ePartner, both team members used a tablet on which the MECA-HEART application was installed. In the condition without ePartner, they could still use this app, but its functionality was limited by disabling all support functions related to the framework presented in Section 4. As a result, they would still have access to resource level information (such as locations of actors or battery levels), but no higher level interpretations of this information were made.

The tablet device used in the experiment by both team members was a Samsung Galaxy Tab S with Android operating system. The participant conducting the role of Albert had to perform the EVA with a rover, in this case this was the Eurobot demonstrator at ESTEC. Other material used for the experiment included two walkie talkies (for communication between Hannah and Albert), five batteries, a drill and an oxygen tank (to load onto the rover and store in the cache), and a pop-up tent (to serve as cache). Additionally, a Wizard of Oz (WoZ) control unit was used, enabling one of the experimenters to inject events in the scenario to simulate, among others, some of the off-nominal situations depicted in Figure 2 (such as a 'wheel failure' and a 'communication failure'). These events were simulated via the WoZ control unit as this was more practical than actually making them happen in the physical world. Especially in these off-nominal situations, the ePartner was expected to have an added value in supporting the team in successfully completing the mission.

During the experiment, data was collected from various sources, including: 1) the low-level interaction logs of the ePartner software (e.g., which tabs are selected?, which buttons are clicked?), 2) the observed behavior and decisions made by the test participant (e.g., how did he perform his tasks?, and how much time did this take?), and 3) questionnaires which indicate the subjective experience of using the software.

Fig. 7. Impression of the pilot experiment at ESTEC. Left: astronaut is interacting with the tablet during the task 'drive to location'. The Eurobot is visible at the background. Right: astronaut is interacting with the tablet during the task 'fix cache'.

6.2   Results

Preliminary results pointed out that the pilot experiment was an effective means to demonstrate the usability of the prototype, and collect relevant feedback from domain experts. In general, the ePartner seemed to be a useful tool to support the participants during a scenario like this. This was confirmed by anecdotal evidence and subjective reports by the participant. For example, when the wheel failure occurred, the ePartner automatically related this to higher level conclusions about the mission status. In turn, the system used these conclusions to propose a number of potential solutions to the participant (such as 'aborting the mission', 'changing the planned location of the cache', and 'replacing the current battery with a reserve battery'), along with a corresponding explanation. These kinds of supportive measures allowed the participant to maintain situation awareness and quickly solve the problem. Instead, in the same situation during the condition without ePartner, the information presented to the participant was substantially less transparent (mainly consisting of low-level warnings, e.g., about the wheel failure). As a result, the participant had more difficulties (and needed more time) to effectively complete the mission. Figure 7 provides an impression of the pilot experiment.

7   Discussion

In the literature on cognitive engineering, the notion of abstraction hierarchy is well-established [16,17,18]. In [8], an overview is provided of studies in which the abstraction hierarchy has been applied to different work domains, varying from process control systems to air traffic control systems. However, in most cases, abstraction hierarchies are used in an informal manner. As a result, the semantics of the underlying knowledge are not represented in an unambiguous manner. Still, there are some exceptions. For example, already in 1994, Bisantz and Vicente [3] developed a formal representation of the abstraction hierarchy that formed the basis of a computer program that reasons about a thermal-hydraulic process. And more recently, Ham [8] proposed a semi-formal framework that combines the use of abstraction hierarchies and living systems theory, and is illustrated by modelling the knowledge of a secondary cooling system of nuclear power plants. Nevertheless, these systems are mainly used *before* the execution of the process that is studied, for instance as guidelines for human engineers during interface design. The current paper goes a step further as it presents a machine-readable representation of abstraction hierarchies that is used by an intelligent system (the ePartner) *during* execution of a mission. In particular, by formalising the information at the different layers of the hierarchy (as well as the relations between them), the system is able to reason about it dynamically, for instance to generate dedicated support at runtime during safety-critical missions. Another advantage is that the current system applies to missions that involve teams of both humans and robots, whereas the approaches mentioned above mainly focus on technology-oriented engineering systems.

As opposed to the area of cognitive engineering, the literature in Artificial Intelligence and Agent Technology contains a number of papers describing applications of personal assistant agents that support humans during a particular task. However, most of these applications are either aimed supporting one single user during a very specific task (e.g., time management [10]), or they present generic conceptual models that have not been implemented within real world applications (e.g., [4]). In contrast, the current paper presented a generic framework that has the ability to address complex human-robot team missions (represented in terms of abstraction hierarchies), and has actually been implemented and tested in a space environment, in interaction with space technology.

Based on the preliminary results of the pilot experiment, the framework seemed to be a suitable tool to support human-robot teams during these kind of space scenarios. The astronaut seemed to process the presented information by the ePartner in the intended way, and was able to use it to effectively adapt to off-nominal circumstances and complete his mission. Also the user interface turned out to be easy to use.

As a follow up, the framework is currently being evaluated more extensively, based on quantitative between-subject experiments involving a large number of participants. Additionally, it will be further developed and extended in various ways, among others by enriching the data models (of resources, tasks, processes, etc.), adding more user interface visualisations, expanding the rule set, and increasing its integration with other services offered by mobile devices.

Acknowledgements. This research was conducted in the context of the MECA-HEART project, funded by the European Space Agency under grant agreement 4000110730/14/NL/LvH. The authors wish to thank Leo Breebaart, Antonio Olmedo Soler, and Joaquim Rosa for their work on the implementation of the software, Jan Willem Baggerman for his contribution to the formal Abstraction Hierarchy framework, and Frank Plassmeier for his input regarding the scenarios.

References

1. van der Aalst, W.M., ter Hofstede, A.H., Weske, M.: Business process management: a survey. In: van der Aalst, W.M., Weske, M. (eds.) BPM 2003. LNCS, vol. 2678, pp. 1–12. Springer, Heidelberg (2003)
2. Baker, C., Naikar, N., Neerincx, M.A.: Engineering planetary exploration systems: integrating novel technologies and the human element using work domain analysis. In: Proceedings of the 59th International Astronautical Congress (IAC 2008)
3. Bisantz, A.M., Vicente, K.J.: Making the abstraction hierarchy concrete. International Journal on Human-Computer Studies **40**, 83–117 (1994)
4. Bosse, T., Duell, R., Hoogendoorn, M., Klein, M., van Lambalgen, R., van der Mee, A., Oorburg, R., Sharpanskykh, A., Treur, J., de Vos, M.: A generic personal assistant agent model for support in demanding tasks. In: Schmorrow, D.D., Estabrooke, I.V., Grootjen, M. (eds.) FAC 2009. LNCS(LNAI), vol. 5638, pp. 3–12. Springer, Heidelberg (2009)
5. Coyne, R.: Wicked problems revisited. Design Studies **26**, 5–17 (2005)
6. Fischer, G., Nakakoji, K.: Beyond the macho approach of artificial intelligence: empower human designers — do not replace them. Knowledge-Based Systems **5**(1), 15–30 (1992)
7. Halpin, T.: Object-role modeling (ORM/NIAM). In: Bernus, P. et al. (eds.) Handbook on Architectures of Information Systems. International Handbooks on Information Systems, pp 81–103. Springer Verlag (2006)
8. Ham, D.-H.: Modelling work domain knowledge with the combined use of abstraction hierarchy and living systems theory. Cognition, Technology & Work, April 2015. Springer Verlag (2015)
9. Johnson, M., Bradshaw, J.M., Feltovich, P.J., Jonker, C.M., van Riemsdijk, M.B., Sierhuis, M.: Coactive Design: Designing Support for Interdependence in Joint Activity. Journal of Human-Robot Interaction **3**(1), 43–69 (2014)
10. Myers, K., Berry, P., Blythe, J., Conley, K., Gervasio, M., McGuinness, D.L., Morley, D., Pfeffer, A., Pollack, M., Tambe, M.: An Intelligent Personal Assistant for Task and Time Management. AI Magazine, Summer **2007**, 47–61 (2007)
11. Neerincx, M.A.: Situated Cognitive Engineering for Crew Support in Space. Personal and Ubiquitous Computing **15**(5), 445–456 (2011)
12. Neerincx, M.A., Bos, A., Olmedo-Soler, A., Brauer, U., Wolff, M.: The mission execution crew assistant: improving human-machine team resilience for long duration missions. In: Proc. of the 59th Int. Astronautical Congress (IAC 2008) (2008)
13. Neerincx, M.A., Grant, T.: Evolution of Electronic Partners: Human-Automation Operations and ePartners During Planetary Missions. Journal of Cosmology **12**, 3825–3833 (2010)

14. Olmedo Soler, A., Smets, N., Neerincx, M.A., van Diggelen, J., Baggerman, J.W., Breebaart, L., Rosa, J., Plassmeier, F.: HEART Requirements. Technical report for the ESA project MECA-HEART (2014). http://www.crewassistant.com/docs/pub/MECA_HEART/MECA_HEART_WP1_D1a_sC ET_report_v2.pdf

15. Plassmeier, F., Baggerman, J.W., Bosse, T., van Diggelen, J., Smets, N.: Mission Simulation Specification. Technical report for the ESA project MECA-HEART (2015). http://www.crewassistant.com/docs/pub/MECA_HEART/MECA_HEART-WP3-D2b-MissionSimulationSpecs.pdf

16. Rasmussen, J., Lind, M.: Coping with complexity. Risø-M-2293, Electronics Department, Risø Nat. Laboratory, Roskilde, Denmark (1981)

17. Vicente, K.J.: Cognitive Work Analysis: Towards safe, productive, and healthy computer-based work. Lawrence Erlbaum Associates, Mahwah (1999)

18. Vicente, K.J.: Ecological interface design: Progress and challenges. Hum. Factors **44**, 62–78 (2002)

Flexible Reward Plans for Crowdsourced Tasks

Yuko Sakurai[1]([✉]), Masato Shinoda[2], Satoshi Oyama[3], and Makoto Yokoo[1]

[1] Kyushu University, Fukuoka, Japan
{sakurai,yokoo}@inf.kyushu-u.ac.jp
[2] Nara Women's University, Nara, Japan
shinoda@cc.nara-wu.ac.jp
[3] Hokkaido University, Sapporo, Japan
oyama@ist.hokudai.ac.jp

Abstract. We develop flexible reward plans to elicit truthful predictive probability distribution over a set of uncertain events from workers. In general, strictly proper scoring rules for categorical events only reward a worker for an event that actually occurred. However, different incorrect predictions vary in quality, and the principal would like to assign different rewards to them, according to her subjective similarity among events; e.g. a prediction of overcast is closer to sunny than rainy.

We propose concrete methods so that the principal can assign rewards for incorrect predictions according to her similarity between events. We focus on two representative examples of strictly proper scoring rules: spherical and quadratic, where a worker's expected utility is represented as the inner product of her truthful predictive probability and her declared probability. In this paper, we generalize the inner product by introducing a reward matrix that defines a reward for each prediction-outcome pair. We first show that if the reward matrix is symmetric and positive definite, both the spherical and quadratic proper scoring rules guarantee the maximization of a worker's expected utility when she truthfully declares her prediction. We next compare our rules with the original spherical/quadratic proper scoring rules in terms of the variance of rewards obtained by workers. Finally, we show our experimental results using Amazon Mechanical Turk.

1 Introduction

Mechanism design is a subfield of game theory and microeconomics that studies how to design mechanisms for good outcomes even when agents act strategically. Studies on mechanism design have been advanced by the AI and multiagent systems research communities. In particular, mechanisms for eliciting or aggregating information about uncertain events from agents is becoming a common research topic due to the expansion of prediction markets and crowdsourcing [5,4,3,8,14,15].

Prediction mechanisms aggregate forecasts of future events from agents to accurately predict uncertain events. Strictly proper scoring rules incentivize an agent to truthfully reveal her predictive probability distribution over uncertain

© Springer International Publishing Switzerland 2015
Q. Chen et al. (Eds.): PRIMA 2015, LNAI 9387, pp. 400–415, 2015.
DOI: 10.1007/978-3-319-25524-8_25

events [2,6,9,13]. A variety of strictly proper scoring rules has been developed for cases where only one alternative event occurs. In such existing rules, a principal rewards an agent for predicting events that actually happened.

Consider an example of forecasting tomorrow's weather, where a requester asks a worker about the probabilities for sunny, overcast, and rainy. The requester sets different similarities for each pair of alternative events. For example, he considers overcast more similar to sunny than to rainy because rainfall largely affects such activities as buying umbrellas or canceling/changing plans. If the weather on the next day is overcast, the requester pays more to the person who predicted a greater chance of sunny (sunny:40%, overcast:50%, and rainy:10%) than one who predicted a greater chance for rain (sunny:10%, overcast:50%, and rainy:40%). Assigning rewards to incorrect predictions is also attractive to workers. In theory, we generally assume that a worker has no preference between a plan that only rewards correct outcomes and one that also rewards incorrect outcomes. However, since various types of people work in crowdsourcing services, we have to consider the existence of workers who prefer rewards for incorrect predictions.

Assigning rewards to incorrect predictions is also attractive to agents. In theory, if an agent is risk neutral, she has no preference between a plan that only rewards the correct outcome and one that also rewards incorrect outcomes. However, various types of people work in crowdsourcing services. Since assuming that all of them are risk neutral is not realistic, we have to consider existence of risk averse agents who will prefer some reward for incorrect predictions.

In this paper, we consider reward plans with which a requester can flexibly design based on the similarity among categorical events/alternatives and generalize strictly proper scoring rules to realize this idea. The requester can also give different reward amounts for different non-actual events, based on the similarity to the actual event. Predicting one outcome among categorical events/alternatives is a well-known task, such as image labeling problems in crowdsourcing services. The similarity among categorical events is determined based on a requester's subjective view in contrast to the case of predicting the outcome of continuous values. We focus on the structure of a worker's expected utility of spherical and quadratic proper scoring rules. In them, we calculate a worker's expected utility by the inner product of her truthful predictions and her declarations. We can set various rewards by generalizing this inner product by introducing a reward matrix. The original proper scoring rules had a diagonal reward matrix that only gives a reward when the worker's prediction matches the real outcome. We generalize them by introducing a non-diagonal reward matrix, where a non-diagonal element represents the payment for a prediction different from the actual outcome. We show that the worker's expected reward is maximized by truthfully declaring her predictive probability distribution if the reward matrix is symmetric and positive definite. We also show that if the ratio of the diagonal element (the reward paid for a correct outcome) to the sum of all the elements does not exceed a certain proportion, e.g., 60%, a worker who gives a predictive probability greater than a certain proportion, e.g., 84%, to the event she considers most probable will receive a reward with smaller variance from our proposed rules than the original rules.

We also experimentally evaluated our generalized spherical proper scoring rules using Amazon Mechanical Turk (MTurk) and posted two types of tasks: predicting highest temperature in a certain city and predicting exchange rate movements. After executing a task, a worker chooses either the original spherical proper scoring rule or our generalized spherical proper scoring rule for calculating her reward. In the task of predicting highest temperature, 60% of 90 workers selected our rule. The average reward from our rule exceeded the original rule, but its variance of reward was lower than the original rule. In the task of predicting exchange rate movements, 52% of 60 workers selected our rule.

2   Related Work

Recently, studies related to proper scoring rules have gathered much attention from AI and multi-agent system researchers. Here, we discuss several existing works that are related to our research, i.e., those exploring extensions of the original proper scoring rules.

Prelec (2004) proposed Bayesian truth serum (BTS) to elicit both an agent's private signal and the distribution prediction of all agent signals when assuming they share a common prior. BTS gives high rewards to answers that are more common than collectively predicted answers. Witkowski and Parkes (2012) developed a robust BTS (RBTS) to elicit binary signals for small populations, since BTS only works with many agents. Padanovic and Faltings (2013) generalized RBTS to elicit non-binary signals for small populations, and Zhang and Chen (2014) proposed knowledge-free peer prediction under weaker assumptions than these previous works. Huang and Shoham (2014) modified the market scoring rule (MSR), which is a sequential scoring rule, with a trade limit to reduce the manipulability of prediction markets even if honest traders aren't aware of the manipulators.

Gneiting and Raftery (2007) proposed a continuous ranked probability score (CRPS) to predict the outcome of continuous variables. Robu et al. (2012) developed a pricing mechanism based on CRPS to incentivize renewable distributed energy resources to declare their production estimates, including the uncertainty in them when they joined a cooperative. Akasiadis and Chalkiadakis (2013) also applied CRPSs for shifting electricity consumption to give incentives to agents to accurately and truthfully report their expected shifting capabilities.

3   Preliminaries

In this section, we explain the model of our problem settings.

Definition 1 (A set of categorical events/alternatives). *We define E as a set of categorical events/alternatives and assume $|E| = m < \infty$. Exactly one event $i \in E$ will occur in the future.*

Definition 2 (Predictive probability distribution). *The predictive probability distribution of a worker over E is an m-tuple $\mathbf{p} = (p_1, \ldots, p_m)$, which means that she predicts that the ith event will occur with probability p_i. $0 \leq p_i \leq 1$ for any i and $\sum_{1 \leq i \leq m} p_i = 1$ have to be satisfied.*

When a requester asks workers to predict tomorrow's weather, E is set to $\{sunny, overcast, rainy\}$. Predictive probability distribution $\mathbf{p} = (0.7, 0.2, 0.1)$ means that the worker considers the *sunny* probability to be 70%, the *overcast* probability to be 20%, and the *rainy* probability to be 10%.

Based on a worker's predictive probability distribution over E, she declares her prediction to a requester.

Definition 3 (Declaration). *The declaration of a worker is an m-tuple $\mathbf{q} = (q_1, \cdots, q_m)$, which means that she declares that the ith event will occur with probability q_i. $\forall i, 0 \leq q_i \leq 1$ and $\sum_{1 \leq i \leq m} q_i = 1$ hold. She need not declare her prediction truthfully and may strategically choose $\mathbf{q}$.*

Thus, $\mathbf{q}$ may not equal $\mathbf{p}$.

A worker determines $\mathbf{q}$ and declares it to the requester, who rewards her based on that declaration.

Definition 4 (Reward function). *Reward function $\mathbf{r}(\cdot)$ takes declaration $\mathbf{q}$ as input and returns $\mathbf{r}(\mathbf{q})$ as a reward:*

$$\mathbf{r}(\mathbf{q}) = \begin{pmatrix} r_1(\mathbf{q}) \\ \vdots \\ r_m(\mathbf{q}) \end{pmatrix},$$

where $r_i(\mathbf{q}) \in \mathbf{R}$ represents the reward for the occurrence of the ith event.

We assume reward function $\mathbf{r}(\cdot)$ is fixed, which a worker knows when she determines her declaration.

A worker's expected utility of prediction $\mathbf{p}$ is calculated as follows.

Definition 5 (Expected utility). *Let $u(\mathbf{p}, \mathbf{q})$ denote a worker's expected utility when her prediction is $\mathbf{p}$ and her declaration is $\mathbf{q}$. $u(\mathbf{p}, \mathbf{q})$ is given by*

$$u(\mathbf{p}, \mathbf{q}) = \sum_{1 \leq i \leq m} p_i r_i(\mathbf{q}) = \mathbf{p} \cdot r(\mathbf{q}).$$

Here, we explain strictly proper scoring rules that have been proposed to give an incentive for each worker to truthfully declare her prediction.

Definition 6 (Strictly proper scoring rule). $\mathbf{r}(\cdot)$ *is said to be a strictly proper scoring rule if*

$$u(\mathbf{p}, \mathbf{p}) > u(\mathbf{p}, \mathbf{q})$$

holds for any $\mathbf{p} \neq \mathbf{q}$.

The above definition of a strictly proper scoring rule means that a worker maximizes her expected utility by the truthful declaration ($\mathbf{q} = \mathbf{p}$) of her prediction.

There exists a variety of strictly proper scoring rules. We introduce two representative examples.

Definition 7 (Spherical proper scoring rule). *A spherical proper scoring rule is defined by*

$$r_i(\mathbf{q}) = \alpha \frac{q_i}{\sqrt{\sum_{1 \leq j \leq m} q_j^2}},$$

where α indicates the maximum amount of the scores.

Definition 8 (Quadratic proper scoring rule). *A quadratic proper scoring rule is defined by*

$$r_i(\mathbf{q}) = \alpha(2q_i - \sum_{1 \leq j \leq m} q_j^2)$$

where α indicates the maximum amount of the scores.

A quadratic proper scoring rule does not always yield a non-negative reward. Thus, the following slightly modified rule, $r_i(\mathbf{q}) = \alpha(2q_i - \sum_{1 \leq j \leq m} q_j^2 + 1)$ guarantees a positive reward, since penalizing a worker is not always feasible or acceptable.

We use an inner product generated by symmetric positive definite matrix A of size $m \times m$:

$$A = \begin{pmatrix} a_{1,1} & \cdots & a_{1,m} \\ \vdots & \ddots & \vdots \\ a_{m,1} & \cdots & a_{m,m} \end{pmatrix}.$$

Definition 9 (Symmetry). *Matrix A is symmetric if $a_{i,j} = a_{j,i}$ holds for any i, j.*

Definition 10 (Positive definiteness). *Matrix A is positive definite if $^t\mathbf{x}A\mathbf{x} > 0$ holds for any $\mathbf{x} \in \mathbf{R}^m$ with $\mathbf{x} \neq \mathbf{0}$.*

When matrix A is symmetric and positive definite, the quadratic form,

$$(\mathbf{x}, \mathbf{y})_A = {}^t\mathbf{x}A\mathbf{y},$$

becomes an inner product. We denote $||\mathbf{x}||_A = \sqrt{(\mathbf{x}, \mathbf{x})_A}$.

4   Generalized Strictly Proper Scoring Rules

In this section, we consider strictly proper scoring rules that enable a requester to design a flexible reward plan based on his subjective similarity among alternative events. We focus on the structure of a worker's expected utility for both spherical and quadratic proper scoring rules. The expected utility can be represented as an inner product of a worker's declaration and her truthful prediction.

4.1 Generalized Spherical/Quadratic Rules

We define a matrix to represent a reward plan determined by a requester based on the similarity among alternative events.

Definition 11 (Reward matrix). *We define an $m \times m$ reward matrix as A. A diagonal element of $a_{i,i}$ represents the reward for correct outcomes, whereas the non-diagonal elements of $a_{i,j}$ ($j \neq i$) represent the reward of an incorrect outcome.*

If a requester gives no reward for events that did not occur, he sets $a_{i,j} = 0$ for any $i \neq j$. If he guarantees non-negative rewards, $a_{i,j} \geq 0$ must be satisfied for any $i, j \in E$.

We assume that this reward matrix A is symmetric and positive definite, which enables us to define an inner product with respect to the reward matrix. We can develop a reward function that gives higher rewards to the worker whose declaration is closer to the truthful declaration by introducing this inner product. As examples of such reward functions, we propose new rules by generalizing the original spherical and quadratic proper scoring rules.

Definition 12 (Generalized spherical proper scoring rule). *We define the generalized spherical scoring rule for the i-th event as*

$$r_i^A(\mathbf{q}) = \alpha \sum_{j=1}^{m} q_j \frac{a_{ij}}{||\mathbf{q}||_A},$$

where α is the maximum amount of the scores.

Theorem 1. *The generalized spherical scoring rule maximizes a worker's expected utility when she truthfully declares her prediction.*

Proof. The expected utility of a worker with prediction $\mathbf{p}$ and declaration $\mathbf{q}$ is given by

$$u_A(\mathbf{p}, \mathbf{q}) = \alpha \sum_{i=1}^{m} p_i r_i^A(\mathbf{q}) = \frac{\alpha}{||\mathbf{q}||_A} \sum_{i=1}^{m} \sum_{j=1}^{m} p_i a_{ij} q_j$$

$$= \alpha \frac{(\mathbf{p}, \mathbf{q})_A}{||\mathbf{q}||_A}.$$

From the Cauchy-Schwarz inequality, we obtain

$$u_A(\mathbf{p}, \mathbf{q}) = \alpha \frac{(\mathbf{p}, \mathbf{q})_A}{||\mathbf{q}||_A} \leq \alpha \frac{||\mathbf{p}||_A \cdot ||\mathbf{q}||_A}{||\mathbf{q}||_A}$$

$$= \alpha ||\mathbf{p}||_A.$$

As a result, we guarantee that the generalized spherical scoring rule is strictly proper, since $u(\mathbf{p}, \mathbf{q})$ is maximized when $\mathbf{q} = \mathbf{p}$ holds.

If a requester sets $A = I$ where I is an $m \times m$ identity matrix, this rule coincides with the original spherical proper scoring rule.

Definition 13 (Generalized quadratic proper scoring rule). *When a worker declares* $\mathbf{q}$, *the reward of the i-th event is calculated by*

$$r_i^A(\mathbf{q}) = \alpha(2(A\mathbf{q})_i - ||\mathbf{q}||_A^2),$$

where α *is the maximum amount of the scores and* $(A\mathbf{q})_i$ *means the i-th coordinate of* $A\mathbf{q}$.

Theorem 2. *The generalized quadratic proper scoring rule maximizes a worker's expected utility when she truthfully declares her prediction.*

Proof. The expected utility of a worker with prediction $\mathbf{p}$ and declaration $\mathbf{q}$ is given by

$$u_A(\mathbf{p}, \mathbf{q}) = \alpha(2\sum_{i=1}^m p_i r_i(\mathbf{q}) - ||\mathbf{q}||_A^2)$$
$$= \alpha(2\mathbf{p}A\mathbf{q} - ||\mathbf{q}||_A^2)$$
$$= \alpha(||\mathbf{p}||_A^2 - ||\mathbf{p} - \mathbf{q}||_A^2) \leq \alpha||\mathbf{p}||_A^2 w.$$

If we regard $u(\mathbf{p}, \mathbf{q})$ as a function of $\mathbf{q}$, it is maximized when $\mathbf{q} = \mathbf{p}$.

If a requester sets $A = I$ where I is an $m \times m$ identity matrix, this rule coincides with the original quadratic proper scoring rule.

We show an example to explain how to determine a reward matrix to satisfy symmetry and positive definiteness. We assume that a worker predicts whether it will be sunny, overcast, or rainy on the next day, i.e., $E = \{sunny, overcast, rainy\}$. If the next day's weather is overcast, he gives less reward for a rainy prediction than a sunny one because the incorrect prediction causes him greater loss. For such case, the requester can design a reward matrix:

$$A = \begin{pmatrix} 1 - s & s & 0 \\ s & 1 - s - t & t \\ 0 & t & 1 - t \end{pmatrix},$$

4.2 Relations with Kernel and Continuous Ranked Probability Scores

Gneiting and Raftery (2007) investigated the conditions where the ways of giving rewards to the declared probability distributions are proper scoring rules. They showed a class of proper scoring rules based on a negative definite kernel (kernel score). The negative definite kernel score is represented as a quadratic form for the declared probabilities with the quantified similarities among the alternatives as the coefficient of the declared probabilities. Real-valued function g on $E \times E$ is said to be a negative definite kernel if it is symmetric in its arguments and

$\sum_{i=1}^{m} \sum_{j=1}^{m} p_i p_j g(i, j) \leq 0$ for all positive integers m and all $p_1, \ldots p_n \in \mathcal{R}$. Here, $g(i, j)$ indicates a function related to the difference between alternatives i and j.

The kernel score is calculated by the sum of average rewards that a worker obtains when she truthfully declares her prediction and a negative definite kernel. In other words, this means that we carry a penalty for incorrect predictions against the average reward she obtains when her declaration is true. A kernel score and our generalized quadratic scoring rule share common features of representation. While the negative definite kernel score carries a penalty based on differences between results and declarations, our rule applies a positive definite and adds the scores based on the similarities among alternatives. In that sense, our generalized quadratic proper scoring rule is one instance of negative definite kernel scores. On the other hand, our spherical proper scoring rule is not a negative definite kernel score, since it is not represented as a quadratic formula.

A continuous ranked probability score (CRPS) is also known to be one instance of kernel scores that predicts the outcome of continuous variables. Its discretized version is considered a special case of our proposed general quadratic scoring rules. A CRPS works on commutative distributions instead of probability distributions. When $\mathbf{p}$ and $\mathbf{q}$ represent the predictive probability distribution and the worker's declared distribution, their commutative distributions are computed by $U\mathbf{p}$ and $U\mathbf{q}$, where U is a lower-triangular matrix whose non-zero elements are all 1. CRPS is equivalent to computing ${}^t(\mathbf{p} - \mathbf{q}){}^t UU(\mathbf{p} - \mathbf{q})$, which is a special case of our generalized quadratic scoring rule where ${}^t UU = A$.

Although CRPS has been extended to give different weights for different cumulative intervals, which correspond to introducing diagonal matrix D and using $A = {}^t UDU$, the requester is given less flexibility in designing a reward matrix than ours. On the other hand, our approach allows a requester to design a reward matrix based on her subjective similarities among events, and it can also be applied to spherical scoring rules as well as quadratic scoring rules.

5   Comparison Between the Original and Our Proposed Rules

In this section, we compare the original proper scoring rules and our generalized scoring rules in terms of the variance of reward. We expect that our proposed rule can reward humans in real-world services. Thus, we give sufficient conditions to satisfy the following: (i) our rules improve the guaranteed minimum reward and (ii) the variance of reward obtained by our rules is lower than the variance of reward obtained by the original rules.

For reward matrix A, we assume that

$$\sum_{j=1}^{m} a_{i,j} = 1 \tag{1}$$

holds for any $i \in E$ and also assume a symmetric positive definite matrix. This condition means that the total reward is constant regardless of i.

In the following, we concentrate on our generalized spherical proper scoring rule defined by Def. 12, since applying it provides more intuitive meaning than the generalized quadratic proper scoring rule. We can prove the theorems for the generalized quadratic proper scoring rule in the same manner. We regard a worker's reward from a spherical rule as

$$r_i^A(\mathbf{p}) = \alpha \frac{(A\mathbf{p})_i}{||\mathbf{p}||_A},$$

by assuming that she declares a truthful prediction, i.e., $\mathbf{q} = \mathbf{p}$, since we already proved that this rule is strictly proper in Theorem 1. Her expected utility is also calculated by

$$u_A(\mathbf{p}, \mathbf{p}) = \alpha \frac{(\mathbf{p}, \mathbf{p})_A}{||\mathbf{p}||_A} = ||\mathbf{p}||_A.$$

For simplicity, in this section, we assume that $\alpha = 1$ and first show that we can improve the guaranteed minimum reward if reward matrix A is non-negative.

Proposition 1. *Assume that a worker truthfully declares* $\mathbf{p} = (p_1, p_2, \ldots, p_m)$. *We set* $k = argmin_{1 \leq i \leq m} p_i$ *and obtain the following:*

(1) $r_i^I(\mathbf{p}) > 0$ *implies* $r_i^A(\mathbf{p}) > 0$,
(2) $r_k^I(\mathbf{p}) \leq r_i^A(\mathbf{p})$ *for any* $i \in E$.

Proof. (1) $a_{i,i} > 0$ for any i, since A is positive definite. Thus, from the assumption of non-negativity, we have

$$r_i^A(\mathbf{p}) = \frac{\sum_{j=1}^m a_{i,j} p_j}{||\mathbf{p}||_A} \geq \frac{a_{i,i} p_i}{||\mathbf{p}||_A} > 0.$$

(2) We first show $||\mathbf{p}||_I \geq ||\mathbf{p}||_A$. From $||\mathbf{p}||_I = \sqrt{\mathbf{p} I \mathbf{p}}$ and $||\mathbf{p}||_A = \sqrt{\mathbf{p} A \mathbf{p}}$, it suffices to show that $\mathbf{p}(I - A)\mathbf{p} \geq 0$. In other words, we want to show that $I - A$ is a positive semi-definite matrix. Since Eq. (1) implies that the maximal eigenvalue of A is 1 , any eigenvalue of $I - A$ is non-negative and $I - A$ is thus positive semi-definite. Using this and $p_j \geq p_k$ for $\forall j$, we obtain

$$r_i^A(\mathbf{p}) = \frac{\sum_{j=1}^m a_{i,j} p_j}{||\mathbf{p}||_A} \geq \frac{\sum_{j=1}^m a_{i,j} p_k}{||\mathbf{p}||_I} = r_k^I(\mathbf{p}).$$

We next show the sufficient conditions to satisfy the following: the variance of reward obtained by our rules is lower than the variance of reward obtained by the original rules. We first present a way of concisely calculating the variance of rewards in a generalized spherical proper scoring rule.

For a generalized spherical scoring rule with reward matrix A, variance of rewards $V^A(\mathbf{p})$ is given by

$$V^A(\mathbf{p})\|\mathbf{p}\|_A = \sum_{i=1}^{m} p_i(r_i^A(\mathbf{p}))^2 - \Big(\sum_{i=1}^{m} p_i r_i^A(\mathbf{p})\Big)^2$$

$$= \sum_{i=1}^{m} p_i(1 - p_i) r_i^A(\mathbf{p})^2 - 2 \sum_{1 \le i < j \le m} p_i p_j r_i^A(\mathbf{p}) r_j^A(\mathbf{p})$$

$$= \sum_{i=1}^{m} p_i \sum_{j \ne i} p_j r_i^A(\mathbf{p})^2 - 2 \sum_{1 \le i < j \le m} p_i p_j r_i^A(\mathbf{p}) r_j^A(\mathbf{p})$$

$$= \sum_{1 \le i < j \le m} p_i p_j (r_i^A(\mathbf{p}) - r_j^A(\mathbf{p}))^2, \tag{2}$$

from Eq. (1). Therefore, if we show the variance of the reward obtained by our proposed rule is lower than the original rule, it suffices to show $|r_i^A(\mathbf{p}) - r_j^A(\mathbf{p})| < |r_i^I(\mathbf{p}) - r_j^I(\mathbf{p})|$ holds for all $i \ne j$, since it implies $V^A(\mathbf{p}) < V^I(\mathbf{p})$.

We show an example where our rule can reduce the variance of reward obtained by a worker.

Example 1. Consider a weather forecast. We set $E = \{sunny, overcast, rainy\}$ and $A = \begin{pmatrix} 0.8 & 0.2 & 0 \\ 0.2 & 0.6 & 0.2 \\ 0 & 0.2 & 0.8 \end{pmatrix}$.

If $\mathbf{p} = (0.7, 0.3, 0)$, then $r^A(\mathbf{p}) = (0.85, 0.44, 0.08)$ and $r^I(\mathbf{p}) = (0.92, 0.39, 0)$. Here, $|r_i^A(\mathbf{p}) - r_j^A(\mathbf{p})| < |r_i^I(\mathbf{p}) - r_j^I(\mathbf{p})|$ holds for all $i \ne j$ since the differences of rewards are reduced among mutual elements, e.g., $0.85 - 0.08 = 0.77 > 0.92 - 0 = 0.92$. From the previous proposition, this inequality implies that $V^A(\mathbf{p}) < V^I(\mathbf{p})$. Thus, our rule reduces the variance of reward.

An agent's reward is determined by her prediction $\mathbf{p}$ and naturally the variance of her reward also depends on her prediction. Therefore, the variance of her rewards cannot always be diminished by just setting an appropriate reward matrix. In Example 1, we consider another agent who predicts $\mathbf{p} = (0.5, 0.5, 0)$. For this agent, our rule cannot reduce the variance of reward since $V^I(\mathbf{p}) = 0$ and $V^A(\mathbf{p}) = 0.005 > 0$ are calculated. In general, if $V^I(\mathbf{p})$ is extremely small, no variance reduction can be attained unless the reward matrix is almost trivial. Therefore, the following theorem shows that for any prediction $\mathbf{p}$, a linear combination of identity and constant matrix A guarantees that the variance of our rules does not exceed the original rule. Intuitively, this means that we have to make all diagonal elements (rewards for correct outcomes) identical to each other and make all non-diagonal elements (rewards for incorrect outcomes) identical to each other to reduce the variance of reward for any outcome.

Theorem 3. *The following statements are equivalent.*

(i) *Reward matrix A is set to*

$$A = sI + \frac{1-s}{m} \begin{pmatrix} 1 & \cdots & 1 \\ \vdots & \ddots & \vdots \\ 1 & \cdots & 1 \end{pmatrix}, \tag{3}$$

where s is a constant value such that $0 < s \leq 1$ holds.

(ii) *For any prediction* $\mathbf{p}$,

$$V^A(\mathbf{p}) \leq V^I(\mathbf{p})$$

holds.

Proof. To prove that (i) $\Longrightarrow$ (ii), we assume that Eq. (3) holds and that we have

$$r_i^I(\mathbf{p}) - r_j^I(\mathbf{p}) = \frac{p_i - p_j}{\|\mathbf{p}\|_I},$$

$$r_i^A(\mathbf{p}) - r_j^A(\mathbf{p}) = \frac{s(p_i - p_j)}{\|\mathbf{p}\|_A}.$$

Furthermore, we obtain

$$\|\mathbf{p}\|_A = \sqrt{{}^t\mathbf{p}A\mathbf{p}} = \sqrt{s\|\mathbf{p}\|_I^2 + \frac{1-s}{sm}} \geq \sqrt{s}\|\mathbf{p}\|_I.$$

From these relations, we have

$$|r_i^A(\mathbf{p}) - r_j^A(\mathbf{p})| \leq \frac{\sqrt{s}(p_i - p_j)}{\|\mathbf{p}\|_I} \leq |r_i^I(\mathbf{p}) - r_j^I(\mathbf{p})|,$$

which induces (i) $\Longrightarrow$ (ii).

To prove (ii) $\Longrightarrow$ (i), we first show $a_{i,i} = a_{j,j}$ for any i, j. For the sake of contradiction, we assume $a_{i,i} \neq a_{j,j}$ holds for some $i \neq j$. We set $\mathbf{p}$ such that $p_i = p_j = \frac{1}{2}$ and $p_k = 0$ for all $k \neq i, j$. Then $V^I(\mathbf{p}) = 0$ holds since $r_i^I(\mathbf{p}) = r_j^I(\mathbf{p}) = \frac{1}{2}$ holds, while $(A\mathbf{p})_i = \frac{a_{i,i} + a_{i,j}}{2}$ and $(A\mathbf{p})_j = \frac{a_{j,i} + a_{j,j}}{2}$ hold. $a_{i,j} = a_{j,i}$ implies $(A\mathbf{p})_i \neq (A\mathbf{p})_j$ which leads to $V^A(\mathbf{p}) > 0$. This is a contradiction.

We next assume that $a_{i,k} \neq a_{j,k}$ for some $i \neq j, k$. We set $\mathbf{p}$ such that $p_i = p_j = p_k = \frac{1}{3}$ holds and obtain $V^I(\mathbf{p}) = 0$. On the other hand, $V^A(\mathbf{p}) > 0$ is satisfied, because $(A\mathbf{p})_i = \frac{1}{3}(a_{i,i} + a_{i,j} + a_{i,k})$, $(A\mathbf{p})_j = \frac{1}{3}(a_{j,i} + a_{j,j} + a_{j,k})$, $a_{i,i} = a_{j,j}$ and $a_{i,j} = a_{j,i}$ imply $(A\mathbf{p})_i \neq (A\mathbf{p})_j$.

We finally give the following sufficient condition that our rule can reduce the variance of reward by setting an assumption about a worker's probability.

Theorem 4. *We assume that a requester sets* $x = \min_{i \in E} a_{i,i}$ *in reward matrix* A *and let* $p = \max_{1 \leq i \leq m} p_i$ *for* $i \in E$. *For a worker who predicts* $\mathbf{p}$ *that satisfies*

$$p(1-p)\frac{(2p-1)^2}{p^2 + (1-p)^2}$$

$$> \left(p(1-p) + \frac{(1-p)^2}{2}\right)\left((2x-1) + \frac{(1-x)}{p}\right) \tag{4}$$

her variance is reduced:

$$V^A(\mathbf{p}) < V^I(\mathbf{p}) \tag{5}$$

holds.

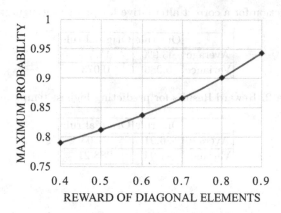

Fig. 1. Threshold Condition

Proof. We assume that $p = p_1$. From Eq. (2), we have

$$V^I(\mathbf{p}) \geq p_1 \sum_{i=2}^{m} p_i \frac{(p_1 - p_i)^2}{\|\mathbf{p}\|_I^2}$$

$$\geq p_1(1 - p_1)\frac{(2p_1 - 1)^2}{p_1^2 + (1 - p_1)^2} \tag{6}$$

On the other hand, we obtain

$$V^A(\mathbf{p}) \leq \sum_{1 \leq i < j \leq m} p_i p_j \frac{((A\mathbf{p})_i - (A\mathbf{p})_j)^2}{\|\mathbf{p}\|_A^2}$$

$$\leq \left(p_1(1 - p_1) + \frac{(1 - p_1)^2}{2}\right) \frac{(A\mathbf{p})_1}{p_1}.$$

From $(A\mathbf{p})_1 \leq a_{1,1}p_1 + (1 - a_{1,1}) = (2p_1 - 1)a_{1,1} + (1 - p_1)$, $(A\mathbf{p})_1$ is a linear function of $a_{1,1}$. Thus, $(A\mathbf{p})_1$ increases along with the increase of $a_{1,1}$ when assuming $p_1 \geq 0.5$ and we have $(A\mathbf{p})_1 \leq (2p_1 - 1) \times x + (1 - p_1)$. Thus, we have

$$V^A(\mathbf{p})$$
$$\leq \left(p_1(1 - p_1) + \frac{(1 - p_1)^2}{2}\right)\left((2x - 1) + \frac{(1 - x)}{p_1}\right). \tag{7}$$

From Eq. (6) and Eq. (7), we obtain Eq. (4).

We can verify the threshold conditions for $a_{i,i}$ and p_i in this theorem, since it shows a sufficient condition. When we set $x = \min_{i \in E} a_{i,i}$ and $p = \max_{1 \leq i \leq m} p_i$, the following figure indicates a pair of (x, p) that satisfies Eq. (4).

Table 1. Prediction for a correct alternative for predicting highest temperature

	Our rule	Original rule
Average	43.9%	41.5%
Variance	0.086	0.073

Table 2. Reward Results for predicting highest temperature

	Our rule	Original rule
Average	26.91	27.03
Variance	41.94	288.21

Theorem 4 gives a sufficient condition where our rule is always guaranteed to be lower than the original rule in terms of the variance of reward. In Fig. 1, if the maximum probability is located above the curve calculated by Eq. (4), the variance of reward of our rule is always lower than that of the original rule. In the original rule, a worker who predicts that a certain alternative will be realized with high probability can obtain a relatively high reward when her prediction is correct. But her reward is reduced when her prediction is incorrect. Thus, the variance of reward of the original rule is large for such a worker. On the other hand, in our rule, we reduce the reward for a correct alternative more than the original rule and reward semi-correct alternatives. As a result, for a worker who has high probability for a certain alternative, her variance of reward becomes small.

If the maximum probability is located below the curve, we consider a worker's knowledge for a task to be ambiguous. Since such a worker's reward obtained in the original rule is relatively low, her variance of reward is not always reduced even if our rule is applied. In other words, in some cases, the variance of reward in our rule exceeds the variance of reward in the original rule. However, this is a tiny fraction of all cases. From Eq. (2), the variance of reward much depends on the maximum value of $p_i r_i^A(\mathbf{p})$. In our rule, when $x = \min a_{i,i}$ is small, p_i and $r_i^A(\mathbf{p})$ cannot be large simultaneously.

6   Experimental Evaluations

We compared the generalized and the original rules by using the Amazon Mechanical Turk (MTurk) and posted two types of tasks. One predicted the highest temperature in a certain city, and the other predicted changes in foreign currency exchange rates. We gathered ten workers for each HIT. Each worker was paid 10 cents per task and could also receive a bonus based on the scoring rule. In this experiment, we adopted a spherical proper scoring rule. A worker is asked to assign probabilities (discretized by 10% intervals) over three alternatives. We rejected results by workers whose probabilities over three alternatives did not add up to 100%. After assigning the probabilities, we also asked workers to choose either our spherical scoring rule or the original scoring rule to calculate their bonus. To make a fair comparison between our proposed rule and an existing rule, we set each reward matrix as follows:

– The original spherical scoring rule:

$$A = \begin{pmatrix} 50 & 0 & 0 \\ 0 & 50 & 0 \\ 0 & 0 & 50 \end{pmatrix}$$

– Our generalized spherical scoring rule:

$$A = \begin{pmatrix} 30 & 15 & 5 \\ 15 & 20 & 15 \\ 5 & 15 & 30 \end{pmatrix}$$

The average reward and variance of our proposed rule are lower than that of the existing rule. We gave workers a concrete formula with which they can calculate their bonus.

6.1   Task of Predicting Highest Temperature

We show the results of the tasks to predict the highest temperature in three cities: Kyoto, London, and New York. For each city, we performed three sets of experiments. We gathered 30 workers for each city; 54 workers selected our scoring rule, and 36 selected the original rule. We show the results summed over the three cities because we did not find any notable difference among the cities.

We show the results regarding the mean of the probabilities assigned to the correct alternative and rewards. As shown in Table 1, the average probability assigned to a correct alternative is higher with our scoring rule than with the original scoring rule. Table 2 shows the results regarding rewards. The average rewards paid to workers were lower with our rule than with the original rule. The variance of rewards was smaller with our results than with the original rule.

6.2   Task of Predicting Exchange Rate Movements

In this subsection, we show the results for tasks that predicted the change in foreign currency exchange rates on two consecutive days. A worker assigns probabilities over three intervals of the percentages of changes from the currency exchange rate of the first day: over 0.02%, $-0.02\% \sim 0.02\%$, or below -0.02%. We conducted two experiments for the exchange rate of Euro against USD and for the exchange rate of JPY against USD, respectively.

We gathered 60 workers in total. 31 workers choose our rule and 29 workers choose the original rule. As shown in Table 3, the average probabilities assigned to a correct alternative was larger for workers who chose the original rule but the difference was not large. However, the average was lower than that of the tasks to predict weather, apparently because predicting currency exchange rates was more difficult than predicting weather. Table 4 shows that the average rewards were larger and their variance was smaller for workers who chose our rule.

Table 3. Prediction for a correct alternative for predicting exchange rate movement

	Our rule	Original rule
Average	32.2%	36.5%
Variance	0.049	0.056

Table 4. Results of rewards for predicting exchange rate movement

	Our rule	Original rule
Average	25.72	24.85
Variance	35.66	123.53

7　Conclusion

We investigated strictly proper scoring rules for truthfully eliciting predictions over categorical events to allow requesters to determine a flexible reward plan based on his subjective similarity among events. In our rule, a requester rewards both a correct and semi-correct outcomes. We utilized the structure of a worker's expected utility for the original quadratic and spherical proper scoring rules and generalized them by applying an inner product generated by a reward plan. The properties of our proposed rules are as follows: (1) If a reward matrix is symmetric and positive definite, our rules are strategy-proof. (2) Our rule incentivize workers to sincerely declare the probabilities of all alternatives. (3) Both average and variance of rewards of our proposed rules are lower than those of the existing scores. If we only care about reducing the variance, as shown in Theorem 3, we have to make all diagonal elements (rewards for correct outcomes) identical to each other and make all non-diagonal elements (rewards for incorrect outcomes) identical to each other. However, this is too restricted and so we propose our score to determine rewards for alternatives more flexibly according to the similarities the requester considers.

Future work will apply our concept to other strictly proper scoring rules and evaluate our rules for various tasks on MTurk. We also will consider an incentive mechanism that is more understandable for workers.

Acknowledgments. This research was partially supported by JSPS KAKENHI Grant Number 24220003, 15H02751, and 15H02782.

References

1. Akasiadis, C., Chalkiadakis, G.: Agent cooperatives for effective power consumption shifting. In: Proceedings of the 27th AAAI Conference on Artificial Intelligence (AAAI 2013), pp. 1263–1269 (2013)
2. Brier, G.W.: Verification of forecasts expressed in terms of probability. Monthly Weather Review **78**(1), 1–3 (1950)

3. Chen, Y., Gao, X.A., Goldstein, R., Kash, I.A.: Market manipulation with outside incentives. In: Proceedings of the 25th AAAI Conference on Artificial Intelligence (AAAI 2011), pp. 614–619 (2011)
4. Chen, Y., Pennock, D.M.: Designing markets for prediction. AI Magazine **31**(4), 42–52 (2010)
5. Conitzer, V.: Prediction markets, mechanism design, and cooperative game theory. In: Proceedings of the 25th Conference on Uncertainty in Artificial Intelligence (UAI 2009), pp. 101–108 (2009)
6. Gneiting, T., Raftery, A.E.: Strictly proper scoring rules, prediction, and estimation. Journal of the American Statistical Association **102**(477), 359–378 (2007)
7. Huang, E.H., Shoham, Y.: Price manipulation in prediction markets:analysis and mitigation. In: Proceedings of the 13th International Conference on Autonomous Agents and Multiagent Systems (AAMAS 2014), pp. 213–220 (2014)
8. Law, E., Ahn, L.V.: Human Computation. Morgan & Claypool Publishers (2011)
9. Matheson, J.E., Winkler, R.L.: Scoring rules for continuous probability distributions. Management Science **22**(10), 1087–1096 (1976)
10. Prelec, D.: A bayesian truth serum for subjective data. Science **306**(5695), 462–466 (2004)
11. Radanovic, G., Faltings, B.: A robust bayesian truth serum for non-binary signals. In: Proceedings of the 27th AAAI Conference on Artificial Intelligence (AAAI 2013), pp. 833–839 (2013)
12. Robu, V., Kota, R., Chalkiadakis, G., Rogers, A., Jennings, N.R.: Cooperative virtual power plant formation using scoring rules. In: Proceedings of the 26th AAAI Conference on Artificial Intelligence (AAAI 2012), pp. 370–376 (2012)
13. Savage, L.J.: Elicitation of personal probabilities and expectations. Journal of the American Statistical Association **66**(336), 783–801 (1971)
14. Witkowski, J., Parkes, D.C.: A robust bayesian truth serum for small populations. In: Proceedings of the 26th AAAI Conference on Artificial Intelligence (AAAI 2012), pp. 1492–1498 (2012)
15. Wolfers, J., Zitzewitz, E.: Prediction markets. Journal of Economic Perspectives **18**(2), 107–126 (2004)
16. Zhang, P., Chen, Y.: Elicitability and knowledge-free elicitation with peer prediction. In: Proceedings of the 13th International Conference on Autonomous Agents and Multiagent Systems (AAMAS 2014), pp. 245–252 (2014)

Majoritarian Group Actions

Daniele Porello[(✉)]

Laboratory for Applied Ontology, ISTC-CNR, Trento, Italy
danieleporello@gmail.com

Abstract. In this paper, we introduce a logic to reason about group actions for groups that are defined by means of the majority rule. It is well known that majoritarian aggregation is subject to irrationality, as the results in social choice theory and judgment aggregation show. The logic of action that we use here for modelling group actions is based on a substructural propositional logic that allows for preventing inconsistent outcome. Agency is modeled by means of a "bringing-it-about" modal logic with coalitions. We show that, in this way, it is possible to obtain a consistent model of agency of groups that are defined in an aggregative manner.

1 Introduction

The rationality of group attitudes, such as beliefs, desires, intentions, and agency is a central issue in the foundation of multiagent system. The concept of group attitudes has been interpreted in different ways by a number of approaches. For instance, Christian List [10] distinguishes between three kinds of collective attitudes: *aggregate*, *common*, and *corporate* group attitudes. We are here interested in the first two kinds. Common attitudes are ascribed to a group by requiring that every member of the group share the same attitude. Common attitudes have been presupposed by the approach to group actions based on collective intentionality and joint action [26,10,12]. In this view, possible disagreements among the members of the group are excluded. By contrast, an aggregative view of group attitudes does not presuppose that the individuals that are members of the group all share the same attitude. A group attitude can be ascribed to the group by solving the disagreement by means of an aggregation procedure such as the majority rule. This view is appealing, since it seems to be capable of accounting for the common attitudes perspective, that implies unanimity, but also for a number of situations in which it is reasonable to define a group attitude without assuming that all the members of the group share a common attitudes. For instance, in case we model parliaments, organizations, committees. Besides being descriptively adequate to a number of modelling scenarios, non-unanimous group attitudes are important also from the point of view of multiagent systems and knowledge representation of group information. Consider the following situations involving artificial agents. Suppose three sensors have been placed in different locations of a room and they are designed to trigger a fire alarm in case they detect smoke. By viewing the three sensors as a group, we may investigate

Q. Chen et al. (Eds.): PRIMA 2015, LNAI 9387, pp. 416–432, 2015.
DOI: 10.1007/978-3-319-25524-8_26

what are the conditions that defines the group action, in this case, "trigger the alarm". By forcing unanimity, that is, by viewing group attitudes as common attitudes, we are assuming that the three sensors as a group trigger the alarm only in the case they all agree in detecting smoke. However, a unanimous view of group actions may lead to lose a lot of relevant information: if the sensors disagree, the alarm is simply not triggered, even if the disagreement may be caused, for instance, by the fact that one of the three sensors is in a location that has not been reached by the smoke yet. Unanimity appears to be a too restrictive requirement in this case [20]. An aggregative view provides the formal means to tailor the concept of group information to the specific scenario, by selecting the appropriate aggregation procedure. Although an aggregative view of group attitudes is desirable for many reasons, several results in social choice theory and judgment aggregation show that many important aggregation procedures are not capable of guaranteeing a rational outcome. One crucial example is the majority rule [11]. As usual in the BDI approach to agency, at least a modicum of rationality has to be presupposed in order to define an agent. An agent cannot hold (synchronically) inconsistent attitudes, such as plans, commitments or beliefs. When the outcome of an aggregation procedure is inconsistent, as in the case of the majority rule, we simply cannot define a majoritarian group as an agent. The solution that has been developed in the literature on judgment aggregation is to give up procedures such as the majority rule and investigate aggregation procedures that guarantee consistency [13].

In this paper, we are interested in pursuing a different strategy. We want to be able to ascribe collective attitudes to groups even in the case individual attitudes are aggregated by means of the majority rule. The motivation is that many real scenarios actually use the majority rule to settle disagreement. Besides, the majority rule has a number of desirable features such as it is simple to understand and implement, preference aggregation is strategy-proof (when consistent) [3], it has been associated to an epistemic interpretation justified by the Condorcet's jury theorem.

In order to avoid the inconsistency, as well as the irrationality caused by the majority rule, we shall weaken the logic that we use to model group rationality in order to ensure general consistency. For instance, we know that the majority rule may return inconsistent sets of judgments. On a closer inspection, the inconsistency is deeply intertwined with the principles of classical logic. In [19], a possibility result for the majority rule has been provided by means of linear logic [7,8]. We will build on that in order to develop a logic for *majoritarian groups* attitudes, that is, groups whose attitudes are aggregatively defined by means of the majority rule. In principle, our treatment can be instantiated to a number of propositional attitudes such as beliefs, desires, intentions. We focus here on action and agency and we model the situation in which a number of agents submit proposals for action that have to be aggregated in a group action.

In order to model action and agency, we shall use a "bringing-it-about" modality whose properties have been investigated for instance by [5,9]. A logic of agency based on intuitionistic linear logic has been presented in [21]. Moreover, a insightful discussion of bringing-it-about modalities for representing coalitional ability has been done in [25]. A closely related work is [2]. There, the authors use judgment aggregation in order to model group attitudes by relying on logics of agency. The significant difference with respect to the present paper is that their treatment applies to aggregation procedures that are known to guarantee consistency, e.g. the premise based procedure [13], whereas here we are interested in approaching the majority rule.

Modelling group actions in case of an aggregative view is simpler than modelling common group actions in a number of aspects. Firstly, we do not need to assume joint intentionality nor a shared goal. By definition of majoritarian group, we are already assuming that individuals do have different goals [10]. For that reason, we are labelling the actions of the group by *group* actions and not by *joint* action. Moreover, it means that intentionality and goals do not need to enter the model for defining what a group action is [12]. That is, the "bringing-it-about" modality is sufficient for this preliminary task.

The remainder of this paper is organized as follows. In the next section, after presenting the basic notions of judgment aggregation, we shall introduce the problem of majoritarian group actions in an informal way by discussing a discursive dilemma [11]. In Section 3, we see the basics of the propositional substructural logic that we are going to use to build our model of group actions. In Section 4, we enrich the propositional substructural logic by means of the modalities for agency. Besides a number of technicalities, the difference with [21] is that we are going to introduce coalitions in the spirit of [25]. Moreover, we are going to establish soundness and completeness of the Hilbert system for our logic. In Section 5, we approach our modelling of group actions and we show how to provide a consistent modellisation of majoritarian aggregation. In particular, we show how to view discursive dilemmas as examples of the complex nature of group actions, rather than a case of mere logical inconsistency. Finally, Section 6 concludes.

2   Background on Judgment Aggregation

We present now the basic definitions of the judgement aggregation (JA) setting [13,6], which provides the formal counterpart of an aggregative view of collective attitudes [10]. We slightly rephrase the definitions for the present application. Let N be a (finite) set of agents. An *agenda* $\mathcal{X}_{\mathcal{L}}$ is a (finite) set of propositions in the language $\mathcal{L}_L$ of a given logic L that is closed under complements. i.e. non-double negations. We let the logic L unspecified here, as we shall see two logics for defining judgment sets. Moreover, we shall assume that the agenda does not contain tautologies or contradictions, this is motivated in a number of papers in JA [13] but it is also motivated here by the fact that we are assuming that it is not meaningful to talk about tautological actions (cf. Section 4.2).

The standard definitions of the JA framework are the following. A *judgement set* J is a subset of $\mathcal{X}_L$ such that J is (wrt L) *consistent* ($J \nvdash_L \bot$), *complete* (for all $\varphi \in \mathcal{X}_L$, $\varphi \in J$ or $\neg\varphi \in J$) and *deductive closed* (if $J \vdash_L \varphi$ and $\varphi \in \mathcal{X}_L$, $\varphi \in J$). The definitions are presented in syntactic terms, by referring to a calculus

$\vdash_L$. The notion of consistency has been rephrased to cope with the logic that we are going to introduce. Note that our definition are equivalent to their usual model-theoretic counterparts.

Denote by $J(\mathcal{X}_L)$ the set of all judgement sets on $\mathcal{X}_L$. A *profile* of judgements sets $\mathbf{J}$ is a vector $(J_1, \ldots, J_n)$, where $n = |N|$. An *aggregator* is then a function $F : J(\mathcal{X}_L)^n \to \mathcal{P}(\mathcal{X}_L)$. The codomain of F is the powerset $\mathcal{P}(\mathcal{X}_L)$, therefore admitting possibly inconsistent sets. Let $N_\varphi = \{i \mid \varphi \in J_i\}$, the majority rule is defined as follows: $m : J(\mathcal{X}_L)^n \to \mathcal{P}(\mathcal{X}_L)$ such that $m(\mathbf{J}) = \{\varphi \in \mathcal{X}_L \mid |N_\varphi| > n/2\}$.

In JA, the collective set $F(\mathbf{J})$ is also assumed to be consistent, complete, and deductively closed wrt. L. This defines the notion of *collective rationality*. The classical results in JA show that the majority rule is not collectively rational. That means that there exists an agenda and a profile of judgment sets such that $F(\mathbf{J})$ is not consistent. We present now a significant example.

We are endorsing an aggregative view of group attitudes, that means that the attitudes that one can ascribe the group are obtained as outcomes of an aggregation procedure [10]. Consider the following case of discursive dilemma [11] on the agenda of propositions $\{A, B, A \wedge B, \neg A, \neg B, \neg(A \wedge B)\}$.

	A	$A \wedge B$	B	$\neg A$	$\neg(A \wedge B)$	$\neg B$
1	yes	yes	yes	no	no	no
2	no	no	yes	yes	yes	no
3	yes	no	no	no	yes	yes
maj.	yes	no	yes	no	yes	no

By majority, the group accepts A, because of 1 and 3, it accepts B, because of 1 and 2, and it also has to accept $\neg(A \wedge B)$. Therefore, one can see that the group is inconsistent since, for instance, A and B entails $A \wedge B$ which contradicts $\neg(A \wedge B)$, i.e. $A \wedge B, \neg(A \wedge B) \vdash \bot$.

We are interested in representing majoritarian group reasoning and the outcomes of an election by means of the bringing-it-about modality E. For instance, suppose the group G is assumed to be the agent who is bringing about the propositions accepted by majority. To express that, we write formulas such as $\mathsf{E}_G A$, $\mathsf{E}_G B$, and $\mathsf{E}_G \neg(A \wedge B)$. By means, of the usual principles of the modality E — for instance the axiom T: $\mathsf{E}_G \varphi \to \varphi$ — we can infer again the inconsistency between $A \wedge B$ and $\neg(A \wedge B)$.

We will see that a fundamental point in order to save collective rationality in case of majoritarian decisions is to keep track of the coalitions that are responsible for supporting the collectively accepted propositions [19]. In order to do that, we want to reason about formulas that indicates that the coalition$\{1, 3\}$ brings about A, coalition $\{1,2\}$ brings about B, and coalition $\{2, 3\}$ does not brings about $(A \wedge B)$. We write such statements as follows: $\mathsf{E}_{\{1,3\}} A, \mathsf{E}_{\{1,2\}} B, \mathsf{E}_{\{2,3\}} \neg(A \wedge B)$. We will see that the inconsistency in discursive dilemmas is caused by mixing propositions that hold because they are supported by a single coalition, e.g. $\mathsf{E}_{\{1,3\}} A$, and propositions that hold because they follow from propositions that are supported by two distinct coalitions: for instance, $\mathsf{E}_{\{1,2,3\}} (A \wedge B)$ that follows from $\mathsf{E}_{\{1,3\}} A$ and $\mathsf{E}_{\{1,2\}} B$.

In the next section, we will introduce a logic that is capable of distinguishing two modes of combinations of propositions supported by coalitions, preventing the majoritarian outcomes from inconsistency.

3   Background on Substructural Logics

We briefly introduce the basics of Linear Logic (LL). LL captures a resource-sensitive reasoning that means that, for instance, wrt linear logic implication $\multimap$, *modus ponens* $A, A \multimap B \vdash B$ is valid only if the right amount of assumptions is given, so that $A, A, A \multimap B \nvdash B$. This implication has been interpreted as a form of *causal* connection between the antecedent and the consequence [8]: the antecedent is *consumed* by the causal process and it is not available for further inferences. In order to achieve resource-sensitivity of the entailment, linear logic rejects the global validity of the structural rules of the sequent calculus: contraction (C) and weakening (W). Rejecting (W) amounts to preventing monotonicity of the entailment and rejecting (C) blocks the possibility of making indistinguishable copies of the assumptions. By rejecting (W) and (C), we are lead to split the classical connectives into two classes: *multiplicatives* and *additives*. For instance, the classical conjunction $\wedge$ splits into two distinct operators: the multiplicative $\otimes$ ("tensor") and the additive & ("with") [7,8]. Since monotonicity fails in general, the tensor conjunction for instance does *not* satisfy $A \otimes B \nmultimap B$ nor $A \otimes B \nmultimap A$, by contrast the additive conjunction does: $A \& B \multimap A$ and $A \& B \multimap B$. Analogous distinction can be made for disjunction. We will use an intuitionistic variant of linear logic, thus we shall have the implication $\multimap$ instead of the multiplicative disjunction. By slightly abusing the notation, we will denote the additive disjunction by $\vee$.

For our purpose, the resource-sensitive nature of linear logic is fundamental as it is capable of handling an important distinction between the truth makers of a proposition: we will see that a formula $A \otimes B$ will be made true by two different coalitions of agents, one supporting A and one supporting B, whereas $A \& B$ will be made true by a single coalition, cf. [19]. For the sake of simplicity, we shall stick to a fragment of intuitionistic linear logic (exponential-free). Moreover, as we shall see in the next section, we assume distributivity of additive connective & over $\vee$. Distributivity is not valid in linear logic. By slightly abusing the notation, we shall call our fragment by ILLD[1]. The motivation for adding distributivity is mainly technical: it is due to the fact that we can still prove soundness and completeness wrt a simple Kripke-like model.

The language of ILLD, $\mathcal{L}_{ILLD}$, then is defined as follows:

$$A ::= 1 \mid p \mid A \otimes A \mid A \& A \mid A \multimap A \mid A \vee A$$

where $p \in Atom$.

---

[1] Note that, since distributivity hold, ILL D is also known as a *contractionless relevance logic* [16], which is a decidable relevance logic [15]. We leave a proper comparison with the families of substructural and relevance logics for future work.

3.1   Hilbert System for ILLD

We introduce the Hilbert system for ILLD, that has been basically developed in [1], see also [24,16]. We define the Hilbert-style calculus by introducing a list of axioms in Table 1 and by defining the following notion of deduction. The concept of deduction of linear logic requires a tree-structure in order to handle the hypothesis in the correct resource-sensitive way. This entails that, in particular, in linear logic, every *modus ponens* application (cf. $\multimap$-rule) applies to a single occurrence of A and of $A \multimap B$.

Table 1. Axioms of ILL

1. $\vdash A \multimap A$
2. $\vdash (A \multimap B) \multimap ((B \multimap C) \multimap (A \multimap C))$
3. $\vdash (A \multimap (B \multimap C)) \multimap (B \multimap (A \multimap C))$
4. $\vdash A \multimap (B \multimap A \otimes B)$
5. $\vdash (A \multimap (B \multimap C)) \multimap (A \otimes B \multimap C)$
6. $\vdash 1$
7. $\vdash 1 \multimap (A \multimap A)$
8. $\vdash (A \& B) \multimap A$
9. $\vdash (A \& B) \multimap B$
10. $\vdash ((A \multimap B) \& (A \multimap C)) \multimap (A \multimap B \& C)$
11. $\vdash A \multimap A \vee B$
12. $\vdash B \multimap A \vee B$
13. $(A \multimap C) \& (B \multimap C) \multimap (A \vee B \multimap C)$
14. $A \& (B \vee C) \multimap (A \& B) \vee (A \& C)$
15. $(A \vee B) \& (A \vee C) \multimap A \& (B \vee C)$

The notion of proof in the Hilbert system is defined as follows.

Definition 1 (Deduction in H-ILLD). *A deduction tree in* H-ILLD $\mathcal{D}$ *is inductively constructed as follows. (i) The leaves of the tree are assumptions* $A \vdash A$, *for* $A \in \mathcal{L}_{\mathsf{ILLD}}$, *or* $\vdash B$ *where* B *is an axiom in Table 1 (base cases).*

(ii) We denote by $\Gamma \overset{\mathcal{D}}{\vdash} A$ *a deduction tree with conclusion* $\Gamma \vdash A$. *If* $\mathcal{D}$ *and* $\mathcal{D}'$ *are deduction trees, then the following are deduction trees (inductive steps).*

$$\frac{\Gamma \overset{\mathcal{D}}{\vdash} A \qquad \Gamma' \overset{\mathcal{D}'}{\vdash} A \multimap B}{\Gamma, \Gamma' \vdash B} \; \multimap\text{-rule} \qquad \frac{\Gamma \overset{\mathcal{D}}{\vdash} A \qquad \Gamma \overset{\mathcal{D}'}{\vdash} B}{\Gamma \vdash A \& B} \; \&\text{-rule}$$

3.2   Models of ILL

A Kripke-like class of models for ILLD is substantially due to Urquhart [27]. A *Kripke resource frame* is a structure $\mathcal{M} = (M, e, \circ, \geq)$, where $(M, e, \circ)$ is a commutative monoid with neutral element e, and $\geq$ is a pre-order on M.

The frame has to satisfy the condition of *bifunctoriality*: if $m \geq n$, and $m' \geq n'$, then $m \circ m' \geq n \circ n'$. To obtain a *Kripke resource model*, a valuation on atoms $V : Atom \rightarrow \mathcal{P}(M)$ is added. It has to satisfy the *heredity* condition: if $m \in V(p)$ and $n \geq m$ then $n \in V(p)$. The truth conditions of the formulas of $\mathcal{L}_{\mathsf{ILLD}}$ in the Kripke resource model $\mathcal{M} = (M, e, \circ, \geq, V)$ are the following:

$m \models_{\mathcal{M}} p$ iff $m \in V(p)$.

$m \models_{\mathcal{M}} \mathbf{1}$ iff $m \geq e$.

$m \models_{\mathcal{M}} A \otimes B$ iff there exist m_1 and m_2 such that $m \geq m_1 \circ m_2$ and $m_1 \models_{\mathcal{M}} A$ and $m_2 \models_{\mathcal{M}} B$.

$m \models_{\mathcal{M}} A \,\&\, B$ iff $m \models_{\mathcal{M}} A$ and $m \models_{\mathcal{M}} B$.

$m \models_{\mathcal{M}} A \vee B$ iff $m \models_{\mathcal{M}} A$ or $m \models_{\mathcal{M}} B$

$m \models_{\mathcal{M}} A \multimap B$ iff for all $n \in M$, if $n \models_{\mathcal{M}} A$, then $n \circ m \models_{\mathcal{M}} B$.

Denote $\|A\|^{\mathcal{M}}$ the extension of A in $\mathcal{M}$, i.e. the set of worlds of $\mathcal{M}$ in which A holds. A formula A is *true* in a model $\mathcal{M}$ if $e \models_{\mathcal{M}} A$.[2] A formula A is *valid* in Kripke resource frames, noted $\models A$, iff it is true in every model. The heredity condition can be straightforwardly proved to extend naturally to every formula, that is: For every formula A, if $m \models A$ and $m' \geq m$, then $m' \models A$. By means of this semantics, it is possible to prove that ILL D is sound and complete wrt to the class of Kripke models [27].

4   Linear Bringing-it-about Logic with Coalitions (Linear BIAT C)

The (non-normal modal) logic of agency of bringing-it-about [5,9] has been traditionally developed on top of classical propositional logic. In [21], a version of bringing-it-about based on ILL has been developed as a logic for modeling resource-sensitive actions of a single agent. In the next section, we will propose a version Linear BIAT with coalitions, based on ILLD. We simply label it Linear BIAT C. The *bringing-it-about* modality has been discussed in particular by [5,9]. For each agent a in a set of agents $\mathcal{A}$, the modality $E_a A$ specifies that agent $a \in \mathcal{A}$ brings about A. The following principles captures the intended notion of agency [5]:

1. If something is brought about, then this something holds.
2. It is not possible to bring about a tautology.
3. If an agent brings about two things concomitantly then the agent also brings about the conjunction of these two things.
4. If two statements are equivalent, then bringing about one is equivalent to bringing about the other.

---

[2] When the context is clear we will write $\|A\|$ instead of $\|A\|^{\mathcal{M}}$, and $m \models A$ instead of $m \models_{\mathcal{M}} A$.

The logical meaning of the four principle is the following. The first item corresponds to the axiom T of modal logics: $\mathsf{E}_i A \multimap A$. It states that bringing-it-about is effective: if an action is brought about, then the action affects the state of the world, i.e. the formula A that represents the execution of the action holds. The second item corresponds to the axiom $\neg\mathsf{E}_i\top$ (notaut) in classical bringing-it-about logic. It amounts to assuming that agents cannot bring about tautologies. The motivation is that a tautology is always true, regardless what an agent does, so if acting is construed as something that affects the state of the world, tautologies are not apt to be the content of something that an agent actually does. Item 3 corresponds to the axiom: $\mathsf{E}_i A \wedge \mathsf{E}_i B \to \mathsf{E}_i(A \wedge B)$. We shall discuss this principle in detail, when we will approach the linear version of this logic. The fourth item allows for viewing bringing it about as a modality, obeying the rule of equivalents: if $\vdash A \leftrightarrow B$ then $\vdash \mathsf{E}_i A \leftrightarrow \mathsf{E}_i B$.

4.1 Axioms of Linear BIAT C

We assume a set of coalitions $\mathbf{C}$ that is closed by disjoint union $\sqcup$. In this version of BIAT logic, agents are replaced by coalition. We admit singleton coalitions, in that case the meaning of a coalition C in $\mathbf{C}$ is $\{i\}$. This move is similar to those made in [25] to discuss coalitional ability. The language of Linear BIAT with coalition, $\mathcal{L}_{\mathsf{LBIATC}}$ simply extends the definition of $\mathcal{L}_{\mathsf{ILLD}}$, by adding a formula $\mathsf{E}_C A$ for each coalition $C \in \mathbf{C}$. The axioms of Linear BIAT C are presented in Table 2. The Hilbert system is defined by extending the notion of deduction in Definition 1 by means of the new axioms in Table 2 and of two new rules for building deduction trees, cf. Definition 2.

A number of important differences are worth noticing, when discussing the principle of agency in linear logics. Principle 1 is captured by Axiom 16, that is, the linear version of T: $\mathsf{E}_a A \multimap A$. Since in linear logics all the tautologies are not provably equivalent, principle 2 changes into an inference rule, that is ($\sim$ nec) in Definition 2: if $\vdash A$, then $E_C A \vdash \bot$. That means that, if a formula is a theorem, a coalition that brings it about implies the contradiction[3]. Moreover, the rule ($\mathsf{E}_C\mathsf{re}$) captures the fourth principle.

The principle for combining actions (Item 3 in the list) is crucial here: it can be interpreted in linear logic in two ways, namely, in a multiplicative way by $\otimes$ (Axiom 18) and in an additive way by & (Axiom 17) The distinction between the two types of combination is crucial for preventing collective irrationality [19]. The point is that the multiplicative combination, in our interpretation, requires two different winning coalitions that support the propositions, whereas the additive combination forces the same coalition to support both propositions. This distinction is reflected by the resource-sensitive nature of the two conjunctions. For instance, one can prove that $C \multimap A, D \multimap B \vdash C \otimes D \multimap A \otimes B$ and $C \multimap A, C \multimap B \vdash C \multimap A \,\&\, B$, that is in the former case the combination of hypotheses $B \otimes C$ is required, whereas in the latter only C is required. Therefore,

---

[3] This amounts to negating $E_C A$, according to intuitionistic negation.

Axiom 17 means that if the same coalition brings about A and brings about B, then the same coalition can bring about the combination of A and B: $A \& B$.

We define the disjoint union of two coalitions $C \sqcup D$ by $C \cup D$, if $C \cap D = \emptyset$ and $C \sqcup D = (C \times \{1\}) \cup (D \times \{0\})$, otherwise. Axiom 18 means that if a coalition C brings about action A and coalition C' brings about action B then, the disjoint union of two coalitions $C \sqcup C'$ brings about the combination of actions $A \otimes B$. It is important to stress that the condition of disjointness of C and C' is crucial for modelling the group actions defined by majority in a consistent way. In particular, the condition shows that the individuals that are member of the coalition are all equally relevant to make the proposition accepted. Take for instance the case of $\mathsf{E}_{\{1,2\}} A$ and $\mathsf{E}_{\{2,3\}}$. If we enable the inference to $\mathsf{E}_{\{1,2,3\}} A \otimes B$, then we would lose the information concerning the possibly crucial contribution of agent 2 in both coalitions.

Axiom 17 and 18 are reminiscence of Coalition Logic [17]. Note that we do not assume any further axiom of coalition logic. For instance, no coalition monotonicity. That is motivated by the fact that we are modelling *profile-reasoning*, that is, we start by a fixed profile of individual attitudes and we want to capture, by means of the modality E, how the group reasons about those propositions that have been accepted by majority in that profile. In this setting, given a profile of individual attitudes, there exists only one coalition that supports a proposition that has been accepted by majority. This is a different perspective wrt coalition logic and logic of coalitional ability [25].

Moreover, the principles for combining actions, such as Axiom 17 and 18, have been criticized on the ground that coalitions C and D may have different goals, therefore it is not meaningful to view the action of $C \sqcup D$ as a joint action. However, the aggregative view of group actions defined by means of the majority rule presupposes that the group is not defined by means of a shared goal. Therefore, Axioms 17 and 18 are legitimate from this point of view.

Table 2. Axioms of Linear BIAT

- All the axioms of ILL (cf. Table 1)
16 $\mathsf{E}_C A \multimap A$
17 $\mathsf{E}_C A \& \mathsf{E}_C B \multimap \mathsf{E}_C (A \& B)$
18 $\mathsf{E}_C A \otimes \mathsf{E}_D B \multimap \mathsf{E}_{C \sqcup D} (A \otimes B)$

The following definition extends the concept of deduction to Linear BIAT C.

Definition 2 (Deduction in Linear BIAT C). *A deduction tree in Linear BIAT C denoted by $\mathcal{D}$ is inductively constructed as follows. (i) The leaves of the tree are assumptions $A \vdash A$, for $A \in \mathcal{L}_{\mathrm{LBIATC}}$, or $\vdash B$ where B is an axiom in Table 2 (base cases).*

(ii) If $\mathcal{D}$ and $\mathcal{D}'$ are deduction trees, then the trees in Definition 1 are also deduction trees in Linear BIAT. Moreover, the following are deduction trees (inductive steps).

$$\frac{\overset{\mathcal{D}}{\vdash A \multimap B} \quad \overset{\mathcal{D}'}{\vdash B \multimap A}}{\vdash \mathsf{E}_C A \multimap \mathsf{E}_C B} \; \mathsf{E}_C \, (re) \qquad \frac{\vdash A}{\vdash \mathsf{E}_C A \multimap \bot} \sim nec$$

4.2 Models of Linear BIAT C

The semantics of the bringing-it-about modality is defined by adding a neighborhood semantics on top of the Kripke resource frame. A neighborhood function is a mapping $N : M \to \mathcal{P}(\mathcal{P}(M))$ that associates a world m with a set of sets of worlds (see [4]). The intuitive meaning of the neighborhood in this setting is that it associates to each world a set of propositions that can be done by coalition C. Neighborhood functions are related to effectivity function introduced in Social Choice Theory [14] for modelling coalitional power.

In order to interpret the modalities in a modal Kripke resource frame, we take one neighborhood function N_C for every coalition $C \in \mathbf{C}$ and we define:

$$m \models \mathsf{E}_C A \text{ iff } ||A|| \in N_C(m)$$

Note that it is possible that $m \models \mathsf{E}_C A$, yet $m' \not\models \mathsf{E}_C A$ for some $m' \geq m$. That is, heredity may fail in the extension of $\models$ for $\mathcal{L}_{LBIATC}$. We will then require our neighborhood function to satisfy the condition that if some set $X \subseteq M$ is in the neighborhood of a world, then X is also in the neighborhood of all the worlds that are above according to $\geq$.

$$\text{if } X \in N_C(m) \text{ and } n \geq m \text{ then } X \in N_C(n) \tag{1}$$

The rule ($\mathsf{E}_C$re) does not require any further condition on Kripke resource frames, it is already true because of the definition of E_C.

The rule ($\sim$ nec) requires:

$$\text{if } (X \in N_C(w)) \text{ and } (e \in X) \text{ then } (w \in V(\bot)) \tag{2}$$

Axiom 16 requires:

$$\text{if } X \in N_C(w) \text{ then } w \in X \tag{3}$$

We turn now to action compositions. Axiom 17 requires:

$$\text{if } X \in N_C(w) \text{ and } Y \in N_C(w), \text{ then } X \cap Y \in N_C(w) \tag{4}$$

Let $X \circ Y = \{x \circ y \mid x \in X \text{ and } y \in Y\}$, the condition corresponding to the multiplicative version of action combination, Axiom 18, requires that the upper closure of $X \circ Y$, denote it by $(X \circ Y)^\uparrow$, is in $N_{C \sqcup D}(x \circ y)$:

$$\text{if } X \in N_C(x) \text{ and } Y \in N_D(y) \text{ , then } (X \circ Y)^\uparrow \in N_{C \sqcup D}(x \circ y) \tag{5}$$

Summing up, Linear BIAT is evaluated over the following models:

Definition 3. *A* modal Kripke resource model *is a structure* $\mathcal{M} = (M, e, \circ, \geq, N_C, V)$ *such that:*

- $(M, e, \circ, \geq)$ *is a Kripke resource frame;*
- *For any* $C \in \boldsymbol{C}$, N_C *is a neighborhood function that satisfies conditions (1), (2), (3), (4), and (5).*
- *V is a valuation on atoms,* $V : Atom \rightarrow \mathcal{P}(M)$.

Heredity is true as well for Linear BIAT C over modal Kripke resource models for modal formulas, as an easy induction shows.

4.3   Soundness and Completeness

We approach now the proof of soundness and completeness of Linear BIAT C wrt Kripke resource frames that satisfy the conditions we put. The proof for the propositional case is mainly due to [27]. A proof of soundness and completeness for Linear BIAT in case of as single agent is provided in [21,22]. The proof that we present here is a simple adaptation of those proofs for the case of the Hilbert system for Linear BIAT C.

Theorem 1 (Soundness of Linear BIAT with Coalitions). *Linear* BIAT C *is sound wrt the class of Kripke resource frames that satisfy (1) (2), (3), (4), and (5): if* $\Gamma \vdash A$, *then* $\Gamma \models A$.

Proof. We only present the cases for axioms 17 and 18. The other cases are handled in similar way in [21].

We show that axiom 17 is valid. That is, for every model, $e \models \mathsf{E}_C A \& \mathsf{E}_C B \multimap \mathsf{E}_C(A \& B)$. That means, by definition of $\multimap$, for every x, if $x \models \mathsf{E}_C A \& \mathsf{E}_C B$, then $x \models \mathsf{E}_C(A \& B)$. If $x \models \mathsf{E}_C A \& \mathsf{E}_C B$, then $x \models \mathsf{E}_C A$ and $x \models \mathsf{E}_C B$, that entails, by definition of E_C, that $||A|| \in N_C(x)$ and $|B|| \in N_C(x)$. Thus, by condition (4), we infer $||A|| \cap ||B|| \in N_C(x)$. That means $x \models \mathsf{E}_C(A \& B)$.

We show that axiom 18 is valid, $e \models \mathsf{E}_C A \otimes \mathsf{E}_D B \multimap \mathsf{E}_{C \cup D}(A \otimes B)$. That is, for every x, if $x \models \mathsf{E}_C A \otimes \mathsf{E}_D B$, then $x \models \mathsf{E}_{C \cup D}(A \otimes B)$. If $x \models \mathsf{E}_C A \otimes \mathsf{E}_D B$, then by definition of $\otimes$, there exist y and z, such that $x \geq y \circ z$ and $y \models \mathsf{E}_C A$ and $z \models \mathsf{E}_D B$. Therefore, $||A|| \in N_C(y)$ and $||B|| \in N_D(z)$, this by condition (5), we infer that $(||A|| \circ ||B||)^\uparrow \in N_{C \cup D}(y \circ z)$. Thus, since $x \geq y \circ z$, by condition (5), $(||A|| \circ ||B||)^\uparrow \in N_{C \cup D}(x)$, that is $x \models \mathsf{E}_{C \cup D}(A \otimes B)$.

We turn now to show completeness. Firstly, we define the canonical model, which is adapted from [21].

In the following, $\sqcup_m$ is the multiset union. Also, we denote by $\Delta^\star = A_1 \otimes \cdots \otimes A_m$, for $A_i \in \Delta$. Moreover, the extension of A in the canonical model is $|A|^c = \{\Gamma \mid \Gamma \vdash A\}$.

Definition 4. *Let* $\mathcal{M}^c = (M^c, e^c, o^c, \geq^c, N^c, V^c)$ *such that:*

- $M^c = \{\Gamma \mid \Gamma \text{ is a finite multiset of formulas}\}$;
- $\Gamma \circ^c \Delta = \Gamma \sqcup_m \Delta$;
- $e^c = \emptyset$;
- $\Gamma \geq^c \Delta$ *iff* $\Gamma \vdash \Delta^*$;
- $\Gamma \in V^c(p)$ *iff* $\Gamma \vdash p$;
- *For every* $C \in \boldsymbol{C}$, $N^c_C(\Gamma) = \{\mid A \mid^c \mid \Gamma \vdash \mathsf{E}_C A\}$.

Lemma 1. $\mathcal{M}^c$ *is a modal Kripke resource model that satisfies (1) (2), (3), (4), and (5).*

Proof. We only show the case of condition (4), and (5), which differs from the proof in [21].

Case of Condition (4). Suppose $X \in N^c_C(\Gamma)$ and $Y \in N^c_C(\Gamma)$. By definition of N^c_C, $X \in \{X = \mid A \mid^c \mid \Gamma \vdash \mathsf{E}_C A\}$, thus $\Gamma \vdash \mathsf{E}_C A$ is provable in the Hilbert system. Analogously, $\Gamma \vdash \mathsf{E}_C B$, where $Y = |B|^c$. Then, we can prove in the Hilbert system that $\Gamma \vdash \mathsf{E}_C A \,\&\, \mathsf{E}_C B$, by means of the &-rule:

$$\frac{\overset{\mathcal{D}}{\Gamma \vdash \mathsf{E}_C A} \qquad \overset{\mathcal{D}'}{\Gamma \vdash \mathsf{E}_C B}}{\Gamma \vdash \mathsf{E}_C A \,\&\, \mathsf{E}_C B} \text{ \&-rule}$$

By axiom 12 and ⊸-rule (i.e. *modus ponens*), we conclude $\Gamma \multimap \mathsf{E}_C(A \,\&\, B)$ as follows:

$$\frac{\Gamma \vdash \mathsf{E}_C A \,\&\, \mathsf{E}_C B \qquad \vdash \mathsf{E}_C A \,\&\, \mathsf{E}_C B \multimap \mathsf{E}_C(A \,\&\, B)}{\Gamma \vdash \mathsf{E}_C A \,\&\, B} \text{ ⊸-rule}$$

Since $\Gamma \vdash \mathsf{E}_c A \,\&\, B$, we have that $\|A \,\&\, B\| \in N^c_C(\Gamma)$. Therefore, we can conclude since $\|A \,\&\, B\| = \|A\| \cap \|B\| = X \cap Y$.

Case of Condition (5). Assume $X \in N^c_C(\Gamma)$, $Y \in N^c_D(\Delta)$. By definition of canonical neighborhood, we have: $\Gamma \vdash \mathsf{E}_C A$, $\Delta \vdash \mathsf{E}_D B$, where $\|A\| = X$ and $\|B\| = Y$. We can prove that $\Gamma, \Delta \vdash \mathsf{E}_C A \otimes \mathsf{E}_D B$ as follows.

$$\frac{\Gamma \vdash \mathsf{E}_C A \qquad \dfrac{\vdash \mathsf{E}_C A \multimap (\mathsf{E}_D B \multimap (\mathsf{E}_C A \otimes \mathsf{E}_D B)) \text{ (ax. 4)}}{\Gamma \vdash \mathsf{E}_D B \multimap \mathsf{E}_C A \otimes \mathsf{E}_D B} \text{ ⊸-rule} \qquad \Delta \vdash \mathsf{E}_D B}{\Gamma, \Delta \vdash \mathsf{E}_C A \otimes \mathsf{E}_C B} \text{ ⊸-rule}$$

By means of axiom 18, we infer $\Gamma, \Delta \vdash \mathsf{E}_{C \sqcup D}(A \otimes B)$.

$$\frac{\Gamma, \Delta \vdash \mathsf{E}_C A \otimes \mathsf{E}_C B \qquad \vdash \mathsf{E}_C A \otimes \mathsf{E}_D B \multimap \mathsf{E}_{C \sqcup D}(A \otimes B) \text{ (ax 13, } C \cap D = \emptyset)}{\Gamma, \Delta \vdash \mathsf{E}_{C \sqcup D} A \otimes B} \text{ ⊸-rule}$$

Therefore, $(\|A\| \circ \|B\|)^\dagger \in N^c_{C \sqcup D}(\Gamma \circ \Delta)$. We conclude by noticing that $(X \circ Y)^\dagger = (\|A\| \circ \|B\|)^\dagger$.

We are ready now to prove the truth lemma. The proof is as usual by induction on the complexity of the formula A and there is no significative difference wrt the proof in [21]. We denote by $\Gamma \models^c A$ the satisfaction relation wrt the canonical model.

Lemma 2 (Truth lemma). *If $\Gamma \models^c A$, then $\Gamma \vdash A$.*

As usual, by means of the truth lemma, one establishes completeness.

Theorem 2 (Completeness of Linear BIAT with Coalitions). *Linear BIAT C is sound wrt the class of Kripke resource frames that satisfy (1) (2), (3), (4), and (5): If $\Gamma \models A$, then $\Gamma \vdash A$.*

5   Aggregative View of Group Attitudes

We want to interpret the relationship between individual and collective attitudes by means of the logic Linear BIAT C. However, the majority rule is not interpreted within the logic by means of a logic formula, as for instance in [23, chapter4]. Recall that in intuitionistic logics, one can define $\sim A = A \multimap \bot$.

We want to associate to each individual judgment set J_i, that contains formulas of an agenda defined in classical logic, a set $\bar{J}_i$ of E_i-formulas of Linear BIAT C. Recall that the *additive connectives* of Linear BIAT C are & and $\vee$ and the *multiplicative connectives* are $\otimes$ and $\multimap$.

If φ is a formula in classical logic, then its *additive translation* in Linear BIAT C is defined as follows: $p' = p$, for p atomic; $(A \wedge B)' = A' \mathbin{\&} B'$ and $(A \vee B)' = A' \vee B'$.

For each individual judgment set J_i, we define the set $\bar{J}_i = \{\mathsf{E}_i\varphi' \mid \varphi \in J_i\}$. That is, we view the elements of the agenda that are supported by an agent i as actions that she/he is proposing to bringing about as a group action. Moreover, it is easy to see that, if J_i is a judgment set (i.e. it is individually rational) according to classical logic, then $\bar{J}_i$ is a judgment set (individually rational) wrt to Linear BIAT C.

Note that any $\bar{J}_i$ cannot contain multiplicative formulas. Firstly, by the additive translation, any φ occurring in $\mathsf{E}_i\varphi$ is additive (i.e. it contains only &, $\vee$, $\sim$). Secondly, $\bar{J}_i$ cannot infer any multiplicative formula of the form $\mathsf{E}_i\varphi$, since that the only axiom that would entail $\mathsf{E}_i\varphi$ where φ is a multiplicative formula is Axiom 18, but that demands making the disjoint union of coalitions, e.g. from $\mathsf{E}_iA, \mathsf{E}_iB$ one can only infer $\mathsf{E}_{i \sqcup i}(A \otimes B)$.

This motivates the role of the additive translation $()'$ in modelling individual attitudes: by means of Linear BIAT C, we can view individual judgment sets as supported by a single coalition, that is, the coalition made by the agent i who is supporting her/his propositions. Therefore, multiplicative formulas cannot be in the individual judgment sets, because they would require the attitudes of at least another agent.

We associate now a set of formulas in Linear BIAT C to the set of formulas obtained by majority $m(\mathbf{J})$ for a given profile $\mathbf{J}$. Denote such a set by J_G. We say that coalition C *supports* φ in profile $\mathbf{J}$ iff $C = N_\varphi$. Thus,

$$\bar{J}_G = \{\mathsf{E}_C\varphi \mid \varphi \in m(\mathbf{J}) \text{ and } C \text{ supports } \varphi \text{ in } \mathbf{J}\} \qquad (6)$$

For instance, in the example of discursive dilemma in Section 2, we have the following sets of formulas of Linear BIAT C:

$$\bar{J}_1 = \{\mathsf{E}_1 A, \mathsf{E}_1 B, \mathsf{E}_1(A \& B)\}$$
$$\bar{J}_2 = \{\mathsf{E}_2 \sim A, \mathsf{E}_2 B, \mathsf{E}_2 \sim (A \& B)\}$$
$$\bar{J}_3 = \{\mathsf{E}_3 A, \mathsf{E}_3 \sim B, \mathsf{E}_3 \sim (A \& B)\}$$
$$\bar{J}_G = \{\mathsf{E}_{1,3} A, \mathsf{E}_{1,2} B, \mathsf{E}_{2,3} \sim (A \& B)\}$$

Note that each set $\bar{J}_i$ is consistent and complete wrt Linear BIAT C.[4] We show that $\bar{J}_G$ is consistent, complete and deductively closed wrt Linear BIAT C.

Definition 5 (Majoritarian group reasoning). *Majoritarian group reasoning is defined as the deductive closure wrt Linear BIAT C of $\bar{J}_G$: $cl(\bar{J}_G)$.*

By adapting the proof in [19], we can show that group reasoning by means of Linear BIAT C is always consistent, that is, for every profile of judgment sets, although $m(\mathbf{J})$ may be inconsistent wrt classical logic, $\bar{J}_G$ is consistent wrt Linear BIAT C.

Theorem 3. *For every profile $\mathbf{J}$, majoritarian group reasoning $cl_l(\bar{J}_G)$ is consistent, complete, and deductively closed wrt Linear BIAT C.*

Proof. In [19], it is proved that, for every agenda of formulas defined in the language of additive linear logic, the majority rule is always consistent, i.e. for any profile $\mathbf{J}$, $m(\mathbf{J})$ is consistent. The proof is based on the fact that, in additive linear logic, every minimally inconsistent[5] set has cardinality 2. This follows from the fact that every deduction in the additive fragment of linear logic contains exactly two formulas $A \vdash B$, therefore every minimally inconsistent set must be of the form $A, \sim B \vdash$.

By means of the characterization in [13,6], one can infer that, if every minimally inconsistent subset of an agenda $\mathcal{X}$ has cardinality less then 3, then the majority rule is consistent for every profile of judgment sets defined on $\mathcal{X}$.

Thus, firstly, we need to show that every minimally inconsistent set in additive linear logic *plus* distributivity (axiom 14 and 15) has cardinality 2. We show that this is the case. If every deduction in the additive fragment of Linear BIAT contains exactly two formulas, then this holds also for the additive fragment plus axioms 14 and 15. It is sufficient to notice that, if $\varGamma \vdash A$ is derivable in the additive fragment, since axioms 14 and 15 are of the form $\varphi_1 \multimap \varphi_2$, by means of them and of the $\multimap$-rule the number of formulas in the derivation does not increase.

In order to conclude, it is enough to notice that if a set of formula S is consistent (and S does not contain a tautology nor a contradiction), then, for

---

[4] Note that $\bar{J}$ is consistent iff it is not the case that $\bar{J} \multimap \bot$.

[5] Recall that a minimally inconsistent set Y is an inconsistent set that does not contain inconsistent subsets.

every i, $S' = \{E_i\varphi \mid \varphi \in S\}$ is also consistent. Therefore, $\bar{J}_G$ is consistent wrt the additive fragment. Thus, $cl(\bar{J}_G)$ is consistent and deductively closed wrt Linear BIAT C.

Therefore, by reasoning in Linear BIAT C about the set of formulas that are obtained by majority, i.e. about $\bar{J}_G$, we can consistently model the actions of a majoritarian group. In order to exemplify that $\bar{J}_G$ is consistent, we can show that we can infer $E_{\{1,2\}\sqcup\{1,3\}}(A \otimes B)$ from formulas in $\bar{J}_G$, however this does not contradict $E_{\{2,3\}} \sim (A \& B)$.

Firstly,

$$\frac{E_{\{1,3\}}A \vdash E_{\{1,3\}}A \text{ (as.)} \qquad \vdash E_{\{1,3\}}A \multimap (E_{\{1,2\}}B \multimap E_{\{1,3\}}A \otimes E_{\{1,2\}}B) \text{ (ax 4)}}{E_{\{1,3\}}A \vdash E_{\{1,2\}}B \multimap E_{\{1,3\}}A \otimes E_{\{1,2\}}B)} \multimap\text{-rule}$$

Then,

$$\frac{E_{\{1,3\}}A \vdash E_{\{1,2\}}B \multimap E_{\{1,3\}}A \otimes E_{\{1,2\}}B) \qquad E_{\{1,2\}}B \vdash E_{\{1,2\}}B \text{ as.}}{E_{\{1,3\}}A, E_{\{1,2\}}B \vdash E_{\{1,3\}}A \otimes E_{\{1,2\}}B} \multimap$$

Finally, by means of Axiom 18 and the $\multimap$-rule:

$$\frac{E_{\{1,3\}}A, E_{\{1,2\}}B \vdash E_{\{1,3\}}A \otimes E_{\{1,2\}}B \qquad \vdash E_{\{1,3\}}A \otimes E_{\{1,2\}}B \multimap E_{\{1,3\}\sqcup\{1,2\}}(A \otimes B)}{E_{\{1,3\}}A, E_{\{1,2\}}B \vdash E_{\{1,3\}\sqcup\{1,2\}}(A \otimes B)}$$

In order to show that $E_{\{1,2\}\sqcup\{1,3\}}(A \otimes B)$ and $E_{\{2,3\}} \sim (A \& B)$ are not contradictory in Linear BIAT C, we can notice that $A \otimes B$ and $\sim (A \& B)$ are *not* inconsistent in linear logic. By looking at the semantics of the two formulas, they in fact state quite different things: the former states that there are two truth-makers x_1 and x_2 one for A and one for B, whereas the latter states that the is no x such that x is both a truth-maker of A and truth-maker of B. The reason why the version of $\bar{J}_G$ in classical logic is inconsistent is that it mixes the two interpretations. Indeed, $\bar{J}_G$ turns inconsistent, if we are able to infer from it, for some combination of coalitions C, $E_C(A \& B)$. But this cannot be the case in Linear BIAT C, because there is no coalition C that supports both A and B in $\bar{J}_G$. Therefore, in this setting, the discursive dilemma shows the complex nature of majoritarian reasoning, instead of being a mere logical inconsistency.

To conclude, our approach shows that it is in principle possible to talk about majoritarian group actions, provided we keep track of the complex internal structure of the alleged group agent, that is, the relationship between its internal coalitions. We may be tempted to define an agent G, the majoritarian group agent, who is responsible for all the group actions, i.e. of the formulas in $\bar{J}_G$. This can be done for instance by means of the following definition: *if* $E_C\varphi$ *is in* $\bar{J}_G$*, for some* C *and* φ*, then* $E_G\varphi$. The agency of G, E_G, needs to be carefully investigated because it has to reflect the complexity of the structure of the coalitions. For instance, we have to prevent axiom 17 to hold for E_G. Otherwise, we will end up facing again inconsistent outcomes: in the example above, $\mathsf{E}_G A$ and $\mathsf{E}_G B$ imply $\mathsf{E}_G(A \,\&\, B)$ and that would contradict $\mathsf{E}_G \neg (A \,\&\, B)$. By contrast, it is possible to prove that a version of axiom 18 is harmless. We need to replace the disjoint union of coalitions with an operation of composition such that it is idempotent on G: $X \bullet Y = X \sqcup Y$, for $X, Y \neq G$ and $G \bullet G = G$. By rephrasing Axiom 18 for G and $\bullet$, we have Axiom 18': $\mathsf{E}_G A \otimes \mathsf{E}_G B \multimap \mathsf{E}_{G \bullet G = G}(A \otimes B)$. The reason why axiom 18' does not lead to inconsistency is that formulas in the scope of E_G other than those introduced by axiom 18' are additive. Therefore, there is indeed a viable notion of majoritarian group agent G, the definition of its agency can be approached by means of a modality E_G that satisfies axiom 16, 18' and rules $(\mathsf{E}_G(\mathrm{re}))$ and $(\sim \mathrm{nec})$ of Definition 2. The actions of the majoritarian group depend on the structure of its coalition and the formulas of linear logic can express such constraints. Suppose that A and B are preconditions for the action O. We have two ways of expressing it, an additive and a multiplicative way: $\mathsf{E}_G(A \,\&\, B) \multimap \mathsf{E}_G O$ and $\mathsf{E}_G(A \otimes B) \multimap \mathsf{E}_G O$. In the former case, O is pursued by the group only if a single coalition of agents would pursue A and B; in the latter case, O is pursued even if the coalitions that support A and B are different. This means that, in the example above, if the additive constraint is assumed, then the group shall not pursue O, whereas in case the multiplicative constraint is chosen, from $\mathsf{E}_G(A \otimes B)$ and $\mathsf{E}_G(A \otimes B) \multimap \mathsf{E}_G O$, we can infer that O is performed. We leave the detailed treatment of E_G and of its further principles for future work.

6   Conclusion

We have seen that there is a viable alternative to classical logic for modelling group actions, when group attitudes are defined by majority. We have used a logic of bringing-it-about agency grounded on a propositional logic that is tailored to reflect fine-grained aspects of majoritarian reasoning. Therefore, we enabled the treatment of majoritarian groups as BDI agents, since we can show that, for any circumstances, the group guarantees a modicum of rationality. Future work concerns the study of the computational complexity of the proposed logic. For instance, the logic of agency based on intuitionistic linear logic is proved to be in PSPACE in [21]. Moreover, we plan to extend the treatment that we have proposed to represent other types of collective propositional attitudes. It is possible to provide decidable first-order versions of substructural logics in order to view preference aggregation within judgment aggregation [18]. For other types of attitude, such as beliefs, we plan to investigate the realm of substructural epistemic logics.

References

1. Avron, A.: The semantics and proof theory of linear logic. Theor. Comput. Sci. **57**, 161–184 (1988)
2. Boella, G., Pigozzi, G., Slavkovik, M., van der Torre, L.: Group intention is social choice with commitment. In: De Vos, M., Fornara, N., Pitt, J.V., Vouros, G. (eds.) COIN 2010. LNCS, vol. 6541, pp. 152–171. Springer, Heidelberg (2011)

3. Campbell, D.E., Kelly, J.S.: A strategy-proofness characterization of majority rule. Economic Theory **22**(3), 557–568 (2003)
4. Chellas, B.: Modal Logic: An Introduction. Cambridge University Press (1980)
5. Elgesem, D.: The modal logic of agency. Nordic J. Philos. Logic **2**(2) (1997)
6. Endriss, U., Grandi, U., Porello, D.: Complexity of judgment aggregation. Journal of Artificial Intelligence Research **45**, 481–514 (2012)
7. Girard, J.-Y.: Linear logic. Theor. Comput. Sci. **50**(1), 1–101 (1987)
8. Girard, J.-Y.: Linear logic: its syntax and semantics. In: Proceedings of the Workshop on Advances in Linear Logic, pp. 1–42. Cambridge University Press, New York (1995)
9. Governatori, G., Rotolo, A.: On the Axiomatisation of Elgesem's Logic of Agency and Ability. Journal of Philosophical Logic **34**, 403–431 (2005)
10. List, C.: Three kinds of collective attitudes. Erkenntnis **79**(9), 1601–1622 (2014)
11. List, C., Pettit, P.: Aggregating sets of judgments: An impossibility result. Economics and Philosophy **18**(1), 89–110 (2002)
12. List, C., Pettit, P.: Group Agency. The possibility, design, and status of corporate agents. Oxford University Press (2011)
13. List, C., Puppe, C.: Judgment aggregation: a survey. In: Handbook of Rational and Social Choice. Oxford University Press (2009)
14. Moulin, H., Peleg, B.: Cores of effectivity functions and implementation theory. Journal of Mathematical Economics **10**(1), 115–145 (1982)
15. Ono, H.: Substructural logics and residuated latticesan introduction. Springer (2003)
16. Paoli, F.: Substructural logics: a primer, vol. 13. Springer Science & Business Media (2002)
17. Pauly, M.: A modal logic for coalitional power in games. J. Log. Comput. **12**(1), 149–166 (2002)
18. Porello, D.: Ranking judgments in arrow's setting. Synthese **173**(2), 199–210 (2010)
19. Porello, D.: A proof-theoretical view of collective rationality. In: IJCAI 2013, Proceedings of the 23rd International Joint Conference on Artificial Intelligence, Beijing, China, August 3–9, 2013 (2013)
20. Porello, D., Endriss, U.: Ontology merging as social choice: Judgment aggregation under the open world assumption. Journal of Logic and Computation **24**(6), 1229–1249 (2014)
21. Porello, D., Troquard, N.: A resource-sensitive logic of agency. In ECAI 2014–21st European Conference on Artificial Intelligence, August 18–22, 2014, Prague, Czech Republic - Including Prestigious Applications of Intelligent Systems (PAIS 2014), pp. 723–728 (2014)
22. Porello, D., Troquard, N.: Non-normal modalities in variants of linear logic (2015). CoRR, abs/1503.04193
23. Rubinstein, A.: Economics and language: Five essays. Cambridge University Press (2000)
24. Troelstra, A.S.: Lectures on Linear Logic. CSLI Publications (1992)
25. Troquard, N.: Reasoning about coalitional agency and ability in the logics of "bringing-it-about". Autonomous Agents and Multi-Agent Systems **28**(3), 381–407 (2014)
26. Tuomela, R.: Social ontology: Collective intentionality and group agents. Oxford University Press (2013)
27. Urquhart, A.: Semantics for relevant logics. J. Symb. Log. **37**(1), 159–169 (1972)

Programming Deliberation Strategies
in Meta-APL

Sam Leask and Brian Logan[✉]

School of Computer Science, University of Nottingham, Nottingham, UK
{svl,bsl}@cs.nott.ac.uk

Abstract. A key advantage of BDI-based agent programming is that agents can deliberate about which course of action to adopt to achieve a goal or respond to an event. However, while state-of-the-art BDI-based agent programming languages provide flexible support for expressing plans, they are typically limited to a single, hard-coded, deliberation strategy (perhaps with some parameterisation) for all task environments. In this paper, we present an alternative approach. We show how both agent programs and the agent's deliberation strategy can be encoded in the agent programming language meta-APL. Key steps in the execution cycle of meta-APL are *reflected* in the state of the agent and can be queried and updated by meta-APL rules, allowing BDI deliberation strategies to be programmed with ease. To illustrate the flexibility of meta-APL, we show how three typical BDI deliberation strategies can be programmed using meta-APL rules. We then show how meta-APL can used to program a novel *adaptive* deliberation strategy that avoids interference between intentions.

1 Introduction

The BDI approach to agent programming has been very successful, and is perhaps now the dominant paradigm in agent language design [8]. In the BDI approach, agents select plans in response to changes in their environment, or to achieve goals. In most BDI-based agent programming languages, plan selection follows four steps. First the set of relevant plans is determined. A plan is relevant if its triggering condition matches a goal to be achieved or a change in the agent's beliefs the agent should respond to. Second, the set of applicable plans are determined. A plan is applicable if its belief context evaluates to true, given the agent's current beliefs. Third, the agent commits to (intends) one or more of its relevant, applicable plans. Finally, from this updated set of intentions, the agent then selects one or more intentions, and executes one (or more) steps of the plan for that intention. This deliberation process then repeats at the next cycle of agent execution.

Current APLs provide considerable syntactic support for steps one and two (determining relevant applicable plans). However, with the exception of some flags, the third and fourth steps can not be programmed in the APL itself. No single deliberation strategy is clearly 'best' for all agent task environments.

© Springer International Publishing Switzerland 2015
Q. Chen et al. (Eds.): PRIMA 2015, LNAI 9387, pp. 433–448, 2015.
DOI: 10.1007/978-3-319-25524-8_27

It is therefore important that the agent developer has the freedom to adopt the strategy which is most appropriate to a particular problem.

Some languages allow the programmer to over-ride the default deliberation cycle behaviour by redefining 'selection functions' in the host language (the language in which the APL is itself implemented), e.g., [2], or by specifying the deliberation strategy in a different language, e.g., [10]. Clearly, this is less than ideal. If often requires considerable knowledge of how the deliberation cycle is implemented in the host language, for example. Moreover, without reading additional code (usually written in a different language), an agent developer cannot tell how a program will be executed.

An alternative approach is to use procedural reflection. A reflective programming language [11] incorporates a model of (aspects of) the language's implementation and state of program execution in the language itself, and provides facilities to manipulate this representation. Critically, changes in the underlying implementation are reflected in the model, and manipulation of the representation by a program results in changes in the underlying implementation and execution of the program. Perhaps the best known reflective programming language is 3-Lisp [12]. However, many agent programming languages also provide some degree of support for procedural reflection. For example, the Procedural Reasoning System (PRS) [9] incorporated a meta-level, including reflection of some aspects of the state of the execution of the agent such as the set of applicable plans, allowing a developer to program deliberation about the choice of plans in the language itself. Similarly, languages such as *Jason* [2] provide facilities to manipulate the set of intentions. However the support for procedural reflection in current state-of-the-art agent programming languages is often partial, in the sense that it is difficult to express the deliberation strategy of the agent directly in the agent programming language.

In this paper, we show how procedural reflection in the agent programming language meta-APL [7] can be used to allow a straightforward implementation of steps three and four in the deliberation cycle of a BDI agent, by allowing both agent programs and the agent's deliberation strategy to be encoded in the same programming language. By exploiting procedural reflection an agent programmer can customise the deliberation cycle to control which relevant applicable plan(s) to intend, and which intention(s) to execute. To illustrate the flexibility of meta-APL, we show how three typical BDI deliberation strategies can be programmed using meta-APL rules. We then show how meta-APL can used to program a novel *adaptive* deliberation strategy that avoids interference between intentions.

2   Specifying Deliberation Strategies

Many deliberation strategies are possible and it is impossible to consider them all in detail. Instead we focus on three deliberation strategies that are representative of deliberation strategies found in the literature and in current implementations of BDI-based agent programming languages. The strategies are based on those presented in [1], however the terminology has been changed to be more consistent with usage in the BDI literature (e.g., 'selecting a planning goal rule' becomes 'selecting a plan' etc.), and the restriction in [1] that plans don't have subgoals has been removed.

The simplest deliberation strategy is a *non-interleaved* (**ni**) deliberation strategy that executes a single intention to completion before adopting another intention. Alternatively, the agent may pursue multiple goals in parallel, choosing and executing plans for several (sub)goals at the same time. In [1] two parallel strategies are described: the *alternating (single action)* (**as**) strategy, and the *alternating (multi action)* (**am**) strategy. The (**as**) strategy first selects a plan for an event (e.g., a belief update or (sub)goal) and then executes a single basic action of one of the agent's current intentitons. One common instantiation of the (**as**) strategy is *round robin* scheduling (RR), in which the agent executes one step of each intention at successive deliberation cycles. (RR) is the default deliberation strategy used by *Jason* [2]. The (**am**) strategy first selects a plan for an event and then executes a single basic action from each of the agent's current current intentions (i.e., it executes multiple actions per deliberation cycle). (**am**) is the deliberation strategy used by 3APL [4].

However none of these strategies (or any other single strategy) is clearly "best" for all agent task environments. For example, the (**ni**) strategy has the advantage that it minimises conflicts between intentions. If the preconditions of plans for each top-level goal are disjoint, and the preconditions for all subplans (and actions) are established by preceding steps in the intention, then, if a set of intentions can be executed at all in a given environment, they can be executed by a (**ni**) strategy. However it has the disadvantage that the agent is unable to respond to new goals until (at least) the intention for the current goal has been executed. In many situations it is desirable that the agent progresses all its intentions at approximately the same rate (i.e., achieves its top-level goals in parallel). For example, if goals correspond to requests from users, we may wish that no user's request is significantly delayed compared to those of other users. Conversely, the (**as**) and (**am**) strategies allow an agent to pursue multiple goals at the same time, e.g., allowing an agent to respond to an urgent, short-duration task while engaged in a long-term task. For example, round robin scheduling attempts to ensure 'fairness' between intentions by executing a one step of each intention in turn at each deliberation cycle. However these strategies can increase the risk that actions in plans in different intentions will interfere with each other. Such conflicts between intentions can sometimes be avoided by using *atomic* constructs that prevent the interleaving of actions in a plan in one intention with actions from plans in other intentions. However, it is difficult for the programmer to ensure that all potential interactions between plan steps are encapsulated within atomic constructs, and excessive use of atomic constructs may reduce the responsiveness of the agent to an unacceptable degree.[1] It is therefore important that the agent developer has the freedom to choose the strategy that is most appropriate to a particular problem.

---

[1] We return to the problem of interference in Section 5.

3   Meta-APL

Meta-APL is a BDI-based agent programming language in which a programmer, in addition to being able to write normal agent programs, can also specify the deliberation cycle. This is achieved by adding to the language the ability to query the agent's plan state and actions which manipulate the plan state.

There are two key goals underlying the design of meta-APL:

- it should be possible to specify a wide range of deliberation cycles, e.g., the deliberation cycles of current, state-of-the art agent programming languages
- it should be simple and easy to use, e.g., it should be easy to specify alternative deliberation strategies

The ability to express deliberation strategies (and other language features) in a clear, transparent and modular way is a flexible tool for agent design. By expressing a deliberation strategy in meta-APL, we provide a precise, declarative operational semantics for the strategy which does not rely on user-specified functions. Even low level implementation details of a strategy, such as the order in which rules are fired or intentions are executed, can be expressed if necessary.

In this section, we briefly introduce meta-APL [7].[2] A meta-APL agent consists of an *agent program* and the *agent state* which is queried and manipulated by the program. The agent program consists of an ordered sequence of sets of rules. The agent's state consists of two main components: the *mental state*, which is a collection of *atom instances*, and the *plan state* which consists of a collection of *plan instances* and their properties. Atom instances are used to represent beliefs, goals, events etc. Plan instances play a role similar to relevant, applicable plans in conventional BDI agent programming languages.

3.1   Meta-APL Syntax

The syntax of Meta-APL is built from atoms, plans, clauses, macros, object rules, and meta-rules, and a small number of primitive operations for querying and updating the mental state and plan state of an agent.

Atoms. Atoms are built of terms. Terms are defined using the following disjoint sets of symbols: *IDs* which is a non-empty totally ordered set of ids, *Pred* which is a non-empty set of predicate symbols, *Func* which is a non-empty set of function symbols, and *Vars* which is a non-empty set of variables.

---

[2] A preliminary version of meta-APL was presented in [6]. The main differences between the verson of meta-APL presented in [6] and that presented here, are that the belief and goal bases have been merged into a single 'mental state', plan instances are automatically deleted if any of the atoms forming the *justification* for the plan (see below) are deleted, and plan instances must be explicitly scheduled for execution (in [6] a single step of the root plan in each intention was executed at each cycle).

The syntax of terms t and atoms a is given by:

$$t =_{def} x \mid f(t_1, \ldots, t_m)$$
$$a =_{def} p(t_1, \ldots, t_n)$$

where $f \in Func$,[3] $p \in Pred$, $x \in Vars \cup IDs$, $n \geq 0$, and $m \geq 0$. For example, a domestic robot (cf. [2]) may represent a belief that its supply of beer has been depleted as:

$$\text{belief}(\text{stock}(\text{beer}, 0))$$

To distinguish between different instances of syntactically identical atoms (e.g., two instances of the same event), each atom instance is associated with a unique $id \in IDs$.

The atom instances comprising the agent's mental state can be queried and updated using the following primitive operations:

- atom(i, a): an instance of the atom a has id i
- add-atom(i, a): create a new instance of the atom a and bind its id to i
- delete-atom(i): delete the atom instance with id i

For brevity, queries may be expressed in terms of atoms rather than atom instances where the id is not important, i.e., the query a is true if the query atom$(\_, a)$ is true.

Plans. A *plan* is a textual representation of a sequence of actions the agent can execute in order to change its environment or its mental state. Plans are built of external actions, mental state tests, reified mental state actions and subgoals composed with the sequence operator ';'. A plan π is defined as:

$$\pi =_{def} \epsilon \mid (ea \mid mt \mid ma \mid sg); \pi$$

where ϵ denotes the empty plan, ea is an external action of the form $e(t_1, \ldots, t_n)$, $e \in ActionNames$ and $t_1, \ldots t_n$, $n \geq 0$ are ground terms, mt is a mental state test of the form $?q$ where q is a (primitive or defined) mental state query, ma is a (primitive or defined) mental state action, and sg is a subgoal of the form $!g(u_1, \ldots, u_m)$ where $g(u_1, \ldots, u_m)$ is an atom and $u_1, \ldots u_m$, $m \geq 0$ are (possibly non-ground) terms. For example, the domestic robot may employ the following plan to scold its owner:

!at(robot, owner);
say("You should drink no more than 3 units of alcohol per day!")

Meta-APL distinguishes between generic plans, which are a static part of the agent program, and plan instances — specific substitutions of generic plans generated during the execution of the program. The plan state of a meta-APL agent may contain multiple instances of the same plan (e.g., if a plan is used to

---

[3] In addition to standard functors, we assume Prolog-style list syntax.

achieve different subgoals). Each plan instance has a unique *id*, a current *suffix* (the part of the instance still to be executed), one or more justifications, a substitution and (at most) one active subgoal. A *justification* is an atom instance *id*. Informally a justification is a 'reason' for executing (this instance of) the plan, e.g., an atom representing a belief or goal. In general, a plan instance may have multiple justifications, and a justification may be the reason for adopting multiple plan instances. The *substitution* $\theta = \{x_1/t_1, \ldots, x_k/t_k\}$ specifies the current binding of variables in the plan instance to terms. A *subgoal* is created by the execution of a subgoal step $!\,g(u_1, \ldots, u_m)$, and is an instance of the atom $g(u_1, \ldots, u_m)$ which shares variables with the subgoal in the plan instance. Each plan instance also has a set of *execution state flags* σ. σ is subset of a set of flags *Flags* which includes at least **intended**, **scheduled**, **stepped** and **failed**, and may contain additional user-defined flags, e.g., some deliberation strategies may require a **suspended** execution state. The **scheduled** flag indicates that the plan instance is selected to be executed at the current deliberation cycle. The **stepped** flag indicates that the plan instance was executed at the last cycle. Finally, the **failed** flag indicates that attempting to execute the plan instance failed, e.g., a mental state test returned false, or attempting to execute an external action failed.

The plan instances comprising the plan state of an agent can be queried and updated using the following primitive operations:

- plan(i, π): i is the *id* of an instance of the plan π
- plan-remainder(i, π): π is the textual representation of the (unexecuted) suffix of the plan instance with *id* i
- justification(i, j): the plan instance with *id* i has the atom instance with *id* j as a justification
- substitution(i, θ): the plan instance with *id* i has substitution θ
- subgoal(i, j): j is the *id* of the subgoal of the plan instance with *id* i, i.e., plan-remainder($i, !\,g; \pi$) and *atom*(j, g) such that j is the *id* of the instance of g created by executing $!\,g$ in i
- state(i, σ): the plan instance with *id* i has execution state flags σ
- set-remainder(i, π) set the (unexecuted) suffix of the plan instance with *id* i to π
- set-substitution(i, θ): set the substitution of the plan instance with *id* i to θ, where θ may be an implicit substitution resulting from the unification of two terms $t(x) = t(a)$
- set-state(i, σ) set the execution state flags of the plan instance with *id* i to σ
- delete-plan(i): delete the plan instance with *id* i, together with its suffix, substitution and subgoal (if any)
- cycle(n): the current deliberation cycle is n

Clauses and Macros. Additional mental state and plan state queries can be defined using Prolog-style Horn *clauses* of the form:

$$q \leftarrow q_1, \ldots, q_n$$

where $q_1, \ldots, q_n$ are mental or plan state queries or their negation. Negation is interpreted as negation as failure, and we assume that the set of clauses is always *stratified*, i.e., there are no cycles in predicate definitions involving negations. Clauses are evaluated as a sequence of queries, with backtracking on failure.

Additional mental state and plan state actions can be defined using *macros*. A macro is a sequence of mental state and/or plan state queries/tests and actions. Macros are evaluated left to right, and evaluation aborts if an action or query/test fails. For example, the mental state action add-atom(a) which does not return an instance *id* can be defined by the macro: add-atom(b) = add-atom(_, b). Macros can also be used to define *type specific* mental state actions, e.g., to add an instance of the atom b as a belief and signal a belief addition event as in *Jason* [2], we can use the macro

$$\text{add-belief}(b) = \text{add-atom}(\text{belief}(b)), \text{add-atom}(+\text{belief}(b))$$

Object Rules. To select appropriate plans given its mental state, an agent uses *object rules*. Object rules correspond to plan selection constructs in conventional BDI agent programming languages, e.g., plans in *Jason* [2], or PG rules in 3APL [4]. The syntax of an object rule is given by:

$$reasons\,[\,:\,context\,] \rightarrow \pi$$

where *reasons* is a conjunction of non-negated primitive mental state queries, *context* is boolean expression built of mental state queries and π is a plan. The context may be null (in which case the ":" may be omitted), but each plan instance must be justified by at least one reason. The reason and the context are evaluated against the agent's mental state and both must return true for π to be selected. Firing an object rule gives rise to a new instance of the plan π that forms the right hand side of the rule which is justified by the atom instances matching the *reasons*. For example, the following object rule selects a plan to brings beer the robot's owner:

has(owner, beer) : available(beer, fridge), not drunk(owner) →
  !at(robot, fridge); open(fridge); get(beer); close(fridge);
  !at(robot, owner); give(beer); ?date(d); add-atom(_, consumed(beer, d))

Meta-rules. To update the agent's state, specify which plan instances to adopt as intentions and select which intentions to execute in a given cycle an agent uses *meta-rules*. The syntax of a meta-rule is given by:

$$meta\text{-}context \rightarrow m_1; \ \ldots \ ; m_n$$

where *meta-context* is a boolean expressions built of mental state and plan state queries and $m_1, \ldots, m_n$ is a sequence of mental state and/or plan state actions. When a meta-rule is fired, the actions that form its right hand side are immediately executed.For example, the following meta-rule selects a 'root' plan for an intention when the agent has no current intention

$$\text{not intention}(\_), \text{plan}(i, \_) \rightarrow \text{add-intention}(i)$$

Meta-APL Programs. A meta-APL program $(D, \mathcal{R}_1, \ldots, \mathcal{R}_k, A)$ consists of a set of clause and macro definitions D, a sequence of rule sets $\mathcal{R}_1, \ldots, \mathcal{R}_k$, and a set of initial atom instances A. Each *rule set* $\mathcal{R}_i$ is a set of object rules or a set of meta-rules that forms a component of the agent's deliberation cycle. For example, rule sets can be used to update the agent's mental and plan state, propose plans or create and execute intentions.

3.2   Meta-APL Core Deliberation Cycle

The meta-APL core deliberation cycle consists of three main phases. In the first phase, a user-defined *sense* function updates the agent's mental state with atom instances resulting from perception of the agent's environment, messages from other agents etc. In the second phase, the rule sets comprising the agent's program are processed in sequence. The rules in each rule set are run to quiescence to update the agent's mental and plan state. Each rule is fired once for each matching set of atom and/or plan instances. Changes in the mental and plan state resulting from rule firing directly update the internal (implementation-level) representations maintained by the deliberation cycle, which may allow additional rules to match in the same or subsequent rule sets. Finally, in the third phase, the next step of all **scheduled** object-level plans is executed. The deliberation cycle then repeats. Cycles are numbered starting from 0 (initial cycle), and the cycle number is incremented at each new cycle.

In the remainder of this section, we briefly summarise how the key steps in the execution of meta-APL are reflected in the agent state — full details are given in [5]. The firing of an object-level rule creates a new plan instance, together with a justification associating the atom instances matching each mental state query in the *reasons* of the object-level rule with the plan instance. The initial substitution of the plan instance is the result of evaluating the mental state queries in the *reason* and *context* of the corresponding object-level rule with the mental state of the agent. The execution of a plan instance updates the agent's mental and plan state. The execution of a mental state query may update the substitution of the plan instance. The execution of a mental state action may add or remove an atom instance from the agent's state. Deleting an atom instance with *id* i also deletes all atom instances that have i as argument. In addition, if any of the justifications of a plan instance are deleted, the plan instance, together with any subgoal of the plan instance are also deleted (recursively). The evaluation of a subgoal creates a new instance of the goal atom (with the substitution of the plan instance applied to any variables in the goal), together with a subgoal relation associating the plan instance and the new instance of the goal atom. Executing an action in a plan instance also updates the plan-remainder of the instance. The firing of a meta-rule immediately executes the meta-actions on the RHS of the rule. The meta actions may add or delete atom instances, set the state or substitution of a plan instance, or delete it.

4 Encoding Deliberation Strategies

In this section, we show how to encode the deliberation strategies given in Section 2 in meta-APL. We assume that we are given a user program expressed as a set of meta-APL object rules $\mathcal{R}_2$, and we show how to execute this program under the three different strategies. The encoding of each strategy takes the form of a meta-APL program $(D, \mathcal{R}_1, \mathcal{R}_2, \mathcal{R}_3, A)$, where D and $\mathcal{R}_1$ are a set of clause and macro definitions and a set of meta-rules common to all deliberation strategies, $\mathcal{R}_2$ is the user program, and $\mathcal{R}_3$ is the encoding of the deliberation strategy itself.

We first define D and $\mathcal{R}_1$. D contains the following clause-definable plan state queries:

- intention(i): the plan instance with id i is intended

$$\text{intention}(i) \leftarrow \text{state}(i, \sigma), \text{ member}(\mathbf{intended}, \sigma)$$

- intended-plan(j, i): the plan instance with id i is the intended means for the reason (e.g., belief or goal event) with id j

$$\text{intended-plan}(j, i) \leftarrow \text{justification}(i, j), \text{ intention}(i)$$

- executable-intention(i): the intention with id i has no subgoal (hence no subintention)

$$\text{executable-intention}(i) \leftarrow \text{intention}(i), \text{ not subgoal}(i, \_)$$

- scheduled(i): a step of the plan instance with id i will be executed at the current deliberation cycle

$$\text{scheduled}(i) \leftarrow \text{state}(i, \sigma), \text{ member}(\mathbf{scheduled}, \sigma)$$

and the macro-definable plan state actions:

- add-intention(i): add the $\mathbf{intended}$ flag to the plan instance with id i

$$\text{add-intention}(i) = \text{state}(i, \sigma), \text{ set-state}(i, \sigma \cup \{\mathbf{intended}\})$$

- schedule(i): add the $\mathbf{scheduled}$ flag to the plan instance with id i

$$\text{schedule}(i) = \text{state}(i, \sigma), \text{ set-state}(i, \sigma \cup \{\mathbf{scheduled}\})$$

$\mathcal{R}_1$ contains meta-rules to remove non-intended plan instances from the previous cycle and to remove completed intentions:

$$
\begin{aligned}
\mathcal{R}_1 = \ & \text{plan}(i, \_), \text{ not intended}(i) \rightarrow \text{delete-plan}(i) \\
& \text{executable-intention}(i), \text{ plan-remainder}(i, \epsilon), \text{ justification}(i, j), \\
& \quad \text{not subgoal}(\_, j) \rightarrow \text{delete-atom}(j) \\
& \text{executable-intention}(i), \text{ plan-remainder}(i, \epsilon), \text{ justification}(i, j), \\
& \quad \text{subgoal}(k, j), \text{ substitution}(k, s), \text{ substitution}(i, s') \\
& \quad \rightarrow \text{set-substitution}(k, s \cup s'), \text{ delete-atom}(j)
\end{aligned}
$$

The first rule removes non-intended plan instances generated at the previous cycle. The second rule removes the 'root' plan of a completed intention and its associated triggering event (reason). The plan must have finished execution (have an empty remainder), and be executable, i.e., have no pending subgoal. (In the case that the plan body is empty but has an active child plans, the plan instance should not be removed because any child plans would also be removed.) The third rule removes a completed 'leaf' plan of an intention. The substitution of the parent plan instance is extended with the substitution of the completed plan instance, and the subgoal justifying the completed plan instance is deleted. We can now define the deliberation strategies.

4.1   Non-interleaved (ni)

In the non-interleaved strategy **(ni)**, the agent executes a single intention at a time. It can be encoded as the following set of meta-rules:[4]

$$\mathcal{R}_3 = \text{not intention}(\_), \text{plan}(i, \_) \rightarrow \text{add-intention}(i)$$
$$\text{subgoal}(\_, j), \text{not intended-plan}(j, \_), \text{justification}(i, j)$$
$$\rightarrow \text{add-intention}(i)$$
$$\text{executable-intention}(i) \rightarrow \text{schedule}(i)$$

The first rule selects a 'root' plan for an intention when the agent has no current intention. The plan is selected non-deterministically from the plan instances that are generated by the execution of the program's object-level rules. The second rule extends an intention by adding a new 'leaf' plan for a subgoal for which there is currently no intended plan. The third rule re-enables the (leaf) intention for execution at the current cycle. Together, these rules ensure that the agent progresses a single intention to completion, even though the meta-APL core deliberation cycle generates all relevant applicable plan instances at each cycle.

4.2   Alternating (Single Action) (as)

In the **(as)** strategy, a plan instance from the set of plan instances generated by the object-level rules is intended, and a single intention is `scheduled` for execution. For the **(as)** strategy defined in [1], in which the intention to be executed is chosen non-deterministically from the set of intentions, two meta-rules suffice for implementation.

$$\mathcal{R}_3 = \text{cycle}(c), \text{not}(\text{selected-plan}(\_, c), \text{intended-plan}(j, \_)), \text{justification}(i, j)$$
$$\rightarrow \text{add-intention}(i), \text{add-atom}(\_, \text{selected-plan}(i, c))$$
$$\text{not scheduled}(\_), \text{executable-intention}(i) \rightarrow \text{schedule}(i)$$

The first rule selects a plan instance for a reason (e.g., (sub)goal) j for which there is no current intention, and adds the plan instance as an intention.

---

[4] Encodings of variants of the **(ni)** and round robin strategies are given in [5].

To ensure that at most one plan instance is intended at each deliberation cycle, we also record the fact that a plan has been selected at this cycle by adding a selected-plan atom to the agent's mental state. The second rule non-deterministically selects an executable intention and schedules it.

For a round robin (RR) strategy, the implementation is slightly more involved. To ensure fairness, we must keep track of which intention has been *least recently executed*. There are several ways in which this could be done. We adopt the the most straightforward approach, which is to explicitly record the cycle at which each intention was last executed in the agent's mental state. We extend D with the clause and macro definitions

– least-recently-executed(i): the intention with id i is least recently executed

$$\text{least-recently-executed}(i) \leftarrow \text{intention}(i), \text{intention}(i'), \text{not } i = i',$$
$$\text{last-executed}(i, c), \text{last-executed}(i', c'), \text{not } c' < c$$

– executed(i, c): record that the intention with id i was executed at cycle c

$$\text{executed}(i, c) = \text{atom}(j, \text{last-executed}(i, \_)), \text{delete-atom}(j),$$
$$\text{add-atom}(\_, \text{last-executed}(i, c))$$

The round robin strategy can then be encoded as:

$$\mathcal{R}_3 = \text{cycle}(c), \text{not}(\text{selected-plan}(\_, c), \text{intended-plan}(j, \_)), \text{justification}(i, j)$$
$$\rightarrow \text{add-intention}(i), \text{add-atom}(\text{selected-plan}(i, c))$$
$$\text{not scheduled}(\_), \text{least-recently-executed}(i), \text{cycle}(c)$$
$$\rightarrow \text{schedule}(i), \text{executed}(i, c)$$

The first rule non-deterministically selects a plan for a reason for which there is no current intention, and is the same as in the simple **(as)** strategy above. The second rule schedules the least recently executed intention, and records the fact that it was last executed at the current deliberation cycle.

4.3   Alternating (Multi-action) (am)

In the alternating multiple **(am)** strategy, a plan instance from the set of plan instances generated by the object-level rules is intended, and a single step of all current intentions are executed at each cycle. This strategy can be encoded as:

$$\mathcal{R}_3 = \text{cycle}(c), \text{not}(\text{selected-plan}(\_, c), \text{intended-plan}(j, \_)), \text{justification}(i, j)$$
$$\rightarrow \text{add-intention}(i), \text{add-atom}(\text{selected-plan}(i, c))$$
$$\text{executable-intention}(i), \text{not scheduled}(i) \rightarrow \text{schedule}(i)$$

The first rule non-deterministically selects a plan for a reason for which there is no current intention and is the same as in the **(as)** strategy. The second rule simply schedules all executable intentions.

5 An Adaptive Deliberation Strategy

It is straightforward to encode variations of the 'standard' deliberation strategies considered in the previous section in meta-APL. For example, it is possible to encode strategies that take preferences regarding plans into account as in [14].

However, in this section we illustrate the flexibility of meta-APL by presenting a novel adaptive deliberation strategy that combines features of both the (ni) and (as) (or (am)) strategies. As noted in Section 2 the (ni) strategy has the advantage that it minimises conflicts between intentions. However it has the disadvantage that the agent is unable to respond to new goals until (at least) the intention for the current goal has been executed. Conversely, the (as) and (am)) strategy allows an agent to pursue multiple goals at the same time. However it can increase the risk that actions in plans in different intentions will interfere with each other. In this section we define an adaptive strategy that interleaves steps in intentions where this does not result in conflicts between intentions. If conflicts are inevitable, it defers execution of one or more intentions in an attempt to avoid the conflict. As such it avoids the need for the programmer to insert *atomic* constructs that prevent the interleaving of actions in a plan in one intention with actions from plans in other intentions.[5]

The adaptive strategy checks for conflicts between the postconditions of the next action in each of the agent's current intentions. If the postconditions conflict, e.g., if the next action in one intention would cause the agent to move to the left while the next action in another intention would cause it move to the right, execution of one of the intentions is deferred. At each deliberation cycle, the strategy:

- computes the effects of the first action in the remainder of each intention
- checks the effects to identify conflicts
- if there are conflicts, defers the execution of one or more intentions

We will now explain how to encode this strategy in meta-APL, starting with techniques for computing the effects of each type of plan element. Mental state tests have no effects on the mental state or environment, and therefore cannot cause a conflict of the kind described above. Similarly subgoals can't give rise to conflicts. Mental state actions are considered to conflict if they add and delete the same atom. (For simplicity, we consider only addition and deletion here. It would be straightforward to extend the check to simple forms of logical inconsistency.) The effects of mental state actions can be determined by inspection of the code and so require no additional information from the programmer. External actions are considered to conflict if they result in incompatible states of the environment, e.g., the fridge being open and it being closed. As this information can't be inferred from the program text, it must be provided by the programmer.

---

[5] As with the use of atomic constructs, the approach we present here does not guarantee that a set of intentions can be executed successfully, e.g., where one intention destroys a precondition required for the execution of another intention and which can't be regenerated.

There are several ways in which this could be done. For simplicity, we assume that each external action has a single postcondition, i.e., actions are deterministic. (This could be extended to, for example, make the postcondition dependent on the agent's current beliefs.) We further assume that the programmer specifies the effect of each external action as an 'effect' unit clause, and provides a definition for a predicate 'conflict' that returns true if two postconditions denote incompatible states of the environment. In the example below, 'conflict' is defined using a set of unit clauses, but again more complex approaches are possible. Lastly, we assume that any macros appearing in plans in the user program are inlined at the call site recursively when the plan suffix is returned by the plan-remainder primitive.

An adaptive deliberation strategy can be encoded as follows. We extend D with the clause definitions

- conflicting(i, i'): the next step in intentions with id i, i' have incompatible effects

$$\text{conflicting}(i, i') \leftarrow \text{intention}(i), \text{ intention}(i'), \text{ not } i = i',$$
$$\text{plan-remainder}(i, s ; \ldots), \text{ plan-remainder}(i', s' ; \ldots),$$
$$\text{conflicts}(s, s')$$

- conflicts(s, s'): the plan steps s and s' have incompatible effects

$$\text{conflicts}(s, s') \leftarrow \text{effect}(s, e), \text{ effect}(s', e'), \text{ conflict}(e, e')$$
$$\text{conflicts}(s, s') \leftarrow \text{effect}(s, e), \text{ effect}(s', e'), \text{ conflict}(e', e)$$

We assume that the definitions of the predicates 'effect' and 'conflict' for external actions are given in the ruleset $\mathcal{R}_2$ containing the user program. The adaptive deliberation strategy itself is encoded as

$$\mathcal{R}_3 = \text{executable-intention}(i), \text{ not } (\text{scheduled}(i), \text{ conflicting}(i, \_))$$
$$\rightarrow \text{schedule}(i)$$
$$\text{executable-intention}(i), \text{ not scheduled}(i), \text{ conflicting}(i, i'), \text{ not } i' < i$$
$$\rightarrow \text{schedule}(i)$$

The first rule schedules all intentions that do not conflict with any other intention. The second rule schedules a single intention from a set of conflicting intentions (chosen arbitrarily to be the one with lowest id). By permitting the execution of one conflicting intention per cycle, we avoid deadlock.

The approach above essentially implements single step lookahead. However in many cases, an external action in a plan establishes a precondition for a later step in the same plan (these are called *p-effects* in [13]). For example, the action of going to a particular location such as the fridge may establish the precondition for a later action which must be performed at that location such as opening the fridge. We can extend the adaptive strategy to avoid this kind of conflict by taking the preconditions of actions into account when evaluating conflicts. We briefly sketch one way in which this can be done below.

The only changes required are to modify the definitions of the predicate 'conflicting' to consider plan suffices rather than the next steps of intentions, and of the predicate 'conflicts' to consider both pre- and postconditions. (For simplicity, we assume that each external action has a single precondition.)

$$\text{conflicting}(i, i') \leftarrow \text{intention}(i), \text{intention}(i'), \text{not } i = i',$$
$$\text{plan-remainder}(i, \pi), \text{plan-remainder}(i', \pi'),$$
$$\text{conflicts}(\pi, \pi')$$
$$\text{conflicts}(\pi, \pi') \leftarrow \text{effects}(\pi, es), \text{conditions}(\pi', cs),$$
$$\text{member}(e, es), \text{member}(c, cs), \text{conflict}(e, c)$$
$$\text{conflicts}(\pi, \pi') \leftarrow \text{effects}(\pi', es), \text{conditions}(\pi, cs),$$
$$\text{member}(e, es), \text{member}(c, cs), \text{conflict}(e, c)$$

The predicates 'effects' and 'conditions' return the set of postconditions and the set of pre- and postconditions of a plan suffix π respectively, and are omitted due to lack of space.

6   Related Work

The Procedural Reasoning System (PRS) [9] had a meta-level, namely the ability to program deliberation about the choice of plans in the language itself. Since PRS, there have been several attempts to make the deliberation cycle of agent programming languages programmable. For example, 3APL enables the programmer to modify 3APL interpreter deliberation cycle [4]. It provides a collection of Java classes for each mental attitude, where each class has a collection of methods representing operations for manipulating this attitude. In order to implement a particular deliberation cycle, the programmer should essentially modify the interpreter to call the methods of those Java classes in a particular order. This idea of extending 3APL with a set of programming constructs which allowed the deliberation cycle to be programmed was proposed in an earlier paper [3], where the authors explicitly consider the option of adding meta-actions to 3APL as basic actions, and programming the interpreter in 3APL itself. However they argued against this approach on the grounds that it would give "too much" expressive power to the programmer and would make the meta-level hard to program. They opted instead for providing a simple separate language for programming deliberation cycle which uses a small set of primitives. The language is imperative and extends that proposed in [10], mainly by adding a primitive to call a planner and generate a new plan. Plans can be compared on the grounds of cost with the gain from achieving the goal, and a plan which has a cost less than gain selected. We share the motivation for providing an ability for the programmer in an agent programming language to change the deliberation cycle on a program-by-program basis, but believe that it is more natural and elegant to do this in the same language, rather than joining together two different languages.

In [7] Doan et al show how *Jason* and 3APL programs (and their associated deliberation strategies) can be translated into meta-APL to give equivalent behaviour under weak bisimulation equivalence.

There has also been a considerable amount of work on avoiding conflicts between intentions in agent programming languages, e.g., [13,15,16]. While such approaches can avoid more conflicts than the approach we present here, this work focus on developing a single deliberation strategy that is 'hardwired' into the the deliberation cycle of an agent programming language, and which cannot be easily adapted by an agent developer to meet the needs of a particular application.

7   Conclusion

In this paper, we showed how procedural reflection in the agent programming language meta-APL [7] can be used to allow a straightforward implementation of the deliberation strategy of a BDI agent. To illustrate the flexibility of meta-APL, we showed how three typical BDI deliberation strategies from [1] can be programmed using meta-APL rules. We also showed how meta-APL can used to program a novel *adaptive* deliberation strategy combines features of both a non-interleaved and an alternating strategy to avoid interference between intentions.

By exploiting procedural reflection an agent programmer can customise the deliberation cycle to control when to deliberate (as in the non-interleaved strategy), which relevant applicable plan(s) to intend, and which intention(s) to execute. We argue this brings the advantages of the BDI approach to the problem of selecting an appropriate deliberation strategy given the agent's current state, and moreover, facilitates a modular, incremental approach to the development of deliberation strategies. In future work, we plan to explore more sophisticated approaches to the selection of plan instances as in, e.g., [14], and intention reconsideration.

References

1. Alechina, N., Dastani, M., Logan, B., John-Jules, C.: Meyer. Reasoning about agent deliberation. Autonomous Agents and Multi-Agent Systems **22**(2), 1–26 (2010)
2. Bordini, R.H., Hübner, J.F., Wooldridge, M.: Programming multi-agent systems in AgentSpeak using Jason. Wiley Series in Agent Technology. Wiley (2007)
3. Dastani, M., de Boer, F., Dignum, F., Meyer, J.J.C.: Programming agent deliberation: an approach illustrated using the 3APL language. In: Proceedings of the 2nd International Joint Conference on Autonomous Agents and Multiagent Systems (AAMAS 2003), pp. 97–104. ACM (2003)
4. Dastani, M., van Riemsdijk, M.B., Meyer, J.-J.C.: Programming multi-agent systems in 3APL. In: Multi-Agent Programming: Languages, Platforms and Applications, pp. 39–67. Springer (2005)
5. Doan, T.T.: Meta-APL: A general language for agent programming. PhD thesis, School of Computer Science, University of Nottingham (2013)

6. Doan, T.T., Alechina, N., Logan, B.: The agent programming language meta-APL. In: Dennis, L.A., Boissier, O., Bordini, R.H. (eds) Proceedings of the Ninth International Workshop on Programming Multi-Agent Systems (ProMAS 2011), pp. 72–87, Taipei, Taiwan, May 2011

7. Doan, T.T., Yao, Y., Alechina, N., Logan, B.: Verifying heterogeneous multi-agent programs. In: Proceedings of the 2014 International Conference on Autonomous Agents and Multi-agent Systems, AAMAS 2014, pp. 149–156. International Foundation for Autonomous Agents and Multiagent Systems, Richland (2014)

8. Georgeff, M., Pell, B., Pollack, M.E., Tambe, M., Wooldridge, M.J.: The belief-desire-intention model of agency. In: Müller, J.P., Rao, A.S., Singh, M.P. (eds.) ATAL 1998. LNCS (LNAI), vol. 1555, pp. 1–10. Springer, Heidelberg (1999)

9. Georgeff, M.P., Lansky, A.L.: Reactive reasoning and planning. In: Proceedings of AAAI 1987, pp. 677–682 (1987)

10. Hindriks, K.V., de Boer, F.S., van der Hoek, W., John-Jules, C.: Meyer. Agent programming in 3APL. Autonomous Agents and Multi-Agent Systems **2**(4), 357–401 (1999)

11. Rivières, J.D., Smith, B.C.: The implementation of procedurally reflective languages. In: Proceedings of the 1984 ACM Symposium on LISP and Functional Programming, pp. 331–347. ACM, New York (1984)

12. Smith, B.C.: Reflection and semantics in lisp. In: Proceedings of the Symposium on Principles of Programming Languages, pp. 23–35. ACM (1984)

13. Thangarajah, J., Padgham, L., Winikoff, M.: Detecting & avoiding interference between goals in intelligent agents. In: Gottlob, G., Walsh, T. (eds.) IJCAI 2003, Proceedings of the Eighteenth International Joint Conference on Artificial Intelligence, pp. 721–726. Morgan Kaufmann, Acapulco (2003)

14. Visser, S., Thangarajah, J., Harland, J., Dignum, F.: Preference-based reasoning in bdi agent systems. Autonomous Agents and Multi-Agent Systems, 1–40 (2015)

15. Waters, M., Padgham, L., Sardina, S.: Evaluating coverage based intention selection. In: Lomuscio, A., Scerri, P., Bazzan, A., Huhns, M. (eds) Proceedings of the 13th International Conference on Autonomous Agents and Multi-agent Systems (AAMAS 2014), pp. 957–964. IFAAMAS (2014)

16. Yao, Y., Logan, B., Thangarajah, J.: SP-MCTS-based intention scheduling for BDI agents. In: Proceedings of the 21st European Conference on Artificial Intelligence, ECCAI. IOS Press, Prague, August 2014

Multi-Context Systems with Preferences

Tiep Le[(⊠)], Tran Cao Son, and Enrico Pontelli

Computer Science Department, New Mexico State University, Las Cruces, USA
{tile,tson,epontell}@cs.nmsu.edu

Abstract. This paper presents an extension of the *Multi-Context Systems (MCS)* framework to allow preferences to be expressed at the context level. The work is motivated by the observation that a casual use of preference logics at a context level in MCS can lead to undesirable outcomes (e.g., inconsistency of the MCS). To address this issue, the paper introduces the notion of a *ranked logic,* suitable for use with multiple sources of preferences, and employs it in the definition of weakly and strongly-preferred equilibria in a *Multi-Context Systems with Preferences (MCSP)* framework. The usefulness of MCSP is demonstrated in two applications: modeling of distributed configuration problems and finding explanations for distributed abductive diagnosis problems.

1 Introduction

The paradigm of *Multi-Context Systems (MCSs)* has been introduced in [9,12, 23,25,30] as a framework for integration of knowledge from different sources. Since then, MCSs have been applied to a variety of domains, such as data integration and multi-agent systems [9,14,17]. Intuitively, a MCS in [9] consists of several theories, referred to as *contexts*—e.g., representing *agents* or *knowledge bases.* The contexts may be heterogeneous, in the sense that each context could potentially rely on a different logical language and a different inference system, such as propositional logic, first order logic, or logic programming. The contexts are interconnected via *bridge rules,* which model the contexts' perception of the environment and the dependencies among different contexts. Bridge rules describe how the knowledge modeled in a context depends on the knowledge of other contexts. The semantics of MCS in [9] is defined in terms of its *equilibria.* Research has been performed to develop efficient distributed algorithms for evaluating MCS, e.g., *DMCS* [14,17], and to generalize the MCS model beyond the original design, e.g., [10,33].

By definition, the MCS framework is general, in that it is not specifically tied to any language, inference system, or implementation. It is therefore necessary to instantiate the framework with specific logics in order to apply it to concrete problems. End-users need to select what logics should be used to encode the different contexts. Observe that each context of a MCS could be viewed as a knowledge base or a belief of an agent, as highlighted by the motivating examples used in the original paper that introduced the MCS framework. In several applications, a context also needs to express the *preferences* of the agent.

© Springer International Publishing Switzerland 2015
Q. Chen et al. (Eds.): PRIMA 2015, LNAI 9387, pp. 449–466, 2015.
DOI: 10.1007/978-3-319-25524-8_28

A natural solution to such requirement is the use of *preference logics,* which have been proposed to represent and reason about preferences—e.g., in default logic [5,7,16], in circumscription [3], in logic programming [4,6,8], or in more general frameworks [11,15,22]. However, previously developed preference logics have been designed for single agents. This raises the question of whether these logics are suitable to express preferences in the context of a MCS, i.e., *how would a MCS whose contexts employ preference logics behave?* The following example highlights the need to address this question.

Example 1 (Dining Out). Consider two friends A and B who want to dine together at a restaurant. A can only eat chicken (c) or lamb (l); B can only eat fish (f) or steak (s). They want to share a bottle of wine. The restaurant sells red (r) and white (w) wines. A knows that white (resp. red) wine could go with chicken (resp. lamb); B knows that fish (resp. steak) should go with white (resp. red) wine. A prefers chicken over lamb and B prefers steak over fish. The two cannot afford two bottles of wine and neither of them can eat two dishes. The story can be easily represented as a MCS (see Fig. 1) whose underlying logics in the contexts of A and B are preference logics. In this example, we will use *CR-Prolog* [4] (a preference logic) and *Answer Set Optimization (ASO)* [11] (a preference logic built over answer set programming) to represent knowledge base of A and B respectively.

	Context of A	Context of B
Choices	$w \leftarrow c$ $r \leftarrow l$ $\leftarrow r, w$ $\leftarrow not\ c, not\ l$ $prefer(r_1, r_2) \leftarrow$	$w \leftarrow f$ $r \leftarrow s$ $\leftarrow w, r$ $s \leftarrow not\ f$ $f \leftarrow not\ s$
Preferences	$r_1 :\ c \overset{+}{\underset{-}{\leftarrow}}$ $r_2 :\ l \overset{+}{\underset{-}{\leftarrow}}$	$s > f \leftarrow$
Bridges	$w \leftarrow (b : w)$ $r \leftarrow (b : r)$	$w \leftarrow (a : w)$ $r \leftarrow (a : r)$

Fig. 1. Two Contexts in CR-Prolog and ASO Logic

The first five rules encode the choice of each person; the sixth and seventh rules in the context of A capture the A's preferences; the sixth rule in the context of B represents the B's preferences. Specifically, in the context of A, the preference rules r_1 and r_2 (i.e., $c \overset{+}{\underset{-}{\leftarrow}}$ and $l \overset{+}{\underset{-}{\leftarrow}}$, respectively) and the fact $prefer(r_1, r_2)$ indicate that either the fact c or l can be added to make A's knowledge consistent, and that adding c is preferred to adding l. Likewise, in the context of B, the preference rule $s > f \leftarrow$ expresses that B prefers to have s than f in its beliefs. The last two lines in each context encode its bridge rules. It is easy to see that this MCS has no equilibrium under the semantics of ASO and CR-Prolog. The context of A has a unique preferred answer set (or *belief set*) $\{c, w, prefer(r_1, r_2)\}$, while B has a unique preferred answer set $\{s, r\}$; neither of them can be used to create an equilibrium. Observe that, if the preferences are removed, the MCS would have two equilibria $(\{c, w, prefer(r_1, r_2)\}, \{f, w\})$ and $(\{l, r, prefer(r_1, r_2)\}, \{s, r\})$. Neither of these equilibria respects both A's and B's preferences. However, these are the **only** possibilities for the two friends to dine together given their preferences; and, all things considered, either of these solutions is a reasonable one.

Observe also that $\{f, w\}$ is an alternative belief set of B but is less preferred than $\{s, r\}$. Furthermore, if $\{f, w\}$ is considered as an alternative belief set of B, then the MCS will have $(\{c, w, prefer(r_1, r_2)\}, \{f, w\})$ as an equilibrium. In this equilibrium, A can have a preferred meal. Likewise, the MCS would have $(\{l, r, prefer(r_1, r_2)\}, \{s, r\})$ as an equilibrium in which B has a preferred meal. $\square$

The above discussion shows that a straightforward use of preference logics in a MCS can easily result in inconsistencies, due to the interactions between preferences. Our overall goal in this paper is to allow each agent (context) to express its preferences and to provide an acceptable semantics for MCS with preferences. As shown in Example 1, the difficulty lies in the interaction between preferences. Example 1 also shows that methods for combining local preference logics are needed. To this end, we define a preference logic that can be easily integrated in the MCS framework. The main contributions of this paper are: **(a)** A general notion, called *ranked logic*, that is suitable for combining preference logics; **(b)** The formal definition of *MCS with preferences (MCSP)* and the notion of strong and weak equilibria; and **(c)** Applications of MCSP in distributed configuration problems and finding explanations for distributed abductive diagnosis problems.

2   Background

In this section, we review the basics of MCSs and two representative preference logics (i.e., Answer Set Optimization and CR-Prolog) that will be used in the later parts. Space limitation prevents additional preference logics to be included.

2.1   Multi-Context Systems

Heterogeneous non-monotonic multi-context systems (MCS) are introduced in [9]. Its definition starts with a generic notion of a logic. A *logic* L is a tuple (KB_L, BS_L, ACC_L) where KB_L is the set of well-formed knowledge bases of L—each being a set of formulae. BS_L is the set of possible belief sets; each element of BS_L is a set of syntactic elements representing the beliefs L may adopt. $ACC_L : KB_L \rightarrow 2^{BS_L}$ describes the *"semantics"* of L by assigning to each element of KB_L a set of acceptable sets of beliefs.

Using the concept of logic, we can introduce the notion of multi-context system. A MCS $M = (C_1, \ldots, C_n)$ consists of contexts $C_i = (L_i, kb_i, br_i)$, $(1 \leq i \leq n)$, where $L_i = (KB_i, BS_i, ACC_i)$ is a logic, $kb_i \in KB_i$ is a specific knowledge base of L_i, and br_i is a set of L_i-bridge rules of the form:

$$s \leftarrow (c_1 : p_1), \ldots, (c_j : p_j), not\ (c_{j+1} : p_{j+1}), \ldots, not\ (c_m : p_m) \qquad (1)$$

where, for each $1 \leq k \leq m$, we have that: $1 \leq c_k \leq n$, p_k is an element of some belief set of L_{c_k}, and $kb_i \cup \{s\} \in KB_i$. Intuitively, a bridge rule r allows us to add s to a context, depending on the beliefs in the other contexts. Given a bridge rule r, we will denote by $head(r)$ the part s of r. The semantics of MCS is described by the notion of belief states. Let $M = (C_1, \ldots, C_n)$ be a MCS. A *belief state* is a sequence $S = (S_1, \ldots, S_n)$ where each S_i is an element of BS_i.

Given a belief state $S = (S_1, \ldots, S_n)$ and a bridge rule r, we say that r is *applicable* in S if $p_v \in S_{c_v}$ for each $1 \leq v \leq j$ and $p_k \notin S_{c_k}$ for each $j+1 \leq k \leq m$. By $app(B, S)$ we denote the set of the bridge rules $r \in B$ that are applicable in S.

The semantics of a MCS M is defined in terms of particular belief states $(S_1, \ldots, S_n)$ that take into account the bridge rules that are applicable with respect to the given belief sets. A belief state $S = (S_1, \ldots, S_n)$ of M is an *equilibrium* if, for all $1 \leq i \leq n$, we have that $S_i \in ACC_i(kb_i \cup \{head(r) \mid r \in app(br_i, S)\})$.

2.2   Logic Programs Under Answer Set Semantics (ASP)

A logic program Π is a set of rules of the form

$$c_1 \mid \ldots \mid c_k \leftarrow a_1, \ldots, a_m, not\, a_{m+1}, \ldots, not\, a_n \qquad (2)$$

where $0 \leq m \leq n$, $0 \leq k$, each a_i or c_j is a literal of a first order language and *not* represents *negation-as-failure (naf)*. For a literal a, *not a* is called a naf-literal. For a rule of the form (2), the left and right hand sides of the rule are called the *head* and the *body*, respectively. Both the head and the body can be empty. When the head is empty, the rule is called a *constraint*. When the body is empty, the rule is called a *fact*.

For a ground instance r of a rule of the form (2), $H(r)$ and $B(r)$ denote the left and right hand side of $\leftarrow$, respectively; $head(r)$ denotes the set $\{c_1, \ldots, c_k\}$; and $pos(r)$ and $neg(r)$ denote $\{a_1, \ldots, a_m\}$ and $\{a_{m+1}, \ldots, a_n\}$, respectively.

Consider a set of ground literals X. X is consistent if there exists no atom a such that both a and $\neg a$ belong to X. The body of a ground rule r of the form (2) is *satisfied* by X if $neg(r) \cap X = \emptyset$ and $pos(r) \subseteq X$. A ground rule of the form (2) with nonempty head is satisfied by X if either its body is not satisfied by X or $head(r) \cap X \neq \emptyset$. In particular, a constraint is *satisfied* by X if its body is not satisfied by X.

For a consistent set of ground literals S and a ground program Π, the *reduct* of Π w.r.t. S, denoted by Π^S, is the program obtained from Π by deleting (i) each rule that has a naf-literal *not a* in its body with $a \in S$, and (ii) all naf-literals in the bodies of the remaining rules.

S is an *answer set (or a stable model)* of a ground program[1] Π [21] if it satisfies the following conditions: (i) If Π does not contain any naf-literal (i.e., $m = n$ in every rule of Π) then S is a minimal consistent set of literals that

---

[1]   A program with variables is viewed as a collection of all ground instances of its rules.

satisfies all the rules in Π; and **(ii)** If Π contains some naf-literal ($m < n$ in some rule of Π), then S is an answer set of Π^S. Note that Π^S does not contain naf-literals, and thus its answer set is defined in case **(i)**. A program Π is said to be *consistent* if it has an answer set. Otherwise, it is inconsistent.

To increase the expressiveness of logic programming and simplify its use in applications, ASP has been extended with several constructs such as:

- Weight constraint atom (e.g., [26]): atoms of the form

$$l \{a_1 = w_1, \ldots, a_n = w_n, not\ b_{n+1} = w_{n+1}, \ldots, b_{n+k} = w_{n+k}\}\ u \quad (3)$$

where a_i and b_j are literals and l, u, and w_j's are integers, $l \le u$. If all $w_j = 1$, the parts "$= w_j$" are omitted. Such an atom is satisfied in a set of literal X if $l \le \sum_{a_i \in X} w_i + \sum_{b_{n+k} \notin X} w_{n+k} \le u$.

- Aggregates atoms (e.g, [19,27,31]): Atoms of the form

$$f(S)\ op\ v \quad (4)$$

where $f \in \{\text{SUM}; \text{COUNT}, \text{MAX}, \text{MIN}\}$; $op \in \{>, <, \ge, \le, =\}$; v is a number; and S is a set-literal that is of the form (*i*) $\{X \mid p(W)\}$ where X is a vector of variables, W is vector of parameters and constants such that each variable in X also occurs in W; or (*ii*) $\{X \mid Y.p(W)\}$ where X and Y are vectors of variables, W is vector of parameters and constants such that each variable in X or Y also occurs in W.

Standard syntax for these types of atoms has been proposed and adopted in most state-of-the-art ASP-solvers such as CLASP [20] and DLV [13].

2.3 Answer Set Optimization (ASO)

An ASO program over a signature Σ [11] is a pair (P_{gen}, P_{pref}), where: P_{gen} is a logic program over Σ, called the *generating program*, and P_{pref} is a *preference program*. P_{gen} is used for generating answer sets and can be of any type. Its semantics is required to be given in terms of sets of literals (or belief sets) that are associated with programs. Given a set of atoms A, a P_{pref} over A is a finite set of preference rules of the form $\Gamma_1 > \cdots > \Gamma_k \leftarrow a_1, \ldots, a_n,\ not\ b_1, \ldots,\ not\ b_m$ where a_i and b_j are literals over A, and Γ_l are boolean combinations over A. A boolean combination is a formula built from atoms in A by means of disjunction, conjunction, strong negation ($\neg$, which appears only in front of atoms), and default negation (*not*, which appears only in front of literals). Given a preference rule r, we denote $body(r) = a_1, \ldots, a_n,\ not\ b_1, \ldots,\ not\ b_m$. An answer set S satisfies the body of r, denoted by $S \models body(r)$ iff S contains $a_1, \ldots, a_n$ and does not contain any $b_1, \ldots, b_m$. The preference rule states that if an answer set S satisfies the body of r, then Γ_1 is preferred to Γ_2, Γ_2 to Γ_3, etc. The *satisfaction degree* of preference rule r in an answer set S (denoted $v_S(r)$) is:

- $v_S(r) = 1$, if **(i)** $S \not\models body(r)$, or **(ii)** $S \models body(r)$ and $S \not\models \Gamma_l$ for each $1 \le l \le k$;
- $v_S(r) = \min\{i : S \models \Gamma_i\}$, otherwise.

Given an ASO program $P = (P_{gen}, P_{pref})$, let S_1 and S_2 be answer sets of P_{gen}, and $P_{pref} = \{r_1, \ldots, r_n\}$. We write $S_1 < S_2$ if **(i)** $v_{S_1}(r_i) \geq v_{S_2}(r_i)$, for $1 \leq i \leq n$, and **(ii)** for some $1 \leq j \leq n, v_{S_1}(r_j) > v_{S_2}(r_j)$. We refer to this ordering as *preference order* between S_1 and S_2.

Example 2. Let us consider the ASO program from the context B. in Example 1, $P^B = (P^B_{gen}, P^B_{pref})$, where P^B_{gen} is the program consisting of the first five rules under answer set semantics and $P^B_{pref} = \{s > f \leftarrow\}$. It is possible to show that P^B has two answer sets $S_1 = \{s, r\}$, $S_2 = \{f, w\}$, and $S_2 < S_1$.

2.4   CR-Prolog

CR-Prolog was introduced in [4]. CR-Prolog introduces an additional type of rules, called *consistency restoring rules* (or *cr-rules*), of the form

$$r: \quad c_1 \mid \ldots \mid c_k \xleftarrow{+} a_1, \ldots, a_m, not\ a_{m+1}, \ldots, not\ a_n \tag{5}$$

where r is the name of the rule and c_i's and a_j's are literals as in the rule (2). Observe that a cr-rule can be viewed as a normal rule by dropping its name and replacing the connective $\xleftarrow{+}$ with $\leftarrow$.

A CR-program P is given by a pair (P^r, P^c) where P^r is a set of rules of the form (2) and P^c is a set of rules of the form (5). Let C be a subset of P^c. By $P^r \cup C$ we denote the program consisting of rules in P^r and the cr-rules in C viewed as normal rules.

The answer sets of P are defined as follows. If P^r is consistent, then any answer set of P^r is an answer set of P. Otherwise, an answer set of P is an answer set of $P^r \cup C$ where C is a minimal subset of P^c such that $P^r \cup \{H(r) \leftarrow B(r) \mid H(r) \xleftarrow{+} B(r) \in C\}$ is consistent.

When multiple rules can be used in restoring the consistency of a program, a *preference* relation in the form of $prefer(r_1, r_2)$ can be added to the program to force the application of more preferred cr-rules in restoring the consistency of the program. It is assumed that *prefer* is a transitive and anti-symmetric relation among cr-rules of a program. The semantics of CR-programs ensures that if $prefer(r_1, r_2)$ is specified then the rule r_2 should be used in restoring the consistency of the program only if no solution containing r_1 is possible and the two rules are never used at the same time.

Given a CR-program $P = (P^r, P^c)$ and S_1 and S_2 be two answer sets of $P^r \cup C_1$ and $P^r \cup C_2$, respectively. S_1 is preferred to S_2, denoted by $S_2 \prec_{cr} S_1$ if there exists some $r_1 \in C_1 \setminus C_2$ and $r_2 \in C_2 \setminus C_1$ such that $prefer(r_1, r_2) \in S_1 \cap S_2$. The requirement on the *prefer* relation ensures that $\prec_{cr}$ is a partial order. Most preferred answer sets of P are maximal elements with respect to the $\prec_{cr}$.

Example 3. The knowledge base in the context of A from Example 1 is the CR-Prolog program $P^A = (P^r, P^c)$ where P^r consists of the first five rules and P^c consists of the 6th and 7th rule. It is possible to show that (P^r, P^c) has two answer sets $U_1 = \{c, w, prefer(r_1, r_2)\}$ and $U_2 = \{l, r, prefer(r_1, r_2)\}$ with $U_2 \prec_{cr} U_1$.

3   Ranked Logics

In this section, we develop the notion of a *ranked logic* that extends preference logics and is suitable for representing and reasoning about preferences in a distributed setting. Observe that preference logics have been extensively studied in several contexts, especially within non-monotonic logics. For example, preferred default theories are investigated in [5,7,16]; circumscription with preferences are studied in [3]; various approaches to dealing with preferences in logic programming can be found in [4,6,8,11,15,22].

In general, preferences are integrated into a logic as follows. Given a logic $L = (KB_L, BS_L, ACC_L)$, a preference logic over L, denoted by $L^<$, is often defined by:

- Extending the language KB_L to allow preferences to be expressed at the language level (e.g., between literals or rules of the language); and
- Modifying ACC_L to create (or define) a new semantics function $ACC_L^\le$ with the following properties:
  - It coincides with ACC_L whenever the input knowledge base does not contain preferences; and
  - It returns a set of belief sets that are the candidate belief sets and are maximal elements with respect to a partial ordering $<$ over the set of candidate belief sets.

The above general approach can be seen clearly from the definition of ASO with respect to answer set programming (ASP). The ASP logic can be abstractly viewed as a triple $(KB_{ASP}, BS_{ASP}, ACC_{ASP})$ where KB_{ASP} is the set of logic programs, BS_{ASP} is the set of sets of literals (or set of answer sets), and ACC_{ASP} is the semantic function that maps each program $kb \in KB_{ASP}$ to its set of answer sets (a member of $2^{BS_{ASP}}$). ASO first extends ASP by adding a component for preference representation: the P_{pref} component. It then defines a partial order among the answer sets of the program.

Example 1 shows that, in order to allow preferences in MCSs, a method for combining preferences is needed. We next propose a general notion of a ranked logic that extends the notion of preference logics to define an ordering among belief sets from different knowledge bases. The intuition behind this ordering is that the set of applicable bridge rules of a context can be different in different equilibria. As such, for the context to be able to express the preferences of an agent (within a context), such a combination of preferences becomes necessary.

Definition 1 (Ranked Logic). *A ranked logic L is a tuple $(KB_L, BS_L, ACC_L, <_L)$ where*

- *(KB_L, BS_L, ACC_L) is an arbitrary logic; and*
- *$<_L \subseteq (KB_L \times BS_L) \times (KB_L \times BS_L)$ is a partial order over pairs of knowledge bases and belief sets satisfying the condition that if $((kb_1, b_1), (kb_2, b_2)) \in <_L$ then $b_i \in ACC_L(kb_i)$ for $i = 1, 2$.*

We will often write $(kb_1, b_1) <_L (kb_2, b_2)$ instead of the $((kb_1, b_1), (kb_2, b_2)) \in <_L$ to describe the ordering $<_L$ in a ranked logic $(KB_L, BS_L, ACC_L, <_L)$. Given

$b_i \in ACC_L(kb_i)$ for $i = 1,2$ such that $(kb_1, b_1) \not<_L (kb_2, b_2)$ and $(kb_2, b_2) \not<_L (kb_1, b_1)$, we say that (kb_1, b_1) and (kb_2, b_2) are *incomparable*, and denote it with $(kb_1, b_1) \sim (kb_2, b_2)$.

For generality, Definition 1 does not require the underlying logic of a ranked logic to be a preference logic. It is, however, sensible to discuss the requirement for a ranked logic whose underlying logic is a preference logic. Ideally, we expect that the ordering expressed by the ranked logic coincides with the ordering of its underlying logic when it is projected on the first component, i.e., $<_L (kb)$ should concede with the preference ordering of the underlying logic. Formally, given a preference logic $L^< = (KB_L, BS_L, ACC_L^<)$ over $L = (KB_L, BS_L, ACC_L)$, we say that a ranked logic $(KB_L, BS_L, ACC_L, <_L)$ *faithfully extends* $L^<$ if $<_L$ contains all pairs of the form $((kb, S_1), (kb, S_2))$ such that $S_1, S_2 \in ACC_L(kb)$ and (S_1, S_2) is a member of the ordering $<$ defined by $ACC_L^<$.

In the following, we will be interested in a ranked logic, denoted by L_{ASO}, defined as follows. Given a signature Σ, $L_{ASO} = (\mathbf{KB_{ASO}}, \mathbf{BS_{ASO}}, \mathbf{ACC_{ASO}}, <_{ASO})$ is a ranked logic over Σ where

- $\mathbf{KB_{ASO}}$ is the set of ASO programs over Σ;
- $\mathbf{BS_{ASO}}$ is the set of answer sets of ASO programs over Σ;
- $\mathbf{ACC_{ASO}}$ maps each ASO program to its possible answer sets;
- $<_{ASO}$ is defined as follows: $(kb_1, S_1) <_{ASO} (kb_2, S_2)$ for $kb_i = (P_{gen}^i, P_{pref})$ and $S_i \in ACC_{ASO}(kb_i)$ where $i = 1, 2$ such that $S_1 < S_2$ with respect to the ASO preference order defined over the set of rules P_{pref}.

Observe that the order $<_{ASO}$ extends the preference order defined by the ASO logic, by considering ASO programs which have different generating programs but the same preference program. It is easy to see that L_{ASO} is indeed a ranked logic that faithfully extends ASO because $(kb, S_1) <_{ASO} (kb, S_2)$ if S_1, S_2 are answer sets of the program kb and $S_1 < S_2$ according to the preference order defined by ASO. For the program in Example 2, we have that $(P^B, S_2) <_{ASO} (P^B, S_1)$.

Example 4. Consider the ASO program $P^B = (P_{gen}^B, P_{pref}^B)$ from the Example 2. P^B has two answer sets $S_1 = \{s, r\}$, $S_2 = \{f, w\}$, and $S_2 < S_1$. Thus, $(P^B, S_2) <_{ASO} (P^B, S_1)$. Furthermore, let $P^{B'} = (P_{gen}^B \cup \{w\}, P_{pref}^B)$ be another ASO program, and $P^{B'}$ has an unique answer set $S_3 = \{f, w\}$. It is possible to see that $(P^{B'}, S_3) <_{ASO} (P^B, S_1)$

As another example for ranked logic, we construct a ranked logic from CR-Prolog. The $\prec_{cr}$ in section 2.4 is given only among answer sets of the same CR-Prolog program (P^r, P^c). Thus, our first step is to define an extension $\prec_{cr'}$ of $\prec_{cr}$ to give preferences among answer sets that are of different knowledge bases. Let us consider two CR-programs $P_i = (P_i^r, P^c)$, where $i = 1, 2$, and let S_1 and S_2 be answer sets of $P_1^r \cup C_1$ and $P_2^r \cup C_2$, respectively (with $C_1 \subseteq P^c$ and $C_2 \subseteq P^c$). S_1 is preferred to S_2, denoted by $S_2 \prec_{cr'} S_1$, if there is $r_1 \in C_1 \setminus C_2$ and $r_2 \in C_2 \setminus C_1$ such that $prefer(r_1, r_2) \in S_1 \cap S_2$.

The preference order $\prec_{cr'}$ enables the definition of a ranked logic $L_{cr'}$, in a similar way L_{ASO} is defined. More precisely, we define the ranked logic $L_{cr'} = (\mathbf{KB_{cr'}}, \mathbf{BS_{cr'}}, \mathbf{ACC_{cr'}}, <_{\mathbf{cr'}})$ over Σ:

- $\mathbf{KB_{cr'}}$ is the set of CR-Prolog programs over Σ;
- $\mathbf{BS_{cr'}}$ is the set of answer sets of CR-Prolog programs over Σ;
- $\mathbf{ACC_{cr'}}$ maps each CR-Prolog program to its possible answer sets;
- $<_{cr'}$ is defined as follows: $(kb_1, S_1) <_{cr'} (kb_2, S_2)$ for $kb_i = (P_i^r, P^c)$ and $S_i \in ACC_{cr'}(kb_i)$ where $i = 1, 2$ such that $S_1 \prec_{cr'} S_2$ with respect to the $\prec_{cr'}$ preference order defined above.

Example 5. Let $P^A = (P^r, P^c)$ be the CR-Prolog program from Example 3. P^A has two answer sets $U_1 = \{c, w, prefer(r_1, r_2)\}$ and $U_2 = \{l, r, prefer(r_1, r_2)\}$. Since $U_2 \prec_{cr'} U_1$ in P^A, we have $(P^A, U_2) <_{cr'} (P^A, U_1)$. Furthermore, let $P^{A'} = (P^r \cup \{r\}, P^c)$ be another CR-Prolog program, and it is possible to see that $P^{A'}$ has a unique answer set $U_3 = \{l, r, prefer(r_1, r_2)\}$, and $(P^{A'}, U_3) <_{cr'} (P^A, U_1)$.

4   MCS with Preferences and Its Applications

In this section we extend the MCS framework with preferences. We achieve this by requiring ranked logics to be used in each context. As it turns out, the only required extension to the framework is a partial order between equilibria. We will then present different applications of the framework.

4.1   MCS with Preferences

With the notion of a ranked logic, we can define the notion of a *Multi-Context Systems with Preferences* (MCSP) as follows.

Definition 2 (Multi-Context Systems with Preferences). *A multi-context system with preferences $M = (C_1, \dots, C_n)$ consists of a collection of contexts $C_i = (L_i, kb_i, br_i)$ where $L_i = (KB_i, BS_i, ACC_i, <_i)$ is a ranked logic, kb_i is a knowledge base $kb_i \in KB_i$, and br_i is a set of L_i-bridge rules.*

By simply replacing "a logic L_i" with "a ranked logic L_i" in the definitions of other notions (e.g., applicable, belief state, or equilibrium) in the MCS framework, we obtain the definitions of their counterparts in the MCSP framework. For brevity, we omit the precise definitions of these notions. From now on, whenever we refer to a context M, we assume that M is given as in Definition 2 if no confusion is possible. Before we continue, let us define an additional notation. For a MCSP M and an equilibrium $S = (S_1, \dots, S_n)$, by kb_i^S we denote the knowledge base $kb_i \cup \{head(r) \mid r \in app(br_i, S)\}$.

Definition 3 (Weakly Preferred). *Let $M = (C_1, \dots, C_n)$ be a MCSP where C_i is a ranked logic $L_i = (KB_i, BS_i, ACC_i, <_i)$. Let $S = (S_1, \dots, S_n)$ and $E = (E_1, \dots, E_n)$ be equilibria of M. We say that*

- S *is* weakly preferred *(or w-preferred) to E, denoted with* $E \prec_w S$, *iff*
  - $(kb_i^E, E_i) <_i (kb_i^S, S_i)$ *or* $(kb_i^S, S_i) \sim (kb_i^E, E_i)$ *for every* i, $1 \leq i \leq n$; *and*
  - $(kb_j^E, E_j) <_j (kb_j^S, S_j)$ *for some* j, $1 \leq j \leq n$.
- S *is* weakly incomparable *(or w-incomparable) to E, denoted with* $S \sim_w E$, *if* $S \not\prec_w E$ *and* $E \not\prec_w S$.

The definition of w-preferred belief sets provides a way for comparing the equilibria. Observe that because ranked logics define a partial order among belief sets, we have that $S \sim_w E$ implies $E \sim_w S$, and $E \prec_w S$ implies that $S \not\prec_w E$. It is easy to see that $\prec_w$ is not transitive in general, since the independence between contexts can create a cycle of the form $S \prec_w U$, $U \prec_w V$, and $V \prec_w S$. We can define a stronger notion of preferred equilibrium as follows.

Definition 4 (Strongly Preferred). *Let* $M = (C_1, \ldots, C_n)$ *be a MCSP where* C_i *is a ranked logic* $L_i = (KB_i, BS_i, ACC_i, <_i)$. *Let* $S = (S_1, \ldots, S_n)$ *and* $E = (E_1, \ldots, E_n)$ *be equilibria of M. We say that*

- S *is* strongly preferred *(or s-preferred) to E, denoted with* $E \prec_s S$, *iff* $(kb_j^E, E_j) <_j (kb_j^S, S_j)$ *for* $1 \leq j \leq n$.
- S *is* strongly incomparable *(or s-incomparable) to E, denoted with* $S \sim_s E$, *iff* $S \not\prec_s E$ *and* $E \not\prec_s S$.

Since the preference relation in a ranked logic is a partial order, the following property holds.

Proposition 1. *Let* $M = (C_1, \ldots, C_n)$ *be a MCSP and* S_1, S_2, S_3 *be three equilibria of M. Then,* $S_1 \prec_s S_2$ *and* $S_2 \prec_s S_3$ *imply* $S_1 \prec_s S_3$.

We note that, in Definition 3 and 4, E_i and S_i (resp. E_j and S_j) are possibly derived from different knowledge bases. Thus, the preference order between E_i and S_i (resp. E_j and S_j) are necessarily determined together with the knowledge bases that they are derived from, like in Definition 1. We will now define the notion of most preferred equilibrium.

Definition 5 (Most Preferred Equilibrium). *Let* M *be a MCSP. An equilibrium* E *of* M *is a* most strongly *(resp.* most weakly*) preferred equilibrium of* M *iff there is no equilibrium* E' *of* M *such that* $E \prec_s E'$ *(resp.* $E \prec_w E'$*).*

The above definition deserves some discussion. In fact, by Definition 5, if an equilibrium S is strongly/weakly-incomparable with all other equilibria, S is most strongly/weakly preferred. From the preference perspective, this is a reasonable view. For the two equilibria $(\{c, w, prefer(r_1, r_2)\}, \{f, w\})$ and $(\{l, r, prefer(r_1, r_2)\}, \{s, r\})$ from Example 1, we have that both are most weakly preferred as well as most strongly preferred. Furthermore, the two are strongly/weakly incomparable. We will now describe two applications of MCSP.

4.2   Distributed Configuration Problems as MCSP

A *Distributed Configuration Problem (DCP)* typically consists of determining arrangements of a set of components that satisfy a set of requirements and constraints on how to connect the components. The components might come from different sources and each source is governed by different entities. A DCP can be specified by an extension of the logic *LoCo* [2]. A specification of a DCP consists of the following:

- **Components**: A component is specified by its name (type), a unique identifier, and a vector of attributes. It is specified by a ground atom of the form $t(id, \boldsymbol{x})$.
- **Connections**: For every ordered set $\{t_i, t_j\}$ of component types which are potentially connected to each other, a predicate symbol $t_i 2 t_j$ representing a connection from t_i to t_j is introduced. For each $t_i(id, \boldsymbol{x})$, its connections to components of type t_j are axiomatized as

$$t_i(id, \boldsymbol{x}) \Rightarrow (\exists^{u_i}_{l_i} ID).[t_i 2 t_j(id, ID) \wedge t_j(ID, \boldsymbol{y}) \wedge \phi(id, ID, \boldsymbol{x}, \boldsymbol{y})] \qquad (6)$$

or

$$t_i(id, \boldsymbol{x}) \Rightarrow (\exists^{u_i}_{l_i} ID).[t_j 2 t_i(ID, id) \wedge t_j(ID, \boldsymbol{y}) \wedge \phi(ID, id, \boldsymbol{y}, \boldsymbol{x})] \qquad (7)$$

where formulas of the form $\phi(id, ID, \boldsymbol{x}, \boldsymbol{y})$ express additional constraints of connecting component id to component ID,[2] and the formula $\exists^u_l x. \gamma(x, \boldsymbol{v})$ says that the number of different x where $\gamma(x, \boldsymbol{v})$ holds is restricted to be within the range $[l, u]$.

- **Preference**: A preference on how to connect a component $t_i(id, \boldsymbol{x})$ with other components of the type t_j (the predicate $t_i 2 t_j$ is assumed to exist) is specified by

$$\begin{array}{c} t_i(id, \boldsymbol{x}) \wedge \bigwedge^k_{\ell=1} t_j(id_{j_\ell}, \boldsymbol{y}_{j_\ell}) \wedge \phi(id, \langle id_{j_\ell} \rangle^k_{\ell=1}, \boldsymbol{x}, \langle \boldsymbol{y}_{j_\ell} \rangle^k_{\ell=1}) \Rightarrow \\ t_i 2 t_j(id, id_{j_1}) > \cdots > t_i 2 t_j(id, id_{j_k}) \end{array} \qquad (8)$$

where $\phi(id, \langle id_{j_\ell} \rangle^k_{\ell=1}, \boldsymbol{x}, \langle \boldsymbol{y}_{j_\ell} \rangle^k_{\ell=1})$ expresses additional constraints for the connection between components id_i and components of type t_j.

A DCP problem $\mathcal{C}$ is defined by a tuple $\langle C, KB, Pre, Prob, Src, \alpha \rangle$ where C is the set of all components of the problem, KB is the set of axioms of the form (6) or (7) over C, Pre is a set of preferences of the form (8), $Prob \subseteq C$, $Srcs$ is a set of locations, and α is a function that assigns to each component $t(id, \boldsymbol{x})$ a unique source $\alpha(id) \in Src$. For simplicity of the presentation, we often assume that $Src = \{1, \ldots, n\}$ where $n = |Src|$ when no confusion is possible.

A *valid configuration* (or configuration) of a problem $\mathcal{C} = \langle C, KB, Pre, Prob, Src, \alpha \rangle$ is S where $Prob \subseteq S$ such that S is subset minimal and $S \cup KB$ is consistent.

Let S be a configuration and r be a preference rule of the form (8). We say that S satisfies r with the degree $v_S(r) = 1$ if $t_i(id, \boldsymbol{x}) \notin S$, there exists no ℓ such

---

[2] $\phi(id, ID, \boldsymbol{x}, \boldsymbol{y})$ might be different from $\phi(ID, id, \boldsymbol{y}, \boldsymbol{x})$.

that $t_i2t_j(id, id_{j_\ell}) \in K$, or the additional constraint $\phi(id, \langle id_{j_\ell}\rangle_{\ell=1}^k, \boldsymbol{x}, \langle \boldsymbol{y}_{j_\ell}\rangle_{\ell=1}^k)$ is not satisfied in S; otherwise, $v_S(r) = l$ if $t_i(id, \boldsymbol{x}) \in S$ and $l = \min\{s \mid t_i2t_j(id, id_{j_s}) \in S\}$. A configuration S_1 is said to be more preferred than a configuration S_2, denoted by $S_2 \prec S_1$, if *(i)* $v_{S_1}(r) \leq v_{S_2}(r)$ for every rule r of the form (8); and *(ii)* $v_{S_1}(r) < v_{S_2}(r)$ for some rule r of the form (8). A *solution* of a DCP problem is a valid configuration S such that there does not exist the valid configuration S' where $S' \neq S$ and $S \prec S'$.

A configuration problem $\mathcal{C} = \langle C, KB, Pre, Prob, \{1, \ldots, n\}, \alpha\rangle$ can be modeled by a MCSP $M(\mathcal{C}) = (M_1, \ldots, M_n)$ and the ranked logic of context M_i is L_{ASO} whose underlying logic is answer set programming.

- Each kb_q consists of:
  - For each $t(id, \boldsymbol{x})$ in C where $\alpha(id) = q$, a fact of the form $t(id, \boldsymbol{x})$, and a preference rule $\neg in(id) > in(id) \leftarrow$.
  - For each rule of the form (6) in KB such that $\alpha(id) = q$, a set of rules of the form:

$$0\{t_i2t_j(id, ID)\}1 \leftarrow t_i(id, \boldsymbol{x}), in(id), t_j(ID, \boldsymbol{y}), \phi_L(id, ID, \boldsymbol{x}, \boldsymbol{y}).$$
$$\leftarrow t_i(id, \boldsymbol{x}), in(id), not\ l_i\{t_i2t_j(id, ID) : t_j(ID, \_)\}u_i.$$
$$(9)$$

    where $\phi_L(id, ID, \boldsymbol{x}, \boldsymbol{y})$ is the encoding in ASP of the formula $\phi(id, ID, \boldsymbol{x}, \boldsymbol{y})$ in (6).
  - For each rule of the form (7) in KB such that $\alpha(id) = q$, a set of rules of the form:

$$0\{t_j2t_i(ID, id)\}1 \leftarrow t_i(id, \boldsymbol{x}), in(id), t_j(ID, \boldsymbol{y}), \phi_L(ID, id, \boldsymbol{y}, \boldsymbol{x}).$$
$$\leftarrow t_i(id, \boldsymbol{x}), in(id), not\ l_i\{t_j2t_i(ID, id) : t_j(ID, \_)\}u_i.$$
$$(10)$$

    where $\phi_L(ID, id, \boldsymbol{y}, \boldsymbol{x})$ is the encoding in ASP of the formula $\phi(ID, id, \boldsymbol{y}, \boldsymbol{x})$ in (7).
  - For each predicate t_i2t_j such that it exists some $t_i(ID, \boldsymbol{x})$ or some $t_j(ID, \boldsymbol{x})$ where $\alpha(ID) = q$, a rule of the form:

$$2\{in(X), in(Y)\}2 \leftarrow t_i2t_j(X, Y)\tag{11}$$

  - For each $t(id, \boldsymbol{x})$ in $Prob$ where $\alpha(id) = q$, a fact of the form $in(id)$.
  - For each rule of the form (8) in Pre such that $\alpha(id_i) = q$, a preference rule of the form

$$t_i2t_j(id, id_{j_1}) > \ldots > t_i2t_j(id, id_{j_k}) \leftarrow t_i(id, \boldsymbol{x}), t_j(id_{j_1}, \boldsymbol{y}_{j_1}), \ldots, t_j(id_{j_k}, \boldsymbol{y}_{j_k}),$$
$$\phi_L(id, \langle id_{j_\ell}\rangle_{\ell=1}^k, \boldsymbol{x}, \langle \boldsymbol{y}_{j_\ell}\rangle_{\ell=1}^k)$$
$$(12)$$

    where $\phi_L(id, \langle id_{j_\ell}\rangle_{\ell=1}^k, \boldsymbol{x}, \langle \boldsymbol{y}_{j_\ell}\rangle_{\ell=1}^k)$ is the ASP encoding of $\phi(id, \langle id_{j_\ell}\rangle_{\ell=1}^k, \boldsymbol{x}, \langle \boldsymbol{y}_{j_\ell}\rangle_{\ell=1}^k)$.
- Each br_q consists of:

○ For each $t_j(id, \boldsymbol{x})$ in C such that $\alpha(id) = m$ and either $t_i 2 t_j$ or $t_j 2 t_i$ occurs in kb_q, a bridge rule of the form

$$t_j(id, \overrightarrow{x})) \leftarrow (m : t_j(id, \overrightarrow{x})) \tag{13}$$
$$t_i 2 t_j(X, Y) \leftarrow (m : t_i 2 t_j(X, Y)) \tag{14}$$
$$t_j 2 t_i(X, Y) \leftarrow (m : t_j 2 t_i(X, Y)) \tag{15}$$

Given an equilibrium $E = (E_1, \ldots, E_n)$ of $M(\mathcal{C})$, let $S(E) = \bigcup_{i=1}^n \{t(id, \boldsymbol{x}) \mid in(id) \in E_i\} \cup \bigcup_{i=1}^n \{t_i 2 t_j(id, id') \mid t_i 2 t_j(id, id') \in E_i\})$. The next proposition relates $M(\mathcal{C})$ and $\mathcal{C}$:

Proposition 2. S *is a solution of* $\mathcal{C}$ *iff there exists some most w-preferred equilibrium* E *of* $M(\mathcal{C})$ *such that* $S = S(E)$.

Let us illustrate the problem using an example.

Example 6 (Harbor problem). Two companies A and B operate their business at harbor H. A needs to transport packages (type p) of different sizes and would like to minimize the cost of renting containers (type c) from company B. B has containers of different sizes as well. Preferably, A wants to use a container as small as possible that fits the package's size. We assume that each container carries at most one package.

- **Components.** A component is either a package (type p) or a container (type c). A package id_i is represented by an atom of the form $p(id_i, s)$ where s is the size of the package. A container id_j is represented by an atom of the form $c(id_j, s)$ where s is the size of the package. For simplicity of the presentation, we often write $p(id_i, size(id_i))$ (resp. $c(id_j, size(id_j))$) to represent a component;
- **Connections.** Let id_i and id_j be two components of the type package and container, respectively. A connection axiom is specified as follows.

$$p(id_i, size(id_i)) \Rightarrow \exists_1^1 id_j. \, [p2c(id_i, id_j) \wedge c(id_j, size(id_j)) \wedge size(id_i) \leq size(id_j)]$$
$$c(id_j, size(id_j)) \Rightarrow \exists_0^1 id_i. \, [p2c(id_i, id_j) \wedge p(id_i, size(id_i)) \wedge size(id_i) \leq size(id_j)]$$

- **Preferences.** A preference for each package id_i is of the form (assume that there are k different containers)

$$p(id_i, size(id_i)) \wedge$$
$$c(id_{j_1}, size(id_{j_1})) \wedge \ldots \wedge c(id_{j_k}, size(id_{j_k})) \wedge$$
$$size(id_{j_1}) \leq \ldots \leq size(id_{j_k}) \Rightarrow p2c(id_i, id_{j_1}) > \ldots > p2c(id_i, id_{j_k})$$

A harbor problem can be given by a DCP problem $\mathcal{C} = \langle C, KB, Pre, Prob, Src, \alpha \rangle$ where C is a collection of packages and containers, KB is a set of connections and preferences, and $Prob \subseteq C$, $Src = \{A, B\}$, and for $x \in C$, $\alpha(x) = A$ if x is a package and $\alpha(x) = B$ otherwise.

4.3   Distributed Diagnosis and MCSP

Abductive diagnosis aims at finding an explanation as *a cause for the observation*. More formally, in finding the most generic diagnoses, we are seeking minimal subsets of hypotheses that explain a collection of observations and respect some background knowledge. Traditionally, diagnosis is considered as a centralized application, i.e., background knowledge is a single knowledge base. Yet, background knowledge is naturally captured by distributed collection of knowledge bases. For example, different departments in the hospital have the best understanding on different types of diseases. They usually need to interact with each other to come up with a final diagnosis for patients, yet a department usually only provides the other departments the necessary information.

Let $M = (C_1, \ldots, C_n)$ be a MCS. In the following, we write $lit(X)$ as the set of all literals that appear in X where X could be the MCS M, a context C_i, a knowledge base kb, or a belief state $E = (E_1, \ldots, E_n)$. For $Y \subseteq lit(M)$ and a kb_i in the context of C_i, $kb_i \oplus Y$ denotes $kb_i \cup (lit(C_i) \cap Y)$. We define $M \oplus Y = (C_1', \ldots, C_n')$ where each $C_i' = (L_i, kb_i \oplus Y, br_i)$. A belief state $E = (E_1, \ldots, E_n)$ entails a set $Y \subseteq lit(M)$, denoted by $E \models Y$, if $Y \cap lit(C_i) \subseteq E_i$ for $i = 1, \ldots, n$. $M \models Y$ if for every equilibrium E of M, $E \models Y$.

Definition 6. *A* distributed abductive diagnosis *(DAD) problem* $\mathcal{D}$ *is defined by a tuple* $\langle M, H, O \rangle$ *where* M *is a MCS,* H *is a finite set of hypotheses, and* O *is a finite set of observations such that* $H, O \subseteq lit(M)$.

We next define the notion of an explanation in DAD.

Definition 7. *Let* $\langle M, H, O \rangle$ *be a DAD. An* explanation *for* O *in* D *is a* subset minimal K *of* H *such that* $M \oplus K$ *has an equilibrium* E *and* $E \models O$.

An explanation for the observations in a DAD problem $\langle M, H, O \rangle$ can be found by adding a set of hypotheses K to M and then check for the entailment $M \oplus K \models O$ and ensure that K is subset minimal. As it turns out, this could be modeled using a MCSP whose underlying logics support the process of generating (the set K) and testing (for other conditions) can be used for computing explanations of DAD problems. We next discuss how this can be done. In this paper, we will use MCSP whose logics are ranked ASO logics over logic program and its extensions.

Given a DAD problem $\mathcal{D} = \langle M, H, O \rangle$ with $M = (C_1, \ldots, C_n)$ and $C_i = (L_i, kb_i, br_i)$, an explanation for $\mathcal{D}$ can be computed via the MCSP $P_{dad}(M, H, O) = (C_1', \ldots, C_n')$, where $C_i' = (L_i, kb_i', br_i')$ and

- $kb_i' = (P_{gen}, P_{pref})$ in which[3]

$$P_{gen} = (kb_i \cup \{1\{\neg h, h\}1 \leftarrow \mid h \in kb_i \oplus H\} \cup \{\leftarrow not\ had(o), not\ o \mid o \in kb_i \oplus O\},$$

  had is a fresh predicate not occurring in M, and $P_{pref} = \{\neg h > h \leftarrow \mid h \in kb_i \oplus H\}$.

---

[3] For simplicity we are using ASP rules to extend the knowledge bases

- $br'_i = br_i \cup \{had(o) \leftarrow (j : o) \mid o \in kb_i \oplus O \wedge o \in kb_j \oplus O, i \neq j\}$.

Given an equilibrium $E = (E_1, \ldots, E_n)$ of $P_{dad}(M, H, O)$, let $S(E) = \bigcup_{i=1}^{n} \{h \mid h \in (H \cap E_i)\}$. We have the following result:

Proposition 3. *For a DAD problem $\mathcal{D} = \langle M, H, O \rangle$, H' is an explanation for $\mathcal{D}$ iff there exists some most w-preferred equilibrium E of $P_{dad}(M, H, O)$ such that $H' = S(E)$*

A concrete example for finding explanations for distributed abductive diagnosis problem will be given in appendix II for space limitation.

5 Discussion

The work proposed in this paper is motivated by the observation that a casual use of preference logics at the context level could make an MCS inconsistent. The use of ranked logics at the context level of MCSs allows us to combine preferences in MCSs without causing that problem. Our work is different from the proposal in [18]. Specifically, while the work in [18] considers inconsistency assessment of MCSs using preferences, our work in this paper aims to combine preferences in MCSs.

Aggregation of preferences in multi-agent systems has been extensively studied in the literature (e.g., [1,28,29,34]) and provides an alternative approach to combining preferences in MCS. It is therefore important to point out the differences between an approach to preferences based on aggregation and the approach proposed in this paper. First, let us observe that the majority of approaches to combining preferences in multi-agent systems focus on the voting problem and the properties satisfied by a certain way of combining preferences. Such a voting mechanism assumes that the aggregate function can access the preferences of *all* agents in the system and is therefore suitable only for MCSs whose sources of knowledge (or agents) can accommodate this requirement. Specifically, an aggregation of preferences can only be applied to MCS when it is possible for all contexts to directly or indirectly (via bridge rules and their propagation) provide their preferences to a selected context, who might or might not be among the contexts of the MCS and who will evaluate the preferences. Since MCSs were originally developed to address the problem of not being able to share all information among different contexts, an approach to combining preferences based on aggregation is generally not suitable for all MCSs. Our approach is general and can be applied to any MCS with preferences.

On the other hand, we observe that there are MCSs whose structure is well suited for use with aggregation of preferences. For example, a hierarchical network of information providers can be represented as a MCS for which preferences can be aggregated bottom-up and compared at the root node; in this case, a method based on aggregation of preferences could be more appropriate. Deciding when and how should an approach combining preferences based on aggregation of preferences be applied to MCSs is an interesting question that we plan to investigate in the future.

Our approach to combining preferences can also be extended to the recently introduced framework for reasoning with heterogeneous knowledge bases [24]. The new proposal removes the explicit bridge rules within contexts. Information exchanges between contexts are specified via shared atoms.

6   Conclusions and Future Works

In this paper, we showed that it is necessary to provide an approach to combining local preferences in MCSs. Specifically, we argued that to maintain the privacy of information in each context and to allow preferences to be expressed at the local level, novel preference logics are needed. We presented an approach to address this problem by defining the notion of a ranked logic and using it in the definition of MCS with preferences. We defined two notions of preference ordering among equilibria of a MCS. We related these two notions and showed how the proposed approach can be applied in modeling distributed configuration problems and in finding explanations for distributed abductive diagnosis problems.

Our goal in this paper was to develop a framework for integrating preferences into MCS. As such, we did not discuss how most strongly/weakly-preferred equilibria can be computed. We note that there have been different implementations of MCSs (e.g., [14,32]). We plan to extend these systems with preferences and experiment with the proposed applications. We are currently investigating the use of MCSP in modeling smartgrid domains where each context encodes a node (e.g., a house, a power station) and the bridge rules represent the energy requirements (e.g., production, loads) at each context. A full version of this paper can be downloaded at http://www.cs.nmsu.edu/~tile/PRIMA15/prima15.pdf.

References

1. Arrow, K.J., Sen, A., Suzumura, K.: Handbook of Social Choice and Welfare, vol. 2. North Holland, Elsevier (2011)
2. Aschinger, M., Drescher, C., Vollmer, H.: Loco – a logic for configuration problems. In: Proceedings of ECAI 2012 (2012)
3. Baker, A., Ginsberg, M.: A theorem prover for prioritized circumscription. In: Proceedingsof IJCAI 1989, pp. 463–467 (1989)
4. Balduccini, M., Gelfond, M.: Logic Programs with Consistency-Restoring Rules, March 2003
5. Brewka, G.: Adding priorities and specificity to default logic. In: MacNish, C., Pearce, D., Pereira, L.M. (eds.) JELIA '94. LNCS, vol. 838, pp. 247–260. Springer, Heidelberg (1994)
6. Brewka, G., Eiter, T.: Preferred answer sets for extended logic programs. Artificial Intelligence 109, 297–356 (1999)
7. Brewka, G., Eiter, T.: Prioritizing default logic. In: Intellectics and Computational Logic, Applied Logic Series, vol. 19, pp. 27–45. Kluwer (2000)

8. Brewka, G.: Preferences in answer set programming. In: Marín, R., Onaindía, E., Bugarín, A., Santos, J. (eds.) CAEPIA 2005. LNCS (LNAI), vol. 4177, pp. 1–10. Springer, Heidelberg (2006)

9. Brewka, G., Eiter, T.: Equilibria in heterogeneous nonmonotonic multi-context systems. In: Proceedings of AAAI 2007, pp. 385–390 (2007)

10. Brewka, G., Eiter, T., Fink, M., Weinzierl, A.: Managed multi-context systems. In: Proceedings of IJCAI 2011, pp. 786–791. AAAI Press (2011)

11. Brewka, G., Niemelä, I., Truszczynski, M.: Answer set optimization. In: Proceedings of IJCAI 2003, pp. 867–872 (2003)

12. Brewka, G., Roelofsen, F., Serafini, L.: Contextual default reasoning. In: Proceedings of IJCAI 2007, pp. 268–273 (2007)

13. Citrigno, S., Eiter, T., Faber, W., Gottlob, G., Koch, C., Leone, N., Mateis, C., Pfeifer, G., Scarcello, F.: The dlv system: model generator and application frontends. In: Proceedings of the 12th Workshop on Logic Programming WLP, pp. 128–137, September 1997

14. Dao-Tran, M., Eiter, T., Fink, M., Krennwallner, T.: Distributed nonmonotonic multi-context systems. In: Proceedings of KR 2010 (2010)

15. Delgrande, J., Schaub, T., Tompits, H.: A framework for compiling preferences in logic programs. Theory and Practice of Logic Programming 3(2), 129–187 (2003)

16. Delgrande, J., Schaub, T.: Expressing preferences in default logic. Artificial Intelligence 123, 41–87 (2000)

17. Drescher, C., Eiter, T., Fink, M., Krennwallner, T., Walsh, T.: Symmetry breaking for distributed multi-context systems. In: Delgrande, J.P., Faber, W. (eds.) LPNMR 2011. LNCS, vol. 6645, pp. 26–39. Springer, Heidelberg (2011)

18. Eiter, T., Fink, M., Weinzierl, A.: Preference-based inconsistency assessment in multi-context systems. In: Janhunen, T., Niemelä, I. (eds.) JELIA 2010. LNCS, vol. 6341, pp. 143–155. Springer, Heidelberg (2010)

19. Faber, W., Leone, N., Pfeifer, G.: Recursive aggregates in disjunctive logic programs: semantics and complexity. In: Alferes, J.J., Leite, J. (eds.) JELIA 2004. LNCS (LNAI), vol. 3229, pp. 200–212. Springer, Heidelberg (2004)

20. Gebser, M., Kaufmann, B., Neumann, A., Schaub, T.: clasp: A conflict-driven answer set solver. In: Baral, C., Brewka, G., Schlipf, J. (eds.) LPNMR 2007. LNCS (LNAI), vol. 4483, pp. 260–265. Springer, Heidelberg (2007)

21. Gelfond, M., Lifschitz, V.: Logic programs with classical negation. In: Proceedings of the Seventh International Conference, pp. 579–597 (1990)

22. Gelfond, M., Son, T.C.: Prioritized default theory. In: Selected Papers from the Workshop on Logic Programming and Knowledge Representation 1997, pp. 164–223 (1998)

23. Giunchiglia, F., Serafini, L.: Multilanguage hierarchical logics, or: How we can do without modal logics. Artif. Intell. 65(1), 29–70 (1994)

24. Lierler, Y., Truszczynski, M.: An abstract view on modularity in knowledge representation. In: Proceedings of AAAI 2015 (2015)

25. McCarthy, J.: Generality in artificial intelligence. Commun. ACM 30(12), 1030–1035 (1987). http://doi.acm.org/10.1145/33447.33448

26. Niemelä, I., Simons, P., Soininen, T.: Stable model semantics for weight constraint rules. In: Gelfond, M., Leone, N., Pfeifer, G. (eds.) Logic Programming and Nonmonotonic Reasoning. LNCS, vol. 1730, pp. 317–331. Springer, Heidelberg (1999)

27. Pelov, N., Denecker, M., Bruynooghe, M.: Partial stable models for logic programs with aggregates. In: Lifschitz, V., Niemelä, I. (eds.) LPNMR 2004. LNCS (LNAI), vol. 2923, pp. 207–219. Springer, Heidelberg (2003)

28. Pini, M.S., Rossi, F., Venable, K.B., Walsh, T.: Aggregating partially ordered preferences. J. Log. Comput. **19**(3), 475–502 (2009)

29. Pozza, G.D., Rossi, F., Venable, K.B.: Multi-agent soft constraint aggregation - A sequential approach. In: Proceedings of ICAART 2011, pp. 277–282 (2011)

30. Roelofsen, F., Serafini, L.: Minimal and absent information in contexts. In: Proceedings of IJCAI 2005 (2005)

31. Son, T., Pontelli, E.: A Constructive Semantic Characterization of Aggregates in Answer Set. Theory and Practice of Logic Programming **7**(03), 355–375 (2007)

32. Son, T.C., Pontelli, E., Le, T.: Two applications of the ASP-Prolog system: decomposable programs and multi-context systems. In: Flatt, M., Guo, H.-F. (eds.) PADL 2014. LNCS, vol. 8324, pp. 87–103. Springer, Heidelberg (2014)

33. Tasharrofi, S., Ternovska, E.: Generalized multi-context systems. In: Proceedings of KR 2014 (2014)

34. Xia, L., Conitzer, V., Lang, J.: Aggregating preferences in multi-issue domains by using maximum likelihood estimators. In: Proceedings of (AAMAS 2010), pp. 399–408 (2010)

A Dynamic-Logical Characterization of Solutions in Sight-Limited Extensive Games

Chanjuan Liu[1,4](✉), Fenrong Liu[2,4], and Kaile Su[3,4]

[1] School of Electronics Engineering and Computer Science,
Peking University, Beijing, China
chanjuan.pkucs@gmail.com
[2] Department of Philosophy, Tsinghua University, Beijing, China
fenrong@tsinghua.edu.cn
[3] Institute for Integrated and Intelligent Systems, Griffith University,
Nathan, Australia
kailepku@gmail.com
[4] Department of Computer Science, Jinan University, Guangzhou, China

Abstract. An unrealistic assumption in classical extensive game theory is that the complete game tree is fully perceivable by all players. To weaken this assumption, a class of games (called *games with short sight*) was proposed in literature, modelling the game scenarios where players have only limited foresight of the game tree due to bounded resources and limited computational ability. As a consequence, the notions of equilibria in classical game theory were refined to fit games with short sight. A crucial issue that thus arises is to determine whether a strategy profile is a solution for a game. To study this issue and address the underlying idea and theory on players' decisions in such games, we adopt a logical way. Specifically, we develop a logic through which features of these games are demonstrated. More importantly, it enables us to characterize the solutions of these games via formulas of this logic. This work not only provides an insight into a more realistic model in game theory, but also enriches the possible applications of logic.

Keywords: Extensive games · Short sight · Dynamic logic · Solution concept

1 Introduction

Game theory has been applied in many real-world domains, including those involving multi-agent systems. In order to embed game-theoretic principles into multi-agent systems, we need to deal with the logical aspects of game theory, such as knowledge representation formalisms, reasoning about rationality and decision making of agents. Indeed, the development of logics for reasoning about game theoretic concepts have recently attracted much attention within the multi-agent systems community [8,15]. In particular, there is much more work on logical reasoning about extensive form games [2,4,5,12,14].

© Springer International Publishing Switzerland 2015
Q. Chen et al. (Eds.): PRIMA 2015, LNAI 9387, pp. 467–480, 2015.
DOI: 10.1007/978-3-319-25524-8_29

Extensive Games with Short Sight (Egss) is a variant of extensive games, in which players may have no access to the complete game structure. The reason for Egss being proposed is as follow: It is known that the assumption of full rationality in classical game theory is too strong. To weaken this assumption, Grossi and Turrini [7] introduced the concept of *short sight*, modelling scenarios in which players cannot see the terminal nodes due to their limited computational power and not being omniscient, especially in large games like chess. To make it clear, we consider a relatively simple game, *Tic-Tac-Toe* [1]. Even for this game, there are 362,880 (i.e., 9!) leaves in the complete game tree, not to mention the number of all the intermediate nodes.

Example 1. Figure 1 shows a part of the Tic-Tac-Toe game tree. There are two players: player $1(\times)$ and player $2(\circ)$. The solid arrows show the moves of player 1, and dotted arrows of player 2. v_0 is the initial state.

Obviously, it is impossible for players to explicitly compute the complete game. In fact, they can only predict a part of the future states at each node. In Figure 1, we use the shaded area to represent the part that player 1 can see at v_0.

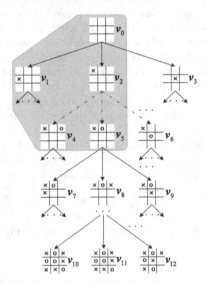

Fig. 1. A Part of Tic-Tac-Toe game.

Games with short sight are of particular importance, as it can be used to model multi-agent systems where agents have limited computational power. Inspired by logics for classical extensive games [10], we aim to develop a logic for reasoning about games with short sight. There are advantages for providing

---

[1] The rule for Tic-Tac-Toe is: Two players take turns to mark the spaces in a 3×3 grid. The player who succeeds in placing three respective marks in a horizontal, vertical, or diagonal row wins the game.

such logical representation for games: First, logical representations are usually succinct, and thus offer convenience for automated reasoning such as theorem proving. It can be combined with model checking techniques to fulfill some tasks such as to check whether a game has a certain property. Second, from the logical perspective, how sight would act on and extend game logics is an interesting exploration. This targeted logic should have the capacity of reasoning about what players prefer, what they see, and what they do, and particularly, of characterizing equilibrium solutions of Egss. Equilibrium solution models patterns of behaviors with the property that no player wishes to deviate given other players' strategies at every state. That is, it models players' behavior in a steady state. It is not only crucial to game theory, but also highly related to the study of other fields or techniques, such as decision problem in computability theory, specification description of model checking and steady states in automata theory. For example, there are two frequently asked decision problems: Membership problem (whether a given strategy profile is a member of the equilibrium concept or not) and Emptiness problem (whether the set of solutions is empty).

Technically, to address the dynamics issues of Egss, we consider the standard Propositional Dynamic Logic (PDL) [9], which was introduced by Fischer and Ladner [6] as a formalism for reasoning about programs. PDL can be used to describe the dynamic evolution of agent-based systems and to characterize players' moves in game theory. However, it cannot express players' preference and observational ability in Egss. In this paper, we extend PDL with several modal operators, resulting in a logic called *Dynamic Logic for Short Sight* (DLS). This logic turns out to be feasible to reason about such game and its equilibrium concept. In addition, we also give a sound and complete axiomatization for it.

The rest of the paper is organized as follows. In the following section, we introduce extensive game with short sight as well as its equilibrium concept. The syntax and semantics, and an axiomatization of DLS are given in Section 3. Section 4 is concerned with the representation of equilibrium concept in Egss by the logic. We discuss its soundness and completeness in section 5. Finally, we conclude this work with issues for further research.

2   Game Theoretical Notions

An extensive game with short sight is defined much like a classical extensive game [10,13]. An essential difference that makes the former more realistic lies in that we specify the players' sights at each non-terminal node. To keep our logical analysis in later sections as perspicuous as possible, we confine our attention to finite extensive games in pure strategies with perfect information.

2.1   Extensive Game with Short Sight

The following definition is adapted from [7].

Definition 1. (Extensive game with short sight). An *extensive game with short sight* (Egss) is a tuple $S = (N, V, A, t, \Sigma_i, \succeq_i, s)$, where

- N is a finite non-empty set of the *players*;

- V is a finite non-empty set of nodes, and $A \subseteq V^2$ a set of edges. (V, A) is a directed, irreflexive tree. For any two nodes v and v', if $(v, v') \in A$, we call v' a *successor* of v, and A is also regarded as the *successor* relation. *Leaves* are nodes having no successors, denoted by $Z \subseteq V$;

- t is a *turn function* assigning a member of N to each non-terminal node;

- Σ_i is a finite set of *strategies* of player i. A *strategy* of player i is a function $\sigma_i : \{v \in V \backslash Z \mid t(v) = i\} \to V$, which assigns a successor of v to each non-terminal node when it is i's turn to move;

- $\succeq_i$, a total order over V, is a *preference* relation[2] for each player $i \in N$;

- s, called *sight function*, is a function $V \backslash Z \to 2^V \backslash \{\emptyset\}$, associating to each node a nonempty set of nodes that players can see from a node in the game.

As usual, we use $\sigma = (\sigma_i)_{i \in N}$ to represent a *strategy profile* which is a combination of strategies from all players and Σ to represent the set of all strategy profiles. We define an *outcome* function $O : \Sigma \to Z$ assigning leaves to strategy profiles. $O(\sigma)$ is the *outcome* when the strategy profile σ is followed by all players. Particularly, $O(\sigma'_i, \sigma_{-i})$ is the *outcome* if player i uses strategy σ' while all other players employ σ.

Sight function s has the following properties.

1. For node v, $s(v) \subseteq V|_v \backslash \{\emptyset\}$ and $|s(v)| < \infty$, where $V|_v$ represents the set of nodes extending v (which includes v itself). The intuition is that sight at v consists of a finite nonempty set of descendants of v.
2. $v' \in s(v)$ implies that $v'' \in s(v)$ for every $v'' \lhd v'$ with $v'' \in V|_v$, i.e. players' sight is closed under predecessors, where relation $\lhd$ is the transitive closure of the successor relation A. We call this property as 'downward closed'.

Remark 1. Note that extensive games with short sight are different from games with imperfect information. In the latter, players may be imperfectly informed about some of the choices that have already been made. For each player, there is a partition I_i of $\{v \in V | t(v) = i\}$, the nodes in any given member of I_i is indistinguishable to player i. While the idea of short sight is that players can distinguish the position they are currently in, but may have no ability to foresee the future completely, i.e., the whole subtree following the current position.

2.2   Solutions for Egss

This section is devoted to introducing the solutions for Egss. First, we address a fact that in Egss, players have a limited vision at each node, and each of the visible part is actually a smaller Egss, called *visible game*.

---

[2] Players' preferences are defined over all vertices rather than over the terminal nodes only. Players are assumed to have preferences over any two nodes, including the internal ones [10].

Definition 2. (*Visible games*) Let $S=(N,V,A,t,\Sigma_i,\succeq_i,s)$ be an Egss. Given any non-terminal node v, agents' sight at v forms an Egss

$$S\lceil_v = (N\lceil_v, V\lceil_v, A\lceil_v, t\lceil_v, \Sigma_i\lceil_v, \succeq_i\lceil_v, s\lceil_v),$$

where

- $N\lceil_v = \{\, i\,|\, t(v) = i \text{ for some } v \in s(v)\}$, is the set of players who will play at some node within the sight at v;
- $V\lceil_v = s(v)$, is the set of nodes within the sight from node v. The *terminal nodes* of $S\lceil_v$ are those without successor nodes in $V\lceil_v$, denoted by $Z\lceil_v$;
- $A\lceil_v = A \cap (V\lceil_v \times V\lceil_v)$;
- $t\lceil_v = V\lceil_v \backslash Z\lceil_v \rightarrow N$ satisfies $t\lceil_v(v') = t(v')$;
- $\Sigma_i\lceil_v$ is the set of strategies that are available at v and restricted to $s(v)$, for each player. It consists of elements $\sigma_i\lceil_v$ such that $\sigma_i\lceil_v(v') = \sigma_i(v')$ for each $v' \in V\lceil_v$ with $t\lceil_v(v') = i$;
- $\succeq_i\lceil_v = \succeq_i \cap (V\lceil_v \times V\lceil_v)$, represents each player i's preference over $V\lceil_v$.
- $s\lceil_v(u) = V|u \cap V\lceil_v$, for any $u \in V\lceil_v$, i.e., the sight of each $u \in V\lceil_v$ is the set of descendants of u restricted to $V\lceil_v$.

We refer to the visible part $S\lceil_v$ at each node v as a *visible game* at v. It is easy to see that a visible game is obtained by restricting all the elements in the whole game to the sight at v. Accordingly, we define the outcome function $O\lceil_v: \Sigma\lceil_v \rightarrow Z\lceil_v$ assigning leaf nodes of $S\lceil_v$ to strategy profiles.

Remark 2. In this paper, we implicitly use $s(v)$ to represent for each node v, player $t(v)$'s sight at v. Therefore, $S\lceil_v$ shows player $t(v)$'s view of the game at v. Moreover, to avoid too much analysis on interactive knowledge of opponents' sights and focus on the logical part, we simply assume that each current player believes that others' sight is the same as hers. However, our work bears future extension with entanglement of such reasoning about the opponents.

Example 2. For the visible game $S\lceil_{v_0}$ shown by the shaded part of Figure 1, we have: $N\lceil_{v_0}=N$; $V\lceil_{v_0}=\{v_0,v_1,v_2,v_4,v_5\}$, $A\lceil_{v_0}=\{(v_0,v_1),(v_0,v_2),(v_2,v_4),(v_2,v_5)\}$; $t\lceil_{v_0}(v_0)=1$, $t\lceil_{v_0}(v_2)=2$; $\Sigma_i\lceil_{v_0}$ is restricted to the states that are within sight $s(v_0)$. E.g., there is a σ, such that $\sigma\lceil_{v_0} = (\sigma_1\lceil_{v_0}, \sigma_2\lceil_{v_0})$, with $O\lceil_{v_0}(\sigma\lceil_{v_0}) = v_5$, where $\sigma_1\lceil_{v_0}(v_0) = v_2$ and $\sigma_2\lceil_{v_0}(v_2) = v_5$; $s\lceil_{v_0}(v_2) = \{v_4,v_5\}$.

Now we introduce the solution concept for Egss [7], matching the notion of *Subgame Perfect Equilibrium* (SPE) for classical extensive games[3]. Intuitively, a sight-compatible SPE is a strategy profile that is in accordance with a SPE of the visible game $S\lceil_v$ for each decision point v:

Definition 3. (Sight-compatible subgame perfect equilibrium) Let $S=(G,s)$ be an Egss and $S\lceil_v$ be the visible game at v. A strategy profile σ^* is a *sight-compatible SPE* of S if for every nonterminal node v, there exists a strategy profile $\sigma\lceil_v$ that is a subgame perfect equilibrium of $S\lceil_v$ and $\sigma_{t(v)}\lceil_v(v) = \sigma^*_{t(v)}(v)$.

---

[3] Since subgame perfect equilibrium is a basic notion in game theory [13], we only give a brief introduction here: A strategy profile σ^* is a *subgame perfect equilibrium* (SPE) of a game G if for every player i, and each node v for which $t(v) = i$, it holds that $O|_v(\sigma^*_i|_v, \sigma^*_{-i}|_v) \succeq_i O|_v(\sigma_i, \sigma^*_{-i}|_v)$, for every strategy σ_i available to i in the subgame $G|_v$ of G that follows node v, where $G|_v$ is the restriction of G to the subtree rooted at v.

3 Dynamic Logic for Short Sight

In this section, we propose a logic called Dynamic Logic for Short Sight (DLS), for representing games with short sight. We enrich the Propositional Dynamic Logic (PDL) with two modal operators: $\langle \leq_i \rangle$ and $\langle \lhd \rangle$, to reason about players' preferences over the possible outcomes, and players' sights respectively.

3.1 Syntax and Semantics

The language $\mathcal{DLS}$ contains a non-empty but countable set of propositional variables P, a non-empty but countable set of labels N, as well as a countable set of labels Σ. The formulas of $\mathcal{DLS}$ is given by the following BNF:

$$\varphi ::= p \mid \neg\varphi \mid \varphi \wedge \varphi \mid \langle \pi \rangle\varphi \mid \langle \leq_i \rangle\varphi \mid \langle \lhd \rangle\varphi$$
$$\pi ::= a \mid \pi;\pi \mid \pi \cup \pi \mid \pi^* \mid \varphi?,$$

where $a \in N \cup \Sigma$, $p \in P$, $i \in N$.

We write $[\pi]\varphi$ to abbreviate $\neg\langle\pi\rangle\neg\varphi$, and the same for other modalities.

The atomic programs in the language $\mathcal{DLS}$ come from Σ or N. That is, any atomic program a is either σ or i, where $\sigma \in \Sigma$ and $i \in N$. The set of all programs consists of atomic programs and the complex programs built out of atomic programs using the following operators:

- $\pi_1; \pi_2$ (Composition): Executing π_1 and π_2 sequentially,
- $\pi_1 \cup \pi_2$ (Choice): Executing π_1 or π_2 non-deterministically,
- π^*(Iteration): Executing π a finite number of times,
- φ?(Test): It tests whether φ holds, and if so, continues; if not, it fails.

Up to games with short sight, the labels in $\mathcal{DLS}$ are interpreted as follows.

- The label N denotes the set of players.
- The label $\leq_i$ encodes player i's preference relation.
- The label $\lhd$ encodes the sight for the current player, with $\langle \lhd \rangle\varphi$ intuitively stating that "φ holds in some node within the current player's sight at the present node v."
- The program $\sigma \in \Sigma$ stands for players' strategies. Intuitively, $\langle \sigma \rangle\varphi$ holds at a vertex v means that φ holds at the next node reached if σ is adopted.
- The program formula $\langle i \rangle\varphi$ is read as "φ holds at one of the successor nodes of the current node where it is player i's turn to move".

To guarantee the above interpretation in games, we can further restrict $\mathcal{DLS}$ with the following features, making it suitable for games with short sight:

N is a non-empty and finite set such that for each $i \in N$, there is correspondingly a player i in the game. Similarly, Σ is a finite set with elements corresponding to profile strategies in the game.

As a modal language, the frames for $\mathcal{DLS}$ can naturally be represented by a kind of Kripke structures:

Definition 4. (Game Frames and Models) Fix an Egss S. A *frame F_S* for $\mathcal{DLS}$ is defined as a tuple $(V, \{R_\pi\}_{\pi \in \Pi}, R_{\leq_i}, R_\lhd)$, where for any player i, any strategy profile σ, and any nodes v, v':

$$
\begin{aligned}
vR_{\leq_i}v' \quad &\text{iff} \quad v' \succeq_i v. \\
vR_\lhd v' \quad &\text{iff} \quad v' \in s(v). \\
vR_\sigma v' \quad &\text{iff} \quad \sigma_{t(v)}(v) = v'. \\
vR_i v' \quad &\text{iff} \quad t(v) = i \text{ and } (v, v') \in A.
\end{aligned}
$$

In frame F_S, the set of worlds V corresponds to the set of nodes in S. The relation R_i, corresponding to a subset of the edges of S, reflects player i's ability to reach some world.

A *model* for $\mathcal{DLS}$ is a pair (F, I), where F is a frame for $\mathcal{DLS}$, and I is an interpretation function $P \to 2^V$.

The truth conditions of modal formulas in $\mathcal{DLS}$ are as follows:

$$
\begin{aligned}
M, v \models p \quad &\text{iff} \quad v \in I(p). \\
M, v \models \neg\varphi \quad &\text{iff} \quad M, v \nvDash \varphi. \\
M, v \models \varphi \wedge \psi \quad &\text{iff} \quad M, v \models \varphi \text{ and } M, v \models \psi. \\
M, v \models \langle \pi \rangle \varphi \quad &\text{iff} \quad \text{for some } v', vR_\pi v', M, v' \models \varphi. \\
M, v \models \langle \leq_i \rangle \varphi \quad &\text{iff} \quad \text{for some } v', vR_{\leq_i}v', M, v' \models \varphi. \\
M, v \models \langle \lhd \rangle \varphi \quad &\text{iff} \quad \text{for some } v', vR_\lhd v', M, v' \models \varphi.
\end{aligned}
$$

A model M is *regular* if the program connectives have the following intuitive interpretations:

$$
\begin{aligned}
R_{\pi_1;\pi_2} &= R_{\pi_1} \circ R_{\pi_2}, \qquad R_{\pi_1 \cup \pi_2} = R_{\pi_1} \cup R_{\pi_2}, \\
R_{\pi^*} &= (R_\pi)^*, \qquad R_{\varphi?} = \{(v, v') : M, v \models \varphi, \text{with } v, v' \in V\},
\end{aligned}
$$

where $R_{\pi_1} \circ R_{\pi_2}$ is the relational composition of R_{π_1} and R_{π_2}, $R_{\pi_1} \cup R_{\pi_2}$ is the non-deterministic choice of R_{π_1} and R_{π_2}, and $(R_\pi)^*$ represents the reflexive transitive closure of R_π. In this paper, we are only interested in regular models.

As usual [1,3], we say that a formula φ is valid in a model M, $M \models \varphi$, if for all states v in the model, $M, v \models \varphi$. φ is valid in F, $F \models \varphi$, if for all interpretation functions I, $(F, I) \models \varphi$. Finally, a formula φ is valid, $\models \varphi$, if for all frames F, $F \models \varphi$.

Example 3. To illustrate the language, take S as the game in Figure 1. Suppose $O(\sigma) = v_{11}$. Let M be the model for S in which $I(p) = \{v_5, v_{11}, v_{12}\}$. Then

- $M, v_2 \models \langle 2 \rangle \neg p$, i.e., p is false at one of the successor nodes of v_2 by strategy of player 2 (namely v_4).
- $M, v_0 \models \langle \lhd \rangle p$, i.e., there is a node v that can be seen from v_0 and that satisfies p (namely, v_5).
- $M, v_8 \models \langle \sigma \rangle \langle \leq_1 \rangle p$, i.e., p is true at some node (namely, v_{12}) that is preferable by player 1 to some node, which is the successor of v_8 by adopting strategy σ (namely, v_{11}).

Definition 5. (Subframe and Submodel) Given an extensive game with short sight S, and any non-terminal node v in S, we can obtain a subframe $F_{S\lceil_v}$ for S at v, where $S\lceil_v = (N\lceil_v, V\lceil_v, A\lceil_v, t\lceil_v, \Sigma_i\lceil_v, \succeq_i\lceil_v)$ is the visible game at v:

$F_{S\lceil v}$ is a tuple $(V\lceil v, R_{\leq_i\lceil v}, R_{\pi\lceil v}, R_{\lhd\lceil v})$, in which for any two nodes u, u' in the game $S\lceil v$, i.e., $u, u' \in V\lceil v$, the accessibility relations are defined as follows.

$uR_{\leq_i\lceil v}u'$ iff $u' \succeq_i\lceil v \ u$.

$uR_{\lhd\lceil v}u'$ iff $u \lhd u'$.

$uR_{\sigma\lceil v}u'$ iff $u' = \sigma_{t(u)}\lceil v(u)$.

$uR_{i\lceil v}u'$ iff $t\lceil v(u) = i$ and $(u, u') \in A\lceil v$.

The intuition behind the definitions of the accessibility relations in subframes is given in Definition 2.

A model $M_{S\lceil v}$ is a pair $(F_{S\lceil v}, I)$ where $F_{S\lceil v}$ is a subframe for $\mathcal{DLS}$ and I is an interpretation function $I : P \to 2^{V\lceil v}$.

3.2   Axiomatization: Expressing Properties

Each frame for extensive games with short sight should satisfy certain properties, which are defined by axiom schemas. Table 1 presents an axiomatization DLS characterizing the validities of the language $\mathcal{DLS}$ in $\mathcal{DLS}$-models[4].

Interpreted on frames for Egss, the axioms in Table 1 have intuitive meanings: K is used in all variants of the standard modal logic. $T_{\leq_i}$ and 4 determine the preference of players to be *reflexive* and *transitive*, and the sight of a player is reflexive. D ensures that the node reachable by a strategy profile σ from a node v is *determined*. P states that the strategy profile contains only the moves that players can perform. E guarantees that whenever a program i is enabled, there exists a σ that is enabled. A shows that at each node only one program is enabled. Re lists the axioms for regular frames.

More interestingly, games with short sight take on some particular patterns. We will put our emphasis on the following properties.

- *$\lhd$-reflexivity*. Players' sight is reflexive, since at every node, the node itself is visible to players.
- *intransitivity*. Usually, the sight of a player is not transitive. Take Figure 1 as an example. Suppose $s_1(v_2) = \{v_4, v_5, v_6\}$. Then it holds that $v_2 \in s_1(v_0)$, $v_6 \in s_1(v_2)$ but $v_6 \notin s_1(v_0)$.
- *totality*.   It means that players' preference is a total order, i.e., for any two siblings v_1 and v_2 (any two children of any node), and any player i, either $v_1 \succeq_i v_2$ or $v_2 \succeq_i v_1$.
- *closure*.   Axiom C makes certain that players' sight is *closed* under predecessors, i.e., *downward closed*. If a node v' is within sight $s_i(v)$, then for any node v'' which locates between v and v', it holds that $v'' \in s_i(v)$.
- *uniformity*.   If a node v_2 is within sight $s_i(v)$, then it must also be within sight $s_i(v_1)$, where v_1 is any intermediate node between v and v_2. E.g., for the nodes v_0, v_2 and v_5 in Figure 1, since player 1 can see v_5 from v_0, he can also see v_5 from v_2.

---

[4] For simplicity, we use $\langle(\sigma)^n\rangle$ to represent applying σ for n times, i.e., $\langle\underbrace{\sigma; \sigma \cdots ; \sigma}_{n}\rangle$

Table 1. Valid Principles of DLS

(1) Normal modal logic axioms		
Name	Axiom schema	Frame property
Taut	any classical tautology	none
K	$[\leq_i](p \to q) \to ([\leq_i]p \to [\leq_i]q)$ $[\pi](p \to q) \to ([\pi]p \to [\pi]q)$ $[\lhd](p \to q) \to ([\lhd]p \to [\lhd]q)$	distribution
(2) Axioms for extensive games		
Name	Axiom schema	Frame property
D	$\langle\sigma\rangle\varphi \to [\sigma]\varphi$	determinism
P	$\langle\sigma\rangle\varphi \to \bigvee_{i\in N}\langle i\rangle\varphi$	performability
E	$\bigvee_{i\in N}\langle i\rangle\top \to \bigvee_{\sigma\in\Sigma}\langle\sigma\rangle\top$	enabled
A	$\langle i\rangle\top \to \bigwedge_{j\in N\setminus\{i\}}[j]\bot$	asynchronization
F	$\bigwedge_{\sigma\in\Sigma}\bigvee_{n\in N}\langle(\sigma)^n\rangle\bot$	finiteness
(3) Axioms for sight function and preference relation		
Name	Axiom schema	Frame property
$T_{\leq_i}$	$[\leq_i]\varphi \to \varphi$	$\leq_i-$ reflexivity
$T_\lhd$	$[\lhd]\varphi \to \varphi$	$\lhd-$reflexivity
4	$[\leq_i]\varphi \to [\leq_i][\leq_i]\varphi$	transitivity
C	$(\langle(\sigma)^n\rangle\varphi \to \langle\lhd\rangle\varphi) \to$ $(\bigwedge_{k<n}\langle(\sigma)^k\rangle\varphi \to \langle\lhd\rangle\varphi)$	closure
U	$(\langle(\sigma)^n\rangle\varphi \to \langle\lhd\rangle\varphi) \to$ $(\langle(\sigma)^n\rangle\varphi \to \bigwedge_{k<n}\langle(\sigma)^k\rangle\langle\lhd\rangle\varphi)$	uniformity
To	$\bigwedge_{i\in N}\bigwedge_{\sigma\in\Sigma}\bigwedge_{\sigma'\in\Sigma}((\langle\sigma'\rangle\varphi \to \langle\sigma\rangle\langle\leq_i\rangle\varphi)$ $\vee(\langle\sigma\rangle\varphi \to \langle\sigma'\rangle\langle\leq_i\rangle\varphi)$	totality
(4) Axioms for regular frames		
Name	Axiom schema	Frame property
Re	$\langle\pi_1;\pi_2\rangle\varphi \leftrightarrow \langle\pi_1\rangle\langle\pi_2\rangle\varphi$ $\langle\pi_1 \cup \pi_2\rangle\varphi \leftrightarrow \langle\pi_1\rangle\varphi \vee \langle\pi_2\rangle\varphi$ $\langle\varphi?\rangle\psi \leftrightarrow (\varphi \wedge \psi)$ $\langle\pi^*\rangle\varphi \leftrightarrow (\varphi \vee \langle\pi\rangle\langle\pi^*\rangle\varphi)$ $[\pi^*](\varphi \to [\pi]\varphi) \to (\varphi \to [\pi^*]\varphi)$	regularity

Inference rules:
Modus Ponens (*MP*), and Necessitation (*Nec*) for operators $[\pi]$, $[\lhd]$ and $[\leq_i]$.

4 Characterizing Solutions

Determining equilibrium solutions of games is a significant issue in game theory. In this section, we illustrate how to characterize equilibrium concept for Egss via formulas of $\mathcal{DLS}$. We find the formula schema φ, s.t. any strategy profile σ is an equilibrium of S iff $F_S \models \varphi$.

Proposition 1. *Let* $\pi(\sigma_{-N_0})$ *(where* $N_0=\{i_0,\cdots,i_k\}\subseteq N$, $\sigma\in\Sigma$*) be an operator with the following semantics:* $M,v \models \langle\pi(\sigma_{-N_0})\rangle\varphi$ *iff there is some* v' *for which* $M,v' \models \varphi$ *and* $v' \in O|_v(\sigma_{-N_0}|v)$*. Then* $\pi(\sigma_{-N_0})$ *is definable in* $\mathcal{DLS}$*.*

Proof. The definition of $\pi(\sigma_{-N_0})$ is given as:

$$\pi(\sigma_{-N_0}) =_{df} (((\langle\sigma\rangle\top)?; (\sigma \cup i_0 \cup i_1 \cup \cdots \cup i_k))^*; (\neg\langle\sigma\rangle\top)?$$

The intuition is: $\pi(\sigma_{-N_0})$ executes non-deterministically one of the programs i ($i \in N_0$) or σ, as longs as σ is enabled. The program terminates when σ is no longer enabled.

Particularly, we define $\pi(\sigma) =_{df} ((\langle\sigma\rangle\top)?; \sigma)^*; (\neg\langle\sigma\rangle\top)?$. In contradistinction, $\pi(\sigma)$ reduces to a deterministic program that repeats σ until it terminates.

The accessibility relations are defined as:

$$vR_{\pi(\sigma)}v' \quad \text{iff } v' = O|_v(\sigma|_v).$$
$$vR_{\pi(\sigma_{-N_0})}v' \text{ iff } v' \in O|_v(\sigma_{-N_0}|_v).$$

$\square$

Proposition 2. *Let* $S = (N, V, A, t, \Sigma_i, \succeq_i, s)$ *be an Egss. Then*

(a) A strategy profile σ is a subgame perfect equilibrium *(SPE) of $S\lceil v$ iff for any formula φ, and any $u \in V\lceil_v \backslash Z\lceil_v$:*

$$F_{S\lceil_v}, u \models \bigwedge_{i \in N}(\langle\pi(\sigma)\rangle\varphi \to [\pi(\sigma_{-i})]\langle\leq_i\rangle\varphi).$$

(b) A strategy profile σ is a sight-compatible SPE *of S iff for any formula φ, and all $v \in V \backslash Z$:*

$$F_{S\lceil_v}, v \models [\lhd](\bigwedge_{i \in N}(\langle\pi(\sigma)\rangle\varphi \to [\pi(\sigma_{-i})]\langle\leq_i\rangle\varphi)).$$

Proof. (a) ($\Rightarrow$) assume $\bigwedge_{i \in N}(\langle\pi(\sigma)\rangle\varphi \to [\pi(\sigma_{-i})]\langle\leq_i\rangle\varphi)$ is invalid at some state u in $F_{S\lceil_v}$. Then for some player i, $\langle\pi(\sigma)\rangle\varphi \to [\pi(\sigma_{-i})]\langle\leq_i\rangle\varphi$ is invalid at u in $F_{S\lceil_v}$. Consequently, $\langle\pi(\sigma)\rangle\varphi \wedge \langle\pi(\sigma_{-i})\rangle[\leq_i]\neg\varphi$ is valid at u. It follows that σ is not a subgame perfect equilibrium of $S\lceil_v$ (refer to the definition of Subgame perfect equilibrium [13]). Proof for ($\Leftarrow$) is similar.

(b) ($\Rightarrow$) assume $[\lhd](\bigwedge_{i \in N}(\langle\pi(\sigma)\rangle\varphi \to [\pi(\sigma_{-i})]\langle\leq_i\rangle\varphi)$ is invalid at the starting point v of $F_{S\lceil_v}$. Then there exists a node v' such that (1) $v' \in s(v)$ and (2) $F_{S\lceil_v}, v' \not\models \bigwedge_{i \in N}(\langle\pi(\sigma)\rangle\varphi \to [\pi(\sigma_{-i})]\langle\leq_i\rangle\varphi)$. By (2), σ is not a SPE of $S\lceil_v$. Then by (1) it follows that σ is not a sight-compatible subgame perfect equilibrium of S. ($\Leftarrow$), assume σ is not a sight-compatible subgame perfect equilibrium of S. Then there exists a state $v \in V$ such that for any SPE σ^* of $S\lceil_v$, $\sigma \neq \sigma^*$. So σ is not a SPE of $S\lceil_v$. Then we have: $\exists u \in V\lceil_v$ such that $F_{S\lceil_v}, u \models \neg\bigwedge_{i \in N}(\langle\pi(\sigma)\rangle\varphi \to [\pi(\sigma_{-i})]\langle\leq_i\rangle\varphi)$. It follows that $F_{S\lceil_v}, v \models \langle\lhd\rangle\neg\bigwedge_{i \in N}(\langle\pi(\sigma)\rangle\varphi \to [\pi(\sigma_{-i})]\langle\leq_i\rangle\varphi)$. By Dual, $F_{S\lceil_v}, v \not\models [\lhd](\bigwedge_{i \in N}(\langle\pi(\sigma)\rangle\varphi \to [\pi(\sigma_{-i})]\langle\leq_i\rangle\varphi)$. $\square$

By now, we have shown that $\mathcal{DLS}$ is well suited for capturing equilibrium solutions in extensive games with short sight.

5   Soundness and Completeness

We now take a position to show the soundness and completeness results of DLS. **Theorem 1.** *DLS is sound w.r.t. the class of all $\mathcal{DLS}$-models.*

Proof. It is trivial to show that the rules preserve logical consequence. So this proof boils down to a check of validity for the given axioms. Here we list the proofs for some of the axioms, since others can be proved similarly.

For *closure*, let $M, w \models (\langle(\sigma)^n\rangle\varphi \rightarrow \langle\lhd\rangle\varphi)$. It means that for any node v, if v can be reached from w by going n steps according to σ, then $v \in s(w)$. Since sight function is downward closed, for any node u, if u can be reached from w by going k ($k \leq n$) steps according to σ, then $u \in s(w)$. That is, $M, w \models (\bigwedge_{k \leq n}\langle(\sigma)^k\rangle\varphi \rightarrow \langle\lhd\rangle\varphi)$.

For *uniformity*, let $M, w \models (\langle(\sigma)^n\rangle\varphi \rightarrow \langle\lhd\rangle\varphi)$. It means that for any node v, if v can be reached from w by going n steps according to σ, then $v \in s(w)$. By uniformity of sight function, we deduce that for any node u, if u is an intermediate node between w and v, i.e., u can be reached from w by k ($k \leq n$) steps, and v can be reached from u by $n - k$ steps, then $v \in s(u)$. Hence, $M, w \models (\langle(\sigma)^n\rangle\varphi \rightarrow \bigwedge_{k \leq n}\langle(\sigma)^k\rangle\langle\lhd\rangle\varphi)$. □

We prove completeness of DLS via finite canonical models [3]. We first explain two notations for later use.

(1) *Fischer-Ladner closure*: The *Fischer-Ladner closure* of a formula ϕ is the least set $FL(\phi)$ of formulas containing ϕ and such that (*i*) $FL(\phi)$ is closed under subformulas and single negations $\sim$. (*ii*) If $\langle\pi_1; \pi_2\rangle\varphi \in FL(\phi)$ then $\langle\pi_1\rangle\langle\pi_2\rangle\varphi \in FL(\phi)$. (*iii*) If $\langle\pi_1 \cup \pi_2\rangle\varphi \in FL(\phi)$ then $\langle\pi_1\rangle\varphi \vee \langle\pi_2\rangle\varphi \in FL(\phi)$. (*iv*) If $\langle\pi^*\rangle\varphi \in FL(\phi)$ then $\langle\pi\rangle\langle\pi^*\rangle \in FL(\phi)$. (*v*) If $\langle\varphi?\rangle\psi \in FL(\phi)$ then $\varphi \in FL(\phi)$ and $\psi \in FL(\phi)$.

(2) *Atoms*: A set of formulas A is an atom over a formula ϕ if it is a maximal consistent subset of $FL(\phi)$. $At(\phi)$ is the set of all atoms over ϕ. Atoms are generalization of maximal consistent sets.

Definition 6. (Canonical model) The *canonical model* M^ϕ over any formula ϕ is the tuple $(At(\phi), \{R_\pi^\phi\}_{\pi \in \Pi}, R_{\leq_i}^\phi, R_\lhd^\phi, I^\phi)$, where $I^\phi(p) = \{A \in At(\phi) \mid p \in A\}$ for all *propositional variables* p, and for all *atoms* $A, B \in At(\phi)$, all *basic programs* a, and any modal operators $\xi \in \{\leq_i, \lhd\}$,

$A R_a^\phi B$ if $\widehat{A} \wedge \langle a\rangle\widehat{B}$ is consistent;

$A R_\xi^\phi B$ if   for all $\psi, \psi \in B$ implies $\langle\xi\rangle\psi \in A$;

For complex programs, inductively define the DLS-relations R_π^ϕ by R_a^ϕ in the usual way using *unions*, *compositions*, and *reflexive transitive closure* and *test*.

We first obtain some useful lemmas.

Lemma 1. *Any canonical model M^ϕ is a $\mathcal{DLS}$-model.*

Proof. It is sufficient to demonstrate that canonical models satisfy the properties of $\mathcal{DLS}$-models. We only show the proofs for some properties.

• *Transitivity*: For any $A, B, C \in At(\phi)$, suppose $(A, B) \in R_{\leq_i}^\phi$ and $(B, C) \in R_{\leq_i}^\phi$. Then for any $\psi \in C$, we have $\langle\leq_i\rangle\psi \in B$, and $\langle\leq_i\rangle\langle\leq_i\rangle\psi \in A$. By axiom 4, i.e., $\langle\leq_i\rangle\langle\leq_i\rangle\psi \rightarrow \langle\leq_i\rangle\psi$, it holds that $\langle\leq_i\rangle\psi \in A$. It follows that $(A, C) \in R_{\leq_i}^\phi$.

- *Regularity*: For composition ;, let A, B be any atoms in $At(\phi)$, suppose $(A, B) \in R^\phi_{\pi_1;\pi_2}$. Then $\widehat{A} \wedge \langle \pi_1; \pi_2 \rangle \widehat{B}$ is consistent. By Axiom Re, we have $\widehat{A} \wedge \langle \pi_1 \rangle \langle \pi_2 \rangle \widehat{B}$ is consistent. Then we can construct an atom C such that $\widehat{A} \wedge \langle \pi_1 \rangle \widehat{C}$ and $\widehat{C} \wedge \langle \pi_2 \rangle \widehat{B}$ are both consistent. By definition of $R^\phi_{\pi_1}$ and $R^\phi_{\pi_2}$, it follows that $(A, C) \in R^\phi_{\pi_1}$, and $(C, B) \in R^\phi_{\pi_2}$. The arguments for $\cup, *, ?$ are similar. $\qquad \Box$

Lemma 2. (*Existence Lemma*) *Let A be an atom and let $\langle \xi \rangle \psi$ be a formula in $FL(X)$ with $\xi \in \{\pi, \leq, \lhd\}$. Then $\langle \xi \rangle \psi \in A$ iff $\exists B$ such that $AR^\phi_\xi B$ and $\psi \in B$.*

Proof. We first prove the $(\Rightarrow)$ direction.

(1) For programs. Suppose $\langle \pi \rangle \psi \in A$. We can build an atom B such that $\psi \in B$ and $AR^\phi_\pi B$. The case of basic programs is trivial by [3].

For complex programs, we only show the case for test. (Please refer to [3] for proofs of other cases): Suppose $\langle \varphi ? \rangle \psi \in A$, then we have $\varphi \in A$ and $\psi \in A$. Then there is an atom $B = A$ such that $AR^\phi_{\varphi?} B$ and $\psi \in B$.

(2) For modalities $\langle \lhd \rangle$ (or $\langle \leq_i \rangle$). Suppose $\langle \lhd \rangle \psi \in A$. We will construct an atom B such that $AR^\phi_\lhd B$ and $\psi \in B$. Let B^- be $\{\psi\} \cup \{\varphi | [\lhd]\varphi \in A\}$. Then B^- is consistent. For suppose not. Then there are $\varphi_1, \cdots, \varphi_n$ such that $\vdash (\varphi_1 \wedge \cdots \wedge \varphi_n) \rightarrow \neg\psi$, and it follows by an easy argument that $\vdash [\lhd](\varphi_1 \wedge \cdots \wedge \varphi_n) \rightarrow [\lhd]\neg\psi$. Hence $\vdash ([\lhd]\varphi_1 \wedge \cdots \wedge [\lhd]\varphi_n) \rightarrow [\lhd]\neg\psi$. Now $[\lhd]\varphi_1 \wedge \cdots \wedge [\lhd]\varphi_n \in A$ thus it follows that $[\lhd]\neg\psi \in A$. Then it holds that $\neg\langle \lhd \rangle \psi \in A$. Contradiction. Then let B be any atom extending B^-. By the process of construction, $\psi \in B$. Furthermore, (a) for all formulas φ, $[\lhd]\varphi \in A$ implies $\varphi \in B$. Hence $AR^\phi_\lhd B$. For suppose not, then there exists ψ such that $\psi \in B$ and $\langle \lhd \rangle \psi \notin A$. However, by (a), we have that $\psi \in B$ implies $\langle \lhd \rangle \psi \in A$. Contradict.

The direction $(\Leftarrow)$ can be proved similarly.

(1) For programs. We prove induction on the structure of π.

(1.1) For basic programs, i.e., $\pi = a$. Suppose there is an atom B such that $AR_a B$ and $\psi \in B$. Then $\widehat{A} \wedge \langle a \rangle \widehat{B}$ is consistent. As ψ is one of the conjuncts in $\widehat{B}$, $\widehat{A} \wedge \langle a \rangle \psi$ is consistent. Since A is an atom and hence maximal consistent in $FL(\phi)$, and $\langle a \rangle \psi$ is in $FL(\phi)$, we have $\langle a \rangle \psi$ must also be in A.

(1.2) For complex programs. In the case of $\pi = \pi_1; \pi_2$, and suppose $AR_{\pi_1;\pi_2} B$ and $\psi \in B$. Thus there is an atom C such that $AR_{\pi_1} C$ and $CR_{\pi_2} B$ and $\psi \in B$. By the Fischer-Ladner closure conditions, $\langle \pi_2 \rangle \psi$ belongs to $FL(\phi)$, hence by the inductive hypothesis, $\langle \pi_2 \rangle \psi \in C$. Similarly, as $\langle \pi_1 \rangle \langle \pi_2 \rangle \psi \in A$, we have $\langle \pi_1; \pi_2 \rangle \psi \in A$ by the properties of atoms. The case of $\pi_1 \cup \pi_2$ is similar.

For test. Suppose $AR_{\varphi?} B$ and $\psi \in B$. By Definition 6 and the above argument for the basic programs, we have $A = B$, $\varphi \in A$ and $\psi \in A$. Thus $\langle \varphi? \rangle \psi$ follows from the property that for all $\langle \psi? \rangle \varphi \in FL(\phi)$: $\langle \psi? \rangle \varphi \in A$ iff $\varphi \in A$ and $\psi \in A$.

For π with the form of ρ^*. Assume $AR_{\rho^*} B$ and $\psi \in B$. Then there is a finite sequence of atoms $C_0, \cdots, C_n$ such that $A = C_0 R_\rho C_1, \cdots, C_{n-1} R_\rho C_n = B$. By a subinduction on n we prove that $\langle \rho^* \rangle \psi \in C_i$ for all i; the required result for $A = C_0$ is then immediate. For base case $n = 0$. This means

$A = B$, and since $\vdash \rho^*\rangle\psi \leftrightarrow \psi \vee \langle\rho\rangle\langle\rho^*\rangle\psi$, we have $\vdash \psi \rightarrow \langle\rho^*\rangle\psi$. Thus $\langle\rho^*\rangle\psi \in A$. For Inductive step. Suppose the result holds for $n \leq k$, and that $A = C_0 R_\rho C_1, \cdots, C_k R_\rho C_{k+1} = B$. By the inductive hypothesis, $\langle\rho^*\rangle\psi \in C_1$. Hence $\langle\rho\rangle\langle\rho^*\rangle\psi \in A$, for $\langle\rho\rangle\langle\rho^*\rangle\psi \in FL(\phi)$. But $\langle\rho^*\rangle\psi \leftrightarrow \psi \vee \langle\rho\rangle\langle\rho^*\rangle\psi$. Hence $\langle\rho^*\rangle\psi \in A$.

(2) The cases for $\langle\leq_i\rangle$ and $\langle\lhd\rangle$ follow from Definition 6.   □

Lemma 3. (*Truth Lemma*) *For any canonical model M^ϕ over ϕ, any atom A, and any formula $\varphi \in FL(\phi)$, $M^\phi, A \models \varphi$ iff $\varphi \in A$.*

Proof. We do this by induction on the number of connectives. The base case and the boolean case is trivial. It remains to deal with the modalities ξ. First, it holds that:
$$M^\phi, A \models \langle\xi\rangle\varphi \text{ iff } \exists B(A R_\xi^\phi B \wedge M^\phi, B \models \varphi) \text{ iff } \exists B(A R_\xi^\phi B \wedge \varphi \in B) \tag{\dag}$$
We now prove the ($\Rightarrow$) direction, the other direction is similar.

(1) For modality $\langle\lhd\rangle$ (or $\langle\leq_i\rangle$), by the definition of $R_\lhd^\phi$ (or $R_{\leq_i}^\phi$), it naturally follows from (†) that $\langle\lhd\rangle\varphi \in A$.

(2) For program π. By (†) and Existence Lemma, it holds that $\langle\pi\rangle\varphi \in A$.   □

The completeness theorem follows directly from the above lemmas:

Theorem 2. *DLS is weakly complete w.r.t the class of all $\mathcal{DLS}$-models.*

Proof. it is sufficient to find, for any consistent formula ϕ, a model M and a state w in M such that $M, w \models \phi$. By Lindenbaum's Lemma [3], there is an atom $A \in At(\phi)$ such that $\phi \in A$. Then by the Lemma 3, $M^\phi, A \models \phi$. So M^ϕ and A are the model and the right state for φ respectively.   □

6   Discussion and Conclusion

By extending the standard PDL, we developed a dynamic logic called DLS for reasoning about Egss and formulating the solutions. Overall, we provided a theoretical analysis and formal characterization of extensive games under a more realistic model, viz., games with short sight. Meanwhile, this work draws a closer connection between the fields of logic and game theory. In the literature, the most related work is [11], which also proposed a logic for game with short sight. But there are apparent differences, since we focused on the dynamic evolution of games along with the interior structure of solutions, while the logic in [11] took strategy profiles as primitive operators and put more emphasis on the final outcomes of strategy profiles.

We have provided formula schemas specifying the features for a strategy profile to be a solution. For further research, we would like to look into the model checking problem on membership of the set of solutions. It should be interesting to investigate the compare the complexity of model checking in games with short sight compared with that in classical game model. To concentrate on the logical part, we put on some restrictions on the game model in this paper. Therefore, it would also be a possible direction to drop all these assumptions and go further towards a complete practical model for games.

Acknowledgments. This work is supported by the China Scholarship Council and NSFC grant No. 61472369.

References

1. van Benthem, J.: Modal Logic for Open Minds. Center for the Study of Language and Information Lecture Notes. Stanford University (2010)
2. van Benthem, J., Pacuit, E., Roy, O.: Toward a theory of play: A logical perspective on games and interaction. Games **2**(1), 52–86 (2011)
3. Blackburn, P., de Rijke, M., Venema, Y.: Modal logic. Cambridge University Press (2001)
4. Bonanno, G., Magill, M., Van Gaasback, K.: Branching time logic, perfect information games and backward induction. Working Papers 9813, University of California, Davis, Department of Economics (2003)
5. Cui, J., Luo, X., Sim, K.M.: A new epistemic logic model of regret games. In: Wang, M. (ed.) KSEM 2013. LNCS, vol. 8041, pp. 372–386. Springer, Heidelberg (2013)
6. Fischer, M.J., Ladner, R.E.: Propositional dynamic logic of regular programs. J. Comput. Syst. Sci. **18**(2), 194–211 (1979)
7. Grossi, D., Turrini, P.: Short sight in extensive games. In: Proceedings of the 11th International Conference on Autonomous Agents and Multiagent Systems (AAMAS 2012), pp. 805–812 (2012)
8. Halpern, J.Y., Pucella, R.: A logic for reasoning about evidence. Journal of Artificial Intelligence Research **26**, 1–34 (2006)
9. Harel, D., Kozen, D., Tiuryn, J.: Dynamic logic. In: Handbook of Philosophical Logic, pp. 497–604. MIT Press (1984)
10. Harrenstein, P., van der Hoek, W., Meyer, J.J.C., Witteveen, C.: A modal characterization of Nash equilibrium. Fundamenta Informaticae **57**(2–4), 281–321 (2003)
11. Liu, C., Liu, F., Su, K.: A logic for extensive games with short sight. In: Grossi, D., Roy, O., Huang, H. (eds.) LORI 2013. LNCS, vol. 8196, pp. 332–336. Springer, Heidelberg (2013)
12. Lorini, E., Moisan, F.: An epistemic logic of extensive games. Electronic Notes in Theoretical Computer Science **278**, 245–260 (2011)
13. Osborne, M.J., Rubinstein, A.: A Course in Game Theory. MIT Press (1994)
14. Ramanujam, R., Simon, S.E.: Dynamic logic on games with structured strategies. In: Principles of Knowledge Representation and Reasoning: Proceedings of the Eleventh International Conference, KR 2008, Sydney, Australia, September 16–19, pp. 49–58. AAAI Press (2008)
15. Shoham, Y., Leyton-Brown, K.: Multiagent Systems: Algorithmic, Game-Theoretic, and Logical Foundations. Cambridge University Press, New York (2008)

Early Innovation Papers

Kinetic Description of Opinion Evolution in Multi-agent Systems: Analytic Model and Simulations

Stefania Monica[(✉)] and Federico Bergenti

Dipartimento di Matematica e Informatica, Università Degli Studi di Parma,
Parco Area Delle Scienze 53/A, 43124 Parma, Italy
{stefania.monica,federico.bergenti}@unipr.it

Abstract. In this paper we consider multi-agent systems where interactions among agents are modeled using a kinetic approach. While kinetic theory aims at studying macroscopic properties of gases starting from microscopic interactions among molecules, we are interested in modeling the global behaviour of multi-agent systems on the basis of local interactions among pairs of agents. In particular, here we study the dynamics of opinion formation. Given a microscopic description of each single interaction, we derive stationary profiles for the global opinion. Analytic results are validated by simulations obtained by implementing the proposed theoretical model.

1 Introduction

In this paper a model for opinion formation in multi-agent systems is considered. Various approaches have been proposed in the literature to describe the opinion evolution in a multi-agent system, among which it is worth recalling those based on graph theory (e.g., [1]), on cellular automata (e.g., [2]), and on thermodynamics (e.g., [3]).

In recent years, social interactions in multi-agent systems have been described according to models inspired by kinetic theory of gases [4]. In particular, agent-based cooperation models, such as that in [5], and large scale systems, such as those in [6], could be modeled according to the kinetic framework. The same approach could be also used in scenarios that involve general-purpose industrial strength technology (see, e.g., [7,8]) and in the context of wireless sensor networks (see, e.g., [9,10]). The literature on this topic gave birth to two new disciplines, known as *econophysics* and *sociophysics* [11]. While econophysics describes the evolution of market economy [12] or wealth distribution in a system [13], sociophysics is aimed at modeling the evolution of social characteristics of the system [14]. According to such new disciplines, exchanges of money or opinion evolution can be modeled using the formalism of kinetic theory that describes the interactions of molecules in a gas. Starting from the microscopic details of the collisions between two molecules, kinetic theory derives macroscopic properties of gases. Similarly, the evolution of a global opinion in a society can be

© Springer International Publishing Switzerland 2015
Q. Chen et al. (Eds.): PRIMA 2015, LNAI 9387, pp. 483–491, 2015.
DOI: 10.1007/978-3-319-25524-8_30

described from a macroscopic viewpoint, starting from a model that describes
the effect of single interactions between a pair of agents [15]. More precisely, we
assume that each agent of the considered system is associated with an opinion v
defined in a given set $I \subseteq \mathbb{R}$. The temporal evolution of the opinion distribution
f is described according to the Boltzmann equation, which typically describes
the evolution of gases. In this paper we investigate the opinion evolution of a
system starting from given stochastic rules that describe the effects of single
interactions. According to [16] each agent can interact with any other agent in
the system and it can change its opinion due to compromise, which is modeled
as a deterministic process, and to a randomly modeled diffusion process.

This paper is organized as follows. Section 2 describes the considered kinetic
model from an analytic viewpoint. Section 3 derives explicit formulas for the
stationary profiles in a specific case and it shows simulation results for different
values of the parameters of the model. Section 4 concludes the paper.

2   Kinetic Model of Opinion Formation

Sociophysics is based on the idea that social interactions among agents can be
described by generalizing the laws which describes binary interactions among
molecules. In kinetic theory, the molecules of a gas are typically associated
with their velocities at each instant t. Similarly, agents can be associated with
attributes that represent their characteristics, such as their richness and their
opinion. In the remaining of this paper, we associate to each agent a single scalar
parameter v in the interval $I = [-1, 1]$ and we assume that it represents the agent's
opinion. With this choice of the interval I, ± 1 represent extremal opinions, while
values close to 0 correspond to moderate opinions. This choice is not restrictive
and the model we consider can be used in any other closed interval.

Following the approach of kinetic theory, the proposed model relies on the
definition of a function $f(v,t)$ which represents the density of opinion v at time
t and which is defined for each opinion $v \in I$ and for each time $t \geq 0$. Since
$f(v,t)$ is a density function, the following equality holds

$$\int_I f(v,t)\mathrm{d}v = 1. \tag{1}$$

In order to describe the opinion evolution using a kinetic approach, we assume
that the function $f(v,t)$ evolves according to the Boltzmann equation. In particular, we consider the following (homogeneus) formulation of the Boltzmann
equation

$$\frac{\partial f}{\partial t} = \mathcal{Q}(f,f)(v,t) \tag{2}$$

where the left-hand side represents the temporal evolution of the distribution
function and $\mathcal{Q}$ is the *collisional operator* which takes into account the effects of
interactions.

In order to derive an explicit formula for the collisional operator $\mathcal{Q}$, the
details of the binary interactions need to be described. In the considered model,

the post-interaction opinions of two interacting agents are obtained by adding to their respective pre-interaction opinions a contribution related to compromise and a contribution related to diffusion, according to the following formula [17]

$$\begin{cases} v' = v + \gamma C(|v|)(w - v) + \eta_* D(|v|) \\ w' = w + \gamma C(|w|)(v - w) + \eta D(|w|) \end{cases} \tag{3}$$

where the pair (v', w') denotes the post-interaction opinions of the two agents whose pre-interaction opinions were (v, w). In (3) the second terms on the right-hand side of the two equations model a compromise process, since they are proportional to the difference between the opinions of the two interacting agents. We consider values of the parameter γ in $(0, \frac{1}{2})$, and the function $C(\cdot)$ is assumed to be a (symmetric) function of the opinion. The third terms are related to diffusion through η and η_*, which are supposed to be two random variables, and function $D(\cdot)$. In the following we assume that the two functions $C(\cdot)$ and $D(\cdot)$ satisfy

$$0 \le C(|v|), D(|v|) \le 1 \qquad \forall v \in I.$$

Moreover, we assume that both functions are nonincreasing with respect to the absolute value of the opinion, coherently with the fact that, typically, extremal opinions are more difficult to change.

Observe that if the diffusion term in (3) is neglected, then the post-interaction opinions are deterministic and they only depend on the choice of γ and $C(\cdot)$. From (3), since both γ and $C(\cdot)$ are positive, the contribution of compromise is positive each time an agent interacts with another agent whose opinion is greater while it is negative otherwise. Hence, the idea of compromise is respected, since the difference between the opinions of the two agents is reduced after the considered interaction. Moreover, the post-interaction opinion of an agent is closer to its pre-interaction opinion than to that of the agent it interacts with because, taking for instance the first equation of (3), since in our assumption $0 \le \gamma C(|v|) \le 1/2$, the following inequality holds

$$|v' - v| = \gamma C(|v|)|w - v| \le (1 - \gamma C(|v|)) = |v' - w|. \tag{4}$$

The contribution of diffusion can be either positive or negative depending on the value of the random variables η and η_*. In the following, we assume that such random variables have the same statistics. In particular, we assume that their average value is 0 and their variance is σ^2 so that, defining their , the following equalities hold

$$\int_{\mathbb{B}} \eta \vartheta(\eta) \mathrm{d}\eta = \int \eta_* \vartheta(\eta_*) \mathrm{d}\eta_* = 0 \qquad \int_{\mathbb{B}} \eta^2 \vartheta(\eta) \mathrm{d}\eta = \int \eta_*^2 \vartheta(\eta_*) \mathrm{d}\eta_* = \sigma^2 \tag{5}$$

where $\mathbb{B}$ is the support of the two random variables η and η_*. The set $\mathbb{B}$ is chosen to ensure that the post-interaction opinions v' and w' always belong to the interval I where the opinion is defined.

Under these assumptions, the explicit expression of the collisional operator Q defined in (2) can be finally written as

$$Q(f,f) = \int_{\mathbb{B}^2} \int_I [\vartheta(\eta)\vartheta(\eta_*)\frac{1}{J}f('v)f('w) - \vartheta(\eta)\vartheta(\eta_*)f(v)f(w)]\mathrm{d}w\mathrm{d}\eta\mathrm{d}\eta_* \quad (6)$$

where $'v$ and $'w$ are the pre-interaction variables which lead to v and w, respectively, $'W$ is the transition rate relative to the quadruple $('v,'w,v,w)$ and J is the Jacobian of the transformation of $('v,'w)$ in (v,w) [16].

Instead of solving (2) we consider its weak form. In functional analysis, the weak form of a differential equation is obtained by multiplying both sides of the considered equation by a test function $\phi(\cdot)$, a smooth function with compact support, and then integrating the obtained equation. The weak form of the Boltzmann equation can be derived from (2) and (6). Using a proper change of variable in the integral, it can be written as:

$$\frac{\mathrm{d}}{\mathrm{d}t}\int_I f(v,t)\phi(v)\mathrm{d}v = \int_{\mathbb{B}^2}\int_{I^2} \vartheta(\eta)\vartheta(\eta_*)f(v)f(w)(\phi(v') - \phi(v))\mathrm{d}v\mathrm{d}w\mathrm{d}\eta\mathrm{d}\eta_*. \quad (7)$$

If we consider $\phi(v) = 1$ in (7) then the following equation is obtained

$$\frac{\mathrm{d}}{\mathrm{d}t}\int_I f(v,t)\mathrm{d}v = 0 \quad (8)$$

as expected from (1). This property is analogous to mass conservation in a gas.

Considering $\phi(v) = v$ as test function in (7) and recalling (3) we obtain

$$\frac{\mathrm{d}}{\mathrm{d}t}\int_I f(w,t)v\mathrm{d}v = \gamma\int_{\mathbb{B}^2}\int_{I^2} \vartheta(\eta)\vartheta(\eta_*)f(v)f(w)C(|v|)(w-v)\mathrm{d}v\mathrm{d}w\mathrm{d}\eta\mathrm{d}\eta_*$$
$$+ \int_{\mathbb{B}^2}\int_{I^2} \vartheta(\eta)\vartheta(\eta_*)f(v)f(w)\eta D(|v|)\mathrm{d}v\mathrm{d}w\mathrm{d}\eta\mathrm{d}\eta_*. \quad (9)$$

Defining the average value of the opinion at time t as

$$u(t) = \int_I f(v,t)v\,\mathrm{d}v \quad (10)$$

the left hand side of (9) corresponds to the derivative $\dot{u}(t)$ of the average opinion. The first integral in the right hand side of (9) can be written in a simplified way by proper manipulation as

$$\gamma\int_I f(v)C(|v|)\mathrm{d}v\int_I vf(v)\mathrm{d}v - \gamma\int_I f(v)C(|v|)v\mathrm{d}v. \quad (11)$$

The second integral in (9) is 0 because the average value of ϑ is 0, according to (5). Therefore, from (9) and (11), it can be obtained that the derivative of the average opinion u can be written as

$$\dot{u}(t) = \gamma u(t)\int_I f(v)C(|v|)\mathrm{d}v - \gamma\int_I f(v)C(|v|)v\mathrm{d}v. \quad (12)$$

Observe that if C is constant then, using (1), the right-hand side of (12) is 0 and equation (12) becomes

$$\dot{u}(t) = 0 \tag{13}$$

i.e., the average opinion is conserved, namely $u(t) = u(0)$. This property corresponds to the conservation of momentum in gases.

We are interested in studying the behaviour of the distribution function $f(v,t)$ for large values of the time t and in deriving stationary profiles. In order to simplify notation we first define a new temporal variable $\tau = \gamma t$ where γ is the coefficient related to compromise which appear in (3). Assuming that γ is small, namely that each interaction causes small opinion changes, the function

$$g(v,\tau) = f(v,t) \tag{14}$$

describes the asymptotic behaviour of $f(v,t)$. If we substitute $f(v,t)$ with $g(v,\tau)$ in (7) and use the Taylor series expansion of $\phi(v)$ around v in (7) [18]:

$$\frac{\partial g}{\partial \tau} = \frac{\lambda}{2} \frac{\partial^2}{\partial v^2}(D(|v|)^2 g) + \frac{\partial}{\partial v}((v-u)g) \tag{15}$$

where

$$\lambda = \sigma^2/\gamma. \tag{16}$$

From now on we assume that the function $C(\cdot)$ is constant and equal to 1. We are now interested in studying stationary solutions of equation (15), which is denoted as g_∞ in the remaining of this paper. The stationary profiles are found by imposing that the derivative of g with respect to τ is 0 and, from (15), they can be found by solving the following second order partial differential equation

$$\frac{\lambda}{2} \frac{\partial^2}{\partial v^2}(D(|v|)^2 g) + \frac{\partial}{\partial v}((v-u)g) = 0. \tag{17}$$

In the following section, the solutions of (17) are analyzed for a specific expression of the diffusion function $D(|v|)$ and for different values of the parameter λ. Analytic results are also compared with simulations.

3 Stationary Behaviour of Opinion Distribution

In this section we derive the stationary profiles g_∞ for the opinion density for a specific diffusion function. As in the analytic derivation in Section 2, the compromise function $C(|v|)$ is assumed to be constant and equal to 1. As observed in Section 2, this choice leads to a constant value of the average opinion $u(t)$. In the following the dependence on t is omitted since $u(t)$ is constant and, therefore, the average opinion is denoted as u.

The stationary profiles are the solutions of (17) and, therefore, they depend on the average opinion u, on the parameter λ (which is related to γ and σ^2), and on the choice of the diffusion function $D(\cdot)$. The results obtained with the distribution function

$$D(|v|) = 1 - |v| \tag{18}$$

are investigated in this paper. This function depends on v through its absolute value, as required in (3). Moreover, it is a decreasing function of $|v|$ and its image is $[0, 1]$, in agreement with the assumptions made in the previous section.

By considering the diffusion function $D(|v|)$ defined in (18) in the system of equations (3), which describes the effect of each single interaction between two agents, one obtains

$$\begin{cases} v' = v + \gamma(w - v) + \eta(1 - |v|) \\ w' = w + \gamma(v - w) + \eta_*(1 - |w|). \end{cases} \tag{19}$$

In this case, we set the support of ϑ equal to $\mathbb{B} = (-(1 - \gamma), 1 - \gamma)$. This choice guarantees that the post-collisional opinions belong to the interval I where they are defined, as shown in [19].

In [19] it is shown that the stationary profile, namely the solution of (17), is

$$g_\infty(v) = c_{u,\lambda}(1 - |v|)^{-2 - \frac{2}{\lambda}} \exp\left(-\frac{2(1 - uv)}{\lambda(1 - |v|)}\right) \tag{20}$$

where $c_{u,\lambda}$ is a proper constant which depends on the parameter of the model, namely on the average opinion u and on λ and which must be set in order to guarantee that g_∞ is a probability density function.

The stationary profile g_∞ defined in (20) is piecewise $\mathcal{C}^1$ and it is non-differentiable in $v = 0$, as $D(|v|)$. Moreover, the following equality holds

$$g_\infty(v; u, \lambda) = g_\infty(-v; -u, \lambda) \tag{21}$$

meaning that the solution is symmetric with respect to the change of v and u with $-v$ and $-u$. In particular, if $u = 0$, equation (21) implies that g_∞ is an even function.

The stationary profile g_∞ can then have one or two stationary points. All the possible cases can be expressed as follows.

- If $u = 0$ then $g'_\infty(v) = 0$ in two points symmetrical with respect to 0, namely $\tilde{v}_{1,2} = \pm\frac{\lambda}{\lambda+1}$.
- If $u > 0$ then the condition $\lambda > -u$ is always satisfied, so that the positive stationary point is always defined. The negative stationary point exists only if $\lambda > u$. These conditions can be summarized as follows:
  - if $0 < \lambda \leq u$ then the unique stationary point is $\tilde{v} = \frac{u+\lambda}{\lambda+1}$ and it is positive;
  - if $\lambda > u$ then there are two stationary points with opposite signs, namely $\tilde{v}_{1,2} = \frac{u\pm\lambda}{\lambda+1}$
- If $u < 0$ then $\lambda > u$ for all possible values of λ so that the negative stationary point is always defined. The positive stationary point, instead, exists only if $\lambda > -u$. These conditions can be summarized as follows:
  - if $0 < \lambda \leq -u$ then the unique stationary point is $\tilde{v} = \frac{u-\lambda}{\lambda+1}$ and it is negative;
  - if $\lambda > -u$ then there are two stationary points with opposite signs, namely $\tilde{v}_{1,2} = \frac{u\pm\lambda}{\lambda+1}$.

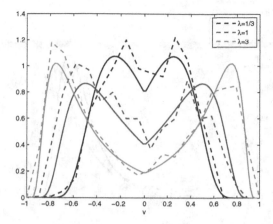

Fig. 1. The stationary profiles g_∞ relative to the average opinion $u = 0$ are shown with solid lines for $\lambda = 1/3$ (blue line), $\lambda = 1$ (red line), $\lambda = 3$ (green line). Simulation results are shown using dashed lines.

Observe that simple manipulations shows that

$$\lim_{v \to 0^+} g'_\infty(v) > 0 \qquad \lim_{v \to 0^-} g'_\infty(v) < 0 \tag{22}$$

and, therefore, $v = 0$ is a non differentiable point. According to (22), the point $v = 0$ can be considered as a point of minimum. Therefore, the stationary points are points of maximum.

In Figs. 1 and 2 the plots of the functions g_∞ defined in (20) are shown (solid lines) for some values of u and λ. More precisely, Fig. 1 is relative to the case with $u = 0$ and $\lambda = 1/3$ (blue line), $\lambda = 1$ (red line), and $\lambda = 3$ (green line). As previously observed, the stationary profiles are even functions and they all have two points of maximum, symmetric with respect to $v = 0$. The points of maximum get closer to the extremes of I as λ increases.

Fig. 1 also shows simulations results (dashed lines). All these results are obtained using 1000 agents. The initial opinion of each agent is randomly initialized in I in such a way that their average is $u = 0$. In order to obtain the stationary profiles, a large number of interactions among agents must be considered. The results shown in Fig. 1 are obtained with 10^6 interactions. At each iteration, two agents, among the 1000, are randomly chosen and their opinions are updated according to (19). The (dashed) lines shown in Fig. 1 are relative to the opinion distribution at the end of the 10^6 interactions. A comparison between solid and dashed lines shows that simulation results fit the analytic plots. As a matter of fact, the trends of the curves obtained by simulation are similar to the curves obtained as analytic solutions of the model.

Fig. 2 shows the stationary profiles g_∞ derived in (20) obtained when the average opinion is $u = 1/2$. As in the previous case, three values of λ are considered, namely: $\lambda = 1/3$ (blue line), $\lambda = 1$ (red line), and $\lambda = 3$ (green line). Observe that if $\lambda = 1/3$, then $\lambda < u$ and the stationary profile has only one

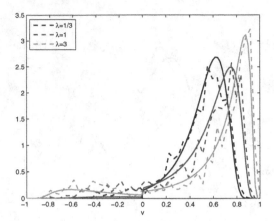

Fig. 2. The stationary profiles g_∞ relative to the average opinion $u = 1/2$ are shown with solid lines for $\lambda = 1/3$ (blue line), $\lambda = 1$ (red line), $\lambda = 3$ (green line). Simulation results are shown using dashed lines.

(positive) point of maximum. If $\lambda = 1$ and if $\lambda = 3$, instead, the stationary profile has two points of maximum, with opposite signs. Moreover, the value of the positive maximum is greater than the negative one, in agreement with the fact that the average opinion is $u = 1/2$.

Fig. 2 also shows the results of simulations obtained, once again, using 1000 agents (dashed lines). Such results are obtained considering 10^6 interactions as in the previous case. At the beginning, the opinions are randomly initialized in I so that their average is $u = 1/2$. In the simulator, pairs of agents are randomly chosen and their opinions are updated according to (19). This process is iterated 10^6 times and the resulting density functions are shown in Fig. 2. As observed when $u = 0$, simulation results are in agreement with analytic plots.

4   Conclusions

In this paper we consider a model for opinion formation in a multi-agent system based on kinetic theory. As a matter of fact, the opinion evolution of the system is described according to the Boltzmann equation and agents are reinterpreted as the molecules of a gas. In the considered model, the opinion of an agent can change because of compromise and diffusion. Assuming that the contribution of compromise is proportional to the difference between the opinions of the two interacting agents, we consider a specific expression for the diffusion process. We analytically derive the asymptotic distribution of the opinion as a function of the parameters of the model. Moreover, we perform simulations which, starting from the microscopic model that describes single interactions between two agents, allows obtaining the large time behaviour of the opinion distribution. Simulation results are in agreement with the analytic framework.

References

1. Tsang, A., Larson, K.: Opinion dynamics of skeptical agents. In: Proceedings of 13th International Conference on Autonomous Agents and Multiagent Systems (AAMAS 2014), Paris, France, May 2014
2. Monica, S., Bergenti, F.: A stochastic model of self-stabilizing cellular automata for consensus formation. In: Proceedings of 15th Workshop "Dagli Oggetti agli Agenti" (WOA 2014), Catania, Italy, September 2014
3. Schweitzer, F., Holyst, J.: Modelling collective opinion formation by means of active brownian particles. European Physical Journal B, 723–732 (2000)
4. Pareschi, L., Toscani, G.: Interacting Multiagent Systems: Kinetic Equations and Montecarlo Methods. Oxford University Press, Oxford (2013)
5. Bergenti, F., Poggi, A., Somacher, M.: A collaborative platform for fixed and mobile networks. Communications of the ACM **45**(11), 39–44 (2002)
6. Bergenti, F., Caire, G., Gotta, D.: Large-scale network and service management with WANTS. In: Industrial Agents: Emerging Applications of Software Agents in Industry, pp. 231–246. Elsevier (2015)
7. Bergenti, F., Caire, G., Gotta, D.: Agents on the move: JADE for Android devices. In: Procs. Workshop From Objects to Agents (2014)
8. Bergenti, F., Caire, G., Gotta, D.: Agent-based social gaming with AMUSE. In: Procs. 5th Int'l Conf. Ambient Systems, Networks and Technologies (ANT 2014) and 4th Int'l Conf. Sustainable Energy Information Technology (SEIT 2014), ser. Procedia Computer Science, pp. 914–919. Elsevier (2014)
9. Monica, S., Ferrari, G.: Accurate indoor localization with UWB wireless sensor networks. In: Proceedings of the 23rd IEEE International Conference on Enabling Technologies: Infrastructure for Collaborative Enterprises (WETICE 2014), Parma, Italy, pp. 287–289. June 2014
10. Monica, S., Ferrari, G.: Optimized anchors placement: an analytical approach in UWB-based TDOA localization. In: Proceedings of the 9th International Wireless Communications & Mobile Computing Conference (IWCMC 2013), Cagliari, Italy, pp. 982–987. July 2013
11. Chakraborti, B.K., Chakrabarti, A., Chatterjee, A.: Econophysics and Sociophysics: Trends and Perspectives. Wiley, Berlin (2006)
12. Cordier, S., Pareschi, L., Toscani, G.: On a kinetic model for simple market economy. Journal of Statistical Physics **120**, 253–277 (2005)
13. Slanina, F.: Inelastically scattering particles and wealth distribution in an open economy. Physical Review E **69**, 46–102 (2004)
14. Sznajd-Weron, K., Sznajd, J.: Opinion evolution in closed community. International Journal of Modern Physics C **11**, 1157–1166 (2000)
15. Weidlich, W.: Sociodynamics: a systematic approach to mathematical modelling in the social sciences. Harwood Academic Publisher, Amsterdam (2000)
16. Toscani, G.: Kinetic models of opinion formation. Communications in Mathematical Sciences **4**, 481–496 (2006)
17. Monica, S., Bergenti, F.: A Kinetic Study of Opinion Dynamics in Multi-Agent Systems. In: Proceedings of 14th Conference of the Italian Association for Artificial Intelligence (AI*IA 2015), Ferrara, Italy, September 2015
18. Toscani, G.: One-dimensional kinetic models of granular flows. ESAIM. Mathematical Modelling and Numerical Analysis **34**, 1277–1291 (2000)
19. Monica, S., Bergenti, F.: Simulations of opinion formation in multi-agent systems using kinetic theory. In: Proceedings of 16th Workshop "Dagli Oggetti agli Agenti" (WOA 2015), Napoli, Italy, pp. 97–102. June 2015

An Agent-Based Model to Study Effects of Team Processes on Compliance with Safety Regulations at an Airline Ground Service Organization

Alexei Sharpanskykh[✉] and Rob Haest

Faculty of Aerospace Engineering, Delft University of Technology,
Kluyverweg 1, 2629 HS Delft, The Netherlands
{o.a.sharpanskykh,r.c.s.haest}@tudelft.nl

Abstract. Maintaining high levels of safety under conditions of ever increasing air traffic is a challenging task. Failures to comply with safety-related regulations are often considered to be important contributors to safety occurrences. To address the issue of compliance, approaches based on external regulation of the employees' behavior were proposed. Unfortunately, an externally imposed control is often not internalized by employees and has a short-term effect on their performance. To achieve a long-term effect, employees need to be internally motivated to adhere to regulations. Theories from social sciences propose that team processes play an important role in the dynamics of individual motivation. In this paper an agent-based model is proposed, by which the impact of social interaction and coordination in teams of platform employees on their individual motivation and compliance with safety regulations at an airline ground service organization are explored. The model was simulated and partially validated by a case study performed at a real airline ground service organization. The model was able to reproduce behavioral patterns of compliance of the platform employees in this study.

Keywords: Compliance · Agent-based model · Motivation · Cognitive models · Social contagion

1 Introduction

The amount of air traffic increases with every passing year. The performance pressures imposed nowadays on the actors in air transportation make it difficult to achieve safety targets formulated by regulatory organizations. According to the aviation statistics [2], most of the safety occurrences happen not during the flight, but on the ground, e.g., during aircraft ground handling operations and aircraft maintenance operations. Decreasing the number of ground safety occurrences has a high priority in many airlines in different countries. To achieve this aim some airlines use Ramp Line Operations Safety Assessments (LOSA) [2] - a monitoring tool for measuring and identifying the adherence to safety regulations on the platform. Unfortunately, the introduction of ramp LOSA in the ground service organization under study did not result in a decrease in the number of ground safety occurrences.

© Springer International Publishing Switzerland 2015
Q. Chen et al. (Eds.): PRIMA 2015, LNAI 9387, pp. 492–500, 2015.
DOI: 10.1007/978-3-319-25524-8_31

To achieve a long-term compliance, employees need to be internally motivated to adhere to regulations [3]. In this paper, based on a theoretical fundament from social sciences we build an agent-based model to explore the role of team processes in individual motivation and compliance of platform employees with safety regulations in an airline ground service organization. In particular we consider a specific task of the aircraft arrival procedure - Foreign Object Damage (FOD) check. Foreign object is any object that should not be located near aircraft as it can damage aircraft or injure personnel. According to [1], the improper execution of FOD checks costs airlines and airports millions of dollars every year. Nevertheless, the ramp LOSA statistics showed that FOD checks are often not performed by platform employees.

The proposed model elaborates the motivation and decision making of the platform employees whether or not to perform the FOD check. In this elaboration, next to social also cognitive and organizational factors are taken into account. Furthermore, the model includes individual and social learning of agents representing the employees and addresses two modes of reasoning of agents – explicit rational and implicit automatic (habits). At the social level we are particularly interested in how coordination influences the motivation and compliance with safety regulations of the agents. In the organization under study, first implicit coordination was used in the teams, when the FOD check task was not explicitly allocated to any team member, but to the team as a whole, and could be executed by any team member who decides to do so. After some time, a new arrival procedure was introduced, which used explicit coordination. In this case, the FOD check task was explicitly assigned to a specific team member. We identified by simulation that in the case of implicit coordination a high level of compliance was maintained in the presence of a high managerial control and the level of compliance dropped quickly when the control decreased to a lower level. On the contrary, in the case of explicit coordination the compliance did not decrease significantly in the presence of low control. These simulation outcomes are well supported by the ramp LOSA statistics from the real ground service organization.

The paper is organized as follows. In the following Section 2 the theoretical basis of the model is described. In Section 3 the proposed agent-based model is provided. Main results from the simulation study are discussed in Section 4. The paper ends with conclusions and discussions.

2   Theoretical Background

The theoretical basis of the model comprises several theories from social sciences described below. These theories address human needs, the way how humans reason about their needs and make choices to act based on this reasoning. All the theories used for the model development have a good empirical support.

Self-determination theory [3] is a theory of human motivation, which addresses people's universal, innate psychological needs and tendencies for growth and fulfillment. Specifically, the theory postulates three types of basic needs:

-    *the need for competence* concerns the people's inherent desire to be effective in dealing with the environment;

-    *the need for relatedness* concerns the universal disposition to interact with, be connected to, and experience caring for other people;
-    *the need for autonomy* concerns people's universal urge to be causal agents, to experience volition.

In line with other motivation theories [6, 7], in addition to the needs listed above, *the need for safety* was added, which is particularly relevant for the ground service organization, in which physical injuries are not uncommon.

Based in needs individual goals can be defined. Higher level individual goals may be refined in goal hierarchies as described in [8]. To achieve or maintain his or her goals, an individual considers different behavioral options (actions or plans). One of the theories that explains why individuals choose one option over another is *the Expectancy Theory of Motivation by Vroom* [7]. According to the theory, when an individual evaluates alternative possibilities to act, he or she explicitly or implicitly makes estimations for the following factors: *expectancy, instrumentality* and *valence.*

Expectancy refers to the individual's belief about the likelihood that a particular act will be followed by a particular outcome (called a first-level outcome). Its value varies between 0 and 1.

Instrumentality is a belief concerning the likelihood of a first level outcome resulting into a particular second level outcome; its value varies between -1 and +1. A second level outcome represents a desired (or avoided) state of affairs that is reflected in the agent's goals.

Valence refers to the strength of the individual's desire for an outcome or state of affairs; it is also an indication of the priority of goals.

Values of expectancies, instrumentalities and valences may change over time, in particular due to individual and social learning. *The motivational force* of an individual i to choose option to act k is calculated as:

$$F_{k,i}(t) = \sum_{l=1}^{n} E_{kl,i}(t) \sum_{h=1}^{m} V_{h,i}(t) I_{klh,i}(t) \qquad (1)$$

Here $E_{kl,i}(t)$ is the strength of the expectancy that option k will be followed by outcome l; $V_{h,i}(t)$ is the valence of the second level outcome (a goal) h; $I_{klh,i}(t)$ is perceived instrumentality of outcome l for the attainment of outcome h for option k.

The Vroom's theory describes the process of rational decision making. However, repetitive actions such as occur during aircraft handling may over time become automatic, i.e., a habit. *The dual process theory* [5] distinguishes System 1 and System 2 thinking. While System 2 is used for rational, rule-based and analytic thinking, System 1 is associated with unconscious, implicit and automatic reasoning. Depending on the dynamics of environmental changes, an individual switches between the systems. Both systems are used in the model and the case study considered in the paper.

3   The Agent-Based Model

To develop the model, an extensive one year study was performed at a real ground service organization. The data were gathered by observation, questionnaires and interviews with employees playing different roles in the organization. The collected data were separated in two data sets. The first set contained data on the organizational context (i.e., formal organizational structures and processes, norms and regulations) and on local processes and characteristics of the organizational agents. This dataset was used for the model initialization. To represent the uncertainty and variability of the components of the model, most of the parameters were specified by intervals with a uniform distribution. The second set contained data describing global organizational or systemic properties (such as ramp LOSA statistics), which were used for the model validation. Because of the space limitations, only a part of the model is described below. For the complete model description please refer to [9].

Specification of Decision Making of Agents

Decision making by the Platform Employee agents whether or not to perform FOD check was modeled by using the Vroom's expectancy theory (Fig. 1). To initialize the expectancies, instrumentalities and valences of the model for each agent three classes of values were introduced: Low, Medium and High. Most of the numerical scales of these parameters were divided equally among the classes: Low for $[0, 0.33)$, Medium for $[0.33, 0.67)$, and High for $[0.67, 1]$.

The expectancy theory model was used for System 2 reasoning. When the same operations were routinely executed by a Platform Employee agent, the agent's System 2 reasoning was gradually shifting to System 1 reasoning – a habit had been formed. This shift was modeled by the dynamics of agent's i openness parameter α_i:

$$\alpha_i(t + \Delta t) = \alpha_i(t) + \zeta(\alpha_i^{min} - \alpha_i(t))\Delta t, \tag{2}$$

where α_i^{min} is the minimum perceptive openness of agent i (set to 0.1 in the simulation), ζ is the rate of transition from System 2 to System 1. It depends on the execution frequency of the operation by the agent, as well as on the agent's personal characteristics. In the simulation $\zeta = 0.015$, meaning that it takes around two months to form a new habit.

When procedural rules change, an agent needs to adapt to a new situation and reconsider options by switching from System 1 to System 2: the agent i's openness is set to its initial value $\alpha_i(0)$ and the process of the new habit formation starts again.

A similar expectancy theory model was created for option 2 – 'Not to perform FOD check'. It has the same types of parameters, but their values are different.

In the simulation, every time when an agent i considers explicitly (System 2) or implicitly (System 1) whether or not to perform FOD check, motivation forces $F_{1,i}$ and $F_{2,i}$ for both options are calculated by (1). Then, the agent performs FOD check with probability $(F_{max}+F_{1,i})/(2F_{max}+F_{1,i}+F_{2,i})$. The normalization with F_{max} is used to compensate for the negative values of the instrumentalities.

Specification of Agent Learning and Social Interaction

Two types of learning were modeled: individual and social learning of agents.

An agent learns individually by observing a feedback from the environment on its action. In the decision making model from Fig. 1, the individual learning was realized by updating values of expectancies (E) based on the following observations:

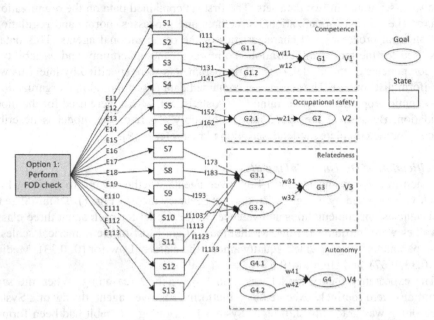

Fig. 1. Decision making model of a Platform Employee agent for performing FOD check based on the Expectancy Theory with expectancies (E), instrumentalities (I), states (S) and valences (V). For readability purposes the time parameter and agent indexes were omitted.

- An agent observes whether or not a reprimand from other agents is provided, when the agent does not comply with regulations (E111, E112, E113).
- After the successful execution of a task, an agent observes how much time it took and how it influenced the execution time of the operation (E11, E12).
- When an agent does not perform a FOD check, a safety occurrence could occur. The agent is able to observe such occurrences (E13, E14).

Furthermore, the Platform Employee agents are able to observe the execution of operations by other agents in their teams and to learn from these agents by verbal communication. Social learning is modeled as the process of social contagion [4]. By this process expectancies $E_{kl,i}(t)$ were updated as:

$$E_{kl,i}(t+\Delta t) = E_{kl,i}(t)+ \delta_{kl,i}(t)\Delta t \qquad (3)$$

Here $\delta_{kl,i}(t) = \sum_{j \in T} \gamma_{j,i}(t)(E_{kl,j}(t) - E_{kl,i}(t))/\sum_{j \in T} \gamma_{j,i}(t)$ is the amount of change of the agent i's state; T is the set of the agents in the team. A weight $\gamma_{j,i} \in [0,1]$ is the degree of influence of agent j on agent i defined as:

$$\gamma_{j,i}(t)=\alpha_i(t)\,\varepsilon_j(t)\,\beta_{ji} \qquad (4)$$

Table 1. The goals and states of the decision making model provided in Fig.1.

Goals	States
G1 Achieve a high level of competence	S1 Action saves time
G1.1 Achieve the highest time efficiency	S2 Action costs additional time
G1.2 Prevent aircraft, equipment and/or infrastructural damage	S3 Action results in aircraft, equipment or infrastructural damage
	S4 Action prevents aircraft, equipment or infrastructural damage
G2 Achieve a high level of occupational safety	S5 Action results in personal injury
	S6 Action prevents personal injury
G2.1 Prevent personal injury	S7 Action is in alignment with the team member norms
	S8 Action is not in alignment with the
G3 Maintain sense of belonging and attachment to colleagues	team norms
G3.1 Maintain high team acceptance	S9 Action is in alignment with sector
G3.2 Maintain high management acceptance	management norms
	S10 Action is not in alignment with sector management norms
G4 Achieve a high control over own behavior and goals	S11 Reprimand received from team member
G4.1 Achieve a high level of freedom in the execution of tasks	S12 Reprimand received from team leader
G4.2 Achieve high psychological ownership of rules	S13 Reprimand received from sector manager

$\alpha_i(t)$ and $\varepsilon_j(t)$ are the agent characteristics – the openness of information recipient agent i and the expressiveness of information provider agent j, and $\beta \in [0,1]$ is the strength of the information channel between the two agents.

Identification of Shared Beliefs, Norms and Values of (Groups of) Agents

By field observations and interviews a team norm was identified. The norm applies to situations in which a team arrives too late at an aircraft stand while the aircraft is waiting for the docking process. To save time, the FOD check is omitted and the arrival procedure starts directly. Field data revealed that employees who execute the check in the described situation get a social reprehension from other team members. This influences the achievement of goal G3.1, which is driven by the alignment of the decision option with the team norms and team leader norms.

The Team Leader agent's and Sector Manager agent's norms are in line with the organizational regulations.

Specification of Coordination Mechanisms in Teams of Agents

Before the introduction of the new arrival procedure the tasks were coordinated implicitly, in an ad-hoc manner. In particular, the FOD check task was executed by different members, who had decided to perform it or was not executed at all. This way of working is described by the model provided above.

After the introduction of the new procedure each agent in the team was assigned a specific task. Field study data indicated that the probability for team member reprimands and team leader reprimands have increased significantly due to the explicit task division. Thus, in the decision making model of the agent responsible for the FOD check the relevant parameters were changed for the new procedure.

4   Simulation Study

We consider a real scenario, which occurred in the past and consists of five periods:

Before the introduction of the new arrival procedure, when implicit coordination was used in the teams:

P1: the first period with a limited managerial control over the execution of the platform operations and limited safety information provision.

P2: the second period (8 weeks) with a high managerial control after many safety occurrences happened in the first period.

P3: the third period in which the release of managerial control occurs over time.

Transition to the new arrival procedure, which includes explicit coordination:

P4: in the fourth period information sessions were organized to explain the purpose and effects of the procedural change to the employees. High managerial control was applied in the first months after the introduction of the new procedure.

P5: in the fifth period after one month after the introduction of the new procedure the intensity of information provision and the managerial control decreased.

A team consists of 5 agents: a team leader and 4 platform employees. In the simulation the agents in the teams communicate with each other in a random order.

In line with the empirical findings, two types of agents in the teams are modeled: more expressive agents with $\varepsilon_i \in [0.5, 0.9]$ and less expressive agents with $\varepsilon_i \in [0.1, 0.5]$. Each agent can be of either type with an equal probability. The openness of an agent α_i is assigned a wide range $[0.1, 0.9]$ to represent the diversity of agents. In each simulation run the agents' parameters are randomly instantiated from the uniformly distributed intervals introduced above.

In the simulation, one simulation day is divided in three shifts. During normal operations, on average, the arrival procedure is executed three times at each shift. The simulated time period is 200 working days.

In the following we discuss the dynamics of the motivational forces obtained in the simulation. In period P1, after the initialization phase, most of the agents have a relatively constant motivational force for both decision options. The motivational forces to perform FOD checks are low as the organization neither sufficiently controls the execution of operations nor creates a sufficient awareness about the importance of FOD checks. Some agents in the team even prefer not to perform the check. By the end of the phase the agents function in System 1 mode of reasoning. In the beginning of P2 the organization introduces more frequent managerial control and reprimands. To adapt to the new circumstances, the agents switch to System 2 mode of reasoning.

Such a change results in an increased motivation to perform FOD checks and a de-creased motivation not to do so of all agents in all teams. The differences in motiva-tion are explained by differences in the individual characteristics of the agents. How-ever, when after 8 weeks the control and information provision is gradually removed, the agents start gradually returning to their previous state. This form of motivated behavior is known in the literature as externally regulated behavior [3]. These beha-vioral patterns were also observed in the organization under study.

The introduction of the new procedure with the explicit coordination results in P4 in a higher motivation levels to perform FOD check and a lower motivation levels not to perform the check than in the previous three phases (Fig.2). Thus, the decision options have become better discriminated than in the previous periods. In P5 the ma-nagerial control is gradually removed. However, the motivational forces not to per-form FOD check do not increase significantly. This effect can partly be explained by a better information provision and the social control.

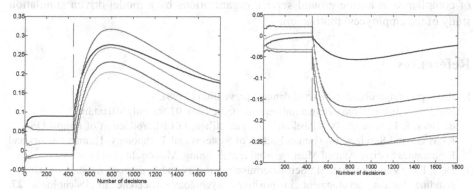

Fig. 2. The motivational forces of the agents in a team to perform FOD check (left) and to not perform FOD check (right) in the periods P4 and P5 with the explicit coordination in the teams. The dashed vertical line indicates the beginning of fourth period (increased control).

The model simulation outcomes were also compared to the ramp LOSA statistics of the FOD checks execution in the ground service organization. The model was able to capture the trends in the real ramp LOSA data. The Student's two-sample t-test performed on real and simulated data for periods P1-P3 supported the null-hypothesis at the significance level 5%. The statistics about periods P4 and P5 is currently insuf-ficient to draw substantiated conclusions. However the gathered data indicated that the compliance has increased substantially, which is in line with the simulation model prediction. The model predicts that the compliance with safety regulations will not drop as much as in P3 after the managerial control is decreased in P5. Thus, according to the model, the agents will not return to the safety-compromising habits.

5   Discussion and Conclusions

In this paper a formal agent-based motivation model is presented, based on an integrated theoretical basis from social sciences. All the theories used for the model development were extensively validated by experiments with human subjects.

In the study presented in the paper a good agreement is demonstrated between the simulated data obtained using the proposed model and the real data from the ground service organization under study. Based on the developed model, global sensitivity analysis was performed to identify parameters with the highest impact on the compliance both in the implicit and explicit coordination case. This analysis indicated that the parameters that define social relations and processes in teams are of the utmost importance in the case of explicit coordination. More detailed results on the sensitivity analysis are presented in [9].

To the best knowledge of the authors, it is a first attempt to approach the problem of compliance in airline ground service organizations by a model-driven simulation study of the employees' motivation.

References

1. Boeing: Foreign object debris and damage prevention (1998).
   http://www.boeing.com/commercial/aeromagazine/aero_01/textonly/s01txt.html
2. de Boer, R.J., Koncak, B., Habekotté, R., van Hilten, G.J.: Introduction of ramp-LOSA at KLM Ground Services. In: Human Factors of Systems and Technology, Human Factors and Ergonomics Society Annual Meeting. Shaker Publishing, Maastricht (2011)
3. Deci, E.L., Vansteenkiste, M.: Self-determination theory and basic need satisfaction: Understanding human development in positive psychology. Ricerche di Psichologia 27, 17–34 (2004)
4. Hegselmann R., Krause, U.: Opinion dynamics and bounded confidence: models, analysis and simulation, J. of Artificial Societies and Social Simulation 5(3) (2002)
5. Kahneman, D.: Thinking, Fast and Slow. Farrar, Straus and Giroux, New York (2011)
6. McClelland, D.C.: Human motivation. CUP Archive (1987)
7. Pinder, C.C.: Work Motivation in Organizational Behavior. Prentice-Hall, NJ (1998)
8. Popova, V., Sharpanskykh, A.: Formal Modelling of Organisational Goals Based on Performance Indicators. Data and Knowledge Engineering 70(4), 335–364 (2011)
9. Sharpanskykh, A., Haest, R.: An agent-based model to study effects of team processes on compliance with safety regulations at an airline ground service organization. Technical report, TU Delft (2015). http://homepage.tudelft.nl/j11q3/papers/tech_report_182014.pdf

Agent-Oriented Programming Languages as a High-Level Abstraction Facilitating the Development of Intelligent Behaviours for Component-Based Applications

Seán Russell[✉], G.M.P. O'Hare, and Rem W. Collier

School of Computer Science, University College Dublin, Dublin, Ireland
{sean.russell,gregory.ohare,rem.collier}@ucd.ie

Abstract. Developing behaviours for complex component based systems is a difficult task. This paper evaluates the use of agent-oriented programming languages as a high level abstraction for performing this task. Evaluation carried out objectively shows that participants completed more tasks and subjectively they perceived that it was easier to use when compared with the same tasks performed using Java.

Keywords: Agent-oriented programming languages · Component based applications · Ease of development

1 Introduction

The development and maintenance of intelligent behaviours for complex systems, such as wireless sensor network applications, is a difficult task. In order to successfully implement these behaviours, a developer may require detailed knowledge of the underlying component system or the application itself.

Previous research has investigated the integration of component frameworks with multi-agent systems [1]. This work utilised agents as both a method of control of the component system as well as a facility for the introduction of intelligent behaviours. This paper has developed the concept further, focusing on the integration of multi-agent systems and a component based wireless sensor network middleware to facilitate the development of intelligent wireless sensor network applications. The main assertion of these works is that the integration provides an accessible means to quickly alter the behaviour of the system.

The purpose of this work is to evaluate the accuracy of this assertion. As such, there is no focus on the intelligence of the agents or the behaviours that they are used to implement. More abstractly, this assertion can be viewed as the use of agent-oriented programming languages as a higher-level abstraction for the addition of behaviours to a component-based application. Intelligent behaviours are introduced through the integration of an environment abstraction technology. A desirable side-effect is that this allows the use of a number of compatible agent-oriented programming languages. Documentation of the environment specifies

© Springer International Publishing Switzerland 2015
Q. Chen et al. (Eds.): PRIMA 2015, LNAI 9387, pp. 501–509, 2015.
DOI: 10.1007/978-3-319-25524-8_32

the interface that is presented by the environment abstraction and behaviours are written with respect to this. As such, it is possible to effect the operation of a complex system with little or no detailed knowledge of the underlying infrastructure.

2   Background

Within this study, students were required to perform a number of tasks based on the development of intelligent behaviours for a component-based system. This section will briefly introduce the technologies involved. Both problems in the evaluation involved the development of behaviours for a wireless sensor network application named WAIST (Waste Augmentation and Integrated Shipment Tracking).

WAIST is an intelligent transportation system that enables the monitoring of waste in transit, with the intention of identifying instances of illegal dumping [2]. The application is built on the SIXTH middleware for the sensor web [3]. The SIXTH middleware is built on the Open Services Gateway Initiative framework (OSGi) [4], which provides a flexible component framework enabling the addition, removal and update of services at runtime.

2.1   OSGi

The OSGi specification describes a modular system and a service platform for the Java programming language [4]. This system implements a complete and dynamic component model, something that does not exist in standalone Java/VM environments. Components, coming in the form of bundles for deployment, can be remotely installed, started, stopped, updated, and uninstalled without requiring a reboot. Application life cycle management is implemented via APIs that allow for remote downloading of management policies. This functionality is quite useful in a sensor network application as it allows the deployment and removal of bundles in line with the addition and removal of sensors.

2.2   SIXTH

SIXTH is a Java-based Sensor Web Middleware incorporating sensed data from diverse sources. This includes physical devices, such as sensors, as well as cyber resources, such as Internet resources [3]. Based on OSGi, applications can be built using SIXTH through the addition of bundles containing application code. SIXTH provides the resources to route and filter the data that is introduced such that additional bundles need only state the type of data that they require. This data is then delivered to specific parts of the application for processing.

SIXTH also provides mechanisms for reconfiguring the operation of the sensors on the fly. The tasking service is provided that can be used to specify the a change in behaviour to a particular sensor (this will be encapsulated into a message and be delivered to the appropriate bundle in the system). A tasking message, if accepted as valid, is translated by an adaptor's message wrapper implementation, which performs transformation into a native messaging format for that platform, which is then passed to the sensor node.

2.3   WAIST

As WAIST is built using the SIXTH middleware it is also based on the OSGi component system. WAIST utilises a number of sensors to track the location and activity of shipments of waste in transit in real time.

- A single GPS sensor attached to the truck carrying the shipment
- Multiple acceleration sensors attached to individual containers of waste within the shipment
- Multiple light sensors attached to individual containers of waste within the shipment
- Contact sensors attached to lids of individual containers

These sensors are combined to maintain a record of the location of the shipment at all times as well as to attempt to determine if illegal dumping has occurred. Pattern recognition is used to determine the state of containers within the shipment and with context of state of other containers as well as location this can be used to determine if illegal dumping has occurred.

3   Agent-Oriented Programming Languages

Agent-oriented programming (AOP) is a software development paradigm aimed at creating entities known as intelligent agents [5] or rational agents [6]. Agents are situated in environments in which they perceive and act. An issue that repeatedly has to be dealt with, from a software development point of view, is how to connect agents to environments. The design and implementation of the interaction between the agents and the environment often requires substantial effort, even though most environments and agent systems are implemented in Java. Commonly this can hinder the exploitation of the full potential of the environment by multi-agent systems [7].

3.1   Environment Abstraction

In order to mitigate the impact of the problem, this work utilises an environment layer to simplify the integration of agents and their environment. The two most well-known environment layer technologies in the area of agent programming are the Environment Interface Standard (EIS) [8] and the Common Artifacts for Agents Open framework (CArtAgO) [9].

CArtAgO was chosen for use within this work due to the difficulties integrating EIS (EIS environments are loaded from the local file space using a dedicated Java class loader). CArtAgO easily integrates with OSGi, which is also designed to manage class loading for the component based system.

3.2 ASTRA

While the integration of CArtAgo and SIXTH is not tied to a single agent-oriented programming language, one was chosen for use during the evaluation of this work. ASTRA, an implementation of Agentspeak(TR), is a logic-based agent programming language that combines AgentSpeak(L) [10] (implementation based on Jason [11]) with Teleo-Reactive [12] functions. ASTRA provides a large number of features, such as typing of variables, support for multiple inheritance [13] and integration with multiple environment abstractions (including CArtAgo). Further detail on the ASTRA language is available in [14].

4 Integration

The integration of the CArtAgo environment abstraction with SIXTH takes the form of a single OSGi bundle. The bundle contributes a number of artifacts, each designed to provide an agent with information about the middleware or allow some measure of control. These artifacts provide functionality and information in a generic manner. In this way they can be useful to all applications built using SIXTH.

4.1 Basic Functionality

The basic integration of CArtAgo and SIXTH provides the following artifacts relevant to the problems in the evaluation: the `BundleArtifact` allowing interactions with OSGi bundles and the `RetaskerArtifact` allowing actuation in the sensor network.

4.2 Expanded Functionality in WAIST

As this system was designed to enable the support of complex applications built using SIXTH, the basic functionality may not provide enough information or control. Figure 1 shows the design of the integration with WAIST. Agents in the system are not only capable of utilising artifacts designed to interact with SIXTH but also those designed to interact with WAIST. This allows the creation of artifacts that are specific to the application and capable of finer detail and control.

This extensibility is exploited in WAIST to provide a number of artifacts that interact directly with the application. The artifacts provided that are relevant to the problems in the evaluations are: the `GPSDataArtifact` which presents the location information of the shipments and the `DeploymentArtifact` which provides information about the shipments and configures messages for the SIXTH tasking service.

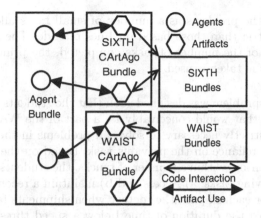

Fig. 1. CArtAgO Artifacts usage Example

5   Evaluation

Evaluating programming languages, methodologies, paradigms and toolkits is a matter of some discussion and debate within the wider software engineering community. For systems like this, the principal aim is to make it easier for developers to perform particular tasks. Specifically, it should facilitate developers in implementing reliable, predictable, understandable behaviours for component based applications.

Commonly, the notion of "programmer effort" is used in attempting to quantify the amount of work a programmer must undertake to complete some programming task. A number of studies have used objective measures to quantify programmer effort. Although not specifically based in the agent domain, these metrics can help inform a choice of metric for agent-oriented programming and have previously been used as such [15].

When performing an evaluation such as this, a common approach is to use two groups of participants. Each group is presented with a common problem to solve, with all factors other than the subject of the evaluation being kept equal [16,17]. This evaluation utilises two independent problems such that the students, cannot gain an advantage by having completed the first problem that would skew the results.

5.1   Problems

Two problems were developed, each containing a number of distinct tasks. The first problem was based on analysing incoming GPS readings and performing actions and the second was based on managing the OSGi bundles of the application. This section will describe both of these problems briefly, however for further detail the full problem specifications have been included in [18]. These include the materials describing how the same precesses can be achieved using Java as were described in the preceding sections.

The design of the problems as a number of small tasks allows the use of a more concrete metric than those based on lines of code. The solutions can be analysed in terms of the number of tasks completed, the principle is the same as in [16] where time taken is used.

Problem 1. This problem was designed such that the students would undertake a number of tasks that would conceivably be a part of the WAIST application. While it was not strictly necessary to solve all problems in the order provided, most tasks have a reliance on the previous task. Based on the concept of GPS and acceleration sensors within a number of trucks, the students were required to complete the following tasks: a) Access and b) maintain a record of the most up to date location for each shipment, c) detect when shipments fall below a speed threshold, d) record the duration of time below a speed threshold, e) activate sensors within a shipment when it is below a speed threshold.

Problem 2. This problem was designed such that the students would undertake a number of tasks based on the management of the bundles in the WAIST application. Based on this premise, the students were required to carry out the following tasks: a) Access and b) maintain a record of all the bundles within the application, c) search for new bundles to be installed, d)install and start new bundles, e) update bundles to newer versions when found.

5.2   Participants

A user trial that was conducted using students from the MSc in Advanced Software Engineering programme in University College Dublin. Twenty participants with average number of years experience in industry of of 7.4 ± 5.1 years were asked to solve two problems relating to the use of the WAIST system. The students all indicated some level of experience with Java and had experience with ASTRA during the class. All students indicate that they had little or no experience with using OSGi and no students had previously used SIXTH.

The students were randomly assigned to one of two groups. Group A attempted the first problem using ASTRA and group B using Java. This was then reversed for the second problem such that all students had attempted one problem in each language. The students had one hour to complete each problem after which they were required to submit the work they had completed. Students were incentivised to complete both problems by requiring them to be finished and submitted as a component of their grades at a later date.

The aim of this work was to reduce the required effort when implementing intelligent behaviours in a complex system. Naturally it can be assumed that a programmer sufficiently competent with the technologies in use could implement the behaviours using those technologies. However, the intention of this work is to show that programmers with a lesser understanding of tools such as SIXTH and OSGi benefit from the higher level abstractions provided through CArtAgO. This study was intended to ascertain whether the use of the system reduced the effort required by a developer to implement a solution.

5.3   Results

The source code of the solutions was analysed in order to measure the number of tasks completed within the allotted time. Table 1 shows the average number of tasks completed for each problem and language combination. The class the participants were studying takes place over a one week period, the evaluation took place on a Friday afternoon and was the last commitment of the students. As such, a number of students did not stay to complete the second problem, which was perceived as the more difficult problem. The students had been randomly distributed into two groups, however 1 student mistakenly believed that he was assigned to group A when he was in fact assigned to group B.

Table 1. Number of tasks completed

Problem	Group	Language	Number of submissions	Number of tasks	Average tasks solved	Standard deviation
1	A	ASTRA	11	5	2.63	1.15
1	B	Java	9	5	0.67	0.47
2	B	ASTRA	4	5	1	0.70
2	A	Java	7	5	0.86	1.72

Table 1 displays an obvious improvement in the number of tasks completed when using ASTRA over the number of tasks completed using Java particularly for the first problem. There still exists an improvement in the second problem, however due to the number of students who did not submit any work, no conclusions can be drawn from this.

5.4   Survey

In order to attain a subjective analysis of the programmer effort involved in the completion of the problems, the students were asked to respond to a survey. Students were asked to indicate their level of agreement with statements relating to their experience level with a number of technologies and their experiences with the problems they completed. The results were captured on a 5 point Likert scale. The following statements relating to the problems were made:

Q1 The supporting information for solving the problem in ASTRA was adequate.
Q2 The supporting information for solving the problem in Java was adequate.
Q3 Using ASTRA made the problems easier to complete.
Q4 ASTRA was easier to use than Java.
Q5 ASTRA was easier to modify than Java.
Q6 My ASTRA solution was more readable than my Java solution.

The responses to the questions are contained in Table 2 where the percentage is given for each of the responses. The average and standard deviation of the responses is calculated, where strongly disagree is 1, agree is 2, neither agree or disagree was 3, agree was 4 and strongly agree is 5. The responses for a number of statements were partially positive, primarily questions 3, 4 & 6.

Table 2. Question responses

Question	Strongly disagree	Disagree	Neither agree or disagree	Agree	Strongly agree	Mean	SD
1	0%	35%	20%	45%	0%	3.1	0.89
2	10%	30%	20%	40%	0%	2.9	1.04
3	0%	10%	30%	45%	15%	3.65	0.85
4	0%	30%	30%	30%	10%	3.2	0.98
5	0%	35%	45%	20%	0%	2.85	0.73
6	0%	20%	30%	35%	15%	3.45	0.97

6   Conclusions and Future Work

A number of methods were utilised to evaluate the efficacy of this work as a means to simplify the implementation of intelligent behaviours. These were based on a class of masters students studying Agent-Oriented Software Engineering as part of an MSc in Advanced Software Engineering.

The first method measured the number of tasks completed by the students within a fixed amount of time. The results of the two problems were detailed, and show that students completed a greater number of tasks when using ASTRA compared to the same tasks completed in Java.

The subjective analysis carried out re-enforces the objective assessment. The results show that there was a perception amongst the students, that using ASTRA rather than Java made the problems easier to complete with 55% of the participants either agreeing or strongly agreeing as opposed to 10% disagreeing.

Further work is required to address issues with the evaluation such as the limited time available to complete the problems and possible bias in the questions of the survey. Ideally a greater number of participants would be found.

Acknowledgments. This research has been supported by the Irish Environmental Protection Agency (EPA) and Science Foundation Ireland (Grant 07/CE/I1147).

References

1. Lillis, D., Collier, R.W., Dragone, M., O'Hare, G.M.P.: An Agent-Based Approach to Component Management. In: Proceedings of the 8th International Conference on Autonomous Agents and Multi-Agent Systems (AAMAS 2009), Budapest, Hungary, International Foundation for Autonomous Agents and Multiagent Systems, pp. 529–536, May 2009
2. Russell, S., O'Grady, M.J., Diamond, D., Ziókowski, B., O'Hare, G.: Monitoring and Validating the Transport of Waste. Pervasive Computing, IEEE **12**(1), 42–43 (2013)
3. Carr, D.: The SIXTH Middleware: Sensible Sensing for the Sensor Web. Ph.D thesis, University College Dublin, Dublin, Ireland (2015)
4. OSGi Alliance: OSGi Specifications. http://www.osgi.org/Specifications/Home Page

5. Jennings, N.R., Wooldridge, M.J.: Applications of Intelligent Agents. In: Jennings, N., Wooldridge, M. (eds.) Agent Technology, pp. 3–28. Springer, Berlin Heidelberg (1998)
6. Wooldridge, M.J.: Reasoning about rational agents. MIT press (2000)
7. Weyns, D., Omicini, A., Odell, J.: Environment as a first class abstraction in multiagent systems. Autonomous Agents and Multi-Agent Systems 14(1), 5–30 (2007)
8. Behrens, T., Hindriks, K.V., Bordini, R.H., Braubach, L., Dastani, M., Dix, J., Hübner, J.F., Pokahr, A.: An interface for agent-environment interaction. In: Collier, R., Dix, J., Novák, P. (eds.) ProMAS 2010. LNCS, vol. 6599, pp. 139–158. Springer, Heidelberg (2012)
9. Ricci, A., Viroli, M., Omicini, A.: CArtAgO: a framework for prototyping artifact-based environments in MAS. In: Weyns, D., Van Dyke Parunak, H., Michel, F. (eds.) E4MAS 2006. LNCS (LNAI), vol. 4389, pp. 67–86. Springer, Heidelberg (2007)
10. Rao, A.S.: AgentSpeak(L): BDI agents speak out in a logical computable language. In: Perram, J., Van de Velde, W. (eds.) MAAMAW 1996. LNCS, vol. 1038, pp. 42–55. Springer, Heidelberg (1996)
11. Bordini, R.H., Hübner, J.F., Wooldridge, M.: Programming multi-agent systems in AgentSpeak using Jason. John Wiley & Sons (2007)
12. Nilsson, N.J.: Teleo-reactive programs for agent control. JAIR 1, 139–158 (1994)
13. Dhaon, A., Collier, R.W.: Multiple inheritance in agentspeak (L)-style programming languages. In: Proceedings of the 4th International Workshop on Programming Based on Actors Agents & Decentralized Control, pp. 109–120. ACM (2014)
14. Collier, R.W.: ASTRA Programming Language. http://astralanguage.com
15. Lillis, D., Collier, R.W., Jordan, H.R.: Evaluation of a conversation management toolkit for multi agent programming. In: Dastani, M., Hübner, J.F., Logan, B. (eds.) ProMAS 2012. LNCS, vol. 7837, pp. 90–107. Springer, Heidelberg (2013)
16. Hochstein, L., Basili, V.R., Vishkin, U., Gilbert, J.: A pilot study to compare programming effort for two parallel programming models. Journal of Systems and Software 81(11), 1920–1930 (2008)
17. VanderWiel, S., Nathanson, D., Lilja, D.: Complexity and performance in parallel programming languages. In: Proceedings Second International Workshop on High-Level Parallel Programming Models and Supportive Environments, pp. 3–12. IEEE Computer. Soc. Press (1997)
18. Russell, S.: Real-time monitoring and validation of waste transportation using intelligent agents and pattern recognition. Ph.D thesis, University College Dublin (2015)

Towards a Taxonomy of Task-Oriented Domains of Dialogue

Tânia Marques[(✉)]

School of Informatics, University of Edinburgh, Edinburgh EH8 9AB, UK
tmarques@inf.ed.ac.uk

Abstract. To deal with a broad spectrum of domains, intelligent agents have to generate their own task-oriented dialogue that stems from the need to interact with another agent when solving their own individual task. Most work created to date has either been focused on the task or on the dialogue, but not on both. A taxonomy that describes how the characteristics of a domain determine the types of dialogue needed would be useful, both for understanding how to create agents that are more adaptable to different domains, and also to facilitate reusing previous work. In this paper, we present a number of dimensions that could be included in such a taxonomy, and illustrate how they could be used to determine the nature of dialogue needed in a particular type of domain.

Keywords: Agent communication · Taxonomy · Task-oriented dialogue

1 Introduction

Creating agents who are able to automatically determine how to function in different domains — in other words, agents who adapt their interactions to the domain-level problem they are facing — would be a useful addition to the state of the art models of interaction, which typically are tuned manually to the specific domain of application. This is only possible if the agents communicate with other agents when the task demands it. To date most of the work in the agents community has focused on creating agents that are very good at solving a given task when communication is not needed [1,2], very good at communicating when recipes to solve the task are given [3,4], or very good only in very specific settings [5,6]. It is necessary to bridge the gap between these trends of research to create more flexible agents, capable of dealing with a broader spectrum of domains.

A taxonomy showing how the characteristics of a particular type of domain influence the dialogue needed can be a useful tool. It would help understand what is required of dialogue when building task-oriented domain-independent agents, adaptable to several tasks and situations. It would make explicit the connection between the task and the potential dialogue, while helping grounding the communication to the physical task-domain. Forging the link between task and the discourse can also be of value for reusing work that was previously done in the literature by understanding how it correlate with the domain task.

© Springer International Publishing Switzerland 2015
Q. Chen et al. (Eds.): PRIMA 2015, LNAI 9387, pp. 510–518, 2015.
DOI: 10.1007/978-3-319-25524-8_33

For instance, if the agents need to perform a joint plan, then work related to argumentation might be relevant for them to exchange arguments about the adequacy of a certain plan.

The purpose of this paper is to discuss the need of a taxonomy that forges a link between the task and dialogue for agent interaction by showing a first attempt to create it, and explaining how this taxonomy could be used. To that end, we describe a number of dimensions that define task-oriented domains in terms of characteristics that might influence the types of dialogue needed in such domains. It should be noted that this is an initial attempt where the simple case of one on one interaction between agents, and a common language is assumed. The dimensions described should not be seen as an exhaustive list of all independent dimensions needed to describe a task-oriented domain. Nor should the taxonomy be seen as the only one that should be used.

This paper is structured as follows: related work is described in Section 2. Section 3 is divided in two parts: we start by presenting a number of dimensions used to characterize task-oriented domains, and then we describe how a taxonomy could be created from the dimensions presented. Some examples illustrating its use can be found in section 4. Section 5 concludes by presenting some limitations of the taxonomy presented here and future work.

2   Related Work

In the literature, several taxonomies were proposed for the classification of speech acts [7,8]. These were intended for describing human language and are unnecessarily expressive for multi-agent systems. The Foundation for Intelligent Physical Agents (FIPA) [9] uses a small subset of those speech acts in the ACL language such as *request* and *inform*. Their focus was on defining a minimal subset of generic models of communication semantics, rather than on how the speech acts can actually be used based on the task being performed. Our taxonomy does not aim to classify speech acts or the minimal set needed to communicate like the previous works do. Instead, it attempts to use the existing classifications and the task being performed to help identify the types of speech acts that might be needed by a particular agent.

In the area of argumentation, Walton and Krabbe [10] have provided a taxonomy to determine which type of dialogue should be used by identifying the goal behind it (see Figure 1). Their dialogue typology is composed of six formal models:

- **Information-Seeking:** agents ask for information from the other party;
- **Inquiry:** the two parties attempt to answer a question whose answer is unknown by both, but may be answered with their joint knowledge;
- **Persuasion:** one party attempts to change the other party's beliefs;
- **Negotiation:** the participants bargain over the allocation of resources;
- **Deliberation:** the parties collaborate to know which course of action should be done in which situation;
- **Eristic:** the participants quarrel verbally to vent grievances.

We are interested in understanding how a similar taxonomy can be created for task-oriented agents where communication is not defined by the goal of the dialogue, but it is instead determined by the characteristics of the domain and the task to be performed.

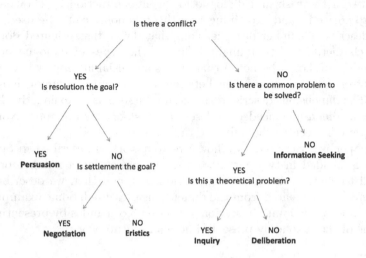

Fig. 1. A categorization to determine the type dialogue, according to Walton and Krabbe pp. 81 [10].

3   Taxonomy

Creating a taxonomy that tells us which type of dialogue is going to be needed by a particular agent can only be achieved if we understand the task and domain where the agent operates. In this section, we look at some dimensions that can be found in the literature, and attempt to understand how they could be used to develop a taxonomy of task-oriented domains of dialogue.

3.1   Finding Dimensions of Task-Oriented Domains

In this section, we present a number of dimensions that characterize task-oriented domains. This allows us to identify how domains determine the communication that is performed by an agent, and consequently, it also tell us something about the implementation requirements behind such an agent. This list is not exhaustive and there is not enough evidence to say that these dimensions are totally independent. In spite of that, we believe that it is representative of the type of dimensions that must be found to create a taxonomy of task-oriented domains of dialogue.

Observability. There is a great incentive to use communication in domains with partial observability and/or incomplete information. Planning for decentralized agents with partial information of the world is significantly more complex than planning for a single agent [11], but if information is shared between agents, the number of possible belief-states is reduced and the problem becomes equivalent to single-agent planning. Cooperative map acquisition by agents is another example where sharing information has been shown to be beneficial [12] to reduce the time needed for acquiring a plausible map. Lack of information is also an issue when the goal of the agents is finding an equilibrium strategy, where no agent could gain from changing strategy, because it might not be possible to find any equilibrium with the known information. In such a scenario, the agents' best choice would be to announce private information [13].

The communication mechanisms in partial observable domains can usually be seen as information-seeking. The questions, however, will depend on the nature of the domain. If the agent needs to acquire knowledge concerning the current state, then this can be seen as a transmission of actions and/or observations using speech acts such as *inform* or *assert*. When the agent seeks to know the likely outcome of the action, then its questions will possibly be requests of the information known by the other agent regarding that action. In the particular case where the questions stem from not knowing the opponent, then the agents will most likely ask about the other's intentions. If it is not possible to confirm the information given by the other agents, then information-seeking will only make sense if the agents are sincere, and sincerity is a rational principle only when the preference functions of the agents align [14].

Types of Actions. The actions that an agent can perform in a determined setting will influence whether dialogue is needed. If there is a finite amount of resources, the agent might want to ask for some of the resources from the other agent (e.g. [15]). This exchange requested is an action that the agent is unable to perform by itself. In a similar fashion, there may also exist actions that the other agent is able to prevent this agent from executing. For example, if the other agent blocks this agent's path. These actions which are naturally dependent of the interaction of the agents are called public in multi-agent planning. They include joint actions, where agents need to synchronize to perform them simultaneously. In contrast, private actions cannot be influenced by other agents and are thus independent of the interaction [16].

Succinctly, we can consider three types of actions: actions that need to be performed by the other agent — usually actions that have to be requested to be executed or avoided — to allow this agent to perform a certain action, private actions that the agent can perform by itself, and joint actions where both agents need to perform it simultaneously. Depending on the action's type, the agents may decide to jointly plan their activity by using a dialogue of deliberation, or may decide to be more competitive and use a process of negotiation [17].

Preferences Over Costs. Communication is not necessarily advantageous in all domains, and it may even be better to avoid it, especially when the cost incurred is too high or the available bandwidth is very restricted. The solution may be to be selective in the type of messages that are exchanged, as for example in [18], where the agents only send the messages that are the most valuable for team performance, or it could even be finding solutions that do not involve communication such as the one proposed in [19], where agents use deduction based on sensory information. However, there are also cases where the cost of the task exceeds the communication cost. For example, in domains presented in [21] where the agents can reduce the walked distance if they exchanged their individual tasks amongst themselves. Depending on the domain, the agent will have a stronger preference over minimizing the cost of the communication or the cost of the task.

Available Interactions. Dialogue is also influenced by the interactions that can be performed between agents in a certain domain. In [20] Tan discusses three types of interaction in cooperative settings: sharing observations, sharing actions that happened, and sharing learned policies or plans. In other settings, exchange of resources (e.g. [15]), or exchange of tasks might also be available (e.g. [21]). The availability of resources is usually scarce and limited, thusly the exchange of resources is more likely to be competitive and require negotiation. On the other hand, the sharing of observations or plans if under an assumption of sincerity is less likely to be competitive, leading to deliberative dialogues.

3.2   Creating a Taxonomy

In section 3.1, we identified four dimensions of task-oriented domains that seem to influence the existence of dialogue and its characteristics: observability, types of actions, preferences over costs, and available interactions. Now, we need to understand how they relate to specific types of dialogue. The categorization of dialogues proposed by Walton and Krabbe [10] mainly focuses on argumentative settings, but can also be used for a broader range of domains due to the heterogeneity of the categories. Most of the speech acts proposed by FIPA (Foundation for Intelligent Physical Agents) in the ACL language [9], the standard language for agent communication, can also be mapped into these categories. For instance some of its speech acts such as *propose* correspond to a dialogue of negotiation, and *query* can be seen in information-seeking dialogue. Therefore, it seems to be justifiable to use this categorization to create an initial model of how a taxonomy for task-oriented domains of dialogue could look like.

From the literature presented, we can see a prevalence of: (*a*) information-seeking, corresponding to information sharing; (*b*) negotiation in competitive settings; and (*c*) deliberation when performing joint tasks. This does not mean that other types of dialogue are not relevant. Negotiation benefits from persuasion and inquiry is a type of information seeking. However, for now, we will focus on the information-seeking, negotiation and deliberation. These categories of dialogue are presented in table 1, along with the a set of speech acts from FIPA associated with each category, the benefit for the agent of using it, and some research fields that might be relevant for creating multi-agent system with that type of dialogue.

Table 1. Types of dialogue used in the taxonomy

Type of Dialogue	FIPA Speech Acts	Benefit	Fields of Interest
Negotiation	propose; accept-proposal; reject-proposal; call-proposals	Reach agreement; Get the best deal to oneself	Automated negotiation; Argumentation; Preferences handling
Deliberation	request; agree; refuse	Reach agreement; Build a joint plan	Argumentation; Shared plans generation; Automated planning
Information-Seeking	inform; query; confirm; disconfirm	Share information; Common understanding of the world	Knowledge representation; Automated reasoning; Belief revision
No Dialogue	—	Avoid cost of dialogue	Centralized multi-agent planning; Offline optimization

Considering the types of dialogue and the dimensions presented, we inferred the relations illustrated in Figure 2. Our reasoning is that an agent might not need to communicate when it has full observability and there are no actions that it cannot perform by itself or that are influenced by other agents. Even so, the agent might decide to communicate if the cost of the task could be decreased by doing so. This is usually possible when an agent may exchange tasks or resources, otherwise the agent will not benefit from the interaction. There are two distinct cases to consider when communication is needed: the case with partial observability and the one with full observability. In the former, the agent's priority will usually be to exchange information if that is possible (e.g. observations, outcomes, intentions). In both cases, the agents would benefit from interacting when performing a joint task. If they are able to exchange plans, then the agents might recur to the use of deliberation, or they might as well simply negotiate tasks and resources if it is not possible to reason cooperatively about the plans to be performed. Even when the agents are not performing a joint task, there might be actions or exchanges that are needed or may affect the agent's goal. This corresponds to the case where the agent needs to communicate, but it is not able to exchange information and it is not performing a joint action. Negotiation of resources or tasks might be suitable in such cases to bargain with the other agent in order to obtain what is needed to reach its goals.

The categories used in the taxonomy are not mutually exclusive and it is possible for agents to require more than one type of dialogue in a certain domain. As stated before, this is only an initial attempt to create a taxonomy for task-oriented domains of dialogue, and more work is needed to fully understand how communication is influenced by the task and the domain. Yet, it is possible to imagine some examples were this taxonomy could be useful. We present two examples of this in the following section.

4   Examples

In this section, we present two examples of how the taxonomy presented could be useful for creating multi-agent systems. In the first example, we use the taxonomy to identify the type of dialogue for a given domain. In the second example,

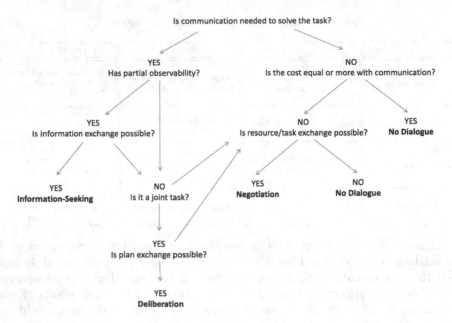

Fig. 2. A categorization to determine the type dialogue that the agents need to perform taking in consideration the domain they inhabit.

we explain how the taxonomy could potentially help in the creation of more flexible agents able to deal with different domains.

Example 1. The most obvious application of the taxonomy is to identify the most adequate type of dialogue for a particular domain. We will exemplify this with two agents whose task is to vacuum a number of rooms separated by walls that are not soundproof. For efficiency purposes, the agents will avoid repeated work. Looking at the taxonomy, it seems that an information-seeking dialogue fits this problem. Communication is needed, because there is partial information (the agents do not see which rooms have been vacuumed), and information exchange is possible (the walls are not soundproof). After knowing the type of dialogue, the concrete speech acts that might be useful can be found in table 1. In this particular case, the speech act inform might be enough for this system. The different types of dialogues are also closely related to certain fields of research. Thusly, it can give us an idea that the work done in knowledge representation and belief revision might be relevant for modeling this multi-agent system.

Example 2. Another potential application of such taxonomy is the creation of more flexible agents that can deal with several domains. Imagine an agent or a set of agents able to generate the different types of dialogue presented in the taxonomy. If the agent was able to identify the dialogue needs from the domain description given, then it could use a subset of algorithms or sub-agents that can deal with such a dialogue. In other words, given a description of a domain and task, the agent would look at the task, and decide if it could solve the task without communication, and if it discovers that it can not, then it would proceed to see if there is partial information in the world, and so on. For this, the agent must have some algorithm to obtain the input needed. For example, if the agent identifies the type of dialogue as negotiation, then it knowns that it needs to create a set of deals with the resources available, and generate a dialogue of negotiation. This is a theoretical abstract use of the taxonomy, but it shows that it might be possible to create more flexible communicative agents, if we identify how the domain correlates with the types of dialogue needed in it.

5   Conclusions and Further Work

In this paper, we presented an initial study of how to create a taxonomy where domains are categorized according to a number of dimensions which determine the dialogue required by agents inhabiting those domains. We believe that such a taxonomy can help identify the requirements for creating more flexible agents able to deal with different domains, and it can give insights of how work created in different areas of research correlate with each other. The taxonomy presented is simple, and there is still a lot of work to be done. For example, it is not easy to understand how preferences over the communication can influence the dialogue. In the future, we plan to look at the literature to identify the different techniques used to reduce or avoid communication overhead and how they influence the types of dialogue. We also intend to drop the assumption regarding the agents' honesty. We imagine that these directions will lead to a more accurate taxonomy, where there might be very little or no dialogue when the communication cost is very high or when trust between agents is not possible. Another possible direction consists of analyzing how dialogue is influenced by the absence of a shared language amongst the agents. We predict that this might increase the negotiation required even in domains where this type of dialogue is not common, due to the need of agreeing on a symbol for a particular object when its definition differs amongst agents. It would also be interesting to explore how the social needs of the other agents may also affect the agent's actions in a certain domain.

Acknowledgments. The research presented in this paper has been funded by the European Community's Seventh Framework Programme (FP7/2007-2013) under grant agreement no. 567652 *ESSENCE: Evolution of Shared Semantics in Computational Environments* (http://www.essence-network.com/).

References

1. Ghallab, M., Nau, D., Traverso, P.: Automated Planning: Theory and Practice. Morgan Kaufmann, San Francisco (2004)
2. Meneguzzi, F., de Silva, L.: Planning in BDI agents: a survey of the integration of planning algorithms and agent reasoning. The Knowledge Engineering Review **30**, 1–44 (2015)

3. Rahwan, I., Simari, G.R. (eds.).: Argumentation in artificial intelligence, vol. 47. Springer (2009)

4. Jennings, N.R., Faratin, P., et al.: Automated negotiation: prospects, methods and challenges. Group Decision and Negotiation 10(2), 199–215 (2001)

5. Nicoletta, F., Viganó, F.: Colombetti. M.: Agent communication and artificial institutions. Autonomous Agents and Multi-Agent Systems 14(2), 121–142 (2007)

6. Goldman, C.V., Zilberstein, S.: Optimizing information exchange in cooperative multi-agent systems. In: the 2nd international joint conference on Autonomous agents and multiagent system, pp. 137–144. ACM (2003)

7. Austin, J.L.: How To Do Things With Words. In: Urmson, J.O., Sbisà, M. (eds.). Oxford, Oxford University Press (1975)

8. Searle, J.R.: A taxonomy of illocutionary acts. Language in Society 5(1–23), 344–369 (1975)

9. O'Brian, P.D., Nicol, R.C.: FIPA: Towards a Standard for Software Agents. BT Technology Journal 16(3), 51–59 (1998)

10. Walton, D.N., Krabbe, E.C.W.: Commitment in Dialogue: Basic Concepts of Interpersonal Reasoning. State University of New York Press, SUNY Series in Logic and Language (1995)

11. Bernstein, D.S., Givan, R., et al.: The complexity of decentralized control of Markov decision processes. Mathematics of Operations Research 27(4), 819–840 (2002)

12. López-Sánchez, M., Esteva, F., et al.: Map generation by cooperative low-cost robots in structured unknown environments. In: Autonomous Agents. Springer (1998)

13. Jackson, M.O., Simon, L.K. et al.: Communication and equilibrium in discontinuous games of incomplete information. Econometrica, pp. 1711–1740 (2002)

14. Asher, N., Lascarides, A.: Strategic Conversation. Semantics and Pragmatics 6(2), 1–62 (2013)

15. Gal, Y., Grosz, B. et al.: Colored Trails: a Formalism for Investigating Decision-Making in Strategic Environments. In: Workshop on Reasoning, Representation and Learning in Computer Games, pp. 25–30. AAAI Press, Menlo Park (2005)

16. Brafman, R.I., Domshlak, C.: From one to many: planning for loosely coupled multi-agent systems. In: The 8th International Conference on Automated Planning and Scheduling, pp. 28–35 (2008)

17. Doran, J.E., Franklin, S.R.J.N., et al.: On cooperation in multi-agent systems. The Knowledge Engineering Review 12(3), 309–314 (1997)

18. Roth, M., Simmons, R., Veloso, M.: What to communicate? Execution-time decision in multi-agent POMDPs. In: Distributed Autonomous Robotic Systems 7, pp. 177–186. Springer (2006)

19. Genesereth, M.R., Ginsberg, M.L., Rosenschein, J.S.: Cooperation without communication, Heuristic Programming Project, Computer Science Department, pp. 51–57. Stanford University (1984)

20. Tan, M.: Multi-agent reinforcement learning: Independent vs. cooperative agents. In: The 10th international conference on machine learning, pp. 330–337 (1993)

21. Rosenschein, J.S., Zlotkin, G.: Rules of Encounter: Designing Conventions for Automated Negotiation Among Computers. MIT Press, Cambridge (1994)

Mechanism Design for Argumentation-Based Information-Seeking and Inquiry

Xiuyi Fan and Francesca Toni[(✉)]

Imperial College London, London, UK
{xf309,ft}@imperial.ac.uk

Abstract. Formal argumentation-based dialogue systems have attracted considerable research interest in the past. Most research in this area introduce "dialectical wrappers" over argumentation formalisms to model verbal interactions amongst agents, resulting in different dialogue models for different types of dialogues, e.g. inquiry or persuasion. In this work, we take a different approach by deploying a single dialogue model for different types of dialogues, focusing in particular on *information-seeking* and *inquiry*, yet equipping agents with different (game-theoretic) strategies and different utility functions in different dialogue types. We prove that the resulting dialogue-based mechanisms implement, in dominant strategies, appropriate social choice functions for the two types of dialogues we consider. Thus, we show the feasibility of studying agents in argumentation-based dialogues in game-theoretic, mechanism design terms.

1 Introduction

Formal argumentation-based dialogue systems have attracted considerable research interest in the past, e.g. see [11,2,9,7]. Work in this area predominantly introduces dialogue protocols connecting dialectical concepts, e.g. utterances and successful dialogues, with argumentation concepts, e.g. arguments and argumentation semantics. Most such existing dialogue models are built for specific types of dialogues, e.g. [11] is built for persuasion and [2] is built for inquiry. In this work, we obtain models for two types of dialogues, i.e. *information-seeking* and *inquiry*, by adapting an existing, generic dialogue model [4,7], based on Assumption-based Argumentation (ABA) [3,12] as the underlying argumentation formalism. This dialogue model is generic in that it is neutral as to which type of dialogues it is applied to. We provide suitable instantiations of this generic model by studying agent strategic behaviours, in two specific types of dialogues we consider.

We view dialogues as games and utterances as actions in these games; agents in different dialogues have different utility profiles and thus choose different actions. Following Walton and Krabbe's characterisation of information-seeking and inquiry dialogues in [13], summarised in Table 1, in these dialogue types, agents can thus be understood as having different objectives, corresponding to different utility profiles, and need to determine the appropriate information to disclose within the utterances they make.

© Springer International Publishing Switzerland 2015
Q. Chen et al. (Eds.): PRIMA 2015, LNAI 9387, pp. 519–527, 2015.
DOI: 10.1007/978-3-319-25524-8_34

Table 1. Information-seeking and inquiry dialogues (from [13]).

	Information-seeking	Inquiry Dialogue
Initial Situation:	Personal ignorance	General ignorance
Main Goal:	Spreading knowledge	Growth of knowledge & agreement
Participant's Aims:	Gain, show or hide knowledge	Find a "proof" or destroy one

By using the dialogue model of [4,7] we choose ABA as the underlying argumentation formalism. ABA is suitable for our proposed model of information-seeking and inquiry dialogues as it allows sub-argument level modelling of agents' knowledge: as we illustrate later, agents are thus able to jointly construct arguments via dialogues. Other forms of structured argumentation, e.g. ASPIC+ [10], would also serve this purpose. We use ABA because it underpins our chosen dialogue model [4,7]. Main building blocks of this dialogue model include *legal-move functions*, defining dialogue protocols, and *strategy-move functions*, defining agent behaviours.

The challenge of this work is twofold. Firstly, in order to study dialogues using game theoretic concepts, we need to map dialogue notions into game notions. It is expected that such a mapping is systematic in the sense that dialogues of different types share a common ground, i.e. generic dialogue models can be mapped to "generic game models". Secondly, to properly model agents in different types of dialogues, different agent utilities need to be defined. The defined utilities need to reflect agents behaviours in these dialogues. We overcome both challenges in this work.

The main contribution of this work is to prove that the game-theoretic analysis we provide results in mechanisms that implement dominant strategies, in a mechanism-design sense [8]. This means that rational agents engaged in these types of dialogues will truthfully disclose information leading to successful outcomes of these dialogues.

2   Background and Preliminaries

In addition to the standard ABA framework definition given in [3], we use the *related* and *rule-related* notions defined in [5].

Agents have private beliefs in some internal representation. When they interact dialectically they exchange information in a shared language. We assume that this language is that of ABA, namely agents exchange rules, assumptions and their contraries, expressed in some shared underlying logical language $\mathcal{L}$. Thus, agents can be thought of as being equipped with ABA frameworks. We will often use the ABA framework an agent is equipped with to denote the agent itself. We will focus on the case of two agents, $\alpha = \langle \mathcal{L}, \mathcal{R}_1, \mathcal{A}_1, \mathcal{C}_1 \rangle$ and $\beta = \langle \mathcal{L}, \mathcal{R}_2, \mathcal{A}_2, \mathcal{C}_2 \rangle$. The *joint framework* (of α and β) is $\mathcal{F}_J = \alpha \uplus \beta = \langle \mathcal{L}, \mathcal{R}_1 \cup \mathcal{R}_2, \mathcal{A}_1 \cup \mathcal{A}_2, \mathcal{C}_J \rangle$, where $\mathcal{C}_J(\alpha) = \mathcal{C}_1(\alpha) \cup \mathcal{C}_2(\alpha)$, for all α in $\mathcal{A}_1 \cup \mathcal{A}_2$.[1] We will assume that α, β and $\alpha \uplus \beta$ are flat, in line with [3]. Intuitively, $\mathcal{F}_J = \alpha \uplus \beta$ amounts to the beliefs that

---

[1] We assume that $\mathcal{C}_i(\alpha) = \{\}$ if $\alpha \notin \mathcal{A}_i$, for $i = 1, 2$.

the two agents would hold collectively, if they were prepared to disclose them truthfully.

We use ABA dialogues given in [4,7], with notions including *legal-move functions*. To generate dialogues fulfilling agents' aims, *strategy-move* functions [5] are used. A *strategy-move function* for agent x is a mapping $\phi : \mathcal{D} \times \Lambda \mapsto 2^{\mathcal{U}^x}$ ($\mathcal{D}$ denotes the set of all dialogues; Λ denotes the set of all legal-move functions; $\mathcal{U}^x$ denotes all possible utterances from x), such that, given $\lambda \in \Lambda$ and $\delta \in \mathcal{D}$: $\phi(\delta, \lambda) \subseteq \lambda(\delta)$. Given a dialogue $\delta = \langle u_1, \ldots, u_n \rangle$ between agents x, y compatible with a legal-move function λ and a strategy-move function ϕ for x, if for all utterances u_m made by x, $u_m \in \phi(\langle u_1, \ldots, u_{m-1} \rangle, \lambda)$, then x *uses* ϕ in δ. If x and y both use ϕ, then δ is *constructed with* ϕ.

There are three particular strategy-move functions we use in this work: *thorough (ϕ_h)*, *non-attack thorough (ϕ_{nh})* and *pass (ϕ_p)* strategy-move functions [5]. Informally:

- A dialogue constructed with ϕ_h contains all information that is relevant to the topic from both agents. Dialogues constructed with ϕ_h have the desirable property that admissible arguments obtained in the dialogue are admissible in the joint ABA framework of the two agents (see Theorem 1 in [5]).
- Agents using ϕ_{nh} utter all rules and assumptions, but not contraries that are related to some utterance in the dialogue.
- Agents using ϕ_p make the claim and utter no rule, assumption or contrary in the dialogue.

We use standard *Mechanism Design* (e.g. see [8]) notions including *type, outcome, social choice function, strategy,* and *dominance*. To study agent behaviours in a framework of games, we map dialogue notions into game-theoretic notions, as follows.

Definition 1. *[6] The types for agents α, β are $\theta_\alpha = \alpha$ and $\theta_\beta = \beta$.*

In ABA dialogues, we view utterances as agents' actions, as follows.

Definition 2. *[6] The action spaces for agent $x \in \{\alpha, \beta\}$ is $2^{\mathcal{U}^x}$.*

We define the *dialogue strategy* for an agent x as the set of utterances made by x in a dialogue.

Definition 3. *[6] Given a dialogue $\mathcal{D}_\alpha^\beta(\chi) = \delta$, the dialogue strategy s_x^δ for agent $x \in \{\alpha, \beta\}$ with respect to δ is such that $s_x^\delta(\theta_x, \delta) = \{u | u = \langle x, \_, \_, \_, \_ \rangle \in \delta\}$.*

Since s_x^δ returns the set of utterances made by x in δ, which is determined by the strategy-move function ϕ used by x, we can thus equate a dialogue strategy used by an agent with the strategy-move function used by this agent in this dialogue.

Given a dialogue δ, the ABA framework drawn from δ captures all information disclosed by both agents in δ. Thus, we let the game-theoretic outcome be the ABA framework drawn from a dialogue, formally:

Definition 4. *[6] The* outcomes *are* $\mathcal{O} = \{\mathcal{F} | \mathcal{F} \in \mathcal{AF}(\mathcal{L})$ *and* $\mathcal{F} = \mathcal{F}_\delta$ *for some* $\delta \in \mathcal{D}\}$.

The *outcome function* maps agent actions to outcomes as follows.

Definition 5. *[6] The* outcome function *for* $\sigma_1 \in \Sigma_1, \sigma_2 \in \Sigma_2$ *is:* $g(\sigma_1, \sigma_2) = \sigma_1 \uplus \sigma_2$.

Note that notions given in this section are generic and do not depend on the types of dialogues agents are engaged in. These notions serve as the common ground for both information-seeking and inquiry dialogues, introduced in the next two sections.

We will illustrate notions/results in the context of the following example (used in [5]), adapted from the movie *Twelve Angry Men*, an example of argumentative reasoning [1]. We focus on the reasoning of two jurors: juror 8, played by Henry Fonda (α), and juror 9, played by Joseph Sweeney (β). These agents need to decide whether to condemn a boy, accused of murder, or acquit him, after a trial where two witnesses have provided evidence against the boy. According to the law, the jurors should acquit the boy if they do not believe that the trial has proven him guilty convincingly.

Example 1. Table 2 gives the ABA frameworks of α and β (as indicated in the rightmost column) as well as their joint framework $\mathcal{F}_J$ (given by the entire leftmost column). The components of these ABA frameworks should be self-explanatory. For example, the first rule says that the boy should be deemed to be innocent if it cannot be proven guilty. This can be assumed (as boy_not_proven_guilty $\in \mathcal{A}_1 = \mathcal{A}_2 = \mathcal{A}_J$) but can be objected to, by proving its contrary (boy_proven_guilty). The second and third rules provide ways to prove this contrary, and they rely upon assumptions in turn, etc.

3   Information Seeking Dialogues

Following [5], we model information-seeking dialogues as engaging a *questioner* agent α posing a topic, χ, and an *answerer* agent β uttering information of relevance to χ. The purpose is to spread knowledge about arguments for χ. We assume that the questioner contributes no information, apart from initiating the dialogue; and the answerer is interested in conveying information *for* χ, but not *against*. In ABA terms, the initial situation is that some $A \vdash \chi$ is in β but is not in α; and the main goal is to find δ such that all $A \vdash \chi$ in β are in $\mathcal{F}_\delta$.

Example 2. (Example 1 continued.) An information-seeking dialogue is shown in Table 3, in which the questioner queries about *w1_not_believable*.

In this example β is the questioner and α is the answerer. Note that here all rules used are known to the answerer only. The (game-theoretic) outcome of this dialogue is the framework $\mathcal{F}_\delta = \langle \mathcal{L}, \mathcal{R}_\delta, \mathcal{A}_\delta, \mathcal{C}_\delta \rangle$, in which:

Table 2. ABA frameworks for Example 1. $\mathcal{L}$ is implicit here and in all examples as it contains all sentences in rules, assumptions, and contraries.

Rules: ($\mathcal{R}_J$)	
boy_innocent ← boy_not_proven_guilty	α, β
boy_proven_guilty ← w1_is_believable	α, β
boy_proven_guilty ← w2_is_believable	α, β
w1_not_believable ← w1_contradicted_by_w2	α
w1_contradicted_by_w2 ←	α
w2_not_believable ← w2_has_poor_eyesight	α
w2_has_poor_eyesight ←	β
w2_is_blond ←	β
w1_is_poor ←	β
Assumptions: ($\mathcal{A}_J$)	
boy_not_proven_guilty	α, β
w1_is_believable	α, β
w2_is_believable	α, β
Contraries: ($\mathcal{C}_J$)	
$\mathcal{C}$(boy_not_proven_guilty) = {boy_proven_guilty}	α, β
$\mathcal{C}$(w1_is_believable) = {w1_is_not_believable}	α, β
$\mathcal{C}$(w2_is_believable) = {w2_is_not_believable}	α, β

Table 3. Information-seeking dialogue for the two agents in example 1.

$\langle \beta, \alpha, 0, claim(w1\_not\_believable), 1 \rangle$
$\langle \alpha, \beta, 1, rl(w1\_not\_believable \leftarrow w1\_contradicted\_by\_w2), 2 \rangle$
$\langle \alpha, \beta, 2, rl(w1\_contradicted\_by\_w2 \leftarrow), 3 \rangle$

$\mathcal{R}_\delta = \{w1\_not\_believable \leftarrow w1\_contradicted\_by\_w2,$
        $w1\_contradicted\_by\_w2 \leftarrow \};$
$\mathcal{A}_\delta = \{\}$; for all $a \in \mathcal{A}_\delta$, $\mathcal{C}(a) = \{\}$.

The instantiation of the mechanism design paradigm to dialogue types requires the definition of suitable utility functions, matching the motivations of agents engaged in the dialogues. In the case of information-seeking, the questioner agent can be deemed to be solely interested in posing the question, whereas the answerer agent is interested in disclosing any argument for the claim in question. This leads to the following definition of information-seeking utilities:

Definition 6. *Given an outcome* $\mathcal{F}_\delta = \langle \mathcal{L}, \mathcal{R}_\delta, \mathcal{A}_\delta, \mathcal{C}_\delta \rangle$ *drawn from* $\delta = \mathcal{D}_\beta^\alpha(\chi)$, *the* information-seeking utilities *of agents* α *and* $\beta = \langle \mathcal{L}, \mathcal{R}_\beta, \mathcal{A}_\beta, \mathcal{C}_\beta \rangle$ *are*

- $v_\alpha(\delta, \alpha) = \begin{cases} 1 & \text{if } \chi \in \mathcal{L}; \\ 0 & \text{otherwise.} \end{cases}$
- $v_\beta(\delta, \beta) = -|U_1| - |U_2|$ *where*[2]
  - $U_1 = \{u \in \mathcal{R}_\beta \cup \mathcal{A}_\beta|$ *there is some* $v \in \mathcal{R}_\delta$ *such that* u *is related to* v *or* χ *but* u *is not in* $\mathcal{F}_\delta\};$ *and*
  - $U_2 = \{u|u$ *is in* $\mathcal{F}_\delta$ *but not in* $\beta\}.$

---

[2] Given a set S, $|S|$ denotes the cardinality of S.

In the remainder of this section, agents are equipped with information-seeking utilities v_α and v_β as in Definition 6.

The following theorem sanctions that for agents with information-seeking utilities, ϕ_p is the dominant strategy for the questioner agent; and ϕ_{nh} is the dominant strategy for the answerer agent.

Theorem 1. *Given $\mathcal{D}_\beta^\alpha(\chi) = \delta$, if δ is constructed with α using ϕ_p and β using ϕ_{nh}, then the dialogue strategy s^δ is dominant.*

We define the social choice function for Information-seeking (IS) as follows:

Definition 7. *The IS social choice function is: $f_{is}(\theta_\alpha, \theta_\beta) = \langle \mathcal{L}, \mathcal{R}_f, \mathcal{A}_f, \mathcal{C}_f \rangle$, in which:*

- *$\mathcal{R}_f = \{\rho \in \theta_\beta | \rho$ is rule-related to χ in $\theta_\beta\}$;*
- *$\mathcal{A}_f = \{a \in \theta_\beta | a$ is rule-related to χ in $\theta_\beta\}$;*
- *$\mathcal{C}_f(a) = \{\}$ for all $a \in \mathcal{A}_f$.*

The intuition of Definition 7 is that the "common good" for both agents in information-seeking can be viewed as the answerer agents putting forward all arguments for the claim in question but nothing else. So truthful information is passed from the answerer agent to the questioner agent.

The next theorem sanctions that the questioner agent using ϕ_p and the answerer agent using ϕ_{nh} not only maximise their own utilities, but also meet the common good.

Theorem 2. *Given $\mathcal{D}_\beta^\alpha(\chi) = \delta$, if δ is constructed with α using ϕ_p and β using ϕ_{nh}, then the mechanism $\mathcal{M} = (\Sigma, s^\delta)$ implements the IS social choice function f_{is}.*

4   Inquiry Dialogues

The specification of inquiry dialogues seen in Table 1 lends itself to several argumentation-based interpretations. In [5] , we consider two such interpretations and accordingly formulate inquiry dialogue in two ways, in I-Type I dialogues, the initial situation is that it is uncertain if χ is admissible in $\mathcal{F}_J$; the main goal is that testing the admissibility of χ in $\mathcal{F}_J$; and in I-Type II dialogues; the initial situation is that there is no argument $A \vdash \chi$ in either α or β; and the main goal is testing whether $A \vdash \chi$ is in $\mathcal{F}_J$.

Example 3. An I-Type inquiry dialogue is shown in Table 4[3]. Here, we can see that the (game theoretic) outcome $\mathcal{F}_\delta$ is the joint framework of the two agents F_J (Table 2).

The utility functions of agents engaged in I-TYPE I dialogues is defined as follows:

---

[3] Here, guilty, W1, not_W1, contradicted, W2, not_W2 are shorthands for boy_proven_guilty, w1_is_believable, w1_not_believable, w1_contradicted_by_w2, w2_is_believable, w2_not_believable, respectively.

Table 4. Inquiry dialogue for the two agents in example 1.

$\langle \alpha, \beta, 0, claim(boy\_innocent), 1 \rangle$
$\langle \beta, \alpha, 1, rl(boy\_innocent \leftarrow boy\_not\_proven\_guilty), 2 \rangle$
$\langle \alpha, \beta, 2, asm(boy\_not\_proven\_guilty), 3 \rangle$
$\langle \beta, \alpha, 3, ctr(boy\_not\_proven\_guilty, guilty), 4 \rangle$
$\langle \alpha, \beta, 4, rl(guilty \leftarrow W1), 5 \rangle$
$\langle \beta, \alpha, 5, asm(W1), 6 \rangle$
$\langle \alpha, \beta, 6, ctr(W1, not\_W1), 7 \rangle$
$\langle \alpha, \beta, 7, rl(not\_W1 \leftarrow contradicted), 8 \rangle$
$\langle \alpha, \beta, 8, rl(contradicted \leftarrow), 9 \rangle$
$\langle \beta, \alpha, 4, rl(guilty \leftarrow W2), 10 \rangle$
$\langle \alpha, \beta, 10, asm(W2), 11 \rangle$
$\langle \beta, \alpha, 11, ctr(W2, not\_W2), 12 \rangle$
$\langle \alpha, \beta, 12, rl(not\_W2 \leftarrow W2\_has\_poor\_eyesight), 13 \rangle$
$\langle \beta, \alpha, 13, rl(W2\_has\_poor\_eyesight \leftarrow), 14 \rangle$

Definition 8. *Given an outcome* $\mathcal{F}_\delta = \langle \mathcal{L}, \mathcal{R}_\delta, \mathcal{A}_\delta, \mathcal{C}_\delta \rangle$ *drawn from some* δ, *the* I-Type I utility *of agent* $x = \langle \mathcal{L}, \mathcal{R}_x, \mathcal{A}_x, \mathcal{C}_x \rangle$ *is* $v_x(\mathcal{F}_\delta, x) = -|U_1| - |U_2|$ *where*

- $U_1 = \{u \in \mathcal{R}_x \cup \mathcal{A}_x \cup \mathcal{C}_x|$ *there is some* $v \in \mathcal{R}_\delta \cup \mathcal{A}_\delta \cup \mathcal{C}_\delta$ *such that* u *is related to* v *but* u *is not in* $\mathcal{F}_\delta\}$; *and*
- $U_2 = \{u|u$ *is in* $\mathcal{F}_\delta$ *but not in* $x\}$.

In the remainder of this section, until Definition 10, agents are equipped with I-Type I utilities v_α and v_β as in Definition 8. Intuitively, this definition of I-Type I utility reflects that agents engaged in this type of dialogues are interested in finding out the acceptability of the claim in question, with respect to the joint knowledge. The following result identifies agent strategy functions that are dominant for agents with I-Type I utility functions.

Theorem 3. *Given* $\mathcal{D}_\beta^\alpha(\chi) = \delta$, *if* δ *is constructed with* ϕ_h, *then the dialogue strategy* s^δ *is dominant.*

In order to characterise the common good for agents in I-Type I dialogues, we define the following social choice function for I-Type I:

Definition 9. *Let* $\mathcal{F}_J = \theta_\alpha \uplus \theta_\beta$. *The* I-Type I social choice function *is:* $f_{i1}(\theta_\alpha, \theta_\beta) = \langle \mathcal{L}, \mathcal{R}_{i1}, \mathcal{A}_{i1}, \mathcal{C}_{i1} \rangle$, *in which:*

- $\mathcal{R}_{i1} = \{\rho \in \mathcal{F}_J|\rho$ *is related to* χ *in* $\mathcal{F}_J\}$;
- $\mathcal{A}_{i1} = \{a \in \mathcal{F}_J|a$ *is related to* χ *in* $\mathcal{F}_J\}$;
- $\mathcal{C}_{i1}(a) = \mathcal{C}_J(a)$ *for all* $a \in \mathcal{A}_{i1}$.

The intuition of Definition 9 is that the common good for agents in I-Type I dialogues is that the acceptability of the claim in question is thoroughly examined with respect to the joint knowledge held by both agents. Thus any information related to the claim in question in one agent's internal knowledge base must be disclosed. The following theorem sanctions that dialogues constructed with ϕ_h meet this common good.

Theorem 4. *Given $\mathcal{D}_\beta^\alpha(\chi) = \delta$, if δ is constructed with ϕ_h, then the mechanism $\mathcal{M} = (\Sigma, s^\delta)$ implements the I Type-I social choice function.*

By altering the utility functions, we can model agents' behaviour in I-Type II agents too, as follows. Since agents in I-Type II aim at jointly finding all arguments for the claim in question, there is no need for them to utter contraries that may lead to arguments attacking the claim.

Definition 10. *Given an outcome $\mathcal{F}_\delta$ drawn from some I-Type II dialogue $\delta = \mathcal{D}_\beta^\alpha(\chi)$, the utility of agent $x = \langle \mathcal{L}, \mathcal{R}_x, \mathcal{A}_x, \mathcal{C}_x \rangle$ is $v_x(\delta, x) = -|U_1| - |U_2|$ where*

- $U_1 = \{u | u \in \mathcal{R}_x \cup \mathcal{A}_x$ *such that u is rule-related to χ but u is not in $\mathcal{F}_\delta\}$; and*
- $U_2 = \{u | u$ *is in $\mathcal{F}_\delta$ but not in $x\}$.*

In the remainder of this section agents are equipped with utilities v_α and v_β as in Definition 10. Similarly to Theorem 3, the following theorem sanctions that ϕ_{nh} is a dominant strategy for both agents in I-Type II dialogues.

Theorem 5. *Given $\mathcal{D}_\beta^\alpha(\chi) = \delta$, if δ is constructed with ϕ_{nh}, then the dialogue strategy s^δ is dominant.*

Similarly to the case of I-Type I dialogues, we define the social choice function for I-Type II dialogues as follows. The common good for agents in I-Type II is on finding all rules and assumptions that form arguments for the claim.

Definition 11. *Let $\mathcal{F}_J = \theta_\alpha \uplus \theta_\beta = \langle \mathcal{L}, \mathcal{R}_J, \mathcal{A}_J, \mathcal{C}_J \rangle$. The I-Type II social choice function is: $f_{i2}(\theta_\alpha, \theta_\beta) = \langle \mathcal{L}, \mathcal{R}_{i2}, \mathcal{A}_{i2}, \mathcal{C}_{i2} \rangle$, in which:*

- $\mathcal{R}_{i2} = \{\rho \in \mathcal{R}_J | \rho$ *is rule-related to χ in $\mathcal{F}_J\}$;*
- $\mathcal{A}_{i2} = \{a \in \mathcal{F}_J | a$ *is rule-related to χ in $\mathcal{F}_J\}$;*
- $\mathcal{C}_{i2}(a) = \{\}$ *for all $a \in \mathcal{A}_{i2}$.*

Dialogues constructed with ϕ_{nh} meet the common good for both agents.

Theorem 6. *Given $\mathcal{D}_\beta^\alpha(\chi) = \delta$, if δ is constructed with ϕ_{nh}, the mechanism $\mathcal{M} = (\Sigma, s^\delta)$ implements the I Type-II social choice function f_{i2}.*

5   Conclusions

Formal argumentation-based dialogue systems have attracted considerable research interest in the past, e.g. see [11,2,9,7]. Different protocols were proposed to model agents in different types of dialogues. Less work has been devoted to understanding agents' strategic behaviours in dialogues. In this work, we study the modelling of information-seeking and inquiry dialogues with game theoretical notions. Continuing our previous work in modelling agents' interests, strategies and actions in persuasion dialogues, we show that a generic correspondence between dialectical concepts and game notions can be established. Thus, this works links argumentation-based dialogues with games. We establish a natural equivalence between agents' dialectical strategies and their game theoretical strategies.

One of the main observations of this work is that by analysing two different types of dialogues, we establish some common ground for modelling dialogues with game-theoretic notions and recognise that altering agents' utility profiles alone is sufficient for modelling different agent behaviours in different types of dialogues. With this setting, we can also look at agent behaviours in a mechanism design perspective in which certain social choices are fulfilled, naturally corresponding to the aims of the dialogues.

We believe that the utility functions we have defined are natural. In any case, in the future, we would like to explore other utility settings for information-seeking and inquiry dialogues and study game theoretical modelling of other types of dialogues, including deliberation and negotiation.

Acknowledgments. This research was supported by the EPSRC TRaDAr project *Transparent Rational Decisions by Argumentation*: EP/J020915/1.

References

1. Alcolea-Banegas, J.: Teaching argumentation theory and practice: the case of *12 angry men*. In: Blackburn, P., van Ditmarsch, H., Manzano, M., Soler-Toscano, F. (eds.) Tools for Teaching Logic. LNCS, vol. 6680, pp. 1–8. Springer, Heidelberg (2011)
2. Black, E., Hunter, A.: An inquiry dialogue system. JAAMAS **19**, 173–209 (2009)
3. Dung, P.M., Kowalski, R.A., Toni, F.: Assumption-based argumentation. In: Argumentation in Artificial Intelligence, pp. 199–218. Springer (2009)
4. Fan, X., Toni, F.: Assumption-based argumentation dialogues. In: Proc. IJCAI (2011)
5. Fan, X., Toni, F.: Agent strategies for ABA-based information-seeking and Inquiry dialogues. In: Proc. ECAI (2012)
6. Fan, X., Toni, F.: Mechanism design for argumentation-based persuasion. In: Proc. COMMA. IOS Press (2012)
7. Fan, X., Toni, F.: A general framework for sound assumption-based argumentation dialogues. Artificial Intelligence **216**, 20–54 (2014)
8. Jackson, M.: Mechanism theory. In: Derigs, U. (ed.) Optimization and Operations Research. EOLSS Publishers, Oxford (2003)
9. McBurney, P., Parsons, S.: Dialogue games for agent argumentation. In: Argumentation in Artificial Intelligence, pp. 261–280. Springer (2009)
10. Modgil, S., Prakken, H.: The ASPIC$^+$ framework for structured argumentation: a tutorial. Argument & Computation **5**(1), 31–62 (2014)
11. Prakken, H.: Formal systems for persuasion dialogue. Knowledge Engineering Review **21**(2), 163–188 (2006)
12. Toni, F.: A tutorial on assumption-based argumentation. Argument & Computation, Special Issue: Tutorials on Structured Argumentation **5**(1), 89–117 (2014)
13. Walton, D, Krabbe, E.: Commitment in Dialogue: Basic concept of interpersonal reasoning. State University of New York Press (1995)

Fair Assessment of Group Work by Mutual Evaluation with Irresponsible and Collusive Students Using Trust Networks

Yumeno Shiba, Haruna Umegaki, and Toshiharu Sugawara[✉]

Department of Computer Science and Communications Engineering,
Waseda University, Tokyo 1698555, Japan
{y.shiba,h.umegaki}@isl.cs.waseda.ac.jp, sugawara@waseda.jp

Abstract. We propose a fair peer assessment method for group work using a multi-agent trust network. Although group work is an effective educational method, accurately assessing individual students is not easy. Mutual evaluation is often used for such assessment, but often presents some potential problems such as irresponsible evaluations and collusion. Our method identifies and excludes such cheating and unfair ratings on the basis of trust networks that are often used to evaluate sellers in e-market places by using customers' ratings. We assume a group-work course in a semester in which students mutually evaluate other group members a few (three to five) times. We introduce the iterative method for alternately generating trust networks using cluster-trust values, which represent similarity of evaluations in a cluster network. We experimentally show that our method can find the irresponsible students and collusive groups and considerably improve accuracy of final marks with only a few chances for mutual evaluations, and thereby, can provide useful information for assessments to instructors.

1 Introduction

Group work is an effective educational method and widely used in universities and at companies. For example, students in a programming course doing group work are divided into a number of groups, and then the individual group members collaboratively work on assignments provided by the instructor. This process of collaboration enables students to obtain knowledge from each other [3], improve their cooperation skills [7], and learn leadership [2,5]. Although group work is an appropriate method to study practical subjects such as programming in which learning-by-doing is more effective than lecture-style rote learning [1], instructors often cannot identify the specific contributions of individual students, especially in large classes. As a result, they tend to give the same scores to all students in the same group by reviewing the group outcome.

However, this often leads to unfair individual assessments, so serious students may complain and lose their motivation to work hard. For example, all the work is sometimes done by only a few students, and less motivated (free-rider) students

© Springer International Publishing Switzerland 2015
Q. Chen et al. (Eds.): PRIMA 2015, LNAI 9387, pp. 528–537, 2015.
DOI: 10.1007/978-3-319-25524-8_35

do not participate in the collaboration at all [5]. Such free-rider students are likely to be more numerous in large classes [8], because instructors cannot monitor all activities. Mutual evaluation by peer assessment is one effective way to reduce such unfairness of assessment because students can observe the activities of other students in the same group. However, there are some issues to be addressed in mutual evaluation, such as irresponsible evaluations, hard/soft ratings, and collusion groups. In addition, correct evaluation is difficult for students because they are required to have enough knowledge for evaluations.

The purpose of this paper is to propose a fair assessment in group work using an iterative-rating method based on trust networks generated from mutual evaluations submitted by students. A trust network is a technique used in e-market places [13] to rate sellers by customers opinions. Because many irresponsible and hostile raters exist, the trust network is often used to identify raters whose comments are trustworthy or not [6]. We use this network: in a trust network, nodes are students, and edges express similarity/consistency of evaluations between nodes. The method then extracts the mutually consistent clusters in the network and only uses evaluations done by students there. The authors [10] already proposed a simple method for fair assessment based on a trust network and demonstrated its effectiveness through a multi-agent simulation. However, our method was not accurate enough, and thereby, assumed less-realistic situations where students evaluate their group members every week (so 15 or 16 chances for mutual evaluations in a semester) [10]; this burdens students, but fewer chances for mutual evaluation decrease the accuracy. We could not address the issue of collusion, either.

The contributions of this paper are two-fold. First, we introduce the iterative trust network generation method and apply it to assessment more accurate than that proposed previously [10]. For this purpose, we introduce a *cluster-trust value*, meaning the degree of mutual trustworthiness within the clusters. The cluster-trust values were originally proposed by Zeng et al. [12], who called them group-trust degree, but we calculate them iteratively, i.e., we build an initial trust network, calculate cluster-trust values, revise the network on the basis of the cluster-trust values, and iterate these processes several times to obtain a stable network. By doing this, we can exclude irresponsible students whose evaluations are incidentally close to the accurate ones in a certain evaluation. Second, we also propose a strategy against groups of colluders, by strategically comparing the submitted evaluations. This method extended from [10] considerably improves the accuracy of the final assessment, so even only three to five chances for evaluation in a semester are enough; this makes our method more realistic and reasonable to give characteristic information for final assessments.

2   Model and Issues

Let $A = \{1, \ldots, n\}$ be a set of agents that correspond to students participating in group work. Classwork in a semester continues for L weeks, and students have to participate in group work every week. A group consists of g_m agents, thus $\lfloor |A|/g_m \rfloor$ groups exist in each classwork (assuming some groups have $g_m +$ 1 agents). The groups are arranged in the first class and may be rearranged (regrouped) a few times during the course of the semester. For agent i, let G_i^k be the group to which i belongs in the k-th week. Thus, agents i and j belong to the same group in the k-th week if $G_i^k = G_j^k$. We define $G_{-i}^k = G_i^k \setminus \{i\}$. We denote the frequency of regrouping in a semester by positive integer, S_G. The agents mutually evaluate other group members S_G times in the final weeks of the current groups. For example, if $S_G = 1$, the group is arranged only once, at the beginning of the course, and the agents evaluate mutually in the final week of the semester. Agent $i \in A$ has parameter γ_i, positive integers ranging from one to 100, representing i's *contribution degree* to the group work. We introduce our simple mutual evaluation scheme using five-point ratings. Ideally, the final ratings must be determined on the basis of γ_i. This correspondence between the value of a contribution and the correct rating is denoted by R_c as listed in Table 1.

Table 1. Correspondence Table

Five-point rating $R_c(\gamma_i)$	5	4	3	2	1
Values of γ_i	$100 - 81$	$80 - 61$	$60 - 41$	$40 - 21$	$20 - 1$

Agents consider the ratings of others in the same group and submit them to the instructors. Agents do not evaluate themselves, and evaluation results are hidden from others. We consider two types of students in evaluation: *responsible* and *irresponsible*. Responsible students try to rate others carefully by considering the contributions to the group work, while irresponsible students rate others without consideration such as random and flat ratings. In addition, there might be a number of collusion groups. Thus, when two or more students in the same collusion group belong to the same working group, they give each other the best rating (five points) regardless of their contributions. We assume no correlation between being (ir)responsible in evaluations and belonging to a collusion group.

Because it is often difficult for responsible agents to give accurate ratings as shown in Table 1, we introduce parameter $\delta_{i,j}^k$, called an *uncertainty factor*, to express inaccuracies caused by such difficulty in mutual evaluation. Thus, responsible agent i gives $R_c(\gamma_j + \delta_{i,j}^k)$ as the (absolute) rating of agent $j \in G_{-i}$ in the k-th week, where $\delta_{i,j}^k$ is selected in accordance with the normal distribution $N(0, \sigma^2)$ at every evaluation opportunity. However, since it is still difficult for students to give an absolute evaluation, we also consider a relative evaluation, where agent i gives the bonus rating denoted as

$$b_i(j_0) = \min\{R_c(\gamma_{j_0} + \delta_{i,j_0}^k) + 1, 5\},$$

to j_0 and $b_i(j_0) - (R_c(\gamma_{j_0} + \delta_{i,j_0}^k) - R_c(\gamma_j + \delta_{i,j}^k))$ to agents $j \in G_{-j_0}^k$, where $j_0 = \arg\max_{j \in G_i^k}(\gamma_j + \delta_{i,j}^k)$, which is the best contributor in G_i^k identified by i.

Hence, j_0 will receive the highest score $b_i(j_0)$ from i, and the others will receive the relative ratings. Behaviors of irresponsible agents are described in Section 4.

We assume that the current evaluation method for group work is based only on the group outcomes, as it is difficult to differentiate individuals in all groups. The final rating of agent i with the conventional evaluation method, c_i, is determined by

$$\forall i \in G^k, c_i = round(\sum_{1 \leq k \leq L} o(G_i^k)/L), \tag{1}$$

where $round$ is the round-off function and $o(G_i^k)$ is the rating of the group outcome in the k-th week. We assume that $1 \leq o(G_i^k) \leq 5$ is determined correctly by instructors. We use the average value of formula (1) as the benchmark for our proposed method.

3   Fair Assessment Using Cluster-Trust and Collusion Strategies

3.1   Initial Trust Network by Submitted Evaluations

A trust network is a graph in which nodes represent agents and edges represent the distance between nodes. We briefly describe the process for generating the trust network since we have already explained it elsewhere [10]. We start from the simplest trust network $N = (A, E)$ whose set of nodes is A and set of edges is empty ($E = \emptyset$). After the mutual evaluation in the k-th week, edge l_{i_1,i_2} between agents i_1 and i_2 in the same group $G_{i_1}^k (= G_{i_2}^k)$ is added to E (if it does not exist) and its k-th distance is defined as

$$d_k(l_{i_1,i_2}) = \frac{\sqrt{\sum_{j \in G_{i_1}^k \setminus \{i_1,i_2\}} (e_{i_1\ j}^k - e_{i_2\ j}^k)^2}}{|G_{i_1}^k \setminus \{i_1,i_2\}|}, \tag{2}$$

where $e_{i\ j}^k$ is agent i's rating for j in the k-th week. At the end of the semester, the $average$ $distance$ of edge l_{i_1,i_2} is calculated as

$$D(l_{i_1,i_2}) = \frac{\sum_{1 \leq k \leq L} M_k(i_1,i_2) \cdot d_k(l_{i_1,i_2})}{\sum_{1 \leq k \leq L} M_k(i_1,i_2)}, \tag{3}$$

where $M_k(i_1,i_2)$ is the $member$ $function$, which is defined as $M_k(i_1,i_2) = 1$ if agents $i_2 \in G_{i_1}^k$, and $M_k(i_1,i_2) = 0$ otherwise. Note that $E = \{l_{i_1,i_2} \mid M_k(i_1,i_2) = 1$ for $1 \leq \exists k \leq L\}$.

Then, we eliminate edges whose average distances are longer than T_s which is called the $separation$ $threshold$:

$$E' = \{l \in E | D(l) < T_s\}.$$

By referring to E', we identify the sets of the connected clusters (connected components), $N_1, N_2, \ldots$, where we denote $N_i = (A_i, E_i)$ and are sorted in descending order (so, $|A_i| \geq |A_{i+1}|$). Then, we find the minimal integer m_s satisfying

$$\sum_{1 \leq i \leq m_s} |A_i| > |A|/2.$$

The set of the selected agents, which is denoted by $Q = \cup_{1 \leq i \leq m_s} A_i$, forms the cluster (sub-network) and is the majority of the non- or less-conflicting evaluations. How to decide the value of separation threshold is describe in [10].

Since mutual evaluation may not be done every week realistically, we define *evaluation-timing function* $P(k) = 1$ if all students have a chance of mutual evaluation in the k-th week, and $P(k) = 0$ otherwise. The evaluation of agent i by other agents up to the k_0-th week is denoted by $u_i(k_0)$, which is defined as

$$s_i^k = \sum_{j \in \tilde{G}_{-i}^k} e_j^k \,_i / |\tilde{G}_{-i}^k| \tag{4}$$

$$u_i(k_0) = round \left(\frac{\sum_{1 \leq k \leq k_0} P(k) \cdot f_e(s_i^k, o(G_i^k))}{\sum_{1 \leq k \leq k_0} P(k)} \right), \tag{5}$$

where $\tilde{G}_{-i}^k = G_{-i}^k \cap Q$, and f_e is the evaluation function ranging from 1 to 5 in accordance with the rating of the group outcome $o(G_i^k)$ and mutual evaluation s_i^k. Function f_e is the evaluation function by the instructor's policy. Thus, the values of s_i^k should be accurate but are actually affected by irresponsibility and collusion. We try to make them more accurate by excluding such assessments.

3.2   Cluster-Trust Value

The cluster set Q in Section 3.1 sometimes includes irresponsible students because their evaluations are incidentally close to the accurate ones in some evaluations. We introduce the concept of *cluster-trust values* to exclude such irresponsible students who are less trusted inside the cluster consisting of many responsible students.

For agent $i \in A$ and the cluster to which i belongs, N_m, the cluster-trust value expresses how much i is trusted by other agents in N_m. The cluster-trust value of i in N_m is calculated as

$$g(i, N_m) = \frac{1}{\sum_{j \in A_m, i \neq j} g(j, N_m)} \sum_{j \in A_m, i \neq j} g(j, N_m) \cdot t_{ji}, \tag{6}$$

where $N_m = (A_m, E_m)$ is the cluster to which i belongs after edges in Section 3.1 have been eliminated. Parameter t_{ji} is the *direct trust degree* from j to i. We define $t_{ji} = 0$ if i and j have no edge between them; otherwise t_{ji} is defined as follows. If i has more neighbor agents in N_m with whom i is connected with high cluster-trust value edges, then $g(i, N_m)$ will become higher. Parameter t_{ji}

corresponds to a normalized value expressing the similarly between evaluations by i and j, and is defined as

$$t_{ji} = \begin{cases} 1 - D(l_{j,i})/2 & \text{if } (D(l_{j,i}) \leq 2), \\ 0 & \text{otherwise.} \end{cases} \tag{7}$$

Note that if the average difference in evaluations is more than two points in our five-point rating scheme, the two agents' attitudes to mutual evaluations are not similar, and thus, they do not trust each other.

3.3   Iterative Calculation of Cluster Values and Trust Networks

Trust networks are iteratively revised by excluding the untrusted agents and adding trusted agents identified by the cluster-trust values. We start with $g(i, N_m) = g_{init}$, which is a certain initial value where $0 \leq g_{init} \leq 1$. Then, we calculate the cluster-trust values for $\forall i \in Q$ by Eq. (6). After that, we exclude the agents with $g(i, N_m) \leq T_{th}$ from their cluster.[1] For all clusters, N_m, we repeat the following excluding steps:

1. Calculate $g(i, N_m)$ for $\forall i \in N_m$.
2. Look for agents whose $g(i, N_m)$ is smaller than T_{th}.
3. If these agents exist, the agent who has the lowest value of $g(i, N_m)$ is excluded from the cluster N_m and returns to the first step.

   In the excluding steps, irresponsible students who were incidentally included in Q are excluded, but a few responsible students may also be excluded. So, we recover such responsible students. Let Z be the set of agent i and cluster N_m where i was excluded from N_m in the excluding steps and Z_h be an empty set. Then, the following recovering steps are repeated for $\forall (i, N_m) \in Z$.

1. Agent i is temporarily added to N_m.
2. Calculate $g(i, N_m)$, and if it is bigger than or equal to T_{th}, add (i, N_m) to Z_h.
3. Remove i from N_m and return to the first step.
4. Finally, for $\forall (i, N_m) \in Z_h$, i is added to N_m.

Then, $Q = \cup_{1 \leq i \leq m_s} A_i$ is calculated again. We iterate the excluding and recovering steps several times until no changes in trust networks are observed.

3.4   Strategies Against Collusive Students

We introduce the strategy against collusive students after generating the trust network. This strategy detects collusive students and excludes their ratings. High-contributing students receive high ratings regardless of whether they collude or not. However, uncooperative or low-contributing students have more

---

[1] We set the value of T_{th} to be appropriate to our method, but this leaves room for improvement.

incentive to collude and might initiate or join collusive groups because they cannot receive high ratings without cheating. Thus, we have to exclude false high ratings given to such students.

We assume that agent i has an incentive to collude if its rating is expected to be low. Let S be the set of agents that satisfy $s_i(L) \leq 3$, and we can assume that agents in S have the incentive, where

$$s_i(k_0) = \frac{\sum_{1 \leq k \leq k_0} P(k) \cdot s_i^k}{\sum_{1 \leq k \leq k_0} P(k)}. \tag{8}$$

Then, for $i \in S$, we look for another agent $j \in Q$ that mutually gave the high (or maximum) rating to i:

$$B_i = \{j \mid \exists k, e_i^k {}_j = e_j^k {}_i = 5\} \text{ and } B = \cup_{i \in S} B_i.$$

If $j \in B_i$, j is the student suspected of colluding student with i. Then, we redefine $\tilde{G}_{-i}^k = G_{-i}^k \cap Q \cap \neg B_i$ in Eq. (4) and re-calculate $u_i(L)$.

4 Experiments

4.1 Experimental Setup

We examined how accuracy can be improved by our proposed method by comparing the resulting marks with those derived by only using the initial trust networks (ITN), which is called the ITN method and corresponds to the method proposed in [10], and by using the conventional method described in Section 2. We also investigated how many ratios of (ir)responsible students can be identified within the limited classes in a semester. In this experiment, we assume that the number of agents ($|A|$) is 500 and groups are randomly created. The contributions γ_i of agents are uniformly selected between one and 100. We also set $L = 16$ and $g_m = 5$. The evaluation of the outcome of a group, G, is defined as $o(G) = R_c(\max_{i \in G} \gamma_i)$ because high-contributing students cannot afford to submit low-quality outcomes and often the outcome is mainly the result of work done by such students. The evaluation policy by the instructor is set to $f_e(s_i^k, o(G_i^k)) = s_i^k \times o(G_i^k)/5$. The cluster-trust values are initially set as $g_{init} = 0.5$.

We introduce four types of irresponsible agents: random, flat, and extremely soft/hard raters. Random raters evaluate others randomly, and flat raters give the same value (but with different values for each evaluation). The extremely hard raters always give 1 or 2 and the extremely soft raters always give 4 or 5. We varied the ratio of irresponsible agents to responsible agents (RIA) from 0% to 45% and assumed (and hoped) that there were fewer irresponsible agents than responsible agents. The four types of irresponsible agents were generated at the same ratios. Note that there is no correlation between capability, contribution, and responsibility in the evaluations. Responsible agents try to but cannot always evaluate others correctly. Variance σ^2 to decide the uncertainty factors was set to 3^2. We also conducted the experiments to evaluate our method for detecting collusive students, but due to the page limitations, the results are omitted here.

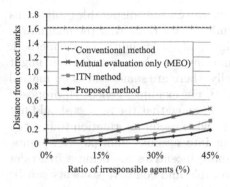 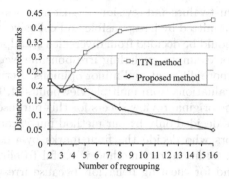

Fig. 1. Distances from correct marks with different methods ($S_G = 5$).

Fig. 2. Distances from correct marks with varying S_G (RIA is 45%).

4.2 Experimental Results and Discussion

Figure 1 plots the average distances between the final marks and the correct marks, which were calculated by $\sum_{i \in A} |R_c(\gamma_i) - u_i(L)| / |A|$. Note that the *mutual evaluation-only* (MEO) method in Fig. 1 indicates the case when students' final marks were decided using all submitted evaluations (by believing all students were responsible). The figure clearly indicates that the assessment by the conventional method was the worst because there were many free-riders and the individual contributions were not considered. In the MEO method, the distances increased almost linearly from 0.038 to 0.481 as RIA increased, because irresponsible evaluations considerably worsened the accuracy of the final marks. However, they were still better than those with the conventional method. The distances lowered between 0.038 and 0.313 in the ITN method. Finally, our proposed method always resulted in the most accurate assessment. In particular, when RIA is large (45%), the proposed method could reduce the distances (0.181) approximately 42% compared with that (0.313) in the ITN method [10]. This result suggested that the proposed method could exclude irresponsible students effectively.

The distances from the correct marks when using the ITN method or the proposed method by changing the frequencies of regrouping, S_G, are plotted in Fig. 2, where RIA was fixed to 45% (the worst case). This figure indicates that the number of regrouping, S_G, and the distances were negatively correlated in the ITN method, because when S_G was large, the resulting networks were complex and thus, the initial trust networks were not accurate enough to decide the marks. Conversely, the distance from correct marks and the number of regrouping, S_G, were positively correlated in the proposed method. We think that mutual evaluation with $S_G = 4$ or 5 is realistic in actual courses, and of course, the proposed method outperformed the ITN method in this case.

The experimental results provide a few suggestions for our method in group work. By introducing the iterative process consisting of calculation of cluster-trust values and revision of trust networks, we can exclude disputable evaluations submitted by irresponsible and collusive students. We think that the final marks should be decided from diversified standpoints and not by only a specific method. For example, excluding irresponsible evaluations must be important but might ignore different and minor opinions. Actually, there are some studies on mutual evaluations from multiple viewpoints [4, 9, 11]. For example, Fellens [4] proposed the original review sheets for this purpose. We know that the ratings should not be decided only by our method but it can provide useful information to instructors who decide the final marks by taking into account multiple viewpoints. In addition, our method is useful to eliminate incentives for being a free-rider and for cheating behavior, because irresponsible and collusive students can be detected with high probability, but the gain by doing so is quite small.

5   Conclusion

We proposed a method for fairly and accurately assessing group work by using mutual evaluation in which some students may evaluate others irresponsibly and collude with some friends. First, we described our model of group work in a multi-agent context where students were represented as agents and also explained the five-point rating that was used in our mutual evaluation. Then, we proposed the fair assessment method through mutual evaluation based on a trust network with cluster-trust values. We experimentally examined how well our proposed method could improve the accuracy of final marks compared with those by the previous method [10] and the conventional method in which instructors decide the final marks only from the outcomes of groups. Students are always flexible and more complex, so instructors should decide the actual final marks from multiple standpoints. We believe that the resulting ratings with our method can be used as a reference for instructors' decisions. Furthermore, our method is suited for computerized education, since it is easy to automate evaluations.

Acknowledgments. This work is partly supported by KAKENHI (25280087).

References

1. Allen, B., Crosky, A., Mcalpine, I., Hoffman, M., Munroe, P.: A blended approach to collaborative learning: can it make large group teaching more student-centred. In: Proceedings of the 23rd Annual ASCILITE Conference, pp. 33–41. University Press (2006)
2. Brutus, S., Donia, M.B.L.: Improving the Effectiveness of Students in Groups With a Centralized Peer Evaluation System. Academy of Management Learning and Education **9**(4), 652–662 (2010). Academy of Management
3. Ettington, D.R., Camp, R.R.: Facilitating Transfer of Skills between Group Projects and Work Teams. Journal of Management Education **26**(4), 356–379 (2002). Sage Publications

4. Fellenz, M.R.: Toward Fairness in Assessing Student Groupwork: A Protocol for Peer Evaluation of Individual Contributions. Journal of Management Education **30**(4), 570–591 (2006). Sage Publications

5. Hall, D., Buzwell, S.: The problem of free-riding in group projects: Looking beyond social loafing as reason for non-contribution. Active Learning in Higher Education (2012)

6. Jiang, S., Zhang, J., Ong, Y.S.: An evolutionary model for constructing robust trust networks. In: Proceedings of the 2013 International Conference on Autonomous Agents and Multi-agent Systems. AAMAS 2013, pp. 813–820. International Foundation for Autonomous Agents and Multiagent Systems, Richland, SC (2013)

7. McCorkle, D.E., Reardon, J., Alexander, J.F., Kling, N.D., Harris, R.C., Iyer, R.V.: Undergraduate Marketing Students, Group Projects, and Teamwork: The Good, the Bad, and the Ugly? Journal of Marketing Education **21**(2), 106–117 (1999). Sage Publications

8. North, A.C., Linley, P.A., Hargreaves, D.J.: Social Loafing in a Co-operative Classroom Task. Educational Psychology **20**(3), 389–392 (2000). Taylor and Fancis

9. Sadler, P.M., Good, E.: The impact of peer-grading on student learning. Educational Assessment **11**(1), 1–31 (2006). Taylor and Fancis

10. Shiba, Y., Sugawara, T.: Fair assessment of group work by mutual evaluation based on trust network. In: Proceedings of the 2014 IEEE Frontiers in Education Conference (FIE), pp. 1–7. IEEE Xplore (2014)

11. Topping, K.J.: Peer Assessment. Theory into Practice **48**(1), 20–27 (2009). Taylor and Fancis

12. Zeng, J., Gao, M., Wen, J., Hirokawa, S.: A hybrid trust degree model in social network for recommender system. In: Proceedings of the 2014 IIAI 3rd International Conference on Advanced Applied Informatics (IIAIAAI), pp. 37–41. IEEE Xplore (2014)

13. Zhang, L., Jiang, S., Zhang, J., Ng, W.K.: Robustness of trust models and combinations for handling unfair ratings. In: Dimitrakos, T., Moona, R., Patel, D., McKnight, D.H. (eds.) IFIPTM 2012. IFIP AICT, vol. 374, pp. 36–51. Springer, Heidelberg (2012)

Modeling the Effects of Personality on Team Formation in Self-assembly Teams

Mehdi Farhangian$^{(\boxtimes)}$, Martin K. Purvis, Maryam Purvis,
and Bastin Tony Roy Savarimuthu

Information Science, University of Otago, Dunedin, New Zealand
Mehdi.farhangian@otago.ac.nz

Abstract. Optimizing the performance of teams in modern organizations is an important managerial function, and particularly so in contexts where new teams must continually be formed voluntarily, such as with software development, crowd-sourcing platforms, and even the formation of scientific collaborative teams. In many such cases, team performance is significantly influenced by the makeup of participant personalities and temperaments and goes beyond the analysis of individual skills. In this study, we present a team-assemblage model that is primarily influenced by knowledge of the past performance of team members and their personalities. Our goal is to provide a model, which can be parameterized for specific organizational contexts, for policy makers and managers to assess potential teams formed in dynamic circumstances. To provide real-world validation for our approach, we extracted data from the Python Enhancement Proposal (PEP) process, which involves the repeated self-assembly of software teams from a common pool of developers. We then used agent-based simulation to enact our model with PEP data to predict team grouping formation and resulting team performances.

Keywords: Multi-agent systems · Social Simulation · Personality · Team performance · Team formation

1 Introduction

Clearly the performance of teams cannot be simply predicted as an extension of individual performance and the issue of predicting team performance is becoming more important with today's increased employment of temporary teams [1]. Examples of temporary teams include crowdsourcing platforms, scientific collaboration teams, open source software development teams, and online games. In today's rapidly evolving world, teams are often assembled from a larger network of related people. But there is little understanding concerning how this self-assembly team formation process should be carried out.

In order to understand the mechanisms governing the composition of social groups, Ruef *et al.* [2] conducted a survey and analysed a data set of organizational teams from a sample of the U.S population. They concluded that homophily and network constraints based on strong ties have the most significant influence on group composition.

© Springer International Publishing Switzerland 2015
Q. Chen et al. (Eds.): PRIMA 2015, LNAI 9387, pp. 538–546, 2015.
DOI: 10.1007/978-3-319-25524-8_36

In addition to such empirical studies, some further studies investigated team assembly mechanisms by using computer simulations. Guimera *et al.* [3] proposed a model for self-assembly in teams based on three parameters: team size, the fraction of newcomers, and the tendency of incumbents to repeat previous collaborations. A team model developed by Johnson *et al.* [4] showed the average tolerance level and attribute range for each population affects individuals' decisions for team coalition.

Since previous collaboration experience is a major factor for self-assembly (as suggested by other researchers i.e. [2]), the model that we present in this paper considers both human factors for group assembly and also knowledge of past performance. In particular, we posit that key human factors arise from personality types, and we consider them in the team-assembly process. Thus, a model is developed on the basis of theoretical and empirical literature on personalities and team behavior. This conceptual model is then implemented as an agent-based computer simulation consisting of simple rules and principles.

Although one might simply posit a model based on the relationship between personality and team performance, the literature in this domain suggests that rules cannot be generalized without considering situational forces such as organizational structure and the types of tasks. Nevertheless, in volatile environments where new teams must be rapidly assembled, some locally-known knowledge must be used to construct the team [11], and this often comes down to local familiarity with past performances and awareness of personality types. We have constructed our model on this basis and have tested it with real-world data from such a team-assembly environment.

The rest of the paper is organized as follows: Section 2 discusses psychological personality models and reviews the literature about the relationship between personality and team performance. Section 3 presents our proposed rules and principles about team-formation mechanisms and our agent-based model. Section 4 is a presentation of some general experiments and results based on our team-formation model. Section 5 is a specification of the model in the domain of small software development teams and serves as both a practical example and a basis for validating the model principles. Section 6 contains the conclusion.

2   Personality

In agent-based modelling, agent personality characterizes agent motivations, behaviour, and thoughts. There have been several simplified schemes developed over the years to profile human personality, the most popular of which seem to be the Five Factor Model (FFM or "Big Five") [5] and the Myer-Briggs Type Indicator (MBTI) scheme [6]. In our work we have employed the MBTI scheme, since (a) it appears to have the most accumulated field data and (b) the FFM model suffers from the disadvantage of identifying and measuring only positive "qualities" of personality. As a consequence, it seems, most people who do not want to be judged are more likely to self-identify their MBTI personality types.

The history of MBTI goes back to Carl Jung, who developed an initial scheme of psychological types that included the notion of introversion and extraversion [7]. Myers added additional elements to this arrangement, and it has evolved into the MBTI scheme [8], which has four "dimensions" of human personality: **Extraversion** vs. **Introversion** (where people focus their attentions), **iNtuition** vs. **Sensing** (the way that people gather information), **Thinking** vs. **Feeling** (the way that people make decisions) **Judgmental** vs. **Perceptive** (the way that people deal with the outer world). The 16 possible type combinations are typically referred to by an abbreviation of four letters—the initial letters of each of their four type preferences. For instance: ISFJ represents introversion (I), sensing (S), feeling (F), and judgmental (J).

In our model, a number between 0 and 100 indicates the personality of agents in each dimension. For example for the Extraversion-Introversion (EI) dimension, a value between 0 and 50 means that a person is extraverted, and a value between 50 and 100 means s/he is introverted.

2.1   Personality and Team Performance

There is interest in evaluating how personality affects team performance, but we recognize that understanding human personality and its effects on performance are enormous subjects in themselves, and we do not pretend to treat this subject in all its depths here. Nevertheless, there are some commonly held notions concerning variations of human temperament and personality that have been developed over the past century, and we take advantage of some of them.

During task activities, the team's personality composition strongly influences the success in finishing a task. Tziner [9] mentioned two social psychological perspectives that account for how team composition affects performance:

- *Similarity theory* predicts that homogeneous teams will be more productive because of the mutual compatibility of the members.
- *Equity theory* predicts team performance is higher in heterogeneous groups because of complementarity among members.

In order to model this aspect of team performance, we introduce two indicators [10] that are used in conjunction with the MBTI measures:

- Team Personality Diversity (**TPD**): the variance with respect to a particular personality trait among team members.
- Team Personality Elevation (**TPE**): a team's mean level for a particular personality trait.

For both similarity and equity theory, TPD, which measures team heterogeneity and homogeneity, is significant. Teams generally high in terms of TPD are described as heterogeneous, whereas teams that are low in terms of TPD are homogeneous. Research findings regarding the relationship between TPD and group effectiveness are mixed. Different tasks have different requirements, for instance, some may require a high level of cognition and complex thinking, while some others may require a high degree of coordination and teamwork. In our environment, we considered two types of tasks:

- *Structured* – tasks that are straightforward and do not require planning.
- *Open-ended* (or 'cognitive') – tasks that require more creativity and imagination (for example, surveying tasks and finding suitable strategies).

Wiersema and Bantel [11], noting that team homogeneity brings about a shared language among team members and improves integration and communication frequency, suggested homogeneous teams are likely to perform better on tasks that require high coordination. In contrast, Bantel [12] predicted that homogeneous teams would perform poorly (because of lack of openness) on tasks requiring new resources of information, and they recommended heterogeneous teams for tasks that require a high level of creativity.

Thus, we know that TPD and TPE do not uniquely predict team performance, but based on the literature discussed above, we assume that for structured tasks low TPDis likely to have a positive effect on team performance. For open-ended tasks, high TPD is likely to positively affect team performance.

3 Proposed Team formation mechanism

In order to develop principles and rules of our agent-based model, we made the following assumptions based on the literature on MBTI personality (i.e. [13]).

iNtuition-Sensing. We assume that intuitive types are more likely to record their past experiences about team performance.

Thinking-Feeling. In our model it is assumed feelers choose new team members based on their familiarity with them, rather than for logical reasons such as experience.

Judging-Perceiving. We assume team members with judging personalities are more likely to refrain from changing their team and prefer to continue with the existing team, while employees with perceiving personalities are more flexible and more likely to change their teammates.

Extraversion-Introversion. We assume employees with extraverted personalities connect with more people in their social network.

In our team formation mechanism, two types of people are involved, which we call requesters and contributors. Requesters start a project and, seeking collaborators from sources such as crowdsourcing platforms, attempt to recruit the required people and complete the work for projects. Contributors are the recruited people who contribute to the tasks. The personality of requesters and contributors determine their team's overall behavior.

To form teams, we proposed a first-price auction-based algorithm, comprising requester and contributor agents. In this system, a virtual currency is assigned to both requesters and contributors. Both of them try to be part of a team that gives the highest chance to increase their wealth in this virtual currency. Their performance in the task is presented in Formula 1:

$$v_{ij}(t) = Performance_b + v_{ij}(t-1) \tag{1}$$

v_{ij} indicates the value that agent i assigns to agent j after performing a task, and $Performance_b$ indicates the performance of the team in task b and presented in Formula 2.

$$Performance_b = 100 - |Heterogeneity_l - Tasktype_b| \tag{2}$$

where $Heterogeinity_l$ indicates the heterogeneity of team l and is calculated based on the average of the standard deviation in each personality dimension and presented in Formula 3. $Tasktype_b$ is the nature of task b that shows the level of how open-ended and structured the task is and can be a number between 0 and 50. 0 indicates that the task is extremely structured, while 50 indicates the task is extremely open-ended. $\overline{S_{EI,j}}$, $\overline{S_{NS,l}}$, $\overline{S_{JP,l}}$ and $\overline{S_{TF,l}}$ represent the standard deviation of team l in Extraverted/Introverted (E-I), iNtutive/Sensing (N-S), Thinking/Feeling (T-F) and Judging/Perceiving (J-P), respectively.

$$Heterogeneity_l = \frac{\overline{S_{EI,l}} + \overline{S_{NS,l}} + \overline{S_{JP,l}} + \overline{S_{TF,l}}}{4} \tag{3}$$

In the agent model, an agent's individual decision about team formation is determined based on two factors: Past success and Familiarity.

- **Past success**: the history of previous team performance.
- **Familiarity**: the history of social interaction of agents.

As mentioned in the assumptions in Section 3, past-success is a more important factor for people with sensing personality, and familiarity is a more important factor for people with feeling personality. So requester j offers C_{ji} to the contributor i as presented in Formula 4.

$$C_{ji} = \frac{(NS_j * v_{ji} + TF_j * familiarity_{ji})}{NS_j + TF_j} \tag{4}$$

In this formula, NS_j is the sensing-intuition personality of the requester j. TF_j is the thinking-feeling personality dimension of the requester j, and $familiarity_{ji}$ represents the interaction of agent j with agent i and is calculated as Formula 5, where G_k improves whenever agent j interacts with agent i as presented in Formula 6.

$$familiarity_{ji} = 10 * e^{G_{kji}} \tag{5}$$

$$e^{G_{kji}} = e^{G_{(k-1)ji}} + 0.1 \tag{6}$$

When contributors receive bids, they select the requester with the highest expected payoff. A_{ij} indicates the payoff of contributor i by joining team j and is presented in Formula 7.

$$A_{ij} = \frac{NS_i * v_{ij} + TF_i * familiarity_{ij}}{NS_i + TF_i} + C_{ji} \tag{7}$$

Apart from performing a task, agents interact with each other. The probability of interaction is based on the extent to which they have an extraverted personality and the probability of leaving a team or firing a contributor is related to the Judging personality index of agents .

4   Experiments and Results

Experiments have been conducted using NetLogo. In the initial settings, agents represent requesters and contributors. Four numbers between 0 and 100 are randomly assigned to each personality dimension for each agent. A number between 0 and 50 represents the degree of a task's being structured or open-ended. The number of required contributors for each task is a random number between 2 and 4. In each time step, new tasks are added to the environment, and the simulation is terminated after 100-time steps. To account foro the randomness of the assigned values, performances are reported as averages over 100 simulation runs.

We were interested in investigating the most popular team compositions. To explore this further, from our simulation data, we added labels to the variables about team personality, such as TPD-EI, TPD-NS, TPD-TF, TPD-JP, TPE-EI, TPE-NS, TPE-TF, TPE-JP, as "Very Low", "Low", "Medium", "High", and "Very High". Observations are summarized in Figure 1. These results will be further discussed and compared in the validation section, where we compare them with the particular domain presented in the next section.

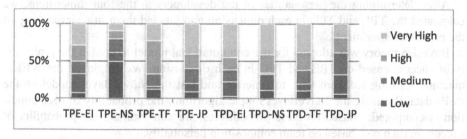

Fig. 1. Team composition (for open-ended tasks)

5   Validation

our model and simulation represent a considerable simplification, and its usefulness needs to be validated with real data. As we mentioned earlier, generating general rules that determine the relationship between team performance and personality is not straightforward. Nevertheless, some further validation would be valuable, and this is always an issue with agent-based modelling. Some researchers have suggested that data mining techniques applied to real projects can be useful in this regard (e.g. [14]). To pursue this idea, we have chosen a specific application domain and investigated a real case study by extracting data from the Python Enhancement Proposal (PEP) process.

A PEP is a document that describes a new feature to be developed by a small team for Python, for which developers use mailing lists as the primary forum for discussion about the Python language's development. We obtained access to 363 PEPs categorized into three labelled categories: process, information, and standard track. There are temporary teams associated with each PEP, where certain team members work together for one task but may change the team for another task.

We are primarily interested to find useful information to show the relationship between personality and performance of teams of developers. In order to identify the personality of developers, some steps were required. Using similar methods as [15], we developed a formula to determine the personality of people from their texts. Initially, the data was extracted from three social networking websites (Quora.com, Reddit.com, and Collegeconfidential.com) where people self-reported their MBTI personalities. After extracting data and texts of 228 users in Quora, we employed the Linguistic Inquiry and Word Count LIWC tool [16] to analyze each textual fragment. After generating the value of all the variables in our Quora samples, we used Pearson correlation to find correlations between personality and these variables, and we considered the variable combinations having their correlation at the 0.01 level to be significant. These correlations were then cross-tested against 25 users in Reddit and 135 users in College Confidential, and they were shown to be 65% and 73% accurate. We then applied our proposed formula to determine the personality of Python developers based on their own texts that were publicly available on the Internet.

After determining the personalities of the developers in the four dimensions, we calculated the TPE and TPD in each dimension and labeled them in a similar way to the previous experiments.

Bayesian theory was adopted for our computational model to predict the probability of success based on TPE and TPD in each dimension. We employed the WEKA machine learning software tool to generate and test the Naïve Bayes model on the PEPs data. By using the NaiveBayesSimple algorithm, the probability of each condition is computed. Based on these probabilities, we can estimate the probability of success in each task based on team composition personality.

New experiments were developed and the roles of requester and contributor were assigned to agents randomly. For each round, agents update their beliefs about success and familiarity with other agents based on their sensing and feeling personalities, respectively. The decision about changing the team is related to the perceiving personality. However, unlike the previous experiments, the performance of each team is not determined by Formula 2. Instead, the performance is determined by the conditional probabilities calculated from data extracted from the PEPs. In summary, apart from the performance calculation, other settings are similar to the previous experiments.

Our interest is to determine the most popular team composition. We assume the nature of tasks in software development is more open-ended and that a higher degree of collaboration is required. The most basic validation is comparing the results about the team composition in the open-ended tasks (Figure 1) and the new results which are summarized in Figure 2.

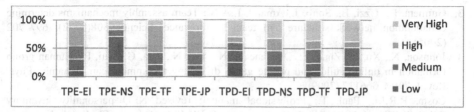

Fig. 2. The composition with data extracted from performance in PEPs

The data shows our model's ability to generate context-dependent behavior. The results show the frequency of team composition in the simulation with open-ended tasks corresponds very well with the simulation results when performance is derived from PEPs. Comparison of Figure 1 and Figure 2 reveals most cases have similar trends, and teams have evolved similarly. If only the comparison of "High" and "Low" is considered as the main criterion, we observe that the model predicts 7 (all variables in the team composition apart from TPD-EI) out of 8 variables correctly and has 87.5 % accuracy. This demonstrates that our model can be used to predict future team formation where teams are formed on a temporary basis.

6   Conclusion

The modeling approach outlined in this research can be used for researchers to have a better understanding about the mechanisms behind the team-formation process. In addition, it can be of use to policy makers whose aim is discovering the most efficient team composition to perform certain types of tasks. We argue that there is no universally successful personality configuration, and success is often significantly related to contextual forces.

We applied our model to a specific domain (PEPs). We determine the personalities of software developers in PEPs. Finally, based on these relationships and employing Bayesian theory, we extracted data about the probability of success in various team composition conditions. We then ran a new set of experiments based on the data extracted from the PEPs. The new results present some similarities with the previous experiments. The observations from two sets of experiments were similar in term of teams' evolutions. These results show the ability of the proposed model in team-formation prediction.

Further experiments and validations must be performed before our results can be generalized. We thus encourage the execution of similar studies of other globally distributed teams to validate our outcomes.

References

1. Contractor, N.: Some assembly required: leveraging Web science to understand and enable team assembly. Philos. Trans. A. Math. Phys. Eng. Sci. **371**(1987), 20120385 (2013)
2. Ruef, M., Aldrich, H., Carter, N.: The structure of founding teams: Homophily, strong ties, and isolation among US entrepreneurs. Am. Sociol. Rev. (2003)

3. Guimerà, R., Uzzi, B., Spiro, J., Amaral, L.A.N.: Team assembly mechanisms determine collaboration network structure and team performance. Science **308**(5722), 697–702 (2005)
4. Johnson, N., Xu, C., Zhao, Z., Ducheneaut, N., Yee, N., Tita, G., Hui, P.: Human group formation in online guilds and offline gangs driven by a common team dynamic. Phys. Rev. E **79**(6), 066117 (2009)
5. Costa, R.R.M., Paul, T.: Professional manual: revised NEO personality inventory (NEO-PI-R) and NEO five-factor inventory (NEO-FFI). Odessa, FL Psychol. Assess. Resour. (1992)
6. Myers, I.: The myers-briggs type indicator. Consult. Psychol. Press (1962)
7. Jung, C.G.: Psychological types: or the psychology of individuation. Harcourt, Brace (1921)
8. Myers, I.B., McCaulley, M.H., Most, R.: Manual: A guide to the development and use of the Myers-Briggs Type Indicator. Consult. Psychol. Press (1985)
9. Tziner, A.: How Team Composition Affects Task Performance: Some Theoretical Insights. Psychol. Rep. **57**(3f), 1111–1119 (1985)
10. Neuman, G.A., Wagner, S.H., Christiansen, N.D.: The Relationship between Work-Team Personality Composition and the Job Performance of Teams. Gr. Organ. Manag. **24**(1), 28–45 (1999)
11. Wiersema, M., Bantel, K.: Top management team demography and corporate strategic change. Acad. Manag. J. (1992)
12. Bantel, K.: Strategic Planning Openness The Role of Top Team Demography. Gr. Organ. Manag. (1994)
13. Bradley, J.H., Hebert, F.J.: The effect of personality type on team performance. J. Manag. Dev. **16**(5), 337–353 (1997)
14. Remondino, M., Correndo, G.: Data mining applied to agent based simulation. In: Proceedings of the 19th European Conference on Modelling and Simulation, Riga, Latvia (2005)
15. Rigby, P., Hassan, A.: What can oss mailing lists tell us? a preliminary psychometric text analysis of the apache developer mailing list. In: Fourth International Workshop on Mining Software Repositories (MSR 2007: ICSE Workshops 2007), pp. 23–23 (2007)
16. Pennebaker, J.: Linguistic inquiry and word count: LIWC 2001. Mahway: Lawrence Erlbaum Associates, p. 71 (2001)

Real-Time Conditional Commitment Logic

Warda El Kholy[1], Mohamed El Menshawy[1,2], Amine Laarej[1],
Jamal Bentahar[1(✉)], Faisal Al-Saqqar[3], and Rachida Dssouli[1]

[1] Concordia Institute for Information Systems Engineering,
Concordia University, Montreal, Canada
w_elkh@encs.concordia.ca, moh_marzok75@yahoo.com, laarej.amine@gmail.com,
bentahar@ciise.concordia.ca, rachida.dssouli@concordia.ca
[2] Faculty of Computers and Information,
Menoufia University, Shibeen El-Kom, Egypt
[3] Faculty of Engineering and Computer Science,
Concordia University, Montreal, Canada
f_alsaqq@encs.concordia.ca

Abstract. A considerably large class of multi-agent systems (MASs) employed in real-time environments requires the possibility to express time-critical properties. In this paper, we develop a system of temporal logic RTCTL^{cc}, an extension of CTL modalities and interval bound until modalities with conditional commitment and their fulfillment modalities. This logic allows us to formally model the interaction among autonomous agents using conditional commitments and to combine qualitative temporal aspects together with real-time constraints (time instants or intervals) in order to permit reasoning about qualitative and quantitative requirements and their specifications. We point out that useful properties of MASs, which are required to express temporal constraints as a fundamental part of functional requirements can be expressed in RTCTL^{cc}. We also argue that time-critical properties expressed in executable action languages in other contributed approaches can be expressed in RTCTL^{cc}.

Keywords: Multi-Agent Systems · Real-time · Conditional commitments · Qualitative and quantitative requirements

1 Introduction

Social and objective commitments among pairs of interacting agents within multi-agent systems (MASs) have been acknowledged as a powerful engineering tool to represent, model, and reason about the content of multi-agent interactions [2,9]. They also provide a fundamental basis for addressing the challenge of checking and validating the compliance of autonomous agents' behaviors with preset specifications [3,8,12]. Temporal logics, such as LTL [16], CTL [3,6,8,12], and CTL* [11] have been successfully extended with temporal modalities to represent and reason about social commitments and some of related commitment actions. What makes commitment languages special is that they include modalities needed for modeling interaction among agents, which cannot be expressed

© Springer International Publishing Switzerland 2015
Q. Chen et al. (Eds.): PRIMA 2015, LNAI 9387, pp. 547–556, 2015.
DOI: 10.1007/978-3-319-25524-8_37

in pure temporal logics. All commitment languages, however, have paid more heed to deal with qualitative temporal commitment properties used to check the correctness of commitment protocols [8,10,12] and business models having social semantics [7,17]. With these specification languages, we can express qualitative commitment properties such as whenever the customer accepts the offer, the merchant conditionally commits to eventually deliver goods provided that the customer sends the payment. This property obviously places no bound constraint on the time that might elapse before the delivery of goods.

Although qualitative properties are in principle desirable to express various formal specifications (e.g., safety and liveness properties [11]), there is a considerably large class of MASs employed in real-time environments. The class requires the possibility to express time-critical properties. Such properties indeed express the occurrences of events at time instants or within time intervals, and play an essential role in verifying the correctness of systems' specifications. The most utilized timing constraint is deadline, i.e., the time instant before which the required result must be actually delivered. Consider the following examples to clarify quantitative properties that are important and relevant in real and practical systems, but ignored in temporal commitment logics. In a business protocol, we might need to affirm a quantitative correctness property such as once the payment is received, the merchant must commit to deliver goods to the customer within bounded time, for instance, 2 time units (days) during which only a certain set of preparation steps is performed. In the car rental business scenario discussed in [4], a customer needs first to sign a contract with a car rental agency. The customer is accordingly obliged to return back the car at a certain bounded time, namely, 5 days from the day of signing the rental contract. In a typical service-level agreement, there is a commitment to maintain network connectivity during bounded times (e.g., at Concordia university, the IT department performs the maintenance process every last Friday in each month).

The current **research questions** are: 1) how temporal deadline constraints can be modeled in the commitment logical languages? 2) how can we define unbounded modalities from bounded ones? and 3) how can we express qualitative and quantitative properties using the same specification commitment logical language? The **contribution** of the paper is the development of an expressive logical language called $RTCTL^{cc}$ that allows us to address these research questions. $RTCTL^{cc}$ particularly extends our CTL^{cc} (CTL plus conditional commitments and their fulfillment modalities [6]) with quantitative modalities in a systematic fashion. We adopt CTL^{cc} as the semantics of conditional commitments and their fulfillment achieve all operational semantic rules commonly agreed on in the literature and meet all Singh's reasoning postulates [16], as shown in [6]. We in fact follow Emerson et al.'s methodology to develop a real-time CTL logic (RTCTL) to deal with different sorts of real-time applications [13].

This work continues as follows. In Section 2, we present the extended version of the interpreted system formalism introduced in our previous work [3,8] and define the syntax and semantics of $RTCTL^{cc}$. In Section 3, we discuss the related work. We conclude and identify future research directions in Section 4.

2 Extended Version of Interpreted Systems and RTCTL^{cc}

The formalism of interpreted systems [14] provides a very popular framework to model MASs. In [3,6,8], we extended this formalism with sets of shared and unshared variables to account for agent communication. Specifically, the extended version of interpreted systems is composed of a set $\mathcal{A} = \{1, \ldots, n\}$ of n agents plus the environment agent e. Each agent $i \in \mathcal{A}$ is characterized by:

1. L_i is a finite set of local states. Each local state l_i represents the whole information about the system that the agent has at a given moment.
2. Var_i is a set of at most $n - 1$ local variables (i.e., $|Var_i| \le n - 1$) to model communication channels through which values are sent and received.
3. Act_i is a finite set of local actions available to the agent including the *null* action in order to account for the temporal evolution of the system.
4. $\mathcal{P}_i : L_i \to 2^{Act_i}$ is a local protocol function, producing the set of enabled actions that might be performed by i in a given local state.
5. $\iota_i \subseteq L_i$ is the set of initial states of the agent i.
6. $\tau_i : L_i \times Act_1 \times \ldots \times Act_n \times Act_e \to L_i$ is a local transition function, defining a local state from another local state and a joint action $a = (a_1, \ldots, a_n, a_e)$, one for each agent and environment agent.

The environment agent e, which captures the information that might not pertain to a specific agent, is characterized by $L_e, Var_e, Act_e, \mathcal{P}_e, \iota_e$ and τ_e. The notion of social state (termed global state in [14]) represents the screenshot of all agents in the system at a certain moment. A social state $s \in S$ is a tuple $s = (l_1, \ldots, l_n, l_e)$ where each element $l_i \in L_i$ represents the i's local state along with the environment state l_e. The set of all social states $S \subseteq L_1 \times \ldots \times L_n \times L_e$ is a subset of the Cartesian product of all local states of all agents and the environment agent. All local transition functions are combined together to define a social transition function $\tau : S \times Act_1 \times \ldots \times Act_n \times Act_e \to S$ in order to give the overall transition function for the system. Let $l_i(s)$ denotes the local state of agent i in the social state s and the value of a variable x in the set Var_i at $l_i(s)$ is denoted by $l_i^x(s)$. A communication channel between i and j does exist iff $Var_i \cap Var_j \neq \emptyset$. For the variable $x \in Var_i \cap Var_j$, $l_i^x(s) = l_j^x(s')$ means the values of x in $l_i(s)$ for i and in $l_j(s')$ for j are the same. Finally, the valuation function $\mathcal{V} : \mathcal{PV} \to 2^S$ defines what atomic propositions are true from the set $\mathcal{PV}$ at system states. To summarize, the extended version of the interpreted system formalism is given by the following tuple $IS^+ = (\{L_i, Var_i, Act_i, \mathcal{P}_i, \tau_i, \iota_i\}_{i \in \mathcal{A}}, \{L_e, Var_e, Act_e, \mathcal{P}_e, \tau_e, \iota_e\}, \mathcal{V})$.

Definition 1 (RTCTL^{cc} models, adopted from [6]). *A conditional commitment model* $M = (S, I, T, \{\sim_{i \to j} \mid (i,j) \in \mathcal{A}^2\}, \mathcal{V})$ *is generated from* $IS^+ = (\{L_i, Var_i, Act_i, \mathcal{P}_i, \tau_i, \iota_i\}_{i \in \mathcal{A}}, \{L_e, Act_e, \mathcal{P}_e, \tau_e, \iota_e\}, \mathcal{V})$ *by synchronising joint actions of* $n + 1$ *composed agent models as follows:*

- $S \subseteq L_1 \times \ldots \times L_n \times L_e$ *is a set of reachable social states for the system.*
- $I \subseteq \iota_1 \times \ldots \times \iota_n \times \iota_e$ *is a set of initial states for the system such that* $I \subseteq S$.

- $T \subseteq S \times S$ is a total temporal relation (i.e., each state has at least one successor) defined by $(s, s') \in T$ iff there exists a joint action $(a_1, \ldots, a_n, a_e) \in ACT = Act_1 \times \ldots \times Act_n \times Act_e$ such that $\tau(s, a_1, \ldots, a_n, a_e) = s'$.
- $\sim_{i \to j} \subseteq S \times S$ is a social accessibility relation defined for each pair $(i, j) \in \mathcal{A}^2$ by $s \sim_{i \to j} s'$ iff the following conditions hold: 1) $l_i(s) = l_i(s')$; 2) $(s, s') \in T$; 3) $Var_i \cap Var_j \neq \emptyset$ and $\forall x \in Var_i \cap Var_j$ we have $l_i^x(s) = l_j^x(s')$; and 4) $\forall y \in Var_j - Var_i$ we have $l_j^y(s) = l_j^y(s')$.
- $\mathcal{V} : \mathcal{PV} \to 2^S$ is a valuation function defined as in IS^+.

Following Emerson et al. [13], each transition in our quantitative temporal model M takes a single time unit for execution from one state to another state. The underlying real-time model is discrete and has a tree-like structure. The model M is unwound into a set of execution paths in which each path $\pi = s_0, s_1, \ldots$ is an infinite sequence of social states increasing simultaneously over time such that $s_i \in S$ and $(s_i, s_{i+1}) \in T$ for each $i \geq 0$. $\pi(k)$ is the k-th state of the path π. The set of all paths starting at s is denoted by $\Pi(s)$.

Definition 2 (Syntax of RTCTL^{cc}). *The syntax of RTCTL^{cc} is as follows:*

$$\varphi ::= p \mid \neg\varphi \mid \varphi \vee \varphi \mid EX\varphi \mid EG\varphi \mid E(\varphi \, U \, \varphi) \mid E(\varphi \, U^{[m..n]} \, \varphi)$$
$$\mid A(\varphi \, U^{[m..n]} \, \varphi) \mid CC \mid Fu$$
$$CC ::= WCC(i, j, \varphi, \varphi) \mid SCC(i, j, \varphi, \varphi)$$
$$Fu ::= FuW(i, WCC(i, j, \varphi, \varphi)) \mid FuS(i, SCC(i, j, \varphi, \varphi))$$

where:

- $p \in \mathcal{PV}$ is an atomic proposition. $\neg$ and $\vee$ are the usual Boolean connectives.
- E and A are the existential and universal quantifiers on paths.
- X, G and U are CTL path modal connectives standing for "next", "globally", and "until", respectively.
- m and $n \in \mathbb{N}^+$ are natural numbers denoting the bounds of time intervals.
- $U^{[m..n]}$ stands for interval bound until. This operator is used to abbreviate other bounded operators (e.g., $F^{[m..n]}$, $U^{\leq n}$ and $U^{=n}$, see Table 1).
- i and $j \in \mathcal{A}$ are two agents. WCC, SCC, FuW and FuS stand for weak and strong conditional commitment and their fulfillments, respectively [6].

From these syntactical rules, the formula $EX\varphi$ is read as "there exists a path such that at the next state of the path φ holds", $EG\varphi$ is read as "there exists a path such that φ holds globally along the path", and $E(\varphi \, U \, \psi)$ is read as "there exists a path such that ψ eventually holds and φ continuously holds until then". $E(\varphi \, U^{[m..n]} \, \psi)$ (respectively, $A(\varphi \, U^{[m..n]} \, \psi)$) can be read as "there exists a path such that (respectively, for all paths) ψ eventually holds at time instant i within the interval $[m..n]$ and φ continuously holds from m until then". We introduce the formula $A(\varphi \, U^{[m..n]} \, \psi)$ in the syntax of RTCTL^{cc} because the equivalent one from E is not compact and depends on other three operators (see Table 1). The formula $WCC(i, j, \psi, \varphi)$ (respectively, $SCC(i, j, \psi, \varphi)$) is read as "agent i weakly (respectively, strongly) commits towards agent j to consequently satisfy φ once the antecedent ψ holds". Intuitively, weak commitments can be activated even if the antecedent will never be satisfied, while strong commitments are solely established when there is a possibility to satisfy their antecedents. The commitment antecedents and consequences can be quantitative and/or qualitative formulae. The formula $FuW(i, WCC(i, j, \psi, \varphi))$ (respectively, $FuS(i, SCC(i, j, \psi, \varphi)))$ is read as "the weak (respectively, strong) conditional commitment $WCC(i, j, \psi, \varphi)$ (respectively, $SCC(i, j, \psi, \varphi)$) is fulfilled".

Definition 3 (Semantics of RTCTL^{cc}). *Given the model M, the satisfaction of RTCTL^{cc} formula φ in a state s, denoted by $(M, s) \models \varphi$, is recursively defined as follows:*

- $(M, s) \models p$ *iff* $s \in \mathcal{V}(p)$,
- $(M, s) \models \neg\varphi$ *iff* $(M, s) \not\models \varphi$,
- $(M, s) \models \varphi \vee \varphi$ *iff* $(M, s) \models \varphi$ *or* $(M, s) \models \varphi$,
- $(M, s) \models EX\varphi$ *iff* $\exists \pi \in \Pi(s)$ *such that* $(M, \pi(1)) \models \varphi$,
- $(M, s) \models EG\varphi$ *iff* $\exists \pi \in \Pi(s)$ *such that* $\forall k \geq 0, (M, \pi(k)) \models \varphi$,
- $(M, s) \models E(\varphi \ U \ \psi)$ *iff* $\exists \pi \in \Pi(s)$ *such that* $\exists k \geq 0, (M, \pi(k)) \models \psi$ *and* $\forall j, 0 \leq j < k, (M, \pi(j)) \models \varphi$,
- $(M, s) \models E(\varphi \ U^{[m..n]} \ \psi)$ *iff* $\exists \pi \in \Pi(s)$ *such that* $\exists i, m \leq i \leq n, (M, \pi(i)) \models \psi$ *and* $\forall j, m \leq j < i, (M, \pi(j)) \models \varphi$,
- $(M, s) \models A(\varphi \ U^{[m..n]} \ \psi)$ *iff* $\forall \pi \in \Pi(s)$ *such that* $\exists i, m \leq i \leq n, (M, \pi(i)) \models \psi$ *and* $\forall j, m \leq j < i, (M, \pi(j)) \models \varphi$,
- $(M, s) \models WCC(i, j, \psi, \varphi)$ *iff* $\forall s' \in S$ *such that* $s \sim_{i \rightarrow j} s'$ *and* $(M, s') \models \psi, (M, s') \models \varphi$,
- $(M, s) \models SCC(i, j, \psi, \varphi)$ *iff* (1) $\exists s' \in S$ *such that* $s \sim_{i \rightarrow j} s'$ *and* $(M, s') \models \psi$, *and* (2) $(M, s) \models WCC(i, j, \psi, \varphi)$,
- $(M, s) \models FuW(i, WCC(i, j, \psi, \varphi))$ *iff* $\exists s' \in S$ *such that* $s' \sim_{i \rightarrow j} s$ *and* $(M, s') \models WCC(i, j, \psi, \varphi)$ *and* $(M, s) \models \varphi \wedge \neg WCC(i, j, \psi, \varphi)$,
- $(M, s) \models FuS(i, SCC(i, j, \psi, \varphi))$ *iff* $\exists s' \in S$ *such that* $s' \sim_{i \rightarrow j} s$ *and* $(M, s') \models SCC(i, j, \psi, \varphi)$ *and* $(M, s) \models \psi \wedge \neg SCC(i, j, \psi, \varphi)$.

With respect to the defined semantics, other propositional connectives can be abbreviated in terms of the above as usual: $\wedge$ for conjunction, $\Rightarrow$ for implication, $\equiv$ for equivalence, and $\top$ for constant true proposition. In Table 1, we define some qualitative and quantitative modalities. From the table, k in the formula $E(\varphi \ U^{\leq k} \ \psi)$ reflects the "maximum number of permitted transitions along a path before the eventuality $\varphi \ U \ \psi$ holds" [13]. In this sense, $EF^{=k} \ \psi$ can be read as "there exists a path such that ψ eventually holds exactly at k time instant along the path". The pressing question is whether or not we can define unbounded modalities from the bounded ones? Following Emerson et al.'s strategy in [13], the unbounded modalities can be defined from the analogous bounded ones when the bounded time exists. For example, $A(\varphi \ U \ \psi) = \exists k \geq 0$ s.t. $A(\varphi \ U^{\leq k} \ \psi)$. We conclude by illustrating how RTCTL^{cc} can be utilized to express the properties that consider an explicit bound on the time instant.

Example 1. Let $q=receivePayment$ and $p=deliverGoods$ be two propositions, then the formula $AG(WCC(Mer, Cus, q, EF^{\leq 3}p))$ specifies that along all paths

Table 1. Some abbreviations of RTCTL^{cc}

Qualitative abbreviations	Quantitative abbreviations
$EF\varphi \triangleq E(\top\ U\ \varphi)$	$EF^{\leq k}\varphi \triangleq E(\top\ U^{\leq k}\ \varphi) \triangleq E(\top\ U^{[0..k]}\ \varphi)$
$AG\varphi \triangleq \neg EF\neg\varphi$	$EF^{[m..n]}\varphi \triangleq E(\top\ U^{[m..n]}\varphi)$
$A(\varphi\ U\ \psi) \triangleq$	$AF^{\leq k}\varphi \triangleq A(\top\ U^{\leq k}\ \varphi) \triangleq A(\top\ U^{[0..k]}\ \varphi)$
$\neg E(\neg\varphi\ U\ (\neg\psi \wedge \neg\varphi)) \wedge \neg EG\neg\varphi$	$AF^{[m..n]}\varphi \triangleq A(\top U^{[m..n]}\varphi)$
$AF\varphi \triangleq A(\top\ U\ \varphi)$	$EG^{\leq k}\varphi \triangleq \neg AF^{\leq k}\neg\varphi$
$AX\varphi \triangleq \neg EX\neg\varphi$	$EG^{[m..n]}\varphi \triangleq \neg AF^{[m..n]}\neg\varphi$
	$AG^{\leq k}\varphi \triangleq \neg EF^{\leq k}\neg\varphi$
	$AG^{[m..n]}\varphi \triangleq \neg EF^{[m..n]}\neg\varphi$
	$E(\varphi\ U^{=k}\ \psi) \triangleq E(\varphi\ U^{[k..k]}\ \psi)$

Fig. 1. shows an RTCTL^{cc} model where the proposition p holds at some future state of every possible path from s_0 to s_4 and the proposition q holds at all states in all paths from s_0 to s_2, formally, $(M, s_0) \models AF^{\leq 4}p \wedge AG^{\leq 2}q$.

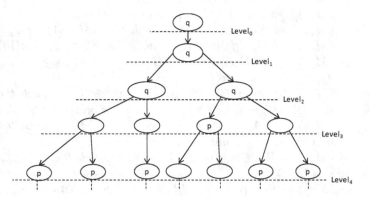

the merchant globally commits to deliver goods to the customer within at most 3 days once she received the agreed payment.

Example 2. Consider the car rental scenario discussed in the introduction.

1. The formula $AG(SCC(Cus, Age, EF\ disposeCar, EF^{=5}returnBackCar))$ expresses that the customer is obliged to return back the rental car to the agency on exactly 5 days as soon as the rental contract is disposed.
2. The customer is obliged to pay the whole rental amount on the first three days of the rental period: $AG(SCC(Cus, Age, EF\ disposeCar, EF^{[1..3]}payment))$. After 2 days from disposing the rental car, the customer sends the agreed payment, which conducts the fulfillment of the commitment: $EF(FuS(Cus, SCC(Cus, Age, EF\ disposeCar, EF^{[1..3]}payment)))$.
3. The agency is committed to the customer to withdraw the broken car and reimburse the remaining days within 2 days from the end of the rental period as soon as the customer notifies for breaking down: $AG(SCC(Age, Cus, EF^{\leq 5}notifyBrokenCar, EF\ withdrawBrokenCar \wedge EF^{[5..7]}reimburse))$.

Other examples in the introduction can be formalized in a similar manner.

3 Related Work

There are only two logical approaches that have defined formal semantics for conditional commitments, a universal type of social commitments, in the literature. The first approach is the one introduced by Singh [16]. In this approach, the author extended LTL with two modalities to represent and reason about two different types of conditional commitments (practical and dialectical). In the second approach, we extended CTL with four modalities to represent and reason about two types of conditional commitments (weak and strong) and their fulfillments [6]. The semantic rules of weak conditional commitments function as the ones introduced in [16]. The resulting logical language is so-called CTL^{cc}. Since unconditional commitments can be treated as a special case of conditional commitments when the antecedent is true: $C(i, j, \varphi) \triangleq WCC(i, j, \top, \varphi) \triangleq SCC(i, j, \top, \varphi)$, we beneath discuss the current approaches that develop only temporal unconditional commitment logics. Among these approaches, El Menshawy et al. [10] developed CTLC, an extension of CTL with unconditional commitment modality. El Menshawy et al. [8] improved the definition of the accessibility relation introduced in [10] to have a new semantics for unconditional commitment and fulfillment modalities. The new logic is called $CTLC^{+}$. The authors in [11] developed a branching time temporal logic called $ACTL^{*c}$ by extending CTL^{*} with temporal modalities to represent and reason about unconditional commitments and all related actions. The authors in [1] introduced a temporal logic called $CTLKC^{+}$, a combination of CTL modalities, knowledge modality and unconditional commitment modality. It is known that temporal logics are time-abstract with regard to the occurrence of events in the past and future without referencing to the precise timing of events. Therefore, temporal-logics-based approaches discussed above are not suitable to represent and reason about deadlines of commitments that incorporate metrics or real-time constraints as in real-life business scenarios. The current approach extends CTL^{cc} with real-time constraints in the bounded operators to rigorously address this limitation.

Mallya et al. [15] enriched CTL with: predicates to reason about commitments and fulfillment and violation actions; and two existential and universal quantifiers to capture temporal deadlines in the commitment consequences. Our interval bound until operators along with existential and universal quantifiers can model their temporal quantifiers in a reasonable way. From Mallya et al.'s approach, let p be a proposition representing a ticket as an offer, so the proposition $[d_1, d_2]p$ denotes that the ticket will be an offer in the interval beginning at d_1 and ending at d_2. In our approach, $WCC(TrCom, Cus, \top, EF^{[1..24]} p))$ means that the travel company weakly commits to a customer to eventually make the ticket as an offer, which is only valid for an entire day (i.e., 24 hours). However, our quantified time intervals are not abstracted as propositions, as done in [15].

In the literature of agent communication, parallel with modeling commitments as temporal modalities, there are executable action languages [4,5], such as event calculus and causal logic C+, which model commitments as fluents. A fluent is a property, which has different values at different time points or can hold within time intervals. The current approaches use Boolean fluents, which have two possible values: true (hence commitments hold) and false (hence commitments do not hold). The operational semantics of commitment actions is defined by a set of axioms. In the event calculus formalism, this operational semantics is as follows: action occurrences are defined by the use of *happens* predicates, the effects of actions are defined by the use of *initiates* and *terminates* predicates and the fluents values are defined by the use of *initially, holdsAt* and *holdsFor* predicates. Although these executable action languages are very easily and efficiently implemented for executable system specifications, the underlying time model is linear (unlike our time branching model) and there is no formal semantics for commitments. Chesani et al. [4] extended the current event calculus formalism with data, variables, and metric time to deal with temporal aspects (e.g., deadlines). Like our approach, the authors argued that metric time is missing in temporal logics (e.g., LTL, CTL and CTL*). From [4], consider the following axiom:

$$create(promise(Ag_1, Ag_2, deliverGoods), C(Ag_1, Ag_2, property(e(T_1, T_2),$$
$$deliverGoods)), T) \leftarrow T_1 \ is \ T + 1, T_2 \ is \ T + 3.$$

Now, suppose we observed the following event: $promise(Mer, Cus, deliverGoods)$ at time 20. Since the signature of this event copes with the description of $create(\ldots)$, then Mer becomes committed to deliver the requested goods between time 21 and time 23: $C(Mer, Cus, property(e(21, 23), deliverGoods))$. The Chesani et al.'s axiom can be defined using our logic as follows: $EF^{=20}promise(Mer, Cus, deliverGoods) \wedge SCC(Mer, Cus, \top, EF^{[21..23]}deliverGoods)$. Our approach can also extend the *content language* expressions in FIPA-ACL with interval operators to express assortment sets of temporal requirements, as done in [18].

4   Conclusion

We have shown how to extend the qualitative conditional commitment logic CTL^{cc} to the quantitative logic called $RTCTL^{cc}$. The new logic is suitable for time-bounded reasoning about real-time MASs computing where the interaction among agents is modeled by conditional commitments and their fulfillment actions. We have also pointed out how quantitative properties expressed in the extended version of event calculus can be rigorously expressed in $RTCTL^{cc}$. As future work, we plan to develop a transformation algorithm to automatically transform the problem of model checking $RTCTL^{cc}$ into the problem of model checking RTCTL [13], so that the use of NuSMV is feasible. Given that, we plan to develop symbolic algorithms for bounded operators and implement them on top of our symbolic model checker MCMAS+ [6] to compare between direct and indirect verification techniques. We also plan to consider arbitrary durations in our model's transitions to have different levels of temporal deadlines and to reduce extra verification work resulting from the use of unit measure steps.

Acknowledgments. The authors would like to thank NSERC (Canada) and Menoufia University (Egypt) for their financial support.

References

1. Al-Saqqar, F., Bentahar, J., Sultan, K., Wan, W., Khosrowshahi, E.: Model checking temporal knowledge and commitments in multi-agent systems using reduction. Simulation Modelling Practice and Theory **51**, 45–68 (2015)
2. Baldoni, M., Baroglio, C., Marengo, E., Patti, V.: Constitutive and regulative specifications of commitment protocols: A decoupled approach. ACM Transactions on Intelligent Systems and Technology **4**(2), 22 (2013)
3. Bentahar, J., El-Menshawy, M., Qu, H., Dssoulia, R.: Communicative commitments: Model checking and complexity analysis. Knowledge-Based Systems **35**, 21–34 (2012)
4. Chesani, F., Mello, P., Montali, M., Torroni, P.: Representing and monitoring social commitments using the event calculus. Autonomous Agents and Multi-Agent Systems **27**(1), 85–130 (2013)
5. Desai, N., Singh, M.: A modular action description language for protocol composition. In: Proceedings of the 22nd AAAI Conference on Artificial Intelligence, pp. 962–967 (2007)
6. El-Kholy, W., Bentahar, J., El-Menshawy, M., Qu, H., Dssouli, R.: Conditional commitments: Reasoning and model checking. ACM Transaction on Software Engineering and Methodology 24, 9:1-9-49 (2014)
7. El-Kholy, W., Bentahar, J., El-Menshawy, M., Qu, H., Dssouli, R.: Modeling and verifying choreographed multi-agent-based web service compositions regulated by commitment protocols. Expert Systems with Applications **41**, 7478–7494 (2014)
8. El-Menshawy, M., Bentahar, J., El-Kholy, W., Dssouli, R.: Reducing model checking commitments for agent communication to model checking ARCTL and GCTL*. Autonomous Agent Multi-Agent Systems **27**(3), 375–418 (2013)
9. El-Menshawy, M., Bentahar, J., Dssouli, R.: Verifiable semantic model for agent interactions using social commitments. In: Dastani, M., El Fallah Segrouchni, A., Leite, J., Torroni, P. (eds.) LADS 2009. LNCS, vol. 6039, pp. 128–152. Springer, Heidelberg (2010)
10. El-Menshawy, M., Bentahar, J., Dssouli, R.: Symbolic model checking commitment protocols using reduction. In: Omicini, A., Sardina, S., Vasconcelos, W. (eds.) DALT 2010. LNCS, vol. 6619, pp. 185–203. Springer, Heidelberg (2011)
11. El-Menshawy, M., Bentahar, J., Kholy, W.E., Dssouli, R.: Verifying conformance of multi-agent commitment-based protocols. Expert Systems with Applications **40**(1), 122–138 (2013)
12. El-Menshawy, M., Benthar, J., Qu, H., Dssouli, R.: On the verification of social commitments and time. In: Sonenberg, L., Stone, P., Tumer, K., Yolum, P. (eds.) AAMAS, pp. 483–490. IFAAMAS (2011)
13. Emerson, E.A., Mok, A.K., Sistla, A.P., Srinivasan, J.: Quantitative temporal reasoning. Real-Time Systems **4**(4), 331–352 (1992)
14. Fagin, R., Halpern, J., Moses, Y., Vardi, M.: Reasoning about Knowledge. MIT Press (1995)
15. Mallya, A.U., Yolum, I., Singh, M.P.: Resolving commitments among autonomous agents. In: Dignum, F.P.M. (ed.) ACL 2003. LNCS (LNAI), vol. 2922, pp. 166–182. Springer, Heidelberg (2004)

16. Singh, M.: Semantical considerations on dialectical and practical commitments. In: Proceedings of 23rd AAAI Conference on Artificial Intelligence, pp. 176–181 (2008)
17. Telang, P., Singh, M.: Specifying and verifying cross-organizational business models: An agent oriented approach. IEEE Transactions on Service Computing 5(3), 305–318 (2012)
18. Verdicchio, M., Colombetti, M.: Dealing with time in content language expressions. In: van Eijk, R.M., Huget, M.-P., Dignum, F.P.M. (eds.) AC 2004. LNCS (LNAI), vol. 3396, pp. 91–105. Springer, Heidelberg (2005)

A Double Auction Mechanism for On-Demand Transport Networks

Malcolm Egan[1], Martin Schaefer[1]([⊠]), Michal Jakob[1], and Nir Oren[2]

[1] Faculty of Electrical Engineering,
Czech Technical University in Prague, Prague, Czech Republic
martin.schaefer@fel.cvut.cz

[2] Department of Computing Science, University of Aberdeen, Aberdeen, UK

Abstract. Market mechanisms play a key role in allocating and pricing commuters and drivers in new on-demand transport services such as Uber, and Liftago in Prague. These services successfully use different mechanisms, which suggests a need to understand the behavior of a range of mechanisms within the context of on-demand transport. In this paper, we propose a double auction mechanism and compare its performance to a mechanism inspired by Liftago's approach. We show that our mechanism can improve efficiency and satisfy key properties such as weak budget balance and truthfulness.

Keywords: Double auction · On-demand transport · Taxis

1 Introduction

Lead globally by Uber, several on-demand transport services—including Grab-Taxi in Singapore and Liftago in Prague[1]—are rapidly making a transition from the traditional taxi model to market-based approaches. These approaches are characterized by dynamic pricing, both for commuters and drivers.

An important, but not widely acknowledged, aspect of the transition to market-based approaches is that different on-demand transport services are using different mechanisms. For instance, Uber utilises a mechanism where commuter prices and driver payments are set using a data-driven approach. On the other hand, companies such as Liftago in Prague and GrabTaxi in Singapore have implemented an auction-based mechanism where drivers bid for commuter journeys. Determining which approach is better is difficult; while both companies are financially viable, they (mainly) operate in different cities.

The success of such different pricing approaches reveals a need to understand how various market mechanisms behave within the context of on-demand transport systems. While auction and posted price mechanisms have been extensively studied in a range of domains, this is not the case for the two-sided markets that arise in on-demand transportation. So far, the only work investigating the properties of these mechanisms is either aligned with Uber's mechanism [1,4,5] or

---

[1] https://www.uber.com/, http://grabtaxi.com, https://www.liftago.com/

© Springer International Publishing Switzerland 2015
Q. Chen et al. (Eds.): PRIMA 2015, LNAI 9387, pp. 557–565, 2015.
DOI: 10.1007/978-3-319-25524-8_38

targeted at on-demand transport services with salaried drivers [3]. In particular, there has not been an evaluation of auction-based mechanisms, such as those adopted by Liftago and GrabTaxi.

In this paper, we introduce a market mechanism for on-demand transport services that aligns more closely with Liftago's approach rather than the one adopted by Uber. In particular, our mechanism is based on a double auction, which means that both commuters and drivers bid for a journey. Although commuter bidding is not widely used at present, double auctions are known to be highly efficient—forming a benchmark for other approaches—and the service is accessible to all commuters when there is not significant financial inequality (e.g., in on-demand transport services targeted at businesses).

In contrast with standard applications of double auctions [6], goods (i.e., journeys) in on-demand transport systems are heterogeneous. Furthermore, on-demand transportation systems are large scale. Therefore, any new approach must be able to both cope with the domain's heterogeneity, and directly address the scalability challenge. To this end, we show that our mechanism naturally decomposes the large-scale market into a number of smaller scale sub-markets, which can be run in parallel. We also provide key properties of our mechanism, including conditions when truthfulness holds. We show via simulations that our mechanism can achieve both a higher number of trades and efficiency, compared with a benchmark auction mechanism inspired by Liftago's approach.

2   System Model

In this section, we develop an agent-based model including commuters, drivers, and the provider (e.g., Uber or Liftago). Our model captures the private preferences of commuter and drivers, and forms the basis for our proposed double auction mechanism, which we describe in Section 3. We consider the common scenario where pre-booking and ridesharing are not supported.

Underlying our model is the road network. This is represented by a directed graph $G = (V, E)$. In the graph, the set of nodes V represents possible pick-up and drop-off locations of commuters. The set of edges E represents the direct routes between locations in V, which can be traversed by the drivers. Associated to each edge $e \in E$ are: a pick-up location $u \in V$; a drop-off location $w \in V$; a cost[2] $c_e \in [0, \infty)$ for a vehicle to traverse edge $e \in E$; and an edge traversal time $\tau_e \in \mathbb{Z}_+$.

We consider a discrete time model, where the market mechanism is run every T minutes. We assume that all commuters are willing to accept a delay of T minutes on top of the time that it takes their allocated driver to reach their pick-up location. This is not a strong assumption when T is sufficiently small; e.g., 10 minutes.

We now detail our assumptions on commuter and driver preferences.

---

[2] Such costs could arise due to fuel consumption and vehicle wear and tear.

2.1   Commuter Preferences

Commuter i desires a journey with immediate pick-up at a location $u_i \in V$ and drop-off location $v_i \in V$, which is reported to the provider. Each commuter i has a maximum price, $p_{i,\max}$, she is prepared to pay for the journey. This is determined by two factors: the distance of the journey; and the maximum price-rate (in euros/km), $r_{i,\max}$, that she is prepared to pay, known only to the commuter. The value of $r_{i,\max}$ reflects commuter i's desire for the journey and her beliefs about how much alternative transportation options will cost. As such, $r_{i,\max}$ captures the effect of competition between providers—if there is an alternative, $r_{i,\max}$ will be less than what the alternative provider is offering.

The maximum price that commuter i will pay for their journey is given by $p_{i,\max} = r_{i,\max} R_i$, where R_i is the distance of the requested journey between pick-up location u_i and drop-off location v_i, dependent on the road network. The maximum price $p_{i,\max}$ determines how much commuter i will bid to be transported in our double auction mechanism (described in Section 3). The utility of commuter i that pays price p is $p_{i,\max} - p$ if allocated and zero otherwise.

2.2   Driver Preferences

Drivers are profit-seeking; that is, each driver j seeks to obtain a minimum profit for each journey. The profit that driver j will receive, S_j, from transporting commuter i is given by $S_j = r_{j,i} R_i - c R_i - c R_{j,i}$, where R_i is the distance of commuter i's requested journey, c is the cost per kilometer (due to fuel consumption as well as vehicle wear and tear), $R_{j,i}$ is the distance from driver j's initial location to commuter i's pick-up location, and $r_{j,i}$ is the price-rate per kilometer that driver j receives for transporting commuter i. The price-rate $r_{j,i}$ is determined by our mechanism detailed in Section 3.

Each driver j is only willing to transport a passenger if a minimum profit target, $S_{j,\min}$, is met; that is if $S_j \geq S_{j,\min}$. The minimum profit $S_{j,\min}$ determines how much driver j will bid for a journey in our double auction mechanism which reflects the expectations of the driver including journey duration. The utility of driver j is $S_j - S_{j,\min}$ if she is allocated and zero otherwise.

3   Proposed Market Mechanism

In this section, we introduce our double auction market mechanism. The purpose of the mechanism is to allocate commuters to drivers and determine how much commuters pay for their journeys as well as the payment drivers receive. In this setting, each commuter's requested journey is treated as a good that is bought by commuters from drivers. Unlike the usual double auction setup [6], journeys are not homogeneous, with each journey different: the pick-up location and journey distance varies from commuter to commuter; and the distance between each driver's initial location and each commuter's pick-up location also differs for each driver-commuter pair.

Journey heterogeneity means that standard double auction mechanisms—designed for homogeneous goods—cannot be directly applied. To deal with this problem, we introduce a market decomposition algorithm in Section 3.1, which decomposes the market into a number of approximately homogeneous sub-markets. This allows us to exploit the desirable properties of the McAfee mechanism [6] in each sub-market, which we describe in Section 3.2. The approximately homogeneous nature of each sub-market causes bidders to behave differently compared with homogeneous markets. The properties of our mechanism are described in Section 3.3.

3.1 Sub-Market Decomposition

The first component of our mechanism is a method to decompose the market (consisting of commuters and drivers) at the time the mechanism is run. The purpose of the decomposition is to generate a number of *approximately* homogeneous sub-markets that can be run in parallel.

To generate the sub-markets, first observe that each driver j's valuation of a journey is in terms of their profit, whereas each commuter i's valuation is in terms of price. In order to compare the bids, the provider converts the bid of commuter i to an effective profit. That is, the net profit received by a potential driver k that serves commuter i will be $S_{k,i} = p_{i,\max} - cR_i - cR_{k,i}$, where $R_{k,i}$ is the distance between the initial location of driver k to the pick-up location of commuter i. Observe that the heterogeneity in the market arises because R_i and $R_{k,i}$ differ for each driver-commuter pair.

To generate a homogeneous sub-market, we need to ensure that R_i and $R_{k,i}$ are the same for each driver-commuter pair. This occurs in two situations: either all commuters are in the same location, have a journey with the same distance, and each driver is at the same distance from each commuter (e.g., an airport); or all drivers are in the same location, and each commuter has the same distance journey with pick-up locations at the same distance from each driver (e.g., a city center).

In practice, the conditions for a homogeneous sub-market will not normally occur *exactly*; instead, we need to settle for approximate homogeneity. This can be achieved for the first situation as follows (illustrated in Fig. 1):

- *Situation I (Commuter-centric):*
    - K commuters are treated as being in the same location if the pick-up locations of all K commuters do not differ by more than a distance δ; i.e., $\|u_k - u_c\| \leq \delta$, $\forall k$, where u_c is the centroid of the pick-up locations of all K commuters.
    - K commuters having the same the journey distance if their journey distances $\{R_i\}$ do not differ pairwise by more than a distance ϵ; i.e., $|R_k - R_l| \leq \epsilon$, $\forall k, l$.
    - N drivers are treated as being at the same distance from the commuters if distances from their initial location to the centroid, u_c, do not differ pairwise by more than a distance γ; i.e., $|R_{k,c} - R_{l,c}| \leq \gamma$, $\forall k, l$, where

$R_{k,c}$ is a distance to the centroid of all pick-up locations from initial position of driver k.

The second driver-centric situation can be formed similarly (we omit details due to space constraints).

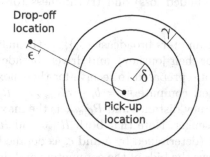

Drop-off location

Pick-up location

Fig. 1. Illustration of sub-market formation in Situation I.

To generate the sub-markets, the parameters ϵ, δ and γ need to be tuned. This will typically rely on statistics from the network. The sub-markets are then formed using an algorithm based on K-mean clustering. We examine the effect of these parameters and the resulting approximate homogeneity on a realistic on-demand transport network in Section 4.

3.2 Double Auction Mechanism

We now detail our proposed double auction mechanism, which consists of two phases:

1. Decompose the on-demand transport market into approximately homogeneous sub-markets using the approach detailed in Section 3.1;
2. Allocate commuters to drivers:
   - While there is a sub-market with at least one commuter and driver in the sub-market, run a double auction in that sub-market using the McAfee rule (detailed below).
   - If there is only one commuter (or driver) in the sub-market, then run a sealed bid second price auction where a trade occurs only if the commuter (or driver) accepts the journey (based on their valuation as detailed in Section 2).

A key feature of our mechanism is that it decomposes the potentially large scale market into a number of sub-markets, which can be run in parallel. As such, we are able to automatically group desirable commuters and drivers together, which is important in practice as it reduces the need for drivers to respond to a large number of commuter offers.

We now detail how commuters and drivers are allocated in the second phase of our mechanism when there is at least one commuter and driver in a sub-market. The basic idea of the allocation is to match the commuters that bid the most to drivers that bid the least, which maximizes the number of efficient trades. The additional steps are based on the McAfee mechanism [6] to ensure high efficiency (with bounded loss) and truthfulness (discussed further in the following sections).

(i) (Initialization) Commuters broadcast $\{b_i\}_{i=1}^{K}$ (the maximum price they are prepared to pay for their journey), and drivers broadcast $\{s_j\}_{j=1}^{N}$ (the minimum profit they are prepared to receive for their next journey).

(ii) For each commuter, compute $b_i' = b_i - cR_{\max} - cR_{0,\max}$, where $R_{\max}$ is the maximum journey distance and $R_{0,\max}$ is the maximum distance of the driver from a passenger. Note that both $R_{\max}$ and $R_{0,\max}$ are parameters of the sub-market (determined by δ and ϵ, as detailed in the previous subsection). This allows the bids of the commuters and drivers to be compared as they are both in terms of profit.

(iii) Sort commuters: $b_{(1)}' \geq b_{(2)}' \geq \cdots \geq b_{(K)}'$; drivers: $s_{(1)} \leq s_{(2)} \leq \cdots \leq s_{(N)}$.

(iv) Compute the number of efficient trades: $k^* = \max\{k : b_{(k)}' \geq s_{(k)},\ b_{(k+1)}' < s_{(k+1)}\}$ and compute $p_0 = \frac{1}{2}(b_{(k+1)}' + s_{(k+1)})$.

(v) Check the McAfee condition:

    (a) If $p_0 \in [s_{(k^*)}, b_{(k^*)}']$, then the actual prices for the drivers and commuters are $s = b' = p_0$ and all k^* efficient pairs are allocated;

    (b) Otherwise the prices for the drivers and commuters are $s = s_{(k^*)}$, $b' = b_{(k^*)}'$ and $k^* - 1$ pairs are allocated.

(vii) Commuters are then required to pay $b' + cR_{\max} + cR_{0,\max}$ and each driver j who transports commuter i is paid $s + cR_i + cR_{j,i}$.

3.3 Mechanism Properties

The approximate homogeneity in the sub-markets that arise in our mechanism means that not all properties of standard double auctions hold. We now state without proof (due to space constraints) the key properties of our mechanism.

Proposition 1. *The mechanism is weak budget balanced and individually rational.*

Proposition 2. *The mechanism is ex interim truthful when agents are risk averse*[3]. *However, the mechanism is not ex post truthful when agents are risk neutral.*

---

[3] Recall that *ex interim* means that agents know their own preferences, but not for the others, and risk averse means that agents act by maximizing their minimum utility (as opposed to the average in the risk neutral case)

Note that the standard McAfee mechanism for homogeneous goods is *ex post* truthful for risk neutral agents [6]. The restriction to *ex interim* truthfulness with risk averse agents is a consequence of approximate homogeneity in each sub-market. These properties suggest that our mechanism is useful in practice as it ensures that the provider does not lose money on each journey (weak budget balance), as well as ensuring that drivers and commuters have incentives to participate (the mechanism is individually rational). In the next section, we investigate the efficiency (i.e., sum of drivers' and commuters' utilities) of our mechanism via simulation and compare with a benchmark mechanism inspired by Liftago's approach.

4   Simulation Results

In this section, we evaluate the efficiency of our mechanism via simulation. Our mechanism is benchmarked against an approach inspired by Liftago's mechanism; namely, a sealed bid second price auction, where the commuter accepts the journey if the second highest bid is less than the maximum price she is prepared to pay. Our simulation study is based on the commuter demand profile in the Mobility Services Testbed [2] for the city of Hague. We assume that there are 20 available drivers and 100 commuters throughout the road network at the beginning of a mechanism run, at a peak hour. We set the time between mechanism runs as 10 minutes and the cost per kilometer as c = 0.3 euros.

In figures 2(a) to 3(b), we evaluate the efficiency and number of trades in a single commuter-centric *sub-market* (as detailed in Section 3.1), and the dependence on the parameter choices (i.e., for δ, γ). Although this does not evaluate the long-term network-wide performance of our mechanism, it provides insight into how the choices of these parameters affect efficiency and how a single sub-market compares to the benchmark. The maximum price-rate that each commuter is prepared to accept and the minimum profit a driver is willing to receive

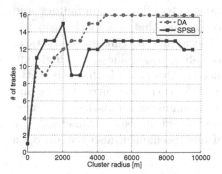

(a) Plot of number of trades vs. the commuter cluster radius, δ.

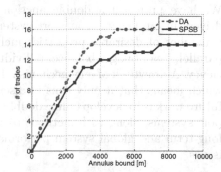

(b) Plot of number of trades vs. width of the driver annulus, γ.

Fig. 2. Effect of sub-market parameters on the number of trades.

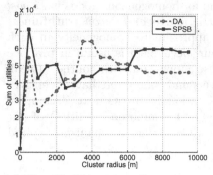
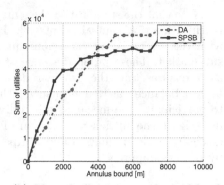

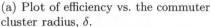

(a) Plot of efficiency vs. the commuter cluster radius, δ.

(b) Plot of efficiency vs. the width of the driver annulus, γ.

Fig. 3. Effect of sub-market parameters on the efficiency (i.e., sum of drivers' and commuters' utilities).

is drawn from the beta distribution (a highly flexible distribution with bounded support), with parameters $\alpha_r = 1, \beta_r = 1$ on support $[0, 2.5]$ (for the price-rate) and $\alpha_s = 1, \beta_s = 2.5$ on support $[0, 10]$ (for the minimum profit). We note that a similar preference model was also used in [3].

Observe in figures 2(a) to 3(b) that using a choice of $\epsilon = \delta = \gamma = 5$ km, our mechanism outperforms the benchmark in terms of both number of trades (i.e., number of commuters served) and the efficiency. Importantly, the number of trades and efficiency is dependent on the parameter choices, which suggests further improvements are possible by optimizing our mechanism to tailor it to a particular city in order to outperform the benchmark.

5 Conclusions

We have proposed a double auction mechanism to allocate commuters and drivers in on-demand transport systems. We showed that our mechanism has a number of desirable properties including the ability to run sub-markets in parallel, weak budget balance, individual rationality, truthfulness, and high efficiency. A drawback of our mechanism introduced in this paper is that it is static, which means that it only runs in discrete time. As such, our current focus and future work is to develop online double auction mechanisms for on-demand transport systems, along with methods to optimize the sub-market parameters. The long-term and global system performance of our mechanism also remain open issues.

Acknowledgments. Supported by the European Commission under MyWay, a collaborative project part of the Seventh Framework Programme for research, technological development and demonstration under grant agreement no 609023. Further supported by the European social fund within the framework of realizing the project

"Support of inter-sectoral mobility and quality enhancement of research teams at Czech Technical University in Prague", CZ.1.07/2.3.00/30.0034. Period of the projects realization 1.12.2012-30.6.2015.

References

1. Borgs, C., Candogan, O., Chayes, J., Lobel, I., Hazerzadeh, H.: Optimal multiperiod pricing with service guarantees. Management Science **60**(7), 1792–1811 (2014)
2. Čertický, M., Jakob, M., Píbil, R.: Analyzing on-demand mobility services by agent-based simulation. Journal of Ubiquitous Systems & Pervasive Networks **6**(1), 17–26 (2015)
3. Egan, M., Jakob, M.: A profit-aware negotiation mechanism for on-demand transport services. In: Proc. European Conference on Artificial Intelligence (ECAI) (2014)
4. Gan, J., An, B., Miao, C.: Optimizing efficiency of taxi systems: scaling-up and handling arbitrary constraints. In: Proceedings of the 14th International Conference on Autonomous Agents and Multiagent Systems (AAMAS 2015) (2015)
5. Gan, J., An, B., Wang, H., Sun, X., Shi, Z.: Optimal pricing for improving efficiency of taxi systems. In: Proceedings of the 23rd International Joint Conference on Artificial Intelligence (IJCAI) (2013)
6. McAfee, R.: Dominant strategy double auction. Journal of Economic Theory **56**(2) (1992)

Exploiting Social Commitments in Programming Agent Interaction

Matteo Baldoni[(✉)], Cristina Baroglio, Federico Capuzzimati,
and Roberto Micalizio

Dipartimento di Informatica, Università degli Studi di Torino, Turin, Italy
matteo.baldoni@unito.it

Abstract. Modeling and regulating interactions among agents is a critical step in the development of Multiagent Systems (MASs). Some recent works assume a normative view, and suggest to model interaction protocols in terms of obligations. In this paper we propose to model interaction protocols in terms of goals and commitments, and show how such a formalization promotes a deliberative process inside the agents. The proposal is implemented via JaCaMo+, an extension of JaCaMo, in which Jason agents can interact, while preserving their deliberative capabilities, by exploiting commitment-based protocols, reified by special CArtAgO artifacts.

Keywords: Social computing · Agent programming · Commitments and goals · Agents & Artifacts · JaCaMo

1 Introduction

Many researchers claim that an effective way to approach the design and development of a MAS consists in conceiving it as a structure composed of four main entities: *Agents*, *Environment*, *Interactions*, and *Organization* [6,13,14]. Such a separation of concerns enjoys many advantages from a software engineering point of view, since it enables a modular development of code that eases code reuse and maintainability. Currently, there are many frameworks that support the realization of one of these components (e.g., [4,8]). To the best of our knowledge, JaCaMo [5] is the the most complete among the well-established proposals, providing a thorough integration of the three components agents, environments, and organizations into a single programming framework.

A recent extension to JaCaMo [25] further enriches the framework by introducing an interaction component. The interaction component allows regulating both agent interactions and the interactions between agents and environment. More precisely, an interaction component encodes –in an automaton-like shape– a *protocol*, in which states represent protocol steps, and transitions between states are associated with (undirected) *obligations*. Such protocols provide a *guideline* of how a given organizational goal should be achieved. Interaction components, as defined in [25], however, present also some drawbacks.

© Springer International Publishing Switzerland 2015
Q. Chen et al. (Eds.): PRIMA 2015, LNAI 9387, pp. 566–574, 2015.
DOI: 10.1007/978-3-319-25524-8_39

Works such as [11] show the importance, for the agents to be autonomous, to reason about the social consequences of their actions by exploiting *constitutive norms* that link the agents' actions to their respective social meanings. However, an interaction component operates as a coordinator that, by relying on obligations, issues commands about what an agent has to do, and when. This impedes agents from reasoning on the normative effects of their actions. On the one hand, obligations are not constitutive norms, on the other hand, the social meaning of such commands is not known to the agents but only implicitly encoded within the protocol. Agents lose part of their deliberative power since, once they join an interaction component, they have no other choice but deciding whether satisfying or not those obligations they are in charge of, while the rationale behind these obligations remains hidden to them. Consequently, this approach does not suit those situations where interaction is not subject to an organizational guideline, such as when interaction is among agents and each agent decides what is best for itself [24], or when guidelines amount to declarative, underspecified constraints that still leave agents the freedom to take strategic decisions on their behavior. We thus propose a complementary approach to [25] which better supports the deliberative capabilities of the agents.

When organizational goals are not associated with corresponding guidelines, agent deliberation is crucial for the achievement of goals. An agent has to act not only upon its own goals, but also upon what interactions could be necessary for achieving these goals. In other terms, an agent has to discover how to fulfill a goal by interacting with others. It is important to underline that when agents can fully exploit their deliberative capabilities, they can take advantage of opportunities (*flexibility*), and can find alternative ways to get their goals despite unexpected situations that may arise (*robustness*). To this aim, we present JaCaMo+, an agent platform, that builds upon JaCaMo [5], where Jason agents engage *commitment-based interactions* which are reified as CArtAgO artifacts. CArtAgO is a framework based on the A&A meta-model [19,23] which extends the agent programming paradigm with the first-class entity of artifact: a resource that an agent can use, and that models working environments. The environment is itself programmable and encapsulates services and functionalities, making it active. JaCaMo+ artifacts represent the *interaction social state* and provide the roles agents enact. The use of artifacts enables the implementation of monitoring functionalities for verifying that the on-going interactions respect the commitments and for detecting violations and violators. The well-known gold miners scenario is used as an example.

2   Social Commitments for Programming

The heart of our proposal is that whenever organization-driven guidelines are missing, the interactions among the agents should be supported by the very fundamental notions of *goal* and *engagement*. So, we propose to complement the interaction protocol in [25], and more in general organizational and normative approaches [12,15,18], with an *interaction artifact* that can be used by the agents as a common ground. Our interaction artifacts encode the notion of engagement as *social commitment* [20]. A social commitment models the directed relation between two agents: a *debtor* and a *creditor*, that are both aware of the existence of such a relation and of its current state: A commitment $C(x, y, s, u)$ captures that agent x (debtor) commits to agent y (creditor) to bring about the consequent condition u when the antecedent condition s holds. Antecedent and consequent conditions are conjunctions or disjunctions of events and commitments. A commitment is autonomously taken by a debtor towards a creditor on its own initiative, instead of dropping from an organization, like obligations. Unlike obligations, commitments are manipulated by agents through the standard operations *create, cancel, release, discharge, assign, delegate* [20]. Since debtors are expected to satisfy their engagements, commitments have a normative value, providing social expectations on the agents' behaviors, as well as obligations.

The choice of commitments is, thus, motivated by the fact that they are taken by an agent as a result of an internal deliberative process, that creates social relationships with a normative flavour. This preserves the autonomy of the agents and is fundamental to harmonize deliberation with goal achievement. The agent does not just react to some obligations, but it rather includes a deliberative capacity by which it creates engagements towards other agents while it is trying to achieve its goals (or to the aim of achieving its goals). Citing Singh [21], an agent would become a debtor of a commitment based on the agent's own communications: either by directly saying something or having another agent communicate something in conjunction with a prior communication of the debtor. That is, there is a causal path from the establishment of a commitment to prior communications by the debtor of that commitment. By contrast, obligations can result from a deliberative process which is outside the agent; this is the case of the interaction component in [25]. This is the reason why we believe that the introduction of a deliberative process on constitutive rules that rely on obligations would not really support the agents' autonomy.

Commitment-based protocols assume that a (notional) *social state* is available and inspectable by all the involved agents. The social state traces which commitments currently exist between any two agents, and the states of these commitments according to the commitments lifecycle. Commitments can be used by agents in their practical reasoning together with beliefs, intentions, and *goals*. In particular, Telang et al. [22] point out that goals and commitments are one another complementary: A commitment specifies how an agent relates to another one, and hence describes what an agent is willing to bring about for another agent. On the other hand, a goal denotes an agent's proattitude towards some condition; that is, a state of the world that the agent should achieve. An agent can create a commitment towards another agent to achieve one of its goals; but at the same time, an agent determines the goals to be pursued relying on the commitments it has towards others.

3   JaCaMo+

JaCaMo [5] is a platform integrating Jason (as an agent programming language), CArtAgO (as a realization of the A&A meta-model [23]), and Moise (as a support to the realization of organizations). JaCaMo+ extends the CArtAgO and Jason components of the standard JaCaMo. Artifacts are enriched with an explicit representation of commitments and of commitment-based protocols. The resulting class of artifacts reifies the execution of commitment-based protocols, including the social state of the interaction, and enables Jason agents both to be notified about the social events and to perform practical reasoning also about the other agents (this is possible thanks to the *social expectations* raised by commitments). Specifically, a JaCaMo+ artifact encodes a commitment protocol, that is structured into a set of roles. By enacting a role, an agent gains the rights to perform social actions, whose execution has public social consequences, expressed in terms of commitments. If an agent tries to perform an action which is not associated with the role it is enacting, the artifact raises an exception that is notified to the violator. Instead, when an agent performs a protocol action that pertains to its role, the social state is updated accordingly by adding new commitments, or by modifying the state of existing commitments. Since an artifact is a programmable, active entity, it can act as a monitor of the interaction in progress, detecting violations that it can ascribe to the violator without the need of agent introspection. By *focusing* on an artifact, an agent registers to be notified of events that are generated inside the artifact: when the social state is updated, the JaCaMo+ artifact provides such information to the focusing JaCaMo+ agents by exploiting proper *observable properties*. Agents are, thus, constantly aligned with the social state.

Jason [8] implements in Java, and extends, the agent programming language AgentSpeak(L). Jason agents have a BDI architecture. Each has a belief base, and a plan library. It is possible to specify *achievement* (operator '!') and *test* (operator '?') goals. Each plan has a triggering event (causing its activation), which can be either the addition or the deletion of some belief or goal. JaCaMo+ extends JaCaMo by allowing the specification of plans whose triggering events involve commitments. JaCaMo+ represents a commitment as a term $cc(debtor, creditor, antecedent, consequent, status)$ where *debtor* and *creditor* identify the involved agents (or agent roles), while *antecedent* and *consequent* are the commitment conditions. *Status* is the commitment state (the set being defined in the commitments life cycle [16]). Commitment operations are realized as *internal operations* of the new class of artifacts we added to CArtAgO. Thus, they cannot be invoked directly by the agents, but the protocol actions will use them as primitives to modify the social state.

A Jason plan is specified as $triggering\_event : \langle context \rangle \leftarrow \langle body \rangle$. The *triggering_event* denotes the events the plan handles, the *context* specifies the circumstances when the plan could be used, the *body* is the course of action that should be taken. Commitments can be used both in the *context* and in the *body*. Otherwise than beliefs, their assertion/deletion can only occur through the artifact, in consequence to a social state change. The following template shows a Jason plan triggered by the addition of a commitment in the social state: $+cc(debtor, creditor, antecedent, consequent, status) : \langle context \rangle \leftarrow \langle body \rangle$. More precisely, the plan is triggered when a commitment, that unifies with the one in the plan head, appears in the social state. The syntax is the standard for Jason plans. *Debtor* and *creditor* are to be substituted by the proper roles. The plan may be devised so as to change the commitment status (e.g. the debtor will try to satisfy the comment), or it may be devised so as to allow the agent to react to the commitment presence (e.g., collecting information). Similar schemas can be used for commitment deletion and for the addition/deletion of social facts. Further, commitments can also be used in contexts and in plans as test goals ($?cc(\ldots)$), or achievement goals ($!cc(\ldots)$). Addition or deletion of such goals can, as well, be managed by plans; for example: $+!cc(debtor, creditor, antecedent, consequent, status) : \langle context \rangle \leftarrow \langle body \rangle$. The plan is triggered when the agent creates an achievement goal concerning a commitment. Consequently, the agent will act upon the artifact so as to create the desired social relationship. After the execution of the plan, the commitment $cc(debtor, creditor, antecedent, consequent, status)$ will hold in the social state, and will be projected onto the belief bases of all agents focusing on the artifact.

4   JaCaMo+ Gold Miners

The CLIMA VII gold miners scenario consisted of developing a multi-agent system to solve a cooperative task in a dynamically changing environment: a grid-like world where agents could move from one cell to a neighbouring cell if it contained no agent or obstacle. Gold could appear in the cells. Agent teams were expected to explore the environment, avoid obstacles and compete with another agent team for collecting as much gold as they could and deliver it to the depot. Each agent can carry one gold nugget at a time (we say that an agent that is not carrying gold is free). Agents had a local view on environment, their perceptions could be incomplete, and their actions could fail.

```
1  @goldpercepted[atomic]
2  +cell(X,Y,gold)  :  free & not gold(X,Y) & enactment_id(My_Role_Id)
3       & not cc(My_Role_Id,_,Assigned,Drop,"DETACHED")
4       <--     +gold(X,Y); commitToDropGold(X,Y).
5  @goldperceptedswitch[atomic]
6  +cell(X,Y,gold)  :  not free & not carrying(_,_)  & not gold(X,Y)
7       & handling_gold(OldX,OldY) & not changed
8       <--    .drop_intention(handle(gold(_,_)));
9       +gold(X,Y); +changed; -handling_gold(OldX,OldY);
10      changeGoldToPursue(X,Y); communicateGoldPosition(OldX,OldY).
11 +cell(X,Y,gold)  :  not gold(X,Y)
12      <--        communicateGoldPosition(X,Y).
13 @commitgoldfree[atomic]
14 +gold(X,Y)  :  free & pos(myX,myY) & not bet(X,Y)
15      <--       jia.dist(X1,Y1,X2,Y2,Dist); bid(X,Y,Dist); +bet(X,Y).
16 +gold(X,Y)  :  not bet(X,Y)
17      <--   ignore(X,Y); +bet(X,Y).
18 @p2gold[atomic]
19 +cc(My_Role_Id,_,_,drop(X,Y),"DETACHED")
20      : enactment_id(My_Role_Id)
21      <-- -free; !init_handle(gold(X,Y)).
```

Listing 1.1. The gold miner agent code in JaCaMo+.

We used four miners, each executing the same code, part of which is reported in Listing 1.1, the code is at http://di.unito.it/2COMM. The four agents are randomly positioned within the map and start searching for gold. A JaCaMo+ commitment protocol artifact is also created and shared by all the miners. All miners focus on the artifact and, thus, will be notified of changes occurred to its observable properties. This simple mechanism is, for instance, used for handling the case when an agent bumps into gold $-cell(X, Y, gold)$, gold perceived by agent in a certain cell– but, since it is already carrying a gold nugget to the depot, it cannot pick it up (11-12). Then, it communicates its discovery to its team mates, so that someone else can handle the newly found gold. To this aim, it invokes the artifact operation $communicateGoldPosition(X, Y)$, which causes the assertion of an observable property in the social state, which is notified to all agents in their belief bases as the belief $gold(X, Y)$. When the agent that finds the gold is free (2-4), it creates ($commitToDropGold(X, Y)$) a detached commitment towards all other agents, $C(My\_Role\_Id, Others, \top, drop(X,Y))$, of which it is the debtor, to bring the newly found gold to the depot. This will, in turn, activate the plan at lines 19-21 to handle that nugget. If, instead, the agent is not free because when it found the gold it was actually aiming at another nugget, the agent will change its plans (6-10), setting as gold to pick up the newly found nugget, and will communicate, through the artifact, the coordinates of the gold it was previously aiming at, so that someone else can handle it. This is done by the operations $changeGoldToPursue(X, Y)$, which withdraws the commitment to drop the assigned nugget and creates a commitment to drop the just perceived one, and $communicateGoldPosition(OldX, OldY)$.

The appearence of the belief $gold(X, Y)$ in an agent's belief base triggers a plan. A free agent (14-15) will execute the artifact operation bid, which causes the creation of a $conditional\ commitment$: if allocated the task, the agent will collect the gold. So, bid creates a social engagement, whose debtor is the bidding miner, and the creditor is the whole class of team mates. The agent is requested to include one or more behaviors for managing such a commitment and, in particular, for managing the case in which it is $Detached$, i.e. when the gold nugget is allocated to the agent. This is possible because bid and the commitment $C(miner_i, all\_miners, allocated(X, Y, miner_i), drop(X, Y))$ are tied by the social meaning of the operation in an explicit way, and this information is available to the programmer who will add to the agent program plans for handling the commitment state changes it needs to handle. Knowing the social meanings of artifact operations is sufficient for coordinating with others correctly. Agents that are not free just ignore the new gold (line 16). It is possible to distinguish the two cases by properly defining the plan context.

Instead, in [7] the relation between bid and nugget allocation (the latter is a consequence of the former), that is fundamental to the programmer, is $hidden$ inside the the leader agent. The miner communicates its bid and the leader tells it if it is allocated the gold. Gold allocation triggers a plan to drop the gold to the depot. The subtle difference with our proposal is that in this case gold allocation is but a $signal$, so the miner is programmed to react to signals.

The *causal* relation, that ties the plan to the event that activates it, is not expressed explicitly; it is in the structure of the protocol for interacting with the leader. So, for instance, it is nothing that can be reasoned about nor it can be exploited for defining a programming methodology [2].

In our case, instead, the connection between the event "commitment detached" and the associated plan is not only causal, but the plan has the aim of satisfying the consequent condition of the commitment that triggers it (*drop(X, Y)*), i.e. of accomplishing an explicit and shared social engagement. The signal that notifies gold allocation is not relevant to the agent, at the point that it does not even appear in the code nor in the commitment. It is the detachment of the commitment itself that causes handling the gold. There is no need of knowing or using logics, that are internal to the protocol (artifact), for programming the agent. Social meanings are the key.

5   Conclusions

We presented JaCaMo+, an extension to JaCaMo that enables social behaviors into its agents. We started from the interaction protocols based on obligations proposed in [25]. However, obligation-based protocols reduce agent interactions to messages that an agent is obliged to send to another agent; that is, social relationships among agents are not handled directly. Thus, an obligation-based protocol can be adopted when an organization gives guidelines about how inter-actions should be carried on, but it is not applicable where similar guidelines are not available. To cope with these challenging situations, our intuition is to define an interaction in terms of goals and commitments. Commitments, in fact, are at the right level of abstraction for modeling directed relationships between agents. Moreover, since commitments have a normative power, they enable the agents to reason about the behavior of others.

One of the strongest points of JaCaMo+ is the *decoupling* between the design of the agents and the design of the interaction – that builds on the decoupling between computation and coordination done by coordination models like tuple spaces. The decoupling allows us to change the definition of the artifact without the need of changing the agents' implementation. So, in the gold miners scenario, allocation can be FIFO, based on the miners' position, or take into account fur-ther contextual information like day time, known differences in the equipment of the miners, difficulty in reaching the nugget location. All these different policies can be implemented in a way that des not have an impact on the miners' code.

JaCaMo (with interaction [25]) and JaCaMo+ do not equally support *auton-omy*. JaCaMo with interaction just offers an agent to follow a predetermined path (a guideline) in which the agent has to fulfill a precise pattern of obligations. JaCaMo+, instead, offers an agent a tool, the interaction artifact, through which it can communicate with other agents and act together with others. The choice, however, of how and when being involved into an interaction remains up to the agents. The adoption of commitments, in fact, assures that an agent assumes the responsibility for a task only when, by its own choice, performs a specific action on the interaction artifact. An interaction that is based only on obligations hin-ders agents when they need to adapt to unforeseen conditions (flexibility) or when they need to react to unwanted situations (robustness). The agent, in fact, is not free to delegate obligations, schedule them differently, etc. All it can do is to perform the actions that, instructed by the interaction protocol, resolve its obligations. Protocols in [25] aim at defining guidelines to the use of resources in an organization. This, however, limits the modularity of *interaction* protocols because protocols depend on operations that are defined in the organization and there is no explicit association of which actions pertain to which roles. JaCaMo+ interaction protocols, instead, include the definitions of the needed operations, and specify which of them will empower the various role players.

The shift from obligations to commitments is beneficial in many respects. First, the autonomy of the agents is better supported because they are free in deciding how to fulfill their goals. It follows that agents are *deliberative*, and this paves the way to self-* applications, including the ability to autonomously take advantage from opportunities, and the ability of properly reacting to unexpected events (self-adaptation). Moreover, the interplay between goals and commitments opens the way to the integration of self-governance mechanisms into organizational contexts. Thus, our concluding claim is that directly addressing social relationships increases the robustness of the whole MAS.

In the future, we intend to investigate how agents can leverage on their deliberative capabilities, and use it not only to program interactions, but to plan social interactions. Moreover, the modular nature of the implementation facilitates the development of extensions for tackling richer, data-aware contexts [9,10,17]. We are also interested in tackling, in the implementation, a more sophisticate notion of social context and of enactment of a protocol in a social context [3], as well as to introduce a typing system along the line of [1].

Acknowledgments. This work was partially supported by the *Accountable Trustworthy Organizations and Systems (AThOS)* project, funded by Università degli Studi di Torino and Compagnia di San Paolo (CSP 2014).

References

1. Baldoni, M., Baroglio, C., Capuzzimati, F.: Typing multi-agent systems via commitments. In: Dalpiaz, F., Dix, J., van Riemsdijk, M.B. (eds.) EMAS 2014. LNCS, vol. 8758, pp. 388–405. Springer, Heidelberg (2014)
2. Baldoni, M., Baroglio, C., Capuzzimati, F., Micalizio, R.: Empowering agent coordination with social engagement. In: Proc. of XIV Int. Conf. of the Italian Association for Artificial Intelligence (2015) (to appear)
3. Baldoni, M., Baroglio, C., Chopra, A.K., Singh, M.P.: Composing and verifying commitment-based multiagent protocols. In: Proc. of 24th Int. Joint Conference on Artificial Intelligence, IJCAI 2015 (2015)
4. Bellifemine, F.L., Caire, G., Greenwood, D.: Developing Multi-Agent Systems with JADE. John Wiley & Sons (2007)
5. Boissier, O., Bordini, R.H., Hübner, J.F., Ricci, A., Santi, A.: Multi-agent oriented programming with JaCaMo. Science of Computer Programming **78**(6), 747–761 (2013)

6. Boissier, O., Hübner, J.F., Ricci, A., Sichman, J.S.: Multi-agent oriented programming, 2015. Tutorial at AAMAS 2015 (2015)
7. Bordini, R.H., Hübner, J.F., Tralamazza, D.M.: Using *Jason* to implement a team of gold miners. In: Inoue, K., Satoh, K., Toni, F. (eds.) CLIMA 2006. LNCS (LNAI), vol. 4371, pp. 304–313. Springer, Heidelberg (2007)
8. Bordini, R.H., Hübner, J.F., Wooldridge, M.: Programming Multi-Agent Systems in AgentSpeak Using Jason. John Wiley & Sons (2007)
9. Chesani, F., Mello, P., Montali, M., Torroni, P.: Representing and monitoring social commitments using the event calculus. Autonomous Agents and Multi-Agent Systems **27**(1), 85–130 (2013)
10. Chopra, A.K., Singh, M.P.: Cupid: commitments in relational algebra. In: Proc. of the 29th AAAI Conf., pp. 2052–2059. AAAI Press (2015)
11. Criado, N., Argente, E., Noriega, P., Botti, V.: Reasoning about constitutive norms in BDI agents. Logic Journal of IGPL **22**(1), 66–93 (2014)
12. Dastani, M., Grossi, D., Meyer, J.-J.C., Tinnemeier, N.: Normative multi-agent programs and their logics. In: Meyer, J.-J.C., Broersen, J. (eds.) KRAMAS 2008. LNCS, vol. 5605, pp. 16–31. Springer, Heidelberg (2009)
13. Demazeau, Y.: From interactions to collective behaviour in agent-based systems. In: Proc. of the 1st. European Conf. on Cognitive Science, Saint-Malo (1995)
14. Hammer, F., Derakhshan, A., Demazeau, Y., Lund, H.H.: A multi-agent approach to social human behaviour in children's play. In: Proc. of the IEEE/WIC/ACM Int. conf. on Intelligent Agent Tech. IEEE Comp. Soc. (2006)
15. Meneguzzi, F., Luck, M.: Norm-based behaviour modification in BDI agents. In: AAMAS, vol. 1, pp. 177–184. IFAAMAS (2009)
16. Meneguzzi, F., Telang, P.R., Singh, M.P.: A first-order formalization of commitments and goals for planning. In: AAAI. AAAI Press (2013)
17. Montali, M., Calvanese, D., De Giacomo, G.: Verification of data-aware commitment-based multiagent system. In: Proc. of AAMAS, pp. 157–164. IFAAMAS/ACM (2014)
18. Okouya, D., Fornara, N., Colombetti, M.: An infrastructure for the design and development of open interaction systems. In: Winikoff, M. (ed.) EMAS 2013. LNCS, vol. 8245, pp. 215–234. Springer, Heidelberg (2013)
19. Omicini, A., Ricci, A., Viroli, M.: Artifacts in the A&A meta-model for multi-agent systems. JAAMAS **17**(3), 432–456 (2008)
20. Singh, M.P.: An ontology for commitments in multiagent systems. Artif. Intell. Law **7**(1), 97–113 (1999)
21. Singh, M.P.: Commitments in multiagent systems some controversies, some prospects. In: The Goals of Cognition. Essays in Honor of Cristiano Castelfranchi, chapter 31, pp. 601–626. College Publications, London (2011)
22. Telang, P.R., Singh, M.P., Yorke-Smith, N.: Relating goal and commitment semantics. In: Dennis, L., Boissier, O., Bordini, R.H. (eds.) ProMAS 2011. LNCS, vol. 7217, pp. 22–37. Springer, Heidelberg (2012)
23. Weyns, D., Omicini, A., Odell, J.: Environment as a first class abstraction in multiagent systems. JAAMAS **14**(1), 5–30 (2007)
24. Yolum, I., Singh, M.P.: Commitment Machines. In: Meyer, J.-J.C., Tambe, M. (eds.) ATAL 2001. LNCS (LNAI), vol. 2333, pp. 235–247. Springer, Heidelberg (2002)
25. Zatelli, M.R., Hübner, J.F.: The interaction as an integration component for the JaCaMo platform. In: Dalpiaz, F., Dix, J., van Riemsdijk, M.B. (eds.) EMAS 2014. LNCS, vol. 8758, pp. 431–450. Springer, Heidelberg (2014)

Social Continual Planning in Open Multiagent Systems: A First Study

Matteo Baldoni(✉), Cristina Baroglio, and Roberto Micalizio

Dipartimento di Informatica, Università degli Studi di Torino, Turin, Italy
{matteo.baldoni,cristina.baroglio,roberto.micalizio}@unito.it

Abstract. We describe a Multiagent Planning approach, named Social Continual Planning, that tackles *open* scenarios, where agents can join and leave the system dynamically. The planning task is not defined from a global point of view, setting a global objective, but we allow each agent to pursue its own subset of goals. We take a *social* perspective where, although each agent has its own planning task and planning algorithm, it needs to get engaged with others for accomplishing its own goals. Cooperation is not forced but, thanks to the abstraction of *social commitment*, stems from the needs of the agents.

Keywords: Continual Planning · Multi-agent Planning · Social commitments

1 Introduction

The ability to plan one's own activities, even in dynamic and challenging scenarios such as Multiagent Systems (MAS), represents a key feature in many real-world applicative domains (see e.g., logistics, air traffic control, rescue missions, and so on). Not surprisingly, planning in MAS is drawing the attention of an ever growing number of researchers, as witnessed by the new series of *Distributed and Multi-Agent Planning Workshops* hosted by ICAPS.

The term Multiagent Planning (MAP) refers to a planning task in which a set of planning agents, each equipped with its own tools and capabilities, has to synthesize a *joint solution* (i.e., a joint multiagent plan). The planning task usually involves a number of interdependent subgoals, so that some form of coordination among the agents is necessary to solve the problem. Different methodologies have been proposed in the literature. Besides centralized approaches (e.g., [3]), which fall outside the above notion of MAP, the other distributed solutions can be categorized into three main families, depending on when the coordination among the agents is actually performed: *after* the planning phase [7], *interleaved* with the planning process [8,9,13], or *before* the planning search [6].

In all the above approaches, the planning task defines a global objective to be achieved by means of a "joint solution" involving the capabilities of the agents. Moreover, the set of agents to be involved is known in advance and cannot change during the planning process; the system is therefore closed. In this paper

© Springer International Publishing Switzerland 2015
Q. Chen et al. (Eds.): PRIMA 2015, LNAI 9387, pp. 575–584, 2015.
DOI: 10.1007/978-3-319-25524-8_40

we deal with a *different planning problem*, and propose a methodology named *Social Continual Planning* (SCP), to tackle it. We consider the planning problem of an agent situated in an open multiagent system. The agent may resort on other agents for solving a task of its own interest. The agent plans both its own actions, and its interactions with others whenever it is not capable, or it deems as not convenient, to execute certain steps in autonomy. The focus is not on negotiation, but on the framework through which an agent seeks the help by the others, and on the *engagements* that bind agents to supporting each other. Interaction is not limited to communication but it is a process through which the involved agents progress each in the solution of its own task. Engagements are binary social relationships, that are established dynamically and that create expectations on the involved agents behavior. An agent autonomously decides (plans) when to bind to another one to do something.

More precisely, we take a *social* perspective in the sense that, even though each agent has its own planning task and uses its own planning algorithm, the agent has still to get engaged with others in order to accomplish its own goals. The interactions that an agent has with others will, in general, allow both parties to get closer to their own goals. Cooperation is not forced to the agents just because their are part of the system, but rather cooperation stems from the needs of the agents within the system, and endures as far as the parties take advantage of it. In other terms, we propose a form of (agent) planning which is *situated* in a multiagent system, where an agent not only has to plan its own actions, but has also to plan its social relationships with other agents. Since the coordination has to be planned, it must be supported by a proper abstraction that enables one agent to create expectations about the behaviors of others. To this end, in this paper we adopt *social commitments* [14]. Interestingly, a recent work by Telang et al. [16] shows how goals and commitments are strongly interrelated by means of a set of practical rules. This supports our intuition that commitments may play a central role, together with beliefs and goals, in the synthesis of a plan in a multiagent setting. [2] describes an early implementation, and exemplifies the approach in a logistic scenario.

2   Related Work and Background

Multiagent Planning. To the best of our knowledge, the SCP problem has not been tackled in the literature, so far. SCP is however rooted in multiagent and distributed planning that, since the seminal work by Boutilier et al. [3], has addressed the problem of finding a coordinated, joint solution to a given planning task. In the early, centralized methodologies to multiagent planning, agents are seen as resources to be managed so as to achieve the global goal. More recently, distributed approaches allow the planning search to be distributed among the agents; however, the definition of the planning task is still centralized; see for instance the MA-STRIPS formalization [4]. Distributed approaches can be distinguished on how the planning and coordination phases are actually carried on. First attempts to coordinating plan *after* the planning phases [7] suffered from a sever drawback: whenever conflicts were detected between any two plans, the agents had to revise their plans accordingly. Thus, the domain knowledge about conflicts and constraints was not used actively during the planning phase, but only *a posteriori* to verify the correctness of the joint solution. This drawback is overcome by approaches (see e.g., [8,9,13]) in which the coordination and planning phases are *interleaved*. These approaches rely on the exchange of various kinds of information, such as partial plans, or states inferred during the search, so that conflicts are discovered as soon as possible, and corrections can be made while the planning phase is still in progress. A last family of approaches set the coordination phase *before* the planning one (see e.g., [6]). Such solutions, however, assume that all the possible conflicts are known in advance and globally defined.

Commitments. As stated in the introduction, SCP is a novel methodology of planning driven by social engagements; in particular, in this paper we focus on social engagements that can be modeled as *social commitments* (simply commitments below), first introduced in [14]. Commitments arise, exist, are satisfied, revoked, or otherwise manipulated, all in a social context (i.e., *social state* below); commitments have therefore a *life cycle* that evolves as a consequence of the operation performed by agents on them [11,12,15]. More formally, a commitment $C(x, y, s, u)$ formalizes a relationship between an agent x, playing the role of *debtor*, and another agent y, playing the role of *creditor*: the debtor is committed towards the creditor to bring about a consequent condition u, whenever an antecedent condition occurs s. Antecedent and consequent conditions are conjunctions or disjunctions of events and commitments and they concern only the *observable behavior* of the agents.

Notably, there have been some recent attempts to integrate commitments in planning problems, see [11,12,15] which as well as our work rely on the rules proposed in [16]. The idea of translating pragmatic rules into a planning language is first proposed in [15], where the Hierarchical Task Network (HTN) formalization is used. HTNs, however, are used at design time to model and verify commitment protocols [11]; thus, the point of view of these works is still centralized. In this work we will consider a STRIPS-like representation of the pragmatic rules, and use them for generative planning in a context where a centralized point of view is missing. In other terms, in this paper the interactions via commitments are not outlined within pre-designed HTNs, but have to be discovered at execution time by the planning search.

Goal Formalization. The notion of *goal* plays an important role not only from the point of view of planning, but also in general whenever one has to design and develop intelligent agents. In this paper, we take advantage of the formalization initially proposed in [17], and subsequently revised in [16]; specifically, a goal G is a tuple $G(x, p, r, q, s, f)$, where x is the agent pursuing G, p is a precondition that must be satisfied before G can be considered active, r is an invariant condition that holds until the achievement of G, q is a post-condition (effect) that becomes true when G is successfully achieved, and finally, s and f are the success and failure conditions, respectively. As well as commitments, goals have a life cycle in which state transitions are triggered by the execution of proper goal actions [16].

Pragmatic Rules. The relation between goals and commitments has been studied in [16], and it has been formalized in terms of practical rules, which capture patterns of pragmatic reasoning, in terms of changes to the configuration of an agent. Specifically, the configuration of an agent x is the tuple $S_x = \langle \mathcal{B}, \mathcal{G}, \mathcal{C} \rangle$ where $\mathcal{B}$ is its set of beliefs about the current snapshot of the world, $\mathcal{G}$ is the set of agent's goals, and $\mathcal{C}$ its set of commitments; i.e., commitments in which x is involved either as debtor or as creditor.

The operational semantics of pragmatic rules is given via guarded rules in which S_i are configurations having form $\frac{S_1 \longrightarrow S_2}{guard}$; where $guard$ is a condition over the current agent's beliefs and commitments; whereas $S_1 \longrightarrow S_2$ is a state transition involving a change in the state of commitments or goals; usually it corresponds to an operation on goals or commitments. Pragmatic rules are distinguished into: (1) rules from goals to commitments, they involve commitments that are used as a means to achieve some goal; and (2) rules from commitments to goals, they involve goals that are used as a means to achieve either the antecedent (if the agent at issue is debtor) or the consequent (if creditor) condition of a commitment. Some rule examples are reported in Table 1 (subscripts denote the state of commitments and goals as discussed in [16]).

For instance, the ENTICE rule tackles the situation in which (only) by creating the commitment can the agent satisfy its goal: If G is active and C is null, x creates an offer to another agent. The DELIVER rule, on the other hand, allows an agent to discharge one of its commitments by activating the goal appearing in the consequent condition: If C becomes detached (i.e., goal G_2 has been satisfied), then debtor x activates a goal G_1 to bring about the consequent.

3 The Social Continual Planning Problem

A *Social Continual Planning (SCP) system* is an open environment inhabited by heterogeneous and independent agents. Each agent has its own planning task, and can perform a specific set of actions. A *Social Continual Planning Problem* is a planning problem of an agent, situated within an SCP system, which, for being solved, requires the agent to plan also a set of engagements, realized as social commitments, with other agents in the system. Agents can join and leave the system dynamically; however, we assume that no agent leaves the system as

Table 1. Examples of practical rules from [16]

Goals-to-Commitments	$\frac{\langle G^A, C^N \rangle}{\text{create}(C)}$	ENTICE		$\frac{\langle G^{T \vee F}, C^A \rangle}{\text{cancel}(C)}$	WITHDRAW OFFER
Commitments-to-Goals	$\frac{\langle G_1^N, C^D \rangle}{\text{consider}(G_1) \wedge \text{activate}(G_1)}$	DELIVER		$\frac{\langle G_2^N, C^C \rangle}{\text{consider}(G_2) \wedge \text{activate}(G_2)}$	DETACH

long as there are active commitments involving it either as debtor or as creditor. More formally, an SCP system is a tuple $\langle \mathcal{U}, \mathcal{A}, \mathcal{S} \rangle$ where:

- $\mathcal{U}$ is a finite set of propositional atoms, whose truth value can be observed by all the agents in the SCP; $\mathcal{U}$ represents a sort of common language through which agents can interact. Atoms in this set are used to describe the state of the environment shared by the agents. In addition, these are the atoms that can appear as antecedents and consequents of the commitments.
- $\mathcal{A}$ is a set of agents; each agent $i \in \mathcal{A}$ is associated with a configuration which extends the agent configuration we have already introduced. Specifically, the agent configuration for agent i is a tuple $\langle \mathcal{B}^i, \mathcal{G}^i, \mathcal{C}^i, Acts^i, Socs^i \rangle$: $\mathcal{B}^i$, $\mathcal{G}^i$, and $\mathcal{C}^i$ are as before; whereas:
    - $Acts^i$ is a set of actions agent i can perform; it is partitioned into:
        Φ^i is a set of "physical" actions; as usual, these actions are defined in terms of preconditions and effects, which can be both conditions on environment atoms (i.e., in $\mathcal{U}$) or on internal (agent-dependent) atoms that are not globally traced (i.e., the internal state of an agent is private).

        Σ^i is a set of *social actions*; preconditions and effects are defined in terms of goals in $\mathcal{G}^i$ and commitments in $\mathcal{C}^i$. More precisely, each social action corresponds to a pragmatic rule from goals to commitments. Indeed, we consider these pragmatic rules as actions because, as we discuss below, they can be used by an automated planner to plan interactions with other agents. Note that while goals in $\mathcal{G}^i$ are *private* (only agent i can see and manipulate them), commitments in $\mathcal{C}^i$ have a *social value*: whenever i changes the state of a commitment in $\mathcal{C}^i$, this change becomes visible to all the other agents in the system (see $\mathcal{S}$).
    - $Socs^i$ is a the set of pragmatic rules from commitments to goals adopted by an agents; from our point of view these rules define the *social strategy* of agent i. Thus, these rules are not used during the planning search, but rather to decide which goals should be pursued.
- $\mathcal{S}$ is the social state shared by all the agents in the SCP system at hand. The social state can be partitioned into two subsets:
    - $\mathcal{S}^{\mathcal{C}}$ is the set of all the active commitments defined between any two agents in $\mathcal{A}$; in particular, for each agent $i \in \mathcal{A}$, $\mathcal{C}^i \subseteq \mathcal{S}$, $\mathcal{C}^i$ is the projection of $\mathcal{S}$ over all the commitments in which i appears either as debtor or as creditor.
    - $\mathcal{S}^{\mathcal{E}}$ is the set of all the propositional atoms describing the environment that hold at a given time; in particular, $\mathcal{S}^{\mathcal{E}} \subseteq \mathcal{U}$.

Given an SCP system $\langle \mathcal{U}, \mathcal{A}, \mathcal{S} \rangle$, let $i \in \mathcal{A}$ be an agent, that is described by the tuple $\langle \mathcal{B}^i, \mathcal{G}^i, \mathcal{C}^i, Acts^i, Socs^i \rangle$. An SCP problem for i amounts to finding a plan, composed by $Acts^i$ and $Socs^i$, to achieve $\mathcal{G}^i$ starting from $\mathcal{B}^i$. In particular:

- $\mathcal{B}^i$ is the initial state of the planning task i is responsible for; such a state is a set of atoms possibly occurring in $\mathcal{U}$, but also occurring in a private set of atoms describing the internal state of i, and hence these atoms are not traced within the SCP system. We only assume that i joins the SCP system iff $\mathcal{S} \cup \mathcal{B}^i \not\models \bot$.

- $\mathcal{G}^i$ is a list of goals the agent has to achieve; each goal can be an atom or a conjunction of atoms in $\mathcal{U}$ and possibly in the private set of agent's atoms. Note that, differently from classical planning, it is not required that all the goals in $\mathcal{G}^i$ hold in a unique system state.
- $\mathcal{C}^i$ is initially empty.
- Φ^i is a set of domain-dependent actions agent i can directly perform whenever their preconditions hold. For instance, in a logistic domain, a truck-agent can perform action drive, whereas a plane-agent can fly.
- Σ^i can be initialized in different ways; in fact, differently from Φ^i, this set needs not to be static; on the contrary, it could change over time according to contextual conditions. In our preliminary implementation, we have adopted a very simple solution. Let us consider the ENTICE rule above[1]. The objective of this rule is to create a commitment of the form $C(i, j, s, u)$, in order to "entice" another agent j to bring about s, which is of interest for i. At this initial stage, however, i cannot know which condition u is of interest for j. Surely enough, i knows which atoms it can directly achieve by performing its physical actions. Thus, for each atom $s \in \mathcal{U}$ such that s never appears as an effect of any action in Φ^i, agent i creates a template entice-s whose effect is the creation of a commitment $C(i, \_, s, u)$, where $\_$ denotes any agent willing to satisfy s, and u is any atom in $\mathcal{U}$ that appears in the effects of at least one physical action in Φ^i. Of course, since the entice-s template can be instanced in different ways, depending on the actual u condition, agent i will offer first the conditions, that from its point of view, are the cheapest to achieve.
- $Socs^i$ is a static set of rules, decided at design time, that defines the social behavior of i; namely, how an agent is reliable for bringing about the consequent and antecedent conditions of the commitments in $\mathcal{C}^i$.

Social Continual Planning: the Strategy. The SCP strategy we propose, sketched in Algorithm 1, is a form of continual planning (see e.g., [5]) in which generative planning is interleaved with plan execution. The main difference with other approaches is that to achieve a goal, an agent plans not only its own actions, but also its engagements with others, and depending on how these interactions carry through, the agent may decide to perform some replanning or to pursue a different goal.

An agent i follows the SCP strategy as far as there are goals in $\mathcal{G}^i$ to be achieved or $\mathcal{C}^i$ is not empty. This second condition assures that an agent does

---

[1] Other rules are treated consequently.

Algorithm 1. Social Continual Planning Strategy

SCP-Strategy($\mathcal{B}^i, \mathcal{G}^i, \mathcal{C}^i, Acts^i, Socs^i$)
1. **while** $\mathcal{G}^i \neq \emptyset \vee \mathcal{C}^i \neq \emptyset$ **do**
2.   **on** $\mathcal{S}$ **change** update $\mathcal{G}^i$ using $Socs^i$
3. $g \leftarrow$ pick up a goal from $\mathcal{G}^i$
4. $\pi \leftarrow$ plan to g
5. $status \leftarrow$ execute π
6.   **if** $status$ equals $success$ **then**
7. $\mathcal{G}^i \leftarrow \mathcal{G}^i \setminus \{g\}$
8.   **end if**
9. **end while**

---

not leave the system when it is still involved in some active commitments.[2] At each iteration, the agent checks for updates in the social state $\mathcal{S}$ (line 2); any change occurring in $\mathcal{S}$, in fact, can have an impact on the set $\mathcal{G}^i$ of goals. For instance, a new commitment $C(j, \_, s, u)$ appearing in $\mathcal{S}^C$ could draw the attention of agent i when u is a condition that i needs but it cannot achieve on its own, and at the same time i knows how to obtain s. In such a case, i could accept to be the *creditor*: s is added to $\mathcal{G}^i$ (i will eventually bring about s). On the other hand, the occurrence of a new atom in $\mathcal{S}^{\mathcal{E}}$ could make the achievement of a goal g in $\mathcal{G}^i$ no longer necessary, so g is dropped. Of course, these agent's decisions are driven by the $Socs^i$ behavioral rules.

Once $\mathcal{G}^i$ has been updated, agent i selects one goal g from $\mathcal{G}^i$ (line 3); and synthesizes a plan π reaching g (line 4). It is worth noting that any off-the-shelf planner can be used to synthesize π since from the point of view of the planner there is no distinction between social and physical actions (both kinds of actions are translated into PDDL, see below). We only assume that in case the used planner produces a partial-order plan (POP), π is one of the possible linearizations of such a POP.

After the planning step, the agent can start the execution of π (line 5), which contains both physical actions in Φ^i, and social actions in Σ^i. The execution of π proceeds one action a at a time and in the order. If a is a physical action, it is immediately executed, and its effects on atoms in $\mathcal{U}$ are made available to all the other agents via $\mathcal{S}^{\mathcal{E}}$. If a is a social action, e.g., an entice-s action, the action execution affects $\mathcal{S}^C$ with the addition of a new commitment $C(i, \_, s, u)$, which has to be picked up by some other agent. The execution of π is therefore suspended; indeed, the entice-s action is part of π only in case the atom s is a precondition for some subsequent action, and hence the plan execution cannot

---

[2] In principle, an agent may remaining situated within the system indefinitely, waiting for agents to cooperate with. For example, in a logistic domain, a shipper has the high-level objective of earn money by offering its transportation facilities. This objective does not immediately translate into an initial goal $\mathcal{G}$, but rather it is better modeled in terms of pragmatic rules (i.e., both social actions in Σ, and behavioral rules in $Socs$), so as the shipper is willing to accept requests from other agents, but also offers itself shipment services to others.

proceeds without s. In case an agent j is interested in u, it accepts the offers by finalizing the commitment in $C(i, j, s, u)$, and eventually it will bring about s. As soon as s is satisfied, i proceeds with the execution of its plan (u will be added to $\mathcal{G}^i$ the next time i checks for changes in S). When all the actions in π are performed, the execution phase terminates in *success* state (i.e., g has been achieved), and hence g is removed from $\mathcal{G}^i$ (line 7).

However, it is also possible that no agent is interested in the service u offered by i. To avoid an indefinite wait, i sets up a timer. As soon as the time runs out, the commitment is canceled from $\mathcal{S}^C$, and the plan execution terminates with a *failure* state. Since g has not been achieved, it is not removed from $\mathcal{G}^i$. At the next iteration of the strategy, i first checks whether g is still required (line 2), and then tries to find an alternative plan reaching it (line 4) that may require a different instantiation for the entice-s action (i.e., with a different condition offered as consequent of the commitment).

Intuitively, the correctness of the approach relies on the coherence and convergence properties discussed in [16]. In particular, the goal convergence property states that in the situation in which agent i has a goal $G_1 = \mathsf{G}(i, p_1, r_1, q_1, s, f_1)$, another agent j has a goal $G_2 = \mathsf{G}(j, p_2, r_2, q_2, s, f_2)$, and there exists a commitment $C_1 = C(i, j, s, u) \in \mathcal{S}^C$, then, there is a finite sequence of pragmatic rules that leads to $G2$'s state equaling $G1$'s state. This means that whenever agent j brings about s, satisfying its internal goal G_2, then, also agent i has its own goal G_1 indirectly satisfied. This demonstrates the correctness of the SCP strategy in the sense that whenever a plan π, synthesized by i, contains an entice action entice-s, which actually creates the commitment C_1, then the plan is:

1. *feasible*: no action a in π has open preconditions (i.e., atoms that are neither provided by the initial state nor by any previous action); this implies that the preconditions that agent i cannot directly produce, are obtained via cooperation with others;
2. *correct*: if each action is performed successfully, g holds in $\mathcal{S}^\mathcal{E}$ at the end of π; as noted above, the execution of social action implies the cooperation with other agents.

4   Discussion and Conclusions

In this paper we addressed the SCP problem, and proposed the SCP strategy as a possible solution. Differently from MAP approaches, where a predefined team of agents has to find a *joint* plan solving a given planning task, here we deal with situations in which each agent is given a planning task which is independent of the others' ones. The challenge, thus, is not to find a joint plan, but to find a plan for each agent that solves the agent's planning task taking advantage of the cooperation with other agents. Moreover, agents are free to join and leave the system dynamically.

The novelties of our proposal are not limited to the openness of the agent team. While in approaches to MAP agents can be thought of as resources used for solving the given planning task, in SCP agents are seen as *autonomous* entities.

This change implies that an agent cannot order another agent to do a job, but the agent can just make an offer, and as we have seen, social commitments come at handy to model this kind of relations. More importantly, however, we have to observe that an agent receiving an offer, being an autonomous entity, can accept or reject the offer depending on its contextual conditions and its local goals. A rational agent, in fact, should accept an offer only if the offer brings along some advantages, otherwise the offer should be put aside. It is worth noting how the SCP strategy supports the *decoupling* of agents, that just share environment objects, whereas they are independent for all the other respects. In particular, each agent can implement its social strategy (i.e., pragmatic rules in *Socs* and Σ) according to local criteria. Moreover, the planning algorithm each agent uses can be tailored to meet optimization functions that are relevant for the agent itself. Note also how the cooperation among the agents do not require that an agent knows the action templates of others (as for instance happens in [13]), and, hence, also the agents' privacy is preserved.

Many lines of research and improvement are possible. In the near future we aim at engineering the implementation of the SCP strategy by exploiting one of the many agents platforms available. In particular, the JaCaMo+ platform [1] seems to be a good candidate since it naturally supports the notions of commitments and social states. In addition, the social behavioral rules in *Socs* could find an easy implementation as Jason plans (used to program JaCaMo+ agents). Also the integration with a planner does not seem to raise too much troubles; as demonstrated in [10] where Jason plans have been integrated with generative planning.

Acknowledgments. This work was partially supported by the *Accountable Trustworthy Organizations and Systems (AThOS)* project, funded by Università degli Studi di Torino and Compagnia di San Paolo (CSP 2014).

References

1. Baldoni, M., Baroglio, C., Capuzzimati, F., Micalizio, R.: Programming with commitments and goals in JaCaMo+. In: Proce. of the International Conference on Autonomous Agents and Multiagent Systems (AAMAS 2015), pp. 1705–1706. International Foundation for Autonomous Agents and Multiagent Systems (2015)
2. Baldoni, M., Baroglio, C., Micalizio, R.: Exploring multiagent cooperation via social continual planning. In: Cortellessa, G., Magazzeni, D., Maratea, M., Serina, I. (eds.) Proc. of 6th Italian Workshop on Planning and Scheduling, IPS 2015, Ferrara, Italy, September 2015. CEUR-WS.org Workshop Proceedings (2015)
3. Boutilier, C., Dearden, R., Goldszmidt, M.: Stochastic dynamic programming with factored representations. Artificial Intelligence **121**(1–2), 49–107 (2000)
4. Brafman, R.I., Domshlak, C.: From one to many: planning for loosely coupled multi-agent systems. In: Proceedings of the Eighteenth International Conference on Automated Planning and Scheduling, ICAPS, Sydney, Australia, pp. 28–35, September 14–18, 2008
5. Brenner, M., Nebel, B.: Continual planning and acting in dynamic multiagent environments. Autonomous Agents and Multi-Agent Systems **19**(3), 297–331 (2009)

6. Buzing, P., Ter Mors, A., Valk, J., Witteveen, C.: Coordinating self-interested planning agents. Autonomous Agents and Multi-Agent Systems 12(2), 199–218 (2006)
7. Cox, J.S., Durfee, E.H., Bartold, T.: A distributed framework for solving the multi-agent plan coordination problem. In: Proceedings of the Fourth International Joint Conference on Autonomous Agents and Multiagent Systems, pp. 821–827. ACM (2005)
8. Durfee, E.H., Lesser, V.R.: Partial global planning: A coordination framework for distributed hypothesis formation. IEEE Transactions on Systems, Man and Cybernetics 21(5), 1167–1183 (1991)
9. Lesser, V., Decker, K., Wagner, T., Carver, N., Garvey, A., Horling, B., Neiman, D., Podorozhny, R., Prasad, M.N., Raja, A., et al.: Evolution of the gpgp/taems domain-independent coordination framework. Autonomous Agents and Multi-Agent Systems 9(1–2), 87–143 (2004)
10. Meneguzzi, F., Luck, M.: Leveraging new plans in AgentSpeak(PL). In: Baldoni, M., Son, T.C., van Riemsdijk, M.B., Winikoff, M. (eds.) DALT 2008. LNCS (LNAI), vol. 5397, pp. 111–127. Springer, Heidelberg (2009)
11. Meneguzzi, F.R., Telang, P.R., Singh, M.P.: A first-order formalization of commitments and goals for planning. In: Proc. of the 27th AAAI Conference on Artificial Intelligence. AAAI Press (2013)
12. Meneguzzi, F.R., Telang, P.R., Yorke-Smith, N.: Towards planning uncertain commitment protocols. In: Proc. of the 2015 Int. Conf. on Autonomous Agents and Multiagent Systems, AAMAS, pp. 1681–1682. ACM (2015)
13. Nissim, R., Brafman, R.I.: Distributed heuristic forward search for multi-agent planning. Journal of Artificial Intelligence Research (JAIR) 51, 293–332 (2014)
14. Singh, M.P.: An ontology for commitments in multiagent systems. Journal of Artificial Intelligence in Law 7(1), 97–113 (1999)
15. Telang, P.R., Meneguzzi, F.R., Singh, M.P.: Hierarchical planning about goals and commitments. In: Int. Conf. on Autonomous Agents and Multi-Agent Systems, AAMAS 2013, pp. 877–884. IFAAMAS (2013)
16. Telang, P.R., Singh, M.P., Yorke-Smith, N.: Relating goal and commitment semantics. In: Dennis, L., Boissier, O., Bordini, R.H. (eds.) ProMAS 2011. LNCS, vol. 7217, pp. 22–37. Springer, Heidelberg (2012)
17. Winikoff, M., Padgham, L., Harland, J., Thangarajah, J.: Declarative & procedural goals in intelligent agent systems. In: Fensel, D., Giunchiglia, F., Mc Guinness, D.L., Williams, M.-A. (eds.) Proc. of the 8th Int. Conf. on Principles and Knowledge Representation and Reasoning (KR-2002), pp. 470–481. Morgan Kaufmann (2002)

Security Games with Ambiguous Beliefs of Agents

Hossein Khani[1][(✉)] and Mohsen Afsharchi[2]

[1] Institute for Advanced Studies in Basic Sciences, Zanjan, Iran
Hossein.Khani8564@gmail.com
[2] University of Zanjan, Zanjan, Iran
Afsharchim@znu.ac.ir

Abstract. Currently the Dempster-Shafer based algorithm and Uniform Random Probability based algorithm are the preferred methods of resolving security games, in which security forces are able to identify attackers and need only to determine their strategies. However this model is inefficient in situations where resources are limited and both the identity of the attackers and their strategies are ambiguous. The intent of this study is to find a more effective algorithm to guide the security forces in choosing which outside forces with which to cooperate given both ambiguities. We designed an experiment where security forces were compelled to engage with outside forces in order to maximize protection of their targets. We introduced two important notions: the behavior of each agent in target protection and the tolerance threshold in the target protection process. From these, we proposed an algorithm that was applied by each security force to determine the best outside force(s) with which to cooperate. Our results show that our proposed algorithm is safer than the Dempster-Shafer based and Uniform Random Probability based algorithm.

Keywords: Ambiguous games · Tolerance threshold · Behavior · Optimistic · Pessimistic · Self-confidence · Security games

1 Introduction

With the current state of politics, economics, and conflicting ideologies, security has become an ever increasing concern and the driving force behind much strategic development. For example, the security game-solving algorithm of DOBSS serves as the core of the ARMOR system, which has been successfully utilized in security patrol schedule at Los Angeles International Airport [1,2].

In such situations, limited resources pose a constant challenge issue to providing full security coverage. Examples of limitations include restricted finances, manpower, supplies, etc. Security forces must often recruit outside forces to aid in the protection of their targets. The situation becomes further exacerbated when information on the outside forces is unavailable or ambiguous. Ambiguous

© Springer International Publishing Switzerland 2015
Q. Chen et al. (Eds.): PRIMA 2015, LNAI 9387, pp. 585–593, 2015.
DOI: 10.1007/978-3-319-25524-8_41

information refers to the uncertainty of security forces in relation to the objective and behavior of outside forces were they to engage in such a cooperation process.

Much literature on the topic of security games attempts to address the issues involved with ambiguous information. In these games, the security forces cannot assign a probability value to how the outside force will respond(i.e., whether these forces will behave more like attackers or security forces in a cooperation process). Here Bayesian models cannot be applied as they require that the security forces be able to assign a precise probability value for the outside forces. Based on the need of security forces to form cooperation processes, and on the ambiguity of the decision framework, we proposed a model that uses the Choquet Expected Utility [3] and two factors to determine which outside forces are selected as appropriate cooperators. From the security forces and outside force's point of view, an appropriate cooperator is one with whom cooperation leads to an increase in payoff for the security forces.

The rest of the article is organized as follows. Section 2 recaps the Choquet Expected Utility and its usage in decision-making. Section 3 introduces our security game as a formal game and proposes an algorithm to solve it. Section 4 describes the experiments conducted to evaluate the performance of the algorithm. Finally, Section 5 concludes our article.

2 Background

This section outlines some background information and describes key components of decision-making in ambiguity. In this study, the cooperation process model is based on that employed by Shehory and Sykara and Sless, Hazon, and Kraus in their respective studies[4, 5].

Marinacci el al. studied details of cooperation of the agents in the presence of ambiguity [6]. The ambiguous setting was described by Paolo Ghirardato [7] as an extension of maximum expected utility which is introduced by Savage[8]. The Ellsberg paradox is an example of an uncertain domain that shows the importance of studying ambiguous situations and how they differ from certain situations[9]. The Ellsberg Paradox concerns subjective probability theory, which fails to follow the expected utility theory. To handle ambiguous situations, computer scientists defined some real-valued function as neo-additive probabilities, called capacities. Using these capacities, the Choquet Expected Utility was introduces as a generalization of expected utility.

In the presence of ambiguity, the majority of agents respond by behaving cautiously. Such cautious behavior is referred to as ambiguity-aversion. Bade [10] explains the effect of ambiguity aversion on equilibrium outcomes based on the relaxation of randomized strategy. In contrast, a minority of agents behave more carelessly, which is referred to as ambiguity-preference. The majority of the time, agents do not act purely in accordance to either ambiguity aversion or ambiguity preference, but rather somewhere in between. Wakker [11] further extends the notions of ambiguity to arbitrary events and characterizes optimistic and pessimistic attitudes. More details can be found in the extended version of this article[12].

The problem in this study is defined in the context of a battlefield in which n security forces try to protect n vital resources, while the enemy tries to penetrate their defense and commit espionage. When the security forces employ outside forces to reinforce their strength, they cannot determine for certain which resources are being targeted. Each security force d is responsible for protecting only one of the targets (t) with the use of its ability (a_d^t), and as a result, it must provide the outside force with compensation (b_d^t) from the owner of the target. The main issue is that both security and outside forces cannot assign a precise probability to one another. we will categorize outside forces into three types: (1) helpful, which help fortify the protection of targets,(2) mildly harmful, which inflict minimal damage such as a minor security breach, and (3) extremely harmful, which cause more severe damage such as extensive physical damage and casualties.

Thus the goal of the security forces become choosing appropriate cooperators among outside forces that will result in an increase in the obtained payoff. Both security and outside forces in the battlefield use two factors to assess the ambiguity of one another. Security force d uses "behavior" and "tolerance threshold" to assess. Behavior is defined as an ordered pair of the amount of energy that the security force assigns to protect the target t and the expected payoff obtained from the owner of target (a_d^t, b_d^t) . "Tolerance threshold" is defined as a number between zero and one which is applied by security force d as a measure to assess the response of others TT_d^t. This value is based on the amount of energy the security force uses in the protection process. For example, suppose security force d wants to choose an outside force p as a cooperator. The security force d assesses its ambiguity about outside force p using the following method:

If $\frac{b_p^t}{a_p^t} \leq TT_d^t$ holds, the security force d can confidently determine the type of outside force p. There is no ambiguity; the assistant is loyal. On the other hand, if $\frac{b_p^t}{a_p^t} > TT_d^t$ holds, the security force d cannot verify the loyalty of the outside force p and ambiguity about type of the outside force is present. The ambiguity degree of security force d in regard to outside force p in a cooperation process to protect target t, $\sigma_{d,p}^t$, can be computed as follows:

$$\sigma_{d,p}^t = \frac{log_2(\frac{b_p^t}{a_p^t} - TT_d^t)}{log_2 TT_d^t} \tag{1}$$

We can verify the behavior of this function by exploring the impact of different variables, such as tolerance threshold.

Suppose the outside force p has a specific behavior (a_p^t, b_p^t) to deal with the target t. The more impatient the security force d is in dealing with the target t, the lower its tolerance threshold becomes and the numerator of the fraction increases. Moreover, a decrease in the tolerance threshold results in a decrease in the denominator. Meanwhile, increase in the numerator and decrease in the denominator lead to an increase in the ambiguity degree of security force d

towards outside force a, $(\sigma_{d,p}^t)$. Inversely, the more patient the security force d is, the higher it's tolerance threshold. In this case, the numerator of the function will be lower and the denominator higher, which translates to a decrease in the ambiguity degree.

3   Methods and Materials

Formal Definition of the Game

Using the information obtained from the framework, we define our game as (N, T, B, S, r, U, PI) such that:

1. $N = (D, P)$ is the set of both security and outside forces, where d shows the set of security forces and p is the set of outside forces.
2. T contains elements of T_i which represents the type set of either security force or outside force i.
3. $B = \{B_i | i \in N\}$ represents the behavior set of security and outside forces.
4. $S = S_d \times S_p$ where $S_d = S_p = \{s_1, s_2, ..., s_n\}$ is the pure strategy set of both security and outside forces representing the different values for each of their respective tolerance thresholds.
5. $r = \{r_i(w, T_j) | i, j \in N\}$ and $r_i(w, T_j)$ is the real payoff obtained by either the security force or outside force i when it cooperates with one of the other members of set N (j). w is the ordered pair of the amount of ability used by j and the amount of ability used by i.
6. $U = \{U_i(s_i, (a_j, b_j)) | i, j \in N \ \& \ s_i \in S_i \ \& \ (a_j, b_j) \in B\}$ is the payoff that i expects to obtain according to strategy profile S while it cooperates with j whose behavior is defined as (a_j, b_j).
7. PI is the set of initial beliefs π of both security and outside forces about one anothers types.

The optimal strategy of the security force is one where the different, possible values for its tolerance threshold are examined and the one that maximizes payoff is selected. In our security game, first the security force commits to al strategy, then the outside forces try to determine a strategy for themselves [13]. Because each security force is responsible for protecting only one target, we suppose that the expected payoff is obtained through all available outside forces in the cooperation. It is also worth mentioning that the expected payoff of the outside force is to be received from the security force, regardless of the attendance of the other outside forces in the cooperation.

The security force finds its optimal strategy in two phases. In the first phase, it needs to recognize which one of the outside forces is willing to participate in the cooperation process. An outside force is willing when the payoff the security force expects to obtain from cooperation is higher than its previously obtained payoff. In the second phase, the security force d compares different strategies on the basis of the amount of payoff it expects.

The security force uses formula (1) to assess how its behavior is ambiguous from the view of the others, and using the following formula it computes the expected payoff for each outside force:

$$U_p(s_p, (a_d, b_d)) = b_p((1 - \sigma_{p,d}^t)\pi(t_p) + \sigma_{p,d}^t[\alpha max_{t_d} r_p(a_d, t_d) + (1 - \alpha)min_{t_d} r_p(a_d, t_d)]). \qquad (2)$$

This formula is a variant of formula (4). Note the difference between the number of arguments of function U_d and U_p. It is important to know that in formula (6) and (8), if $\sigma_{p,d}^t = 0$, these formulas are reduced to Savage Expected Utility. If $\alpha = 0$ both security and outside forces are pessimistic and if $\alpha = 1$, they are optimistic.

The security force then compares, for each outside force, the different strategies that the outside force can choose on the basis of its corresponding expected payoff and determines whether it's the optimal strategy. The security force finds, for each prospective cooperation, optimal strategy and corresponding expected payoff of each outside force using:

$$U_p(s_p^*, (a_d, b_d)) \geq U_p(s_p', (a_d, b_d)) \quad \forall s_p' \in S_p \qquad (3)$$

In the second phase, the security force evaluates its options through a similar process used in the first phase. Using formula (5), it quantifies ambiguity degrees and from formula (6) the corresponding expected payoff for each strategy.

$$u_d(s_d, (a_p, b_p)) = (1 - \sigma_{d,p}^t)\pi(t_p) + \sigma_{d,p}^t[\alpha max_{t_p} r_d(a_p, t_p) + (1 - \alpha)min_{t_p} r_d(a_p, t_p)]. \qquad (4)$$

In this formula, $\sigma_{d,p}^t$ is the ambiguity degree of the security force in relation to the outside force p. This value can be computed by formula (5). $\pi(t_p)$ is the initial belief the security force has in regard to the types of the outside force p, t_p represent a specific type from all available types of the outside forces. α is the degree of optimism, which shows how optimistic the security force is in its computations.

Suppose the set of outside forces who cooperate with the security force to protect the target t is shown by C_t; thus, the total payoff which is obtained by security force d to protect target t is represented by:

$$U_d((s_d, s_p), B) = b_d^t \times \Sigma_{i \in C_t} u_d(s_d, b_i) \qquad (5)$$

Given the security force's strategy s_d, if the optimal response strategies of the outside force are s_a^*, then s_d^* is the security forces optimal strategy if:

$$U_d(s_d^*, s_p^*, B) \geq U_d(s_d', s_p^*, B) \quad \forall s_d' \in S_d \qquad (6)$$

The time complexity of the algorithm is computed in the theorem below.

Theorem 1. In security games with ambiguous force types, the complexity of finding optimal pure strategies of a selected security force, is $O(\#players, \#outcomes)$.

Proof. Each pure strategy to which the (first security or outside) force may commit will induce a subgame for the remaining forces. We can solve each such subgame recursively to find all of its optimal strategy profiles; each of these will give the original first (first security or outside) force some utility. Those that give the first (first security or outside) force maximum utility correspond exactly to the optimal strategy profiles of the original game.

Note that if the security force d assesses the type of the outside force p as a cooperator inaccurately, i.e. T_p is the extremely harmful but the security force miscategorizes it as a helpful type, the real obtained payoff by the security force would decrease.

4 Experiments

In this section, we evaluate our model via experimentation. One of the more realistic works is done by Zhang and his colleagues[14]. To see a more concrete discussion about the details visit the extended version of this article[12].

We begin by evaluating the impact of changing the quantity of both security and outside forces on the outcome of our proposed algorithm (CEU-based solution algorithm) and D-S theory based algorithm. We observe that in the worst case, the number of true detections in our algorithm is more than the number of true detections in D-S theory based algorithm. In one scenario we assume both security and outside forces have ambiguity-preference (the degree of optimism of all agents are high) and in another scenario we assume both security and outside forces have neither ambiguity aversion nor ambiguity preference(the degree of optimism of both security and outside forces are moderate). Figure 1 shows that having ambiguity aversion or preference has no impact on the CEU-based algorithm. Figure 2 evaluates the impact of changing the number of strategies both security and outside forces can choose from the output of two (D-S based and CEU-based) algorithms. We also show the differences in sensitivity of these two algorithms in Figure 3. We find the sensitivity measure using the following:

$$Sensitivity = \frac{\#of\ True\ Positives}{\#of\ True\ Positives + \#of\ False\ Negatives} \qquad (7)$$

To explore the errors in the two (D-S based and CEU-based) algorithms, we use MRSE measure (Mean Root Square Error). We find the normalized MRSE value for each algorithm and refer to the difference between them as the distance of the worst penalties(Figure (4)).

Observation 1. Our model guarantees more safety than the model based on D-S theory even when taking varying degrees of optimism into account.

Observation 2. The Choquet Expected Utility solution based algorithm is safer than the model based on D-S theory, even when considering varying number of types and strategies for each agent.

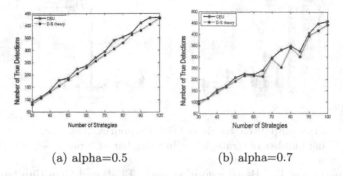

(a) alpha=0.5   (b) alpha=0.7

Fig. 1. Comparison of the performance of CEU-based solution algorithm with D-S theory based solution algorithm.(number of types=3, number of strategies=8)

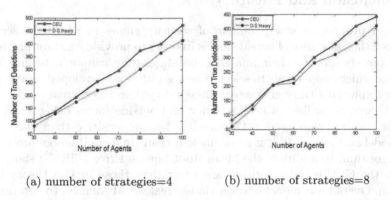

(a) number of strategies=4   (b) number of strategies=8

Fig. 2. Comparison of the performance of CEU-based solution algorithm with D-S theory based solution algorithm considering varying number of types and strategies for each agent.(number of types=4)

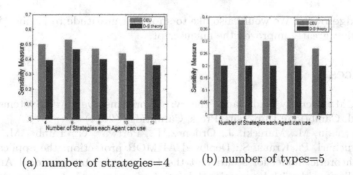

(a) number of strategies=4   (b) number of types=5

Fig. 3. Comparison of the sensitivity of D-S Based algorithm and CEU-Based algorithm considering a varying number of types for each agent(number of agents=40).

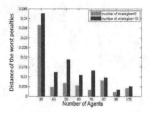 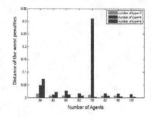

(a) Comparison by vary-   (b) Comparison by varying number of strategies   ing number of types

Fig. 4. Comparison of D-S Based algorithm and CEU-Based algorithm based on distance of the worst penalties.

5   Conclusion and Future Work

This paper proposes a new paradigm of security games in which the security forces need the assistance of outside forces in order to provide constant protection of their targets, due to their limited capabilities,they cannot determine with confidence which cooperators to select. The algorithm we developed based on the Choquet Expected Utility guarantees more safety than the current model based on D-S theory, regardless of both security and outside forces being ambiguity-averse or ambiguity-preference. Our model is more sensitive than D-S theory based model and as a result it is more efficient than Uniform Random probability based algorithm. In addition, the Mean Root Square Error (MRSE) shows that errors in the CEU-based algorithm are fewer than those in D-S theory based algorithm. Overall our model offers a viable, real world solution to determining the best course of action in the presence of ambiguous information.

As the future works we are going to deal with equilibria issues in our preposed framework and show how that different types of contingent ambiguity affect equilibrium behavior.

Acknowledgement. We would also like to show our gratitude to Fariba Massah for comments that greatly improved the manuscript.

References

1. Tambe, M.: Security And Game Theory: Algorithms, Deployed Systems. Lessons Learned. Cambridge University Press, Cambridge (2011)
2. Pita, J., Jain, M., Marecki, J., Ordonez, F., Portway, C., Tambe, M., Western, C., Paruchuri, P., Kraus, S.: Deployed ARMOR protection: the application of a game theoretic model for security at the Los Angeles International Airport. In: Proceedings of the 7th International Joint Conference on Autonomous Agents and Multiagent Systems: Industrial Track, pp. 125–132 (2008)
3. Marinacci, M.: Ambiguous Games. Games and Economic Behavior **31**(2), 191–219 (2000)

4. Shehory, O., Sykara, S.: Multi-agent Coordination through Coalition Formation. In: Rao, A., Singh, M., Wooldridge, M. (eds.) ATAL1997. LNCS(LNAI), vol. 1365, pp. 143–154. Springer, Heidelberg (1997)

5. Sless, L., Hazon, N., Kraus, S., Wooldridge, M.: Forming coalitions and facilitating relationships for completing tasks in social networks, AAMAS (2014)

6. Marinacci, M., Montrucchio, L.: Introduction to the Mathematics of Ambiguity. Dipartimento di Statistica e Matematica Applicata and ICER Universit di Torino (2003)

7. Ghirardato, P.: Ambiguity. Universita di Torino, Dipartimento di Matematica Applicata and Collegio Carlo Alberto (2010)

8. Savage, L.J.: The Foundations of Statistics. Wiley, New York (1954)

9. Segal, U.: The Ellsberg Paradox and Risk Aversion: An Anticipated Utility Approach. University of Toronto, Department of Economics (1985)

10. Bade, S.: Ambiguous act equilibria. Games and Economic Behavior **71**(2), 246–260 (2011)

11. Wakker, P.: Testing and characterizing properties of nonadditive measures through violations of the sure thing principle. Econometrica **69**, 1039–1060 (2001)

12. abs/1508.02035 [cs.AI]

13. Pita, J., Jain, M., Ordonez, F., Portway, C., Tambe, M., Western, C., Paruchuri, P., Kraus, S.: Using game theory for Los Angeles airport security. AI Magazine **30**(1), 43–57 (2009)

14. Zhang, Y., Luo, X., Ma, W.: Security Games with Ambiguous Information about Attacker Types. In: Cranefield, S., Nayak, A. (eds.) AI 2013. LNCS, vol. 8272, pp. 14–25. Springer, Heidelberg (2013)

Introducing Preference-Based Argumentation to Inconsistent Ontological Knowledge Bases

Madalina Croitoru[1], Rallou Thomopoulos[2], and Srdjan Vesic[3]([envelope])

[1] INRIA, LIRMM, University Montpellier 2, Montpellier, France
[2] INRA GraphIK, Montpellier, France
[3] CRIL, CNRS - University of Artois, Lens, France
vesic@cril.fr

Abstract. Handling inconsistency is an inherent part of decision making in traditional agri-food chains – due to the various concerns involved. In order to explain the source of inconsistency and represent the existing conflicts in the ontological knowledge base, argumentation theory can be used. However, the current state of art methodology does not allow to take into account the level of significance of the knowledge expressed by the various ontological knowledge sources. We propose to use preferences in order to model those differences between formulas and evaluate our proposal practically by implementing it within the INRA platform and showing a use case using this formalism in a bread making decision support system.

1 Introduction

Querying several heterogeneous data sources while taking into account the ontological information [19] recently received growing interest both from academia and from industry. Consider the platform developed in the French Institute for Research in Agronomy (INRA) to link agronomy insights with socio-economic developments and behaviour of various stakeholders involved: farmers, consumers, biologists or industrial partners[1].

In such practical applications, the knowledge (obtained from several sources) might be inconsistent. Different inconsistency methods have been devised in order to reason with such knowledge [7,18]. *Argumentation theory* [16] is another method for dealing with inconsistent knowledge [5,22]. It not only allows to resolve inconsistency; furthermore, the reasons why certain formulas are not compatible can be highlighted and presented to a user in form of arguments. The logic-based argumentation ontological instantiation using the Datalog+/- family of languages has already shown the practical interest in using argumentation for query answering explanation in OBDA [2,3].

While argumentation-based techniques have already been successfully applied in agronomy (for instance in traditional agri-food chains [25] or packaging conception [24]) the current state of art methodology does not allow to take

---

[1] see e.g. the MEANS initiative, http://www6.inra.fr/means_eng/.

© Springer International Publishing Switzerland 2015
Q. Chen et al. (Eds.): PRIMA 2015, LNAI 9387, pp. 594–602, 2015.
DOI: 10.1007/978-3-319-25524-8_42

into account the degree of significance of the knowledge expressed by the various knowledge sources. In the INRA platform handling preferences is fundamental, since not all participants provide information of equal importance, regarding the scope, priority and urgency of the issues considered. Such handling needs to be generic: presupposing a total order (or any property) of the preference relation would induce some loss of generality that will limit the practical applicability.

The research task of this paper is to define the first preference-based argumentation system that works with inconsistent ontologies, study its properties and apply it to a bread conception scenario within INRA.

2   Knowledge Representation

We consider the well known rule-based Tuple-Generating Dependencies (Datalog+/-) family of languages that generalise certain subsets of Description Logics [4,12]. Here we restrict ourselves to Datalog+/- classes where the skolemised chase is finite (Finite Expansion Sets). Due to the space restrictions, we do not recall the technical details of this language. The interested reader is referred to the technical report [14] containing all the definitions, proofs, more explanations and more examples, which can be found on-line at http://www.cril.fr/~vesic.

Example 1. Consider a knowledge base $\mathcal{K} = (\mathcal{F}, \mathcal{R}, \mathcal{N})$ where:

- $\mathcal{F}$ contains the following facts:
  - $F_1 = Bread(bleuette) \wedge ContaminantFree(bleuette)$
  - $F_2 = \exists\, e\ ExtractionRate(e, bleuette)$
  - $F_3 = \exists\, f\ (FiberContent(f, bleuette) \wedge High(f))$
- $\mathcal{R}$ consists of the following rules:
  - $R_1 = \forall\ x,y\ (Bread(x) \wedge ExtractionRate(y,x) \wedge PesticideFree(x) \rightarrow Moderate(y))$
  - $R_2 = \forall\ x,y,z\ (Bread(x) \wedge ExtractionRate(y,x) \wedge FiberContent(z,x) \wedge High(z)$
$$\rightarrow Intensive(y))$$
  - $R_3 = \forall\ x\ (Bread(x) \wedge ContaminantFree(x)$
$$\rightarrow PesticideFree(x) \wedge MycotoxinFree(x))$$
- $\mathcal{N}$ contains the following negative constraint:
  - $N = \forall\ x\ (Intensive(x) \wedge Moderate(x)) \rightarrow \perp$

$\mathcal{K}$ is inconsistent since $(\mathcal{F}, \mathcal{R}) \models N$. Indeed, F_1 and R_3 allow to deduce *PesticideFree(bleuette)*. Combined to F_2 and R_1 we obtain *Moderate(e)*. F_1, F_2, F_3 and R_2 deduce *Intensive(e)*, violating the negative constraint N.

If a knowledge base $\mathcal{K} = (\mathcal{F}, \mathcal{R}, \mathcal{N})$ is inconsistent, everything is entailed from it. A common solution for knowledge bases where preferences are not considered [7,18] is to construct maximal (with respect to set inclusion) consistent subsets of facts, called *repairs*. We define $Repair(\mathcal{K}) = \{\mathcal{F}' \subseteq \mathcal{F} \mid \mathcal{F}'$ is maximal for $\subseteq$ $\mathcal{R}$-consistent set$\}$. In Example 1, we have three repairs: $\{F_1, F_2\}$, $\{F_2, F_3\}$ and $\{F_1, F_3\}$.

2.1   Argumentation

For a set of formulae $\mathcal{G} = \{G_1, \ldots, G_n\}$, notation $\bigwedge G$ is used as an abbreviation for $G_1 \wedge \ldots \wedge G_n$.

Definition 1. *An argument (w.r.t. $\mathcal{K}$) is a tuple $a = (F_0, F_1, \ldots, F_n)$ where:*

- *$(F_0, \ldots, F_{n-1})$ is a derivation sequence with respect to $\mathcal{K}$*
- *F_n is an atom, a conjunction of atoms, the existential closure of an atom or the existential closure of a conjunction of atoms such that $F_{n-1} \models F_n$.*

Example 2 (Example 1 Cont.). As an example of an argument, built with F_1 and R_3, consider $a = (\{Bread(bleuette) \wedge ContaminantFree(bleuette)\}, \{Bread(bleuette) \wedge ContaminantFree(bleuette), PesticideFree(bleuette) \wedge MycotoxinFree(bleuette)\}, PesticideFree(bleuette)).$

For an argument $a = (F_0, \ldots, F_n)$ we denote $\mathtt{Supp}(a) = F_0$ and $\mathtt{Conc}(a) = F_n$. For a set $S \subseteq \mathcal{F}$ of facts, $\mathtt{Arg}(S)$ is defined as the set of all arguments a such that $\mathtt{Supp}(a) \subseteq S$. For a set $\mathcal{E}$ of arguments, $\mathtt{Base}(\mathcal{E}) = \bigcup_{a \in \mathcal{E}} \mathtt{Supp}(a)$.

Definition 2. *Let $\mathcal{K}$ be a knowledge base and let a and b be two arguments. The argument a attacks argument b, denoted $(a, b) \in Att$, if and only if there exists $\varphi \in \mathtt{Supp}(b)$ such that the set $\{Conc(a), \varphi\}$ is $\mathcal{R}$-inconsistent.*

Given a knowledge base $\mathcal{K}$, the *corresponding argumentation framework* $\mathcal{AF}_K$ is $(\mathcal{A} = \mathtt{Arg}(\mathcal{F}), Att)$ where $\mathcal{A}$ is the set of arguments that can be constructed from $\mathcal{F}$ and Att is the corresponding attack relation as specified in Definition 2. The notion of conflict-freeness and the semantics are defined in the usual way [16]. For an argumentation framework $AS = (\mathcal{A}, Att)$ we denote by $Ext_\sigma(AS)$ the set of its extensions with respect to semantics σ. (All the definitions are available in the technical report [14].)

3   Preference Handling

A preference based knowledge base is a 4-tuple $\mathcal{K} = (\mathcal{F}, \mathcal{R}, \mathcal{N}, \geq)$ composed of four finite sets of formulae: a set $\mathcal{F}$ of facts, a set $\mathcal{R}$ of rules, a set $\mathcal{N}$ of constraints and a set $\geq$ of preferences. The preference relation $\geq$ is defined over the facts $\mathcal{F}$. We put no constraints on the preference relation except that it has to be reflexive and transitive.

Example 3. Let us consider the following preference-based knowledge base:

- $\mathcal{F}$ contains the following facts:
    - $F_1 = ExtractionRate(T65, bleuette)$
    - $F_2 = Bread(p) \wedge ExtractionRate(\tau, p) \wedge Moderate(\tau)$
    - $F_3 = Bread(p) \wedge SaltAdjunction(s, p) \wedge Reduced(s)$
    - $F_4 = Bread(p) \wedge ExtractionRate(\tau, p) \wedge Intensive(\tau)$
    - $F_5 = Bread(p) \wedge Crusty(p) \wedge SaltAdjunction(s, p) \wedge Maintained(s)$

- $\mathcal{R}$ consists of the following rules:
  - $R_1 = \forall\ x,y\ (Bread(x) \wedge ExtractionRate(y,x) \wedge Moderate(y) \rightarrow Digestible(x))$
  - $R_2 = \forall\ x,z\ (Bread(x) \wedge SaltAdjunction(z,x) \wedge Reduced(z) \rightarrow LowSalt(x))$
  - $R_3 = \forall\ x,y\ (Bread(x) \wedge ExtractionRate(y,x) \wedge Moderate(y) \rightarrow Pesticide\text{-}Free(x))$
  - $R_4 = \forall\ x,y\ (Bread(x) \wedge ExtractionRate(y,x) \wedge Intensive(y) \rightarrow High\text{-}Fiber(x))$
  - $R_5 = \forall\ x,z\ (Bread(x) \wedge Crusty(x) \wedge SaltAdjunction(z,x) \wedge Maintained(z) \rightarrow ConsumerFriendly(x))$
- $\mathcal{N}$ contains the following negative constraints:
  - $N_1 = \forall\ x\ (Intensive(x) \wedge Moderate(x)) \rightarrow \perp$
  - $N_2 = \forall\ x\ (Reduced(x) \wedge Maintained(x)) \rightarrow \perp$
- $\geq$ is defined by the experts as follows:
  F_3 and F_4 express nutritional concerns, F_2 expresses a sanitary concern, F_5 a sensorial concern, while F_1 is neutral.
  In the PNNS programme recommendation, nutritional concerns take priority over sanitary ones, which take priority over sensorial ones.
  The preference relation $\geq$ is thus defined by:
  $F_3 \sim F_4 > F_2 > F_5$, while F_1 is incomparable with the other facts.

The preferences on the facts are used to refine the set of repairs of an inconsistent knowledge base. Consider here the three notions introduced by Staworko et al. [23]: locally optimal (LO), Pareto optimal (PO) and globally optimal (GO). We denote the set of LO (resp. PO, GO) repairs of $\mathcal{K}$ by $Repair^{lo}(\mathcal{K})$ (resp. $Repair^{po}(\mathcal{K})$, $Repair^{go}(\mathcal{K})$).

Definition 3 ([23]). *Let* $\mathcal{K} = (\mathcal{F}, \mathcal{R}, \mathcal{N}, \geq)$ *be a knowledge base and* $A' \in Repair(\mathcal{K})$ *one of its repairs.*

- *A' is a locally optimal repair iff there exist no $\varphi \in A'$ and $\psi \in \mathcal{F} \setminus A'$ such that $\psi > \varphi$ and $(A' \setminus \{\varphi\}) \cup \{\psi\}$ is an $\mathcal{R}$-consistent set*
- *A' is a Pareto optimal repair iff there exist no $X \subseteq A'$, $X \neq \emptyset$ and $\psi \in \mathcal{F} \setminus A'$ such that*
  - *for every $\varphi \in X$ we have $\psi > \varphi$*
  - *$(A' \setminus X) \cup \{\psi\}$ is an $\mathcal{R}$-consistent set.*
- *A' is a globally optimal repair iff there exist no $X \subseteq A'$, $X \neq \emptyset$ and $Y \subseteq \mathcal{F} \setminus A'$ such that*
  - *for every $\varphi \in X$ there exists $\psi \in Y$ such that $\psi > \varphi$*
  - *$(A' \setminus X) \cup Y$ is an $\mathcal{R}$-consistent set.*

4 Preference Ranking

First note that the attack relation considered in this paper does not depend on the preference relation $\geq$. Its goal is to underline the conflicts between the arguments coming from conflicts from the knowledge base. Those conflicts still exist even if some piece of information is preferred to another one. So in our framework all attacks succeed.

Definition 4. *Let* $\mathcal{K} = (\mathcal{F}, \mathcal{R}, \mathcal{N}, \geq)$ *be a knowledge base,* $\mathcal{AF}_K$ *the corresponding argumentation framework, let* σ *be a semantics and* $\mathcal{E}$ *an extension with respect to* σ.

- $\mathcal{E}$ *is a locally optimal (LO) extension iff there exists no* $\varphi \in \text{Base}(\mathcal{E})$ *and* $\psi \in \mathcal{F} \setminus \text{Base}(\mathcal{E})$ *such that* $\text{Arg}((\text{Base}(\mathcal{E}) \setminus \{\varphi\}) \cup \{\psi\})$ *is a conflict-free set and* $\psi > \varphi$.
- $\mathcal{E}$ *is a Pareto optimal (PO) extension iff there exists no* $X \subseteq \text{Base}(\mathcal{E})$ *and* $\psi \in \mathcal{F} \setminus \text{Base}(\mathcal{E})$ *such that* $X \neq \emptyset$ *and* $\text{Arg}((\text{Base}(\mathcal{E}) \setminus X) \cup \{\psi\})$ *is a conflict-free set and for every* $\varphi \in X$ *we have* $\psi > \varphi$.
- $\mathcal{E}$ *is a globally optimal (GO) extension iff there exists no* $X \subseteq \text{Base}(\mathcal{E})$ *and* $Y \subseteq \mathcal{F}$ *such that* $X \neq \emptyset$ *and* $\text{Arg}((\text{Base}(\mathcal{E}) \setminus X) \cup Y)$ *is a conflict-free set and for every* $\varphi \in X$ *there exists* $\psi \in Y$ *such that* $\psi > \varphi$.

We denote by $\text{Ext}^{lo}_{\sigma}(\mathcal{AF}_K)$ (resp. $\text{Ext}^{po}_{\sigma}(\mathcal{AF}_K)$, $\text{Ext}^{go}_{\sigma}(\mathcal{AF}_K)$) the sets of locally (resp. Pareto, globally) optimal extensions under semantics σ.

Example 4 (Example 3 Cont.). We obtain the following stable / preferred extensions :
$ext_1 = \text{Arg}(\{F_1, F_2, F_3\})$, $ext_2 = \text{Arg}(\{F_1, F_2, F_5\})$, $ext_3 = \text{Arg}(\{F_1, F_3, F_4\})$, $ext_4 = \text{Arg}(\{F_1, F_4, F_5\})$.

In this example, extension ext_3 is the best according to all criteria (LO, PO, GO). Selecting this extension yields the following conclusions: *ExtractionRate(T65,bleuette)*, *Bread(p)*, *SaltAdjunction(s,p)*, *Reduced(s)*, *ExtractionRate(τ,p)*, *Intensive(τ)*, *LowSalt(p))*, *HighFiber(p))*.

5   Theoretical Evaluation

This section contains the theoretical evaluation of our proposal. It shows that the result returned by the argumentation system is equivalent to that returned by using repairs. We also show that our argumentation framework satisfies the postulates for instantiated argumentation systems. Finally, we study the properties of our system in case when the preference relation is total.

We now show that there is a full correspondence between the result obtained by using our preference-based argumentation system and the result obtained by using the repairs of the given inconsistent ontological knowledge base.

Proposition 1. *Let* $\mathcal{K} = (\mathcal{F}, \mathcal{R}, \mathcal{N}, \geq)$ *be a knowledge base and* $\mathcal{AF}_K$ *the corresponding preference-based argumentation system. Let* σ *be preferred or stable semantics and* $\beta \in \{lo, po, go\}$. *Then:*

$$\text{Ext}^{\beta}_{\sigma}(\mathcal{AF}_K) = \{\text{Arg}(A') \mid A' \text{ is a } \beta \text{ repair of } \mathcal{K}\}.$$

We can show that the preference-based argumentation framework we propose in this paper satisfies the rationality postulates for instantiated argumentation frameworks [13]: direct and indirect consistency and closure. The details are omitted due to space restrictions, but can be found in the technical report [14].

In the case when $\geq$ is total, Pareto optimal and globally optimal repairs coincide. Furthermore, it can be shown that PO repairs (and GO repairs) coincide with preferred subtheories [11] of $\mathcal{K}$. However, using LO repairs may still yield a different result. For the exact definitions and the proofs, the reader is referred to the technical report [14].

The next example shows that LO repairs do not coincide with PO repairs even in the case when $\geq$ is a total order.

Example 5. Let $\mathcal{K} = (\mathcal{F}, \mathcal{R}, \mathcal{N}, \geq)$ with $\mathcal{F} = \{whiteBread(B),\ wholeWheat\text{-}Bread(B),\ organicWholeWheatBread(B)\}$, $\mathcal{R} = \emptyset$, $\mathcal{N} = \{\forall x\ (whiteBread(x) \wedge wholeWheatBread(x) \rightarrow \bot),\ \forall x\ (whiteBread\ (x) \wedge organicWholeWheatBread(x) \rightarrow \bot)\}$, and let $whiteBread(B) \geq wholeWheatBread(B) \geq organicWholeWheat\text{-}Bread(B)$.

Set $A' = \{wholeWheatBread(B),\ organicWholeWheatBread(B)\}$ is a locally optimal repair but is not a Pareto optimal repair.

6   Qualitative Evaluation

The evaluation of the implemented system was done via a series of interviews with domain experts. The first point to highlight is that our initial approach with experts included no preference expression. The experts themselves raised the question of the importance attached to the different pieces of knowledge modeled in the system. Moreover, in some cases experts hesitated on the relevance of some facts or rules. From that first step of the project, the need to take into account different levels of importance among arguments became obvious. Preferences were introduced from that point.

The knowledge and reasoning procedures were implemented using the COGUI knowledge representation tool, with an extension of 2000 lines of supplemental code. Three experts have validated our approach: two researchers in food science and cereal technologies of the French national institute of agronomic research, specialists respectively of the grain-to-flour transformation process and of the breadmaking process, and one industrial expert - the Director of the French National Institute of Bread and Pastry.

Four scenarios were evaluated. These scenarios concern four kinds of consumers: obeses (fiber preference), people with iron deficiency (micronutrient preference), people with cardiovascular disease (decreased salt preference) and vegetarians (limited phytic acid), which produces different sets of goals. For each scenario, the system proposes several output recommendations. The audience for decreasing salt tips the balance in favour of a recommendation for the T80 bread, while the audience for decreasing phytic acid pushes to specify recommendations towards a natural sourdough bread or a conservative T65 bread. The results were considered as explainable by experts, but not obvious, since many considerations had to be taken into account.

Let us focus on the case of vegetarians. Phytic acid, which is contained in the outer layers of the wheat grain, is known to limit the bioavailability of cations, including essential minerals such as coper, zinc or iron, which must be preserved especially for vegetarians. Therefore the conservative solution of T65 bread can be explained by the fact that the current T65 bread contains few outer grain layers, thus limiting the phytic acid risks. However, natural sourdough bread has a lower pH level. This acidity interferes with the activity of phytic acid, thus avoiding the decrease of mineral bioavailability. Now why chose one solution rather than another one? This point could be highlighted by the system. Indeed, the choice depends on the ordering of consumer preferences. Favouring organoleptic aspects of bread (e.g. crusty, white, honeycombed bread) leads to chose the T65 solution, whereas favouring nutritional aspects (e.g. fibers, vitamins, satiety) leads to the natural sourdough solution.

7   Conclusion and Related Work

We introduced the first preference-based argumentation system that works with inconsistent ontological knowledge bases and studied its properties. We also applied it to an agronomy scenario.

A two-step approach for preference-based argumentation was proposed recently [1]. In that work, the authors propose a general argumentation framework that can be instantiated in different ways. They propose to take into account both attacks and preferences in the first phase; the second phase uses only preferences to refine the result. The main difference is that we show it is possible to define an instantiation in which taking attacks and preferences into account is done in completely separated phases: namely, in our approach the first phase (inconsistency resolution) is done without looking at the preferences.

The links between argumentation semantics (stable, preferred, grounded) and different semantics in inconsistent ontological knowledge bases, such as AR, IAR or ICR were recently studied [15]. The present paper is more general since it also takes into account the preference relation between the sources.

The ASPIC+ system [22] has also recently studied using preferences and structured argumentation. This approach imposes restrictions on the preference relation and, of course, does not consider equivalence results with the inconsistent ontology query answering semantics or preference based repair selection. Another related contribution comprises constructing an argumentation framework with ontological knowledge allowing two agents to discuss the answer to queries concerning their knowledge without one agent having to copy all of their ontology to the other [10]. However the authors do not consider preferences. Let us also mention the work of Kaci [17], which only considers symmetrical attack relations.

Binas and McIlraith [9] use argumentation in order to answer inconsistent queries. The authors use the similar definitions of argument and attack as in this paper but only consider propositional logic. Benferhat et al. [6] consider that a formula should be deduced if no stronger reasons for deducing its negation exist. Recently, in OBDA, preference handling methods have been extended to Datalog+/- families and DL-Lite knowledge bases [8, 20, 21].

References

1. Amgoud, L., Vesic, S.: Rich preference-based argumentation frameworks. International Journal of Approximate Reasoning **55**, 585–606 (2014)
2. Arioua, A., Tamani, N., Croitoru, M.: On conceptual graphs and explanation of query answering under inconsistency. In: Hernandez, N., Jäschke, R., Croitoru, M. (eds.) ICCS 2014. LNCS, vol. 8577, pp. 51–64. Springer, Heidelberg (2014)
3. Arioua, A., Tamani, N., Croitoru, M., Buche, P.: Query failure explanation in inconsistent knowledge bases using argumentation. In: Proceedings of the Fifth International Conference on Computational Models of Argument (COMMA 2014), pp. 101–108 (2014)
4. Baader, F., Brandt, S., Lutz, C.: Pushing the EL envelope. In: Proceedings of the 19th International Joint Conferences on Artificial Intelligence (IJCAI 2005), pp. 364–369 (2005)
5. Benferhat, S., Dubois, D., Prade, H.: Argumentative inference in uncertain and inconsistent knowledge bases. In: Proceedings of the 9th Conference on Uncertainty in Artificial intelligence (UAI 1993), pp. 411–419 (1993)
6. Benferhat, S., Dubois, D., Prade, H.: Some syntactic approaches to the handling of inconsistent knowledge bases: a comparative study part 2: the prioritized case. In: Logic at Work: Essays Dedicated to the Memory of Helen Rasiowa, vol. 24, pp. 437–511. Physica-Verlag (1999)
7. Bienvenu, M.: On the complexity of consistent query answering in the presence of simple ontologies. In: Proceedings of the 26th Conference on Artificial Intelligence (AAAI 2012), pp. 705–711 (2012)
8. Bienvenu, M., Bourgaux, C., Goasdoué, F.: Querying inconsistent description logic knowledge bases under preferred repair semantics. In: Proceedings of the 28th Conference on Artificial Intelligence (AAAI 2014), pp. 996–1002 (2014)
9. Binas, A., McIlraith, S.A.: Peer-to-peer query answering with inconsistent knowledge. In: Proceedings of the 11th International Conference on Principles of Knowledge Representation and Reasoning (KR 2008), pp. 329–339 (2008)
10. Black, E., Hunter, A., Pan, J.Z.: An argument-based approach to using multiple ontologies. In: Godo, L., Pugliese, A. (eds.) SUM 2009. LNCS, vol. 5785, pp. 68–79. Springer, Heidelberg (2009)
11. Brewka, G.: Preferred subtheories: an extended logical framework for default reasoning. In:1 Proceedings of the 11th International Joint Conference on Artificial Intelligence (IJCAI 1989), pp. 1043–1048 (1989)
12. Calvanese, D., De Giacomo, G., Lembo, D., Lenzerini, M., Rosati, R.: Tractable reasoning and efficient query answering in description logics: the DL-lite family. Journal of Automated Reasoning **39**(3), 385–429 (2007)
13. Caminada, M., Amgoud, L.: On the evaluation of argumentation formalisms. Artificial Intelligence Journal **171**(5–6), 286–310 (2007)
14. Croitoru, M., Thomopoulos, R., Vesic, S.: Introducing preference-based argumentation to inconsistent ontological knowledge bases. CNRS - University of Artois, Technical report, CRIL (2015)
15. Croitoru, M., Vesic, S.: What can argumentation do for inconsistent ontology query answering? In: Liu, W., Subrahmanian, V.S., Wijsen, J. (eds.) SUM 2013. LNCS, vol. 8078, pp. 15–29. Springer, Heidelberg (2013)

16. Dung, P.M.: On the acceptability of arguments and its fundamental role in non-monotonic reasoning, logic programming and n-person games. Artificial Intelligence Journal **77**, 321–357 (1995)
17. Kaci, S.: Refined preference-based argumentation frameworks. In: Proceedings of the Third International Conference on Computational Models of Argument (COMMA 2010), pp. 299–310 (2010)
18. Lembo, D., Lenzerini, M., Rosati, R., Ruzzi, M., Savo, D.F.: Inconsistency-tolerant semantics for description logics. In: Hitzler, P., Lukasiewicz, T. (eds.) RR 2010. LNCS, vol. 6333, pp. 103–117. Springer, Heidelberg (2010)
19. Lenzerini, M.: Data integration: a theoretical perspective. In: Proceedings of the 21st Symposium on Principles of Database Systems (PODS 2002), pp. 233–246 (2002)
20. Lukasiewicz, T., Martinez, M.V., Simari, G.I.: Inconsistency handling in Datalog+/- ontologies. In: Proceedings of the 20th European Conference on Artificial Intelligence (ECAI 2012), pp. 558–563 (2012)
21. Lukasiewicz, T., Martinez, M.V., Simari, G.I.: Complexity of inconsistency-tolerant query answering in Datalog+/-. In: Informal Proceedings of the 26th International Workshop on Description Logics, pp. 791–803 (2013)
22. Modgil, S., Prakken, H.: A general account of argumentation and preferences. Artificial Intelligence Journal **195**, 361–397 (2013)
23. Staworko, S., Chomicki, J., Marcinkowski, J.: Preference-driven querying of inconsistent relational databases. In: Grust, T., Höpfner, H., Illarramendi, A., Jablonski, S., Fischer, F., Müller, S., Patranjan, P.-L., Sattler, K.-U., Spiliopoulou, M., Wijsen, J. (eds.) EDBT 2006. LNCS, vol. 4254, pp. 318–335. Springer, Heidelberg (2006)
24. Tamani, N., Croitoru, M., Buche, P.: Conflicting viewpoint relational database querying: An argumentation approach. In: Proceedings of the 13th International Conference on Autonomous Agents and Multi-agent Systems (AAMAS 2014), pp. 1553–1554 (2014)
25. Thomopoulos, R., Croitoru, M., Tamani, N.: Decision support for agri-food chains: a reverse engineering argumentation-based approach. Ecological Informatics (2014)

Compliant Business Processes with Exclusive Choices from Agent Specification

Francesco Olivieri[1], Matteo Cristani[1], and Guido Governatori[2]($\boxtimes$)

[1] Department of Computer Science, University of Verona, Verona, Italy
[2] NICTA, Queensland Research Laboratory, Spring Hill, Australia
guido.governatori@nicta.com.au

Abstract. In this paper we analyse the problem of synthesising compliant business processes from rules-based declarative specifications for agents. In particular, we consider the approach by [1,2] and we propose computationally efficient algorithms to combine plans extracted from the deliberation of an agent to generate the corresponding business processes with exclusive choice patterns.

1 Introduction

The standard architectures for cognitive agents (e.g., the BDI architecture) distinguish three phases: the deliberation phase where agents deliberate what are their goals; then in the plan selection phase, the agent selects, based on the outcome of the first phase, which plan to actuate from her plan library; finally, in the last phase, the agent executes the selected plan. [1,2], in addition to the inclusion of norms, propose a different approach where an agent is defined by a set of rules describing the environment where the agent is situated, the capabilities of the agent (the actions or tasks the agent can perform, the conditions under which the agent can perform them, and the effects they generate), the aims of the agent, and the norms the agent is subject to. Given a set of facts describing a situation, the agent deliberates using its rule base to determine whether a particular outcome is attainable without violating the relevant norms. Given the information in the rule base, the deliberation contains information about the tasks to be performed (and the relative order in which they have to be executed) to reach the objective. Thus, the deliberation effectively generates a plan. [3,4] propose an efficient algorithm to extract such plans and to visualise them in form of business process models.

A business process model is a compact (graphical) representation of a set of activities and the order in which they have to be executed to reach a business objective. The tasks or activities are connected by control flow connectors. In particular, the basic control flow connectors are: sequence (task t' directly follows task t), AND split or parallel split (all tasks in all the branches are executed),

G. Governatori—NICTA is funded by the Australian Government through the Department of Communications and the Australian Research Council through the ICT Centre of Excellence Program.

Q. Chen et al. (Eds.): PRIMA 2015, LNAI 9387, pp. 603–612, 2015.
DOI: 10.1007/978-3-319-25524-8_43

exclusive choice or X-OR split (only the tasks in one of the branches are executed), AND join (all tasks in the incoming branches must have been executed), and X-OR join (one branch must have been executed). A business process model can be seen as a set of sequences of tasks, which corresponds to a set of plans. One of the advantages of business process models being that they provide an intuitive (graphical) representation that can be understood by the stakeholders of the business process, and that they can be executed by workflow engines. While rules (and, in general, declarative specifications) can provide powerful and flexible representation languages, and the individual rules can be easily understood by stakeholders and domain experts (including rules modelling norms), it can be daunting to understand what is going on with large knowledge bases. To mitigate this problem, [3,4] propose to translate a case (set of facts) into a business process model (i.e., a model guaranteed to comply with the applicable norms and fulfilling the predefined objective).

The approach in [3,4] has the limitation that it synthesises business processes without exclusive choices. This is due to the following two factors: the logic underlying the declarative agent specifications (Defeasible Logic, a sceptical non-monotonic logic) and the use of a consistent set of facts as input for the case. However, nothing prevents us from considering different (and incompatible) sets of facts as input. For each set, we can generate the resulting business process and we could join them using each business processes as a branch in a global X-OR block. However, this would defy the purpose of aiming at compact representations. In this paper, we address the problem of how to generate business process models with exclusive choice patterns starting from a set of cases (each represented by a set of facts encoding, for example, standard configurations and most common choices) and a set of declarative specifications for an agent.

2 Logic

The aim of this section is to give some basic notions of the logic presented in a series of works [1,2] and to make the reader acquainted with the intuitions behind such a logic apparatus while avoiding instead the technicalities.

DL is typically sceptical, meaning that it allows rules for opposite conclusions. In the situation where rules for opposite literals are activated (may *fire*), the logic does not produce any inconsistency but it simply does not draw any conclusion unless a preference (or superiority) relation states that one rule prevails over the other. A *defeasible theory* D is defined as a structure $(F, R, >)$, where (i) F is a set denoting simple pieces of information that are considered to be always true (e.g., a fact is that "Sylvester is a cat", formally $cat(Sylvester)$), (ii) R contains two finite sets of rules: defeasible rules and defeaters, (iii) $> \subseteq R \times R$ is a binary relation. A rule is an expression $r : A(r) \hookrightarrow C(r)$, and consists of: (i) a unique name r, (ii) the antecedent $A(r)$ which is a finite set of (modal) literals, (iii) an *arrow* $\hookrightarrow \in \{\Rightarrow, \leadsto\}$ denoting, respectively, defeasible rules and defeaters, and (iv) its consequent $C(r)$ which is a single literal (or a chain of modal literals, see below). A *defeasible* rule can be defeated by contrary evidence; for example the rule representing "cats typically eat birds" is "$cat(X) \Rightarrow eat\_birds(X)$", means that if something is a cat, then we may conclude that it eats birds, unless there is evidence proving otherwise. *Defeaters* are special rules whose only purpose is to defeat defeasible rules by producing contrary evidence. The *superiority relation* $>$ is used to define when one rule may override the conclusion of another one, e.g., given the rules "$r : cat(X) \Rightarrow eat\_birds(X)$" and "$s : domestic\_cat(X) \Rightarrow \neg eat\_birds(X)$", if we state that "$s > r$", then Sylvester does not to eat birds.

A defeasible conclusion is a tagged literal and can have one of the following form: (1) $+\partial q$ which means that q is defeasibly provable in D, and (2) $-\partial q$ which means that q is refuted, or not defeasibly provable in D. The idea of $+\partial$ derivation being that a given literal q is defeasibly provable if either it is definitely provable, or we argue by using the defeasible part of the theory. In the latter case, $\sim q$ must be not definitely provable, and there must exist an applicable strict or defeasible rule for q. Finally, every attack on such a rule is either discarded, or defeated by a stronger rule supporting q.

The logic of [1,2] is equipped with modal rules and operators to capture the obligations an agent has to comply with and the goal-like mental attitudes of the agent. However, such components are not needed to synthesis the plans an agent commits to, and, for the purpose of this paper they can be considered as simple conditions literals.

Given a defeasible theory D, we define the set of positive and negative conclusions as the *extension* of the theory. The positive extension is noted by $E^+(D)$, the negative one by $E^-(D)$. More formally the positive and negative extensions are defined as follows: $E^+(D) = \{p|D \vdash +\partial p\}$ and $E^-(D) = \{p|D \vdash -\partial p\}$.

Observation. *An extension is characteristic of a specific set of facts: fixed the rules and the superiority relation, two different sets of facts may lead to two distinct extensions.*

Exclusive Choice Patterns. Here we describe three possible variants to effectively model exclusive choice patterns in defeasible logic.

When we consider only a single literal t, a *choice pattern* is a set of rules proving t. Typically, such rules have distinct sets of antecedents. On the contrary, an *exclusive choice pattern* must not consider a single literal, but a set of distinct literals, $t_1, \ldots, t_n$. These literals must share, to a certain extent, the same sets of antecedents (activation elements). What do we mean by *to a certain extent*? Recall that literals in our theory are conceptually divided between condition- and task-literals. Hence, $t_1, \ldots, t_n$ must have a common set of activation task-literals, while differing on the activation condition-literals. For instance, in the following scenario

$$r_1: a, b, c_1 \Rightarrow t_1 \qquad r_2: a, b, c_2 \Rightarrow t_2,$$

t_1 and t_2 share the set of common activation task-literals (a and b), while the distinctive activation condition-literals are c_1 for t_1, and c_2 for t_2. Hereafter, condition-literals are denoted by cs with a subscript notation.

The key distinction between a choice and an exclusive choice is that, in the former, every alternative can be executed at the same time while, in the exclusive choice, once an alternative is executed, none of the others can. Thus, the logic must exhibit structures to prevent the execution of all the other alternatives once a choice is made. This can be easily handled by the use of defeater rules.

Variant 1 sees a preferred task (say t_1) while all the other alternatives are of equal importance with respect to one another. Formally,

$$r_1 : \Delta \Rightarrow t_1$$
$$r_i : \Delta, \Gamma_i \Rightarrow t_i \quad \text{for } 1 < j \leq n$$
$$d_{1j} : t_1 \rightsquigarrow \sim t_j \quad \text{for } 1 < j \leq n$$
$$d_{ij} : t_i \rightsquigarrow \sim t_j \quad \text{for } 1 \leq i, j \leq n, \ i \neq j.$$

Δ the set of common activation task-literals; Γ_i denotes the set of condition-literals distinctive for task-literal t_i. Task t_1 is the default choice: as such, no activation conditions are needed. Defeaters d_{1i} and d_{ij} ensure that once an alternative is chosen, no other can.

Variant 2 considers none of the tasks involved to be preferred to the others.

$$r_i : \Delta, \Gamma_i \Rightarrow t_i \qquad d_{c_{ij}} : t_i \rightsquigarrow \sim t_j \quad \text{for } 1 \leq i, j \leq n, \ i \neq j.$$

A different form of this second variant excludes sets Γ_is from playing a role in the choice of which branch to run. We think that such a variation is conceptually weak given that there should always be some way to discriminate why running an alternative instead of another. Nonetheless, in the following algorithms, it will be trivially calculated.

Variant 3 There are situations where a branch of the exclusive choice pattern does not actually perform any action, but it is just used to skip the run to the end of the X-OR join gate (we can see it like an empty branch).

$$r_1 : \Delta, \Gamma_1 \Rightarrow t_1$$
$$r_i : \Delta, \Gamma_i \Rightarrow t_i \quad \text{for } 1 < i \leq n$$
$$r_{i1} : t_i \Rightarrow t_1 \quad \text{for } 1 < i \leq n$$
$$d_{1j} : \Gamma_1 \rightsquigarrow \sim t_i \quad \text{for } 1 < i \leq n$$
$$d_{ij} : t_i \rightsquigarrow \sim t_j \quad \text{for } 1 < i, j \leq n \text{ and } i \neq j.$$

Here, the execution of t_1 prevents the execution of any other t_i.

3   Algorithms

In [3, 4], we presented methodologies to compute a process graph starting by a set of declarative specifications being able to describe: (i) the system's environment, (ii) the active norms and (iii) a set of goals (called outcomes) the system aims to achieve. The execution of that step was possible upon previous computations on a series of algorithms which efficiently compute which actions the system is meant to perform in order (i) to achieve a set of goals (ii) while it does not to violate certain norms (or to compensate all the violated ones) [1,2]. The input of [1,2]'s algorithms was (1) the underlying modal logic (of the type of the one presented in Section 2), and (2) an assignment to the set of facts. The output was an extension. We recall that, fixed the rules, distinct set of facts (typically) generate different extensions. Given a set of facts, some rules are activated to produce certain effects and these effects may, in turn, activate other rules which produce other effects (and so on). Therefore, the positive extension represents all the *active* literals. This means that if the literal stands for a condition, such a condition is fulfilled (for instance, the norm is not violated or compensated); if the literal stands for a task, that task will be executed in the corresponding process.

The algorithms of [3,4] started from a single extension. The focus, and novelty, of the present research being that such an assignment to the set of facts may well not be the only one resulting in a compliant situation. This is typical in business practices as we argued above where, instead of a single case, we consider multiple (possibly incompatible) cases corresponding to scenarios the agent has to deal with. Before showing the algorithmic results for the exclusive choice pattern computation, we briefly describe of how [3,4]'s algorithms work. The idea of those algorithms is to start from a set of *proved* goals and from each one of them to navigate backwards the derivation tree by considering only those literals in the positive extension. This procedure is then recursively iterated on each of those literals. This schema naturally captures the three main features of a process graph: (1) *sequence*, given a literal p, if a belongs to a certain $A(r)$ such that $C(r) = p$, then in the graph there is an edge linking node A to node P; (2) *parallel execution*, if also literal b is in $A(r)$ then it is natural that nodes A and B are linked to P by and AND JOIN gate; (3) *choice*, many rules proving p represent different alternatives to obtain p and we link them to P through an OR JOIN gate. Once this backwards phase ended, the process graph is synthesised by recognising *co-occurrence* patterns and by removing condition-literals, substituted by labelled edges.

X-OR Pattens Algorithms. The algorithms we describe hereafter recognise exclusive choice patterns. Algorithm 1 (X-OR) has been designed to be a procedure invoked by the main algorithm of [3,4] after the condition-task elimination has taken place. Let us understand the basic principles behind it by helping us with the following examples.

Example 1. Let D be the theory, with empty superiority relation, such that

$$r_1 : a, c_1 \Rightarrow t_1 \quad r_2 : a, c_2 \Rightarrow t_2 \quad r_3 : t_1 \Rightarrow b \quad r_4 : t_2 \Rightarrow b \quad d_{12} : t_1 \rightsquigarrow \sim t_2 \quad d_{21} : t_2 \rightsquigarrow \sim t_1.$$

Here, if we have the two distinct assignments $F' = \{a, c_1\}$ and $F'' = \{a, c_2\}$, then task-literals t_1 and t_2 are in an exclusive choice pattern. Indeed, (i) t_1 is proved only when using F' (and symmetrically for t_2 with F''), (ii) t_1 and t_2 share the activation task a, (iii) c_1 (resp. c_2) is the unique activation condition for t_1 (resp. t_2), and (iii) the activation of one task defeats the activation of the other through the presence of defeaters d_{12} and d_{21}. Finally, both t_1 and t_2 derive b. We can thus close the pattern by linking T_1 and T_2 to an X-OR JOIN gate-node, which in turn is followed by B.

Exclusive choice variants described in Section 2 are useful to define some theoretical properties and to give the reader an understanding of which differences distinguish one variant from another. Their common, focal point being that the tasks in the exclusive choice share a set of activation task-literals while other sets of condition-literals are characteristic of which choice-branch to run. Given that Algorithm 1 X-OR's execution begins after the condition nodes have been removed from the graph, to gather for such activation requirements is not trivial, as following Example 2 points out.

Example 2. Let D be the theory, with empty superiority relation, such that

$$r_1 : b, c_3 \Rightarrow t_1 \quad r_2 : d \Rightarrow t_1 \quad r_3 : a \Rightarrow c_1$$
$$r_4 : c_1 \Rightarrow c_3 \quad r_5 : t_1 \Rightarrow e \quad r_6 : a, b, d, c_2 \Rightarrow t_2$$
$$r_7 : t_2 \Rightarrow e \quad r_8 : e \Rightarrow f \quad d_{12} : t_1 \rightsquigarrow {\sim}t_2 \quad d_{21} : t_2 \rightsquigarrow {\sim}t_1.$$

Given two assignments to the set of facts (e.g., $F' = \{a, b, d, c_3\}$ and $F'' = \{a, b, d, c_2\}$), are t_1 and t_2 in an exclusive choice pattern? Yes, they are. Apparently, the immediately previous activation task-literals of t_1 are b and d only (resp. due to r_1 and r_2), while for t_2 are a, b and d. What about a for t_1? a is the antecedent of r_3 for proving c_1 which, in turn, is used by r_4 to prove c_3. Recall that, once the process graph is made, synthesis Phase 2 sees nodes C_1 and C_3 being removed from the graph and substituted by a labelled arc connecting A *directly* to AND-J$_{r_1}$. Thus, task-node A can be seen as an activation task of T_1. Therefore, activation tasks of t_1 are the same of t_2 even if, in case of t_1, they come from four distinct rules, while in case of t_2 from the single r_5. Is that nonetheless correct? Again, the answer is yes, provided that, for every each t_i in the exclusive choice pattern, all its activation literals are derived in the same extension.

Before the detailed description of the algorithms, we introduce the two last preliminary notions. A task dependency graph is essentially a dependency graph where we consider task-literals only. The *task dependency graph* of D, $TDG(D)$, is the directed graph defined as follows: the set of vertices is $V_{TDG(D)} = \{t | t$ is a task-literal in $D\}$. The set of arcs is $E_{TDG(D)} = \{(a, b) | \exists r \in R_{sd}[b] : a \in A(r)$ and $a, b \in V_{TDG(D)}$; or $\exists r_1, \ldots, r_n \in R_s d : a \in A(r_1), b = C(r_n), C(r_j) \notin V_{TDG(D)}$ $j < n$, and $C(r_i) \in A(r_{i+1})\}$. Given the task dependency graph $TDG(D)$ and a task-literal l in it, define *Reachability(l)* as the set of nodes reachable from a l. Formally *Reachability(l)* $= \{M \in V_{TDG(D)} | \exists M_1, \ldots M_n :$ $(L, M_1), (M_i, M_{i+1}) \in E_{TDG(D)}$ and $M = M_n\}$. Notice that computing the task dependency graph and the set of reachable nodes is quadratic in the number of vertices.

Algorithm 1 (X-OR) is the main procedure, which invokes its subroutines Algorithm 2 (BACKWARDTASKSPROJ) and Algorithm 3 (IFX-OR). Algorithm 1

Algorithm 1. X-Or

```
1: Compute the task-dependency graph TDG
2: alreadyXed ← ∅, conditionsLabels ← ∅, XJoin ← ∅
3: for T ∈ V \ alreadyXed. ∃i, j. t ∈ E_i^+(D) and t ∉ E_j^+(D) with i, j ≤ m, i ≠ j do
4:     backwardTasks ← BACKWARDTASKSPROJ(T)
5:     XORtasks ← IFX-OR(T, i, backwardTasks)
6:     if XORtasks ≠ ∅ then
7:         XJoin(T_l) ← Reachability(t_l)
8:         closure ← ⋂_{1≤l≤n} XJoin(T_l)
9:         closure ← closure \ {P ∈ closure | P depends on Q ∈ closure or P is not a task-node}
10:        T_{final} ← XORtasks ∩ closure
11:        V ← V ∪ {XOR-S_{T_1,...,T_n}, XOR-J_{T_1,...,T_n}} with T_1,...,T_n ∈ XORtasks
12:        for T_l ∈ XORtasks \ {T_{final}} do
13:            E ← E ∪ {(L, XOR-S_{t_1,...,t_n}) | L ∈ in_V(T_i)} \ {(L, T_i)}
14:            E ← E ∪ {e = (XOR-S_{T_1,...,T_n}, T_i)}
15:            label(e) ← conditionLabels(T_i)
16:        if closure ≠ ∅ then
17:            if T_{final} ≠ null then
18:                E ← E ∪ {(XOR-J_{T_1,...,T_n}, T_{final})} ∪ {(L, XOR-J_{T_1,...,T_n}) | ∃1 ≤ j ≤ n. L ∈
       in_V(T_{final}) ∩ XJoin(T_j)} \ {(L, T_{final}) | L ∈ in_V(T_{final}) ∩ XJoin}
19:            else
20:                for P ∈ closure do
21:                    E ← E ∪ {(L, XOR-J_{T_1,...,T_n}) | ∃1 ≤ j ≤ n. L ∈ in_V(P) ∩ XJoin(T_j)} \
       {(L, P) | L ∈ in_V(P) ∩ XJoin} ∪ {(XOR-J_{T_1,...,T_n}, P)}
22:        alreadyXed ← alreadyXed ∪ XORtasks
```

is conceptually divided in two phases. During the first phase of the main algorithm, it collects the tasks appearing in an exclusive choice pattern. The second phase starts if an X-OR has been found and manages the graph operations needed to insert the X-OR SPLIT and X-OR JOIN into the process graph.

In the first phase, for every task-node, Algorithm 1 gathers (a) the activation tasks and (b) the activation conditions. It stores the tasks in the set *backwardTasks* and the conditions in *conditionLabels*. *conditionLabels* is an array of arrays and will be afterwards used to label edges: for each task that will be present in the X-OR pattern, there is a set where to store all the activation conditions.

Steps (a) and (b) are performed by Algorithm 2: it stores all nodes with an outgoing edge towards the node under examination in the set *premises* (T in the algorithm). The information about such nodes is provided by $in_V(T)$. We say that, for any node X, $in_V(X) = \{Y \in V \mid (Y, X) \in E\}$ denotes the set of all nodes reaching X. All elements stored in *premises* are now analysed. For every of such element P, if P is a task node, then we do not need to further analyse P's predecessors: we simply save it in *bwTasks* and update *conditionLabels*(T). We update *conditionLabels*(T) by adding to it the label of each edge e connecting P to a node previously analysed (that is, a node in *pastPrem*). The edge labelling process recursively collects conditions occurring between tasks, as illustrated in Example 2. In case P is an AND-J_r or an OR-J_N node, we update *premises* with P's immediate predecessors $(in_V(P))$. In case P is an OR-J node, we update *conditionLabels* as the previous case, while in case is an AND-J_r node, we also

---

Algorithm 2. BACKWARDTASKSPROJ

1: **procedure** BACKWARDTASKSPROJ(node T)
2:      $bwTasks \leftarrow \emptyset$, $premises \leftarrow in_V(T)$, $pastPrem \leftarrow T$
3:      **while** $premises \neq \emptyset$ **do**
4:          Let P be the first element of $premises$
5:          **switch** (Node type of P)
6:              **case** P is a task node:
7:                  $conditionLabels(P) \leftarrow conditionLabels(P) \cup labels(e)$ for each $e \in \{e' \in E \mid e' = (P, L)$ and $L \in pastPrem\}$
8:                  $premises \leftarrow premises \setminus \{P\}$
9:                  $bwTasks \leftarrow bwTasks \cup \{P\}$
10:             **case** P is and AND-J$_r$ node:
11:                 $conditionLabels(P) \leftarrow conditionLabels(P) \cup \{c$ is condition-literal $\mid c \in A(r)\} \cup labels(e)$ for each $e \in \{e' \in E \mid e' = (P, L)$ and $L \in pastPrem\}$
12:                 $premises \leftarrow premises \cup in_V(P) \setminus \{P\}$
13:             **case** P is and OR-J$_P$ node:
14:                 $conditionLabels(P) \leftarrow conditionLabels(T) \cup labels(e)$ for each $e \in \{e' \in E \mid e' = (P, L)$ and $L \in pastPrem\}$
15:                 $premises \leftarrow premises \cup in_V(P) \setminus \{P\}$
16:         **end switch**
17:         $pastPrem \leftarrow pastPrem \cup \{P\}$
18:     **return** $bwTasks$

---

add to *conditionLabels* all the condition-literals present in $A(r)$. Notice that subscript r uniquely identifies the corresponding AND-J node.

Once Algorithm 2 has done collecting such information, the execution returns to Algorithm 1 which invokes Algorithm 3 to discover whether an exclusive choice pattern actually exists. To do so, Algorithm 3 searches for all eligible task nodes. A node T' is eligible if (i) task-literal t' is in (at least) a positive extension E_j^+ "not used" by any other task in the X-OR pattern. For instance, let us assume we are considering an X-OR pattern between T_1, T_2 and T_3, and we know that there are five extensions. If t_1 is in E_1^+, while t_2 is in E_2^+ and E_3^+, then t_3 must have been proved in E_4^+ or E_5^+.

If T' is eligible, Algorithm 2 is invoked to compute whether the activation tasks of T' are the same of T's. If that is the case, Algorithm 3 lastly inspects whether a suitable defeaters' structure exists. The execution now returns to Algorithm 1: if an exclusive choice pattern has been found, the algorithm passes to the second phase and performs the operations described hereafter, otherwise it proceeds in controlling the next candidate node. The computation of tasks in *XORtasks* gives knowledge of where to insert the X-OR SPLIT gate-node (X-OR-S$_{T_1,...,T_n}$ in notation, where T_1–T_n are the nodes in the exclusive choice pattern). We now need to understand where to insert the X-OR JOIN gate-node (X-OR-J$_{T_1,...,T_n}$ in notation). For each task T_l in *XORtasks* we store in *XJoin* (a set of sets) the task-nodes reached by T_l. If the intersection of such T_ls (*closure*) is not empty, the exclusive choice pattern is well structured; otherwise the declarative specifications were poorly written and, consequently, no X-OR-J can be inserted into the process graph.

When *closure* is not empty, we need to remove from it all the gate-nodes along with those nodes that depend on nodes in *closure*. The operations described

---

Algorithm 3. IFX-OR

1: **procedure** IFX-OR(task T, index i, set $TbwTasks$)
2:     $Xtasks \leftarrow \{T\}$, $extensions \leftarrow \{i\}$
3:     **for** $T' \in V \setminus alreadyXed \setminus Xtasks$ s.t. $\exists j \notin extensions$. $t' \in E_j^+(D)$ **do**
4:         $TjTasks \leftarrow$ BACKWARDTASKSPROJ(T', j)
5:         **if** $TjTasks = TbwTasks$ **then** $Xtasks \leftarrow Xtasks \cup \{T'\}$, $extensions \leftarrow extensions \cup \{j\}$
6:     $supp \leftarrow \emptyset$
7:     **if** $\exists!T_i \in Xtasks$ s.t. $conditionLabels = \emptyset$ **then**
8:         **for** $T_j \in Xtasks$ with $j \neq i$ **do**
9:             **if** $\exists d \in R_{dft}[\sim t_j].A(d) = \{t_i\}$ **then**
10:                 **for** $T_k \in Xtasks$ with $k \neq i, j$ **do**
11:                     **if** $\exists d \in R_{dft}[\sim t_j].A(d) = \{t_k\}$ **then** $supp \leftarrow supp \cup \{T_j\}$
12:     **if** $\left(supp \neq \emptyset\right)$ **then return** $supp$
13:     $supp \leftarrow \emptyset$
14:     **for** $T_j \in Xtasks$ **do**
15:         **for** $T_k \in Xtasks$ with $k \neq j$ **do**
16:             **if** $\exists d \in R_{dft}[\sim t_j].A(d) = \{t_k\}$ **then**
17:                 **if** $\exists d \in R_{dft}[\sim t_k].A(d) = \{t_j\}$ **then** $supp \leftarrow supp \cup \{T_j\}$
18:     **return** $supp$

---

above serve exactly to this purpose: to eliminate nodes like F from *closure*. Finally, if one of the task in *closure* belongs to *XORtasks* as well, we have an instance of Variant 3. We first identify such a task-node (T_{final} in notation), and then we link the X-OR-$J_{T_1,...,T_n}$ to it (Lines 17–18). In both circumstances, edges from a node in *Xjoin* towards a node in *closure* are erased and substituted to proper connect them to the new inserted X-OR-$S_{T_1,...,T_n}$ node (resp. Lines 18 and 21).

The structure of the algorithms and the operations used in the algorithms indicate that the complexity of the problem investigated in this paper remains polynomial. A thorough analysis is left for future work.

4 Conclusion and Related Work

In this paper we addressed the theoretical issue of how to synthesise compliant business process models incorporating exclusive choice patterns from declarative agent specifications. We proposed computationally efficient algorithms to merge alternative plans into a single business process model. The suitability of the approach to model real life applications is left for future work.

Our approach departs from the standard BDI architecture and agent programming languages implementing it [5,6], and extensions with norms in several respects [7]. While in the above mentioned approaches the agent has to select predefined plans from a library, we propose that the agent generates on the fly a set of plans to meet the objectives without violating the norms. [8] present *norm-aware agents*; a norm-aware agent can deliberate on its goals, norms, and sanctions before deciding which plan to select and execute. In this respect, our agents are norm-aware. [9] provide an account of goals by integrating BDI failure mechanisms with HTN planning techniques. HTN planing is notoriously undecidable even if no variables are allowed, or PSPACE-hard if some restrictions are given. The main feature of their CAN^A is that, if a plan fails, alternative plans are tried. Compared to theirs, our framework has the advantage that we generate all the possible plans at design time. [10] "force" the notion of obligation within the STRIPS framework for agent planning. Their framework is lacking in at least two aspects if compared to ours: (i) they cannot specify the motivational aspects of BDI agents, (ii) their framework cannot generate alternative plans or process graph as we do.

References

1. Governatori, G., Olivieri, F., Rotolo, A., Scannapieco, S., Cristani, M.: Picking up the best goal. In: Morgenstern, L., Stefaneas, P., Lévy, F., Wyner, A., Paschke, A. (eds.) RuleML 2013. LNCS, vol. 8035, pp. 99–113. Springer, Heidelberg (2013)
2. Governatori, G., Olivieri, F., Scannapieco, S., Rotolo, A., Cristani, M.: The rationale behind the concept of goal. Theory and Practice of Logic Programming (in Press)
3. Olivieri, F., Governatori, G., Scannapieco, S., Cristani, M.: Compliant business process design by declarative specifications. In: Boella, G., Elkind, E., Savarimuthu, B.T.R., Dignum, F., Purvis, M.K. (eds.) PRIMA 2013. LNCS, vol. 8291, pp. 213–228. Springer, Heidelberg (2013)
4. Olivieri, F.: Compliance by design: Synthesis of business processes by declarative specifications. Ph.D. thesis, Griffith University and University of Verona (2015)
5. Dastani, M.: 2APL: a practical agent programming language. Autonomous Agents and Multi-Agent Systems 16(3), 214–248 (2008)
6. Bordini, R.H., Hübner, J.F.: BDI Agent programming in agentspeak using *Jason* (Tutorial Paper). In: Toni, F., Torroni, P. (eds.) CLIMA 2005. LNCS (LNAI), vol. 3900, pp. 143–164. Springer, Heidelberg (2006)
7. Andrighetto, G., Governatori, G., Noriega, P., van der Torre, L.W.N., eds.: Normative Multi-Agent Systems. Leibniz-Zentrum fuer Informatik
8. Alechina, N., Dastani, M., Logan, B.: Programming norm-aware agents. In: van der Hoek, W., Padgham, L., Conitzer, V., Winikoff, M., eds.: AAMAS, IFAAMAS, pp. 1057–1064 (2012)
9. Sardiña, S., Padgham, L.: A BDI agent programming language with failure handling, declarative goals, and planning. Autonomous Agents and Multi-Agent Systems 23(1), 18–70 (2011)
10. Panagiotidi, S., Vázquez-Salceda, J.: Towards practical normative agents: a framework and an implementation for norm-aware planning. In: Cranefield, S., van Riemsdijk, M.B., Vázquez-Salceda, J., Noriega, P. (eds.) COIN@AAMAS& WI-IAT. LNCS, vol. 7254, pp. 93–109. Springer, Heidelberg (2012)

Probabilistic Perception Revision
in AGENTSPEAK(L)

Francisco Coelho[✉] and Vitor Nogueira

Departamento de Informática, Escola de Ciências e Tecnologia,
Universidade de Évora, Alentejo, Portugal
{fc,vbn}@di.uevora.pt

Abstract. Agent programming is mostly a symbolic discipline and, as such, draws little benefits from probabilistic areas as machine learning and graphical models. However, the greatest objective of agent research is the achievement of autonomy in dynamical and complex environments — a goal that implies embracing uncertainty and therefore the entailed representations, algorithms and techniques. This paper proposes an innovative and conflict free two layer approach to agent programming that uses already established methods and tools from both symbolic and probabilistic artificial intelligence. Moreover, this method is illustrated by means of a widely used agent programming example, GoldMiners.

1 Introduction and Motivation

Agent autonomy is a key objective in Artificial Intelligence (AI). Complex environments, like the physical world where robots must delve, impose a degree of uncertainty that challenges symbolic processing. But while a probabilistic approach, currently expressed in Machine Learning (ML) and Probabilistic Graphical Models (PGMs) [14], is required for certain aspects of autonomy, a great deal of agent programming is better handled by declarative programming (*e.g.* PROLOG) and more specifically, Beliefs, Desires and Intentions (BDI) architectures for autonomous agents, part of symbolic AI.

Symbolic and probabilistic areas of AI are not necessarily incompatible. Consider for example distribution semantics [18] and markov logic [8]. From there two paths exist towards the interplay of symbolic and probabilistic AI: extending PGMs with logical representations, in Statistical Relational Learning (SRL) [18], and extending logic programming languages with probability, in Probabilistic Logic Programming (PLP) [11,12]. For autonomous agents the symbolic *vs.* probabilistic division persists. Symbolic architectures, such as BDI, describe agent behavior on the basis of metaphors (*e.g.* goals, beliefs, plans) drawn from human behavior while the principle of Maximum Expected Utility (MEU) guides probabilistic AI but there is only seminal work blurring that division.

Concerning agents programming JASON [6] is a popular AGENTSPEAK(L) (ASL) [17] interpreter and framework, triggering a considerable amount of research (*e.g.* [5]). The BDI architecture in general, including ASL and JASON

© Springer International Publishing Switzerland 2015
Q. Chen et al. (Eds.): PRIMA 2015, LNAI 9387, pp. 613–621, 2015.
DOI: 10.1007/978-3-319-25524-8_44

in particular, outline a set of symbolic data structures and processes with more or less detailed semantics. However we can see these agents in trouble when their environment becomes stochastic. This assertion is supported by the experiment plotted in Figure 3: the GoldMiners (GM) is a virtual scenario used in the 2006 Multi-Agent Programming Contest [3] edition, now part of JASON's examples. The two playing teams reach scores that are clearly reduced even with a small amount of sensor misreadings. It turns out that Bayesian Networks (BNs) are representations of dependency of random variables and, thus, natural candidates to represent probabilistic beliefs. But replacing symbolic beliefs by BNs is not trivial in part because changing the symbolic nature of beliefs entails reconsiderations about the BDI architecture (e.g. the beliefs base must unify with plans contexts; changing these to a distribution will break the semantic of such unifications).

Our proposal is, at large, to wrap a layer of probabilistic techniques around certain symbolic processes without altering those processes or associated semantics. Here we illustrate this approach by focusing on the perception. In a stochastic environment, with a certain probability, values reported by sensors differ from the actual value. If sensor reported values are directly used by the deliberation process then performance suffers a penalty that results from the illusions about the truth of the environment. But sensor misreadings can be partially corrected under certain conditions using probabilistic methods. Our task is to find out if with such corrections performance degradation is attenuated and the added complexity has little impact in the deliberation cycle.

The remainder of this paper is organized as follows: next are provided the main concepts of these areas, followed, in section 2, by a general description of the percept-correction function (PCF) in the BDI architecture and a specific instantiation for the GM scenario extended with sensor misreadings. Section 3 presents a particular experiment on that scenario and respective results. In the last section the authors draw some conclusions on that experiment and outline future research.

1.1 State of the Art

Here we outline the groundwork of our proposal: the ASL language, its interpreter JASON, together with PGMs, Dynamic Bayesian Networks (DBNs), and Hidden Markov Models (HMMs).

AGENTSPEAK(L) and JASON. BDI is the predominant architecture used for defining intelligent agents. ASL [17] can be described as a logic programming based language geared towards the BDI architecture. JASON [4,6] implements the operational semantics of an extension of ASL and its deliberation cycle is depicted in Figure 1. In this cycle, the environment generates percepts that are processed by a belief-revision function (BRF). Each change in the beliefs base generates an event. Goals in the set of events represent different desires that the agent selects by the function $S_{\mathcal{E}}$. The selected event entails applicable plans (options) instantiated from the plans library. Selection of a plan among applicable ones is performed by the function $S_{\mathcal{O}}$ and included in the set of (current)

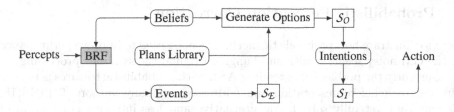

Fig. 1. The JASON deliberation process outlined, with the BRF highlighted. Percepts are processed to generate events and update the beliefs base. Available options are instantiated plans triggered by one event (selected by $S_\mathcal{E}$) and compatible with the current beliefs. One option (defined by $S_\mathcal{O}$) is then appended to the intentions, where $S_\mathcal{I}$ chooses an action.

intentions. Finally function $S_\mathcal{I}$ selects one action from the set of intentions the one (action). Although the BRF evaluation is not part of the ASL specification it is a necessary component of the architecture. The default one that comes with JASON "simply updates the belief base and generates the external events in accordance with current percepts. In particular, it does not guarantee belief consistency." [4] (nevertheless, in [1], the authors present a polynomial-time belief revision algorithm that restores belief base consistency when there are derived inconsistencies). JASON is used as the ASL framework and scenario simulator in this work.

Hidden Markov Models and Dynamic Bayesian Networks. HMM is a well-known framework to deal with latent variables in stochastic processes [2, 14, 16]. A (discrete) system state at time step t is described by a random variable $X^{(t)}$ that verifies the markov condition $\Pr(X^{(t+1)} \mid X^{(0:t)}) = \Pr(X^{(t+1)} \mid X^{(t)})$. This distribution is the *transition model* of the system. If $X^{(t)}$ is hidden but a *sensor model* $\Pr(Y^{(t)} \mid X^{(t)})$ is known then the *filter problem* is to compute the distribution of $X^{(t)}$ given an *initial state*, $x^{(0)}$, and a *sequence of observations*, $y^{(1:t)}$. The *forward* algorithm is a common procedure to compute $\Pr(X^{(t)})$ that requires a belief about the previous environment state, $\hat{x}^{(t-1)}$, updates it with the transition model and corrects that update with the sensor model and current sensor reading, $y^{(t)}$. The major problem with a naïve approach of HMMs is that the size of the transition model is quadratic in the number of system states. DBNs tries to minimize this problem by exploiting independences in the *structure* of the system to, hopefully, produce smaller representations of the transition and sensor models. The general HMM and DBN frameworks can be used directly to describe agent related problems. Perceptions are represented by the observation model and actions by an observed variable, say $a^{(t)}$. The transition model becomes $\Pr(X^{(t)} \mid X^{(t-1)}, A^{(t)})$ and the sensor model $\Pr(Y^{(t)} \mid X^{(t)}, A^{(t)})$. DBN are used in this work to correct agent perceptions. In this specific case the transition and sensor models have many independence relations that are exploited to obtain "small" matrices. The next section describes the construction of such models.

2 Probabilistic Perception Correction

Here we illustrate how probabilistic methods can be used to improve performance in the GM noisy scenario without changing original the symbolic processing.

Currently the problem of extending ASL with probabilistic features is mostly directed to belief representation and addressed by many authors [9,10,13,15, 19] but isn't yet fully solved. An alternative and less intrusive application of probabilistic AI to ASL, proposed here, targets the processes instead of the data structures. Bounding probabilistic techniques to the computation of certain ASL functions (e.g. the BRF, $\mathcal{S}_{\mathcal{E}}, \mathcal{S}_{\mathcal{O}}, \mathcal{S}_{\mathcal{I}}$ functions, as in figure 1) promises a number of advantages. Since the computations of those functions are unspecified in ASL (and overwritable in JASON), probabilistic techniques can be used there without invalidating previous work. So symbolic and probabilistic AI have clearly separated roles and each is used to solve "familiar" problems in the respective domain while both simultaneously contribute to the agent behavior. Symbolic programming uses unchanged ASL programs to define high level agent behavior, with plans, beliefs, *etc.* while probabilistic algorithms process low level noisy signals — with BNs, influence diagrams, *etc.*

Defining certain functions of ASL as tasks to be solved by probabilistic techniques seems a promising technique to address open problems in agent autonomy, using already known theory and tools. Next we describe the setup of an example of this interplay of symbolic and probabilistic techniques. This experiment uses original ASL programs designed for a (mostly) deterministic scenario; adds sensor misreadings, the respective rate being defined by a parameter; re-defines the computation of the BRF with the help of a probabilistic process and records the performance of agents. The outcome of the first two steps is depicted in Figure 3 where performance degradation is associated with increased sensor misreadings.

Problem Statement: (Noisy) GoldMiners. The GM competition is described in [7]. A miner is equipped with a 3×3 grid of sensors, $Y_{0:8}$, that scans its neighborhood. Each sensor reports the content of a cell, that can be one of *empty, obstacle, gold* or *miner*. The miner can also select one action of *up, down, left, right, pick, drop* and *skip*. Non-determinism is present as incomplete perception and action failure and in the examples in JASON noise increases the probability of action failure in proportion to current cargo. Values depicted in Figure 3 result from the JASON simulator with noisy sensors. The "noise" parameter is the rate of cell misreadings. Sensors are independent but equally parameterized: the value reported by each sensor depends only on the noise parameter and cell content.

Proposal: Percept-Correction Function. Our proposal to recover agent performance is to prepend a percept-correction function (PCF) to the BRF applying probabilistic knowledge of the environment (see Figure 2). Correction of perceptions is an inference problem in the framework of HMMs and DBNs .

The formal problem statement is: *In the GM simulation extended with sensor noise parameter θ, update the estimate of cells content $\hat{x}'_{0:8}$ given the previous estimate $\hat{x}_{0:8}$, current action $A' = a'$ and sensor readings $Y'_{0:8} = y'_{0:8}$.* For notation

Detail current belief revision...   ...to include perception correction before symbolic BRF.

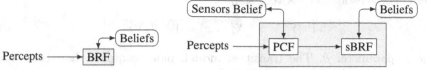

Fig. 2. Inclusion of percept-correction function (PCF) before the original, symbolic, BRF (denoted by sBRF) to correct noisy perceptions. The Sensors Belief is a distribution of sensor values and independent of the (symbolic) beliefs used in the BDI deliberation.

Table 1. Neighbors in the grid sensor. The function $N(i)$ defines the set of neighbors of sensor i. From this topology follow independence statements of the form $X'_i \perp \perp X_{\setminus N(i)} \mid X_{N(i)}$ where $\setminus N(i)$ is a short-hand to $1:8 \setminus N(i)$.

$$N(0) = \{0,1,3\} \quad N(1) = \{0,1,2,4\} \quad N(2) = \{1,2,5\}$$
$$N(3) = \{0,3,4,6\} \quad N(4) = \{1,3,4,5,7\} \quad N(5) = \{2,4,5,8\}$$
$$N(6) = \{3,6,7\} \quad N(7) = \{4,6,7,8\} \quad N(8) = \{5,7,8\}$$

simplicity we write $X = X^{(t-1)}_{0:8}, X' = X^{(t)}$, etc. A resolution is as follows. Given the previous estimate $\hat{x}$, current action a' and sensor reading y', the update is

$$\Pr(X' \mid \hat{x}, a', y') \propto \Pr(y' \mid X') \Pr(X' \mid \hat{x}, a') \tag{1}$$

and perception correction is the *maximum a posteriori* (MAP) of each sensor,

$$\hat{x}'_i = \arg_s \max \Pr(X'_i = s \mid \hat{x}, a', y') \tag{2}$$

where s ranges over all (four) sensor values. The $\arg_s$ max computation doesn't require normalizing the right side of Equation 1, a welcome simplification but direct calculation doesn't scale to the grid sensor. Each location has four different values so the state space has 4^9 and for each action the corresponding transition has $4^{9 \times 2}$ parameters. Numbers of this magnitude render intractable a direct HMM approach. Fortunately, the grid sensor entails many independence statements that reduce the number of transition and observation parameters to a convenient size:

1. Sensor values are independent between them so instead of a "big" transition we only need to deal with nine "small" transitions, one for each sensor;
2. Updated values of each sensor depend only on the action and the previous values of neighbor sensors, defined in Table 1. This can be further refined when the action is considered (e.g. for the "up" action the "bottom" neighbors are irrelevant);
3. The observed value of a sensor depends only on the corresponding cell content;

Using these independence statements the transition and observation models can be described by relatively small matrices and the computations of Equations 1 and 2 become acceptable for the inclusion of the PCF in the BDI deliberation process. The sensor model is very simple:

$$\Pr(Y_i' = x \mid X_i' = x) = 1 - \theta, \; \forall x \tag{3}$$

for noise parameter θ. The transition model, more complex than the sensor model, is explained in the next sub-section.

Resolution: Transition Model. The transition model is based on a few simplifying assumptions about the environment:

1. The state of the environment only changes by effect of the miner's actions. In particular detected miners do not move and gold doesn't "appear" in empty cells;
2. The miner never moves to "obstacle" or "miner" cells;
3. The content of unscanned cells is uniformly distributed over all possible values;

The state of a sensor depends only on the action and previous values of the neighbors. Different actions entail different schemes for the transition parameters, easier to describe one action at a time.

Action "skip". In this case the miner doesn't change the environment state;

Action "pick". The miner removes a gold from its location, if one exists;

Action "drop". The miner adds a gold in its location, if that cell is empty;

Action "up". The miner moves up and the sensors that enter unscanned cells are $\{0, 1, 2\}$. For these cells the scanned value is uniformly distributed. Each one of the other sensors scans the cell previously above it;

Remaining actions ("right", "down" and "left".) These are similar to "up";

These descriptions can be easily translated into conditional probabilities that completely define the transition model for the sensor grid. That model can be used by the forward algorithm outlined before and Equations 1 – 2 to correct perceptions.

3   Results

The proposed approach requires support on the effect it may have on agents performance. Our option was to gather empirical evidence to guide further research.

Implementation Notes. JASON already provides a simulator for the original GM. Its object-oriented nature helps the construction of a noisy variant by overriding some classes and methods. Computation of the PCF uses two libraries developed by the authors, one (at https://github.com/fmgc/jpgm) targeted to the sparse representation of matrices and related operations and a second one (at https://github.com/fmgc/ngm) bridging the operations of the first library to the noisy GM scenario. These are minimal libraries providing only the necessary support here.

Empirical Results. Evaluation of the effect of the PCF uses three teams: a

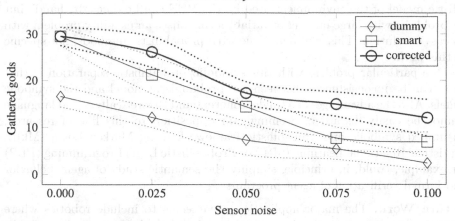

Fig. 3. Sensor noise (horizontal axis) *vs.* agent performance measured by gathered golds (vertical axis). Performance of the "dummy", "smart" and "corrected" teams under various levels of sensor noise are plotted. Each data point summarizes the number of gathered golds by team in a given noise value and consists of the mean (black line) and standard variation (band of dotted lines) of ten samples. The results of the "corrected" team are clearly above the others.

"dummy" team that barely uses any ASL features; a "smart" team that makes heavy use of ASL but not the PCF and a "corrected" team that has the same ASL programs of the "smart" team and uses the PCF. Performance of each team is the number of gathered golds after a given number of time-steps and the sensor noise rate is set at five values: 0.000, 0.025, 0.050, 0.075 and 0.100. A run is defined by a team and a noise value and simulates the GM scenario for 700 time-steps. At the end the number of gathered golds is recorded. Each run (team, noise) is launched ten times and those runs are summarized by the mean and standard variation of the number of gathered golds. The final result are fifteen pairs of (mean, standard variation), plotted in Figure 3.

4   Conclusion

These results provide empirical support to further research the interplay of symbolic and probabilistic AI specifically concerning BDI agent architectures.

There seems to be no major *theoretical* obstacles to generalize this method to other domains and applications. However probabilistic inference in general is intractable [2] despite factorization methods and efficient algorithms for specific graph structures (e.g. DBN, Junction Tree). Probabilistic *learning* was not considered here, although *unsupervised bayesian learning* seems tailored to suit autonomous agents since the benefits of self-reconfiguration might prove critical. Again, adoption of such features stumbles into the computational complexity of the problem.

For relatively simple scenarios the definition of the transitions of the probabilistic model of the environment used by the PCF can be done "by hand" but for problems with large number of variables this raises an usability problem with no easy resolution. This is also an issue with probabilistic methods, not specific to this work.

One particular problem with this symbolic/probabilistic separation is that there can be inconsistencies between the probabilistic model and the symbolic beliefs. Also the advantages of a single, coherent and theoretically sound language cannot be easily discarded. Seemingly in opposition to this line of research, an unified symbolic and probabilistic framework using Markov Logic (MkL), Statistical Relational Learning (SRL) or Probabilistic Logic Programming (PLP) for example, could, in principle, simplify the semantic study of agent behavior and formal verification of agent programs.

Future Work. The major application area seems to include robotics where intrinsically noisy perception is one of the major obstacles to symbolic controls. Hopefully this line of research might facilitate such integration. Further development of this work folds into four major lines: *formal specification and semantics* to support verification of agent programs, guaranteed behavior, *etc*; *further applications of probabilistic methods* to symbolic agent programming (*e.g.* use of influence diagrams to sort actions in the intention selection); *simulations* in virtual environments is a key step in robotics. JASON already provides a large set of scenarios ready to explore in the lines of the GM example presented here; *deployment in physical robots* like the ardrone or twopi is a major challenge given the (usual) computation and real-time constraints of such platforms.

Acknowledgments. The people around us, the flow of life, the internet. And, of course, the gracious money provider, Fundação para a Ciência e Tecnologia.

References

1. Alechina, N., Bordini, R.H., Hübner, J.F., Jago, M., Logan, B.: Belief revision for agentspeak agents. In: Proceedings of the Fifth International Joint Conference on Autonomous Agents and Multiagent Systems AAMAS 2006 (2006)
2. Barber, D.: Bayesian reasoning and machine learning. Cambridge University Press (2012)
3. Behrens, T., Dix, J., Köster, M., Hübner, J.: Special issue about multi-agent-contest II. Ann. Math. Artif. Intell. **61** (2011)
4. Bordini, R.H., Hübner, J.F.: BDI agent programming in agentspeak using *jason* (Tutorial Paper). In: Toni, F., Torroni, P. (eds.) CLIMA 2005. LNCS (LNAI), vol. 3900, pp. 143–164. Springer, Heidelberg (2006)
5. Bordini, R.H., Hübner, J.F.: Semantics for the jason variant of agentspeak (plan failure and some internal actions). In: ECAI, pp. 635–640 (2010)
6. Bordini, R.H., Hübner, J.F., Wooldridge, M.: Programming multi-agent systems in AgentSpeak using Jason. Wiley (2007)
7. Dastani, M., Dix, J., Novák, P.: The second contest on multi-agent systems based on computational logic. In: Inoue, K., Satoh, K., Toni, F. (eds.) CLIMA 2006. LNCS (LNAI), vol. 4371, pp. 266–283. Springer, Heidelberg (2007)

8. Domingos, P., Kok, S., Poon, H., Richardson, M., Singla, P.: Unifying logical and statistical AI. AAAI **6**, 2–7 (2006)
9. Fagundes, M.S.: Integrating BDI model and Bayesian Networks. Master's thesis, Universidade Federal do Rio Grande do Sul (2007)
10. Fagundes, M.S., Vicari, R.M., Coelho, H.: Deliberation process in a BDI model with bayesian networks. In: Ghose, A., Governatori, G., Sadananda, R. (eds.) PRIMA 2007. LNCS, vol. 5044, pp. 207–218. Springer, Heidelberg (2009)
11. Fierens, D., den Broeck, G.V., Renkens, J., Shterionov, D., Gutmann, B., Thon, I., Janssens, G., Raedt, L.D.: Inference and learning in probabilistic logic programs using weighted boolean formulas, pp. 1304–6810 (04 2013). http://arxiv.org/abs/1304.6810
12. Gutmann, B., Thon, I., De Raedt, L.: Learning the parameters of probabilistic logic programs from interpretations. In: Gunopulos, D., Hofmann, T., Malerba, D., Vazirgiannis, M. (eds.) ECML PKDD 2011, Part I. LNCS, vol. 6911, pp. 581–596. Springer, Heidelberg (2011)
13. Kieling, G.L., Vicari, R.M.: Insertion of probabilistic knowledge into BDI agents construction modeled in bayesian networks. In: 2011 International Conference on Complex, Intelligent and Software Intensive Systems (CISIS), pp. 115–122. IEEE (2011)
14. Koller, D., Friedman, N.: Probabilistic graphical models: principles and techniques. The MIT Press (2009)
15. Luz, B., Meneguzzi, F., Vicari, R.: Alternatives to threshold-based desire selection in bayesian BDI agents. In: 1st International Workshop on Engineering Multi-Agent Systems (2013)
16. Murphy, K.P.: Machine learning: a probabilistic perspective. MIT press (2012)
17. Rao, A.S.: AgentSpeak(L): BDI agents speak out in a logical computable language. In: Van de Velde, W., Perram, J.W. (eds.) Agents Breaking Away. LNCS, vol. 1038, pp. 42–55. Springer, Heidelberg (1996)
18. Sato, T.: A statistical learning method for logic programs with distribution semantics. In: Proceedings of the 12th International Conference on Logic Programming (ICLP 1995) (1995)
19. Silva, D.G., Gluz, J.C.: AgentSpeak(PL): A new programming language for BDI agents with integrated bayesian network model. In: International Conference on Information Science and Applications (2011)

Adaptive Multi-stage Optimisation for EV Charging Integration into Smart Grid Control

Christopher-Eyk Hrabia(✉), Tobias Küster, Marcus Voß,
Francisco Denis Pozo Pardo, and Sahin Albayrak

Faculty of Electrical Engineering and Computer Science, DAI-Labor,
Technische Universität Berlin, Ernst-Reuter-Platz 7, 10587 Berlin, Germany
christopher-eyk.hrabia@dai-labor.de

Abstract. The increasing amount of both, renewable energy production
and electric vehicle usage, puts considerable stress on smart grids, making it necessary to synchronize vehicle charging with energy production,
but also allowing to use those vehicles as additional energy storages. In
this paper, we combine machine learning and evolutionary algorithms to
create near-optimal vehicle charging schedules from incomplete information. Using multi-agent systems and process modelling techniques, the
different stages can easily be combined and distributed. The result is
a reusable and extensible solution that is used for optimizing charging
schedules in many different project settings.

Keywords: Multiagent systems · Distributed information systems ·
Optimisation · Charge scheduling · Smart grids · Machine learning

1 Introduction and Problem Statement

To avoid the "long tailpipe", a sustainable electrified transport needs to be
powered by energy coming from renewable energy resources. Therefore many
countries are setting targets for both, the penetration of electric vehicles (EV)
and a higher share of renewable energy [2]. However, this poses new challenges to
the energy system, namely due to the high volatility of energy production and
consumption and its distribution on lower voltage levels of the grid. Further,
a high share of EV – especially with fast charging technologies – may impose
substantial strains on local parts of the electricity grid. As a response, more
intelligence is emerging on all levels of the energy system into the so-called *smart
grid*. Smaller confined parts of the smart grid, which are behaving from the grid's
perspective as a single producer or load, are referred to as *microgrids* [6]. They
are characterized by a large share of distributed (renewable) energy resources
(DER), storage, and an intelligent control system, enabling microgrids to be
even capable of acting (temporarily) independent of the surrounding distribution

This work was partially funded by the German government under the funding reference numbers 16SBB005C (NaNu!), 16SBB016E (Micro Smart Grid EUREF) and
16SBB014A (Smart E-User).

© Springer International Publishing Switzerland 2015
Q. Chen et al. (Eds.): PRIMA 2015, LNAI 9387, pp. 622–630, 2015.
DOI: 10.1007/978-3-319-25524-8_45

grid (*islanding*). Moreover, a quantification of benefits for optimisation efforts in EV charging showed savings up to 45% [4].

This problem domain of combining the energy system with a sustainable transportation was investigated in several applied research projects [12]. The solution discussed here affects three ongoing research projects. First, *MSG EUREF* focuses on software architectures and optimisation procedures for micro-grids and smart distribution feeders. The EUREF site encompasses several producers (photovoltaic plants, wind plants, and a combined heat and power plant (CHP)) and consumers (different smaller buildings, a immersion heater, and most importantly 22 EV charging points), as well as about 150 kWh of storage. Due to missing EV usage data we need to predict when vehicles will be connected, and how much they will need to charge, such that those charges can then be scheduled optimally depending on the current scenario (*peak shaving, economic optimisation, renewable usage, islanding*). In contrast *NaNu!* has to cope with a system of exchangeable batteries for medium-weight delivery trucks. The test scenario is being evaluated with a 12t carrier vehicle with a maximum capacity for 8 batteries. The goal of the project is to optimize the allocation of batteries to vehicles as well as the actual charging times to ensure that the vehicles will have enough energy to accomplish their routes and at the same time reducing overall charging costs. Vehicle usage prediction is not an issue here, since the delivery routes are known in advance. The project *Smart E-User* focuses on integrating electric fleets in companies, combining dynamic route planning and energy management. The route planning component selects the most energy-efficient routes; the energy management system then has to optimize and coordinate the charging times of different locations, taking into account the restrictions imposed by the routing system, but also by electrical requirements of each location.

All projects are going to be integrated into real world test-beds with different smart grid configurations. As a consequence, we are dealing with a large amount of different system setups, which we are aiming to address in one generic modular solution. Due to new and varying requirements in current projects we had to extend former solutions [11] to the one presented in this paper. By implementing a high modular system we can for instance cope in a flexible manner with changing optimisation goals such as aligning EV charging with renewable production, flattening EV charging loads, supporting islanding operation, or decreasing charging costs. In contrast, the previous solution was more monolithic and less flexible and missing data was not addressed.

Different authors have proposed similar systems for optimizing vehicle charging in smart micro grids (e.g., [8,9,13]). Often, they employ one agent per vehicle and their agents negotiate the charging times in a decentralized way. While our system is also distributed, the optimisation itself is centralized. Also, optimisation focuses mostly on a single aspect, e.g., load smoothness, while in our work we are using a multi-criterion optimisation, balancing several conflicting goals. There are limited studies that present models for learning EV usage data for smart charging integration, which could be argued with the lack of good data sets. Hence, Ashtari et al. collected data for 75 vehicles to evaluate their stochastic driving behaviour model [1]. Goebel and Voß use the publicly available data set of 445 non-electric vehicles of the Puget Sound Regional Council [14] to analyse the distribution of the first daily departure time for application in intelligent charge control. They apply a sliding window approach, which produced suitable accuracy only to a sub-class of commuters [5].

In this work we are focusing on the experience made in the three aforementioned German research projects from the Electromobility Showcase initiative Berlin-Brandenburg or "Schaufenster Elektromobilität Berlin-Brandenburg". In particular we are introducing our solution for a modular and adaptive charge scheduling solution (Sections 2 and 3) that can cope with a variety of requirements induced by different scenarios and contexts. The evaluation of parts of the system with over a year of historic data is shown in Section 4.

2   System Architecture

The implemented architecture is based on our common energy domain model [12] and takes into account required forecasts, resource allocation, integration with other Supervisory Control and Data Acquisition (SCADA) components and demand scheduling. As stated in the problem description, it was an important requirement to design a common modular solution, able to adapt to dynamic environments and varying operation modes. Hence, it was a natural choice to follow a multiagent approach and split different modules into roles or behaviour units, i.e. agent descriptions. Following this paradigm allows for using available frameworks with their provided low-level infrastructure. The motivation for splitting the optimisation process into several stages has following objectives:

- To structure and simplify the complex multi-objective optimisation process with a wide spectrum of scenario descriptions by using a division into smaller and more specific domains.
- To enable a flexible configuration and orchestration at runtime, allowing the online deployment of improvements or different scenarios.
- To transparently distribute the several components of the system as well as the different stages of the optimisation to different machines on the network.
- To enable additional potentials for future extensions like integrating competing optimisation strategies, running in parallel on distributed machines.
- To allow for simplified parallelisation and improved robustness of the optimisation via distribution to different redundant agents [11].

These stages are specified with interfaces that are implemented by one or more agents for each stage. Moreover, it is possible to have several different instances of one stage running in sequence or parallel, for instance of enabling a multi-level prediction or integrating feedback loops. Thereby, some stages are mandatory and some are optional. Those four stages are:

1. Enhancing input information with prognoses and heuristics [optional]
2. Allocation of resources
3. Meta-heuristic optimisation of the schedule
4. Post-optimisation for special requirements [optional]

In the first stage, the process is initiated with a scheduling request, containing information about availability of resources, time period and other meta information. The first stage aims for enhancing the scheduling request by using predictions or heuristics to make assumptions about missing or incomplete data, like the availability of EV. Further, it allows to forecast non-deferrable consumption and renewable energy, as well as predicting the controllability of the CHP. The second stage takes all available information about the resources including given constraints and allocates an EV for each booking, batteries (if exchangeable) to an EV, and EVs to charging points, which can be complex or trivial, depending on the scenario. The third stage takes care of the optimisation, resulting in a charging schedule. The fourth stage can be used to integrate further post-processing steps.

Figure 1 shows the optimisation process modelled with the Business Process Modelling Notation (BPMN). Using our "Visual Service Design Tool" process editor (VSDT), the stages can be orchestrated visually to facilitate an improved end-user experience. The diagram is directly executable, and is deployed to a JIAC agent, which is interpreting the process diagram and invoking the different optimisation stages accordingly [7, 10].

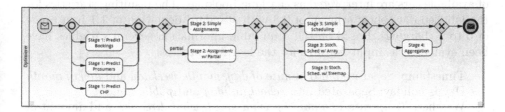

Fig. 1. Orchestrating the optimisation stages with BPMN process modelling

A stage, or agent, can be added, removed, replaced or reconfigured during runtime at any time. This allows for comparison of different configuration against each other. Moreover, we are able to run particular optimisation components in a central location (MSG EUREF) or distributed directly to the charging station (Smart E-User). Moreover, we are able to adjust this configuration during runtime in order to deal with connection problems or maintenance requirements.

3 Implementation of Optimisation Stages

The four optimization stages have been implemented in different ways, according to the requirements in the different projects.

- *Vehicle availability prediction (Stage 1)*: Using machine learning to predict bookings, and thus when to expect charging vehicles, from historical data.
- *Prosumer prediction (Stage 1)*: Using machine learning to predict production of PV and wind, as well as non-deferrable consumption.
- *Allocation of resources (Stage 2)*: Allocation of vehicles to bookings, batteries to vehicles (if applicable), and charging stations to batteries.
- *Meta-heuristic optimisation of the schedule (Stage 3)*: Optimization of charging schedules using evolutionary algorithms, quality assessment of results.
- *Heuristic baseline algorithm (Stage 3)*: Naive 'baseline' algorithm, charging as soon as a vehicle is connected to the charging station.
- *Post-optimisation (Stage 4)*: Aggregation of results, data conversion, etc.

In the following, we will take a closer look at the two most relevant stages: Vehicle prediction and stochastic optimization.

3.1   Stage 1: Vehicle Availability Prediction

In order to deal with the missing booking information in the project MSG EUREF we have trained a model of the EV usage behaviour at our test site that enables long-term scheduling without any vehicle booking information. The learning process is using an ANN (artificial neural network) with two hidden layers, similar to [15], and was developed on historical data from 15 months with a resolution of 3 minutes. We used information about consumption of charging stations to determine whether a car was available/connected at a time slot based on a minimal consumption threshold (consumption > 0.5kW). The period of available cars are interpreted as charging bookings. The resulting statistics for the labelled data show a mean of 0.8 with standard deviation of 1.1 in a range of 0 to 7 chargings. Based on the acquirable information several variables have been evaluated as input features for the learning process:

- Timestamp: Separated into *minute of day, month, weekday* and *day of month*
- Day is holiday: Separated into *school holiday* and *public holiday*
- Weather: *Temperature, humidity, wind speed, wind direction* and amount of *precipitation* and *insolation*

The most effective features have been selected with an exhaustive search using all available feature combinations and time aggregations from 3min (original resolution), 15min, 30min and 60min. We received the best results with 3min resolution and the features *minute of day, day of week, month, school holiday* and *public holiday*. Furthermore, the ANN configuration with 100 training cycles, a learning rate of 0.5 and momentum of 0.2 was determined through manual selection. The model has been trained with a 10-fold cross-validation using stratified sampling on normalized data. Training and testing was executed on the set of 12 months, while keeping 3 months for evaluation (see Section 4.1).

During runtime the model serves as initial prognosis model that is adapted in short-term by using feedback from external *Operation & Control*. The adaptation adjusts the initial prediction for a certain time period and decaying influence with the difference between predicted value and real life measurement.

3.2   Stage 3: Meta-Heuristic Optimisation of the Schedule

For finding the optimal charging schedule, we make use of evolutionary algorithms [3], particularly a variant of $(\mu/\rho + \lambda)$ *evolution strategy*. That means, in each iteration, starting with μ parents, λ offspring are created, whereas each offspring is *recombined* from ρ randomly chosen parents and afterwards *mutated*. The resulting offspring are assessed and the best μ are selected as parents for the next generation. This is repeated until the quality converges.

Implementation of Optimisation Algorithm. The evolutionary algorithm itself is generic; only *recombine* and *mutate* functions are domain specific. Those are selected randomly amongst several variations. Generally speaking, recombination happens *between* charging intervals, while mutation happens *within*.

- For recombination, different charging intervals are taken from different parents,whereas either all charging intervals for one storage, or all intervals within a certain time frame are taken from the same parent. This way, charging intervals that "co-evolved" remain together.
- For mutation, one charging interval is selected randomly and modified, e.g., by changing the charging power or start/end times. There can be more than one charging (or discharging) event within one charging interval.

Quality Assessment. In order to determine the *best* schedule with the highest *quality* the charging process is simulated, keeping track of different metrics:

- *Missed Booking*: Fulfilment of requested kWh of bookings
- *Overcharging*: Storages charged beyond their maximum capacity
- *Changes in Charging Power*: Total number of changes in charging power
- *Sum Energy Cons.*: Sum and difference of energy consumption per step
- *Energy Price*: Total energy cost according to current (variable) tariff
- *Green Energy*: Total percentage of "green" energy used
- *Drawn from/Fed into Grid*: Total energy drawn from/fed into the grid
- *Similarity*: A measure of similarity to the previous schedule

All of those metrics m_i are weighted with a factor w_i and combined in a fitness function $f(x) = \sum w_i \cdot m_i(x)$. The optimization result is determined by the selected weights, focusing on one aspect or using a well-balanced combination.

4   Evaluation

The feasibility of the optimised schedule is highly dependent on the quality of the booking prognoses. Thus, we evaluate the different stages individually, so that the quality of the prognoses does not affect the optimisation. The evaluation uses the configuration and historical data from the MSG EUREF project.

4.1   Booking Prognoses

We applied the trained model, as described in Section 3.1, to an evaluation set of unknown data of three months (June to August 2014), reaching an overall accuracy of 61.54%. Figure 2 visualises the model applied on averaged input attributes from the period of one year. Since the testbed is located on an industry campus, most charging activity is during day time. The diagram shows that the data has high variability, and that our model is hence only able to provide a general trend over a week approaching daily peaks during work days. Furthermore, it needs to be considered that our model is formulated to predict integer numbers, as this is the currently needed input for the optimisation.

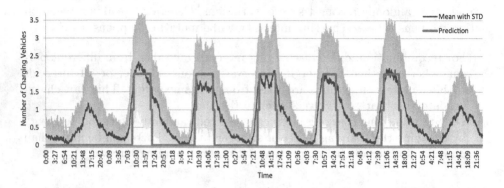

Fig. 2. Prognosis of the number of charged EV of a mean weak (Sun. to Sat.) over the period of Oct. 2013 to Oct. 2014 in comparison to the historical mean with STD.

Although the model is not able to give an accurate prediction from a problem independent perspective, it gives still a lot of useful information we did not have before. As shown in Figure 2, our model gives a conservative prediction of the number of available vehicles in general. Such underestimation of how many cars are available for the optimisation is still superior to load optimisation without having any information about available EVs at all. Furthermore, we are able to predict the time with no available vehicles with good performance.

4.2   Charge Scheduling Optimisation

For the evaluation of the optimisation algorithm (Section 3.2) we used four different configurations: *Simple* uses the heuristic baseline algorithm, charging vehicle batteries directly on plug in and using local storages to myopically buffer and retrieve surplus energy. This closely resembles the regular process at the site. *No Vehicle information* uses the *Simple* algorithm for vehicle batteries and the optimisation for local storages. Representing the worst case, with no available vehicle bookings and manually charged vehicles. *Full Vehicle information* uses the optimisation for scheduling vehicle batteries and local storages, corresponding to the highest degree of freedom for optimisation and accurate booking prognoses. *Vehicle Consumption information* models vehicle usage as uncontrollable consumer, but with accurate prognosis, optimising local storages only.

In Table 1 the results of our evaluation w.r.t our quality metrics are given. Optimising stationary batteries only, while vehicles are charged unpredictably, has the worst performance, due to interferences, like charging EVs while having heavy load or low production. Providing information about EV usage and making them controllable allows to outperform the simple algorithm. Surprisingly, modelling EV usage just as consumer forecast has superior performance relative to the others, even though it has fewer degrees of freedom. However, in that last case the first four metrics and thus the overall quality are not entirely comparable with the others, due to the missing bookings and generally lower number of total charging events. Further, our scenario does not consider EVs with vehicle-to-grid capabilities, as they are not yet commonly available.

Table 1. Normalised charge scheduling quality as mean over 30 randomly selected test periods of 24 hours in a period of one year. 0=best, 1=worst result

	Missed Bookings	Overcharging	Changes in Charging Power	Changes in Charging Signum	Energy Cons. Squared	Energy Cons. Delta Squared	Energy Price	Drawn from Grid	Fed into Grid
Simple	1.00	**0.59**	1.00	1.00	0.75	0.56	0.97	0.97	**0.10**
No Vehicle information	1.00	0.61	0.69	**0.84**	1.00	1.00	1.00	1.00	0.68
Full Vehicle Information	**0.96**	1.00	**0.45**	1.00	0.60	**0.29**	1.00	0.98	1.00
Vehicle Consumption Information	n/a	**0.01**	**0.18**	**0.15**	**0.45**	**0.29**	**0.75**	**0.76**	0.75

In summary, our evaluation shows that modelling the vehicle booking or consumption behaviour is crucial to achieve good optimisation results, but if EV bookings are not available, then predicting EV usage as simple consumption forecast can be sufficient. However, this comparison will have to be reconsidered once the system is fully deployed in real life in cooperation with the *operation & control* module and the complete adaptation feedback loop.

5 Conclusion

In this paper, we presented an agent-based solution for integrating the EV charging processes within the operations of a wide set of smart micro-grid setups, enabling the required level of modularity and adaptive capabilities. The evaluation shows that having different stages to accomplish different tasks in the optimisation process helps to enhance the results, enabling better response times and balancing the served charges. However, there are still open issues related to this context. For validating this work, different configurations of this system will be tested in real environments. In particular, we will develop an alternative implementation for stage 1 that focuses on predicting pure vehicle consumption instead of complete booking behaviour. Furthermore, based on the not yet deployed NaNu! project, it will be possible to specifically evaluate the resource allocation stage, as well as the evaluation of all stages working together.

References

1. Ashtari, A., Bibeau, E., Shahidinejad, S., Molinski, T.: PEV charging profile prediction and analysis based on vehicle usage data. IEEE Transactions on Smart Grid 3(1), 341–350 (2012)
2. Bundesregierung: Energiekonzept für eine umweltschonende, zuverlässige und bezahlbare Energieversorgung, September 2010. http://www.bundesregierung. de/ContentArchiv/DE/Archiv17/_Anlagen/2012/02/energiekonzept-final.pdf (accessed April 1, 2015)
3. Eiben, A., Smith, J.: Introduction to Evolutionary Computing. Natural Computing Series. Springer, Heidelberg (2003)
4. Goebel, C.: On the business value of ICT-controlled plug-in electric vehicle charging in California. Energy Policy 53, 1–10 (2013)
5. Goebel, C., Voß, M.: Forecasting driving behavior to enable efficient grid integration of plug-in electric vehicles. In: IEEE Online Conference on Green Communications (GreenCom), pp. 74–79. IEEE (2012)
6. Hatziargyriou, N., Asano, H., Iravani, R., Marnay, C.: Microgrids. IEEE Power and Energy Magazine 5(4), 78–94 (2007)
7. Hrabia, C.-E., Pardo, F.D.P., Küster, T., Albayrak, S.: Multi-stage smart grid optimisation with a multiagent system (demonstration). In: Proc. of 14th Int. Conf. on Autonomous Agents and Multiagent Systems (AAMAS 2015) (2015)
8. Kamboj, S., Pearre, N., Kempton, W., Decker, K., Trnka, K., Kern, C.: Exploring the formation of electric vehicle coalitions for vehicle-to-grid power regulation. In: Proceedings of the 1st International Workshop on Agent Technologies for Energy Systems (ATES 2010), Toronto, Canada, pp. 1–8 (2010)
9. Kempton, W., Udo, V., Huber, K., Komara, K., Letendre, S., Baker, S., Brunner, D., Pearre, N.: A test of vehicle-to-grid (V2G) for energy storage and frequency regulation in the pjm system. Technical report, University of Delaware, November 2008
10. Küster, T., Lützenberger, M., Albayrak, S.: A formal description of a mapping from business processes to agents. In: Proc. of 3nd Int. Workshop on Engineering Multi-Agent Systems (EMAS) (2015)
11. Küster, T., Lützenberger, M., Voß, M., Freund, D., Albayrak, S.: Applying heuristics and stochastic optimization for load-responsive charging in a smart grid architecture. In: Proc. of 5th IEEE PES Innovative Smart Grid Technologies (ISGT) European 2014 Conference (2014)
12. Lützenberger, M., Masuch, N., Küster, T., Keiser, J., Freund, D., Voß, M., Hrabia, C.-E., Pozo, D., Fähndrich, J., Trollmann, F., Albayrak, S.: Towards a holistic approach for problems in the energy and mobility domain. Procedia Computer Science 32, 780–787 (2014)
13. Markel, T., Bennion, K., Kramer, W., Bryan, J., Giedd, J.: Field testing plug-in hybrid electric vehicles with charge control technology in the Xcel energy territory. Technical report, National Renewable Energy Laboratory, August 2009
14. Puget Sound Regional Council. Traffic choices study: Summary report (2008)
15. Zhang, H.-T., Xu, F.-Y., Zhou, L.: Artificial neural network for load forecasting in smart grid. In: 2010 International Conference on Machine Learning and Cybernetics (ICMLC), vol. 6, pp. 3200–3205, July 2010

Collaborative Judgement

Ewa Andrejczuk[1,2]([✉]), Juan Antonio Rodriguez-Aguilar[1], and Carles Sierra[1]

[1] Artificial Intelligence Research Institute (IIIA-CSIC), Barcelona, Spain
[2] Change Management Tool S.L., Barcelona, Spain
{ewa,jar,sierra}@iiia.csic.es

Abstract. In this paper we introduce a new ranking algorithm, called Collaborative Judgement (CJ), that takes into account *peer opinions* of agents and/or humans on objects (e.g. products, exams, papers) as well as *peer judgements* over those opinions. The combination of these two types of information has not been studied in previous work in order to produce object rankings. We apply CJ to the use case of scientific paper assessment and we validate it over simulated data. The results show that the rankings produced by our algorithm improve current scientific paper ranking practice based on averages of opinions weighted by their reviewers' self-assessments.

1 Introduction

In many areas of our lives we are used to the process of assessing and being assessed. We pass exams at the University, we go through job interviews, we undergo research project reviews, we are evaluated by our employers, etc. Artificial Intelligence research has focused on the assessment process for long and a number of algorithms have been developed to assist in assessing the performance of humans or artificial agents. Indeed large number of trust and reputation models have been proposed [3,12,15–17].

Surprisingly, to our knowledge, no significant effort has been put in the development of algorithms that use *judgement* information over such assessments. We consider exam marks unjust, interview outcomes biased, and review reports unfair, and we normally comment about these opinions on our performance with friends and relatives. We think that this kind of information is very important as it can be key to build the reputation of assessors. A bad assessor can be detected by the assessing community if they were allowed to simply express their opinions about the bad assessor. Actually, in many social networks this kind of information is collected ("was this recommendation useful to you?"), and they present this information to users but how the sites use this information to rank recommendations is never clearly explained if it is used at all.

Similarly, in the area of multiagent systems, agents' performance is key to build teams and coalitions [10]. Team formation and coalition formation are key for many applications related to multiagent cooperation, e.g. RoboCup rescue team [8,13], Unmanned Aerial Vehicles (UAVs) operations [5], team formation in social networks [7]. Both team formation and coalition formation focus on

© Springer International Publishing Switzerland 2015
Q. Chen et al. (Eds.): PRIMA 2015, LNAI 9387, pp. 631–639, 2015.
DOI: 10.1007/978-3-319-25524-8_46

forming the *best* possible group of agents (be it either a team or a coalition) to accomplish some tasks of interest given some limited resources. Hence, it is key in these processes to count on an assessment of the *expected capabilities* of the agents to recruit. With this aim, many trust models have been developed in the past to model agent behaviour [9,11], but judgements have again never been used to our knowledge.

In this paper we present an algorithm, called *Collaborative judgement* (CJ), which wants to go a step further in the use of judgements. CJ takes into account judgements on opinions to build reputation values on assessors and then use them as the basis to aggregate the opinions of a group of assessors. In current recommender systems the opinions about an object are aggregated using weights or not. When no weights are used, the final opinion is just an average of all the opinions (e.g. Amazon, TripAdvisor). When they are used the aggregated opinion is a weighted average using self-assigned weights. This is very common in Conference Management Systems like Confmaster or Easychair. In this paper we will compare CJ with the standard algorithm that weights opinions with the assessors self-assessments. We will call this simple algorithm *Self-Assessment Weighted Algorithm* (SAWA).

Here we will particularize the problem of peer judgement to the case of Conference Paper reviewing. The need to improve the way conferences (and to some extend journals) assess papers is key for scientific progress and its pitfalls have been discussed recently, see for instance the NIPS experiment: http://blog.mrtz. org/2014/12/15/the-nips-experiment.html. Some researchers have been trying to ameliorate the situation by improving the paper assignment process [1]. However, there is a growing phenomenon in which reviews are not made nor supervised by the expert member of the program committee but by someone to whom the reviewing task was delegated (e.g. a PhD student). This would invalidate this potential improvement. Here we propose to adapt CJ to detect those non-expert reviewers and dismiss their opinions from the final decision on accepting a paper. Henceforth, the notation we will use will be based on the ontology of a conference: papers, reviewers, marks, ...

In Section 2 we present the ranking algorithm that we benchmark in Section 4 against SAWA, presented in Section 3. Then, in Sections 5 and 6 we discuss the results and summarise our main achievement and outline our future work.

2   Collaborative Judgement

We first introduce the notation (focused on the case of paper assessment), which we will use in the rest of the paper.

Definition 1. *A conference is a tuple* $\langle P, R, E, o, v \rangle$, *where*

- $P = \{p_i\}_{i \in \mathcal{P}}$ *is a set of papers.*
- $R = \{r_j\}_{j \in \mathcal{R}}$ *is a set of reviewers.*
- $E = \{e_i\}_{i \in \mathcal{E}} \cup \{\perp\}$ *is a totally ordered evaluation space, where* $e_i \in \mathbb{N}$ *and* $e_i < e_j$ *iff* $i < j$ *and* $\perp$ *stands for the absence of evaluation.*

- $o : R \times P \to E$ *is a function giving the opinions of reviewers on papers.*
- $v : R \times R \times P \to E$ *is a function giving the judgements of reviewers over opinions on papers.*[1] *Therefore, a judgement is a reviewer's opinion about another reviewer's opinion.*

In general we might have different dimensions of evaluation, that is a number of E spaces over which to express opinions and judgements. For instance, originality, soundness, etc. but for simplicity reasons we will assume that the evaluation of a paper is made over a single dimension. Actually, the 'overall' opinion is what is aggregated in real systems.

The steps of the CJ algorithm applied over a conference $\langle P, R, E, o, v \rangle$ are as follows:

1. Compute the *agreement level* between reviewers r_i and r_j, $a : R \times R \to [0, 1] \cup \{\perp\}$. If the reviewers had some papers to review in common then the judgements on the opinions, in case they exist, and the similarity between the opinions over the common papers are combined as follows:

$$a(r_i, r_j) = \begin{cases} \frac{\sum_{p_k \in P} s(r_i, r_j, p_k)}{|P_{ij}| \cdot d} & \text{if } P_{ij} = \{p_k \in P | o(r_i, p_k) \neq \perp, o(r_j, p_k) \neq \perp\} \neq \emptyset \\ \perp & \text{otherwise} \end{cases}$$

where d is the maximum distance in the evaluation space and:

$$s(r_i, r_j, p_k) = \begin{cases} v(r_i, r_j, p_k) & \text{if } v(r_i, r_j, p_k) \neq \perp \\ Sim(o(r_i, p_k), o(r_j, p_k)) & \text{otherwise} \end{cases}$$

and Sim stands for an appropriate similarity measure. When no explicit judgements are given, the similarity in opinions is considered a good heuristic for them. The more similar a review is to my opinion, the better I judge that opinion.

2. Compute a complete *Trust Graph* as an adjacency function matrix $C = \{c_{ij}\}_{i,j \in R}$.

$$c_{ij} = \begin{cases} a(r_i, r_j) & \text{if } a(r_i, r_j) \neq \perp \\ \max_{h \in chains(r_i, r_j)} \prod_{(k,k') \in h} a(r_k, r_{k'}) & \text{otherwise} \end{cases}$$

where $chains(r_i, r_j)$ is the set of sequences of reviewer indexes connecting i and j. Formally, a chain h between reviewers i and j is a sequence $\langle l_1, \ldots, l_{n_h} \rangle$ such that $l_1 = i$, $l_{n_h} = j$, and $a(r_k, r_{k+1}) \neq \perp$ for each pair $(k, k + 1)$ of consecutive values in the sequence. To compute this step we use a version of Dijkstra's algorithm that instead of looking for the shortest path (using $+$ and min) it looks for the path with the largest arc product (using $\cdot$ and max). The running time of the Dijkstra algorithm can take $O(n \log n)$, where $n = |R|$, if using priority queues [2].

---

[1] In tools like ConfMaster (www.confmaster.net) this information could be gathered by simply adding a private question to each paper review, answered with elements in E, one value in E for the judgement on each fellow reviewer's review.

3. Compute a *reputation* for each reviewer in R, $\{t_i\}_{i \in R}$, by using Eigentrust [6]. In order for this to be applicable we need to guarantee that the graph C is aperiodic and strongly connected. In this step we obtain a global trust value for each reviewer. In vectorial notation, the trust vector is assessed as $\bar{t} = \lim_{k \to \infty} \bar{t}^{k+1}$ with $\bar{t}^{k+1} = C^T \bar{t}^k$ and $\bar{t}^0 = \bar{e}$ being $\bar{e}_i = 1/|\bar{e}|$. The complexity of the Eigentrust algorithm used in this step is $O(n^2)$. In our case, we cannot force the values in a row of C to add up to 1, as required by the Eigentrust algorithm, so we do normalize the trust vector as generated after each step to guarantee convergence.

4. Compute the *final opinion* on objects as a weighted average of the opinions of those that expressed an opinion. The weights are the reputation of those expressing an opinion:

$$o_{CJ}(p_j) = \frac{\sum_{i \in \{i \in R | o(r_i, p_j) \neq \perp\}} \bar{t}_i \cdot o(r_i, p_j)}{\sum_{i \in \{i \in R | o(r_i, p_j) \neq \perp\}} \bar{t}_i}$$

3   The SAWA Algorithm

We will benchmark CJ against the algorithm used by the conference management systems mentioned in the introduction, which we call in this paper SAWA. We assume there is a function $r : R \times P \mapsto [0,1]$ that keeps how confident each reviewer feels about her opinion on a paper. So the aggregated opinion on a paper is computed as:

$$o_{SAWA}(p_j) = \frac{\sum_{i \in \{i \in R | o(r_i, p_j) \neq \perp\}} r(i, p_j) \cdot o(r_i, p_j)}{\sum_{i \in \{i \in R | o(r_i, p_j) \neq \perp\}} r(i, p_j)}$$

4   Evaluation

In this section we validate the algorithm via simulation. We show that CJ behaves according to expectations with respect to SAWA. The hypotheses we are interested in are:

H1 **CJ rankings get closer to the true quality of a paper when the number of good reviewers increase.**[2]

H2 **Ceteris paribus, the better the reviewers, the larger the improvement of CJ with respect to SAWA.**

H3 **The overall trust on reviewers positively correlates with the number of good reviewers.**

We next explain the experimental setting and three experiments providing support to these hypotheses.

---

[2] See next subsection for our representation of a good reviewer.

4.1   Experimental Setting

We assume a set $P = \{p_1, \ldots, p_n\}$ of papers and a function for their true qual-ity in a range $[0, 1]$,[3] $q : P \rightarrow [0, 1]$. We use the following evaluation space $E = \{1, 2, 3, 4, 5, 6, 7, 8, 9, 10\}$, which is rather common in the context of paper reviewing. We assume two types of reviewers: good and bad, with the following behaviour:

- *Good Reviewer.* She provides fair opinions and fair judgements. Her opinion on any paper p_k is always close to its true quality $q(p_k)$. We assume the absolute value of the difference between the opinion of a reviewer and the true quality (as a percent) follows a beta distribution, $Beta(\alpha, \beta)$, very positively skewed, for instance with $\alpha = 1$ and $\beta = 30$. For each paper p_k reviewed by a good reviewer, we sample the reviewer's associated beta distribution for a percentage difference, apply it to the paper quality $q(p_k)$ (up or down randomly) and round the result to fit an element in E. Her judgements on someone's opinion are close to 0 if the opinion is far from the true quality of the paper, and close to 1 otherwise. We implement this as the following function:

$$v(r_i, r_j, p_k) = 1 - |o(r_j, p_k) - q(p_k)|$$

and self-judgements from $Beta(5, 2)$, slightly negatively skewed.
We assume that when a good reviewer judges a bad reviewer she samples a value in E from a beta distribution rather positively skewed: $Beta(2, 40)$. The intuition is that good reviewers poorly mark bad reviews.

- *Bad Reviewer.* She provides unfair opinions, because she is incompetent, but provides reasonable judgements as she can interpret the opinions of others as being informative or not. Thus, we sample opinions from $Beta(20, 12)$ — rather central with a slight negative skew, judgements for good reviews and self-judgements from $Beta(5, 2)$ as for good reviewers —negatively skewed, and judgements on bad reviews from $Beta(2, 5)$ —slightly positively skewed. The overall idea is that bad reviewers stay mostly in the central area of the evaluation space.

We use $Sim(x, y) = (|E| - 1 - |\tau(x) - \tau(y)|)/(|E| - 1)$ as a simple linear similarity function where τ is a function that gives the position of an element in the ordered set E.

Experiment 1: We set an increasing percentage of good reviewers, from none to 100%. We plot the improvement, that is, the error reduction, using the Mean Absolute Error of the values generated by the two ranking meth-ods (CJ and SAWA) and the true quality of the papers. That is, we plot $(1 - (MAE(O_{CJ}, q)/MAE(O_{SAWA}, q))) \cdot 100$ where

$$MAE(f, g) = \frac{\sum_{p_j \in P} |f(p_j) - g(p_j)|}{|P|}.$$

---

[3] Assessing the true quality of an object may be difficult and it is certainly a domain dependent issue.

In Figure 1 we see this improvement for 10 runs of the algorithms. We observe that CJ improves SAWA and the improvement becomes larger than 10% and statistically significant for percentages of good reviewers between 20% and 80%. These results support H1.

Fig. 1. Percentage of error improvement of CJ over SAWA with the error measured as the Average Mean Absolute Error with respect to the true quality of papers for increasing percentages of good reviewers. The parameters are those explained in the experimental setup.

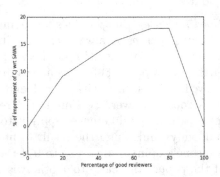

Experiment 2: As mentioned before, we model good reviewers' opinions with a $Beta(\alpha, \beta)$ very positively skewed from which we sample the difference between the reviewer's opinion and the true quality. With $\alpha = 1$ and $\beta > 30$ the expert is frequently telling the true quality in her opinions (specially because we discretise the sampled values into our evaluation space —i.e. almost all the distribution mass is rounded to a distance of 0 with respect to the true quality). In figure 2 we plot the improvement of CJ with respect to SAWA for $\alpha = 1$ and increasing values of β (better reviewer behaviour). We observe that the improvement asymptotically grows to 16%, and hence this supports Hypothesis H2.

Fig. 2. Improvement of CJ over SAWA as the reviewers' quality increases (with fixed $\alpha = 1$ and increasing β values). This plot is for a population with 50% good reviewers and 50% bad reviewers.

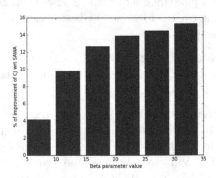

Experiment 3: In Figure 3 we see the increasing mutual trust between reviewers as the average of all values in matrix C with respect to an increasing percentage of good reviewers. This supports Hypothesis H3.

Fig. 3. Increasing mutual trust of reviewers for an increasing percentage of good reviewers.

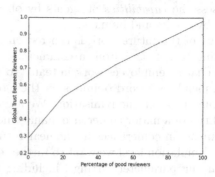

5 Discussion

One issue worth discussing is the feasibility of getting real data to model $q(\cdot)$. We mentioned before that this is obviously a domain dependent issue and that it can be difficult to obtain. For instance, in the case of paper review, what is the true quality of a paper? It seems impossible to answer this question. We could get data on impact of papers and assume that impact relates to quality. This can be done for the papers that were accepted and published, but not for those that were rejected. Therefore, the validation of the algorithm results will necessarily be partial. This will always be controversial as the use of any quality metric would always be debatable. It is in this context that our algorithm contributes since the key assumption of our algorithm is: *when there is no clear-cut method to determine the quality of an object, then the true quality can be determined by the social acceptance of the opinions expressed by experts.*

Another issue worth mentioning is that reviewer quality depends on the particular subarea of a conference. In general, our opinions are fair or not depending on our competences. Thus, CJ should consider this dimension as many existing trust models do [10,14]. The inclusion of a semantic dimension on trust and reputation requires defining an ontology of the domain and semantic distances between the elements in the vocabulary. This represents no technical problem and will basically increase the complexity of the computation proportionally to the granularity of the vocabulary.

6 Conclusions and Further Work

In this paper we introduced CJ. It is a new ranking algorithm that takes into account *peer opinions* of agents and/or humans as well as *peer judgements* over those opinions. We applied CJ to the use case of scientific paper assessment and we validated it over simulated data. The results show that the rankings produced by this new algorithm (under (reasonable) assumptions on reviewer behaviour) improve current scientific paper ranking practice. The use of this algorithm in the context of agent team formation is key as it will provide a sound method to assess the *capabilities* of agents by observing peer opinions and judgements made by agents and humans.

Part of the future work is centred on evaluating CJ over real data. We are planning to get data from a commercial bank about the skills of team members. That is, employees work in teams to solve tasks that require specific skills. Team members record opinions on their team-mates' skills and judgements on the opinions after anonymisation. We are also discussing the extension of functionalities of a major conference management system so that we can get data on judgements in conferences in the near future.

At simulation level we want to further explore the sensitiveness of the results for varying parameter settings, including the impact of similarity functions as these have not been relevant in the reported experiments. Finally, the modelling of *malicious* reviewers (those who know the quality of a paper and deliberately lie about it) will be considered. We expect that our method might help in detecting those reviewers.

In many settings, including conference paper rankings, the actual numerical value is not the key element but the order between alternatives. CJ produces a *partial ranking* among alternatives, that is, there can be ties between objects (e.g. papers). We plan to compare CJ vs SAWA using the generalisation of the Kendall Tau distance proposed in [4] to compare partial rankings.

Finally, this algorithm is an important milestone on our path to develop methods to build agent and human teams to solve complex tasks that balance capabilities and mutual relationships.

Acknowledgments. The first author is supported by an Industrial PhD scholarship from the Generalitat de Catalunya. This work is also supported by the CollectiveMind project (Spanish Ministry of Economy and Competitiveness, grant number TEC2013-49430-EXP) and the COR project (TIN2012-38876-C02-01).

References

1. Charlin, L., Zemel, R.S., Boutilier, C.: A framework for optimizing paper matching. CoRR, abs/1202.3706 (2012)
2. Cormen, T.H., Stein, C., Rivest, R.L., Leiserson, C.E.: Introduction to Algorithms, 2nd edn. McGraw-Hill Higher Education (2001)
3. de Alfaro, L., Shavlovsky, M.: Crowdgrader: Crowdsourcing the evaluation of homework assignments. Thech. Report 1308.5273, arXiv.org (2013)
4. Fagin, R., Kumar, R., Mahdian, M., Sivakumar, D., Vee, E.: Comparing and aggregating rankings with ties. In: Proceedings of the Twenty-Third ACM SIGMOD-SIGACT-SIGART Symposium on Principles of Database Systems, PODS '04, pp. 47–58. ACM, New York (2004)
5. Haque, M., Egerstedt, M., Rahmani, A.: Multilevel coalition formation strategy for suppression of enemy air defenses missions. Journal of Aerospace Information Systems **10**(6), 287–296 (2013)
6. Kamvar, S.D., Schlosser, M.T., Garcia-Molina, H.: The eigentrust algorithm for reputation management in p2p networks. In: Proceedings of the 12th International Conference on World Wide Web, WWW '03, pp. 640–651. ACM, New York (2003)

7. Lappas, T., Liu, K., Terzi, E.: Finding a team of experts in social networks. In: Proceedings of the 15th ACM SIGKDD International Conference on Knowledge Discovery and Data Mining, KDD '09, pp. 467–476. ACM, New York (2009)

8. Nair, R., Tambe, M., Marsella, S.C.: Team formation for reformation in multiagent domains like RoboCupRescue. In: Kaminka, G.A., Lima, P.U., Rojas, R. (eds.) RoboCup 2002. LNCS (LNAI), vol. 2752, pp. 150–161. Springer, Heidelberg (2003)

9. Osman, N., Gutierrez, P., Sierra, C.: Trustworthy advice. Knowl.-Based Syst. **82**, 41–59 (2015)

10. Osman, N., Sierra, C., McNeill, F., Pane, J., Debenham, J.K.: Trust and matching algorithms for selecting suitable agents. ACM TIST **5**(1), 16 (2013)

11. Osman, N., Sierra, C., Sabater-Mir, J.: Propagation of opinions in structural graphs. In: Coelho, H., Studer, R., Wooldridge, M. (eds.) ECAI 2010–19th European Conference on Artificial Intelligence, Lisbon, Portugal, 16–20 August 2010. Frontiers in Artificial Intelligence and Applications, vol. 215, pp. 595–600. IOS Press (2010)

12. Piech, C., Huang, J., Chen, Z., Do, C., Ng, A., Koller, D.: Tuned models of peer assessment in moocs. In: Proc. of the 6th International Conference on Educational Data Mining (EDM 2013) (2013)

13. Ramchurn, S.D., Farinelli, A., Macarthur, K.S., Jennings, N.R.: Decentralized coordination in robocup rescue. Comput. J. **53**(9), 1447–1461 (2010)

14. Sierra, C., Debenham, J.K.: Trust and honour in information-based agency. In: Nakashima, H., Wellman, M.P., Weiss, G., Stone, P. (eds.) 5th International Joint Conference on Autonomous Agents and Multiagent Systems (AAMAS 2006), Hakodate, Japan, 8–12 May 2006, pp. 1225–1232. ACM (2006)

15. Walsh, T.: The peerrank method for peer assessment. In: Schaub, T., Friedrich, G., O'Sullivan, B. (eds.) ECAI 2014–21st European Conference on Artificial Intelligence, 18–22 August 2014, Prague, Czech Republic - Including Prestigious Applications of Intelligent Systems (PAIS 2014). Frontiers in Artificial Intelligence and Applications, vol. 263, pp. 909–914. IOS Press (2014)

16. Wu, J., Chiclana, F., Herrera-Viedma, E.: Trust based consensus model for social network in an incompletelinguistic information context. Applied Soft Computing (2015)

17. Zhang, J., Ghorbani, A.A., Cohen, R.: A familiarity-based trust model for effective selection of sellers in multiagent e-commerce systems. Int. J. Inf. Sec. **6**(5), 333–344 (2007)

Model Checking Resource Bounded Systems with Shared Resources via Alternating Büchi Pushdown Systems

Nils Bulling[1](✉) and Hoang Nga Nguyen[2](✉)

[1] Delft University of Technology, Delft, The Netherlands
N.Bulling@tudelft.nl
[2] School of Computer Science, University of Nottingham, Nottingham, UK
Hoang.Nguyen@nottingham.ac.uk

Abstract. It is well known that the verification of resource-constrained multi-agent systems is undecidable in general. In many such settings, resources are private to agents. In this paper, we investigate the model checking problem for a resource logic based on Alternating-Time Temporal Logic (ATL) with shared resources. Resources can be consumed and produced up to any amount. We show that the model checking problem is undecidable if two or more of such unbounded resources are available. Our main technical result is that in the case of a single shared resource, the problem becomes decidable. Although intuitive, the proof of decidability is non-trivial. We reduce model checking to a problem over alternating Büchi pushdown systems. An intermediate result connects to general automata-based verification: we show that model checking Computation Tree Logic (CTL) over (compact) alternating Büchi pushdown systems is decidable.

1 Introduction and Related Work

Research on resource-constrained multi-agent systems has become a popular topic in recent years, e.g. [1–3,7,8,13]. In particular, the verification of strategic agents acting under resource-constraints has been investigated by researchers; many of these approaches extend the alternating-time temporal logic (ATL) [4] with actions that, in the general case, consume or produce resources. If no bound on the possible amount of resources is given the model checking problems are easily undecidable [8]. Exceptions are possible if restrictions are imposed on the language [3] or on the semantics [1,13]. In many settings, resources are private to agents, each agent has its own set of resources. In [13] resources are shared and a resource money is used to claim resources. The authors present a decidable model checking result which is possible as the amount of resources is bounded. In this paper we are interested in the model checking problem where resources are shared and *unbounded*; resources can be consumed and produced without an upper bound on the total number of resources. The setting is rather natural. Resources are shared in e.g., the travel budget of a computer science department.

© Springer International Publishing Switzerland 2015
Q. Chen et al. (Eds.): PRIMA 2015, LNAI 9387, pp. 640–649, 2015.
DOI: 10.1007/978-3-319-25524-8_47

All departmental members compete for the travel budget. Parts of the travel money of a successful grant application will be credited to the department's budget; there is no a priori bound on the total budget.

In this paper, we show that the model checking problem for the resource agent logic RAL [8] considered here is undecidable in general when there are more than two of such unbounded shared resources. This result follows as a corollary from [3,8] where model checking resource bounded systems with private, unbounded resources has been proved undecidable. Secondly, we show that model checking RAL is decidable in case of a single shared, unbounded resource. Although this seems intuitive, as a single unbounded resource can intuitively be encoded by a single stack/counter, its proof is (technically) non-trivial and is based on a reduction to alternating Büchi pushdown systems [5,15]. We first introduce compact alternating Büchi pushdown systems (CABPDSs) to encode the resource bounded models of our logic such that the runs of the automaton can be related to execution trees of a given set of agents in the model. We show that model checking CTL over these systems is decidable using results of [15]. Finally, we reduce model checking RAL to model checking CTL over CABPDSs. These results extend work on model checking CTL over pushdown systems where atomic propositions can be given by regular languages [15]. The latter results, in turn, are based on [5] where reachability of alternating pushdown systems and model checking problems over pushdown systems with standard labelling functions are investigated. Model checking CTL over pushdown systems and its computational complexity have also been considered in [6]. Our model checking problem is also related to reachability in Büchi games [10]. Many complexity results about ABPDSs and their variants are known and established in the above mentioned pieces of work. In our future research we plan to determine the exact computational complexity of the model checking problem for resource agent logic (RAL) over 1-unbounded resource bounded models.

The paper is organised as follows. In Section 2 we introduce our version of resource agent logic with shared resources. In Section 3 we recall alternating Büchi pushdown systems (ABPDSs) and variants thereof. We propose compact ABPDSs for encoding our models. We show that model checking CTL over them is decidable. In Section 4 we give our main decidability result for a single unbounded resource and also conclude undecidability for the general setting with more than 1-unbounded shared resource. Finally, we conclude in Section 5. Due to lack of space, we have to skip details and proofs. An extended version of this paper can be found in [9].

2   Resource Agent Logic

In this section we define the logic *resource agent logic* RAL and resource-bounded models. The framework is essentially based on [3]. But, in this paper we are intersted in *shared resources*. There is a common pool of resources and agents compete for them. There are more dimensions along which resources can be classified [9], one of these dimensions is *boundedness*. A resource is called *unbounded* if there is no a priori bound on the number of available resources, in principle they can be produced without limit. Settings with only bounded resources are often decidable [8]. In the following we consider unbounded resources and assume that $\mathcal{R}es$ is a finite non-empty set of such unbounded, shared resource types. A *(shared) endowment (function)* $\eta : \mathcal{R}es \to \mathbb{N}_0$ specifies the available shared resources of the resource types $\mathcal{R}es$ in the system; i.e., $\eta(r)$ is the number of shared resources of type r. With En we denote the set of all possible endowments. A special minimal endowment function is denoted by $\bar{0}$. It expresses that there are no resources at all.

Syntax. Resource agent logic (RAL) is defined over a set of agents Agt and a set of propositional symbols Π. RAL-formulae[1] are essentially generated according to the grammar of ATL [4] as follows: $\varphi ::= \mathsf{p} \mid \neg\varphi \mid \varphi\wedge\varphi \mid \langle\!\langle A \rangle\!\rangle^{\downarrow}\mathbf{X}\varphi \mid \langle\!\langle A \rangle\!\rangle^{\downarrow}\varphi\mathbf{U}\psi \mid \langle\!\langle A \rangle\!\rangle^{\downarrow}\mathbf{G}\varphi$ where $\mathsf{p} \in \Pi$ is a proposition and $A \subseteq$ Agt is a set of agents.

A formula $\langle\!\langle A \rangle\!\rangle^{\downarrow}\varphi$ is called *flat* if φ contains no cooperation modalities. The operators $\mathbf{X}$, $\mathbf{U}$, and $\mathbf{G}$ denote the standard temporal operators expressing that some property holds in the *next* point in time, *until* some other property holds, and *now and always* in the future, respectively. The *eventually* operator is defined as macro: $\mathbf{F}\varphi = \top\mathbf{U}\varphi$ (*now or sometime in the future*). The cooperation modality $\langle\!\langle A \rangle\!\rangle^{\downarrow}$ assumes that *all* agents in Agt act under resource constraints. The reading of $\langle\!\langle A \rangle\!\rangle^{\downarrow}\varphi$ is that *agents A have a strategy compatible with the currently available resources* to enforce φ. This means that the strategy can be executed given the agents' resources. Thus, it is necessary to keep track of resource production and consumption during the execution of a strategy.

Semantics. We define the models of RAL as in [3]. We also introduce a special class of these models in which agents have an *idle action* in their repertoire that neither consumes nor produces resources. Note that a model with idle actions is a special case of the general model.

Definition 1 (RBM, iRBM, Unbounded). *A resource-bounded model (RBM) is given by* $\mathfrak{M} = (\text{Agt}, Q, \Pi, \pi, Act, d, o, \mathcal{R}es, t)$ *where* $\mathcal{R}es$ *is a set of shared, unbounded resources,* $\text{Agt} = \{1, \ldots, k\}$ *is a set of agents;* $\pi : \Pi \to 2^Q$ *is a valuation of propositions; Act is a finite set of actions; and the function* $d : \text{Agt} \times Q \to 2^{Act} \setminus \{\emptyset\}$ *indicates the actions available to agent* $a \in \text{Agt}$ *at state* $q \in Q$. *We write* $d_a(q)$ *instead of* $d(a, q)$, *and use* $d(q)$ *to denote the set* $d_1(q) \times \ldots \times d_k(q)$ *of action profiles in state* q. *Similarly,* $d_A(q)$ *denotes the action tuples available to A at q. o is a transition function which maps each state* $q \in Q$ *and action profile* $\boldsymbol{\alpha} = (\alpha_1, \ldots, \alpha_k) \in d(q)$ *(specifying a move for each agent) to another state* $q' = o(q, \boldsymbol{\alpha})$. *Finally, the function* $t : Act \times \mathcal{R}es \to \mathbb{Z}$ *models the resources consumed and produced by actions. We define* $\mathsf{prod}(\alpha, r) := \max\{0, t(\alpha, r)\}$ *(resp.* $\mathsf{cons}(\alpha, r) := \min\{0, t(\alpha, r)\}$*) as the amount of resource r produced (resp. consumed) by action* α. *For* $\boldsymbol{\alpha} = (\alpha_1, \ldots, \alpha_k)$, *we use* $\boldsymbol{\alpha}_A$ *to*

---

[1] Note that we slightly change the notation in comparison with [8] where $\langle\!\langle A \rangle\!\rangle^{\downarrow}$ has the meaning of $\langle\!\langle A \rangle\!\rangle^{\downarrow}_{\text{Agt}}$. Moreover, we only use operators that refer to the currently available resources in the system.

denote the sub-tuple consisting of the actions of agents $A \subseteq$ Agt. *We call an* **RBM** k*-unbounded if* $|\mathcal{R}es| = k$ *for a natural number* k.

An **RBM** with idle actions, **iRBM** *for short, is an* **RBM** $\mathfrak{M}$ *such that for all agents* a, *all states* q, *there is an action* $\alpha \in d_a(q)$ *such that for all resource types* r *in* $\mathfrak{M}$ *we have that* $t(\alpha, r) = 0$. *We refer to this action (or to one of them if there is more than one) as the* idle action *of* a *and denote it by* idle.

A *path* $\lambda \in Q^{\omega}$ is an infinite sequence of states such that there is a transition between two adjacent states. A *resource-extended* path $\lambda \in (Q \times$ En$)^{\omega}$ is an infinite sequence over $Q \times$ En such that the restriction to states (the first component), denoted by $\lambda|_Q$, is a path in the underlying model. The projection of λ to the second component of each element in the sequence is denoted by $\lambda|_{\mathsf{En}}$. We define $\lambda[i]$ to be the $i + 1$-th element of λ, and $\lambda[i, \infty]$ to be the suffix $\lambda[i]\lambda[i + 1] \ldots$. A *strategy*[2] for a coalition $A \subseteq$ Agt is a function $s_A : (Q \times$ En$)^+ \to Act^A$ such that $s_A((q_0, \eta_0) \ldots (q_n, \eta_n)) \in d_A(q_n)$ for $(q_0, \eta_0) \ldots (q_n, \eta_n) \in (Q \times$ En$)^+$. Such a strategy gives rise to a set of (resource-extended) paths that can emerge if agents follow their strategies. A (q, η, s_A)-*path* is a resource-extended path λ such that for all $i = 0, 1, \ldots$ with $\lambda[i] := (q_i, \eta_i)$ there is an action profile $\boldsymbol{\alpha} \in d(\lambda|_Q[i])$ such that: (i) $q_0 = q$ and $\eta_0(r) = \eta(r)$ for all $r \in \mathcal{R}es$ (describes initial configuration); (ii) $s_A(\lambda[0, i]) = \boldsymbol{\alpha}_A$ (A follow their strategy); (iii) $\lambda|_Q[i + 1] = o(\lambda|_Q[i], \boldsymbol{\alpha})$ (transition according to $\boldsymbol{\alpha}$); (iv) for all $\boldsymbol{\alpha}' \in Act_{\mathsf{Agt} \setminus A}$ and for all $r \in \mathcal{R}es$: $\eta_i(r) \geq \sum_{a \in \mathsf{Agt} \setminus A} \mathsf{cons}(\boldsymbol{\alpha}'_a, r) + \sum_{a \in A} \mathsf{cons}(\boldsymbol{\alpha}_a, r)$ (enough resources to perform the actions are available); and (v) $\eta_{i+1}(r) = \eta_i(r) + \sum_{a \in \mathsf{Agt}} \mathsf{prod}(\boldsymbol{\alpha}_a) - \sum_{a \in \mathsf{Agt}} \mathsf{cons}(\boldsymbol{\alpha}_a)$ for all $r \in \mathcal{R}es$. Condition (iv) models that the opponents have priority when claiming resources.

The (q, η, s_A)-*outcome* of a strategy s_A in q, $out(q, \eta, s_A)$, is defined as the set of all (q, η, s_A)-paths starting in q. We also refer to this set as an *execution tree* of A. Truth is defined over an **RBM** $\mathfrak{M}$, a state $q \in Q$, and an endowment η. The *semantics* is given by the satisfaction relation $\models$. Here, we only present clauses for two types of formulae: $\mathfrak{M}, q, \eta \models$ p iff p $\in \Pi$ and $q \in \pi(\mathsf{p})$; and $\mathfrak{M}, q, \eta \models \langle\!\langle A \rangle\!\rangle^{\downarrow} \psi \mathbf{U} \varphi$ iff there exists a strategy s_A for A such that for all $\lambda \in out(q, \eta, s_A)$, there is an i with $i \geq 0$ and $\mathfrak{M}, \lambda|_Q[i], \lambda|_{\mathsf{En}}[i] \models \varphi$ such that for all j with $0 \leq j < i$ it holds that $\mathfrak{M}, \lambda|_Q[j], \lambda|_{\mathsf{En}}[j] \models \psi$. The other clauses are given analogously, cf. [9]. The *model checking problem* is to determine whether $\mathfrak{M}, q, \eta \models \varphi$ holds.

Example. We illustrate the framework by extending the introductory example on the departmental travelling budget. Consider a department which consists of a dean d, two professors p_1, p_2 and three lecturers l_1, l_2, and l_3. The department's travel budget is allocated annually and can be spent to attend conferences. There are three categories to request money: premium, advanced, and economic. All options are available to the dean, the last two to professors, and only the last one to the lecturers. For instance, if the cost of attending PRIMA is, depending

---

[2] We note that differently from [1,3,8], our notion of strategy takes the history of states as well as the history of endowments into account. In the setting considered here such strategies are more powerful than strategies only taking the state-component into account.

on the category, \$2000, \$1000, and \$500, respectively, then with an available budget of \$4000 not all lecturers can be sure to be able to attend PRIMA. Because, the dean and the professors could all decide to attend PRIMA and to request the advanced category. In that case, only \$1000 would remain, not enough for all lecturers to attend; formally specified, $\langle\langle d, p_1, p_2 \rangle\rangle^{\downarrow} \mathbf{F}(\mathsf{d} \wedge \mathsf{p_1} \wedge \mathsf{p_2} \wedge \neg \langle\langle \{l_1, l_2, l_3\} \rangle\rangle^{\downarrow} \mathbf{F}(\mathsf{l_1} \wedge \mathsf{l_2} \wedge \mathsf{l_3}))$ is true where a proposition x expresses that "person" x is attending PRIMA. Equivalently, $\neg \langle\langle \{l_1, l_2, l_3\} \rangle\rangle^{\downarrow} \mathbf{F}(\mathsf{l_1} \wedge \mathsf{l_2} \wedge \mathsf{l_3}))$ is true; this highlights that the opponents have priority in claiming resources. However, by collaborating with the professors, they have a strategy which allows all lecturers to attend, independent of the actions of the dean: i.e., $\langle\langle \{p_1, p_2, l_1, l_2, l_3\} \rangle\rangle^{\downarrow} \mathbf{F}(\mathsf{l_1} \wedge \mathsf{l_2} \wedge \mathsf{l_3})$.

3   Model Checking CTL over Büchi Pushdown Systems

We first review existing results on alternating Büchi pushdown systems (ABPDSs). Then, we use these results to give an automata-theoretic approach to model check CTL-formulae over *compact* ABPDSs. The latter will be used to encode **RBMs** in Section 4.

3.1   Alternating Büchi Pushdown Systems

An *alphabet* Γ is a non-empty, finite set of symbols. Γ^* denotes the set consisting of all finite words over Γ including the empty word ϵ. Typical symbols from Γ are denoted by $a, b, \ldots$ and words by $w, v, u, \ldots$. We read words from left to right. As before, we assume that Π denotes a finite, non-empty set of propositions. We use words to represent the stack content. We say that word $w = a_1 \ldots a_n$ is on the stack if a_1 is the lowest symbol, followed by a_2 and so forth. The symbol on top is a_n. An *alternating pushdown system* (APDS) is a tuple $\mathcal{P} = (P, \Gamma, \Delta)$ where P is a non-empty, finite set of control states, Γ a non-empty, finite (stack) alphabet, and $\Delta \subseteq (P \times \Gamma) \times 2^{P \times \Gamma^*}$ a transition relation [5,16]. We call $\mathcal{P}$ a *pushdown system* (PDS) if $(s, a)\Delta X$ implies $|X| = 1$ where $X \in 2^{P \times \Gamma^*}$. An *alternating Büchi pushdown system* (ABPDS) $\mathcal{B} = (P, \Gamma, \Delta, F)$ is defined as a APDS but a set of accepting states $F \subseteq P$ is added. In the following we focus on ABPDSs, but most of the definitions do also apply to APDSs and PDSs with obvious changes. A transition $(p, a)\Delta\{(p_1, w_1), \ldots, (p_n, w_n)\}$ represents that if the system is in state p and the top-stack symbol is a then the ABPDS $\mathcal{B}$ is copied n-times where the ith copy changes its local state to p_i, pops a from the stack and pushes w_i on the stack, $1 \le i \le n$. For a transition rule $(p, a)\Delta\{(p_1, w_1), \ldots, (p_n, w_n)\}$ and a stack content $w \in \Gamma^*$ we say that (p, wa) is an *immediate predecessor* of $\{(p_1, ww_1), \ldots, (p_n, ww_n)\}$. We write $(p, wa) \Rightarrow_{\mathcal{B}} \{(p_1, ww_1), \ldots, (p_n, ww_n)\}$. A *configuration* of $\mathcal{B}$ is a tuple from $\mathsf{Cnf}_{\mathcal{B}} = P \times \Gamma^*$. A *c-run* ρ of $\mathcal{B}$, where c is a configuration of $\mathcal{B}$, is a tree in which each node is labelled by a configuration such that the root of the tree is labelled by c. If a node labelled by (p, w) has n (direct) child nodes labelled by $(p_1, w_1), \ldots, (p_n, w_n)$, respectively, then it is required that $(p, w) \Rightarrow_{\mathcal{B}} \{(p_1, w_1), \ldots, (p_n, w_n)\}$. We use $\mathcal{R}_{\mathcal{B}}(c)$ to denote the set of all c-runs and $\mathcal{R}_\mathcal{B} = \bigcup_{c \in \mathsf{Cnf}_\mathcal{B}} \mathcal{R}_\mathcal{B}(c)$. We note that a run in a PDS $\mathcal{P}$ is simply a linear sequence of configurations. A ρ-path, $\rho \in \mathcal{R}_\mathcal{B}(c)$, is a maximal length branch $\kappa = c_0 c_1 \ldots$ of ρ starting at the root node c. We shall identify ρ with its set of paths and write $\kappa \in \rho$ to indicate that κ is a ρ-path. Again, in the case of a PDS $\mathcal{P}$ a run and a path in it are essentially the same. We say that $\kappa \in \rho$ is *accepting* if a state of F occurs infinitely often in configurations on κ. A run is accepting if each path $\kappa \in \rho$ is accepting; and a configuration c is accepting if there is an accepting run $\rho \in \mathcal{R}_\mathcal{B}(c)$. The *language* accepted by $\mathcal{B}$, $L(\mathcal{B})$, is the set of all accepting configurations.

A nice property of an ABPDS is that its set of accepting configurations is regular, in the sense that it is accepted by an appropriate automaton which is defined next. An *alternating automaton* [5] is a tuple $\mathcal{A} = (S, \Sigma, \delta, I, S_f)$ where S is a finite, non-empty set of states, $\delta \subseteq S \times \Sigma \times 2^S$ is a transition relation, Σ an input alphabet, $I \subseteq S$ a set of initial states, and $S_f \subseteq S$ a set of final states. The automaton *accepts* $(s, w) \in S \times \Sigma^*$ iff $s \in I$ and each state reached after the automaton has read w is a final state. The language accepted by $\mathcal{A}$ is denoted by $L(\mathcal{A})$. A language is called *regular* if it is accepted by an alternating automaton. We recall the following result from [15]:

Theorem 1 ([15]). *For any ABPDS $\mathcal{B}$ there is an effectively computable alternating $\mathcal{B}$-automaton $\mathcal{A}$ such that $L(\mathcal{A}) = L(\mathcal{B})$.*

3.2   Model Checking CTL Over ABPDSs

We first consider model checking *Computation Tree Logic* (CTL) over PDSs. We assume that the reader is familiar with CTL and refer to [9,12] for details. Essentially, the cooperation modalities of RAL are replaced by the existential and universal path quantifiers E and A, respectively. The formula $\mathsf{E}\varphi$ expresses that there is a path along which φ holds; analogously, $\mathsf{A}\varphi$ expresses that φ holds along all paths. The problem of CTL model checking over PDSs has been considered in, e.g., [5,6,15]. We now recall from [15] how the problem is defined. First, the PDS is extended with a labelling function lab to give truth to propositional atoms. In [15] two alternatives are considered. The first alternative assigns states to propositions, $\mathsf{lab} : \Pi \to 2^P$. The second alternative assigns configurations to propositions, $\mathsf{lab} : \Pi \to 2^{P \times \Gamma^*}$. In the following we only consider the second, more general alternative as this is the one we shall need for model checking RAL. For this type of labelling function we need a finite representation. We call lab *regular* if there is an alternating automaton $\mathcal{A}_\mathsf{p}$ with $L(\mathcal{A}_\mathsf{p}) = \mathsf{lab}(\mathsf{p})$ for each $\mathsf{p} \in \Pi$. We are ready to give the semantics of CTL-formulae over a PDS $\mathcal{P} = (P, \Gamma, \Delta)$, $c \in \mathsf{Cnf}_\mathcal{P}$, and a regular labelling function $\mathsf{lab} : \Pi \to 2^{P \times \Gamma^*}$. The semantic clauses are defined in the usual way, due to space contraints we present one clause only and refer to [9] for further details: $\mathcal{P}, c, \mathsf{lab} \models \mathsf{EG}\varphi$ iff there is a c-run $\rho = c_0 c_1, \ldots \in \mathcal{R}_\mathcal{P}(c)$ such that $\mathcal{P}, c_i, \mathsf{lab} \models \varphi$ for all $i \geq 0$.

The authors of [15] give a model checking algorithm which uses ABPDSs. They construct from $\mathcal{P}$, lab and φ, an ABPDS $\mathcal{B}_{\mathcal{P},\varphi}$ such that $\mathcal{P}, (p, w), \mathsf{lab} \models \varphi$ iff $((p, \varphi), w) \in L(\mathcal{B}_{\mathcal{P},\varphi})$. The ABPDS is essentially the product of the PDS $\mathcal{P}$

with the closure $\mathsf{cl}(\varphi)$ of φ^3, in particular states of $\mathcal{B}_{\mathcal{P},\varphi}$ are tuples $(p, \psi) \in P \times \mathsf{cl}(\varphi)$. The existential and universal path quantifiers of the formula cause the alternation of the ABPDS.

For our later results, we need to be able to define the truth of CTL-formulae over ABPDSs rather than PDSs. Let an ABPDS $\mathcal{B}$ be given. We first discuss what it means that $\mathcal{B}, c, \mathsf{lab} \models \mathsf{E}\varphi$. As before, we interpret it as: there is a *run* $\rho \in \mathcal{R}_{\mathcal{B}}(c)$ on which φ holds. However, given that ρ is a tree in the case of ABPDSs (or a set of paths) we need to explain how to evaluate φ on trees. We require that φ must be true on *each* path $\kappa \in \rho$ on the run. This can nicely be illustrated if $\mathcal{B}$ is considered as a two player game where player one decides which transition to take, and player two selects one of the child states. Thus, $\mathsf{E}\varphi$ expresses that player one has a strategy in the sense that it can enforce a run ρ such that player two cannot make φ false on any path $\kappa \in \rho$. For a given configuration $c \in \mathsf{Cnf}_{\mathcal{B}}$, and a regular labelling lab, the semantic rules have the following form [9]: $\mathcal{B}, c, \mathsf{lab} \models \mathsf{EG}\varphi$ iff there is a c-run $\rho \in \mathcal{R}_{\mathcal{B}}(c)$ such that for all paths $c_0 c_1 \ldots \in \rho$ it holds that $\mathcal{B}, c_i, \mathsf{lab} \models \varphi$ for all $i \geq 0$.

Our reduction of model checking RAL to an acceptance problem over ABPDSs relies on an encoding of an 1-unbounded **iRBM** as an ABPDS. Roughly speaking, the stack is used to keep track of the shared pool of resources. A technical difficulty is that an action may consume several resources at a time, whereas an ABPDS can only read the top stack symbol. Therefore, we introduce a more compact encoding of an ABPDS which allows to read (and pop) more than one stack symbol at a time.

Given a natural number $r \geq 1$, an r-*compact* ABPDS (CABPDS) is a tuple $\mathcal{C} = (P, \Gamma, \Delta, F, r)$ where all ingredients have the same meaning as in an ABPDS with the exception that $\Delta \subseteq P \times \Gamma^{\leq r} \times 2^{P \times \Gamma^*}$ where $\Gamma^{\leq r} = \bigcup_{i=1}^{r} \Gamma^i$ denotes the set of all non-empty words over Γ of length at most r. This models that the selection of the next transition can depend on up to the top r stack symbols. All notions introduced so far are also used for CABPDSs. A CABPDS is no more expressive than a "standard" ABPDS. In [9] we show how to construct an ABPDS $\mathcal{B}(\mathcal{C})$ from a given CABDS $\mathcal{C}$ such that $c \in L(\mathcal{C})$ iff $c \in L(\mathcal{B}(\mathcal{C}))$, for all configurations $c \in P \times \Gamma^*$. As for ABPDSs, we can use CABPDSs as models for CTL. We obtain the following result:

Theorem 2. *For a given CABPDS $\mathcal{C}$, a regular labelling function lab, and a CTL-formula φ there is an effectively computable alternating automaton $\mathcal{A}_{\mathcal{C},\varphi}$ such that for all configurations $c = (p, w) \in \mathsf{Cnf}_{\mathcal{C}}$ the following holds: $\mathcal{C}, c, \mathsf{lab} \models \varphi$ iff $((p, \varphi), w) \in L(\mathcal{A}_{\mathcal{C},\varphi})$.*

4   (Un-)Decidable Model Checking Result

First, we consider the general case of k-unbounded **iRBMs**[4] with $k \geq 2$. In [3,8] it is shown that most variants of RAL with two resource types are

---

[3] The closure $\mathsf{cl}(\varphi)$ is the set of all subformulae of φ.

[4] Note that undecidability proofs wrt. **iRBMs** are stronger than those for **RBMs**.

undecidable. This has been proved by reductions of the halting problem of two-counter automata [14] to the different model checking problems. Two counter automata are finite automata extended with two counters. The undecidability proofs of [3,8] can be adapted to our setting. We obtain the following result:

Proposition 1 (Corollary of [3,8]). *Model checking* RAL *(with shared resources) over k-unbounded* **iRBM***s with* $k \geq 2$ *is undecidable.*

Second, we show decidability over 1-unbounded **RBM**s. In the following we assume that $\mathfrak{M} = (\mathbb{A}\mathrm{gt}, Q, \Pi, \pi, Act, d, o, \mathcal{R}es, t)$ consists of of a single unbounded shared resource. Moreover, let A be a set of agents and $\bar{A} = \mathbb{A}\mathrm{gt} \backslash A$. As there is only one resource, we can simplify the notation. We write η for $\eta(r)$, $\mathsf{cons}(\alpha)$ instead of $\mathsf{cons}(\alpha, r)$ and so on. Also, for an action profile $\boldsymbol{\alpha}_A$ we use $\mathsf{cons}(\boldsymbol{\alpha}_A)$ (resp. $\mathsf{prod}(\boldsymbol{\alpha}_A)$) to refer to $\sum_{a \in A} \mathsf{cons}(\alpha_a)$ (resp. $\sum_{a \in A} \mathsf{prod}(\alpha_a)$). Furthermore, for a natural number x, $[x]_1$ is used to refer to a sequence $|| \ldots |$ of x lines each representing one element on the stack, i.e. $[x]_1$ corresponds to the *unary encoding* of x. We write $[0]_1 = \epsilon$. Similarly, we use $[y]_{10}$ to refer to the *ternary encoding* of $y = [x]_1$ for a natural number x. We define the following auxiliary functions where q is a state in $\mathfrak{M}$, $\boldsymbol{\alpha}_A$ a joint action of A and $\boldsymbol{\alpha}_{\bar{A}}$ a joint action of $\bar{A}$: $\Delta\mathsf{max}_{\bar{A}}(q) = \max\{\mathsf{cons}(\boldsymbol{\alpha}_{\bar{A}}) \mid \boldsymbol{\alpha}_{\bar{A}} \in d_{\bar{A}}(q)\}$; $\Delta\mathsf{con}_A(q, \boldsymbol{\alpha}_A) = \mathsf{cons}(\boldsymbol{\alpha}_A) + \Delta\mathsf{max}_{\bar{A}}(q)$; and $\Delta\mathsf{prd}_A(q, \boldsymbol{\alpha}_A, \boldsymbol{\alpha}_{\bar{A}}) = \Delta\mathsf{max}_{\bar{A}}(q) - \mathsf{cons}(\boldsymbol{\alpha}_{\bar{A}}) + \mathsf{prod}((\boldsymbol{\alpha}_A, \boldsymbol{\alpha}_{\bar{A}}))$. The number $\Delta\mathsf{max}_{\bar{A}}(q)$ denotes the worst case consumption of resources of the opponents at q, that is the maximal amount of resources they could claim. The number $\Delta\mathsf{con}_A(q, \boldsymbol{\alpha}_A)$ is the consumption of resources if A executes $\boldsymbol{\alpha}_A$ and the opponents choose their actions with the worst case consumption; this models a pessimistic view. This is valid as the proponents can never be sure to have more resources available. Finally, $\Delta\mathsf{prd}_A(q, \boldsymbol{\alpha}_A, \boldsymbol{\alpha}_{\bar{A}})$ denotes the number of resources that need to be produced after $(\boldsymbol{\alpha}_A, \boldsymbol{\alpha}_{\bar{A}})$ was executed at q. It is the sum of the number of resources produced by $(\boldsymbol{\alpha}_A, \boldsymbol{\alpha}_{\bar{A}})$, and the difference between the consumption of the estimated worst case behavior of the opponents and the consumption of the actions which were actually executed by $\bar{A}$.

From $\mathfrak{M}$ and A, we define an r-compact ABPDS where $r = [\max_{q, \boldsymbol{\alpha}_A, \boldsymbol{\alpha}_{\bar{A}}}\{\Delta\mathsf{con}_A(q, \boldsymbol{\alpha}_A), \Delta\mathsf{prd}_A(q, \boldsymbol{\alpha}_A, \boldsymbol{\alpha}_{\bar{A}})\}]_1$ is the maximal number which is ever *consumed* or *produced*.

Definition 2 ($\mathcal{C}_{\mathfrak{M},A}$). *The* r*-compact ABPDS* $\mathcal{C}_{\mathfrak{M},A}$ *is the CABPDS* $(S, \Gamma, \Delta, F, r)$ *where* $S = F = Q$, $\Gamma = \{|\}$, *and for all* $q \in Q$, $\boldsymbol{\alpha}_A \in d_A(q)$ *we have that*
$(q, [\Delta\mathsf{con}_A(q, \boldsymbol{\alpha}_A)]_1) \Delta \{(o(q, (\boldsymbol{\alpha}_A, \boldsymbol{\alpha}_{\bar{A}})), [\Delta\mathsf{prd}_A(q, \boldsymbol{\alpha}_A, \boldsymbol{\alpha}_{\bar{A}})]_1) \mid \boldsymbol{\alpha}_{\bar{A}} \in d_{\bar{A}}(q)\}$.

The CABPDS $\mathcal{C}_{\mathfrak{M},A}$ encodes the outcome sets $out(q, s_A, \eta)$ for any state q and strategy s_A. To show our main decidable result, we need to extend **RBM**s with regular labelling functions $\pi : \Pi \to 2^{Q \times \mathsf{En}}$ as done in Section 3.2 for PDSs. Now, suppose that we want to model check $\mathfrak{M}, q_0, \eta \models \langle\!\langle A \rangle\!\rangle^{\downarrow}\varphi$ where $\langle\!\langle A \rangle\!\rangle^{\downarrow}\varphi$ is a flat formula. Firstly, we construct the CABPDS $\mathcal{C}_{\mathfrak{M},A}$ which accepts the outcome sets of A. Let lab be the labelling function defined as: $(q, [\eta]_1) \in$

lab(p) iff $(q, \eta) \in \pi(p)$. Then, we have that: $\mathfrak{M}, q_0, \eta \models \langle\!\langle A \rangle\!\rangle^\downarrow \varphi$ if, and only if, $\mathcal{C}_{\mathfrak{M},A}, (q_0, [\eta]_1), \mathsf{lab} \models \mathsf{E}\varphi$. By Theorem 2 this can be efficiently solved by constructing an alternating automaton $\mathcal{A}_{\mathcal{C}_{\mathfrak{M},A}, \mathsf{E}\varphi}$ that accepts $((q_0, \mathsf{E}\varphi), [\eta]_1)$ iff the above equivalence is true.

Finally, this procedure can be combined with the standard bottom-up model checking approach used for **CTL***[11]. Firstly, the innermost (flat) formulae ψ of φ are considered. We can compute the regular set of configurations at which each of these subformulae ψ hold and replace the subformula by a fresh propositions p_ψ. Then, we extend the regular labelling of $\mathfrak{M}$ such that p_ψ is assigned the configurations at which ψ is true (Theorem 2). Applied recursively, we obtain:

Theorem 3. *The model-checking problem for* RAL *(with shared resources) over* 1-*unbounded* **RBM***s is decidable.*

5   Conclusions

In this paper, we have introduced a variant of resource agent logic RAL [8] with shared resources, which can be consumed and produced. We showed that the model checking problem is undecidable in the presence of at least two unbounded resource types. Our main technical result is a decidability proof of model checking RAL with one shared, unbounded resource type. Otherwise, we impose no restrictions, in particular nested cooperation modalities do not reset the resources available to agents. This property is sometimes called *non-resource flatness*. In order to show decidability, we first show how CTL can be model-checked with respect to (compact) alternating Büchi pushdown systems extending results on model checking CTL over pushdown and alternating pushdown systems [5,15]. A compact alternating Büchi pushdown system allows to read and to pop more than one symbol from its stack at a time. It is used for encoding resource bounded models in order to apply the automata-based model checking algorithm.

Acknowledgments. We would like to thank Natasha Alechina and Brian Logan for the many discussions on this topic and their valuable comments.

References

1. Alechina, N., Logan, B., Nguyen, H.N., Raimondi, F.: Decidable model-checking for a resource logic with production of resources. In: Proceedings of the 21st European Conference on Artificial Intelligence (ECAI-2014), pp. 9–14. ECCAI. IOS Press (2014)
2. Alechina, N., Logan, B., Nguyen, H.N., Rakib, A.: Resource-bounded alternating-time temporal logic. In: Proceedings of the 9th International Conference on Autonomous Agents and Multiagent Systems (AAMAS 2010), pp. 481–488. IFAA-MAS (2010)
3. Alechina, N., Bulling, N., Logan, B., Nguyen, H.N.: On the boundary of (un)decidability: decidable model-checking for a fragment of resource agent logic. In: Proceedings of the Twenty-Fourth International Joint Conference on Artificial Intelligence, IJCAI 2015, Buenos Aires, Argentina, 25–31 July 2015, pp. 1494–1501 (2015)

4. Alur, R., Henzinger, T., Kupferman, O.: Alternating-time temporal logic. Journal of the ACM **49**(5), 672–713 (2002)
5. Bouajjani, A., Esparza, J., Maler, O.: Reachability analysis of pushdown automata: application to model-checking. In: Mazurkiewicz, A., Winkowski, J. (eds.) CONCUR 1997. LNCS, vol. 1243, pp. 135–150. Springer, Heidelberg (1997)
6. Bozzelli, L.: Complexity results on branching-time pushdown model checking. Theoretical Computer Science **379**(1), 286–297 (2007)
7. Bulling, N., Farwer, B.: Expressing properties of resource-bounded systems: the logics RTL* and RTL. In: Dix, J., Fisher, M., Novák, P. (eds.) CLIMA X. LNCS, vol. 6214, pp. 22–45. Springer, Heidelberg (2010)
8. Bulling, N., Farwer, B.: On the (un-)decidability of model checking resource-bounded agents. In: Proceedings of the 19th European Conference on Artificial Intelligence (ECAI 2010), vol. 215, pp. 567–572. IOS Press (2010)
9. Bulling, N., Nguyen, H.N.: Model checking resource bounded systems with shared resources via alternating Büchi pushdown systems. Technical report. ArXiv e-prints (2015)
10. Cachat, T.: Symbolic strategy synthesis for games on pushdown graphs. In: Widmayer, P., Triguero, F., Morales, R., Hennessy, M., Eidenbenz, S., Conejo, R. (eds.) ICALP 2002. LNCS, vol. 2380, p. 704. Springer, Heidelberg (2002)
11. Clarke, E., Grumberg, O., Peled, D.: Model Checking. MIT Press (1999)
12. Clarke, E.M., Emerson, E.A.: Design and synthesis of synchronization skeletons using branching time temporal logic. In: Kozen, D. (ed.) Logics of Programs. LNCS, vol. 131, pp. 52–71. Springer, Heidelberg (1981)
13. Della Monica, D., Napoli, M., Parente, M.: Model checking coalitional games in shortage resource scenarios. In: Proceedings of the 4th International Symposium on Games, Automata, Logics and Formal Verification (GandALF 2013). EPTCS, vol. 119, pp. 240–255 (2013)
14. Hopcroft, J.E., Ullman, J.D.: Introduction to Automata Theory, Languages, and Computation. Addison-Wesley (1979)
15. Song, F., Touili, T.: Efficient CTL model-checking for pushdown systems. Theoretical Computer Science **549**, 127–145 (2014)
16. Suwimonteerabuth, D., Schwoon, S., Esparza, J.: Efficient algorithms for alternating pushdown systems with an application to the computation of certificate chains. In: Graf, S., Zhang, W. (eds.) ATVA 2006. LNCS, vol. 4218, pp. 141–153. Springer, Heidelberg (2006)

Integrating Conversation Trees and Cognitive Models Within an ECA for Aggression De-escalation Training

Tibor Bosse[1,2(✉)] and Simon Provoost[1]

[1] Department of Computer Science, VU University Amsterdam,
De Boelelaan 1081, 1081 HV Amsterdam, The Netherlands
{t.bosse,s.j.provoost}@vu.nl
[2] Department of Training and Performance Innovations, TNO,
Kampweg 5, 3769 DE Soesterberg, The Netherlands

Abstract. Traditionally, Embodied Conversational Agents communicate with humans using dialogue systems based on conversation trees. To enhance the flexibility and variability of dialogues, this paper proposes an approach to integrate conversation trees with cognitive models. The approach is illustrated by a case study in the domain of aggression de-escalation training, and a preliminary evaluation in the context of a practical application is presented.

Keywords: Virtual training · Aggression de-escalation · Cognitive modelling

1   Introduction

Embodied Conversational Agents (ECAs) can be defined as computer-generated characters 'that demonstrate many of the same properties as humans in face-to-face conversation, including the ability to produce and respond to verbal and nonverbal communication' [7]. ECAs have been put forward as a promising means for the training of social skills [11]. Indeed, in recent years, various systems have been designed involving ECAs that enable users to develop their social abilities (e.g., [12]).

An important requirement to effectively train users in developing their social skills, is *believability* of ECAs, as believable agents permit their conversation partners to 'suspend their disbelief', which is an important condition for learning [3]. In [8], believability is defined by three dimensions, namely aesthetic, functional, and social qualities of agents, which can be related, respectively, to the agent's physical appearance, behaviour, and interaction style. With respect to physical appearance and interaction style, much progress has been made in recent years: graphics are becoming increasingly realistic, and the mechanisms to interact with ECAs are changing from purely text-based systems to sophisticated multi-modal interfaces [17].

With respect to the behaviour of ECAs, some steps forward have been made as well, regarding both verbal and non-verbal aspects. For non-verbal behaviour, recent work addresses systems to generate realistic facial expressions, head movements, and body gestures [13]. Instead, the focus of the current work is on verbal behaviour, i.e., on dialogues. The traditional approach to drive the verbal behaviour of ECAs during

© Springer International Publishing Switzerland 2015
Q. Chen et al. (Eds.): PRIMA 2015, LNAI 9387, pp. 650–659, 2015.
DOI: 10.1007/978-3-319-25524-8_48

a human-agent dialogue is to use *conversation trees*, i.e. tree structures representing all possible developments of the dialogue, where users can decide between different branches using multiple choice. Although this approach can be successful due to its transparency, an important limitation of conversation trees is that they are quite rigid. Consequently, the resulting behaviour of the ECAs is often perceived as stereotypical and predictable. This can be overcome by constructing large conversation trees with many branches, but this approach is highly labour-intensive and difficult to re-use.

As an alternative, several authors have proposed the use of cognitive models to endow ECAs with more sophisticated behaviour (e.g., [10,14,16]). Using such models, agents base their behaviour not only on their current observations (or input), but also on internal states, such as their emotions and personality. As a consequence, this approach potentially results in more varied and human-like behaviour from the perspective of the human conversation partner. Elaborating upon these ideas, the current research attempts to further bridge the gap between traditional approaches based on conversation trees (which are transparent, but rigid), and more novel approaches based on cognitive models (which are flexible, but abstract). It does so by presenting an approach that not only enables flexible dialogues, but that can also easily be integrated with existing systems in the gaming industry based on conversation trees. The approach is illustrated by a specific case study in the domain of simulation-based training for aggression de-escalation.

The remainder of this paper is structured as follows. In Section 2, the context in which this research was conducted is described, namely a project on aggression de-escalation training. Next, Section 3 introduces the underlying dialogue system that is used within this project, and Section 4 presents an approach to integrate the system with a cognitive model. Section 5 describes a practical application that has been used to test the resulting behaviour of the system. Section 6 concludes the paper with a discussion.

2   Aggression De-escalation Training

In domains such as law enforcement and public transport, aggressive behaviour against employees is an ongoing concern. According to a recent study in the Netherlands, around 60% of the employees in the public sector have been confronted with such behaviour in the last 12 months [1]. Being confronted with (verbal) aggression has been closely associated with psychological distress, which in turn has a negative impact on work performance. Responses to aggression range from emotions like anger and humiliation through intent to leave the profession. In case of severe incidents, employees may even develop post-traumatic stress syndrome [4].

To deal with aggression, a variety of techniques are available that may prevent escalation [2,5]. These include verbal and non-verbal communication skills, conflict resolution strategies, and emotion regulation techniques. The current paper is part of a project that explores to what extent simulation-based training using ECAs can be an effective method for employees to develop these types of social skills[1]. In the

---

[1] More information on this project can be found at http://stress.few.vu.nl.

envisioned training environment, a trainee will be placed in a virtual scenario involving verbal aggression, with the goal of handling it as adequately as possible. The scenarios emphasise dyadic (one-on-one) interactions. For instance, the trainee plays the role of a tram driver, and is confronted with a virtual passenger who starts intimidating him in an attempt to get a free ride. The trainee observes the behaviour of the ECA, and has to respond to it by selecting the most appropriate responses from a multiple choice menu[2]. Additionally, the trainee is 'monitored' during the task by an 'intelligent tutor', i.e. a piece of software that observes his behaviour and provides personalised support.

The main learning goal of the training system is to help trainees develop their *emotional intelligence*: they should be able to recognise the emotional state of the (virtual) conversation partner, and choose the right communication style. In this respect, an important factor is the distinction between *reactive* and *proactive* aggression that is made within psychological literature: reactive aggression is characterised as an emotional reaction to a negative event that frustrates a person's desires (e.g. a passenger becomes angry because the tram is late), whereas proactive aggression is the instrumental use of aggression to achieve a certain goal (e.g. a passenger intimidates the driver in an attempt to ride for free) [15]. Hence, one of the key differences between these two types is the presence or absence of anger. To decide whether they are dealing with a reactive or a proactive aggressor, trainees should pay attention to specific cues that point to the presence or absence of emotion in the (virtual) conversation partner, such as a trembling voice or frequent arm gestures.

Based on the type of aggressive behaviour that is observed, the trainee should select the most appropriate communication style. More specifically, when dealing with a reactive aggressor, empathic, *supportive* behaviour is required to de-escalate a situation, for example by ignoring the conflict-seeking behaviour, by actively listening to what the aggressor has to say, and by showing understanding for the situation. Instead, when dealing with a proactive aggressor, a more dominant, *directive* type of intervention is assumed to be most effective. In this case, one should make it clear that aggressive behaviour is not acceptable, and that such behaviour will have consequences [2,5]. By ensuring that the ECAs respond in an appropriate manner to the chosen responses (e.g. a reactive aggressor calms down when approached in a supportive manner, but becomes even more angry when approached in a directive manner), the system will provide implicit feedback on the chosen communication style.

3   Dialogue System

The proposed training system is based on the InterACT software, developed by the company IC3D Media[3]. InterACT is a software platform that has been specifically designed for simulation-based training. It uses state-of-the-art game technology that builds upon recent advances in the entertainment gaming industry. Unlike most existing software, it focuses on smaller situations, with high realism and detailed

---

[2] Although our research as a whole explores a variety of modalities (such as speech, facial expressions and gestures), the current paper has an emphasis on text-based interaction.

[3] See http://www.interact-training.nl/ and http://ic3dmedia.com/.

interactions with virtual characters. True-to-life animations and photo-realistic characters are used to immerse the player in the game. An example screenshot of a training scenario for the public transport domain is shown in Figure 1. In this example, the user plays the role of the tram driver that has the task of calming down an aggressive virtual passenger.

To enable users to engage in a conversation with an ECA, a dialogue system based on conversation trees is used. The system assumes that a dialogue consists of a sequence of spoken sentences that follow a turn-taking protocol. That is, first the ECA says something (e.g. "I forgot my public transport card. You probably don't mind if I ride for free?"). After that, the user can respond, followed by a response from the ECA, and so on. In InterACT, these dialogues are represented by conversation trees, where vertices are either atomic ECA behaviours or decision nodes (enabling the user to determine a response), and the edges are transitions between nodes.

Fig. 1. Example screenshot of the InterACT environment.

The atomic ECA behaviours consist of pre-generated fragments of speech, synchronised with facial expressions and possibly extended with gestures. Scenario developers can generate their own fragments using the motion capture software Face-Shift[4], using a Microsoft Kinect camera. As the recorded fragments are independent from a particular avatar, they can be projected on arbitrary characters.

Each decision node is implemented as a multiple choice menu that allows the user to choose between multiple sentences. In the current version, for every decision node, four options are used, which can be classified, respectively, as *letting go*, *supportive*, *directive*, and *call for support*. Here, the supportive and directive option relate to the communication styles explained earlier. The other two options are more 'extreme' interventions, which according to a national protocol for aggression management should be applied, respectively, in case the aggressor has calmed down or in case the aggression is about to escalate into physical violence [5]. Figure 1 illustrates how

---

[4] See http://www.faceshift.com/

these four options can be instantiated in terms of concrete sentences (option A-D). Additionally, the choice of the user determines how the scenario continues (or whether it ends immediately) by triggering a corresponding branch in the tree.

Although this approach works well, there is a risk that the behaviour of the ECAs becomes predictable in the long term. For example, in the situation shown in Figure 1, choosing option C (the 'directive' option) will always result in the ECA becoming irritated, no matter how often the scenario is played, or what has happened before. This problem can be overcome by endowing the agent with *internal states* [6] that are either set beforehand (e.g. whether the agent is a reactive or a pro-active aggressor) or are the result of earlier interactions (e.g. a state of anger that gradually increases during the scenario). Our approach to realise this will be explained next.

4   Integration with a Cognitive Model

To endow the ECAs with internal states, an existing cognitive model of aggression is used [5,18]. Although the details of the model are left out of the current paper, a high-level overview of the knowledge on which the model is based is shown in Table 1. This table describes how the agent's mental state changes depending on the type of de-escalation approach that it observes (which is similar to [19]).

Table 1. Impact of various de-escalation approaches on the agent's mental state.

observed approach	reactive aggression	proactive aggression
letting go	*remains constant*	*remains constant*
supportive	*decreases*	*increases*
directive	*increases*	*decreases*
call for support	*remains constant*	*remains constant*

Our approach to connect this model of aggression to the dialogue system is depicted in Figure 2. The integrated system consists of three elements (dialogue system, human user, and cognitive model) that interact based on the following information flow:

- *from dialogue system to user*: The dialogue system continuously keeps track of which node in the conversation tree is active. As mentioned in Section 3, nodes are either atomic ECA behaviours or decision nodes (implemented as multiple choice menus). In a typical conversation tree, each ECA behaviour is followed by a decision node. This means that whenever the dialogue system shows information to the user, an ECA behaviour fragment is presented (i.e. the virtual character says something, accompanied with facial expressions and gestures) right before the multiple choice menu is displayed.

- *from user to cognitive model (1)*: Next, the user has to select an option from the multiple choice menu. The options correspond to the different types of observations used in the cognitive model (i.e., [letting_go, supportive, directive, call_for_support]).

- *from user to cognitive model (2)*: In addition, the user's emotional state is provided as input to the cognitive model as well. One of the simplest ways of achieving this is to ask the user to provide a subjective indication of how much emotion (s)he experiences during every interaction. A more advanced solution (which will be used in other stages of the current project) is to determine the user's emotional state based on various sensor measurements like heart rate, electrodermal activity, and facial expressions.

- *from cognitive model to dialogue system*: Based on the observed verbal and non-verbal behaviour of the user, the cognitive model determines the level of aggressiveness of the verbal and non-verbal behaviour to be produced by the ECA. Next, these two variables (aggression intensity values of verbal and non-verbal behaviour) are transferred to the dialogue system, which uses them to decide how the conversation continues. Currently, this is done by defining for each point in the dialogue, a number of alternative sentences with varying levels of aggressiveness. For example, in case the user (playing the tram driver) has just chosen the sentence 'Your chip card is out of credit', and the ECA's verbal behaviour should have an aggressiveness level between 0 and 0.2, then it will respond with a statement like 'I understand that sir, but unfortunately I am in a hurry. Could you please let me hitch a ride?'. Instead, when it should have an aggressiveness level between 0.8 and 1, it will respond with 'Seriously? What do you want me to do, miss this ride? Come on, it's just one stop, man!'. In a similar manner, the variable for the ECA's non-verbal behaviour determines its amount of emotional expression (e.g. by using more arm gestures).

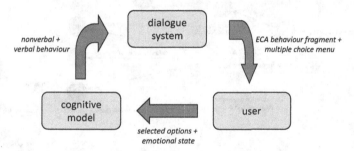

Fig. 2. Overview of the integrated system.

5   Practical Application

The integrated system as described in the previous section is currently being implemented in the InterACT environment. To already get an idea of the proposed mechanism's performance, its behaviour has been studied in the context of a practical application. To this end, a 'light' version of the system has been implemented in Matlab[5]. Basically, the application follows the same information flow as depicted in Figure 2, only the behaviour of the ECA is not visualised in a graphical environment; instead, its utterances and non-verbal behaviour are described in a textual format.

---

[5] The application can be downloaded from http://www.cs.vu.nl/~tbosse/STRESS.

Additionally, a simple feedback module has been implemented. The goal of this module is to provide the user with feedback on his or her performance at the end of a training scenario. Essentially it checks whether the situation was successfully de-escalated or not, and in the latter case, it analyses what the cause of this unsuccessful de-escalation was. In this analysis, several types of mistakes are distinguished such as 1) the user failed to judge the type of aggression (i.e. reactive or proactive) correctly, 2) the user failed to apply the appropriate communication style (supportive or directive), and 3) the user failed to control his or her own emotional state. The decision tree that is used by the module is shown in Figure 3. Here, a green end state indicates successful de-escalation, whereas a red end state indicates unsuccessful de-escalation. Based on the specific end state a corresponding feedback message is generated, represented by the numbers in the figure. For example, in case a scenario is classified as category (6), the following feedback is presented:

6. The user applies the wrong approach towards a proactive aggressor.
"You correctly judged the nature of the aggression, but you used the wrong verbal approach. A proactive aggressor should always be approached in a directive manner. Acting supportively is likely to make the aggressor think he can walk all over you, and that his aggressive behaviour is going to get him what he wants."

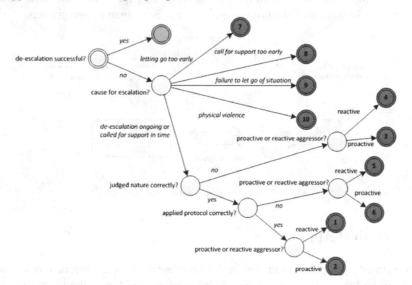

Fig. 3. Overview of the feedback system.

To test the Matlab application, a specific scenario has been worked out in the context of a man who is running late for the custody hearing for his daughter, and has no cash money to pay for a tram ticket. A group of users (students and researchers in Artificial Intelligence) have extensively played the scenario, by systematically varying the parameter settings of the cognitive model. A complete overview of the scenario, as well as an illustration of some of the resulting conversations, is provided in [18].

Based on this preliminary evaluation, we can conclude that the application was evaluated positively, in the sense that no instances of unrealistic dialogue flow were reported. This is a nice finding in itself, but it becomes more valuable in combination with the observation that the proposed approach allowed us to create a large variation in scenarios with relatively limited effort. This has to do with the fact that cognitive models enrich an ECA with internal states, and that these states basically keep track of the *history* of the conversation. To start with, we can now use threshold values to determine which verbal response to activate when the ECA has a certain internal emotional state. Moreover, by designing additional verbal statements that contain language of an increasingly aggressive nature but otherwise carry the same message, *every* user choice can now be followed by a wider variety of ECA responses. Lastly, adjusting the parameter settings that regulate the rate at which the ECA's internal state changes, makes it possible to endow the ECA with a virtually unlimited number of personality types. A more extensive explanation of these benefits is presented in [6].

6   Discussion

The current paper presented a system for simulation-based training of aggression de-escalation skills using Embodied Conversational Agents. By integrating a cognitive model of aggression within a dialogue system based on conversation trees, the system benefits from the advantages of both methods: on the one hand, the use of the dialogue system (based on pre-recorded conversation fragments) guarantees highly realistic animations. This is particularly important for a domain like aggression de-escalation, in which the ECAs ideally induce some kind of 'stress response' in their human conversation partners. On the other hand, the use of a cognitive model ensures that the ECAs are endowed with internal states, which enables them to take the history of the interaction into account when generating their behaviour. As a result, the resulting conversations provide more variation, and are therefore perceived as less predictable. Our first results based on the Matlab application pointed out that users indeed appreciated the conversations as interesting and not too predictable on the longer term.

This is by no means the first paper that attempts to enrich ECAs with more flexible behaviour. Without trying to provide an exhaustive overview, some related approaches are presented in [10,14,16]. The current paper does not attempt to compete with the above approaches in the sense that it claims to generate more variation in scenarios. Instead, one of the main assets of the proposed approach is its simplicity: it allows designers to generate variation in scenarios using a relatively light-weight and easy to use cognitive model. At the same time, it is compatible with state-of-the-art software in the gaming industry that uses traditional conversation trees, such as the InterACT environment. As a result, the approach takes the best of both worlds: on the one hand it can be connected to graphically realistic 3D environments, yet it offers more flexibility than most pre-scripted approaches that are typically used in industry. Another contribution is the fact that the approach has been implemented and tested in the context of a real world domain: aggression de-escalation.

Note that the approach is based on the deliberate decision to work with pre-generated conversation fragments. An interesting alternative is to generate utterances 'at runtime' using a combination of natural language generation techniques and text-to-speech software [9]. Such an approach has the advantage that it results in even less predictable ECA behaviour (from the user's perspective), but a drawback is that it is difficult to guarantee a natural development of the conversation, and that the resulting speech is typically perceived as less realistic by the user.

Regarding the interaction in the other direction (i.e., from user to ECA), our current system uses the easily controllable, but relatively rigid method of multiple choice menus. In ongoing research, we are exploring the possibilities to give the user more freedom by taking an intermediate approach: the user is still asked to choose between certain options; however these options are not completely pre-defined sentences, but 'classes of responses' corresponding to the different communication styles [letting_go, supportive, directive, call_for_support]. Using this approach, the user is free to choose his or her preferred wording, as long as it fits in a category. A sentiment analysis module will then relate the utterance to the right category, allowing for snatural continuation of the dialogue. In addition to such extensions, future work will address a more extensive evaluation of the approach. This will not only be done with the presented Matlab application, but also with the complete ECA-based training system and with end users.

Acknowledgements. This research was supported by funding from the National Initiative Brain and Cognition, coordinated by the Netherlands Organisation for Scientific Research (NWO), under grant agreement No. 056-25-013. The authors would like to thank Karel van den Bosch for a number of fruitful discussions.

References

1. Abraham, M., Flight, S., Roorda, W.: Agressie en geweld tegen werknemers met een publieke taak (in Dutch). DSP, Amsterdam (2011)
2. Anderson, L.N., Clarke, J.T.: De-escalating verbal aggression in primary care settings. Nurse Pract. **21**(10), 95, 98, 101–102 (1996)
3. Bates, J.: The role of emotions in believable agents. Communications of the ACM **37**(7), 122–125 (1994)
4. Bonner, G., McLaughlin, S.: The psychological impact of aggression on nursing staff. Br. J. Nurs. **16**(13), 810–814 (2007)
5. Bosse, Tibor, Provoost, Simon: Towards aggression de-escalation training with virtual agents: a computational model. In: Zaphiris, Panayiotis, Ioannou, Andri (eds.) LCT. LNCS, vol. 8524, pp. 375–387. Springer, Heidelberg (2014)
6. Bosse, Tibor, Provoost, Simon: On conversational agents with mental states. In: Brinkman, Willem-Paul, Broekens, Joost, Heylen, Dirk (eds.) IVA 2015. LNCS, vol. 9238, pp. 60–64. Springer, Heidelberg (2015)
7. Cassell, J., Sullivan, J., Prevost, S., Churchill, E.: Embodied Conversational Agents. MIT Press, Cambridge (2000)
8. De Angeli, A., Lynch, P., Johnson, G.: Personifying the e-market: a framework for social agents. In: Hirose, M. (ed.) Proc. of Interact 2001, pp. 198–205. IOS Press (2001)

9. van Deemter, K., Krenn, B., Piwek, P., Klesen, M., Schroeder, M., Baumann, S.: Fully generated scripted dialogue for embodied agents. Artificial Intelligence 172(10), 1219–1244 (2008)
10. Gebhard, Patrick, Kipp, Michael, Klesen, Martin, Rist, Thomas: Adding the emotional dimension to scripting character dialogues. In: Rist, Thomas, Aylett, Ruth S., Ballin, Daniel, Rickel, Jeff (eds.) IVA 2003. LNCS (LNAI), vol. 2792, pp. 48–56. Springer, Heidelberg (2003)
11. Kenny, P., Hartholt, A., Gratch, J., Swartout, W., Traum, D., Marsella, S., Piepol, D.: Building interactive virtual humans for training environments. In: Proc. of 2007 Interservice/Industry Training, Simulation and Education Conference, Orlando, FL (2007)
12. Kim, J., Hill, R.W., Durlach, P., Lane, H.C., Forbell, E., Core, C., Marsella, S., Pynadath, D., Hart, J.: BiLAT: A game-based environment for practicing negotiation in a cultural context. International Journal of AI in Education 19(3), 289–308 (2009)
13. Lee, Jina, Marsella, Stacy C.: Nonverbal behavior generator for embodied conversational agents. In: Gratch, Jonathan, Young, Michael, Aylett, Ruth S., Ballin, Daniel, Olivier, Patrick (eds.) IVA 2006. LNCS (LNAI), vol. 4133, pp. 243–255. Springer, Heidelberg (2006)
14. Mateas, M., Stern, A.: Façade: an experiment in building a fully-realized interactive drama. In: Game Developers Conference (GDC 2003), San Jose, CA, USA (2003)
15. Miller, J.D., Lyna, D.R.: Reactive and proactive aggression: Similarities and differences. Personality and Individual Differences 41(8), 1469–1480 (2006)
16. Muller, T.J., Heuvelink, A., van den Bosch, K., Swartjes, I.: Glengarry glen ross: using BDI for sales game dialogues. In: The Eighth Annual AAAI Conference on Artificial Intelligence and Interactive Digital Entertainment (2012)
17. Nijholt, A., Heylen, D.: Multimodal Communication in Inhabited Virtual Environments. International Journal of Speech Technology 5(4), 343–354 (2002)
18. Provoost, S.: A computational model of aggression de-escalation. M.Sc. Thesis, VU University Amsterdam (2014). http://hdl.handle.net/1871/50480
19. Smith, C., et al.: Interaction Strategies for an Affective Conversational Agent. Presence 20(5), 395–411 (2011)

Checking WELTLK Properties of Weighted Interpreted Systems via SMT-Based Bounded Model Checking

Agnieszka M. Zbrzezny(✉) and Andrzej Zbrzezny

IMCS, Jan Długosz University, Al. Armii Krajowej 13/15,
42-200 Częstochowa, Poland
{agnieszka.zbrzezny,a.zbrzezny}@ajd.czest.pl

Abstract. We present a SMT-based bounded model checking (BMC) method for weighted interpreted systems (i.e. interpreted systems in which every agent includes a weight function that associates with each local action a weight, which is an arbitrary natural number) and for properties expressible in the existential fragment of a weighted linear temporal logic with epistemic components (WELTLK). We implemented the standard BMC algorithm and compared it with the SAT-based BMC method for the same systems and the same property language on two multi-agent systems: a weighted bit transmission problem and a weighted generic pipeline paradigm. For the SAT-based BMC we used the PicoSAT solver and for the SMT-based BMC we used the Z3 solver.

1 Introduction

The problem of model checking [2] is to check automatically whether a structure $\mathcal{M}$ defines a model for a given modal (temporal, epistemic, etc.) formula. Bounded model checking (BMC) is a verification technique designed for finding counterexamples, and whose main idea is to consider a model curtailed to a specific depth to search for an execution (or a set of executions) of a system under consideration of some length k, which constitutes a counterexample for a tested property.

Multi-agent systems (MAS) are composed of many intelligent agents that interact with each other. The agents can share a common goal or they can pursue their own interests. Also, the agents may have deadline or other timing constraints to achieve intended targets. As it was shown in [3], knowledge is a useful concept for analysing the information state and the behaviour of agents in multi-agent systems.

Partly supported by National Science Centre under the grant No. 2014/15/N/ST6/05079.

The study is co-funded by the European Union, European Social Fund. Project PO KL "Information technologies: Research and their interdisciplinary applications", Agreement UDA-POKL.04.01.01-00-051/10-00.

© Springer International Publishing Switzerland 2015
Q. Chen et al. (Eds.): PRIMA 2015, LNAI 9387, pp. 660–669, 2015.
DOI: 10.1007/978-3-319-25524-8_49

The formalism of *interpreted systems* (IS) was introduced in [3] to model multi-agent systems (MAS) [7], which are intended for reasoning about the agents' epistemic and temporal properties. The formalism of weighted interpreted systems (WIS) [9] extends IS to make the reasoning possible about not only temporal and epistemic properties, but also about agents's quantitative properties.

SMT-based bounded model checking (BMC) consists in translating the existential model checking problem for a modal logic and for a model to the satisfiability modulo theory problem (SMT-problem) of a quantifier-free first-order formula.

The original contributions of the paper are as follows. First, we propose a SMT-based BMC technique for WIS and for WELTLK. Second, we report on the implementation of the proposed BMC method as a new module of a verification system, and evaluate it experimentally by means of a modified *generic pipeline paradigm* [6] and a modified *bit transmission problem* [4].

2 Preliminaries

In this section we explain some notations used through the paper, and recall the definition of weighted interpreted systems [8] and the syntax and semantics of WELTLK[8]. In what follows we omit the operators $\overline{D}_\Gamma$, $\overline{E}_\Gamma$, and $\overline{C}_\Gamma$ since the syntax, the semantics and the translations of them can be found in [9], and moreover, we do not use them in the benchmarked formulae.

WIS. Let $Ag = \{1, \ldots, n\}$ denote a non-empty and finite set of agents, and $\mathcal{E}$ be a special agent that is used to model the environment in which the agents operate and $\mathcal{PV} = \bigcup_{c \in Ag \cup \{\mathcal{E}\}} \mathcal{PV}_c$ be a set of propositional variables, such that $\mathcal{PV}_{c_1} \cap \mathcal{PV}_{c_2} = \emptyset$ for all $c_1, c_2 \in Ag \cup \{\mathcal{E}\}$. The *weighted interpreted system* (WIS) is a tuple

$$(\{L_c, Act_c, P_c, t_c, \mathcal{V}_c, d_c\}_{c \in Ag \cup \{\mathcal{E}\}}, \iota),$$

where L_c is a non-empty set of *local states* of the agent c, $S = L_1 \times \ldots \times L_n \times L_{\mathcal{E}}$ is the set of all global states, $\iota \subseteq S$ is a non-empty set of initial states, Act_c is a non-empty set of *possible actions* of the agent c, $Act = Act_1 \times \ldots \times Act_n \times Act_{\mathcal{E}}$ is the set of *joint actions*, $P_c : L_c \to 2^{Act_c}$ is a *protocol function* that define rules according to which actions may be performed in each local state, $t_c : L_c \times Act \to L_c$ is a (partial) *evolution function*, $\mathcal{V}_c : L_c \to 2^{\mathcal{PV}}$ is a *valuation function* assigning to each local state a set of propositional variables that are assumed to be true at that state, and $d_c : Act_c \to \mathbb{N}$ is a *weight function*.

For a given WIS we define: (1) a set of all *possible global states* $S = L_1 \times \ldots \times L_n \times L_{\mathcal{E}}$; by $l_c(s)$ we denote the local component of agent $c \in Ag \cup \{\mathcal{E}\}$ in a global state $s = (\ell_1, \ldots, \ell_n, \ell_{\mathcal{E}})$; and (2) a *global evolution function* $t : S \times Act \to S$ as follows: $t(s, a) = s'$ iff for all $c \in Ag$, $t_c(l_c(s), a) = l_c(s')$ and $t_{\mathcal{E}}(l_{\mathcal{E}}(s), a) = l_{\mathcal{E}}(s')$. In brief we write the above as $s \xrightarrow{a} s'$.

Now, for a given weighted interpreted system we define a *weighted model* (or simply a *model*) as a tuple $\mathcal{M} = (Act, S, \iota, \mathcal{V}, d)$, where:

$-Act = Act_1 \times \ldots \times Act_n \times Act_\mathcal{E}$ is the set of all the joint actions,
$-S = (L_1 \times \ldots \times L_n \times L_\mathcal{E})$ is the set of all the *global states*
$-\iota = (\iota_1 \times \ldots \times \iota_n \times \iota_\mathcal{E})$ is the set of all the *initial* global states,
$-\mathcal{V} : S \to 2^{\mathcal{PV}}$ is the valuation function defined as $\mathcal{V}(s) = \bigcup_{c \in Ag \cup \{\mathcal{E}\}} \mathcal{V}_c(l_c(s))$,
  $T \subseteq S \times Act \times S$ is a transition relation defined by the global evolution function
  as follows: $(s, a, s') \in T$ iff $s \xrightarrow{a} s'$.
$-d : Act \to \mathbb{N}$ is the "joint" weight function defined as follows: $d((a_1, \ldots, a_n, a_\mathcal{E})) = d_1(a_1) + \ldots + d_n(a_n) + d_\mathcal{E}(a_\mathcal{E})$.

Given a WIS one can define the indistinguishability relation $\sim_c \subseteq S \times S$ for agent **c** as follows: $s \sim_c s'$ iff $l_c(s') = l_c(s)$. Further, a *path* in $\mathcal{M}$ is an infinite sequence $\pi = s_0 \xrightarrow{a_1} s_1 \xrightarrow{a_2} s_2 \xrightarrow{a_3} \ldots$ of transitions. For such a path, and for $j \le m \in \mathbb{N}$, by $\pi(m)$ we denote the m-th state s_m, by π^m we denote the m-th suffix of the path π, which is defined in the standard way: $\pi^m = s_m \xrightarrow{a_{m+1}} s_{m+1} \xrightarrow{a_{m+2}} s_{m+2} \ldots$. Next, by $\pi[j..m]$ we denote the finite sequence $s_j \xrightarrow{a_{j+1}} s_{j+1} \xrightarrow{a_{j+2}} \ldots s_m$ with $m - j$ transitions and $m - j + 1$ states, and by $D\pi[j..m]$ we denote the (cumulative) weight of $\pi[j..m]$ that is defined as $d(a_{j+1}) + \ldots + d(a_m)$ (hence 0 when $j = m$). By $\Pi(s)$ we denote the set of all the paths starting at $s \in S$, and by $\Pi = \bigcup_{s^0 \in \iota} \Pi(s^0)$ we denote the set of all the paths starting at initial states.

WELTLK. Let I be an interval in $\mathbb{N}$ of the form: $[a, b)$ or $[a, \infty)$, for $a, b \in \mathbb{N}$ and $a \ne b$. The WELTLK is the existential fragment of WLTLK [9], defined by the following grammar:
$$\varphi ::= \textbf{true} \mid \textbf{false} \mid p \mid \neg p \mid \varphi \wedge \varphi \mid \varphi \vee \varphi \mid \mathbf{X}_I \varphi \mid \varphi \mathbf{U}_I \varphi \mid \varphi \mathbf{R}_I \varphi \mid \overline{\mathbf{K}}_c \varphi$$
The semantics of the WLTLK is the following. A WLTLK formula φ is true along the path π (in symbols $\mathcal{M}, \pi \models \varphi$) iff $\mathcal{M}, \pi^0 \models \varphi$, where:

$\mathcal{M}, \pi^m \models \alpha \wedge \beta$ iff $\mathcal{M}, \pi^m \models \alpha$ and $\mathcal{M}, \pi^m \models \beta$,
$\mathcal{M}, \pi^m \models \alpha \vee \beta$ iff $\mathcal{M}, \pi^m \models \alpha$ or $\mathcal{M}, \pi^m \models \beta$,
$\mathcal{M}, \pi^m \models \mathbf{X}_I \alpha$ iff $D\pi[m..m+1] \in I$ and $\mathcal{M}, \pi^{m+1} \models \alpha$,
$\mathcal{M}, \pi^m \models \alpha \mathbf{U}_I \beta$ iff $(\exists i \ge m)(D\pi[m..i] \in I$ and $\mathcal{M}, \pi^i \models \beta$ and
    $(\forall m \le j < i)\mathcal{M}, \pi^j \models \alpha)$,
$\mathcal{M}, \pi^m \models \alpha \mathbf{R}_I \beta$ iff $(\forall i \ge m)(D\pi[m..i] \in I$ implies $\mathcal{M}, \pi^i \models \beta)$ or $(\exists i \ge m)$
    $(D\pi[m..i] \in I$ and $\mathcal{M}, \pi^i \models \alpha$ and $(\forall m \le j \le i)\mathcal{M}, \pi^j \models \beta)$,
$\mathcal{M}, \pi^m \models \mathbf{K}_c \alpha$ iff $(\forall \pi' \in \Pi)(\forall i \ge 0)(\pi'(i) \sim_c \pi(m)$ implies $\mathcal{M}, \pi'^i \models \alpha)$,
$\mathcal{M}, \pi^m \models \overline{\mathbf{K}}_c \alpha$ iff $(\exists \pi' \in \Pi)(\exists i \ge 0)(\pi'(i) \sim_c \pi(m)$ and $\mathcal{M}, \pi'^i \models \alpha)$.

The satisfiability relation $\models$ which indicates truth of a WELTLK formula in the model $\mathcal{M}$ at some state s of $\mathcal{M}$ is defined as in [9]. A WLTLK formula φ *holds* in the model $\mathcal{M}$ (denoted $\mathcal{M} \models \varphi$) iff $\mathcal{M}, \pi \models \varphi$ for some path $\pi \in \Pi$. The *model checking problem* asks whether $\mathcal{M} \models \varphi$.

3   SMT-Based Bounded Model Checking

In this section we present an outline of the bounded semantics for WELTLK and define a SMT-based BMC for WELTLK, which is based on the BMC encoding presented in [8]. The main difference between the SAT-based encoding and the SMT-base encoding is the representation of symbolic states, symbolic actions, and symbolic weights. In effect, the SMT-based encoding is the generalization of the propositional encoding. Both the SAT-based BMC and SMT-based BMC are based on the notion of the bounded semantics, the definition of which requires the concept of k-paths and loops.

3.1   Bounded Semantics

Let $\mathcal{M}$ be a model, and $k \in \mathbb{N}$ a bound. A k-path π_l is a pair (π, l), where π is a finite sequence $s_0 \xrightarrow{a_1} s_1 \xrightarrow{a_2} \dots \xrightarrow{a_k} s_k$ of transitions. A k-path π_l is a *loop* if $l < k$ and $\pi(k) = \pi(l)$. Note that if a k-path π_l is a loop, then it represents the infinite path of the form uv^ω, where $u = (s_0 \xrightarrow{a_1} s_1 \xrightarrow{a_2} \dots \xrightarrow{a_l} s_l)$ and $v = (s_{l+1} \xrightarrow{a_{l+2}} \dots \xrightarrow{a_k} s_k)$. $\Pi_k(s)$ denotes the set of all the k-paths of $\mathcal{M}$ that start at s, and $\Pi_k = \bigcup_{s^0 \in \iota} \Pi_k(s^0)$.

The bounded satisfiability relation $\models_k$ which indicates k-truth of a WELTLK formula in the model $\mathcal{M}$ at some state s of $\mathcal{M}$ is also defined in [8]. A WELTLK formula φ is k-*true* in the model $\mathcal{M}$ (in symbols $\mathcal{M} \models_k \varphi$) iff φ is k-true at some initial state of the model $\mathcal{M}$.

The *model checking problem* asks whether $\mathcal{M} \models \varphi$, but the *bounded model checking problem* asks whether there exists $k \in \mathbb{N}$ such that $\mathcal{M} \models_k \varphi$. The following theorem states that for a given model and a WELTLK formula there exists a bound k such that the model checking problem ($\mathcal{M} \models \varphi$) can be reduced to the bounded model checking problem ($\mathcal{M} \models_k \varphi$).

Theorem 1. *Let $\mathcal{M}$ be a model and φ a WELTLK formula. Then, the following equivalence holds: $\mathcal{M} \models \varphi$ iff there exists $k \leq |\mathcal{M}| \cdot |\varphi| \cdot 2^{|\varphi|}$ such that $\mathcal{M} \models_k \varphi$.*

Proof. The theorem can be proved by induction on the length of the formula φ (for details one can see [8]).

3.2   Translation to SMT

SMT-solvers extend the capabilities of SAT-solvers by allowing for the first order formulae that can be defined over several built-in theories, and types other than Booleans. To encode the BMC problem for WELTLK and WIS by means of SMT, we consider a very weak fragment of logics that can be handled by modern SMT solvers: quantifier-free logic with individual variables ranging over the natural numbers.

Let $\mathcal{M}$ be a model, φ a WELTLK formula, and $k \geq 0$ a bound. The presented SMT encoding of the BMC problem for WELTLK is based on the BMC encoding of [9, 10], and it relies on defining the quantifier-free first-order formula: $: [\mathcal{M}, \varphi]_k := [\mathcal{M}^{\varphi, \iota}]_k \wedge [\varphi]_{\mathcal{M}, k}$ which is satisfiable if and only if $\mathcal{M} \models_k \varphi$ holds.

The definition of $[\mathcal{M}^{\varphi,\iota}]_k$ assumes that the states and the join actions of $\mathcal{M}$, and the sequence of weights associate to the join actions are encoded symbolically, which is possible, since both the set of states and the set of joint actions are finite. Formally, each state $s \in S$ is represented by a vector

Let $\mathbf{c} \in Ag \cup \{\mathcal{E}\}$. The definition of the formula $[\mathcal{M}, \varphi]_k$ assumes that

- each global state $s \in S$ is represented by a valuation of a *symbolic state* $\overline{\mathbf{w}} = (w_1, \ldots, w_n, w_{\mathcal{E}})$ that consists of *symbolic local states* and each symbolic local state $w_{\mathbf{c}}$ is an individual variable ranging over the natural numbers;
- each joint action $a \in Act$ is represented by a valuation of a *symbolic action* $\overline{a} = (a_1, \ldots, a_n, a_{\mathcal{E}})$ that consists of *symbolic local actions* and each symbolic local action $a_{\mathbf{c}}$ is an individual variable ranging over the natural numbers;
- each sequence of weights associated with the joint action is represented by a valuation of a *symbolic weights* $\overline{d} = (d_1, \ldots, d_{n+1})$ that consists of *symbolic local weights* and each symbolic local weight $d_{\mathbf{c}}$ is an individual variable ranging over the natural numbers.

Further, in order to define $[\mathcal{M}^{\varphi,\iota}]_k$ we need to specify the number of k-paths of the model $\mathcal{M}$ that are sufficient to validate φ. To calculate this number, we use the following auxiliary function ([9]) $f_k : WELTLK \to \mathbb{N}$ that is defined as follows: $f_k(\mathbf{true}) = f_k(\mathbf{false}) = f_k(p) = f_k(\neg p) = 0$, for $p \in \mathcal{PV}$; $f_k(\alpha \wedge \beta) = f_k(\alpha) + f_k(\beta)$; $f_k(\alpha \vee \beta) = max\{f_k(\alpha), f_k(\beta)\}$; $f_k(\mathbf{X}_I \alpha) = f_k(\alpha)$; $f_k(\alpha \mathbf{U}_I \beta) = k \cdot f_k(\alpha) + f_k(\beta) + 1$; $f_k(\alpha \mathbf{R}_I \beta) = (k+1) \cdot f_k(\beta) + f_k(\alpha) + 1$; $f_k(\overline{\mathbf{K}}_{\mathbf{c}} \alpha) = f_k(\alpha) + 1$.

Now, since in the BMC method we deal with the existential validity, the number of k-paths sufficient to validate φ is given by the function $\widehat{f}_k : WELTLK \to \mathbb{N}$ that is defined as $\widehat{f}_k(\varphi) = f_k(\varphi) + 1$.

Given the above, the j-th symbolic k-path π_j is defined as the following sequence of transitions: $\overline{\mathbf{w}}_{0,j} \xrightarrow{\overline{a}_{1,j}, \overline{d}_{1,j}} \overline{\mathbf{w}}_{1,j} \xrightarrow{\overline{a}_{2,j}, \overline{d}_{2,j}} \ldots \xrightarrow{\overline{a}_{k,j}, \overline{d}_{k,j}} \overline{\mathbf{w}}_{k,j}$, where $\overline{\mathbf{w}}_{i,j}$ are symbolic states, $\overline{a}_{i,j}$ are symbolic actions, and $\overline{d}_{i,j}$ are sequences of *symbolic weights*, for $0 \leq i \leq k$ and $1 \leq j \leq \widehat{f}_k(\varphi)$.

Let $\overline{\mathbf{w}}$ and $\overline{\mathbf{w}}'$ be two different symbolic states, $\overline{d}$ a sequence of symbolic weighs, $\overline{a}$ a symbolic action, and u be a symbolic number. We assume definitions of the following auxiliary quantifier-free first-order formulae: $p(\overline{\mathbf{w}})$ - encodes the set of states of $\mathcal{M}$ in which $p \in \mathcal{PV}$ holds, $I_s(\overline{\mathbf{w}})$ - encodes the state s of the model $\mathcal{M}$, $H_{\mathbf{c}}(w_{\mathbf{c}}, w'_{\mathbf{c}})$ - it encodes equality of two local states, such that $w_{\mathbf{c}} = w'_{\mathbf{c}}$ for $\mathbf{c} \in Ag \cup \mathcal{E}$; $\mathcal{T}(\overline{\mathbf{w}}, (\overline{a}, \overline{d}), \overline{\mathbf{w}}')$ - encodes the transition relation of $\mathcal{M}$, $\mathcal{D}^I_{a,b;c,d}(\pi_n)$ for $a \leq b$ and $c \leq d$ - if $a < b$ and $c < d$, then it encodes that the weight represented by the sequences $\delta_{a+1,n}, \ldots, \delta_{b,n}$ and $\delta_{c+1,n}, \ldots, \delta_{d,n}$ belongs to the interval I; if $a = b$ and $c < d$, then it encodes that the weight represented by the sequence $\delta_{c+1,n}, \ldots, \delta_{d,n}$ belongs to the interval I; if $a < b$ and $c = d$, then it encodes that the weight represented by the sequence $\delta_{a+1,n}, \ldots, \delta_{b,n}$ belongs to the interval I; if $a = b$ and $c = d$, then $\mathcal{D}^I_{a,b;c,d}(\pi_n)$ is true iff $0 \in I$.

The formula $[\mathcal{M}^{\varphi,\iota}]_k$, which encodes the unfolding of the transition relation of the model $\mathcal{M}$ $\widehat{f}_k(\varphi)$-times to the depth k, is defined as follows:

$$[\mathcal{M}^{\varphi,\iota}]_k := \bigvee_{s \in \iota} I_s(\overline{\mathbf{w}}_{0,0}) \wedge \bigvee_{j=1}^{\widehat{f}_k(\varphi)} \overline{\mathbf{w}}_{0,0} = \overline{\mathbf{w}}_{0,j} \wedge \bigwedge_{j=1}^{\widehat{f}_k(\varphi)} \bigvee_{l=0}^{k} l = u_j \wedge \quad (1)$$

$$\bigwedge_{j=1}^{\widehat{f}_k(\varphi)} \bigwedge_{i=0}^{k-1} \mathcal{T}(\overline{\mathbf{w}}_{i,j}, (\overline{a}_{i,j}, \overline{d}_{i,j}), \overline{\mathbf{w}}_{i+1,j})$$

where $\overline{\mathbf{w}}_{i,j}$, $\overline{a}_{i,j}$, $\overline{d}_{i,j}$, and u_j are, respectively, symbolic states and actions, and sequences of symbolic weights and numbers, for $0 \leq i \leq k$ and $1 \leq j \leq \widehat{f}_k(\varphi)$.

Let $F_k(\varphi) = \{j \in \mathbb{N} \mid 1 \leq j \leq \widehat{f}_k(\varphi)\}$, and $[\varphi]_k^{[m,n,A]}$ denote the translation of φ along the n-th symbolic path $\boldsymbol{\pi}_n^m$ with the starting point m by using the set $A \subseteq F_k(\varphi)$. Then, the next step is a translation of a WELTLK formula φ to a quantifier-free first-order formula $[\varphi]_{\mathcal{M},k} := [\varphi]_k^{[0,1,F_k(\varphi)]}$.

Definition 1 (Translation of the WELTLK formulae). *Let $\mathcal{M}$ be a model, φ a WELTLK formula, and $k \geq 0$ a bound. We define inductively the translation of φ over a path number $n \in F_k(\varphi)$ starting at the symbolic state $\overline{\mathbf{w}}_{m,n}$ as shown below, where $n' = min(A)$, $h_{\mathbf{U}} = h_{\mathbf{U}}(A, f_k(\beta))$, and $h_R = h_R(A, f_k(\alpha))$.*

$[\mathbf{true}]_k^{[m,n,A]} := \mathbf{true}, \qquad [\mathbf{false}]_k^{[m,n,A]} := \mathbf{false},$

$[p]_k^{[m,n,A]} := p(\overline{\mathbf{w}}_{m,n}), \qquad [\neg p]_k^{[m,n,A]} := \neg p(\overline{\mathbf{w}}_{m,n}),$

$[\alpha \wedge \beta]_k^{[m,n,A]} := [\alpha]_k^{[m,n,g_l(A,f_k(\alpha))]} \wedge [\beta]_k^{[m,n,g_r(A,f_k(\beta))]},$

$[\alpha \vee \beta]_k^{[m,n,A]} := [\alpha]_k^{[m,n,g_l(A,f_k(\alpha))]} \vee [\beta]_k^{[m,n,g_l(A,f_k(\beta))]},$

$[\mathbf{X}_I \alpha]_k^{[m,n,A]} := \begin{cases} \overline{d}_{m,n} \in I \wedge [\alpha]_k^{[m+1,n,A]}, & \text{if } m < k \\ \bigvee_{l=0}^{k-1}(\overline{d}_{l,n} \in I \wedge \overline{\mathbf{w}}_{k,n} = \overline{\mathbf{w}}_{l,n} \wedge [\alpha]_k^{[l+1,n,A]}), & \text{if } m = k \end{cases}$

$[\alpha \mathbf{U}_I \beta]_k^{[m,n,A]} := \bigvee_{j=m}^{k}((\overline{d}_{m+1,n} + \ldots + \overline{d}_{j,n}) \in I \wedge [\beta]_k^{[j,n,h_{\mathbf{U}}(k)]} \wedge$

$\bigwedge_{i=m}^{j-1}[\alpha]_k^{[i,n,h_{\mathbf{U}}(i)]}) \vee (\bigvee_{l=0}^{m-1} l = u_n \wedge \overline{\mathbf{w}}_{k,n} = \overline{\mathbf{w}}_{l,n} \wedge$

$\bigvee_{j=0}^{m-1}(j > u_n \wedge [\beta]_k^{[j,n,h_{\mathbf{U}}(k)]} \wedge \bigvee_{l=0}^{m-1}(l = u_n \wedge \mathcal{D}_{m,k;l,j}^I(\boldsymbol{\pi}_n))$

$\wedge \bigwedge_{i=0}^{j-1}(i > u_n \to [\alpha]_k^{[i,n,h_{\mathbf{U}}(i)]}) \wedge \bigwedge_{i=m}^{k}[\alpha]_k^{[i,n,h_{\mathbf{U}}(i)]}),$

$[\alpha \mathbf{R}_I \beta]_k^{[m,n,A]} := \bigvee_{j=m}^{k}((\overline{d}_{m+1,n} + \ldots + \overline{d}_{j,n}) \in I \wedge [\alpha]_k^{[j,n,h_R(k)]} \wedge$

$\bigwedge_{i=m}^{j}[\beta]_k^{[i,n,h_R(i)]}) \vee (\bigvee_{l=0}^{m-1}(l = u_n \wedge \overline{\mathbf{w}}_{k,n} = \overline{\mathbf{w}}_{l,n}) \wedge$

$\bigvee_{j=0}^{m-1}(j > u_n \wedge [\alpha]_k^{[j,n,h_R(k)]} \wedge \bigvee_{l=0}^{m-1}(l = u_n \wedge \mathcal{D}_{m,k;l,j}^I(\boldsymbol{\pi}_n))$

$\wedge \bigwedge_{i=0}^{j}(i > u_n \to [\beta]_k^{[i,n,h_R(i)]}) \wedge \bigwedge_{i=m}^{k}[\beta]_k^{[i,n,h_R(i)]}) \vee$

$((\overline{d}_{1,n} + \ldots + \overline{d}_{k,n}) \geq \mathbf{right}(I) \wedge \bigwedge_{j=m}^{k}((\overline{d}_{m+1,n} + \ldots + \overline{d}_{j,n})$

$\in I \to [\beta]_k^{[j,n,h_R(k)]})) \vee ((\overline{d}_{1,n} + \ldots + \overline{d}_{k,n}) < \mathbf{right}(I)$

$\wedge \bigwedge_{j=m}^{k}((\overline{d}_{m+1,n} + \ldots + \overline{d}_{j,n}) \in I \to [\beta]_k^{[j,n,h_R(k)]}) \wedge$

$\bigvee_{l=0}^{k-1}[(\overline{\mathbf{w}}_k = \overline{\mathbf{w}}_l) \wedge \bigwedge_{j=l}^{k}(\mathcal{D}_{m,k;l,j}^I(\boldsymbol{\pi}_n) \to [\beta]_k^{[j,n,h_R(k)]})]),$

$[\overline{\mathbf{K}}_{\mathbf{c}} \alpha]_k^{[m,n,A]} := \bigvee_{s \in \iota} I_s(\overline{\mathbf{w}}_{0,n'}) \wedge \bigvee_{j=0}^{k}([\alpha]_k^{[j,n',g_s(A)]} \wedge H_{\mathbf{c}}(\overline{\mathbf{w}}_{m,n}, \overline{\mathbf{w}}_{j,n'})),$

The theorem below states the correctness and the completeness of the translation. It can be proven by induction on the complexity of the given WELTLK formula.

Theorem 2. *Let $\mathcal{M}$ be a model, and φ a WELTLK formula. Then for every $k \in \mathbb{N}$, $\mathcal{M} \models_k \varphi$ if, and only if, the propositional formula $[\mathcal{M}, \varphi]_k$ is satisfiable.*

4   Experimental Results

We have performed the experiments using two benchmarks: the *weighted generic pipeline paradigm* (WGPP) WIS model [8,9] and the *weighted bit transmission problem* (WBTP) WIS model [9]. For computing the experimental results we used a computer equipped with Intel i7-3770 3.4 GHz processor, 32 GB of RAM, and the operating system Linux with the kernel 4.0.5. We set the CPU time limit to 1800 seconds. Moreover, in order to compare the SMT-based BMC method (SMT-BMC for short) with with the SAT-based BMC method (SAT-BMC for short), we have asked the authors of [9] to provide us the binary version of their implementation of SAT-BMC and we have obtained the requested binaries. Furthermore, our SMT-based BMC algorithm is implemented as a standalone program written in the programming language C++. For SAT-BMC we used the state of the art SAT-solver PicoSAT [1], and for the SMT-BMC we used the state of the art SMT-solver Z3. [5].

Let Min denote the minimum cost needed to ensure that Consumer receives the data produced by Producer. Further, let $a \in \mathbb{N}$ and $b \in \mathbb{N}$ be the costs of sending, respectively, bits by Sender and an acknowledgement by Receiver. The specifications we consider for the WGPP and WBTP systems, respectively, are:

- $\varphi_1 = \mathrm{K}_P \mathbf{G}_{[Min,Min+1)} ConsReceived$, which expresses that Producer knows that always the cost of receiving by Consumer the commodity is Min.
- $\varphi_2 = \mathrm{K}_P \mathbf{G}(ProdSend \rightarrow \mathbf{F}_{[0,Min-d_P(Produce))} ConsReceived)$, which states that Producer knows that always if she/he produces a commodity, then Consumer receives the commodity and the cost is less than $Min - d_P(Produce)$.
- $\varphi_3 = \mathrm{K}_P \mathbf{G}(ProdSend \rightarrow \mathrm{K}_C \mathrm{K}_P \mathbf{F}_{[0,Min-d_P(Produce))} ConsReceived)$, which states that Producer knows that always if she/he produces a commodity, then Consumer knows that Producer knows that Consumer has received the commodity and the cost is less than $Min - d_P(Produce)$.
- $\varphi_4 = \mathrm{K}_C \mathbf{G}(ProdReady \rightarrow \mathbf{X}_{[d_P(Produce),d_P(Produce)+1)} ProdSend)$, which expresses that Consumer knows that the cost of producing of a commodity by Producer is $d_P(Produce)$.
- $\psi_1 = \mathbf{G}_{[a+b,a+b+1)}(\mathbf{recack} \rightarrow \mathrm{K}_{Send}(\mathrm{K}_{\mathcal{R}}(\bigvee_{i=0}^{2^n-2} i)))$ - the property says that if an ack is received by $Send$, then $Send$ knows that Rec knows at least one value of the n-bit numbers except the maximal value, and the cost is $a + b$.
- $\psi_2 = \mathbf{G}_{[a+b,a+b+1)}(\mathrm{K}_{Send}(\bigvee_{i=0}^{2^n-1}(\mathrm{K}_{\mathcal{R}}(i))))$ – the property says that $Send$ knows that Rec knows the value of the n-bit number and the cost is $a + b$.

Note, that we describe specifications as universal formulae, for which we verify the corresponding counterexample formulae that are interpreted existentially and belong to WELTLK. Moreover, for every specification given, the corresponding WELTLK formula holds in the model of the benchmark.

4.1 Performance Evaluation

The experimental results show that the SMT-BMC is sensitive to scaling up the size of the benchmarks, but it is not sensitive to scaling up the weights, while the SAT-based BMC is more sensitive to scaling up the weights.

From Fig. 1 one can observe that the SAT-BMC is able to verify the formula φ_1 for WGPP with 65 nodes and basic weights (bw for short) and is able to verify the same formula for WGPP with 45 nodes and bw multiplied by 1000000, whereas the SMT-BMC is able to verify the formula φ_1 for WGPP with 35 nodes

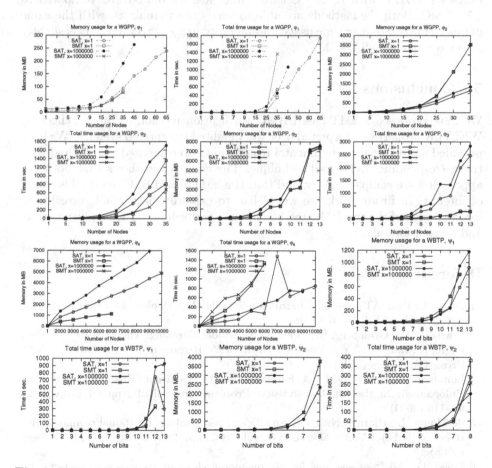

Fig. 1. SMT- and SAT-based BMC: WGPP with n nodes, WBTP with n bits integer value.

regardless of the bw. Moreover, the memory usage for SMT-BMC is lower than for SAT-BMC for the considered formula. Both the SAT-BM and SMT-BMC are able to verify the formulae φ_2 and φ_3 for WGPP with the same number of nodes. For φ_2 the memory usage by the SMT-BMC is three times higher than by the SMT-BMC, yet the SMT-BMC method consumes less time. For the formula φ_3 both the SAT-BMC and SMT-BMC use almost the same amount of memory, but the total time usage for the SAT-BMC is up to six times higher than for the SMT-BMC. The SAT-BMC is able to verify the formula φ_4 9000 for WGPP with 10000 nodes and bw and for WGPP with 9000 nodes and bw multiplied by 1000000, whereas the SMT-BMC is able to verify the formula φ_4 only for WGPP with 8000 nodes regardless of the basic weights. However, SMT-BMC consumes three times less memory than SAT-BMC.

The SAT-BMC is able to verify the formula ψ_1 for WBTP with 13 bits, whereas SMT-BMC is able to verify ψ_1 for WBTP with 12 bits, however time usage for WBTP with 12 bits is three times less for SMT-BMC compared to SAT-BMC. Both the methods are able to verify the formula ψ_2 with the same number of bits, however time usage and memory usage for SMT-BMC is slightly larger compared to SAT-BMC.

5   Conclusions

We have proposed a SMT-based BMC verification method for model checking WELTLK properties interpreted over the weighted interpreted systems. We have provided a preliminary experimental results and also compared our method with the corresponding SAT-based technique. The comparison shows that both the approaches are complementary, and that the SMT-based BMC method is worth of interest. In future work, we would like to explore whether it is possible to foresee which of the two BMC methods might perform better for a given system and a given formula.

References

1. Biere, A.: PicoSAT essentials. Journal on Satisfiability, Boolean Modeling and Computation (JSAT) **4**, 75–97 (2008)
2. Clarke, E.M., Grumberg, O., Peled, D.A.: Model Checking. The MIT Press (1999)
3. Fagin, R., Halpern, J.Y., Moses, Y., Vardi, M.Y.: Reasoning about Knowledge. MIT Press, Cambridge (1995)
4. Lomuscio, A., Sergot, M.: A Formalisation of Violation, Error Recovery, and Enforcement in the Bit Transmission Problem. Journal of Applied Logic **2**(1), 93–116 (2004)
5. de Moura, L., Bjørner, N.S.: Z3: An efficient SMT solver. In: Ramakrishnan, C.R., Rehof, J. (eds.) TACAS 2008. LNCS, vol. 4963, pp. 337–340. Springer, Heidelberg (2008)
6. Peled, D.: All from one, one for all: on model checking using representatives. In: Courcoubetis, C. (ed.) CAV 1993. LNCS, vol. 697, pp. 409–423. Springer, Heidelberg (1993)

7. Wooldridge, M.: An Introduction to Multi-Agent Systems, 2nd edn. John Wiley & Sons (2009)
8. Woźna-Szcześniak, B.: SAT-based bounded model checking for weighted deontic interpreted systems. In: Correia, L., Paulo Reis, L., Cascalho, J. (eds.) EPIA 2013. LNCS, vol. 8154, pp. 444–455. Springer, Heidelberg (2013)
9. Woźna-Szcześniak, B., Zbrzezny, A.M., Zbrzezny, A.: SAT-based bounded model checking for weighted interpreted systems and weighted linear temporal logic. In: Boella, G., Elkind, E., Savarimuthu, B.T.R., Dignum, F., Purvis, M.K. (eds.) PRIMA 2013: Principles and Practice of Multi-Agent Systems. LNCS, vol. 8291, pp. 355–371. Springer, Heidelberg (2013)
10. Zbrzezny, A.: A New Translation from ECTL* to SAT. Fundamenta Informaticae 120(3–4), 377–397 (2012)

Games with Communication: From Belief to Preference Change

Guillaume Aucher[1](✉), Bastien Maubert[2](✉), Sophie Pinchinat[3](✉),
and François Schwarzentruber[4](✉)

[1] IRISA - INRIA / Université de Rennes 1, Rennes, France
guillaume.aucher@inria.fr
[2] LORIA - CNRS / Université de Lorraine, Nancy, France
bastien.maubert@gmail.com
[3] IRISA / Université de Rennes 1, Rennes, France
sophie.pinchinat@irisa.fr
[4] IRISA - ENS Rennes, Rennes, France
francois.schwarzentruber@ens-rennes.fr

Abstract. In this work we consider simple extensive-form games with two players, Player **A** and Player **B**, where Player **B** can make announcements about his strategy. Player **A** has then to revise her preferences about her strategies, so as to better respond to the strategy she believes Player **B** will play. We propose a generic framework that combines methods and techniques from belief revision theory and social choice theory to address this problem. Additionally, we design a logic that Player **A** can use to reason and decide how to play in such games.

1 Introduction

Communication between players is a notion that arises naturally in a variety of contexts in game theory, and that led to the theory of games where players can communicate [4,5,11]. We are interested in non-cooperative games with two players, say Player **A** and **B**, in which Player **B** makes announcements about his strategy, before the game starts. Just as the *cheap talks* in [4], this preliminary communication round does not directly affect the payoffs of the game.

We illustrate our research problem with a classic example from [11] in which communication between players improves the payoff of both players. The extensive form game is described in Figure 1. Player **A** can go left or right. If **A** goes left, she gets 1$ and **B** gets 0$. If **A** goes right, player **B** can in turn choose to go left or right. If **B** goes left, he gets 100$ and **A** gets 0$, if **B** goes right both get 99$. The solution given by the classic backward induction algorithm, which relies on the hypothesis that players are rational, is the following: **A** thinks that if she goes right, **B** will go left to maximize his payoff, and **A** will get 0$. Therefore, **A** prefers to move left, and gets 1$.

On the other hand, let us assume that the players communicate and trust each other, and that **B** tells **A**: "If you move right, I will move right". As a consequence, **A** thinks she would better move right since she would collect 99$ instead of 1$: as such, **A** has revised her preferences about her own strategies.

© Springer International Publishing Switzerland 2015
Q. Chen et al. (Eds.): PRIMA 2015, LNAI 9387, pp. 670–677, 2015.
DOI: 10.1007/978-3-319-25524-8_50

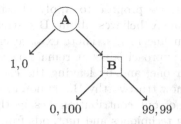

Fig. 1. Motivating example

Notice that in this example, **B**'s announcement could have been reflected by pruning the game, in the spirit of Public Announcement Logic [9]: we could have removed the moves (in the example, just one) of **B** that do not conform to his announcement, in this very case by ruling out his left move, and have recomputed a strategy of **A** by backward induction in the pruned game.

However, the pruning technique, although attractive in practice, has some serious limitations. First, we cannot guarantee that in any game, every announcement of **B** amounts to pruning the game, in particular those relying on conditional statements. Second, **B** can make a series of successive announcements, possibly conflicting each other. In that case, **A** will need to aggregate these announcements in order to revise her beliefs on what **B** will play. This phenomenon cannot be represented straightforwardly by means of a series of destructive prunings of the game, and we propose to work on the level of **B**'s strategies instead.

Preliminary announcements can be motivated by various reasons, such as trying to coordinate with the other player or to mislead him in order to get a better payoff. After these announcements, Player **A** needs to revise her strategy so as to better respond to what Player **B** pretends to play. Notice that depending on the context, the confidence Player **A** has on Player **B**'s commitment about his annoucements varies widely. In this work, like in belief revision theory [6], we assume that Player **A** always trusts Player **B**'s last announcement, which has also priority over the previous announcements.

The question we consider is the following:

> How can Player **A** take into account the announcements of Player **B** about his strategy in order to update her preferences on her strategies?

This question can be decomposed into:

> **Question 1:** How can Player **A** revise her beliefs about Player **B**'s preferences on his strategies?
> **Question 2:** How can Player **A** update her preference about her strategies on the basis of these beliefs?

Regarding Question 1, we propose to apply classical belief-revision techniques[1] to represent what **A** believes about **B**'s strategy and update these beliefs when **B** makes announcements. There exist several ways to perform this update/revision, but our approach aims at remaining as general as possible by not selecting a particular one, and by leaving the choice to peak the update mechanism that reflects how trustworthy **B**'s announcements are considered.

The main originality of our contribution lies in the solution we offer for Question 2, by combining techniques and methods from game theory and from social choice theory [2]: informally, each possible strategy of **B** is seen as a voter, who votes for strategies of **A** according to the payoff **A** would obtain in the play defined by both strategies. Individual votes are then aggregated to define the new preferred strategy of **A**. Here again we do not choose a particular type of ballot nor a precise aggregation method, but rather leave it open and free to be set according to the kind of strategy one wants to obtain: for instance, one that has best average payoff against **B**'s most plausible strategies, or one that is most often a best response.

The paper is organized as follows. In Section 2, we set up the mathematical framework we use to model games and communication/announcements. In Section 3, we develop the solution to the revision of beliefs, and in Section 4 we expose our proposal for the revision of preferences. Based on the developed setting, we propose in Section 5 a logic that Player **A** can use to reason and decide how to play. Section 6 illustrates our framework on a more complex example.

2   Games and Announcements

We consider two-player extensive-form games in which at each decision node two distinct moves are available. A *finite rooted binary tree* (simply called *tree* from now on) is a prefix-closed finite set $T \subset \{0,1\}^*$. Elements of T are called *nodes*, ϵ is the *root*, if $w \cdot a \in T$, with $a \in \{0,1\}$, then w is called the *parent* of $w \cdot a$ and $w \cdot a$ is called the *left* (resp. *right*) *child* of w if $a = 0$ (resp. $a = 1$). If a node has no child, it is a *leaf*, otherwise it is an *interior node*. A tree is called *complete* if every interior node has exactly two children. If T, T' are trees such that $T \subseteq T'$, we say that T is a *subtree* of T'.

A *game* between **A** and **B** is a tuple $G = (T, \nu_{\mathbf{A}}, \nu_{\mathbf{B}})$ where T is a complete tree, and if we note $L \subseteq T$ the set of leaves of T, then $\nu_{\mathbf{A}} : L \to \mathbb{N}$ is the *utility function* for **A**, $\nu_{\mathbf{B}} : L \to \mathbb{N}$ is the utility function for **B**. Interior nodes are partitioned between nodes of **A** ($N_{\mathbf{A}}$) and those of **B** ($N_{\mathbf{B}}$), such that $T = N_{\mathbf{A}} \uplus N_{\mathbf{B}} \uplus L$.

Given a game $G = (T, \nu_{\mathbf{A}}, \nu_{\mathbf{B}})$, a *strategy*[2] for **A** (resp. **B**) is a subtree $\sigma_{\mathbf{A}}$ (resp. $\sigma_{\mathbf{B}}$) of T such that every node in $\sigma_{\mathbf{A}} \cap N_{\mathbf{A}}$ (resp. $\sigma_{\mathbf{B}} \cap N_{\mathbf{B}}$) has exactly

---

[1] Typically, **A** initially believes that **B** will play one of the strategies given by the classical backward-induction algorithm. Then **B** may announce a piece of information that is in contradiction with this belief, which thus needs to be revised.

[2] To be precise these are reduced strategies, but they are sufficient for what we present here.

one child, and every node in $\sigma_{\mathbf{A}} \cap N_{\mathbf{B}}$ (resp. $\sigma_{\mathbf{B}} \cap N_{\mathbf{A}}$) has exactly two children. Two strategies $\sigma_{\mathbf{A}}$ and $\sigma_{\mathbf{B}}$ define a unique path, hence a unique leaf in the tree T, that we shall write $\sigma_{\mathbf{A}}\hat{\sigma}_{\mathbf{B}}$. We note $\Sigma_{\mathbf{A}}$ and $\Sigma_{\mathbf{B}}$ the set of all strategies for $\mathbf{A}$ and $\mathbf{B}$, respectively.

For a strategy $\sigma_{\mathbf{A}} \in \Sigma_{\mathbf{A}}$, we define its *value* $\mathrm{val}(\sigma_{\mathbf{A}})$ as the minimum utility it can bring about for $\mathbf{A}$: $\mathrm{val}(\sigma_{\mathbf{A}}) := \min_{w \in L} \nu_{\mathbf{A}}(w)$. The value of a strategy for Player $\mathbf{B}$ is defined likewise.

The language Player $\mathbf{B}$ uses to make the announcements about his strategies is the bimodal language $\mathcal{L}_2$, the syntax of which is:

$$\psi ::= p \mid \neg\psi \mid \psi \wedge \psi \mid \Diamond_i \psi$$

where $p \in \{turn_{\mathbf{A}}, turn_{\mathbf{B}}\}$ and $i \in \{0, 1\}$.

For $i \in \{0, 1\}$, we write $\top$ for $\neg(p \wedge \neg p)$, $\Box_i \psi$ for $\neg\Diamond_i\neg\psi$, $\Box\varphi$ for $\Box_0\varphi \wedge \Box_1\varphi$, and *move$_i$* for $\Diamond_i\top$, meaning that the strategy at this point chooses direction i.

Example 1. For instance, in the example of Figure 1, the strategy of $\mathbf{B}$ consisting in playing the action leading to 99, 99 is $\Diamond_1\Diamond_1\top$.

Given a game $G = (T, \nu_{\mathbf{A}}, \nu_{\mathbf{B}})$, a strategy σ can be seen as a Kripke structure with two relations (one for left child, one for right child). The valuations of propositions $turn_{\mathbf{A}}$ and $turn_{\mathbf{B}}$ are given by the partition between positions of Player $\mathbf{A}$ and Player $\mathbf{B}$. Formally, the truth conditions are defined inductively as follows:

$$\sigma, w \models turn_a \quad \text{if } w \in N_a,\ a \in \{\mathbf{A}, \mathbf{B}\}$$
$$\sigma, w \models \neg\psi \qquad \text{if } \sigma, w \not\models \psi$$
$$\sigma, w \models \psi \wedge \psi' \quad \text{if } \sigma, w \models \psi \text{ and } \sigma, w \models \psi'$$
$$\sigma, w \models \Diamond_i\psi \qquad \text{if } w \cdot i \in \sigma \text{ and } \sigma, w \cdot i \models \psi$$

3 Belief Revision: From Announcements to Beliefs

We now represent the beliefs $\mathbf{A}$ has about what $\mathbf{B}$ is more likely to play, and how these beliefs evolve as $\mathbf{B}$ makes new announcements.

From a purely semantic point of view, the framework of belief revision theory [1,7] can be roughly described as follows. Given a universe $\mathcal{U}$ of possible worlds, a player ranks each possible world via a *ranking function* $\kappa : \mathcal{U} \to \mathbb{N}$, also called *belief state*, such that $\kappa^{-1}(0) \neq \emptyset$. This ranking induces a plausibility preorder between possible worlds: among two possible worlds, the one with the lowest rank is considered to be more plausible than the other by the player. Given a ranking function κ, the set of *most plausible worlds* for the player is the set $\kappa^{-1}(0)$.

The impact of a new piece of information on these beliefs is modelled by a *revision function* which takes a ranking function together with the new information, and returns the revised ranking function that induces the new belief state of the player. Many such revision functions exist in the literature, that correspond amongst other things to various degrees in the trust put in the received information, the reluctance to modify one's beliefs, etc (see *e.g.* [10]). Formally, if one chooses say formulas of propositional logic PL to represent new pieces of information, a revision function is a binary function $* : (\mathcal{U} \to \mathbb{N}) \times PL \to (\mathcal{U} \to \mathbb{N})$, and given $F \in PL$, a belief state κ is changed into $\kappa * F$.

In our framework, the universe $\mathcal{U} = \Sigma_\mathbf{B}$ is the set of Player $\mathbf{B}$'s strategies, and the new pieces of information are modal formulas of $\mathcal{L}_2$, representing $\mathbf{B}$'s announcements about his strategy. For a belief state κ, $\kappa^{-1}(0)$ is then what $\mathbf{A}$ believes $\mathbf{B}$ is the most likely to play. Initially, we assume that $\mathbf{A}$ has an *a priori* belief, represented by κ_0, that may for example arise from the very values of the strategies:

$$\kappa_0(\sigma_\mathbf{B}) := \max_{\sigma'_\mathbf{B} \in \Sigma_\mathbf{B}} \text{val}(\sigma'_\mathbf{B}) - \text{val}(\sigma_\mathbf{B}) \tag{1}$$

The revision function signature is now $(\Sigma_\mathbf{B} \to \mathbb{N}) \times \mathcal{L}_2 \to (\Sigma_\mathbf{B} \to \mathbb{N})$, and we can use any kind of revision function. For example here, we present the classic *moderate revision* [8,10], written $*_m$, and defined by: for κ, $\psi \in \mathcal{L}_2$ and $\sigma \in \Sigma_\mathbf{B}$,

$$(\kappa *_m \psi)(\sigma) = \begin{cases} \kappa(\sigma) - \min_{\sigma' \models \psi} \kappa(\sigma') & \text{if } \sigma \models \psi \\ \max_{\sigma' \models \psi} \kappa(\sigma') + 1 + \kappa(\sigma) \\ \quad - \min_{\sigma' \not\models \psi} \kappa(\sigma') & \text{if } \sigma \not\models \psi \end{cases}$$

The moderate revision makes all the possible worlds that verify the announcement ψ more believed than those which do not; it preserves the original order of preference otherwise.

4   Voting: From Beliefs to Preferences

The belief Player $\mathbf{A}$ has about $\mathbf{B}$'s strategy induces some preference over $\mathbf{A}$'s strategies. We describe a mechanism that, given a belief state κ, computes a *preference set* $\mathcal{P}_\kappa \subseteq \Sigma_\mathbf{A}$. This preference set is made of all the strategies that should be preferred by $\mathbf{A}$ if she believes that $\mathbf{B}$ will play a strategy in $\kappa^{-1}(0)$. This mechanism relies on voting systems.

A plethora of different voting systems have been proposed and studied [3], verifying different properties one may want a voting system to verify (majority criterion, Condorcet criterion etc). Since we are interested in quantitative outcomes, we argue that a relevant choice is to use a *cardinal voting system* [12]. In a cardinal voting system, a voter gives each candidate a *rating* from a set of grades; we take here grades in $\mathbb{N}$. Take a set of n candidates, $C = \{c_1, \ldots, c_n\}$, and a set of m voters, $V = \{v_1, \ldots, v_m\}$. A *ballot* is a mapping $b : C \to \mathbb{N}$ and a *voting correspondence* is a function $r^C : (C \to \mathbb{N})^m \to 2^C \setminus \{\emptyset\}$ that takes a vector $(b_1, b_2, \ldots, b_m)$ of ballots (one for each voter) and returns a nonempty set of *winning* candidates[3]. In this work we take as an example the *range voting system*, but the method is generic and any other cardinal voting system can be used. Range voting works as follows: for each candidate, we sum the grades obtained in the different ballots, and the set of winners is the set of candidates

---

[3] It is called a voting rule if there is a unique winner.

who share the highest overall score: if b_i is voter i's ballot, for $i \in \{1, \ldots, m\}$, r^C is defined by

$$r^C(b_1, \ldots, b_m) := \operatorname*{argmax}_{c \in C} \sum_{i=1}^{m} b_i(c).$$

We aim at electing the strategies of Player **A** that she should prefer with regard to the most plausible strategies of Player **B**. Therefore, the set of candidates consists in Player **A**'s possible strategies ($C = \Sigma_{\mathbf{A}}$), and each of Player **B**'s most plausible strategie is seen as a voter ($V = \kappa^{-1}(0)$). We assume that Player **A** prefers strategies that in average give her the best payoff, which leads us to define ballots as follows. For each strategy $\sigma_{\mathbf{B}} \in \kappa^{-1}(0)$, we let $b_{\sigma_{\mathbf{B}}}$ be the ballot that assigns to each $\sigma_{\mathbf{A}} \in \Sigma_{\mathbf{A}}$ the payoff of **A** in the play $\sigma_{\mathbf{A}}\hat{\ }\sigma_{\mathbf{B}}$, that is $b_{\sigma_{\mathbf{B}}}(\sigma_{\mathbf{A}}) = \nu_{\mathbf{A}}(\sigma_{\mathbf{A}}\hat{\ }\sigma_{\mathbf{B}})$. In other words, each voter ranks the candidates according to the corresponding payoff for Player **A**. The voting system aggregates these "individual" preferences in order to obtain a "collective" preference $\mathcal{P}_\kappa$ against all strategies of $\kappa^{-1}(0)$, defined by:

$$\mathcal{P}_\kappa := r^C(b_{\sigma_{\mathbf{B}}^1}, \ldots, b_{\sigma_{\mathbf{B}}^m}), \text{ whenever } \kappa^{-1}(0) = \{\sigma_{\mathbf{B}}^1, \ldots, \sigma_{\mathbf{B}}^m\}.$$

Remark 1. Note that we could use more of the information we have by letting all strategies in $\Sigma_{\mathbf{B}}$ vote, and weigh their votes according to their respective plausibility.

5 A Logic for Strategies, Announcements and Preferences

We present the formal language $\mathcal{L}_{SAP}$, where SAP stands for "Strategies, Announcements and Preferences", to reason about Player **A**'s preferences concerning her strategies, and how these evolve while Player **B** makes announcements about his strategy. The syntax of $\mathcal{L}_{SAP}$ is the following:

$$\varphi ::= \psi \mid \neg\varphi \mid \varphi \wedge \varphi \mid P_{\mathbf{A}}\varphi \mid [\psi!]\varphi$$

where $\psi \in \mathcal{L}_2$.

The formula $P_{\mathbf{A}}\varphi$ reads as 'φ holds in all the preferred strategies of Player **A**'; $[\psi!]\varphi$ reads as 'φ holds after Player **B** announces that her strategy satisfies ψ'.

$\mathcal{L}_{SAP}$ formulas are evaluated in models of the form $(\kappa, \sigma_{\mathbf{A}})$, where κ is the *belief state* of Player **A** and $\sigma_{\mathbf{A}} \in \Sigma_{\mathbf{A}}$ is the strategy **A** is considering. The truth conditions are given inductively as follows:

$$
\begin{aligned}
(\kappa, \sigma_{\mathbf{A}}) &\models \psi & &\text{if } (\sigma_{\mathbf{A}}, \epsilon) \models \psi \\
(\kappa, \sigma_{\mathbf{A}}) &\models \neg\varphi & &\text{if } (\kappa, \sigma_{\mathbf{A}}) \not\models \varphi \\
(\kappa, \sigma_{\mathbf{A}}) &\models \varphi \wedge \varphi' & &\text{if } (\kappa, \sigma_{\mathbf{A}}) \models \varphi \text{ and } (\kappa, \sigma_{\mathbf{A}}) \models \varphi' \\
(\kappa, \sigma_{\mathbf{A}}) &\models P_{\mathbf{A}}\varphi & &\text{if for all } \sigma_{\mathbf{A}}' \in \mathcal{P}_\kappa, (\kappa, \sigma_{\mathbf{A}}') \models \varphi \\
(\kappa, \sigma_{\mathbf{A}}) &\models [\psi!]\varphi & &\text{if } (\kappa *_m \psi, \sigma_{\mathbf{A}}) \models \varphi
\end{aligned}
$$

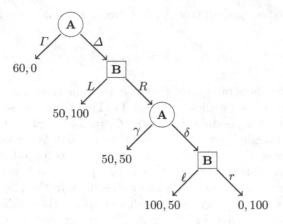

Fig. 2. Second example game

6   Example

Consider the game in Figure 2. By backward induction, we get that **B** chooses r, **A** thus chooses γ, **B** chooses L, and finally **A** chooses Γ, obtaining 60\$ while **B** gets nothing. **B** would therefore like **A** to change her mind and play Δ on the first move, so that he can play L and get 100. The problem is that if he announces that he will do so, then **A** will stick to her strategy, as she will know that changing it will give her a payoff of 50 instead of 60. So **B** announces, instead, that he commits to play either L, or R and then ℓ (we note this strategy $R\ell$), but not Rr. This announcement can be described by the following $\mathcal{L}_2$-formula:

$$\psi = \Box(turn_\mathbf{B} \to move_0) \vee \Box\Box\Box(turn_\mathbf{B} \to move_0)$$

Consider now the following $\mathcal{L}_{SAP}$-formula:

$$\varphi = turn_\mathbf{A} \wedge P_\mathbf{A}move_0 \wedge [\psi!]P_\mathbf{A}move_1$$

φ expresses that it is Player **A**'s turn to play, and that in all her preferred strategies she goes left (*i.e.* she plays Γ), but in case Player **B** announces ψ, Player **A** prefers to play differently, namely moving right.

Now, considering this game, moderate revision, range voting, with the initial belief ranking κ_0 of Equation (1) on Page 674, and any strategy $\sigma_\mathbf{A} \in \Sigma_\mathbf{A}$, one can check that indeed we have:

$$(\kappa_0, \sigma_\mathbf{A}) \models \varphi$$

This is because going right ensures **A** a better mean-payoff against **B**'s most plausible strategies after the announcement ψ, which are L and Rl. However, consider now the classic plurality voting system, where each voter only gives one voice to its preffered candidate (here, the one that ensures **A** the best outcome), and where the winner is the one with most votes for him. This amounts to electing **A**'s strategy that is most often a best response against **B**'s most plausible strategies. Using this instead of range voting system, one can verify that after the announcement, the vote results into a tie, with strategy Γ of **A** obtaining one vote (from **B**'s strategy L), and strategy $\Delta\delta$ receiving the other one (from strategy Rl). Therefore, $P_{\mathbf{A}}move_1$ does not hold in the state resulting from the announcement, so that we have:

$$(\kappa_0, \sigma_{\mathbf{A}}) \not\models \varphi$$

7 Conclusion

Our work contributes to the study of games with communication. We have defined a generic framework that uses belief revision techniques to take into account communication, and voting for choosing strategies to play. A specific revision function and voting system may characterize the behavior of Player **A** (trustful, optimistic, etc), and the kind of strategies she wants (best mean pay-off, most often best-response...). Investigating the theoretical properties of the agent's behavior in terms of combinations of revision and voting mechanisms is left for future work.

References

1. Alchourrón, C.E., Gärdenfors, P., Makinson, D.: On the logic of theory change: Partial meet contraction and revision functions. J. Symb. Log. **50**(2), 510–530 (1985)
2. Arrow, K.J., Sen, A.K.: Handbook of social choice and welfare, vol. 19. North Holland (2002)
3. Brams, S.J., Fishburn, P.C.: Voting procedures. Handbook of social choice and welfare **1**, 173–236 (2002)
4. Crawford, V.P., Sobel, J.: Strategic information transmission. Econometrica: Journal of the Econometric Society, pp. 1431–1451 (1982)
5. Farrell, J., Rabin, M.: Cheap talk. The Journal of Economic Perspectives, 103–118 (1996)
6. Gärdenfors, P.: Knowledge in Flux (Modeling the Dynamics of Epistemic States). Bradford/MIT Press, Cambridge (1988)
7. Gärdenfors, P., Rott, H.: Belief revision. Handbook of Logic in Artificial Intelligence and Logic Programming, vol. 4, pp. 35–132 (1995)
8. Nayak, A.C.: Iterated belief change based on epistemic entrenchment. Erkenntnis **41**(3), 353–390 (1994)
9. Plaza, J.: Logics of public communications. Synthese **158**(2), 165–179 (2007)
10. Rott, H.: Shifting priorities: simple representations for twenty-seven iterated theory change operators. Towards mathematical philosophy, pp. 269–296 (2009)
11. van Benthem, J.: Logical dynamics of information and interaction. Cambridge University Press (2011)
12. Vasiljev, S.: Cardinal voting: the way to escape the social choice impossibility. Available at SSRN 1116545 (2008)

Design Patterns for Environments in Multi-agent Simulations

Philippe Mathieu, Sébastien Picault[✉], and Yann Secq

SMAC Team, CRIStAL UMR CNRS 9189,
University of Lille – Science and Technology, 59655 Villeneuve d'Ascq Cedex, France
{philippe.mathieu,sebastie.picault,yann.secq}@univ-lille1.fr
http://cristal.univ-lille.fr/SMAC

Abstract. In the field of multi-agent based simulation (MABS), the concept of environment is omnipresent, though poorly defined. We argue here that depending on the modeling of space and of relations between agents, only a few efficient implementations can be set up. We aim at formalizing the core functions of environments, so as to highlight the computational answers to possible modeling choices. This unifying approach leads to the identification of four paradigmatic *Design Patterns*, associated with specific *atomic environments*, which can be composed in order to tackle complex situations.

Keywords: Environments · Modeling · Parsimony · Engineering · Design patterns

1   Introduction

In this paper, we focus on the definition and on the implementation of the concept of "environment" in MABS. It is generally admitted that agents act "in an environment" [1,2], and most of the time "environments are simply *assumed* as given" [3]. Indeed everybody is *supposed to know* what an environment is, but this implicit reference to common sense makes the environment the neglected concept in MABS design. Hence, the term itself refers to heterogeneous realities, from an abstract description of an "habitat" (in an ecological sense) where the agents "live", to the hardware/software execution infrastructure of a platform [4] and interoperability issues [5,6]. Some exceptions are found in Agent-Based Simulation, where the issue is crucial [7,8]. Several criteria for characterizing environments have been proposed by [2, ch. 2] (e.g. accessibility, determinism, static vs. dynamic, continuous vs. discrete), yet a close reading shows that they are not exactly environment features, but rather perception, cognition and action capabilities *of the agents* that are situated in it.

In contrast, [4] addresses crucial issues such as eliciting the link between agents and environments, the need for a taxonomy of environments, or the essential role of topological relations. Indeed, in order to act each agent needs to know on which other agents it can perform actions (including communication). As the

© Springer International Publishing Switzerland 2015
Q. Chen et al. (Eds.): PRIMA 2015, LNAI 9387, pp. 678–686, 2015.
DOI: 10.1007/978-3-319-25524-8_51

agent has only a limited (local) perception, it can (must) interact only with its *neighbors. Thus, the main issue is: how does an agent determine its neighbors? Essentially, the environment* ought *to be an answer to this question.*

Our goal in this paper is to search for a minimal, formal definition of what the term "environment" can mean in a MABS, and to show how to reduce the diversity of environments found in existing MABS to a few combinable *patterns*, as suggested by [9]. We argue that the choice of appropriate techniques for modeling environments only depends on a very limited number of criteria, as in the classical Design Patterns used in software engineering [10].

In the following, *each entity of the simulation model is represented by an agent* as suggested in [11,12]. We also assume *discrete time,* so that, at each time step, the MABS contains a set of agents, denoted by $\mathcal{A}_t$. At this stage we do not assume any special hypothesis regarding the capabilities of action, perception or cognition of those entities. From the environment indeed, "objects", "artifacts" or "agents" are undiscernible (proactivity being an internal feature). Obviously though, *everything* is not meant to be reified by agents: depending on the analysis level required in the model, there is a *granularity level, beyond which would-be entities are modeled by an aggregated information* (see § 2.2).

In the next section, we propose a minimal abstract definition of a MABS environment; then, we describe four patterns induced by modeling and implementation choices; finally, we explain how those patterns may be composed for building usual MABS environments.

2   Formalizing the Concept of Environment

We advocate that there are two main roles devoted to the environment in a MABS: first, *to place agents* so as to define neighborhood and accessibility relationships; second, *to provide spatial information*, which reflects underlying levels that would not be reified through agents.

2.1   First Purpose: Placing Agents

We suppose a set E composed of "places" which can host agents, and can be *arbitrarily chosen* w.r.t the nature of the world to be modeled. To determine accessibility relations from one place to the others, we also suppose a distance function $\mathbf{d} : \mathbf{E} \times \mathbf{E} \to \mathbb{R}^+ \cup \{+\infty\}$, so that (E, d) is a *metric space* in which the distance induces a *topology*. This minimalistic description covers many situations, e.g. the usual 3D space $(E = \mathbb{R}^3)$ with the euclidean distance; a 2D grid with the Moore neighborhood $(E = \mathbb{Z}^2$, d being the Chebychef distance); a continuous 2D "toric" space of width w and height h (quotient space $E = \mathbb{R}^2/(w\mathbb{Z} \times h\mathbb{Z})$); an acquaintance network (graph, i.e. a set E of nodes, endowed with the geodesic distance); etc. "Non situated" agent corresponds to a singleton $E = \{p\}$, endowed with the trivial distance $\forall x, y\ d(x, y) = 0$. Generally only a subset $\mathcal{E} \subset E$ is used in the simulation.

Since the first purpose of the environment is to locate agents, $\mathcal{E}$ must be endowed with a function designed to provide the agents with a *position* at each time step: $pos_t : \mathcal{A}_t \to \mathcal{E}$. Then, an *environment* can be defined as *a subset $\mathcal{E}$ of a metric space (E, d) endowed with a family of functions $(pos_t)_{t \in [0, T_{\max}]}$ which give the successive positions of agents within $\mathcal{E}$.* Those functions can often be specified only in *extension*; besides, each agent a is responsible for handling the value of $pos_t(a)$ (e.g. as an attribute). Moreover, the transition between pos_t and pos_{t+1} is itself the consequence of the behavior of each agent. Nevertheless, this function-based description also covers cases where positions can be specified in *intension* (e.g. trajectories following physical laws). We also define the *reciprocal function* of the position, i.e. the *content* of a point of the environment, as follows: $\forall p \in \mathcal{E}, cont_t(p) = \{a \in \mathcal{A}_t \mid pos_t(a) = p\}$.

From this formalization, we claim that two features can discriminate between several kinds of environments and their possible implementation: first, the *nature of the metric space (E, d)* (continuous, lattice, graph, singleton...), and second, the *decision (or need) to provide explicitly those functions*, especially $cont_t$. Indeed, the behavior of agents crucially depends on their *neighborhood function*, devoted to *identifying their neighbors*, i.e. with whom they can interact, namely $\nu_t : \mathcal{A}_t \to \wp(\mathcal{A}_t)$. Among an infinite variety of possible functions, a simple example is the *topological ball* centered on the position of a and of radius r: $\nu_t^r(a) = \{a' \in \mathcal{A}_t \smallsetminus \{a\} \mid d(pos_t(a), pos_t(a')) \leq r\}$. The *computational cost* of computing a neighborhood may require a time/space compromise between algorithmic efficiency and data structures. Thus a given neighborhood function may be implemented through several forms, as explained in section 3.

2.2   Second Purpose: Providing Information

Depending on the modeling scale, some underlying levels may require a macroscopic approximation. For instance, pheromones, as entities (molecules) should be represented by agents (endowed with physico-chemical behaviors: brownian motion, evaporation, degradation). But, in practice, they are usually aggregated numerically (like the concentration in chemistry) and mapped to a discretized space (the cells of a grid), in the mere intend of reducing the computational cost of handling a large number of entities, but at the expense of approximating diffusion phenomena. The MAS literature does not agree on any convention for naming such a purely informational representation. The concept of *field*, already used in reactive navigation or for pheromones (*Potential Fields* [13] and *Mean Fields* [14]) seems a convenient way of modeling *any kind of "information" afforded by the environment* (e.g. gravitation forces, temperature, obstacles) and *not reified by agents*. A field is thus a function which maps points of $\mathcal{E}$ to any set of information pieces $\mathcal{I}$; e.g. the pheromone level in grid cells would be: $phero_t : \mathbb{Z}^2 \to \mathbb{R}^+$, defined in *extension* and changing at each time step through a classical diffusion-evaporation algorithm [15]. A field can sometimes be defined in *intension*, e.g. the gravity field in the usual 3D space $g : \mathbb{R}^3 \to \mathbb{R}^3$ which maps each point to an acceleration vector.

We especially emphasize this representation of spatial information through field functions, because the modeling decision (or needs) of representing those functions in an explicit way or not, leads to specific constraints regarding the implementation of the environment.

3   Four Fundamental Patterns

We intend to show that a limited number of implementation families can be identified for MABS environments, depending on the nature of the metric space (E, d), and on the choice of reifying (or not) $cont_t$. Our point here is not to aim at a normative approach, nor at a comprehensive listing of cases, but rather at describing recurrent typical usages and their distinctive features. We introduce below the four fundamental *patterns* we have identified, with their principles, advantages and drawbacks. We show how to handle efficiently the search for neighbors and the motion of agents, i.e. how to actually compute the values of the functions ν_t^r and pos_{t+1} for each agent (resp. neighbors(a,r) and move_to(a,p)). Finally, we indicate when each pattern is best suited.

3.1   The "AgentSet" Pattern

Principle. Each agent is endowed with an attribute pos containing $pos_t(a)$. The environment is reduced to a set of agents ($\mathcal{A}_t$) and the distance function d.

Algorithm 1. Calculation of the neighbors of an agent (AgentSet pattern)

---

neighbors(a_i, r):
N ← ∅
for $a_j \in \mathcal{A}_t, a_j \neq a_i$ do
$\quad$ if $d(pos_t(a_i), pos_t(a_j)) \leq r$ then
$\quad\quad$ N ← N ∪ $\{a_j\}$
$\quad$ end
end
return N

Advantages and Drawbacks. Only the function pos_t is explicitly reified. Conversely, the computational complexity of neighbor perception in the simulation is in $\mathcal{O}(n^2)$, where $n = |\mathcal{A}_t|$. Indeed, each agent has to check its distance to the $(n-1)$ other agents (algorithm 1). However, when an agent moves, it only has to modify its pos attribute as follows: move_to(a_i, p) : $pos_{t+1}(a_i) \leftarrow p$.

Usages. The AgentSet pattern proves convenient for implementing plain environments containing a *small number of agents*, otherwise finding the neighbors is costly. It is also suited for fields given in intension, since the corresponding functions have just to be implemented together with the set of agents and the distance function.

3.2   The "StandardGrid" Pattern

Principle. In many models, the environment to build is a discrete space organized as a geometric *lattice*, indexable by a system of discrete coordinates of dimension k (such as $E = \mathbb{Z}^k$). The discrete positions can also be seen as "cells".

To implementation such environments, the structure of the latter pattern is endowed with a *grid*, i.e. a tessellation of the environment, through a k-dimension array containing sets of agents. This explicit reification of function $cont_t$ provides a direct access to all agents situated on any point (or "cell") p. Besides, all points adjacent to p are retrieved easily, either by their coordinates or by cross-references between cells: hence, an immediate calculation of the neighbor points of p (neighborhood in algorithm 2).

Algorithm 2. Neighbors calculation (StandardGrid pattern)

neighbors(a_i, r):
N $\leftarrow \emptyset$
neighborhood $\leftarrow \{p \in E \mid d(pos_t(a_i), p) \leq r\}$
for $c \in$ neighborhood do
| N $\leftarrow$ N $\cup$ $cont_t(c)$
end
return N$\setminus\{a_i\}$

Algorithm 3. Movement of an agent (StandardGrid pattern)

move_to(a_i, p):
if $pos_t(a_i) \neq p$ then
| $cont_{t+1}(pos_t(a_i)) \leftarrow$
| $cont_t(pos_t(a_i)) \setminus \{a_i\}$
| $cont_{t+1}(p) \leftarrow cont_t(p) \cup \{a_i\}$
end
$pos_{t+1}(a_i) \leftarrow p$

Advantages and Drawbacks. Direct access to all agents on a point provides a considerable speed-up of neighbors search, since they are necessarily on the same cell as a_i or on adjacent cells. Finding the neighbors of n agents within a radius of r (algorithm 2), has a cost in $\mathcal{O}(n.r^k)$ (e.g., with a Moore neighborhood and $k = 2$, neighbors are in a square of $(2r + 1)^2$ cells). Conversely, moving an agent requires more complicated updates than in the previous pattern, in order to ensure consistency between pos_{t+1} and $cont_{t+1}$ (algorithm 3).

Usages. This pattern fits environments based on *integer coordinates*, especially if the average perception radius $\bar{r}$ of the agents (within which they search their neighbors) fulfils $\bar{r}^k \ll n$. It is also well suited to *represent field functions* even when given in extension (yet, assuming that those fields are defined on discrete coordinates): the values of the field on each point are held by a k-dimension array as well. This pattern also handles obstacles easily, when represented either by agents (which prevent the access to their cell), or by fields, or by the distance function (topology of the cells). Noteworthy, this grid-based approach is obviously *not limited to square tessellations*; many simulations e.g. in geography use hexagons [16], which also constitute a lattice of $\mathbb{R}^2$. We can also mention a very frequent *simplification* of this pattern: when the model assumes that two agents cannot occupy the same position, then the grid is simply a k-dimension array of agents (instead of a set of agents).

3.3   The "AggregateGrid" Pattern

Principle. The previous pattern cannot be used when the environment is based on a continuous space, because of the practical impossibility to provide exhaustive adjacency relations. Yet, if the function $cont_t$ cannot be reified as such, a discrete approximation can be build by *"projecting" the continuous positions in E on a discrete space* $\mathbb{E} \subset E$. Therefore, a discretization of E, depending on a mesh size m, must be defined: $cell_m : E \to \mathbb{E}$. In other words we need: $\forall c \in \mathbb{E}, \exists c' \in \mathbb{E}, c' \neq c$ such that $d(c, c') \leq m$. For instance, taking $E = \mathbb{R}^2$, it is quite natural to choose $\mathbb{E} = \mathbb{Z}^2$; then a simple discretization function would be: $\forall (x, y) \in \mathbb{R}^2, cell^m(x, y) = (\lfloor \frac{x}{m} \rfloor, \lfloor \frac{y}{m} \rfloor)$ (where $\lfloor u \rfloor$ denotes the floor of u). An "aggregate" form of the function $cont_t$ can then be defined, so as to calculate the set of all agents situated in a "cell" c: $\forall c \in \mathbb{E}, cell\_cont_t^m(c) = \{a \in \mathcal{A}_t \mid cell^m(pos_t(a)) = c\}$.

Now, the function $cell\_cont_t^m$ can be reified exactly like in the previous pattern, through a k-dimension array `cell_cont` which contains sets of agents (the set of all agents situated in cell $cell_m(p)$).

Algorithm 4. Neighbors calculation (**AggregateGrid** pattern)	**Algorithm 5.** Movement of an agent (**AggregateGrid** pattern)

`neighbors`(a_i, r):
$\text{N} \leftarrow \emptyset$
$c_0 \leftarrow cell^m(pos_t(a_i))$
`neighborhood` $\leftarrow \{p \in \mathbb{E} \mid d(c_0, p) \leq \lceil \frac{r}{m} \rceil\}$
for $c \in$ `neighborhood` **do**
    for $a_j \in cell\_cont_t^m(c), a_j \neq a_i$ **do**
        if $d(a_i, a_j) \leq r$ **then**
            $\text{N} \leftarrow \text{N} \cup \{a_j\}$
        end
    end
end
return N
	`move_to`(a_i, p):
	if $cell^m(pos_t(a_i)) \neq cell^m(p)$ **then**
	    $cont\_cell_{t+1}(pos_t(a_i)) \leftarrow$
	    $cont\_cell_t(pos_t(a_i)) \setminus \{a_i\}$
	    $cont\_cell_{t+1}(p) \leftarrow$
	    $cont\_cell_t(p) \cup \{a_i\}$
	end
	$pos_{t+1}(a_i) \leftarrow p$

Advantages and Drawbacks. Due to the discretization of the continuous space, this pattern benefits from the computational speed-up of a grid structure (cf. algorithm 4). At the same time, the arbitrary size of the mesh m allows a fine tuning of this discretization if needed: the computational cost of neighbors detection for n agents, within a radius of r, is in $\mathcal{O}(n.(\lceil \frac{r}{m} \rceil)^k.q)$ (where $\lceil u \rceil$ denotes the ceiling of u and q the *density* of agents i.e. the average number of agents in each cell). Again, the counterpart is a more complicated technique for updating the content of cells when agents move (cf. algorithm 5).

Usages. This pattern is relevant for modeling continuous environments containing a large number of agents. It can be also useful for implementing a *discrete* environment where the "natural" mesh size of 1 would be quite inefficient (i.e. when $\bar{r} \gg 1$). Like in the **StandardGrid** pattern, the representation of fields is quite straightforward, provided that the mesh size m leads to a realistic approximation w.r.t. the spatial scale of the field. This approach can be extended to other tessellation methods (e.g. hexagons in the plane), including partition methods suited for heterogeneous spatial distribution of agents (e.g. Voronoi, quadtrees, etc.): the key principle is that each cell must have direct access to adjacent cells.

3.4   The "SocialNet" Pattern

Principle. Each agent owns an attribute `acquaintances` which contains the set of all agents it *knows* and can interact with. Then pos_t is bijective, i.e. the key issue is not knowing the places where the agents are situated, but rather the accessibility relations between places. Here, the *topology* of the environment comes first, because acquaintances relations are equivalent to the adjacency matrix of a graph (possibly directed if some acquaintances are not reciprocal): $\forall i, j, e_{ij} = 1$ if $a_j \in$ acquaintances$_t(a_i)$, 0 otherwise.

Thus, two very different situations may occur. If agents are allowed to interact *with their own acquaintances only*, the `neighbors`(a_i, r) function is defined only for $r = 1$, and trivially returns the `acquaintances` attribute. The environment can be considered "virtual" (or "purely communicating" [1]), being distributed through the acquaintances lists. On the contrary, if agents are allowed to interact *within a wider range*, then the cost of the corresponding breadth-first search of "neighbors" within a radius of r, is in $\mathcal{O}(\bar{q}^r)$ (with $\bar{q}$ the average size of acquaintances lists). Instead, the distance function can be reified through a distance matrix (δ_{ij}) where $\forall i, j \ \delta_{ij} = d(pos_t(a_i), pos_t(a_j))$. It gives the shortest paths in the graph (computed using e.g. the Floyd-Warshall algorithm [17]). Then, the determination of the neighbors follows the same method as in the `AgentSet` pattern (algorithm 1).

Advantages and Drawbacks. The trivial case is quite simple to implement. In the second situation, using a distance matrix provides the ability for any agent to interact with neighbors within an arbitrary radius. Yet, if changes occur in the acquaintances relations, this matrix has to be updated by recomputing the shortest paths, which is in $\mathcal{O}(n^3)$ in the Floyd-Warshall algorithm.

Usages. This pattern is naturally suited to "social" environments though it actually only assumes *topological* hypotheses regarding the accessibility relations between agents, regarded as nodes of a graph. Obviously, the approach can be extended with few transformations in situations where acquaintances are associated with *weights*.

4   Combining Patterns

The pattern-based approach to environments we defend here, is rather a continuation of the method sketched in [9], than an attempt to build a unique, complex, monolithic first-class abstraction which is able to deal with all concerns at the same time as proposed in [18]. Without prejudging the interest of such integrated models for the analysis, design or implementation of MAS, we prefer to follow an orthogonal approach which ensures on the contrary a clear separation of concerns (in the same sense as in software engineering). Therefore we argue that it is more advisable to *combine several of those fundamental patterns*.

For instance, in a case where simulated robots have to explore a building, they are indeed situated in a continuous environment where they find obstacles (other entities), and at the same time may exchange information with their peers (the network of their acquaintances). Thus, "the" environment is actually a combination between the "AggregateGrid" and the "SocialNet" patterns. The neighbors of a robot is composed of, on the one hand, the entities perceived in the 3D surrounding space, and on the other hand, other robots that can be reached through radio communications.

Noteworthy, a multi-agent based simulation platform like NetLogo [19] actually provides an implementation for each of the patterns we propose, although not explicitly identified as such. The "AgentSet" is a native data type in the NetLogo language, which contains the collection of all agents of a kind. The "StandardGrid" pattern is a built-in feature due to the existence of NetLogo *patches*, which are 1×1 square cells discretizing the environment. The "AggregateGrid" pattern is realized by the fact that each NetLogo "turtle", which is endowed with floating-point coordinates, is located on a single patch (hence patches implement the two patterns simultaneously). The "SocialNet" pattern is provided by the ability to build *links* between turtles (and use them to detect "link-neighbors"). Besides, those NetLogo concepts do not imply any special use either as physical or social features, and are meant to be used together for implementing the various needs of a simulation model.

Thus, we note that our pattern-based approach leads to a unification of concepts of physical and social environments, that are usually kept distinct. Besides, it also pushes the designer to decompose "the" environment of the MAS, which is usually seen as a rather complex whole, into as many atomic environments as needed, each one with a univocal purpose and implementation.

5 Conclusion and Perspectives

In this paper, we assume two main purposes for an "atomic environment": the spatial or social placement of agents, and the provision of information that cannot be represented by agents at the chosen modeling scale. Thus, an atomic environment is defined primarily as a *space*, endowed with a distance measure, with positioning and content functions, and aimed at finding agents and neighbors of agents: those features lead to a limited number of *design patterns*. The four patterns presented here seem to cover a wide range of applications in agent-based simulation.Besides, instead of modeling a single, complex environment in a MAS, we recommend to rather combine several patterns with a clear separation of concerns and purposes.

References

1. Ferber, J.: Multi-Agent Systems. An Introduction to Distributed Artificial Intelligence. Addison Wesley (1999)

2. Russell, S., Norvig, P.: Artificial Intelligence. Prentice Hall (1995)
3. Okuyama, F.Y., Bordini, R.H., da Rocha Costa, A.C.: ELMS: an environment description language for multi-agent simulation. In: Weyns, D., Van Dyke Parunak, H., Michel, F. (eds.) E4MAS 2004. LNCS (LNAI), vol. 3374, pp. 91–108. Springer, Heidelberg (2005)
4. Weyns, D., Van Dyke Parunak, H., Michel, F., Holvoet, T., Ferber, J.: Environments for multiagent systems state-of-the-art and research challenges. In: Weyns, D., Van Dyke Parunak, H., Michel, F. (eds.) E4MAS 2004. LNCS (LNAI), vol. 3374, pp. 1–47. Springer, Heidelberg (2005)
5. Ricci, A., Viroli, M., Omicini, A.: CArtAgO: a framework for prototyping artifact-based environments in MAS. In: Weyns, D., Van Dyke Parunak, H., Michel, F. (eds.) E4MAS 2006. LNCS (LNAI), vol. 4389, pp. 67–86. Springer, Heidelberg (2007)
6. Behrens, T.M., Hindriks, K.V., Dix, J.: Towards an environment interface standard for agent platforms. Ann. Math. Artif. Intell. **61**(4), 261–295 (2011)
7. Helleboogh, A., Vizzari, G., Uhrmacher, A., Michel, F.: Modeling dynamic environments in multi-agent simulation. J. Auton. Agents and Multi-Agent Systems (JAAMAS) **14**(1), 87–116 (2007)
8. Weyns, D., Holvoet, T.: A reference architecture for situated multiagent systems. In: Weyns, D., Van Dyke Parunak, H., Michel, F. (eds.) E4MAS 2006. LNCS (LNAI), vol. 4389, pp. 1–40. Springer, Heidelberg (2007)
9. Schelfthout, K., Coninx, T., Helleboogh, A., Holvoet, T., Steegmans, E., Steegmans, E., Weyns, D.: Agent implementation patterns. In: Workshop on Agent-Oriented Methodologies, 17th Annual ACM Conf. on Object-Oriented Programming, Systems, Languages, and Applications (OOPSLA), pp. 119–130 (2002)
10. Gamma, E., Helm, R., Johnson, R., Vlissides, J.: Design Patterns, Elements of Reusable Object-Oriented Software. Addison Wesley (1994)
11. Kubera, Y., Mathieu, P., Picault, S.: Everything can be agent! In: 9th Int. Joint Conf. on Auton. Agents and Multi-Agent Systems (AAMAS), pp. 1547–1548 (2010)
12. Picault, S., Mathieu, P.: An interaction-oriented model for multi-scale simulation. In: 22nd Int. Joint Conf. on Artificial Intelligence (IJCAI), pp. 332–337. AAAI (2011)
13. Latombe, J.C.: Robot Motion Planning. Kluwer Academic Publishers (1991)
14. Van Dyke Parunak, H.: Between agents and mean fields. In: Villatoro, D., Sabater-Mir, J., Sichman, J.S. (eds.) MABS 2011. LNCS, vol. 7124, pp. 113–126. Springer, Heidelberg (2012)
15. Colorni, A., Dorigo, M., Maniezzo, V.: Distributed optimization by ant colonies. In: 1st European Conf. on Artifical Life (ECAL), pp. 134–142. Elsevier (1991)
16. Sanders, L., Pumain, D., Mathian, H., Guérin-Pace, F., Bura, S.: SIMPOP: a multi-agents system for the study of urbanism. Environment and Planning B **24**, 287–305 (1997)
17. Floyd, R.: Algorithm 97: shortest path. Communications of the ACM **5**(6), 345 (1962)
18. Weyns, D., Omicini, A., Odell, J.: Environment as a first class abstraction in multiagent systems. J. Auton. Agents and Multi-Agent Systems (JAAMAS) **14**(1), 5–30 (2007)
19. Wilensky, U.: Netlogo. Center for Connected Learning and Computer-Based Modeling, Northwestern University, Evanston, IL (1999). http://ccl.northwestern.edu/netlogo/

Commitments, Expectations, Affordances and Susceptibilities: Towards Positional Agent Programming

Giovanni Sileno[✉], Alexander Boer, and Tom van Engers

Leibniz Center for Law, University of Amsterdam, Amsterdam, The Netherlands
{g.sileno,aboer,vanengers}@uva.nl

Abstract. The paper introduces an agent architecture centered around the notions of commitment, expectation, affordance, and susceptibility. These components are to a certain measure at the base of any agent system, however, inspired by research in explanation-based decision making, this contribution attempts to make explicit and start organizing under the same operationalization neglected figures as negative commitment, negative expectation, etc.

Keywords: Cognitive architectures · Positional programming · PACK · Reactive systems · Petri nets

1 Introduction

As the myth tells, even if he knew that all sailors who had done it went lost into the open sea, Ulysses wanted to hear the voices of the Sirens. To achieve this goal, the sail direction set, he put some wax in his companions' ears and asked them to bind him to the mainmast with the strongest rope. He also ordered not to follow any of his requests before destination. Eventually, he succeeded, and we, listening to his story, can understand why. However, are we able to fully represent it with current agent-based languages? The story refers to notions as *conditional persistent commitment* (Ulysses desiring to jump off towards the Sirens, and insisting on trying it even if bound to the mainmast), *positive expectation* (about the fact that the sirens were along that specific path), which find some correspondence in most common BDI representations. However, in modeling those characters, we may easily identify other notions at stake, as e.g. *negative affordance* (associated with the overall plan *preventing* Sirens' effect), *disability* (Ulysses bound to the mast), *negative susceptibility* (the sailors to Ulysses' requests) and *no-susceptibility* (the sailors to Sirens' voices). The purpose of the present work is to identify and consider these "neglected" *positions* as first-class citzens, and to start operationalizing them in practical reasoning terms.

1.1 Background and Motivation

The initial idea behind this contribution grew out from our work in institutional modeling (see e.g. [1]). In a formal institution, each actor is bound to other

© Springer International Publishing Switzerland 2015
Q. Chen et al. (Eds.): PRIMA 2015, LNAI 9387, pp. 687–696, 2015.
DOI: 10.1007/978-3-319-25524-8_52

actors according to the legal relationships derived from the role he is enacting. Hohfeld [2], for instance, identified positions as *duty, claim, power* and *liability* as the fundamental components to describe the legal configurations holding between two parties.[1] Being our general objective to model complex institutional scenarios, including scenarios of non-compliance, the composition of mere institutional roles is however not satisfactory (e.g. a seem-to-be normal sale may hide a money-laundering scheme). Roles need to be enriched with an explicit intentional component, or, in other words, with an explicit link between *motives* and institutional aspects. This requirement brought us to the exploration of the *agent-role* concept [3].

Reflecting on the interactions between the institutional and agent components, we discovered deeper underlying connections between the two domains: *where institutional positions identify extrinsic commitments and abilities, agentic positions identify intrinsic commitments and abilities.*[2] In practice, the *correlativeness* of the institutional positions of two parties can be put in analogy to the correlativeness between agent and environment. This epistemological leap allowed us to explore figures that are usually overlooked in agent modeling, but which are important in the legal domain. For instance, *negative action* – in the two forms of lack of action or actively preventing another outcome – is equally relevant to attribute responsibility [4].

To confirm this representational need, we attempted to review other agent languages/platforms considering the categories we will introduce in the paper. Except Jason [6], built upon AgentSpeak(L) [7], those considered (2APL [8], GOAL [9], ALP [10] and DALI [11]) refer only to default negation and introduce some form of declarative goals. Losing the difference between *null* and *negative* polarity, all negative positions we will introduce conflate. On the other hand, without declarative goals, modeling mutual interactions between goals is much more complex. Even if these and other representational limits may be overcome with adequate extensions, our idea is to approach the issue from an alternative direction: to start from stronger representational requirements, and to construct the reasoning platform on top of those. Rather than rational choice theory, the foundations of our contribution are to be found in cognitive research as e.g. [5], focusing on *explanation-based* decision making.

The paper proceeds as follows. First, we define the foundations of the modeling language, i.e. the notion of position and the two types of negation (§ 2). Second, we analyze in some detail the position types (§ 3). Third, we briefly draft their operationalization in a practical reasoning framework (§ 4). Discussion and future developments end the paper.

---

[1] These relations bring specific inter-dependencies: e.g. if a party has a duty to perform a certain action, then there is another party that has a claim towards the first. At the same time, if a party is in a certain position (e.g. duty to A), this precludes the same party to be in another position (e.g. no-duty to A).

[2] Extrinsic means that it is the result of social, normative forces, external to the agency: the agent cannot change such position, even if he may still neglect or overlook it. Intrinsic means that the agent has in principle control over it.

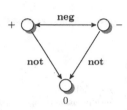

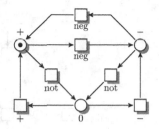

(a) *positive*, *negative*, *null* positions and *negation* operators.

(b) positional triple as a Petri net.

Fig. 1. Triangle of contrariety and relative Petri net model.

2   Modeling Language: Positions and Negations

The proposed modeling language is centered around the notion of *position*. In general, a position is a local state of the system that can be related to other positions in dimensional terms. For instance, in a classic logic system, each proposition can be put in relation with its negation. In this framework, however, we consider the dimensional characterization associated to the *triangle of contrariety*.[3] In addition to positive $(+)$ and negative $(-)$ polarities, we consider a *null* (0) polarity. For instance, black is certainly *not* white, but e.g. gray is *not* white as well. Similarly, prohibition is the *opposite* of obligation, but they are both *not* the same as faculty. Different operators can then be considered for those negations: **neg** and **not**, illustrated in Fig. 1a. The first corresponds to classic negation (or *strong negation*), relying on the duality/opposition of two notions (e.g. black/white, obligation/prohibition). The second operator removes the polarity; the null position states a certain qualification cannot be concluded neither positively, nor negatively. In other words, restricting ourselves to the terms proposed by that bipolar frame, *undecidability* holds. To a certain extent, this can be associated to *default negation*.

Using this pattern, given any position, we can construct a triple of positions. Only one of the three may hold at a certain time. The three symbols $+$, $-$, 0, can be interpreted both in *state* and *transition* terms: i.e. as identifying a certain local state of this positional triple, or as identifying the event bringing about that state. Exploiting this two-fold interpretation, and the focus on local states, we ground our language to the computational model given by the Petri net notation, as in Fig. 1b (see e.g. [14] for an introduction to Petri nets).

3   Cognitive Components

3.1   Commitment

Commitment identifies a general motivational component, i.e. an internal cognitive mechanism which eventually converges or plays a role in driving towards

---

[3] The triangle of contrariety (with nodes A, E, Y) can be derived from the Aristotelian square (A, E, O, I), with $Y = O \wedge I$, see e.g. [12,13]. In relation to Hohfeld, see [1].

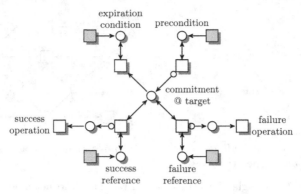

Fig. 2. Operational structure of commitment

action or action avoidance. Following the triangle of contrariety, commitment can be declined into the positions of *positive commitment, negative commitment* and *no-commitment*.

Positive Commitment. A positive commitment position can be specified via the elements illustrated in Fig. 2.[4]

The *target* identifies what the agent is committed to. The *precondition* represents the situation in which the commitment is instantiated. If the precondition is present, the resulting element is a *conditional commitment*, as in 'If I listen to the Sirens' voice, I want to follow them'. The *success reference* corresponds to the specification on how to recognize its satisfaction (usually a proxy of the target). The *success operation* describes what to perform after the commitment is recognized as satisfied. The *failure reference/operation* identify how to recognize/what to do when the commitment fails. These may be used to instantiate *backup* commitments. The *expiration condition* expresses situations that remove the commitment, independent from the ones defined in success or failure.

The structure allows to distinguish easily *achievement goals* from *maintenance goals*, depending on the presence in success operation of the removal the commitment (cf. [15]). Similarly, a commitment is called *non-persistent* instead of *persistent* if it nullifies itself after that the failure is recognized (cf. [16] for analogous institutional notions). For instance, Ulysses' intent to reach the sirens is persistent, as he continues to strive even when he acknowledges of not being able to be freed from the rope.

Negative Commitment. A negative commitment reflects a negative position of the agent towards a reference. In practice, the agent is committed to *avoid* the situation expressed in the target. The structure is the same as the previous one, apart that the recognition of the target situation (what the agent does *not* want) is encoded in the *failure* field this time. On the other hand, the *success* field reference is a situation in which this "negative" desire has been respected.

---

[4] The gray transitions are not part of this module, but highlight that *this structure is operational only if some mechanism evaluates the associated expressions.*

The positive and negative specifications of commitment offer two different frames to the modeler. For instance, in 'I want to listen to the sirens before we arrive at destination', reaching the destination can be interpreted as an event making explicit the failure of the commitment. If we consider a rephrasing the previous statement 'I do not want to arrive at destination before listening to the sirens', the success and failure fields are the same of the previous case. As a human reader, however, we recognize that the two phrases transport a different *pragmatic* meaning. The first case is clearly a matter of direct planning; in the second, there is an implicit reference to something that is blocking the path towards the desired outcome. See § 4.1.

No Commitment. A no commitment position corresponds to the absence of commitment towards the reference. Consequently, there are no failures, no successes to be accounted.

3.2 Expectation

If commitments are essential for the definition of the *subject*, expectations reflect the *situatedness* of the subject in the world. What the agent expects from the world is what he believes the world is, *actually* and *potentially*.

Positive Expectation. The structure of expectation is the same as that of commitment, and, therefore, a similar analysis of the components applies. If there is no precondition, the expectation is a *belief* about what is currently holding. The target defines the propositional content of the belief. The precondition specifies how the expectation can be formed. The success/failure referents are used to specify the means to verify/defeat the expectation, and they are usually built upon primitive perceptions or on other expectations. Differently, the expiration condition can be used to put a limit to such expectations, e.g. 'after the rain, the wind flows for a couple of hours'.

Negative Expectation. A negative expectation specifies what the agent thinks it is not the case or impossible. For instance 'Sirens do not exist'. It can be used to include constraints in the knowledge base of the agent.

No Expectation. This position states that the agent has not constructed any belief about the matter: it is an *agnostic* position. For instance, 'I do not know whether sirens exist', or 'I don't know whether people follow the sirens when they hear their voice'.

3.3 Affordance

In its traditional form, an *affordance* reifies the possibility of the agent to adopt a certain behaviour in certain conditions to achieve a certain result [17]. Affordances interact with commitments to define which behaviour the agent will perform.

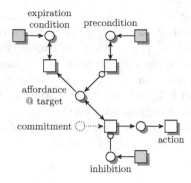

Fig. 3. Operational structure of affordance.

Positive Affordance. The structure to specify affordances is illustrated in Fig. 3. Its components can be compared to those of action languages: the precondition is basically a *pre* element, while the target identifies what the agent would achieve with that action, a subset of a traditional *post* element. Precondition and expiration elements are like in the previous structures. The *action* element corresponds to a plan of actions. The *inhibition* field identifies a situation in which the affordance, although available, cannot be used. This can be exploited to solve conflicts raised at motivational level. See § 4.1.

Negative Affordance. Negative affordance, or negative power, reflects on the ability of the agent to adopt a certain plan to *prevent* to reach a certain state of affairs. For instance, Ulysses perceives that his plan provides him with a negative affordance about falling for the sirens. In principle, the situation expressed by the target represents what is going to occur if the action is not performed.

Disability. The absence of any type of association between the behaviour of the agent to a certain target corresponds to *disability*. In general, given a certain action, infinite disabilities can be expressed (all of that cannot be achieved via that action). This would be redundant and uninteresting information to be maintained. When disability is expressed explicitly, usually it is because it settles domain limitations to an existing ability.

3.4   Susceptibility

The positional triple correlative to affordance is susceptibility. The agent is susceptible to a certain event if he has some reaction to its occurrence, at least at epistemic level.

Positive Susceptibility. Positive susceptibility describes the attention of the agent around a potential situation, identified by the target, whose occurrence is associated to a certain *reaction*. The structure is similar to that of affordance, apart from the renaming of action with reaction. Interestingly, all conditional positions can be transformed using susceptibility. A more general mechanism is then unveiled: all situations accounted in the structures have to be aligned with adequate susceptibilities. See § 4.2.

Negative Susceptibility. At the opposite polarity, we find negative susceptibility. If the stimulus described by the *target* occurs, then the agent generates a negative commitment towards what is specified in the reaction field. The sailors on Ulysses' boat receives orders from their captain to untie him. While usually they would have followed those, now they avoid doing what he asks.

No Susceptibility. The absence of susceptibility is *unresponsiveness* or no susceptibility. For instance, because of the wax in the ears, sailors are unresponsive to the voice of the Sirens. As with no-affordance, this serves to define the boundaries of an existing domain of susceptibility.

4   Operationalization

4.1   From Commitment to Action

To operationalize the connection between commitment and action, we relate these four cognitive components using the *prevent-acquire-cure-keep* (PACK) psychological framework [18]: the presence/absence of a positive/negative condition guides the agent to select a certain behaviour, in order to promote/demote such condition. This can be translated with the following rules:

Acquire (A). If you have a commitment towards a certain target, not holding at the moment, and an associated affordance is available, then use it.

Keep (K). If you have a commitment towards a certain target, which is holding at the moment, and you have a negative affordance associated with its negation, then use it. Furthermore, if there are available affordances that may produce this outcome as expected side-effect, inhibit them.[5]

Prevent (P). If you have a negative commitment towards a certain target, which is not holding at the moment, and you have a negative affordance towards it, then use such affordance. Similarly to the *keep* case, we also have to consider to inhibit affordances with undesired side-effects.

Cure (C). If you have a negative commitment towards a certain target, which is holding at the moment, and you have the affordance associated with its negation, then use such affordance.

Current agent platforms focus mostly on the first reasoning pattern. Integrating the others, however, we are able to explain the pragmatic difference between the two rephrasing of commitment given in § 3.1. The positive characterization triggers a mechanism A targeting the goal; the negative one a mechanism P in order to avoid not to bring about the goal. The two frames activate and interact with different distributions of affordances and expectations.

---

[5] This solution is simplistic: mutually excluding commitments would inhibit both affordances. A natural correction would be to introduce priorities between commitments.

4.2 From Commitment to Monitoring

Not all what the agent may perceive or infer from his knowledge is *relevant* to his commitments. The relevance relation can be extracted from the commitment specifications, considering two directions: *forward*, i.e. identifying potential situations enabling changes, because of preconditions, expiration conditions related to current positions and potential positions addressed by the PACK; *backward*, i.e. circumscribing success and failure references, necessary to readdress the current configuration. Both forward and backward components are required for the viability of the system. The first allows to respond adequately to changes in the environment. The second provides the means for steering, enabling repair, and for reifying errors in expectations, useful for adaptation purposes.

Identifying the primitive expectations relevant to a certain commitment configuration is however not sufficient. Expectations may for instance expire, the agent still requiring such knowledge. Agents have typically to start a specific course of action to retrieve missing information. This evidence-oriented focus is particularly relevant for our intended institutional applications (see § 1.1).

5 Discussion and Further Developments

The paper traces an outline of an agent architecture based on commitments, expectations, affordances, and susceptibilities, distinguished in positive, negative and null positions. For reasons of space, it overlooks technical details, preferring to give a wide overview of the system. A preliminary proof-of-concept of the architecture is being developed at the moment, and we are evaluating further elements (for instance, the suspension of commitments, cf. [19]).

Our aim is to fill a representational gap experienced while modeling complex institutional scenarios with current agent-based platforms. Such models are intended to be used for simulation, and for model-based diagnosis or similar abductive processes. Interestingly, the resulting architecture may be used as well to model characters in narratives, as the proposed Ulysses' story.

The agents we target are *non-reflective*: they cannot modify their own scripts. However, contrary to what the Petri net notation may suggest, they may show proactivity, as a consequence of maintenance goals.

Another important issue we are confronted with is of a computational nature. Kowalski et al. have convincingly argued that there are widespread confusions about the different natures of production and declarative rules [20], which we think can be aligned with some of the problems observable in e.g. deontic logic with contrary-to-duty obligations, in analytic philosophy with dispositions, etc. Our hypothesis is that, focusing on a computational model like Petri nets, constructed upon the notion of causation (and therefore, on local states), we are able to put aside the problem, still exploiting the advantage of formal grounding.

In the past, other authors worked already on connecting agents with Petri nets [21–23], especially for model checking reasons, but the models they proposed do not primarily focus on agent cognition. This work essentially aims to start filling this gap.

References

1. Sileno, G., Boer, A., van Engers, T.: On the interactional meaning of fundamental legal concepts. In: Proc. Int. Conf. Legal Knowledge and Information Systems - JURIX 2014, pp. 39–48 (2014)
2. Hohfeld, W.N.: Fundamental legal conceptions as applied in judicial reasoning. The Yale Law Journal 26(8), 710–770 (1917)
3. Boer, A., van Engers, T.: An agent-based legal knowledge acquisition methodology for agile public administration. In: Proc. Int. Conf. on Artificial Intelligence and Law - ICAIL 2011, pp. 171–180 (2011)
4. Lehmann, J., Breuker, J.A., Brouwer, P.W.: Causation in AI & Law. Artificial Intelligence and Law 12(4), 279–315 (2004)
5. Pennington, N., Hastie, R.: Reasoning in explanation-based decision making. Cognition 49, 123–163 (1993)
6. Bordini, R.H., Hübner, J.F., Wooldridge, M.: Programming multi-agent systems in AgentSpeak using Jason. John Wiley & Sons Ltd. (2007)
7. Rao, A.S.: AgentSpeak (L): BDI agents speak out in a logical computable language. In: Proc. Workshop on Modelling Autonomous Agents in a Multi-Agent World (1996)
8. Dastani, M.: 2APL: a practical agent programming language. Autonomous Agents and Multi-Agent Systems 16(3), 214–248 (2008)
9. Hindriks, K.V.: Programming rational agents in GOAL. In: Multi-agent Programming: Languages, Platforms and Applications, pp. 119–157 (2009)
10. Kowalski, R., Sadri, F.: From Logic Programming towards Multi-agent systems. Annals of Mathematics and Artificial Intelligence 25, 391–419 (1999)
11. Costantini, S., Tocchio, A.: DALI: An Architecture for Intelligent Logical Agents. In: Proc. Workshop on Architectures for Intelligent Theory-Based Agents (AITA) (2008)
12. Blanché, R.: Sur l'opposition des concepts. Theoria 19(3), 89–130 (1953)
13. Béziau, J.Y.: The Power of the Hexagon. Logica Universalis 6(1–2), 1–43 (2012)
14. Bobbio, A.: System modelling with Petri nets. In: Systems Reliability Assessment, pp. 102–143 (1990)
15. Hindriks, K.V., van Riemsdijk, M.B.: Satisfying maintenance goals. In: Baldoni, M., Son, T.C., van Riemsdijk, M.B., Winikoff, M. (eds.) DALT 2007. LNCS (LNAI), vol. 4897, pp. 86–103. Springer, Heidelberg (2008)
16. Governatori, G., Rotolo, A.: Norm compliance in business process modeling. In: Dean, M., Hall, J., Rotolo, A., Tabet, S. (eds.) RuleML 2010. LNCS, vol. 6403, pp. 194–209. Springer, Heidelberg (2010)
17. Gibson, J.: The ecological approach to visual perception. Houghton Mifflin, Boston (1979)
18. Ogilvie, D.M., Rose, K.M.: Self-with-other representations and a taxonomy of motives: two approaches to studying persons. Journal of Personality 63(3), 643–679 (1995)
19. Meneguzzi, F., Telang, P., Singh, M.: A first-order formalization of commitments and goals for planning. In: Proc. 27th AAAI Conference on Artificial Intelligence, pp. 697–703 (2013)
20. Kowalski, R., Sadri, F.: Integrating logic programming and production systems in abductive logic programming agents. In: Polleres, A., Swift, T. (eds.) RR 2009. LNCS, vol. 5837, pp. 1–23. Springer, Heidelberg (2009)

21. Behrens, T., Dix, J.: Model checking with logic based petri nets. In: Proc. of CLIMA (2007)
22. Celaya, J.R., Desrochers, A.A., Graves, R.J.: Modeling and analysis of multi-agent systems using petri nets. Journal of Computers 4(10), 981–996 (2009)
23. Purvis, M., Cranefield, S.: Agent modelling with petri nets. In: Proc. Computational Engineering in Systems Applications - CESA 1996, pp. 602–607 (1996)

Using Conceptual Spaces for Object Recognition in Multi-agent Systems

João Mario Lopes Brezolin[✉], Sandro Rama Fiorini,
Marcia de Borba Campos, and Rafael H. Bordini

Pontifical Catholic University of Rio Grande do Sul (PUCRS), Porto Alegre,
Rio Grande do Sul, Brazil
joao.brezolin@acad.pucrs.br, srfiorini@gmail.com,
{marcia.campos,rafael.bordini}@pucrs.br

Abstract. The development of a system to support the mobility of blind
or visually impaired users requires the development of an agent capable
of performing the recognition of perceived objects as well as determining their location within the physical space. Taking into account the
principle that conceptual representations can improve the object recognition process, the work presented here proposes the integration of a
conceptual-space level into the BDI agent architecture. Such integration
is developed on top of the resources of the Jason agent platform and
the CSML API for conceptual-space models. In this paper, we present a
practical example showing how to integrate conceptual representations
into the agent reasoning cycle.

Keywords: BDI architecture · Conceptual spaces · CSML API · Jason

1 Introduction

The development of a system to support the mobility of blind or visually
impaired users requires the development of an agent capable of performing the
recognition of perceived objects as well as determining their location within the
physical space. Conceptual spaces is a framework for concept representation that
allows one to represent similarity between objects and concepts [7]. It is particularly interesting for object recognition and classification. Conceptual spaces can
be thought of as geometric spaces, in which points represent objects and regions
represent concepts. The dimensions of a conceptual space denote the qualities in
which these entities can be compared. The distance metric encodes the similarity
between object/concepts. In order to improve the agent's abilities in regards to
object recognition, our work proposes the integration of a level of representation
based on conceptual spaces into the architecture of BDI agents. We extend and
use the Jason platform [3] to support the design of systems that incorporate
such conceptual inference processes into the agent reasoning cycle. In our work,
the representation of conceptual spaces is established with the aid of the Conceptual Space Markup Language (CSML). Based on the algebra proposed by

Q. Chen et al. (Eds.): PRIMA 2015, LNAI 9387, pp. 697–705, 2015.
DOI: 10.1007/978-3-319-25524-8_53

Adams and Raubal [1], CSML allows users to specify conceptual databases and manage them with the aid of a programming interface.

This paper presents the first results towards the integration of these resources and its contribution to the development of a system to support the mobility of blind or visually impaired users. First, we review the main aspects of the BDI architecture, the theory of conceptual spaces, and the role of the computational platforms used in our implementation. Next, we present a practical example, through which we detail the customisations made on the existing platforms to enable our proposed conceptual inference integration. We then draw conclusions from this study.

2   BDI Architecture, Conceptual Spaces, and Related Computational Platforms

The BDI (Beliefs, Desires, Intentions) architecture is a commonly used approach for the development of systems of rational agents situated in complex and dynamic environments [15]. Agents are active entities able to analyse and act on their environment. The BDI (Beliefs, Desires, Intentions) architecture established the basis for the development of the AgentSpeak(L) programming language.

The Jason platform for the development of multi-agent systems [3] was developed based on an extended version of the AgentSpeak language. It supports inter-agent communication through performatives based on the theory of speech acts [11]. Following on ideas from the AgentSpeak language, also in the Jason variant an agent is defined through the specification of the initial state of its belief base and its plan library. In addition to supporting the basic syntax of the language AgentSpeak, Jason has support for additional features such as the use of annotations in beliefs and plans, support to customised functions developed in Java and incorporated as internal actions, a Java class for environment specification, and the possibility of customisation of agent architectural features.

In the conceptual spaces approach, concepts are represented by regions in a multidimensional geometric space where objects are projected as points or as vectors of points [7]. Conceptual space is structured by quality dimensions that are endowed with a geometric structure and a specific metric that allows one to measure distances between objects. This mechanism enables inferences on degrees of similarity between the objects represented in the space. That is, two objects may have a high degree of similarity if the computed distance between the points which represent them is small in relation to a domain-specific threshold. Otherwise, if this threshold is exceeded, these objects may not be considered (sufficiently) similar. The decomposition of space into convex regions is determined by the existence of a cell that intersects a set of half-plans and establishes the point containing the most representative element of the region. Decomposition of space into regions provides the basis for the notions of property and concept. A *property* is represented as a convex region of a domain in a conceptual space (e.g., a region denoting the red colour), while *concepts* are represented as sets of regions in a number of domains. For example, the concept of apple is composed of regions in domains such as colour, shape, and texture, among others. An individual object is represented by a vector that indexes points in regions of the conceptual space.

Seeking to motivate the development of real applications based on the theory of conceptual spaces, Adams and Raubal [1] proposed an algebraic model for conceptual spaces. This algebra laid the foundation for the development of the CSML language, which supports the hierarchical representation of the elements composing a conceptual space according to the algebra they proposed in [2]. For example, the definition of concepts is followed by the definition of the domain regions composing it. Along with the definition of the concept ID is the definition of its prototype instance as shown in the code snippet below:

```
<csml:Concept csml:ID="#RedApple"
  csml:prototypeID="#RedApplePrototype">
  <csml:Region
    csml:ID="#RedAppleColorRegion"
    csml:domainID="#Color">
      <csml:AMatrix> ... </csml:AMatrix>
      <csml:qVector> ... </csml:qVector>
      <csml:bVector> ... </csml:bVector>
    </csml:Region>
    ...
</csml:Concept>
```

Along with the language specification, the authors developed an API to support the use of CSML files. The API provides resources to create, compare, manipulate, and validate CSML content with the aid of a reasoner. Available under GPL license, the API also allows customisation of its code to suit the need of a particular system. This API serves for the purpose of this work due to its features and the fact that integration with the Jason framework is facilitated because both software platforms were developed in the same programming language.

3   Integration of a Conceptual Space Model into the Reasoning Cycle of BDI Agents

This study is largely driven by the goal of developing a system to aid the mobility of those who are visually impaired. Orientation and mobility (O&M) skills help people who are blind or visually impaired know where they are, where they want to go (orientation), and how to get there safely and independently by walking or using some form of transportation (mobility). The identification of landmarks and obstacles are examples of information that is extracted from the environment by the individual in order to establish their spatial orientation [10]. The objects perceived in the environment are identified by their peculiar characteristics (e.g., colour, shape, size) and by their position in the physical space. Both types of information are used to help those who are visually impaired in the development of their *cognitive map*.

In our proposal, conceptual spaces sit between the symbolic belief base and the perceptual level of the agent. The conceptual inference process involves determining the appropriate conceptual representation to identify objects perceived in the environment. This process can be initiated at the subconceptual level where the *percepts* (i.e., units of sensorial representation) received by the agent are mapped into domains of the conceptual space. As a result, a vector that indexes points of regions of the conceptual space is generated, establishing a conceptual representation for an observed object, which can be associated with a symbolic belief that can in turn be manipulated by the agent. It should be also noted that the process of recognising objects is noisy, and also at times the properties observed from an object may not be sufficient to categorise it. In our current work, the agents will have to manage observations that represent concepts with partial descriptions.

In regards to the architecture of BDI agents, it can be said that the process of belief acquisition is one of the essential building blocks on which the conceptual reasoning for BDI agents can be implemented. In its default method, a Jason agent receives information from the environment then stores it in a list of percepts. The new elements of this list are then compared to the elements of the agent's belief base. If a belief is present in the percept list but is not present in the belief base, it is added to the latter. If a belief is found in the belief base but is no longer in the list of percepts, it must be removed from the agent's belief base [3]. To allow conceptual inference, it is necessary to modify this process by adding new features to it, since it is now necessary to evaluate if new perceptions received by the agent's sensorial apparatus can compose a complete conceptual description of the observed object through the conceptual space representation. Thus, it is necessary to project the data captured by the sensors of the agent onto domains of the conceptual space, with the help of the CSML API.

The customised code used to execute this task in the belief acquisition process is detailed in Algorithm 1. When a percept is received, and before it is added to the belief base, it is necessary to check whether it refers to an object property. If it does, information must be extracted to identify from which object this perception was originated (line 4). This will allow us to recover a list of the previously stored percepts that also refers to the same object (line 8). This list is created with the aid of Jason's (BeliefBase class) method getPercepts, which recovers from the agent's belief base all beliefs marked as originating from perception of the environment (line 5). The set composed of information extracted from previous and current beliefs allows the generation of a temporary CSML specification of a concept instance that can be compared to concept specifications stored in the CSML database (lines 6–10). From the percepts stored in the belief base it is possible to extract information about domains and points to which each one of these percepts refer and add it to the temporary concept instance (lines 7–10). Next, it is necessary to compare the conceptual structure of the built instance to the structure of the concepts in the CSML model. With the aid of the CSML API's reasoner, a set of candidate concepts is generated by comparing the shared domains between the temporary instance and the concepts in

Algorithm 1. Attempt to Recognise an Object through a Newly Perceived Property

```
 1: function RECOGNISE(literal l)
 2:     Elected ← null
 3:     if isObjectProperty(l) then
 4:         id ← extractID(l)
 5:         P ← getPercepts()
 6:         I ← CreateInstance()
 7:         for all p ∈ P do
 8:             I ← buildInstance(p, id)
 9:         end for
10:         I ← buildInstance(l)
11:         C ← getConcepts()
12:         N ← sharedDomains(C, I)
13:         Elected ← ClosestConcept(I, N)
14:         if (distance(Elected, I) > threshold) then
15:             Elected ← null
16:         end if
17:         if (Elected) then
18:             for all p ∈ P do
19:                 removeBel(p, id)
20:             end for
21:             cl ← createLiteral(Elected(id))
22:             cl ← AddAnnot(TPercept, csmlDB, csmlIns(I))
23:         end if
24:     end if
25:     if (Elected) then
26:         return(cl)                                    ▷ object was recognised as cl
27:     else
28:         return(l)                                     ▷ no recognition was possible
29:     end if
30: end function
```

the CSML specification (line 12). If this set is non-empty, the distances between the projected points of the temporary instance and the prototypes of each concept in that set are computed and the concept with the smallest distance is selected (line 13). The value computed for the distance between the elected concept and the temporary instance is compared to a predefined domain-threshold. If the value is above such threshold, the chosen concept receives a null value (lines 14–16). Otherwise, the respective concept is chosen to represent the perceived object. All previous beliefs about proprieties of the object used to classify it can then be removed from the agent's belief base because they will be replaced by the concept representation just chosen (lines 18–20). A new belief that represents the object as a concept instance is then generated (line 21). For example, if the elected concept was "apple", the new belief will state that an instance of this concept were found in the environment (e.g., `apple(obj2)`, where `obj2` is the object ID). It is important to preserve the (meta) information that this new belief was originated from perception of the environment. This will aid in future interactions of the agent because it will be able to retrieve information about this object from the list of perceptual beliefs. It is also important to associate information about the conceptual space model and the instance that originated this object/concept belief (line 22). This will help the agent in recovering the object properties in future interaction processes if necessary. Last, it is checked whether the current or the generated belief should be returned to be (re)included in the belief base (lines 25–29). If the selection of a representative concept was not possible, then the object property itself is returned to be, as usual, added to the agent's belief base as any other (perceptual) belief referring to a property of that (so far) unrecognised object.

Besides the object classifications, the conceptual level can also be useful to retrieve information about objects that were already recorded in the CSML Database. One intuitive way to do this is by using a Jason internal action as described in Algorithm 2.

Algorithm 2. getCSMLObject Internal Action

1: **function** GETCSMLOBJECT($Term\ ObjI, ObjC, ObjD, ObjQ, ResV$)
2:    $I \leftarrow getInstances(ObjC)$
3:    **for all** $i \in I$ **do**
4:        **if** $sameID(i, ObjI)$ **then**
5:            $N \leftarrow getQDimension(i, ObjD)$
6:            $v \leftarrow getQValue(N, ObjQ)$
7:        **end if**
8:    **end for**
9:    $return\ unifies(v, ResV)$;
10: **end function**

Initially, the function receives five arguments that allow us to set the parameters to retrieve information from the CSML database: the object instance about which the information is required, the name of the concept that was assigned to the object instance in question, the domain, and its respective quality dimension. The last parameter will be used to return a result to the AgentSpeak plan calling this internal action. The first argument helps determine the CSML file that will be used to recover the required instance information (lines 2–8). When the instance is found (line 4), it is necessary to select the specific domain having the quality dimension required (line 5). Finally, from set of quality dimensions of the domain it is possible to filter the specific quality dimension and get its respective point value (line 6). The value recovered is then unified with the last argument received by the function for the result of the execution of this function to be returned to the AgentSpeak plan. An example of the use of both algorithms is presented in the next section.

4   A Practical Example of the Use of Conceptual Information in Multi-agent Systems

To exemplify how conceptual information can be used by an agent, consider the following scenario implemented in Jason where an agent has the goal of helping a visually impaired user to find a specific object in a room (in this case, a red apple). To achieve this goal, the agent has first to identify where the object of interest is, as well as to determine the path to its location.

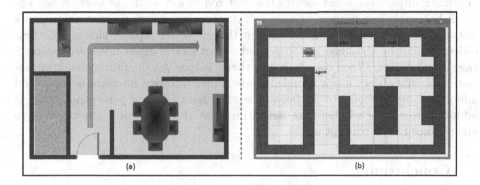

Fig. 1. Target Object Recognition Scenario

Figure 1(a) shows the expected movement of the agent in the environment and the location of the objects recognised by the agent. Figure 1(b) shows how this scenario was adapted to a Jason environment. To get closer to the objects to be checked, the agent has to help the user to get at the end of the hall.

In order to execute this task, the agent has first to determine the depth of the hall. This information is already present in the CSML database and can be recovered with the aid of the customised internal action described in the previous section, which is called by the plan shown in the code snippet below:

```
1:  +at(hall,hall1) :
2:  <- myp.getCSMLObject(hall,hall1,shape,depth,D);
3:     -+hall_depth(D);
```

First, the agent realises that it is in a location "hall1" that was already classified as a "hall". This enables the agent to use an internal action to retrieve the required information from the CSML database (line 2). When the internal action is called, the following parameters are informed: the object instance (hall1), the concept name (hall), the domain (shape) and its respective quality dimension (depth). As a result of the execution of the internal action, the information retrieved from the CSML Database is added or updated as an agent belief (line 3). When the user reaches the end of the hall, the agent performs a new reading of the environment. On the left-hand side, the agent finds a green object that does not correspond to the characteristics expected of the desired object, but it might be used as a landmark. On the right-hand side, the agent will find two red objects which might be the object desired by the visually impaired user. The agent only perceived the objects' positions and colors and try to classify each one of them by executing Algorithm 1, but those objects cannot yet be classified. Both objects are therefore recorded as unrecognised. By checking those objects positions on the grid, the agent can determine that the desired objects are to the right of the green object. The green object also allows them to find a safe path to get near the unrecognised objects. When the user gets next to the landmark object, the agent assigns the first red object as the nearest. When the agent becomes close to the first object, it receives information about the object's shape. The information does not match the expected (apple) shape. The first object cannot be classified as the desired object so the agent needs to approach the second object. When the agent gets there, it receives the perceptual information that this object has a rounded shape. The similarity measure is computed and the value is found to be below the threshold. A new perceptual belief is added to the agent's belief base indicating that this particular object refers to an instance of the concept apple.

5   Conclusion

In this paper, we described initial steps towards integrating a knowledge representation level based on the conceptual spaces paradigm into a BDI agent architecture. We have also shown how this integration can contribute towards the development of a system to support the mobility of blind or visually impaired users. In our approach, we used the Jason platform and the CSML API to build the necessary infrastructure to establish a process of conceptual inference for BDI agents. We proposed and demonstrated the use of an algorithm establishing the similarity of concept representations based on the use of a function that computes the distance between the spatial representations of an observation and prototypical instances of candidate concepts to represent that observed object. Finally, we exemplified how information from the conceptual database can be retrieved by using a Jason internal action that we developed.

References

1. Adams, B., Raubal, M.: A metric conceptual space algebra. In: Hornsby, K.S., Claramunt, C., Denis, M., Ligozat, G. (eds.) COSIT 2009. LNCS, vol. 5756, pp. 51–68. Springer, Heidelberg (2009)
2. Adams, B., Raubal, M.: Conceptual Space Markup Language (CSML): Towards the cognitive semantic web. In: International Conference on Semantic Computing (2009)
3. Bordini, R.H., Hübner, J.F., Wooldridge, M.: Programming Multi-Agent Systems in AgentSpeak Using Jason. Wiley and Sons, New York (2007)
4. Bratman, M.E.: Intention, Plans, and Practical Reason. Harvard University Press, Cambridge (1999)

5. Bratman, M.E., Israel, D.J., Pollack, M.E.: Plans and resource-bounded practical reasoning. Computational Intelligence (1988)
6. Edelman, S., Shahbazi, R.: Renewing the respect for similarity. Front. Comput. Neurosci. **6**, 45 (2012)
7. Gärdenfors, P.: Conceptual Spaces: The Geometry of Thought. MIT Press, Cambridge (2000)
8. Gärdenfors, P.: The Dynamics of Thought. Springer, Dordrecth (2005)
9. Giudice, N.A., Legge, G.E.: Blind navigation and the role of technology. In: Engineering Handbook of Smart Technology for Aging, Disability, and Independence. Wiley and Sons, New York (2008)
10. Long, R.G., Giudice, N.A.: Establishing and maintaining orientation for orientation and mobility. In: Foundations of Orientationand Mobility. American Foundation for the Blind, New York (2010)
11. Moreira, Á.F., Vieira, R., Bordini, R.H.: Extending the operational semantics of a BDI agent-oriented programming language for introducing speech-act based communication. In: Leite, J., Omicini, A., Sterling, L., Torroni, P. (eds.) DALT 2003. LNCS (LNAI), vol. 2990, pp. 135–154. Springer, Heidelberg (2004)
12. Rao, A.S.: AgentSpeak(L): BDI agents speak out in a logical computable language. In: Proceedings of the 7th European Workshop on Modelling Autonomous Agents in a Multi-agent World: Agents Breaking Away (1996)
13. Steels, L., Baillie, J.: Shared grounding of event descriptions by autonomous robots. Robotics and Autonomous Systems (2003)
14. Wassermann, R.: Revising Concepts. In: Fifth Workshop on Logic, Language, Information and Comunication (WoLLIC) (1998)
15. Wooldridge, M.J.: Introduction to Multiagent Systems. Wiley and Sons, New York (2002)
16. Klapiscak, T., Bordini, R.H.: JASDL: a practical programming approach combining agent and semantic web technologies. In: 6th International Workshop on Declarative Agent Languages and Technologies VI (2008)

Author Index

Printed in the United States
By Bookmasters